Reprinted 1985 by Historical Times, Inc.

Distributed by   Broadfoot Publishing Company
Historical Times, Inc.
Morningside House

THE REPUBLICATION, in its entirety, of the *War of the Rebellion: Official Records of the Union and Confederate Armies*, is a service project undertaken by the National Historical Society in the interest of libraries and scholars who have long needed a reissue of this indispensable work. Each of the 128 volumes is published in full, including the *Index*, and all are heavily bound in buckram for long and continued use. This and other volumes of the set are available only from the National Historical Society.

ISBN 0-918678-07-2

LC No. 72-176712

THE NATIONAL HISTORICAL SOCIETY
Harrisburg, PA 17105

Printed on 45 lb. Glatfelter Acid-Free
Paper by Edwards Brothers, Ann Arbor, MI 48106

The National Historical Society seeks to expand and enrich knowledge of the American past and, through its programs and services, to bring its members a fuller appreciation and deeper understanding of the people and events that came together to create the great history that is our heritage.

THE

WAR OF THE REBELLION:

A COMPILATION OF THE

OFFICIAL RECORDS

OF THE

UNION AND CONFEDERATE ARMIES.

PREPARED UNDER THE DIRECTION OF THE SECRETARY OF WAR, BY BVT. LIEUT. COL. ROBERT N. SCOTT, THIRD U. S. ARTILLERY,

AND

PUBLISHED PURSUANT TO ACT OF CONGRESS APPROVED JUNE 16, 1880.

SERIES I—VOLUME V.

WASHINGTON:
GOVERNMENT PRINTING OFFICE.
1881.

PREFACE.

By an act approved June 23, 1874, Congress made an appropriation "to enable the Secretary of War to begin the publication of the Official Records of the War of the Rebellion, both of the Union and Confederate Armies," and directed him "to have copied for the Public Printer all reports, letters, telegrams, and general orders not heretofore copied or printed, and properly arranged in chronological order."

Appropriations for continuing such preparation have been made from time to time, and the act approved June 16, 1880, has provided "for the printing and binding, under direction of the Secretary of War, of 10,000 copies of a compilation of the Official Records (Union and Confederate) of the War of the Rebellion, so far as the same may be ready for publication, during the fiscal year"; and that "of said number, 7,000 copies shall be for the use of the House of Representatives, 2,000 copies for the use of the Senate, and 1,000 copies for the use of the Executive Departments."

This compilation will be the first general publication of the military records of the war, and will embrace all official documents that can be obtained by the compiler, and that appear to be of any historical value.

The publication will present the records in the following order of arrangement:

The **1st Series** will embrace the formal reports, both Union and Confederate, of the first seizures of United States property in the Southern States, and of all military operations in the field, with the correspondence, orders, and returns relating specially thereto, and, as proposed, is to be accompanied by an Atlas.

In this series the reports will be arranged according to the campaigns and several theaters of operations (in the chronological order of the events), and the Union reports of any event will, as a rule, be immediately followed by the Confederate accounts. The correspondence, &c., not embraced in the "reports" proper will follow (first Union and next Confederate) in chronological order.

The **2d Series** will contain the correspondence, orders, reports, and returns, Union and Confederate, relating to prisoners of war, and (so far as the military authorities were concerned) to State or political prisoners.

The **3d Series** will contain the correspondence, orders, reports, and returns of the Union authorities (embracing their correspondence with the Confederate officials) not relating specially to the subjects of the *first* and *second* series. It will set forth the annual and special reports of the Secretary of War, of the General-in-Chief, and of the chiefs of the several staff corps and departments; the calls for troops, and the correspondence between the National and the several State authorities.

The **4th Series** will exhibit the correspondence, orders, reports, and returns of the Confederate authorities, similar to that indicated for the Union officials, as of the *third* series, but excluding the correspondence between the Union and Confederate authorities given in that series.

ROBERT N. SCOTT,
Major, Third Art., and Bvt. Lieut. Col.

WAR DEPARTMENT, *August* 23, 1880.

Approved:

ALEX. RAMSEY,
Secretary of War.

CONTENTS.

CHAPTER XIV.

v

CONTENTS OF PRECEDING VOLUMES.

VOLUME I.

VOLUME II.

VOLUME III.

VOLUME IV.

CHAPTER XIV.

OPERATIONS IN MARYLAND, NORTHERN VIRGINIA, AND WEST VIRGINIA.

August 1, 1861–March 17, 1862.

---

* Of some of the minor conflicts noted in this "Summary" no circumstantial reports are on file, the only record of such events being references to them on muster rolls or returns.

† Neither the date when General Lee assumed command in "Western Virginia" nor the nature of that command is shown by the records; but see Davis to Johnston, August 1, 1861, in the "Correspondence, etc.," *post*.

‡ Better known as the Army of the Potomac.

§ Date taken from memorandum in A. G. O. See Dix to Williams, November 19, 1861, in "Correspondence, etc.," *post*.

Aug. 28–30, 1861.—Skirmishes near Bailey's Corners (or Cross-Roads), Va.
      31, 1861.—Skirmish at Munson's Hill, or Little River Turnpike, Va.
Sept.   1, 1861.—Skirmish at Blue Creek, W. Va.
              Skirmish at Boone Court-House, W. Va.
              Skirmish at Burlington, W. Va.
        2, 1861.—Skirmish near the Hawk's Nest, W. Va.
              Skirmish at Worthington, W. Va.
              Skirmish at Beller's Mill, near Harper's Ferry, W. Va.
        4, 1861.—Skirmish at Great Falls, Md.
        6, 1861.—Skirmish at Rowell's Run, W. Va.
        9, 1861.—Skirmish at Shepherdstown, W. Va.
       10, 1861.—Engagement at Carnifix Ferry, W. Va.
              Skirmish near Lewinsville, Va.
       11, 1861.—Reconnaissance from Chain Bridge to Lewinsville, Va., and action
              at that place.
   11–17, 1861.—Operations in Cheat Mountain, West Virginia, including actions
              and skirmishes at Cheat Mountain Pass, Cheat Summit, Point
              Mountain Turnpike, and Elk Water.
       12, 1861.—Skirmish at Petersburg, W. Va.
              Skirmish near Peytona, W. Va.
   12–17, 1861.—Arrest of members of the Maryland Legislature and other citizens
              of that State.
       15, 1861.—Skirmish at Pritchard's Mill, Va., near Antietam Ford, Md.
       16, 1861.—Skirmish opposite Seneca Creek, Md.
              Action at Princeton, W. Va.
              Skirmish at Magruder's Ferry, Va.
       18, 1861.—Skirmish near Berlin, Md.
       19, 1861.—Department of Western Virginia constituted.
       20, 1861.—Skirmish opposite Seneca Creek, Md.
       21, 1861.—General Robert E. Lee, C. S. Army, in immediate command of
              forces in the valley of the Kanawha.
       23, 1861.—Skirmish at Cassville, W. Va.
   23–25, 1861.—Descent upon Romney, W. Va., including affairs at Mechanics-
              burg Gap and Hanging Rock Pass.
       24, 1861.—Skirmish at Point of Rocks, Md.
       25, 1861.—Engagement at Freestone Point, Va.
              Reconnaissance to and skirmish near Lewinsville, Va.
              Action at Kanawha Gap, near Chapmanville, W. Va.
              Brig. Gen. Henry A. Wise, C. S. Army, relieved from command in
              West Virginia.
              Maj. Gen. Gustavus W. Smith, C. S. Army, assigned to command
              of Second Corps, Army of the Potomac.
       28, 1861.—Affair near Vanderburgh's house, Munson's Hill, Va.
       29, 1861.—Skirmish at Berlin, Md.
Oct.   1, 1861.—Confederate Council of War at Centreville, Va.
        2, 1861.—Skirmish at Springfield Station, Va.
        3, 1861.—Engagement at Greenbrier River, W. Va.
              Expedition to Pohick Church, Va.
              Skirmish at Springfield Station, Va.
        4, 1861.—Skirmish near Edwards Ferry, Md.
       11, 1861.—Brig. Gen. William S. Rosecrans, U. S. Army, assumes command
              of the Department of Western Virginia.
              Skirmish at Harper's Ferry, W. Va.
       13, 1861.—Skirmish at Cotton Hill, W. Va.
       15, 1861.—Skirmish on Little River Turnpike, Va.

Oct.   16, 1861.—Skirmish at Bolivar Heights, near Harper's Ferry, W. Va.

        18, 1861.—Reconnaissance towards Occoquan River, Va.

        19–Nov. 16, 1861.—Operations in the Kanawha and New River region, W. Va.

        20, 1861.—Reconnaissance to Hunter's Mill and Thornton Station, Va.

    21–24, 1861.—Operations on the Potomac, near Leesburg, Va., including engagement at Ball's Bluff and skirmish on Leesburg road (October 21), and action near Edwards Ferry (October 22).

        22, 1861.—Brig. Gen. Benjamin F. Kelley, U. S. Army, assigned to command of the Department of Harper's Ferry and Cumberland.

Department of Northern Virginia constituted, under command of General Joseph E. Johnston, C. S. Army. General Beauregard and Major-Generals Holmes and Jackson assigned, respectively, to command of the Potomac, Aquia, and Valley Districts.

Affairs around Budd's Ferry, Md.

    23–27, 1861.—Reconnaissance in the Kanawha Valley, W. Va.

        26, 1861.—Action at Romney, W. Va.

Skirmish at South Branch Bridge, W. Va.

Skirmish near Springfield, W. Va.

        28, 1861.—Skirmish near Budd's Ferry, Md.

        31, 1861.—Skirmish at Greenbrier, W. Va.

Nov.   1, 1861.—Maj. Gen. George B. McClellan supersedes Lieut. Gen. Winfield Scott in command of the Armies of the United States.

    1– 3, 1861.—Skirmishes near Gauley Bridge, or Cotton Hill, W. Va.

    3–11, 1861.—Expedition into Lower Maryland.

    4, 1861–Feb. 21, 1862.—Operations in the Valley District.

        5, 1861.—General Robert E. Lee, C. S. Army, assigned to command of the Department of South Carolina, Georgia, and East Florida.

        9, 1861.—Expedition to Mathias Point, Va.

      10, 1861.—Affair at Guyandotte, W. Va.

      12, 1861.—Reconnaissance to Pohick Church and Occoquan River, Va.

      13, 1861.—Skirmish near Romney, W. Va.

      14, 1861.—Affair at the mouth of Mattawoman Creek, Md.

Skirmish on road from Fayetteville to Raleigh, W. Va.

Skirmish at McCoy's Mill, W. Va.

    14–22, 1861.—Expedition through Accomac and Northampton Counties, Va.

      16, 1861.—Capture of Union foraging party at Doolan's Farm, Va.

      18, 1861.—Skirmish on road from Falls Church to Fairfax Court-House, Va.

      26, 1861.—Skirmish near Vienna, Va.

    26–27, 1861.—Expedition to Dranesville, Va., and skirmish.

      27, 1861.—Skirmish near Fairfax Court-House, Va.

      30, 1861.—Skirmish near mouth of Little Cacapon River, W. Va.

Dec.   2, 1861.—Skirmish at Annandale, Va.

        4, 1861.—Skirmish at Burke's Station, Va.

        6, 1861.—Expedition to Gunnell's Farm, near Dranesville, Va.

        8, 1861.—Skirmish near Romney, W. Va.

Skirmish at Dam No. 5, Chesapeake and Ohio Canal.

      11, 1861.—Skirmish at Dam No. 4, Chesapeake and Ohio Canal.

      12, 1861.—Skirmish at Greenbrier River, W. Va.

      13, 1861.—Engagement at Camp Alleghany, W. Va.

      15, 1861.—Affair in Roane County, W. Va.

Capture of the sloop Victory.

    15–17, 1861.—Operations on the Lower Potomac.

    15–21, 1861.—Expedition to Meadow Bluff, W. Va.

    17–21, 1861.—Jackson's operations against Dam No. 5, Chesapeake and Ohio Canal.

Dec. 18, 1861.—Reconnaissance to Pohick Church, Va.
      19, 1861.—Skirmish at Point of Rocks, Md.
      20, 1861.—Engagement at Dranesville, Va.
  24–25, 1861.—Scout towards Fairfax Court-House, Va.
      25, 1861.—Skirmish at Cherry Run, W. Va.
              Skirmish at Fort Frederick, Md.
      28, 1861.—Beckley (Raleigh Court-House), W. Va., occupied by Union forces.
  29–30, 1861.—Capture of Suttonville (Braxton Court-House), and skirmishes in
              Clay, Braxton, and Webster Counties, W. Va.
Jan.   3, 1862.—Descent upon and skirmish at Huntersville, W. Va.
   3– 4, 1862.—Skirmishes at Bath, W. Va.
       4, 1862.—Skirmishes at Slane's Cross-Roads, Great Cacapon Bridge, Sir
              John's Run, and Alpine Depot, W. Va.
   5– 6, 1862.—Bombardment of Hancock, Md.
       7, 1862.—Skirmish at Hanging Rock Pass, or Blue's Gap, W. Va.
       8, 1862.—Skirmish on the Dry Fork of Cheat River, W. Va.
       9, 1862.—Skirmish near Pohick Run, Va.
  12–23, 1862.—Expedition to Logan Court-House and the Guyandotte Valley,
              W. Va.
      26, 1862.—General G. T. Beauregard, C. S. Army, ordered from the Potomac
              District to Columbus, Ky.
      29, 1862.—Affair at Lee's house, on the Occoquan, Va.
Feb.   3, 1862.—Reconnaissance to Occoquan Village, Va.
       7, 1862.—Expedition to Flint Hill and Hunter's Mill, Va.
       8, 1862.—Skirmish at the mouth of the Blue Stone, W. Va.
      14, 1862.—Affair at Bloomery, W. Va.
      22, 1862.—Expedition to Vienna and Flint Hill, Va.
      24, 1862.—Affair at Lewis' Chapel, near Pohick Church, Va.
  25–May 6, 1862.—Operations in Loudoun County, Va.
Mar.   3, 1862.—Skirmish at Martinsburg, W. Va.
       5, 1862.—Skirmish at Bunker Hill, Va.
              Skirmish near Pohick Church, Va.
       7, 1862.—Skirmish near Winchester, Va.
   7– 9, 1862.—Withdrawal of the Confederate forces from Evansport, Dumfries,
              Manassas, and Occoquan, Va.
   7–11, 1862.—Advance of the Union forces to Centreville and Manassas, Va.
       8, 1862.—Occupation of Leesburg, Va., by the Union forces.
       9, 1862.—Skirmish at Sangster's Station, Va.
      11, 1862.—Major-General McClellan relieved from command of the Armies
              of the United States—retaining command of the Army of the
              Potomac.
              The Department of Western Virginia merged into the Mountain
              Department.
              Skirmish at Stephenson's Station, near Winchester, Va.
  11–12, 1862.—Winchester, Va., abandoned by the Confederates and occupied
              by the Union forces.
      13, 1862.—Army Corps organized in the Army of the Potomac, and Generals
              McDowell, Sumner, Heintzelman, Keyes, and Banks assigned
              as commanders.
              General Robert E. Lee "charged with the conduct of military
              operations in the Armies of the Confederacy."
      14, 1862.—Brigadier-General Rosecrans, U. S. Army, assumes command of
              the Mountain Department.
  14–16, 1862.—Reconnaissance to Cedar Run, Va.

GENERAL REPORTS.

No. 1.—Maj. Gen. George B. McClellan, U. S. Army, of the operations of the Army of
the Potomac from July 27, 1861, to March 17, 1862.

No. 2.—Brig. Gen. William F. Barry, Chief of Artillery, Army of the Potomac, of the
organization and operations of the artillery of that army from July 25,
1861, to September 1, 1862.

No. 3.—Maj. Albert J. Myer, Chief Signal Officer U. S. Army, of the signal service in
the Army of the Potomac from August 14, 1861, to March 23, 1862, and of
signal detachments in other commands.

No. 4.—Surg. Charles S. Tripler, Medical Director Army of the Potomac, of the operations of the medical department of that army from August 12, 1861, to
March 17, 1862.

No. 1.

*Extract, embracing the "First Period," from Maj. Gen. George B. McClellan's
report of the operations of the Army of the Potomac from July 27, 1861,
to November 9, 1862.*

CHAPTER I.

NEW YORK, *August* 4, 1863.

SIR: I have the honor to submit herein the official report of the operations of the Army of the Potomac while under my charge. Accompanying it are the reports of the corps, division, and subordinate commanders pertaining to the various engagements, battles, and occurrences of the campaigns, and important documents connected with its
organization, supply, and movements. These, with lists of maps and
memoranda submitted, will be found appended, duly arranged, and
marked for convenient reference.*

Charged in the spring of 1861 with the operations in the Department
of the Ohio, which included the States of Illinois, Indiana, Ohio, and
latterly Western Virginia, it had become my duty to counteract the
hostile designs of the enemy in Western Virginia, which were immediately directed to the destruction of the Baltimore and Ohio Railroad
and the possession of the Kanawha Valley, with the ultimate object of
gaining Wheeling and the control of the Ohio River.

The successful affairs of Philippi, Rich Mountain, Carrick's Ford, &c.,
had been fought, and I had acquired possession of all Western Virginia
north of the Kanawha Valley, as well as of the lower portion of that
valley.

I had determined to proceed to the relief of the Upper Kanawha
Valley as soon as provision was made for the permanent defense of the
mountain passes leading from the east into the region under our control, when I received at Beverly, in Randolph County, on the 21st of
July, 1861, intelligence of the unfortunate result of the battle of Manassas, fought on that day.

---

* Only such of the subordinate reports, &c., as relate more particularly to operations from August 1, 1861, to March 17, 1862, will be found in this volume. The others
will appear in the chapters embracing the operations covered by the second and third
and by the fourth periods of General McClellan's report, viz, the Peninsular and the
first Maryland campaigns.

On the 22d I received an order by telegraph directing me to turn over my command to Brigadier-General Rosecrans and repair at once to Washington.*
I had already caused reconnaissances to be made for intrenchments at the Cheat Mountain Pass, also on the Huntersville road, near Elkwater, and at Red House, near the main road from Romney to Grafton. During the afternoon and night of the 22d I gave the final instructions for the construction of these works, turned over the command to Brigadier-General Rosecrans, and started on the morning of the 23d for Washington, arriving there on the afternoon of the 26th. On the 27th I assumed command of the Division of the Potomac, comprising the troops in and around Washington, on both banks of the river.

With this brief statement of the events which immediately preceded my being called to the command of the troops at Washington I proceed to an account, from such authentic data as are at hand, of my military operations while commander of the Army of the Potomac.

The subjects to be considered naturally arrange themselves as follows: The organization of the Army of the Potomac; the military events connected with the defenses of Washington from July, 1861, to March, 1862; the campaign on the Peninsula, and that in Maryland.

The great resources and capacity for powerful resistance of the South at the breaking out of the rebellion, and the full proportions of the great conflict about to take place, were sought to be carefully measured, and I had also endeavored by every means in my power to impress upon the authorities the necessity for such immediate and full preparation as alone would enable the Government to prosecute the war on a scale commensurate with the resistance to be offered.

On the 4th of August, 1861, I addressed to the President the following memorandum, prepared at his request :

MEMORANDUM.

The object of the present war differs from those in which nations are usually engaged mainly in this, that the purpose of ordinary war is to conquer a peace and make a treaty on advantageous terms. In this contest it has become necessary to crush a population sufficiently numerous, intelligent, and warlike to constitute a nation. We have not only to defeat their armed and organized forces in the field, but to display such an overwhelming strength as will convince all our antagonists, especially those of the governing, aristocratic class, of the utter impossibility of resistance. Our late reverses make this course imperative. Had we been successful in the recent battle (Manassas), it is possible that we might have been spared the labor and expenses of a great effort.

Now we have no alternative. Their success will enable the political leaders of the rebels to convince the mass of their people that we are inferior to them in force and courage, and to command all their resources. The contest began with a class ; now it is with a people. Our military success can alone restore the former issue.

By thoroughly defeating their armies, taking their strong places, and pursuing a rigidly protective policy as to private property and unarmed persons, and a lenient course as to private soldiers, we may well hope for a permanent restoration of a peaceful Union. But in the first instance the authority of the Government must be supported by overwhelming physical force.

Our foreign relations and financial credit also imperatively demand that the military action of the Government should be prompt and irresistible.

The rebels have chosen Virginia as their battle-field, and it seems proper for us to make the first great struggle there. But, while thus directing our main efforts, it is necessary to diminish the resistance there offered us by movements on other points both by land and water.

Without entering at present into details, I would advise that a strong movement be made on the Mississippi, and that the rebels be driven out of Missouri.

* See Vol. II of this series, p. 753.

As soon as it becomes perfectly clear that Kentucky is cordially united with us, I would advise a movement through that State into Eastern Tennessee, for the purpose of assisting the Union men of that region and of seizing the railroads leading from Memphis to the East. The possession of those roads by us, in connection with the movement on the Mississippi, would go far towards determining the evacuation of Virginia by the rebels. In the mean time all the passes into Western Virginia from the East should be securely guarded, but I would advise no movement from that quarter towards Richmond, unless the political condition of Kentucky renders it impossible or inexpedient for us to make the movement upon Eastern Tennessee through that State. Every effort should, however, be made to organize, equip, and arm as many troops as possible in Western Virginia, in order to render the Ohio and Indiana regiments available for other operations.

At as early a day as practicable it would be well to protect and reopen the Baltimore and Ohio Railroad. Baltimore and Fort Monroe should be occupied by garrisons sufficient to retain them in our possession.

The importance of Harper's Ferry and the line of the Potomac in the direction of Leesburg will be very materially diminished so soon as our force in this vicinity becomes organized, strong, and efficient, because no capable general will cross the river north of this city when we have a strong army here ready to cut off his retreat.

To revert to the West: It is probable that no very large additions to the troops now in Missouri will be necessary to secure that State.

I presume that the force required for the movement down the Mississippi will be determined by its commander and the President. If Kentucky assumes the right position, not more than 20,000 will be needed, together with those that can be raised in that State and Eastern Tennessee, to secure the latter region and its railroads, as well as ultimately to occupy Nashville.

The Western Virginia troops, with not more than 5,000 to 10,000 from Ohio and Indiana, should, under proper management, suffice for its protection.

When we have reorganized our main army here 10,000 men ought to be enough to protect the Baltimore and Ohio Railroad and the Potomac ; 5,000 will garrison Baltimore, 3,000 Fort Monroe, and not more than 20,000 will be necessary at the utmost for the defense of Washington.

For the main army of operations I urge the following composition:

	Men.
250 regiments of infantry, say	225,000
100 field batteries, 600 guns	15,000
28 regiments of cavalry	25,500
5 regiments engineer troops	7,500
Total	273,000

The force must be supplied with the necessary engineer and pontoon trains, and with transportation for everything save tents. Its general line of operations should be so directed that water transportation can be availed of from point to point by means of the ocean and the rivers emptying into it. An essential feature of the plan of operations will be the employment of a strong naval force, to protect the movement of a fleet of transports intended to convey a considerable body of troops from point to point of the enemy's sea-coast, thus either creating diversions and rendering it necessary for them to detach largely from their main body in order to protect such of their cities as may be threatened, or else landing and forming establishments on their coast at any favorable places that opportunity might offer. This naval force should also cooperate with the main army in its efforts to seize the important seaboard towns of the rebels.

It cannot be ignored that the construction of railroads has introduced a new and very important element into war, by the great facilities thus given for concentrating at particular positions large masses of troops from remote sections, and by creating new strategic points and lines of operations.

It is intended to overcome this difficulty by the partial operations suggested, and such others as the particular case may require. We must endeavor to seize places on the railways in the rear of the enemy's points of concentration, and we must threaten their seaboard cities, in order that each State may be forced, by the necessity of its own defense, to diminish its contingent to the Confederate army.

The proposed movement down the Mississippi will produce important results in this connection. That advance and the progress of the main army at the East will materially assist each other by diminishing the resistance to be encountered by each.

The tendency of the Mississippi movement upon all questions connected with cotton is too well understood by the President and Cabinet to need any illustration from me.

There is another independent movement that has often been suggested, and which has always recommended itself to my judgment. I refer to a movement from Kansas and Nebraska through the Indian Territory upon Red River and Western Texas, for the purpose of protecting and developing the latent Union and free-State sentiment well known to predominate in Western Texas, and which, like a similar sentiment in Western Virginia, will, if protected, ultimately organize that section into a free State. How far it will be possible to support this movement by an advance through New Mexico from California is a matter which I have not sufficiently examined to be able to express a decided opinion. If at all practicable it is eminently desirable, as bringing into play the resources and warlike qualities of the Pacific States, as well as identifying them with our cause and cementing the bond of union between them and the General Government.

If it is not departing too far from my province, I will venture to suggest the policy of an intimate alliance and cordial understanding with Mexico; their sympathies and interests are with us—their antipathies exclusively against our enemies and their institutions. I think it would not be difficult to obtain from the Mexican Government the right to use, at least during the present contest, the road from Guaymas to New Mexico. This concession would very materially reduce the obstacles of the column moving from the Pacific. A similar permission to use their territory for the passage of troops between the Panuco and the Rio Grande would enable us to throw a column of troops by a good road from Tampico, or some of the small harbors north of it, upon and across the Rio Grande, without risk, and scarcely firing a shot.

To what extent, if any, it would be desirable to take into service and employ Mexican soldiers is a question entirely political, on which I do not venture to offer an opinion.

The force I have recommended is large; the expense is great. It is possible that a smaller force might accomplish the object in view, but I understand it to be the purpose of this great nation to re-establish the power of its Government and restore peace to its citizens in the shortest possible time.

The question to be decided is simply this: Shall we crush the rebellion at one blow, terminate the war in one campaign, or shall we leave it as a legacy for our descendants?

When the extent of the possible line of operations is considered, the force asked for for the main army under my command cannot be regarded as unduly large; every mile we advance carries us farther from our base of operations and renders detachments necessary to cover our communications, while the enemy will be constantly concentrating as he falls back. I propose, with the force which I have requested, not only to drive the enemy out of Virginia and occupy Richmond, but to occupy Charleston, Savannah, Montgomery, Pensacola, Mobile, and New Orleans; in other words, to move into the heart of the enemy's country and crush the rebellion in its very heart.

By seizing and repairing the railroads as we advance the difficulties of transportation will be materially diminished. It is, perhaps, unnecessary to state that, in addition to the forces named in this memorandum, strong reserves should be formed, ready to supply any losses that may occur.

In conclusion, I would submit that the exigencies of the Treasury may be lessened by making only partial payments to our troops when in the enemy's country, and by giving the obligations of the United States for such supplies as may there be obtained.

GEO. B. McCLELLAN,
Major-General.

I do not think the events of the war have proved these views upon the method and plans of its conduct altogether incorrect. They certainly have not proved my estimate of the number of troops and scope of operations too large. It is probable that I did underestimate the time necessary for the completion of arms and equipments. It was not strange, however, that by many civilians intrusted with authority there should have been an exactly opposite opinion held on both these particulars.

The result of the first battle of Manassas had been almost to destroy the *morale* and organization of our Army, and to alarm Government and people. The national capital was in danger; it was necessary, besides holding the enemy in check, to build works for its defense strong and capable of being held by a small force.

It was necessary also to create a new army for active operations, and to expedite its organization, equipment, and the accumulation of the material of war, and to this not inconsiderable labor all my energies for the next three months were constantly devoted.

Time is a necessary element in the creation of armies, and I do not therefore think it necessary to more than mention the impatience with which many regarded the delay in the arrival of new levies, though recruited and pressed forward with unexampled rapidity, the manufacture and supply of arms and equipments, or the vehemence with which an immediate advance upon the enemy's works directly in our front was urged by a patriotic but sanguine people.

The President, too, was anxious for the speedy employment of our Army, and, although possessed of my plans through frequent conferences, desired a paper from me upon the condition of the forces under my command and the immediate measures to be taken to increase their efficiency. Accordingly, in the latter part of October I addressed the following letter to the Secretary of War:

SIR: In conformity with a personal understanding with the President yesterday, I have the honor to submit the following statement of the condition of the army under my command, and the measures required for the preservation of the Government and the suppression of the rebellion:

It will be remembered that in a memorial I had the honor to address to the President soon after my arrival in Washington, and in my communication addressed to Lieutenant-General Scott under date of 8th of August,* in my letter to the President* authorizing him, at his request, to withdraw the letter written by me to General Scott, and in my letter of the 8th of September,† answering your note of inquiry of that date, my views on the same subject are frankly and fully expressed.

In these several communications I have stated the force I regarded as necessary to enable this army to advance with a reasonable certainty of success, at the same time leaving the capital and the line of the Potomac sufficiently guarded not only to secure the retreat of the main army in the event of disaster, but to render it out of the enemy's power to attempt a diversion in Maryland.

So much time has passed and the winter is approaching so rapidly, that but two courses are left to the Government, viz, either to go into winter quarters or to assume the offensive with forces greatly inferior in numbers to the army I regarded as desirable and necessary. If political considerations render the first course unadvisable, the second alone remains. While I regret that it has not been deemed expedient, or perhaps possible, to concentrate the forces of the nation in this vicinity (remaining on the defensive elsewhere), keeping the attention and efforts of the Government fixed upon this as the vital point where the issue of the great contest is to be decided, it may still be that, by introducing unity of action and design among the various armies of the land, by determining the courses to be pursued by the various commanders under one general plan, transferring from the other armies the superfluous strength not required for the purpose in view, and thus re-enforcing this main army, whose destiny it is to decide the controversy, we may yet be able to move with a reasonable prospect of success before the winter is fairly upon us.

The nation feels, and I share that feeling, that the Army of the Potomac holds the fate of the country in its hands. The stake is so vast, the issue so momentous, and the effect of the next battle will be so important thoughout the future as well as the present, that I continue to urge, as I have ever done since I entered upon the command of this army, upon the Government to devote its energies and its available resources towards increasing the numbers and efficiency of the army on which its salvation depends.

A statement, carefully prepared by the chiefs of engineers and artillery of this army, gives as the necessary garrison of this city and its fortifications 33,795 men, say 35,000.

The present garrison of Baltimore and its dependencies is about 10,000. I have sent the chief of my staff to make a careful examination into the condition of these troops, and to obtain the information requisite to enable me to decide whether this number can be diminished or the reverse.

At least 5,000 men will be required to watch the river hence to Harper's Ferry and its vicinity; probably 8,000 to guard the Lower Potomac.

As you are aware, all the information we have from spies, prisoners, &c., agrees in showing that the enemy have a force on the Potomac not less than 150,000 strong, well drilled and equipped, ably commanded, and strongly intrenched. It is plain, therefore, that to insure success, or to render it reasonably certain, the active army should not number less than 150,000 efficient troops, with 400 guns, unless some material change occurs in the force in front of us.

The requisite force for an advance movement by the Army of the Potomac may be thus estimated:

---

*That letter and resulting correspondence, found since this volume was stereotyped, will be printed in Series I, Vol. XI, Part III.
† See p. 587.

	Men.	Guns.
Column of active operations	150,000	400
Garrison of the city of Washington	35,000	40
To guard the Potomac to Harper's Ferry	5,000	12
To guard the Lower Potomac	8,000	24
Garrison for Baltimore and Annapolis	10,000	12
Total effective force required	208,000	488

or an aggregate, present and absent, of about 240,000 men, should the losses by sickness, &c., not rise to a higher percentage than at present.

Having stated what I regard as the requisite force to enable this army to advance, I now proceed to give the actual strength of the Army of the Potomac. The aggregate strength of the Army of the Potomac, by the official report on the morning of the 27th instant, was 168,318 officers and men of all grades and arms. This includes the troops at Baltimore and Annapolis, on the Upper and Lower Potomac, the sick, absent, &c. The force present for duty was 147,695. Of this number 4,268 cavalry were completely unarmed, 3,163 cavalry only partially armed, 5,979 infantry unequipped, making 13,410 unfit for the field (irrespective of those not yet sufficiently drilled), and reducing the effective force to 134,285, and the number disposable for an advance to 76,285. The infantry regiments are, to a considerable extent, armed with unserviceable weapons. Quite a large number of good arms, which had been intended for this army, were ordered elsewhere, leaving the Army of the Potomac insufficiently and, in some cases, badly armed. On the 30th of September there were with this army 228 field guns ready for the field. So far as arms and equipments are concerned, some of the batteries are still quite raw, and unfit to go into action. I have intelligence that eight New York batteries are *en route* hither; two others are ready for the field. I will still (if the New York batteries have six guns each) be 112 guns short of the number required for the active column, saying nothing for the present of those necessary for the garrisons and corps on the Potomac, which would make a total deficiency of 200 guns.

I have thus briefly stated our present condition and wants. It remains to suggest the means of supplying the deficiencies:

First. That all the cavalry and infantry arms, as fast as procured, whether manufactured in this country or purchased abroad, be sent to this army until it is fully prepared for the field.

Second. That the two companies of the Fourth Artillery, now understood to be *en route* from Fort Randall to Fort Monroe, be ordered to this army, to be mounted at once; also that the companies of the Third Artillery, *en route* from California, be sent here. Had not the order for Smead's battery to come here from Harrisburg to replace the battery I gave General Sherman been so often countermanded, I would again ask for it.

Third. That a more effective regulation may be made authorizing the transfer of men from the volunteers to the regular batteries, infantry and cavalry, that we may make the best possible use of the invaluable regular "skeletons."

Fourth. I have no official information as to the United States forces elsewhere, but from the best information I can obtain from the War Department and other sources I am led to believe that the United States troops are:

In Western Virginia, about	30,000
In Kentucky	40,000
In Missouri	80,000
In Fortress Monroe	11,000
Total	161,000

Besides these, I am informed that more than 100,000 are in progress of organization in other Northern and Western States.

I would, therefore, recommend that, not interfering with Kentucky, there should be retained in Western Virginia and Missouri a sufficient force for defensive purposes, and that the surplus troops be sent to the Army of the Potomac, to enable it to assume the offensive; that the same course be pursued in respect to Fortress Monroe, and that no further outside expeditions be attempted until we have fought the great battle in front of us.

Fifth. That every nerve be strained to hasten the enrollment, organization, and armament of new batteries and regiments of infantry.

Sixth. That all the battalions now raised for new regiments of regular infantry be at once ordered to this army, and that the old infantry and cavalry *en route* from California be ordered to this army immediately on their arrival in New York.

I have thus indicated in a general manner the objects to be accomplished and the means by which we may gain our ends. A vigorous employment of these means will, in my opinion, enable the Army of the Potomac to assume successfully this season the offensive operations which, ever since entering upon the command, it has been my anxious desire and diligent effort to prepare for and prosecute. The advance should not be postponed beyond the 25th of November, if possible to avoid it.

Unity in councils, the utmost vigor and energy in action, are indispensable. The entire military field should be grasped as a whole, and not in detached parts. One plan should be agreed upon and pursued; a single will should direct and carry out these plans.

The great object to be accomplished, the crushing defeat of the rebel army (now) at Manassas, should never for one instant be lost sight of, but all the intellect and means and men of the Government poured upon that point. The loyal States possess ample force to effect all this and more. The rebels have displayed energy, unanimity, and wisdom worthy of the most desperate days of the French revolution. Should we do less?

The unity of this nation, the preservation of our institutions, are so dear to me, that I have willingly sacrificed my private happiness with the single object of doing my duty to my country. When the task is accomplished, I shall be glad to return to the obscurity from which events have drawn me. Whatever the determination of the Government may be, I will do the best I can with the Army of the Potomac, and will share its fate, whatever may be the task imposed upon me.

Permit me to add that, on this occasion, as heretofore, it has been my aim neither to exaggerate nor underrate the power of the enemy, nor fail to express clearly the means by which, in my judgment, that power may be broken.

Urging the energy of preparation and action, which has ever been my choice, but with the fixed purpose by no act of mine to expose the Government to hazard by premature movement, and requesting that this communication may be laid before the President, I have the honor to be, very respectfully, your obedient servant,

GEO. B. McCLELLAN,
Major-General.

Hon. Simon Cameron, *Secretary of War.*

When I assumed command in Washington, on the 27th of July, 1861, the number of troops in and around the city was about 50,000 infantry, less than 1,000 cavalry, and 650 artillerymen, with nine imperfect field batteries, of thirty pieces. On the Virginia bank of the Potomac the brigade organization of General McDowell still existed, and the troops were stationed at and in rear of Fort Corcoran, Arlington, and Fort Albany, Fort Runyon, Roach's Mill, Cole's Mill, and in the vicinity of Fort Ellsworth, with a detachment at the Theological Seminary. There were no troops south of Hunting Creek, and many of the regiments were encamped on the low grounds bordering the Potomac, seldom in the best positions for defense, and entirely inadequate in numbers and condition to defend the long line from Fort Corcoran to Alexandria. On the Maryland side of the river, upon the heights overlooking the Chain Bridge, two regiments were stationed, whose commanders were independent of each other. There were no troops on the important Tennallytown road, or on the roads entering the city from the south. The camps were located without regard to purposes of defense or instruction, the roads were not picketed, and there was no attempt at an organization into brigades.

In no quarter were the dispositions for defense such as to offer a vigorous resistance to a respectable body of the enemy, either in the position and numbers of the troops or the number and character of the defensive works. Earthworks, in the nature of *têtes-de-pont*, looked upon the approaches to the Georgetown Aqueduct and Ferry, the Long Bridge, and Alexandria, by the Little River turnpike, and some simple defensive arrangements were made at the Chain Bridge. With the latter exception not a single defensive work had been commenced on the Maryland side. There was nothing to prevent the enemy shelling the city from heights within easy range, which could be occupied by a hostile column almost without resistance. Many soldiers had deserted, and the streets of Washington were crowded with straggling officers and men, absent from their stations without authority, whose behavior indicated the general want of discipline and organization.

I at once designated an efficient staff, afterwards adding to it as opportunity was afforded and necessity required, who zealously co-operated with me in the labor of bringing order out of confusion, reassigning troops and commands, projecting and throwing up defensive works, receiving and organizing, equipping and providing, for the new levies arriving in the city.

The valuable services of these officers in their various departments during this and throughout the subsequent periods of the history of the Army of the Potomac can hardly be sufficiently appreciated. Their names and duties will be given in another part of this report, and they are commended to the favorable notice of the War Department.

The restoration of order in the city of Washington was effected through the appointment of a provost-marshal, whose authority was supported by the few regular troops within my command. These troops were thus in position to act as a reserve, to be sent to any point of attack where their services might be most wanted. The energy and ability displayed by Col. A. Porter, the provost-marshal, and his assistants, and the strict discharge of their duty by the troops, produced the best results, and Washington soon became one of the most quiet cities in the Union.

The new levies of infantry, upon arriving in Washington, were formed into provisional brigades, and placed in camp in the suburbs of the city, for equipment, instruction, and discipline. As soon as regiments were in a fit condition for transfer to the forces across the Potomac they were assigned to the brigades serving there. Brig. Gen. F. J. Porter was at first assigned to the charge of the provisional brigades. Brig. Gen. A. E. Burnside was the next officer assigned to this duty, from which, however, he was soon relieved by Brig. Gen. S. Casey, who continued in charge of the newly-arriving regiments until the Army of the Potomac departed for the Peninsula, in March, 1862. The newly-arriving artillery troops reported to Brig. Gen. William F. Barry, the chief of artillery, and the cavalry to Brig. Gen. George Stoneman, the chief of cavalry.

By the 15th of October the number of troops in and about Washington, inclusive of the garrison of the city and Alexandria, the city guard, and the forces on the Maryland shore of the Potomac below Washington, and as far as Cumberland above, the troops under the command of General Dix at Baltimore and its dependencies, were as follows:

Total present for duty 133,201
Total sick 9,290
Total in confinement 1,156

Aggregate present 143,647
Aggregate absent 8,404

Grand aggregate 152,051

The following table exhibits similar data for the periods stated, including the troops in Maryland and Delaware:

| Date. | Present. | | | Absent. | Total present and absent. |
	For duty.	Sick.	In confinement.		
December 1, 1861	169,452	15,102	2,189	11,470	198,213
January 1, 1862	191,480	14,790	2,260	11,707	219,707
February 1, 1862	190,806	14,363	2,917	14,110	222,196
March 1, 1862	193,142	13,167	2,108	13,570	221,987

For convenience of reference the strength of the Army of the Potomac at subsequent periods is given:

Date.	Present.						Aggregate.	Absent.			Grand aggregate, present and absent.
	For duty.		Sick.		In arrest or confinement.			By authority.	Without authority.		
	Officers.	Men.	Officers.	Men.	Officers.	Men.					
April 30....	4,725	104,610	233	5,385	41	356	115,350	11,037	....	*126,387	
June 20....	4,665	101,160	496	10,541	44	320	117,226	27,700	887	†145,813	
July 10	3,834	85,715	685	15,959	60	213	106,466	34,638	3,782	‡144,886	

* Including Franklin.
† Including McCall, not Dix.
‡ Including two brigades of Shields' division, absent, 5,354 men.

In organizing the Army of the Potomac and preparing it for the field, the first step taken was to organize the infantry into brigades of four regiments each, retaining the newly-arrived regiments on the Maryland side until their armament and equipment were issued and they had obtained some little elementary instruction before assigning them permanently to brigades. When the organization of the brigades was well established and the troops somewhat disciplined and instructed, divisions of three brigades each were gradually formed, as is elsewhere stated in this report. Although I was always in favor of the organization into army corps as an abstract principle, I did not desire to form them until the army had been for some little time in the field, in order to enable the general officers first to acquire the requisite experience as division commanders on active service and that I might be able to decide from actual trial who were best fitted to exercise these important commands. For a similar reason I carefully abstained from making any recommendations for the promotion of officers to the grade of major-general.

When new batteries of artillery arrived, they also were retained in Washington until their armament and equipment were completed and their instruction sufficiently advanced to justify their being assigned to divisions. The same course was pursued in regard to cavalry. I regret that circumstances have delayed the chief of cavalry, General George Stoneman, in furnishing his report upon the organization of that arm of service. It will, however, be forwarded as soon as completed, and will doubtless show that the difficult and important duties intrusted to him were efficiently performed. He encountered and overcame, as far as it was possible, continual and vexatious obstacles arising from the great deficiency of cavalry arms and equipments and the entire inefficiency of many of the regimental officers first appointed. This last difficulty was, to a considerable extent, overcome in the cavalry, as well as in the infantry and artillery, by the continual and prompt action of courts-martial and boards of examination.

As rapidly as circumstances permitted every cavalry soldier was armed with a saber and revolver, and at least two squadrons in every regiment with carbines.

It was intended to assign at least one regiment of cavalry to each division of the active army, besides forming a cavalry reserve of the regular regiments and some picked regiments of volunteer cavalry. Circumstances beyond my control rendered it impossible to carry out this intention fully, and the cavalry force serving with the army in the field was never as large as it ought to have been.

It was determined to collect the regular infantry to form the nucleus of a reserve. The advantage of such a body of troops at a critical moment, especially in an army constituted mainly of new levies, imperfectly disciplined, has been frequently illustrated in military history, and was brought to the attention of the country at the first battle of Manassas. I have not been disappointed in the estimate formed of the value of these troops. I have always found them to be relied on. Whenever they have been brought under fire they have shown the utmost gallantry and tenacity. The regular infantry, which had been collected from distant posts and which had been recruited as rapidly as the slow progress of recruiting for the regular service would allow, added to the small battalion with McDowell's army which I found at Washington on my arrival, amounted on the 30th of August to 1,040 men; on the 28th of February, 1862, to 2,682, and on the 30th of April, to 4,603. On the 17th of May, 1862, they were assigned to General Porter's corps for organization as a division, with the Fifth Regiment New York Volunteers, which joined May 4, and the Tenth New York Volunteers, which joined subsequently. They remained from the commencement under the command of Brig. Gen. George Sykes, major Third Infantry, U. S. Army.

ARTILLERY.

The creation of an adequate artillery establishment for an army of so large proportions was' a formidable undertaking, and had it not been that the country possessed in the regular service a body of accomplished and energetic artillery officers, the task would have been almost hopeless.

The charge of organizing this most important arm was confided to Major (afterwards Brig. Gen.) William F. Barry, chief of artillery, whose industry and zeal achieved the best results. The report of General Barry is appended among the accompanying documents. By referring to it it will be observed that the following principles were adopted as the basis of organization :*

* * * * * * *

The zeal and services of Maj. A. S. Webb, assistant to General Barry, entitle him to especial praise. At the close of the Peninsular campaign General Barry assumed the duties of chief of artillery of the defenses of Washington, and was relieved in his former position by Col. Henry J. Hunt, who had commanded the artillery reserve with marked skill, and brought to his duties as chief of artillery the highest qualifications. The services of this distinguished officer in reorganizing and refitting the batteries prior to and after the battle of Antietam, and his gallant and skillful conduct on that field, merit the highest encomium in my power to bestow. His assistant, Major Doull, deserves high credit for his services and gallantry throughout both campaigns.

The designations of the different batteries of artillery, both regular and volunteer, follow within a few pages.

The following distribution of regiments and batteries was made, as a preliminary organization of the forces at hand, shortly after my arrival in Washington. The infantry, artillery, and cavalry, as fast as collected and brought into primary organization, were assigned to brigades and divisions, as indicated in the subjoined statements :

---

* For portion here omitted see Report No. 2, paragraphs numbered 1 to 7, and [13], [15], and [16], pp. 67–69.

Organization of the Division of the Potomac, August 4, 1861.

Brigadier-General Hunter's brigade.—Twenty-third, Twenty-fifth, Thirty-fifth, and Thirty-seventh Regiments New York Volunteers.

Brigadier-General Heintzelman's brigade.—Fifth Regiment Maine Volunteers, Sixteenth, Twenty-sixth, and Twenty-seventh Regiments New York Volunteers, and Tidball's battery (A), Second U. S. Artillery.

Brig. Gen. W. T. Sherman's brigade.—Ninth and Fourteenth Regiments Massachusett's Volunteers, De Kalb [Forty-first] Regiment New York Volunteers, Fourth Regiment Michigan Volunteers, Hamilton's battery (E), Third U. S. Artillery, and Company I, Second U. S. Cavalry.

Brigadier-General Kearny's brigade.—First, Second, and Third Regiments New Jersey Volunteers, Greene's battery (G), Second U. S. Artillery, and Company G, Second U. S. Cavalry.

Brigadier-General Hooker's brigade—First and Eleventh Regiments Massachusetts Volunteers, Second Regiment New Hampshire Volunteers, and Twenty-sixth Regiment Pennsylvania Volunteers.

Colonel Keyes' brigade.—Twenty-second, Twenty-fourth, and Thirtieth Regiments New York Volunteers, and Fourteenth Regiment New York State Militia [Eighty-fourth Volunteers].

Brigadier-General Franklin's brigade.—Fifteenth, Eighteenth, Thirty-first, and Thirty-Second Regiments New York Volunteers, Platt's battery (M), Second U. S. Artillery, and Company C [First], New York (Lincoln) Cavalry.

Colonel Blenker's brigade.—Eighth and Twenty-ninth Regiments New York Volunteers, Twenty-seventh Regiment Pennsylvania Volunteers, and Garibaldi Guard [Thirty-ninth], New York Volunteers.

Colonel Richardson's brigade.—Twelfth Regiment New York Volunteers and Second and Third Regiments Michigan Volunteers.

Brigadier-General Stone's brigade.—Thirty-fourth and Tammany [Forty-second] Regiments New York Volunteers, First Regiment Minnesota Volunteers, and Second Regiment New York State Militia [Eighty-second Volunteers].

Col. William F. Smith's brigade.—Second and Third Regiments Vermont Volunteers, Sixth Regiment Maine Volunteers, Thirty-third Regiment New York Volunteers, Company H, Second U. S. Cavalry, and Captain Mott's New York battery.

Colonel Couch's brigade.—Second Regiment Rhode Island Volunteers, Seventh and Tenth Regiments Massachusetts Volunteers, and Thirty-sixth Regiment New York Volunteers.

The Second Regiment Maine, the Second Regiment Wisconsin, and the Thirteenth Regiment New York Volunteers, stationed at Fort Corcoran.

The Twenty-first Regiment New York Volunteers, stationed at Fort Runyon.

The Seventeenth Regiment New York Volunteers, stationed at Fort Ellsworth.

By October the new levies had arrived in sufficient numbers, and the process of organization so far carried on that the construction of divisions had been effected.

The following statement exhibits the composition of the Army, October 15, 1861:

Organization of the Army of the Potomac, October 15, 1861.

1. *Brig. Gen. George Stoneman's cavalry command.*—Fifth U. S. Cavalry, Fourth Pennsylvania Cavalry, Oneida Cavalry (first company), Eleventh Pennsylvania Cavalry (Harlan's), and Barker's Illinois Cavalry (one company).

2. *Col. H. J. Hunt's artillery reserve.*—Batteries L, A, and B, Second U. S. Artillery; Batteries K and F, Third U. S. Artillery; Battery K, Fourth U. S. Artillery; Battery H, First U. S. Artillery, and Battery A, Fifth U. S. Artillery.

3. CITY GUARD, BRIG. GEN. ANDREW PORTER.

Cavalry.—Companies A and E, Fourth U. S. Cavalry.
Artillery.—Battery K, Fifth U. S. Artillery.
Infantry.—Second and Third battalions U. S. Infantry, Company — Eighth and Company — First U. S. Infantry, and Sturges' rifles (Illinois Volunteers).

4. BANKS' DIVISION.

Cavalry.—Four companies Third Regiment New York Cavalry (Van Alen's).
Artillery.—Best's battery (F), Fourth U. S. Artillery; detachment Ninth New York

Artillery; Matthews' battery (F), First Pennsylvania Artillery; Tompkins' battery (A), First Rhode Island Artillery.

Infantry.—Abercrombie's brigade: Twelfth Massachusetts, Twelfth and Sixteenth Indiana, and Thirtieth Pennsylvania Volunteers. Stiles' brigade: Third Wisconsin, Twenty-ninth Pennsylvania, and Thirteenth Massachusetts Volunteers, and Ninth New York State Militia [Eighty-third Volunteers]. Gordon's brigade: Second Massachusetts, Twenty-eighth and Nineteenth New York, Fifth Connecticut, Forty-sixth and Twenty-eighth Pennsylvania, and First Maryland Volunteers.

M'DOWELL'S DIVISION.

Cavalry.—Second New York Cavalry (Harris' Light), Colonel Davies.
Artillery.—Battery M, Second, and Battery G, First, U. S. Artillery.
Infantry.—Keyes' brigade: Fourteenth New York State Militia [Eighty-fourth Volunteers], and Twenty-second, Twenty-fourth, and Thirtieth New York Volunteers. Wadsworth's brigade: Twelfth, Twenty-first, Twenty-third, and Thirty-fifth New York Volunteers. King's brigade: Second, Sixth, and Seventh Wisconsin, and Nineteenth Indiana Volunteers.

HEINTZELMAN'S DIVISION.

Cavalry.—First New Jersey Cavalry, Colonel Halsted.
Artillery.—Thompson's battery (G), U. S. Artillery.
Infantry.—Richardson's brigade: Second, Third, and Fifth Michigan, and Thirty-seventh New York Volunteers. Sedgwick's brigade: Third and Fourth Maine and Thirty-eighth and Fortieth New York Volunteers. Jameson's brigade: Thirty-second, Sixty-third, Sixty-first, and Forty-fifth Pennsylvania Volunteers, and Wild Cat Reserves (Pennsylvania Volunteers).

F. J. PORTER'S DIVISION.

Calvary.—Third Pennsylvania Cavalry, Colonel Averell, and Eighth Pennsylvania Cavalry, Colonel Gregg.
Artillery.—Battery E, Second, and Battery E, Third, U. S. Artillery.
Infantry.—Morell's brigade: Thirty-third Pennsylvania, Fourth Michigan, Ninth Massachusetts, and Fourth New York Volunteers. Martindale's brigade: Thirteenth New York, Second Maine, and Eighteenth Massachusetts Volunteers, and De Kalb [Forty-first] Regiment New York Volunteers. Butterfield's brigade: Fiftieth New York, Eighty-third Pennsylvania, Seventeenth and Twenty-fifth New York Volunteers, and Stockton's Independent Michigan [Sixteenth] Regiment.

FRANKLIN'S DIVISION.

Cavalry.—First New York Cavalry, Colonel McReynolds.
Artillery.—Batteries D and G, Second U. S. Artillery, and Hexamer's battery (New Jersey Volunteers).
Infantry.—Kearny's brigade: First, Second, Third, and Fourth New Jersey Volunteers. Slocum's brigade: Sixteenth, Twenty-sixth, and Twenty-seventh New York, and Fifth Maine Volunteers. Newton's brigade: Fifteenth, Eighteenth, Thirty-first, and Thirty-second New York Volunteers.

STONE'S DIVISION.

Cavalry.—Six companies Third New York (Van Alen) Cavalry.
Artillery.—Kirby's battery (I), First United States; Vaughn's battery (B), First Rhode Island Artillery, and Bunting's Sixth New York Independent Battery.
Infantry.—Gorman's brigade: Second New York State Militia [Eighty-second Volunteers], First Minnesota, Fifteenth Massachusetts, and Thirty-fourth New York Volunteers, and Tammany [Forty-second] Regiment New York Volunteers. Lander's brigade: Nineteenth and Twentieth Massachusetts, and Seventh Michigan Volunteers, and a company of Massachusetts Sharpshooters. Baker's brigade: Pennsylvania Volunteers (First, Second, and Third California).

BUELL'S DIVISION.

Artillery.—Batteries D and H, First Pennsylvania Artillery.
Infantry.—Couch's brigade: Second Rhode Island, Seventh and Tenth Massachusetts, and Thirty-sixth New York Volunteers. Graham's brigade: Twenty-third and

Thirty-first Pennsylvania, and Sixty-seventh (First Long Island) and Sixty-fifth (First U. S. Chasseurs) New York Volunteers. Peck's brigade: Thirteenth and Twenty-first Pennsylvania and Sixty-second (Anderson Zouaves) and Fifty-fifth New York Volunteers.

M'CALL'S DIVISION.

Cavalry.—First Pennsylvania Reserve Cavalry, Colonel Bayard.
Artillery.—Easton's battery (A), Cooper's battery (B), and Kerns' battery (G), First Pennsylvania Artillery.
Infantry.—Meade's brigade: First Rifles, Pennsylvania Reserves, Fourth, Third, Seventh, Eleventh, and Second Pennsylvania Reserve Infantry. ——— brigade: Fifth, First, and Eighth Pennsylvania Reserve Infantry. ——— brigade: Tenth, Sixth, Ninth, and Twelfth Pennsylvania Reserve Infantry.

HOOKER'S DIVISION.

Cavalry.—Eight companies Third Indiana Cavalry, Lieutenant-Colonel Carter.
Artillery.— Elder's battery (E), First U. S. Artillery.
Infantry.— ——— brigade: First and Eleventh Massachusetts, Second New Hampshire, Twenty-sixth Pennsylvania, and First Michigan Volunteers. Sickles' brigade: First, Second, Third, Fourth, and Fifth Regiments Excelsior Brigade [Seventieth, Seventy-first, Seventy-second, Seventy-third, and Seventy-fourth], New York Volunteers.

BLENKER'S BRIGADE.

Cavalry.—Fourth New York Cavalry (mounted rifles), Colonel Dickel.
Artillery.—One battery.
Infantry.—Eighth and Twenty-ninth New York, Twenty-seventh and Thirty-fifth Pennsylvania Volunteers, Garibaldi Guard, and Cameron Rifles ([Thirty-ninth and Sixty-eighth] New York Volunteers).

SMITH'S DIVISION.

Cavalry.—Fifth Pennsylvania Cavalry (Cameron Dragoons), Colonel Friedman.
Artillery.—Ayres' battery (F), Fifth U. S. Artillery; Mott's Second New York Independent battery, and Barr's battery (E), First Pennsylvania Artillery.
Infantry.— ——— brigade: Second, Third, Fourth, and Fifth Vermont Volunteers. Stevens' brigade: Thirty-third and Forty-ninth New York and Sixth Maine Volunteers, and Seventy-ninth New York State Militia [Seventy-ninth Volunteers]. Hancock's brigade: Forty-seventh and Forty-ninth Pennsylvania, Forty-third New York, and Fifth Wisconsin Volunteers. Companies B and E, Berdan Sharpshooters.
Casey's Provisional Brigades.—Fifth, Sixth, and Seventh New Jersey Volunteers, Roundhead Regiment ([One hundredth] Pennsylvania Volunteers), Battalion District of Columbia Volunteers, Fortieth Pennsylvania, Eighth New Jersey, and Fourth New Hampshire Volunteers.

5. GARRISONS.

Alexandria.—Brigadier-General Montgomery, military governor. Cameron Guard ([Eighty-eighth] Pennsylvania Volunteers).
Fort Albany.—Fourteenth Massachusetts Volunteers.
Fort Richardson.—Fourth Connecticut Volunteers.
Fort Washington.—Company D, First U. S. Artillery; Companies H and I, Thirty-seventh New York Volunteers, and United States recruits unassigned.

6. DIX'S DIVISION, BALTIMORE.

Cavalry.—Company of Pennsylvania cavalry.
Artillery.—Battery I, Second U. S. Artillery, Second Massachusetts Light Battery, and a battery of New York artillery.
Infantry.—Third, Fourth, and Fifth New York, Seventeenth and Twenty-fifth Massachusetts, Twenty-first Indiana, Sixth Michigan, Fourth Wisconsin, Seventh Maine, Second Maryland Battalion, and Reading City Guard, volunteers.

[Battery E, Third U. S. Artillery, the Seventy-ninth New York State Militia, the Forty-seventh Pennsylvania Volunteers, and the Roundhead Regiment were transferred to General Sherman's expedition.]

2 R R—VOL V

On the 8th of March, 1862, the President directed, by the following order, the organization of the active portion of the Army of the Potomac into four army corps, and the formation of a fifth corps from the divisions of Banks and Shields.

The following is the text of the President's order:

PRESIDENT'S GENERAL WAR ORDER, No. 2.	EXECUTIVE MANSION, Washington, March 8, 1862.

Ordered, 1. That the major-general commanding the Army of the Potomac proceed forthwith to organize that part of the said army destined to enter upon active operations (including the reserve, but excluding the troops to be left in the fortifications about Washington) into four army corps, to be commanded according to seniority of rank, as follows:

First Corps to consist of four divisions, and to be commanded by Maj. Gen. I. McDowell.

Second Corps to consist of three divisions, and to be commanded by Brig. Gen. E. V. Sumner.

Third Corps to consist of three divisions, and to be commanded by Brig. Gen. S. P. Heintzelman.

Fourth Corps to consist of three divisions, and to be commanded by Brig. Gen. E. D. Keyes.

2. That the divisions now commanded by the officers above assigned to the commands of army corps shall be embraced in and form part of their respective corps.

3. The forces left for the defense of Washington will be placed in command of Brig. Gen. James S. Wadsworth, who shall also be military governor of the District of Columbia.

4. That this order be executed with such promptness and dispatch as not to delay the commencement of the operations already directed to be undertaken by the Army of the Potomac.

5. A fifth army corps, to be commanded by Maj. Gen. N. P. Banks, will be formed from his own and General Shields' (late General Lander's) divisions.

ABRAHAM LINCOLN.

The following order, which was made as soon as circumstances permitted, exhibits the steps taken to carry out the requirements of the President's War Order, No. 2:

GENERAL ORDERS, No. 151.	HEADQUARTERS ARMY OF THE POTOMAC, Fairfax Court-House, Va., March 13, 1862.

In compliance with the President's War Order, No. 2, of March 8, 1862, the active portion of the Army of the Potomac is formed into army corps, as follows:

First Corps, Maj. Gen. Irvin McDowell, to consist for the present of the divisions of Franklin, McCall, and King.

Second Corps, Brig. Gen. E. V. Sumner; divisions, Richardson, Blenker, and Sedgwick.

Third Corps, Brig. Gen. S. P. Heintzelman; divisions, F. J. Porter, Hooker, and Hamilton.

Fourth Corps, Brig. Gen. E. D. Keyes; divisions, Couch, Smith, and Casey.

Fifth Corps, Maj. Gen. N. P. Banks; divisions, Williams and Shields.

The cavalry regiments attached to divisions will for the present remain so. Subsequent orders will provide for these regiments, as well as for the reserve artillery, regular infantry, and regular cavalry. Arrangements will be made to unite the divisions of each army corps as promptly as possible.

The commanders of divisions will at once report in person, or, where that is impossible, by letter to the commander of their army corps.

By command of Major-General McClellan:

A. V. COLBURN,
Assistant Adjutant-General.

I add a statement of the organization and composition of the troops on April 1, commencing with the portion of the Army of the Potomac which went to the Peninsula, giving afterwards the regiments and batteries left on the Potomac and in Maryland and Virginia after April 1, 1862:

Troops of the Army of the Potomac sent to the Peninsula in March and early in April, 1862.

1st. Cavalry reserve, Brig. Gen. P. St. G. Cooke.—Emory's brigade: Fifth U. S. Cavalry; Sixth U. S. Cavalry; Sixth Pennsylvania Cavalry. Blake's brigade: First U. S. Cavalry; Eighth Pennsylvania Cavalry; Barker's squadron Illinois cavalry.

2d. Artillery reserve, Col. Henry J. Hunt: Graham's battery (K and G), First U. S., six Napoleon guns; Randol's battery (E), First U. S., six Napoleon guns; Carlisle's battery (E), Second U. S., six 20-pounder Parrott guns; Robertson's battery, Second U. S., six 3-inch ordnance guns; Benson's battery (M), Second U. S., six 3-inch ordnance guns; Tidball's battery (A), Second U. S., six 3-inch ordnance guns; Edwards' battery (L and M), Third U..S., six 10-pounder Parrott guns; Gibson's battery (C and G), Third U. S., six 3-inch ordnance guns; Livingston's battery (F and K), Third U. S., four 10-pounder Parrott guns; Howe's battery (G), Fourth U. S., six Napoleon guns; De Russy's battery (K), Fourth U. S., six Napoleon guns; Weed's battery (I), Fifth U. S., six 3-inch ordnance guns; Smead's battery (K), Fifth U. S , four Napoleon guns; Ames' battery (A), Fifth U. S., six (four 10-pounder Parrott and two Napoleon) guns; Diedrich's battery (A), New York artillery battalion, six 20-pounder Parrott guns; Voegelie's battery (B), New York artillery battalion, four 20-pounder Parrott guns; Knieriem's battery (C), New York artillery battalion, four 20-pounder Parrott guns; Grim's battery (D), New York artillery battalion, six 32-pounder howitzer guns; total, 100 guns.

3d. Volunteer engineer troops, General Woodbury: Fifteenth New York Volunteers, Fiftieth New York Volunteers. Regular engineer troops, Captain Duane: Companies A, B, and C, U. S. Engineers. Artillery troops, with siege trains: First Connecticut Heavy Artillery, Colonel Tyler.

4th. Infantry reserve (regular brigade), General Sykes: Nine companies Second U. S. Infantry, seven companies Third U. S. Infantry, ten companies Fourth U. S. Infantry, ten companies Sixth U. S. Infantry, eight companies Tenth and Seventeenth U. S. Infantry, six companies Eleventh U. S. Infantry, eight companies Twelfth U. S. Infantry, nine companies Fourteenth U. S. Infantry, and Fifth New York Volunteers, Colonel Warren.

SECOND CORPS, GENERAL SUMNER.

Cavalry.—Eighth Illinois Cavalry, Colonel Farnsworth, and one squadron Sixth New York Cavalry.

RICHARDSON'S DIVISION.

Artillery.—Clarke's battery (A and C), Fourth U. S., six Napoleon guns; Frank's battery (G), First New York, six 10-pounder Parrott guns; Pettit's battery (B), First New York, six 10-pounder Parrott guns; Hogan's battery (A), Second New York, six 10-pounder Parrott guns.

Infantry.—Howard's brigade: Fifth New Hampshire, Eighty-first Pennsylvania, and Sixty-first and Sixty-fourth New York Volunteers. Meagher's brigade: Sixty-ninth, Sixty-third, and Eighty-eighth New York Volunteers. French's brigade: Fifty-second, Fifty-seventh, and Sixty-sixth New York and Fifty-third Pennsylvania Volunteers.

SEDGWICK'S DIVISION.

Artillery.—Kirby's battery (I), First U. S., six Napoleon guns; Tompkins' battery (A), First Rhode Island, six (four 10-pounder Parrott and two 12-pounder howitzer) guns; Bartlett's battery (B), First Rhode Island, six (four 10-pounder Parrott and two 12-pounder howitzer) guns; Owen's battery (G), six 3-inch ordnance guns.

Infantry.—Gorman's brigade: Second New York State Militia, Fifteenth Massachusetts, Thirty-fourth New York, and First Minnesota Volunteers. Burns' brigade: Sixty-ninth, Seventy-first, Seventy-second, and One hundred and sixth Pennsylvania Volunteers. Dana's brigade: Nineteenth and Twentieth Massachusetts, Seventh Michigan, and Forty-second New York Volunteers.

NOTE.—Blenker's division detached, and assigned to the Mountain Department.

THIRD CORPS, GENERAL HEINTZELMAN.

Cavalry.—Third Pennsylvania Cavalry, Colonel Averell.

PORTER'S DIVISION.

Artillery.—Griffin's battery (D), Fifth U. S., six 10-pounder Parrott guns; Weeden's battery (C), Rhode Island; Martin's battery (C), Massachusetts, six Napoleon guns; Allen's battery (E), Massachusetts, six 3-inch ordnance guns.

Infantry.—Martindale's brigade: Second Maine, Eighteenth and Twenty-second Massachusetts, and Twenty-fifth and Thirteenth New York Volunteers. Morell's brigade: Fourteenth New York, Fourth Michigan, Ninth Massachusetts, and Sixty-second Pennsylvania Volunteers. Butterfield's brigade: Seventeenth, Forty-fourth, and Twelfth New York, Eighty-third Pennsylvania, and Stockton's [Sixteenth] Michigan Volunteers.
First Berdan Sharpshooters.

HOOKER'S DIVISION.

Artillery.—Hall's battery (H), First U. S., six (four 10-pounder Parrott and two 12-pounder howitzer) guns; Smith's battery, Fourth New York, six 10-pounder Parrott guns; Bramhall's battery, Sixth New York, six 3-inch ordnance guns; Osborn's battery (D), First New York Artillery, four 3-inch ordnance guns.
Infantry.—Sickles' brigade: First, Second, Third, Fourth, and Fifth Excelsior, New York. Naglee's brigade: First and Eleventh Massachusetts, Twenty-sixth Pennsylvania, and Second New Hampshire Volunteers. Colonel Starr's brigade: Fifth, Sixth, Seventh, and Eighth New Jersey Volunteers.

HAMILTON'S DIVISION.

Artillery.—Thompson's battery (G), Second U. S., six Napoleon guns; Beam's battery (B), New Jersey, six (four 10-pounder Parrott and two Napoleon) guns; Randolph's battery (E), Rhode Island, six (four 10-pounder Parrott and two Napoleon) guns.
Infantry.—Jameson's brigade: One hundred and fifth, Sixty-third, and Fifty-seventh Pennsylvania and Eighty-seventh New York Volunteers. Birney's brigade: Thirty-eighth and Fortieth New York and Third and Fourth Maine Volunteers. —— brigade: Second, Third, and Fifth Michigan and Thirty-seventh New York Volunteers.

FOURTH CORPS, GENERAL KEYES.

COUCH'S DIVISION,

Artillery.—McCarthy's battery (C), First Pennsylvania, four 10-pounder Parrott guns; Flood's battery (D), First Pennsylvania, four 10-pounder Parrott guns; Miller's battery (E), First Pennsylvania, four Napoleon guns; Brady's battery (F), First Pennsylvania, four 10-pounder Parrott guns.
Infantry.—Graham's brigade: Sixty-seventh (First Long Island) and Sixty-fifth (First U. S. Chasseurs) New York, and Twenty-third, Thirty-first, and Sixty-first Pennsylvania Volunteers. Peck's brigade: Ninety-eighth, One hundred and second, and Ninety-third Pennsylvania, and Sixty-second and Fifty-fifth New York Volunteers. —— brigade: Second Rhode Island, Seventh and Tenth Massachusetts, and Thirty-sixth New York Volunteers.

SMITH'S DIVISION.

Artillery.—Ayres' battery (F), Fifth U. S., six (four 10-pounder Parrott and two Napoleon) guns; Mott's battery, Third New York, six (four 10-pounder Parrott and two Napoleon) guns; Wheeler's battery (E), First New York, four 3-inch ordnance guns; Kennedy's battery, First New York, six 3-inch ordnance guns.
Infantry.—Hancock's brigade: Fifth Wisconsin, Forty-ninth Pennsylvania, forty-third New York, and Sixth Maine Volunteers. Brooks' brigade: Second, Third, Fourth, Fifth, and Sixth Vermont Volunteers. Davidson's brigade: Thirty-third, Seventy-seventh, and Forty-ninth New York and Seventh Maine Volunteers.

CASEY'S DIVISION.

Artillery.—Regan's battery, Seventh New York, six 3-inch ordnance guns: Fitch's battery, Eighth New York, six 3-inch ordnance guns; Bates' battery (A), First New York, six Napoleon guns; Spratt's battery (H), First New York, four 3-inch ordnance guns.
Infantry.—Keim's brigade: Eighty-fifth, One hundred and first, and One hundred and third Pennsylvania and Ninety-sixth New York Volunteers. Palmer's brigade: Eighty-fifth, Ninety-eighth, Ninety-second, Eighty-first, and Ninety-third New York Volunteers. —— brigade: One hundred and fourth and Fifty-second Pennsylvania, Fifty-sixth and One hundredth New York, and Eleventh Maine Volunteers.

5th. Provost guard: Second U. S. Cavalry; battalions Eighth and Seventeenth U. S. Infantry.

At general headquarters: Two companies Fourth U. S. cavalry, one company Onedia cavalry (New York volunteers), and one company Sturges' rifles (Illinois volunteers).

The following troops of the Army of the Potomac were left behind or detached on and in front of the Potomac for the defense of that line April 1, 1862. Franklin's and McCall's divisions, at subsequent and different dates, joined the active portion of the army on the Peninsula. Two brigades of Shields' division joined at Harrison's Landing:

FIRST CORPS, GENERAL McDOWELL.

Cavalry.—First, Second, and Fourth New York, and First Pennsylvania.
Sharpshooters.—Second Regiment Berdan Sharpshooters.

FRANKLIN'S DIVISION.

Artillery.—Platt's battery (D), Second U. S., six Napoleon guns; Porter's battery (A), Massachusetts, six (four 10-pounder Parrott and two 12-pounder howitzer) guns; Hexamer's battery (A), New Jersey, six (four 10-pounder Parrott and two 12-pounder howitzer) guns; Wilson's battery (F), First New York Artillery, four 3-inch ordnance guns.
Infantry.—Kearny's brigade: First, Second, Third, and Fourth New Jersey Volunteers. Slocum's brigade: Sixteenth and Twenty-seventh New York, Fifth Maine, and Ninety-sixth Pennsylvania Volunteers. Newton's brigade: Eighteenth, Thirty-first, and Thirty-second New York, and Ninety-fifth Pennsylvania Volunteers.

M'CALL'S DIVISION.

Artillery.—Seymour's battery (C), Fifth U. S., six Napoleon guns; Easton's battery (A), First Pennsylvania, four Napoleon guns; Cooper's battery (B), First Pennsylvania, six 10-pounder Parrott guns; Kerns' battery (G), First Pennsylvania, six (two 10-pounder and four 12-pounder) Parrott guns.
Infantry.—Reynolds' brigade: First, Second, Fifth, and Eighth Pennsylvania Reserve Regiments. Meade's brigade: Third, Fourth, Seventh, and Eleventh Pennsylvania Reserve Regiments. Ord's brigade: Sixth, Ninth, Tenth, and Twelfth Pennsylvania Reserve Regiments. First Pennsylvania Reserve Rifles.

KING'S DIVISION.

Artillery.—Gibbon's battery (B), Fourth U. S., six Napoleon guns; Monroe's battery (D), First Rhode Island, six 10-pounder Parrott guns; Gerrish's battery (A), New Hampshire, six Napoleon guns; Durell's battery, Pennsylvania, six 10-pounder Parrott guns.
Infantry.— —— brigade: Second, Sixth, and Seventh Wisconsin, and Nineteenth Indiana Volunteers. Patrick's brigade: Twentieth, Twenty-first, Twenty-Third, and Twenty-fifth New York State Militia. Augur's brigade: Fourteenth New York State Militia [Eighty-fourth Volunteers], and Twenty-second, Twenty-fourth, and Thirtieth New York Volunteers.

FIFTH CORPS, GENERAL BANKS.

Cavalry.—First Maine, First Vermont, First Michigan, First Rhode Island, Fifth and Eighth New York, Keys' battalion of Pennsylvania, eighteen companies of Maryland, one squadron of Virginia.
Unattached.—Twenty-eighth Pennsylvania Volunteers and Fourth Regiment Potomac Home Brigade (Maryland Volunteers).

WILLIAMS' DIVISION.

Artillery.—Best's battery (F), Fourth U. S., six Napoleon guns; Hampton's battery, Maryland, four 10-pounder Parrott guns; Thompson's battery, Maryland, four 10-pounder Parrott guns; Matthews' battery (F), Pennsylvania, six 3-inch ordnance guns; Cothran's battery (M), First New York, six 10-pounder Parrott guns; Knap's battery, Pennsylvania, six 10-pounder Parrott guns; McMahon's battery, New York, six 3-inch ordnance guns.

Infantry.—Abercrombie's brigade: Twelfth and Second Massachusetts, and Sixteenth Indiana, First Potomac Home Brigade (Maryland), one company Zouaves d'Afrique (Pennsylvania) Volunteers. —— brigade: Ninth New York State Militia, [Eighty-third Volunteers], and Twenty-ninth Pennsylvania, Twenty-seventh Indiana, and Third Wisconsin Volunteers. —— brigade: Twenty-eighth New York, Fifth Connecticut, Forty-sixth Pennsylvania, First Maryland, Twelfth Indiana, and Thirteenth Massachusetts Volunteers.

SHIELDS' DIVISION.

Artillery.—Clark's battery (E), Fourth U. S., six 10-pounder Parrott guns; Jenks' battery (A), First Virginia, four 10-pounder Parrott and two 6-pounder guns; Davey's battery (B), First Virginia, two 10-pounder Parrott guns; Huntington's battery (A), First Ohio, six 13-pounder James guns; Robinson's battery (L), First Ohio, two 12-pounder howitzers and four 6-pounder guns, and —— battery, Fourth Ohio Artillery.

Infantry.— —— brigade: Fourteenth Indiana, Fourth, Eighth, and Sixty-seventh Ohio, Seventh Virginia, and Eighty-fourth Pennsylvania Volunteers. —— brigade: Fifth, Sixty-second, and Sixty-sixth Ohio, Thirteenth Indiana, and Thirty-ninth Illinois Volunteers. —— brigade: Seventh and Twenty-ninth Ohio, Seventh Indiana, First Virginia, and One hundred and tenth Pennsylvania Volunteers. Andrew S. S.

GENERAL WADSWORTH'S COMMAND.

Cavalry.—First New Jersey Cavalry at Alexandria, and Fourth Pennsylvania Cavalry east of the Capitol.

Artillery and Infantry.—Tenth New Jersey Volunteers, Bladensburg road; One hundred and fourth New York Volunteers, Kalorama Heights; First Wisconsin Heavy Artillery, Fort Cass, Virginia; three batteries of New York artillery, Forts Ethan Allen and Marcy; depot of New York Light Artillery, Camp Barry; Second District of Columbia Volunteers, Washington City; Twenty-sixth Pennsylvania Volunteers, G-street wharf; Twenty-sixth New York Volunteers, Fort Lyon; Ninety-fifth New York Volunteers, Camp Thomas; Ninety-fourth New York and detachment of Eighty-eighth Pennsylvania Volunteers, Alexandria; Ninety-first Pennsylvania Volunteers, Franklin Square Barracks; Fourth New York Artillery, Forts Carroll and Greble; One hundred and twelfth Pennsylvania Volunteers, Fort Saratoga; Seventy-sixth New York Volunteers, Fort Massachusetts; Fifty-ninth New York Volunteers, Fort Pennsylvania; detachment of Eighty-eighth Pennsylvania Volunteers, Fort Good Hope; Ninety-ninth Pennsylvania Volunteers, Fort Mahon; Second New York Light Artillery, Forts Ward, Worth, and Blenker; One hundred and seventh and Fifty-fourth Pennsylvania Volunteers, Kendall Green; Dickenson's Light Artillery, Eighty-sixth New York, and detachment of Eighty-eighth Pennsylvania Volunteers, east of the Capitol; Fourteenth Massachusetts (Volunteers) Heavy Artillery and Fifty-sixth Pennsylvania Volunteers, Forts Albany, Tillinghast, Richardson, Runyon, Jackson, Barnard, Craig, and Scott; detachments of Fourth U. S. Artillery and Thirty-seventh New York Volunteers, Fort Washington; Ninety-seventh, One hundred and first, and Ninety-first New York, and Twelfth Virginia Volunteers, Fort Corcoran.

In camp near Washington.—Sixth and Tenth New York, Swain's New York, and Second Pennsylvania Cavalry, all dismounted.

These troops (3,359 men) were ordered to report to Colonel Miles, commanding the railroad guard, to relieve 3,306 older troops ordered to be sent to Manassas to report to General Abercrombie.

GENERAL DIX'S COMMAND, BALTIMORE.

Cavalry.—First Maryland Cavalry and detachment of Purnell Legion Cavalry.

Artillery.—Battery I, Second U. S.; battery —, Maryland; battery L, First New York, and two independent batteries of Pennsylvania artillery.

Infantry.—Third, and Fourth New York, Eleventh, Eighty-seventh, and One hundred and eleventh Pennsylvania, detachment Twenty-first Massachusetts, Second Delaware, Second Maryland, First and Second Eastern Shore (Maryland) Home Guards, and Purnell Legion (two battalions) Maryland Volunteers.

In a staff charged with labors so various and important as that of the Army of the Potomac, a chief was indispensable to supervise the various departments and to relieve the commanding general of details. The office of chief of staff, well known in European armies, had not been considered necessary in our small peace establishment. The functions of the office were not defined, and so far as exercised had been included in the Adjutant-General's Department. The small number of officers in this department, and the necessity for their employment in other duties, have obliged commanding generals during this war to resort to other branches of the service to furnish suitable chiefs of staff.

On the 4th of September, 1861, I appointed Col. R. B. Marcy, of the Inspector-General's Department, chief of staff, and he entered upon service immediately, discharging the various and important duties with great fidelity, industry, and ability from this period until I was removed from command at Rectortown. Many improvements have been made during the war in our system of staff administration, but much remains to be done.

Our own experience and that of other armies agree in determining the necessity for an efficient and able staff. To obtain this, our staff establishment should be based on correct principles, and extended to be adequate to the necessities of the service, and should include a system of staff and line education.

The affairs of the Adjutant-General's Department, while I commanded the Army of the Potomac, were conducted by Brig. Gen. S. Williams, assisted by Lieut. Col. James A. Hardie, aide-de-camp. Their management of the department during the organization of the Army in the fall and winter of 1861 and during its subsequent operations in the field, was excellent. They were during the entire period assisted by Capt. Richard B. Irwin, aide-de-camp, and during the organization of the Army by the following-named officers : Capts. Joseph Kirkland, Arthur McClellan, M. T. McMahon, William P. Mason, and William F. Biddle, aides-de-camp.

My personal staff, when we embarked for the Peninsula, consisted of Col. Thomas M. Key, additional aide-de-camp; Col. E. H. Wright, additional aide-de-camp and major Sixth U. S. Cavalry; Col. T. T. Gantt, additional aide-de-camp; Col. J. J. Astor, jr., volunteer aide-de-camp; Lieut. Col. A. V. Colburn, additional aide-de-camp, and captain Adjutant-General's Department; Lieut. Col. N. B. Sweitzer, additional aide-de-camp, and captain First U. S. Cavalry; Lieut. Col. Edward McK. Hudson, additional aide-de camp, and captain Fourteenth U. S. Infantry; Lieut. Col. Paul Von Radowitz, additional aide-de-camp; Maj. H. von Hammerstein, additional aide-de-camp; Maj. W. W. Russell, U. S. Marine Corps ; Maj. F. LeCompte, of the Swiss Army, volunteer aide-de-camp; Capts. George A. Custer, Joseph Kirkland, Arthur McClellan, L. P. D'Orleans, R. D'Orleans, M. T. McMahon, William P. Mason, jr., William F. Biddle, and E. A. Raymond, additional ades-de-camp.

To this number I am tempted to add the Prince de Joinville, who constantly accompanied me through the trying campaign of the Peninsula, and frequently rendered important services. Of these officers Captain McMahon was assigned to the personal staff of Brigadier-General Franklin, and Captains Kirkland and Mason to that of Brig. Gen. F. J. Porter during the siege of Yorktown. They remained subsequently with those general officers. Major LeCompte left the Army during the siege of Yorktown ; Colonels Gantt and Astor, Maj. Russell, Capts. L. P. D'Orleans, R. D'Orleans, and Raymond, at the close of the Peninsular campaign. Before its termination Capts. W. S. Abert and Charles R. Lowell, of the Sixth U. S. Cavalry, joined my staff as aides-de-camp, and remained with me until I was relieved from the command of the Army of the Potomac. All of these officers served me with great gallantry and devotion; they were ever ready to execute any service, no matter how dangerous, difficult, or fatiguing.

INSPECTOR-GENERAL'S DEPARTMENT.

The highly important duties of this department were performed by Col. D. B. Sacket and Maj. N. H. Davis to my entire satisfaction. They introduced many valuable changes in the system of inspections and in the forms of reports, and so systematized the labors of the inspectors of corps and divisions that excellent results were obtained. The intelligent and energetic performance of their duties by these officers enabled me to keep myself well informed of the condition of the troops and to correct evils promptly.

ENGINEERS.

When I assumed command of the Army of the Potomac I found Maj. J. G. Barnard, U. S. Engineers, subsequently brigadier-general of volunteers, occupying the position of chief engineer of that army. I continued him in the same office, and at once gave the necessary instructions for the completion of the defenses of the capital, and for the entire reorganization of the department. Under his direction the entire system of defenses was carried into execution. This was completed before the army departed for Fort Monroe, and is a sufficient evidence of the skill of the engineers and the diligent labor of the troops.

For some months after the organization of the Army of the Potomac was commenced there were no engineer troops with it. At length, however, three companies were assigned. Under the skillful management of Capt. J. C. Duane, U. S. Engineers, these new companies rapidly became efficient, and, as will be seen, rendered most valuable service during the ensuing campaigns.

The number of engineer troops being entirely inadequate to the necessities of the army, an effort was made to partially remedy this defect by detailing the Fifteenth and Fiftieth New York Volunteers, which contained many sailors and mechanics, as engineer troops. They were first placed under the immediate superintendence of Lieut. Col. B. S. Alexander, U. S. Engineers, by whom they were instructed in the duties of pontoniers, and became somewhat familiar with those of sappers and miners. Previous to the movement of the army for the Peninsula this brigade was placed under the command of Brig. Gen. D. P. Woodbury, major U. S. Engineers.

The labor of preparing the engineer and bridge trains devolved chiefly upon Captain Duane, who was instructed to procure the new model French bridge train, as I was satisfied that the India-rubber pontoon was entirely useless for the general purposes of a campaign.

The engineer department presented the following complete organization when the army moved for the Peninsula:

Brig. Gen. J. G. Barnard, chief engineer; First Lieut. H. L. Abbot, Topographical Engineers, aide-de-camp. Brigade volunteer engineers, Brigadier-General Woodbury commanding; Fifteenth New York Volunteers, Col. J. McLeod Murphy; Fiftieth New York Volunteers, Col. C. B. Stuart. Battalion three companies U. S. Engineers, Capt. J. C. Duane commanding; companies respectively commanded by First Lieuts. C. B. Reese, C. E. Cross, and O. E. Babcock, U. S. Engineers. The chief engineer was ably assisted in his duties by Lieut. Col. B. S. Alexander, and First Lieuts. C. B. Comstock, M. D. McAlester, and Merrill, U. S.

Engineers. Capt. C. S. Stewart and Second Lieut. F. U. Farquhar, U. S. Engineers, joined after the army arrived at Fort Monroe.

The necessary bridge equipage for the operations of a large army had been collected, consisting of bateaux with the anchors and flooring material (French model), trestles, and engineer's tools, with the necessary wagons for their transportation.

The small number of officers of this corps available rendered it impracticable to detail engineers permanently at the headquarters of corps and divisions. The companies of regular engineers never had their proper number of officers, and it was necessary, as a rule, to follow the principle of detailing engineer officers temporarily whenever their services were required.

TOPOGRAPHICAL ENGINEERS.

To the corps of topographical engineers was intrusted the collection of topographical information and the preparation of campaign maps. Until a short time previous to the departure of the army for Fort Monroe Lieut. Col. John N. Macomb was in charge of this department, and prepared a large amount of valuable material. He was succeeded by Brig. Gen. A. A. Humphreys, who retained the position throughout the Peninsula campaign. These officers were assisted by Lieuts. H. L. Abbot, O. G. Wagner, N. Bowen, John M. Wilson, and James H. Wilson, Topographical Engineers. This number, being the greatest available, was so small that much of the duty of the department devolved upon parties furnished by Professor Bache, Superintendent of the Coast Survey, and other gentlemen from civil life.

Owing to the entire absence of reliable topographical maps the labors of this corps were difficult and arduous in the extreme. Notwithstanding the energy and ability displayed by General Humphreys, Lieutenant-Colonel Macomb, and their subordinates, who frequently obtained the necessary information under fire, the movements of the army were sometimes unavoidably delayed by the difficulty of obtaining knowledge of the country in advance. The result of their labors has been the preparation of an excellent series of maps, which will be invaluable to any army traversing the same ground.

During the campaign it was impossible to draw a distinct line of demarkation between the duties of the two corps of engineers, so that the labors of reconnaissance of roads, of lines of intrenchments, of fields for battle, and of the position of the enemy, as well as the construction of siege and defensive works, were habitually performed by details from either corps, as the convenience of the service demanded.

I desire to express my high appreciation of the skill, gallantry, and devotion displayed by the officers of both corps of engineers, under the most trying circumstances.

During the Maryland campaign I united the two corps under Capt. J. C. Duane, U. S. Engineers, and found great advantages from the arrangement.

MEDICAL DEPARTMENT.

For the operations of the medical department I refer to the reports, transmitted herewith, of Surg. Charles S. Tripler and Surg. Jonathan Letterman, who, in turn, performed the duties of medical director of the Army of the Potomac, the former from August 12, 1861, until July 1, 1862, and the latter after that date. The difficulties to be overcome in organizing and making effective the medical department were very great, arising principally from the inexperience of the regimental medical officers, many of whom were physicians taken suddenly from civil life, who, according to Surgeon Tripler, "had to be instructed in their duties from the very alphabet," and from the ignorance of the line officers as to their relations with the medical officers, which gave rise to confusion and conflict of authority. Boards of examination were instituted, by which many ignorant officers were removed, and by the successive exertions of Surgeons Tripler and Letterman the medical corps was brought to a very high degree of efficiency. With regard to the sanitary condition of the army while on the Potomac, Dr. Tripler says that the records show a constantly increasing immunity from disease. "In October and November, 1861, with an army averaging 130,000 men, we had 7,932 cases of fever of all sorts. Of these about 1,000 were reported as cases of typhoid fever. I know that errors of diagnosis were frequently committed, and therefore this must be considered as the limit of typhoid cases. If any army in the world can show such a record as this, I do not know when or where it was assembled." From September, 1861, to February, 1862, while the army was increasing, the number of sick decreased from 7 per cent. to 6.18 per cent. Of these the men sick in the regimental and general hospitals were less than one-half; the remainder were slight cases, under treatment in quarters. "During this time, so far as rumor was concerned, the army was being decimated by disease every month." Of the sanitary condition of the army during the Peninsular campaign, up to its arrival at Harrison's Landing, Dr. Tripler says:

During this campaign the army was favored with excellent health. No epidemic disease appeared. Those scourges of modern armies—dysentery, typhus, cholera—were almost unknown. We had some typhoid fever and more malarial fevers, but even these never prevailed to such an extent as to create any alarm. The sick reports were sometimes larger than we cared to have them, but the great majority of the cases reported were such as did not threaten life or permanent disability. I regret that I have not before me the retained copies of the monthly reports, so that I might give accurate statistics. I have endeavored to recover them, but have been unsuccessful. My recollection is that the whole sick report never exceeded 8 per cent. of the force, and this including all sorts of cases, the trivial as well as the severe. The Army of the Potomac must be conceded to have been the most healthy army in the service of the United States.

His remarks at the conclusion of his report upon our system of medical administration and his suggestions for its improvement are especially worthy of attention.

The service, labors, and privations of the troops during the seven days' battles had of course a great effect on the health of the army after it reached Harrison's Landing, increasing the number of sick to about 20 per cent. of the whole force. The nature of the military operations had also unavoidably placed the medical department in a very unsatisfactory condition. Supplies had been almost entirely exhausted or necessarily abandoned, hospital tents abandoned or destroyed, and the medical officers deficient in numbers and broken down by fatigue. All the remarkable energy and ability of Surgeon Letterman were required to restore the efficiency of his department, but before we left Harrison's Landing he had succeeded in fitting it out thoroughly with the supplies it required, and the health of the army was vastly improved by the sanitary measures which were enforced at his suggestion.

The great haste with which the army was removed from the Peninsula made it necessary to leave at Fort Monroe, to be forwarded afterwards, nearly all the baggage and transportation, including medical stores and ambulances, all the vessels being required to transport the troops themselves and their ammunition; and when the Army of the Potomac returned to Washington after General Pope's campaign, and the medical department came once more under Surgeon Letterman's control, he found it in a deplorable condition. The officers were worn-out by the labors they had performed, and the few supplies that had been brought from the Peninsula had been exhausted or abandoned, so that the work of reorganization and resupplying had to be again performed, and this while the army was moving rapidly, and almost in the face of the enemy. That it was successfully accomplished is shown by the care and attention which the wounded received after the battles of South Mountain and Antietam.

Among the improvements introduced into his department by Surgeon Letterman, the principal are the organization of an ambulance corps, the system of field hospitals, and the method of supplying by brigades, all of which were instituted during the Maryland campaign, and have since proved very efficient.

QUARTERMASTER'S DEPARTMENT.

On assuming command of the troops in and around Washington I appointed Capt. S. Van Vliet, assistant quartermaster (afterwards brigadier-general), chief quartermaster to my command, and gave him the necessary instructions for organizing his department and collecting the supplies requisite for the large army then called for.

The disaster at Manassas had but recently occurred, and the army was quite destitute of quartermaster's stores. General Van Vliet with great energy and zeal set himself about the task of furnishing the supplies immediately necessary, and preparing to obtain the still larger amounts which would be required by the new troops, which were moving in large numbers towards the capital. The principal depot for supplies in the city of Washington was under charge of Col. D. H. Rucker, assistant quartermaster, who ably performed his duties. Lieut. Col. R. Ingalls, assistant quartermaster, was placed in charge of the department on the south side of the Potomac. I directed a large depot for transportation to be established at Perryville, on the left bank of the Susquehanna, a point equally accessible by rail and water. Capt. C. G. Sawtelle, assistant quartermaster, was detailed to organize the camp, and performed his duties to my entire satisfaction. Capt. J. J. Dana, assistant quartermaster, had immediate charge of the transportation in and about Washington, as well as of the large number of horses purchased for the use of the artillery and cavalry. The principal difficulties which General Van Vliet had to encounter arose from the inexperience of the majority of the officers of his department in the new regiments and brigades. The necessity of attending personally to minor details rendered his duties arduous and harassing in the extreme. All obstacles, however, were surmounted by the untiring industry of the chief quartermaster and his immediate subordinates, and when the army was prepared to move, the organization of the department was found to be admirable.

When it was determined to move the army to the Peninsula, the duties of providing water transportation were devolved by the Secretary of War upon his assistant, the Hon. John Tucker. The vessels were ordered to Alexandria, and Lieutenant-Colonel Ingalls was placed in immediate charge of the embarkation of the troops, transportation, and material of every description. Operations of this nature on so extensive a scale had no parallel in the history of our country.

The arrangements of Lieutenant-Colonel Ingalls were perfected with remarkable skill and energy, and the army and its material were embarked and transported to Fort Monroe in a very short space of time and entirely without loss.

During the operations on the Peninsula, until the arrival of troops at Harrison's Landing, General Van Vliet retained the position of chief quartermaster, and maintained the thorough organization and efficiency of his department. The principal depots of supplies were under the immediate charge of Lieutenant-Colonels Ingalls and Sawtelle.

On the 10th of July, 1862, General Van Vliet having requested to be relieved from duty with the Army of the Potomac, I appointed Lieutenant-Colonel Ingalls chief quartermaster, and he continued to discharge the duties of that office during the remainder of the Peninsula and the Maryland campaigns in a manner which fully sustained the high reputation he had previously acquired.

The immense amount of labor accomplished, often under the most difficult circumstances, the admirable system under which the duties of the department were performed, and the entire success which attended the efforts to supply so large an army, reflect the highest credit upon the officers upon whom these onerous duties devolved. The reports of General Van Vliet and Lieutenant-Colonel Ingalls, with the accompanying documents, give in detail the history of the department from its organization until I was relieved from the command of the Army of the Potomac.

SUBSISTENCE DEPARTMENT.

On the 1st of August, 1861, Col. H. F. Clarke, commissary of subsistence, joined my staff, and at once entered upon his duties as chief commissary of the Army of the Potomac. In order to realize the responsibilities pertaining to this office, as well as to form a proper estimate of the vast amount of labor which must necessarily devolve upon its occupant, it is only necessary to consider the unprepared state of the country to engage in a war of such magnitude as the present, and the lack of practical knowledge on the part of the officers with reference to supplying and subsisting a large and at that time unorganized army. Yet notwithstanding the existence of these great obstacles, the manner in which the duties of the commissary department were discharged was such as to merit and call forth the commendation of the entire army.

During the stay of the Army of the Potomac in the vicinity of Washington, prior to the Peninsular campaign, its subsistence was drawn chiefly from the depots which had been established by the Commissary Department at Washington, Alexandria, Forts Corcoran and Runyon. In the important task of designating and establishing depots of supplies Colonel Clarke was ably seconded by his assistants, Col. Amos Beckwith, commissary of subsistence, U. S. Army; Lieut. Col. George Bell, commissary of subsistence, U. S. Army; Lieut. Col. A. P. Porter, commissary of subsistence, U. S. Army; Capt. Thomas Wilson, commissary of subsistence, U. S. Army; Capt. Brownell Granger, commissary of subsistence, U. S. Volunteers; Capt. W. H. Bell, commissary of subsistence, U. S. Army; Capt. J. H. Woodward, commissary of subsistence, U. S. Volunteers; and Capt. W. R. Murphy, commissary of subsistence, U. S. Volunteers.

For a full knowledge of the highly creditable manner in which each and all of the above-mentioned officers discharged their duties I invite attention to the detailed report of Colonel Clarke. The remarks and suggestions contained in his report are worthy of attention, as affording valuable rules for the future guidance of the Subsistence Department in supplying armies in the field. The success of the subsistence department of the Army of the Potomac was in a great measure attributable to the fact that the Subsistence Department at Washington made ample provision for sending supplies to the Peninsula, and that it always exercised the most intelligent foresight. It moreover gave its advice and countenance to the officers charged with its duties and reputation in the field, and those officers, I am happy to say, worked with it and together in perfect harmony for the public good. During the entire period that I was in command of the Army of the Potomac there was no instance within my knowledge where the troops were without their rations from any fault of the officers of this department.

ORDNANCE DEPARTMENT.

This very important branch of the service was placed under the charge of Capt. C. P. Kingsbury, Ordnance Corps, colonel and aide-de-camp. Great difficulty existed in the proper organization of the department for the want of a sufficient number of suitable officers to perform the duties at the various headquarters and depots of supply. But far greater obstacles had to be surmounted, from the fact that the supply of small-arms was totally inadequate to the demands of a large army, and a vast proportion of those furnished were of such inferior quality as to be unsatisfactory to the troops and condemned by their officers. The supply of artillery was more abundant, but of great variety. Rifled ordnance was just coming into use for the first time in this country, and the description of gun and kind of projectile which would prove most effective, and should therefore be adopted, was a mere matter of theory. To obviate these difficulties, large quantities of small-arms of foreign manufacture were contracted for; private enterprise in the construction of arms and ammunition was encouraged, and by the time the army was ordered to move to the Peninsula the amount of ordnance and ordnance stores was ample. Much also had been done to bring the quality both of arms and ammunition up to the proper standard. Boards of officers were in session continually during the autumn and winter of 1861 to test the relative merits of new arms and projectiles.

The reports of these boards, confirmed by subsequent experience in the field, have done much to establish the respective claims of different inventors and manufacturers. During the campaigns of the Peninsula and Maryland the officers connected with the department were zealous and energetic and kept the troops well supplied, notwithstanding the perplexing and arduous nature of their duties. One great source of perplexity was the fact that it had been necessary to issue arms of all varieties and calibers, giving an equal diversity in the kinds of ammunition required. Untiring watchfulness was therefore incumbent upon the officers in charge to prevent confusion and improper distribution of cartridges. Colonel Kingsbury discharged the duties of his office with great efficiency until the — day of July, 1862, when his health required that he should be relieved. First Lieut. Thomas G. Baylor, Ordnance Corps, succeeded him, and performed his duty during the remainder of the Peninsular and Maryland campaigns with marked ability and success.

The want of reports from Colonel Kingsbury and Lieutenant Baylor renders it impossible for me to enter at all into the details of the organization of the department.

PROVOST-MARSHAL'S DEPARTMENT.

Immediately after I was placed in command of the Division of the Potomac, I appointed Col. Andrew Porter, Sixteenth U. S. Infantry, provost-marshal of Washington. All the available regular infantry, a battery, and a squadron of cavalry were placed under his command, and by his energetic action he soon corrected the serious evils which existed and restored order in the city.

When the army was about to take the field General Porter was appointed provost-marshal-general of the Army of the Potomac, and held that most important position until the end of the Peninsular campaign, when sickness, contracted in the untiring discharge of his duties, compelled him to ask to be relieved from the position he had so ably and energetically filled.

The provost-marshal-general's department had the charge of a class of duties which had not before in our service been defined and grouped under the management of a special department. The following subjects indicate the sphere of this department:

Suppression of marauding and depredations, and of all brawls and disturbances, preservation of good order, and suppression of disturbances beyond the limits of the camps.
Prevention of straggling on the march.
Suppression of gambling-houses, drinking-houses, or bar-rooms, and brothels.
Regulation of hotels, taverns, markets, and places of public amusement.
Searches, seizures, and arrests. Execution of sentences of general courts-martial involving imprisonment or capital punishment. Enforcement of orders prohibiting the sale of intoxicating liquors, whether by tradesmen or sutlers, and of orders respecting passes.
Deserters from the enemy.
Prisoners of war taken from the enemy.
Countersigning safeguards.
Passes to citizens within the lines and for purposes of trade.
Complaints of citizens as to the conduct of the soldiers.

General Porter was assisted by the following-named officers:
Maj. W. H. Wood, Seventeenth U. S. Infantry; Capt. James McMillan, acting assistant adjutant-general, Seventeenth U. S. Infantry; Capt. W. T. Gentry, Seventeenth U. S. Infantry; Capt. J. W. Forsyth, Eighteenth U. S. Infantry; Lieut. J. W. Jones, Twelfth U. S. Infantry; Lieut. C. F. Trowbridge, Sixteenth U. S. Infantry; and Lieut. C. D. Mehaffey, First U. S. Infantry.

The provost guard was composed of the Second U. S. Cavalry, Major Pleasonton, and a battalion of the Eighth and Seventeenth U. S. Infantry, Major Willard. After General Porter was relieved Major Wood was in charge of this department until after the battle of Antietam, when Brigadier-General Patrick was appointed provost-marshal-general.

COMMANDANT OF GENERAL HEADQUARTERS.

When the army took the field, for the purpose of securing order and regularity in the camp of headquarters and facilitating its movements, the office of commandant of general headquarters was created, and assigned to Maj. G. O. Haller, Seventh U. S. Infantry. Six companies of infantry were placed under his orders for guard and police duty. Among the orders appended to this report is the one defining his duties, which were always satisfactorily performed.

JUDGE-ADVOCATE.

From August, 1861, the position of judge-advocate was held by Col.

Thomas T. Gantt, aide-de-camp, until compelled by ill-health to retire, at Harrison's Landing, in August, 1862. His reviews of the decisions of courts-martial during this period were of great utility in correcting the practice in military courts, diffusing true notions of discipline and subordination, and setting before the army a high standard of soldierly honor. Upon the retirement of Colonel Gantt the duties of judge-advocate were ably performed by Col. Thomas M. Key, aide-de-camp.

SIGNAL CORPS.

The method of conveying intelligence and orders, invented and introduced into the service by Maj. Albert J. Myer, Signal Officer, U. S. Army, was first practically tested in large operations during the organization of the Army of the Potomac.

Under the direction of Major Myer a Signal Corps was formed by detailing officers and men from the different regiments of volunteers and instructing them in the use of the flags by day and torches by night.

The Chief Signal Officer was indefatigable in his exertions to render his corps effective, and it soon became available for service in every division of the army. In addition to the flags and torches, Major Myer introduced a portable insulated telegraph wire, which could be readily laid from point to point, and which could be used under the same general system. In front of Washington, and on the Lower Potomac, at any point within our lines not reached by the military telegraph, the great usefulness of this system of signals was made manifest. But it was not until after the arrival of the army upon the Peninsula, and during the siege and battles of that and the Maryland campaigns, that the great benefits to be derived from it on the field and under fire were fully appreciated.

There was scarcely any action or skirmish in which the Signal Corps did not render important services. Often under heavy fire of artillery, and not unfrequently while exposed to musketry the officers and men of this corps gave information of the movements of the enemy and transmitted directions for the evolutions of our own troops. The report of the Chief Signal Officer, with accompanying documents, will give the details of the services of this corps, and call attention to those members of it who were particularly distinguished.

TELEGRAPHIC.

The telegraphic operations of the Army of the Potomac were superintended by Maj. Thomas T. Eckert, and under the immediate direction of Mr. ——— Caldwell, who was, with a corps of operators, attached to my headquarters during the entire campaigns upon the Peninsula and in Maryland. The services of this corps were arduous and efficient. Under the admirable arrangements of Major Eckert they were constantly provided with all the material for constructing new lines, which were rapidly established whenever the army changed position, and it was not unfrequently the case that the operatives worked under fire from the enemy's guns, yet they invariably performed all the duties required of them with great alacrity and cheerfulness, and it was seldom that I was without the means of direct telegraphic communication with the War Department and with the corps commanders. From the organization of the Army of the Potomac up to November 1, 1862, including the Peninsular and Maryland campaigns, upwards of 1,200 miles of military telegraph line had been constructed in connection with the operations of the army, and the number of operatives and builders employed was about 200.

To Professor Lowe, the intelligent and enterprising æronaut, who had the management of the balloons, I was greatly indebted for the valuable information obtained during his ascensions.

I have more than once taken occasion to recommend the members of my staff, both general and personal, for promotion and reward. I beg leave to repeat these recommendations, and to record their names in the history of the Army of the Potomac as gallant soldiers, to whom their country owes a debt of gratitude, still unpaid, for the courage, ability, and untiring zeal they displayed during the eventful campaigns in which they bore so prominent a part.

CHAPTER II.

On the 15th of October the main body of the Army of the Potomac was in the immediate vicinity of Washington, with detachments on the left bank of the Potomac as far down as Liverpool Point and as far up as Williamsport and its vicinity. The different divisions were posted as follows: Hooker at Budd's Ferry, Lower Potomac; Heintzelman at Fort Lyon and vicinity; Franklin near the Theological Seminary; Blenker near Hunter's Chapel; McDowell at Upton's Hill and Arlington; F. J. Porter at Hall's and Miner's Hills; Smith at Mackall's Hill; McCall at Langley; Buell at Tennallytown, Meridian Hill, Emory's Chapel, &c., on the left bank of the river; Casey at Washington; Stoneman's cavalry at Washington; Hunt's artillery at Washington; Banks at Darnestown, with detachments at Point of Rocks, Sandy Hook, Williamsport, &c.; Stone at Poolesville, and Dix at Baltimore, with detachments on the Eastern Shore.

On the 19th of October, 1861, General McCall marched to Dranesville with his division, in order to cover reconnaissances to be made in all directions the next day, for the purpose of learning the position of the enemy and of covering the operations of the topographical engineers in making maps of that region.

On the 20th, acting in concert with General McCall, General Smith pushed strong parties to Freedom Hill, Vienna, Flint Hill, Peacock Hill, &c., to accomplish the same purpose in that part of the front. These reconnaissances were successful.

On the morning of the 20th I received the following telegram from General Banks' headquarters:

DARNESTOWN, *October* 20, 1861.

SIR: The signal station at Sugar Loaf telegraphs that the enemy have moved away from Leesburg. All quiet here.

R. M. COPELAND,
Acting Assistant Adjutant-General.

General MARCY.

Whereupon I sent to General Stone, at Poolesville, the following telegram:

CAMP GRIFFIN, *October* 20, 1861.

General McClellan desires me to inform you that General McCall occupied Dranesville yesterday and is still there. Will send out heavy reconnaissances to-day in all directions from that point. The general desires that you will keep a good lookout upon Leesburg, to see if this movement has the effect to drive them away. Perhaps a slight demonstration on your part would have the effect to move them.

A. V. COLBURN,
Assistant Adjutant-General.

Brig. Gen. C. P. STONE, *Poolesville.*

Deeming it possible that General McCall's movement to Dranesville, together with the subsequent reconnaissances, might have the effect of inducing the enemy to abandon Leesburg, and the dispatch from Sugar Loaf appearing to confirm this view, I wished General Stone, who had only a line of pickets on the river—the mass of his troops being out of sight of and beyond range from the Virginia bank—to make some display of an intention to cross, and also to watch the enemy more closely than usual. I did not direct him to cross, nor did I intend that he should cross the river in force for the purpose of fighting.

The above dispatch was sent on the 20th, and reached General Stone as early as 11 a. m. of that day. I expected him to accomplish all that was intended on the same day; and this he did, as will be seen from the following dispatch, received at my headquarters in Washington from Poolesville on the evening of October 20:

Made a feint of crossing at this place this afternoon, and at the same time started a reconnoitering party towards Leesburg from Harrison's Island. The enemy's pickets retired to intrenchments. Report of reconnoitering party not yet received. I have means of crossing 125 men once in ten minutes at each of two points. River falling slowly.

C. P. STONE,
Brigadier-General.

Major-General McCLELLAN.

As it was not foreseen or expected that General McCall would be needed to co-operate with General Stone in any attack, he was directed to fall back from Dranesville to his original camp, near Prospect Hill, as soon as the required reconnaissances were completed. Accordingly he left Dranesville on his return at about 8.30 a. m. of the 21st, reaching his old camp at about 1 p. m.

In the mean time I was surprised to hear from General Stone that a portion of his troops were engaged on the Virginia side of the river, and at once sent instructions to General McCall to remain at Dranesville, if he had not left before the order reached him. The order did not reach him until his return to his camp at Langley. He was then ordered to rest his men and hold his division in readiness to return to Dranesville at a moment's notice, should it become necessary. Similar instructions were given to other divisions during the afternoon.

The first intimation I received from General Stone of the real nature of his movements was in a telegram, as follows:

EDWARDS FERRY, *October* 21—11.10 a. m.

Major-General McCLELLAN:

The enemy have been engaged opposite Harrison's Island; our men behaving admirably.

C. P. STONE,
Brigadier-General.

At 2 p. m. General Banks' adjutant-general sent the following:

DARNESTOWN, *October* 21, 1861—2 p. m.

General R. B. MARCY:

General Stone safely crossed the river this morning. Some engagements have taken place on the other side of the river; how important is not known.

R. M. COPELAND,
Acting Assistant Adjutant-General.

General Stone sent the following dispatches on the same day at the hours indicated:

EDWARDS FERRY, *October* 21, 1861—2 p. m.

Major-General McCLELLAN:

There has been sharp firing on the right of our line, and our troops appear to be advancing there under Baker. The left, under Gorman, has advanced its skirmishers nearly 1 mile, and, if the movement continues successful, will turn the enemy's right.

> C. P. STONE,
> *Brigadier-General.*

EDWARDS FERRY, *October* 21, 1861—4 p. m.

General MCCLELLAN:

Nearly all my force is across the river. Baker on the right; Gorman on the left. Right sharply engaged.

> C. P. STONE,
> *Brigadier-General.*

EDWARDS FERRY, *October* 21, 1861—9.30 p. m.

Major-General MCCLELLAN:

I am occupied in preventing further disaster, and try to get into a position to re-deem. We have lost some of our best commanders—Baker dead, Cogswell a prisoner or secreted. The wounded are being carefully and rapidly removed, and Gorman's wing is being cautiously withdrawn. Any advance from Dranesville must be made cautiously.

All was reported going well up to Baker's death, but in the confusion following that, the right wing was outflanked. In a few hours I shall, unless a night attack is made, be in the same position as last night, save the loss of many good men.

> C. P. STONE,
> *Brigadier-General.*

Although no more fully informed of the state of affairs, I had during the afternoon, as a precautionary measure, ordered General Banks to send one brigade to the support of the troops at Harrison's Island, and to move with the other two to Seneca Mill, ready to support General Stone if necessary. The 9.30 p. m. dispatch of General Stone did not give me an entire understanding of the state of the case.

Aware of the difficulties and perhaps fatal consequences of recrossing such a river as the Potomac after a repulse, and from these telegrams supposing his whole force to be on the Virginia side, I directed General Stone to intrench himself, and hold the Virginia side at all hazards until re-enforcements could arrive, when he could safely withdraw to the Maryland side or hold his position on the Virginia side, should that prove advisable. General Banks was instructed to move the rest of his division to Edwards Ferry, and to send over as many men as possible before daylight to re-enforce Stone. He did not arrive in time to effect this, and was instructed to collect all the canal-boats he could find and use them for crossing at Edwards Ferry in sufficient force to enable the troops already there to hold the opposite side.

On the 22d I went to the ground in person, and reaching Poolesville, learned for the first time the full details of the affair.

The following extract from the evidence of General Stone before the Committee on the Conduct of the War, on the 5th of January, 1862, will throw further light on this occurrence:

General Stone says he received the order from my headquarters to make a slight demonstration at about 11 a. m. on the 20th, and that, in obedience to that order, he made the demonstration on the evening of the same day.

In regard to the reconnaissance on the 21st, which resulted in the battle of Ball's Bluff, he was asked the following questions:

Question. Did this reconnaissance originate with yourself or had you orders from the General-in-Chief to make it?

To which he replied: "It originated with myself—the reconnaissance."

Question. The order did not proceed from General McClellan?

Answer. I was directed the day before to make a demonstration; that demonstration was made the day previous.

Question. Did you receive an order from the General-in-Chief to make the reconnaissance?
Answer. No, sir.

Making a personal examination on the 23d, I found that the position on the Virginia side at Edwards Ferry was not a tenable one, but did not think it wise to withdraw the troops by daylight. I therefore caused more artillery to be placed in position on the Maryland side to cover the approaches to the ground held by us, and crossed the few additional troops that the high wind permitted us to get over, so as to be as secure as possible against any attack during the day. Before nightfall all the precautions were taken to secure an orderly and quiet passage of the troops and guns. The movement was commenced soon after dark, under the personal supervision of General Stone, who received the order for the withdrawal at 7.15 p. m. By 4 a. m. of the 24th everything had reached the Maryland shore in safety.

A few days afterward I received information, which seemed to be authentic, to the effect that large bodies of the enemy had been ordered from Manassas to Leesburg to cut off our troops on the Virginia side. Their timely withdrawal had probably prevented a still more serious disaster.

I refer to General Stone's report of this battle, furnished the War Department, and his published testimony before the Committee on the Conduct of the War, for further details.*

The records of the War Department show my anxiety and efforts to assume active offensive operations in the fall and early winter. It is only just to say, however, that the unprecedented condition of the roads and Virginia soil would have delayed an advance until February, had the discipline, organization, and equipment of the Army been as complete at the close of the fall as was necessary, and as I desired and labored against every impediment to make them.

While still in command only of the Army of the Potomac—namely, in early September—I proposed the formation of a corps of New Englanders for coast service in the bays and inlets of the Chesapeake and Potomac, to co-operate with my own command, from which most of its material was drawn.

On the 1st of November, however, I was called to relieve Lieutenant-General Scott in the chief and general command of the armies of the Union. The direction and nature of this coast expedition, therefore, were somewhat changed, as will soon appear in the original plan submitted to the Secretary of War and the letter of instructions later issued to General Burnside, its commander. The whole country, indeed, had now become the theater of military operations from the Potomac to beyond the Mississippi, and to assist the Navy in perfecting and sustaining the blockade it became necessary to extend these operations to points on the sea-coast, Roanoke Island, Savannah, and New Orleans. It remained also to equip and organize the armies of the West, whose condition was little better than that of the Army of the Potomac had been. The direction of the campaigns in the West and of the operations on the seaboard enabled me to enter upon larger combinations and to accomplish results the necessity and advantage of which had not been unforeseen, but which had been beyond the ability of the single army formerly under my command to effect.

The following letters and a subsequent paper, addressed to the Sec-

---

* See "Operations on the Potomac," etc., October 21-24, *post;* and Fry to McDowell, October 24, 1861, etc., in "Correspondence, etc.," *post.*

retary of War, sufficiently indicate the nature of those combinations to minds accustomed to reason upon military operations:

HEADQUARTERS ARMY OF THE POTOMAC,
Washington, September 6, 1861.

SIR: I have the honor to suggest the following proposition, with the request that the necessary authority be at once given me to carry it out—to organize a force of two brigades, of five regiments each, of New England men, for the general service, but particularly adapted to coast service, the officers and men to be sufficiently conversant with boat service to manage steamers, sailing vessels, launches, barges, surf-boats, floating batteries, &c.; to charter or buy for the command a sufficient number of propellers or tug-boats for transportation of men and supplies, the machinery of which should be amply protected by timber; the vessels to have permanent experienced officers from the merchant service, but to be manned by details from the command: a naval officer to be attached to the staff of the commanding officer; the flank companies of each regiment to be armed with Dahlgren boat guns and carbines with waterproof cartridges; the other companies to have such arms as I may hereafter designate; to be uniformed and equipped as the Rhode Island regiments are; launches and floating batteries with timber parapets of sufficient capacity to land or bring into action the entire force. The entire management and organization of the force to be under my control, and to form an integral part of the Army of the Potomac.

The immediate object of this force is for operations in the inlets of Chesapeake Bay and the Potomac. By enabling me thus to land troops at points where they are needed, this force can also be used in conjunction with a naval force operating against points on the sea-coast. This coast division to be commanded by a general officer of my selection; the regiments to be organized as other land forces; the disbursements for vessels, &c., to be made by the proper department of the Army upon the requisitions of the general commanding the division, with my approval.

I think the entire force can be organized in thirty days, and by no means the least of the advantages of this proposition is the fact that it will call into the service a class of men who would not otherwise enter the Army.

You will immediately perceive that the object of this force is to follow along the coast and up the inlets and rivers the movements of the main army when it advances.

I am, very respectfully, your obedient servant,

GEO. B. McCLELLAN,
Major-General, Commanding.

Hon. SIMON CAMERON, <i>Secretary of War.</i>

Owing chiefly to the difficulty in procuring the requisite vessels and adapting them to the special purposes contemplated, this expedition was not ready for service until January, 1862. Then in the chief command, I deemed it best to send it to North Carolina, with the design indicated in the following letter:

HEADQUARTERS OF THE ARMY,
Washington, January 7, 1862.

GENERAL: In accordance with verbal instructions heretofore given you, you will, after uniting with Flag-Officer Goldsborough, at Fort Monroe, proceed under his convoy to Hatteras Inlet, where you will, in connection with him, take the most prompt measures for crossing the fleet over the bulkhead into the waters of the sound. Under the accompanying general order, constituting the Department of North Carolina, you will assume command of the garrison at Hatteras Inlet, and make such dispositions in regard to that place as your ulterior operations may render necessary, always being careful to provide for the safety of that very important station in any contingency.

Your first point of attack will be Roanoke Island and its dependencies. It is presumed that the Navy can reduce the batteries on the marshes and cover the landing of your troops on the main island, by which, in connection with a rapid movement of the gunboats to the northern extremity as soon as the marsh battery is reduced, it may be hoped to capture the entire garrison of the place. Having occupied the island and its dependencies, you will at once proceed to the erection of the batteries and defenses necessary to hold the position with a small force. Should the flag-officer require any assistance in seizing or holding the debouches of the canal from Norfolk, you will please afford it to him.

The commodore and yourself having completed your arrangements in regard to Roanoke Island and the waters north of it, you will please at once make a descent on New Berne, having gained possession of which and the railroad passing through it, you will at once throw a sufficient force upon Beaufort, and take the steps necessary to reduce Fort Macon and open that port. When you seize New Berne, you will endeavor to seize the railroad as far west as Goldsborough, should circumstances favor such a movement. The temper of the people, the rebel force at hand, &c., will go far towards determining the question as to how far west the railroad can be safely occupied and held. Should circumstances render it advisable to seize and hold Raleigh, the main north and south line of railroad passing through Goldsborough should be so effectually destroyed for considerable distances north and south of that point as to render it impossible for the rebels to use it to your disadvantage. A great point would be gained, in any event, by the effectual destruction of the Wilmington and Weldon Railroad.

I would advise great caution in moving so far into the interior as upon Raleigh. Having accomplished the objects mentioned, the next point of interest would probably be Wilmington, the reduction of which may require that additional means shall be afforded you. I would urge great caution in regard to proclamations. In no case would I go beyond a moderate joint proclamation with the naval commander, which should say as little as possible about politics or the negro; merely state that the true issue for which we are fighting is the preservation of the Union and upholding the laws of the General Government, and stating that all who conduct themselves properly will, as far as possible, be protected in their persons and property.

You will please report your operations as often as an opportunity offers itself.

With my best wishes for your success, I am, &c.,

GEO. B. McCLELLAN,
Major-General, Commanding in Chief.

Brig. Gen. A. E. Burnside, *Commanding Expedition.*

The following letters of instruction were sent to Generals Halleck, Buell, Sherman, and Butler; and I also communicated verbally to these officers my views in full regarding the field of operations assigned to each, and gave them their instructions as much in detail as was necessary at that time:

HEADQUARTERS OF THE ARMY,
Washington, D. C., November 11, 1861.

General: In assigning you to the command of the Department of the Missouri, it is probably unnecessary for me to state that I have intrusted to you a duty which requires the utmost tact and decision. You have not merely the ordinary duties of a military commander to perform, but the far more difficult task of reducing chaos to order, of changing probably the majority of the *personnel* of the staff of the department, and of reducing to a point of economy, consistent with the interests and necessities of the State, a system of reckless expenditure and fraud, perhaps unheard-of before in the history of the world.

You will find in your department many general and staff officers holding illegal commissions and appointments not recognized or approved by the President or Secretary of War. You will please at once inform these gentlemen of the nullity of their appointment, and see that no pay or allowances are issued to them until such time as commissions may be authorized by the President or Secretary of War.

If any of them give the slightest trouble, you will at once arrest them and send them, under guard, out of the limits of your department, informing them that if they return they will be placed in close confinement. You will please examine into the legality of the organization of the troops serving in the department. When you find any illegal, unusual, or improper organizations, you will give to the officers and men an opportunity to enter the legal military establishment under general laws and orders from the War Department, reporting in full to these headquarters any officer or organization that may decline.

You will please cause competent and reliable staff officers to examine all existing contracts immediately, and suspend all payments upon them until you receive the report in each case. Where there is the slightest doubt as to the propriety of the contract, you will be good enough to refer the matter with full explanation to these headquarters, stating in each case what would be a fair compensation for the services or materials rendered under the contract. Discontinue at once the reception of material or services under any doubtful contract. Arrest and bring to prompt trial all officers who have in any way violated their duty to the Government. In regard to the political conduct of affairs, you will please labor to impress upon the inhabitants of Missouri and the adjacent States that we are fighting solely for the integrity of the Union, to uphold the power of our National Government, and to restore to the nation the blessings of peace and good order.

With respect to military operations, it is probable, from the best information in my possession, that the interests of the Government will be best served by fortifying and holding in considerable strength Rolla, Sedalia, and other interior points, keeping strong patrols constantly moving from the terminal stations, and concentrating the mass of the troops on or near the Mississippi, prepared for such ulterior operations as the public interests may demand.

I would be glad to have you make, as soon as possible, a personal inspection of all the important points in your department, and report the result to me. I cannot too strongly impress upon you the absolute necessity of keeping me constantly advised of the strength, condition, and location of your troops, together with all facts that will enable me to maintain that general direction of the armies of the United States which it is my purpose to exercise. I trust to you to maintain thorough organization, discipline, and economy throughout your department. Please inform me as soon as possible of everything relating to the gunboats now in process of construction, as well as those completed.

The militia force authorized to be raised by the State of Missouri for its defense will be under your orders.

I am, general, &c.,

GEO. B. McCLELLAN,
Major-General, Commanding U. S. Army.

Maj. Gen. H. W. HALLECK, U. S. A., *Comdg. Dep't of Missouri.*

HEADQUARTERS OF THE ARMY,
Washington, November 7, 1861.

GENERAL: In giving you instructions for your guidance in command of the Department of the Ohio, I do not design to fetter you. I merely wish to express plainly the general ideas which occur to me in relation to the conduct of operations there. That portion of Kentucky west of the Cumberland River is by its position so closely related to the States of Illinois and Missouri, that it has seemed best to attach it to the Department of the Missouri. Your operations, then (in Kentucky), will be confined to that portion of the State east of the Cumberland River. I trust I need not repeat to you that I regard the importance of the territory committed to your care as second only to that occupied by the army under my immediate command. It is absolutely necessary that we shall hold all the State of Kentucky; not only that, but that the majority of its inhabitants shall be warmly in favor of our cause, it being that which best subserves their interests. It is possible that the conduct of our political affairs in Kentucky is more important than that of our military operations. I certainly cannot overestimate the importance of the former. You will please constantly bear in mind the precise issue for which we are fighting. That issue is the preservation of the Union and the restoration of the full authority of the General Government over all portions of our territory. We shall most readily suppress this rebellion and restore the authority of the Government by religiously respecting the constitutional rights of all. I know that I express the feelings and opinions of the President when I say that we are fighting only to preserve the integrity of the Union and the constitutional authority of the General Government.

The inhabitants of Kentucky may rely upon it that their domestic institutions will in no manner be interfered with, and that they will receive at our hands every constitutional protection. I have only to repeat that you will in all respects carefully regard the local institutions of the region in which you command, allowing nothing but the dictates of military necessity to cause you to depart from the spirit of these instructions.

So much in regard to political considerations.

The military problem would be a simple one could it be entirely separated from political influences. Such is not the case. Were the population among which you are to operate wholly or generally hostile, it is probable that Nashville should be your first and principal objective point. It so happens that a large majority of the inhabitants of Eastern Tennessee are in favor of the Union. It therefore seems proper that you should remain on the defensive on the line from Louisville to Nashville, while you throw the mass of your forces by rapid marches, by Cumberland Gap or Walker's Gap, on Knoxville, in order to occupy the railroad at that point, and thus enable the loyal citizens of Eastern Tennessee to rise, while you at the same time cut off the railway communication between Eastern Virginia and the Mississippi. It will be prudent to fortify the pass before leaving it in your rear.

Brig. Gen. D. C. BUELL.

HEADQUARTERS OF THE ARMY,
Washington, November 12, 1861.

GENERAL: Upon assuming command of the department I will be glad to have you make as soon as possible a careful report of the condition and situation of your troops and of the military and political condition of your command. The main point to which I desire to call your attention is the necessity of entering Eastern Tennessee as soon as it can be done with reasonable chances of success, and I hope that you will, with the least possible delay, organize a column for that purpose, sufficiently guarding at the same time the main avenues by which the rebels may invade Kentucky. Our conversations on the subject of military operations have been so full and my confidence in your judgment is so great, that I will not dwell further upon the subject, except to urge upon you the necessity of keeping me fully informed as to the state of affairs, both military and political, and your movements. In regard to political matters, bear in mind that we are fighting only to preserve the integrity of the Union and to uphold the power of the General Government. As far as military necessity will permit, religiously respect the constitutional rights of all. Preserve the strictest discipline among the troops, and while employing the utmost energy in military movements, be careful so to treat the unarmed inhabitants as to contract, not widen, the breach existing between us and the rebels.

I mean by this that it is the desire of the Government to avoid unnecessary irritation by causeless arrests and persecution of individuals. Where there is good reason to believe that persons are actually giving aid, comfort, or information to the enemy, it is of course necessary to arrest them; but I have always found that it is the tendency of subordinates to make vexatious arrests on mere suspicion. You will find it well to direct that no arrest shall be made except by your order or that of your generals, unless in extraordinary cases, always holding the party making the arrest responsible for the propriety of his course. It should be our constant aim to make it apparent to all that their property, their comfort, and their personal safety will be best preserved by adhering to the cause of the Union.

If the military suggestions I have made in this letter prove to have been founded on erroneous data you are of course perfectly free to change the plans of operations.

Brig. Gen. D. C. BUELL, Comdg. Dep't of the Ohio.

HEADQUARTERS OF THE ARMY,
Washington, February 14, 1862.

GENERAL: Your dispatches in regard to the occupation of Dawfuskie Island, &c., were received to-day. I saw also to-day, for the first time, your requisition for a siege train for Savannah.

After giving the subject all the consider,ation in my power, I am forced to the conclusion that, under present circumstances, the siege and capture of Savannah do not promise results commensurate with the sacrifices necessary. When I learned that it was possible for the gunboats to reach the Savannah River above Fort Pulaski, two operations suggested themselves to my mind as its immediate results:

First. The capture of Savannah by a *coup de main*—the result of an instantaneous advance and attack by the Army and Navy.

The time for this has passed, and your letter indicates that you are not accountable for the failure to seize the propitious moment, but that, on the contrary, you perceived its advantages.

Second. To isolate Fort Pulaski, cut off its supplies, and at least facilitate its reduction by a bombardment.

Although we have a long delay to deplore, the second course still remains open to us; and I strongly advise a close blockade of Pulaski, and its bombardment as soon as the 13-inch mortars and heavy guns reach you. I am confident you can thus reduce it. With Pulaski you gain all that is really essential; you obtain complete control of the harbor; you relieve the blockading fleet, and render the main body of your force disposable for other operations.

I do not consider the possession of Savannah worth a siege after Pulaski is in our hands. But the possession of Pulaski is of the first importance. The expedition to Fernandina is well, and I shall be glad to learn that it is ours.

But, after all, the greatest moral effect would be produced by the reduction of Charleston and its defenses. There the rebellion had its birth; there the unnatural hatred of our Government is most intense; there is the center of the boasted power and courage of the rebels.

To gain Fort Sumter and hold Charleston is a task well worthy of our greatest efforts and considerable sacrifices. That is the problem I would be glad to have you study. Some time must elapse before we can be in all respects ready to accomplish that purpose. Fleets are *en route* and armies in motion which have certain preliminary objects to accomplish before we are ready to take Charleston in hand, but the time will before long arrive when I shall be prepared to make that movement. In the mean time it is my advice and wish that no attempt be made upon Savannah, unless it can be carried with certainty by a *coup de main*.

Please concentrate your attention and forces upon Pulaski and Fernandina. Saint Augustine might as well be taken by way of an interlude, while awaiting the preparations for Charleston. Success attends us everywhere at present.

Very truly, yours,

GEO. B. McCLELLAN,
Major-General, Commanding U. S. Army.

Brig. Gen. T. W. SHERMAN, *Comdg. at Port Royal, &c.*

HEADQUARTERS OF THE ARMY,
Washington, February 23, 1862.

GENERAL: You are assigned to the command of the land forces destined to co-operate with the Navy in the attacks upon New Orleans. You will use every means to keep your destination a profound secret, even from your staff officers, with the exception of your chief of staff and Lieutenant Weitzel, of the Engineers. The force at your disposal will consist of the first thirteen regiments named in your memorandum handed to me in person, the Twenty-first Indiana, Fourth Wisconsin, and Sixth Michigan (old and good regiments from Baltimore).

The Twenty-first Indiana, Fourth Wisconsin, and Sixth Michigan will await your orders at Fort Monroe.

Two companies of the Twenty-first Indiana are well drilled as heavy artillery. The cavalry force already *en route* for Ship Island will be sufficient for your purposes.

After full consultation with officers well acquainted with the country in which it is proposed to operate, I have arrived at the conclusion that two light batteries fully equipped and one without horses will be all that are necessary. This will make your force about 14,400 infantry, 275 cavalry, 580 artillery; total, 15,255 men. The commanding general of the Department of Key West is authorized to loan you, temporarily, two regiments; Fort Pickens can, probably, give you another, which will bring your force to near 18,000.

The object of your expedition is one of vital importance—the capture of New Orleans. The route selected is up the Mississippi River, and the first obstacle to be encountered (perhaps the only one) is in the resistance offered by Forts Saint Philip and Jackson. It is expected that the Navy can reduce these works; in that case you will, after their capture, leave a sufficient garrison in them to render them perfectly secure; and it is recommended that, on the upward passage, a few heavy guns and some troops be left at the pilot station (at the forks of the river) to cover a retreat in the event of a disaster. These troops and guns will of course be removed as soon as the forts are captured. Should the Navy fail to reduce the works, you will land your forces and siege train, and endeavor to breach the works, silence their fire, and carry them by assault.

The next resistance will be near the English Bend, where there are some earthen batteries. Here it may be necessary for you to land your troops and co-operate with the naval attack, although it is more than probable that the Navy unassisted can accomplish the result. If these works are taken, the city of New Orleans necessarily falls. In that event, it will probably be best to occupy Algiers with the mass of your troops, also the eastern bank of the river above the city. It may be necessary to place some troops in the city to preserve order, but if there appears to be sufficient Union sentiment to control the city, it may be best for purposes of discipline to keep your men out of the city.

After obtaining possession of New Orleans, it will be necessary to reduce all the works guarding its approaches from the east, and particularly to gain the Manchac Pass.

Baton Rouge, Berwick Bay, and Fort Livingston will next claim your attention. A feint on Galveston may facilitate the objects we have in view. I need not call your attention to the necessity of gaining possession of all the rolling stock you can on the different railways and of obtaining control of the roads themselves. The occupation of Baton Rouge by a combined naval and land force should be accomplished as soon as possible after you have gained New Orleans. Then endeavor to open your communication with the northern column by the Mississippi, always bearing in mind the necessity of occupying Jackson, Miss., as soon as you can safely do so, either after or before you have effected the junction. Allow nothing to divert you from obtaining full possession of all the approaches to New Orleans. When that object is accomplished to its fullest extent, it will be necessary to make a combined attack on Mobile, in order to gain possession of the harbor and works, as well as to control the railway terminus at the city. In regard to this I will send more detailed instructions as the operations of the northern column develop themselves.

I may briefly state that the general objects of the expedition are, first the reduction of New Orleans and all its approaches; then Mobile and its defenses; then Pensacola, Galveston, &c. It is probable that by the time New Orleans is reduced it will be in the power of the Government to re-enforce the land forces sufficiently to accomplish all these objects. In the mean time you will please give all the assistance in your power to the army and navy commanders in your vicinity, never losing sight of the fact that the great object to be achieved is the capture and firm retention of New Orleans.

I am, &c.,

GEO. B. McCLELLAN,
Major-General, Commanding U. S. Army.

Maj. Gen. B. F. BUTLER, *U. S. Volunteers.*

The plan indicated in the above letters comprehended in its scope the operations of all the armies of the Union, the Army of the Potomac as well. It was my intention, for reasons easy to be seen, that its various parts should be carried out simultaneously, or nearly so, and in co-operation along the whole line. If this plan was wise, and events have failed to prove that it was not, then it is unnecessary to defend any delay which would have enabled the Army of the Potomac to perform its share in the execution of the whole work. But about the middle of January, 1862, upon recovering from a severe illness, I found that excessive anxiety for an immediate movement of the Army of the Potomac had taken possession of the minds of the administration. A change had just been made in the War Department, and I was soon urged by the new Secretary, Mr. Stanton, to take immediate steps to secure the reopening of the Baltimore and Ohio Railroad, and to free the banks of the Lower Potomac from the rebel batteries, which annoyed passing vessels. Very soon after his entrance upon office I laid before him verbally my design as to the part of the plan of campaign to be executed by the Army of the Potomac, which was to attack Richmond by the Lower Chesapeake. He instructed me to develop it to the President, which I did. The result was that the President disapproved it, and by an order of January 31, 1862, substituted one of his own. On the 27th of January, 1862, the following order was issued, without consultation with me:

PRESIDENT'S GENERAL WAR ORDER,   EXECUTIVE MANSION,
                No. 1.   *Washington, January* 27, 1862.

Ordered, That the 22d day of February, 1862, be the day for a general movement of the land and naval forces of the United States against the insurgent forces. That especially the army at and about Fortress Monroe; the Army of the Potomac; the Army of Western Virginia; the army near Munfordville, Ky.; the army and flotilla at Cairo, and a naval force in the Gulf of Mexico, be ready to move on that day.

That all other forces, both land and naval, with their respective commanders, obey existing orders for the time, and be ready to obey additional orders when duly given.

That the heads of Departments, and especially the Secretaries of War and of the Navy, with all their subordinates, and the General-in-Chief, with all other commanders and subordinates of land and naval forces, will severally be held to their strict and full responsibilities for prompt execution of this order.

                                                  ABRAHAM LINCOLN.

The order of January 31, 1862, was as follows:

PRESIDENT'S SPECIAL WAR ORDER,   EXECUTIVE MANSION,
                No. 1.   *Washington, January* 31, 1862.

Ordered, That all the disposable force of the Army of the Potomac, after providing safely for the defense of Washington, be formed into an expedition for the immediate object of seizing and occupying a point upon the railroad southwestward of what is known as Manassas Junction, all details to be in the discretion of the Commander-in-Chief, and the expedition to move before or on the 22d day of February next.

                                                  ABRAHAM LINCOLN.

I asked his excellency whether this order was to be regarded as final, or whether I could be permitted to submit in writing my objections to his plan and my reasons for preferring my own. Permission was accorded, and I therefore prepared the letter to the Secretary of War which is given below.

Before this had been submitted to the President he addressed me the following note:

                    EXECUTIVE MANSION, *Washington, February* 3, 1862.

MY DEAR SIR: You and I have distinct and different plans for a movement of the Army of the Potomac—yours to be down the Chesapeake, up the Rappahannock to Urbana, and across land to the terminus of the railroad on the York River; mine to move directly to a point on the railroads southwest of Manassas.*

---

*For the President's memorandum accompanying this note, see under same date in "Correspondence, etc.," *post.*

If you will give me satisfactory answers to the following questions I shall gladly yield my plan to yours:

1st. Does not your plan involve a greatly larger expenditure of *time* and *money* than mine?

2d. Wherein is a victory *more certain* by your plan than mine?

3d. Wherein is a victory *more valuable* by your plan than mine?

4th. In fact, would it not be *less* valuable in this, that it would break no great line of the enemy's communications, while mine would?

5th. In case of disaster, would not a retreat be more difficult by your plan than mine?

Yours, truly,

ABRAHAM LINCOLN.

Major-General McClellan.

These questions were substantially answered by the following letter of the same date to the Secretary of War:

HEADQUARTERS OF THE ARMY,
Washington, February 3, 1862.

SIR: I ask your indulgence for the following paper, rendered necessary by circumstances.

I assumed command of the troops in the vicinity of Washington on Saturday, July 27, 1861, six days after the battle of Bull Run.

I found no army to command—a mere collection of regiments cowering on the banks of the Potomac, some perfectly raw, others dispirited by the recent defeat.

Nothing of any consequence had been done to secure the southern approaches to the capital by means of defensive works; nothing whatever had been undertaken to defend the avenues to the city on the northern side of the Potomac. The troops were not only undisciplined, undrilled, and dispirited; they were not even placed in military positions. The city was almost in a condition to have been taken by a dash of a regiment of cavalry.

Without one day's delay I undertook the difficult task assigned to me; that task the honorable Secretary knows was given to me without my solicitation or foreknowledge. How far I have accomplished it will best be shown by the past and the present.

The capital is secure against attack, the extensive fortifications erected by the labor of our troops enable a small garrison to hold it against a numerous army, the enemy have been held in check, the State of Maryland is securely in our possession, the detached counties of Virginia are again within the pale of our laws, and all apprehension of trouble in Delaware is at an end; the enemy are confined to the positions they occupied before the disaster of the 21st July. More than all this, I have now under my command a well-drilled and reliable army, to which the destinies of the country may be confidently committed. This army is young and untried in battle, but it is animated by the highest spirit and is capable of great deeds.

That so much has been accomplished, and such an army created in so short a time from nothing, will hereafter be regarded as one of the highest glories of the administration and the nation.

Many weeks, I may say many months, ago, this Army of the Potomac was fully in condition to repel any attack; but there is a vast difference between that and the efficiency required to enable troops to attack successfully an army elated by victory and intrenched in a position long since selected, studied, and fortified.

In the earliest papers I submitted to the President I asked for an effective and movable force far exceeding the aggregate now on the banks of the Potomac. I have not the force I asked for.

Even when in a subordinate position I always looked beyond the operations of the Army of the Potomac. I was never satisfied in my own mind with a barren victory, but looked to combined and decisive operations. When I was placed in command of the Armies of the United States I immediately turned my attention to the whole field of operations, regarding the Army of the Potomac as only one, while the most important, of the masses under my command. I confess that I did not then appreciate the total absence of a general plan which had before existed, nor did I know that utter disorganization and want of preparation pervaded the Western armies. I took it for granted that they were nearly, if not quite, in condition to move towards the fulfillment of my plans. I acknowledge that I made a great mistake.

I sent at once, with the approval of the Executive, officers I considered competent to command in Kentucky and Missouri. Their instructions looked to prompt movements. I soon found that the labor of creation and organization had to be performed there; transportation, arms, clothing, artillery, discipline, all were wanting. These things required time to procure them.

The generals in command have done their work most creditably, but we are still delayed. I had hoped that a general advance could be made during the good weather of December. I was mistaken. My wish was to gain possession of the Eastern Tennessee Railroad as a preliminary movement, then to follow it up immediately by an attack on Nashville and Richmond, as nearly at the same time as possible.

I have ever regarded our true policy as being that of fully preparing ourselves, and then seeking for the most decisive results. I do not wish to waste life in useless battles, but prefer to strike at the heart.

Two bases of operation seem to present themselves for the advance of the Army of the Potomac:

I. That of Washington—its present position—involving a direct attack upon the intrenched positions of the enemy at Centreville, Manassas, &c., or else a movement to turn one or both flanks of those positions, or a combination of the two plans.

The relative force of the two armies will not justify an attack on both flanks; an attack on his left flank alone involves a long line of wagon communication, and cannot prevent him from collecting for the decisive battle all the detachments now on his extreme right and left.

Should we attack his right flank by the line of the Occoquan, and a crossing of the Potomac below that river, and near his batteries, we could perhaps prevent the junction of the enemy's right with his center (we might destroy the former); we would remove the obstructions to the navigation of the Potomac, reduce the length of wagon transportation by establishing new depots at the nearest points of the Potomac, and strike more directly his main railway communication.

The fords of the Occoquan below the mouth of the Bull Run are watched by the rebels; batteries are said to be placed on the heights in the rear (concealed by the woods), and the arrangement of his troops is such that he can oppose some considerable resistance to a passage of that stream. Information has just been received to the effect that the enemy are intrenching a line of heights extending from the vicinity of Sangster's (Union Mills) towards Evansport. Early in January Spriggs' Ford was occupied by General Rodes with 3,600 men and eight guns. There are strong reasons for believing that Davis' Ford is occupied. These circumstances indicate or prove that the enemy anticipates the movement in question and is prepared to resist it. Assuming for the present that this operation is determined upon, it may be well to examine briefly its probable progress. In the present state of affairs our column (for the movement of so large a force must be made in several columns, at least five or six) can reach the Accotink without danger. During the march thence to the Occoquan our right flank becomes exposed to an attack from Fairfax Station, Sangster's, and Union Mills. This danger must be met by occupying in some force either the two first-named places, or, better, the point of junction of the roads leading thence to the village of Occoquan. This occupation must be continued so long as we continue to draw supplies by the roads from this city or until a battle is won.

The crossing of the Occoquan should be made at all the fords from Wolf Run to the mouth, the points of crossing not being necessarily confined to the fords themselves. Should the enemy occupy this line in force, we must, with what assistance the flotilla can afford, endeavor to force the passage near the mouth, thus forcing the enemy to abandon the whole line, or be taken in flank himself.

Having gained the line of the Occoquan, it would be necessary to throw a column by the shortest route to Dumfries, partly to force the enemy to abandon his batteries on the Potomac, partly to cover our left flank against an attack from the direction of Aquia, and lastly, to establish our communications with the river by the best roads, and thus give us new depots. The enemy would by this time have occupied the line of the Occoquan above Bull Run, holding Brentsville in force, and perhaps extending his lines somewhat farther to the southwest.

Our next step would then be to prevent the enemy from crossing the Occoquan between Bull Run and Broad Run, to fall upon our right flank while moving on Brentsville. This might be effected by occupying Bacon Race Church and the cross-roads near the mouth of Bull Run, or still more effectually by moving to the fords themselves, and preventing him from debouching on our side.

These operations would possibly be resisted, and it would require some time to effect them, as nearly at the same time as possible we should gain the fords necessary to our purposes above Broad Run. Having secured our right flank, it would become necessary to carry Brentsville at any cost; for we could not leave it between our right flank and the main body. The final movement on the railroad must be determined by circumstances existing at the time.

This brief sketch brings out in bold relief the great advantage possessed by the enemy in the strong central position he occupies, with roads diverging in every direction, and a strong line of defense enabling him to remain on the defensive, with a small force on one flank, while he concentrates everything on the other for a decisive action.

Should we place a portion of our force in front of Centreville, while the rest crosses the Occoquan, we commit the error of dividing our army by a very difficult obstacle, and by a distance too great to enable the two parts to support each other, should either be attacked by the masses of the enemy while the other is held in check.

I should perhaps have dwelt more decidedly on the fact that the force left near Sangster's must be allowed to remain somewhere on that side of the Occoquan until the decisive battle is over, so as to cover our retreat in the event of disaster, unless it should be decided to select and intrench a new base somewhere near Dumfries, a proceeding involving much time.

After the passage of the Occoquan by the main army, this covering force could be drawn into a more central and less exposed position—say Brimstone Hill or nearer the Occoquan. In this latitude the weather will for a considerable period be very uncertain, and a movement commenced in force on roads in tolerably firm condition will be liable, almost certain, to be much delayed by rains and snow. It will therefore be next to impossible to surprise the enemy or take him at a disadvantage by rapid maneuvers. Our slow progress will enable him to divine our purposes and take his measures accordingly. The probability is, from the best information we possess, that the enemy has improved the roads leading to his lines of defense, while we will have to work as we advance.

Bearing in mind what has been said, and the present unprecedented and impassable condition of the roads, it will be evident that no precise period can be fixed upon for the movement on this line, nor can its duration be closely calculated; it seems certain that many weeks may elapse before it is possible to commence the march. Assuming the success of this operation, and the defeat of the enemy as certain, the question at once arises as to the importance of the results gained. I think these results would be confined to the possession of the field of battle, the evacuation of the line of the Upper Potomac by the enemy, and the moral effect of the victory—important results, it is true, but not decisive of the war, nor securing the destruction of the enemy's main army; for he could fall back upon other positions and fight us again and again, should the condition of his troops permit. If he is in no condition to fight us again out of the range of the intrenchments at Richmond, we would find it a very difficult and tedious matter to follow him up there, for he would destroy his railroad bridges and otherwise impede our progress through a region where the roads are as bad as they well can be, and we would probably find ourselves forced at last to change the whole theater of war, or to seek a shorter land route to Richmond, with a smaller available force, and at an expenditure of much more time than were we to adopt the short line at once. We would also have forced the enemy to concentrate his forces and perfect his defensive measures at the very points where it is desirable to strike him when least prepared.

II. The second base of operations available for the Army of the Potomac is that of the Lower Chesapeake Bay, which affords the shortest possible land route to Richmond, and strikes directly at the heart of the enemy's power in the east.

The roads in that region are passable at all seasons of the year. The country now alluded to is much more favorable for offensive operations than that in front of Washington (which is very unfavorable), much more level, more cleared land, the woods less dense, the soil more sandy, and the spring some two or three weeks earlier. A movement in force on that line obliges the enemy to abandon his intrenched position at Manassas, in order to hasten to cover Richmond and Norfolk. He must do this; for should he permit us to occupy Richmond; his destruction can be averted only by entirely defeating us in battle, in which he must be the assailant. This movement, if successful, gives us the capital, the communications, the supplies of the rebels. Norfolk would fall, all the waters of the Chesapeake would be ours, all Virginia would be in our power, and the enemy forced to abandon Tennessee and North Carolina. The alternative presented to the enemy would be to beat us in a position selected by ourselves, disperse, or pass beneath the Caudine Forks.

Should we be beaten in battle, we have a perfectly secure retreat down the Peninsula upon Fort Monroe, with our flanks perfectly covered by the fleet. During the whole movement our left flank is covered by the water. Our right is secure, for the reason that the enemy is too distant to reach us in time. He can only oppose us in front. We bring our fleet into full play.

After a successful battle our position would be: Burnside forming our left, Norfolk held securely; our center connecting Burnside with Buell, both by Raleigh and Lynchburg; Buell in Eastern Tennessee and North Alabama; Halleck at Nashville and Memphis. The next movement would be to connect with Sherman on the left, by reducing Wilmington and Charleston; to advance our center into South Carolina and Georgia; to push Buell either towards Montgomery or to unite with the main army in Georgia; to throw Halleck southward to meet the naval expedition from New Orleans. We should then be in a condition to reduce at our leisure all the Southern sea ports; to occupy all the avenues of communication; to use the great outlet of the Mississippi; to re-establish our Government and arms in Arkansas, Louisiana, and Texas; to force the slaves to labor for our subsistence instead of that of the rebels; to bid defiance to all foreign interference. Such is the object I have ever had in view; this is the general plan which I hope to accomplish.

For many long months I have labored to prepare the Army of the Potomac to play its part in the programme. From the day when I was placed in command of all our armies I have exerted myself to place all the other armies in such a condition that they, too, could perform their allotted duties.

Should it be determined to operate from the Lower Chesapeake, the point of landing which promises the most brilliant result is Urbana, on the Lower Rappahannock. This point is easily reached by vessels of heavy draught; it is neither occupied nor observed by the enemy; it is but one march from West Point, the key of that region, and thence but two marches to Richmond. A rapid movement from Urbana would probably cut off Magruder in the Peninsula, and enable us to occupy Richmond before it could be strongly re-enforced. Should we fail in that, we could, with the co-operation of the Navy, cross the James and throw ourselves in the rear of Richmond, thus forcing the enemy to come out and attack us, for his position would be untenable with us on the southern bank of the river. Should circumstances render it not advisable to land at Urbana, we can use Mob Jack Bay; or, the worst coming to the worst, we can take Fort Monroe as a base, and operate with complete security, although with less celerity and brilliancy of results, up the Peninsula.

To reach whatever point may be selected as a base a large amount of cheap water transportation must be collected, consisting mainly of canal-boats, barges, wood boats, schooners, &c., towed by small steamers, all of a very different character from those required for all previous expeditions. This can certainly be accomplished within thirty days from the time the order is given. I propose, as the best possible plan that can, in my judgment, be adopted, to select Urbana as a landing place for the first detachments; to transport by water four divisions of infantry with their batteries, the regular infantry, a few wagons, one bridge train, and a few squadrons of cavalry, making the vicinity of Hooker's position the place of embarkation for as many as possible; to move the regular cavalry and reserve artillery, the remaining bridge trains and wagons, to a point somewhere near Cape Lookout; then ferry them over the river by means of North River ferry-boats, march them over to the Rappahannock (covering the movement by an infantry force near Heathsville), and to cross the Rappahannock in a similar way. The expense and difficulty of the movement will then be very much diminished (a saving of transportation of about 10,000 horses), and the result none the less certain.

The concentration of the cavalry, &c., on the lower counties of Maryland can be effected without exciting suspicion, and the movement made without delay from that cause.

This movement, if adopted, will not at all expose the city of Washington to danger.

The total force to be thrown upon the new line would be, according to circumstances, from 110,000 to 140,000. I hope to use the latter number by bringing fresh troops into Washington, and still leaving it quite safe. I fully realize that in all projects offered time will probably be the most valuable consideration. It is my decided opinion that, in that point of view, the second plan should be adopted. It is possible, nay, highly probable, that the weather and state of the roads may be such as to delay the direct movement from Washington, with its unsatisfactory results and great risks, far beyond the time required to complete the second plan. In the first case we can fix no definite time for an advance. The roads have gone from bad to worse. Nothing like their present condition was ever known here before; they are impassable at present. We are entirely at the mercy of the weather. It is by no means certain that we can beat them at Manassas. On the other line I regard success as certain by all the chances of war. We demoralize the enemy by forcing him to abandon his prepared position for one which we have chosen, in which all is in our favor, and where success must produce immense results.

My judgment as a general is clearly in favor of this project. Nothing is certain in war, but all the chances are in favor of this movement. So much am I in favor of the southern line of operations, that I would prefer the move from Fortress Monroe as a base as a certain though less brilliant movement than that from Urbana to an attack upon Manassas.

I know that his excellency the President, you, and I all agree in our wishes; and that these wishes are to bring this war to a close as promptly as the means in our possession will permit. I believe that the mass of the people have entire confidence in us. I am sure of it. Let us then look only to the great result to be accomplished and disregard everything else.

I am, very respectfully, your obedient servant,

GEO. B. McCLELLAN,
Major-General, Commanding.

Hon. E. M. STANTON, *Secretary of War.*

This letter must have produced some effect upon the mind of the President, since the execution of his order was not required, although it was not revoked as formally as it had been issued. Many verbal conferences ensued, in which, among other things, it was determined to collect as many canal-boats as possible, with a view to employ them largely in the transportation of the army to the Lower Chesapeake. The idea was at one time entertained by the President to use them in forming a bridge across the Potomac near Liverpool Point, in order to throw the army over at that point; but this was subsequently abandoned. It was also found by experience that it would require much time to prepare the canal-boats for use in transportation to the extent that had been anticipated.

Finally, on the 27th of February, 1862, the Secretary of War, by the authority of the President, instructed Mr. John Tucker, Assistant Secretary of War, to procure at once the necessary steamers and sailing craft to transport the Army of the Potomac to its new field of operations.

The following extract from the report of Mr. Tucker, dated April 5, will show the nature and progress of this well-executed service:

*   *   *   *   *   *   *

I was called to Washington by telegraph on 17th January last by Assistant Secretary of War Thomas A. Scott. I was informed that Major-General McClellan wished to see me. From him I learned that he desired to know if transportation on smooth water could be obtained to move at one time, for a short distance, about 50,000 troops, 10,000 horses, 1,000 wagons, 13 batteries, and the usual equipment of such an army. He frankly stated to me that he had always supposed such a movement entirely feasible until two experienced quartermasters had recently reported it impracticable in their judgment. A few days afterwards I reported to General McClellan that I was entirely confident the transports could be commanded, and stated the mode by which his object could be accomplished. A week or two afterwards I had the honor of an interview with the President and General McClellan, when the subject was further discussed, and especially as to the time required.

I expressed the opinion that as the movement of the horses and wagons would have to be made chiefly by schooners and barges; that as each schooner would require to be properly fitted for the protection of the horses and furnished with a supply of water and forage, and each transport for the troops provided with water, I did not deem it prudent to assume that such an expedition could start within thirty days from the time the order was given.

The President and General McClellan both urgently stated the vast importance of an earlier movement. I replied that if favorable winds prevailed, and there was great dispatch in loading, the time might be materially diminished.

On the 14th of February you (Secretary of War) advertised for transports of various descriptions, inviting bids. On the 27th February I was informed that the proposed movement by water was decided upon. That evening the Quartermaster-General was informed of the decision. Directions were given to secure the transportation, and any assistance was tendered. He promptly detailed to this duty two most efficient assistants in his department. Col. Rufus Ingalls was stationed at Annapolis, where it was then proposed to embark the troops, and Capt. Henry C. Hodges was directed to meet me in Philadelphia, to attend to chartering the vessels. With these arrangements I left Washington on the 28th February.

*   *   *   *   *   *

I beg to hand herewith a statement, prepared by Captain Hodges, of the vessels chartered, which exhibits the prices paid and parties from whom they were taken:

113 steamers, at an average price per day-------------------------------------- $215 10
188 schooners, at an average price per day------------------------------------   24 45
88 barges, at an average price per day---   14 27

In thirty-seven days from the time I received the order in Washington (and most of it was accomplished in thirty days) these vessels transported from Perryville, Alexandria, and Washington to Fort Monroe (the place of departure having been changed, which caused delay) 121,500 men, 14,592 animals, 1,150 wagons, 44 batteries, 74 ambulances, besides pontoon bridges, telegraph materials, and the enormous quantity of equipage, &c., required for an army of such magnitude. The only loss of which I have heard is eight mules and nine barges, which latter went ashore in a gale within a few miles of Fort Monroe, the cargoes being saved. With this trifling exception not the slightest accident has occurred, to my knowledge.

I respectfully but confidently submit that, for economy and celerity of movement, this expedition is without a parallel on record.

*   *   *   *   *   *

JOHN TUCKER,
Assistant Secretary of War.

In the mean time the destruction of the batteries on the Lower Potomac, by crossing our troops opposite them, was considered, and preparations were even made for throwing Hooker's division across the river, to carry them by assault. Finally, however, after an adverse report from Brig. Gen. J. G. Barnard, chief engineer, given below, who made a reconnaissance of the positions, and in view of the fact that it was still out of the power of the Navy Department to furnish suitable vessels to co-operate with land troops, this plan was abandoned as impracticable. A close examination of the enemy's works and their approaches, made after they were evacuated, showed that the decision was a wise one. The only means, therefore, of accomplishing the capture of these works, so much desired by the President, was by a movement by land, from the left of our lines, on the right bank of the Potomac—a movement obviously unwise.

The attention of the Navy Department, as early as August 12, 1861, had been called to the necessity of maintaining a strong force of efficient war vessels on the Potomac:

HEADQUARTERS DIVISION OF THE POTOMAC,
Washington, August 12, 1861.

SIR: I have to-day received additional information which convinces me that it is more than probable that the enemy will, within a very short time, attempt to throw a respectable force from the mouth of Aquia Creek into Maryland. This attempt will probably be preceded by the erection of batteries at Mathias and White House Points. Such a movement on the part of the enemy, in connection with others probably designed, would place Washington in great jeopardy. I most earnestly urge that the strongest possible naval force be at once concentrated near the mouth of Aquia Creek, and that the most vigilant watch be maintained day and night, so as to render such passage of the river absolutely impossible.

I recommend that the Minnesota and any other vessels available from Hampton Roads be at once ordered up there, and that a great quantity of coal be sent to that vicinity, sufficient for several weeks' supply. At least one strong war vessel should be kept at Alexandria, and I again urge the concentration of a strong naval force on the Potomac without delay.

If the Naval Department will render it absolutely impossible for the enemy to cross the river below Washington, the security of the capital will be greatly increased.

I cannot too earnestly urge an immediate compliance with these requests.

I am, sir, very respectfully, your obedient servant,
GEO. B. McCLELLAN,
Major-General, Commanding.

Hon. GIDEON WELLES, *Secretary of the United States Navy.*

It was on the 27th of September, 1861, that General Barnard, chief engineer, in company with Captain Wyman, of the Potomac flotilla, had been instructed to make a reconnaissance of the enemy's batteries as far as Mathias Point. In his report of his observations he says:

Batteries at High Point and Cockpit Point, and thence down to Chopawamsic, *cannot* be prevented. We may, indeed, prevent their construction on *certain* points, but along here somewhere the enemy can establish, in spite of us, as many batteries as he chooses. What is the remedy? Favorable circumstances, not to be anticipated nor made the basis of any calculations, might justify and render successful the attack of a particular battery. To suppose that we can capture *all*, and by mere attacks of this kind prevent the navigation being molested, is very much the same as to suppose that the hostile army in our own front can prevent us building and maintaining field works to protect Arlington and Alexandria by capturing them, one and all, as fast as they are built.

In another communication upon the subject of crossing troops for the purpose of destroying the batteries on the Virginia side of the Potomac General Barnard says:

The operation involves the forcing of a very strong line of defense of the enemy and all that we would have to do if we were really opening a campaign against them there.

It is true we hope to force this line by turning it, by landing on Freestone Point. With reason to believe that this may be successful, it cannot be denied that it involves a risk of failure. Should we, then, considering all the consequences which may be involved, enter into the operation merely to capture the Potomac batteries? I think not. Will not the Ericsson, assisted by one other gunboat capable of keeping alongside these batteries, so far control their fire as to keep the navigation sufficiently free as long as we require it? Captain Wyman says yes.

It was the opinion of competent naval officers, and I concur with them, that had an adequate force of strong and well-armed vessels been acting on the Potomac from the beginning of August, it would have been next to impossible for the rebels to have constructed or maintained batteries upon the banks of the river. The enemy never occupied Mathias Point nor any other point on the river which was out of supporting distance from their main army.

When the enemy commenced the construction of these batteries the Army of the Potomac was not in a condition to prevent it. Their destruction by our army would have afforded but a temporary relief, unless we had been strong enough to hold the entire line of the Potomac. This could be done either by driving the enemy from Manassas and Aquia Creek by main force or by maneuvering to compel them to evacuate their positions. The latter course was finally pursued, and with success.

About the 20th of February, 1862, additional measures were taken to secure the reopening of the Baltimore and Ohio Railroad. The preliminary operations of General Lander for this object are elsewhere described.

I had often observed to the President and to members of the Cabinet that the reconstruction of this railway could not be undertaken until we were in a condition to fight a battle to secure it. I regarded the possession of Winchester and Strasburg as necessary to cover the railway in the rear, and it was not until the month of February that I felt prepared to accomplish this very desirable but not vital purpose.

The whole of Banks' division and two brigades of Sedgwick's division were thrown across the river at Harper's Ferry, leaving one brigade of Sedgwick's division to observe and guard the Potomac from Great Falls to the mouth of the Monocacy. A sufficient number of troops of all arms were held in readiness in the vicinity of Washington, either to march via Leesburg or to move by rail to Harper's Ferry, should this become necessary in carrying out the objects in view.

The subjoined notes from a communication subsequently addressed to the War Department will sufficiently explain the conduct of these operations:

NOTES.

When I started for Harper's Ferry I plainly stated to the President and Secretary of War that the chief object of the operation would be to open the Baltimore and Ohio Railroad by crossing the river in force at Harper's Ferry; that I had collected the material for making a permanent bridge by means of canal-boats; that from the nature of the river it was doubtful whether such a bridge could be constructed; that if it could not, I would at least occupy the ground in front of Harper's Ferry, in order to cover the rebuilding of the railroad bridge, and finally, when the communications were perfectly secure, move on Winchester.

When I arrived at the place I found the batteau bridge nearly completed; the holding ground proved better than had been anticipated; the weather was favorable, there being no wind. I at once crossed over the two brigades which had arrived, and took steps to hurry up the other two, belonging respectively to Banks' and Sedgwick's divisions. The difficulty of crossing supplies had not then become apparent. That night I telegraphed for a regiment of regular cavalry and four batteries of heavy artillery to come up the next day (Thursday), besides directing Keyes' division of infantry to be moved up on Friday.

Next morning the attempt was made to pass the canal-boats through the lift-lock, in order to commence at once the construction of a permanent bridge. It was then found for the first time that the lock was too small to permit the passage of the boats, it having been built for a class of boats running on the Shenandoah Canal, and too narrow by some four or six inches for the canal-boats. The lift-locks above and below are all large enough for the ordinary boats. I had seen them at Edwards Ferry thus used. It had always been represented to the engineers by the military railroad employés and others that the lock was large enough, and, the difference being too small to be detected by the eye, no one had thought of measuring it or suspecting any difficulty. I thus suddenly found myself unable to build the permanent bridge. A violent gale had arisen, which threatened the safety of our only means of communication. The narrow approach to the bridge was so crowded and clogged with wagons, that it was very clear that, under existing circumstances, nothing more could be done than to cross over the baggage and supplies of the two brigades. Of the others, instead of being able to cross both during the morning, the last arrived only in time to go over just before dark. It was evident that the troops under orders would only be in the way should they arrive, and that it would not be possible to subsist them for a rapid march on Winchester. It was therefore deemed necessary to countermand the order, content ourselves with covering the reopening of the railroad for the present, and in the mean time use every exertion to establish as promptly as possible depots of forage and subsistence on the Virginia side, to supply the troops, and enable them to move on Winchester independently of the bridge. The next day (Friday) I sent a strong reconnaissance to Charlestown, and under its protection went there myself. I then determined to hold that place, and to move the troops composing Lander's and Williams' commands at once on Martinsburg and Bunker Hill, thus effectually covering the reconstruction of the railroad. Having done this, and taken all the steps in my power to insure the rapid transmission of supplies over the river, I returned to this city, well satisfied with what had been accomplished. While up the river I learned that the President was dissatisfied with the state of affairs, but on my return here understood from the Secretary of War that upon learning the whole state of the case the President was fully satisfied. I contented myself, therefore, with giving to the Secretary a brief statement, as I have written here.

The design aimed at was entirely compassed, and before the 1st of April, the date of my departure for the Peninsula, the railroad was in running order. As a demonstration upon the left flank of the enemy, this movement no doubt assisted in determining the evacuation of his lines on the 8th and 9th of March.

On my return from Harper's Ferry, on the 28th of February, the preparations necessary to carry out the wishes of the President and Secretary of War in regard to destroying the batteries on the Lower Potomac were at once undertaken. Mature reflection convinced me that this operation would require the movement of the entire army, for I felt sure that the enemy would resist it with his whole strength. I undertook it with great reluctance, both on account of the extremely unfavorable condition of the roads and my firm conviction that the proposed movement to the Lower Chesapeake would necessarily, as it subsequently did, force the enemy to abandon all his positions in front of Washington. Besides, it did not forward my plan of campaign to precipitate this evacuation by any direct attack, nor to subject the army to any needless loss of life and material by a battle near Washington, which could produce no decisive results. The preparations for a movement towards the Occoquan to carry the batteries were, however, advanced as rapidly as the season permitted, and I had invited the commanders of divisions to meet at headquarters on the 8th of March, for the purpose of giving them their instructions and receiving their advice and opinion in regard to their commands, when an interview with the President indicated to me the possibility of a change in my orders.

His excellency sent for me at a very early hour on the morning of the 8th, and renewed his expressions of dissatisfaction with the affair at Harper's Ferry and with my plans for the new movement down the Chesapeake. Another recital of the same facts which had before given satisfaction to his excellency again produced, as I supposed, the same result. The views which I expressed to the President were re-enforced by the result of a meeting of my general officers at headquarters. At that meeting my plans were laid before the division commanders, and were approved by a majority of those present. Nevertheless, on the same day two important orders were issued by the President, without consultation with me. The first of these was the General War Order, No. 2, directing the formation of army corps and assigning their commanders.*

I had always been in favor of the principle of an organization into army corps, but preferred deferring its practical execution until some little experience in campaign and on the field of battle should show what general officers were most competent to exercise these high commands; for it must be remembered that we then had no officers whose experience in war on a large scale was sufficient to prove that they possessed the necessary qualifications. An incompetent commander of an army corps might cause irreparable damage, while it is not probable that an incompetent division commander could cause any very serious mischief. These views had frequently been expressed by me to the President and members of the Cabinet. It was therefore with as much regret as surprise that I learned the existence of this order.

The first order has been given above; the second order was as follows:

PRESIDENT'S GENERAL WAR ORDER,   EXECUTIVE MANSION,
       No. 3.   Washington, March 8, 1862.

Ordered, That no change of the base of operations of the Army of the Potomac shall be made without leaving in and about Washington such a force as, in the opinion of the General-in-Chief and the commanders of army corps, shall leave said city entirely secure.

That no more than two army corps (about fifty thousand troops) of said Army of the Potomac shall be moved *en route* for a new base of operations until the navigation of the Potomac from Washington to the Chesapeake Bay shall be freed from enemy's batteries and other obstructions, or until the President shall hereafter give express permission.

That any movement as aforesaid, *en route* for a new base of operations, which may be ordered by the General-in-Chief, and which may be intended to move upon the Chesapeake Bay, shall begin to move upon the bay as early as the 18th March instant, and the General-in-Chief shall be responsible that it moves as early as that day.

Ordered, That the Army and Navy co-operate in an immediate effort to capture the enemy's batteries upon the Potomac between Washington and the Chesapeake Bay.

                                   ABRAHAM LINCOLN.

L. THOMAS, *Adjutant-General.*

After what has been said already in regard to the effect of a movement to the Lower Chesapeake, it is unnecessary for me to comment upon this document, further than to say that the time of beginning the movement depended upon the state of readiness of the transports, the entire control of which had been placed by the Secretary of War in the hands of one of the Assistant Secretaries, and not under the Quartermaster-General, so that, even if the movement were not impeded by the condition imposed in regard to the batteries on the Potomac, it could not have been in my power to begin it before the 18th of March, unless the Assistant Secretary of War had completed his arrangements by that time.

Meanwhile important events were occurring which materially modified the designs for the subsequent campaign. The appearance of the Merrimac off Old Point Comfort, and the encounter with the United States squadron on the 8th of March, threatened serious derangement

---

* See p. 18.

of the plan for the Peninsula movement. But the engagement between the Monitor and Merrimac on the 9th of March demonstrated so satisfactorily the power of the former, and the other naval preparations were so extensive and formidable, that the security of Fort Monroe as a base of operations was placed beyond a doubt, and although the James River was closed to us, the York River with its tributaries was still open as a line of water communication with the Fortress. The general plan, therefore, remained undisturbed, although less promising in its details than when the James River was in our control.

On Sunday, the 9th of March, information from various sources made it apparent that the enemy was evacuating his positions at Centreville and Manassas as well as on the Upper and Lower Potomac. The President and Secretary of War were present when the most positive information reached me, and I expressed to them my intention to cross the river immediately, and there gain the most authentic information prior to determining what course to pursue.

The retirement of the enemy towards Richmond had been expected as the natural consequence of the movement to the Peninsula, but their adoption of this course immediately on ascertaining that such a movement was intended, while it relieved me from the results of the undue anxiety of my superiors and attested the character of the design, was unfortunate in that the then almost impassable roads between our positions and theirs deprived us of the opportunity for inflicting damage usually afforded by the withdrawal of a large army in the face of a powerful adversary.

The retirement of the enemy and the occupation of the abandoned positions which necessarily followed presented an opportunity for the troops to gain some experience on the march and bivouac preparatory to the campaign, and to get rid of the superfluous baggage and other "impedimenta" which accumulates so easily around an army encamped for a long time in one locality.

A march to Manassas and back could produce no delay in embarking for the Lower Chesapeake, as the transports could not be ready for some time, and it afforded a good intermediate step between the quiet and comparative comfort of the camps around Washington and the rigors of active operations, besides accomplishing the important object of determining the positions, and perhaps the future designs, of the enemy, with the possibility of being able to harass their rear.

I therefore issued orders during the night of the 9th of March for a general movement of the army the next morning towards Centreville and Manassas, sending in advance two regiments of cavalry under Colonel Averell, with orders to reach Manassas if possible, ascertain the exact condition of affairs, and do whatever he could to retard and annoy the enemy if really in retreat; at the same time I telegraphed to the Secretary of War that it would be necessary to defer the organization of the army corps until the completion of the projected advance upon Manassas, as the divisions could not be brought together in time. The Secretary replied, requiring immediate compliance with the President's order; but on my again representing that this would compel the abandonment or postponement of the movement to Manassas, he finally consented to its postponement.

At noon on the 10th of March the cavalry advance reached the enemy's lines at Centreville, passing through his recently-occupied camps and works, and finding still burning heaps of military stores and much valuable property.

Immediately after being assigned to the command of the troops around

Washington I organized a secret-service force, under Mr. E. J. Allen, a very experienced and efficient person. This force, up to the time I was relieved from command, was continually occupied in procuring from all possible sources information regarding the strength, positions, and movements of the enemy. (Mr. Allen Pinkerton was the trustworthy and efficient chief of the secret-service corps mentioned under the assumed name of E. J. Allen.)

All spies, "contrabands," deserters, refugees, and many prisoners of war coming into our lines from the front were carefully examined, first by the outpost and division commanders, and then by my chief of staff and the provost-marshal-general. Their statements, taken in writing, and in many cases under oath, from day to day, for a long period, previous to the evacuation of Manassas, comprised a mass of evidence which, by careful digests and collations, enabled me to estimate with considerable accuracy the strength of the enemy before us. Summaries showing the character and results of the labors of the secret-service force accompany this report, and I refer to them for the facts they contain, and as a measure of the ignorance which led some journals at that time, and persons in high office, unwittingly to trifle with the reputation of an army, and to delude the country with quaker-gun stories of the defenses and gross understatements of the numbers of the enemy.

The following orders were issued for the examination of persons coming from the direction of the enemy:

[CIRCULAR.]   HEADQUARTERS ARMY OF THE POTOMAC,
                                   Washington, December 16, 1861.

The Major-General Commanding directs that hereafter all deserters, prisoners, spies, "contrabands," and all other persons whatever coming or brought within our lines from Virginia shall be taken immediately to the quarters of the commander of the division within whose lines they may come or be brought, without previous examination by any one, except so far as may be necessary for the officer commanding the advance guard to elicit information regarding his particular post; that the division commander examine all such persons himself, or delegate such duty to a proper officer of his staff, and allow no other persons to hold any communication with them; that he then immediately send them, with a sufficient guard, to the provost-marshal in this city for further examination and safe-keeping, and that stringent orders be given to all guards having such persons in charge not to hold any communication with them whatever; and, further, that the information elicited from such persons shall be immediately communicated to the major-general commanding or to the chief of staff, and to no other person whatever.

The Major-General Commanding further directs that a sufficient guard be placed around every telegraph station pertaining to this army, and that such guards be instructed not to allow any person, except the regular telegraph corps, general officers, and such staff officers as may be authorized by their chief, to enter or loiter around said stations within hearing of the sound of the telegraph instruments.

By command of Major-General McClellan:

                                           S. WILLIAMS,
                                      Assistant Adjutant-General..

———

GENERAL ORDERS, }   HEADQUARTERS ARMY OF THE POTOMAC,
    No. 72.   }   *Washington, February* 26, 1862.

*   *   *   *   *   *   *

All deserters from the enemy, prisoners, and other persons coming within our lines will be taken at once to the provost-marshal of the nearest division, who will examine them in presence of the division commander, or an officer of his staff designated for the purpose. This examination will only refer to such information as may affect the division and those near it, especially those remote from general headquarters.

As soon as this examination is completed—and it must be made as rapidly as possible—the person will be sent, under proper guard, to the provost-marshal-general, with a statement of his replies to the questions asked. Upon receiving him the provost-marshal-general will at once send him, with his statement, to the chief of staff of the Army of the Potomac, who will cause the necessary examination to be made. The provost-marshal-general will have the custody of all such persons. Division commanders will at once communicate to other division commanders all information thus obtained which affects them.

   *   *   *   *   *   *   *

By command of Major-General McClellan:

S. WILLIAMS,
Assistant Adjutant-General.

In addition to the foregoing orders the division commanders were instructed, whenever they desired to send out scouts towards the enemy, to make known the object at headquarters, in order that I might determine whether we had the information it was proposed to obtain, and that I might give the necessary orders to other commanders, so that the scouts should not be molested by the guards.

It will be seen from the report of the chief of the secret-service corps, dated March 8, that the forces of the rebel Army of the Potomac, at that date, were as follows:

	Men.
At Manassas, Centreville, Bull Run, Upper Occoquan, and vicinity	80,000
At Brooks' Station, Dumfries, Lower Occoquan, and vicinity	18,000
At Leesburg and vicinity	4,500
In the Shenandoah Valley	13,000
	115,500

About 300 field guns and from 26 to 30 siege guns were with the rebel army in front of Washington. The report made on the 17th of March, after the evacuation of Manassas and Centreville, corroborates the statements contained in the report of the 8th, and is fortified by the affidavits of several railroad engineers, conductors, baggage-masters, &c., whose opportunities for forming correct estimates were unusually good. These affidavits will be found in the accompanying reports of the chief of the secret-service corps.

A reconnaissance of the works at Centreville, made by Lieutenant McAlester, U. S. Engineers, on March 14, 1862, and a survey of those at Manassas, made by a party of the U. S. Coast Survey, in April, 1862, confirmed also my conclusions as to the strength of the enemy's defenses. Those at Centreville consisted of two lines, one facing east and the other north. The former consisted of seven works, viz: one bastion fort, two redoubts, two lunettes, and two batteries, all containing embrasures for 40 guns, and connected by infantry parapets and double *caponnières*. It extended along the crest of the ridge a mile and three-quarters from its junction with the northern front to ground thickly wooded and impassable to an attacking column.

The northern front extended about one and one-fourth miles to Great Rocky Run, and thence three-fourths of a mile farther to thickly-wooded, impassable ground in the valley of Cub Run. It consisted of six lunettes and batteries, with embrasures for 31 guns, connected by an infantry parapet in the form of a *crémaillère* line with redans. At the town of Centreville, on a high hill commanding the rear of all the works within range, was a large hexagonal redoubt with ten embrasures.

Manassas Station was defended in all directions by a system of detached works, with platforms for heavy guns arranged for marine carriages, and often connected by infantry parapets. This system was rendered complete by a very large work, with sixteen embrasures, which commanded the highest of the other works by about 50 feet.

Sketches of the reconnaissances above referred to will be found among the maps appended to this report.

From this it will be seen that the positions selected by the enemy at Centreville and Manassas were naturally very strong, with impassable streams and broken ground, affording ample protection for their flanks, and that strong lines of intrenchments swept all the available approaches.

Although the history of every former war has conclusively shown the great advantages which are possessed by an army acting on the defensive and occupying strong positions, defended by heavy earthworks, yet at the commencement of this war but few civilians in our country, and indeed not all military men of rank, had a just appreciation of the fact.

New levies that have never been in battle cannot be expected to advance without cover under the murderous fire from such defenses and carry them by assault. This is work in which veteran troops frequently falter and are repulsed with loss. That an assault of the enemy's positions in front of Washington, with the new troops composing the Army of the Potomac, during the winter of 1861-'62, would have resulted in defeat and demoralization, was too probable.

The same army, though inured to war in many battles, hard-fought and bravely won, has twice, under other generals, suffered such disasters as it was no excess of prudence then to avoid. My letter to the Secretary of War, dated February 3, 1862, and given above, expressed the opinion that the movement to the Peninsula would compel the enemy to retire from his position at Manassas and free Washington from danger, When the enemy first learned of that plan, they did thus evacuate Manassas. During the Peninsular campaign, as at no former period, Northern Virginia was completely in our possession and the vicinity of Washington free from the presence of the enemy. The ground so gained was not lost, nor Washington again put in danger, until the enemy learned of the orders for the evacuation of the Peninsula, sent to me at Harrison's Bar, and were again left free to advance northward and menace the national capital. Perhaps no one now doubts that the best defense of Washington is a Peninsula attack on Richmond.

My order for the organization of the army corps was issued on the 13th of March. It has been given above.

While at Fairfax Court-House, on March 12, I was informed through the telegraph by a member of my staff that the following document had appeared in the National Intelligencer of that morning:

PRESIDENT'S WAR ORDER, }   EXECUTIVE MANSION,
        No. 3.   }   *Washington, March* 11, 1862.

Major-General McClellan having personally taken the field at the head of the Army of the Potomac, until otherwise ordered he is relieved from the command of the other military departments, he retaining command of the Department of the Potomac.

Ordered further, That the departments now under the respective commands of Generals Halleck and Hunter, together with so much of that under General Buell as lies west of a north and south line indefinitely drawn through Knoxville, Tenn., be consolidated and designated the Department of the Mississippi, and that, until otherwise ordered, Major-General Halleck have command of said department.

Ordered also, That the country west of the Department of the Potomac and east of the Department of the Mississippi be a military department, to be called the Mountain Department, and that the same be commanded by Major-General Frémont.

That all the commanders of departments, after the receipt of this order by them, respectively report severally and directly to the Secretary of War, and that prompt, full, and frequent reports will be expected of all and each of them.

                                             ABRAHAM LINCOLN.

Though unaware of the President's intention to remove me from the position of General-in-Chief, I cheerfully acceded to the disposition he saw fit to make of my services, and so informed him in a note on the 12th of March, in which occur these words:

I believe I said to you some weeks since, in connection with some Western matters, that no feeling of self-interest or ambition should ever prevent me from devoting myself to the service. I am glad to have the opportunity to prove it, and you will find that, under present circumstances, I shall work just as cheerfully as before, and that no consideration of self will in any manner interfere with the discharge of my public duties. Again thanking you for the official and personal kindness you have so often evinced towards me, I am, &c.

On the 14th of March a reconnaissance of a large body of cavalry, with some infantry, under command of General Stoneman, was sent along the Orange and Alexandria Railroad to determine the position of the enemy, and, if possible, force his rear across the Rappahannock, but the roads were in such condition that, finding it impossible to subsist his men, General Stoneman was forced to return after reaching Cedar Run.

The following dispatch from him recites the result of this expedition:*

*   *   *   *   *   *   *

The main body of the army was on the 15th of March moved back to the vicinity of Alexandria, to be embarked, leaving a part of General Sumner's corps at Manassas until other troops could be sent to relieve it. Before it was withdrawn a strong reconnaissance, under General Howard, was sent towards the Rappahannock, the result of which appears in the following dispatch:

WARRENTON JUNCTION, *March* 29, 1862.
General S. WILLIAMS:

Express just received from General Howard. He drove the enemy across the Rappahannock Bridge, and is now in camp on this bank of and near the Rappahannock River. The enemy blew up the bridge in his retreat. There was skirmishing during the march, and a few shots exchanged by the artillery, without any loss on our part. Their loss, if any, is not known. General Howard will return to this camp to-morrow morning.

E. V. SUMNER,
Brigadier-General.

The line of the Rappahannock and the Manassas Gap Railroad was thus left reasonably secure from menace by any considerable body of the enemy.

On the 13th of March a council of war was assembled at Fairfax Court-House to discuss the military status. The President's Order, No. 3, of March 8, was considered. The following is a memorandum of the proceedings of the council:

HEADQUARTERS ARMY OF THE POTOMAC,
Fairfax Court-House, March 13, 1862.

A council of the generals commanding army corps at the headquarters of the Army of the Potomac were of the opinion:

I. That the enemy having retreated from Manassas to Gordonsville, behind the Rappahannock and Rapidan, it is the opinion of the generals commanding army corps that the operations to be carried on will be best undertaken from Old Point Comfort, between the York and James Rivers, provided—

1st. That the enemy's vessel, Merrimac, can be neutralized;

2d. That the means of transportation sufficient for an immediate transfer of the force to its new base can be ready at Washington and Alexandria to move down the Potomac; and

3d. That a naval auxiliary force can be had to silence, or aid in silencing, the enemy's batteries on the York River.

---

* For report here omitted see "Reconnaissance to Cedar Run," March 14–16, in Reports, *post.*

4th. That the force to be left to cover Washington shall be such as to give an entire feeling of security for its safety from menace. (Unanimous.)

II. If the foregoing cannot be, the army should then be moved against the enemy, behind the Rappahannock, at the earliest possible moment, and the means for reconstructing bridges, repairing railroads, and stocking them with materials sufficient for supplying the army should at once be collected for both the Orange and Alexandria and Aquia and Richmond Railroads. (Unanimous.)

N. B.—That with the forts on the right bank of the Potomac fully garrisoned and those on the left bank occupied a covering force in front of the Virginia line of 25,000 men would suffice. (Keyes, Heintzelman, and McDowell.) A total of 40,000 men for the defense of the city would suffice. (Sumner.)

This was assented to by myself and immediately communicated to the War Department. The following reply was received the same day:

WAR DEPARTMENT, *March* 13, 1862.

The President having considered the plan of operations agreed upon by yourself and the commanders of army corps, makes no objection to the same, but gives the following directions as to its execution:

1. Leave such force at Manassas Junction as shall make it entirely certain that the enemy shall not repossess himself of that position and line of communication.

2. Leave Washington entirely secure.

3. Move the remainder of the force down the Potomac, choosing a new base at Fortress Monroe, or anywhere between here and there, or, at all events, move such remainder of the army at once in pursuit of the enemy by some route.

EDWIN M. STANTON,
Secretary of War.

Maj. Gen. GEORGE B. McCLELLAN.

My preparations were at once begun in accordance with these directions, and on the 16th of March the following instructions were sent to Generals Banks and Wadsworth:

HEADQUARTERS ARMY OF THE POTOMAC,
March 16, 1862.

SIR: You will post your command in the vicinity of Manassas, intrench yourself strongly, and throw cavalry pickets well out to the front.

Your first care will be the rebuilding of the railway from Washington to Manassas and to Strasburg, in order to open your communications with the valley of the Shenandoah. As soon as the Manassas Gap Railway is in running order, intrench a brigade of infantry, say four regiments, with two batteries, at or near the point where the railway crosses the Shenandoah. Something like two regiments of cavalry should be left in that vicinity to occupy Winchester and thoroughly scour the country south of the railway and up the Shenandoah Valley, as well as through Chester Gap, which might perhaps be advantageously occupied by a detachment of infantry, well intrenched. Block-houses should be built at all the railway bridges. Occupy by grand guards Warrenton Junction and Warrenton itself, and also some little more advanced point on the Orange and Alexandria Railroad as soon as the railway bridge is repaired.

Great activity should be observed by the cavalry. Besides the two regiments at Manassas, another regiment of cavalry will be at your disposal to scout towards the Occoquan, and probably a fourth towards Leesburg.

To recapitulate, the most important points which should engage your attention are as follows:

1. A strong force, well intrenched, in the vicinity of Manassas—perhaps even Centreville; and another force (a brigade), also well intrenched, near Strasburg.

2. Block-houses at the railway bridges.

3. Constant employment of the cavalry well to the front.

4. Grand guards at Warrenton Junction, and in advance as far as the Rappahannock, if possible.

5. Great care to be exercised to obtain full and early information as to the enemy.

6. The general object is to cover the line of the Potomac and Washington.

The above is communicated by command of Major-General McClellan.

S. WILLIAMS,
Assistant Adjutant-General.

Maj. Gen. N. P. BANKS,
Commanding Fifth Corps, Army of the Potomac.

HEADQUARTERS ARMY OF THE POTOMAC,
March 16, 1862.

SIR: The command to which you have been assigned, by instructions of the President, as military governor of the District of Columbia, embraces the geographical limits of the District, and will also include the city of Alexandria, the defensive works south of the Potomac from the Occoquan to Difficult Creek, and the post of Fort Washington. I inclose a list of the troops and of the defenses embraced in these limits.

General Banks will command at Manassas Junction, with the divisions of Williams and Shields, composing the Fifth Corps, but you should nevertheless exercise vigilance in your front, carefully guard the approaches in that quarter, and maintain the duties of advance guards. You will use the same precautions on either flank.

All troops not actually needed for the police of Washington and Georgetown, for the garrisons north of the Potomac, and for other indicated special duties, should be moved to the south side of the river.

In the center of your front you should post the main body of your troops, and proper proportions at suitable distances towards your right and left flanks. Careful patrols will be made, in order thoroughly to scour the country in front from right to left.

It is specially enjoined upon you to maintain the forts and their armaments in the best possible order, to look carefully to the instruction and discipline of their garrisons, as well as all other troops under your command, and by frequent and rigid inspections to insure the attainment of these ends.

The care of the railways, canals, depots, bridges, and ferries within the above-named limits will devolve upon you, and you are to insure their security and provide for their protection by every means in your power. You will also protect the depots of the public stores and the transit of stores to troops in active service.

By means of patrols you will thoroughly scour the neighboring country south of the Eastern Branch, and also on your right; and you will use every possible precaution to intercept mails, goods, and persons passing unauthorized to the enemy's lines.

The necessity of maintaining good order within your limits, and especially in the capital of the nation, cannot be too strongly enforced.

You will forward and facilitate the movement of all troops destined for the active part of the Army of the Potomac, and especially the transit of detachments to their proper regiments and corps.

The charge of the new troops arriving in Washington and of all troops temporarily there will devolve upon you. You will form them into provisional brigades, promote their instruction and discipline, and facilitate their equipment. Report all arrivals of troops, their strength, composition, and equipment, by every opportunity.

Besides the regular reports and returns which you will be required to render to the Adjutant-General of the Army, you will make to these headquarters a consolidated report of your command every Sunday morning and monthly returns on the first day of each month.

The foregoing instructions are communicated by command of Major-General McClellan.

S. WILLIAMS,
Assistant Adjutant-General.

Brig. Gen. J. S. WADSWORTH,
Military Governor of the District of Columbia.

The Secretary of War had expressed a desire that I should communicate to the War Department my designs with regard to the employment of the Army of the Potomac in an official form. I submitted, on the 19th of March, the following:

HEADQUARTERS ARMY OF THE POTOMAC,
Theological Seminary, Va., March 19, 1862.

SIR: I have the honor to submit the following notes on the proposed operations of the active portion of the Army of the Potomac.

The proposed plan of campaign is to assume Fort Monroe as the first base of operations, taking the line of Yorktown and West Point upon Richmond as the line of operations, Richmond being the objective point. It is assumed that the fall of Richmond involves that of Norfolk and the whole of Virginia; also that we shall fight a decisive battle between West Point and Richmond, to give which battle the rebels will concentrate all their available forces, understanding, as they will, that it involves the fate of their cause. It therefore follows—

1st. That we should collect all our available forces and operate upon adjacent lines, maintaining perfect communication between our columns.

2d. That no time should be lost in reaching the field of battle.

The advantages of the Peninsula between York and James Rivers are too obvious to need explanation. It is also clear that West Point should as soon as possible be reached and used as our main depot, that we may have the shortest line of land transportation for our supplies and the use of the York River.

There are two methods of reaching this point:

1st: By moving directly from Fort Monroe as a base, and trusting to the roads for our supplies, at the same time landing a strong corps as near Yorktown as possible, in order to turn the rebel lines of defense south of Yorktown; then to reduce Yorktown and Gloucester by a siege, in all probability involving a delay of weeks, perhaps.

2d. To make a combined naval and land attack upon Yorktown the first object of the campaign. This leads to the most rapid and decisive results. To accomplish this, the Navy should at once concentrate upon the York River all their available and most powerful batteries. Its reduction should not in that case require many hours. A strong corps would be pushed up the York, under cover of the Navy, directly upon West Point, immediately upon the fall of Yorktown, and we could at once establish our new base of operations at a distance of some 25 miles from Richmond, with every facility for developing and bringing into play the whole of our available force on either or both banks of the James.

It is impossible to urge too strongly the absolute necessity of the full co-operation of the Navy as a part of this programme. Without it the operations may be prolonged for many weeks, and we may be forced to carry in front several strong positions, which by their aid could be turned without serious loss of either time or men.

It is also of first importance to bear in mind the fact, already alluded to, that the capture of Richmond necessarily involves the prompt fall of Norfolk, while an operation against Norfolk, if successful, as the beginning of the campaign, facilitates the reduction of Richmond merely by the demoralization of the rebel troops involved, and that after the fall of Norfolk we should be obliged to undertake the capture of Richmond by the same means which would have accomplished it in the beginning, having meanwhile afforded the rebels ample time to perfect their defensive arrangements; for they would well know, from the moment the Army of the Potomac changed its base to Fort Monroe, that Richmond must be its ultimate object.

It may be summed up in few words, that for the prompt success of this campaign it is absolutely necessary that the Navy should at once throw its whole available force, its most powerful vessels, against Yorktown. There is the most important point—there the knot is to be cut. An immediate decision upon the subject-matter of this communication is highly desirable, and seems called for by the exigencies of the occasion.

I am, sir, very respectfully, your obedient servant,

GEO. B. McCLELLAN,
Major-General.

Hon. E. M. STANTON, *Secretary of War.*

In the mean time the troops destined to form the active army were collected in camps convenient to the points of embarkation, and every preparation made to embark them as rapidly as possible when the transports were ready.

A few days before sailing for Fort Monroe, while still encamped near Alexandria, I met the President by appointment on a steamer. He there informed me that he had been strongly pressed to take General Blenker's division from my command and give it to General Frémont. His excellency was good enough to suggest several reasons for not taking Blenker's division from me. I assented to the force of his suggestions, and was extremely gratified by his decision to allow the division to remain with the Army of the Potomac. It was therefore with surprise that I received on the 31st the following note:

EXECUTIVE MANSION,
Washington, March 31, 1862.

MY DEAR SIR: This morning I felt constrained to order Blenker's division to Frémont, and I write this to assure you that I did so with great pain, understanding that you would wish it otherwise. If you could know the full pressure of the case I am confident you would justify it, even beyond a mere acknowledgment that the Commander-in-Chief may order what he pleases.

Yours, very truly,

ABRAHAM LINCOLN.

Major-General McCLELLAN.

To this I replied in substance that I regretted the order, and could ill afford to lose 10,000 troops which had been counted upon in forming my plan of campaign, but as there was no remedy, I would yield, and do the best I could without them. In a conversation with the President a few hours afterwards I repeated verbally the same thing, and expressed my regret that Blenker's division had been given to General Frémont from any pressure other than the requirements of the national exigency. I was partially relieved, however, by the President's positive and emphatic assurance that I might be confident that no more troops beyond these 10,000 should in any event be taken from me or in any way detached from my command.

At the time of the evacuation of Manassas by the enemy Jackson was at Winchester, our forces occupying Charlestown, and Shields' reaching Bunker Hill on the 11th. On the morning of the 12th a brigade of General Banks' troops, under General Hamilton, entered Winchester, the enemy having left at 5 o'clock the evening before, his rear guard of cavalry leaving an hour before our advance entered the place. The enemy having made his preparations for evacuation some days before, it was not possible to intercept his retreat. On the 13th the mass of Banks' corps was concentrated in the immediate vicinity of Winchester, the enemy being in the rear of Strasburg. On the 19th General Shields occupied Strasburg, driving the enemy 20 miles south to Mount Jackson. On the 20th the first division of Banks' corps commenced its movement towards Manassas, in compliance with my letter of instructions of the 16th. Jackson probably received information of this movement, and supposed that no force of any consequence was left in the vicinity of Winchester, and upon the falling back of Shields to that place, for the purpose of enticing Jackson in pursuit, the latter promptly followed, whereupon ensued a skirmish on the 22d, in which General Shields was wounded, and an affair at Winchester on the 23d, resulting in the defeat of Jackson, who was pursued as rapidly as the exhaustion of our troops and the difficulty of obtaining supplies permitted. It is presumed that the full reports of the battle of Winchester were forwarded direct to the War Department by General Banks.

It being now clear that the enemy had no intention of returning by the Manassas route, the following letter of April 1 was written to General Banks:

HEADQUARTERS ARMY OF THE POTOMAC,
On Board the Commodore, April 1, 1862.

GENERAL: The change in affairs in the valley of the Shenandoah has rendered necessary a corresponding departure, temporarily at least, from the plan we some days since agreed upon.

In my arrangements I assume that you have with you a force amply sufficient to drive Jackson before you, provided he is not re-enforced largely. I also assume that you may find it impossible to detach anything towards Manassas for some days, probably not until the operations of the main army have drawn all the rebel force towards Richmond.

You are aware that General Sumner has for some days been at Manassas Junction with two divisions of infantry, six batteries, and two regiments of cavalry, and that a reconnaissance to the Rappahannock forced the enemy to destroy the railway bridge at Rappahannock Station, on the Orange and Alexandria Railroad. Since that time our cavalry have found nothing on this side the Rappahannock in that direction, and it seems clear that we have no reason to fear any return of the rebels in that quarter. Their movements near Fredericksburg also indicate a final abandonment of that neighborhood. I doubt whether Johnston will now re-enforce Jackson with a view of offensive operations. The time is probably past when he could have gained anything by doing so. I have ordered in one of Sumner's divisions (that of Richardson, late Sumner's) to Alexandria for embarkation. Blenker's has been detached from the Army of the Potomac and ordered to report to General Frémont. Abercrombie is probably at Warrenton Junction to-day. Geary is at White Plains. Two regiments of cavalry have been ordered out and are now on the way to relieve the two regiments of Sumner.

Four thousand infantry and one battery leave Washington at once for Manassas. Some 3,000 more will move in one or two days, and soon after some 3,000 additional. I will order Blenker to march on Strasburg and to report to you for temporary duty, so that, should you find a large force in your front, you can avail yourself of his aid as soon as possible. Please direct him to Winchester, thence to report to the Adjutant-General of the Army for orders; but keep him until you are sure what you have in front.

In regard to your own movements, the most important thing at present is to throw Jackson well back, and then to assume such a position as to enable you to prevent his return. As soon as the railway communications are re-established it will be probably important and advisable to move on Staunton, but this would require secure communications and a force of from 25,000 to 30,000 for active operations. It should also be nearly coincident with my own move on Richmond; at all events, not so long before it as to enable the rebels to concentrate on you and then return on me. I fear that you cannot be ready in time, although it may come in very well with a force less than that I have mentioned, after the main battle near Richmond. When General Sumner leaves Warrenton Junction, General Abercrombie will be placed in immediate command of Manassas and Warrenton Junction under your general orders. Please inform me frequently by telegraph and otherwise as to the state of things in your front.

I am, very truly, yours,

GEO. B. McCLELLAN,
Major-General, Commanding.

P. S.—From what I have just learned it would seem that the regiments of cavalry intended for Warrenton Junction have gone to Harper's Ferry. Of the four additional regiments placed under your orders, two should as promptly as possible move by the shortest route on Warrenton Junction.

I am, sir, very respectfully, your obedient servant,

GEO. B. McCLELLAN,
Major-General, Commanding.

Maj. Gen. N. P. Banks, *Commanding Fifth Corps.*

This letter needs no further explanation than to say that it was my intention, had the operations in that quarter remained under my charge, either to have resumed the defensive positions marked out in the letter of March 16, or to have advanced General Banks upon Staunton, as might in the progress of events seem advisable.

It is to be remembered that when I wrote the preceding and following letters of April 1 I had no expectation of being relieved from the charge of the operations in the Shenandoah Valley, the President's War Order, No. 3, giving no intimation of such an intention, and that so far as reference was made to final operations after driving Jackson back and taking such a position as to prevent his return, no positive orders were given in the letter, the matter being left for future consideration when the proper time arrived for a decision.

From the following letter to the Adjutant-General, dated April 1, 1862, it will be seen that I left for the defenses of the national capital and its approaches, when I sailed for the Peninsula, 73,456 men, with 109 pieces of light artillery, including the 32 pieces in Washington alluded to but not enumerated in my letter to the Adjutant-General. It will also be seen that I recommended other available troops in New York (more than 4,000) to be at once ordered forward to re-enforce them:

HEADQUARTERS ARMY OF THE POTOMAC,
Steamer Commodore, April 1, 1862.

GENERAL: I have to request that you will lay the following communication before the honorable Secretary of War:

The approximate numbers and positions of the troops left near and in rear of the Potomac are as follows:

General Dix has, after guarding the railroads under his charge, sufficient to give him 5,000 for the defense of Baltimore and 1,988 available for the Eastern Shore, Annapolis, &c. Fort Delaware is very well garrisoned by about 400 men.

The garrisons of the forts around Washington amount to 10,600 men; other disposable troops now with General Wadsworth about 11,400 men.

The troops employed in guarding the various railways in Maryland amount to some 3,359 men. These it is designed to relieve, being old regiments, by dismounted cavalry, and to send forward to Manassas.

General Abercrombie occupies Warrenton with a force which, including Colonel Geary at White Plains and the cavalry to be at his disposal, will amount to some 7,780 men, with 12 pieces of artillery.

I have the honor to request that all the troops organized for service in Pennsylvania and New York and in any of the Eastern States may be ordered to Washington. I learn from Governor Curtin that there are some 3,500 men now ready in Pennsylvania. This force I should be glad to have sent to Manassas. Four thousand men from General Wadsworth I desire to be ordered to Manassas. These troops, with the railroad guards above alluded to, will make up a force under the command of General Abercrombie of something like 18,639 men.

It is my design to push General Blenker's division from Warrenton upon Strasburg. He should remain at Strasburg long enough to allow matters to assume a definite form in that region before proceeding to his ultimate destination.

The troops in the valley of the Shenandoah will thus, including Blenker's division, 10,028 strong, with 24 pieces of artillery; Banks' Fifth Corps, which embraces the command of General Shields, 19,687 strong, with 41 guns; some 3,652 disposable cavalry and the railroad guards, about 2,100 men, amount to about 35,467 men.

It is designed to relieve General Hooker by one regiment, say 850 men, being, with some 500 cavalry, 1,350 men on the Lower Potomac.

To recapitulate—

	Men.
At Warrenton there is to be	7,780
At Manassas, say	10,859
In the valley of the Shenandoah	35,467
On the Lower Potomac	1,350
In all	55,456

There would thus be left for the garrisons and the front of Washington, under General Wadsworth, some 18,000, inclusive of the batteries under instruction. The troops organizing or ready for service in New York, I learn, will probably number more than 4,000. These should be assembled at Washington, subject to disposition where their services may be most required.

I am, very respectfully, your obedient servant,
GEO. B. McCLELLAN,
Major-General, Commanding.

Brig. Gen. L. THOMAS, *Adjutant-General, U. S. Army.*

The following letter from General Barry shows that thirty-two field guns, with men, horses, and equipments, were also left in Washington City when the army sailed. These were the batteries under instruction referred to above:

HEADQUARTERS INSPECTOR OF ARTILLERY,
Washington, December 16, 1862.

GENERAL: It having been stated in various public prints, and in a speech of Senator Chandler, of Michigan, in his place in the United States Senate, quoting what he stated to be a portion of the testimony of Brigadier-General Wadsworth, military governor of Washington, before the joint Senate and House Committee on the Conduct of the War, that Major-General McClellan had left an insufficient force for the defense of Washington, and not a gun on wheels—

I have to contradict this charge as follows:

From official reports made at the time to me (the chief of artillery of the Army of the Potomac), and now in my possession, by the commanding officer of the light artillery troops left in camp in the city of Washington by your order, it appears that the following-named field batteries were left:

Battery C, First New York Artillery, Captain Barnes, two guns; Battery K, First New York Artillery, Captain Crounse, six guns; Battery L, Second New York Artillery, Captain Robinson, six guns; Ninth New York Independent Battery, Captain Morozowicz, six guns; Sixteenth New York Independent Battery, Captain Locke; Battery A, Second Battalion New York Artillery, Captain Hogan, six guns; Battery B, Second Battalion New York Artillery, Captain McMahon, six guns; total, seven batteries, thirty-two guns.

With the exception of a few horses, which could have been procured from the Quartermaster's Department in a few hours, the batteries were all fit for immediate service, excepting the Sixteenth New York Battery, which having been previously ordered,

on General Wadsworth's application, to report to him for special service, was unequipped with either guns or horses.

I am, general, very respectfully, your obedient servant,

W. F. BARRY,
Brigadier-General, Inspector of Artillery, U. S. Army.

Major-General McCLELLAN, *U. S. Army.*

It is true that Blenker's division, which is included in the force
enumerated by me, was under orders to re-enforce General Frémont,
but the following dispatch from the Secretary of War, dated March 31,
1862, will show that I was authorized to detain him at Strasburg until
matters assumed a definite form in that region, before proceeding to his
ultimate destination; in other words, until Jackson was disposed of.
And had he been detained there, instead of moving on to Harper's
Ferry and Franklin, under other orders, it is probable that General
Banks would have defeated Jackson, instead of being himself obliged
subsequently to retreat to Williamsport:

WAR DEPARTMENT,
Washington, D. C., March 31, 1862.

The order in respect to Blenker is not designed to hinder or delay the movement of
Richardson or any other force. He can remain wherever you desire him as long as
required for your movements and in any position you desire. The order is simply
to place him in position for re-enforcing Frémont as soon as your dispositions will
permit, and he may go to Harper's Ferry by such route and at such time as you shall
direct. State your own wishes as to the movement, when and how it shall be made.

EDWIN M. STANTON,
Secretary of War.

Major-General McCLELLAN.

Without including General Blenker's division, there were left 67,428
men and eighty-five pieces of light artillery, which, under existing circumstances, I deemed more than adequate to insure the perfect security
of Washington against any force the enemy could bring against it, for
the following reasons:

The light troops I had thrown forward under General Stoneman in
pursuit of the rebel army, after the evacuation of Manassas and Centreville, had driven their rear guard across Cedar Run, and subsequent
expeditions from Sumner's corps had forced them beyond the Rappahannock. They had destroyed all the railroad bridges behind them,
thereby indicating that they did not intend to return over that route.
Indeed, if they had attempted such a movement, their progress must
have been slow and difficult, as it would have involved the reconstruction of the bridges; and if my orders for keeping numerous cavalry
patrols well out to the front, to give timely notice of any approach of
the enemy, had been strictly enforced (and I left seven regiments of
cavalry for this express purpose), they could not by any possibility
have reached Washington before there would have been ample time to
concentrate the entire forces left for its defense, as well as those at
Baltimore, at any necessary point.

It was clear to my mind, as I reiterated to the authorities, that the
movement of the Army of the Potomac would have the effect to draw
off the hostile army from Manassas to the defense of their capital, and
thus free Washington from menace. This opinion was confirmed the
moment the movement commenced, or rather as soon as the enemy
became aware of our intentions, for with the exception of Jackson's
force of some 15,000, which his instructions show to have been intended
to operate in such a way as to prevent McDowell's corps from being
sent to re-enforce me, no rebel force of any magnitude made its appearance in front of Washington during the progress of our operations on

the Peninsula, nor until the order was given for my return from Harrison's Landing was Washington again threatened.

Surrounded as Washington was with numerous and strong fortifications, well garrisoned, it was manifest that the enemy could not afford to detach from his main army a force sufficient to assail them.

It is proper to remark, that just previous to my departure for Fort Monroe I sent my chief of staff to General Hitchcock, who at that time held staff relations with his excellency the President and the Secretary of War, to submit to him a list of the troops I proposed to leave for the defense of Washington, and the positions in which I designed posting them. General Hitchcock, after glancing his eye over the list, observed that he was not the judge of what was required for defending the capital; that General McClellan's position was such as to enable him to understand the subject much better than he did, and he presumed that if the force designated was in his judgment sufficient, nothing more would be required. He was then told by the chief of staff that I would be glad to have his opinion, as an old and experienced officer. To this he replied, that as I had had the entire control of the defenses for a long time, I was the best judge of what was needed, and he declined to give any other expression of opinion at that time.

On the 2d of April, the day following my departure for Fort Monroe, Generals Hitchcock and Thomas were directed by the Secretary of War to examine and report whether the President's instructions to me of March 8 and 13 had been complied with. On the same day their report was submitted, and their decision was—

That the requirement of the President that this city (Washington) shall be left entirely secure has not been fully complied with.

The President, in his letter to me on the 9th of April, says:

And now allow me to ask, do you really think I should permit the line from Richmond via Manassas Junction to this city to be entirely open except what resistance could be presented by less than 20,000 unorganized troops?

In the report of Generals Hitchcock and Thomas, alluded to, it is acknowledged that there was no danger of an attack from the direction of Manassas, in these words:

In regard to occupying Manassas Junction, as the enemy have destroyed the railroads leading to it, it may be fair to assume that they have no intention of returning for the reoccupation of their late position, and therefore no large force would be necessary to hold that position.

That, as remarked before, was precisely the view I took of it, and this was enforced by the subsequent movements of the enemy.

In another paragraph of the report it is stated that 55,000 men was the number considered adequate for the defense of the capital. That General McClellan, in his enumeration of the forces left, had included Banks' army corps, operating in the Shenandoah Valley, but whether this corps should be regarded as available for the protection of Washington they decline to express an opinion. At the time this report was made the only enemy on any approach to Washington was Jackson's force, in front of Banks, in the Shenandoah Valley, with the Manassas Gap Railroad leading from this valley to Washington; and it will be admitted, I presume, that Banks, occupying the Shenandoah Valley, was in the best position to defend, not only that approach to Washington, but the road to Harper's Ferry and above. The number of troops left by me for the defense of Washington, as given in my letter to the Adjutant-General, were taken from the latest official returns of that date, and these, of course, constituted the most trustworthy and authentic source from which such information could be obtained.

Another statement made by General Hitchcock before the Committee on the Conduct of the War in reference to this same order should be noticed. He was asked the following question:

Do you understand now that the movement made by General McClellan to Fort Monroe and up the York River was in compliance with the recommendation of the council of generals commanding corps and held at Fairfax Court-House on the 13th of March last, or in violation of it?

To which he replied as follows:

I have considered, and do now consider, that it was in violation of the recommendation of that council in two important particulars, one particular being that portion of this report which represents the council as agreeing to the expedition by way of the Peninsula, provided the rebel steamer Merrimac could first be neutralized. That important provision General McClellan disregarded.

*   *   *   *   *   *   *

The second particular alluded to by General Hitchcock was in reference to the troops left for the defense of Washington, which has been disposed of above.

In regard to the steamer Merrimac I have also stated that so far as our operations on York River were concerned the power of this vessel was neutralized. I now proceed to give some of the evidence which influenced me in coming to that conclusion.

Previous to our departure for the Peninsula, Mr. Watson, Assistant Secretary of War, was sent by the President to Fort Monroe to consult with Flag-Officer Goldsborough upon this subject. The result of that consultation is contained in the following extract from the evidence of Admiral Goldsborough before the Committee on the Conduct of the War, viz:

I told Mr. Watson, Assistant Secretary of War, that the President might make his mind perfectly easy about the Merrimac going up York River; that she could never get there, for I had ample means to prevent that.

Capt. G. V. Fox, Assistant Secretary of the Navy, testifies before the committee as follows:

General McClellan expected the Navy to neutralize the Merrimac, and I promised that it should be done.

General Keyes, commanding Fourth Army Corps, testifies as follows before the committee:

During the time that the subject of the change of base was discussed I had refused to consent to the Peninsula line of operations until I had sent word to the Navy Department and asked two questions: First, whether the Merrimac was certainly neutralized or not. Second, whether the Navy was in a condition to co-operate efficiently with the Army to break through between Yorktown and Gloucester Point. To both of these answers were returned in the affirmative; that is, the Merrimac was neutralized, and the Navy was in a condition to co-operate efficiently to break through between Yorktown and Gloucester Point.

Before starting for the Peninsula I instructed Lieut. Col. B. S. Alexander, of the U. S. Corps of Engineers, to visit Manassas Junction and its vicinity, for the purpose of determining upon the defensive works necessary to enable us to hold that place with a small force. The accompanying letters from Colonel Alexander will show what steps were taken by him to carry into effect this important order. I regret to say that those who succeeded me in command of the region in front of Washington, whatever were the fears for its safety, did not deem it necessary to carry out my plans and instructions to them. Had Manassas been placed in condition for a strong defense and its communications secured, as recommended by Colonel Alexander, the result of General Pope's campaign would probably have been different:

WASHINGTON, D. C., *April* 2, 1862.

SIR: You will proceed to Manassas at as early a moment as practicable, and mark on the ground the works for the defense of that place on the positions which I indicated to you yesterday. You will find two carpenters experienced in this kind of work ready to accompany you, by calling on Mr. Dougherty, the master carpenter of the Treasury Extension. The general idea of the defense of this position is to occupy the fringe of elevation which lies about half way between Manassas depot and the junction of the railroad with a series of works open to the rear, so that they may be commanded by the work hereafter to be described. There will be at least four of these works, three of them being on the left of the railroad leading from Alexandria, at the positions occupied by the enemy's works; the other on the right of this road, on the position we examined yesterday. The works of the enemy to the north of this latter position, numbered 1 and 2 on Lieutenant Comstock's sketch, may also form a part of the front line of our defense, but the sides of these works looking towards Manassas Station should be leveled, so that the interior of the works may be seen from the latter position. Embrasures should be arranged in all these works for field artillery. The approaches should be such that a battery can drive into the works. The number of embrasures in each battery will depend upon its size and the ground to be commanded. It is supposed there will be from four to eight embrasures in each battery.

The other works of the enemy looking towards the east and south may be strengthened, so as to afford sufficient defense in these directions. The work No. 3 in Lieutenant Comstock's sketch may be also strengthened and arranged for field artillery when time will permit. This work is in a good position to cover a retreat, which would be made down the valley in which the railroad runs towards Bull Run. At Manassas Station there should be a fort constructed. The railroad might pass through this fort, and the depot, if there should be one built, should be placed in its rear. This latter work should be regarded as the key to the position. It should be as large as the nature of the ground will permit.

By going down the slopes, which are not steep, it may be made large enough to accommodate 2,000 or 3,000 men. The top of the position need not be cut away; it will be better to throw up the earth into a large traverse, which may also be a bomb-proof. Its profile should be strong and its ditches should be flanked. It should receive a heavy armament of 24 or 32 pounders, with some rifled (Parrott) 20 or 30 pounders. Its guns should command all the exterior works, so that these works could be of no use to the enemy should he take them. In accommodating the fort to the ground this consideration should not be lost sight of.

After tracing these works on the ground you will make a sketch embracing the whole of them, showing their relative positions and size. This sketch should embrace the junction of the railroads and the ground for some distance around the main work. It need not be made with extreme accuracy. The distances may be paced or measured with a tape-line. The bearings may be taken by compass.

Having located the works and prepared your sketch, you will report to Capt. Frederick E. Prime, of the Corps of Engineers, who will furnish you the means of construction.

It is important that these works should be built with the least possible delay. You will therefore expedite matters as fast as possible.

Very respectfully, your obedient servant,

B. S. ALEXANDER,
Lieutenant-Colonel, Aide-de-Camp.

Capt. FRED. R. MUNTHER, *Present.*

WASHINGTON, *April* 6, 1862.

SIR: I inclose you herewith a copy of the instructions which I gave to Captain Munther in reference to the defenses of Manassas.

As there has been a new department created (that of the Rappahannock), it is possible that you and I, as well as General McClellan, are relieved from the further consideration of this subject at the present time.

I will, however, state for your information, should the subject ever come before you again, that in my opinion the communication with Manassas by land should be secured.

To effect this in the best manner, so far as my observations extend, I think the bridge over Bull Run near Union Mills and just above the railroad bridge should be rebuilt or thoroughly repaired, and that a small work or two or three open batteries should be erected on the adjacent heights to protect it as well as the railroad bridge.

The communication by land would then be through or near Centreville, over the road used by the enemy.

I write this for fear something should detain me here, but I hope to leave here to join you to-morrow. My health is much improved.
Very respectfully, your obedient servant,

B. S. ALEXANDER,
Lieutenant-Colonel, Aide-de-Camp.

Brig. Gen. J. G. BARNARD,
  Chief Engineer, Army of the Potomac.

I may be permitted also to mention that the plans (also unexecuted by my successor) indicated in my letter of instructions to General Banks, dated March 16, 1862, for intrenching Chester Gap and the point where the Manassas Railroad crosses the Shenandoah, were for the purpose of preventing even the attempt of such a raid as that of Jackson in the month of May following.

MILITARY INCIDENTS OF THE FIRST PERIOD.

Before taking up the history of the embarkation and Peninsula campaign, I should remark that during the fall and winter of 1861-'62, while the Army of the Potomac was in position in front of Washington, reconnaissances were made from time to time, and skirmishes frequently occurred, which were of great importance to the education of the troops, accustoming them to the presence of the enemy, and giving them confidence under fire. There were many instances of individual gallantry displayed in these affairs. The reports of them will be found among the documents which accompany this report.

One of the most brilliant of these affairs was that which took place at Dranesville, on December 20, 1861, when the third brigade of McCall's division, under Brig. Gen. E. O. C. Ord, with Easton's battery, routed and pursued four regiments of infantry, one of cavalry, and a battery of six pieces.

The operations of Brig. Gen. F. W. Lander, on the Upper Potomac, during the months of January and February, 1862, frustrated the attempts of General Jackson against the Baltimore and Ohio Railroad, Cumberland, &c., and obliged him to fall back to Winchester. His constitution was impaired by the hardships he had experienced, and on the 2d March the fearless General Lander expired, a victim to the excessive fatigue of the campaign.

*   *   *   *   *   *   *

I am, sir, very respectfully, your obedient servant,

GEO. B. McCLELLAN,
Major-General, U. S. Army.

Brig. Gen. L. THOMAS,
  Adjutant-General U. S. Army.

No. 2.

Report of Brig. Gen. William F. Barry, Chief of Artillery, Army of the Potomac, of the organization and operations of the artillery of that army from July 25, 1861, to September 1, 1862.

WASHINGTON, *September 1, 1862.*

GENERAL : In compliance with the orders of Major-General McClellan, I have the honor to give some account of the history, organization, and operations of the artillery of the Army of the Potomac from July, 1861, to September, 1862, the period during which I was its chief.

When Major-General McClellan was appointed to the command of the Division of the Potomac (July 25, 1861), a few days after the first battle of Bull Run, the whole field artillery of his command consisted of no more than parts of nine batteries or thirty pieces of various and in some instances unusual and unserviceable calibers. Most of these batteries were also of mixed calibers, and they were insufficiently equipped in officers and men, and in horses, harness, and material generally.

My calculations were based upon the expected immediate expansion of the "Division of the Potomac" into the "Army of the Potomac," to consist of at least 100,000 infantry. Considerations of the peculiar character and extent of the force to be employed, of the probable field and character of operations, of the utmost efficiency of the arm, and of the limits imposed by the as yet undeveloped resources of the nation, led to the following general propositions offered by me to Major-General McClellan, and which received his full approval:

1st. That the proportion of artillery should be in the ratio of at least two and a half pieces to 1,000 men, to be expanded if possible to three pieces to 1,000 men.

2d. That the proportion of rifled guns should be restricted to the system of the U. S. Ordnance Department, and of Parrott and the smooth bore (with the exception of a few howitzers for special service) to be exclusively the 12-pounder gun of the model of 1857, variously called the "gun howitzer," the "light 12-pounder," or the "Napoleon."

3d. That each field battery should, if practicable, be composed of six guns, and none to be less than four guns, and in all cases the guns of each battery should be of uniform caliber.

4th. That the field batteries were to be assigned to divisions and not to brigades, and in the proportion of four to each division, of which one was to be a battery of regulars, the remainder of volunteers; the captain of the regular battery to be the commander of artillery of the division. In the event of several divisions constituting an army corps, at least one-half of the divisional artillery was to constitute the reserve artillery of the corps.

5th. That the artillery reserve of the whole army should consist of 100 guns, and should comprise, besides a sufficient number of light mounted batteries, all of the guns of position, and until the cavalry was massed all the horse artillery.

6th. That the amount of ammunition to accompany the field batteries was not to be less than 400 rounds per gun.

7th. A siege train of fifty pieces. This was subsequently expanded (for special service at the siege of Yorktown) to very nearly 100 pieces, and comprised the unusual calibers and enormously heavy weight of metal of two 200-pounders, five 100-pounders, and ten 13-inch sea-coast mortars.

8th. That instruction in the theory and practice of gunnery, as well as in the tactics of the arm, was to be given to the officers and non-commissioned officers of the volunteer batteries by the study of suitable text-books and by actual recitations in each division, under the direction of the regular officer commanding the divisional artillery.

9th. That personal inspections, as frequent as the nature of circumstances would permit, should be made by me, to be assured of the strict observance of the established organization and drill and of the special regulations and orders issued from time to time under the authority of the commanding general, and to note the progressive improvement of the officers and enlisted men of the volunteer batteries, and the actual fitness for field service of the whole, both regular and volunteer.

[10th.] A variety of unexpected circumstances conspired to compel in some degree trifling modifications of these general propositions, but in the main they scrupulously formed the basis of the organization of the artillery of the Army of the Potomac. This sudden and extensive expansion of the artillery arm of the nation taxed far beyond their capacities the various arsenals and private founderies which had hitherto exclusively supplied to the United States the requisite ordnance material. The Ordnance Department promptly met my requisitions by enlarging as far as possible the operations of the arsenals of supply and construction and by the extensive employment of private contractors. The use of contract work, while it gave increased facility in meeting promptly the suddenly-increased demand, was the unavoidable cause of introducing into the service much inferior ordnance material. The gun-carriages were particularly open to this objection, and their bad construction was in more than one instance the unfortunate occasion of the loss of field guns.

[11th.] It affords me great satisfaction to state that the Ordnance Department in the main kept the supply constantly up to the demand, and by cheerful and ready attention to complaints and the prompt creation of the requisite means enabled me to withdraw inferior material and substitute such as was found to be more reliable.

[12th.] To Lieutenant-Colonel Ramsay, in command of Washington Arsenal, to Lieutenant Bradford, his assistant, and to Captain Benton, in the office of the Chief of Ordnance, these remarks in particular apply. To their promptness, industry, and active general co-operation am I indebted in a great degree for the means which enabled me to organize such an immense artillery force in so short a time.

[13th.] As has been before stated, the whole of the field artillery of the Army of the Potomac July 25, 1861, was comprised in nine imperfectly-equipped batteries of 30 guns, 650 men, and 400 horses. In March, 1862, when the whole army took the field, it consisted of ninety-two batteries of 520 guns, 12,500 men, and 11,000 horses, fully equipped and in readiness for active field service. Of the whole force thirty batteries were regulars and sixty-two batteries volunteers. During this short period of seven months all of this immense amount of material was issued to me and placed in the hands of the artillery troops after their arrival in Washington. About one-quarter of all the volunteer batteries brought with them from their respective States a few guns and carriages, but they were nearly all of such peculiar caliber as to lack uniformity with the more modern and more serviceable ordnance with which I was arming the other batteries, and they therefore had to be withdrawn and replaced by more suitable material. While about one-sixth came supplied with horses and harness, less than one-tenth were apparently fully equipped for service when they reported to me, and every one of those required the supply of many deficiencies of material and very extensive instruction in the theory and practice of their special arm.

[14th.] When the Army of the Potomac on the 1st of April embarked for Fort Monroe and the Virginia Peninsula the field-artillery force which had been organized was disposed of as follows, viz:

	Batteries.	Guns.
Detached for service in the Department of South Carolina	2	12
Detached for service in the Department of North Carolina	1	6
Detached for service in the Department of the Gulf	1	6
Detached for service in the command of Major-General Dix	3	20
Detached for service in the Mountain Department (division Blenker)	3	18
First Corps (Major-General McDowell)	12	68
Fifth Corps (Major-General Banks)	13	59
Defenses of Washington (Brigadier-General Wadsworth)	7	32
	42	221
Embarked March 15 to April 1, 1862, for the Peninsula	52	299

[15th.] The operations on the Peninsula by the Army of the Potomac commenced with a field-artillery force of fifty-two batteries, of 299 guns. To this must be added the field artillery of Franklin's division of McDowell's corps, which joined a few days before the capture of Yorktown, but was not disembarked from its transports for service until after the battle of Williamsburg, and the field artillery of McCall's division of McDowell's corps (four batteries, 22 guns), which joined in June, a few days before the battle of Mechanicsville, June 26, 1862, making a grand total of field artillery at any time with the army on the Peninsula of sixty batteries, of 343 guns. With this large force, serving in six corps d'armée of eleven divisions and the artillery reserve, the only general and field officers were 1 brigadier-general, 4 colonels, 3 lieutenant-colonels, and 3 majors, a number obviously insufficient, and which impaired to a great degree (in consequence of the want of rank and official influence of the commanders of corps and divisional artillery) the efficiency of the arms. As this faulty organization can be suitably corrected only by legislative action, it is earnestly hoped that the attention of the proper authorities may be at an early day invited to it.

[16th.] When there were so many newly-organized volunteer field batteries, many of whom received their first and only instruction in the intrenched camps covering Washington during the three or four inclement months of the winter of 1861–'62, there was, of course, much to be improved. Many of the volunteer batteries, however, evinced such zeal and intelligence and availed themselves so industriously of the instructions of the regular officer, their commander, and of the example of the regular battery, their associate, that they made rapid progress and attained a degree of proficiency highly creditable.

[17th.] Special detailed reports have been made and transmitted by me of the general artillery operations at the siege of Yorktown, and by their immediate commanders of the services of the field batteries at the battles of Williamsburg, Hanover Court-House, and those severely contested ones comprised in the operations in front of Richmond. To these several reports I respectfully refer the commanding general for details of services as creditable to the artillery of the United States as they are honorable to the gallant officers and brave and patient enlisted men, who with but few exceptions, struggling through difficulties, overcoming obstacles, and bearing themselves nobly on the field of battle, stood faithfully to their guns, performing their various duties with a steadiness, a devotion, and a gallantry worthy of all commendation.

[18th.] For the artillery of the Army of the Potomac it is but simple justice to claim that, in contributing its aid to the other two arms as far as lay in its power, it did its whole duty faithfully and intelligently, and that on more than one occasion (the battle of Malvern particularly) it confessedly saved the army from serious disaster.

I am, general, very respectfully, your obedient servant,

WILLIAM F. BARRY,

Brigadier-General, late Chief of Artillery Army of the Potomac.

Brig. Gen. S. WILLIAMS, *Assistant Adjutant-General.*

No. 3.

Report of Maj. Albert J. Myer, Chief Signal Officer, U. S. Army, of the signal service in the Army of the Potomac, from August 14, 1861, to March 23, 1862, and of signal detachments in other commands.

OFFICE OF THE SIGNAL OFFICER,
Washington, D. C., October 21, 1862.

GENERAL: The Chief Signal Officer, then serving at headquarters Department of Virginia, was, by Special Orders, No. 26, directed to report for duty at the headquarters of the then Division of the Potomac, on August 14, 1861. This order was consequent upon information which had been received that our forces on the Upper Potomac needed intercommunication between the different divisions, and also to the fact that attention had been called at that part of our lines and along our front before Washington to the telegraphic field signals of the enemy. The general commanding the then Division of the Potomac required a signal line to connect the right of his army with the forces surrounding Washington. Orders to this effect were received on the same day, verbally, from the general commanding the army and by the letter herewith from the Assistant Secretary of War.

The organization of the signal corps of the Army of the Potomac was commenced on the issue of the order herewith. On this order officers and men were collected from various regiments and were gathered at small camps of instruction, which were formed at Pooles-ville, Md., then the headquarters of General Stone; on the top of Sugar Loaf Mountain, a prominent mountain in Maryland, and at Hyatts-town, then the headquarters of General Banks. These camps were respectively in charge of Lieuts. Theodore S. Dumont, Fifth New York Volunteers, and acting signal officer; Evan Thomas, Fourth Artillery, U. S. Army, and acting signal officer, and Leonard F. Hepburn, Fourth New York Volunteers, and acting signal officer, who, instructed and previously serving at Fortress Monroe, Va., had been ordered to aid in the formation of this party. The course of instruction in signal duty was commenced at the camps mentioned while the officers there stationed had communication by signals between them.

On the 31st August, 1861, the central signal camp of instruction was established at Red Hill, Georgetown, D. C. The detachment of officers and men detailed for signal duty from the Pennsylvania Reserve Volunteer Corps and on examination approved for instruction was the first received at this camp.

On the 12th of September, 1861, the approved officers and men of the detachments from the Upper Potomac were here concentrated. The next day the new camp was organized, the courses of instruction were decided upon, and the central signal camp of instruction in Georgetown became the school for all the acting signal officers of the Army.

For the successful management and control of this camp of instruction much credit is due to the efficient co-operation of the then First Lieutenant Samuel T. Cushing, Second Infantry, U. S. Army, acting signal officer, who, from the day of its formation until it was abandoned, associated with the Chief Signal Officer, labored zealously and with perseverance to fit the officers and men there under instruction to honorably bear their parts in the campaigns of the war then just opening.

The organizing, instructing, disciplining, and retaining for service the signal corps of the Army of the Potomac (from which all other detachments of the signal corps in the United States have directly or indirectly sprung) was attended with many circumstances of interest and many of difficulty. It was a work of no ordinary toil to originate and to put in the field in the time of such a war a corps before unknown. There were duties to be performed in the face of prejudices which were childish, and in spite of oppositions born of ignorance. The narrative of these early days and the recital of the modes in which step by step the signal corps won its way will form a part of a general report to the Chief Signal Officer.

At the signal camp of instruction the officers and men were taught the manual of the signal apparatus, and they were practiced to send messages of any kind and of any number of words by telegraphic signals. The apparatus used is now well known to the general commanding. It is sufficient, therefore, to say that, by the motions of a single flag, attached to a staff, held and worked by the hands of one man, in the day, or by the similar motions of a lighted torch, fastened to the staff instead of a flag, at night, a single man is converted into a semaphore, useful for any distances at which the signs made are visible either with the naked eye or with telescopes.

The officers were instructed in countersign signals, by which to distinguish friendly regiments, and in the employment of colored lights and rockets as signals. They were habituated by constant use to the management of the telescope. They were taught the drill of the flagman. They learned to ride, and were instructed how to provide for themselves and their parties in the field. They were taught some duties of reconnaissance. They were fresh from civil life; it was aimed to give them something of the feeling and habits of soldiers.

It was from the beginning the intention to place in charge of this corps the flying or field electric telegraphs, for use upon the field of battle or in the immediate presence of the enemy. These were to be similar in their general construction to those telegraphic trains at a later day brought into use on the Peninsula. The efforts to procure these trains were thwarted to some extent by the actions of persons who seemed to greatly desire that all the duties of electric telegraphy should be in the hands of civilians, and in part, perhaps, by the hesitation of officers in authority to become responsible by favoring it for the success of what was then an experiment in our service. I did all I could to obtain authority and the means to properly fit such trains to accompany the army on the march. In the early days of the war I could not obtain the asked permission to organize a party or to draw on the Departments for supplies. Later, when I submitted plans and further requests on this subject, they were either not answered or received non-committal replies. Estimates accompanying my annual report of November 10, 1862, were not acted upon.

With embarrassments of this nature the work could not be successfully carried on. It was only when the Army was fairly in the field that the plans began to receive some favorable attention and some support. One train was, however, partially completed, and the officers of the corps were familiarized with its use. This was the first movable telegraphic train of which there is record, as made for the United States Army.

COUNTERSIGN SIGNALS.

On October 17, 1861, the order for the adoption of countersign signals in the Army of the Potomac was issued at the suggestion of the Chief Signal Officer. To acquire a thorough knowledge of the use of these signals, to procure and issue the necessary supplies, and to instruct the designated officers in the two hundred and fifty regiments and organizations comprised in the Army of the Potomac occupied much of the attention and employed much of the time of the forming corps until late in December. The theory of these signals was good; the apparatus was convenient; the modes of making the signals were practicable. Experience has shown, however, that in a new army these signals will not be safely used unless an organized corps of signal officers accompany such an army. The failure of Congress to organize a signal corps during the session of 1861-'62 led, on the recommendation of the Chief Signal Officer, to the suspension, in October, 1862, of the use of counter-sign signals in the Army of the Potomac. They were of practical use on some few occasions, and it is probable beneficially influenced the army, in so far as, by leading the men to presume that signals would always distinguish their enemies from their friends, they prevented the stampedes and panic firings which by their sad results had early in the war so moved the nation. I am of the opinion that, with the improving organization of the armies of the United States, this use, first tested in the Army of the Potomac, will be perfected and made general.

OUTPOST AND SCOUT SIGNALS.

In December, 1861, the Chief Signal Officer was ordered to prepare a plan for outpost and scout signals, or signs by which troops upon outposts and with scouting parties might recognize friendly forces. These signals were for some months used along the lines in front of and near Washington and after the army had taken the field on the Peninsula. The very general use attempted to be made of them in so great an army was always of doubtful value. There was danger that troops widely separated, of different intelligence and of different nations, could not be rightly instructed. The proper employment of signals of this character is for especial occasions and for especial troops. Their use (from the beginning neglected) was formally abandoned while the army was upon the Chickahominy, in June, 1862.

Early in January, 1862, the force at the signal camp of instruction, at Georgetown, D. C., was largely increased by a detail of 3 officers and 6 men, ordered from each brigade of the Army of the Potomac, which had not previously furnished its quota. Fifty per cent. of the officers thus ordered failed to report.

ORIGIN OF THE SIGNAL CORPS OF THE ARMY.

The officers and men detailed for signal service manifested interest in the study of their duties, and as a corps early attained an advanced preparation. The character of their employment attracted much attention. Small signal parties had been left stationed at Poolesville, on Sugar Loaf Mountain, and at Seneca, Md. These points were in daily communication. The simplicity of the apparatus with which the officers conversed; their power of communicating at distances of many miles and in the night as well as in the day; the incomprehensible orders given by the officers to the flagmen, and the seemingly more incomprehensible evolutions with flags and torches, were, in and out of the army, subjects of ceaseless comment.

Like comment was elicited by the work of officers sent out to practice in the vicinity of Washington, and who were found at all hours of the night as well as day scattered about the country, miles from camp, on towers or on prominent heights, busily telegraphing, and with airs of sage importance and mystery, messages as lessons of practice. In the newspaper histories of the war the signal camp of instruction will be found to have a special mention.

The organization of the signal corps of the Army of the Potomac (then the grand army of the United States) became a fact of general knowledge. As other armies were formed or expeditions were prepared, skilled officers and men sent from the parent camp formed with these armies, with other officers and men by them instructed, the different detachments of the acting signal corps which, serving in the various geographical departments, have carried the signal flag on so many fields in this war. The details for this purpose from the Army of the Potomac were as follows, viz:

DETACHMENTS.

Early in the month of October, 1861, the expedition of the combined land and naval forces, afterwards styled the "Port Royal Expedition," was contemplated. On the application of General Thomas W. Sherman, commanding the expedition, the Chief Signal Officer was ordered to detail signal officers to accompany it. A party of 7 signal officers, with 14 men, equipped, commanded by Lieut. E. J. Keenan, Eleventh Pennsylvania Reserve Volunteer Corps, and acting signal officer, joined the expedition for duty a few days before it sailed from Annapolis. The brilliant success of this party, achieved by the gallantry and the labor of the officers and men composing it, contributed to the success of the expedition and to the advancement of the corps. The detachment of the signal corps now serving in South Carolina had hence its origin.

In December, 1861, an application was made by Major-General Buell, then commanding the Department of the Ohio, for a detail of signal officers to be sent to him. There was some vacillation about the movement of this party, the order to send and to retain it being for a time alternated. At last, however, a detachment of 5 officers and 10 men, equipped, was sent to General Buell. The signal party now commanded by Capt. Jesse Merrill, Seventh Pennsylvania Reserve Volunteer Corps, and acting signal officer, and serving with General Rosecrans in the Department of the Cumberland, took its origin from this detail. The difficulties encountered by this party, in the unfavorable character of the country, the situation and condition of the forces, the want of experience of the officers composing it, and the semi-official opposition of other officers, who knew nothing of its duties, have not been surpassed. That the corps through all its difficulties maintained its organization and has attained the position it now holds under General Rosecrans has proven some intrinsic value in its duties and much merit in the officers who organized and have composed it.

A few days before the sailing of the Burnside expedition for North Carolina there was received the application, made by General Burnside, for a signal party to be detailed to his army, and the order to make the detail. Three officers and 6 men, equipped, and commanded by Lieut. Joseph Fricker, Eighth Pennsylvania Reserve Volunteer Corps, and acting signal officer, reported at Annapolis to accompany this expedition. A class of 22 officers was there detailed and its instruction commenced. At this time there was in the hands of the signal officer, to supply the whole Army of the United States, the sum of $208.94. Such scanty equipment as could be gathered was hurried to this party as it was embarking from Annapolis. It accompanied the expedition. Twenty-five officers, with their men, were crowded in one small schooner. They were driven off the coast in the gale which so severely damaged the Burnside fleet, and among their earliest experiences in the service was that of a sea voyage of three weeks' duration from Fortress Monroe to Hatteras. Arriving at last at Hatteras, they were at once in action at Roanoke Island. The care with which the usefulness of this party was developed by General Burnside was repaid by their services in every engagement in his department. They originated the detachment of the signal corps now in North Carolina.

On the 10th of March, 1862, after the return of the Army of the Potomac to Alexandria, following the evacuation of Manassas, two detachments, each of 3 officers and 6 men, equipped and supplied with extra stores, were ordered to report, the one in charge of Lieut. J. B. Ludwick, Ninth Pennsylvania Reserve Volunteer Corps, and acting signal officer, to Maj. Gen. H. W. Halleck, then commanding the Department of the Mississippi at Saint Louis, the other in charge of Lieut. E. H. Russell, Ninth Pennsylvania Reserve Volunteer Corps, and acting signal officer, to Maj. Gen. B. F. Butler, commanding the Department of the Gulf.

The party reporting to General Halleck formed under the orders of that officer a class of 20 officers and 40 men. This party was instructed, equipped, and prepared to take the field. A detachment from it served at Fort Saint Charles, White River.

At the time the whole party was reported for duty in the field and for some weeks after the Army of the Mississippi lay before Corinth. The country was unfavorable for their operations, and it was, perhaps, not contemplated that that army was to move, or that there might be service on the banks of the Mississippi and the incurrent rivers. The officers composing the party were ordered by the general commanding to rejoin their regiments, and the organization was thus on the 30th of June, 1862, broken up. The operations of the fall and winter of 1862-'63 have made it necessary to repeat the labor of the past spring, and to instruct and form anew the party of the Mississippi Valley.

The detachment detailed for the Department of the Gulf reached, after many delays, the headquarters of General Butler after the capture of New Orleans. A party was organized and instructed for service in this department. It served successfully at the battle of Bayou La Fourche. It constitutes now a part of the corps serving under General N. P. Banks.

From the date of the first order, in August, 1861, a party of 8 officers and 16 men, commanded by Lieut. W. W. Rowley, Twenty-eighth New York Volunteers, and acting signal officer, was left to serve with the forces under General Banks. During the fall and through the winter and until the advance of the force of that general into the valley of the Shenandoah, this party held stations of observation and communication on Maryland Heights, on the heights at Point of Rocks, on Sugar Loaf Mountain, at Poolesville, Md., and on the ridge at Seneca. The labors and the usefulness of this party elicited the thanks of the general under whom it served.

Early in February, 1862, a movement of the forces under General Hooker on the Lower Potomac was contemplated. They were, it was said, to cross the river for an advance upon the enemy. A detachment of 8 officers and 25 men, equipped and mounted, commanded by Lieut. B. F. Fisher, Third Pennsylvania Reserve Volunteer Corps, and acting signal officer, reported to General Hooker for service in the expected engagement. The enemy abandoned their batteries before an attack was made, and the river was crossed without opposition. The party rejoined the main Army of the Potomac in Alexandria in April, and accompanied it to the Peninsula.

MOVEMENT OF THE CORPS TO ACCOMPANY THE ARMY.

In the early days of March, 1862, the improving condition of the roads indicating that a movement of the army would be soon practicable, the corps was mobilized.

At midnight on the 9th of March, 1862, the order of the general commanding the army, directing the corps to take the field, was received at the signal camp of instruction.

At 1 a. m. on the 10th of March an order was received directing the field telegraphic train to be on the Little River turnpike, ready to move with the commanding general at daylight. This train had not been completed and was not ready for the field.

The camp was struck before daylight. On the evening of the 10th of March the different sections had either arrived at the points indicated in Special Orders, No. 41, or were so near those positions that the chiefs of sections had reported in person to the different generals. One section alone was prevented by impassable roads from reporting before daylight on the morning of the 11th. The headquarters of the signal corps were established on the night of the 10th at Fairfax Court-House, Va.

On the morning of the 11th information was received that the enemy had evacuated Manassas and were rapidly falling back towards the Rappahannock. On the morning of the 12th signal stations were established on the heights at Centreville and among the ruins, yet smoking, at Manassas. The advance station at Manassas, in charge of Lieut. J. B. Ludwick, acting signal officer, was some miles beyond our pickets, and with no guard. These stations were held with some risk and much labor while the army lay at Fairfax Court-House.

An effort was made to connect Manassas Junction and Union Mills by a line of signals. The attempt failed because it was found that to do so would require more stations than officers could be spared to command.

In the reconnaissances made by signal officers of our army there was found a station occupied by the signal officers of the rebel army before and at the time of the first battle of Manassas. There is perhaps no country better formed by nature for the successful use of signal communication than on and near this battle-field. It was a subject of regretful remembrance that the Army of the United States had not secured for it in that battle such aid as signals might have given it.

On the 14th of March headquarters of the Army of the Potomac were established near Alexandria, Va. The detachments of the signal corps were quartered in that village.

BATTLE OF WINCHESTER.

While the army lay here the report of the battle of Winchester, fought by General Banks in the valley of the Shenandoah, was received. Mention of this battle is made in this report for the reason that the corps commanded by General Banks was at that time a part of the Army of the Potomac, and that the signal corps serving with him was a part of that originally formed for that army. Stations were established in this action on the right, the left, and the center of the line engaged, and also to the rear, communicating with the general commanding at Winchester. The full reports of Lieut. W. W. Rowley, Twenty-eighth New York Volunteers, and acting signal officer, and his officers, clearly define the positions taken by them on that field and the services they rendered. Lieutenant Rowley has mentioned in his report the names of Lieuts. D. A. Taylor, Third New York Artillery, and acting signal officer; S. D. Byram, Sixteenth Indiana Volunteers, and acting signal officer; W. L. Larned, First Minnesota Volunteers, and acting signal officer; J. H. Spencer, First Minnesota Volunteers, and acting signal officer; J. H.

Fralick, Thirty-fourth New York Volunteers, and acting signal officer; F. N. Wicker, Twenty-eighth New York Volunteers, and acting signal officer; I. J. Harvey, Second Pennsylvania Reserve Volunteer Corps, and acting signal officer; B. N. Miner, Thirty-fourth New York Volunteers, and acting signal officer; E. A. Briggs, Forty-third New York Volunteers, and acting signal officer; E. L. Halsted, Fortieth New York Volunteers, and acting signal officer, for their parts at this battle.

The officers and men of this detachment again elicited the official commendation of General Banks on the retreat from the valley of the Shenandoah. This signal party, as was the case of that commanded by Lieutenant Wilson, acting signal officer, detailed to the corps commanded by General McDowell, served with the army corps to which they were attached throughout the summer and until (in September) the forces in front of Washington were consolidated in the Army of the Potomac for the defense of that city.*

*   *   *   *   *   *   *

Very respectfully, general, your obedient servant,
                        ALBERT J. MYER,
                    Signal Officer, Major U. S. Army,
                and *Chief Signal Officer Army of Potomac.*
The ADJUTANT-GENERAL ARMY OF THE POTOMAC.

No. 4.

Report of Surg. Charles S. Tripler, Medical Director of the Army of the Potomac, of the operations of the medical department of that Army from August 12, 1861, to March 17, 1862.

                        DETROIT, MICH., *February* 7, 1863.

GENERAL: In compliance with your instructions, I have the honor to submit the following report of the operations of the medical department of the Army of the Potomac during the time I was connected with it as medical direction:

This time naturally divides itself into two periods: the first embracing the time from the beginning of the organization of that army to that of its taking the field; the second from the latter time to the completion of the change of base to Harrison's Landing, on the James River.

I joined the Army of the Potomac August 12, 1861, and was immediately charged with the organization of the medical department. At that time the three months' volunteers were mustered out of service, and the new levies were being rapidly assembled in Washington and its vicinity. A number of camps were formed on both sides of the Potomac, and the construction of the field works had been commenced. There were some five or six hotels, seminaries, and infirmaries in Washington and Georgetown occupied as general hospitals, and one or two in Alexandria, the fruits of the exigencies of the three-months' campaign. These were under capable officers, well regulated and well conducted, but with no system in reference to the admission or discharge of patients. Every regimental surgeon sent what men he pleased to the general hospitals, without knowing whether there was room for them or not, and men were discharged from the hospitals with no means pro-

----

* Continuation of the report in operations of March 17–September 2, 1862.

vided to insure their return to their regiments. It was not an unusual circumstance for sick men to pass the night in the ambulances, wandering about the streets from hospital to hospital seeking admission. I could find no information anywhere as to what regiments were present or whether they had medical officers or not.

My first effort was to endeavor to find out who were the medical officers of the several regiments, how the hospital departments were supplied, what was the strength of the regiments, how many of the men were sick, and what were the prevailing diseases. For this purpose I applied for and had an order issued directing all the medical officers to report to me in person without delay. From them I required the other items of information I have indicated. A singular state of things was revealed. In General Orders, No. 25, War Department, May 25, 1861, the President had directed that a surgeon and an assistant surgeon should be appointed for each regiment of volunteers by the governors of their respective States, and that these officers should be examined by a board, to be appointed by the governors, as to their qualifications; the appointments to be subject to the approval of the Secretary of War. The third section of the act of August 6, 1861, required vacancies among the volunteer officers to be filled by the governors in the same manner as the original appointment. Some of the States had promptly appointed these boards, but many others had entirely neglected it. The Secretary of War had also accepted what were termed independent regiments, the colonels of which asserted a right to appoint their own medical officers, and, notwithstanding the act of Congress, to fill vacancies. In other instances colonels of State regiments refused to receive the medical officers appointed in conformity with the law and the orders of the President, and went so far as to put these gentlemen out of their camps by force when they reported in obedience to the orders of the governors and of the headquarters of the Army of the Potomac. The State authorities, especially of New York and Pennsylvania, remonstrated strongly against this course, and I used every effort to arrest it, but in vain. I was at last officially notified, on the 19th of November, 1861, that the medical officers of regiments accepted directly by the Secretary of War had acquired rights that could not be set aside by the governors of the States. These irregularities created great embarrassment and confusion in organizing my department, and many regiments were thus left to take their chances with surgeons as to whose competency nothing was known.

In other instances regiments or parts of regiments were sent on without their medical officers, the colonels assuming authority to leave them at home under various pretexts. To meet a case of this kind I addressed the following letter to the surgeon-general of Pennsylvania:

HEADQUARTERS ARMY OF THE POTOMAC,
Medical Director's Office, Washington, September 7, 1861.

SIR: The First Regiment Pennsylvania Cavalry has sent seven companies to this city without a medical officer. I have the honor to request you will send a duly-commissioned surgeon and assistant to this regiment immediately. I am informed a Dr. Harlan is surgeon, but has never joined the regiment. The surgeons of regiments in the field are intended for service and not for ornament. The Government cannot wait the convenience of Dr. Harlan.

Very respectfully, your obedient servant,

CHAS. S. TRIPLER,
Surgeon and Medical Director Army of the Potomac.

H. H. SMITH, M. D., *Surgeon-General of Pennsylvania.*

Another source of embarrassment was, that neither the law nor orders had provided medical officers for batteries or detachments of cavalry.

In these cases I could only direct that such bodies should be attended to by the medical officers of the regiments nearest to them.

To remedy the irregular and doubtful appointments made by colonels, and to give the troops confidence in their medical officers, I determined to assemble boards for the examination of all such as rapidly as their cases were brought to my notice. This I did under authority of General Orders, No. 35, War Department, June 20, 1861. September 7, 1861, I assembled such a board and ordered twelve medical officers before it for examination. From that time forward, whenever a medical officer was complained of for incompetency, a board was ordered. In many cases the complaints were ascertained to be well founded and the officers were discharged.

The third section of the act of July 22, 1861, having provided for a surgeon to each brigade, a board was assembled in Washington to examine candidates for that appointment. A number of the appointees under that act were assigned to duty with the Army of the Potomac. The act had not defined the duties of these officers, nor had any regulation in reference to them emanated from the War Department. Their position was doubtful, and it was necessary to define it. The regimental medical officers were for the most part physicians, taken suddenly from civil life, with no conception whatever of their duties. These had to be taught them from the very alphabet. The line officers were equally ignorant with themselves in this respect, and hence confusion, conflicts of authority, discontent, and very seriously impaired efficiencies in the medical department. The general idea seemed to be that it was the duty of the doctor to physic every man who chose to report sick and to sign such papers as the colonel directed him to sign. To superintend the sanitary condition of the regiment, to call upon the commanding officers to abate nuisances, to take measures for the prevention of disease was in many instances considered impertinent and obtrusive, and the suggestion of the medical officers to those ends were too frequently disregarded and ignored.

It occurred to me that the brigade surgeons, being very generally taken from those who had seen some service in the three-months' campaign, might be made useful in remedying these evils and in carrying out my views for increasing the efficiency of the department. Bearing the commission of the President, I was of opinion that they were the superior officers of the State surgeons, and had authority to control them in their own department; I therefore assigned these gentlemen to the staffs of the several brigadiers, and prepared an order defining their duties. (See Appendix A.)

By conversation with the brigade surgeons I endeavored to impress upon them the importance of the trust confided to them, and show them how much the efficiency of the army depended upon the fidelity and success with which they should discharge their duties. Every item of the order was explained to them, and they were urged to be active and zealous in imbuing the regimental surgeons with a thorough understanding and just appreciation of the hygienic suggestions it contained. It was impossible for me to see and instruct such a number of regimental officers as our army included, and I was therefore obliged to rely upon the brigade surgeons to attend to the training of these officers in their routine duties. This arrangement was the most promising I could command, and I hoped its advantages would be readily seen and appreciated; still some were found to place impediments in the way of these officers in the performance of their duties. In reply to a complaint made by one of them I wrote him as follows:

HEADQUARTERS ARMY OF THE POTOMAC,
Medical Director's Office, Washington, September 20, 1861.

SIR: Your duplicate report, which was very properly made, has been received. The brigade commander will no doubt issue the proper orders to correct the evils which you represent. In relation to your complaint that the colonel of the Thirty-third Pennsylvania Volunteers does not recognize your official relations to him, I have to say that those relations depend upon your commission from the President of the United States and not upon the recognition or non-recognition of any individual officer under the President's command.

Very respectfully, your obedient servant,

CHAS. S. TRIPLER,
Medical Director Army of the Potomac.

Brigade Surgeon PRINCE, *Graham's Brigade.*

I had thus established a hierarchy, which, though imperfect, enabled me to keep myself tolerably well informed of the condition of the medical department of the army. The irregularities prevailing in relation to the sending of men to the general hospitals and discharging them therefrom were corrected by paragraphs 4 to 9 of General Orders, No. 9, Army of Potomac, September 9, 1861. (See Appendix B.)

In suggesting this order I had also another object in view, to control and to diminish as far as possible the number of men sent from the regimental to the general hospitals. The experience of all armies has shown, and my personal observation has convinced me of the fact, that the sick do much better in these regimental than in the general hospitals. I consider general hospitals general nuisances, to be tolerated only because there are occasions when they are absolutely necessary, as, for instance, when an army is put in motion and cannot transport its sick. It is a singular fact, but one as to which I believe all military surgeons of experience will agree with me, that the sick report of a regiment under ordinary circumstances is a constant quantity; that after a regiment has been in the field a month that quantity will be ascertained, and that if the regimental hospital is evacuated in a short time, it will be found to contain again its habitual number of inmates; so that we may have as many successive crops of sick as we choose by repeating the process of evacuating the regimental upon the general hospitals. A leading object with me was to keep up the fighting force to its maximum, and therefore, as well as for the more speedy recovery of the men themselves, I discouraged the practice of sending them to the general hospitals. If I had permitted the practice I found existing to continue —that of sending men promiscuously and without restraint to the general hospitals—the only limit to the number and extent of these would have been what was required to contain the whole army. I stopped it, and thus kept a healthy army in the field.

Having thus established some order and system in the *personnel* of the medical department and some method in instructing the officers in their duties, my attention was turned to the means of keeping them supplied with medicines, instruments, stores, &c. In this I met with many difficulties. The volunteer medical officers being many of them country doctors, accustomed to a village nostrum practice, could not readily change their habits and accommodate themselves to the rigid system of the army in regard to their supplies. To meet this difficulty I attempted within reasonable limits to disregard supply tables, and to give the surgeons articles of medicine and hospital stores to suit even their caprices, if in my judgment such articles could be of any avail in the treatment of disease. In this effort I first felt the inconvenience of being in Washington. The medical purveyor was bound by the regulations, and although my order ought to have been sufficient to have relieved him from all responsibility, still, to be perfectly safe, he would refer such requisitions to the Surgeon-General. The consequence was my orders were countermanded, and I was finally ordered by the Surgeon-General not to issue anything not allowed by the supply table without his sanction, previously obtained.

The pressure upon the purveyor consequent upon the influx of so large a body of troops caused great delay in the issuing of supplies. Complaints of this delay were made to me as early as the beginning of September. I offered the purveyor more assistance if it would expedite his issues. That officer replied on the 6th of September that "any additional aid to that now employed is unnecessary, and would in nowise facilitate the matter." Subsequently a different conclusion was arrived at, and additional aid was furnished.

Another difficulty was encountered in getting the supplies to the regiments after they were put up. Ordinarily the purveyor turns over his supplies to the quartermaster, and it is the duty of that officer to transport them to their destination. It was soon perceived that this mode would not answer in the confusion then reigning in Washington. The regular quartermasters were charged with duties considered of more importance, and the volunteer quartermasters did not know how to perform what we required. We were therefore obliged to require the medical officers to call for and transport their own supplies to their camps. Much was accomplished in this way, though in many instances great negligence and indifference were manifested on the part of the surgeons themselves. Another difficulty to overcome was the supplying the regiments with hospital tents. I determined to issue three of these tents to a regiment. These would accommodate comfortably thirty men. The demand for tents and the scarcity of canvas made it necessary to reduce the allowance to the minimum that could be made to suffice. I approved of requisitions for this number whenever they were presented, and I ordered requisitions to be made in all cases where I discovered it had been neglected. These tents, however, were frequently taken by arbitrary authority for other purposes, such as store tents, guard tents, and the like. Whenever an abuse of this sort was brought to my notice I took every means in my power to correct it, and I believe, from the best information I could get, that when the army moved to Fairfax Court-House every regiment in it had its full supply of hospital tents. When the medical officers reported to me I required them to submit to me an inventory of the supplies of all sorts they had on hand. These were carefully revised, and whenever they were defective, requisitions were immediately called to meet the deficiencies. Great difficulty was experienced in enforcing obedience to this simple requirement. By firmness and patience I believe it was overcome, so that I had every assurance short of personal inspection, which was impossible, that nearly every regiment in the army was fully supplied for three months at the time we moved. A few had succeeded in neglecting this duty and escaping the vigilance of the inspectors and brigade surgeons. These applied for issues during the few days we remained at Alexandria after our return from Fairfax. My purveyor was then engaged in packing and shipping his stores for Fort Monroe. Of course I could not arrest this work to remedy the faults of half a dozen idlers.

My next step was an attempt to improve the condition of the camps, so as to promote the health of the army, by correcting hygienic errors and by removing as far as practicable the causes of disease. On the 19th of August I directed all the prisoners at the Capitol Prison to be vaccinated, a bath to be fitted up for their use, and such outdoor exercise to be allowed them as was consistent with their safe-keeping. On the 22d of August I sent a surgeon to remedy the defects in the police of the camp of the Pennsylvania cavalry, on Seventh street. This camp at the time was a nuisance. On the same day I recommended the removal of the troops encamped upon the flats near Arlington to the higher grounds, if practicable. Thirty-three per cent. of some of the regiments there were reported sick with diarrhea, intermittent, and typhoid fevers. The chief surgeon of McDowell's division, who had been some weeks at Arlington, expressed his doubts to me, in a report on the subject, whether the flats were more insalubrious than the high woodlands of that district. I represented to the Adjutant-General that I acknowledged these doubts to be well founded within certain limits— that malarial fevers do prevail on the slope towards the river—but I thought it practicable to remove the camps beyond the first crest, so as to afford the protection of the hills against infected currents of air. Ascertaining by personal inquiry and inspection that the men were turned out long before sunrise and were hours waiting for their break- fasts, and feeling persuaded that this had much to do with the preva- lence of malarial fevers, I asked for and obtained an order that reveille should not be beat till after sunrise, and that hot coffee should be issued to the men immediately after roll-call. Soon after this you directed me to provide a reasonable allowance of cots for the sick in the regi- mental hospitals. I ordered them to be purchased immediately, and as soon as they were procured I directed the regimental surgeons to send to the purveyor for their quota. Strange to say, I experienced a good deal of difficulty in making these officers send in. As late as December 27 I was obliged to compel some of the surgeons to supply themselves.

The want of military experience of the medical officers and their consequent helplessness made it extremely difficult to discover the real causes of disease, sometimes the nature of the diseases themselves, and to enforce the means of preventing these when discovered. A week after the hot coffee was ordered a regimental surgeon complained to me that green coffee was issued to his men, without the means of prop- erly roasting it, and that they could not get the "extra" rations ordered. Colonel Clarke, to whom I referred the complaint, promptly replied that green coffee was always issued; that it should be roasted in a mess-pan, or a Dutch-oven, or other vessel, purchased with the company fund; that the quantity issued was fixed by law, and was deemed ample; and so it was, but it required the exercise of a little judgment to discover it. I made constant and diligent inquiries of the surgeons as to their opinion of the causes of disease in their regiments, and whenever an undue proportion of sick was reported in any regi- ment a special report was invariably called for. If I had had compe- tent inspectors at that time the health of the army might have been more rapidly improved and myself saved much labor and anxiety.

First among the causes assigned for the numbers on the sick report, and the one as to which there was a general concurrence of opinion, was the recklessness with which the men had been enlisted. General Orders, No. 51, War Department, August 3, 1861, commanded that when volunteers were mustered in they should be minutely examined by the surgeon and assistant surgeon of the regiment as to their physical qualifications. I doubt whether this most important order has ever received the slightest attention from the persons whose duty it was to execute it. So notorious was the neglect of its behests, or the incompetency of those who pretended to obey it, that another general order from the same authority was demanded and issued December 3 of the same year, which declares that the evidence was abundant that this duty was neglected, and threatens to make the derelict officers pecuniarily responsible for it if not amended. The effect of this neglect, incompetency, or dishonesty has been always to swell essentially the ratio of the sick to the whole force. The surgeon of the Sixty-first New York reported to me as a reason for his large sick report that he had a large number of broken-down men—many 60 to 70 years old, many affected with hernia, old ulcers, epilepsy, and the like. Another brigade surgeon reports that there had been no medical examination of many of the regiments before they were enrolled. Another that there were eighty men with hernia and epilepsy in the Fifth New York Cavalry.

During the months of October, November, and December 3,939 men were discharged from the Army of the Potomac upon certificates of disability. Of these 2,881 were for disabilities that existed at the time the men were enlisted. These men cost the Government not less than $200 each, making nearly $200,000 a month out of which the people had been defrauded in a single army through the faithlessness of those to whom the duty of bringing none but able-bodied men into the field had been confided. It seemed as if the army called out to defend the life of the nation had been made use of as a grand eleemosynary institution for the reception of the aged and infirm, the blind, the lame, and the deaf, where they might be housed, fed, paid, clothed, and pensioned, and their townships relieved of the burden of their support.

The general prevalence of the measles was another accident increasing the ratio of the sick. I know of no means of preventing the occurrence of this disease. In more than thirty years' experience and observation I can only say that I have rarely seen a regiment of irregular troops in which it did not appear sooner or later after they had been assembled in camp. In many of our regiments it broke out before they left their homes. Some were more severely scourged than others, but nearly all suffered to some extent. Among regular soldiers it is rarely seen. I do not doubt that it is due to the difficulty of securing the same attention to police, to cooking, to clothing, to ventilation of tents, &c., among volunteers that is habitual with regular soldiers.

Complaints were made to me in several instances of the inferior quality of the blankets issued to the men. This was perhaps to some degree a cause of disease, but I knew it to be irremediable. It was impossible for the clothing department to furnish the heavy army blankets instantaneously to 600,000 men. The same remarks apply to a considerable proportion of the tents in use. Some regiments suffered for want of good and sufficient clothing. A singular circumstance presents itself in this connection. On the 8th of November, 1861, the surgeon of the Eighth Illinois Cavalry reported to me that 200 of the men had received no overalls from the United States. Many of them were reduced to their drawers. He had three hospital tents floored and furnished with stoves. His regiment was unusually healthy; no death had occurred in it for three months. The location of the regiment was afterwards changed. It was encamped in low grounds, that became intolerably muddy in the course of the winter. The part occupied by the horses was a perfect quagmire, never policed at all. The men became discouraged and careless, and in January, 1862, there were 207 cases of typhoid fever among them. These were removed to the general hospital in Alexandria, but the sick list remained large, and in

March, when preparing to take the field, 132 men of that regiment were reported unfit for duty.

Another cause of disease was the heavy details for labor in the field works and the severe nature of the labor; another, the exposure incident to picket duty. Regular officers and soldiers know how to make themselves comfortable on picket duty; volunteers do not. The 'frequent alarms in some portions of our lines were considered by some of the medical officers as a cause of disease. This was particularly the case in front of some of the Vermont troops in Brooks' brigade. It is possible this may have had an unfavorable effect upon men predisposed to disease from other causes.

The principal causes of disease, however, in our camps were the same that we have always to deplore and find it so difficult to remedy, simply because citizens suddenly called to the field cannot comprehend that men in masses require the attention of their officers to enforce certain hygienic conditions without which health cannot be preserved. The individual man at home finds his meals well cooked and punctually served, his bed made, his quarters policed and ventilated, his clothing washed and kept in order without any agency of his own, and without his ever having bestowed a thought upon the matter. The officer in ninety-nine cases in a hundred has given no more reflection than the private to these important subjects. When the necessity for looking after these things is forced upon his attention, he is at a loss how to proceed. Too frequently he lacks the moral courage and the energy to make his men do what neither he nor they stipulated for or understood when they entered the service. To bad cooking, bad police, bad ventilation of tents, inattention to personal cleanliness, and unnecessarily irregular habits we are to attribute the greater proportion of the diseases that actually occurred in the army.

My attention was given to these evils from the beginning. By precept and by orders the necessity and the methods of correcting them were urged upon the commanders and the medical officers of the several regiments. When the brigade surgeons were assigned, the first paragraph of the order defining their duties impressed the paramount importance of hygienic morality upon their consciences, and no occasion was let slip by me of urging upon both commanders and surgeons their obligations in this respect. Some of the regimental surgeons I know faithfully performed this duty. Copies of reports made to their commanding officers, creditable alike to their intelligence and their zeal, were sent to me. The attention of commanding officers is earnestly called in these reports to the drainage of their camps, the clothing and cleanliness of their men, to the situation of their sinks, and the like. One surgeon reports that he cannot strike the tents as I had enjoined, because they were too old, and urges his colonel to get new ones, if possible.

The prophylactic use of quinine and whisky having been suggested as a means of preventing malarial disease, I determined to try its efficacy. There being no warrant for such an issue in the Regulations of the Army, I procured a small quantity from the Sanitary Commission, and received favorable reports of its effects. Upon representing this to the Surgeon-General, I was authorized to issue it in reasonable quantities to regiments whose condition seemed most to demand it. I required reports as to the effect. These reports were generally favorable; so much so, that I was induced to keep it constantly on hand afterwards in the purveyor's store. The surgeon of the Cameron Dragoons reported that by its use he had reduced his sick report from 126 to 74 in two weeks. The surgeon of the Sixty-second Pennsylvania reported equally favorably, and stated that two companies of the regiment who had used it faithfully for two weeks presented a sick report of only four men. Much prejudice and aversion, however, had to be overcome in inducing the men to take it, and I scarcely think it would have been practicable to have forced it upon the whole army. Fortunately there was no necessity for this.

In order to secure some comforts for the sick in the regimental hospitals I attempted to show the surgeons how to create and to use a hospital fund. The regimental commissaries strenuously opposed this, on account of the inconvenience to themselves. The first paragraph of General Orders, No. 9, Army of the Potomac, September 9, 1861, however, enjoined this upon them as a duty, and in the course of some four or five months we succeeded in getting the system pretty generally established.

As cold weather came on I judged it necessary to make some provision for warming the tents. A very ingenious plan having been proposed by Brigade Surgeon McRuer, which had received the approval of General Heintzelman and other officers of experience, I directed Dr. McRuer to visit every division of the army, and to construct one of his furnaces for a model. This duty he performed. Some of course were found to object to it, but it was generally well received and found to contribute much to the comfort of the men. Some, however, still used the Crimean pit, and others succeeded in getting stoves. A cheap and convenient stove, and one readily transported, the make of Mr. Hainsworth, of Newport, Ky., was introduced into the army and found to answer well. It was the general understanding that the army was not to go into winter quarters, and therefore I did not recommend the housing of the men until the middle of January, 1862; but in December, 1861, learning that some of the regiments were excavating pits in the ground and covering them with their tents, I hastened to object strenuously to this plan. I suggested inclosures of rails or palisades some three feet high, to be roofed over with the tents. The excavations could not be kept dry or well ventilated, and certainly would not be kept in good police; all of which objections would be obviated by the above-ground inclosure. This plan was adopted in a number of camps I visited, and they presented an air of comfort that was very gratifying. Later in the season I recommended the Chester hut, with roof ventilation, as used so successfully at Balaklava.

Protection of the men against the contagion of small-pox of course received constant attention. While the Army of the Potomac was in process of organization small-pox was prevailing rather extensively in several of the districts from which the troops were being drawn. It was unsafe to travel without protection over any railway in the country. The city of Washington was infected, as I knew from the number of applications made to me by the authorities for the use of our small-pox ambulances to convey city patients to the pest-house. An eruptive-fever hospital had been established before I took charge of the army. Under the excellent arrangements made in that establishment by Dr. Thomas, the surgeon in charge, but little risk was incurred of the propagation of the disease to the camps. Orders were issued and reiterated for the vaccination of all volunteers unprotected. I also recommended that an order should be published requiring that all recruits for the Army of the Potomac should be vaccinated before they were put en route from their rendezvous, and that they should be carefully inspected as to this immediately upon their arrival. Not satisfied with what had been done, I asked for and obtained another order, in December, 1861, requiring the division and brigade commanders to cause the brigade surgeons to rein-spect all the men, vaccinating such as were still unprotected, and to report the results to me. At this late period most of the brigades were found to have some men unprotected; in a few the number was serious. In Slocum's brigade there were 1,500, in Blenker's 1,250, and in Sickles' 750. Crusts were furnished and the vaccination completed. As the result, small-pox, though rife in the community, never gained any foot-hold in the army. A sporadic case would occasionally occur, sometimes in the most unaccountable way. There are individuals so susceptible, that neither vaccination nor a former attack of small-pox secures them against the disease. An alarming report of the dangers to which the army was exposed from the system adopted at the hospital, having been made by the Sanitary Commission, with suggestions of some few modi-fications to suit their views, I inquired into the statistics of the disease in our army up to that time, and found that in seven months we had had but 168 cases, the majority of whom were ill with the disease when they reached Washington. I adopted such of the suggestions of the Commission as were not already in use, but with no perceptible effect. In fact, the precautions always adopted had made the cases, considered in reference to the size of the army, too insignificant to give the least uneasiness to any one at all informed on the subject.

I had always been solicitous to get possession of a few experienced regular medical officers, to be employed as inspectors of the field hos-pitals, through whom I might be assured that the measures devised for the preservation of the health of the men were faithfully and intelligently carried out. This was accomplished at last. In the middle of Novem-ber, 1861, two officers were assigned to me for that purpose and some weeks afterwards a third. I prepared instructions for them and set them at work at once. (See Appendix C.) These inspections extended from Budd's Ferry to Cumberland. They included Lander's division at Cumberland and Burnside's expedition fitting out at Annapolis. From the reports made by these officers I was enabled to correct many errors in hygiene, as well as to improve the discipline of my department and to keep it always in readiness for an advance. All faults in police, cooking, clothing, location of camps, &c., were promptly reported by me to the Adjutant-General, and by him as promptly ordered to be cor-rected.

I come now to speak of the regimental and brigade hospitals. The Regulations of the Army recognized only regimental and general hospi-tals. The regimental hospitals in the field were established in tents or in such buildings as might chance to be within the limits or in the im-mediate vicinity of each camp. The general hospitals available for the Army of the Potomac were the few old hotels or other similar buildings occupied as hospitals in the cities of Alexandria, Washington, George-town, and a small portion of the Naval Academy building at Annapolis. There was no authority for any hospital establishments in the vicinity of the divisions or brigades that might relieve the hospital tents if crowded or that might keep the men near their camps, so that they could be readily returned to duty when sufficiently recovered. It is true I might have authorized such establishments, but I was dependent upon the provisions of the regulations for the necessary stewards, cooks, and nurses for the service. Several intelligent and zealous brigade sur-geons pressed these hospitals upon my attention. Their advantages were obvious, and I determined, when I could get the buildings, to put them in operation. I required, however, that the necessary *personnel* should be furnished from the regimental details authorized by the regulations, and that the brigade hospitals should be considered and conducted as aggregations of the regimental hospitals; that their stewards, &c., should be mustered on the regimental rolls. In this way a number of them were organized and served. Brigade Surgeon Suckley organized one for Kearny's brigade near Alexandria, another was fitted up for Blenker's brigade at Hunter's Chapel, another in Hooker's division at Budd's Ferry, afterwards others in Fitz-John Porter's division, and several more. A very nice building was put up at Poolesville for Stone's command, upon plans furnished by Brigade Surgeon Crosby and approved by yourself.

About the 1st of February, 1862, my attention was called by General Williams to the condition of Lander's division at Cumberland. This was the first intimation I had had that there were any troops there. I sent one of my inspectors immediately to examine into the facts, with authority to provide at once for their necessities, to hire buildings, or to put up hospital huts if required.

On the 5th of February Brigade Surgeon Suckley was assigned to Lander's division, and instructed to use every exertion to put things in order. He was informed that the condition of the sick in that division was represented as scandalous, and that no effort must be spared to reform it. On the 8th I received the report of the inspector. It confirmed all that had been reported as to the shocking state of affairs. The regiments composing the command were scattered in all directions for some 40 miles over the hills. The sick, numbering 1,200, were abandoned in the city of Cumberland, and were in a wretched condition. They were "quartered in close, compact, ill-ventilated rooms, where the police is bad, food badly cooked and improperly served out; men of different regiments reeling and staggering through the streets with fevers, seeking shelter and medical attendance." The inspector had succeeded in getting comfortable and roomy quarters for 500 of the sick at the time of his report, had employed a number of women in making bed-sacks, and had contracted for some hundred bunks.

Dr. Suckley was in position on the 7th. On the 9th he had collected 1,079 of the sick; on the 11th he had 1,400. He found things in the town in a wretched condition; no discipline, no system. The commissary had no funds. There were nineteen regiments of infantry, besides cavalry and artillery, in the division. On the 18th he asked authority to build two shanties, to contain 50 patients each. This was immediately granted. On the 20th he had succeeded in making things more comfortable, had procured eight Sisters of Charity for nurses, had classified his patients, and had provided proper medical attendance. He reported also that the mortality and the gravity of disease were diminishing. He had received authority to build as many shanties as were necessary.

Measures were taken by me upon receipt of these reports to provide instantly for all the necessities of the case. I applied to the Commissary-General to place funds in the hand of the commissary. On the 19th Colonel Taylor informed me he had sent $5,000. I ordered a supply of ambulances to be forwarded, loaded with bedding, from Baltimore. Medical and hospital stores were also forwarded by myself as well as the Surgeon-General. March 3 I received a telegram from the railroad agent at Wheeling, informing me that 149 boxes of hospital stores would be at Cumberland the next day. There was no more trouble with that establishment. The brigade and field hospitals of the Army of the Potomac were at last organized and in working order.

The next subject I shall glance at is that of ambulance transportation. Previously to this war the Army of the United States had never been supplied with carriages expressly designed for the transportation of the sick and wounded. A board assembled by the Secretary of War some two years before the rebellion had adopted a four-wheeled carriage and two models of two-wheeled carriages for experiment. The four-wheeled carriage had been tested upon the plains in an expedition to New Mexico, and had been favorably reported upon by the medical officer in charge of it. The two-wheeled carriages, though a few had been built, had never been tried. Some doubts were entertained as to their suitableness for their purposes, but they were adopted and recommended as the best for "badly-wounded men." Experience, however, has shown that they are utterly unfit for any such purpose. When the present exigencies came upon us, the Quartermaster's Department lost no time in having the carriages built as rapidly as possible. They were of course ordered in the proportions recommended by the board—i. e., 5 two-wheeled to 1 four-wheeled. The two-wheeled were the basis of the system—a most unfortunate decision. It was my duty, however, to supply the Army of the Potomac with as many of these carriages as would suffice for probable necessities if they could be had. A considerable number of the two-wheeled had already been accumulated in Washington before my arrival and had been distributed to the several camps. I found them in general use as pleasure carriages for idlers and accommodation cabs for conveying officers and men from their camps to the city of Washington. A large number of them had already been broken down in this service. This was immediately stopped. An order was promulgated directing all ambulances, with the exception of 1 two-wheeled to each regiment, to be turned in to the Quartermaster's Department in Washington, and the use of that one was strictly limited to the service for which it was intended. We were enabled by this means to find out what we had and to keep most of them in order.

October 5, 1861, the depot quartermaster reported 109 two-wheeled and 12 four-wheeled ambulances in use, and 224 two-wheeled and 38 four-wheeled not in use. The unphilosophical idea of a two-wheeled being an easier carriage than a four-wheeled had been exaggerated in providing the vehicles. The quartermaster had issued 228 two-wheeled since July 1; 119 of these carriages had disappeared in a little more than three months, showing both how recklessly they had been used and how incapable they were of standing the hard work of our campaigns. December 31, 1861, there were in Washington 314 two-wheeled and 71 four-wheeled ambulances. Each regiment had its own two-wheeled in addition to these.

The two-wheeled carriages being so generally condemned, I endeavored to have a number of *cacolets* collected to replace them in the Army of the Potomac. The Quartermaster-General had already procured some of them, made after the French model. They weigh 140 pounds. I thought this too heavy, and that their weight might be materially reduced without compromising their strength or durability. This I recommended to be done. Several other models were presented to me afterwards that were much lighter, and I requested the Quartermaster's Department to procure a limited number of 2 of them. I thought I had secured 200 altogether for our army, but I received but 40, and most of these not until we had reached the Chickahominy. As early as August 21, 1861, I requested the Quartermaster-General to introduce these litters in the proportion of 1 to a regiment. On the 8th of

October I asked for 50 of Davies' plan, and on the 19th of November I recommended Kohlen's to the attention of General Van Vliet. I instituted some experiments with these, from which I was led to doubt whether they could entirely replace the two-wheeled ambulances. There was more motion than I expected when the litters were placed horizontally; in a sitting posture the wounded man could ride very comfortably. They have the advantage of being readily carried wherever a horse or mule can be led, and the disadvantage of affording no protection against the weather.

In a report upon the distribution of ambulances, dated January 7, 1862, I recommended that a suitable number of horses should be trained to carry these litters, and February 13 I repeated this suggestion. This was approved and ordered to be carried into effect, but for some reason it was not done.

I append my report of January 7 to show the policy pursued in relation to ambulances while we were in Washington and the reasons for it. This report was approved by yourself, and its suggestions directed to be observed. (See Appendix D.)

In estimating the number of ambulances required for the Army of the Potomac it was at once apparent that the army allowance was altogether in excess of what could be obtained or what could be managed, even if it were to be had. This allowance would have made a train of four-wheeled ambulances 5 miles in length, and of two-wheeled ambulances about 20, making a total train of 25 miles. To mention this shows how preposterous the thing would be. The schedule was never intended for an army of 100,000 men, but for a regiment or detachment, making a long march over the plains or in an Indian country. Still, great discontent was manifested by a number of officers, whose responsibilities were limited to a single regiment or brigade, that the whole number was not furnished. After a careful consideration of the matter I made a report on the subject, which will be found in the appendix marked E. Here I estimated for 250 four-wheeled. I hoped this number might be obtained. It was, however, never reached; and I was obliged afterwards to contrive the best I could to make the number actually furnished go as far as possible. The events on the Peninsula convinced me that my original estimate was the minimum that would have enabled us to get along without serious discomfort. The atrocious roads in that region destroyed a considerable portion of those we had, embarrassing the operations of my department very materially.

General Van Vliet having reported the number of ambulances of both sorts he had in depot and in the possession of the troops, after comparing the latter with the reports of my inspectors I found he could furnish only 12 of the four-wheeled and 22 of the two-wheeled to each division of the army, with a proportionate number to commands of less size. I accordingly submitted that plan of distribution to General Williams on the 5th of March, and in the same letter I repeated an estimate I had made on the 27th of February for 1 ordinary transportation wagon to each regiment, for the conveyance of medicines, stores, mess-chests, and hospital tents. The latter was ordered and very generally furnished. On the 10th of March, 1862, having received orders to move the ambulances to Fairfax Court-House, I called upon General Van Vliet to make the distribution according to my plan, and inclosed him a copy of my letter to General Williams as his guide. I moved with the headquarters to Fairfax Court-House the next day. When the army was assembled there the ambulances were not in position.

The army being ordered to fall back upon Alexandria, I hastened to

Washington, and had an interview with General Van Vliet on this subject. He informed me he had ordered 36 four-wheeled ambulances from Perryville to Fort Monroe, and that he would send on 86 more from Washington. That would have given us 177 for the whole army, including McDowell's corps and Blenker's division. This was too few, but it was the best that could be done with the number reported on hand. Colonel Ingalls being under the impression that there was still a large number at Perryville, I telegraphed to Washington to have 50 more added to our allotment, but I did not get them. In fact, the last of the original 86 did not reach us till the 1st of May; 12 were received April 9, 16 April 15, and 58 May 1.

In the mean time the divisions of Stone at Poolesville, Banks at Sandy Hook, Lockwood on the Eastern Shore of Maryland, and Lander at Cumberland, had been furnished with as many carriages of each sort as we could spare and they were likely to need. Stone had 59 two-wheeled, 7 four-wheeled, and 67 transport carts. They proved amply sufficient to remove his wounded after the action at Ball's Bluff with the greatest speed and safety to his hospitals. This affair was misrepresented by some volunteer philanthropist to the Sanitary Commission. My report from Brigade Surgeon Crosby, who conducted the hospital administration on that occasion—an officer who has no superiors in the corps to which he belongs—shows that his carriages were promptly as near the field as they could be brought. He could not very well cross either the canal or the Potomac River with his train.

The most feasible plan for organizing a force to act as an ambulance corps engaged my attention at an early period. Several propositions were made by foreigners to raise and command such a corps. They were mere repetitions of the Continental systems, and however serviceable they might have promised to be, they could not under the then existing laws have been raised for our army. The only plan that appeared to be within my reach was that adopted and established by the sixth paragraph of Orders No. 20. The regulations of the army authorized a detail of 10 men from each regiment for hospital attendants. The bands of regiments had long been used for the purpose I wanted them for in time of action in our service, and I could by the plans indicated expect to command about 25 men to a regiment to serve as ambulance attendants when wanted. They required, however, to be instructed in that duty, and with that view they were ordered to be drilled regularly every day by the medical officers under the superintendence of the brigade surgeons. Whenever this order was obeyed, the progress of the men in the drill was quite satisfactory. It was at least a beginning of an ambulance corps. Perhaps a distinct ambulance corps may yet be made a part of our military establishment. I am satisfied it would contribute essentially to the efficiency of the hospital department. The surgeon-general of Pennsylvania, under date of September 19, 1861, requested authority to organize such a corps at Camp Curtin for the troops of his State. I indorsed his proposal favorably and referred it to the Secretary of War, but no action was taken upon it. An elaborate project for an ambulance corps was submitted to the Surgeon-General by a Mr. Pfersching, and by him referred to me for examination in March, 1862. Upon this plan I made the report marked F in the appendix.

GENERAL HOSPITALS.

When I took charge of the Army of the Potomac I supposed that the general hospitals within the limits of that army were under my control, and that it devolved upon me so to extend their capacity as to provide accommodation for the number of sick and wounded that we should be likely to have. The buildings already provided and occupied were seen at once to be totally inadequate. The entire hospital establishment in Washington, Georgetown, Alexandria, Baltimore, and Annapolis contained but 2,700 beds. The Sanitary Commission being in session in Washington about the 1st of September, an invitation was extended to me to assist, which I accepted. They were then discussing the subject of general hospitals. They seemed to be of the opinion that there should be as many as 5,000 beds in Washington. I explained to the gentlemen at some length my views on the subject, and endeavored to show them that 20,000 beds at least would be required. After several days' consideration the Commission appointed a committee to wait upon the Secretary of War, to request him to have frame buildings erected sufficient to accommodate 15,000 men, and to request your approval of the same. The subject was brought to your notice in a letter from Mr. Gibbs, one of the Commission, which letter was referred to me, and was the occasion of my first report to you in reference to general hospitals. This report, dated September 9, 1861, will be found in the appendix, marked G.

I had at that time taken some steps to increase the existing establishment to meet immediate wants, when I was informed by the Surgeon-General that the Secretary of War had charged him with the superintendence and control of this matter, and that he should have all that was necessary provided in due season. My report, however, with a letter from the Sanitary Commission, was submitted by you to the Secretary of War, accompanied by a letter from yourself. In the course of the month it was returned to you, with authority to make your own arrangement for providing hospitals. I was then directed by you to go on with this work, but first to submit my plans to you. I was, as I stated in my first report, decidedly in favor of putting up cheap frame buildings, expressly designed for hospitals, in preference to relying upon hotels, school-houses, and the like, as seemed to be the existing plan. I fully believed suitable buildings could be erected at a cost not exceeding $25 per bed. I had seen such a plan in the possession of Dr. Harris, of the Commission, and had been promised a copy of it. The Commission, however, objected to his furnishing it, agreeing to send me a much better plan, and one sufficiently economical to suit my views. After tedious delays their drawings were at last sent to Washington. They were the design of an architect in New York, taken from the general plan of the Lariboisiere in Paris, excellent in itself, but too costly I feared for our purposes. The expense, as estimated by the architect, was $75 per bed. Time pressing, and it being too late to wait for other plans, I reluctantly determined to adopt it, after having made certain modifications that would not impair its advantages, but would reduce the cost to about $60 per bed—i. e., if the architect's estimate could be relied on. I submitted the plan to you, accompanied with a report. (See Appendix H.) I adhered in this report to my original estimate for 20,000 men as a minimum. To the plan proposed you objected on account of the expense in the then condition of the Treasury, but you thought that one-fourth of the buildings I had recommended might be put up. I then proposed to go to Annapolis, Baltimore, and Philadelphia, to see what could be done there to increase our accommodations, hoping that by evacuating all our hospitals in the vicinity of Washington, with the addition of the 5,000 beds to be provided in the new buildings, we might be able to get along with tolerable comfort in the event of a battle. Upon my return I submitted the report in Appendix I.

When the Quartermaster-General advertised for proposals to put up the new buildings, instead of $15,000 for each 200 beds, as estimated by the architect, the bids ranged from about $30,000 to $80,000. This expense could not be incurred, and two only of the buildings, sufficient for 400 men, were attempted, and it was many months before they were completed. In the mean time some of the Philadelphia hospitals were put in order. In February, 1862, 900 beds were ready in that city. In November, 1861, a new hospital in Alexandria was prepared, capable of receiving 900 patients. In the same month Minnesota Row was taken and ordered to be fitted up, and I succeeded in securing 200 beds in the Saint Elizabeth Asylum. These hospitals were fitted up with great care, and made as comfortable as such buildings could be made. They were well organized, and provided with competent medical staffs and good nurses. They gave us a total accommodation of about 6,000 beds, and were sufficient to receive the sick of the Army of the Potomac when it was put en route for the Peninsula. It was a source of deep regret to me that I was unable to accomplish at least so much of my original plan as had received your approval, but at that time such a thing was impossible in Washington. Anywhere else it could and would have been done. Subsequent events have shown that if it had been done, much inconvenience and suffering might have been spared.

The sanitary condition of the army during this period was very satisfactory. My records show a constantly-increasing immunity from disease. I regret that I am not in possession of the retained copies of my monthly reports of sick and wounded made to the Surgeon-General. I left a locked chest, containing my official documents and correspondence, in one of the military stores in Washington when we took the field. Through the kindness of General Meigs what remains of those records has been transmitted to me. The assistant quartermaster in whose care the chest was left informs me it was ordered to the Surgeon-General's Office, opened, and some of the papers removed. I miss from it the reports of my inspectors, the duplicates of my sick reports, my records of killed and wounded in the skirmishes in front of Washington, and various other papers. Fortunately what has been permitted to remain will suffice to give a very good idea of the sanitary history of your army up to March 1, 1862.

The Army of the Potomac during this period included the divisions of Stone at Poolesville, Banks at Harper's Ferry and Frederick, Dix at Baltimore, and the forces in the vicinity of Washington. August 22, 1861, 33 per cent. of the troops encamped on the flats near Arlington were reported sick with diarrhea and malarial fever. I have already alluded to the action taken in reference to these men; they belonged to McDowell's division. On the 13th February, 1862, this same division had but 9 serious cases in a force of 10,000 men; there were, in addition, some 200 cases of catarrh and a few of measles. There had been in the mean time, as in other portions of the army, some typhoid fever, but at the last date it had almost entirely disappeared.

I have already remarked upon the constantly-recurring outbreaks of measles among the volunteers. We had more or less of it among different commands during this whole period. In February, 1862, it was prevailing in the Railroad Brigade. In January it was rife in Dix's division, in Baltimore. September 14, 1861, Stone had 6,000 men at Poolesville, with but 54 sick in hospital, one-fifth of whom had measles, the remainder typhoid and intermittent fever. September 21, 9,000 men are reported at Poolesville, with 91 in hospital and 254 in quarters. February 3, 1862, measles alone kept up the number of men in hospitals

in Fitz-John Porter's division. On the 8th of the same month measles
are reported as having disappeared, while the number of sick in quarters
is reported as materially reduced, notwithstanding the inclemency of
the weather. Typhoid fever appeared in some of the camps during the
autumn, but gradually disappeared as winter advanced. This disease is
now and has been for years endemic in the United States. We could
not hope to escape it altogether. In some few regiments, under peculiar circumstances, there were a good many cases, but taken as a whole,
and considering the number of men in the camps, the cases were so few,
we might almost ignore it altogether. In Hunt's artillery reserve during the last quarter of 1861 it prevailed to some extent, but in January
it had entirely disappeared. This command had during this time one
of the largest sick reports in the army. On the 31st January, 1862,
the prevalent diseases in it were reported to be catarrh and bronchitis,
attributed to the effects of the rains and thaws.

In October and November, 1861, with an army averaging 130,000
men, we had 7,932 cases of fevers of all sorts. Of these about 1,000
were reported as cases of typhoid fever. I know that errors of diagnosis were frequently committed, and therefore this must be considered
as the limit of typhoid cases. If any army in the world can show such
a record as this, I do not know when and where it was assembled.

The most striking contrasts were exhibited in the relative health of
the troops from different States and sometimes among regiments from
the same State. Thus, in November, 1861, with a mean ratio of 6.5 per
cent. sick in the whole army, twelve Massachusetts regiments gave an
average of 50 sick each; five Vermont, an average of 144 each, and
thirty-five Pennsylvania, an average of 61 each. In January, 1862, the
Twelfth Massachusetts, 1,005 strong, had but 4 sick; the Thirteenth,
1,008 strong, but 11; while the Fifteenth, 809 strong, had 68. In the
same month the Fifth Vermont, 1,000 strong, had 271 sick; the Fourth,
1,047 strong, had 244 sick; while the Second, 1,021 strong, had but 87,
and the Third, 900 strong, had but 84. All these regiments were in the
same brigade and encamped side by side. The Tenth Pennsylvania
Reserves, 965 strong, had 7 sick; the First Pennsylvania Rifles, 889
strong, had 67 sick; and the First Pennsylvania Cavalry, 890 strong,
had 96 sick.

The health of some of the regiments, under adverse hygienic circumstances, seemed to set all reasoning at defiance. Thus, in February,
1862, Colonel Geary's Pennsylvania regiment, of Banks' division, that
had been serving all summer upon the banks of the Potomac and the
canal, had but 2.5 per cent. sick. There was a constant improvement
in the health of the whole army as the season progressed, and at the
time the march to Fairfax Court-House was ordered, with a very few
exceptions, every regiment in it was in the most satisfactory condition.
Some of them showed a most extraordinary improvement. Thus, in
four regiments of Pennsylvania troops in McCall's division, there were
but 68 men on the sick report on the 1st of March, 1862.

The records in my possession show that in—

September, 1861, among 84,788 men, we had 6,007 sick=7 per cent.
October, 1861, among 116,763 men, we had 7,443 sick=6.07 per cent.
November, 1861, among 142,577 men, we had 9,281 sick=6.50 per
cent.
January, 1862, among 181,082 men, we had 11,225 sick=6.18 per cent.

Of these the men sick in the regimental and general hospitals were
less than one-half; the remainder were slight cases, under treatment in
quarters. The health of particular regiments was at this time very re-

markable. Thus, the Second Rhode Island had but .45 per cent. sick, the Seventh Massachusetts 1.99, the Ninety-eighth Pennsylvania 1.21, the First Long Island 1.46, and the mean of Keyes' division was but 3.29. During this time, so far as rumor was concerned, the Army of the Potomac was being decimated by disease every month. The reports from the regimental headquarters were only less erroneous than rumor. The statistics I have given are from the weekly and monthly reports of medical officers. It was ascertained to be the general habit of the captains to report every man sick who found it convenient to report himself so. The difference between these reports and the facts is illustrated in my letter to General Williams of January 28, 1862, a copy of which is appended, marked K. I append also a report in relation to that subject made to the Surgeon-General of the Army January 4, 1862 (L).

During this period there were frequent skirmishes, giving a number of wounded men. Two affairs of importance took place : On the 21st of October, 1861, the battle of Ball's Bluff, and on the 20th of December, General Ord's affair at Dranesville. In the former, 280 men were reported wounded ; in the latter, 34. Of the wounds at Ball's Bluff 93 were in the head and face—a very large proportion—showing the accuracy of fire of the enemy, as well as the skill with which they availed themselves of the advantage they possessed on that occasion.

This concludes the first period. I hope to resume the subject and to report upon the second period in a few days.

Very respectfully, your obedient servant,

　　　　　　　　　　　　　　　　　CHAS. S. TRIPLER,
　　　　　　　　　　　　　　　　　　　Surgeon, U. S. Army.

Maj. Gen. GEORGE B. MCCLELLAN, *U. S. Army.*

[Appendix A.]

GENERAL ORDERS, }　　　HDQRS. ARMY OF THE POTOMAC,
　　No. 20.　　　 }　　　　　　*Washington, October 3, 1861.*

The following regulations respecting the duties of brigade surgeons are published for the government of all concerned :

I. The brigade surgeons will frequently inspect the police, cooking, clothing, and cleanliness of the camps and men in their respective brigades ; the position and condition of the sinks, the drainage of the camp grounds, the ventilation of the tents, &c.; making written reports to the brigade commanders whenever, in their opinion, any errors in these respects require correction, and sending duplicates of these reports to the medical director of the army.

II. They will see that the medicines, hospital stores, instruments, and dressings of the several regimental surgeons are kept constantly sufficient in quantity in good order, and always ready for active service.

III. They will collect from the several regimental surgeons and transmit every Saturday morning to the medical director a copy of their morning report made to the commanding officer of their regiment, and will accompany these with remarks showing the character of the principal diseases prevailing.

IV. They will promptly report to the medical director all changes in station or location of themselves or of any of the medical officers in their brigades, with the number, date, and authority of the order by which such changes were made.

V. They will inspect carefully all men receiving certificates of disability for discharge, and if they approve, they will countersign such certificates.

VI. The hospital attendants, to the number of 10 men to a regiment, and the regimental bands, will be assembled under the supervision of the brigade surgeons, and will be drilled one hour each day, except Sunday, by the regimental medical officers, in setting up and dismantling the hand-stretchers, litters, and ambulances; in handling men carefully; placing them upon the litters and ambulance beds; putting them into the ambulances, taking them out, &c.; carrying men upon the hand-stretchers (observing that the leading bearer steps off with the *left* foot and the rear bearer with the *right*); in short, in everything that can render this service effective and the most comfortable for the wounded who are to be transported.

VII. Brigade surgeons will see that the orders of the commanding general in relation to the uses to which ambulances are to be applied are strictly obeyed, and they will report promptly to the brigade commanders all infractions of these orders.

VIII. Whenever a skirmish or affair of outposts occurs in which any portion of their brigades is engaged, they will see that the ambulances and stretchers, properly manned with the drilled men, are in immediate attendance to bring off the wounded, and that the regimental medical officers are at their posts, with their instruments, dressings, and hospital knapsacks in complete order and ready for immediate use, so that no delay may occur in rendering the necessary surgical aid to the wounded.

IX. They will report in writing to the medical director, within twenty-four hours after any affair with the enemy, the name, rank, and regiment of each of the wounded, the nature and situation of the wound, and the surgical means adopted in the case.

X. Brigade surgeons will be held responsible that the hospital service in their brigades is kept constantly effective and in readiness for any emergency. No remissness in this respect will be tolerated or overlooked.

By command of Major-General McClellan:

S. WILLIAMS,
Assistant Adjutant-General.

NOTE.—The medical director desires that exsection of the shoulder and elbow joint shall be resorted to in preference to amputation in all cases offering a reasonable hope of success, and that Pirigoff's operation at the ankle should be preferred to Chopart's or to amputation above the ankle, in cases that might admit of a choice.

[Appendix B.]

GENERAL ORDERS }   HDQRS. ARMY OF THE POTOMAC,
   No. 9.   }   *Washington, September* 9, 1861.

I. The attention of brigade and regimental commissaries of subsistence and of officers acting as such is directed to paragraphs 20, 21, and 22, Subsistence Regulations, or paragraphs 1073, 1074, and 1075, Army Regulations, 1857. Subsistence officers must make issues to the hospital, and keep the accounts of the hospital funds in strict conformity with the requirements of the regulations cited.

II. All changes of station of medical officers are to be promptly reported to the medical director at these headquarters, and the authority given by which the change was made.

III. Leaves of absence to medical officers are prohibited, unless granted at these headquarters.

IV. Patients will not be sent from the regimental to the general hospitals without the authority of the medical director. Applications for this authority must be made in writing, specifying the names and diseases of the patients, and be handed in to the office of the medical director between the hours of 9 and 10 a. m.

V. When a soldier is sent to general hospital, his company commander shall certify and send with him his descriptive list and account of pay and clothing.

VI. Male nurses and cooks for general hospitals are to be detailed from the privates of the army, regular and volunteer. The allowance will be 1 nurse to 10 patients, and 1 cook to 30. Where women are employed, the number of men to be called for will not exceed the number sufficient to make up the whole force to the allowance above authorized. Hired nurses and cooks will be forthwith discharged.

VII. Men reported at the general hospitals for duty will be sent by the surgeons in charge to the office of the medical director at 10 a. m. for the passes necessary for them to rejoin their regiments.

VIII. Medical officers joining this army for duty, with or without troops, will report promptly to the medical director in person. If with troops, they will report the number of men, the state of their supplies, and ambulance transportation.

IX. Ambulances will not be used for any other than the specific purpose for which they are designed, viz, the transportation of the sick and wounded, except by the written authority of the brigade commander, the medical director of the army, and the quartermasters in charge of them in the city of Washington. The provost-marshal is directed to see that the provisions of this order are carried out, and will arrest every officer and confine every private and non-commissioned officer who is found violating it.

X. All Government ambulances now in possession of regiments or separate corps will be turned in to the chief quartermaster, with the exception of 1 two-wheeled ambulance to each regiment. One two-wheeled transport cart will be allowed to each general hospital for the conveyance of marketing and hospital stores.

XI. The reveille will not be beaten until after sunrise, and hot coffee will be issued to the troops immediately after reveille roll-call, as a preventive of the effects of malaria.

By command of Major-General McClellan:

S. WILLIAMS,
Assistant Adjutant-General.

[Appendix C.]

HEADQUARTERS ARMY OF THE POTOMAC,
Medical Director's Office, Washington, November 25, 1861.

The inspectors of hospitals assigned to duty with the Army of the Potomac will proceed to the camps of such divisions of the army as they may be directed to visit from time to time, and will institute careful and rigid inspections as to the following points:

I. Whether there is a brigade surgeon on duty with the brigade; what is his name and date of commission; whether he is active, competent, and attentive to his duties; whether the duties assigned to brigade surgeons in General Orders, No. 20, are fully comprehended and faithfully carried out.

II. Whether each regiment in any brigade is provided with a surgeon and assistant surgeon; what are their names, dates of commission, and dates of mustering in; whether they are present and for duty with their regiments; if absent, by what authority, for what reasons, and how long.

III. The number of hospital tents; how many have been received, and from what source; whether they are used for the sick; if diverted to any other use, by what authority this was done; whether the hospital tents are properly located, sufficiently warmed and ventilated, furnished with bunks and bedding, and kept in good police.

IV. Whether there is a competent hospital steward and a sufficient number of hospital attendants; whether these men are well selected, and attentive to their duties.

V. How many men are sick in hospital; how many in quarters? What are the prevailing diseases in each?

VI. Whether there is a brigade hospital; if so, how is it situated; how served; stewards, attendants, &c. What kind of building is it? Is it comfortable, in good repair, and sufficiently provided with bunks and bedding? Can it be advantageously dispensed with? Should any of the patients be sent to the general hospitals? How many patients does it contain, and what are the diseases? Is the building sufficiently ventilated and warmed?

VII. What is the condition of medicines, hospital stores, instruments, and dressings? Are they sufficient to enable the regiment to take the field? If deficient, in what respect? Has any record been kept of the supply received? Have they been judiciously and faithfully used?

VIII. Has the hospital fund been kept in accordance with paragraph 1, General Orders, No. 9; if not, who is responsible for the neglect?

IX. How many and what kind of ambulances are on hand; what is their condition; from what source were they received? Is their use strictly confined to the transportation of the sick and the ambulance drills; if not, who is to blame?

X. Are the records of the hospitals properly kept? Do the surgeons send in their weekly reports to the brigade surgeons for the medical director?

XI. What is the condition of the camp? Is it well located; if not, can its location be advantageously changed? Is it well drained and well policed? Are the tents in good order and well ventilated?

XII. Are the men well clothed? Are their persons kept clean?

XIII. How is the cooking done? Are the messes inspected, and by whom? Are the provisions good?

XIV. Are the men's sinks properly located and attended to?

XV. What means are resorted to for warming the camps and are they effective?

XVI. What is the strength of the regiments?

XVII. What is the general sanitary condition of the regiment? How many would have to be sent to the general hospitals if the regiment were ordered to march?

Upon all these points a systematic report will be made to the medical director immediately after each inspection. Where the inspectors perceive hygienic errors to exist, they will call the attention of the proper authority to them at once, and state in the report of the inspection that they have done so. The inspectors will also examine the medical officers upon their duties, to ascertain whether they understand them, taking the regulations as their guide. They will instruct the medical officers in their duties, being careful to correct any errors they may have imbibed, and to point out to them the scope and correct manner of performing their duties.

The surgeon's call should be beaten in the presence of the inspector, to enable him to judge whether the men understand it, whether the men attending it correspond with the official reports, and whether they are judiciously treated. The inspectors will also institute an inquiry into the cases of the men who are recommended for discharge. The number of certificates sent to headquarters indicates either great facility in granting these discharges or great carelessness in the inspection of the men at the time of their enlistment. It is the desire of the general that a thorough medical inspection of the army be made as speedily as possible, that no possible deficiency may exist in the medical department when it advances upon the enemy, and to this end he commands all officers, of whatever rank, to afford to the inspectors of hospitals every facility in conducting their inspections.

CHAS. S. TRIPLER,
Surgeon and Medical Director Army of the Potomac.

[Appendix D.]

HEADQUARTERS ARMY OF THE POTOMAC,
Medical Director's Office, January 7, 1862.

GENERAL: In reference to the letter of Brigade Surgeon Stocker, inclosing requisitions for ambulances and transport carts furnished by the State of Pennsylvania for McCall's brigade, I have the honor to report that the quartermaster in charge of these carriages informs me he has receipted to Lieutenant-Colonel Crosman for all that have arrived here up to December 31, 1861. I am further informed upon inquiry that he has no transport carts on hand. Upon the inspection of General McCall's division by Dr. Milhau, inspector of hospitals, on the 5th of December, they had 22 two-wheeled and 2 four-wheeled ambulances and 1 transport cart. Four of the two-wheeled are reported broken at this date, but as fifteen days elapsed before they were wanted, they must have been repaired if proper attention was given to their condition. There have been reported to me 34 men wounded in General Ord's late action. I suppose this to be correct, as the brigade surgeons are required by General Orders, No. 20, of 1861, to report to me within twenty-four hours after an action the names, &c., of the wounded, and I have always found General McCall's brigade surgeons very punctual in the performance of their duties. There was then in General McCall's camp sufficient transportation for the wounded. Why it was not sent to the battle-field I don't know.

We have at this point 48 four-wheeled ambulances in use and 23 in depot, and 84 two-wheeled in use and 230 in depot. Of the four-wheeled we want 20 here constantly. That will leave 28 for distribution, if it should be decided upon.

But it has been the policy to withdraw these carriages from distribution to the camps in this vicinity, because in case of an action in front they can be readily sent in a few hours to any point or points where they may be required and in suitable numbers to different points. If distributed, those on the extreme right might be wanted on the extreme left or the reverse, and thus delay would be incurred in commanding them; whereas if kept here a telegram or a mounted orderly would put them in their proper position in a few hours. Again, if distributed, for want of shelter and want of care they would inevitably get out of order in a short time. I am confirmed in this opinion by Dr. Stocker's letter. With all his care he reports them as being uncomfortable for the wounded, because they have been used to carry articles never intended to go in them. Because we have now for the first time ambulances in the army it does not follow that they are to be used, or rather abused, by employing them as baggage-wagons. For carrying tents, cooking utensils, and provisions ordinary wagons should be used. Transport carts are intended for the field supply of medicines and stores and stretchers on a march. If there are no transport carts, these articles must be transported in common wagons. Ambulances should never be used for this purpose. The sooner the volunteer medical officers learn this the better. I cannot advise any increased ambulance transportation to be issued to divisions within reach of me in a few hours until this lesson is learned. It must be observed that whatever indulgences are accorded to one division must be accorded to another, and however careful General McCall's officers may be, it is possible even they may not be able to prevent the abuses I have adverted to above. I know that in one of the best divisions of the army an ambulance was loaded with ammunition by order of a colonel of a regiment of volunteers to go to a sham fight. We shall want all our ambulances, and want them in good order, at some not distant day, and if I can preserve them in such order I will endeavor to do it.

For troops at a greater distance from this center I think a greater issue of ambulance transportation is necessary; accordingly General Banks' and General Stone's divisions have been supplied. On the 11th of December, in a letter to you, I recommended an increased issue to Hooker's division. I have not been informed if it was ordered. If not, I beg leave to repeat that recommendation. For the brigades in our front I should prefer the present arrangement, with orders that when an action occurs I should be called upon by telegraph or by a mounted orderly to send any additional supply of ambulances that may be needed; but if the general commanding should disagree with me in opinion, then I propose the issue of one four-wheeled ambulance to each brigade and one additional two-wheeled ambulance to each regiment.

In this connection I would mention that we now have a number of *cacolets*, or horse-litters, on hand. To render these serviceable, it is necessary that a suitable number of good horses should be trained to carry them. I would, therefore respectfully and earnestly recommend that this should be undertaken by careful and competent men without delay. After the horses are properly trained, one *cacolet* and horse should be sent to each brigade for the ambulance drill.

Very respectfully,

CHAS. S. TRIPLER,
Medical Director.

General S. WILLIAMS.

[Appendix E.]

HEADQUARTERS ARMY OF THE POTOMAC,
Medical Director's Office, February 22, 1862.

GENERAL: I have the honor to acknowledge the receipt of the statement of four-wheeled ambulances in the Army of the Potomac, referred by you to me for my opinion as to the sufficiency of the supply. The statement does not agree with the reports made to me by the inspectors of hospitals in several instances, but that may be accounted for by the wagons being in possession of the quartermaster and not brought to the notice of the inspectors, and, further, it is probable that many of these ambulances are wagons furnished by the several States and claimed as regimental property. If, however, they are available as ambulances, this is of little consequence; but there are other inaccuracies, as, for instance, in General Banks' division, where I know that 10 four-wheeled ambulances, new and of the army pattern, are or ought to be in possession of the quartermaster. In addition to this, I know that some of his regiments have four-wheeled ambulances furnished by their States. I regret that we have not received the returns of casualties at Fort Donelson, as they would assist me in estimating for the probable wants of this army. My estimate should be a minimum for several obvious reasons; still it would not be prudent to make it too small. The ambulance board estimated for 2 four-wheeled and 10 two-wheeled ambulances for a regiment. These would give transportation for 40 men, or 4 per cent. of the assumed force. At this rate we should have 500 four-wheeled ambulances for this army and 2,500 two-wheeled. This would require a train of four-wheeled ambulances 5 miles long, and yet it would carry but 5,000 wounded; whereas in a general engagement, with a force of 200,000 men, we might expect 60,000 wounded. If one-half of these require ambulance transportation, it would take 3,000 four-wheeled army ambulances to carry them, and the train would be 30 miles long. I mention all this to show how inadequate any attainable train must be to provide for possible wants. Let us have a reasonable train, and if needs be it must be sent back and forth as often as may be necessary to remove the wounded from the field to the hospital.

The two-wheeled ambulances are universally condemned, and we cannot rely upon them for the road. They are in my opinion indispensable as tenders to the four-wheeled ambulances. They can be run with comparative ease where it would be impracticable to carry a four-wheeled ambulance; therefore, to bring men off the field to the road or to the hospitals on the field or for any distance not exceeding 2 miles, they will be found very useful. Combined with the *cacolets* and the hand-stretchers they will and must suffice for field purposes during an action. We have some 250 of these two-wheeled ambulances and about 200 *cacolets*. These in my opinion are sufficient of that kind of transportation for the army. The *cacolet* will answer for the road in case of necessity, and perhaps some classes of wounds might be transported to the hospitals in the two-wheeled carts.

I am furnished, then, with a basis of 250 regiments on which to found my estimate for the four-wheeled ambulances. After much reflection I have concluded that one of these of the army pattern should be provided for each regiment or separate battalion. These would give transportation for 2,500 men (if 250 in number), and would make a train 2½ miles in length. Upon the advance of course they would not be assembled in one body, but in sending the wounded back to the general hospitals it is possible they may be, and the train would then be as long and convey as many people as would probably be sent at one time to the hospitals. I would therefore respectfully recommend that the number of four-wheeled ambulances to be provided for the army be one to a regiment or separate corps, and that it be of the army pattern.

Very respectfully, your obedient servant,

CHAS. S. TRIPLER,
Surgeon and Medical Director Army of the Potomac.

General S. WILLIAMS,
Assistant Adjutant-General, Army of the Potomac.

[Appendix F.]

HEADQUARTERS ARMY OF THE POTOMAC,
Medical Director's Office, Washington, March 6, 1862.

SIR: I have the honor to report that, in obedience to your instructions, I have examined the plan of organization of an ambulance corps submitted by Ch. Pfersching. However desirable a regularly-organized ambulance corps may be for an army, it is now too late to raise, drill, and equip so elaborate an establishment as this for our service. There is nothing new in the plan, nothing that has not been thought of and even weighed years ago in connection with our own organization, unless it be the arsenal of pistols and hatchets with which the men are to be loaded. As we have no ambulance corps proper, an attempt has been made to instruct a certain number of men in each regiment in the duties appertaining to such a corps. An order providing for the drilling of ten men and the band of each regiment to the ambulance service was issued from these headquarters on the 3d October, 1861. This has been generally faithfully done, and we now have a tolerably well-instructed body of men for this duty. Instructions for the distribution and employment of these men during an action have been prepared by me, and were submitted to General Williams, adjutant-general of the Army of the Potomac, for the action of General McClellan, some ten days ago. I hope they will soon be printed and circulated. When that is done, all necessary and practicable arrangements for the transportation of our wounded will have been made. I am therefore of opinion that the plan of Mr. Pfersching is neither needed nor available for our service at the present time.

Very respectfully, your obedient servant,

CHAS. S. TRIPLER,
Surgeon and Medical Director.

Surg. Gen. C. A. FINLEY, U. S. A.

[Appendix G.]

HEADQUARTERS ARMY OF THE POTOMAC,
Medical Director's Office, Washington, September 9, 1861.

MAJOR: In reference to the letter of Mr. George Gibbs, referred to me by direction of Major-General McClellan, I have to state that the subject of suitable provision for the reception of the wounded at this position has engaged my attention for the last three weeks. I had commenced arrangements by providing a hotel in Baltimore and ordering it to be fitted up. I had also asked authority to take the Riggs house, near the Circle, with the purpose of converting it into a hospital. I had also other arrangements in view, when I was informed by the Surgeon-General that under the direction of the Secretary of War he had taken all the general hospitals under his exclusive supervision and control, and that he intended making extensive arrangements for the reception of all the sick and wounded that this army would afford; that in case of an action I would find accommodations in readiness for the wounded.

At a meeting of the Sanitary Commission, at which I was present, last week, a resolution was passed appointing a committee to wait upon the Secretary of War, to request him to have frame buildings erected sufficient for the reception of 15,000 men, and also to request General McClellan's approval of the same. The committee had not been able to see General McClellan up to last night. I have now the honor to say that, in my opinion, frame huts, such as were finally constructed in the Crimea, are much better adapted to hospital purposes than large buildings of masonry, such as hotels, colleges, and the like. They admit of more perfect ventilation, can be kept in better police, are more convenient for the sick and wounded and their attendants, admit of a ready distribution of patients into proper classes, and are cheaper. The Quartermaster-General informed me some time since that he would put up any buildings that might be required. So far as I am informed, there are about 2,700 beds in the general hospitals on the Potomac and in Maryland. Notwithstanding unremitted efforts, I have not been able to get reports of the number of sick in all the regiments of the army, but in forty-eight regiments that have reported there were on the 31st August 916 sick in hospital and 1,546 in quarters. Of the strength of these regiments I have no accurate information. Assuming them to average 800, we have an aggregate of 38,400. Again, assuming that all the sick in hospitals and one-half of those in quarters would require to be sent to a general hospital in case of an advance on our part, we should require 1,689 beds for their accommodation. This gives a ratio of 1 to 23.33 nearly, or between 4 or 5 per cent. I think we may estimate for 5 per cent. of any force intended to leave here as sure to require hospital accommodation. If this army attains a strength of 200,000, we shall then want 10,000 beds immediately available.

Again, should this army of 200,000 men have a general engagement with anything like equal numbers, and the action be well contested upon the side of the enemy, we may calculate upon casualties reaching 60,000 as a maximum. Of these, should the battle be fought principally with artillery, one-half would be killed or mortally wounded. It is scarcely to be expected or apprehended that anything like so great a slaughter will really be endured by the troops on either side, but I do not think it an unreasonable estimate to say that we should have hospital accommodation for 20,000 wounded. This number ought to be reached of our own men and those of the enemy that will fall into our hands.

Now, if this estimate is at all reasonable, it is easily seen that there are not buildings enough in Washington that are likely to or can be procured to meet our wants. There is no question in my mind as to the absolute superiority of temporary huts of suitable size and properly constructed over all other buildings that can be had for our purposes. The cost of the buildings will be about one-half or less of what we are now paying for rents of hotels, colleges, and seminaries. If the matter were in my hands, I should recommend the building of these huts at once.

Very respectfully, your obedient servant,
CHAS. S. TRIPLER,
Surgeon and Medical Director Army of the Potomac.
Maj. S. WILLIAMS,
Assistant Adjutant-General, Headquarters Army of Potomac.

[Appendix H.]

HEADQUARTERS ARMY OF THE POTOMAC,
Medical Director's Office.

GENERAL: In obedience to the instructions of Major-General McClellan, I have the honor to report that I have carefully considered the subjects referred to me, and now submit the following plans:

My attention having been invited to the views of the general commanding and those of the honorable Secretary of War, as conveyed in his indorsement upon Major-General McClellan's letter, it seems to me I am required to submit my views upon the organization of an ambulance corps as well as upon an increase of hospital accommodation.

1. *The immediate organization of an ambulance corps, to act under the medical director's command.*—I submitted some weeks since for the action of the General a plan for the only kind of ambulance corps I think we can raise under existing laws. That plan was to take the hospital attendants to the number of 10 men to each regiment and the band, and have them drilled daily for one hour under the medical officers, in the whole manipulation of ambulances of all sorts, the handling of men, the carrying of them upon litters, placing them in the carriages and taking them out, and the like. I propose that these men shall accompany the ambulances upon the march, and in time of action shall man the litters to bear the wounded to the rear, and act as guides to such of the wounded as can walk to the field or principal hospitals. These men should carry upon their persons a suitable supply of lint, a few bandages and pins, a field tourniquet, and a small canteen of whisky or brandy, and should be instructed in the proper use of all these articles, that they may be ready to apply them judiciously in case of emergency. This is not such an ambulance corps as I would prefer, but it is the best I can devise under existing laws and circumstances. An efficient ambulance corps should be composed of men enlisted for that purpose, and should be organized into companies and battalions, with commissioned and non-commissioned officers. They should be uniformed so that they might be known, armed with revolvers, and drilled under the direction of the medical officers in all duties pertaining to their corps. Companies or detachments of the corps could then be assigned to brigades, divisions, or corps d'armée, as occasion might require. They would move under command of their own officers, could perform their duties promptly, intelligently, and efficiently, and obviate all necessity or excuse for the men in the ranks to fall out to assist the wounded.

But it is obvious these detachments should be under the command of the principal medical officer, and such is the plan proposed by Major-General McClellan. To effect this, it will be necessary to modify the law in relation to the rank of medical officers. I would suggest that the Medical Department of the Army be placed upon the same military footing precisely as the Quartermaster's Department, with the same grades, titles, and ranks, simply substituting the word "surgeon" for "quartermaster" wherever it occurs. If this were done, it would clear away at once the rubbish that has so long embarrassed the operations of the department, and now stands in the way of its efficiency at a time when every energy of every man's mind and body is called into requisition to meet the pressing necessities of the public service.

2. The employment of an adequate corps of male and female nurses by the medical director, to act under his supervision. This being another important suggestion of the Sanitary Commission, and recommended by Major-General McClellan, I have to remark upon it that the sixth section of the act approved August 3, 1861, has provided for the employment of female nurses whenever desired by the medical director or the surgeon in charge of a permanent hospital. In the plan to be submitted for hospitals it will be seen that a due proportion of male and female nurses is provided for. We can get female nurses through Miss Dix and from among the Sisters of Charity. It is a very damaging position for any one to take and avow, but in the honest discharge of

my duties, though a Protestant myself, I do not hesitate to declare that in my opinion the latter are far preferable to the former, being better disciplined, more discreet and judicious, and more reliable. In the arrangement of the hospitals it might be judicious to assign one section to the Sisters of Charity and the other to the Protestant nurses.

Male nurses are most readily obtained by detail from the troops. There are many men in the ranks who are the subjects of infirmities, disqualifying them for the active duties of the field, who could be usefully employed as nurses in the hospitals. Numbers have been enlisted with hernia and cirsocele, and are being discharged on account of these, who would be very capable of doing the duties of nurses.

3. *Plan for the extension of hospital accommodations at Washington, D. C.*—I assume that this army will number 200,000 men, of whom 30,000 will garrison Washington and its defenses, and 170,000 will be mobilized. We had on the 18th September 84,778, of whom 6,007 were reported sick; this is a little in excess of 6 per cent. of the whole force. The sanitary condition of the army has been constantly improving for the last six weeks. The ratio of sick is increased by the condition of a few corps. Some of the regiments arrived with large sick reports; others have suffered from being encamped in unhealthy locations; but even these are improving, and I am confident we shall not have to leave in hospital more than five per cent. when the grand army is put in motion. This would require 8,500 beds for the 170,000. We have now 1,163 beds, exclusive of the eruptive-fever hospital, leaving 7,337 to be provided for. I have not estimated for the sick of the garrison of Washington, as they can be taken care of in their field hospitals. Many of those left sick in the general hospitals would be able in a short time to serve in the works in case of an attack upon Washington, and they might be considered as forming a part of the garrison to be left; so that we estimate that the whole complement of 170,000 will be put in motion.

If the 170,000 should fight anywhere within seventy-two hours' transportation of Washington, I should recommend that the wounded be sent back to this city. If we have a well-contested series of battles within that time of Washington we may have 56,666 casualties. The Army of Mexico left Pueblo 10,500 strong, and the killed and wounded in the valley exceeded 3,000. We have no right to rely upon a less proportionate loss, though no one expects it to occur.

The proportion of the killed to the whole loss is a difficult problem to investigate. We are yet to experience the destructive power of rifled muskets and cannon. I do not know how well the enemy may be supplied with either, or how well they may be able to serve them if they have them. We used to estimate the proportion of the killed with the old weapons to be 25 per cent. of the whole loss. It has been estimated since the introduction of the new arms that that proportion is now inverted—*i. e.*, that of 100 casualties 75 will now be fatal. I think that extravagant. But let us estimate one-half of the loss as likely to require hospital accommodation, and we shall then want 28,333 beds for the wounded, making, with the sick, a grand total of 35,670.

Now, the General knows his own plans and I am ignorant of them. It may be the great battle may be fought nearer Fort Monroe than Washington, or nearer Richmond than either. Our hospitals at Washington in either case would be to a great extent unavailable. I cannot, therefore, make more than an approximate estimate of what will be required here. From the data I have adduced the General can form a better judgment than myself. I think, however, assuming 200,000 as the strength of the army, that 10 per cent., or 20,000 men, ought to be provided for in the hospitals.

But 20,000 patients will require 2,000 nurses, 666 cooks, and 1,000 matrons; 200 medical officers, and as many stewards and ward-masters, will also be required. The number of cooks may be reduced materially, but the number of matrons cannot, as I include the laundresses under that head. I think 300 cooks will be sufficient. Whatever extent of hospital establishment may be determined upon finally may find its administrative force adjusted by this scale. For the medical officers required as *internes,* I rely upon the States that have appointed medical boards of examiners. They must be employed by contract. The commissioned medical officers of the army or volunteers cannot supply the necessary force.

The buildings for this establishment will necessarily be large and expensive, but I am satisfied the demands of economy and humanity will be met by the adoption of the plans herewith submitted. All experience has shown that dwelling-houses, hotels, and the like are unfit for military hospitals. It is impossible to ventilate them properly, and their interior is always so arranged that, while there is great waste of space, the sick are always crowded, and at the same time a larger number of surgeons, cooks, stewards, &c., are required for their administration than in the well-arranged hospitals that modern science and experience have devised. The single-floor pavilion hospital is the one that now unites the opinions of the scientific and humane throughout the world in its favor. Such a plan has been prepared by an architect under the supervision of the Sanitary Commission, and is herewith submitted. This is a design for one building, and is calculated to accommodate 200 patients, with the necessary administrative force. It will require 100 of these buildings for the number of patients I have supposed we shall have. The accompanying memoir of the Sanitary Commission contains the specifications for the building.*

Under ordinary circumstances I would not undertake to modify this plan in any way. It meets my views fully as it stands. But as I think we may save both time and money in the construction by some modifications, I would suggest—

1. That the buildings should rest upon timber instead of masonry supports.

2. That the wards should be but 12 instead of 14 feet high.

This will give each man 1,260 cubic feet, an ample space, considering the excellent arrangements for ventilation in the plan.

3. The upper windows in the plan may be dispensed with if we make the other windows 8 feet high, and reaching from within 1 foot of the ceiling to 3 feet of the floor. The upper sash should let down. The lower sash may be made "French fashion," or to lift, but it should be furnished with a lock, so that it could not be opened without the orders of the surgeon.

4. The administration building may be reduced in size by omitting two of the 14 by 20 rooms on each floor. The remaining rooms will be sufficient for the necessary *personnel* of the building. For sites for these buildings I propose to occupy the grounds of Mr. Stone on Fourteenth street, opposite Columbian College. He has two lots, one of 87 acres, the other of 40, both of which he has placed at the disposal of the Government for this purpose. The grounds lie well, are well drained, and well supplied with excellent water. There are three springs upon

---

* Not found.

the place, at present furnished with pumps, and as many more may readily be sunk as the necessities of the buildings may require. These lots will afford room for about one-fourth of the proposed buildings. We have a lease of 100 acres at Kalorama. This land is similarly circumstanced with that of Mr. Stone as to its general features and the water supply. It will afford room for 20 buildings. We shall want about 250 acres more for the remaining buildings. There is plenty of unoccupied land upon the heights about Washington that might be procured for this purpose. I apprehend the Quartermaster's Department will find little difficulty in effecting leases of as much as will be required.

There will thus be some three or four large hospital towns at some distance from each other. Each assemblage of buildings or hospital section will require one experienced, active, and energetic surgeon of the Army as superintendent; one assistant commissary of subsistence, and one assistant quartermaster at least will be required, and perhaps more. The guards can be furnished by the troops occupying this military position. They should be required to enforce the orders of the chief surgeon.

There being no fund within the control of the Medical Department from which suitable hospital clothing can be furnished for the inmates of this establishment, we must rely for a time upon the contributions of the Sanitary Commission for that purpose, and I am happy to say they are now taking measures to meet this demand. But it is reasonable to suppose that the time during which they will be called upon to supply this want will be limited; for the hospital fund, well managed, ought to be sufficient in the course of two months to provide all necessary comforts for the sick.

Very respectfully, your obedient servant,

CHAS. S. TRIPLER,
Surgeon and Medical Director Army of the Potomac.

Brig. Gen. S. WILLIAMS,
Assistant Adjutant-General, Army of the Potomac.

[Appendix I.]

HEADQUARTERS ARMY OF THE POTOMAC,
Medical Director's Office, October 29, 1861.

GENERAL: I have the honor to report that, in obedience to the orders of Major-General McClellan, I proceeded to Annapolis, Baltimore, Philadelphia, and New York for the purpose of making arrangements for the sick of the Army of the Potomac. I wished, if possible, to evacuate all the hospitals upon the Potomac, at Annapolis, and Baltimore upon Philadelphia and New York, and also to ascertain how much hospital accommodation could be depended upon at Annapolis and Baltimore. At Annapolis a portion only of the public buildings is at present occupied for hospital purposes. I would recommend that all the buildings at that point should be fitted up as hospitals, and the establishment could then accommodate 1,200 patients. At Baltimore there are two hotels and three dwelling-houses now occupied. These buildings can receive in cold weather, when windows and doors are to be kept closed, but 310 patients. The rents paid for them amount to $12,900. At such an extravagant rate I did not think it advisable to negotiate for any extension of hospital accommodation in Baltimore.

I then proceeded to Philadelphia and made inquiries for buildings suitable for our purposes. Several large and small buildings were suggested to me as available. I estimated for about 4,000 beds as likely to be wanted in Philadelphia and New York, and therefore, after procuring the assistance of the quartermaster and some of my professional friends in looking up convenient buildings, I went to New York to see what could be done there. In that city I was unable to accomplish anything. After several days' delay, I could only procure one offer, and that was to accommodate 250 men in the New York Hospital at $5 per week each. This I considered altogether too high. The commissioners of emigration have six buildings on Staten Island, capable of accommodating 125 men each, that they have placed at the disposal of the governor of the State for barracks for volunteers. These buildings the quartermaster-general of the State told me we might occupy, provided the United States would put up rough board barracks for the accommodation of the volunteers. I did not think it best to accept this offer. If we are to build, it would be better to build here than there. It would be both hazardous to the men and expensive to the Treasury to send patients to Staten Island. It would involve the increased cost of transportation from Philadelphia to New York and back in each case, and the additional cost of a steamer to convey the men from the depot at Jersey City to the island. The distance of the island from the city also would create great difficulty in subsisting the men there. For these reasons I felt obliged to give up the idea of availing ourselves of any assistance from New York. Upon my return to Philadelphia I visited, examined, and requested the quartermaster to hire the following buildings and to fit them up for hospitals:

1st. The National Hall, on Market, below Thirteenth street. It will accommodate 350 patients. The rent is $425 per month.

2d. The Reading Railroad Depot, corner of Broad and Arch streets. It will accommodate 400 patients. The rent is $1,750 per annum.

3d. A paper factory, corner of Twenty-second and Wood streets. Will accommodate 275 patients. Rent not ascertained.

4th. The State Arsenal. Will accommodate 350 patients. For this I think no rent will be demanded. It is under the control of General Patterson, who told me he would write to the governor on the subject, and that I might rely upon having it.

5th. A silk factory, corner of Twenty-second and South streets. It will accommodate 160 patients. Rent, $150 per month.

6th. The Summit House. It will accommodate 100 patients. Rent, $150 per month.

In addition to these accommodations, we are offered 150 beds at St. Joseph's Hospital, and 150 at the Pennsylvania Hospital, at $3.50 per week each. This, after a careful calculation, I find to be about what it costs to furnish any hospital accommodation to our men. The sum asked includes everything—medicines, stores, fuel, lights, medical attendance, &c. I therefore earnestly recommend that these offers be accepted immediately. We can avail ourselves of them at once, to relieve our crowded hospitals in Washington.

This gives a total accommodation of 1,935 beds. When prepared, this will just about relieve the present general hospitals on the Potomac, in Annapolis, and Baltimore. The rents are very reasonable, averaging about $9 per man per annum, whereas in Baltimore the average is more than $40.

To carry out these plans the authority of the Quartermaster-General for hiring the buildings and making the necessary improvements is required. I respectfully ask that it may be obtained.

For the bedding, furniture, and medical attendance the action of the

Surgeon-General will be necessary. It was my intention to ask for the appointment of Dr. John Neill, of Philadelphia, as brigade surgeon, and to place him in charge of the whole Philadelphia establishment, giving him for assistants a suitable number of young physicians, to be employed by contract. These can be procured in Philadelphia at $50 per month each. The economy and efficiency of the whole arrangement I hope will be perceived.　　　＊　　　＊　　　＊

Very respectfully, your obedient servant,

CHAS. S. TRIPLER,
Surgeon and Medical Director Army of the Potomac.

General S. WILLIAMS,
Assistant Adjutant-General, Army of the Potomac.

[Appendix K.]

HEADQUARTERS ARMY OF THE POTOMAC,
Medical Director's Office, January 28, 1862.

GENERAL: In obedience to instructions in your letter of January 21 I have the honor to submit the following report:

Having the reports of the inspectors of hospitals as to the sanitary condition of nearly all the divisions of the army in this vicinity, showing their conditions at periods varying from December 5 to the present date, and having also the weekly reports of the brigade surgeons of nearly all the brigades up to January 18, for the purpose of laying before the general what I conceive to be the true state of the hospitals of this army, I hasten to present this letter in anticipation of the completion of all the inspections ordered. The importance of the subject seems to me to demand this, in order to allay unnecessary apprehensions and to afford an opportunity for correcting certain existing irregularities, as well as to offer suggestions as to the means of preventing as far as practicable any increase of disease during the winter and spring.

I am able from the reports in my hands to compare the true sick lists in brigades with those sent in to the Adjutant-General's Office. Among the brigades to which my attention was directed are the following. I arrange them in tabular form, to show how widely the reports of the brigade surgeons differ from those in the table appended to your letter:

Brigades.	General Williams' table, January 10.	Brigade surgeon's report.	Date.
	Per cent.	*Per cent.*	
Slocum's	14. 34	6. 8	January 21
Howard's	12. 44	9. 3	Januar 18
Richardson's	11. 19	6. 7	January 18
Jameson's	10. 95	6. 4	January 18
French's	9. 6	6. 3	January 11
Morell's	9. 17	3. 4	January 18
Hancock's	17. 1	10. 9	January 18
Brooks'	29. 75	14. 52	January 11
Brannan's	9. 36	5. 82	January 11
Steinwehr's	11. 8	5. 2	January 18
Palmer's	12. 56	6. 5	January 22
Sykes'	9. 95	6. 5	January 25

The above are sufficient for my present purpose, which is to show that numbers of men are reported sick by their captains who are not found upon the reports of the medical officers of their regiments. The true number of the sick is large enough to give me much concern, but I am unwilling it should be represented to be larger than it really is through the careless manner in which company reports are too frequently made out. Considering the season of the year and the unfavorable state of the weather it cannot be disputed that this is the most healthy army the world has ever seen. The general health of the whole force is rather improving than deteriorating; still, certain corps are at a stand-still, while others are sadly falling off.

I have observed in several instances that regiments after arriving here speedily exhibited a wretched sanitary condition. The maximum, however, was soon reached, and they have steadily improved until their sick lists would compare favorably with the rest. This might be accounted for by acclimation, by gradual improvement in discipline and police, by becoming better acquainted with the wants of a soldier in camp, and with the means of meeting those wants. But other troops, and those, too, from particular sections of country, have not improved. The Vermont regiments in Brooks' brigade are examples of this. They give us the largest ratio of sick of all the troops in this army, and that ratio has not essentially varied for the last three months. They suffered in the first place from measles. In this they simply shared the lot of all irregular troops. Since then they have been and are the subjects of fevers (remittent and typhoid).

The inspector of hospitals (Surgeon Keeney) reports the police of all these regiments as good, their clothing good, their tents good, with the exception of the Second and Third Regiments, and, strange to say, those two regiments are in decidedly the best sanitary condition. The locations of the camps of the Fifth and Sixth are reported as bad, but that of the Third is also bad. The soil is clay; the face of the country rolling, but presenting many plains sufficiently extensive for camps. These plains have been selected, and in consequence the difficulties of drainage, always great in a clay soil, have been increased.

While writing I have received another weekly report from the Vermont brigade, which shows a large increase of sick over that of the preceding week. The Berdan Sharpshooters are also in a bad sanitary condition, and not improving. Their camp, however, is badly located. I shall visit this brigade personally.

We have now successfully passed through the season of malarious fevers. The sanitary arrangements of this army have been successful in warding off the diseases of summer and autumn. We are now called upon to guard against those of winter and spring. The principal diseases we have to fear are typhus and typhoid fevers and pneumonia. These diseases prevail in this district during the present and approaching season. Already a number of cases have occurred, some of which have been fatal. These diseases arise from foul air, bad clothing, imperfect shelter, exposure to cold and wet, imperfectly-drained and badly-policed camps, &c. The indispensable conditions for securing the health of men in the field are good shelter, good clothing, good food, and good water, dry camp grounds, and an abundant supply of pure air.

For the shelter of our men we are to choose between tents and huts. There are clusters of buildings at several places within our limits that might be occupied by our troops, but having been erected for a different purpose, they are in nowise adapted to this. They are ill-constructed, ill-ventilated, too crowded, and generally out of position. I should prefer, if it is practicable, the "Chester hut," as used at Balaklava.

the plans for which will be found in the Report of the English Sanitary Commission. These huts, with the independent roof ventilation, were found well adapted for hospitals as well as quarters, and the results of their employment were altogether satisfactory; but it will take time to erect them, and our necessities seem to be too pressing to admit of this delay. They might, however, be put up to some extent in the worst of our camping grounds, if military necessity requires that our men shall be kept in those positions.

Next to these huts I would invite attention again to the plan of improving our tents that I recommended in mine of the 11th December last, and perhaps in other letters, i. e., to build a pen of logs and slabs the size of the base of the tent, some 3 feet high, and then to secure the tent upon this for a roof. This plan is now in use in several camps, and wherever it has been adopted it has been found to contribute very much to the comfort of the men. In some of the camps the pit has been dug, as in the Crimea, and the tent placed over that. This I condemned emphatically in the letter alluded to, and I repeat it, it is totally inadmissible. I should add to what I said before that in my opinion board floors should be furnished to all the tents and fresh straw or hay for the men to sleep upon. These tents must not be overcrowded. This is the tendency of all armies, and is a pernicious practice. The ventilation of tents, again, is a more difficult matter than is generally supposed. This should be secured by windows, as they are termed, in the tent, and by frequently opening the tent doors or keeping them open during the day.

Most of the subsoil upon the Potomac is of clay. This is particularly so in the camps presenting the largest sick reports, and therefore the greater attention is required to be paid to its drainage. I do not believe such a soil can be sufficiently well drained in a wet season to enable us to dispense with floors to the tents, but to secure as good a drainage as practicable I would recommend each company ground should be surrounded by a ditch not less than 12 inches deep at its shallowest parts; this ditch to be 4 feet from the outside border of the tents, and to be laid out and dug under the superintendence of a competent engineer; otherwise it will be imperfectly done, and be productive of more harm than good. Supplementary ditches a few inches in depth should also surround the tents, and be carefully conducted into the main ditch. I would further suggest that the floors of the tents should be raised some three inches from the ground; that lime or charcoal should be strewed over the surface of the ground, and then the floor laid without pinning, that it may be readily taken up and the ground under it policed.

Pure air cannot exist without good police. To secure this as much as possible I recommend that all impurities collected in the camps and all other impurities shall be buried not less than 12 inches below the surface. In cavalry camps the manure must be got rid of in some way, or the men will get sick. Camping grounds long occupied seem frequently to get saturated with putrescent exhalations that engender and aggravate disease. A change of ground will often be found to arrest or diminish an endemic for a while until a new saturation of the new soil sets it in motion again. This was exemplified in Brooks' brigade. A change of camp seemed to have checked the endemic in one of his worst regiments. Gradually, however, it reappeared.

The camping ground of Berdan Sharpshooters I think should be changed on this principle, as well as that its drainage is bad. This regiment is suffering from measles, and lately severe lung complications have accompanied the disease. A fresh and a dry camp, therefore, is in my opinion decidedly necessary for the command. If a suitable ground is selected and the tents put up in the way I have suggested, I should look for favorable results.

Allow me to insert here what I have omitted in its proper place, that the tent foundations should not be permitted to be banked up with dirt. You can never have a dry soil under the tent floors where this practice obtains.

I respectfully recommend an immediate change of the camping grounds of all the brigades that show an undue proportion of sick; that these grounds shall be selected upon proper principles in relation to their drainage capabilities, their exposure to storms, and the vicinity of marshes; that they shall be ditched in the mode I have pointed out, and that the tents shall be fitted up as I have suggested.

The food of our men is now good, and they are gradually improving in their cooking. We have no pernicious dysenteries or diarrheas in our camps. The clothing of the men is generally good. I do not think any deficiency in this respect has anything to do with the fevers that scourge our Vermont troops. If it were practicable, it would be desirable that our men should be furnished with the high water-proof boots, that their feet and legs might be kept dry when compelled to walk through the deep mud of the Virginia side of the Potomac.

I recommended in September that hot coffee should be issued to the men immediately after reveille. This was enjoined in general orders. I doubt whether it is now observed, but I think it important, and it should be reiterated. Picket duty is very severe at this season. The *tente d'abris*, if not used, might be used much to the comfort of the men exposed. I would give a whisky ration twice a day to men thus exposed, and they certainly should be furnished with the long boots I have suggested.

A little contrivance might provide them a comparatively dry bivouac. India-rubber blankets to spread upon the ground would be advisable. I think if we do all this, or as much of it as is possible, we shall have done all we can to secure the health of our men. I do not expect it will meet the whole difficulty in the Vermont cases, but it will go far to alleviate it. I believe there is a nostalgic element in those regiments affecting them unfavorably. This we cannot remedy, except in so far as it may be aggravated by the spectacle of so many of their comrades being sick and dying. We shall diminish disease by the course I have pointed out, and this will react favorably upon the other men. The process of acclimation has been more tedious in these troops than in any others. It does, however, progress. Most of the sickness in these regiments occurs among the recruits, and those regiments which have been longest here are the best off. All this in encouraging.

While upon this subject, I ask leave to suggest that it is advisable to forbid soldiers coming into the cities of Washington or Georgetown unless upon duty with written orders. Small-pox is quite prevalent in these cities, and I have reason to believe that the cases that have occurred of late among our men have originated from exposure in town. Vaccination has been pushed as actively as possible among our troops, but still cases of this disease do occur. Men have become its subjects who have been vaccinated and revaccinated very recently. Such occurrences set all calculations at defiance, and I know no other means of preventing them than keeping our men out of the way of infection altogether. I also earnestly recommend that all recruits intended for this army shall be revaccinated before they leave the rendezvous where they are enlisted to join their regiments. Hundreds of recruits have joined this army lately who have never been vaccinated. It is notoriously unsafe to travel over any railroad in the country at the present day unprotected.

The brigade of General Hamilton is in General Banks' division. As soon as the inspection of the few remaining commands in this vicinity is completed an inspector will be sent to that brigade.

I have written this report before I am able to communicate all the information required in your instructions, because the exigency seemed urgent. The inspections will be pressed forward, and the results communicated as rapidly as possible.

Very respectfully, your obedient servant,

CHAS. S. TRIPLER,
Surgeon and Medical Director Army of the Potomac.

Brig. Gen. S. WILLIAMS,
Assistant Adjutant-General, Army of the Potomac.

[Appendix L.]

HEADQUARTERS ARMY OF THE POTOMAC,
Medical Director's Office, January 4, 1862.

SIR: I have the honor to submit the following report of the sanitary condition of the Army of the Potomac, deduced from the reports received at this office for the months of October and November:

This army having been hastily assembled, and its medical officers of all grades appointed from civil life, and necessarily without military experience, it has been no easy task to collect the proper reports. Up to the month of October but a small proportion of the regiments made reports, and few of those received were made out with sufficient accuracy to be considered useful or reliable. As the medical officers learn more of their duties, I am happy to say that greater punctuality is observed in this respect. I received for the month of October reports from 129 regiments, 7 battalions, 14 batteries, and 8 general hospitals. The aggregate strength of the forces from which these reports were received is 116,763. Of these 38,248 were under treatment during the month in the field and general hospitals; 27,983 were returned to duty; 295 died, and 7,443 remained under treatment at the end of the month; 510 were discharged on surgeon's certificate of disability. These men never should have been enlisted; they were simply impositions upon the Government, and were received through the carelessness or incompetency of the recruiting or inspecting officers. The same remarks may apply to those who will be presently noticed as having been discharged in November. The ratio of the sick remaining at the end of the month to the whole force was 6.07 per cent. The ratio of deaths is 3.03 per cent. per annum.

For the month of November I have reports from 156 regiments, 6 battalions, 20 batteries, and 8 general hospitals. From the division commanded by General Dix I have no reports.

The aggregate strength of the forces from which I have received reports is 142,577. Of these, 47,836 have been under treatment in the field and general hospitals, 35,915 of whom have been returned to duty, and 281 have died; 9,281 remained under treatment at the end of the month; 618 have been discharged upon surgeons' certificates of disability. The number remaining is considered the constant diminution of force due to sickness. This is 6.5 per cent. Of these, however, more than one-half are probably capable of taking the field, and would do so in case of an advance or an attack. The proportion of serious cases to the whole number treated is about one-third, and this I should consider as the true number of the sick who would be unfit for any duty at any given time. This would give 2.3 per cent. as inefficient.

The deaths have been in November 281, which gives a mortality for the whole force of 2.36 per cent. per annum.

The diseases from which our men have suffered most have been continued remittent and typhoid fevers, measles, diarrhea, dysentery, and the various forms of catarrh. Of all the scourges incident to armies in the field I suppose that chronic diarrheas and dysenteries have always been the most prevalent and the most fatal. I am happy to say that in this army they are almost unknown. We have but 280 cases of chronic diarrhea and 69 of chronic dysentery reported in the month of November. No other army that has ever taken the field can show such a record. We have 1,331 cases of measles reported in November. This disease almost invariably appears among irregular troops in a few weeks after they are assembled in camp. The regiments among whom these cases have occurred are those recently arrived. Most of them reached this city with the disease prevailing. It has been generally of a mild form, soon running through the regiment, and then disappearing. I don't consider its propagation under these circumstances as due to contagion. On the contrary, it springs up from local causes, to which all the men are equally exposed, and those susceptible become its subjects as a matter of course. Among regular troops it is very rarely seen.

Of fevers of all sorts we have had 7,932 cases. Of these 4,051 were remittents and typhoids. The proportion of the latter to the former is stated to be 1 to 2.3. I have every reason to believe that this is greatly exaggerated from error in diagnosis. I do not look upon typhoid fever to the extent it has prevailed in this army as being of any great moment. From the report of inspectors of hospitals, as far as inspections have yet been made, I am satisfied this disease, if it ever prevailed to that extent, is now considerably declining. The regiments that have suffered most from fevers in November have been the Vermont, one from Maine, one or two from Pennsylvania, and one from Indiana. In all these regiments disease is now sensibly abating, and we have every reason to hope that in a few months their sanitary condition will be equally as good as that of the rest of the army.

I think there is abundant reason to be satisfied with the progress that has been made in this army in introducing something of a system of hygiene; in instructing its medical officers in their duties; in keeping them supplied with sufficient medicines, hospital stores, and instruments; in exacting from them a proper accountability for public property, and insisting upon its being used with economy; in preventing the army from being burdened with articles that, however convenient they may be, are not absolutely necessary, and cannot be transported in any possible supply train when the men are required to march; in requiring reports at short intervals of the sanitary condition of the regiments, and in instituting regular and thorough sanitary inspections, by officers of experience of the medical department of the army, who are competent to perform that duty, who understand what is necessary and what superfluous, and upon whose reports we can undertake to correct errors and abuses understandingly.

The result of all this great effort is seen in the statistics above recorded. While the ratio of cases of disease to the whole force does not differ for the two months reported, the ratio of mortality is .67 per cent.

per annum less in November than in October—a difference which, if secured in civil life, would make the fortune of an insurance company.

Important information is being constantly received from the inspectors of hospitals as to all matters relating to the comfort and health of the troops, thus affording opportunities for correcting errors and irregularities wherever they may be found to exist. A satisfactory progress has been made in improving the sanitary condition of the Army of the Potomac, and there is no reason to fear that this progress will not continue to be made until the health of this army will be such as will leave nothing to be desired.

Very respectfully, your obedient servant,

CHAS. S. TRIPLER,
Surgeon and Medical Director Army of the Potomac.

Surg. Gen. C. A. FINLEY, U. S. A.

AUGUST 18, 1861.—Scout to Accotink and skirmish at Pohick Church, Va.

REPORTS.

No. 1.—Brig. Gen. William B. Franklin, U. S. Army.
No. 2.—Capt. William H. Boyd, First New York Cavalry.

No. 1.

Report of Brig. Gen. William B. Franklin, U. S. Army.

ALEXANDRIA, VA., *August* 18, 1861.

The company of Lincoln [First New York] Cavalry sent out this morning met a party of the enemy's cavalry at Pohick Church, about 12 miles from here, numbering about 20. They charged the enemy, scattered them in all directions, and wounded two of them. One of our men was killed, and 2 are missing, who were thrown from their horses.

The enemy's horses far outstripped ours, so that no prisoners could be made. I have learned nothing definite about Springfield. Our scouts were 1½ miles from there last night. Saw their pickets; so there is no doubt that they are there. General Kearny thinks the force there is a variable one. So report his scouts.

W. B. FRANKLIN,
Brigadier-General, Commanding.

Maj. S. WILLIAMS.

No. 2.

Report of Capt. William H. Boyd, First New York Cavalry.

CAMP ELIZABETH, *Alexandria, Va., August* 18, 1861.

SIR: Your orders of this a. m., "to proceed on a scout down the Mount Vernon road and vicinity of Accotink, to capture, if possible, 27 cavalry of the enemy," have, as far as circumstances would permit, been obeyed. At about 10 o'clock a. m., accompanied by Lieutenant Gibson, Second Dragoons, U. S. Army, Lieutenant Hanson, Dr. Herrick, and 46 of my own company, I proceeded towards Accotink, interrogating all pedestrians and examining all houses and outbuildings on our way thither, until we reached Accotink, where we learned that a number of cavalry of the enemy were this morning at Pohick Church, whither we immediately proceeded. Our advanced pickets, upon nearing the church, thought they discovered a whole army, and immediately retreated, communicating directly with the men instead of me, thereby causing a stampede. After a little delay I succeeded in rallying our men together, and immediately retraced our steps. The road being narrow, we were unable to proceed to much advantage. Being in advance myself, upon getting up to the main road I was suddenly brought face to face with the enemy, whom I should judge to have been about 20 strong. The enemy were the first to challenge, and were evidently prepared to meet us, as they were in line at the side of the road (they being apprised of our coming by our advanced pickets, who had been previously challenged). After the usual war salutations I gave the order to charge, and our men shouted, cheered, and charged.

Immediately beyond the church are cross-roads. The enemy separated on the three roads, and our men divided and followed in hot pursuit. One party pursued within a short distance of Occoquan, both parties shooting as they rode. At the cross-roads were three men in ambush, and it is believed that these were the men who fired on us. Our loss is one killed (Jacob Erwen, shot through the body), and two missing (Williams and Lancaster), who were thrown from their horses. We cannot say whether the enemy lost any or not, but it is said one of the enemy was shot in the arm, and another fell on his horse's neck, and seemed to be unable to manage his horse. The enemy were well mounted, had very superior horses, and were enabled to outfoot us, and thus make their escape. It is my opinion that had we some infantry with us we would have been able to outflank them and taken some prisoners. Our dead we brought home with us.

I desire to make honorable mention of our guide, Lieutenant Gibson, Second Dragoons, U. S. Army.

I am, sir, very respectfully, your obedient servant,

WM. H. BOYD,
Captain Company C, Lincoln Cavalry.

Brigadier-General FRANKLIN.

AUGUST 23, 1861.—Engagement between Confederate Batteries at mouth of Potomac Creek, Virginia, and U. S. Steamers Yankee and Release.

Report of Colonel R. M. Cary, Thirtieth Virginia Infantry.

HEADQUARTERS, MARLBOROUGH POINT,
August 23, 1861.

COLONEL : I have the honor to report that this afternoon at about 4.30 o'clock the enemy's steamer Yankee and a tug were seen standing in the mouth of Potomac Creek. I ordered down to the point the siege rifled gun (Betty Holmes) and a section (rifle) of Walker's battery.

The enemy fired the first shot, not aimed at this point, however. Smith's battery replied. As soon as our field pieces opened the U. S. steamer Release (ice-boat) stood in and engaged us.

The officers in charge of the pieces and the men behaved with proper coolness and deliberation. They were Lieutenants Hagerty, Pegram, and Dabney.

The enemy's fire was very accurate, frequently bursting his shell in close proximity to our pieces. It is believed that both the Yankee and the Release were hit; the former more than once. No one was hurt on our side.

The action lasted about forty minutes, during which we fired some twenty-five shot and shell; the enemy as many more. Capt. R. L. Walker was present, in immediate command of all the pieces.

I am, colonel, very respectfully, your obedient servant,

> R. M. CARY,
> *Thirtieth Virginia Infantry, Commanding.*

D. H. MAURY,
  Asst. Adjt. Gen., Dep't of Fredericksburg, Brooke's.

AUGUST 25, 1861.—Skirmish near Piggot's Mill, West Virginia.

Report of Brig. Gen. Henry A. Wise, C. S. Army.

HEADQUARTERS WISE'S LEGION, *August 27*, 1861.

SIR : On Saturday, as I informed you, I in person reconnoitered and found the enemy, and stationed guards on the turnpike, in advance of the Saturday road, at Tyree's, perfectly covering that and other roads. I left that point, near Westlake's, about 4 o'clock, with my men well posted. It seems that after I left (and certainly unknown to me, without the least notice to my command) a corps of your cavalry, about 175 strong, came down the Saturday road and advanced on the turnpike, under the command of Acting Colonel Jenkins, aided by Major Reynolds. They relieved my guard, who had scouted and were well acquainted with the ground. This was done by Colonel Jenkins, without notice to me or Colonel Davis, in command of the cavalry, or to Captain Brock, in command of the company. The result of this unexpected accession of force from your camp is known. The men not having sufficiently scouted the ground, and being badly supplied with ammunition, were ambuscaded and routed, with loss and a demoralizing flight. I met men with their subordinate officers flying at 5 miles distance from the enemy, and so panic-struck, that even there they could not be rallied or led back to look after the dead and wounded. Colonel Jenkins and Major Reynolds, on the spot of the ambuscade, tried bravely to rally them, but it was in vain. Eighteen of my cavalry, who were picketed in view of the scene, on a neighboring hill (Brock's troop), rushed to the rescue, and lost 1 killed and 5 wounded. Colonel Jenkins was hurt by the fall of his horse, and is here still, somewhat disabled. Major Reynolds, though in my camp, made no report to me, and has left with his command. His men and officers, whom I met flying, utterly failed to obey my orders, delivered in person, under the threat of the pistol, and did not return, from sheer cowardice, to the scene from which the enemy had rapidly retired. The appearance of this force on my outposts was the more unexpected, inasmuch as you had ordered me to send you 100 cavalry, which I did.

And now I beg leave, most respectfully, to protest that nothing but disaster can follow such interference with my immediate command, without notice, and with orders from you to me which led me to expect the very contrary of what has occurred. I deplore the disaster which has occurred, but am not in the least responsible for it. I beg that in future you will notify me of any movement under your orders on the lines you have left me to defend.

Very respectfully, your obedient servant,

HENRY A. WISE,
Brigadier-General.

Brigadier-General FLOYD, *Commanding, &c.*

P. S.—My camp is severely disabled by measles, and I send you a copy of a report, by Colonel Richardson, of the reduced condition of his regiment, the best under my command. I also send to you a copy of a report, made to me by Colonel Henningsen, showing the necessity of keeping my whole force for the present in position on this turnpike, and of watching the advance of the enemy on the Chestnutburg road. I respectfully submit whether I shall move a regiment to Carnifix Ferry. I will await your further orders, feeling, as I do, the necessity of keeping all my remaining force here.

HENRY A. WISE,
Brigadier-General.

[Inclosures.]

HDQRS. FIRST REGIMENT INFANTRY, WISE'S BRIGADE,
Camp Dogwood, Va., August 26, 1861.

GENERAL: I have the honor to report that the remnant of my command will be ready to move to-morrow morning by 9 o'clock. I regret that I have to offer an excuse for my regiment, but really think that it is not advisable to send it off crippled as it is. If it should be called into action in its present condition the result might not prove satisfactory, and I feel that I should be censurable if I did not report these facts. I wish the command to do itself credit, and do not doubt that it will do so under any circumstances, but think it best just to give it a trial at first in its original strength. I beg leave herewith to submit the actual strength of my regiment, as per report of the company commanders: Company A, 39; Company B, 47; Company C, 29; Company D, 41; Company E, 19; Company F, 47; Company G, 30; Company H, 39; Company I, 41; Company K, 39, amounting in the aggregate to 371 effective men, a little upwards of one-third of the whole command, the measles daily reducing the ranks at the rate of at least 25 a day. According to the report of the surgeon of the regiment, it is owing to exposure and fatigue incident to rapid and forced marches. I have presented these facts as a matter of duty, and offer them for your consideration.

Very respectfully, your obedient servant,

J. H. RICHARDSON,
Lieut. Col. Forty-sixth Reg't, P. A. C. S., Comdg. First Inf., W. B.

Brig. Gen. H. A. WISE.

CAMP AT DOGWOOD GAP, VA.,
August 26, 1861.

GENERAL: In your dispatch of this morning you order me to maintain my position at Dogwood Gap, as the best to cover the turnpike, and as the best from which to move to the support of General Floyd.

You warn me at the same time that this position is threatened from the New River, and you conclude by saying:

Thus you have to guard the turnpike. Be ready to move with all your force to Carnifix Ferry, and to take commanding position against the enemy in the opposite direction.

You add:

This raises the question, "Have you more than force enough to do any one of these essential services?"

In reply, I beg leave to state that the strength of the three regiments of infantry and of the artillery comprised in my command at Dogwood Camp is this morning reported at 1,386 privates and non-commissioned officers present and fit for duty. Colonel Davis, commanding the cavalry, who, as you are aware, does not report to me, told me yesterday that the horses were so worn with scouting, and had suffered so much from want of shoes, that he had only 50 efficient cavalry. Of these, 5 were killed and wounded yesterday endeavoring to aid Colonel Jenkins in his unfortunate skirmish. Less than 1,440 men, with five guns, is, therefore, as far as I am aware, the total force here present at your disposal. Undivided, by the aid of artillery used in positions where artillery is available, and with the assistance of position, this force is sufficient, by the exercise of great vigilance, to effect one, and probably two, of the objects you specify, and partially to cover them all. I mean that of guarding the turnpike road and preventing the enemy from getting on our rear by crossing the New River. This, in my opinion, can only be securely done by occupying Dogwood Gap. If driven thence, or compelled to abandon this position, all the other objects you specify might, and probably would, be frustrated; that is to say, the defense of the Lewisburg road, the safety of your command, and your ability to succor General Floyd or cover his rear in case of reverse to his arms, or even otherwise, would be jeopardized.

I learned from you to-day that by reliable accounts the enemy had about 1,000 men at Gauley Bridge; 1,000 up the turnpike; 700 at the Hawk's Nest, and 500 at Cotton Hill. This information has since been confirmed to me, with the addition that the force at Cotton Hill is 1,000 men.

The enemy, I am satisfied, is perfectly cognizant of our strength, or rather weakness, and immediately informed of all our movements. The moment we abandon Dogwood Gap, or leave it in a defenseless condition, even if he had received no further re-enforcements, he may, and doubtless would, advance along the turnpike and occupy or force the gap and hold it. In this case our communication, if we moved to Carnifix Ferry, or that of such portion of our force as moved thither, and also the communication of General Floyd with the turnpike, would be cut off, and the Legion, or a portion of it, starved into dispersion, while the remainder would become abortively weak. On the contrary, by holding Dogwood Gap, which with the present force may be successfully defended even if attacked in front and rear (considering that an attack from the rear could not be carried on for more than two or three days, even if General Floyd's column was cut off from the ferry), the Legion would be strengthened every day. In the first place, reconnoitering and slight intrenchments will so strengthen the position as to require less force for secure defense. In the next few days rest for men and horses will much increase the efficiency of the now exhausted force, to say nothing of its augmentation by re-enforcements under way and of sick returning to their companies and collecting already on the road.

Further, from a secure position like Dogwood Gap comparatively rapid marches may be made within striking distance with the efficiency of double the number of men without this stronghold to fall back upon, because, leaving the baggage and provision in security, such marches may be made with what the men carry in their haversacks, or with one wagon, with picked team, per regiment, instead of with a number of under-horsed wagons, requiring the expedition force to guard them and delaying their advance. Hence with a secure possession of the gap, 400 or 500 men, and in a few days a much larger number, may be detached with impunity and efficiency, either to operate on the Sunday Road, or up to Carnifix Ferry, or toward the Fayetteville road and New River. This, if the force be divided, by detachment (beyond reach) of even one regiment, would become impossible. Without a nucleus to fall back upon nothing, in my opinion, can be effected—and it is little more than a nucleus now, although a valuable one. Dividing at this time would be like breaking up an army into isolated files. Not only the future efficiency and the present usefulness but the actual safety of the Legion would be unwarrantably imperiled under present circumstances by any but a very prudent course, and I must respectfully put on record my protest against the execution of certain orders which you have mentioned, and which, I am sure, could only have been conceived under erroneous impressions as to the strength and condition of the corps.

I am, general, respectfully, yours,

C. F. HENNINGSEN.

Brig. Gen. H. A. WISE, *Commanding Wise's Legion.*

AUGUST 26, 1861.—Action at Cross-Lanes, near Summersville, W. Va.

Reports of Brig. General William S. Rosecrans, U. S. Army.

CLARKSBURG, *August* 28, 1861.

General Cox reports, under date 27th, Seventh Ohio, under Tyler, advanced regiment at Cross-Lanes, below Summersville, was surprised by Floyd while eating his breakfast, and dispersed. Baggage trains saved and half the regiment come in. Other half continues to straggle in. Floyd, with five regiments and three guns, at Cross-Lanes, 5 miles below Summersville. Wise, with about the same force, on New River. General reports give Lee and Loring 10,000 men at Huntersville. Troops sickly. Reynolds endeavoring to get close information to-day. News not in yet. I have twenty-two companies infantry, one of cavalry, two guns at Sutton, and Mack's battery; one regiment of ten companies at Bulltown to-night; ten companies more and mountain-howitzer battery will probably reach there to-morrow; eight companies of infantry to-morrow night; fifteen companies now on rail for this place, to go down as soon as possible; total, sixty-five infantry. They will be down there by Saturday evening. This will be all I can spare, unless news from Cheat Mountain indicates the possibility of using some of the eight regiments there.

ROSECRANS.

Col. E. D. TOWNSEND.

AUGUST 28, 1861.

Dispatch from General Cox says "that Seventh Ohio, 5 miles below Summersville, on Gauley road, was overpowered by superior numbers and scattered." A good many missing, but thinks the casualties not great. Expects them all in. Has orders in full to hold his position at Gauley. Thinks he can do it. Enemy estimated at from 5,000 to 10,000. Am moving down all available force to Sutton. Will have fitty-five companies there by to-morrow evening. Expect to attack the enemy on Friday or Saturday, and crush his column, if possible, at or near Summersville.

ROSECRANS.

AUGUST 28–30, 1861.—Skirmishes near Bailey's Corners (or Cross-Roads), Va.

REPORTS, ETC.

No. 1.—Maj. Stephen G. Champlin, Third Michigan Infantry.
No. 2.—Capt. Louis Dillman, Second Michigan Infantry.
No. 3.—Letter of commendation from General McClellan to Major Champlin.

No. 1.

Report of Maj. Stephen G. Champlin, Third Michigan Infantry.

HEADQUARTERS,
Hunter's Chapel, August 30, 1861.

I have the honor to report that this morning, while reconnoitering from the top of Mrs. Hunter's house, the enemy was observed to send off from the top of the hill lying north of Bailey's Corners two companies of infantry, who numbered about 200 men, who were marched in the direction of our pickets, stationed northeast of Bailey's Corners and on the right of Captain Dillman's position. I started immediately for Bailey's Corners, to inform Captain Dillman and take steps for defense. I found that Captain Dillman was acquainted with the movement of the enemy.

A few moments after my arrival about 100 of the enemy attacked our pickets on the right side of the road, and occupying the Bailey out-houses and premises adjoining. An attack was also made on our line of pickets, extending as far as the first house on the direct road from Arlington Mill to Bailey's Corners. The pickets returned the fire and retreated back on Captain Dillman's command and upon the reserve stationed half way from Arlington Mill to Bailey's Corners. I directed Captain Dillman to march one company of his men on the table-land to his right to a point opposite the enemy in the woods and deploy them as skirmishers, advance them across the road, and engage the enemy on their flank, while I brought up and engaged the enemy's front with the reserve stationed half way to the mill, under command of Lieutenant Morris, and also with a portion of Captain Judd's command, stationed near Arlington Mill. The order was executed, and the enemy retreated before the skirmishers, and would not and did not wait an engagement. Our pickets were re-established, and the forces of both sides are again in the same position they respectively occupied this morning. Our loss none [killed]; wounded, 1 or 2 slightly. The enemy were observed to carry off 3 of their own men, who were either killed or wounded.

Throughout the whole of this affair both officers and men behaved with great coolness and bravery, and I think the retreat was timely for the enemy, for had they waited the advance, they must have been repulsed with considerable loss.

I have the honor to be, &c., your obedient servant,

S. G. CHAMPLIN,
Major, Commanding Special Detachment.

Col. I. B. RICHARDSON, *Commanding Fourth Brigade.*

———

2.

Report of Capt. Louis Dillman, Second Michigan Infantry.

CAMP SECOND MICHIGAN REG'T, NEAR ARLINGTON,
September 3, 1861.

On Thursday, August 28, in compliance with your order of same date, I left Hunter's Chapel with a detachment of 250 men from the Second Michigan Regiment for Bailey's Cross-Roads, to occupy and hold the same against the encroachments of the enemy's forces in that vicinity. I reached the Cross-Roads at 10 a. m., and at once threw out pickets on the line shown by the map accompanying this report.* The rebel pickets opened their fire at once, and kept it up until about 10 p. m., ceasing at that time until daylight next morning, when it was again opened by them quite briskly along the whole line, but with no return from our pickets. Emboldened by our silence, a detachment of about 80 men was sent out from their camp, apparently with the intention of driving in pickets on the right of my line, thus cutting off all communication with the headquarters of the regiment. In this sally they were partially successful. The pickets were driven from their posts, but, rallying, and being supported by a detachment of 40 skirmishers hurriedly thrown out, under Captain Humphrey, the rebels were checked and driven back, with a loss of 6 or 8 killed and wounded.

The firing was kept up from both sides through the day with considerable effect from our side, the enemy carrying off some twelve men killed and wounded. Darkness closed the firing, to be reopened at daylight the next (Sunday) morning. It commenced on the left, and gradually worked along to the right until the whole line was warmly engaged. The firing continued through the day with but little intermission. The enemy were seen to carry a number off the field. Our loss was 1 wounded—a private in Company G. He has since died from the effect of the wound.

Sunday but little firing, except morning and evening.

Monday the same.

Two privates of Company D—J. Austin and P. F. Walworth—straying from camp, passed through the enemy's lines and up to within some forty rods of the rear of their earthwork on Munson's Hill. Seeing two rebels near, they watched their chance, each picked his man, fired, and brought him to the ground. They returned safely to camp. They report seeing about 500 men around the works. There were no tents in sight, but some twelve or fifteen wagons and two pieces of artillery were lying on the back of the hill. They also report seeing a large number of field officers busy looking over their maps and charts.

In concluding this report, allow me to say of the officers and men under my charge that they behaved as soldiers, were cool in their de-

———
* Not found.

portment. willingly and cheerfully performed every duty assigned them, and were found ever faithful at their posts. That we were able to keep up a continued skirmish of five days with the loss of but one man attests sufficiently to the general good conduct and faithfulness of both officers and men.

I have the honor, &c.,

L. DILLMAN,
Captain, Comdg. Detachment Second Reg't Mich. Infantry.
General RICHARDSON.

No. 3.

Letter of commendation from General McClellan to Major Champlin.

HEADQUARTERS ARMY OF THE POTOMAC,
Washington, September 5, 1861.

GENERAL: Major General McClellan has received Maj. S. G. Champlin's report of his reconnaissance and skirmish on the 30th ultimo. The general is much pleased with Major Champlin's dispositions on the occasion, which he deems eminently proper, and he desires you to convey his thanks to Major Champlin for the efficient manner in which this service was performed.

I have the honor to be, very respectfully, your obedient servant,

S. WILLIAMS,
Assistant Adjutant-General.

Brig. Gen. I. B. RICHARDSON, *Commanding Brigade, &c.*

AUGUST 31, 1861.—Skirmish at Munson's Hill, on Little River Turnpike, Va.

Report of Col. George W. Taylor, Third New Jersey Infantry.

CAMP OF THE THIRD REGIMENT NEW JERSEY VOLS.,
Bivouac at Intersection, September 2, 1861.

GENERAL: The pickets of the enemy having for some time been extremely annoying to our outposts on the Little River turnpike and on the road leading from thence to Chestnut Hill, I decided on making a reconnaissance in person, with a small force, with the view of cutting them off. Accordingly I marched with 40 men, volunteers from two companies of my regiment, on the morning of the 31st August, at 3 a. m., and keeping to the woods, arrived soon after daylight at or near the point (a little beyond) at which I desired to strike the road and cut them off. Here we were obliged to cross a fence and a narrow corn field, where the enemy, who had doubtless dogged our approach through the woods, lay in considerable force. While in the corn we were suddenly opened upon by a rapid and sharp fire, which our men, whenever they got sight of the enemy, returned with much spirit. Scarce two minutes elapsed when I found 3 men close to me had been shot down. The enemy being mostly hid, I deemed it prudent to order my men to fall back to the woods, distant about 30 yards, which I did. At the same time I ordered enough to remain with me to carry off the wounded, but they did not hear or heed my order except two. With these we got all off, as I supposed (the corn being thick), but Corporal Hand, Company I, who, when I turned him over, appeared to be dying. I took his musket, also the musket of one of the wounded, and returned to the woods to rally the men. I regret to say that none of them could be found, nor did I meet them until I reached the blacksmith-shop, three-quarters of a mile distant.

Here I found Captain Regur, Company I, with his command. Re-enforcing him with 25 men of the picket, then in charge of Captain Vickers, Third Regiment New Jersey Volunteers, with the latter he immediately marched back to bring in Corporal Hand and any others still missing. He reports that on reaching the ground he found the enemy in increased force, and did not re-enter the corn field, in which I think he was justified.

I should have stated that quite a number of the enemy were in full view in the road when we jumped the fence and charged them, and that each man in the charge, Captain Regur leading by my side, seemed eager to be foremost; nor did one, to my knowledge, flinch from the contest until my order to fall back to the woods, which, unfortunately, they misconstrued into a continuous retreat to our pickets. The enemy seemed to have retreated very soon after, as the firing had ceased before I left.

The 3 wounded men are doing well, except 1.* As near as I can ascertain there were 3 of the enemy shot down. The whole affair did not last ten minutes.

The officers with me were Captain Regur, Company I, First Lieutenant Taylor, and Second Lieutenant Spencer, both of the same company.

All of which I have the honor, respectfully, to report.

GEO. W. TAYLOR,
Colonel Third Regiment New Jersey Volunteers.

Brig. Gen. P. KEARNY, *Commanding Brigade.*

SEPTEMBER 2, 1861.—Skirmish near the Hawk's Nest, W. Va.

Reports of Brig. Gen. Henry A. Wise, C. S. Army.

AT TYREE'S, KANAWHA TURNPIKE, VIRGINIA,
September 4, 1861.

From Carnifix Ferry I returned to Dogwood Gap, and finding my men very weary with their march to and from the ferry, I rested them for the night, and gave orders for them to move early in the morning upon the Hawk's Nest. Stripping each regiment of infantry down to six companies, or 300 men, with three pieces of artillery, and about 250 cavalry (making in all about 1,250), I marched the day before yesterday morning down to Hamilton's, within half a mile of the Hawk's Nest. Feeling our way cautiously, late in the evening I advanced upon Turkey Creek, leading the advance guard myself in person. About dusk we arrived at McGraw's bridge, over Turkey Creek, and were then fired upon (a very short time hotly) by the enemy, concealed in the corn fields and brush-wood on both sides, and just as we were crossing the bridge. I am proud to say that the guard (Captain Summers' company) stood

---

* Nominal list of casualties shows 2 killed and 3 wounded.

their ground and behaved handsomely, returning the fire promptly, and I led them across the bridge, the enemy disappearing before us on the quick advance of our column. Night coming on, I thought it prudent to rest on our arms for the time, and it is well we did, for the next day (yesterday) I found him in ambuscade and intrenched very strongly at Big Creek. At McGraw's I ascertained his position. The turnpike downwards towards McGraw's turns to the right, descending a long hill on the margin of Big Creek. Crossing the creek over a narrow bridge, it passes up the right bank of the creek some 400 yards, and then turns through a gap, directly back, towards New River, around a high and isolated spur of mountain, and just at the turn a mountain road comes in to the turnpike from Rich Creek, on the Gauley. There, on the hills in front, at the junction of the roads, and around the sharp angle of the turnpike, back of the mountain, I found the enemy in considerable force, impossible to be told, from their being perfectly concealed. Seeing no other alternative to drive them out, I determined to drop a battalion across the creek, and charge them in the front, on the mountain side, which was bravely done by parts of three companies, Summers', Ryan's, and Janes' (about 120 men). They crossed silently until they rose the hill, and then, with a shout, drove the enemy to the top, they flying most cowardly, dropping guns, hats, canteens, &c., until my men reached the top and got above them. I then brought up a howitzer, and with shot and shell soon cleared the front and sides of the mountain next to us, but soon found that the enemy were thick in the gorges of the creek running up towards Rich Creek Gap. There was danger then of their turning my right flank, and I found it hazardous to pass the gap in face of their rifled cannon, which they had played over our heads for some time.

Having sent the companies of the Second Regiment up Turkey Creek, to come around the head of Big Creek, in their rear or left flank, I paused to wait for Colonel Anderson to come upon them and to feel their position and numbers still further. In this time they were reenforced with six companies and several pieces of artillery from Gauley. They had 1,250 in position, and their re-enforcements increased their numbers to 1,800 men of all arms, cavalry as well as infantry and artillery. They had about 75 horses.

Having attained my object, to secure Miller's Ferry and Liken's Mill (both essential to our uses), I fell back to Hamilton's, and am encamped there and at Westlake's Creek, guarding the ferry, the boat of which I have raised and am now repairing. But, sir, this point is liable to attack at all times from the rear by paths which converge from Gauley and Rich Creek at Sugar Gap, and come down to the turnpike at this place and at Shade Creek. I have left but six companies at Dogwood Gap, with two pieces of artillery, and have but three here to guard the three essential points. As your forces are now near 3,000 men, I beg that you will return to my Legion the corps of artillery, with their guns belonging to it, which you have, the measles having so thinned my ranks that I need all the men belonging to my command and double as many more. I have ordered Caskie, with General Beckley's militia, down the Loop, and by this time they are there. The day before yesterday they fought the enemy at Cotton Hill, and drove them within 2 miles of Montgomery's Ferry. General Chapman has arrived there now with about 1,600 men, and our communication with him will be opened to-day or to-morrow. Some days ago you asked for Colonel Croghan. I now send him to you, to be transferred to your brigade if

you desire it.   If you will advance upon Gauley, I will amuse the enemy in front upon this road.
    Very respectfully,
                                            HENRY A. WISE,
                                                    Brigadier-General.
Brigadier-General FLOYD, *Commanding, &c.*

—

                            CAMP NEAR HAWK'S NEST, VA.,
                                        September 5, 1861.
    GENERAL: Yours of August 31 was received last evening.   It is very gratifying to me to receive the approbation with which you commend my humble command, and particularly coming from you; but, sir, pardon me for saying that it does not meet my complaint that I am continually harassed with orders to do nothing but hard marching, to no end or purpose but to distract and dishearten all independent effort and action of my Legion.   Before I was marched to Carnifix, to march back again under orders which were changed four times in forty-eight hours, and after every appointment of co-operation essential to safety and success had been counteracted by General Floyd, precisely the same wrong has been repeated.   On the 31st ultimo General Floyd informed me that the enemy had abandoned Gauley Bridge, and were then advancing upon him, and said if this information was correct I should send him my strongest regiment to the top of the hill, near Gauley, with a good battery, so as to be perfectly in reach of him in case of need; and that I should at once advance with the remainder of my command and take possession of the camp at the mouth of the Gauley.   He asked me also to send him two companies of efficient cavalry (his had been cut to pieces, under Colonel Jenkins, interferring with my immediate command, and he had sent them to Greenbrier recruiting, and was measurably without dragoon force, though I had sent him 100 troopers already).   Such was the order of the morning of that day.
    On the same day, at 5 p. m., I received from him another note, dated at 12 noon, saying that he had received information through scouts that the enemy were advancing from Gauley Bridge in that (his) direction; that they were within 12 miles of him, and ordered that I would send him without delay 1,000 of my infantry, my best battery, and one squadron of horse.   This note was received at 5 p. m., and I marched the next morning again to Carnifix, with two out of the three regiments of infantry, three out of five pieces of artillery (having sent him three before out of eight pieces), and two troops of cavalry.   This left, for this entire turnpike and the old State road, from Gauley to Lewisburg (with innumerable and indescribable mountain paths leading into the rear everywhere), one regiment of infantry, two pieces of artillery, and about 100 efficient horse, and ·this, too, when General Floyd was re-enforced by Tompkins' two regiments (800 strong), another of his own brigade, just arrived (from 600 to 800 strong), and three pieces of artillery and 61 men from my Legion, making his force, in all (his own 1,200, re-enforcements 1,600) 2,800 men, with five pieces of artillery, in an intrenched and almost impregnable position, while my force left at Dogwood, with which I was to take the camp at the mouth of Gauley, was reduced by measles and the re-enforcement of him to about 500 infantry, two pieces of artillery, with 60 men, and about 100 efficient horse, in all, 660 men.   Yet again I marched to Carnifix, through stalling roads, and just reached the river and was descending to the ferry-boat

when General Floyd's adjutant put into my hands another note, of September 1, saying that it was doubtful whether the movement of the enemy required the union of my force with his, and I would retain my force in camp (meaning at Dogwood) until further orders.

To this note was also added a sneering order at Colonel Henningsen, my senior colonel of infantry, too small to be indited here. Justly vexed at this vacillation of command, I ordered my men back immediately, and announced to them my resolution to take Hawk's Nest, without delay, in order to command Liken's Mill (to grind wheat and corn for them) and Miller's Ferry (to communicate with Generals Chapman and Beckley), and take possession of Cotton Hill, south side of New River. It was night before I reached Dogwood Camp, and my men were weary, and some of my wagons broken down. I therefore rested my men for the night, waited for the wagons, and, on the morning of the 2d, marched for the Hawk's Nest. Between Hamilton's and that point we met their pickets, who retired. We paused to refresh and scouted ahead. In that pause some of our men were fired upon at McGraw's Bridge, over Honey Creek. Dinner over, I advanced, taking command of the advance guard in person, in order to look to untried men, who had never been under fire before. At about dusk, with one company, I cautiously reached the bridge, and just then the enemy opened a hot fire, for a very short time, upon us. The guard were disturbed a moment by the horse of Captain Swank, who was in advance with me, but Captain Summers, of the guard, rallied them in a moment, and, at a word from me, they advanced firmly, returning the fire, and, rushing over, as the column advanced, we swept the field on the right, the river guarding our left. It turned out to be a force of from 30 to 50 of the enemy, who fled at our approach, and disappeared in bushes and darkness. But 2 of our men were wounded, and they slightly. I then halted, posted guards, and slept on arms. Then I found the true position of the enemy. From the Hawk's Nest the turnpike leads, first, over Turkey Creek, then over Honey or McGraw's Creek, all emptying into New River, and heading with Rich Creek, and emptying into Gauley, thus:

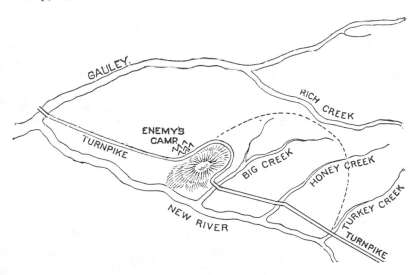

I learned their force was three companies regularly posted, and 1,000 lately advanced to re-enforce them, making in all about 1,250 infantry, 75 troopers, and several pieces of artillery, intrenched on the west side of Big Creek. The road there passes down a hill nearly north to the bridge, on the east side of Big Creek, crosses and passes up on the west side, nearly to its forks, through deep gorges, and then cuts at an acute angle, sharp and sudden, around a terrapin-backed mountain, very steep, and runs quite back to New River, making the position very strong, and suddenly bringing my advancing column exposed to a full sweep of artillery. On the north terminus of the mountain we found the advance of the enemy posted. My force was three regiments of infantry, reduced to six companies each (by forces left at Dogwood), and these companies, reduced by measles to about 50 each, effective men, making 900 infantry, and three pieces of artillery (a howitzer, a rifle, and smooth bore 6 pounder), and about 300 effective horse, of no use in the attack.

Moreover, I reduced my force to two regiments by sending Colonel Anderson, with the Second, back to Turkey Creek, to take a trace-road, leading from Turkey Creek to the mountain ridge, and thence around head of Big Creek, to fall on the enemy's left flank. To contest the bridge and the angle of the road there I had but 600 infantry and 3 pieces of artillery. I tried the enemy by passing a few men over unmolested, and thereby I knew he meant to entrap us. Determined to feel his very pulse, I passed three companies straight across Big Creek to the opposite side of a steep mountain, and drove him up and over. They fled incontinently, dropping guns, hats, canteens, &c., and my men gained the summit, and looked down into their very camps, keeping upon them an irregular skirmish fire. They were studiously hid on the other side, but we saw their tents, cannon, and baggage train in close gun-shot. I then shelled the mountain side, and drove them from the point of the road next to me, and they answered my howitzer with a rifled gun. Clearing the mountain side, we paused for Anderson. Unfortunately he lost his way, and returned, effecting nothing. I then fell back and encamped so as to cover Miller's Ferry and Liken's Mill, near the Hawk's Nest, and here I am determined to incubate a brood of results in that eyrie, if I can, in co-operation with Generals Chapman and Beckley. I have sent Caskie (of cavalry) already down Loop Creek, below the Falls of Kanawha, to strike a blow, and on the 2d the militia drove the enemy across Montgomery's Ferry. I will mount my rifled 6-pounder on Cotton Hill in a day or two and salute their camp at Gauley Bridge, where they are said to have eighteen pieces of all calibers. I omitted to say, while waiting for Anderson, that the enemy were re-enforced by six companies and several pieces of artillery from Gauley. When Anderson came up we would have had to attack 1,800 or 2,000 (double our number), and, having gained my point, I fell back. I shall cross New River with part of my forces, and I repeat my request to be defended from these vexatious orders of General Floyd. Let me get out of the way of these, and I will enter the Kanawha Valley near Charleston.

I beg you to order me south of New River. Now that General Floyd has two regiments added to his command from Georgia and North Carolina, he will have near 4,000 troops without me, and can defend this turnpike and Carnifix, too, without my Legion; and he will not be without it either, for my movement on Charleston will weaken the enemy at Gauley in every way more than anything else can. Please take command of me. I had rather have your censure then than your compliments now, acting under and not co-operating with General Floyd.

Colonel Tompkins begs me to apply to you, too, to have his regiment and himself transferred to my Legion. I earnestly urge his request, that they be incorporated with my independent command. I do not wish them if they are merely to be attached. If incorporated General Floyd will have added or attached to his command McCausland's and I will have incorporated Tompkins' regiment with mine. Thus let us divide the balance of State forces, and then let us part in peace. I feel, if we remain together, we will unite in more wars than one. I will try to be patient and peaceable, as you command, but I lay these facts before you, sir, and appeal to a soldier's pride and sense of honor.

With the highest respect, yours, faithfully,

HENRY A. WISE.

General R. E. LEE, *Commanding, &c.*

P. S.—The enemy now in the valley and adjacent parts is 5,800 strong, and has the measles badly. He cannot fight more than 5,000, probably.

THURSDAY MORNING, *September* 6, 1861.

Capt. R. A. Caskie has just arrived from the other side of the New River, and reports having heard from the enemy, through persons (ladies) who had been permitted to visit their camp and pass through to a funeral, that one shot from the howitzer, which took effect on an old house, killed and wounded 60 who had been stationed therein. It is very certain that one gun did very good execution.

SEPTEMBER 4, 1861.—Skirmish at Great Falls, Md.

Report of Brig. Gen. George A. McCall, U. S. Army.

HEADQUARTERS PENNSYLVANIA RESERVE,
Camp Tennally, September 5, 1861.

GENERAL: In relation to my command, I have the honor to report that the enemy having opened fire on the Seventh Infantry of this brigade at Great Falls at 8.30 a. m. yesterday, with two 24-pounder howitzers and three rifle cannon, it was ascertained that our guns did not reach their position (the intrenchment in rear of Dickey's house, already reported), and Colonel Harvey having reported these facts to me, I immediately sent forward two rifle cannon and the Eighth Infantry to support the Seventh, but afterwards recalled the Eighth, as instructed. At 1 o'clock, however, the Eighth was again put in motion. I afterwards learned that the enemy, after throwing about 50 shells and shot, mostly too high, ceased firing at 11 a. m., which up to 5 p. m. had not been resumed. I have as yet received no report of later date. My brigade was kept ready to move during the day and night.

The work on the redoubt will probably be finished to-day. One gun is mounted, and should the pintles arrive to-day I hope to have them all mounted. Will you please order a 20-pounder rifle gun for this work.

Colonel Campbell desires that two companies of his regiment of artillery now encamped in rear of the Capitol be sent here, as we have ample drill ground, and I rather approve his request, as the Sixth Regiment, recently removed from that camp, has suffered greatly from typhoid fever, no doubt contracted there.

Since the above was written I have received Colonel Harvey's report up to 7 a. m. He had received two rifle guns from General Banks besides those I sent. The enemy had thrown up another small earthwork, but had not opened upon our position since 11 a. m. yesterday. His guns were still in position.

With great respect, your obedient servant,

GEO. A. McCALL,
Brigadier-General, Commanding.

Maj. Gen. GEORGE B. McCLELLAN, *Commanding, &c.*

SEPTEMBER 10, 1861.—Engagement at Carnifix Ferry, Gauley River, West Virginia.

REPORTS, ETC.

No. 1.—Brig. Gen. William S. Rosecrans, U. S. Army, commanding Army of Occupation.
No. 2.—Brig. Gen. Henry W. Benham, U. S. Army, commanding First Brigade.
No. 3.—Col. William H. Lytle, Tenth Ohio Infantry.
No. 4.—Lieut. Col. Carr B. White, Twelfth Ohio Infantry.
No. 5.—Capt. James D. Wallace, Twelfth Ohio Infantry.
No. 6.—Col. William S. Smith, Thirteenth Ohio Infantry.
No. 7.—Col. Robert L. McCook, Ninth Ohio Infantry, commanding Second Brigade.
No. 8.—Lieut. Col. Charles Sondershoff, Ninth Ohio Infantry.
No. 9.—Col. Augustus Moor, Twenty-eighth Ohio Infantry.
No. 10.—Col. Frederick Poschner, Forty-seventh Ohio Infantry.
No. 11.—Capt. F. Schambeck, Chicago Dragoons.
No. 12.—Col. Eliakim P. Scammon, Twenty-third Ohio Infantry, commanding Third Brigade.
No. 13.—Col. Hugh Ewing, Thirtieth Ohio Infantry.
No. 14.—Return of casualties in Union forces.
No. 15.—Brig. Gen. John B. Floyd, C. S. Army, commanding Army of the Kanawha, and response of the Secretary of War.
No. 16.—Brig. Gen. Henry A. Wise, C. S. Army, covering the operations of his command from June to September 25.

No. 1.

Reports of Brig. Gen. William S. Rosecrans, U. S. Army, commanding Army of Occupation, West Virginia.

CAMP SCOTT, *September* 11, 1861—p. m.

We yesterday marched 17½ miles, reached the enemy's intrenched position in front of Carnifix Ferry, driving his advanced outposts and pickets before us. We found him occupying a strongly intrenched position, covered by a forest too dense to admit its being seen at a distance of 300 yards. His force was five regiments, besides the one driven in. He had probably sixteen pieces of artillery.

At 3 o'clock we began a strong reconnaissance, which proceeded to such length we were about to assault the position on the flank and front, when, night coming on and our troops being completely exhausted, I drew them out of the woods and posted them in the order of battle behind ridges immediately in front of the enemy's position, where they rested on their arms till morning.

Shortly after daylight a runaway contraband came in and reported that the enemy had crossed the Gauley during the night by means of the ferry and a bridge which they had completed.

Colonel Ewing was ordered to take possession of the camp, which he did about 7 o'clock, capturing a few prisoners, two stands of colors, a considerable quantity of arms and quartermaster's stores, messing and camp equipage.

The enemy having destroyed the bridge across the Gauley, which here rushes through a deep gorge, and our troops being still much fatigued, and having no material for immediately repairing the bridge, it was thought prudent to encamp the troops, occupy the ferry and the captured camp, sending a few rifle-cannon shots after the enemy to produce a moral effect.

Our loss would probably amount to 20 killed and 100 wounded. The enemy's loss has not been ascertained, but from report it must have been considerable.

W. S. ROSECRANS,
Brigadier-General, Commanding.

Col. E. D. TOWNSEND.

—

HEADQUARTERS A. O. W. VA.,
Cross-Lanes, September 21, 1861.

SIR: By telegram I have advised you of the movements of the column under my command up to the evening of the 9th instant. On the evening of the 11th I announced those of the 10th and the battle of Carnifix Ferry, which resulted in dislodging Floyd from his intrenched camp and the capture of two stands of colors, a quantity of ammunition and camp and garrison equipage. I have now the honor to submit, for the information of the Commander-in-Chief, a more detailed report of the battle, accompanied by the reports of the brigade, regimental, and detachment commanders who took part in the action, with a list of the killed and wounded, and a plan of the intrenchments, exhibiting the position of our forces when night put a stop to our operations.*

Having driven the enemy's pickets before us from Big Birch, we bivouacked 8 miles above Summersville. The column began to move at 4.15 on the morning of the 10th, and reached Summersville at 8 o'clock, having been delayed by a burned bridge. Found the town evacuated by a regiment of infantry and a company of cavalry, which had retreated towards the intrenched camp. Two cavalry prisoners, stragglers from their company, were captured, from whom we found that Floyd was strongly intrenched and confident of holding his position against great odds in front of Carnifix Ferry.

From this point the column moved cautiously but rapidly forward over 4 miles of very bad roads, forming almost a defile, and then over more open country, until the head of it reached a point where the first road leading to the ferry diverges from the lower road to Gauley Bridge, on which we were marching. Reached there about 2 o'clock, and halted for half an hour for the column and train to close up, and then began to move down towards the rebels' position, said to be about 2½ miles distant. Picket-firing commenced at the head of the column within three-quarters of a mile. The First Brigade, under General

---

* To appear in Atlas.

Benham, the Tenth Ohio ahead, led the column, and soon reached a camp which had been abandoned, leaving some camp equipage and private baggage, which gave rise to the impression in the mind of the brigade commander that the enemy 'were in full retreat. Satisfied however, that we should find it was not so, I directed Brigadier-General Benham to move forward with his brigade slowly and cautiously into the woods, for the purpose of reconnoitering. He was directed to be very careful to feel the enemy closely, but not to engage him unless he saw an evident opening. Orders were dispatched to the other brigades to follow. The Tenth Ohio followed the road shown on the accompanying plan. The Thirteenth Ohio closed up behind. The Twelfth Ohio, as soon as the head of it arrived at the woods at the deserted camp, as shown on the accompanying plan, was directed to take a beaten path leading to the left of the road, but apparently nearly parallel to it. Twenty-five minutes after the column left the deserted camp terrific volleys of musketry and the roar of the rebels' artillery told that we were upon them, and indicated the right of their position, a point to which the Twelfth Ohio was directed to proceed.

A message from General Benham reached me at the deserted camp, announced that an engagement had commenced, and that he wanted help. Having the Tenth and Thirteenth with him, McMullin's howitzer battery and two rifled cannon were sent forward to the head of the column, and he was informed that the Twelfth had been ordered to his left, on the right of the rebels' works. Orders were dispatched to hasten the coming up of the Second and Third Brigades, under Colonels McCook and Scammon, and I proceeded to the head of the column to ascertain the position of the First Brigade and reconnoiter the rebels' works more closely. Arrived there, I found the Tenth Ohio and the batteries in the position indicated on the accompanying plan, the Thirteenth and a portion of the Twelfth in the valley in the rear of the position marked twenty-eighth on this plan. I proceeded into the valley to examine the right of the rebels' position, and afterwards to the corn field, in the rear of which was the Tenth, to examine that portion of the rebels' works visible from that point. I then awaited report of a reconnoitering party which had gone through the woods still farther to the enemy's left, entirely invisible from our position. Heavy volleys of musketry and the discharge of artillery soon told that this party had made its appearance in front of an unknown part of the rebels' position. Meanwhile our skirmishers kept up a well-directed fire along the whole of the enemy's left, while Schneider's rifled* battery, taking a more advantageous position, and McMullin's howitzer battery continued to play on the rebels' guns at the battery shown on the plan.

Meanwhile Col. W. S. Smith, of the Thirteenth, and Captain Margedant, acting engineer, reported the practicability of reaching the rebels' extreme right, if not turning it. Orders were accordingly given that Col. W. S. Smith, with the Thirteenth Ohio and four companies of the Twelfth, re-enforced by the Twenty-eighth from the Second Brigade, and four companies of the Twenty-third of the Third Brigade, which had been directed by Captain Margedant to reconnoiter the rebels' extreme right and had reached the position shown on the plan, to make the attack on that point. Lieutenant-Colonel Korff, with the Tenth and a portion of the Twelfth which had become detached from the remainder and passed over to our right, was directed to advance to the right of the corn field to attack the rebel center and left. (See plan.)

The storming column of eight companies of the Ninth and six companies of the Forty-seventh was formed in the position shown on the plan. By this time it became dusk, the men were exhausted, the brush thick and tangled, and the strength and condition of the rebels, as well as the extent of their works, very imperfectly known. At the same time came a report from Col. W. S. Smith, stating that it would be impossible for his command to make their way through the brush and attack from the position which they occupied, as shown on the plan, owing to the darkness; a like report came to me from Lieutenant-Colonel Sondershoff, commanding the Ninth, who, while avowing himself ready to obey orders, stated that he did not believe the men in their present state of exhaustion would be able to make the assault.

Under these circumstances I deemed it prudent to withdraw our forces from the woods to the open fields in rear of the intrenched camp. (See bottom of the plan.) To cover this withdrawal, the batteries which had discontinued firing were ordered into position, and directed, in a tone of voice intended to be heard by the enemy, to give them "Hail Columbia," and with the same intention the Ninth was called for and ordered to ambush them well. The regimental commanders were then ordered to lead their men quietly out by the flank, while the Ninth and the Third Brigade, including Mack's battery, were directed from their position, as shown in the plan, to dispose themselves to cover the movement and prevent the mischief which might have been done by a vigorous sortie. Captain Hartsuff directed the columns as they withdrew through the narrow roads and amidst the darkness and separated the commands in the fields in rear of the Third Brigade; after which, all my staff being worn-out, I arranged the troops in order of battle on ground still farther to the rear, looked after the train which remained at the point of our halt, and at 2 o'clock retired to an oat loft to sleep, leaving Colonel Ewing in command of the advanced guard posted in the woods.

The wounded were conveyed to a barn and house immediately in rear of the troops, with the exception of a few who fell near the rebels' works and were not found till the next day. More exhausted troops I never saw than ours. Early the next morning one of our sentries brought a runaway negro, who reported that the enemy had abandoned their camp during the night, crossed the Gauley, and destroyed their boats. I ordered Colonel Ewing with his troops to verify the truth of the statement, which he soon did, returning with a stand of colors. Having taken possession of the camp and a few sick prisoners, I proceeded to the extremity of the camp, and saw that the ferry was gone, foot-bridge destroyed, and the enemy's column out of sight, with the exception of a few wagons. The Gauley here runs through a deep gorge, a continuous fall for 12 or 15 miles, with here and there a small pool. The descent to the ferry from this side is by a narrow wagon track, winding around a rocky hill-side. The ascent from the other side is by a road passing up the Meadow River, which is in a deep rocky gorge, the bottom being little wider than the bed of the river and the side ascending precipitously to the height of nearly 300 feet. For 2 miles the road gradually ascends until it reaches the top of the hill, when the country becomes high, rolling, and partially cultivated.

Finding we had no means whatever of crossing the ferry, which is here 370 feet wide, pursuit was impossible, though much desired. The rebels, aware of this, left a body of skirmishers to occupy the cliffs along Meadow River down to the ferry to prevent small parties from crossing. Orders were therefore given to go into camp, that the troops might rest. Camp Gauley, the captured camp, was occupied, and the captured property taken care of, a return of which is herewith inclosed. Orders were given to Colonel McCook to drive the rebels from the other side of the river, take possession of the heights with two or three companies, and Brigadier-General Benham was directed to repair the roads and ferry. General Cox had been instructed, on hearing the fire of our cannon, to operate a diversion with all his disposable troops in this direction. In expectation that our cannon would be heard, it was anticipated that he would open communication with us at least by the evening of the 11th, when, not hearing from him, messengers were dispatched towards Gauley, but had such difficulty in passing his pickets that it was not until the morning of the 12th that the defeat of Floyd and his escape from us reached him. Dispatches directed him to advance with all his available force on the Lewisburg road, but cautiously, until he should find whether the rebels were in retreat or in force.

Papers found in camp showed that Floyd's force consisted of at least five regiments, two batteries, and a battalion of cavalry, and that a Georgia and a North Carolina regiment were waiting him on the Lewisburg road, and had expected to join him within a day. Wise's force not having been put at less than 2,000, I feared they might fall on and crush Cox before we could cross. I was speedily relieved from these fears by a report from him from the mouth of Sunday road, saying that the rebels were in full retreat, and he had been within two hours of their rear guard. By this time one of the small ferry-boats had been got up, and Colonel McCook's brigade was passed over to re-enforce Cox; since which you have been advised of our movements by telegraph.

I cannot close this report without bearing testimony to the patience, perseverance, and indomitable energy of the troops, both officers and men, under my command in this column, most of whom had been in motion over rugged mountains and rough roads for the last two months, sleeping in heavy dews and cold rains, not unfrequently without tents, and several of whom had averaged 20 miles a day for the last two weeks previous to the commencement of this march. That on the day of battle they should have marched 17½ miles and then fought a battle of three hours, struggling through dense forests covered with undergrowth, is a most convincing proof of these virtues, which I doubt not will excite the admiration of the Commander-in-Chief.

I beg leave also to signalize Col. W. H. Lytle for the gallantry with which he led his troops into action; Col. W. S. Smith for the great energy and perseverance with which he pushed the reconnaissance on the enemy's left and for his coolness and courage in leading his column to the attack, and Capt. G. L. Hartsuff, Assistant Adjutant-General, who, by his presence at the head of the column and the energy and promptitude with which he directed messengers and conveyed orders, as well as the good judgment evinced in giving directions during my absence while I was reconnoitering and in separating and placing the troops as they emerged from the woods, deserves especial mention.

For details I refer you to the reports of Brigadier-General Benham, First Brigade; Col. R. L. McCook, Second Brigade; Col. E. P. Scammon, Third Brigade; to which, respectively, are appended the lists of the killed and wounded, amounting in the aggregate to 16 killed and 100 wounded.*

Very respectfully, your obedient servant,

W. S. ROSECRANS,
Brigadier-General, U. S. Army.

Col. E. D. TOWNSEND, *Adjutant-General, Washington, D. C.*

---

* See report No. 14, p. 146.

No. 2.

Report of Brig. Gen. Henry W. Benham, U. S. Army, commanding First Brigade.

HEADQUARTERS FIRST BRIGADE, A. O. W. VA.,
Camp Scott, September 12, 1861.

SIR: I have the honor to report as follows in relation to the operation of my brigade in the battle at the rebel intrenchments at Carnifix Ferry on the 10th instant.

As previously stated to you, the head of my brigade started from the camp, 8 miles north of Summersville, at about 4 a. m., reaching that place before 8 a. m. in good order, and with the men eager for the continuance of the march toward the enemy, who we there ascertained were well intrenched and determined to resist us near Carnifix Ferry. After a halt of nearly two hours about 1 mile short of the Cross-Lanes, we moved rapidly forward toward the position of the enemy, until our arrival at the site of this camp, about 1 mile from their intrenchments, a little past 2 o'clock, when, after a reconnaissance by you, myself accompanying you, I was authorized to move forward with my brigade, using my best discretion in the case. Upon receiving this order, and with the mass of my brigade well closed up, which had been accomplished during our reconnaissance, I moved carefully forward, with the Tenth Ohio Regiment leading, having our skirmishers well ahead and at the flanks for nearly three-fourths of a mile, when we discovered through the opening of the woods on our left their intrenchments in an open space beyond a deep and steep valley and crowning the crest of the opposite hill.

Having no engineer officer with my brigade, and no other that I knew of to replace one, I kept with the head of the regiment to avoid ambuscade and to judge myself of their position and arrangements. After advancing about one-fourth of a mile to the end of the woods I halted the command, and could perceive that a heavy cross-fire had been prepared for us at the open space at the debouch from the woods, and I at once forbid the advance of the regiment beyond this point. Within some five minutes after this time (nearly 3.30 o'clock), while carefully examining the earthworks on the road in front and their log breastworks on our left, a tremendous fire of musketry was opened on us, which in a few minutes was followed by a discharge of grape and spelter-canister from a battery of some six pieces of artillery. This caused a break in the line for a few minutes, though for a few minutes only, for the men immediately returned to the ranks under the lead of their officers to their former position, where I retained them, as I was certain that the fire at us through the close woods was without direct aim, and because they were needed for the protection of our artillery, which I immediately ordered up. The two rifled guns of Captain Schneider, and Captain McMullin, with his four mountain howitzers, immediately followed, throwing their shells well into their intrenchments on our left with excellent effect.

A further examination of their position convinced me that their weak part and our true point of attack was on the right flank across the deep valley from our position, upon which orders were immediately sent to Colonel Smith, of the Thirteenth Regiment, and to Colonel Lowe, of the Twelfth Regiment, to advance and pass the valley on our left, under cover of the woods, to that attack. Neither of these regiments was to be found in their proper position on the road in my rear as I had expected, though after a short time Colonel Smith was met with on our right, where he had been drawn into the woods by the belief, from the sound of the firing, that the attack was upon our right. Upon receipt of my order, however, Colonel Smith moved rapidly across the main road down the ravine valley on our left, where he fortunately struck upon the most advantageous route, and thence he moved up the opposite hill, entirely past the right flank of the enemy. But as I had been unable to find the Twelfth Regiment to send to his support (though I have since learned that three companies under Lieutenant-Colonel White had joined him), his movement became principally a reconnaissance, from which he soon after returned, reporting to me his opinion of the entire practicability of a successful attack upon the rebel intrenchments at that point, he having entirely passed by the breastwork on the right, approaching within about one hundred yards of their lines, pouring a fire into them which it is since satisfactorily ascertained cleared that part of that breastwork of the enemy.

As I was still unable to ascertain the position of the Twelfth Regiment, which it has been reported to me had been ordered into the woods by the commanding general, I sent one of my staff to Colonel McCook, commanding the Second Brigade, to ask him to aid the Thirteenth in this attack with his Ninth Regiment, to which request a reply was returned to me that there were other orders from the commanding general, as stated to my aide by Assistant Adjutant-General Captain Hartsuff. In this state of affairs I could only hold my position in front with the Tenth Regiment protecting the artillery, which was endeavoring to silence the cannon of the enemy, which was to a considerable extent accomplished after the first fifteen or twenty minutes, their guns being removed to other positions, as was then done also with one-half of Schneider's and McMullin's pieces, to enfilade the crest of the hill from the edge of the woods on our right, which gave a fair view of their battery at some 380 yards' distance.

At about this time, or one hour after the commencement of the action, Colonel Lytle, of the Tenth, though not ordered by me, and while I was still endeavoring to obtain troops for the attack from our left, made a very gallant attempt to approach their battery through the cleared space in front of it with a portion of his command, which of course failed from the smallness of his force in that exposed situation, he himself being severely wounded and compelled to retire, with the loss of several of his men killed and wounded.

Colonel Lowe, of the Twelfth, also at a subsequent period made a similar attempt, and, as far as I can learn, without orders, in which, I regret to say, he fell, being instantly killed by a discharge of canister from the enemy.

The above comprises the sum of the action of the portion of my brigade that was with me until you arrived on the field and assumed the direction of affairs; some time after which arrival you also arranged for and directed this attack upon their right with Colonel Smith's regiment and a part of the Twelfth and the Forty-seventh, Colonel Moor. This attack, as having been directed by myself, you will recollect, I offered to lead upon the enemy, recommending at the same time a simultaneous demonstration or attack by the Ninth and Twelfth Regiments under cover of the woods from our right. The command moved forward, however, under direction of Colonel Smith, but from the lateness of the hour it was compelled to return without attempting anything, and the lateness of the hour then seemed to forbid further operations for the day.

There remains now but the grateful duty of acknowledging the valuable services of the different commanders and other officers as far as known to me in this brigade, provisionally assigned to me within the past week only.

The personal gallantry and chivalrous daring of Colonel Lytle are attested by his wound and the exposed position in which he received it; and the soldierly conduct and bravery of his lieutenant-colonel (Korff) and his major (Burke) I myself personally witnessed many times during the action.

In Col. W. S. Smith, of the Thirteenth Ohio Regiment, I have found one of the most valuable and efficient officers I have ever known. His great intelligence, knowledge of his profession, skill and caution, coolness and excellent judgment on all occasions, both previous to and during the action, merit my highest praise. His lieutenant-colonel (Mason), wounded during the attack upon their right flank, I saw bravely ready to guide the way to the second attack, and the major (Hawkins), both in this action and on all other occasions since my connection with this regiment, has shown himself a most courageous and valuable officer; and Lieutenant-Colonel White, of the Twelfth, I found during the action earnestly seeking the opportunity to advance against the lines of the enemy, which he soon found in joining Colonel Smith with his three companies of the Thirteenth, where he rendered most efficient service.

Of Captain Schneider, commanding the two rifled pieces of the Thirteenth Ohio Regiment, and of Captain McMullin, commanding the mountain-howitzer battery, I can speak in the highest terms for their courage and soldierly skill in the conduct of their batteries, which repeatedly silenced the artillery fire of the enemy and forced it to change positions.

And of my staff officers, but recently connected with me on such duty, I have the most satisfactory report to make. Lieut. James O. Stanage, Thirteenth Ohio, as acting assistant adjutant-general, has constantly rendered most valuable services in the performance of his proper duties, and, together with my aide, Lieut. S. B. Warren, Twenty-third Ohio, were constantly by my side through the hottest of the fire, while not bearing orders to the different parts of the field; and Mr. W. L. Mallory, the acting commissary and quartermaster of the brigade, rendered during the early part of the day most valuable service in arranging the advance of the column, and in accompanying the skirmishers, a duty fully as exposed and dangerous as that upon this battle-field. In coming upon the first deserted camp of the enemy, some half a mile short of the battle-field, I regretted to have to leave him in charge of the property captured there, by which during the action I lost his services, which from my knowledge of him I know would have been most useful to me.

The cavalry companies of Captains West and Gilmore, being held in reserve for emergencies, were thus prevented from having their share in the action.

I have the honor to inclose herewith the reports of Colonel Smith, Thirteenth Ohio; Lieutenant-Colonel Korff,* now commanding Tenth Ohio; Lieutenant-Colonel White, now commanding Twelfth Ohio Regiment, and of Captain McMullin,* of the howitzer battery, the reports of the killed and wounded in each command having been previously forwarded.†

Very respectfully, your most obedient servant,

H. W. BENHAM,
Brigadier-General, Commanding First Brigade O. V. M.
Capt. GEORGE L. HARTSUFF, *Assistant Adjutant-General.*

---

* Not found.   †Embodied in report No. 14, p. 146.

No. 3.

Report of Col. William H. Lytle, Tenth Ohio Infantry.

HDQRS. MONTGOMERY REGIMENT, TENTH O. V.,
Camp Scott, Carnifix Ferry, September 11, 1861.

SIR : I have the honor to report that, agreeably to your orders, I proceeded with my command on yesterday, September 10, at 3 o'clock, to reconnoiter the position of the enemy, supposed to be in force in the neighborhood of Gauley River, yourself accompanying and directing the advance with me. Our road led uphill through a densely-timbered forest, and as I then sent out flanking parties to the right and left and skirmishers in advance of my column. After passing through the woods for half a mile our skirmishers were suddenly engaged in front, and I pushed on to their relief until I reached a cleared space on the summit of the hill, where for the first time the enemy came in view, posted in force behind an extensive earthwork, with twelve guns in position, sweeping the road for over a mile. A ravine separated the hill by which we approached from the right of the breast-works of the enemy, which were composed of logs and fence rails and extended for over a mile to the right and left of their intrenchments, affording secure protection to their infantry and riflemen.

When the head of my column reached a point opposite the right center of their earthworks their entire battery opened on us with grape and canister with almost paralyzing effect, my men falling around me in great numbers. I ordered the colors to the front for the purpose of making an assault on their battery, perceiving which, the entire fire of the enemy was directed towards us. The men rallied gallantly on the hill-side under withering volleys of grape and canister with small-arms, and a part of three companies, A, E, and D, actually moved up within pistol-shot of the intrenchments, and for some time maintained a most unequal contest. Both my color-bearers were struck down. The bearer of the State color, Sergeant Fitzgibbons, had the staff shot away and his hand shattered, and in a few moments afterwards was shattered in both thighs while waving his colors on the broken staff. The bearer of the national color, Sergeant O'Connor, at the same time was struck down by some missile, but recovered himself in a short time, and kept waving his color in front of the enemy's lines.

About this time I received a wound in the leg, the ball passing through and killing my horse. Perceiving the fearful odds against us, I directed the men to place themselves under cover. A portion rallied behind two log houses in front of the battery and kept up a spirited fire for at least one hour before any other regiment came into action, and the remaining portion of the right wing, under command of Lieutenant-Colonel Korff, resumed in good order its position under cover of a corn field in front of the right of the battery, from which position, having been soon after supported by artillery, a steady fire was maintained against the enemy until night, after which Companies G, H, I, and K, and a great portion of D and E, by order of General Rosecrans, remained on the ground during the night, throwing out their pickets, under command of Lieutenant-Colonel Korff.

While the right wing of the regiment under my command engaged the enemy on their center, a portion of the left wing, consisting of Companies I, F, K, and C, under command of Major Burke, pushed through the woods on the left of the road and assailed the stockades of the enemy's infantry, a deep ravine intervening. This portion of the command held its position, in face of a terrific fire, until every round of ammunition was expended and the companies relieved by artillery, when it rejoined the right wing, already in position in front of the enemy's battery, the men dragging our guns through the woods in their progress and helping to place them in position.

For men for the first time under fire the conduct of the regiment was highly creditable. Having been disabled in the early part of the action I was necessarily separated from a greater portion of the command, but among those who came under my own notice I would especially mention Capt. S. J. McGroarty, commanding the color company; Lieut. Jno. S. Mulroy, Company D; Lieutenant Fanning, Company A. Both Lieutenant Fanning and Captain McGroarty were severely wounded, the latter while rallying his men around his colors and the former in leading his men to the attack. Captains Steele and Tiernon are also worthy of special mention for their gallantry. I would also mention the name of Corporal Sullivan, Company E, who in the midst of a galling fire went across the front of the enemy's batteries and returned with water for the wounded.

Of the portion of the regiment under Major Burke that officer makes highly honorable mention of the names of Captain Ward, Company I; Captain Robinson, Company K; Captain Hudson and Lieutenant Hickey, Company C; Captain Moore, Company D; Sergeant-Major Knox, for their gallantry and intrepidity under a most destructive fire, and also of the chaplain, Rev. W. T. O'Higgins, who remained on the field during the action in performance of his sacred duties.

I beg leave to inclose a list of killed and wounded of the command.* All of which is respectfully submitted.

WM. H. LYTLE,
Colonel Tenth Ohio Regiment, U. S. V. I.

Brigadier-General BENHAM, U. S. A.,
Commanding First Brigade.

No. 4.

Report of Lieut. Col. Carr B. White, Twelfth Ohio Infantry.

CAMP SCOTT, VA., *September* 11, 1861.

SIR: On the 10th instant, 2 miles from the enemy's intrenchments at Carnifix Ferry, Va., the Twelfth Regiment Ohio Volunteers were detached from the column of advance, by order of General Rosecrans, to skirmish the wood to the left of the road, and after completing the work and returning to the road the regiment had not advanced more than half a mile when the firing from the advance on the enemy's lines commenced. The regiment moved at a double-quick to the enemy's encampment in a field on the left, where General Rosecrans' staff were stationed, when it was diverted to the left from the main road through the field and wood in direction of the enemy's fire. Advancing some 200 yards, it was deployed as skirmishers, facing by the rear rank, with the order from the assistant adjutant-general (George L. Hartsuff) to draw on the fire, close in, and charge the enemy's lines. The underbrush was so thick it was impossible to maintain a line, and it being im-

----

* Embodied in report No. 14, p. 146.

possible to communicate with Col. J. W. Lowe, the left wing was pushed forward to the enemy's right and the attack there made—the Thirteenth Regiment Ohio Volunteers, under Col. W. S. Smith, to our left, and the artillery to our right. Finding but little effect could be made on the enemy from this position, Adjutant Pauly was sent to you to notify you of our position and subject to your order. Afterwards I reported to you in person for orders, in the mean time keeping up a fire on the enemy when he discovered himself above the breastworks. Still later Adjutant Pauly reported to you for orders, when we were attached to the Thirteenth and Twenty-eighth Regiments, under Colonels Smith and Moor, to attack the enemy on his extreme right, of which movement Colonel Smith will report. The movements and operations of the right wing will be reported to you by senior Capt. J. D. Wallace, who assumed command after Col. J. W. Lowe was killed.

Respectfully submitted.

C. B. WHITE,
Lieutenant-Colonel, Commanding Twelfth Regiment Ohio Vols.
Brigadier-General BENHAM.

No. 5.

Report of Capt. James D. Wallace, Twelfth Ohio Infantry.

CAMP SCOTT, *September* 13, 1861.

SIR : On the 10th instant the Twelfth Ohio Regiment, commanded by Col. J. W. Lowe, advanced through an old encampment on its way to the battle-field at this point. An order was given by Captain Hartsuff, of General Rosecrans' staff, to advance through the woods towards the enemy's fire. The right wing of the regiment, viz, Companies A, F, K, and E, advanced through the woods, under the command of Colonel Lowe, towards the enemy's fire, and in front of one of his batteries we crossed the fence of a corn field, entered the field, and were ordered by Colonel Lowe to deploy to the right, and advance through the field towards some houses. The order was obeyed. Colonel Lowe had advanced but a few steps when he was killed.

Up to this time I received all orders from Colonel Lowe. After his death I took command of the right wing, and advanced towards the enemy's breastworks. I sheltered the men in the best manner I could. I sent Lieutenant Fisher, of Company A, to General Rosecrans for orders. I was directed through the general's order to advance to the right and front of the enemy's breastworks. I obeyed the order, crossed a by-road, and halted within easy musket-shot of their works at the edge of the woods. I directed the fire of the rifles at the enemy wherever he exposed himself. Discovering our fire was ineffectual, as the enemy sheltered behind their works, I ordered the fire to cease, and sheltered the men in the woods from the enemy's fire. I again sent for orders, and received through our adjutant, Lieutenant Pauly, an order from the commanding general to advance farther to the right My command passed through the woods, crossed a hollow, and ascended to the right of the enemy's flag-staff, passing through a thick growth of underbrush until we arrived near the top of the hill, and distant about 50 feet from their breastworks, when the enemy delivered a severe fire, at the same time screening themselves behind the breastworks. The men lay flat on the ground. Being unsupported, and finding I could effect nothing there (the enemy having fired a second volley at us), I withdrew the men, and formed them under the hill, at which place I received an order from Lieutenant-Colonel White to join the left wing of the regiment under his command. I obeyed the order, and advanced to the main road below our batteries, where I was ordered by one of your staff to halt my command on the side of the road to await further orders, which I did. I did not see the left wing of the regiment until evening, nor do I personally know how or why the regiment was separated.

Respectfully submitted.

J. D. WALLACE,
Captain, Commanding Company A, Twelfth Regiment.

Brigadier-General BENHAM.

No. 6.

Report of Col. William S. Smith, Thirteenth Ohio Infantry.

HEADQUARTERS THIRTEENTH REG'T O. V. INFANTRY,
Camp Scott, Va., September 11, 1861.

SIR: I have the honor to submit the following statement of the part taken by my regiment in the action near Carnifix Ferry yesterday:

At about 11 o'clock a. m. on the 10th instant, a general halt of the whole column having been ordered at a point about 2½ miles distant from the enemy's intrenchments, my regiment was ordered by General Benham to form in line of battle behind the crest of a hill on the right flank of the position then being occupied by the Second and Third Brigades, it having appeared that they were about to be attacked. My line was just deployed when I received an order from General Rosecrans to move forward, which I did, taking my place in line according to our previous order of march, the Tenth Ohio, McMullin's battery, my own section of two rifled cannon, and yourself, with Gilmore's and West's cavalry, leading in their order. We closed upon the head of the column, and marched thus until we had reached a point within two-thirds of a mile of the enemy's position, when I was again halted by an order from the rear.

We remained halted in this position for about ten minutes, and until the enemy opened fire upon the head of our column. I was then ordered to move forward, which I did, until I was induced by the heavy firing apparently on our right to move in that direction with my regiment until my line was fairly deployed, when I received an order from General Benham to move forward to the left. My regiment was then moved forward by the left flank down the ravine to our left running nearly parallel with the enemy's front, then up the right-hand slope until I saw the works of the enemy from my position at the head of my regiment.

I then moved to the left along the skirt of the woods in front of the enemy's line, and about 200 yards from it, until I reached his extreme right flank, moving all the while behind the summit of the hill which sheltered it from his fire. The enemy's line from his battery at the center to the right flank was completely revealed to us during this flank movement under cover. When we reached the enemy's extreme right we received his fire from behind the breastwork of logs and rails, distant now about 100 yards. The order was immediately given to my regiment to fall down and creep up to the crest of the hill, where we opened fire and maintained it briskly, driving the enemy in upon his center. Having been ordered to make a reconnaissance, not an attack, we ceased firing, and lay in our position to await further orders, sending Lieutenant-Colonel Mason to report the result of our reconnaissance to Generals Benham and Rosecrans. I have since learned through a prisoner taken by us that our fire cleared the enemy from his works on the right and drove him in on his center.

After waiting as I supposed a sufficient length of time, and fearing that Colonel Mason had lost his way in the thick underbrush, I drew down my eight companies into the ravine and back into the main road, and then went in person to report to Generals Benham and Rosecrans. This I did, and requested that a brigadier might lead us to an attack upon the enemy's extreme right. A brigade, consisting of the Twenty-eighth Ohio, eight companies of the Thirteenth Ohio, three of the Twenty-third Ohio, and two of the Twelfth Ohio Regiments, was extemporized by General Rosecrans, and I was placed in command and ordered to carry the works on the right by assault. I formed the command as above constituted in the ravine, and was then ordered by General Rosecrans to halt and await further orders. We remained in this position for about one hour, when General Rosecrans ordered me to move forward to the attack. I reached the head of my column and started just at dusk. Before we could march down the ravine through which we had passed before and countermarched up the right-hand slope, so as to draw out my line on the flank and in front of a portion of the enemy's line, it became so dark and the men so weary, having marched from 3 o'clock in the morning, that it was found impossible to ascend to their line. The ground was covered with rocks and a dense undergrowth of laurel, and Colonel Moor reported that it would take until 2 o'clock in the morning to get two companies of his regiment up.

I then ordered the whole column to face about, and march out just as it had marched in, and crossed the ravine to the rear of the column to lead it out, when a shot or two from the enemy's skirmishers, or an accidental shot from one of our own pieces, caused the whole column, doubled as it was into a "U" shape, to open fire, killing two and wounding about thirty of our own men. The melancholy mistake was at once discovered, and the column extricated and marched back by the left into the main road, and so on back to the grounds selected for our encampment.

At the beginning of the action my section of two rifled cannon, under command of Captain Schneider, and supported by his company (E, Thirteenth Regiment), was ordered by General Benham to take position in the road by which our columns approached, and at a point about 400 yards distant from the enemy's works. Several shots were fired from this position with good effect. Captain Schneider then found a better position for his guns about 100 paces to the right, and cut a road to it with his sword and one hatchet, and from this new position, in full view of the enemy's battery, he fired 75 rounds of solid shot and 15 of shells. His shot plowed through the parapet of the enemy's battery, spreading consternation among those who served the pieces. Captain Schneider and his men behaved with great gallantry, delivering their fire with coolness and accuracy, although exposed to a brisk fire from the enemy's battery and from his musketry. The same may be said of my whole regiment, which was kept in perfect order throughout the day.*

Respectfully submitted.

W. S. SMITH,
Colonel Thirteenth Regiment O. V. I.

Lieut. JAMES O. STANAGE,
Acting Assistant Adjutant-General.

No. 7.

*Report of Col. Robert L. McCook, Ninth Ohio Infantry, commanding
Second Brigade.*

HEADQUARTERS SECOND BRIGADE A. O. W. V.,
Camp Cox, September 21, 1861.

SIR: I have the honor to submit the following as the report of the Second Brigade, in relation to the action at Carnifix Ferry on the 10th instant:

In the afternoon of that day, whilst the Second and Third Brigades were halted east of the forks of the Summersville and Cross-Lanes roads, firing was heard in the direction of the supposed fortifications of the enemy. By order of the general commanding, I formed the Second Brigade in line of battle east of the forks of the road, covering the hills on either side of the Summersville road with the Ninth and Twenty-eighth Regiments, holding the Forty-seventh and Schambeck's cavalry as a reserve, and there awaited orders. Subsequently I was ordered to advance with the brigade to the top of the hill near the woods, which extended to the enemy's fortifications. This I did, and again formed it in line of battle in the same order as before, with the exception that it fronted the noise of the battle. I remained with the brigade thus formed awaiting orders until 3.30 p. m., when Captain Hartsuff appeared and ordered the brigade to proceed to the intrenchments of the enemy for the purpose of storming them. I put in motion the Ninth Ohio in advance, followed by the Twenty-eighth and Forty-seventh, Captain Hartsuff leading the way for the purpose of showing the road and the point at which the works were to be stormed.

After three of the companies of the Ninth had passed the corn field in front of the enemy's works and had deployed into the bush, Captain Hartsuff informed me that the order to charge the works had been countermanded. I immediately placed the brigade in such position as to be most available and under cover from the enemy's fire. This was done as follows: Seven companies of the Ninth Ohio on the path back of the crest of the hill occupied by McMullin's battery, the Twenty-eighth in their rear, and the Forty-seventh on the main road leading to the enemy's works.

.At the time this was being done the three companies of the Ninth, which had deployed before the order to storm the works had been countermanded, were engaging the enemy at that portion of the left flank west of the corn field. They were ordered to retire as soon as the sound of a bugle could be heard above the roar of the cannon and musketry,

---

* In separate reports Colonel Smith specially notices the gallant conduct of Maj. Joseph G. Hawkins, Lieuts. James B. Doney and Joseph T. Snider, Corp. James H. Scott, and Privates Henry Conover and Jefferson Gongwer, of same regiment.

which they did, and joined the regiment at the point where it was stationed. As to the extent and particulars of their engagement, I refer to the report of Lieutenant-Colonel Sondershoff, of the Ninth Ohio, herewith forwarded.

After the brigade had occupied the above positions for some time the enemy seemed to change the range of his cannon, so that it covered the position occupied by the Ninth Ohio. I ordered it to retire to the clear place west of the last field on the right of the road leading to the enemy's works, and then awaited orders. About 7 in the evening it was again determined by the general commanding to storm, the enemy's works. The Ninth Ohio was ordered to the junction of the path with the main road near the east side of the corn field, in front of the enemy's works, and then halted. The Twenty-eighth was detached with portions of the Twelfth, Twenty-third, and Thirteenth Ohio. The Forty-seventh was formed in the main road leading to the works. Of the unfortunate casualty which occurred by the Thirteenth Regiment firing into the Twenty-eighth I desire to say nothing, but refer to the detailed report thereof by Colonel Moor, of the Twenty-eighth Ohio.

Darkness soon set in, so that it became impossible with any degree of safety to our troops to make an attack in the night. I was ordered with my brigade to cover the return of the artillery and ambulances from the field. This, too, I did with the Ninth Ohio, and at 9 p. m. in the night all the artillery and ambulances were brought from the field of battle to camp, and I marched the Second Brigade to the point where we had left at 3.30 p. m. to charge the enemy's works.

Yours, respectfully,

ROBERT L. McCOOK,
Colonel Ninth Ohio Volunteers, Commanding Second Brigade.
Capt. GEORGE L. HARTSUFF, *Assistant Adjutant-General.*

No. 8.

Report of Lieut. Col. Charles Sondershoff, Ninth Ohio Infantry.

The regiment was led into action by Lieut. Col. Charles Sondershoff, by direction of Adjutant-General Hartsuff, at 3.30 p. m., under orders to charge the enemy's works. It was ordered to advance to that point of the enemy's works lying to the left of the corn field. After Companies A, B, and C had passed the corn field and deployed to the enemy's left the order to charge the fortifications was countermanded by the general commanding, and the balance of the regiment was ordered to occupy the crest of the hill immediately in the rear of McMullin's battery. Before the order countermanding that to charge the works could be transmitted to Companies A, B, and C, they had advanced through the thick brush some 300 or 400 feet, when they came to the point where the enemy had cut the brush in front of their main works, which were about 300 yards distant, from which the enemy opened a strong fire of musketry, grape, and canister. After the companies had advanced a short distance towards the main works, sheltering themselves by trees and brush as best they could, all the men returning fire when anything was visible to shoot at, it was soon discovered by Companies A and B that immediately to their right, and about 50 yards distant, there was a wing of the enemy's works extending to the woods at almost right angles with the main works, when they immediately deployed for the purpose of attacking it. At this moment the enemy opened a severe fire from this wing of their works, which was returned by the companies. Companies A and B advanced to within about 100 feet of this wing of the works.

Whilst Companies A and B were thus engaged Company C approached the main works parallel with the corn field, and had got within 100 yards of the work. A signal was sounded to retire, which they did in good order, and proceeded to join the balance of the regiment. The wounded in this engagement is shown by tabular statement attached.* After the regiment had been together some time in the rear of Mc-Mullin's battery, Colonel McCook ordered it to fall farther back, to avoid the grape and canister shots to which its position exposed it. It then retired to the clear space on the east side of the next field to await orders. In about one hour the regiment was again ordered forward to charge the enemy's works, and proceeded to a point about 200 yards west of the corn field aforesaid and a short distance to the right of the main road leading to the enemy's works, where it was halted until night-fall. Then the regiment was ordered to cover the return of the artillery from the woods to camp. One-half of the regiment was deployed through the woods on the right of the road, the balance on the road to the left. After the artillery and all the ambulances were brought from the field, the regiment, about 9 o'clock, joined the balance of the Second Brigade, and went into camp at the place from which it had started at 3.30 o'clock p. m. to charge the enemy's works.

CHAS. SONDERSHOFF,
Lieutenant-Colonel, Comdg. Ninth Regiment Ohio Volunteers.

No. 9.

Report of Col. Augustus Moor, Twenty-eighth Ohio Infantry.

SIR: In obedience to your order I took the position in line of battle assigned to my regiment on the left of the road towards Cross-Lanes and in rear of the road leading to the rebels' works, detaching Captain Ewald, Company B, on the left into the woods, to skirmish and guard against surprise. About 2.35 p. m. I was ordered to send one field officer, with five companies, to Cross-Lanes for observation. I detailed Lieutenant-Colonel Becker, who started forthwith. Soon after, the firing becoming quite lively, I was ordered forward in double-quick. I came up with Lieutenant-Colonel Becker's command, drawn up in line on the right of the road, ordered him to fall in with the regiment, and moved forward to the rear and left of the artillery.

After 5 o'clock, the fire slacking somewhat, I was ordered by General Rosecrans, in person, to move my regiment, with four companies of the Thirteenth and a detachment of the Twenty-third Ohio Regiments, guided by Colonel Smith, in a direction to the left of our position, and after rounding a hill to our right to charge and take the works of the rebels about sunset, an attack from our right to be made at the same time. I marched the column down the ravine as directed, halted, and waited for Colonel Smith to guide the column. One hour and twenty minutes after my arrival at the foot of the hill Colonel Smith brought the verbal order from headquarters to start. I commenced the ascent in two ranks over very steep and slippery rocks, through thick under-

---

* Embodied in report No. 14, p. 146.

growth and thorns.   After half an hour's climbing, Captain Schache, Colonel Smith, and myself, with about thirty of the best climbers of Company A, reached the top, when the adjutant came up and informed us that the whole command could not be brought up before 2 o'clock.

It was now pitch dark in the thicket.   The men had been on their legs since 3 o'clock in the morning, without a drop of water in their canteens, and, although willing, utterly exhausted.   Colonel Smith and myself concluded to descend again, fall back into the ravine, and make the assault at daybreak.   The column was cautioned to face about and descend with as little noise as possible, and continued to do so for about ten minutes, when, after a peculiar kind of whistling, firing suddenly commenced from the direction of the rebels, striking down many of my men.   Instantly the whole extended line of my command was one sheet of fire, which lasted for some time, when, after finding the firing opposite us to cease, I, assisted by Lieutenant-Colonel Becker and Adjutant Bohlender, succeeded in collecting and forming our men again in the ravine, where I found to my surprise detachments of the Thirteenth and Twenty-third Regiments on my left flank instead of on the extreme left of the column, as directed, which disregard of dispositions made three-fourths of an hour before might have brought on an indiscriminate slaughter among troops of the same army.   I, with Lieutenant-Colonel Becker, became disabled by tumbling down some steep cliff, when I turned over the command to Captain Weselowski, who marched the regiment to the camp ground.   Annexed you will find a list of the killed and wounded.*

I am, most respectfully, your most obedient servant,

A. MOOR,
Colonel Twenty-eighth Ohio Regiment U. S. Infantry.

Col. ROBERT L. McCOOK,
Ninth Reg't Ohio Vols., Comdg. 2d Brigade A. O. W. Va.

No. 10.

Report of Col. Frederick Poschner, Forty-seventh Ohio Infantry.

CAMP COX, *September* 19, 1861.

The Forty-seventh Regiment formed in line of battle with the Second Brigade, Col. R. L. McCook commanding.   Marched afterwards with the brigade near the fortifications.   Formed with the Ninth Regiment Ohio Volunteers, the storming column, and retired with the same at night. None killed, wounded, or missing. †

F. POSCHNER,
Colonel, Commanding.

No. 11.

Report of Capt. F. Schambeck, Chicago Dragoons.

While on the march to the battle-field the company was sent ahead to destroy a ferry.   While there some of the enemy, having crossed the river by way of the ferry, fired on the company, and they returned the fire.

---

* Embodied in report No. 14, p. 146.
† Force engaged foots up 18 officers and 367 enlisted men.

One man, Herrmann Reichert, from Chicago, a private, was wounded in the leg. When the troops were formed in line of battle the company was placed in the rear of the Second Brigade, and afterward advanced with the same into the woods, but were ordered back, and took no more part in the action, except some of the men, who were employed as carriers of dispatches.

F. SCHAMBECK, *Captain.*

No. 12.

Report of Col. Eliakim P. Scammon, Twenty-third Ohio Infantry, commanding Third Brigade.

HEADQUARTERS THIRD BRIGADE, A. O. W. VA.,
Camp Scott, September 13, 1861.

SIR: In reference to the operations of the 10th instant I have to report that the Third Brigade, acting as a reserve corps, was not actively engaged. About 4 o'clock p. m. the brigade was ordered to form in line of battle on a hill fronting the right of the enemy's position. It was formed in two lines, the Twenty-third Regiment in front, and a detachment of the Thirtieth, under Colonel Ewing, in rear; Mack's battery of howitzers a little in advance of the infantry. Shortly after taking position, in odedience to orders from the commanding general, Major Hayes and four companies of the Twenty-third Regiment moved to the right of the enemy's intrenchments, taking position in a dense thicket, and advanced toward the enemy's works. Two of his men were wounded at this point. Their names are given below. About dark the brigade was ordered to advance along the road leading to the front of the enemy's works and await orders. The movement was executed immediately, and after waiting an hour and a half for orders to advance, it having become quite dark, orders were received to withdraw the column. We bivouacked on the hill now occupied by our camp. The names of the wounded are: Richmond Shaw, Company K, Twenty-third Regiment Ohio Volunteers, severe wound in the right leg; Timothy C. Wood, Company K, Twenty-third Regiment Ohio Volunteers, slightly wounded in the shoulder.

For a report of the subsequent service performed by Colonel Ewing's detachment of the Thirtieth Regiment, I refer you to his report, herewith inclosed.

Very respectfully, your obedient servant,

E. P. SCAMMON,
Colonel, Commanding Third Brigade.

Capt. GEORGE L. HARTSUFF, *Assistant Adjutant-General.*

No. 13.

Report of Col. Hugh Ewing, Thirtieth Ohio Infantry.

HEADQUARTERS THIRTIETH REGIMENT O. V.,
Camp Scott.

SIR: On the 10th instant three of the four companies of the Thirtieth Regiment attached to the advancing army were ordered from the rear, where they were under my command guarding the train, to join the Third Brigade, at that time (4 p. m.) forming the reserve of the army in its attack on the enemy's intrenchments at Eagle's Nest. I marched my men at quick-step from the rear, and took the position assigned me by Col. E. P. Scammon, commanding the brigade, where we remained until near dark, when, with the remainder of the reserve, we moved to a position in the woods opposite the enemy's center, and remained there an hour and a half, and were ordered back to near our former position, then becoming the camp of the army. My companies, with two of the Twenty-third, formed the guard of the camp, which was placed under my direction.

At daylight on the 11th a fugitive slave from the enemy's intrenchments reported the flight of the rebels, when the general commanding directed me to verify the report. I entered the intrenchments with one of my companies, finding them deserted save a few stragglers, whom I sent to the rear. I placed a guard over the abandoned property, took down the flag of the enemy and placed ours in its stead, and reported to the general commanding. On the morning of the 12th I handed in a list of the prisoners, thus turning them over to the charge of the officer of the guard. My men were not under fire.

Respectfully submitted.

HUGH EWING,
Colonel Thirtieth Regiment.

Col. E. P. SCAMMON, *Commanding Third Brigade.*

No. 14.

Statement of the killed and wounded at the battle of Carnifix Ferry, September 10, 1861.

[By Asst. Surg. Horace R. Wirtz, U. S. A., acting medical director during the action.]

Command.	Killed.	Wounded.
Ninth Ohio Volunteers	1	8
Tenth Ohio Volunteers	9	50
Twelfth Ohio Volunteers	1	1
Thirteenth Ohio Volunteers	1	12
Twenty-eighth Ohio Volunteers	2	29
Ohio artillery (McMullin's)		4
Ohio cavalry	3	37
Total	17	141

No. 15.

Report of Brig. Gen. John B. Floyd, C. S. Army.

HEADQUARTERS ARMY OF THE KANAWHA,
Camp on the Road, September 12, 1861.

SIR: Information had reached me for some number of days that a heavy force was advancing towards my position from the direction of Clarksburg, in the northwestern part of the State. As these rumors became a certainty I made an effort to strengthen myself, first by re-enforcement, and secondly by intrenchments sufficient to withstand the very large force of the enemy. My orders to General Wise I send you copies of, and also copies of his replies.*

---

* See Floyd to Wise, September 9 (2); Wise to Floyd, September 9, 4 p. m.; Floyd to Wise, September 10; Wise to Floyd, September 10, 6.30 a. m. and 12.30 p. m., in "Correspondence, etc.," *post.*

I failed in procuring re-enforcement, but succeeded somewhat better in the construction of a temporary breastwork. At 3 o'clock in the evening of the 10th of September the enemy, under command of General Rosecrans, as we learned through prisoners, of whose advance I was fully aware, at the head of ten regiments, made his appearance before intrenchments, when the battle instantly commenced. Our lines were necessarily very extended for the purpose of protecting our position, and when manned left not one man for reserve. The assault was made with spirit and determination with small-arms, grape, and round shot from howitzers and rifled cannon. There was scarcely an intermission in the conflict until night put an end to the firing. The enemy's force is estimated certainly between 8,000 and 9,000 men, whilst our force engaged was less than 2,000. Upon the close of the contest for the night I discovered that it was only a question of time when we should be compelled to yield to the superiority of numbers. I therefore determined at once to recross the Gauley River and take position upon the left bank, which I accomplished without the loss of a gun or any accident whatever. Our loss, strange to say, after a continued firing upon us by cannon and small-arms for nearly four hours, was only 20 men wounded. The loss of the enemy we had no means of accurately estimating, but we are satisfied, from report of prisoners and other sources of information, it was very heavy. We repulsed them in five distinct and successive assaults, and at nightfall had crippled them to such an extent that they were in no condition whatever to molest us in our passage across the river.

I will only say that our men, without distinction, behaved with the greatest coolness, determination, and presence of mind, and while it is impossible to give praise to one portion of the force engaged over another, it is but proper to say that the artillery behaved with the greatest bravery and efficiency; that under the command of Captain Guy, who had reached me only two days before and were for the first time under fire, behaved themselves in a manner worthy of all praise.

I am very confident that I could have beaten the enemy and have marched directly to the valley of Kanawha if the re-enforcements from General Wise's column had come up when ordered and the regiments from North Carolina and Georgia could have reached me before the close of the second day's conflict. I cannot express the regret which I feel at the necessity, over which I had no control, which required that I should recross the river. I am confident that if I could have commanded the services of 5,000 men instead of 1,800, which I had, I could have opened the road directly into the valley of the Kanawha. It would seem now as if the object so nearly accomplished can only be attained by an advance upon the enemy by the left bank of the Kanawha River with a sufficient force at any time to give him battle. This force, if possible, ought to be collected from Tennessee and Kentucky. Their close correspondence shows distinctly enough the urgent necessity of so shaping the command in the valley of Kanawha as to insure in the future that unity of action upon which alone can rest any hope of success in military matters.

I have not thought proper to take any other notice of these transactions than to bring them to the notice of the President and Secretary of War of the Confederate States. The reasons which have induced me to take this course I am sure will not be misunderstood by either.

I apprehend the course the enemy proposes to pursue is to carry out the plans indicated by General Rosecrans to General Tyler for the invasion of the interior of the State and the seizure of Lewisburg, set forth in an intercepted letter of the latter a month ago. To prevent this I am in command of an actual force of 4,200 men. This force will be required to oppose the advance of General Cox and General Rosecrans, if their forces, as they undoubtedly will, number at least 12,000 men. This disparity in numbers is too great, although I will certainly give battle to the invading army at some such strong point in the mountain passes as I may hope will equalize to some extent our numbers. This may occur within the next three days, but should 'it be deferred for any length of time, I hope the Department will find itself able to strengthen us with re-enforcements. In the mean time, should General Lee attack and repulse the enemy at Rich Mountain, I will hold myself in position to fall upon his flank or rear, as circumstances may allow or my force authorize.

I have the honor to be, with the highest respect, your obedient servant,

JOHN B. FLOYD,
Brigadier-General, Commanding Army of Kanawha.
By WILLIAM E. PETERS,
Assistant Adjutant-General Floyd Brigade.

Hon. L. P. WALKER, *Secretary of War.*

This is signed by Adjutant Peters, because an injury prevents my holding a pen.

———

WAR DEPARTMENT, C. S. A.,
Richmond, September 20, 1861.

Brig. Gen. JOHN B. FLOYD :

SIR : I have the honor to acknowledge the receipt of your letter of the 12th instant, containing report of the repulse by the troops under your command of the attack made by the army of General Rosecrans with greatly superior forces. I take great pleasure in communicating to you the congratulations of the President, as well as my own, on this brilliant affair, in which the good conduct and steady valor of your whole command were so conspicuously displayed. I regret that the attack should have occurred before the arrival of any of the four regiments that were on their way to re-enforce you, and that you were thus deprived of the ability to reap the fruits of your successful repulse of the attack made on you. This Department is making efforts to send you still further re-enforcements as speedily as possible.

I inclose copy of an order issued by the President's instructions to General Wise, by virtue of which his whole command is turned over to you.

Your obedient servant,

J. P. BENJAMIN,
Acting Secretary of War.

[Inclosure.]

WAR DEPARTMENT, C. S. A.,
Richmond, September 20, 1861.

Brig. Gen. HENRY A. WISE,
Gauley River, via Lewisburg, Va. :

SIR : You are instructed to turn over all the troops heretofore immediately under your command to General Floyd, and report yourself in person to the Adjutant-General in this city with the least delay. In making the transfer to General Floyd you will include everything under your command.

By order of the President:

J. P. BENJAMIN,
Acting Secretary of War.

No. 16.

Reports of Brig. Gen. Henry A. Wise, C. S. Army, covering the operations of his command from June to September 25.

DOGWOOD GAP CAMP, VA.,
September 11, 1861—7 p. m.

GENERAL: Disasters have come, and disasters are coming, which you alone, I fear, can repair and prevent. As I predicted, General Floyd, after a hard fight, from 3 p. m. to 7 p. m. yesterday, has given way, recrossed Carnifix Ferry, before a force of some 5,000, re-enforced from Gauley, to what extent is not known. He thinks the enemy has 9,000; I think from 4,000 to 6,000 men. He lost no lives and but few slightly wounded; but his breastworks were near woods all around except in front, and the enemy could approach him quite near. There was severe cannonading on both sides; the enemy had rifled guns of bad range at first but beginning to tell seriously as the fight ended on the breastworks. Owing to inadequacy of transportation and ferriage, he lost in his retreat last night considerable baggage, tents, cooking utensils, fat cattle, and horses, and one caisson. I was detained by the enemy in my front from going to his relief on yesterday. They indicated a purpose to turn my flank at the Hawk's Nest, and to march a considerable force to Carnifix Ferry, in General Floyd's rear. But, receiving peremptory orders last night, I moved my whole force to re-enforce him, got a few miles, found he had retreated to this side of Gauley, and for the third time met his messenger, countermanding my march and ordering my return to this road. My baggage was all sent back to this camp guarded by a small force, and when I reached within a mile of this place I found General Floyd on the road-side, slightly wounded in the right fore-arm. I asked for orders. He said he did not know what orders to give. I urged the necessity of defending Miller's Ferry, on the New River, which, when called away, I left guarded by General Chapman's militia. He mistook me, and thought I spoke of Carnifix Ferry, and replied that now he took no interest in that plan of movement; and then I learned that he had left this side of that ferry wholly undefended and unguarded, and since I hear that the enemy crossed it this morning on prepared bridges. This renders both his and my commands critically exposed. The enemy may fall on our rear between this and Lewisburg by either the Sunday, or the Wilderness, or the Bracken's Creek roads. I am without orders, without command, with wholly inadequate force of my own, with his force greatly impaired, himself stunned by the blow, and obliged to appeal to you.

I solemnly protest that my force is not safe under his command, and I ask to be allowed to co-operate with some other superior. I had for forage and from policy sent nearly all my cavalry to Loop Creek and Coal River across the New River, and to penetrate the Kanawha. I now must recall them (if allowed to do so) to scout my rear. The whole policy of moving on the Lower Kanawha is now defeated, and my confident opinion is that a retreat ought to be ordered to Meadow Bluff, or you will be compelled to move backward towards Lewisburg, and the foe in your front will be thereby given the opportunity to advance on your rear. This all may seem too critical to me, but I nevertheless submit it to you, and ask you to relieve me. In order that you may judge the better, I send you copies of our entire correspondence. At 12 o'clock last night I received General Floyd's last note, peremptorily ordering my whole force to Carnifix, and, marching this morning at 11 a. m., I received a verbal message from him ordering me to fall back, he getting to this point before I did, without having lost a man, and without leaving a guard at the ferry behind him. This makes further retreat eastward inevitable and the necessity for it early and urgent. I fear your reply will be too late.

With the highest respect and esteem, I am, sir, your obedient servant,

HENRY A. WISE,
Brigadier-General.

General R. E. LEE, *Commanding, &c.*

—

RICHMOND, VA., *October* 26, 1861.

SIR: On the 28th ultimo I arrived at Richmond in obedience to an order of the President through the Secretary of War, which order I obeyed to the letter, and without any delay, from Camp Defiance, on Big Sewell, to this city, reported myself at the War Department. I was called from the field of action most unexpectedly, and had to reach Richmond before I could learn the cause of my recall and of the transfer of my command.

The day after my arrival here I was stricken down with severe illness, caused by actual and severe exposure in the service. On the 2d instant I was furnished with a copy of the report of General Floyd, "relative to the battle therein named," which was transmitted to me by direction of the Secretary of War, and from that time to this I have been unable to prepare any reply to that report. Regarding it now as the only matter or thing which I am called upon to answer, I proceed in the most succinct manner to notice its statements of complaint against me and my command.

I am now unable to prepare a reply in detail, and am therefore compelled to furnish the President, through the Department of War, the entire body of my correspondence with Generals Lee and Floyd.*

General Floyd's report to the Secretary of War of September 12 says [No. 15]: "My orders to General Wise I send you copies of, and also copies of his replies." I have not been furnished with the copies which he says he sent, but the President and the Department can now judge whether he sent copies of all the originals. I now send copies of all my correspondence with both Generals Lee and Floyd.

However, before I proceed to answer this special report, I beg leave to make a few preliminary observations. It will be remembered that General Floyd was commissioned prior to the date of my commission, and thus became my senior in rank. Thus, too, he began, weeks before I was commissioned, to raise his command in the southwest. I never contemplated originally the command of a brigade department, but had

---

*No inclosures found with this report; but the communications referred to by General Wise appear entire in the "Reports" or in the "Correspondence, etc.," *post.*

asked specially for an independent partisan command, subject only to the general laws and orders of the service. When I came to Richmond late in May from a sick bed the President himself changed the destination of my command. I was called by him to take a commission at once as brigadier-general, not to await the raising of my partisan brigade, but to command the Middle Department of the West, the State volunteer forces, under Colonel Tompkins, in the valley of the Kanawha, to be attached to my Legion.

Very early in June I left Richmond an invalid, without a man or a gun, and departed for Charleston, Kanawha, and commenced raising the forces which since I have commanded. In June and July Colonel Tompkins' volunteer force was increased from 600 to about 1,800 men, and the Legion was raised to the number of about 2,850; making in all an effective force of about 3,600 men.

By a dispatch from Adjutant-General S. Cooper, dated July 18, 1861, I was ordered to move up toward Covington and communicate with General Floyd, who was ordered to proceed in that direction. This order being in part discretionary, I awaited events and further orders before I proceeded to act under it. Soon afterwards I received a letter from General Robert E. Lee, dated July 24, directing me to look to the security of my rear, keep my command concentrated, and be prepared to unite with General Loring or operate as circumstances on my line of communication might dictate. He gave me permission to increase the strength of my Legion, but warned me that re-enforcements could not be sent to me from Richmond, from the necessity of restricting the operations of the enemy, if possible, north of Pocahontas, and of strengthening the armies of the Potomac. He had hoped that the good citizens of the Kanawha Valley would have rallied under my standard and given me the force I desired, not knowing the utter demoralization and denationalization of a large majority of the good citizens of Kanawha Valley, and ignorant also that even among some of those who professed to be true to the State of Virginia a conspiracy had been raised against my taking command of the valley of the Kanawha. Thus, whilst my aim was upon the enemy, every step was amid the rattlesnakes of treason to the South or petty serpents of jealousy in the disaffection of my own camp. Yet with the aid of Colonel Tompkins, a gentleman, a soldier, and a patriot, I magnified our command by nearly trebling his original numbers and adding the whole number of the Legion, making in all nearly eight times the force we began with.

General Lee also regretted that he could not furnish the ammunition and arms which were incessantly called for by Colonel Tompkins and myself; and it was a secret which neither of us dared to tell in the Kanawha Valley, that at no time of the whole sixty days while we were marching and countermarching, posting and counterposting, scouting and fighting, day in and day out, in a valley the hardest to defend and the easiest to be attacked in the topography of the country, could we at any time have fired in any general action ten rounds of ammunition in our joint commands. Thus distant from the metropolis, thus unofficered and unorganized, thus unsupplied with either arms, ammunition, clothing, or tents, we increased our forces, maintained our positions, and it was only when the order to fall back was repeated that we moved in the direction of Covington, as ordered.

Whatever may have been said or may be said of that retreat from Charleston, from Coal River, and Tyler Mountain, Two Mile, Elk River, and Gauley, I aver, if anything was done which ought not to have been done, or omitted which ought not to have been omitted, or was lost which ought to have been saved, that it was in each and every instance because of violations of my express orders; and upon the whole I aver further that for raw troops, unofficered and unorganized, in various detachments, at distances not supporting each other, in front of a foe more than double their number, the retreat was creditable. My reasons for concurring in the orders to retreat are to be found in my letters to General Lee, of August 1, 1861* (dated at Bunger's Mill, 4 miles west of Lewisburg), and August 4, from the White Sulphur Springs, the latter in reply to his, dated at Huntersville, August 3. In those letters I was caused to report to General Lee an error as to the number of desertions from the State volunteers. Many of the officers and men who were reported as deserters had received written furloughs, unknown to me, from some of their commanding officers.

The main confusion and difficulty in retreating from the Kanawha was owing to the erroneous impression which most of the men had taken up that they were not bound to march out of the valley of the Kanawha or to fight elsewhere than there, which idea was both inculcated and encouraged by many of their officers, several of whom ultimately tendered their resignations, and were obviously bent on impairing if not breaking up my command. Happily their efforts had no effect upon the Legion, but only upon a few of the State volunteers, and the two regiments of Colonels Tompkins and McCausland were reduced to less than 400 men each, while the Legion was unimpaired except by measles and typhoid fever, but the most of the men of the State volunteers proved ultimately to be pure patriots and proud soldiers. Most continued on duty, and many who were said to have deserted returned to duty after the expiration of furloughs actually received; but both Colonel Tompkins' command and mine, both the Legion and the State volunteers, were extremely worn and worsted by two months of excessively hard service. When they arrived at the White Sulphur they had worn-out everything and were supplied with nothing, and required at least one month for refreshment and refitting. The infantry and artillery alone were taken there, and the cavalry, under Colonel Davis, was left as a rear guard of the passes from Fayetteville, Gauley, and Summersville. The cavalry alone, with other precautions, effectually checked the advance of the enemy; all of which was approved by General Lee in his letter dated Huntersville, August 5. It was here, at the White Sulphur, that both Colonel Tompkins and myself hoped and implored to be permitted to refit our commands.

During all this time that our forces were worn and torn by the service for more than sixty days General Floyd was raising his command and fitting it out with every supply he could procure, and at last, when he arrived at the White Sulphur, he brought with him less than 1,200 men, all told. He required us, panting with the fatigue of service, to hasten back over grinding roads, over which our men had just marched almost barefooted, almost shirtless, and quite tentless. His very first approach to my command was nothing less than one of reproach, which, in manner as well as substance, was wounding to those who had been doing their utmost to serve the cause of the State and of the Confederacy. He had not re-enforced us in the valley of the Kanawha, but required me, tattered and torn by service, to turn upon an ordered retreat and to re-enforce him, with but two regiments under his command. I begged for delay. I protested against the necessity of hurrying unsupplied and unprovided men back to a fruitless contest

---

* In Chap. IX, Vol. II, of this series, p. 1011.

with a foe more than triple our numbers, in fastnesses that could be re-enforced at any time in any number by an enemy holding the navigation of the Kanawha, and an enemy, too, who, after the battle of Manassas and the retirement of McClellan from the field to Washington, and by our timely escape from the valley, were so staggered that they manifested no disposition to advance, but paused to fortify themselves at Gauley; when, too, it was our policy to draw them to the eastern verge of the Fayette wilderness, force upon them 40 miles of mountain transportation, instead of our driving on to the western verge of that wilderness and taking upon ourselves with inferior force the loss and cost and risk of that same wilderness mountain transportation. This policy I presented to General Lee, and he in advance emphatically approved it. On the 6th of August General Floyd was within 2 miles of the White Sulphur. That evening he visited me in camp, and notified me that on the morning of the 7th of August he would move to Lewisburg. He wanted to drive the enemy across the Gauley in less than a week, and by his blunt and blatant manner caused me to write to General Lee my letter of August 7.

The first two letters of my correspondence with General Floyd I file for no present purpose of this report. They may explain some matters in future. From Camp Arbuckle, near Lewisburg, August 8, he called upon me for a full detail of my command, the number of men, arms, and ammunition fit for use, the amount of transportation, &c. I replied by mine of the same date from the White Sulphur Springs, August 8, 6 o'clock p. m. On the 10th of August I informed General Lee of additional re-enforcements sent to General Floyd besides my cavalry force of about 500, and that I would follow as soon as possible from day to day—so soon as I could clothe my men and fit them for a march and provide ammunition; and I beg leave to call the attention of the President to this letter to General Lee as containing a proposition to stop the enemy on or near the eastern verge of the Fayette wilderness. See also my two letters to General Lee of August 11 and my letter to General Floyd of August 9 as to my disposition to co-operate with General Floyd. In reply to my letters of the 10th and 11th August, General Lee complimented me for re-enforcing General Floyd so promptly, and added:

Your reasons for our troops not advancing to Gauley at present are conclusive, and your plan of stopping the enemy on the eastern verge of the wilderness you describe is concurred in. Until ready to open and penetrate the Kanawha Valley, whence you may draw your supplies, the line of defense you propose, embracing points of strength, is the best.

Such were the wise instructions of the superior of both General Floyd and myself, and when I found General Floyd running directly counter to this policy, it would have been no wonder if I had leaned to my own judgment thus indorsed by General Lee; but notwithstanding this, the President and Secretary of War will see that I followed my immediate superior in the vain attempt to force the Gauley.

On the 12th August General Floyd assumed command of the forces of the Army of the Kanawha and the country adjacent thereto, appointed Colonel Heth acting inspector-general, and ordered him at once to inspect the forces composing the command, commencing with the Wise Legion. My letter to General Floyd of the 11th August shows my hurry to co-operate with him. On the 13th August General Floyd sent me a communication from Colonel Davis, and called for a battery of artillery and such other forces as I could spare. In mine of the 13th I promised him in the shortest possible time some 1,500 men. On the 13th August, also, he sent me a curiously-worded demand for the regiment of volunteers from beyond New River commanded by Colonel McCausland—a regiment that had been worse torn to pieces than any other by traitorous desertion, by furloughs issued without my authority, and by disaffection and conspiracy of officers who did not wish to leave the valley of the Kanawha. In my letter of August 13 I assigned him the reasons why it was impossible to comply with this request, and I presented these orders to Colonel Tompkins, who on the 14th directed to me his official protest, and I gave him orders according to the reason and just proprieties of the case.

Again, however, under date of the 13th, General Floyd urged me to bring up all my force, and to furnish one of his companies with arms. This was received by me on the 14th, and on the same day I wrote to him that his orders should be promptly and punctually obeyed. I started forces that morning to Meadow Bluff (nearly all the Legion), appointed Colonel Tompkins commandant of the post at the White Sulphur, and left him with his two volunteer regiments to be refitted and to wait for transportation. Strange to say, General Floyd, also on the 14th, at 5 o'clock a. m., wrote his dispatch No. 8, ordering me "peremptorily" to march at once with all my force to join him at Meadow Bluff. His Nos. 7 and 8 were received nearly at the same time. I answered them by saying (on the 14th, at 9.30 o'clock a. m.) that his peremptory order should be executed as promptly as possible so soon as forces and means of transportation could be made available. On the 14th also he sent to me for ammunition, which order was complied with. On the 14th also, at 11 o'clock a. m., I told him that I was doing my best to hasten my march by all the means in my power; that the quartermaster had not half enough wagons, and was unable to procure them. I asked him to send back to me some of his wagons to assist the expedition of my march to join him. In his letter No. 10, of August 15, he declined to send the wagons. On the 13th August I wrote to General Lee, informing him of the demands made upon me by General Floyd—informed him that I was very desirous to promptly obey General Floyd, and to preserve the harmony of our respective brigades. General Floyd had already commenced to violate my command by passing orders to my officers without issuing those orders through me, and I asked from General Lee two general orders: 1st, that no order be passed from General Floyd to my brigade except through me; 2d, that the separate organization and command of my brigade, subject of course to General Floyd's priority of rank and orders for service, should not be interfered with; and I inquired of General Lee about the relations of the State volunteers under Colonel Tompkins and of the militia under Generals Beckley and Chapman to my command.

From General Lee I received his of the 14th August complimenting me upon my rapid progress of preparation, expressing confidence in my zealous and cordial co-operation in every effort against the common enemy, and saying :

As regards the command of your brigade, the military propriety of communicating through you all orders for its movement is so apparent, that I think no orders on the subject necessary. I have always supposed that it was the intention of the President to give a distinct organization to your Legion, for it to be under your command, subject, of course, to the service under the orders of a senior officer. As regards the troops serving hitherto with your Legion, it is within the province of the commanding general to continue them as hitherto under your command, to brigade them separately, or detach them, as the good of the service may demand.

Thus the President will see that I took the utmost pains to define my powers and those of General Floyd. He will see that I had reason to do this, for General Floyd's design—obvious to me—was to destroy my command, and not only transfer to himself the State volunteers and militia, but by constant detachments of my Legion, to merge it also in his brigade, to be commanded by his field officers, and be torn to pieces by maladministration, and to sink me, the second in command, even below his majors and captains. Therefore it was that I obtained from General Lee the distinct law of our relations : That General Floyd could not discontinue my command of the Legion ; that he could not brigade the regiments of the Legion separately; that he could detach them only as the good of the service might demand ; and that, whether de tached or not, I was still in command of all the forces of the Legion.

On the 14th August also I informed General Lee that, though I did not credit the rumors about the approach of the enemy, I should move my entire available force at once to join General Floyd at Meadow Bluff; that I should counsel an advance to the western side of Little Sewell ; that I should take eight pieces of artillery ; that my howitzer was without ammunition ; that in less than three days I could put forward 1,500 and in five days 2,500 men; that General Floyd had his own force, something less than 1,200, my whole cavalry (550), and a detachment of artillery with two 6-pounders—in all, say, 1,800 men; and that within three days his force should be increased to 3,500 or 4,000 men.

On the 15th I informed General Lee that ammunition for my howitzer had arrived late on the 14th, and at 4 o'clock a. m. on the 15th I had moved a corps of artillery, with eight pieces, including a howitzer and three 6-pounders, with three companies of artillery under Major Gibbes, and three regiments of infantry of my Legion, in all about 2,000 men, to join General Floyd at Meadow Bluff on the evening of that day. My corps of cavalry (550 strong) and 50 artillery, with two pieces belonging to the State volunteers, were already with him, and two companies of the State volunteer cavalry would join him by the morrow, making my re-enforcement about 2,600 men—more than double his own force—and making his whole force by the 16th about 3,800 men. This was enough to check the enemy until I could have the State volunteer regiments ready for marching orders. This will show whether I was prompt beyond promise in re-enforcing General Floyd. And I call attention to this entire letter of mine to General Lee of August 15 to justify the failure to send on two regiments of State volunteers, and my protest of a desire for a harmony of co-operation in every sense of cheerful as well as healthful service. But I informed General Lee distinctly that I could not in honor submit to have my brigade mutilated without his orders. I appealed to General Lee not only in behalf of myself, but in behalf of Colonel Tompkins, a soldier of sixteen years' standing in the Regular Army of the United States, for common justice.

I call attention to the letter of General Floyd of August 16 and my reply of August 17, in relation to the propriety of the mode of issuing orders to my command. These letters were written on the top of Big Sewell, on the 17th, 40 miles west of Lewisburg, where I had then already joined and re-enforced General Floyd. On August 17 General Floyd ordered me to occupy the camp vacated by him on the top of Big Sewell, and to remain there until further orders. Again, in his letter (No. 13), he addressed me on the subject of the mode of issuing orders to my command. On the 19th August I replied to that communication, taking the positions authorized by General Lee. On the 18th he notified me that he had fallen back from Tyree's to the camp on Sewell, and on the 19th he ordered me to take up the line of march at 7.30 o'clock on the morning of the 20th, and to proceed with all the forces under my command in the direction of the Kanawha Valley by way of the James River and Kanawha turnpike, and he undertook to prescribe the order of my march. I showed him that it was impossible to comply with his order, and asked again for wagons, with which request he could not comply. The same day, afterwards, he countermanded his orders as to the time of marching, and detached from my command all the forces not belonging to the Legion. One of my ammunition wagons was broken down, which delayed my advance at the hour ordered, but I hastened on to the front to relieve my cavalry from where General Floyd had ordered it, and where it was in danger of being cut off. They had charged the enemy at about 1½ miles beyond Piggot's, at the foot of the Saturday road, and the second encounter occurred at about 2 o'clock p. m. near Hamilton's, about half a mile this side of the Hawk's Nest. I informed General Floyd that they would be in strong force that night at Hawk's Nest, and that a good force of artillery should be posted at Dogwood Gap, at the foot of the Sunday and Hopping roads, and that we should advance that night. He advanced all the forces of his and my command in front of the enemy at Piggot's, near the foot of the Saturday road. What occurred there is detailed in my correspondence with General Lee, to which I will presently refer. On the 18th August I wrote to General Lee again, asking for the necessary orders defining the relations and laws of the command. I beg leave to call attention to that letter and its detail of complaints. Under date of the 21st August General Lee, according to my request, issued special orders placing the Twenty-second and Twenty-third Regiments of Virginia Volunteers subject to the assignment of the commanding general of the Army of the Kanawha, and confirming my immediate command (that of the Wise Legion) as organized by direction of the War Department. On the evening of the 21st of August our commands were united at the foot of Gauley Mountain, where the foe was found in force; and in my letter to General Lee of August 24, 1861, you will see a detailed report of a conference between General Floyd and myself of the orders which I received to move to Carnifix Ferry, while he was to cover the front on the turnpike; the manner in which I executed the order, arriving at Carnifix on the 22d; the manner in which his movements contradicted every conclusion of the conference; the manner in which his orders vacillated and contradicted themselves four times within forty-eight hours, and the manner in which all the baggage trains of both commands and a portion of the artillery were left by him at the mercy of the enemy.

On the 22d August, at Carnifix, General Floyd ordered me to send him four pieces of my artillery, in addition to his own two pieces; also one of my regiments, the strongest; also to send him early the next day, at 7 o'clock, 100 of my most efficient horse; and he ordered me, with the remainder of the force under my command, to take such a position as would enable me to watch the enemy and to check any advance by them. He also ordered me to forward on the regiments of Colonels Tompkins and McCausland to him, but should the force under my command, after making the above deductions, be deemed insufficient for the purpose of watching the enemy and checking his advance, I should retain under my command the regiment of Colonel Tompkins. After writing the above he added that, on conference with Colonel Heth, he was induced to recall his request for one of my regiments. He would try to make good his position with his own force and with my guns. In lieu of the regiment he asked only for 100 horse.

Leaving him a corps of artillery, with three pieces, and 100 horse, I marched back to Dogwood Gap, to which place he addressed the special orders of General Lee, Nos. 1, 2, and 3, under date of August 24. On the same day General Floyd wrote to me that he had good reasons to believe that the enemy had abandoned all idea of crossing the Gauley River in force; that he doubted the intention of the enemy to make an attack upon him, adding, "but I am fully able to defend myself against the combined force of General Cox and Colonel Tyler both together, and court their assault." He alluded to what he called "silly rumors among the teamsters and camp followers" about the danger of his being surrounded and cut off, and asked me to correct these rumors. By the 25th he would be ready to cross the Gauley with his artillery. The truth was that on the 23d General Floyd did lose the only little ferry-boat he had, with four men drowned, and he was in danger of being cut off. I had to obtain nails and plank to construct a new and better boat.

By this time General Floyd had the first two regiments he brought into the field, 1,200; Colonel Wharton's regiment, about 400; Corn's and Beckett's cavalry, 100; two pieces and about 40 men of the State volunteer artillery; three pieces and 61 men of my artillery, and Colonels Tompkins' and McCausland's regiments, little less than 800 men, making in all 2,600 men, less the number sick and on furlough.

On the 24th of August, at 8.30 o'clock p. m., I wrote to him fully, showing him how closely I had scouted the enemy, having been myself in person, pistol in hand, in their camp at Westlake's. On the same day, however, he informed me that on that evening he had received information that 500 of the enemy were encamped within 5 miles of Camp Gauley, and he ordered that I would send him at once one of my regiments—the strongest. He also called for an iron howitzer, ordered 40 rounds of cartridges for the infantry and 100 for the howitzer. This note was received by me at 2.30 o'clock a. m. August 25, and on the same day I replied that an order issued by him to Captain Jenkins, in command of his cavalry, interfering and conflicting with my command, had caused Jenkins to be ambuscaded and badly routed by the enemy, and that the disaster had called out my infantry in force, and had delayed my sending my regiment on the evening of the 25th. (In my letter of the 27th of August, addressed to General Floyd, will be found a description of the ambuscade and rout of Captain Jenkins.) I promised him the required re-enforcements for the morning of the 26th, and that I would hold my whole force ready to re-enforce him. Again, on the 25th of August, General Floyd wrote to me that if all the forces from Gauley advanced upon him I ought to give him the benefit of my whole force, but said that with one of my regiments at the river and my others at Dogwood Gap, ready to march at a moment's warning, he would look upon his position there as nearly impregnable. Again, on the same day, he wrote at 3 o'clock p. m.:

> The enemy are very near us; their advance guard within 3 miles. You will dispatch your strongest regiment to my support, and hold your entire command, if you can do this, within supporting distance.
>
> P. S.—3.30 o'clock p. m. Enemy advancing in battle array.

On examining my infantry after returning from the relief of Colonel Jenkins, learning the movement of the enemy on the turnpike, seeing the danger of the enemy going up the Saturday road to Carnifix to General Floyd's rear, I called for reports from Colonels Henningsen and Richardson, showing the reasons why my forces should not be reduced, meager as they were from the measles, and showing also that it was best for the safety of General Floyd's command that I should not move without further orders. Accordingly, on the 27th, I wrote to General Floyd and asked for further orders. Events proved that I was right. The advance guard of the enemy was but one regiment (that of Tyler), a set of lubberly Dutchmen, whom General Floyd surprised at breakfast, and routed them without losing a man. They were doubtless sent forward to induce the concentration of my forces at Carnifix and to catch General Floyd's and my forces both in the same trap at the same time. And on the 29th August General Floyd addressed to me his letter No. 25, saying that since his signal success and the utter dispersion and demoralization of the enemy, he thought I might then advantageously move towards Gauley Bridge and take possession of the strong position at and about the Hawk's Nest; that in all probability the enemy were likely to retire down the Kanawha, and that I should be close at hand to annoy their retiring columns. He did not reprove me for exercising a sound discretion in this instance; on the contrary, he approved my action, and ordered me still farther from his position. But I regret to say that this letter could not be concluded without a wanton sneer at the senior officer of my infantry, Colonel Henningsen.

From the first mention of the occupation of Carnifix Ferry I urged upon General Floyd the importance of that ferry, as commanding the stem of all the roads to the rear on the turnpike. To this end we could hold it on the left bank or south side of Gauley with a very small force, say 250 men, if their rear were well covered, so as to prevent the approach of the enemy towards them from the turnpike. By holding that stem and advancing our forces to the foot of the Saturday road, and to where the Chesnutburg road enters the turnpike (the mouths of the Saturday and Chesnutburg roads being near each other on opposite sides), we could have forced the enemy to approach on the turnpike alone in single column, and could have met him with our concentrated defenses without much danger of having our flanks turned. It was utterly unmilitary to have crossed Carnifix Ferry, unless General Floyd had force enough to advance. I warned him that this would compel him to divide his command, already too weak when combined; that if he crossed, the enemy might advance upon him from Summersville, from Gauley Bridge up the Gauley, and from Gauley Bridge up the Saturday road, thus attacking him with superior numbers front, flank, and rear. Whilst he would be too weak to withstand the front and flank attack on the right bank of the Gauley, I would be too weak, perhaps, to prevent the enemy from falling on his rear on the left bank of the Gauley; that his ferriage, too, was insufficient for the retreat of his command; whereas, if we took the position I advised, we would hold Miller's Ferry also, on the New River, and could spur the enemy at Cotton Hill, Montgomery's Ferry, at the Loop and from Coal River, all the way down the left bank of the Kanawha, and compel the enemy to withdraw a considerable portion of his forces from Gauley Bridge; that as long as he insisted on crossing that ferry, and thus exposing himself, it would be impossible for me to re-enforce him from across the river, without exposing the safety of both commands to the same disaster of having our retreat cut off. But no; all this obvious reasoning was in vain. Cross he would, and cross he did. I asked, *Cui bono?*—to what end?—to what result? If he wanted to hold Carnifix Ferry, he could do it with one-tenth the number of men on this side. But that was not the sole object. The answer I got was that the President desired the destruction of the trestle-work of the Baltimore and Ohio Railroad, or it was to "break the line of the enemy," or it was to go down Gauley to Twenty Mile—go up Twenty Mile to Bell Creek—go up Bell Creek to its head, and thence to Hughes' Creek, and down Hughes' Creek to the

Kanawha Valley, 15 miles only below Gauley Bridge. All these views were about equally absurd. The idea that he would be attacked either from Sutton or from Birch Mountain he utterly scouted, and the battle of knives and forks at Cross-Lanes had elated my senior to such an extent, that he thought himself impregnable in his position and capable of accomplishing impossibilities. I made it my business to do as he bade me—to watch the enemy and to protect General Floyd's rear; also to keep General Lee advised of my movements.

In my letter to General Lee of the 28th August the President and Secretary of War will see my full report of the first movement to Carnifix. On the 31st August General Floyd notified me that the enemy had abandoned Gauley Bridge and were advancing on him; that I should send him the strongest of my regiments to the top of the hill near Gauley (meaning the cliffs of Carnifix Ferry), and that I should at once advance with the remainder of my force (about 900 or 1,000 men), and take possession of the enemy's camp at the mouth of the Gauley. He also asked me to send him two companies of cavalry—his, since their stampede, having been sent all the way back to Greenbrier. These orders were given to me, notwithstanding he had but little doubt of the retreat of the enemy from Gauley Bridge, and although he much doubted their intention to march in his direction. The absurdity of these orders caused me to address to him my letter from Dogwood Gap of August 31, 10 o'clock p. m. Again, on the 31st August, 12 o'clock m., he addressed me another letter, in which he said that the enemy were advancing upon him in full force from Gauley Bridge, were within 12 miles of him, and calling upon me for 1,000 of my infantry, my best battery, and one squadron of horse. This was received by me between 4 and 5 o'clock a. m. of September 1. That morning I moved again in full force towards Carnifix, leaving a mere guard at Dogwood ; got to the cliffs of Carnifix, and was descending the road to the ferry, when one of his officers put into my hands his order of September 1, saying that from more recent information he doubted whether the movements of the enemy required the union of my force with his, as embraced in his last order, and commanded me to retain my forces in camp (at Dogwood) until further orders, and sneered another insult about the report of Colonel Henningsen.

I was so disgusted by these vacillating and harassing orders, that I determined at once with promptitude and dispatch to drive the enemy as far as possible back upon the turnpike towards their camp at Gauley Bridge. I returned to Dogwood on the evening of September 1, rested my men that night, and the next day (September 2) drove the enemy back west of Big Creek, and gained an advance of more than 13 miles upon the turnpike. With what gallantry and skill this was done by my men and officers you will see in my report to General Floyd of September 4. I have just ascertained an error in my estimate of the enemy's force on that occasion. I now learn from a perfectly reliable source that their force was larger than I had supposed, reaching an aggregate of 3,000 men.

On the same day I addressed to him a second letter, asking him to re-enforce me with the whole or a part of Colonel Tompkins' regiment and by returning to me my corps of artillery.

On the 6th of September I repeated the request, giving him very serious reasons for doing so. On the same day he actually re-enforced me with Colonel Tompkins' regiment, and sent back my two pieces of artillery and 61 men, under Lieutenant Hart, for which I thanked him by a letter of the same date.

In my letter to General Lee of September 5, 1861, you will see a full and detailed account of the battle at Big Creek and of my critical position at the Hawk's Nest.

On September 8 orders were interrupted by General Floyd's most extraordinary letter of that date, accusing one of my officers of having seized upon a rifled gun at Jackson's River, and taking it to the White Sulphur Springs; informing me that he had sent to arrest him, promising to order a court-martial for his trial when he could ascertain his rank, and requiring me to furnish him with a list of my officers and the dates of their commissions, that he might select from among them such names as he would like to be placed upon the court-martial. My answer is dated September 9, 1.15 o'clock p. m. The whole matter is explained in the report of Capt. B. Roemer, of my artillery, of September 12, and in my letter to General Lee of September 9, 10 o'clock a. m.

On the 7th of September General Floyd sent me Colonel Tompkins' regiment. On the morning of the 9th he announced the enemy approaching him, as I expected he would, from Sutton, 6,000 strong, and the apprehension of a considerable force also approaching from the direction of Gauley Bridge. I call your attention to my letter to General Lee of September 9, and to Colonel Tompkins' letter accompanying the same.

At about 8.30 o'clock a. m., September 9, I received a letter from General Floyd, dated 1 o'clock a. m., announcing the advance upon him of the enemy from Sutton, and that they were within 12 miles of Summersville. He stated that his strength, including the regiment of Colonel McCausland, did not exceed 1,600 men, and called for the return of Colonel Tompkins' regiment, and for me at the same time to send one of my own regiments, saying that I, with the remainder of my force, could maintain my position, and that if I could not, I must call on General Chapman across New River for re-enforcements. This surprised me as to his forces. He brought out two regiments, little less than 1,200; was then joined by Colonel Wharton's regiment, 400; then by McCausland's and Tompkins' regiments, 800; making 2,400 men; and two additional regiments, one from North Carolina and one from Georgia, were within a day's march of him. At the time that I dispatched Colonel Tompkins to him, in my letter of September 9, addressed to General Floyd, I assigned unanswerable reasons why I could not send a regiment of the Legion. I was reduced by measles to a force of infantry and artillery of about•1,050 efficient men. It was very hazardous to remain where I was with this force. If one-third of it were taken away I could not prevent the enemy from approaching Carnifex Ferry by the Saturday road. I would have to fall back again to Dogwood Gap, lose all I had gained by driving the enemy beyond Big Creek, lose Miller's Ferry, and all opportunity of communicating with Generals Chapman and Beckley, and all the advantages of Likens', a first-class mill, to grind meal and flour for my men; but, above all, the governing reason was that I could not defend General Floyd's rear, if I had re-enforced him with my whole force and crossed Carnifix Ferry. By his estimate he would have had but 2,700 men, and by my estimate about 3,500, to have fought what I estimated at 6,000, and he at 9,000, in his front, with from 2,500 to 3,000 in our rear to cut off all retreat, and he was in intrenchments most unskillfully traced, behind works not worthy of Chinese. I begged him, therefore, to relieve me from the order to send him one of my fragments of regiments, and appealed to him to allow me to await further events and orders and the removal of the immediate pressure of the enemy upon me. The fact was, I had been already twice fooled in going to Carnifix, and there was great danger in my falling back at all, with the probability of being ordered again to remain in camp.

But again, September 9, General Floyd addressed to me another dispatch, saying that the enemy at 5 o'clock p. m. of that day were advancing, about 4,000 strong, this side of Powell's Mountain; called upon me to hurry up Colonel Tompkins, and to send him at once 1,000 of my own men with one of my batteries. Again, September 9, in his dispatch No. 37, the enemy were advancing upon him through Webster under Rosecrans, and he ordered me to station my regiment for which he had sent at Dogwood Gap. Thus there was another perfect confusion of orders. No. 36 was received at 2.15 a. m., No. 37 at 2 p. m., September 10. (See the notes of verbal messages made by Mr. Lewis attached to dispatches 34 and 35.) I wrote to General Floyd September 10, 6.30 a. m., in answer to all these orders and dispatches, and at 10 a. m. I informed him that the enemy were advancing upon me. The same day he dispatched to me his order No. 38, in which he reprimanded my delay, and ordered me to send him 1,000 of my infantry and one battery of artillery; he also required me to reply, state the hour of receiving his order and that of starting my reply. I was then within half a mile of the Hawk's Nest, mounted, directing the advance of my van-guard against the enemy. This order was received at five minutes past 12 o'clock, and at 12.30 o'clock, by his own messenger, Mr. Carr, I returned him my answer No. 38, dated September 10, telling him the hour at which his letter was received, that it found me meeting an advance of the enemy threatening my picket at the Hawk's Nest, and that all my force of three regiments of infantry, four companies of artillery, and two companies of cavalry were under arms, to prevent, if possible, the success of an obvious attempt to turn our right flank and to pass us up the turnpike, most probably to the Saturday road, to gain Carnifix Ferry in his rear. I should therefore exercise a sound discretion in obeying his orders or not.

At 12 or 1 o'clock at night, September 10 and 11, Mr. Carr and Major Glass returned with General Floyd's dispatch No. 39, dated September 10, 8 p. m., ordering me on the receipt of it to dispatch to him all of my available force save one regiment, with which I would occupy my position, unless I deemed it expedient to fall back to a more eligible one. He informed me that the enemy had attacked him in strong force; the battle had been raging for three hours—from 4 till 7 p. m.; that he still held his position, and thought the enemy would renew the attack by daylight in the morning with perhaps increased force.

Accordingly, the next morning I started to re-enforce him, and received verbal orders, when about half way to the ferry, to turn back to Dogwood Gap. General Floyd had given up his position, without the loss of a man, after fighting successfully for three hours, and in the act of being re-enforced by nearly my whole command, and by the two regiments from North Carolina and Georgia, in all reinforcements amounting to upwards of 2,000 men.

On September 11, at 7 o'clock p. m., I addressed to General Lee a letter, giving a report of General Floyd's retreat from Carnifix without loss of life or limb, but with considerable loss of public property.

On the same day I met General Floyd, just beyond Dogwood Gap, prostrate upon the ground, by the side of the turnpike. I rode up to him in the presence of several officers and asked him for orders. He replied that he did not know what orders to give. I had other conversation with him, particularly detailed in my last-mentioned letter to General Lee.

On the 12th September General Floyd issued several unimportant orders about guards and scouts, and about nightfall I received from him an invitation to a conference to determine upon a definite line of action. The result of the consultation was a retreat to the top of Big Sewell. Some unimportant correspondence occurred up to September 16, when myself and officers were called again to General Floyd's headquarters for consultation. As early as practicable, about 5 o'clock p. m., I went, accompanied by Major Tyler, Captain Stanard, Captain Wise, and Colonel Jackson. A memorandum of that conference will be found immediately following General Floyd's dispatch No. 45, addressed to me.

On the same evening, within half an hour after I left his camp, I was informed by him that it was determined to fall back again to the most defensible point between Meadow Bluff and Lewisburg; he would put his column in motion at once, and I would hold my command in readiness to bring up the rear.

On the 18th he inquired why I had not obeyed his order to fall back. On the same day, at 10.30 o'clock a. m., I replied that I had obeyed his order to the letter; that I had held my command in readiness to bring up his rear; that I considered the almost impregnable position I then occupied as essential to protect his rear, and that neither the condition of the roads nor the health of my men would permit me to move them without great inhumanity to man and beast. In the next place, by moving back I would lose the command of Bowyer's Ferry and the old State road. I respectfully requested permission to remain where I was, as best obeying his orders. I refer the President and the Secretary of War to the report of my quartermaster, F. D. Cleary, to my letter of September 18, addressed to General Floyd, and to his of the 19th September to me, respecting wagons and transportation, and to my letter to General Floyd of September 19, 11.30 o'clock p. m., about the policy of falling back.

On September 19, 2 o'clock a. m., I notified General Floyd of the advance of the enemy upon my position. He replied by his letter from Meadow Bluff, dated September 19. I replied by my letter of September 19, 9.45 a. m. The only reply that I received from him was his letter of September 22, ordering me to send him a piece of artillery, a 10-pounder gun manufactured on the Kanawha; this was instead of re-enforcements. I answered this call for the gun on September 23d; and that is the last letter which I have been obliged to write to General Floyd.

On the 21st of September General Lee addressed me a letter from the camp at Meadow Bluff. I replied to this on the 21st, at 5 o'clock p. m. (referring to his seeming reprimand of my failure to be united with General Floyd at Meadow Bluff), that I considered my force already united with General Floyd for the most effectual co-operation; and I gave my reasons for his examining my position and determining between that and General Floyd's. He visited my camp, examined the ground, announced no conclusions upon the subject, but returned to General Floyd's camp.

On September 23 Major Tyler, under my instructions, addressed to General Lee two communications, announcing the approach of the enemy. On the same day General Lee addressed to me his letter of the 23d. On the same day I replied, announcing to him that the enemy were in strong force on top of Big Sewell. On the 24th he addressed me again. That day I advised him that the enemy were advancing upon me from Big Sewell, and at 7.30 o'clock a. m. I again addressed him in writing. On the same day he arrived at my position with a re-enforcement of four regiments. My advance guard had met that of the enemy on Monday, Tuesday, and Wednesday. By this time the enemy had received re-enforcements swelling their numbers probably to more than 6,000, and their scouts pushed close to our lines, occasioning frequent sharp skirmishes, in all of which our men and officers acquitted themselves to my entire satisfaction. Indeed, from the time that I first marched under General Floyd's orders until the moment of my recall my command was engaged, almost without intermission, in constant skirmishes, severely testing their courage, coolness, and endurance, and tending in a great degree to restrain the advance, embarrass the movements, and prevent the concentration of the enemy's forces. I am proud to say that every instance of attack and defense has only tended to increase my confidence in their efficiency.

At about 4.30 o'clock p. m. September 25 I received, while under fire on the field, the President's order to leave my command, transfer it to General Floyd, and to report at Richmond with the least delay. After a moment's reflection, at 5 o'clock I addressed to General Lee my last letter to him, received his counsel, indorsed upon my note, advising me to obey the order with the least delay, and I left the camp immediately—took time only to pack my baggage—started the next morning, and did not stop until I arrived at Richmond.

I have now made as full and detailed a report as it is possible for me to make in my present prostrated state of health. To recapitulate, then : In reply to General Floyd's report of September 12, of which he gave me no notice when he sent it to the Department, I aver that I did not fail to render him the best assistance in my power; that I defended his rear on this side of Carnifix Ferry ; that had I obeyed his order and crossed the ferry, neither man nor beast of his command or mine would have escaped capture, wounds, imprisonment, or death. I aver the fact that he did not succeed so well in the construction of his temporary breastworks as he did in my defense of his rear. I aver that his intrenchment was not worthy of any command, either in site or construction, and that his facilities for retreat were wholly neglected and inadequate; that wantonly and unnecessarily he lost a large amount of public property, and would have lost all his artillery but for the good conduct and courage of Colonel Tompkins. I aver that if he ought to have crossed that ferry and remained in those intrench-ments one hour to await the approach of a superior force of the enemy, and to fight the enemy for three hours without the loss of a single man killed, he ought to have awaited another attack the next day and the re-enforcements that were marching to his relief. He estimates the enemy's force at between eight and nine thousand, when they were not more than 6,000. Upon the close of the contest at night it was not, as he says it was, a mere question of time—it was impossible for him to discover whether it was a question of time merely—when he should be compelled to yield to the superiority of numbers. He had had plenty of time to have constructed his ferry and amply sufficient breastworks. He says, therefore, that he determined at once to recross the Gauley River and take position on the left bank, which he says he accom-plished without the loss of a gun or any accident whatever. I aver that if he took position on the left bank of the Gauley he did not hold it, and ultimately—almost immediately—he left the left bank of the Gauley totally unprotected. Whether he lost a gun or not is yet to be ascertained. It is certainly credibly reported that he did lose one caisson, 30,000 rounds of ammunition, a large amount of camp equipage and clothing, as well as supplies and provisions, his own personal baggage and arms in part, and ninety-odd fat cattle, and that some of his pickets were cut off.

He says it was strange that his loss was only 20 men wounded. It is stranger still that he should have retreated with so few men wounded and none killed. His men behaved with decided gallantry, and I have no doubt would proudly have stood the brunt of another day's contest. If he had crippled the enemy to such an extent that they were in no condition to molest him in his passage across the river, he might well have stood the brunt of their crippled forces in one more bout. Nothing but extreme ignorance of the forces of the enemy and of the topography of the country could have engendered the belief that he could have beaten the enemy and marched directly to the valley of the Kanawha if he had been re-enforced before the close of the second day's conflict by General Wise's column and the North Carolina and Georgia regiments. General Wise's column and the North Carolina and Georgia regiments were moving up under his orders. Why did he not await a second day's conflict with the enemy? The necessity for his recrossing the river is not made plain, but contradicted by his own statement. He says he is confident that if he could have commanded the services of 5,000 men instead of 1,800, he could have opened the road directly into the valley of the Kanawha. Let me say that General Floyd is more efficient in commanding a force of 1,800 than one of 5,000 men. According to my estimate he had more than 1,800; he had 2,400 men; and as to opening the road directly into the valley of the Kanawha, that road is open already in a dozen places to any force, great or small. My cavalry, 240 strong only, had opened a road into the valley of the Kanawha within 12 miles of Charleston, killing as many of the enemy as General Floyd's whole force did at Carnifix, and this on the 12th September, the very date of General Floyd's report. At any time that General Floyd will attempt to enter the Kanawha Valley in the way that he proposed—by Twenty Mile, Bell's, and Hughes' Creeks, or by Gauley Bridge—General Rosecrans, if permitted, will open the road for him to enter it. He says:

This close correspondence shows distinctly enough the urgent necessity of so shaping the command in the valley of the Kanawha as to insure in the future that unity of action upon which alone can rest any hope of success in military matters.

I aver that the hope of success in military matters ought not to rest on the command of General Floyd. I am not content that my command shall be transferred to him. I will confidently abide by my correspondence with him to show who ought to be the commander. If called upon to give advice to my superiors, I would say General Floyd ought to be confined in his command to the Kentucky border, under some able superior, and that the command of the Department of the Kanawha ought to be given to Col. C. Q. Tompkins, who is a soldier by education and natural qualifications, a gentleman, and a man who has an important stake in the country where he commands. He ought to be promoted to that command, with the rank of brigadier-general; and my Legion ought to be transferred to my immediate command somewhere in the East, leaving in the West such companies as prefer to remain there, and allowing me the privilege to supply their place.

Whenever General Floyd shall think proper to take any other or further notice of these transactions, I will, if I think proper, take further notice of him. It is not so certain that the reasons which have induced him to take the course which he has will be correctly understood either by the President or by the Secretary of War. General Floyd selected no strong point in the mountain passes. On the contrary, he fell back from the mountains, dug a ditch in a meadow marsh covered by every hill around, and the breastworks of which the first rain covered over with a swelling flood. He cannot fight a superior force in any intrenchments that he has selected or constructed. General Lee is now in command, and his counsel had better be taken as to what policy ought to be pursued. I only ask that, if these explanations are not sufficient, I may have the opportunities of defense. If they are sufficient, I ask that my command may be transferred back to me, and that we be separated from the command of General Floyd. I refer to the accompanying charts of my positions at Camp Defiance and at Dogwood and to the map elucidating my explanations.* I beg that, besides favoring this with your own attention, you will do me the kindness to bring this report and accompanying papers without delay to the immediate notice of the President.

I have the honor to be, very respectfully, your obedient servant,

HENRY A. WISE,
Brigadier-General.

Hon. J. P. BENJAMIN, *Secretary of War.*

SEPTEMBER 10, 1861.—Skirmish near Lewinsville, Va.

REPORTS.

No. 1.—Capt. David Ireland, Seventy-ninth New York Infantry.
No. 2.—Capt. Elisha C. Hibbard, Fifth Wisconsin Infantry.

No. 1.

Report of Capt. David Ireland, Seventy-ninth New York Infantry.

HDQRS. SEVENTY-NINTH REGIMENT NEW YORK,
Camp Advance, Va., September 10, 1861.

SIR: In accordance with the following instructions from the brigadier-general commanding,

You will assume command of the expedition which leaves your present camp at 1.30 a. m. to-morrow morning. It is the wish of the brigadier-general commanding this post that you place your men in ambush at Rush's (at or near where the road from Langley to Falls Church crosses Pirnett Run) a little before daylight to-morrow, to co-operate with another column which will cross the road between you and Lewinsville. You will place 75 men in good position as close to the road as possible, leaving 75 men in reserve a short distance in the rear. Your duty then will be to disable any bodies of the enemy's cavalry or artillery which may pass that way. If artillery, let the fire of your men be destructive to the horses and afterwards upon the men who man the pieces. Should you be attacked by superior numbers you will fall back, making as obstinate resistance as possible. Do not leave your cover in the woods under any circumstances. You will hold your position, if possible, for one hour after daylight. Guides will be furnished you. See that the men of your command have no caps upon their guns until you get into position. If you find scouts or pickets of the enemy, either capture them or destroy them by a bayonet charge. Be careful to create no alarm by firing before you are in position. Should you hear firing upon your right, you will hurry forward and occupy your position as soon as you can.

I have the honor to report that, with a detail of 160 officers, non-commissioned officers, and privates, ordered for that purpose by Colonel Stevens, commanding the regiment, and placed under my command, I

---

* Not found.

left camp at 1 o'clock a. m., and proceeded to the place designated through various by-paths, without disturbing the enemy's pickets, and arrived there at daybreak. The command was divided into two wings, to guard the approach of the enemy. Soon after the men had been posted firing was heard in the direction of Lewinsville, and a body of cavalry came from the direction of Falls Church, and when endeavoring to pass where we were posted our men were ordered to fire, which they did, causing the enemy to retreat. Previous to their retreating, which was caused by a well-directed fire from the left wing, under command of Capt. John Falconer, the enemy fired on us, killing one private, John Dowee, of the eighth company. At the same time the right wing captured a prisoner who was wounded, and who had on, when captured, a major's shoulder-straps. His name is Hobbs, of Colonel Stuart's regiment of cavalry.

Having successfully accomplished the mission we were ordered on, viz, preventing the pickets at Lewinsville being re-enforced and the enemy having retreated and the alarm being sounded in all the enemy's camps in the neighborhood, we left our position and arrived in camp by way of Langley at 10.30 o'clock a. m. The lowest estimate of the enemy's loss is four killed, two wounded, and one prisoner. Much of the success of this expedition is owing to the exertions of our guide, Mr. Sage. Lieut. Alexander Graham, of the eighth company, was conspicuous for his coolness and bravery during the engagement. Mr. Hazard Stevens (volunteer) distinguished himself in this expedition by his usefulness and bravery during the engagement, and with these remarks I beg to submit the above report.

I have the honor to be, sir, very respectfully, your obedient servant,

DAVID IRELAND,
Captain, Seventy-ninth Regiment.

Col. ISAAC I. STEVENS,
Acting Assistant Adjutant-General Smith's Brigade.

No. 2.

Report of Capt. Elisha C. Hibbard, Fifth Wisconsin Infantry.

CAMP ADVANCE, *September* 10, 1861.

SIR : The detachment from the Fifth Regiment Wisconsin Volunteers, consisting of Company B, Lieutenant Oliver commanding, Company C, Captain Berens, and Company G, Captain Bugh, ordered to proceed to Lewinsville, and there capture or break up a body of the enemy known to be there, left camp precisely at 11 o'clock, under the guidance of Captain Mott. After having passed our advanced picket this side of Langley, I ordered a sergeant and 8 men to advance 100 yards ahead, divided each side of the road. Taking the road to the right of Langley, we pressed forward in perfect silence and order through Commodore Jones' property into a field beyond, where we lay until daylight. About 4.30 o'clock in the morning we left the field, passing through an open plot of ground into a corn field which lay just in rear of Lewinsville. The scout was sent forward, and on his return reported a portion of the enemy, consisting of cavalry, picketed there.

I took 50 men of Company B, and passing across the road running south, tried to gain the west road; but while so doing the alarm was given by two of the pickets. I immediately ordered the company back into the road, and ordered them to fire and charge. Company C, Captain

Berens, took position across the road in rear of Company B; Company G, Captain Bugh, having deployed by the flank behind the fence near our old position. Company B fired and charged down the road, wound-ing, it is supposed, 2 men, killing 1 horse, capturing 2, and 1 of the rebels.´ We divided and pursued a portion towards Falls Church and the wounded towards Vienna, but they escaped through a corn field and wood, and we fell back on our reserve.

Having heard firing of musketry on the Falls Church road, forming by platoon in close column, with the prisoner and horses, we advanced towards Langley, and soon fell in with Lieutenant Hasbrouck's gun and a detachment of infantry, who brought up our rear. We reached camp at 8 o'clock, having marched all of 20 miles. I should judge there were 10 cavalry in the squad. Had it not been for the splendid management of Captain Mott, assisted by his own men and the scout, the whole expedition would have proved a failure. Captains Berens and Bugh, and Lieutenants Oliver, Ross, and Strong, together with the men, conducted themselves with coolness and judgment.

Respectfully, your obedient servant,

E. C. HIBBARD,
Captain Company B, Commanding Detachment.

Brigadier-General SMITH, *Commanding.*

SEPTEMBER 11, 1861.—Union reconnaissance from Chain Bridge to Lew-insville, Va., and action at that place.

REPORTS, ETC.

No. 1.—Maj. Gen. George B. McClellan, U. S. Army, with letter restoring the colors of the Seventy-ninth New York Infantry.
No. 2.—Brig. Gen. William F. Smith, U. S. Army.
No. 3.—Col. Isaac I. Stevens, Seventy-ninth New York Infantry, commanding ex-pedition.
No. 4.—Lieut. Orlando M. Poe, U. S. Topographical Engineers.
No. 5.—Col. Solomon Meredith, Nineteenth Indiana Infantry.
No. 6.—Lieut. Col. Alexander Shaler, Sixty-fifth New York Infantry.
No. 7.—Capt. David Ireland, Seventy-ninth New York Infantry.
No. 8.—Lieut. Samuel R. Elliott, Seventy-ninth New York Infantry.
No. 9.—Lieut. Col. George J. Stannard, Second Vermont Infantry.
No. 10.—Col. Breed N. Hyde, Third Vermont Infantry.
No. 11.—Capt. Thaddeus P. Mott, Third New York Battery.
No. 12.—Capt. Charles Griffin, Fifth U. S. Artillery.
No. 13.—Lieut. William McLean, Fifth U. S. Cavalry.
No. 14.—William Borrowe, Acting Aide-de-Camp.
No. 15.—General Joseph E. Johnston, C. S. Army, with congratulatory orders.
No. 16.—Brig. Gen. James Longstreet, C. S. Army.
No. 17.—Col. James E. B. Stuart, First Virginia Cavalry.

No. 1.

Report of Maj. Gen. George B. McClellan, U. S. Army, with letter restor-ing the colors of the Seventy-ninth New York Infantry.

SMITH'S HEADQUARTERS, NEAR CHAIN BRIDGE,
September 11, 1861.

General Smith made reconnaissance with 2,000 men to Lewinsville; remained several hours, and completed examination of the ground.

When work was completed and the command had started back, the enemy opened fire with shell, killing 2 and wounding 3. Griffin's battery silenced the enemy's battery. Our men came back in perfect order and excellent spirits. They behaved most admirably under fire. We shall have no more Bull Run affairs.

GEO. B. McCLELLAN,
Major-General, Commanding.

General WINFIELD SCOTT.

—

HEADQUARTERS ARMY OF THE POTOMAC,
Washington, September 14, 1861.

General WILLIAM F. SMITH, *Chain Bridge:*

The colors of the New York Seventy-ninth will be sent to you tomorrow. Please return them to the regiment, with the remark that they have shown by their conduct in the reconnaissance of the 11th instant that they are worthy to carry the banner into action, and the commanding general is confident they will always in future sustain and confirm him in the favorable opinion he has formed of them.*

GEO. B. McCLELLAN,
Major-General, Commanding.

———

No. 2.

Report of Brig. Gen. William F. Smith, U. S. Army.

HEADQUARTERS CAMP ADVANCE, *September* 13, 1861.

CAPTAIN: I inclose herewith the report of Colonel Stevens, commanding the escort of Lieutenant Poe (also the latter's report and sketch), during the reconnaissance of the 11th instant. I heard the firing from camp, and proceeded to take command, after leaving verbal instructions for such troops as could be spared from here to follow me. On the way out I met Captain Mott, with a section of his battery, practicing his horses on the road, and gave him an order to follow, which he and his men obeyed with alacrity. On arriving on the field I found the command retreating in good order, the men in good spirits, and professing themselves ready for anything. After I arrived Captain Griffin had two sections of his battery in use for a little while, but his fire was not replied to. Captain Mott used his section in two positions for a few rounds. The dead and wounded were all brought in, but a lieutenant and 2 men of the Nineteenth Indiana had wandered from their proper places and were captured.

A man who has come in through the lines informs me that he heard the Confederate troops say they lost 4 men killed and several horses. I give the report for what it is worth. I do not doubt but that strong forces had been brought from Flint Hill and Falls Church, and that a hope existed of causing our troops to attack. A fair opportunity was given them to attack us even while retreating, which was done without hurry and with great deliberation, but their artillery firing was stopped, and only glimpses were caught of their cavalry and infantry, and no disposition was evinced to come within range of our guns.

---

* See Colburn to A. Porter, August 14, 1861, in "Correspondence, etc.," *post.*

The infantry of our command bore the artillery fire of the enemy without a chance to reply, and but three or four muskets were fired from our side.

Colonel Stevens' report will show you that great confidence may be placed in the troops who were with him, and that neither my presence nor that of the re-enforcements I ordered were necessary to bring to a successful termination the objects of the expedition.

Very respectfully, your obedient servant,

WM. F. SMITH,
Brigadier-General.

Capt. A. V. COLBURN, *Asst. Adjt. Gen., Washington.*

No. 3.

Report of Col. Isaac I. Stevens, Seventy-ninth New York Infantry, commanding expedition.

CAMP ADVANCE, VA., *September* 13, 1861.

SIR: In command of a force consisting of the Seventy-ninth Regiment New York State Militia; four companies of the First Regiment U. S. Chasseurs, Lieutenant-Colonel Shaler commanding; two companies of the Third Vermont Regiment, Lieutenant-Colonel Stannard; five companies of the Nineteenth Indiana, Colonel Meredith; four guns of Griffin's battery, Captain Griffin; a detachment of 50 regular cavalry, Lieutenant McLean commanding, and one of 40 volunteer cavalry, Captain Robinson commanding, constituting an aggregate force of about 1,800 men, I started from your headquarters on the 11th instant, about 7.30 o'clock, with instructions to cover and protect a reconnaissance of the village of Lewinsville and vicinity, to determine all the facts that would be required for its permanent occupation and defense. In execution of this duty I proceeded quietly and steadily with my command, throwing out skirmishers in advance, and exploring the ground on both flanks to the distance of a mile, entered the village about 10 o'clock, and examined in person the several approaches to it. At Langley I sent forward twenty of Robinson's cavalry, under command of Lieutenant [Seal] on the road to Leesburg, and to proceed to Lewinsville by a cross-road. This duty he performed, and reported that, judging from the appearance of the road, a force of from 100 to 200 of the enemy's cavalry had occupied it on the preceding night.

There are five roads which concentrate at Lewinsville—one on which we approached, a second coming from the north and connecting the pike from camp to Leesburg with the village, a third coming from Falls Church on the south, a fourth coming from Vienna on the west, the four making the cross-roads of the village, and a fifth road about parallel to and southward of the Vienna road, known as the new road to Vienna, and having its junction with the road to Falls Church about 800 yards from the village. I caused to be placed in position to cover the reconnaissance the guns of Griffin's battery, with proper infantry supports and with skirmishers well thrown out on all the assailable points. One gun was placed on a commanding point west of the road leading to the Leesburg pike on the north, supported by the Nineteenth Indiana, disposed as skirmishers and in reserve. A second gun was placed on a commanding point on the road leading directly from the cross-roads of the village to Vienna, and controlling also the approaches on the new road to Vienna and the intervening country. A third gun was placed on the road leading directly to Falls Church, and the fourth was held in reserve. The approaches on the two roads from Vienna and the road from Falls Church were covered by skirmishers from the Vermont Third and one company of the Indiana Nineteenth, besides which a heavy body of skirmishers was placed in the wood between the road to Falls Church and the New road to Vienna, as well as in the road eastward to our rear and northward to the road running north. In fact, the whole position for more than a mile was thoroughly enveloped and watched by skirmishers, who were well thrown out to the number of some 500 men. The two companies of the Vermont Second were specially held as a central reserve to Griffin's battery. The Chasseurs and Highlanders were halted about one-third of a mile from the village, and a heavy body of the latter were thrown out as skirmishers to cover the country towards Falls Church, and they were actually extended to the road leading directly from Lewinsville to Falls Church, and made a perfect connection with the pickets in that quarter.

These dispositions were early made, and the reconnaissance of the position went on entirely uninterrupted. I was most vigilant in seeing that the approaches were well watched, and was ably seconded by all the commanders. Single individuals and small bodies of men were seen to be observing us at safe distances. A picket of 50 cavalry was driven in by Lieutenant McLean, of the regular cavalry. All the information possible was gained as to the position of the enemy. The reconnaissance was completed about 2.15 o'clock. The skirmishers were now recalled, and the order was given to form the•column for a return to Camp Advance.

It will be well here to mention that early notice was given to each body of skirmishers, through a commissioned officer, that they must be ready to obey promptly the recall which would be given when the reconnaissance was finished. The skirmishers, however, thrown out from the regiment of Highlanders towards Falls Church were not recalled till time enough had elapsed to collect and bring in the skirmishers covering the approach on the other roads. They were considered by me to occupy the critical point of the position, and I had given great attention to impress vigilance upon the skirmishers in that quarter. Considerable delay occurred in collecting the skirmishers thrown forward in the new road to Vienna and advanced into the wood between that road and the road to Falls Church. Indeed, skirmishers from the Indiana regiment, seeing the approach of the enemy's infantry, allowed themselves to be drawn forward to fire at them, and forgot their office of sending back information of the approach of the enemy. Three men of this body—Lieutenant Hancock, Sergeant Goodwin, and Private Hubbell—were surrounded and cut off.

Some forty minutes elapsed between sounding the recall and getting together those skirmishers. In the mean time some progress was made in withdrawing the skirmishers covering the approach through the open glade extending from the Falls Church road to our rear, when the enemy's skirmishers crept up, fired upon the pickets of the Highlanders, still near Gilbert's house, planted a battery, and opened its fire upon our rear. Simultaneously another body of their skirmishers advanced from the new Vienna road through the woods, which we had watched all day, and fired upon our withdrawing skirmishers in the village. At this juncture all the commands were formed, nearly all the skirmishers had fallen in, and each command was about taking its place in column.

Immediately on the opening of the enemy's fire from the position occupied by the skirmishers of the Highlanders, I ordered Captain Griffin to advance a section of his battery as soon as possible, place it in position, and open fire upon the enemy. I sent Lieutenant Poe, of the Topographical Engineers, and Lieutenant Borrowe, of Griffin's battery, to make the necessary arrangements to protect the rear, and went in person to the point immediately threatened by the enemy and upon which he had opened his artillery. Our troops were in fine spirits, and obeyed their orders with alacrity. Meanwhile the whole command was withdrawn from the village in perfect order, although exposed to a heavy fire of artillery, and placed in suitable position either to continue the march to Camp Advance, which the firing of the enemy had interrupted, or to advance upon and attack him in the event of his offering battle, or to receive in good order his attack, according to circumstances. Griffin's battery fired with great spirit and rapidity, and soon both silenced the enemy's guns and drove his infantry from their position. Moving to the head of the column, I had indicated new positions for the two sections of Griffin's battery—one at Cook's place, the other on the opposite side of the road—and had given the necessary orders, the position being an admirable battle-field for the command, when you arrived upon the ground and assumed command. I now assumed command of the Seventy-ninth Regiment, which had up to this time been acting with the Chasseurs, the whole under the command of Lieutenant-Colonel Shaler, and placed it as a support to the battery of Captain Mott, just stationed at Cook's place. On Mott's change of position to the hill on the other side of the road, I stationed the Highlanders in the road, and remained there till it was withdrawn, when the Highlanders became the rear guard of the column. I was then directed by you to cross into the fields to the right, and make for a cross-road which led from Falls Church to Langley, and in which it was feared the enemy might advance to annoy our flank. This duty was executed by the Highlanders in most excellent spirit and most of the time on the double-quick. No enemy was found in the cross-road. The Seventy-ninth was then marched to your headquarters and thence conducted to the camp with the Chasseurs, both under the command of Lieutenant-Colonel Shaler, as they were marched out.

The reports from commanders accompanying this will best explain the details of the affair. The steadiness and good conduct of the troops under fire and throughout the day were most gratifying, and is an earnest of the good service their country has to expect from them. Every order was obeyed with alacrity. There was no flinching from fire. I felt throughout the day the most perfect confidence in the troops, and believe they could have been easily handled against a greatly superior force of the enemy. The arrangements of the pickets and skirmishers left nothing to be desired in the way of covering the reconnaissance. I myself served as an officer of Engineers in the second conquest of Mexico, and I present the operations of the 11th as a beautiful specimen of a reconnaissance in presence of the enemy. The operations of Lieutenant Poe showed me that the Engineers had lost none of their ancient skill. Griffin was most gallant and prompt in the conduct of his battery. I examined with him and Lieutenant Poe the entire position of Lewinsville. It has great natural advantages, is easily defensible, will require but a small amount of ordnance, and should be permanently occupied without delay.

In returning my special thanks to commanders, officers, and men I will be pardoned if I present my particular obligations to Captain

Griffin and Lieutenant Borrowe. The latter acted as my aide throughout the day, made the reconnaissance of the village before I advanced the troops, and placed in position the skirmishers on the south and west of the village. I call particular attention to his report, herewith submitted. Lieutenant-Colonel Cameron and Lieutenant Poe, of the Engineers, afforded me most valuable assistance.

Appended to this are the reports by commanders, &c.,

I am, sir, very respectfully, your most obedient servant,

ISAAC I. STEVENS,
Colonel, Commanding.

Brigadier-General SMITH,
Commanding Brigade, Camp Advance.

No. 4.

Report of Lieut. Orlando M. Poe, U. S. Topographical Engineers.

CAMP ADVANCE, September 12, 1861.

SIR: By your direction I was, a few minutes after the enemy commenced firing upon our flank, placed in command of the rear guard of the column led by yourself. I formed the battalion of the Nineteenth Indiana Regiment in rear of the section of 12-pounders, and immediately changed that disposition by allowing it to pass them, my object being to use the guns against the cavalry of the enemy should they attempt to charge us. No such attempt was made. After passing the section of rifled guns the 12-pounders were put in position, but not by myself, as, General Smith having arrived upon the ground, I was detached for duty under his immediate direction.

The conduct of our troops was good, there appearing no disposition to fall into confusion.

Respectfully, your obedient servant,

ORLANDO M. POE,
First Lieutenant, Topographical Engineers.

Col. ISAAC I. STEVENS.

No. 5.

Report of Col. Solomon Meredith, Nineteenth Indiana Infantry.

HEADQUARTERS NINETEENTH INDIANA VOLUNTEERS,
Camp Advance, September 12, 1861.

SIR: In pursuance of your order, received this morning, I herewith submit a report of the part taken by my command in the reconnoitering expedition of the 11th:

Five companies of my command, viz, Company A, Captain May; Company D, Captain Jacobs; Company F, Captain Lindley; Company H, Captain Kelly, and Company I, Lieutenant Baird, formed a part of the expedition which left this place at 7.30 a. m. Nothing special occurred to my command till we reached Lewinsville, 5 miles from camp.

One company (Captain Kelly's) was then left in reserve, while three companies under my immediate charge were sent on the road running north towards the Leadingsburg [Leesburg] turnpike to support a section of Griffin's battery. I here threw out two parties of skirmishers—one a half mile west, one a half mile north—and placed the remainder under cover. Lieutenant-Colonel Cameron was ordered to take Company I down the road leading to Falls Church, with instructions to deploy them as skirmishers in a piece of pine wood commanding the road on the right. When the survey was finished and the recall sounded I called in the skirmishers first detached and moved them with the piece we were protecting down to the cross-roads. When we halted temporarily, Lieutenant-Colonel Cameron, discovering that Company I did not return when recalled, sent a mounted sergeant after them, and as he did not return for some time, Lieutenant-Colonel Cameron followed himself and met them coming out of the woods. At this juncture a heavy body of infantry opened fire upon them.

I may here mention that their delay was thus occasioned: Lieutenant Hancock and four men had left the line of skirmishers, and advanced nearly a half mile to get a shot at two larger bodies of infantry who were discovered deploying down the side of a large hill covered with timber. After a sharp firing, by which a number of the enemy were killed, one of the party, Private Hiram Antibus, though hotly pursued and continually fired on for a long distance, escaped with loss of shoes and cartridge-box, but bringing off his gun, while Lieutenant Hancock, Sergt. S. M. Goodwin, and Private Oliver Hubbell were shot down, being either killed or seriously wounded, nor have they since been heard of.

Having formed my command in line, while waiting orders we suffered from a heavy fire proceeding from a strip of timber and adjoining corn field, killing Private W. H. H. Wood, of Company D, by a shot through the head, and seriously, if not mortally, wounding Private Asbury Inlow, of the same company, by a ball through the left cheek, which passed out behind the ear. In resting I was ordered to cover the rear and protect a portion of Griffin's battery, Lieutenant McLean, with a company of dragoons, following me. Thus we proceeded for half a mile towards camp under a terrific shower of shell, causing to my own command, however, no casualty, while other regiments were less fortunate. The position of the enemy's guns being ascertained, our guns were placed in battery, and we with the rest of the infantry were formed in line, my command still covering the rear. Here a spent ball from an enemy concealed in the woods wounded in the foot Private John Hamilton, of Company D. After a considerable interval, our batteries having silenced those of the enemy and recalled his cavalry, we quietly returned to camp, still covering the rear, till we met re-enforcements.

My men were under fire about two hours, and during the whole of that time behaved with the utmost coolness and gallantry, obeying all orders promptly and with but little confusion, their chief anxiety seeming to be that the enemy's infantry might advance from their cover or that they might have a chance to try their hand on Stuart's cavalry. Though discrimination seems almost invidious when all behaved well, yet I cannot close my report without adverting to the conduct of Lieutenant-Colonel Cameron, whose courage and coolness were conspicuous throughout the whole of this affair. While shells were bursting around us he rode the lines, giving orders with an equanimity which was not even disturbed when one of them passed so close that his horse, sinking under him, with difficulty recovered the shock.

Very respectfully, your obedient servant,

S. MEREDITH,
Colonel Nineteenth Regiment Indiana Volunteers.

Colonel STEVENS,
Commanding Reconnoitering Expedition.

No. 6.

Report of Lieut. Col. Alexander Shaler, Sixty-fifth New York Infantry.

HEADQUARTERS FIRST REGIMENT U. S. CHASSEURS,
Camp Advance, September 11, 1861—8 p. m.

SIR: I have the honor to report that, in compliance with special orders from headquarters, I reported myself at your quarters with four companies of the First Regiment U. S. Chasseurs at 5.45 o'clock this morning, and was placed by you in command of a reserve composed of the Seventy-ninth Regiment and the four companies of the Chasseur Regiment. Shortly afterwards this reserve was reported to General Smith at his headquarters, and assigned a position in the column to be moved towards Lewinsville. On arriving there we took up a position and threw out pickets under your direction. At 2 o'clock p. m., on the recall being sounded, our pickets returned and were formed in line. The battalion of Chasseurs and the Seventy-ninth were countermarched by the right flank on the ground they respectively occupied, which brought the Seventy-ninth in rear. Line of battle was formed faced to the front, and while in this position, waiting for the column then in rear to move forward to the right, a deadly fire of shell from the enemy's guns was opened upon us, the first bursting in the road near the right of the line. This surprise created as a matter of course considerable excitement, but the cover furnished by the fence on the road-side and the coolly-exercised authority of the company officers effectually prevented the men from becoming seriously alarmed, notwithstanding a rapid fire was continued for half an hour before Griffin's battery could be got in position to bear on the enemy.

By your command the detachment was moved forward until met by General Smith with two howitzers of heavy caliber. They at once took position on a prominence on the left of the road, and by your command the Seventy-ninth was detailed to protect them, while the battalion of Chasseurs was ordered to advance and protect a section of Griffin's battery, which had taken position a little in advance and on the right of the road. From this the battalion was ordered farther down the road to protect another section, and again by General Smith's command moved on to the rear of a section stationed at Langley's Tavern. The guns of the enemy having been silenced, we were directed to proceed homeward, which we did, as along the whole route, in regular order, right in front. We were joined at the headquarters of General Smith by the Seventy-ninth, and returned to quarters about 5.30 p. m. without the loss of a single man.

The conduct of the officers and men of the Seventy-ninth while under my command was in the highest degree praiseworthy. They gave undoubted evidence of their bravery and resoluteness. Great credit is also due to the young and inexperienced officers and soldiers of the Chasseur Battalion. Considering that this was the first fire to which they were ever exposed, their conduct was surprisingly cool and deliberate. I commend them, therefore, to your favorable notice, in connection with the noble Highlanders.

With high regard, &c., I have the honor to subscribe myself, your very obedient servant,

ALEXANDER SHALER,
Lieutenant-Colonel First Regiment U. S. Chasseurs.

Colonel STEVENS,
Commanding Detachment on Special Service.

No. 7.

Report of Capt. David Ireland, Seventy-ninth New York Infantry.

HDQRS. SEVENTY-NINTH REGIMENT N. Y. S. M.,
Camp Advance, September 12, 1861.

SIR: I have the honor to submit the following report of the operations of the Seventy-ninth Regiment Highlanders whilst forming a portion of the reserve under your command in the expedition to Lewinsville and vicinity:

I joined the regiment about a mile beyond Langley, and immediately assumed command. At the same time two companies were posted as skirmishers, the sixth, under command of Lieutenant McNie, and the tenth, under Lieutenant Elliott. This latter was posted on the road to Falls Church communicating with the road to Lewinsville, and the left resting at Gilbert's house. The sixth company was thrown out in advance. After remaining in that position until the object of the expedition was evidently accomplished, the recall was sounded. When the skirmishers were retiring from Gilbert's house they were fired upon by the enemy's skirmishers, who had crept up as our men retired, also by a battery of artillery that was posted on the right of Gilbert's house, and which could not have been more than fifteen yards from them at the time they opened fire, but which caused no damage to our men at that time. The skirmishers then took position in line. The enemy's cannonading at this time was very severe, both of shot and shell, wounding 3 of our men, viz: James Van Riper, first company, in the knee; James Elliott, second company, in the ribs; and John Colgan, sixth company, in the foot. The column was then ordered forward, the Highlanders covering the retreat, which they did in firm order, the men being cool and behaving bravely. We were halted several times to support batteries in position, and when drawn up in line of battle in the rear of Captain Cook's house to support Mott's battery, Colonel Stevens assumed command, General Smith taking command of the column.

The conduct of the officers and men on this occasion was all that could be desired. They were cool and collected, behaving as well as if on parade, and more like veteran troops than volunteers. Where all did so well it would be wrong to individualize.

I herewith inclose the report to me of Lieutenant Elliott, in command of the skirmishers.

I have the honor to remain, sir, respectfully, your obedient servant,
DAVID IRELAND,
Captain, Commanding Seventy-ninth Regiment N. Y. S. M.

Lieutenant-Colonel SHALER,
Commanding Reserve, Expedition to Lewinsville.

No. 8.

Report of Lieut. Samuel R. Elliott, Seventy-ninth New York Infantry.

CAMP ADVANCE, LEFT WING SEVENTY-NINTH REGIMENT,
September 12, 1861.

Soon after coming to a halt I received orders to post a picket on the left flank from Gilbert's house, right and left, extending the whole length of the column, in order to give warning of any approach in that direction. Reserving six of the first platoon as a reserve to be stationed at the house, I proceeded to post the remainder. The right extended to the cavalry picket on the Falls Church road, and the left extended considerably beyond the rear of the column. The men, whenever practicable, were placed under cover, and Lieutenant Lusk and myself kept moving along the line to see that they were on the alert. Up to the time when they sounded the recall nothing occurred to attract our attention, although the people of the house told us that the enemy's cavalry picket had left their gate just as our column appeared beyond the corn field.

Just as the bugle was sounding an officer rode up and ordered me to move the picket parallel with the column at the same distance out and preserving the same intervals, so as to protect the flank from surprise. I immediately started for the guide to aid me in carrying out the order, but before I could find him another order came to recall the picket as soon as possible. Lieutenant Lusk started to call in the picket, and in his over-eagerness attempted to call in both platoons, which caused him to be late with his own wing.

As soon as the men stationed by the Falls Church road began to come in, I observed a number of men without uniforms emerge from the wood at the side of that road and creep on their hands and knees along the fence to the gate where the cavalry had been stationed; they then trailed into the wood on the right of Gilbert's house. Forming the men as quickly as I could, I made a signal for the left wing, under Lieutenant Lusk, to retreat through the corn field, as they were cutting us off, and started with what remained of my command down the lane to rejoin our regiment, our pace being somewhat accelerated by the sight of some men unlimbering, as I thought, a gun in a small spot of rising ground behind the corn field and somewhat to the rear of the house. We had not moved fifty paces from the house when a volley of musketry was directed obliquely at us from the left, and at almost the same instant the gun opened fire on the right. Looking back, I saw Lieutenant Lusk, who had not understood my signal, returning with the last of his men into the very yard where the enemy's skirmishers were. By this time nothing would have been easier than to have taken them prisoners, instead of which the skirmishers, apparently thinking themselves surprised, in turn fired at them and retreated by the side of the house. Lieutenant Lusk, with considerable adroitness, leaped the fence, followed by his two sergeants, and retreated under cover of the corn field in safety to his regiment. The men throughout behaved admirably; even after it became certain that those crouching forms were the enemy's advance they showed less trepidation than perhaps I might have wished for the sake of celerity.

Very respectfully,

SAML. R. ELLIOTT,
Lieutenant, Company K.

Captain IRELAND, *Commanding Highlanders.*

No. 9.

Report of Lieut. Col. George J. Stannard, Second Vermont Infantry.

CAMP ADVANCE, VA., NEAR CHAIN BRIDGE,
September 12, 1861.

SIR : On the 11th instant I went to Lewinsville, agreeably to orders received the evening previous, with Companies A and F, of the Second

Vermont Regiment. The position assigned us was to act as guard or reserve to protect the artillery, which they did well. The command obeyed all orders promptly, and kept the ranks closed during the march on the way back to camp while under the rake of the fire of the enemy. While at a halt, in range of the enemy's fire, a shell burst near them and tore the clothes of several but wounded none. They remained cool, showing no desire to leave the position until proper orders were received. As for myself, I have only to say that I was at or near my command during the whole time to receive and communicate orders and see that they were properly executed, and aimed to do my duty.

Respectfully, yours,

GEO. J. STANNARD,
Lieutenant-Colonel Second Vermont Regiment.

Colonel STEVENS.

No. 10.

Report of Col. Breed N. Hyde, Third Vermont Infantry.

CAMP ADVANCE, CHAIN BRIDGE, VA.,
Headquarters Third Regiment V. V., September 12, 1861.

COLONEL: I have the honor to report that while your command, of which my regiment formed a part, was advancing to Lewinsville yesterday I threw out several companies as skirmishers and in advance of the column on the right and left. The skirmishers on the left, about three-fourths of a mile from Lewinsville, discovered several mounted men, evidently the enemy's pickets, who fled precipitately at their approach. At a point 1½ miles beyond Lewinsville they met the enemy's infantry pickets and drove them in after a few moments' skirmish, in which 1 of our men was slightly wounded. In the afternoon, having received your order to march back to camp, my battalion was put in motion. The enemy having placed a battery commanding the road and nearly enfilading it, we were soon in the line of its fire. We received no serious damage till my left had arrived at the point most exposed, when a shell exploded nearly in the center of Company C, Captain Corbin's, killing and wounding several men, a list of whom is given below.*

It is with much pride that I refer to the steady, soldier-like bearing of my regiment under their first fire. I beg leave to speak of the good behavior of the Seventy-ninth Regiment New York Highlanders, immediately preceding my own. In passing up and down the regiments I saw nothing but good order, steadiness, and even cheerfulness under the trying fire of the enemy.

Respectfully submitted.

B. N. HYDE,
Colonel Third Regiment V. V.

Col. ISAAC I. STEVENS,
Commanding Expedition.

---

* The list shows 1 killed and 8 wounded.

No. 11.

Report of Capt. Thaddeus P. Mott, Third New York Battery.

SEPTEMBER 12, 1861.

SIR: In pursuance to your orders I proceeded to the scene of action yesterday (September 11) near Lewinsville, taking up my position on a wooded hill on the right side of the road, about 1 mile from Lewinsville, controlling that place and the surrounding country. I immediately directed fire towards the smoke from the enemy's battery and in the direction of Captain Griffin's shells. As soon as their battery ceased firing I ordered the shells to be thrown into a clump of woods, believing that I saw the enemy in large numbers therein. The order was well carried out by Lieut. William Stuart, commanding the section, the shells landing directly in the wood, which immediately caused its evacuation by, I should think, some 700 cavalry, a number of riderless horses, and some infantry.

Receiving orders to change my position, I used the privilege given me by yourself to exercise my discretion in case I could do them any material damage. I therefore kept up the fire on them, after their leaving the wood across a corn field and into another wood, I should think much to their sorrow. I then moved by your orders to the position before occupied by Captain Griffin, with orders not to unlimber unless for some good object; but seeing a number of them, say from 400 to 500, on their retreat to the new-cut road, I could not resist the temptation of having a farewell blow at them. I think the gunners did a great deal of execution, as I could see with my glass great confusion created amongst them, large breaches being made in their ranks, especially by the 32-pounder shrapnel, the paper fuse at the 10-pounder Parrott guns not acting well.

I take pleasure in being able to testify to the gallant and military bearing of the infantry in my vicinity.

Yours, respectfully, &c.,

THAD'S P. MOTT,
Captain, Artillery, Smith's Brigade.

Brig. Gen. WILLIAM F. SMITH.

No. 12.

Report of Capt. Charles Griffin, Fifth U. S. Artillery.

BATTERY D, FIFTH ARTILLERY,
Camp near Chain Bridge, September 12, 1861.

SIR: Yesterday, after the enemy opened fire on the troops under your command, in accordance with your instructions, two rifled pieces of Battery D, Fifth Artillery, were placed in position some 1,800 yards from the enemy's battery and opened fire, and continued firing until the enemy ceased firing or until Lieutenant Hasbrouck placed two more pieces in position some 600 yards to the rear, on the road towards our camp. The two pieces first placed in battery were then limbered up and moved to a position in rear of Lieutenant Hasbrouck. Some time after Lieutenant Hasbrouck placed his pieces in battery the remaining two pieces of the battery under Lieutenant Hazlett joined and came into battery. The enemy at this time had ceased firing and the cannoneers were resting for the want of a target. Some twenty or thirty minutes after this the enemy showed himself in a little cleared place, whence a round from the guns started him in a full run. From the first position of the rifled pieces some 40 rounds were fired, all shell, and from the second position some 18, to which the enemy made no reply.

The conduct of the lieutenants (Hazlett and Hasbrouck) was that of gallant soldiers, and of the men of the battery all that could be desired. It affords me much gratification to testify to the coolness and handsome deportment of the Vermont Third and some 80 men of the Second Vermont, who were ordered to support the battery. They were for about an hour under a very warm fire from the enemy's artillery.

I am, very respectfully, your obedient servant,

CHAS. GRIFFIN,
Captain, Fifth Artillery, Commanding Battery D.

Col. ISAAC I. STEVENS.

No. 13.

Report of Lieut. William McLean, Fifth U. S. Cavalry.

HEADQUARTERS CAMP ADVANCE,
September 12, 1861.

SIR: By order of General Smith I was placed under your command yesterday, and in accordance with your directions I led my party as the advance guard to Lewinsville, sent 10 men on the road to Falls Church, 4 on the road to Vienna, and 2 on the road to Alexandria. Soon after my arrival I was ordered to send an officer and 10 men to repulse the enemy's mounted pickets on the road towards Vienna. Having no officer present, I led them myself and performed the required duty, dispersing the rebel cavalry to the number of 50 men. I would especially notice the gallantry and firmness of George Hicks, of my command, who bravely faced the enemy previous to my arrival and rendered good service throughout. We returned to Camp Advance in the rear of the column without suffering any loss.

All of which is respectfully submitted, by your obedient servant,

WM. McLEAN,
First Lieutenant, Company H, Fifth Cavalry.

Colonel STEVENS, *Commanding Expedition.*

No. 14.

Report of William Borrowe, acting aide-de-camp.

CAMP NEAR CHAIN BRIDGE, VA., *September* 12, 1861.

SIR: Having been ordered by you to see that Lewinsville was clear of the enemy, so that we could occupy it without danger of falling on their pickets, I took with me the cavalry, under Lieutenant McLean, and two companies of the Third Vermont as skirmishers, and throwing them around the woods, advanced with the cavalry. Finding all clear at the cross-roads, I sent 10 of the cavalry on the road to Falls Church to scout it for the distance of half a mile, and 4 on the road to Vienna, with the same directions. I then advanced the skirmishers to a ridge about a quarter of a mile from Lewinsville to the left, and where we commanded the valley looking towards Vienna as well as a portion of the turnpike road from Falls Church and crossing the road to Vienna in our front and right. The men did their duty entirely to my satisfaction, being entirely concealed, and where all that passed before them could be seen. At the time it was reported that some 50 of their cavalry were seen advancing over the hill, and Lieutenant McLean, with some 12 of his cavalry, were ordered up to support us until others could be sent forward, should they be needed. In the mean time one of our cavalry pickets had ridden into the field and towards them within sufficient distance to discharge his carbine, but with what effect we could not tell. They turned at this and galloped off to the left and towards Falls Church, and, as I afterwards learned from a woman at a house beyond our lines, to give information to the enemy at that place of our being in force at Lewinsville.

The men approaching to us before we saw them made me uneasy for the woods to our left, and which were but slightly guarded, and I posted, with your permission, one company from the Nineteenth Indiana through them, covering us, so that no approach could be made in that direction for more than a mile without being discovered. At 2 o'clock, according to orders, the skirmishers were called in, and I waited fifteen minutes for some stragglers who had wandered off, and, not finding them, marched the men to their commands. At this moment the enemy opened his fire on us with one gun, soon increased to four, and a body of infantry advanced up the road from Falls Church and fired at our men from the road and woods. At this point 1 man of the Nineteenth Indiana was killed, being shot through the head. Fearing an advance of their cavalry, which we had seen in considerable numbers, I placed one of the guns from Lieutenant Hasbrouck's section in the rear, supported by one company of the Nineteenth Indiana and the regular cavalry, and in this order advanced on the road, and though much exposed to their fire for the distance of a half a mile, fortunately none were lost but 2 of the Third Vermont, who were killed by the explosion of a shell. General Smith coming up at this point, I resigned the orders to his aides.

I must, in conclusion, speak of the splendid behavior of the Third Vermont, who stood the fire with the greatest coolness, as well as the Nineteenth Indiana, obeying all orders with a promptness that was extraordinary.

I have the honor to be, your obedient servant,

W. BORROWE,
Acting Aide, Second Lieutenant, Griffin's Battery.

Col. ISAAC I. STEVENS.

No. 15.

Report of Gen. Joseph E. Johnston, C. S. Army, with congratulatory orders.

HEADQUARTERS NEAR FAIRFAX CROSS-ROADS,
Near Fairfax Station, September 14, 1861.

SIR: Herewith I inclose two reports (of Brigadier-General Longstreet and of Colonel Stuart) of the affair of Lewinsville [Nos. 16 and 17]. I am much gratified at having this opportunity of putting before the Department of War and the President this new instance of the boldness and skill of Colonel Stuart and the courage and efficiency of our troops.

Connected with this communication and these reports is a recommendation from General Longstreet, General Beauregard, and myself for forming a cavalry brigade and putting Colonel Stuart at its head. A new organization of the cavalry arm of our service is greatly needed, and greater strength as well as an effective organization. Our numbers in cavalry are by no means in due proportion to our infantry and artillery, yet without cavalry in proper proportion victory is comparatively barren of results ; defeat is less prejudicial ; retreat is usually safe.

You will observe that I propose that Colonel Stuart shall be withdrawn from the immediate command of the First Regiment of Virginia Cavalry. Should this be done, as I hope it will be, other arrangements are necessary in the regiment. As they have served immediately under my eye, and as I thus know them thoroughly, I feel it my duty to make further suggestions.

The regiment so far is exclusively Virginian. By all means keep it so, where it can be done without prejudice in other respects. State pride excites a generous emulation in the Army, which is of inappreciable value in its effect on the spirit of the troops. I therefore recommend that Capt. William E. Jones, who now commands the strongest troop in the regiment and one which is not surpassed in discipline or spirit by any in the army, be made colonel. He is a graduate of West Point, served for several years in the Mounted Rifles, and is skillful, brave, and zealous in a very high degree. It is enough to say that he is worthy to succeed J. E. B. Stuart. For the lieutenant-colonelcy I repeat my recommendation of Capt. Fitzhugh Lee. He belongs to a family in which military genius seems an heirloom. He is an officer of rare merit, capacity, and courage. Both of these officers have the invaluable advantage at this moment of knowledge of the ground which is now the scene of operations.

I do not recommend Maj. Robert Swan of that regiment for promotion in it, because, though personally known to me as a capable and gallant officer, yet his service and experience in the Army heretofore have been in the infantry. I am informed that he would prefer that branch of the service. I therefore recommend his transfer to it. Being a Marylander, it would be preferable to place him in a Maryland regiment. He would be likely thus to serve our cause most effectively.

Most respectfully, your obedient servant,

J. E. JOHNSTON,
General.

Gen. S. COOPER, *Adjt. and Inspr. Gen., Richmond, Va.*

—

GENERAL ORDERS, }   HDQRS. ARMY OF THE POTOMAC,
    No. 19.   }   *September* 12, 1861.

The commanding general has great satisfaction in making known the excellent conduct of Col. J. E. B. Stuart, and of the officers and men of his command, in the affair of Lewinsville, on the 11th instant, on which occasion Colonel Stuart, with Major [James B.] Terrill's battalion (Thirteenth Virginia Volunteers), two field pieces of the Washington Artillery (Louisiana), under Captain [T. L.] Rosser and Lieutenant [C. H.] Slocomb, and Captain Patrick's company of cavalry (First Virginia), attacked and drove from that position in confusion three regiments of infantry, eight pieces of artillery, and a large body of cavalry, inflicting severe loss, but incurring none.

By command of General Johnston:

THOS. G. RHETT,
Assistant Adjutant-General.

No. 16.

Report of Brig. Gen. James Longstreet, C. S. Army.

HDQRS. ADVANCED FORCES, ARMY OF POTOMAC,
September 12, 1861.

COLONEL: I have the honor to submit herewith the report of Col. J. E. B. Stuart of his affair of yesterday. My arrangements had been made to cut off the enemy at Lewinsville by moving a heavy force down during the night. It is probably better that Colonel Stuart did not receive my instructions, and drove the enemy back to his trenches at once. My movement was intended to be made at night, and the heavy rains of last night would have prevented anything of the kind. The enemy are so famous at burrowing, that the command would probably have been well covered before I could have reached it and might have cost us several men.

Colonel Stuart has been at Munson's Hill since its occupation by our troops. He has been most untiring in the discharge of his duties at that and other advanced positions, after having driven the enemy from Mason's, Munson's, and Upton's Hills. In these and other less important skirmishes he has been entirely successful. Where he has lost a man, he has brought in at least two of the enemy, dead or alive.

The affair of yesterday was handsomely conducted and well executed. He makes handsome mention of Major Terrill, Captain Rosser, and Lieutenant Slocomb, and others of his command. It is quite evident that the officers and men deserve much credit for their handsome conduct, one and all. It is difficult to say whether the handsome use of his light infantry by Major Terrill or the destructive fires of the Washington Artillery by Captain Rosser and Lieutenant Slocomb, is the most brilliant part of the affair.

Colonel Stuart has, I think, fairly won his claim to brigadier, and I hope the commanding generals will unite with me in recommending him for that promotion.

I am, sir, very respectfully, your most obedient servant,

JAMES LONGSTREET,
Brigadier-General, Commanding.

Col. THOMAS JORDAN, *Adjutant-General.*

Since making the above report Colonel Stuart reports 2 other prisoners and another body found in the field, besides additional evidences of havoc in the ranks of the enemy. Killed and prisoners, 11. Not even a horse of ours hurt.

Respectfully,

JAMES LONGSTREET,
Brigadier-General.

[Indorsement.]

We think with Brigadier-General Longstreet that Colonel Stuart's laborious and valuable services, unintermitted since the war began on this frontier, entitle him to a brigadier generalcy. His calm and daring courage, sagacity, zeal, and activity qualify him admirably for the command of our three regiments of cavalry, by which the outpost duty of the Army is performed. The Government would gain greatly by promoting him.

J. E. JOHNSTON,
General.
G. T. BEAUREGARD,
General, Commanding First Corps, Army of the Potomac.

No. 17.

Report of Col. James E. B. Stuart, First Virginia Cavalry.

HEADQUARTERS, MUNSON'S HILL, *September* 11, 1861.

GENERAL: I started about 12 o'clock with the Thirteenth Virginia Volunteers, commanded by Major Terrill (305 men), one section of Rosser's battery, Washington Artillery, and a detachment of the First Cavalry, under Captain Patrick, for Lewinsville, where I learned from my cavalry pickets the enemy were posted with some force. My intention was to surprise them, and I succeeded entirely, approaching Lewinsville by the enemy's left and rear, taking care to keep my small force an entire secret from their observation. I at the same time carefully provided against the disaster to myself which I was striving to inflict upon the enemy, and felt sure that, if necessary, I could fall back successfully before any force the enemy might have, for the country was favorable to retreat and ambuscade.

At a point nicely screened by the woods from Lewinsville, and a few hundred yards from the place, I sent forward, under Major Terrill, a portion of his command stealthily to reach the woods at a turn of the road and reconnoiter beyond. This was admirably done, and the major soon reported to me that the enemy had a piece of artillery in position in the road just at Lewinsville, commanding our road. I directed him immediately to post his riflemen so as to render it impossible for the cannoneers to serve the piece, and, if possible, capture it. During subsequent operations the cannoneers tried ineffectually to serve the piece, and finally, after one was shot through the head, the piece was taken off.

While this was going on a few shots from Rosser's section at a cluster of the enemy a quarter of a mile off put the entire force of the enemy in full retreat, exposing their entire column to flank fire from our piece. Some wagons and a large body of cavalry first passed in hasty flight, the rifled piece and howitzer firing as they passed. Then came flying a battery, eight pieces of artillery (Griffin's), which soon took position about 600 yards to our front and right, and rained shot and shell upon us during the entire engagement, but with harmless effect, although striking very near. Then passed three regiments of infantry at double-quick, receiving in succession as they passed Rosser's unerring salutation, his shells bursting directly over their heads, and creating the greatest havoc and confusion in their ranks. The last infantry regiment was followed by a column of cavalry, which at one time rode over the rear of the infantry in great confusion. The field, general, and staff officers were seen exerting every effort to restore order in their broken ranks, and my cavalry vedettes, observing their flight, reported that they finally rallied a mile and a half below and took position there, firing round after round of artillery from that position up the road where they supposed our columns would be pursuing them.

Captain Rosser, having no enemy left to contend with, at his own request was permitted to view the ground of the enemy's flight, and found the road plowed up by his solid shot and strewn with fragments of shells; 2 men left dead in the road, 1 mortally wounded, and 1 not hurt taken prisoner. The prisoners said the havoc in their ranks was fearful, justifying what I saw myself of the confusion. Major Terrill's sharpshooters were by no means idle, firing wherever a straggling Yankee showed his head, and capturing a lieutenant (captured by Major Terrill himself), 1 sergeant, and 1 private, all belonging to the Nineteenth Indiana, Colonel Meredith. The prisoners reported to me that General McClellan himself was present, and the enemy gave it out publicly that the occupancy of Lewinsville was to be permanent. Alas for human expectations!

The officers and men behaved in a manner worthy the general's highest commendation, and the firing done by the section under direction of Captain Rosser and Lieutenant Slocomb, all the time under fire from the enemy's battery, certainly for accuracy and effect challenges comparison with any ever made. Valuable assistance was rendered me by Chaplain Ball, as usual, and Messrs. Hairston and Burks, citizens attached to my staff, were conspicuous in daring. Corporal Hagan and Bugler Freed are entitled to special mention for good conduct and valuable service.

Our loss was not a scratch to man or horse. We have no means of knowing the enemy's, except it must have been heavy, from the effects of the shots. We found in all 4 dead or mortally wounded, and captured 4. Of course they carried off all they could.

Your attention is especially called to the inclosed, which was delivered to me at Lewinsville, and to my indorsement.* I send a sketch also.* Please forward this report to Gen. Johnston. I returned here with my command after re-establishing my line of pickets through Lewinsville.

Most respectfully, your obedient servant,

J. E. B. STUART,
Colonel, Commanding.

General JAMES LONGSTREET.

SEPTEMBER 11–17, 1861.—Operations in Cheat Mountain, West Virginia, including actions and skirmishes at Cheat Mountain Pass, Cheat Summit, Point Mountain Turnpike, and Elk Water.

REPORTS, ETC.

No. 1.—Brig. Gen. Joseph J. Reynolds, U. S. Army.
No. 2.—Col. Nathan Kimball, Fourteenth Indiana Infantry.
No. 3.—Col. George D. Wagner, Fifteenth Indiana Infantry.
No. 4.—Lieut. Col. Richard Owen, Fifteenth Indiana Infantry.
No. 5.—Capt. David J. Higgins, Twenty-fourth Ohio Infantry.
No. 6.—Col. Albert Rust, Third Arkansas Infantry.
No. 7.—General Lee's orders.

No. 1.

Report of Brig. Gen. Joseph J. Reynolds, U. S. Army.

HEADQUARTERS FIRST BRIGADE, A. O. W. VA.,
Elk Water, September 17, 1861.

GENERAL: The operations of this brigade for the past few days may be summed up as follows: On the 12th instant the enemy, 9,000 strong,

----

* Not found.

with eight to twelve pieces of artillery, under command of General R. E. Lee, advanced on this position by the Huntersville pike. Our advanced pickets, portions of the Fifteenth Indiana and Sixth Ohio, gradually fell back to our main picket station, two companies of the Seventeenth Indiana, under Colonel Hascall, checking the enemy's advance at the Point Mountain turnpike, and then falling back on the regiment, which occupied a very advanced position on our right front, and which we now ordered in. The enemy threw into the woods on our left front three regiments, who made their way to the right and rear of Cheat Mountain, took a position on the road leading to Huttonsville, broke the telegraph wire, and cut off our communication with Colonel Kimball, Fourteenth Indiana, commanding on Cheat Summit. Simultaneously another force of the enemy, of about equal strength, advanced by the Staunton pike in the front of Cheat Mountain, and threw two regiments to the right and rear of Cheat, which united with the three regiments from the other column of the enemy. The two posts, Cheat Summit and Elk Water, are 7 miles apart by a bridle-path over the mountains, and 18 miles by the wagon-road, via Huttonsville; Cheat Mountain Pass, the former headquarters of the brigade, being at the foot of the mountain, 10 miles from the summit. The enemy advancing towards the pass, by which he might possibly have obtained the rear or left of Elk Water, was there met by three companies of the Thirteenth Indiana, ordered up for that purpose, and by one company of the Fourteenth Indiana, from the summit. These four companies engaged and gallantly held in check greatly superior numbers of the enemy, foiled him in his attempt to obtain the rear or left of Elk Water, and threw him in the rear and right of Cheat Mountain, the companies retiring to the pass at the foot of the mountain. The enemy, about 5,000 strong, now closed in on Cheat Summit, and became engaged with detachments of the Fourteenth Indiana, Twenty-fourth and Twenty-fifth Ohio, from the summit, in all only about 300, who, deployed in the woods, held in check and killed many of the enemy, who did not at any time succeed in getting sufficiently near the field redoubt to give Daum's battery an opportunity of firing into him.

So matters rested at dark on the 12th, with heavy forces in front and in plain sight of both posts, communication cut off, and the supply train for the mountains, loaded with provisions which were needed, waiting for an opportunity to pass up the road. Determined to force a communication with Cheat, I ordered the Thirteenth Indiana, under Colonel Sullivan, to cut their way, if necessary, by the main road, and the greater part of the Third Ohio and Second Virginia, under Colonels Marrow and Moss, respectively, to do the same by the path. The two commands started at 3 o'clock a. m. on the 13th, the former from Cheat Mountain Pass and the latter from Elk Water, so as to fall upon the enemy, if possible, simultaneously. Early on the 13th the small force of about 300 from the summit engaged the enemy, and with such effect that, notwithstanding his greatly superior numbers, he retired in great haste and disorder, leaving large quantities of clothing and equipments on the ground, and our relieving force, failing to catch the enemy, marched to the summit, securing the provision train and reopening our communication. While this was taking place on the mountain, and as yet unknown to us, the enemy, under Lee, advanced on Elk Water, apparently for a general attack. One rifled 10-pounder Parrott gun from Loomis' battery was run to the front three-fourths of a mile and delivered a few shots at the enemy, causing him to withdraw out of convenient range and doing fine execution. Our relative position remained unchanged until near dark, when we learned the result of the movements on the mountain, as above stated, and the enemy retired somewhat for the night.

On the 14th, early, the enemy was again in position in front of Elk Water, and a few rounds, supported by a company of the Fifteenth Indiana, were again administered, which caused him to withdraw as before. The forces that had been before repulsed from Cheat returned, and were again driven back by a comparatively small force from the mountain. The Seventeenth Indiana was ordered up the path to open communication and make way for another supply train, but, as before, found the little band from the summit had already done the work. During the afternoon of the 14th the enemy withdrew from before Elk Water, and is now principally concentrated some 10 miles from this post at or near his main camp. On the 15th he appeared in stronger force than at any previous time in front of Cheat and attempted a flank movement by the left, but was driven back by the ever-vigilant and gallant garrison of the field redoubt on the summit. To-day the enemy has also retired from the front of Cheat, but to what precise position I am not yet informed.

The results of these affairs are that we have killed near 100 of the enemy, including Col. John A. Washington, aide-de-camp to General Lee, and have taken about 20 prisoners. We have lost 9 killed, including Lieutenant Junod, Fourteenth Indiana, 2 missing, and about 60 prisoners, including Capt. James Bense and Lieutenants Gilman and Scheiffer, of the Sixth Ohio, and Lieutenant Merrill, of the Engineers. I append the reports of Colonel Kimball, Fourteenth Indiana; Captain Higgins, Twenty-fourth Ohio; Lieutenant-Colonel Owen and Colonel Wagner, of the Fifteenth Indiana.

> J. J. REYNOLDS,
> *Brigadier-General, Commanding First Brigade.*

L. THOMAS,
Adjutant-General U. S. Army, Washington, D. C.

No. 2.

Report of Col. Nathan Kimball, Fourteenth Indiana Infantry.

CAMP, CHEAT MOUNTAIN SUMMIT, WEST VIRGINIA,
September 14, 1861.

GENERAL: On the morning of September 12 I started my train (teams from the Twenty-fourth Ohio Regiment) to your camp. When about three-fourths of a mile out they were attacked by a party of the enemy. Information being at once brought to me, I proceeded to the point of attack, accompanied by Colonel Jones, of the Twenty-fifth Ohio, and Lieutenant-Colonel Gilbert, of the Twenty-fourth Ohio, and Companies C (Captain Brooks) and F (Captain Williamson), of the Fourteenth Indiana. I at first supposed the attack was made by a scouting party of the enemy, and sent Captains Brooks and Williamson into the woods, deployed as skirmishers. They soon overhauled the enemy, numbering 2,500. My captains immediately opened fire, and informed me the enemy were there in great force. I ordered them to hold their position. They did so, and soon had the pleasure of seeing the whole force of the enemy take to their heels, throwing aside guns, clothing, and everything that impeded their progress. In the mean time I had detailed a guard of 90 men to be sent forward to relieve Captain Coons, of the Fourteenth Indiana, who had been stationed as a picket on the path between Elk Water Camp and my own. This detail was from the Fourteenth Indiana, Twenty-fourth Ohio, and Twenty-fifth Ohio, under Captain Higgins, Lieutenants Green and Wood. They had proceeded about 2 miles from the point of first attack when they met the Tennessee brigade, gave them battle, and drove them back. Captain Coons, of the Fourteenth Indiana, had met this same force earlier in the morning and undertook to resist them, and did so until driven back. He then came in their rear whilst they were engaged with the command under Captain Higgins, Company C, Twenty-fourth Ohio, Lieutenant Green, of the Fourteenth Indiana, and Lieutenant Wood, of the Twenty-fifth Ohio.

At this juncture I was informed that the enemy was moving in my front above the hill east of my camp, where we have usually had a picket station, which point was occupied by Lieutenant Junod, Company E, Fourteenth Indiana. The enemy surrounded Junod's command, consisting of 35 men, with a force 500 strong, and killed Lieutenant Junod and 1 private. The others have all come into camp. I soon found that Captains Brooks and Williamson were driving the enemy to my right flank. I then dispatched two companies, one from the Fourteenth Indiana, Company A, Captain Foote, and one from the Twenty-fourth Ohio, Captain ———, up Cheat River, to cut off the enemy's retreat. My captains met the enemy 2 miles above the bridge, scattering them and killing several, capturing 2 prisoners, and retaking one of the wagoners taken early in the morning. The enemy's force on my right flank consisted of the Twenty-fifth Virginia, Colonel Heck, Twenty-third, Thirty-first, and Thirty-seventh, and also one battalion of Virginians, under command of Colonel Taliaferro. The force which met Captain Higgins and Lieutenants Green and Wood consisted of the First Tennessee, Col. George Maney; the Seventh Tennessee, Col. R. Hatton; the Fourteenth Tennessee, Colonel Forbes, mustering in all 3,000, commanded by General Anderson. The aggregate of the enemy's force was near 5,500; ours, which engaged and repulsed them, was less than 300. We killed near 100 of the enemy, and wounded a greater number, and have 13 prisoners. We recaptured all our teamsters and others whom the enemy had captured in the morning. We have lost a few noble fellows killed, among whom is Lieutenant Junod, Company E, Fourteenth Indiana. I append a list of killed, wounded, and missing of my command.*

General, I think my men have done wonders, and ask God to bless them.

The woods are literally covered with the baggage, coats, and haversacks, &c., of the enemy. Though almost naked, my command are ready to move forward.

Your obedient servant,

NATHAN KIMBALL,
Colonel Fourteenth Indiana Volunteers, Commanding Post.
Brig. Gen. JOSEPH J. REYNOLDS, *Commanding.*

---

* Not found.

No. 3.

Report of Col. George D. Wagner, Fifteenth Indiana Infantry.

HDQRS. FIFTEENTH REGIMENT INDIANA VOLUNTEERS,
September 12, 1861.

DEAR SIR : On the 9th of the present month I ordered Captain Templeton to take Companies D and F and take possession of and hold the Point Mountain pike at its junction with the Huntersville pike, supported by Major Christopher, of the Sixth Regiment Ohio, with 100 men, at Conrad's Mill, 2 miles in the rear. The first position was about 8 miles in advance of my camp and 4 miles from the enemy's encampment.

On morning of the 11th Captain Templeton's pickets were attacked by the enemy's column, advancing down the road. They fell back on the main force. The enemy still advancing in force, Captain Templeton dispatched a dragoon for re-enforcements. I immediately sent the left wing of the Fifteenth Indiana, under command of Major Wood, with orders to hold the position; but soon after a scout, who had been posted 3 miles east of Captain Templeton, with instructions to report to me any movements of the enemy on the left flank, came in and reported a column of 2,000 troops marching in this direction, with the evident intention of cutting off Captain Templeton and Major Christopher. I immediately sent orders for the entire force to fall back on the main force, which they did in good order, bringing off their wounded, having 2 men killed, 1 taken prisoner, and 3 wounded. Privates Kent and Bealer killed, of Company F, Captain White; T. Spoonmore, of same company, was taken prisoner. The wounded are Corporal Clark and Private Richards, both seriously, Clark having been hit by four balls. Both will recover, but Richards has had his leg amputated. Private Hovey is slightly wounded. All of Company D, of my regiment.

At this time you arrived on the ground and took command.

Let me say that officers and men all did their duty, and I must be allowed to commend to your notice Sergeant Thompson, of Company D, who having command of the first party engaged, as well as the men with him, stood and fought until half of the party was shot down before they would fall back.

I have the honor to be, your most obedient servant,

G. D. WAGNER,
Colonel.

Brig. Gen. JOSEPH J. REYNOLDS.

No. 4.

Report of Lieut. Col. Richard Owen, Fifteenth Indiana Infantry.

CAMP, ELK WATER, RANDOLPH COUNTY, VIRGINIA,
September 18, 1861.

SIR : In accordance with your order to proceed on the Marlin turnpike until I met the enemy, but not to bring on a general engagement, I marched my command of 285 infantry and 4 dragoons (the latter designed to be used as messengers) on Sunday, the 8th September, at noon, out of camp, under the guidance of Dr. Singer, a Union Virginian, who, having formerly practiced in this and adjoining counties, was thoroughly acquainted with all the localities. The infantry consisted of portions of Company B, Captain Wing, Third Ohio; Company A, Captain Rice; Company C, Captain Comparet; Company E, Captain Lambe; Company K, Captain McCutchen, and Company H, under Lieutenant Warren, all of the Fifteenth Indiana Volunteers. Lieutenant Driscoll, of the Third Ohio, volunteered to lead a scouting party consisting of 10 Ohio and 10 Indiana riflemen. Lieutenant Bedford, acting captain of our scouts, volunteered to accompany the expedition. The cavalry was taken from Captain Bracken's Indiana company.

Sleeping the first night on our arms, with half the command awake at a time, with no fires and perfect silence, after picketing wherever the cross-roads pointed out by Dr. Singer seemed to demand it, we proceeded at 4 a. m. on the 9th instant towards the Confederate camp at Marshall's store, carefully scouting the laurel bushes. Immediately after the main body, with Captain Wing in the advance guard, emerged from a dense thicket which lined each side of the road, our scouts commenced firing, having come so close to the enemy and so suddenly that a hand-to-hand scuffle ensued between Private Edwards, of the Fifteenth Indiana, and a North Carolina secessionist, while another Fifteenth Indiana scout, Private J. F. Morris, surprised four dragoons at their breakfast in a house which proved to be on the farm of Henry Thomas, about three-quarters of a mile north of their camp. In accordance with instructions previously given to my command, I ordered them to fire by section, and countermarch to reform and load in the rear. This was carried out in good order, and with such execution that, as prisoners afterwards taken by Colonel Sullivan, of the Thirteenth Indiana, informed him, we killed 15 and wounded about as many more. An officer, who proved to be Major Murray, of the Virginia troops, was shot, it is believed by Lieutenant Bedford, with an Enfield rifle.

Knowing that, although there were but three full companies in sight, the enemy was in strong force at a short distance, I considered it prudent, in accordance with your instructions, to retire the command after all firing on the part of the enemy had ceased, forming for some time as before, faced to the front, but afterwards marching in common time to our camp 11¼ miles, delaying long enough on the route to dress the wounds of one of our men, Private Frank Conner, of Company G, Third Ohio, who was wounded in two places, besides receiving a ball through his haversack, but is now doing well.

The force represented by the prisoners as being in camp near Marshall's store amounted to 8,000 men, and they also report that two pieces of artillery and two regiments of infantry were ordered out in pursuit, doubtless the same a portion of which next day attacked the two companies of your regiment occupying the outposts on that road, viz, Company D, Captain Templeton, and Company F, under Lieutenant Dean, who so successfully and creditably sustained themselves.

The above brief report of our skirmish is submitted with the hope that we carried out your instructions in the manner you designed.

Very respectfully, your obedient servant,

RICHARD OWEN,
Lieutenant-Colonel Fifteenth Indiana Volunteers.

Col. G. D. WAGNER,
Commanding Fifteenth Regiment Indiana Volunteers.

No. 5.

Report of Capt. David J. Higgins, Twenty fourth Ohio Infantry.

CAMP, CHEAT MOUNTAIN SUMMIT, VIRGINIA,
September 17, 1861.

I have the honor to submit the following report of the operations of my command at the skirmish which occurred 4 miles from camp on the 12th instant:

My command was composed of 90 men, detailed 30 each from the Twenty-fourth and Twenty-fifth Ohio Infantry and the Fourteenth Indiana, accompanied by Lieut. John T. Wood, Company H, Twenty-fifth Ohio, and Lieut. M. N. Green, Company B, Fourteenth Indiana. I was ordered to proceed with haste to the relief of Captain Coons, of the Fourteenth Indiana, who the evening of the 11th instant had been ordered to guard a pass 5 miles northwest from camp, leading from the main road to Elk River. Half a mile from camp I found three wagons, whose horses and drivers had that morning been taken by the rebels, who during the night had lain in large force near the camp. Hastening on, we were met by a cavalry soldier leading a wounded horse, who stated that the enemy had collected at the entrance of the pass, had shot his horse, and that Captain Coons and party were doubtless cut off. Sending a squad of men into the woods on both sides of the road, I proceeded cautiously within sight of the spot where the horse had been shot, when I sent Lieutenant Green with his men to deploy on the left of the road and Lieutenant Wood with his men on the right, holding the detail of the Twenty-fourth on the right near the road on line with the others as reserve to check any advance of the enemy on the road, ordering the whole line to move cautiously, covering themselves by trees. The right had proceeded about 3 rods in this manner when it was saluted by a volley of at least 100 guns, with no loss on our side. We returned the volley, and immediately advanced upon the ambush, receiving and returning a second volley.

The rebels fled up from the right to the road, where Lieutenant Green came in sight of them, and poured in a destructive fire. At this moment we saw a large body of men in utter confusion pressing back upon what seemed a larger force in line of battle, in spite of all efforts of officers to rally them. Lieutenant Green, seeing so large a force, fell back upon the reserve, bringing in 2 wounded men—Private Leonard Daum, wounded in the arm, and Private John Killgannon both of Company B, Fourteenth Indiana. I directed the line to be deployed again, but to make no advance, determining to hold the position until the arrival of re-enforcements.

After waiting half an hour Major Harrow, of the Fourteenth Indiana, came up with two companies. He immediately sent forward a squad of men to reconnoiter. These returned, bringing in two prisoners, who reported the force in our front to be General Anderson's brigade of Tennesseeans, numbering 3,000; that we had fallen upon the left wing of his line, and that his was one of three columns of rebel infantry which during the night had collected at three points to attack the camp. Learning these facts, Major Harrow ordered me to draw in my men and post them as advanced guard 2 miles nearer camp. This I did, and held the place unmolested until morning, when I was relieved.

From the most reliable information I can get the rebels have lost in that engagement at least 50 killed, besides many wounded. The actual skirmishing lasted about thirty minutes, but the whole time we held the ground was one hour.

I wish to call the attention of the colonel commanding this post to the general bravery and coolness of all the men under my command during the engagement. Particularly I wish to notice the gallant conduct of Lieut. M. N. Green, of Company B, Fourteenth Indiana, and Lieut. John T. Wood, of Company H, Twenty-fifth Ohio, whose steady coolness and daring example had great force in keeping the deployed line unbroken and in causing so destructive a fire to be poured upon the enemy.

I have the honor to be, colonel, very respectfully, your obedient servant,

DAVID J. HIGGINS,
Captain Company C, Twenty-fourth Ohio Infantry, Comdg. Scout.
Col. NATHAN KIMBALL, *Commanding Post.*

No. 6.

Report of Col. Albert Rust, Third Arkansas Infantry.

CAMP BARTOW, *September* 13, 1861—10 p. m.

GENERAL : The expedition against Cheat Mountain failed. My command consisted of between 1,500 and 1,600 men. Got there at the appointed time, notwithstanding the rain. Seized a number of their pickets and scouts. Learned from them that the enemy was between 4,000 and 5,000 strong, and they reported them to be strongly fortified. Upon a reconnaissance their representations were fully corroborated. A fort or block-house on the point or elbow of the road, intrenchments on the south, and outside of the intrenchments and all around up to the road heavy and impassable abatis, if the enemy were not behind them. Colonel Barton, my lieutenant-colonel, and all the field officers declared it would be madness to make an attack. We learned from the prisoners, they were aware of your movements, and had been telegraphed for re-enforcements, and I heard three pieces of artillery pass down toward your encampment while we were seeking to make an assault upon them.

I took the assistant commissary, and for one regiment I found upon his person a requisition for 930 rations ; also a letter indicating they had very little subsistence. I brought only one prisoner back with me. The cowardice of the guard (not Arkansian) permitted the others to escape. Spies had evidently communicated our movements to the enemy. The fort was completed, as reported by the different prisoners examined separately, and another in process of construction. We got near enough to see the enemy in the trenches beyond the abatis. The most of my command behaved admirably. Some I would prefer to be without upon any expedition.

General Jackson requests me to say that he is in possession of the first summit of Cheat Mountain, and hopes you are doing something in Tygart's Valley, and will retain command of it until he receives orders from your quarters. My own opinion is that there is nothing to be gained by occupying that mountain. It will take a heavy force to take the pass, and at a heavy loss. I knew the enemy had four times my force; but for the abatis we would have made the assault. We could not get to them to make it. The general says, in his note to me, his occupying Cheat Mountain may bring on an engagement, but he is prepared, and will whip them if they come. I see from the postscript that he requests his note to me to be inclosed to you. I can only say that all human power could do towards success in my expedition failed of success. The taking of the picket looked like a providential interposition. I took the first one myself, being at the head of the column when I got to the road.

In great haste, very respectfully, your obedient servant,

A. RUST,
Colonel, &c.

General LORING, *Commanding, &c.*

[Inclosure.]

DEAR COLONEL: Return into camp with your command. So soon as you arrive address a letter to General Loring, explaining the failure and the reasons of it. Show this to Captain Niell, quartermaster, and let him at once furnish an express ready to take your letter by the near route. If possible, get the postmaster, Mr. Abagast, to go, and go rapidly, and at once. Say in your letter that I am in possession of first summit of Cheat Mountain, and am in hopes of something going on in Tygart's Valley, and shall retain command of it until I receive orders from headquarters. It may bring on an engagement, but I am prepared, and shall whip them if they come.

Very truly,

H. R. JACKSON.

P. S.—I cannot write here. Inclose this scrawl in your own letter. You had better return yourself at once to camp, leaving your command to follow. We had several skirmishes yesterday and killed several of the enemy.

No. 7.

General Lee's orders.

SPECIAL ORDERS, }   HEADQUARTERS OF THE FORCES,
No. —.   }   *Valley Mountain, W. Va., September 9, 1861.*

The forward movement announced to the Army of the Northwest in Special Orders, No. 28, from its headquarters, of this date, gives the general commanding the opportunity of exhorting the troops to keep steadily in view the great principles for which they contend and to manifest to the world their determination to maintain them. The eyes of the country are upon you. The safety of your homes and the lives of all you hold dear depend upon your courage and exertions. Let each man resolve to be victorious, and that the right of self-government, liberty, and peace shall in him find a defender. The progress of this army must be forward.

R. E. LEE,
General, Commanding.

SPECIAL ORDERS, }   HEADQUARTERS,
No. —.   }   *Camp on Valley River, Va., September 14, 1861.*

The forced reconnaissance of the enemy's positions, both at Cheat Mountain Pass and on Valley River, having been completed, and the character of the natural approaches and the nature of the artificial defenses exposed, the Army of the Northwest will resume its former position at such time and in such manner as General Loring shall direct, and continue its preparations for further operations. The commanding general experienced much gratification at the cheerfulness and alacrity displayed by the troops in this arduous operation. The promptitude with which they surmounted every difficulty, driving in and capturing the enemy's pickets on the fronts examined and exhibiting that readiness for attack, gives assurance of victory when a fit opportunity offers.

R. E. LEE,
General, Commanding.

SEPTEMBER 12–17, 1861.—Arrest of members of the Maryland Legislature and other citizens of that State.

REPORTS, ETC.

No. 1.—Instructions from Secretary of War to General Banks.
No. 2.—Report of Maj. Gen. John A. Dix.
No. 3.—Letter from General Dix to Maj. Gen. John E. Wool.
No. 4.—Reports of Major-General Banks of arrests at Frederick, Md.
No. 5.—Report of Mr. Allen Pinkerton of arrests at Baltimore, Md.
No. 6.—Letter from General Wool to commanding officer Fort Lafayette, New York.
No. 7.—Letter from Governor Hicks to General Banks.

No. 1.

Instructions from Secretary of War to General Banks, U. S. Army.

WAR DEPARTMENT,
Washington, September 11, 1861.

Maj. Gen. N. P. BANKS, *Commanding near Darnestown, Md.:*

GENERAL : The passage of any act of secession by the legislature of Maryland must be prevented. If necessary, all or any part of the members must be arrested. Exercise your own judgment as to the time and manner, but do the work effectively.

Very respectfully, your obedient servant,
SIMON CAMERON,
Secretary of War.

No. 2.

Report of Maj. Gen. John A. Dix, U. S. Army.

HEADQUARTERS DEPARTMENT OF PENNSYLVANIA,
Baltimore, Md., September 11, 1861—11 p. m.

Hon. SIMON CAMERON, *Secretary of War:*

SIR : Your letter was handed to me half an hour ago by Mr. Allen,* who is of the opinion that, in consideration of the lateness of the hour and the uncertainty of finding all the parties, the arrests should be

---

* Not found; but see report No. 5, following.

deferred till to-morrow night. I will detain the steamer, so that they can be taken directly on board. No effort or precaution will be spared to carry your order into execution promptly and effectually.

I am, very respectfully, your obedient servant,

JOHN A. DIX,
Major-General, Commanding.

No. 3.

Letter from General Dix to Maj. Gen. John E. Wool.

HEADQUARTERS DEPARTMENT OF PENNSYLVANIA,
Baltimore, Md., September 13, 1861.

GENERAL: Lieut. W. M. Wilson, of the Fourth Cavalry, will leave these headquarters this evening with the following gentlemen, who have been taken in custody by order of the Government: George William Brown, mayor of the city of Baltimore; members-elect of the legislature, S. Teakle Wallis, Henry M. Warfield, Charles H. Pitts, T. Parkin Scott, Lawrence Sangston, Ross Winans, John Hanson Thomas, William G. Harrison, Leonard G. Quinlan, and Robert M. Denison; Henry May, member of Congress; F. Key Howard, Andrew A. Lynch, and Thomas W. Hall, citizens of Baltimore. The direction of the Secretary of War is to keep them in close custody, suffering no one to communicate with them, and to convey them at once to Fort Monroe, there to remain in close custody until they shall be forwarded to their ultimate destination. The prisoners are in charge of Lieutenant Wilson, who will return with the detachment of the Third Regiment New York Volunteers, sent as a guard to the prisoners, to these headquarters by the first steamer.

I am, very respectfully, your obedient servant,

JOHN A. DIX,
Major-General, Commanding.

Maj. Gen. JOHN E. WOOL,
Commanding Department of Virginia.

No. 4.

Reports of Major-General Banks of arrests at Frederick, Md.

DARNESTOWN, MD., *September* 18, 1861.
To Governor SEWARD:

But four present at opening yesterday. Eighteen s—— only in town. Twelve secured up to 5 p. m. Probably all last night.

N. P. BANKS.

—

HEADQUARTERS, CAMP NEAR DARNESTOWN,
September 20, 1861.

SIR: I have the honor to report, in obedience to the order of the Secretary of War, and the general commanding the Army of the Potomac, transmitted to me by letter of the 12th instant,* that all the members of the Maryland Legislature assembled at Frederick City on the 17th in-

---

* These instructions cannot be found.

stant known or suspected to be disloyal in their relations to the Government have been arrested.

The opening of the session was attended chiefly by Union men, and after rigid examination but nine secession members were found in the city. These were arrested, with the clerk of the senate, and sent to Annapolis, according to my orders, on the 18th instant, under guard, and safely lodged on board a Government steamer in waiting for them. Of their destination thence I had no direction. The names of the parties thus arrested and disposed of were as follows, viz: B. H. Salmon, Frederick; R. C. McCubbin, Annapolis; William R. Miller, Cecil County; Thomas Claggett, Frederick; Josiah H. Gordon, Alleghany County; Clark J. Durant, Saint Mary's County; J. Lawrence Jones, Talbot County; Andrew Kessler, jr., Frederick; Bernard Mills, Carroll County; J. W. Brecolt, chief clerk of the senate.

No meeting of the senate occurred; but three senators were in town, and those were Union men. Three subordinate officers of the senate, the chief clerk and printer of the house, and one or two others were also arrested, but released after the departure of the members for Annapolis upon taking the oath of allegiance.

Milton Kidd, clerk of the house, is in the last stages of consumption, beyond the power of doing harm, and was released upon taking the oath and making a solemn declaration to act no further with the legislature under any circumstances whatever. This course was adopted upon the urgent solicitation of the Union members present. The same parties desired the release of R. C. McCubbin, of Annapolis, upon the same condition. I telegraphed to the commander of the steamer that he might be left at Annapolis under sufficient guard until the orders of the Government could be ascertained.

Colonel Ruger, Third Wisconsin Regiment; Lieutenant Copeland, my aide-de-camp, and a detachment of police rendered efficient aid.

Sufficient information was obtained as to preparations for board, &c., to lead to the belief that the attendance of members would have been large had not the arrest of some of the leaders been made at Baltimore on Saturday and Monday before the day of meeting.

I regret the attempt at Frederick was not more successful.

I have the honor to be, with great respect, your obedient servant,

N. P. BANKS,
Major-General, Commanding Division.

Col. R. B. MARCY, *Chief of Staff, &c.:*

No. 5.

Report of Mr. Allen Pinkerton of arrests at Baltimore, Md.

WASHINGTON, D. C., *September 23, 1861.*

SIR: On the 11th instant, in pursuance of the orders of the Hon. Simon Cameron, Secretary of War, and Major-General McClellan, I went to Baltimore, accompanied by a sufficient number of my detective force, and Lieut. W. M. Wilson, of the Fourth United States Cavalry. On arriving in Baltimore I proceeded to Fort McHenry, and delivered to Major-General Dix an order from the War Department for the arrest of T. Parkin Scott, S. Teakle Wallis, Frank Key Howard, T. W. Hall, Henry May, and H. M. Warfield. The said order mentioned to General Dix that I was instructed to conduct the arrests, also to search for and seize the correspondence of the above-named parties.

On consultation with General Dix it was deemed advisable, as it was now about midnight, to postpone the attempt to arrest until the following night, as it was impossible to tell if the parties to be arrested were in town or at their respective houses. General Dix directed me to call on Provost-Marshal Dodge and Assistant Provost-Marshal McPhail, of Baltimore, who would furnish me all the police force necessary to make the arrests. On the morning of the 12th instant I called on Messrs. Dodge and McPhail. I found them to be highly intelligent and able men for their respective positions, and arrangements were at once entered into between us for procuring the necessary information in relation to the probable whereabouts of the parties named to be arrested, and the hour of midnight was fixed upon as the time to make the descent, Mr. McPhail detailing a sufficient police force to accompany my own force to each house.

At about 9.30 p. m., while at the provost-marshal's office, an order was received from Major-General Dix, addressed to Provost-Marshal Dodge, directing the arrest of George W. Brown, W. G. Harrison, Lawrence Sangston, Ross Winans, J. Hanson Thomas, Andrew A. Lynch, C. H. Pitts, L. G. Quinlan, and Robert M. Denison. Arrangements were at once made for the arrest of the above-named parties, which was accomplished during the night, and early on the following day (13th) they were all committed to Fort McHenry.

At about midnight the several divisions moved simultaneously upon the places where we had discovered Scott, Wallis, F. Key Howard, Hall, May, and Warfield, and at that time all the above named were arrested within fifteen minutes, their clothing thoroughly searched, and immediately thereafter they were forwarded to Fort McHenry in separate carriages. My force made diligent search for all correspondence on the premises of each of the parties, all of which was seized.

Frank Key Howard being one of the editors of the Baltimore Exchange newspaper and T. W. Hall editor of The South, I construed the order to search for and seize correspondence of a treasonable nature in the possession of the parties arrested a sufficient warrant for me to enter and search the editorial and press rooms of the Exchange and South, which I did, seizing the correspondence found therein.

All the correspondence found I brought with me to Washington, and now beg leave respectfully to submit to you briefs of the same, which I have had carefully prepared, retaining the originals in my possession subject to your order.*

Very respectfully, your obedient servant,

ALLEN PINKERTON.

Hon. WM. H. SEWARD, *Secretary of State, Washington, D. C.*

No. 6.

Letter from General Wool to Commanding Officer Fort Lafayette, N. Y.

HEADQUARTERS DEPARTMENT OF VIRGINIA,
Fort Monroe, September 24, 1861.

SIR : By direction of Lieutenant-General Scott, I forward to you for custody and safe-keeping at Fort Lafayette the following political prisoners, arrested in Baltimore, 14 in number, viz :†

*   *   *   *   *   *   *

---

* Not furnished from the State Department.
† List omitted, embraces all the names given in No. 3, p. 194, except that of Ross Winans.

I presume you will receive instructions in regard to them from the proper quarters. In the mean time, according to the recommendation of the Secretary of State to me, "they will be allowed decent fare and the privileges of air and exercise compatible with their safe-keeping," not going out of the fort. They must be watched during their confinement, and allowed to receive no visitors not authorized by the authorities in Washington, and when visited a commissioned officer must be present.

You will acknowledge the receipt of this communication and of the prisoners named in it. Such acknowledgment, in writing, will be handed to Captain Coster, the bearer of this letter, who will deliver the prisoners into your own custody.

I am, very respectfully, your obedient servant,

JOHN E. WOOL,
Major-General.

To the COMMANDING OFFICER,
Fort Lafayette, New York Harbor.

No. 7.

Letter from Governor Hicks to General Banks.

STATE OF MARYLAND, EXECUTIVE CHAMBER,
Annapolis, September 20, 1861.

DEAR SIR : We have some of the product of your order here in the persons of some eight or ten members of the State Legislature, soon, I learn, to depart for healthy quarters. We see the good fruit already produced by the arrests.

We can no longer mince matters with these desperate people. I concur in all you have done.

With great respect, your obedient servant,

THO. H. HICKS.

Maj. Gen. N. P. BANKS.

SEPTEMBER 15, 1861.—Skirmish at Pritchard's Mill, Va., near Antietam Ford, Md.

Report of Col. John W. Geary, Twenty-eighth Pennsylvania Infantry.

POINT OF ROCKS, MARYLAND,
September 17, 1861.

SIR : On the night of the 13th instant I received reliable information that about 2,200 rebels were stationed in an offensive attitude between the Shenandoah and Shepherdstown, on the Virginia shore of the Potomac. This force was composed of infantry (the greater portion of them being in the neighborhood of the Old Furnace and Pritchard's Mill. The number of them actually engaged is variously estimated at from 500 to 600, while they had a reserve of 1,500 or 1,600 within a short distance behind the hills and along the railroad in the direction of Martinsburg), cavalry, and artillery, with four pieces of cannon. Their object seemed to be to attack the right of my command, resting about 3 miles above Harper's Ferry, on the Maryland side of the river, and threatened that they would turn that position, gain the rear of my pickets, and capture a considerable portion of my command, consisting of two companies of the Thirteenth Massachusetts Regiment. This information reached me at 11 o'clock at night; and one hour after I proceeded from my camp at this place with three companies of riflemen (B, I, and L) of my regiment, a section of the New York Ninth Battery, with two rifled cannon, commanded by Lieut. J. W. Martin. After a very rapid and, owing to the extreme [heat] of the weather, fatiguing march of 12 miles I reached Harper's Ferry about daylight on the morning of the 14th. I found the rebels then engaged in making an attack upon the troops stationed above my command near Sharpsburg. Those troops made a handsome defense, and before I could proceed to their assistance the rebels retired, under pretense of having received orders to report at once at Manassas.

On the morning of the 15th I acquired considerable knowledge of the position of the enemy, and, desiring to assure myself more particularly with regard to their movements, I detailed scouting parties to such points as the rebels were said to be, to ascertain the truth. One of these parties, consisting of an officer (Lieutenant Brown), 1 sergeant, and 6 privates, all of the Thirteenth Massachusetts Regiment, mounted, by my direction pushed forward as far as Antietam Ford; this party, returning, while opposite Pritchard's Mill, were fired upon suddenly from the Virginia side of the river by a volley of about 50 muskets from a body of men perfectly concealed. One man of the party was instantly killed on the spot, and, owing to a continuous fire kept [up] on the remaining portion of the party, it was impossible for them to move from the position to which they had taken themselves to prevent further losses as the enemy deployed down the river.

About the same time a number of the enemy made their appearance on the apex brow of the Loudoun Heights, also on the road leading around its base to Harper's Ferry, and commenced firing. At the same [time] a considerable number of them opened fire from the heights back of Harper's Ferry and from all parts of the railroad along the river up to Pritchard's Mill. The latter were deployed, well covered behind the embankments of the railroad and bushes, and secreted in houses, barns, and lime quarries.

I stationed Company L, under command of Captain Barr, of my regiment, upon that portion of the Baltimore and Ohio Railroad below the abutment of the burnt bridge, in the direction of Sandy Hook, with instructions to clear the Loudoun Heights and the road at their base, which they did, causing the enemy quickly to retire, leaving 5 or 6 killed and wounded on the ground. I stationed a company and a half of the Thirteenth Massachusetts Regiment, commanded by Major Gould, from the bridge upward to the first lock on the canal, a distance of about 1½ miles, to defend against attacks from the town and surrounding heights. I also left one piece of artillery with Major Gould's detachment in such position as to sweep the several streets of Harper's Ferry. I placed Company B, Captain Warden, of my regiment, above the lock, where the right of Major Gould's command rested, and deployed it along the river about 1 mile. This company rendered very efficient service by its good marksmen at long range and seriously galled the enemy. I then advanced with one piece of artillery, commanded by Lieutenant Martin; half of Company I, Thirteenth Massachusetts Regiment, commanded by Captain Shriber; and Company I, commanded by Captain McDonough, Twenty-eighth Pennsylvania Volunteers. The combined advance, numbering about 130 men, took possession of several dry basins along the canal and a point known as Maryland Ore Banks, which afforded an excellent shelter to my men. Thus situated, a very spirited fire was maintained for something over two hours, the fire of the enemy gradually slackening as they were dislodged by our artillery and sharpshooters, until about 6 o'clock the firing entirely ceased. (The enemy were driven from every point they occupied and sullenly retired beyond the range of our guns toward the interior). During this affair considerable damage was done to the mill, houses, and barns in which the rebels had taken shelter within reach of our cannon.

As far as can be ascertained through Virginia sources deemed reliable there were 18 of the rebels killed and about 25 wounded. It is impossible to ascertain exactly what the casualties of the enemy were, from the fact [that] the river divided us from them, and we have partly to rely upon the Virginians themselves for our information. Our loss was 1 killed and 3 slightly wounded. The wounds all occurred from fragments detached from the bands around the James shell, discharged by our own artillery.

The efficiency and long range of our Enfield rifles has been fully proved in this affair, and I am pleased to state they have verified our fullest expectations. Their superior accuracy and length of range over those of the enemy account in part for the small number of casualties on our side.

I am much gratified to be able to state that the troops under my command, without exception, behaved with the most admirable bravery and coolness. And I would be derelict of duty if I did not state that the highest meed of praise is due to the company officers for the gallant manner in which they carried out every order issued and the noble emulation which animated them during the action. Several small skirmishes have occurred since, but owing to the smallness of the numbers engaged would not justify a detailed statement.

A skirmish occurred this evening near Harper's Ferry between the rebels and a portion of troops, resulting successfully to our arms. Several of the enemy are reported killed and wounded.

A small skirmish occurred above this place, in which, it is said, one of the rebels was killed.

Respectfully submitted.

[JOHN W. GEARY,
Colonel Twenty-eighth Regiment Pennsylvania Volunteers.]
Capt. ROBERT WILLIAMS, *Assistant Adjutant-General.*

Casualties of the enemy: 18 killed and 25 wounded.
Casualties of my command: 1 killed; 3 slightly wounded.
Articles captured: 2 iron cannon (12-pounders); 2 fine bay mules; 2 small brass mortars; 1 wagon; 1 prisoner, William S. Engles, second lieutenant Company K, Second Virginia Volunteers.

SEPTEMBER 16, 1861.—Skirmish opposite Seneca Creek, Maryland.

Report of Maj. Gen. Nathaniel P. Banks, U. S. Army.

DARNESTOWN, *September 17, 1861.*

All quiet here. Nothing unusual at Poolesville up to this evening, nor above, so far as we can learn. Last night a party of the Thirty-fourth New York, Colonel La Dew, crossed the river at Seneca Creek, and encountered a force of three companies, losing 2 or 3 men out of 15. This morning they shelled the rebel camp and drove them back. Nothing else has occurred, and nothing is indicated on the part of the enemy.

N. P. BANKS.

Hon. THOMAS A. SCOTT, *Assistant Secretary of War.*

SEPTEMBER 23–25, 1861.—Descent upon Romney, W. Va., including affairs at Mechanicsburg Gap and Hanging Rock Pass.

REPORTS.

No. 1.—Col. Angus W. McDonald, C. S. Army.
No. 2.—Col. E. H. McDonald, Seventy-seventh Virginia Militia.
No. 3.—Col. A. Monroe, One hundred and fourteenth Virginia Militia.
No. 4.—Maj. O. R. Funsten, C. S. Army.
No. 5.—Lieut. J. H. Lionberger, C. S. Army.

No. 1.

Reports of Col. Angus W. McDonald, C. S. Army.

HEADQUARTERS,
Romney Va., October 20, 1861.

GENERAL: Inclosed you have my report of the conflict of the 24th and 25th ultimo. I regret the necessity which compels me to invite your perusal of so long a report of so unimportant an affair. Feeling deeply, however, the importance of holding this post, and anxious that the Department should appreciate the hazard of attempting to do so against greatly superior forces both in numbers and equipments, I have indulged in details combining action and description, that the great extent of my line of defense may be more strikingly manifest.

You will perceive from my report that the two passes through which my position was attacked are distant from each other some 6 miles. Besides these, 2 miles below the Hanging Rock Pass there are three fords and a bridge over the South Branch. The passage over any one of these would place the enemy within the portals of my line. Nine miles south of Romney is a third gap, through which the valley of the South Branch may be entered and the river forded. If my force stationed at any one of the passes or fords should be opposed by over-whelming numbers of the enemy, re-enforcements from either of the other passes could only be received by a march of from 2 to 7 miles.

This statement is, I am sure, sufficient to show by what a precarious tenure, with the handful of force I have, I now hold this place. The printed slip which I inclose, clipped from a Wheeling paper, is from the pen of one who well understands the subject upon which he has written. I will add to it: From Romney to the mouth of Little Cacapon is 25 miles; to the mouth of the South Branch, 18 miles; to the town of Cumberland, 27 miles; to New Creek Station, 18 miles; to Piedmont and Bloomington, each 25 miles. All of these are points on the Baltimore and Ohio Railroad, and any one of them may be attacked by a day's march from Romney. The distance from the mouth of the Little Cacapon to Bloomington is about 60 miles. The mean distance from Romney to the railroad is about 20 miles.

It is, I presume, impossible that either army can winter on the top or at the foot of Cheat Mountain. Jackson's force added to mine could hold the rich valleys of the South Branch and Patterson's Creek, and draw from them abundant supplies during the winter, and always have the power to prevent the use—safe use at least—by the enemy of either the Baltimore and Ohio Railroad or Chesapeake and Ohio Canal.

If my command is to winter here, it is time to provide quarters for them. In less than fifteen days inclement weather will compel us to strike our tents, if the cowardice of the enemy, now outnumbering us five times, will permit us so long to hold this post. Two-fifths of my regiment are now, by the requirements of the Department, in Berkeley and Jefferson. If I had a regiment of volunteers and three additional pieces of artillery my camp would be defended by them, whilst my mounted men could at any time strike some point on the railroad or canal, and prevent their available use by the enemy.

I beg to be informed if I must prepare winter quarters at Romney.

I have the honor to be, respectfully, yours to command,

ANGUS W. McDONALD,
Colonel, Commanding Brigade, &c.

General S. Cooper.

—

HEADQUARTERS,
Romney, Va., October 8, 1861.

General: On the night of the 23d September last, about 11.30 o'clock, the intelligence was received by me that our picket, stationed 2 miles beyond the Mechanicsburg Pass, on the old road leading to Paddytown (now New Creek Station), had been fired upon and driven in by the advance guard of a large force of the enemy moving upon Romney. I at once sent an order to Major Funsten, commanding that portion of the cavalry regiment under my command at this place, to detach the companies of Captains Sheetz, Bowen, Miller, and Harper to the Mechanicsburg Pass, with orders to occupy it and hold it against the approach of the enemy, and to order Captain Myers' company to the Hanging Rock Pass, to co-operate with Col. E. H. McDonald, commanding the Seventy-seventh Regiment of Virginia Militia, in charge of this pass, in holding it against the enemy. At the same time Lieutenant Lionberger was directed to proceed to the Mechanicsburg Pass with the howitzer, under command of Major Funsten.

I learned upon return of my aide, Lieutenant McDonald, that my orders had been anticipated so far as the sending of Captain Myers with his company to the Hanging Rock Pass and Captain Sheetz to the Mechanicsburg Pass. Colonel Monroe, commanding the One hundred and fourteenth Regiment Virginia Militia, was ordered to march his regiment (then reported to be 140 to 150 strong, and encamped at Church Hill, 3 miles east of Romney, on the Northwestern turnpike road) to a point just east of Romney, and, as a reserve, there to await further orders. Captain Jordan was ordered to deploy his company along the eastern base of the mountain in which are the above-named passes, so as to give timely notice should the enemy attempt the passage of the mountain between them. The rifled 6-pounder and the 4-pounder were not removed from camp, retaining them until subsequent events should demonstrate what position for them would be most advantageous. Captains Winfield and Shands' companies of cavalry were also directed to remain in camp, which is about 200 yards back of and on the inland slope of Cemetery Hill, awaiting orders.

It is proper, in order to give you an understanding of the ground upon which the main attack was expected, that you should have before you a brief outline of the positions occupied by my command. The town of Romney is situated upon a plateau elevated some 150 feet above the level of the South Branch, which washes the base of a high bluff. The western terminus of the plateau, 1 mile west of Romney, is the South Branch Mountain, in which are the Mechanicsburg and Hanging Rock Passes; the former 3 miles southwest, the latter 4 miles northwest, from Romney. After having made the disposition of my forces as above detailed, I proceeded to the Mechanicsburg Pass. Before arriving there I heard several volleys of musketry, which proceeded from the western entrance. Arriving there, I found the detachment under Major Funsten; a portion of it strongly posted behind a breastwork formed of rock, and a dam across a mill creek, which flows through the pass, whilst another portion of it was deployed as skirmishers upon both sides of the pass. Whilst here sharp firing occurred between the advance of the enemy and our skirmishers.

At about 6 o'clock in the morning, the firing having ceased at the Mechanicsburg Pass, I returned to town. In the mean time we had been quiet at the Hanging Rock Pass. At about 6.30 several volleys of musketry were distinctly heard coming from this pass. I had been confident up to this time that the attack which had been made at the Mechanicsburg Pass was only a feint to mask the main attack, which was to be made at the other. At this time the fog was so dense as to obscure completely every object beyond a distance of 50 yards and so continued until 10 or 10.30 o'clock.

Immediately upon hearing the firing from the Hanging Rock Pass I sent an order to Colonel Monroe to leave 50 of his men as a reserve, and with the remainder to move without delay to the support of Col. E. H. McDonald. Captain Myers had deployed his company along the east bank of the river, stationing pickets at the ford at the west end of the pass. As the enemy advanced across the ford the pickets halted them at a distance of 40 yards, so dense was the fog, supposing them to be friends. After parleying for some moments they were fired upon by the enemy. This part of Captain Myers' company returned the fire, and retired to their reserve station at the east end of the pass. The enemy then advanced between the river and the rocks, which at points overhang the road. When their cavalry had advanced under these rocks, and the position occupied by Col. E. H. McDonald, whose command, owing to the company of Captain Inskeep being upon detached service, consisted of only 27 men, a destructive fire was opened by this force upon them. Without waiting to reload their guns, the men were ordered to throw rocks upon them which had been previously collected for the purpose. This unexpected and novel attack produced the greatest confusion; the cavalry, stampeded, were driven back upon the infantry, many of whom jumped into the river; some managed to escape to the other side by swimming, but many were drowned. Owing, however, to the dense fog which still enshrouded and obscured everything, the effect of this attack, repulsing the enemy and driving him back out of the pass and across the river, was not discovered, and the vedettes of Col. E. H. McDonald, posted in his rear, giving him the incorrect information that the enemy were crossing upon his right in the attempt to outflank him, he returned with his command towards Romney.

About 7 o'clock I received information from Captain Myers that the enemy were advancing with a large force of infantry and cavalry up the river. Lieutenant-Colonel Lupton, who had been left by Colonel Monroe with 50 men as a reserve, was then ordered to support Colonel Monroe, which order was promptly executed.

Waiting anxiously upon a point upon the river bluff, Cemetery Hill, which commanded a view of the valley between the two passes, for the clearing up of the fog, so as to be able to ascertain the position and force of the enemy, at about 8 o'clock I received a second dispatch from Captain Myers, informing me of the advance of the enemy from Hanging Rock Pass in overwhelming force. Confirmed then that the main attack was to come from this point, I immediately dispatched an order to Major Funsten, directing him to withdraw the force under his command from the Mechanicsburg Pass to Cemetery Hill, and there await further orders.

From this time until about 11.30 o'clock there was no appearance of the enemy either above or below us. At about 11.30 o'clock the enemy made their appearance on the mountain side just below the Mechanicsburg Pass. Major Funsten was directed, with the companies of Captains Bowen and Miller, together with the howitzer given in charge of Captain Bowen, to take position in some woods opposite the bridge, so as to command the bridge and ford. The rifled 6-pounder was then put in position on Cemetery Hill, under charge of Lieutenant Lionberger, so as to command additionally the bridge and ford and the road leading from these points to Romney. The enemy, however, instead of attempting the passage of the river at this point, after saluting us with a few harmless rounds from his cannon, directed towards Major Funsten's command, retired out of sight.

About 12 m. I again received information that the enemy were advancing from the Hanging Rock Gap. Major Funsten was directed to withdraw the detachment under his command from the position commanding the bridge, except Captain Bowen's company and the howitzer, and with all the force of mounted men, together with the 4-pounder, to go to the support of Captains Myers and Jordan, the latter having previously moved to sustain Captain Myers.

Shortly after this order was given the enemy appeared on the hill about 1½ miles north of the town, but seemed to hesitate to attack. At about 3.30 o'clock p. m. a movement was made by the enemy as if he designed to get possession of the Winchester road. This movement was observed also by Major Funsten, who promptly took the steps detailed in his report to prevent it.

By about 4.30 o'clock the enemy had disappeared. I then supposed they were moving in the direction of the Winchester road, and fearing lest the baggage train of the regiment should be cut off, which I had before understood had been removed some two miles from town, and which by my orders had been further removed through a narrow defile to Church Hill, in order to obtain ground upon which the train could be turned if necessary, I gave the order for the cavalry regiment to retire by the Winchester road, and to the commandants of militia who were in the rear of the cavalry to retire to Hanging Rock, 16 miles east of Romney, on the Winchester road, the latter order being countermanded when the command reached Church Hill. Before reaching the church, and when about 2 miles from town, we were overtaken by a messenger, informing us that the enemy had retreated and recrossed the river.

Arrived at the church, and having understood that the baggage train was 3 miles farther down the road, at Frenchtown, where it had been removed by order of Major Funsten, in order to secure it against the expected attack at Churchville, it was decided by a council, composed of the captains of the cavalry commanded by Major Funsten and myself, to encamp the cavalry regiment at Frenchtown. Early the next morning I directed the whole force under my command to prepare to return to Romney whilst preparations were being made for the march.

At about 8.30 o'clock a. m. a courier arrived from Romney, bringing the intelligence that the enemy had returned to Romney and were then in possession of the town. I immediately gave orders directing Major Funsten to take the mounted men under his command, together with the howitzer and rifled gun under charge of Lieutenant Lionberger, and attack the enemy. I sent orders to Colonel Monroe to move as rapidly as possible the forces under his command to the church, and there await further orders, holding in reserve the 4-pounder, the gunner of which was directed to follow on with it, to be put in position as events might decide to be best. During the time that the enemy were in town I understand that they were fired upon by Private Blue, of the Seventy-seventh Regiment, and by Private Picket, of the cavalry regiment, killing one man and wounding others; by a company of the Seventy-seventh Regiment, under Captain Inskeep, and also that some of the One hundred and fourteenth Regiment fired upon some of their cavalry that were drawn about three fourths of a mile from town in pursuit of some horsemen. This firing resulted in some loss to the enemy, killing 1 of the cavalry and wounding others. A short time after the cavalry had been fired into, the enemy commenced to retreat from town, where a halt had been called, and some of them were obtaining something to eat whilst preparations were being made for carrying off all the stock—horses, cattle, &c.—convenient to the road.

Whilst thus engaged an immense cloud of dust rising from the Cemetery Hill announced the rapid approach of the mounted men of the command, gallantly led by Major Funsten. Immediately the enemy, startled by apparent numbers, commenced a rapid retreat. Their rear had not proceeded more than 200 yards from the bridge when the column headed by Major Funsten fearlessly and impetuously charged upon them under a heavy fire from their cannon and musketry. Our column coming up within short shot-gun range, successively delivered their fire with telling effect. The rear of our column, as they crossed the river, filing to the left, commenced a raking fire upon the left flank of the enemy as they passed along the road. Lieutenant Lionberger at this time came up with the howitzer, and putting it in position so as to command their left flank, did effective work.

Fearing lest the enemy might have occupied Mechanicsburg Pass, the pursuit of the enemy, stampeded by the charge, was not pressed within it, but Lieutenant Lionberger was ordered by Major Funsten to shell it with the rifled 6-pounder. After this had been done, the companies of Captains Sheetz and Winfield were sent forward as an advance to reconnoiter. At this time I reached the head of the column, and learned of the sending forward of the companies of Captains Sheetz and Winfield. From one-half to three-quarters of an hour was gained by the enemy in the necessary delay at the pass. The pursuit was now renewed, and at about 6 miles from town the enemy made another short stand, but were immediately put to flight again upon being fired into by the companies of Captains Sheetz and Winfield, and with the loss of several of their number. Such, however, was the character of the country through which the road lay, that the progress of the pursuing column was necessarily cautious, the deep defiles and thick underbrush frequently affording favorable opportunities for successful ambuscade, which had to be provided against by skirmishing and reconnoitering parties.

At Sheetz's Mill, 9 miles from Romney, the enemy again made a short stand. I directed Lieutenant Lionberger to open upon them with shell from his 6-pounder. A single shot was fired, when, discovering a more favorable position, I directed him to it. Whilst the position of the 6-pounder was being changed our shot was returned by shell from the gun of the enemy, passing to our right. Before our gun could be got into its new position the infantry of the enemy were again in rapid retreat, their cavalry lingering in their rear. Under a heavy fire from the carbines of the cavalry the gun was again got into position. Knowing the direction of the road up which the enemy were retreating, and which was concealed by a low wood ridge, I gave Lieutenant Lionberger the range, and he again opened upon them with shell. Some of the shell falling amid the fleeing mass committed fearful havoc amongst them. In the mean time there had been a rapid interchange of shots between their cavalry and ours, but, being at long range, without much effect.

Upon the suggestion of Captain Sheetz I directed Major Funsten to send forward the companies of Captains Sheetz, Myers, Winfield, and Miller by a shorter route, with a view to intercept the retreat of the enemy by ambuscade. Owing, however, to the rapid flight of the enemy, and to a mistake having been made as to the point of intersection of the two roads, the main body of the enemy, with their artillery and baggage train, had passed before the detachment got into position to attack them. At this point we captured 4 stragglers, and, night coming on, I sent an order to Major Funsten, directing the pursuit to cease, having pursued them to within 2 miles of New Creek Station, a distance of 15 miles.

Returning to Romney, at Sheetz's Mill we met the militia, to whom I had given orders just before leaving Mechanicsburg Pass to follow the cavalry as fast as possible, with a view to supporting them if necessary. From Sheetz's Mill the whole command returned to Romney, where it arrived about 2 o'clock in the morning.

Great credit is due to Major Funsten and the officers and men under his command for the impetuous and daring charge which was made upon the enemy just beyond the bridge. A panic seems there to have stricken them, from which they were never afterwards permitted to recover during the whole pursuit.

Our loss during the two days was remarkably small—5 wounded (2 by our own men), to which is to be added the killing of 5 horses and the wounding of 2 or 3 others. Of the loss of the enemy I cannot speak with certainty. Five were captured. From information derived from persons I should estimate the killed and wounded at from 50 to 80. Among this number many were drowned on the morning of the 24th, when driven back from the Hanging Rock Pass. Five of the bodies of those drowned have been recovered.

The pursuit would have been much more effective and destructive had any of the companies of the command at this post been armed in addition to their guns with sabers and pistols. The two companies so armed belonging to this regiment are absent on detached service in Jefferson. None of the companies here have either sabers or pistols. I can but regret the necessity which deprives the officers and men of my command of the weapons adapted to a cavalry charge, and which they have shown themselves so well qualified to make daring and effective use of, especially so when they are opposed to an enemy well equipped in all these particulars, and whom if they meet in a hand-to-hand conflict they must oppose with clubbed rifles and shot-guns against revolvers and sabers.

The force under my command was upon the 24th about 300 mounted men and about 250 infantry—the militia of the county and unmounted men of my regiment. On the 25th the infantry was increased by accessions to the militia to about 350. The strength of the enemy in the two days' fight could not have fallen short of 1,500, in which are included about 75 cavalry.

Before concluding I am obliged to make acknowledgments of the efficient services rendered by Mr. Crane and Robert A. Tilden, connected with the quartermaster's department; Mr. James V. Clark, volunteer, and Lieut. Angus W. McDonald, my aide, in bearing my orders with promptitude to the many distant points at which detachments of my command were posted during the 24th and 25th September. Mr. Tilden, bravely joining in the charge of the cavalry on the 25th, was severely wounded, having his arm broken by a Minie ball, from which he is yet in danger of losing his limb, perhaps his life.

Of all the force engaged the statements made in my report sufficiently attest the gallantry and effective conduct of those to whom they pertain.

I have the honor to be, respectfully, yours to command,

ANGUS W. McDONALD,
Colonel, Commanding Brigade, &c.

General S. COOPER.

No. 2.

Report of Col. E. H. McDonald, Seventy-seventh Virginia Militia.

CAMP BUFFALO, *October* 3, 1861.

SIR: In compliance with your written order of the 2d instant I report the operations of the forces under my command on the 24th and 25th ultimo.

On the morning of the 24th, at 12.30 o'clock, I received your order to hold my command under marching orders. At 1 o'clock I received your order to occupy the lower pass with my available force and co-operate with Captain Myers in its defense. Arriving there at 2 o'clock with 27 infantry and 7 mounted men, I found Captain Myers posted under the rocks. I then took my position with my infantry on the top of the rocks which overhang the road and almost the river, and sent my mounted men to picket a road which ran in the rear of the rocks, known as the Old Ferry Road.

At 4 o'clock a. m. I heard the enemy crossing the ford about one-half mile below, and from the length of time occupied in crossing I supposed them to number 700 infantry and 200 cavalry. As soon as their advance guard had crossed the river Captain Myers' pickets fired upon them. They returned the fire by a volley, and advanced, shouting. Captain Myers then fell back beyond my position. When the enemy had advanced up under where we were posted, they commenced to fire upon us, as I suppose, to draw our fire, as it was impossible, owing to the fog which then prevailed, to see us.

I could restrain my men no longer, and we commenced our attack upon them, some discharging their pieces, others rolling stones down on them. This we kept up, under a heavy fire of musketry, until my pickets reported that the enemy were flanking us upon our right. I then ordered my men to fall back to a position upon the mountain. Owing to the heavy fog, we were not aware that we had driven them back across the ford. I hastened to join you at Romney. Arriving there at 12 m., we ascertained the enemy were renewing their attack in the direction of the bridge. We then took our position on the hill in rear of the howitzer, and remained there until the enemy retired.

Returning to Romney at 6 o'clock p. m. I received your order to join you at Church Hill, but my men were so much fatigued that I found it necessary to encamp for the night with a portion of Colonel Monroe's command upon the outskirts of Romney. During our engagement with the enemy at the rocks our showers of ball and stone threw them into the utmost confusion, their own cavalry riding over their infantry, crowding them into the river, thus drowning many of them—how many we have not been able to ascertain, but we have recovered 5 dead bodies, and learned from our citizens whom they made prisoners that they carried off with them 1 dead and 11 wounded, while on our side no one was hurt. We obtained 5 blankets and 2 muskets, which they threw away on their retreat.

On the morning of the 25th ultimo, about 8 o'clock, the enemy was reported approaching Romney in considerable force. We then fell back to a position east of the town, and exchanged shots with them whenever they ventured within reach of our guns. This position we maintained until the enemy was charged upon by Major Funsten with the cavalry, when we followed as far as Sheetz's Mill, but were unable to come up with them afterward.

The troops spoken of above were commanded by Captain Roberson and Lieutenant Blue, and behaved in a manner which reflected great credit upon themselves and their officers. Lieutenant Blue deserves a special notice for his coolness and bravery. One company of my command, under the charge of Capt. J. V. Inskeep, was stationed at Frankfort, upon special service, whom I could not reach with orders, but as soon as they heard their services were needed, started by a circuitous route for the scene of action. Arriving at Romney on the morning of the 25th, they met the enemy approaching the town. Retiring upon the hills east of them, they fired upon their advance, and thus opened the engagement of that day. They deserve great praise for the promptness and zeal with which they came unbidden to the scene of action.

For the report of that portion of my command detailed to work the artillery I refer you to the report of Lieutenant Lionberger, under whose command they were placed.

Respectfully submitted.

E. H. McDONALD,
Colonel Seventy-seventh Regiment Virginia Infantry.
Col. ANGUS W. McDONALD, *Commanding Brigade.*

No. 3.

Report of Col. A. Monroe, One hundred and fourteenth Virginia Militia.

ROMNEY, VA., *September 28, 1861.*

SIR: After a delay that I hope you will excuse, I have the honor to submit the following report:

At 3 o'clock on the morning of the 24th instant, in obedience to your order, I left my camp at the Branch Mountain, with all the men then there under my command, which, after leaving a small guard at the encampment, amounted about 145 men, but the number was increased during the day to 200. When I reached Romney I heard firing at the Hanging Rock, to which point we started on double-quick. On arriving at the curve in the road south of Colonel Parsons' I learned from a messenger that the enemy had passed the gap, and that the cavalry was advancing up the road very rapidly, and would meet me but a short distance below Parsons' house. I then left the road, passing through his upland fields in a direct line, crossing a deep ravine, and took position on the crest of the bluff facing the bottom, my left wing opposite Parsons' house and within fifty yards of the road, though the fog then was so dense we could scarcely see it.

When the fog had disappeared I discovered that our cavalry had fallen back and were drawn up in line of battle south of the stone house. I also discovered that I could occupy a much more advantageous position a little in advance of the cavalry opposite the house. I then marched my regiment back and took position there. After remaining there a short time I was informed by one of your officers that a large column of the enemy's infantry was on the ridge between Parsons' house and Inskeep's, and moving rapidly towards the mountain. I then divided my command into four detachments, assigning Lieutenant-Colonel Lupton to the command of one, Major Gineven to another, Major Diaver to another, and taking the command of the fourth myself on foot, ordered that all should be deployed as skirmishers as rapidly as possible towards the top of the mountain, following the top of Black's Ridge. The enemy kept in our sight for about a mile and a half up the mountain, though not within rifle shot. As soon as they discovered we had outflanked them they changed their course toward the branch, falling behind the ridge, and I saw no more of them. On learning that they had retreated through the gap, I returned with my detachment to Romney about 4 o'clock, where I remained till after 10 o'clock p. m., expecting Col. E. H. McDonald to bring on a re-enforcement from Frenchburg.

Having been told that you desired me to meet you at Frenchburg I left my men under the command of Col. Isaac Parsons and reached Frenchburg about midnight, where I found Messrs. Lupton, Gineven, and Diaver with their respective commands, together with about 100 additional troops, belonging to my regiment, on their way to join me.

On the morning of the 25th I received orders from you to return with my regiment to the top of the Branch Mountain, and remain there until further ordered, but before reaching said point I was met by a runner, who informed me that the enemy was in Romney. Forgetting your order entirely, which I hope you will pardon, I advanced as fast as possible to meet them, and just as my advance reached Kercheval's field I saw the enemy's cavalry advancing up the road and then retreating. I then dismounted, formed my men on the hill-side in a line parallel with the road and about 30 yards from it, all hands hoping that "Mr. Yankee" would just come on. We had 4 men on horseback, who were maneuvering to induce their cavalry to pursue them far enough to come within proper range of all our guns.

At about 9 a. m. the enemy made a charge, but when they had come within about 400 yards of my advance companies they parted and commenced firing on some of the boys, who were so extremely eager to get a shot at them that they would keep constantly exposed to full view. Believing that they would not advance any farther, my men opened a fire, but not more than 100 fired, for it was thought that our guns could not reach them, and we did not wish to waste our fire; but from the most reliable information I have been able to gather we wounded 5 and killed 1, one man receiving three balls. After their cavalry had retreated they commenced firing cannon, and kept it up for some time, but fortunately, though their bullets and grape flew thick, not one of my men received a scratch.

As a just tribute to my men permit me to say that I did not see a cheek blanched or a hand that trembled, and as a further proof of their valor many who, owing to a mistake with our wagons, had not tasted bread for forty-eight hours were in the front ranks in pursuing the enemy to Patterson's Creek.

I have the honor to be, sir, your obedient servant,

A. MONROE,
Colonel One hundred and fourteenth Reg't Virginia Militia.

ANGUS W. MCDONALD,
Colonel, Commanding Cavalry, C. S. Army.

P. S.—I had about 350 men on the 25th. Since making the above report I learn that some of the men who fired were stationed on the ridge north of Lanier Cooper's house and within less than 300 yards of the enemy.

No. 4.

Report of Maj. O. R. Funsten, C. S. Army.

CAMP FUNSTEN, NEAR ROMNEY,
September 28, 1861.

COLONEL: On the night of the 23d instant, about 11.30 o'clock, our pickets on the Sheetz Mill road from Mechanicsburg Pass came to camp, and informed me that they had been fired upon by a body of cavalry about 2 miles beyond the mouth of the pass, and that they believed that a large body of the enemy was advancing towards the pass from that directiom. I immediately ordered Captain Sheetz to march his company to the vicinity of the point where the enemy was discovered, to ascertain as far as possible their strength and position, and to skirmish them if they were advancing. I also ordered Captain Myers with his company to Hanging Rock Pass, with similar instructions in case the enemy appeared in that direction. I also ordered Lieutenant Lionberger to take his howitzer to Mechanicsburg Pass, and to hold his other guns in readiness to move. At this time you arrived at camp, and directed me to take Captains Bowen's, Harper's, and Miller's companies, in addition to Captain Sheetz's, and occupy and hold Mechanicsburg Pass.

I proceeded at once to execute this order. Arriving at the head of the pass I met Captain Sheetz, who informed me that the enemy were about half a mile above, but that he was unable, from the nature of the ground, to ascertain with accuracy their strength. I then ordered a strong party of skirmishers on the side of the mountain down the pass, and having dismounted, the whole command occupied a very strong point in the pass, with the howitzer supported by the dismounted riflemen, and awaited the approach of the enemy.

In a short time a squad of the enemy's cavalry was driven back by our skirmishers at the head of the pass, which was soon followed by volleys fired by the enemy into the side of the mountain, where our skirmishers were safely located behind rocks and trees. After several hundred shots were exchanged the firing of the enemy became irregular. and a dense fog having raised in the mean time, it ceased.

The enemy evidently intended to march through the pass. Their loss must have been considerable at this point. Our skirmishers, being well protected, suffered no injury. The men who were supporting the howitzer remained in position all night, expecting an attack and feeling confident of defending the pass against an attack from ten times their number.

At 8.30 a. m. Lieutenant McDonald brought me your order "to march my command to a point between the bridge and Romney, and hold myself in readiness to march to Hanging Rock Pass, from which point the enemy was advancing in large numbers, and that you expected the principal attack from that direction." I called in my skirmishers and marched to the positions indicated. In the course of an hour or two the enemy was seen in the road to Mechanicsburg Pass. I then directed Captain Bowen, by your order, to take position with his company and Captain Miller's, and with the assistance of the howitzer to dispute the passage of the bridge and fort. The enemy then opened fire upon us from a cannon in the road on the mountain side, above the bridge, but without injury to us.

I then received your order to march to the support of Captains Myers and Jordan, against whom were advancing an overwhelming force from the direction of Hanging Rock Pass. I marched the companies of Captains Winfield, Harper, Sheetz, and Shands with the utmost speed. Within half a mile of town I met the 4-pounder cannon, and directed the officer in charge of it to advance and take a position which I would designate. Meeting afterwards Captain Myers, he informed me of the estimated strength of the enemy, who were but a short distance down the road, but concealed by a hill, and although they outnumbered us six or seven times, I determined to give them a fight, and proceeded to select my ground to meet their approach. Having done this to my satisfaction, I awaited them. Reconnoitering parties of the enemy were in the mean time visible on the ridge a mile and a half in front of us.

In a short time the glistening of guns could be seen in the underwood which covered the before-mentioned ridge, moving in the direction of the Winchester road, distant about 3 miles. I saw at once that the object of the movement was either to take possession of the narrow pass or the Winchester road, adjacent to town, or to make a feint in that direction, with a view to drawing off part of our force from the position we held. I ordered Captain Sheetz to move rapidly with his company by the way of the Winchester road, to advance upon them, and to skirmish them in front. I also ordered the train which I understood had been ordered up the Winchester road to the point which was now threatened to move farther up the road. I also ordered Captain Winfield to skirmish on their right flank, and watch and report their movement. Captain Winfield promptly executed my order, and soon commenced skirmishing them.

In a short time Lieutenant Pennybacker rode back rapidly with a message from Captain Winfield, informing me that the enemy were advancing in a large body toward the Winchester road, and would soon reach it if not attacked. I immediately ordered Captains Jordan, Myers, and Harper to the point on the Winchester road at which I expected the enemy would enter it. I also ordered the officer commanding the 4-pounder to march with us with his gun. I marched three companies and the piece of artillery rapidly to the church at the summit of the ridge, and there found Captain Sheetz, who had ordered part of his company to reconnoiter from an intermediate road. I ordered him to take the remainder of his company and reconnoiter in another direction, and report to me at a point below. I then marched the other companies to the point designated, and there awaited Captain Sheetz. In a short time he returned and informed me that he had not found the enemy, and being satisfied that they had changed their line of march when they observed our movement in that direction, I marched back to Romney. At the edge of town I met the companies which I had left marching out, and was informed that you had given orders for the regiment to retire, and that the enemy was not in sight of Romney. I called a halt and proceeded to town, when I met you, and, returning with you, ordered the column to march at the summit of the ridge, 3½ miles from town. We ascertained that the train had halted at French's, 2½ miles beyond, where we marched and encamped for the night.

Early the next morning I received your order to have the train ready to move in the direction of Romney. The quartermaster was preparing to execute this order when a messenger arrived from Romney, between 8.30 and 9 o'clock, informing us that the enemy had returned and was then in Romney. I then received your order to take command of the regiment and march against the enemy. I did so without delay. Arriving in sight of the enemy as they were marching across the bridge, I ordered the column to charge, which was responded to in the most gallant manner. The enemy commenced retreating rapidly and in confusion up the mountain by the northwestern road. Passing under the bridge we received the fire of their rear guard, but dashed on until we came within pistol and shotgun range, when we returned their fire with coolness and precision. The rear of our column filed to the left and opened fire upon their flank. In the mean time the enemy fired canister from their cannon. Fortunately for us nineteen out of twenty of their balls passed high above our heads.

The fight lasted fifteen or twenty minutes, when the enemy were again put in motion. Lieutenant Lionberger, who had been detained by one of the wheels of his rifled cannon coming off, came up at the time with the howitzer and opened a spirited fire on the retreating enemy, and with a telling effect, as I have since learned. In this engagement our loss was trifling, in consequence of their bad aiming, amounting to the wounding of 2 men and the killing and wounding of 5 or 6 horses.

I then ordered the officer in charge of the rifled cannon to move his gun to an eminence in front of Mechaniesburg Pass and to shell the enemy from it. This order was handsomely executed by Lieutenant Lionberger, who came up in the mean time, and a few well-directed shells opened the pass to us, and broke the line which the enemy had formed above its mouth, when we again commenced the pursuit. I then sent Captains Winfield and Sheetz forward with their companies to skirmish the enemy and bring them to a fight. At Gilbert's, about 3 miles beyond the pass, these companies came up with the rear of the enemy and opened a spirited fire on it, but had not the effect of checking the speed of the flight of their main body. The fight continued for some minutes, when they again got out of our sight. At Sheetz's Mill, 2 miles beyond, we again came in reach of them, and fired on their rear and flank and gave them two or three shells from the rifled cannon.

At this point Captain Sheetz rode up and informed me that he was well acquainted with the surrounding country, and would cut off their retreat by taking a shorter road, provided he could be aided by two or three companies. All of the companies, excepting Captains Jordan's and Powers' and a part of Captain Shands', received orders to move in that direction, and I continued the pursuit with the last-named companies and two pieces of artillery. About 5 miles beyond Sheetz's Mill, when I believed we were only a few hundred yards in rear of the enemy, the head of our column was fired into from a dense thicket on our right, and instantly an order was given in a loud voice to cease firing, as they were firing on their friends, and soon two of the companies which took the nearer route advanced from the bushes. No blame should attach to the officers of these companies, as the gap between the enemy and ourselves was small, and the mistake was a natural one.

By this unfortunate occurrence we had 2 of our regiment slightly wounded and 1 of the artillerymen badly but not mortally wounded. The delay occasioned by this accident enabled the enemy to increase the distance between us. The pursuit was continued to the base of the Knobly Mountain, within 2 miles of New Creek, from which point the rear of the enemy was seen crossing the summit of the mountain. It was then twilight, and deeming an attack on New Creek at that time imprudent, I discontinued the pursuit and returned to this camp, where we arrived about 2 o'clock at night, after having been thirty-three out of the fifty hours in the saddle.

The aggregate strength of this regiment engaged in the service was 328. The strength of the enemy was not less than 1,300 and probably reached 1,500 men, including artillery and 75 cavalry, the whole command being armed in the best manner. So completely were they demoralized by our first charge, that they must have been cut to pieces had the country been favorable to the operations of cavalry, the road by which they retreated being through mountain passes and deep defiles.

The loss of the enemy in killed and wounded was not less than 50, besides 5 prisoners, 9 horses, and some arms captured. Our loss was trifling, considering the intrepidity of our charges and the very unfavorable ground for attack; it amounted to only 2 wounded and some 10 or 12 horses killed and wounded.

The conduct of the officers and men deserves great praise, and I might cite instances of individual daring deserving especial notice, but as all were disposed to do their duty, I will make no distinctions.

Very respectfully, yours,

O. R. FUNSTEN,
Major, Commanding.

Col. ANGUS W. McDONALD.

No. 5.

Report of Lieut. J. H. Lionberger, C. S. Army.

CAMP FUNSTEN, NEAR ROMNEY, VA., *October* 4, 1861.

On the night of the 23d of September last, about a quarter before 12 o'clock, shortly after the information of the approach of the enemy had reached the camp, I received orders from Major Funsten to repair with the howitzer under my charge at once to the Mechanicsburg Pass, which I did, and remained there until about 8.30 o'clock, when I was directed by Major Funsten to withdraw the howitzer from the pass and take position upon the Cemetery Hill, there to await further orders. Upon arriving at the Cemetery Hill I found my rifled 6-pounder in position upon the hill so as to command the bridge and the ford and the road leading from these points to Romney. By your order my howitzer was sent, under charge of Captain Bowen, to the hill opposite the bridge, so as additionally to command the bridge and the ford, while the 4-pounder, through your order (as I have understood), was sent and placed in position by the gunner upon an eminence north of the town, commanding the road leading from the Hanging Rock Pass to Romney.

About 4.30 o'clock I received your order to retire with the guns in my charge, in company with the whole command, by the Winchester road, which I did, and encamped with the command at Frenchburg.

Early in the morning of the 24th I received your order to prepare to return to Romney with all of the guns under my charge. About 8.30 o'clock I received your order to repair at once to Romney with the howitzer and the rifled 6-pounder, leaving behind the 4-pounder. Without any delay I proceeded to execute this order. Arriving in Romney we learned that the enemy was at the bridge. Whilst passing through the town one of the wheels of the 6-pounder came off. Without waiting for it to be put on again, I proceeded as rapidly as possible to the bridge with the howitzer. Arriving at the bridge I discovered that the enemy had made a stand beyond it. Getting the howitzer into position on the island to do effective service, I was prevented from firing by the charge of our own cavalry.

Changing the position of the gun to a field opposite the enemy and within 300 yards of them, I opened fire. The first shot was too high; the second broke their lines, and produced the greatest confusion, which was soon followed by a retreat. I immediately crossed the river, when I was informed by Major Funsten that he had sent the rifled gun to a hill opposite the mouth of the Mechanicsburg Pass, and directing me to take charge of it and shell the pass, selecting a position which commanded a view of the whole pass, and from which I could see the enemy's line of battle across the upper end of the pass. Before the gun could be used, however, the canister with which it was charged had to be withdrawn and a shell inserted.

In the mean time the enemy had broken line and were in retreat, but again formed higher up the pass. Having fired at them with a shell, which, exploding amongst them, again broke their line and scattered them in great confusion, I continued to shell them from this point until they had passed, as I thought, entirely out of range, when I hastened with the gun to join Major Funsten, changing horses at the mill a mile east of the pass. I afterwards joined the column in the pass. At Patterson's Creek we again came in sight of the enemy, and turning by your order into a field on the right, fired one shot at them, when I received your order to change the position of the gun (the rifled) to one about three-fourths of a mile in advance upon a hill. Here the gun was aimed by you in the direction of the road over which the enemy were retreating, and several shots were fired, and, as I have since learned, with great effect.

Continuing the pursuit, about 3 miles from this point we were fired upon by our own men from the woods by the road-side. Supposing it to be the enemy, I at once ordered my men to unlimber and get ready for action, which order was quickly and bravely responded to; but before firing, the mistake was discovered, but not too soon to show the coolness and courage of the men at this gun. By this unfortunate mistake one of my men was wounded in the arm.

From this point we continued the pursuit about 2 miles, but saw nothing more of the enemy, when your order was received to cease the pursuit. Thence we returned by Sheetz's Mill to Romney, where we arrived about 2 o'clock. Since the chase the guns, carriages, &c., have undergone a thorough cleansing and repairing, and are now ready for use.

Respectfully submitted.

J. H. LIONBERGER,
Lieutenant, and Acting Captain of Artillery.

Col. ANGUS W. McDONALD,
Commanding C. S. Forces at Romney.

SEPTEMBER 24, 1861.—Skirmish at Point of Rocks, Maryland.

Report of Col. John W. Geary, Twenty-eighth Pennsylvania Infantry.

CAMP TYNDALE, *September* 24, 1861.

SIR: There seems to be a lull in the storm which has broken on our lines with abortive violence by the rebel forces in Virginia. They have marched up and down the Potomac, and have felt almost every part of my line from Pritchard's Mill, 3 miles above Harper's Ferry, and having found every point well guarded, they have not dared to assault us. Yet there are reconnaissances or menaces with the recurrence of every favorable opportunity, and I am well aware that only by our vigilance and promptitude will our advantages and position be maintained. Only three days since I discovered them surveying my camp from every available point, purposing, as I have reason to believe, to assault us by artillery from an eligible position on the table or plateau on the Virginia side. Accordingly I moved my entire camp 250 yards eastward, sheltered from sight and assault by a forest on the west, a more healthy place, and affording an excellent site for the artillery just to the right, within range of all points from which the enemy could advance.

Simultaneously with the changing of camp I pushed my pickets forward on Heter's Island, a mile long and standing within a few yards of the Virginia shore, thus affording an unbroken view along the enemy's line, and also of fordings which are in almost every case contiguous to the islands. I have also taken possession of Noland's Island, at the lower end of which is the ferry of the same name, and from which about 1 mile is reported to be secreted in the woods a camp of the enemy, whose pickets line the river. Our enemy, if not so savage as the Indian, purposes to emulate his vigilance.

Allow me to state that I design to occupy all the other serviceable islands within the parallel of my lines and where nature has not provided shelter to make by art.

By this occupation of the islands I am enabled to present a double point, or, in other words, points of reserve, and hold my forces more available to any arising exigencies.

At this moment the enemy are in detachment in view, reconnoitering (9.30 a. m.).

When occasion requires, I will not fail to communicate.

2.30 p. m.—The reconnaissance proved to be an attack by from 100 to

200 of the enemy, supported by about 400 secreted in the woods. The attack was made by musketry, from the opposite side of the river, in the vicinity of the ruins of the bridge at Point of Rocks. They fired about 200 shots, nearly all of which fell short and without injury. We answered promptly with shell and rifles and silenced them in a few minutes; what loss on their side I cannot say positively.

I detached four brave fellows, under cover of artillery, to the opposite side, to burn two vacant houses and a stable, the constant resort of the enemy. They did their work effectually, and, though fired at by several of the concealed enemy, returned in safety.

The enemy being nowhere discoverable, a detachment went across to the Virginia side, but discovered no traces of them, they having either entirely withdrawn or secreted themselves, as usual.

I have just returned, calling in all except the pickets. All is quiet and no appearance of the enemy.

I may conclude by saying that in my opinion there is no position along the line of the Potomac more eligible for artillery firing than the Virginia side of the Point of Rocks.

Very respectfully, &c.,

JOHN W. GEARY,
Colonel Twenty-eighth Pennsylvania Volunteers.

Capt. ROBERT WILLIAMS, *Assistant Adjutant-General.*

SEPTEMBER 25, 1861.—Engagement at Freestone Point, Virginia.

Report of Col. Louis T. Wigfall, First Texas Infantry.

DUMFRIES, *September* 25, 1861.

President JEFFERSON DAVIS:

The fleet lying in this portion of the river sent an armed tug to feel our batteries. She fired ten shots into the point occupied by Hampton's battery before they were returned. The battery then drove her off. The war steamers then opened. We fired thirty shots, the enemy twenty-two. General Whiting ordered the firing to continue after they ceased, to show them we could drive them. The fleet is now divided—part above Powell's Run and part below. When Stevens' batteries are ready they will stop the lower detachment of the fleet. The infantry supports are active and ready. If the enemy land, our knowledge of the ground will make us equal to ten times our numbers. All are cheerful, and the army will send you its congratulations if a serious action results.

Your friend,

LOUIS T. WIGFALL.

SEPTEMBER 25, 1861.—Reconnaissance to Lewinsville, Va., and skirmish near that place.

Report of Brig. Gen. William F. Smith, U. S. Army.

HEADQUARTERS, CAMP ADVANCE, VA., *September* 27, 1861.

SIR: I have the honor to report to you that at 9 o'clock on Wednesday morning, September 25, I moved towards Lewinsville, the right wing under Colonel Taylor, leaving on the hill commanding Langley, on the Leesburg turnpike, one section of Captain Mott's battery, supported by three companies of the Nineteenth Indiana; advancing on the road to Lewinsville, on a knoll covering the country to the right, the center section of the same battery, with four companies of the Second Wisconsin; and one mile farther on the remaining section, under the immediate command of Captain Mott, the Thirty-third New York, and the company of Kentucky cavalry, Captain Robinson, all at Mackall's House; the Third Vermont and the remainder of the Nineteenth Indiana being thrown out as skirmishers on the left and acting as a reserve, I placed the Pennsylvania battery, Captain Barr, with five companies of the Sixth Maine, about 300 men, and in advance to their right one section of Captain Griffin's battery, with three companies of the Fifth Wisconsin, and in the edge of the wood the second battalion of the First California Regiment. Captain Griffin's remaining sections occupied the hill, about one mile and a half from Lewinsville, covering the country to the left and road in front with the first battalion of the First California, Colonel Baker, five companies of the Fifth Wisconsin, the Berdan Sharpshooters, two companies of the Philadelphia Zouaves, and Lieutenant Drummond's company of the regular cavalry forming the center; six companies of the Seventy-ninth New York, half a mile in advance as skirmishers, supported by the two remaining companies of the Seventy-ninth and the Second Vermont; our force in all 5,100 infantry, 16 pieces of artillery, and 150 cavalry.

There being at this time no signs of the enemy, with the exception of a few cavalry scouts, I ordered the quartermaster to load his wagons, ninety in number, all of which was accomplished by 3 o'clock, and got them well on their way home with all the forage they could possibly carry. I then sent orders to draw in the skirmishers, and at 4 o'clock, as they were moving in, some of the men of the Seventy-ninth Regiment captured a prisoner purporting to be an acting aide of Colonel Stuart, who he stated to be within a mile of us. Word at this moment was sent to me that the enemy were approaching, and we could see advancing over the hills from the Falls Church road what seemed to be a large regiment, marching rapidly in close column and others deployed as skirmishers, with the apparent intention of turning our flank. At the same time they opened fire with seemingly one gun on our extreme left, but at too great distance for any effect, which soon ceased entirely; at which I ordered the center section of Griffin's battery back to the California regiment in the wood, and covering the ground for our retreat, should it be necessary. Their cavalry was seen in small bodies, moving through the corn fields and woods to our left and on the Lewinsville road. At 4.30 they had placed two guns in position to our right at about 2,500 yards, and opened on Mott's section at Mackall's, which was at once replied to by Griffin's and the rifled piece of Mott's section. After firing some thirty rounds, some of our shell exploding just in front of them, they limbered to the rear, and we could see their dust as they retreated on the Falls Church road.

At 5.30 I ordered Colonel Taylor, with Mott's section, to fall back slowly on the road to Langley, ready to come into battery should they follow him (there then being no signs of the enemy), and I retired the center and reserve by the fields, marching in columns by the flank, to the road within a mile of my quarters, arriving at camp by 7 o'clock. Just after dusk word was brought in that four or five shots had been fired into Langley, they having brought one piece to the hill commanding the cross-road at that place; but by the time a scout could be sent out all had retired, and the road was clear for the distance of a mile and a half.

The firing from Griffin's section was most excellent, and I would particularly notice Lieutenant Hazlett, in command of the section, who proved himself a most accomplished artillerist in pointing his guns, his shells bursting apparently right among them. The conduct of the troops was all that I could desire, standing with perfect coolness when their shot was falling, as it did at one time, all about them, one shell bursting over the California regiment and wounding one man slightly in the arm, and their cheers must have been heard by the enemy every time our shell seemed to reach their mark.

Very respectfully, your obedient servant,
WM. F. SMITH,
Brigadier-General, Commanding at Chain Bridge.
Col. R. B. MARCY, *Chief of Staff.*

SEPTEMBER 28, 1861.—Affair near Vanderburgh's house, Munson's Hill, Virginia.

REPORTS.

No. 1.—Col. Edward D. Baker, Seventy-first Pennsylvania Infantry.
No. 2.—Col. Dennis O'Kane, Sixty-ninth Pennsylvania Infantry.
No. 3.—Lieut. Col. Isaac J. Wistar, Seventy-first Pennsylvania Infantry.

No. 1.

Report of Col. Edward D. Baker, Seventy-first Pennsylvania Infantry.

HEADQUARTERS BAKER'S BRIGADE,
Near Monocacy, October 6, 1861.

GENERAL: I have the honor to inclose the reports of the officers commanding two regiments in the brigade under my command. It is only necessary for the commanding general to peruse them to be satisfied that the casualties which occurred on the night of the 28th ultimo were inevitable results of causes over which the troops themselves had no control. The circumstances were peculiarly trying, and the confusion, though great, did not impair the courage or steadiness of most of the officers and men.

As the California regiment was most exposed, I deem it proper to speak in terms of high commendation of Lieutenant Colonel Wistar, commanding, who evinced peculiar coolness and intrepidity.

The command is under great obligations to Captain Harvey, assistant adjutant-general of the brigade, for his excellent conduct on the occasion, and the adjutant of the California regiment, Lieutenant Newlin, deserves the praise bestowed on him by his commanding officer.

The field officers of the other regiments of the brigade also evinced high personal bravery, and I have no reason to doubt, from the conduct of officers and men generally, that the losses they sustained are not to be attributed to any want of soldierly qualities, and will in nowise diminish their confidence either in their officers or themselves. Having been absent on duty at the time the events in question took place, I form these opinions after a careful examination, and am confident of their general correctness.

I have the honor to be, general, respectfully, your obedient servant,
E. D. BAKER,
Colonel, Commanding Brigade.
The ADJUTANT-GENERAL, *Army of Potomac, Washington.*

No. 2.

Report of Lieut. Col. Dennis O'Kane, Sixty-ninth Pennsylvania Infantry.

HEADQUARTERS SECOND REGIMENT, BAKER'S BRIGADE,
Camp Advance, Va., September 29, 1861.

SIR: On Saturday morning, the 28th instant, the Second Regiment received orders to prepare two days' cooked provisions, and to strike tents and be in line with the First and Third Regiments of the brigade by 8 o'clock a. m. of the 29th instant, to march to Poolesville, which order was being promptly carried out.

Tattoo was beat at the usual hour on the evening of the 28th, and the regiment had retired to rest, when at 11.15 o'clock General Smith rode up to the quarters of the lieutenant-colonel commanding the regiment, and demanded why it was not in line, to which the lieutenant-colonel replied he had received no orders to that effect, but that the regiment had been ordered to form at 8 o'clock next morning to march to Poolesville, at which General Smith expressed surprise that the regiment had received no orders to form in line that evening, and ordered it to be done at once, ammunition issued, and the regiment marched along the road through camp and over the hill by Fort Baker, and that the direction to be taken would be pointed out by pickets as regiments passed. These were all the instructions received, no orders in writing having been issued to this regiment. The line was immediately formed, ammunition issued, and the regiment put in motion before 12 o'clock.

The officers were in entire ignorance of the purpose or direction of the movement. After marching about an hour, firing was heard in front of the column, which has been attributed to the pickets firing upon the line, and by which several lives were lost. The regiment moved steadily on, and in about thirty minutes was brought to a halt and was resting in line, when three dragoons rode rapidly along, and when about the center of the regiment one of them fired his revolver, exclaiming, "Take care, boys; here they come." Simultaneously a number of skirmishers suddenly appeared from the adjoining woods on the road, when some of our men, supposing the secessionists were on them, discharged their pieces, which led to a general alarm and firing along the line, which unfortunately resulted in the death of Sergeant Gillan, of Company B, and the wounding of 2 more of this regiment. Order was promptly restored, the line reformed, and no further casualties occurred during the night. The regiment was then marched a short distance and formed in line of battle on the outskirts of a wood flanking the road, where they remained in good order until about 11 o'clock a. m., when they were ordered to march back to camp.

The above report is respectfully submitted.

DENNIS O'KANE,
Lieutenant-Colonel, Commanding.

Capt. FRED'K HARVEY, *A. A. G., U. S. Army, Hdqrs. Baker's Brigade.*

No. 3.

Report of Lieut. Col. Isaac J. Wistar, Seventy-first Pennsylvania Infantry.

HEADQUARTERS CALIFORNIA REGIMENT,
Camp Advance, Va., September 29, 1861.

COLONEL: In compliance with orders received last evening from General Smith, during your absence, I marched with my regiment about 9.30

p. m., arriving opposite Vanderburgh's house about 11 p. m. Here I was detained about two hours by the necessity of clearing away a number of trees felled across the road. During the interval I took the head of the column, as directed by General Smith, with the first battalion of my regiment, consisting of nine companies. I was followed by a battery of four guns, and then by my second battalion of seven companies, under Major Parrish.

My instructions from General Smith were to proceed without advance guard or flankers until I should pass Colonel Burnham, who with his regiment was near the next cross-roads, and after passing him, he being the most advanced of our forces, to throw out three companies deployed as skirmishers across the road, and follow them with the column at a distance of, say, 150 yards, connecting the head of the column with the center of the skirmishers by a file of men at intervals of 10 paces. This had just been accomplished, when General Smith himself, with his staff, overtook me, and the whole was immediately put in motion. After proceeding a short distance I was surprised to find a picket guard of a New York regiment, having supposed we had passed all of our own outposts. At the first turn to the right, which occurred within a quarter of a mile after the deployment of my skirmishers, they began to come in collision with picket guards, who said they belonged to the Fourth Michigan. The road at this point was lined with thick woods on both sides. At the turn of the road was stationed in the road a picket of, say, 20 men; 30 yards beyond was another of, say, 6 men, and the head of the column had not progressed more than 50 yards past the latter, the skirmishers being ahead and on both flanks entangled among the pickets in the woods on the left, when a regular volley was fired into the second and third companies of my line from immediately behind the fence which lined the woods on my left. The head of the column having now passed the woods on our right, the latter was replaced by open fields, exposing us to the light of the rising moon, while the woods on our left, whence an invisible enemy continued to pour his fire, was in deep shade.

Considerable confusion took place in the column thus suddenly attacked. Nothing was visible in the woods but the flashes of their guns; but, convinced the firing was the mistake of friends, I rode between my men, who had instantly faced towards the woods whence the firing proceeded, vainly calling upon all parties to cease firing. At this moment my horse was shot and rendered nearly unmanageable, and notwithstanding my exertions, firing commenced among my own men, who could bear it no longer, and continued perhaps for two minutes, when the party in the woods retired. I now ordered my killed and wounded to be carried to the rear and dressed my line, and was endeavoring to reassure all parties, when the parties in the woods, having returned suddenly, threw in another volley from not less than forty pieces, as I should judge, which my men instantly returned without orders, the distance being the width of the road—say 6 yards. This time the firing extended nearly as far back in the road as the rear of my first battalion, producing a panic among the artillery horses, who turned and dashed off to the rear, breaking loose from the guns, and producing great confusion in my second battalion by rushing over them at full speed. A number were shot, and the remainder turned off the road, which soon restored order.

After sending my killed and wounded to the rear, I put my command in the woods which concealed the firing party, whoever they may have been, thoroughly scoured and took possession of it, and with the valuable aid of Adjutant Newlin drew up in line of battle along its front to hold the road, at the same time stationing my second battalion, under command of Major Parrish, who was of very great assistance during the whole night and whose perfect coolness during such general confusion was very gratifying, in the woods at the right, so as to cross fires with the first battalion on the road in front, and then, after rallying my skirmishers and distributing them as pickets all around our front, reported these dispositions to General Smith, who was pleased to approve them. On the following afternoon, at 4. p. m., I left the position by General Smith's order, and marched back to this camp, where I arrived, without further incident, at dark.

My whole loss was 4 killed and 14 wounded, as appears by the surgeon's report, a copy of which, marked A, is herewith returned.*

I have the honor to be, colonel, very respectfully, your obedient servant,

ISAAC J. WISTAR,
Lieutenant-Colonel, Commanding California Regiment.

Col. E. D. BAKER, *Commanding Brigade.*

OCTOBER 3, 1861.—Engagement at Greenbrier River, West Virginia.

REPORTS, ETC.

No. 1.—Brig. Gen. Joseph J. Reynolds, U. S. Army.
No. 2.—Col. Nathan Kimball, Fourteenth Indiana Infantry.
No. 3.—Lieut. Col. William P. Richardson, Twenty-fifth Ohio Infantry.
No. 4.—Casualties in the Union forces.
No. 5.—Brig. Gen. Henry R. Jackson, C. S. Army, and response from Secretary of War.
No. 6.—Col. William B. Taliaferro, Twenty-third Virginia Infantry.
No. 7.—Col. Albert Rust, Third Arkansas Infantry.
No. 8.—Capt. L. M. Shumaker, C. S. Army.
No. 9.—Congratulatory orders from Brig. Gen. W. W. Loring, C. S. Army.

No. 1.

Report of Brig. Gen. Joseph J. Reynolds, U. S. Army, commanding First Brigade.

HEADQUARTERS FIRST BRIGADE, A. O. W. VA.,
Elk Water, October 4, 1861.

SIR: On the night of the 2d October, at 12 o'clock, I started from the summit of Cheat Mountain to make an armed reconnaissance of the enemy's position on the Greenbrier River, 12 miles in advance. Our force consisted of Howe's battery, Fourth regular artillery; Loomis' battery, Michigan volunteer artillery; part of Daum's battery, Virginia volunteer artillery; Twenty-fourth, Twenty-fifth, and Thirty-second Ohio Regiments; Seventh, Ninth, Thirteenth, Fourteenth, Fifteenth, and Seventeenth Indiana Regiments (the last four being reduced by continuous hard service and sickness to about half regiments); parts of Robinson's company of Ohio, Greenfield's Pennsylvania, and Bracken's Indiana cavalry; in all about 5,000. Milroy's Ninth Indiana drove in the enemy's advanced pickets and deployed to our right, driving the enemy on that flank into his intrenchments. Kimball's Fourteenth Indiana was advanced directly to the enemy's front and right, to drive

------

* Not found.

his advanced regiment from a position suitable for our artillery. This was soon done in gallant style, and our batteries promptly took their positions within about 700 yards of the intrenchments and opened fire. Some of the enemy's guns were visible and others concealed. We disabled three of his guns, made a thorough reconnaissance, and after having fully and successfully accomplished the object of the expedition retired leisurely and in good order to Cheat Mountain, arriving at sundown, having marched 24 miles and been under the enemy's fire four hours. The enemy's force was about 9,000, and we distinctly saw heavy re-enforcements of infantry and artillery arrive while we were in front of the works.

We took 13 prisoners. The number of killed and wounded could not be accurately ascertained, but from those actually counted in the field and estimated in the trenches, which could be seen from the heights, it is believed the number reached at least 300. Our loss was surprisingly small—8 killed and 32 wounded—most of them slightly, the proximity of our batteries to the intrenchments causing many shots to pass over us.*

Very respectfully, &c.,

J. J. REYNOLDS,
Brigadier-General, Commanding.

L. THOMAS, *Adjutant-General of the Army, Washington, D. C.*

No. 2.

Report of Col. Nathan Kimball, Fourteenth Indiana Infantry.

CHEAT MOUNTAIN SUMMIT, VA., *October* 4, 1861.

SIR: In obedience to your orders, the Fourteenth Regiment Indiana Volunteers proceeded from this point at 1 a. m. on the 3d instant, as part of the force in making the armed reconnaissance of the enemy's position at Greenbrier River, near the Alleghany Mountains.

My command, on arriving near the front of the enemy's position, took post in their front near the main road and awaited your arrival. By your order I deployed one company (C), Captain Brooks, forward as skirmishers, to open up the way for a position for Loomis' battery. They had proceeded only a few hundred yards when they came in contact with the enemy's infantry, 600 in number. I immediately ordered the rest of my companies forward, and deploying left companies over mountains which were occupied by the enemy, my whole command was soon engaged, and I am proud, rejoiced, to know that they drove the enemy back.

As the whole of this action was under your immediate observation, I need not tell you how gallantly my men behaved. Having succeeded in clearing the point, Captain Loomis soon had his guns in battery and opening on the enemy. I then moved my regiments forward, one company supporting Howe's battery in the road, my right resting in a meadow, directly in front of the enemy. At this time Captain Daum brought one gun forward and took position near my left. He behaved with great gallantry, attending his gun in person, doing good execution, amid a perfect storm of shot and shell.

I directed my line up the hill and to the rear of Daum's piece. We

---

* See report No. 4, p. 223.

occupied this position during the whole cannonading, the men being exposed to the continuous fire from the enemy's batteries. And, general, I am proud to say my men stood firm. They had never before been subjected to the hail-storms of ball and shell, yet they did not waver.

Our position was held until we were ordered to deploy to the enemy's right of the mountain, as skirmishers. I moved with seven companies; the other three were deployed over the summit directly over the face of the mountain, exposed to the fire from the enemy's batteries. Here I was halted near the enemy's right by other regiments, which were on my left. Here I formed a junction with Colonel Wagner, and while endeavoring to move forward we were met by a portion of the regiments returning. We remained in this position for one-half hour awaiting the movement of the regiment in our advance; but seeing all of our forces being drawn off, I marched my command in good order back to its former position in the road and retired in front of the enemy's heavy fire.

General, you witnessed the conduct of my command during most of the day, and it is unnecessary for me to praise them to you. All I will say is, that the Fourteenth were true soldiers, and acted up to their profession and in accordance with their motto, which is, "Keep cool and a steady fire."

I must not fail to mention that my major (W. Harrow) and adjutant (John J. P. Blinn) were with me, and acted with great gallantry and bravery, and deserve the highest praise. My lieutenant-colonel, owing to severe sickness, did not arrive until towards the withdrawal of the forces.

I have to report the loss of 3 killed and 4 wounded. Two of those reported killed died after we returned to camp. One sergeant (J. Urner Price), Company A, lost his left leg by a fraction of a shell. Price was a noble fellow, and died a Christian, as he had lived one. The other (Harrison Myers), of Company H, had a spherical-case shot in his thigh, which was extracted, but he died immediately afterwards. Amos Boyd, of Company C, was killed on the field by the explosion of a shell from the enemy's guns. I recapitulate my loss as follows:

Killed: J. Urner Price, Company A; Amos Boyd, Company C; Harrison Myers, Company H.

Wounded: Capt. L. A. Foote, Company A, and private John D. Lyon, Company E.

General, we are ready again, and hope that the Fourteenth will do as well as they have done heretofore.

Very respectfully and obediently,

NATHAN KIMBALL,
Colonel, Commanding Fourteenth Regiment Indiana Volunteers.

Brig. Gen. JOSEPH J. REYNOLDS, *Commanding.*

No. 3.

Report of Lieut. Col. William P. Richardson, Twenty-fifth Ohio Infantry.

HDQRS. TWENTY-FIFTH REGIMENT OHIO VOLUNTEERS,
Camp, Cheat Mountain Summit, October 6, 1861.

SIR: When the reserve was ordered up in the affair of the 3d instant I understood your order to me to be to push forward the head of my column to the barn and house in front, and there to wait until I saw the movement commenced on the right, which I understood to be a charge, and then to charge in front, and that I was to occupy the right in front. I did precisely what I was ordered to do, so far as putting my regiment in the assigned position and waiting for the commencement of the charge upon the enemy's right flank. I waited some twenty minutes, and saw nothing like a charge upon the right, but concluded to proceed to execute your order as I understood it, and had already given the command forward when Lieutenant-Colonel Wilder came up and asked me why I did not move forward. I repeated what I believed to be your order. He said I was mistaken; that your order was that I should proceed around the enemy's right, and that if I did not immediately proceed he would occupy my place. Afraid, from the fact that I saw no such movement on the right as you had indicated as my guide, that I had mistaken your order, I at once complied with the demand of Lieutenant-Colonel Wilder, and moved up on the hill around the enemy's right flank as far as I could get without passing other regiments that I found there, which I supposed were intended to precede me. I remained there until several regiments had passed me, making a retrograde movement. I inquired of several of the officers why they were going back, but could elicit no information until Colonel Kimball came along with his regiment. He said the order was "To about face and march off the hill." Having no other information, I waited until all the regiments had passed and then brought my regiment off of the hill. Seeing some confusion among some of the regiments, I drew mine up near where one of the guns had been, by the road, and sent my adjutant forward to you for orders. Of the rest of my conduct and that of my regiment you have been apprised by my official report.*

If I misunderstood your order, and thereby in any manner embarrassed the proceedings of the day, no one can regret it more than myself. If, on the other hand, I correctly understood you, I hope this frank explanation will to some extent exonerate me from blame.

I am, very respecfully, yours, &c.,

WM. P. RICHARDSON,
Lieutenant-Colonel, Twenty-fifth Ohio.

Brig. Gen. JOSEPH J. REYNOLDS.

No. 4.

Return of casualties in the Union forces in the engagement on Greenbrier River, West Virginia, October 3, 1861.†

Command.	Killed.		Wounded.		Aggregate.
	Officers.	Enlisted men.	Officers.	Enlisted men.	
Seventh Indiana			1	7	8
Ninth Indiana		2		6	8
Thirteenth Indiana		1		1	2
Fourteenth Indiana		1	1	5	7
Seventeenth Indiana		1		3	4
Twenty-fourth Ohio		2		3	5
Twenty-fifth Ohio				3	3
Howe's (Fourth U. S.) battery		1		5	6
Total		8	2	33	43

* Not found.   † Compiled from records of Adjutant-General's Office.

No. 5.

Reports of Brig. Gen. Henry R. Jackson, C. S. Army, and response from Secretary of War.

CAMP BARTOW, GREENBRIER RIVER, *October* 3, 1861.

The enemy attacked us at 8 o'clock this morning in considerable force, estimated at 5,000, and with six pieces of artillery of longer range than any we have. After a hot fire of four and a half hours, and heavy attempts to charge our lines, he was repulsed, evidently with considerable loss. We had no cavalry to pursue him on his retreat. The loss on our side has been inconsiderable. A fuller report will be given through the regular channels, but for several days my correspondence with General Loring has been interrupted. The enemy's force was much superior to ours, but we had the advantage in position.

H. R. JACKSON,
Brigadier-General, Commanding.

SECRETARY OF WAR.

—

CAMP BARTOW, GREENBRIER RIVER, *October* 7, 1861.

COLONEL : In my note of the 3d instant I gave you a brief account of the attack made that day upon our position by the enemy. Advancing along the turnpike with a heavy column, composed of infantry, artillery, and cavalry, numbering, at a safe estimate, from 6,000 to 7,000 men, he drove in our advance pickets at an early hour in the morning. About 7 o'clock he encountered the main body of the advance guard, re-enforced to about 100 strong, and posted on the right side of the turnpike, 1 mile from our lines, by Col. Edward Johnson, of the Twelfth Georgia Regiment, who took command in person. You will find this position designated upon the accompanying map by the capital letter E.

It is but justice to this superior officer and to the gallant band whose movements he directed to say that it would not have been possible for so small a force to have been more skillfully handled, or to have exhibited more obstinate courage in the face of numbers so overwhelming. They held the column of the enemy in check for nearly an hour, pouring into the head of it a galling fire, not withdrawing until six pieces of artillery had opened briskly upon them, and full battalions of infantry were outflanking them on the right, and then retiring in such order and taking such advantage of the ground as to reach our camp with but trifling loss. To this brilliant skirmish, in which Colonel Johnson had his horse killed under him, is doubtless to be ascribed in a measure the exhilarated spirit manifested by our troops during the remainder of the day. Before taking leave of it and referring to former dispatches, I would beg once again to direct to Col. Edward Johnson the special attention of the commanding general, not simply for this peculiarly brilliant service, but for his gallant and efficient conduct throughout the entire engagement. So soon as it had become apparent that the enemy contemplated a systematic attack upon our camp, I disposed of my entire force to meet it. To convey a correct idea, not simply of that disposition, but of the subsequent action, I must pray reference to the accompanying map, for which I am indebted to Lieutenant-Colonel Barton, of the Third Arkansas Regiment.

As I have already reported to you, our position is not by nature a commanding one. The causes of its weakness are the necessity of defending extended lines on our front (not less than a mile) and on our flanks, and the fact that there are points in our rear which, in possession of an enemy, might give us great trouble. The works essential to our safety were in progress of construction at the time of the attack, but were only partially completed, nothing whatever having been done to strengthen our right flank or our rear.

I am happy to say that during the last three days, through the indefatigable efforts of Lieutenant-Colonel Barton, in immediate charge of the works, backed by the cheerful labor of the men, we are already in condition to defy an approach from any quarter. Not doubting that the attack upon us had been to some extent invited by our commencing to fortify ourselves against it, and fearing that the enemy might have been fully advised of our weak points until he had actually begun his retreat, my mind could not dispossess itself of the idea that he had sent another column over the mountains to turn our right flank. To prepare for this danger I held the First Georgia Regiment, so far as that could be done, in reserve for what I apprehended would be a desperate struggle. I also sent expresses to Colonel Baldwin, whom I had previously ordered to the top of the Alleghany Ridge, directing him to move the Fifty-second Virginia Regiment as rapidly down as possible, and to fall upon the rear of the enemy should he undertake to fall upon ours. That gallant regiment responded, as I have learned, most heartily to the call, and when halted upon the road by the tidings that the day had already been won, despite of its not-to-be-doubted patriotism, could not entirely conceal its chagrin.

The two brigades in this camp, weakened by the absence of the several corps on detached service, the Fifth having been reduced from this cause and from sickness to scarce one-third of its legitimate number, I posted in the following order: The First Georgia Regiment upon our extreme right, under command of Major Thompson, Colonel Ramsey, the field officer of the day, having been cut off from us by the enemy while discharging his duty upon the road; next to it was placed the Twelfth Georgia Regiment—both of these regiments designed for the immediate command of Colonel Johnson. At an early moment I threw out what few mounted men were available, under Captain Sterrett, of the Churchville Cavalry, to different points along the valley upon our right, for the purpose of bringing us timely notice of an approach by the enemy, and I also strengthened considerably the picket guards advanced in that direction. The center I intrusted to the Fifth Brigade, under command of Colonel Taliaferro, composed of the Forty-fourth Virginia Regiment, Colonel Scott; the Twenty-third Virginia Regiment, Lieutenant-Colonel Taliaferro, and Major Reger's battalion [Twenty-fifth Virginia], commanded in his absence from sickness by senior Captain John C. Higginbotham. This brigade was reduced in the course of the action by the detachment of 100 men, under Major Jones, of the Forty-fourth, to re-enforce our left wing. This detachment marched in gallant style under the enemy's fire to the position assigned it in line. The troops on this wing, which from the character of the ground were widely dispersed, fell under the general command of Colonel Rust, of the Third Arkansas Regiment, and consisted of his own command, the Thirty-first Virginia Volunteers, Lieutenant-Colonel Jackson, and the battalion of Lieutenant-Colonel Hansbrough, commanded in his absence on account of sickness by senior Capt. J. A. Robertson. Upon this flank also two field pieces had already been placed in battery, enfilading the Huntersville road, which runs at right angles, if, indeed, those terms can be applied to serpentine mountain roads, from the turnpike. These guns were under the immediate charge of Capt. P. B. Anderson, and the zeal, skill, and determination of that officer leave no doubt that they would have done great execution had the enemy ventured to call them into action. Captain Shumaker's battery, consisting of four pieces (6-pounders), one of them rifled, and one 6-pounder, under Captain Rice, was held in readiness for the front and right flank. The places occupied by these various corps you will find specified upon the map.

Our forces were all in position, when at about 8 o'clock the enemy opened a heavy fire from six pieces of different caliber, placed in a field upon the right-hand side (to them) of the turnpike road, and bearing upon our front and center. This number was subsequently increased by two other pieces placed on the opposite side of the turnpike, one near it and the other upon the rise of the hill. This fire (of round shot, spherical case, shell, and occasionally, upon our left wing, of canister) was continued with extraordinary rapidity and without intermission for upwards of four hours, the eight guns constituting the well-known field batteries of Howe and of Loomis.

The hill occupied by Colonel Taliaferro's brigade, invitingly exposed to all of these batteries, received the greater share of their attention, and but for the protection afforded by the ditch and embankment running along its brow, and constructed under the immediate supervision of Colonel Taliaferro himself, we should doubtless have had inflicted upon us a very severe loss indeed. This fire was returned with great energy and, as the result has proved, with signal effect by the guns of Captain Shumaker and Captain Rice and by one piece detached from Captain Anderson's battery and placed upon the hill occupied by Lieutenant-Colonel Jackson. Lieutenant Massie, its proper chief, being quite indisposed, although he maintained his position near his piece, it was placed under the command of Captain Deshler, aide-de-camp to Colonel Johnson.

From the fact that the rifled gun of Captain Shumaker soon became useless to us (for the cause of this great misfortune see his own report addressed to myself), at no time could we bring more than five pieces into action to return the fire of the enemy's eight. Yet that fire was returned, and that with so much spirit and energy, as to make this artillery duel, rendered peculiarly interesting by the character of the field and its mountain surroundings, ever memorable by those who beheld it. That the casualties among our cannoneers should have been so few is a subject of sincere congratulation, and is very much ascribable to the sound judgment of Captain Shumaker, who repeatedly changed the position of his guns when those of the enemy had obtained his range. For a minuter description of the action in this its most striking phase I take great pleasure in referring to the report of that consummately cool and skillful officer. From it you will learn why it was that our pieces, at the close of the four hours' interchange of fire, were temporarily withdrawn, inducing our friends upon our extreme left and evidently the enemy to suppose that they had been silenced.

At about 9.30 a strong column of infantry was seen to move towards our left flank. Having crossed the so-called river (in fact, a shallow stream of about 20 yards in width), near the point designated on the map by the capital letter A, it undertook to turn our position in that direction. Soon, however, it encountered a portion of the Third Arkansas Regiment, which drove it precipitately back with a destructive fire. The enemy subsequently turned two of his pieces upon this portion of our left wing, pouring out canister and shell in large volumes, but fortunately, on account of the protection afforded by the woods, with but little execution. Simultaneously with this movement towards our left another column of infantry ascended the wooded hill before our right wing at the point designated upon the map by the capital letter B.* Having become at its head involved in a slight skirmish with one of our picket guards, it was immediately and strongly re-enforced. Subsequently to the repulse of the column from our left flank it proceeded in the same general direction, ascending the hill at the point designated by the letter C,* and swelling the force, which now began to threaten seriously our front and right, to some 4,000 men. They moved along the side of the hill, opening upon our lines a desultory fire of rifled musketry, which was continued until the close of the action. So soon as the designs of this column were fully developed I ordered the Twelfth Georgia Regiment to take position near the stream, where a small detachment of it, under Lieutenant Dawson, had already been posted, with instructions to engage the enemy whenever he should attempt to cross it.

From the fact that this movement was made in full face of largely-superior numbers, armed with a superior weapon, and protected by cover of the forest, it was made with an alacrity and a regularity which deserve high commendation, as does also the cool determination with which this command, protecting itself as best it might against enemy's fire, received it, but returned scarce a shot. Not long thereafter 1 ordered Captain Shumaker to open upon the same column, directing his fire to where he supposed the head of it to be. This he promptly did with two of his pieces, and so effectively, that in a short time the unmistakable evidence of their rout became apparent. Distinctly could their officers be heard, with words of mingled command, remonstrance, and entreaty, attempting to rally their battalions into line and to bring them to the charge; but they could not be induced to reform their broken ranks nor to emerge from the cover of the woods in the direction of our fire. Rapidly and in disorder they returned into the turnpike, and soon thereafter the entire force of the enemy—artillery, infantry, and cavalry—retreated in confusion along the road and adjacent fields, leaving behind them at different points numbers of their killed, guns, knapsacks, canteens, &c. Among other trophies taken were a stand of United States colors, which are held subject to the order of the commanding general.

This engagement lasted from 7 in the morning to 2.30 o'clock in the afternoon, at which time the enemy, who had come with artillery to bombard and demoralize us, with infantry to storm our camp, with cavalry to rout and destroy us, and with four days' cooked rations in his haversacks to prosecute a rapid march either toward Staunton or toward Huntersville, was in precipitate retreat back to his Cheat Mountain fastness; and it is certainly a matter not unworthy of mention that while his first insolent advances were received with defiant cheers, running from one end to the other of our line, he was permitted to take his departure under the simple reports of our pieces firing upon him so long as he continued within their range. The relative weakness of our force and the entire absence of cavalry prevented our pursuing him, and thereby realizing the legitimate fruits of our triumph.

His loss in killed and wounded is estimated at from 250 to 300, among them an officer of superior rank. Our own, I am happy to say, was very inconsiderable, not exceeding 50 in all. This most gratifying

---

* Not indicated on original sketch.

result is to be attributed in a great degree to the remarkable coolness of regimental and company officers, who never seemed for a moment to lose their presence of mind, never allowed their men unnecessarily to expose themselves, and profited by every advantage of ground and position to shield them from danger.

In conclusion, I take great pride in saying that the bearing of all the troops, both officers and men, with but few exceptions, was highly creditable to themselves and to the army. Among those who enjoyed the opportunity coveted by all of attracting special notice, in addition to the name of Colonel Johnson, I would mention those of Captain Shumaker, who was wounded at his battery, and to whom I have already had repeated occasion to refer; of Capt. William H. Rice, of whom Captain Shumaker speaks in the following emphatic language: "He had been working his piece beautifully for two hours, and too much praise cannot be given him for the deliberate manner with which he loaded and fired his piece, loading and firing by detail for an hour in the midst of a storm of shot and shell from the enemy," until he was stricken to the earth severely wounded; of Captain Deshler, who directed a rapid fire with marked effect, and of Sergeant Graves, who fell mortally wounded in the cool and gallant discharge of his duty. Peculiarly distinguished among the advance guard, where all were distinguished, must be recorded the names of Lieutenant Gibson, of the Third Arkansas Regiment, the officer in immediate command; of Private Slayton, of the Thirty-first Virginia Regiment, who was severely wounded, and of Private J. W. Brown, of Company F, First Georgia Regiment, who, upon hearing the order to fall back, exclaimed, "I will give them one more shot before I leave," and while ramming down his twenty-ninth cartridge fell dead at his post. Nor can I omit mention in this connection of Lieutenant-Colonel Barton, who, in the absence of engineer staff officers, designed and was in active prosecution of the works to which we are so much indebted for the defense of our position, and who has shown himself at all times prompt to render cheerful and efficient service.

It is hardly necessary to add that Colonel Taliaferro, whose marked coolness and energy could not fail to inspire his men, and Colonel Rust, in command of the left wing, from which the enemy was first repelled, discharged their responsible duty successfully and well. Finally, my own thanks are specially due to my aides, Maj. F. S. Bloom and Lieut. W. D. Humphries, C. S. Army, for the gallant and efficient manner in which they responded to the peculiar and exposing calls made upon them. It is but justice to add that Cadet Henry Jackson, C. S. Army, drew notice to himself by his gallantry under fire.

I have the honor to inclose herewith a list of casualties.

I am, sir, very respectfully, your obedient servant,

H. R. JACKSON,
Brigadier-General, Commanding.

Col. C. L. STEVENSON,
Adjutant General, N. W. A.

[Inclosures.]

List of casualties at the battle of Greenbrier River, October 3, 1861.

Command.	Killed.		Wounded.		Missing.		Aggregate.
	Officers.	Enlisted men.	Officers.	Enlisted men.	Officers.	Enlisted men.	
Third Arkansas		2		9		4	15
First Georgia		1		1			2
Twelfth Georgia		1		4			5
Twenty-third Virginia				2			2
Thirty-first Virginia		1	1	2		9	13
Forty-fourth Virginia			1	4			5
Rice's battery		1	1	4			6
Shumaker's battery			1	3			4
Total		6	4	29		13	52

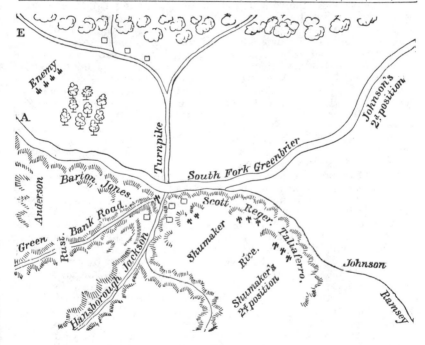

CAMP BARTOW, GREENBRIER RIVER,
October 26, 1861.

SIR: Your kind favor of the 12th instant [following] came duly to hand. How much needed by this branch of the army, by soldiers as well as by officers, some expression of approval was can only be known by one personally familiar with the campaign in this part of Virginia, unequaled in its peculiar hardships, in the asperities of country and climate which have been encountered, in sickness and suffering, in disappointed hopes and untoward events, fate seeming at times to have decreed a terrible antithesis—the misery and obscurity here, the sympathy and the glory elsewhere.

As you must be aware, this command is mainly composed of the wrecks of General Garnett's army, and the annals of warfare might be searched in vain to find a more pitiable picture of suffering, destitution, and demoralization than they presented at the close of their memorable retreat. It has required the untiring efforts of the most energetic officers and all the encouragement which could be brought to bear upon them to restore the troops to anything like the efficiency of which they were originally capable.

In the battle to which you have been pleased to refer in complimentary terms the disparity of numbers between our force and that of the enemy was greater than has been assumed. I did not think it advisable to expose our real condition of weakness. The strongest of our regiments (Colonel Fulkerson's) had been previously withdrawn to protect Colonel Gilham's flank. The reports of the morning preceding the 3d did not show more than 1,800 men for duty, and the pickets and guards which our position requires us to keep up in all directions had taken many of these from the line. Considerably more than trebling us in numbers, doubling us in artillery of superior character, and confident of success, the enemy was repulsed simply by the happy disposition of our forces, the boldness of our movements, and the cool determination of officers and men. What would have been the results of our defeat who can fully estimate? And yet, because it was comparatively bloodless, for the achievement of the victory who will ever give us full credit?

You will discern in what I have now said some reason for the detail character of my report and for the mention by me of so many names. It was necessary as well as proper, and if it be deemed of any importance to foster the spirit of this division of the Army some appreciation of meritorious service must be exhibited.

I would remark, in the same connection, that I delayed acknowledging the receipt of your letter because I contemplated a course of action in reference to certain newspaper publications which I knew would fail to meet your approval. Such publications may be disregarded by the statesman or the soldier of established reputation, but they can do much to wound the officers and men of a young corps like the one I command, who have endured the sufferings without being adjudged the laurels of veterans. Fully sensible, however, of the impropriety of complicating public position with personal feuds, I delayed writing you for the purpose of asking permission to retire from the Army so soon as the winter should withdraw this branch of it from the field. Circumstances of which it is unnecessary to speak have intervened to thwart my intention for the present.

Begging to return my thanks to the President and to yourself for your kind expressions toward my command and toward me, I have the honor to remain, sir, very respectfully, your obedient servant,

H. R. JACKSON.

Hon. J. P. BENJAMIN, *Acting Secretary of War.*

—

WAR DEPARTMENT, C. S. A.,
Richmond, October 12, 1861.

SIR: I have received through the Adjutant-General your report of the action of 3d instant at Greenbrier River. I congratulate both yourself and the officers and men under your command for your brilliant conduct on this occasion and your successful defense of the important position held by you against a force so superior. The President joins me in the expression of the satisfaction we both feel in finding our confidence in you and your command so fully justified. In this connection I beg to say that the President submitted to my perusal your private letter to him in relation to a newspaper report relating to the affair at Cheat Mountain. He has answered your letter, as he informs me. It gives me pleasure to assure you that there is not a syllable in General Lee's report that reflects in the remotest manner any discredit on you, and I hope you will not feel offended at my expressing surprise that you should attach any importance, or feel any sensitiveness in relation to sensation articles or reports in the newspapers. I have the pleasure of seeing my own action and opinions almost daily misconceived or misrepresented on "the most reliable information" with perfect equanimity, and you may well trust to your own well-earned reputation as a perfect shield against all anonymous attacks.

Very respectfully, your obedient servant,

J. P. BENJAMIN,
Acting Secretary of War.

Brig. Gen. HENRY R. JACKSON,
Headquarters, Greenbrier River.

No. 6.

Report of Col. William B. Taliaferro, Twenty-third Virginia Infantry.

HDQRS. FIFTH BRIGADE, ARMY OF NORTHWEST,
Camp at Greenbrier River, October 4, 1861.

GENERAL: I have the honor, in obedience to your orders, to make a report of the operations of the troops under my immediate command in the action between your forces and the enemy on yesterday.

According to your instructions my command, consisting of the Twenty-third and Forty-fourth Virginia Regiments and a battalion of the Twenty-fifth Virginia Regiment, supported by Shumaker's and Rice's light batteries, occupied the center of your line of defense.

As soon as it became manifest that the enemy were approaching in force I ordered the infantry to occupy the lines of trenches defending the front approach and the artillery to be placed in position to command the turnpike and meadow on the left and front of our position.

After a gallant resistance by our picket guard, re-enforced by a detachment headed by Colonel Johnson, who maintained an extraordinary struggle with an overwhelming force of the enemy, their troops in great numbers were seen to debouch from the turnpike and from across the river flat, whilst a heavy column was seen to occupy the hills on the right of the road. Very soon after this their batteries were established in the meadow and on the road, and opened upon our position, and poured without intermission a storm of shot and shell for four hours and a quarter upon it. Our batteries replied with remarkable spirit and determination, and with telling effect, as soon as the enemy approached within range of our pieces.

The infantry of the enemy fell back just without range and made an effort to turn our left flank, but could soon be seen recrossing the river and concentrating upon the left of their lines. Leaving a supporting force with their artillery, they formed on the slope of the hills overlooking the road, and evidently made all these dispositions and preparations either for attacking our center by seeking the shelter of the wooded hills until they could approach our front at the nearest point of range, when they would cross the river and attack our front, or otherwise continuing along the right bank to attempt to turn our right flank. Advancing to a point opposite the center of my position their column halted, being menaced by the troops of your right wing, and marched down the hill-side to the meadow, for the purpose of attempting the assault upon our works. Here they opened preparatory to an assault a fire upon us with their long-range muskets, but our artillery being directed upon them with terrible effect at this moment they were thrown into confusion, and notwithstanding the efforts of their officers, whose words of command and entreaties could be distinctly heard, could not be reformed, and after some time being spent in the effort to bring them to the charge fell back to the hills, and under such cover as they afforded from our artillery, which played upon them during the whole time, regained the turnpike, and withdrew their batteries and retired.

The loss to the enemy must have been very great, as their force, as far as I could estimate, exceeded 5,000, which, whenever it ventured within range, received a storm of missiles from our batteries. The loss sustained by my command was very small.

I cannot speak in too great praise of the conduct of the officers and men of my command. All evinced under the heavy fire to which they were subjected extraordinary coolness and gallantry.

The artillery, which was unprotected by epaulements, behaved with unflinching bravery. Captain Rice, commanding one of the batteries, distinguished by his intrepidity, had his leg carried away by a round shot while nobly encouraging his men to their duty, and the conduct of Private Brookes, of his battery, deserves especial notice. Captain Shumaker and Lieutenant Wooding distinguished themselves by their skill and gallantry, and Sergeant Jones, who commanded the piece on the right of my line, deserves the highest praise. Colonel Scott, commanding Forty-fourth; Lieut. Col. A. G. Taliaferro, commanding Twenty-third, and Captain Higginbotham, commanding Twenty-fifth Regiment, exhibited great coolness, determination, and anxiety to be engaged in action, which was shared by their officers and men.

I take occasion to notice the admirable conduct of Surgeon Daily, of the Twenty-third Regiment, who amid the heaviest fire administered relief to the wounded, and the good conduct of Lieutenant Pendleton, acting assistant adjutant-general. Captain Anderson's battery, part of my brigade, was assigned to duty with the command on the left, when Captain Shumaker's was temporarily transferred to my command. The report of the operations of the former will be made by the officer who commanded on the left, while the casualties in Captain Shumaker's command will be communicated by the officer commanding the brigade to which he is attached.

I append a list of the killed and wounded of my brigade, amounting to 2 killed and 6 wounded.*

I have the honor to be, very respectfully, your obedient servant,

WM. B. TALIAFERRO,
Colonel Twenty-third Regiment, Commanding Brigade.

General HENRY R. JACKSON,
Commanding Monterey Line.

---

* Not found, but see p. 229.

No. 7.

Report of Col. Albert Rust, Third Arkansas Infantry.

BRIGADE HEADQUARTERS, *October 3,* 1861.

GENERAL: This morning, about 7 o'clock, hearing of the advance of the enemy upon us in force, I ordered my men, the Third Arkansas Regiment, to get ready to repel an attack from him, and obeyed a summons to report myself to you at your quarters. You placed me in command of the left wing of our forces, composed of my own regiment, Lieutenant-Colonel Jackson's Virginia Regiment, Hansbrough's Virginia battalion, and Anderson's two pieces of artillery, and ordered me on no account to allow the enemy to turn our left flank, and suggested the disposition to be made of the most of the infantry under my command, the artillery having already been planted. After forming my men, and while marching them to the position designed for them, the enemy commenced a rapid firing of artillery, and before I had satisfactorily formed that portion of the men under my immediate command between the river and the terminus of abatis to the right of Anderson's battery on the Greenbank road, the advance guard of a column of the enemy, marching by flank, had crossed the river some distance below us, as had been anticipated, and upon ascending the first mountain came upon the left flank of my force, which promptly fired a volley into them, which caused them instantly to retire, recross the river, rapidly traverse the meadow, unite with another force, with which a like attempt was made to turn our right flank with a similar result, and, as you are already aware, rapidly and in disorder retreated from the field.

Before the retreat of the enemy began, and while I supposed he was advancing beyond the position occupied by my command, I sent a lieutenant to Lieutenant-Colonel Barton, of my own regiment, who was on my right, to close up my line by falling down the river some 60 or 80 yards, until he united with me, preparatory to making a charge upon the rear and flank of the enemy across the river and meadow beyond it. The lieutenant returned and reported Colonel Barton not present, which I have ascertained was not true, as he was not absent from his post for a moment during the engagement, and had conceived the same idea of attacking the enemy in flank as myself. However, as the enemy had fully eight times as many infantry in the meadow and in the skirt of the woods beyond it as I could have assailed him with, supported by six or seven pieces of artillery, which kept up a continuous and extraordinarily rapid fire during the whole time, the propriety of making the attack is very questionable.*

The men and officers, with one or two exceptions, behaved admirably.

Very respectfully, your obedient servant,

A. RUST,
Colonel, Commanding.

General HENRY R. JACKSON, *Commanding Brigade.*

No. 8.

Report of Capt. L. M. Shumaker, C. S. Army, commanding light battery.

CAMP AT GREENBRIER RIVER, *October 4,* 1861.

SIR: In obedience to your oral order I have the honor to report that at daybreak yesterday, October 3, in pursuance of your instruc-

---

* Nominal list of casualties omitted. See tabulated statement, p. 229.

tions, given in person, I proceeded to get my battery ready for action. I placed my rifled piece in position on a hill in rear of Yager's house, just vacated by Captain Anderson, and then returned to my camp, and sent Lieutenant Wooding to take charge of it. Before getting my other pieces in position word was brought that the rifled gun was useless, a ball having lodged in it near the muzzle. I galloped to the place at once, and had it withdrawn to a position where the men could drive the ball up. I then ordered Lieutenant Wooding to take a gun and go across the river and report to Colonel Johnson, who had sent for it to support his skirmishers. I then brought up one of my bronze 6-pounder guns to the position occupied by the rifled piece, and directed fire upon three of the guns of the enemy in battery in a meadow about 800 yards distant. At this time the enemy had opened a steady and well-directed fire upon position from six guns of different caliber. After the men had succeeded in ramming home the ball lodged in the rifled piece I brought it up to the front and opened fire upon the enemy's caissons; but, unfortunately, the balls would lodge, owing to the close fit and to the gun's fouling easily. Finding the last ball hopelessly lodged, as I supposed, I sent it to the rear, out of the way.

At this time the fire of the enemy was very severe, and so well aimed as to make it necessary to change my position several times. About this time Lieutenant Wooding returned and informed me that the skirmishers had all fallen back, and that Colonel Johnson had directed him to return across the river, and that he had broken his lanyard. I ordered him to take position in front of Yager's house, where he could enfilade the road leading to our position, and to open fire upon the enemy's batteries, changing his position whenever the range of their fire made it necessary. At this time we were replying to them with only four pieces—two of my own, one of Captain Rice's, who commanded his piece, and a gun on a high hill to my left under the command of Captain Deshler. I galloped at once to the rear and brought up my fourth gun, under command of Sergt. Joseph H. Jones, and placed it in the best position that the nature of the ground and the tents of the infantry encampments would allow. The fire of the enemy had now become so severe as to compel me to order the removal of every gun a few feet after every third fire, and I sent word to Captain Rice (who had been working his piece beautifully for two hours, and to whom too much praise cannot be given for the deliberate manner with which he loaded and fired his piece, loading and firing by detail for an hour in the midst of a storm of shot and shell from the enemy) to change his position at once. He withdrew to a position about 250 feet in rear, and rested his men and awaited the cooling of his gun.

Observing at this time that the enemy had been driven back from the river to our left by a fire from Colonel Rust's regiment, and that they were forming in two lines for a demonstration in front, I ordered the fire to cease, and directed my chiefs of piece to rest their men, cool their guns, then load their pieces with canister, and await my order to fire. The enemy meanwhile had been moving down to our right flank to the number of 2,000, when I heard two guns open to my left. I galloped to the point and found my men in confusion, all of Captain Rice's gone but 2, 1 man dying, and was told that Captain Rice and 1 of my corporals were badly wounded. I reprimanded the sergeant, and he informed me that Colonel Johnson and Colonel Taliaferro ordered him to fire, and that he told them he had orders from me not to fire. Colonels Johnson and Taliaferro were not with the guns when I came up. I found two of Captain Rice's drivers, and ordered them to take the harness off one of the wounded horses, and get another, and take their gun to the rear. I called upon several of Colonel Scott's men, who came forward and assisted us in getting the gun off. Having no men that I could spare to work this gun, I sent it over the hill to a place of safety. I then returned to the gun on our right, and awaited the appearance of the enemy, who was evidently preparing to charge across the river. Just then your aide, Lieutenant Humphries, brought me your order to open fire upon them, when I supposed the head of their column was in evident confusion. I at once opened with two guns, and at the third fire they broke and ran from the woods in the wildest confusion. I continued to fire upon them with shot and spherical case as long as they were in range, when I ordered my men to wash out their guns, get water, and lie down to rest.

In a short time I was satisfied that the day was won, and that the enemy were in full retreat. The casualties were 3 men wounded: Private Alexander M. Earles, bullet from shell through the thigh; Corporal Calvin H. P. Eaton, flesh torn from the thick part of thigh by round shot, and Joseph R. Dickerson, shot from shell through the side, neither of them dangerously. Thomas A. Elliott was knocked down by a piece of shell, but soon recovered and kept his place by his gun. Thomas Winsey (a driver) was struck by a Minie ball on the thigh, only a bruise; Sergeant Jones had his horse shot; one of the wheels of my guns was injured in the hub, and two of the caisson wheels had spokes knocked out of them. These constitute the injury sustained by my command.

I take pleasure in calling attention to the officers and men who were with me, and whose gallantry and good conduct has won for themselves and their company the praise of the good and true all over our beloved country. Lieutenant Wooding went promptly wherever I ordered him, and kept up a galling fire upon the enemy's batteries and columns during the engagement, firing about ninety rounds, and for a while with only four men to work his gun. Sergeant Jones behaved with great coolness and judgment, and obeyed every order with promptness, managing his gun himself. His gun fired only forty rounds, being for much of the time out of range, but his fire was very destructive. Sergeant Brently, owing to his youth and temperament, was not efficient as a sergeant; yet the gun was well managed by Corporal Calvin H. P. Eaton until he was wounded, and then by Corporal Oliver P. Carter, who came back from the rifle piece to assist. This gun was worked more than either of the others under my command. My first sergeant, Timothy H. Stamps, was, unfortunately for myself and the company, at Monterey. I had to send him with my company wagons to buy or press forage for my horses. He started when he heard the first gun fired, and reached us just as the fight was over. Had he been with us, I am satisfied that much of the difficulty with our long-range gun would have been avoided, as he succeeded in getting the ball up soon after he came. My first lieutenant, Lanier, was absent on recruiting service, and Second Lieutenant Brown was at home collecting supplies of winter clothing for the men. Serg. William H. Parham was with Lieutenant Wooding, and did his duty well. Corporals Oliver P. Carter, John Q. Adams, and Calvin H. P. Eaton did their duty like brave men and good soldiers. Privates Alexander M. Earles, John H. Welles, James Royster, James T. Williams, Andrew L. Crutchfield, James G. Covey, James M. Terry, Romulus S. Gaines, Thomas A. Elliott, Martin Crawley, Hermann Mantel, Benjamin W. Walton, Samuel

Prescott, and John Murphy deserve especial praise for their bravery and good conduct. The drivers managed their horses well and kept them in place in the midst of a most terrific fire.

Very respectfully,

L. M. SHUMAKER,
Captain, Commanding Light Battery, C. S. Army.

Brig. Gen. HENRY R. JACKSON,
Commanding Force Monterey Line.

No. 9.

Congratulatory orders from Brig. Gen. W. W. Loring, C. S. Army.

GENERAL ORDERS, }   HDQRS. ARMY OF THE NORTHWEST,
No. 11.   }   *Sewell Mountain, October 7, 1861.*

The general commanding has the pleasure to announce to the Army of the Northwest a signal defeat of the enemy from the fortifications of Cheat Mountain by the division of Brigadier-General Jackson.

After three attempts of four and a half hours to force our lines in front and on both flanks with a superior force of artillery, some with longer range, he was repulsed with a considerable loss.

The general commanding tenders his thanks to Brigadier-General Jackson, his officers and soldiers, for their gallant conduct in this engagement, and assures them that they will have the grateful remembrance of our people.

By command of Brigadier-General Loring:

C. L. STEVENSON,
Assistant Adjutant-General.

OCTOBER 3, 1861.—Expedition to Pohick Church, Virginia.

Report of Brig. Gen. Henry W. Slocum, U. S. Army.

HEADQUARTERS SECOND BRIGADE,
Alexandria, Va., October 6, 1861.

SIR: I received information on the 3d instant that a body of the enemy's cavalry was at Pohick Church, about 12 miles from these headquarters, together with such other information as led me to suppose that the force could be captured without difficulty. The plan of an expedition for this purpose was fully matured and was verbally communicated to Colonel Christian, Twenty-sixth New York Volunteers, who was detailed to the command. An order was then issued of which I herewith inclose a copy.

The expedition proved an entire failure, and this result I am informed and believe is to be attributed to the fact that my orders relative to the manner of the execution were not obeyed; and what is still more annoying to me and disgraceful to my command, is the fact that instead of being marched back to the camp in good order, a large portion of the command was allowed to disband beyond our line of pickets, and, as might have been anticipated from such a proceeding, this force sent to operate against the troops of the enemy was converted into a band of marauders, who plundered alike friend and foe.

I deem it my duty to lay these facts before the commanding general, and to suggest that a court of inquiry be convened for the purpose of a thorough investigation of all the circumstances attending the expedition.

I am, sir, very respectfully, your obedient servant,

H. W. SLOCUM,
Brigadier-General Volunteers, Commanding.

Maj. S. WILLIAMS, *Assistant Adjutant-General.*

[Inclosure.]

HEADQUARTERS SECOND BRIGADE,
October 3, 1861.

Col. WILLIAM H. CHRISTIAN:

SIR: You will take command of a detachment of 300 infantry from the regiments composing this brigade and one company of cavalry, and will endeavor to cut off and take prisoners a body of the enemy's cavalry, numbering probably 50 men, stationed at or near Pohick Church.

You will proceed with 225 infantry, according to verbal directions already given you, to certain points in the rear of the enemy's position, and will make your attack at precisely 6 o'clock to-morrow morning.

You will send out 75 infantry and the company of cavalry on the Richmond road, with instructions for them to be at Potter's store, 4 miles from Pohick Church, and 6 miles from these headquarters, at 5.45 o'clock, driving in the enemy's pickets and advancing as rapidly as possible towards Pohick Church, in order to cut off the enemy or to render assistance to the other detachments of your command.

The object of the expedition being accomplished, you will return without delay.

By order of Brigadier-General Slocum :

JOSEPH HOWLAND,
Assistant Adjutant-General.

OCTOBER 3, 1861.—Skirmish at Springfield Station, Va.

Report of Brig. Gen. William B. Franklin, U. S. Army.

OCTOBER 3, 1861.

Eight hundred men of Newton's brigade, under the command of Colonel Pratt, Thirty-first New York Regiment, went out to Springfield to-day with a train for wood and sleepers. They drove in the enemy's pickets at Springfield with no loss, and brought off thirty-two car loads of wood and sleepers. They heard rumors of a large force of the enemy at Annandale, some 8,000, but I do not think the information reliable. Colonel Pratt conducted the expedition with great judgment.

W. B. FRANKLIN.

General McCLELLAN.   *Brigadier-General.*

OCTOBER 4, 1861.—Skirmish near Edwards Ferry, Maryland.

Report of Brig. Gen. Charles P. Stone, U. S. Army.

POOLESVILLE, *October* 4, 1861—3.15 p. m.

The enemy opened fire on our lookout near Edwards Ferry at 9 a. m. His firing was wild and without effect. I returned his fire with three Parrott 10-pounders, and he retired.

At the time of the firing a battalion or more of infantry and some artillery were visible going towards Leesburg, on the turnpike.

CHAS. P. STONE,
Major-General McCLELLAN.   *Brigadier-General.*

OCTOBER 15, 1861.—Skirmish on Little River Turnpike, Virginia.

Report of Lieut. Col. Isaac M. Tucker, Second New Jersey Volunteers.

CAMP SEMINARY, NEW JERSEY BRIGADE,
Wednesday, October 16, 1861.

SIR: I reported at orderly hours yesterday, at your headquarters, as brigade officer of the day, and immediately thereafter proceeded to visit the pickets, stationed as follows:

*   *   *   *   *   *   *

A few moments previous to my visit to Company A, First Regiment, stationed at the negro house on the Little River turnpike, about 11 a. m., a rebel dragoon had been discovered on the turnpike talking with a workman in Minor's corn field, about a half mile beyond our picket Station. Upon receiving this information I took the picket and went through the corn-field. Two grown white boys and one negro man were at work in the field, one of whom admitted to me that the dragoon had inquired of him concerning our pickets, pretending, however, that he gave them no information. I thought proper to arrest them all, and accordingly sent them in to headquarters.

About 5 p. m. 6 men from this station were on the turnpike about a quarter of a mile beyond the station, when a detachment of about 20 rebel cavalry surprised and fired on them. They promptly returned the fire, retreating as best they could towards the station, where the men had been extended by Lieutenant Tillou across the road. Several shots were exchanged during the retreat, the rebels pursuing our picket until nearly within musket range of the skirmishers at the station, when they turned and passed rapidly up the turnpike. Private Jordan Silvers, Company A, First Regiment, was killed in the affair, but not until with a deliberate aim he had killed a rebel officer. Private James Donnelly and Alphonso Nichols, of the same company, are missing. Lieutenant Tillou reports to me that 4 or 5 of the rebels were seen to fall from their horses, which statement was confirmed by all the men.

A scout of 10 men sent out by Captain Young from Company F, Second Regiment, was returning when the firing was heard, but did not reach the ground in time to assist our men. They found a dead horse belonging to the rebels, a sword considerably marked with blood, a new Springfield rifled musket, and a blanket, and brought in the sword, musket, and blanket. They also brought in the dead body of Private Silvers. This party went out as far as the tavern, and were there when the rebels to the number of about 100 were this side of them. The proprietor of the tavern endeavored to get them in his house by strong importunity, evidently intending to detain them for capture, but to no purpose.

During the night I made the grand rounds, and found everything quiet and the pickets unusually vigilant.

Respectfully submitted.

I. M. TUCKER,
Lieut. Col. Second Reg't N. J. Vols., Brigade Officer of the Day.
Brigadier-General KEARNY, *Comdg. New Jersey Brigade.*

[Indorsement.]

HEADQUARTERS NEW JERSEY BRIGADE,
October 16 [1861].

In forwarding this report I have to mention the prompt conduct of my aide, Captain Wilson, who, hurrying to the spot, took the guards near by and swept the ground of combat.

P. KEARNY,
Brigadier-General, Commanding.

OCTOBER 16, 1861.—Skirmish at Bolivar Heights, near Harper's Ferry, W. Va.

REPORTS.

No. 1.—Maj. Gen. Nathaniel P. Banks, U. S. Army.
No. 2.—Col. John W. Geary, Twenty-eighth Pennsylvania Infantry.
No. 3.—Maj. J. P. Gould, Thirteenth Massachusetts Infantry.
No. 4.—Capt. Henry Bertram, Third Wisconsin Infantry.
No. 5.—Capt. George J. Whitman, Third Wisconsin Infantry.
No. 6.—Lieut. Moses O'Brien, Third Wisconsin Infantry.
No. 7.—Lieut. Col. Turner Ashby, C. S. Army.

No. 1.

Report of Maj. Gen. Nathaniel P. Banks, U. S. Army.

HEADQUARTERS CAMP NEAR DARNESTOWN,
October 20, 1861.

SIR : I have the honor to forward for the information of the commanding-general a report in detail, received last evening from Colonel Geary, of the skirmish at Harper's Ferry on the 16th instant. The repulse of the rebel forces was complete, and the work for which our troops occupied the town was successfully carried out.

I have the honor to be, with respect, your obedient servant,

N. P. BANKS,
Major-General, Commanding Division.

Brigadier-General MARCY, *Chief of Staff, &c.*

No. 2.

Report of Col. John W. Geary, Twenty-eighth Pennsylvania Infantry.

HDQRS. TWENTY-EIGHTH REGIMENT PA. VOLS,
Camp Tyndale, Point of Rocks, Md., October 18, 1861.

SIR : On the 8th instant Maj. J. P. Gould, of the Thirteenth Massachusetts Volunteers, acting under orders of Major-General Banks, crossed the Potomac at Harper's Ferry to seize a quantity of wheat held by the rebels at that point. Three companies of the Third Wisconsin Volunteers, and a section of the Rhode Island battery, under Captain Tompkins, were ordered to report to Major Gould, for the purpose of assisting in and covering the necessary movements of the operation.

On the 10th instant the major called on me to aid him with men and cannon, but as the necessity for them seemed to have vanished, the order was countermanded. Again, on Sunday, the 13th, I received reliable information that the rebel forces were concentrating in the direction of Harper's Ferry, and I also learned from Major Gould that he required assistance. In the evening, accompanied by Governor Sprague, of Rhode Island, and Colonel Tompkins, of the Rhode Island Artillery, I went to Sandy Hook, with two companies of my regiment and one piece of cannon. On Monday I entered into Virginia, and on that day and the following one aided in the removal of the wheat, and held in check the gathering forces of the enemy.

The troops under my command were four companies (A, D, F, and G) of the Twenty-eighth Regiment Pennsylvania Volunteers, three companies (C, I, and K) of the Thirteenth Massachusetts Volunteers, and three companies of the Third Wisconsin Regiment, numbering in all 600 men, and two pieces of cannon, under command of Captain Tompkins, of the Rhode Island Battery, and two pieces of the Ninth New York Battery, under Lieutenant Martin. About 100 men of the Massachusetts regiment were left on the north side of the Potomac River, and the two pieces of the Rhode Island Battery were placed on the Maryland Heights, one of the New York guns on the railroad opposite Harper's Ferry, and the other to command the approach from Pleasant Valley, in Virginia, where three companies of rebel cavalry were stationed. The command of all the troops thus left I confided to Major Gould.

The object for which the river had been crossed having been accomplished, on Tuesday night I had determined to recross the river on Wednesday and permit the troops to return to their various regiments; but about 7 o'clock on the morning of the 16th my pickets stationed on the heights above Bolivar, extending from the Potomac to the Shenandoah River, about 2½ miles west of Harper's Ferry, were driven into the town of Bolivar by the enemy, who approached from the west in three columns, consisting of infantry and cavalry, supported by artillery.

I was upon the ground in a few minutes, and rallied my pickets upon the main body of our troops in Bolivar. In a short time the action became general. The advanced guard of the rebels, consisting of several hundred cavalry, charged gallantly towards the upper part of the town, and their artillery and infantry soon took position upon the heights from which my pickets had been driven. The enemy's three pieces of artillery were stationed on and near the Charlestown road where it crosses Bolivar Heights. They had one 32-pounder columbiad, one steel rifled 13-pounder, and one brass 6-pounder, all of which were served upon the troops of my command with great activity, the large gun throwing alternately solid shot, shell, and grape, and the others principally fuse shell.

While these demonstrations were being made in front a large body of men made their appearance upon Loudoun Heights, with four pieces of cannon and sharpshooters stationed at the most eligible points of the mountain, to bombard our troops, and greatly annoy us in the use of the ferry on the Potomac. The commencement of the firing upon our front and left was almost simultaneous.

In order to prevent the enemy from crossing the Shenandoah, I detached a company of the Thirteenth Massachusetts Regiment, under command of Captain Shriber, for the defense of the fords on that river. He took position near the old rifle works, and during the action rendered good service there. There then remained under my immediate command about 450 men. With these the fierce charge of the enemy's cavalry was soon checked and turned back. A second and a third charge was made by them, increasing in impetuosity with each repetition, during which they were supported, in addition to the artillery, by long lines of infantry stationed on Bolivar Heights, who kept up a continuous firing. They were repulsed each time with effect. Under this concentrated fire our troops held their position until 11 o'clock, when Lieutenant Martin, by my order, joined me with one rifled cannon, which had been placed to cover the ferry, he having crossed the river with it under a galling fire of riflemen from Loudoun Heights.

I then pushed forward my right flank, consisting of two companies (A and G) of the Twenty-eighth Regiment Pennsylvania Volunteers. They succeeded in turning the enemy's left near the Potomac, and gained a portion of the heights. At the same time Lieutenant Martin opened a well-directed fire upon the enemy's cannon in our front, and Captain Tompkins succeeded in silencing some of the enemy's guns on Loudoun Heights. These services, simultaneously rendered, were of great importance, and the turning of the enemy's flank being the key to the success of the action, I instantly ordered a general forward movement, which terminated in a charge, and we were soon in possession of the heights from river to river. There I halted the troops, and from that position they drove the fugitives with a well-directed aim of cannon and small-arms across the valley in the direction of Halltown. If any cavalry had been attached to my command the enemy could have been cut to pieces, as they did not cease their flight until they reached Charlestown, a distance of 6 miles.

Immediately after the capture of the heights Major Tyndale arrived with a re-enforcement of five companies of my regiment from Point of Rocks, two of which he ordered to report to Major Gould at Sandy Hook, and soon joined me with the others on the field. The standard of the Twenty-eighth Regiment Pennsylvania Volunteers—the flag of the Union—was then unfurled on the soil of Virginia, and planted on an eminence of Bolivar Heights, and under its folds we directed the fire of our artillery against the batteries and forces on Loudoun Heights, and soon succeeded in silencing every gun and driving away every rebel that could be seen.

The victory was complete. The loss of the enemy in killed and wounded is generally conceded to be about 150, which they carried back in wagons and on horses as rapidly as they fell. We took 4 prisoners, among whom is Rev. Nathaniel Green North, chaplain of Colonel Ashby's command. He is said to have been present at every battle that has occurred in Virginia. The fine 32-pounder columbiad, mounted on an old-fashioned gun-carriage, was captured, together with a quantity of ammunition for it, consisting of ball, shell, and grape shot, for the transportation of which a wagon was used as a caisson. These were immediately transferred to the north side of the Potomac, and the gun is placed in position against its late proprietors. One of their small guns used at Bolivar Heights was disabled, having one of the wheels shot from the gun carriage by a well-directed shot from Lieutenant Martin. They succeeded in dragging it from the field.

Our loss is 4 killed, 7 wounded, and 2 taken prisoners, a list of whom is hereto attached.* The greater part of the loss occurred in the Wisconsin companies, who gallantly sustained the position of our left flank throughout the contest. One of the soldiers taken by the enemy

---

* Nominal list omitted.

was Private Edgar Ross, of Company C, Third Wisconsin Regiment, who was wounded in the action. The other, Corporal Beniah Pratt, of Company A, Twenty-eighth Regiment Pennsylvania Volunteers, was accidentally taken by a few of the enemy, whom he mistook for Massachusetts men, their uniform corresponding in all respects to that of the latter. The four men who were killed were afterwards charged upon by the cavalry and stabbed through the body, stripped of all their clothing, not excepting their shoes and stockings, and left in perfect nudity. One was laid in the form of a crucifixion, with his hands spread out, and cut through the palms with a dull knife. This inhuman treatment incensed my troops exceedingly, and I fear its consequences may be shown in retaliatory acts hereafter.

I visited the iron foundery at Shenandoah City, and ascertained that it was used by the rebels for casting shot and shell of all kinds. I ordered it to be burned, which was done the same night.

The acts of individual gallantry are so numerous in the whole command that it would be impossible to give each an appropriate mention, but I do not hesitate to say that every corps behaved with the coolness and courage of veteran troops.

It affords me pleasure to mention that Hon. Daniel McCook, father of General McCook, as an amateur soldier, gun in hand, volunteered and rendered much service during the engagement. I also mention like service rendered by Benjamin G. Owen, esq., of Saint Louis. Both of these gentlemen were greatly exposed during the action.

I am informed by authority deemed reliable that the enemy's forces consisted of the following troops, viz: The Thirteenth and Nineteenth Mississippi Regiments, the Eighth Virginia Regiment of Infantry, Colonel Ashby's regiment of cavalry, and Rogers' Richmond battery of six pieces and one 32-pounder columbiad, all commanded by General Evans in person.

Bolivar Heights were taken at 1.30 p. m. I directed our troops to rest there until 12 o'clock at night, when we fired a farewell shot into Halltown, and as there was no longer any necessity to remain on that side of the Potomac, our errand having been crowned with the fullest success, I marched my command to the Ferry, and in five hours it was safely landed in Maryland. There being no immediate apprehensions of the enemy there, I ordered the Wisconsin companies to report to Colonel Ruger, their commander, in Frederick, and returned to this place with part of my regiment and the two guns of the New York battery, leaving Captain Tompkins' guns and one company of my own regiment with Major Gould, to guard against any further outbreak.

A flag of truce was sent to me on the morning of the 17th by Colonel Ashby, commander of the rebel cavalry, with a letter dated at Charlestown, inquiring concerning Rev. Mr. North. He stated that, as Mr. North's horse had gone home wounded, his family feared he had been killed. The colonel requested that, as he was a non-combatant, he hoped I would release him. The testimony against him from other sources not being quite so satisfactory, I have determined to retain him, and forward him with the others to such destination as the general may designate. I received assurances from the bearer of the flag that Corporal Pratt was well, and that every attention was being given to the wound of Private Edgar Ross, and that he did not consider his case a dangerous one.

On this morning a few of the enemy in citizens' dress came secretly to Harper's Ferry, by way of the Shenandoah road, burned Herr's mill, from which a great portion of the wheat had been taken, and immediately retired.

The foregoing is a correct official statement of the engagement at Bolivar Heights October 16, 1861.

JNO. W. GEARY,
Colonel Twenty-eighth Regiment Pennsylvania Volunteers.

Capt. R. MORRIS COPELAND,
Acting Assistant Adjutant-General.

No. 3.

Report of Maj. J. P. Gould, Thirteenth Massachusetts Infantry.

SIR: At your request I write you what I saw and heard on Wednesday, October 16 [1861], the day of the Bolivar skirmish. On the night previous—a delightful moonlight night—I went out on our line of picket guards, and did not return to the mill till 12 o'clock, when I bunked down in the counting-room and remained till 6 in the morning, when I arose, examined the remaining grain of the mill, the quarters of Company I, Thirteenth Massachusetts, near the mill; quarters of Companies K and C, near the ferry. I then went upon Camp Hill, and visited all the public buildings where the Wisconsin and the Pennsylvania troops were quartered, and observed all things quiet, and was informed by the officer of the day that all had been quiet during the night. Captain Bertram had served as officer of the day.

I then came across the river to the Maryland side to supervise the further progress of the boating of the wheat and laying the large cable across, for greater conveniences. Whilst taking breakfast at my quarters I heard a cannonading, and immediately sent an agent to learn of it; the firing was being done by our troops. I was soon informed that the enemy were advancing. I sent a telegram to the Point of Rocks to hold all cars in readiness to take troops here. I then repaired to the locks, and gave orders in regard to the boating, laying the cable, and relative to firing the cannon, if opportunity offered. By order of the colonel, sent for Captain Meyer's company, and passed over the other side to supervise with regard to arrangements then necessary at the landing. I then received the order from the colonel to order up Major Tyndale and his force. I returned and gave this order by telegraph. At this time, learning that the cavalry were advancing from the woods, I ordered Captain Tompkins' battery to fire upon them. Again I passed over to Virginia, and passed most up Camp Hill, when I received an order by the colonel to send over two horses and more ammunition. This order I returned to execute. While effecting it Major Tyndale came up with his force. I took the liberty, as I said to him, to order over the river two-thirds of his force. He asked what the exact orders of the colonel were, for he wished to be governed by the colonel's orders strictly, but afterwards the colonel sent for this part of the force. Whilst this force and the ammunition were passing the river the rebels fired upon them from the Loudoun Heights by rifle shots. I ordered one of our iron guns to fire upon them with cannister; two shots silenced them. I ordered one iron gun to play upon the guns on Loudoun Heights, from which they were throwing shells on to and over the mill, with slugs, and I learn that it seemed to have some good effect. A large body of cavalry was seen in Loudoun, opposite Sandy Hook. I ordered down half of a company of the Pennsylvania men, and the cavalry dispersed. The shells were thrown regularly from Loudoun Heights, till their cessation, over the mill and Hall's Rifle Works, where were posted Company I and part of Company K of the Thirteenth Regiment.

At past 2 o'clock, after the firing from Loudoun Heights had ceased, the colonel ordered over the New York battery. This order I received while going up Camp Hill to go on to field at Bolivar. The Rhode Island Battery continued to fire until I learned that his shell were falling short of the enemy and among our own men, when I ordered a close.

This comprises what I actually saw at a distance—the retreat and advance of our right. It seemed to be a premeditated attack. Indeed, I learn since that it was much of a concerted affair. The names of the killed and wounded I have been unable to obtain.

J. P. GOULD, Major.

Earlier I should have sent this statement; but, besides being quite unwell, there was much necessary and pressing business connected with the closing up of this adventure, every part of which needed my personal attention. But, from the accounts I see in the papers, I infer that there is no Major Gould at this post, and, if here, he is only an intruder; nor had he anything to do with getting the wheat. Indeed, his name does not occur in a long whole-column article of to-day's Baltimore paper. Let Cæsar have his own.

Most obediently,

J. P. GOULD.

Col. JOHN W. GEARY.

———

No. 4.

Report of Capt. Henry Bertram, Third Wisconsin Infantry.

FREDERICK CITY, MD., October 18, 1861.

COLONEL: I have the honor to report that on the 16th instant, while Company A, Third Regiment Wisconsin Volunteers, under my command, was in quarters at Harper's Ferry, cannonading was heard early in the morning in the direction of Halltown; and soon after our pickets were driven in by the advancing enemy. I formed company immediately, and moved out toward Bolivar; was there met by Colonel Geary, who ordered me to protect the left flank and road on the Shenandoah.

In obedience to this, I deployed company as skirmishers, left resting on the Shenandoah, the enemy mean time throwing shells upon us from Loudoun Heights. Having but limited range of observation, I ascended the hill under which my men were covered, and, reconnoitering, saw a column of the enemy's infantry, with Confederate colors flying, marching down the road to Bolivar, followed by a corps of artillerymen with a heavy piece of artillery. On bringing forward my left flank I sent in a galling fire, just as the enemy had planted their cannon, covered by a large brick house from the fire of our battery on the Maryland Heights. After sustaining our fire for some fifteen minutes the enemy retreated, taking with them their cannon. I followed in pursuit, a heavy ground and deep gully being between me and the enemy. On coming to the road, I was joined by Lieutenant O'Brien with Company C, Third Regiment Wisconsin Volunteers, and moved on together under a heavy fire from our right and front, and took possession of the brick house, one company of the Thirteenth Massachusetts being in our rear. After half an hour, the house not affording a favorable position to fire with much effect upon the enemy, we advanced upon the road toward the enemy, who had retreated to a ridge covered with timber; saw the enemy's cannon in the road; charged upon it with parts of Companies A and C (about 40 men in all). As we commenced, the enemy attempted to haul off their gun, but in their hasty attempts broke the axle-tree. As we approached the gun we saw one of the men spiking it and the others left it and sought cover, when a tremendous fire upon us from a masked breastwork compelled us to seek cover. We sustained and answered the fire for some fifteen minutes, saw our men falling, and were obliged to retreat, closely pursued by the enemy's cavalry. We rallied, after falling back some 50 rods, and fired upon the enemy's cavalry, driving them back and covering the retreat of our wounded and those who were aiding them off the field; then slowly retreated to the main body.

Company H, Third Regiment Wisconsin, having joined us, we formed a complete line of skirmishers from Bolivar main street to the Shenandoah, and awaited the arrival of artillery. At 1 o'clock p. m., the artillery having arrived, we moved the line slowly forward, by command of Colonel Geary, firing as we advanced, the enemy slowly falling back. On our arrival at the outskirts of Bolivar we advanced rapidly, the enemy having retreated behind the hill; and passing in our advance the gun which had been disabled, we established our line on Bolivar Heights, the enemy having retreated to a belt of wood about three-quarters of a mile away in the direction of Halltown. Captured the chaplain of one of the enemy's regiments, and sent him, along with the captured gun, to the ferry, by order of Colonel Geary.

In the charge upon the gun the following-named men of my command were killed and wounded, which was the only loss suffered by us in the action.*

I take this occasion to make favorable mention of the fearless and judicious conduct of Lieut. Ed. E. Bryant, of Company A, Third Regiment Wisconsin Volunteers, in the action.

I am, sir, very respectfully, your obedient servant,

HENRY BERTRAM,
Captain, Commanding Company A, Third Reg't Wis. Vols.

Col. JOHN W. GEARY, &c.

No. 5.

Report of Capt. George J. Whitman, Third Wisconsin Infantry.

I have the honor of making the following report to Colonel Geary, commanding at Harper's Ferry October 16, 1861:

On the morning of October 9, 1861, at 4 o'clock, Company H, with Companies A and C, of the Third Wisconsin Volunteers, left camp at Frederick City, and marched to the Junction, and took the cars for Sandy Hook; arrived there at 8 o'clock a. m.; crossed the river to Harper's Ferry, and were quartered in Government buildings. On the morning of the 10th had a slight skirmish with a company of cavalry. The company was employed in moving wheat across the river and doing picket duty.

---

* List shows 2 killed and 3 wounded.

October 15, 30 men were detailed to do duty at the mill, and 23, under my command, detailed to act as a reserve, and stationed near the outposts on the Charlestown road. On the morning of October 16, being officer of the day, went to headquarters, leaving First Sergeant J. T. Marvin in command. At 7.30 o'clock the pickets were fired upon by the enemy advancing on the Charlestown road. The reserve went to their support, and joining a company of the Pennsylvania Twenty-eighth, (Captain Copeland), [F], engaged the enemy's cavalry, firing and falling back through the timber. During this time the enemy were throwing shell from the hill beyond, which fell in their midst, and their infantry, advancing up the road, cut them off from their camp, and were obliged to leave their overcoats and blankets, which fell into the hands of the enemy. Advancing up through Bolivar with the rest of the company (Wisconsin), joined by the reserve, deploying to the right and advancing up the hill, intending to flank under the protection of one battery on the other side of the river, but were ordered back to the village by Colonel Geary and then to fall back across the ravine. Soon after were ordered to take position on the Shenandoah, to cut off the enemy's advance on our left, under continual fire from the enemy's battery on Loudoun Heights until it was silenced by the battery on Maryland Heights. Remained there until the arrival of the New York Ninth Artillery, when we were ordered to join the line, and advanced to the ridge formerly occupied by our pickets, the enemy retreating over the ridge beyond; lay on our arms until 11 o'clock, when we were ordered back to and across the river. Marched to Sandy Hook, and remained, waiting for a train to take us to Frederick, until 5.30 p. m.; took the train, and arrived at Frederick at 8 o'clock p. m. October 17, 1861.

Very respectfully,

GEO. J. WHITMAN,
Captain Company H, Third Regiment Wisconsin Volunteers.

Col. JOHN W. GEARY.

No. 6.

Report of Lieut. Moses O'Brien, Third Wisconsin Infantry.

OCTOBER 18, 1861.

COLONEL: I have the honor to report that on the 16th instant the company under my command—Company C, Third Regiment Wisconsin Volunteers—was quartered in town at Harper's Ferry, and at about 7 o'clock a. m. a cannonading was heard, appearing to emanate beyond the heights known as the Bolivar Heights. I forthwith ordered the company to prepare for action, and [as] soon as in ranks, I moved out upon the road in the direction of the firing. Meeting Colonel Geary, was ordered by him to protect the left flank to the right and rearward of Captain Bertram's Company (A), Third Regiment Wisconsin Volunteers, my right on the Halltown turnpike; company into skirmish line. Then, on reconnoitering, I observed a column of infantry and also a squadron of cavalry advancing toward Bolivar from the Shenandoah road, and also another column of infantry and cavalry and a heavy piece of artillery. The enemy's right was bearing down towards Captain Bertram. I then advanced at double-quick to his assistance. At this time the enemy commenced shelling us from a battery on Loudoun Heights. The enemy gained the outskirts of the town of Bolivar and planted their gun behind a large brick house, well covered from our batteries, and supported by a large force of infantry. I opened fire upon them just as they began [to] retreat from the house under a heavy fire from Captain Bertram; then advanced, and my line connected with Captain Bertram, as we gained possession of the brick house. The enemy opened a heavy cross-fire upon us as we advanced upon the house from our right and front, their skirmishers being deployed along and behind a ridge northward of Bolivar. Our musketry not having effect upon the enemy from the cover of the brick house, we deployed again to the left, and advanced along the turnpike toward the enemy. Advancing, observed their gun planted ahead of us in the road and watched by artillerists; charged upon it, in concert with Captain Bertram, which the enemy perceiving, endeavored in haste to haul off their gun. In so doing the axle-tree was broken, and they were forced to leave after spiking.

As we drew near the gun, the enemy being strongly intrenched to our right upon the ridge, opened upon us a terrible fire of musketry and rifle, under which we were forced to seek shelter of trees and hillocks and to lie upon our faces. Not being supported, and the right flank not closing in to dislodge [the] enemy, we fell back out of the fire. As we commenced retreat, the enemy's cavalry dashed upon us, almost surrounding a portion of our small force. I saw their danger, and ordered [the] foremost in retreat to rally to repel cavalry and cover [the] flight of our men. They did so gallantly, and poured a volley into the cavalry that threw into confusion and drove them from the field, several saddles empty. We then retreated into Bolivar upon main body, and held our ground under cannonade from enemy from Loudoun Heights and from high ridge beyond the town. We waited the arrival of artillery, which came to our assistance. We then advanced in skirmish line toward enemy by Colonel Geary's command. The enemy fled back under the fire of our artillery, and we advanced rapidly upon their position, they falling behind the ridge. In our advance we passed the gun the enemy could not remove, and occupied the position on the ridge. The enemy fell back upon Halltown, and were out of sight.

In our advance upon the brick house, Private Steward E. Mosher, Company C, was killed; and in the charge upon the gun, Private Henry Raymond, Company C, was killed, and Corporal George Gray and Corporal William H. Foster, of Company C, were each wounded in the leg, and Private Edgar Ross, of Company C, was wounded and taken prisoner, and Private Thomas Hader, Company C, slightly wounded in the leg, which comprise the whole loss of my command.

I was the only commissioned officer in the company. My men behaved gallantly, evincing great bravery and coolness under galling fire.

I am, sir, very respectfully, your obedient servant,

MOSES O'BRIEN,
First Lieutenant of Company C, Third Wisconsin Volunteers.

Col. JOHN W. GEARY, &c.

No. 7.

Report of Lieut. Col. Turner Ashby, C. S. Army.

CAMP EVANS, NEAR HALLTOWN, VA., *October* 17, 1861.

MY DEAR SIR: I herewith submit the result of an engagement had with the enemy on yesterday (the 16th) at Bolivar Hill. The enemy occupying that position have for several days been committing depredations in the vicinity of their camp. Having at my disposal only 300 militia, armed with flint-lock muskets, and two companies of cavalry

(Captains Turner's and Mason's) of Colonel McDonald's regiment, I wrote to General Evans to co-operate with me, taking position upon Loudoun Heights, and thereby prevent re-enforcements from below, and at the same time to drive them out of the Ferry, where they were under cover in the buildings.

On the evening of the 15th I was re-enforced by two companies of Colonel McDonald's regiment (Captain Wingfield's), fully armed with Minie rifles, and mounted; Captain Miller's, about 30 men mounted, the balance on foot, armed with flint-lock guns. I had one rifled 4-pounder gun, one 24-pounder gun badly mounted, which broke an axle in Bolivar, and I had to spike it. My force upon the morning of the attack consisted of 300 militia, part of two regiments commanded by Colonel Albert, of Shenandoah, and Major Finter, of Page. I had 180 of Colonel McDonald's cavalry (Captain Henderson's men), under command of Lieutenant Glynn; Captain Baylor's mounted militia; Captain Hess, about 25 each. The rifled gun was under command of Captain Avirett, the 24-pounder under Captain Comfield.

I made the attack in three divisions, and drove the enemy from their breastworks without loss of a man, and took position upon the hill, driving the enemy as far as Lower Bolivar. There the large gun broke down, and this materially affected the result. The detachment from the large gun was transferred to the rifled piece, and Captain Avirett was sent to Loudoun Heights with message to Colonel Griffin.

The enemy now formed and charged with shouts and yells, which the militia met like veterans. At this moment I ordered a charge of cavalry, which was handsomely done, Captain Turner's in the lead. In this charge 5 of the enemy were killed. After holding this position for four hours the enemy were re-enforced by infantry and artillery, and we fell back in order to the position which their pickets occupied in the morning. The position which Colonel Griffin held upon Loudoun was such as to be of very little assistance to us, not being so elevated as to prevent them from controlling the crossing.

My main force is now at Camp Evans, while I hold all the intermediate ground. The enemy left the Ferry last night, and are encamped upon the first plateau on Maryland Heights.

My loss is 1 killed and 9 wounded. Report from the Ferry states the loss of the enemy at 25 killed and a number wounded. We have 2 Yankee prisoners and 8 Union men co-operating with them. We took a large number of blankets, overcoats, and about one dozen guns.

I cannot compliment my officers and men too highly for their gallant bearing during the whole fight, considering the bad arms with which they were supplied and their inexperience. I cannot impress too forcibly the necessity of perfect organization of my artillery and the forwarding at a very early day of the other guns promised. These guns are drawn by horses obtained for the occasion, and are worked by volunteers. We are in want of cavalry arms and long-range guns, and would be glad to have an arrangement made to mount my men.

I herewith submit Surgeon West's report,* and cannot compliment him too highly, and respectfully submit his name as one worthy of an appointment. He is temporarily employed by me as a surgeon.

Casualties: Wounded, 13.

Your obedient servant,

TURNER ASHBY,
Lieutenant-Colonel, C. S. Army, Comdg. in Jefferson County.

Hon. Mr. Benjamin, *Acting Secretary of War.*

---

* Not found.

P. S.—I am without ammunition for rifled cannon (4-pounder rifled to Parrott), also without friction primers. I am without a regular quartermaster, and consequently have my movements greatly embarrassed. If I am to continue with this command I would be glad to have the privilege to recommend for appointment, so that I can organize according to what I believe most efficient condition.

OCTOBER 18, 1861.—Reconnaissance towards Occoquan River, Virginia.

Report of Brig. Gen. Israel B. Richardson, U. S. Army.

HEADQUARTERS RICHARDSON'S BRIGADE,
October 19, 1861.

SIR: In obedience to your instructions, I left this camp yesterday at 3.30 p. m. to make a reconnaissance in the direction of Occoquan, my force consisting of two regiments of infantry, one half battery of artillery, and one company of cavalry. The command proceeded as far as Accotink Creek, taking the Telegraph road. On reaching this stream I came to a halt, and sent half a company of cavalry to Pohick Church, the other half to the Accotink Village, and posted a company of infantry to our right on the road leading up the creek. This company on moving up the road fell in with the enemy's pickets, who immediately ran into their camp across the creek and gave the alarm. The long roll beat some 20 minutes from three different camps on our right, showing that they were there in some force. After resting the command half an hour I sent to order in both detachments of cavalry, who soon came in, finding no enemy at the village or at the church. The enemy occupy the valley on the right of the road leading from the crossing to the church. From what I could learn, the road from Pohick Church to Occoquan is clear, and but few troops are at the latter place. Having finished the object of the expedition, I moved the command back to camp, where it arrived at 12 o'clock, having marched some 20 miles. I took this opportunity of moving forward our pickets, who now occupy a direct line from Windsor Hill to the mouth of Dogue Creek.

I have the honor to be, very respectfully, your obedient servant,
I. B. RICHARDSON,
Brigadier-General.

Brig. Gen. S. P. HEINTZELMAN, *U. S. Army.*

[Indorsement.]

HEADQUARTERS DIVISION, FORT LYON,
October 19, 1861.

This reconnaissance shows that the rebels are in force between Long Branch and Accotink Run, above the Telegraph road. If there are any south of this road it is not probable that they are in force. Our pickets now extend from the mouth of Dogue Run to Windsor's Hill, which is a commanding position and overlooks the valley. Accotink Village was abandoned, as well as Pohick Church, several days ago.

Respectfully forwarded.

S. P. HEINTZELMAN,
Brigadier-General Volunteers, Commanding.

The rebels are believed to belong to General Ewell's brigade.

OCTOBER 19–NOVEMBER 16, 1861.—Operations in the Kanawha and New River Region, West Virginia.

SUMMARY OF THE PRINCIPAL EVENTS.

Oct. 19–21, 1861.—Skirmishes on New River.
    23, 1861.—Skirmish at Gauley.
Nov. 1– 3, 1861.—Skirmishes near Gauley Bridge.
    6–15, 1861.—Operations at Townsend's Ferry, New River.
    10–11, 1861.—Skirmishes at Blake's Farm, Cotton Hill.
    12, 1861.—Skirmish on Laurel Creek, Cotton Hill.
    14, 1861.—Skirmishes near McCoy's Mill.

REPORTS, ETC.

No. 1.—Brig. Gen. William S. Rosecrans, U. S. Army, with dispatches.
No. 2.—Brig. Gen. Jacob D. Cox, U. S. Army, of skirmishes at Blake's Farm.
No. 3.—Maj. Samuel W. Crawford, Thirteenth U. S. Infantry, of operations at Townsend's Ferry.
No. 4.—Brig. Gen. Henry W. Benham, U. S. Army, of operations from November 11–16.
No. 5.—Col. Carr B. White, Twelfth Ohio Infantry, of skirmish on Laurel Creek.
No. 6.—Col. William S. Smith, Thirteenth Ohio Infantry, of skirmishes on Laurel Creek and near McCoy's Mill.
No. 7.—Brig. Gen. John B. Floyd, C. S. Army.

No. 1.

Reports of Brig. Gen. William S. Rosecrans, U. S. Army, with dispatches.

CAMP GAULEY, VA., *November* 11, 1861.

Since last night rebels have fallen back to within 3 miles of Fayette. The river too high to cross our force at the ferry above. Their position regarded as impracticable, but which we are prepared to use. Three men attempting to escape from that side of the river came down to cross to our side. Two crossed, and our concealed guard foolishly sprang out, took them prisoners, alarming the other, on whom they fired, and he ran away. The enemy was discovered breaking his camp about 8 o'clock, taking position within 2 or 3 miles of the ferry crossing. At which General Schenck nevertheless is unwilling to advance. Benham will occupy position on their front and flank to-morrow morning, reconnoiter, and engage them. If they stand, I think General Schenck will cross over in their rear and we will bag them.

W. S. ROSECRANS,
Brigadier-General.

Maj. Gen. GEORGE B. MCCLELLAN.

—

CAMP GAULEY, *November* 15, 1861.

Confirming news of my No. 8* I report that General Benham pursued rebels 15 miles beyond Fayette; overtook a rear guard of infantry and cavalry; skirmished with them, and having no train or provisions to enable him to go farther, desisted from pursuit and is returning to Fayette.

Floyd's forces reported to have been eight regiments and 700 cavalry. They left considerable camp equipage, ammunition, and knapsacks.

—————————
* Not found.

The fortifications at Dickerson's farm were very respectable and extensive. The line of Floyd's stockade a mile long; a *crémaillere* line for infantry 700 yards. Two embrasure batteries to defend passage across Miller's Ferry and front attack. Our success in concealing real point of attack was perfect. Continued high water alone prevented a perfect success and capture; and fatal want of nerve and inaction caused the second plan to fail, which would have been equally successful, as we learned. They now draw their supplies from a new depot, established at Newbern, east of Wytheville, on railroad. Rumor of re-enforcement to Floyd from General Davis appears tolerably authentic. Effect of this defeat on the whole to be seen. Believe it will be the last attempt to force Gauley Pass. Propose at once to brigade troops and dispose them to hold winter quarters.

W. S. ROSECRANS.

Major-General McCLELLAN.

—

CAMP GAULEY, *November* 16, 1861.

Since my No. 9 [next preceding] Fayetteville is occupied by General Schenck. Road to Bowyer's Ferry reconnoitered. Enemy's tents left hidden have been burned. Country being examined with a view to its defense, and an advance by pack-mules to Newbern, the new depot of the rebels. Benham's brigade returned to its camp, 6 miles below the mouth of Gauley. Enemy said to have had 500 wagons running from Raleigh to Newbern. Roads in bad condition. Country above Fayette more open than any on the Philippi road, which you remember. Floyd had engaged Huddleston house, 3 miles from Gauley Bridge, for his winter quarters. It wanted nothing but a vigorous execution of plans in all respects successful to have secured his entire army. I am in the utmost need of regular officers for an aide and for an inspector general in place of Major Slemmer, sick. Also, some ordnance officers at headquarters.

I perceive in the paper a new arrangement of departments, whereby, as I understand it, General Kelley is detached from my command. Any arrangement that will conduce to the public interest will be satisfactory to me, but I respectfully call your attention to the fact that I have to draw all my supplies from Cincinnati. My staff are now left in another department; an anomaly which ought not to exist. I have to use Gallipolis as a hospital station and depot for stores, also in another department. I have no control, therefore, over my sick who go there and no right to order officers there. I am obliged to resort to Marietta and the Muskingum Valley for forage, and have a quartermaster stationed at Marietta, where is a depot for receiving horses worked down in the service. The only ordnance officer I have is at Bellaire, in Ohio. I have also 35 miles of telegraph line, connecting line down this valley by Point Pleasant with Hamden, saving forty cents on every ten words transmitted either east or west. It seems to me Ohio is a much more necessary part of this department than of that of Cumberland. Should you think otherwise, I beg you at least to issue such orders as will secure what I have spoken of as necessary beyond the question of interference. The anomalous position of my staff at Cincinnati has prevented me from having the services of Assistant Adjutant-General McLean, though much needed. While though apparently under my command he has been receiving orders and discharging duties directed by another general officer. What is much more important to public service is, I want for the efficient use of the troops here two or three efficient brigadiers. It will also be most desirable to replace several of the regiments here broken down by sickness, allowing them to recruit health and numbers.

Floyd's forces, though beaten and demoralized, are not destroyed, and must be watched. The roads, which become very bad by usage, dry up and become good very quickly, making the county open for enterprises during the winter. Have just returned from Fayette. Will write you in the morning.

W. S. ROSECRANS,
Brigadier-General.

Major-General McClellan.

—

HEADQUARTERS DEPARTMENT WESTERN VIRGINIA,
Camp Gauley Mountain, November 25, 1861.

SIR: My current series of dispatches has informed the commanding general of the principal military events in this department, including those which have occurred on this line since our return from Sewell; but to give the whole connectedly and in detail I now respectfully submit a report, consisting of abstract, details, map, and appendix:*

ABSTRACT.

The first thing after the battle of Carnifix was to unite the forces on the Lewisburg road and follow it up as far as practicable. This was done; the enemy's intrenched position beyond Big Sewell reconnoitered, his force ascertained, and on the 5th of October the troops fell back towards Gauley Bridge, to be near their clothing and supplies. The next thing was to clothe, equip, and pay the troops. This was progressing vigorously when Floyd, with eight regiments, 700 cavalry, and several pieces of artillery, variously stated from two to eight, appeared in the angle west of New River, on the Fayette road, while it was stated, on information entitled to great weight, that Lee was preparing to combine an attack on our front, while Floyd was to cut off our communications down the Kanawha.

It now became necessary to guard against Lee, secure our communications, dislodge, and, if possible, cut off Floyd's forces. The operations for this purpose took up the time from the 1st of November to the 15th of November. One of the plans for capturing Floyd failed on account of the high water, and the other, while it was successful in dislodging the rebels and driving them from this part of the country, failed to capture and destroy their force for want of vigorous and energetic execution of plans confided to General Benham.

The special history of these movements is given in the subjoined details, illustrated by the map and appendix.

REPORT OF DETAILS.

After the battle of Carnifix the troops brought down by the Summersville line passed over on to the Lewisburg road, uniting with the Kanawha Brigade. The head of this column advanced to the top of Big Sewell, 34 miles from Gauley Bridge, on the 28th of September.

---

*Appendix consists of the subordinate reports following.

Two and a half regiments, under Generals Schenck and Benham, came as far as the foot of Sewell to support the advance, which acted as a corps of observation. After reconnoitering the enemy's fortified position from 2 to 4 miles in front on top of Sewell, on Lewisburg road, supported by fortifications at Meadow Bluff, 15 miles this side of Lewisburg, ascertaining his strength to be from twelve to fourteen thousand, and finding that the country beyond was measurably stripped of forage and subsistence, our force (5,200) retired towards Gauley Bridge gradually, and encamped at the positions shown on the accompanying map; Schenck's Brigade being 10 miles from Gauley Bridge, McCook's 8 miles, Benham's 6 miles, while General Cox was posted, one regiment at Tompkins' farm and remainder at Gauley Bridge, with detachments for guarding steamboat landing below.

Our object in taking this position, as reported, was to be near enough to water transportation to enable our transportation to bring forward not only forage and subsistence, but the clothing of the troops. Orders were also immediately dispatched to have the paymasters come and pay them, none having received any since they entered the service. The clothing of all, with the exception of the cavalry, was completed by the 1st of November. The paying went on much more slowly, in consequence of the difficulties in getting the rolls and the inexperience of the paymasters, and is not yet completed.

No military movements were or could be undertaken that would interfere with these primary objects. The enemy's motions at Meadow Bluff were watched. The militia, which all summer long had occupied the region west of the New River and south of the Loop Creek Hills, (see map and accompanying memoir, marked A),* showed themselves opposite Miller's Ferry, near McCook's brigade, about the 18th of October, when they were, as we learned, to be assembled at Fayette for the purpose of being paid off, but as we then supposed and since ascertained with the real object of rallying them if possible. Colonel McCook was therefore directed to pass over with a sufficient force to capture or disperse them, and occupy or treat the country as circumstances might indicate to him best. He passed over, had a slight skirmish with a small militia force, occupied Fayette, reconnoitered the roads in the vicinity, satisfied himself that there was no force except the bushwhacking militia, secession residents of the country, and retired over Miller's Ferry without leaving a guard on the other side. On reporting the result of his expedition the commanding general expressed a regret that he did not leave a company to cover Miller's Ferry on the other side. Esteeming it of little consequence, he was so dilatory, that when he attempted it he found the cliffs occupied by a force of sharpshooters, which rendered crossing dangerous to a small force, and so reported to me. This was about the 25th of October.

Meanwhile the paying and clothing of the troops was going on, and it was deemed best to complete that before occupying the Fayetteville side of New River in force. It was, moreover, judged best to allow whatever force the rebels could gather to assemble and gain some confidence before attempting anything against them which would be something more than a chase. About the 27th of October information reached me that Floyd was moving from Raleigh down to cut off my communications, and these rumors, coupled with a knowledge of the country west of the Kanawha and below us, soon rendered it certain that whatever the rebel force was, it would come in by Fayetteville. It

---

* Memoir not found. Map to appear in Atlas.

was therefore determined to draw them in and capture them. This would not interfere in the least with having our troops clothed and paid.

Camps and smoke began to appear opposite Miller's Ferry and signs of considerable force. The New River gorge and the crests of the adjacent hills protected their encampment and movements from observation, but we learned that Floyd had about 4,000 men; at the same time that orders had been given at Meadow Bluff to Loring and Tompkins to make a secret move, and Lee had said to a person who told him I had intended to occupy Kanawha valley, very significantly, *"if he can."* A flag of truce also came from Meadow Bluff, the headquarters of Lee, signed by Col. J. Lucius Davis, showing that Lee was absent.

These and other circumstances rendered it probable that the enemy was about to attempt to dislodge us from this position, and as a combined movement on both sides of the river above appeared most likely to succeed, it became necessary to provide for that contingency.

On the 29th of October the rebels chased our outposts on the Fayette road down near the mouth of Great Falls Creek, and on the 1st of November appeared on the heights of Cotton Hill, opposite Gauley Bridge, with a 6-pounder rifled piece and with another opposite Montgomery's Ferry (see map), and opened fire with shot and shell. We discontinued running the ferry during the day, for fear it might be struck. General Cox was directed to put pieces in position which replied to the fire. The trains were passed during the night, to avoid exposure.

The plan of operations was now decided as follows : McCook opposite Miller's Ferry, to remain for the purpose of threatening a passage there, while his force would serve to hold in check anything that Lee would bring on the Lewisburg road; Schenck to prepare for and effect a crossing above at Bowyer's Ferry or some point this side; Benham encamped below McCook, whose camp could be moved without exciting suspicion to pass down by night to Gauley, and thence to a point nearly opposite the mouth of Loop Creek, where he was to cross over, be re-enforced, and reconnoiter the roads which by way of Loop Creek would lead to the flanks and rear of the enemy's position. A contingency was that if a scout then out and to return on the night he moved down should report the enemy's force and access thereto favorable, Benham's brigade, with General Cox's force, might cross at the falls. Result of scout was unfavorable to this. General Benham's force passed below, crossed the river, and occupied, as directed, the mouth of Loop Creek and the road 6 or 7 miles up beyond Taylor's.

MOVEMENTS OF GENERAL SCHENCK'S BRIGADE.

Reconnaissances showed but three accessible points of crossing above Miller's Ferry, viz : Bowyer's Ferry, 17 miles up, 15 miles from Sewell, guarded by a force of infantry, and provided with but one boat—an old canoe; crossing called Townsend's Ferry, 5½ miles up, apparently unknown and unthought of; Claypoole's Hole, between that and Miller's Ferry, coming out near the enemy's camp.

November 6, I detached Major Crawford, as acting aide, to report to General Schenck and examine Townsend's Ferry. He found the accesses exceedingly difficult, but evidently unwatched. Determined the possibility of constructing, by means of 'wagon beds and canvas, and by bull-boats and some skiffs, the apparatus for crossing the troops. This apparatus was completed on the 9th instant. (See Crawford's report) [No. 3]. Meanwhile the river rose so as to be impassable, and its condition was watched with solicitude from hour to hour. General Schenck, whose judgment in the matter I relied upon, being unwilling to abandon the plan of crossing his force in the enemy's rear, no movement was made in front that would preclude this, which promised, if effected, the most complete success.

On the 10th I dispatched to General Schenck as follows:

Benham concealed near mouth of Loop Creek with 3,000 men, posting himself on all the roadways. If you can cross above, he will attack them in front and left flank, while you will take the rear. If you cannot cross, you will come down and attack by front, while Benham will cut off their retreat.

BENHAM'S MOVEMENTS.

Benham's movements from the 3d to the 10th were regulated as far as they could be by a series of twenty-three telegraphic dispatches and one written, all appended hereto, the general tenor and object of which was to inform him that he would be re-enforced by detachments from the Seventh, Thirty-seventh, and Forty-fourth Ohio Regiments; that he was to cross over to Loop Creek, occupy it up as far as Taylor's, establish himself firmly, make his men comfortable, see that they were well supplied with rations from three to five days ahead, reconnoiter the passes from Loop Creek to the enemy's position by Cassidy's Mill, and to his rear by the same, and up Loop Creek by Kincaid's, Carter's, and Light's Mill to the Raleigh road, and to hold himself in readiness to act as soon as it was determined whether we could cross New River above Schenck's position. On the 6th General Benham crossed with his brigade. In short, the whole tenor of the dispatches from November 5 to November 8, as will be seen by reference to them, was to enforce upon his attention the necessity of knowing the passes from his position to the flank and rear of the enemy, especially the one by Cassidy's Mill; that, if Schenck could cross to take enemy in rear, his work would be to attack by that route on the flank or by the front and flank, and that, should the river prevent Schenck's passage, he would be called down and would operate in a combined attack on the front, flank, and rear, or flank and rear; that is, as it might be found more or less practicable to move Schenck's troops directly by the Fayette road or by the way of Cassidy's Mill. These points appear in dispatch No. 23, November 9, appended hereto, wherein it is said, among other things:

In that case Schenck will cross 3,000 men, seize Fayette, and advance down the road. You will take them by the Laurel Creek route only or by the Nugent path only, or by both, as may be determined by the nature of the ground, which you will learn from your scouts, and communicate to me your opinion thereon when they come in as soon as practicable.

POSITION OF THE TROOPS ON THE MORNING OF THE 10TH.

Schenck at Camp Ewing; means of crossing ready; river too high. McCook at Camp Anderson; enemy in force at Dickerson's, opposite Miller's Ferry, firing at the ferry, as for the last twenty days. General Cox, with the Second Kentucky, at Tompkins' farm; remainder at Gauley. General Benham at mouth of Loop Creek with main body; strong detachment up Loop, in vicinity of Taylor's and on road towards Cassidy's Mill. Rebels ceased firing with their cannon at Gauley and Tompkins' farm and McCook's camp, which they had tried two or three times to disturb by firing shot and shell across the river.

On that morning General Cox detached Colonel De Villiers with 200 men to cross New River at a ferry which he had rigged just above the mouth of Gauley, and Lieutenant-Colonel Enyart, with 200 of the First Kentucky to cross the lower ferry, to reconnoiter and occupy if practicable the Fayette road as far up as possible. Colonel De Villiers crossed, and after a sharp skirmish drove the enemy from the front hills and beyond Blake's farm. The rebels re-enforced this outpost 200 strong and repelled De Villiers to the margin of the woods near Blake's farm, where he remained until evening, when six companies of the Second Kentucky passed over and re-enforced him, and during the night drove the enemy entirely from the hills in front of New River and occupied the ridge.

On the morning of the 11th Colonel De Villiers, with the Eleventh Ohio and Second Kentucky troops, by General Cox's orders, pushed forward and drove the enemy from the heights towards Cotton Hill, where his baggage train was seen moving on the Fayette turnpike from the camp which he had occupied at Huddleston's, 1½ miles from the river up the Fayette road, supposed to be about two regiments. A party of the First Kentucky followed up the Fayette road at the same time until the main force occupied the position marked T (Exhibit B.)* Thus, after a vigorous and brilliant skirmish, with intervals, during thirty hours, about 700 men of General Cox's brigade drove the rebels from the front of Cotton Hill and their camp at Huddleston's, and held the entire ground for near 3 miles between the Fayette road and New River, with a loss of 2 killed, 1 wounded, and 6 missing. One of the missing was afterwards retaken, having lost an arm.

About 9 o'clock on the morning of the 11th, the other troops remaining in position, the enemy was seen to break camp at Laurel Creek and retire to Dickerson's, where they were observed busily fortifying. As soon as the movement of the enemy's camp was observed, information thereof was dispatched to Generals Schenck and Benham.

All movements up to this time had been made with a view to dispose our troops to hold in check any attempt that might be made on the Lewisburg road, and to make sure of beating and capturing the rebel force on the Fayette side, either by Schenck crossing above taking them in rear while Benham should attack them in front and flank, the latter always insisted on as preferable, or should Schenck's crossing fail, to bring his brigade down to aid in the front and flank attack while Benham should take his rear. (See dispatches Nos. 22, 25, 26, to Benham [*post*], and dispatch of 10th to General Schenck.)†

The occupation of the hills between the Fayette road and New River was a preliminary tightening of the chain, securing to us the debouches for a front attack and feeling the enemy to see if he had force enough to press well down against us. His movement to Dickerson's alarmed me, lest he should retreat; his commencing to fortify there in some degree reassured me. I therefore, on the 11th, after informing General Benham of the enemy's position and our occupancy of Cotton Hill, directed him to occupy as soon as practicable Cassidy's Mill with 1,000 men, and dispose the rest of his force to move, stating to him that I only awaited the information from him as to the practicability of the Cassidy's Mill route to say whether he was to come in on the north side of Cotton Hill on their front or take them in flank and rear. Failing to furnish the information called for, and for which final orders for the movement of his main body had been deferred, he was informed at 11

---

*Inclosure to General Cox's report, No. 2.
† Quoted on p. 255.

o'clock at night that General Schenck had by no means abandoned the plan of crossing at Townsend's Ferry, and directed as soon as practicable to occupy Cotton Hill, which movement began early on the morning of the 12th instant.

His failure to furnish me with the information so often required about the roads by Cassidy's and other routes to the enemy's rear, and many other signs of unsteadiness, had impaired my confidence in his management.   Nevertheless, after the reiterated dispatches sent him, I indulged the hope that he would fully appreciate his position and the decisive results to be expected from a movement by the enemy's left flank to his rear on the Fayetteville road.

Here referring to former instructions directing him on his arrival to open immediate communication with his force at Cassidy's Mill and to know well the route between there and beyond, I informed him that if General Schenck could not cross by the evening of the 12th, he would be ordered down and cross below.

General Benham received these general directions in the afternoon of the 11th.   He was informed that Major Leiper would report to him at the mouth of the Fayette road, and explain to him what he knew of the rebels and the position occupied by the troops of General Cox.

About 3 o'clock p. m. of the 12th General Benham's main force reached the extremity of Cotton Hill, 8 miles from Loop, towards Fayette. About the same time his detachment, which did not march as had been ordered on the previous day, swelled by some mistake from 1,000 to 1,300, reached Cassidy's Mill.

A slight skirmish ensued between a few advanced companies of General Benham's brigade and the rebels.   The command of General Benham halted, and bivouacked on their arms.   General Benham reported to me by a courier, stating his position, and complaining of the weakness of his main force compared with the supposed force of the enemy, and asking re-enforcements, that he might attack them, evidently uneasy at his position, and apparently apprehensive that he might be attacked before he could get re-enforcements.   Calling his attention to former dispatches and the Cassidy's Mill route, informing him the enemy was still at Dickerson's, I directed him again to watch the enemy's movements closely, saying if he did not move, our success was certain; if he did, which I thought he ought to do, General Benham should intercept him by the rear, and throw his entire force, except 500 men, by the way of Cassidy's Mill, on the Raleigh pike.   The enemy's intrenchments were but from 2½ to 3 miles from General Benham's position.   By some mistake he had at Cassidy's Mill 1,300 instead of 1,000 men.   This mill was but from 2½ to 3 miles from the Fayette road.

General Benham had been instructed *ad nauseam* to look to that way of cutting off the enemy's retreat, which began at 9 o'clock on that night.   General Benham did not find it out, according to his report, until 4.30 o'clock the next afternoon.   That is to say, while the last remnant of the rebel force had left Fayette early in the morning of the 13th, according to General Benham's report, his boldest scouts were desperately engaged from daylight until late in the afternoon in finding their way over a distance of 2½ miles that separated his bivouac from the enemy's deserted intrenchments.   His force at Cassidy's Mill had a company in Fayetteville at 9 o'clock next morning fully informed of the retreat of the enemy, and, as the captain of that company states, he dispatched messengers back to Cassidy's Mill and to General Benham immediately; yet General Benham did not learn of the retreat, though only 2½ miles off, until 4.30 p. m. of the 13th, and did not reach Fayette until 12 o'clock at night of the 13th, being twenty-seven hours from the time Floyd commenced his movement. So little attention had he paid to the reiterated instructions, all tending to enforce the one idea that the real blow ought to be struck at the enemy's rear by the Cassidy's Mill route and that a front attack was only desirable in case General Schenck could cross above or in case the enemy stood fight, and that even in this latter event General Schenck was to attack him in front while he was to attack the flank and rear he ordered the entire force from Cassidy's Mill, instead of striking across to the Raleigh road, to join him by moving down Laurel Creek and then to Fayette, thus imposing on it a fatiguing march of 7 or 8 miles.

Advised of all this, and knowing the wretched condition of the roads, and taught by experience that orders for carrying three or more days' rations were never obeyed, I looked upon the game as up and the pursuit of Floyd as not promising much; but, on the suggestion of General Benham that they might have stopped to sleep, dispatched him to use his discretion in the pursuit.

General Schenck had moved down on the 13th, crossed the Kanawha, and bivouacked at Huddleston's, on the Fayette road, and sent forward messengers to General Benham announcing his position. General Benham pursued and overtook some of the enemy's rear guard about 9.30 o'clock in the forenoon of the 14th, killed Colonel Croghan, reported at 11.30 o'clock that the enemy was in force, and asked General Schenck to come up, who had made a forced march to reach Fayette after having marched all the preceding day. At 4 o'clock in the afternoon General Benham had reached a point about 12 or 14 miles from Fayetteville without overtaking them. Dispatched General Schenck that the roads were so bad and his men so weary that it was impossible to pursue them farther; that he proposed to bivouac on the ground, and if General Schenck deemed it advisable, and it were possible to come forward, they might drive the enemy through Raleigh. Nevertheless he says that there was a report from one of the lieutenants of Stewart's cavalry that he had seen a train of wagons coming on the Bowyer's Ferry road, according with information of a negro at McCoy's Mill, which indicated that Lee was coming down with a force of 5,000 men to re-enforce Floyd and attack. He therefore concluded that as this was possible, it might be better for him (General Benham) to return, unite with General Schenck, and drive Lee.

General Schenck, knowing that General Benham's troops were about if not altogether out of provisions, and that none could be brought up in time on the roads, and presuming that Floyd, with twenty-seven hours the start, would not be very easily caught, directed General Benham, after pursuing thus far, to return, which he accordingly did on the 15th instant.

CONCLUSION.

At the close of these details I respectfully submit to the commanding general that, considering the weather and the roads, the operations of this column have been as active as those in any other department. The troops have suffered from the climate severely. They have submitted to many privations with cheerfulness and performed their duties with alacrity. If they have not accomplished all that could have been desired in the annihilation of Floyd's force, they have practically driven the enemy not only from the Kanawha, but from all the country west of Meadow Bluff and north of Raleigh, and the country is now more nearly pacified and disposed to return to the Union than they ever have been since the commencement of the war.

It has been with great regret that I have found it necessary to censure a general officer for the failure to capture the rebel forces who were justly ours.

It is a great pleasure to say to the commanding general that I have found General Cox prudent, brave, and soldierly, and I specially commend his prudence and firmness in occupying Cotton Hill, details of which are given in his report in the appendix.

I bear cordial testimony to the courage and promptitude of General Schenck, and only regret that his exposure, when he first came here, has deprived me for the present of his services. It is my duty also highly to commend Major Crawford, not only for the signal ability with which he reconnoitered Townsend's Ferry and prepared the means of crossing, laboring day and night in the most inclement weather to get everything in readiness. To his exertions mainly the accomplishment of this difficult and arduous task is chiefly due. I have also made special mention of the daring reconnaissance made by Sergeant Haven, of the Twenty-third Regiment Ohio Volunteer Infantry, who crossed the river at the ferry, and reconnoitered alone the road the other side, clear into the enemy's camp at Fayetteville. For the mention of others especially distinguished I refer to the subreports in the appendix; and if I have forborne to signalize the individual members of my staff, it is not because they do not deserve special mention, but because such mention as that has become stereotyped, and everybody expects to see it at the close of a report.

I have the honor to be, very respectfully, your obedient servant,

W. S. ROSECRANS,
Brigadier-General, U. S. Army, Commanding.

Brig. Gen. L. THOMAS, *Adjutant-General, Washington, D. C.*

[Inclosure No. 1.]

HEADQUARTERS DEPARTMENT WESTERN VIRGINIA,
Camp Gauley Mountain, November 2, 1861.

You will immediately prepare to cross the river for an operation either up Paint or Loop Creek. The steps thereto are rest for the men, boats to cross, ammunition in sufficient quantities. Tyler will be ordered to send you 500 picked men, Woods 500, and Siber 500. It will take probably two days to organize this movement. We hope to cross at or near Miller's Ferry in force, at the same time we make a strong demonstration or attack on their front. Let everything be done to secure supplies; every facility made use of. Advise me of your progress.

W. S. ROSECRANS,
Brigadier-General, U. S. Army.

Brig. Gen. H. W. BENHAM, *care of General Cox, Gauley.*

[Inclosure No. 2.]

HEADQUARTERS DEPARTMENT WESTERN VIRGINIA,
Camp Gauley Mountain, November 3, 1861.

Colonel Woods has been ordered to you temporarily for duty. Assign him to command Tenth Regiment. Let Captain Amis and a portion of his men come up to serve the guns. Sent him an order to-day. You will have to get guides below. None here to be got.

W. S. ROSECRANS,
Brigadier-General, U. S. Army.

Brig. Gen. H. W. BENHAM, *Camp Huddleston.*

[Inclosure No. 3.]

NOVEMBER 3, 1861.

Your dispatch received. A boat has been ordered up, but to make sure a large paulin will be sent down to you, with which, spread under a lot of wagon-beds, you will be able to make a large scow. The wagon-beds will have to be lashed crosswise, laid on two poles, and having two poles over them; rope lashing to go between. Telegraph down to Charleston for plenty of bed-cord, in case we should not have plenty here. Woods, Siber, and Tyler must clear the other side of the river and prevent firing on teams immediately.

W. S. ROSECRANS,
Brigadier-General, U. S. Army.

Brig. Gen. H. W. BENHAM, *Camp Huddleston.*

[Inclosure No. 4.]

HEADQUARTERS DEPARTMENT WESTERN VIRGINIA,
Camp Gauley Mountain, November 4, 1861.

Your dispatch received. Three boats will be sent you this evening. You will find the wagon-body arrangement makes a solid and capacious float of great capacity, and may be rowed across with double oars or sweeps. Have the poles 25 feet long and 4 or 5 inches in diameter. Take 6 wagon-bodies. A single wagon-body and tent-fly doubled under it makes a good boat. Conceal your movements, and clear everything up to Loop Creek.

W. S. ROSECRANS,
Brigadier-General, U. S. Army.

Brig. Gen. H. W. BENHAM, *Camp Huddleston.*

[Inclosure No. 5.]

NOVEMBER 4, 1861.

The commanding general expects you to go up Loop Creek in force or else this side, closing the mouth of it. Will likely give final orders to-morrow morning. Push information as far as possible. Will telegraph Major Leiper to see if he can send you scout.

JOSEPH DARR, JR.,
Major, First Virginia Cavalry, A. A. A. G.

Brig. Gen. H. W. BENHAM, *Camp Huddleston.*

[Inclosure No. 6.]

HEADQUARTERS DEPARTMENT WESTERN VIRGINIA,
Camp Gauley Mountain, November 4, 1861.

Take what bread you need. Will not the hawser of the boat or picket rope answer? You can keep the Victor and the scow. Retain Silver Lake until the Victor comes. It was so intended. Boats are expected up that may bring the rope required. You can move over the river to-morrow with your tents, leaving a company or two on this side for a camp guard. Tyler's and Gilbert's men will come up unless something occurs to prevent them, which I do not anticipate. Final orders will be given when both ends are ready.

W. S. ROSECRANS,
Brigadier-General, U. S. Army.

Brig. Gen. H. W. BENHAM, *Camp Huddleston.*

[Inclosure No. 7.]

NOVEMBER 4, 1861.

Can you get ready to move by to-morrow night? If so, McMullin's battery, or a part of it, will be sent down to-night. What report have you from the scouts sent out by you?

W. S. ROSECRANS,
Brigadier-General, U. S. Army.

Brig. Gen. H. W. BENHAM, *Camp Huddleston.*

[Inclosure No. 8.]

HEADQUARTERS DEPARTMENT WESTERN VIRGINIA,
Camp Gauley Mountain, November 4, 1861.

I fear your scouting parties will alarm the enemy; they are so large. However, let them go. We have had scouting party up Loop Creek. The upper end of it is well picketed by the rebels. Have you all your preparations made? Push everything, and let me know how soon you can get ready. I think cavalry would be in your way. For artillery I cannot decide until I hear your report about the road. Presume two mountain howitzers, possibly McMullin's battery entire, if the rifled artillery comes up this way. It leaves Camp Enyart this morning.

W. S. ROSECRANS,
Brigadier-General, U. S. Army.

Brig. Gen. H. W. BENHAM, *Camp Huddleston.*

[Inclosure No. 9.]

NOVEMBER 5, 1861.

The general desires to know about the route as to practicability of sending artillery. He thinks the number of rebels reported to be nearer from 4,000 to 6,000. Glad to hear that McMullin can pass. The general desires to know something of road that leads to Laurel Creek to left of Loop. The commanding general wishes to know if you are over the river.

JOSEPH DARR, JR.,
Major, First Virginia Cavalry, A. A. A. G.

Brig. Gen. H. W. BENHAM, *Camp Huddleston.*

[Inclosure No. 10.]

HEADQUARTERS DEPARTMENT WESTERN VIRGINIA,
Camp Gauley Mountain, November 5, 1861.

It was intended that you should have gone over to-day, and that all would be snug there. Keep the Victor and the scow in the vicinity for service. Final orders will be given you in due time. A sketch map will be sent you, embodying such information as we possess. I wish you to be very careful in your inquiries about the nature of road up Loop. You will find that when you get up to a certain point it forks left over the ridge on the Big Mill Creek, coming in front of their position, right going around and coming into Fayette. You will be able to find guides and get posted by to-morrow. Every other man have coffee in canteens. Some whisky and quinine bitters should be provided if it could be so carried as to be safe. Some nurses must be detailed to go with the surgeons. Don't fear numbers. I shall not send you without strong co-operation.

W. S. ROSECRANS,
Brigadier-General, U. S. Army.

Brig. Gen. H. W. BENHAM, *Camp Huddleston.*

[Inclosure No. 11.]

NOVEMBER 6, 1861.

I regret you did not cross with your forces yesterday. Do so as soon as practicable. Indications are that we shall make a move in force up that creek; therefore you will establish yourself solidly on that position. Men up the creek must have their tents; your supplies of provisions must be ample, and Paint Creek must be kept well scouted by hired countrymen   Offer them liberal pay for good work. Maps and letters by messengers.

W. S. ROSECRANS,
Brigadier-General, U. S. Army.

Brig. Gen. H. W. BENHAM, *Camp Huddleston.*

[Inclosure No. 12.]

HEADQUARTERS DEPARTMENT WESTERN VIRGINIA,
Camp Gauley Mountain, November 6, 1861.

I do not consider your crossing the river in the rain-storm with your command practicable, but it is desirable to have them over and well and warmly encamped, with every attention to their comfort, as soon as possible. This should be done with all your troops, and with caution and secrecy. At Loop Creek it may require only cautious and careful picketing. You know what the object is, and I leave that to your judgment. The roads should be in such repair that we can send provisions if needed up Loop Creek. Couriers just started with written instructions and map.

W. S. ROSECRANS,
Brigadier-General, U. S. Army.

Brigadier-General BENHAM, *Camp Huddleston.*

[Inclosure No. 13.]

NOVEMBER 6, 1861.

The commanding general directs me to say, in reply to your dispatch No. 2, that it is now too late to make crossing very practicable to-night. You have instructions as to the object of crossing, and know what the general desires to accomplish. He expects you to use your discretion, and holds you responsible for the results. Here it is distinctly stated that he considers it too late to cross to-night. As to position in Loop Creek, it is expected to be at or near best place, so as to command its mouth.

JOSEPH DARR, JR.,
Major, First Virginia Cavalry, A. A. A. G.

Brigadier-General BENHAM, *Camp Huddleston.*

[Inclosure No. 14.]

HEADQUARTERS DEPARTMENT WESTERN VIRGINIA,
Camp Gauley Mountain, November 6, 1861.

The commanding general has no objections to your remaining on this side to-night. Make sure preparations to communicate with this side. Have a boat for that purpose and other arrangements made with that view. McMullin's battery goes down to-night.

JOSEPH DARR, JR.,
Major, First Virginia Cavalry, A. A. A. G.

Brig. Gen. H. W. BENHAM, *Camp Huddleston.*

[Inclosure No. 15.]

NOVEMBER 6, 1861.

Nos. 3, 4, 5, 6, and 7 received. Make the men comfortable. Have five days' rations. Send your pioneer party up Loop. Carry out instructions so far as to know the road from Taylor's over to Laurel without alarming the enemy. McMullin, with two of his howitzers, will be down to-night. Your directions to Schneider are good. When you leave you will have to leave a small camp guard, which will be able to secure the Fayette road up the bank of the river. Must probably hold the road above Taylor's. It may prove best to close the Taylor road and follow up the Kincaid route. Endeavor by scouts and others to ascertain this. We shall have further communication before final orders for the combined movement are given. Study well the map and memoir. Be cautious in whose presence you speak, otherwise it will leak out among the soldiers right away. Favorable news came in to-night.

W. S. ROSECRANS,
Brigadier-General, U. S. Army.

Brig. Gen. H. W. BENHAM, *Camp Huddleston.*

[Inclosure No. 16.]

HEADQUARTERS DEPARTMENT WESTERN VIRGINIA,
Camp Gauley Mountain, November 6, 1861.

We must have Loop Creek up beyond Taylor's and the ridge between it and the valley of the Fayette road. Secure this with as little discomfort to the men as is consistent with the firm execution of the purpose. Will send such sketch and information of it as we possess. See that everything is held with a firm hand; that you have plenty of everything needful.

W. S. ROSECRANS,
Brigadier-General, U. S. Army.

Brig. Gen. H. W. BENHAM, *Camp Huddleston.*

[Inclosure No. 17.]

NOVEMBER 7, 1861.

The commanding general is waiting to hear the result of your scouts to-day. Is your way clear, and which appear best routes?

JOSEPH DARR, JR.,
Major, and A. A. A. G.

Brigadier-General BENHAM, *Camp Huddleston.*

[Inclosure No. 18.]

NOVEMBER 8, 1861.

Yours received. You appear to be doing well, but it seems to me the place where paths lead out into Fayette road ought not to bring us out at Huddleston's. If so, what are we to gain over going up the river? You must try and know that route by Laurel spoken of in the memoir. Send me the corrected distances and positions. Where did the scouts see the enemy's camp? Refer to map and name corrections.

W. S. ROSECRANS,
Brigadier-General, U. S. Army.

Brigadier-General BENHAM, *Camp, Loop Creek Mouth.*

[Inclosure No. 19.]

HEADQUARTERS DEPARTMENT WESTERN VIRGINIA,
Camp Gauley Mountain, November 8, 1861.

Your two dispatches and copy of Lieutenant-Colonel Creighton's just received. When the other scouts come in from Colonel Siber collate carefully all the information they have, and from them ascertain the exact nature of the roads or paths the troops have to pass over, and, if possible, the immediate approaches to the enemy's camp. Our information goes to show a small camp at Dickerson's and a larger one in the immediate vicinity of Warner's Mill. So far as at present informed there is where the main body is. You want to know what the road is to this point; what paths, if any, diverge right and left from the one you would follow down Laurel, and what room there is for the display of your troops; also, whether there is any path leading from the top of your line to the top of Cotton Hill. It would be necessary to have the command and we might probably want the use of such path. I should like a report as early in the day as possible, because I want to arrange definitely details of the operations, if possible, for to-night and to-morrow. We have no information of firing from above. No movement was authorized.

Brigadier-General BENHAM, *Camp, Loop Creek Mouth.*

[Inclosure No. 20.]

HEADQUARTERS DEPARTMENT WESTERN VIRGINIA,
Camp Gauley Mountain, November 8, 1861.

Schenck's boats will not be ready to-night. Scouts from Lookout and Bowyer's Ferry report no indications of approaching force. There is a scout out to-night to go up towards Sewell. I want Nugent's located on our map and to hear from your scouts above. We may be obliged to seize Cotton Hill by the front if strongly opposed and unable to cross above. I hope to hear again from your scouts to-night as to the road over to Laurel Creek, &c. I hope, general, you will be reserved in discussing our plans and caution the staff. A dispatch came to me in cipher to you from Lander.

Brigadier-General BENHAM, *Camp, Loop Creek Mouth.*

[Inclosure No. 21.]

Nos. 14 and 15 received. Everything you report noted and so far satisfactory. What I want to know is what sort of a road or path you will have to go over to reach Warner's Mill and what sort of ground you could form or debouch on. The details of that should be well studied. If your front is narrow, the difficulties will of course increase. If you can form out of sight and deploy so as to cover the ground right and left of their position, it would be better. If the passway is clear in the center and positions can be found for the two mountain howitzers to enfilade or even play on their camp, better still. Proceed with great caution and secrecy to get these details as far as possible. The scouts have seen the camp at a distance, as Dives saw Lazarus, but there may be a great gulf between them. Appearances indicate that your brigade, with support from Gauley properly timed, could whip them, but let us try to make a certainty. The distance of 2 miles given by the scouts, as mentioned in No. 15, must be a mistake. It is 4 miles from the mouth of Loop to the Fayette road, mouth of Big Mill, and between these is that immense ridge, on top of which they certainly are not. You say nothing of Cassidy's Mill. Our information shown on the sketch indicates it as a key-point. Give that a little of your attention early to-morrow. Fifteen dragoons have been ordered to report to you.

[Inclosure No. 22.]

HEADQUARTERS DEPARTMENT WESTERN VIRGINIA,
Camp Gauley Mountain, November 9, 1861.

Yours (No. 16) received. This rain is very untoward. General Schenck's report not yet in. Rain may prevent his crossing. He will not be ordered down until we find that it must be abandoned. I have from the beginning had but one intention about your command. It must hold and occupy that side of the river until we have disposed of the rebels, or get possession of Cotton Hill, or been driven back. Your position prevents them from going farther down to play the game they have played above; it threatens them front and rear. Hence, referring to former dispatches pointing out the primary objects of your crossing and enjoining you to establish your command solidly, hold firmly, examine thoroughly, and to make your men comfortable, to keep up your supplies, to take cooking utensils along, &c., &c., I have now to say that, in carrying out these instructions, you must use your discretion to do it effectually and insure the comfort of your men. I see no reason why they should want for cooked provisions. Why not issue them rations? No reason they should have half enough tents. I directed you to take the minimum of baggage, not that could be taken, but that would suffice. If you could not get tents up to all these men, withdraw those who have none until they can be supplied or the weather improves. I look to your dispatches for accurate information of the route to the rebels' camp. None so far say what paths the scouts followed, nor where they came out on the rebels, nor how nor where their pickets. Please let me hear all about these points as far as you know them. You will observe in all my dispatches great stress laid on this, without which we must act in the dark. Awaiting early report.

Brig. Gen. H. W. BENHAM, *Camp, Loop Creek Mouth.*

[Inclosure No. 23.]

HEADQUARTERS DEPARTMENT WESTERN VIRGINIA,
Camp Gauley Mountain, November 9, 1861.

Yours (No. 18) received. Major Crawford just returned, and reports the river too high to cross to night, but falling; will be ready by to-morrow night. We leave three companies scouting the front of Cotton Hill opposite the ferries. Your scouts' reports and these will determine if we are to move at once or wait until to-morrow night. In that case Schenck will cross 3,000 men, and will seize Fayette and advance down the road, and you will take them by the Laurel Creek route only or by the Nugent path only, or by both, as may be determined by the *partieres* of the ground, which you will learn from your scouts, and communicate to me, with your opinion thereon, as soon after they come in as practicable. I have been informed that the area between you and Mill Creek Valley, up which the Fayette road passes, consists of flat-topped rolling surface, over which our scouts can go whenever they please. This was my impression, but it has been so flatly contradicted that I gave up until to-day.

Brigadier-General BENHAM, *Camp, Loop Creek Mouth.*

[Inclosure No. 24.]

NOVEMBER 10, 1861.

Your dispatch received. The Eleventh, 200 strong, is over the river; holds the crests and path well up. The First Kentucky has sent over 200, who hold farther down to near the Fayette road. Schenck will hardly be able to cross to-night, but if the rebels try to dislodge our men, you may be called on to take them in rear. Hold everything in hand. Have your men inspected, to see that no one is without ammunition or provisions. Floyd over on the hill, anxious. Will give you further orders soon.

[Inclosure No. 25.]

HEADQUARTERS DEPARTMENT WESTERN VIRGINIA,
Camp Gauley Mountain, November 10, 1861.

Major Crawford says he thinks those two regiments, or a part of them at least, are moved down again this side of Warner's, on the south side of the mountain; if so, it is a reason for combining strongly. Expect more from above.

Brigadier-General BENHAM, Camp, Loop Creek.

[Inclosure No. 26.]

Yours (No. 20) received. Mine you will find was No. 18. Your suggestions all enter into the plan. You know we hold the hills from Montgomery's Ferry to Gauley, and have a ferry across New River. Everything is going on at General Schenck's to cross the river to-morrow night. If it can be done, your way is by Nugent's, I should suppose, but if he must come down here, then you must make Fayette, and on the Raleigh road above, to cut him off. Scouts will inform you of his movements. If he begins a retreat, you must be ready to intercept him the moment you are certain of it. If he tries to dislodge us on the hills, we will work him well in. You will stand steady until the co-operation is arranged, and then will try him on Laurel Creek.

[Inclosure No. 27.]

Yours (No. 22) just received. We will not move to-night. Our troops here occupy heights between New River and the Fayette road. Your scouts ought to capture that picket guard to-night. Will telegraph you further. Schenck's boats all down; will be ready for use to-morrow.

[Inclosure No. 28.]

HEADQUARTERS DEPARTMENT WESTERN VIRGINIA,
Camp Gauley Mountain, November 11, 1861.

Inform me as early as possible how long it will take you to move from your present position with your entire force to reach Nugent's. Secondly, how long it would take you to reach Cassidy's Mill. How far from there to Warner's, and what difficulties you know of in the way. Can you reach the Raleigh road by Light's Mill? How long will it take you? Will provisions and everything be ready to-day for either route?

Brigadier-General BENHAM, Camp, Loop Creek Mouth.

[Inclosure No. 29.]

NOVEMBER 11, 1861.

What news from you? McCook says they are breaking up camp, but many men there still; more than he ever saw before. One regiment passed up by Fayetteville this morning, and forty-five wagons and five ambulances. Hope soon to receive reply from dispatches of this morning.

[Inclosure No. 30.]

HEADQUARTERS DEPARTMENT WESTERN VIRGINIA,
Camp Gauley Mountain, November 11, 1861.

Yours (No. 25) received. No. 24 not received. The information asked for about the other roads to Fayette and Raleigh not received. Retreat spoken of in my No. 19 has been reported to you so far as we can see at this side of the river. Had hopes you would be better informed than we were. Our skirmishing last night and this morning was necessary. As I told you, an attempt to dislodge us. We did not draw him in. It will be of no use for you to come in at Nugent's in his front on this side of Cotton Hill, if you can succeed in cutting off his retreat by reaching Fayette or the Raleigh road. That question I asked you this morning; and if I could only know, would be able to give you orders immediately. If that cannot be done, then it will be necessary for you to seize the Fayette road at the most convenient point, and push steadily and firmly, taking due precautions against ambuscade. General Cox has now over some 700 men, and they are pushing in towards Cotton Hill quietly. This gives you what information we have. Let me hear from you as soon as possible. In reply to my dispatch No. 16, General Schenck just telegraphs me by no means give up crossing Townsend's Ferry, and will telegraph further soon. Should his dispatch confirm plan of crossing Townsend's, you had better come in on the Fayette pike. Cannot find that the enemy has passed Fayette.

If there is any reliance to be placed on our information, Cassidy's Mill would be the strategic point, provided the road is practicable at all. Answer soon.

Brigadier-General BENHAM, *Camp, Loop Creek Mouth.*

[Inclosure No. 31.]

HEADQUARTERS DEPARTMENT WESTERN VIRGINIA,
Camp Gauley Mountain, November 11, 1861.

Dispatch from our lookout on Bushy Knob above Schenck's says rebels have stopped at Camp Dickerson. If this be so, and local information does not forbid, send about 1,000 men to occupy Cassidy's Mill. Arrange rapid communication with your headquarters. This place, according to our information, is not 5 miles from Fayette, which is 3 miles in rear of their present position. Covering your camp by a strong picket up Loop may at once dispose your troops to move. I only await your report of the practicability of the Cassidy's Mill route to determine whether you are to come in on the north side of Cotton Hill in front of them or take them flank and rear. Look well to the provisions for your troops, and report as soon as you possibly can.

Brigadier-General BENHAM, *Camp, Loop Creek Mouth.*

[Inclosure No. 32.]

HEADQUARTERS DEPARTMENT WESTERN VIRGINIA,
Camp Gauley Mountain, November 11, 1861.

Dispatches just received from General Schenck confirm previous ones. The enemy is concentrated in camp extending from Dickerson's to near Fayette. Has been throwing up some rail and earth intrenchments at Dickerson's and at Jones', a mile above. Appears to hold intersection of Fayette pike and Miller's Ferry road. Under these circumstances you will proceed as follows: Supposing you have proceeded to occupy Cassidy's Mill with 1,000 men, with all provisions and with directions to push forward from that position strong scouting parties on the most practicable road to Fayette, and established an outpost to watch the Loop Creek road, I have directed General Cox to order Major Leiper, who commands the troops on Cotton Hill, to report to you at the intersection of the Ridge road with the Fayette pike. It is about two miles and a half from the ferry. You will proceed with your command by the River road and occupy Cotton Hill to-night, pushing forward as far towards Fayette as you can, and have a strong position. Bivouac your troops. Send forward strong reconnoitering party, with orders to drive in the enemy's pickets and find out if they are retreating. Open communication with your detachment at Cassidy's Mill, in order that you may receive from them the earliest intimation of the enemy's movements. Schneider, with one piece, and McMullin's two howitzers will cross with the Kentucky troops to-night and report to you for orders. What we now have to do is first to occupy Cotton Hill and reconnoiter the enemy, working on his left flank if he retains his position and falling on his flank if he moves. Generals Schenck and McCook remain in position to-night watching. If a rebel force comes down on this side they will fall back, and our movements on your side be governed by circumstances. If the enemy retreat, Schenck will cross at Townsend's and McCook cover this line. I regret that circumstances seem to bring you in front. My great desire has been to cut off his communications. The road by Light's Mill seems now the only one that would do it. Perhaps you may yet be able to make a flank movement as soon as we have got thorough possession of Cotton Hill.

Brigadier-General BENHAM, *Camp, Loop Creek Mouth.*

[Inclosure No. 33.]

HEADQUARTERS DEPARTMENT WESTERN VIRGINIA,
Camp Gauley Mountain, November 11, 1861.

Your 27 received. By waiting it will probably be 11 before you get this. This defeats my plan, which was to have you on Cotton Hill by 10 o'clock to-night by the river road, with strong reconnoitering party, to watch the enemy's movements. If the enemy retreat to-night, he cannot be pursued with any chance of capturing him. If he stands, we shall have to engage him on the front and flank. In his present position he so nearly covers Townsend's Ferry, that Schenck cannot cross to co-operate unless rebels move down or up. If you come in with all your force at Fayette, you will be opposite Townsend's. I cannot send you any men, because I have none to send without calling them down from McCook or General Schenck. This will be the work of a day, and will delay the movement twenty-four hours. All reasonable chance of taking advantage of the enemy's retreat being cut off, the next best thing seems to be that you should let your troops rest to-night. Have everything that can be done to prepare for this movement. Carry out your previous orders, sending such troops as you think best by 6 in the morning. Then carry out the orders you have received, sending such troops as you deem best to Cassidy's Mill, and arranging to communicate with them by Nugent's. You will reach Cotton Hill and Warner's Mill by the time they get to Cassidy's, and can send them word if the rebels have retreated or are standing. You will also send a signal flag to some point opposite my camp to let me know. If they stand, the flag will be raised twice; if they run, only once. Major Leiper has orders to send you word if his scouts report a retreat to-night. Pfau's dragoons will report to you too. You will, on learning what the rebels do, make such disposition of your force on the Fayette road and give such orders to those at Cassidy's Mill as circumstances may require.

Brigadier-General BENHAM, *Camp, Loop Creek Mouth.*

[Inclosure No. 34.]

HEADQUARTERS DEPARTMENT WESTERN VIRGINIA,
Camp Gauley Mountain, November 12, 1861.

Your dispatches Nos. 27 and 28—latter 5 a. m.—received. You say you did not receive my orders until 11. Your dispatch acknowledging receipt was dated 7 p. m. I understand the guard at Taylor's to be 100 men. The only other detachment from your forces is that which occupies Cassidy's Mill. When you get to the top of Cotton Hill, and ascertain where the rebels are and what they are doing, you will be able to take necessary precautions. The objects of our movement have been fully set forth by previous dispatches.

Brigadier-General BENHAM, *Camp, Loop Creek.*

[Inclosure No. 35.]

The commanding general has had no advices from you since this morning. Desires you to report your itinerary, present condition, and position of your forces and those which have been directed to report to you, with all information of the position and movements of the rebels. He also informs you that New River rose last night so as to prevent the stretching of the rope across Townsend's Ferry, which appears to be still unwatched. From your position movements have been seen at Dickerson's farm, but if you occupy Cottton Hill to-night you will be able to know all about the enemy's position and movements, which I understand can be seen from it. Report at your earliest convenience in reply and give the hour. Send for your tents.

[Inclosure No. 36.]

HEADQUARTERS DEPARTMENT WESTERN VIRGINIA,
Camp Gauley Mountain, November 12, 1861—9 p. m.

Your No. 29 received; also Lieut. William H. Mills' verbal report. I am much gratified to hear of your progress and the position you have taken; also that you have sent to communicate at once with Cassidy's Mill. I trust you will find no great loss from the skirmish. Send for your tents and provisions. Get accurate information of the route from your position to Cassidy's Mill, and thence to Raleigh pike in rear of Fayette. Our best information shows that the road from Cassidy's is practicable, not exceeding 3 or 4 miles long, and intersects the Raleigh pike 2 miles in rear of Fayette. The rebels were fortifying on Dickerson's farm at the junction of Miller's Ferry and Fayette roads this afternoon, evidently designing to cover themselves against attack from the Miller's Ferry and Fayette roads. If they will only hold that position our success will be certain. You hold now the key of that country. Their camp is within range of rifle if not Parrott guns. You have probably force enough to whip them now if it could be transferred at once to the Fayette road. Make every exertion to render such a movement easy. Were it possible to find out whether the enemy commences a retreat to-night or not, which I think he certainly ought to do, you ought to move with all your force, except, say, 500 men, by Cassidy's Mill, and intercept them. Hoping he may not do so, Schenck's brigade will be ordered down, and will pass over to-morrow night. Advise me the very best road to reach the Raleigh pike from the falls, by Nugent's, by Loop Creek, or by some point near you across by Cassidy's Mill. Meanwhile give your troops as much rest and refreshment as possible. Communicate frequently with me. If no movements are necessary to-morrow morning, look for good position for a regiment to hold Cotton Hill.

Brigadier-General BENHAM.

[Inclosure No. 37.]

HEADQUARTERS DEPARTMENT WESTERN VIRGINIA,
Camp Gauley Mountain, November 13, 1861.

I hope your camp equipage has been ordered up. Make every arrangement to occupy the hill, and make your troops comfortable until others come over. Keep up your supplies of provisions, so as to have three days ahead. Next ascertain the routes by which the Raleigh road may be reached in the best ways from any point between your position and the mouth of Loop.

Brigadier-General BENHAM.

[Inclosure No. 38.]

Information from Bushy Knob shows the enemy have retreated, and the proper way is to send word to the troops at Cassidy's Mill to press on them and push up the Fayette road.

[Inclosure No. 39.]

HEADQUARTERS DEPARTMENT WESTERN VIRGINIA,
Camp Gauley Mountain, November 13, 1861—5.30 p. m.

Your No. 32, dated 2 p. m., just received. The commanding general does not think the rebels have entirely gone, but what their force may be is unknown. General Schenck, with his entire brigade, comes over to-night to re-enforce you. Being the senior, he will assume command until the commanding general comes over. You will therefore report to him, and, after stating fully the position of everything, act under his orders. The general understands you have ordered the force from Cassidy's Mill. Its withdrawal is in face of his express orders for its occupation, and what seems to him a plain military advantage requires something more in explanation than has been reported to him to justify it, which he awaits. He does not wish to attack Floyd by the front only, but if we can get his left flank and rear we shall succeed in crushing him.

Brigadier-General BENHAM.

[Inclosure No. 40.]

HEADQUARTERS DEPARTMENT WESTERN VIRGINIA,
Camp Gauley Mountain, November 13, 1861.

Your 33 received at 7 p. m. This goes by Miller's Ferry. Regret that the detachment at Cassidy's Mill was not pushed forward towards

Fayette. Your idea that the rebels may be sleeping is a good one, and strikes me favorably. Much will depend whether you shall pursue them on the condition and strength of your troops and the provisions you have. Of these things I know nothing. A question of pursuit is therefore left to your discretion. You can now send by Miller's Ferry, which will much shorten the line of communication. I shall start for Fayette by 8 to-morrow morning, and hope to hear from you whatever you deem proper before that time. General Schenck with his entire brigade is already in camp at Huddleston's. If, therefore, there were a chance to overtake the flying foe, your support is certain. You have more than one-fourth as many troops as the retreating foe.

Brigadier-General BENHAM, *Fayetteville.*

[Addenda.]

NOVEMBER 12, 1861.

Brig. Gen. R. C. SCHENCK, *Camp Ewing, W. Va.:*

The commanding general directs you to break your camp at Ewing to-morrow morning and proceed with your command across the river at Gauley Bridge to the Cotton Hill. The troops should have two days' rations in their haversacks. Their baggage should follow under command of the rear guard, which may be composed of your advanced pickets. You will order Captain Mack to report to Colonel McCook for temporary duty. West's cavalry will come down and encamp at or below Gauley. The troops should move early, and get, if possible, past McCook's camp before the fog gets off the river. Colonel McCook will remain in command of the troops covering the position on this side. Give orders to have all the material that can be saved brought away from Townsend's Ferry. If the boats can be hidden for a few days, I think they may be hidden as well as the pieces for the bull-boat. This is on the supposition that we cannot cross at Townsend's Ferry, while we know we can cross down here. A trusty man should be sent to-night to ascertain whether the river will fall sufficiently; and in case it does not, to be provided with the necessary help and give the necessary directions.

JOSEPH DARR, JR.,
Acting Assistant Adjutant-General.

—

NOVEMBER 13, 1861—9.45 p. m.

Brig. Gen. R. C. SCHENCK, *Camp Huddleston, W. Va.:*

Your dispatch of 8 p. m. received. You will probably not be required to advance much farther. Fayette Court-House is ours. Benham has orders to consider the condition of his men and use his discretion as to pursuit. The last of the rebels passed Fayette at daylight this a. m. You will hear from him during the night if he can find any one; if not, send for sledges—that is, stone-hammers, picks, and shovels—and put pioneers on the road to repair it.

W. S. ROSECRANS,
Brigadier-General, U. S. Army, Commanding.

—

NOVEMBER 14, 1861.

Brig. Gen. R. C. SCHENCK (*care of Colonel McCook*):

Your dispatches received, inclosing one from General Benham. Commanding general's opinion of the pursuit is, that all that could be accomplished could have been done by General Benham's force. Commanding general fears your troops will suffer. Colonel McCook has been ordered to clear out Miller's Ferry road. Everything will be done to help you. In case of necessity you will have to come down to Dickerson's and get some from McCook. Your tents will be taken over the river and pitched near Huddleston, to which camp you will return as soon as you get advices from General Benham, showing, as I doubt not they will, that no advantage is to be gained by carrying your men farther, beyond the reach of subsistence.

JOSEPH DARR, JR.,
Acting Assistant Adjutant-General.

—

NOVEMBER 15, 1861.

Brig. Gen. R. C. SCHENCK, Camp Union:

The commanding general, without having any means to judge of the propriety of ordering the troops back from towards Raleigh, presumes that you acted with sound discretion.

JOSEPH DARR, JR.

———

No. 2.

Report of Brig. Gen. Jacob D. Cox, U. S. Army, of skirmishes at Blake's
farm, November 10–11.

HEADQUARTERS KANAWHA BRIDGE,
Gauley Bridge, November 13, 1861.

GENERAL : I have the honor to report that on the morning of the 10th instant I ordered Colonel De Villiers, of the Eleventh Regiment Ohio Volunteers, to take 200 men (being all of his regiment fit for duty), and after reconnoitering the mountains skirting New River on the other side to occupy and hold the crests, if possible, so as to prevent any further attempts on the part of the enemy to destroy the ferry at this place from the battery lately held by them opposite to us. At the same time I ordered Lieutenant-Colonel Enyart, commanding First Regiment Kentucky Volunteers, to cross the river below the falls with 200 men, and occupy the mills, the spurs of the mountains near there, and reconnoiter the Fayette road, and hold, if possible, the position lately occupied by the enemy's guns opposite the First Kentucky camp. Colonel De Villiers threw over at first a party of 40, of which half was sent along the hills down the Kanawha from the crossing place, a few rods above the bridge piers, where I had previously established a ferry capable of crossing 500 men per hour. The other half of the party the colonel conducted himself along a path by the river side under the cliffs to a ravine leading up to the Blake farm, about 1 mile up New River. At Blake's farm some 50 or 60 of the enemy were discovered and immediately attacked. Being surprised, they were driven into the woods upon the hill-sides above with the loss of several killed, who were dragged away in sight of our men. The enemy was immediately re-enforced by about 200, and the advanced party of the Eleventh retired to the margin of Blake's farm, where, by stationing themselves behind a fence at the edge of a ravine, they were able to hold the rebels in check until the remainder of the party of the Eleventh arrived. The enemy was then driven back up the hills, and our men took a line of defense leading diagonally up the hills from Blake's house to the crest above the battery opposite this point.

Shortly after dark six companies of the Second Kentucky Regiment had crossed the river by my order to re-enforce Colonel De Villiers. The enemy seemed to be collecting forces on the ridge, and about 9 o'clock the left wing of the Eleventh, under Major Coleman, was driven back from Blake's farm about a quarter of a mile, but, upon being re-enforced by two companies of the Second Kentucky, he drove back the enemy and reoccupied his former position. Meanwhile the enemy made a succession of attacks upon the remainder of our force, which was pushing its way up to the mountain crest along the whole line from Blake's to the Kanawha, and a brisk skirmishing fight was kept up until after midnight, when we had secured the ridge as far as Blake's.

During the day the party from the First Kentucky Regiment had occupied the other side of the Kanawha from the mouth of the Fayette road up to the positions of the Eleventh Ohio, and pushed a scouting party a mile up the road towards Fayette, reconnoitering the mountain sides without finding the enemy.

At daybreak of the next day (the 11th instant) Colonel De Villiers, being ordered by me to push the enemy still farther back towards Cotton Hill, collected the larger part of his force and drove in the enemy's pickets on the mountain ridge in his front, and pushed steadily along the crest up the New River. The enemy, several hundred in number, kept up a scattering, skirmishing fight as they retired, but made no persistent stand. As the advance party, under Colonel De Villiers (consisting at this time chiefly of the Second Kentucky Regiment), approached Cotton Hill the enemy was seen moving their baggage train over the hill along the Fayette turnpike from their camping ground above Huddleston's, 1½ miles from the Kanawha, where the scouts had reported a camp of two regiments the evening before. The advance of our men was stopped before reaching Cotton Hill, as I was satisfied the enemy was greatly superior in number to Colonel De Villiers' party, and they seemed to be retiring with the supposition that his force was only the advance guard of a larger body following him. I therefore thought it unwise to have him descend from the wooded ridges and reveal the smallness of his command.

During the afternoon of Monday, the 11th instant, a second party from the First Kentucky Regiment, of 150 men, under Major Leiper, followed the enemy up the Fayette turnpike, crossed Cotton Hill, and took up their position at Laurel Creek, where they remained till evening, then retired half a mile, and remained until General Benham's brigade reached that point, at about 3 o'clock in the afternoon of Tuesday, the 12th, the enemy being in force at Dickerson's, some 2 miles beyond.

In the fighting upon the New River Mountains our men distinctly saw from 20 to 30 of the enemy dragged away dead or badly wounded. Only 1 dead body of the rebels was found by our men on the ground next day. Our own loss was 2 killed, 1 wounded, and 6 missing, all of the Eleventh Ohio Regiment, besides several contusions received by men who fell accidentally in climbing the rocks. The missing are supposed to have been taken prisoners, being a small post stationed on the ridge near where the enemy made a brisk attack about midnight of the 10th.

The whole ground is exceedingly difficult to climb, the mountain sides being very rocky, and in many places almost perpendicular, and the most determined bravery and perseverance were evinced by the troops

18 R R—VOL V

in scaling the heights in the presence of an enemy who held the ridge and were perfectly familiar with the paths.

Very respectfully, your obedient servant,

J. D. COX, *Brigadier-General.*

Brig. Gen. W. S. ROSECRANS,
Commanding Department Western Virginia, Gauley Mountain.

[Inclosure.]

EXPLANATION.

A and B.—Position of Confederate cannon.
C.—The ferry.
D D.—Union position November 10, midnight.

E E.—Confederate position Nov'ber 10, midnight.
F.—Union position November 11, noon.
G.—Confederate position November 11, noon.

No. 3.

Report of Maj. Samuel W. Crawford, Thirteenth U. S. Infantry, of operations at Townsend's Ferry.

HEADQUARTERS DEPARTMENT WESTERN VIRGINIA,
Camp Gauley Mountain, November 21, 1861.

SIR: In reply to your communication of the 20th instant I have the honor to submit the following report of the operations conducted by me at Townsend's Ferry and my subsequent connection with the expedition sent against the forces under Brigadier-General Floyd:

Having been appointed a special aide-de-camp of the commanding general for this expedition, I reported on Wednesday, the 6th instant, to Brigadier-General Schenck, commanding the Third Brigade. It had been determined, if possible, to throw a body of troops under General Schenck across New River, at some point above the enemy's position, in order to strike his rear. For this purpose a neglected ferry, known as Townsend's Ferry, was selected, and a bold and successful reconnaissance of the opposite side was made by Sergeant Haven, of the Twenty-third Regiment Ohio Volunteers, who succeeded in making his way at night within a short distance of the town of Fayette, 1¼ miles from the ferry. It was determined to attempt a crossing of the troops under General Schenck at this point, a distance of 5½ miles from their encampment. To effect this, it was necessary to construct the means of crossing the river, which was at the ferry about 80 or 90 yards across. Four skiffs were sent up from Gauley, and the duty of constructing floats and transferring them and the skiffs to the water's edge was assigned to me. The floats were thus constructed: Two wagon beds, 9½ by 4 feet, were placed upon frames a distance of 3½ feet apart, and secured by wedges and pins. Thus constructed, they were placed upon a duck paulin, which was drawn up tightly around the beds and secured. Light planks were then laid over the wagon beds, and the whole secured by ropes, which, while holding it firmly together, served to control and guide it. A bull-boat, substituting canvas for hides, was constructed by Capt. W. F. Raynolds, Topographical Engineers. These floats and boats were in readiness on Thursday, the 7th instant, and sent on Thursday night to the mountain.

On Wednesday a reconnaissance of the path leading down the mountain on this side of the river was made by me. It was found to be utterly impracticable for the passage of boats or material of any sort, and it became necessary to seek at once for an avenue by which the material prepared might be sent down the mountain. I repaired to the mountain on Thursday, and after a laborious search I marked out a road by which I hoped to send down upon sledges our boats and floats. A steep perpendicular cliff ran along the mountain for half a mile. A point was found where the cliff opened, leaving a smooth rock 12 feet high, over which the boats were sent. In some places the entire material had to be carried over rocks to the heads of steep ravines, down which the skiffs and wagon beds were sent by means of ropes. A detail of pioneers was furnished by the Third Brigade, and subsequently fatigue parties, until the evening of Saturday, when three of the skiffs and two of the wagon-beds were drawn up at a short distance from the water's edge and concealed. The men worked in the rain during the whole period.

On Saturday night a guard, consisting of an officer, a non-commissioned officer, and 10 men, were stationed over the boats, with directions to show no light, to kindle no fires, and to preserve the utmost quiet. Shortly after daylight three men made their appearance on the opposite bank, and launched a small boat made of rough planks. Being too small to hold the three, two of the men came across. When within a few rods of the shore they discovered the guard, and signaling them not to fire, they came ashore and delivered themselves up. The man who remained upon the opposite shore, seeing his comrades taken prisoners, attempted to escape, and was fired upon.

The work, however, was carried on, and by Monday evening the entire material was at the water's edge. Soon after dark the bull-boat and wagon floats were put together and floated, the skiffs were launched, and everything was in readiness. It was now deemed proper by me to make an attempt to throw a rope across the river. Owing to the very heavy and almost incessant rains the river had commenced to rise early in the day and was now much swollen. I directed three experienced oarsmen to enter one of the skiffs and attempt to cross, towing a small rope. When about the middle of the river they were seized by the current and carried swiftly down the river to the rapids, and only returned to this side by great exertions. At the same moment a courier reached me with the intelligence from Captain Piatt, assistant adjutant-general Third Brigade, that no attempt would be made to cross the command that night. The skiffs and floats were then hauled up behind rocks and concealed. Up to the moment of quitting the bank of the river at midnight of the 11th I could detect no sound from the opposite bank or the slightest indication that we were observed. Leaving a small guard at the boats, I returned to headquarters. The river continued to rise during the night. It fell slowly during the day, but at 6 p. m. of Tuesday, the 12th instant, it was visited by Captain Piatt, who reported it impassable.

On the 13th, the Third Brigade, in accordance with previous orders, left their encampment and crossed the Kanawha in the vicinity of Gauley. At 6.30 p. m. I joined the command at its camp at Huddleston's, near the forks of Falls Creek. A communication had been sent by General Schenck to General Benham, commanding the Second Brigade, and who was supposed to be with his force at or near Laurel Creek, a distance of — miles from Fayette. In order, however, to obtain more precise intelligence of the movements and condition of General Benham's force, I was requested by General Schenck to go forward to General Benham, inform him that General Schenck had crossed the river and assumed command, and to learn from General Benham the immediate condition of his command, his position, and the result of his scouts, and to direct him not to go forward unless there was an immediate prospect of coming up with the enemy, in event of which General Schenck would move forward with his whole force; otherwise he would remain at Laurel Creek until General Schenck's arrival in the morning. I left at 7.30 p. m. The road was miry, and in many places almost impassable for wagons. Knots of soldiers were straggling along after their regiments, and in some instances, tired of the pursuit, they had turned aside to bivouac for the night. At a point known as the Widow Stauridge's, where the road from Cassidy's Mill joins the turnpike from Fayette to Gauley, I encountered a large body of men at a halt. At 9 o'clock p. m. I overtook General Benham at Dickerson's farm house, where he had halted with a portion of his command, and was resting until the regiments and stragglers in rear should come up. I found General Benham, and informed him of the object of my visit. He did not understand that General Schenck was to take command, but that their forces were to act conjointly. He stated to me that the enemy's train was just ahead of him, and that he was to start in an hour in pursuit. I informed him that General Schenck had crossed the river and had assumed command, and that he had sent me to him (General B.) to learn the position he was occupying, the disposition he had made of his troops, what information of the enemy's movements and position he had obtained from his scouts, and also to inform him that General Schenck would join him at or near Laurel Creek in the morning. I informed him also that General Schenck desired that he (General

B.) would not move forward unless there was an immediate prospect of meeting the enemy or overtaking them in case they had retreated, when, upon being apprised of this, General Schenck would move forward with his whole command at once to his (General B.'s) support.

General Benham replied to me that he had just dispatched a courier to General Schenck, to say to him that the enemy's train was just ahead, and that he could overtake it; that he was resting his men an hour at Dickerson's, when he should push on to Fayette. He stated to me that the enemy were making a most precipitate retreat, throwing out their baggage, &c.; that his command got nothing on a previous occasion, and that he was determined they should be the first on this. I asked him if the force at Cassidy's Mill had definite instructions. He replied that he had sent his aide-de-camp to that point with directions to use his discretion in reference to the route to be pursued by the command there, and that he (the aide-de-camp) had withdrawn them to the rear, and that he (General B.) was only awaiting their arrival to join his command.

I laid before him a map with the positions marked on it, and remarked to him that the importance of the position at Cassidy's Mill could not be overestimated, and that both General Rosecrans and General Schenck regarded it as the most important point in the whole position, as it threatened the enemy's rear, and the force there could fall upon his flank in a short march of 3½ miles if he retreated. He replied that he had no maps, but he was confident that he would overtake their train anyhow, and that he hoped General Schenck would come on at once.

At 9.15 I left for General Schenck's headquarters at Huddleston's. I arrived at 11 o'clock, and found the command under orders to move in an hour. I found a large number of stragglers making their way towards Dickerson's. These men appeared not to know where they were going or where their regiments were. In an hour the Third Brigade was in motion, and arrived at Dickerson's about daylight. It was raining heavily, the men were without tents or blankets, and the provision train had not been able to pass the roads. A short halt was ordered. We moved on towards Fayette in an hour, when, from information we received that the enemy were far in advance and in consideration of the state of the roads and the condition of the men, tired out by a night's march, and without rations or blankets, it was decided to remain at Fayette and communicate with the force under General Benham, who had left Fayette about nine hours before.

I remained during the day at Fayette, and made an examination of the ascent from the crossing at Townsend's Ferry. It is perfectly practicable for infantry; the ascent, although steep, is open, and leads to open woods upon the sides of the mountain to the table-land above. It passes through open fields to a road that leads directly to Fayette, and there was no evidence of the slightest effort made to protect it or to prevent a crossing at the ferry.

I returned on the morning of the 15th with dispatches, and reported to the commanding general.

Very respectfully, your obedient servant,

S. W. CRAWFORD,

Major, Thirteenth Infantry, U. S. Army, Act. Insp. Gen.

Maj. JOSEPH DARR, Jr.,

Acting Assistant Adjutant-General.

No. 4.

Report of Brig. Gen. Henry W. Benham, U. S. Army, of operations from November 11–16.

FAYETTEVILLE COURT-HOUSE, VA.,
November 16, 1861.

SIR : I have the honor to report as follows in relation to the expedition from which I have this afternoon returned by the order of General Schenck from the pursuit of General Floyd upon the road to Raleigh, by which he escaped by a most rapid and arduous march last night.

Upon the night of the 11th instant, while at a kind of a bivouac at Loop Creek Mouth, where I have been with part of my command by the directions of General Rosecrans since the 4th and 5th instant, I received your orders to proceed as early as practicable with the force then at that point, about 1,500 men of the Tenth, Twelfth, and Thirteenth Regiments, to occupy Cotton Hill, there having been previously stationed by his orders under my direction the Thirty-seventh Regiment of 700 men at Loop Creek Forks, about 4 miles up, and in detachments up to 10 miles from the mouth of the creek; also about 320 of the Forty-fourth Regiment and 430 of the Seventh Regiment about 1 mile up on the left fork.

About the time of marching from Loop Creek, however, I had directed, as he had ordered me, about 1,000 men from these last three regiments to occupy Cassidy's Mill, about 6 miles up from the left fork towards this place, and the remainder, being part of the Thirty-seventh Regiment, to endeavor to reach me at Cotton Hill by a march to the left of Cassidy's Mill by Nugent's.

On the morning of the 12th, in accordance with the directions given, with the first-named force and four mountain howitzers and two rifled 6-pounders, we moved up the left bank of the Kanawha, 4 miles from the mouth of Loop Creek, to Gauley Falls, thence to the right some 5 miles over Cotton Hill to Herscliberger's by 3 p. m., where at Laurel Creek we met the advance pickets of the enemy in force, as it was afterwards ascertained, in a most strong position, prepared with abatis, and after skirmishing with them with the greater part of the Thirteenth Regiment until dark, we went into bivouac in the open air on the escarped mountain road, with but few fires and but little water, myself and staff lying on the bare rocks, with our horses held below us.

Our loss in this skirmish was 1 man killed and 4 wounded; that of the enemy 2 at least killed and about 7 wounded. The enemy were completely driven from the ground they occupied, but not much farther, as a large re-enforcement was seen coming to them (I have since learned four regiments and one piece of artillery were sent), and with only 1,640 men, for Colonel Siber's detachment had not fully joined, I did not think it would be safe to draw on a battle with the whole rebel force, reported by General Rosecrans to me to be from 4,000 to 6,000 men, and, as I heard after, with nine to eleven guns, although, as reported to him that night, I felt I could hold my position on the mountain secure against their force.

During the night, at about 2.30 a. m. of the 13th, it was reported to me by a scout I had sent out to watch the rebel camp that the wheels of heavy wagons or artillery were heard rumbling in the direction of the camp, but as they became no fainter, it was uncertain whether they were retreating or receiving re-enforcements. I immediately sent directions to Colonel Smith, of the Thirteenth Regiment, to send out two other scouts, to ascertain if the movement was a retreat; but most unfortunately (as Colonel Smith informed me in the morning), he did not understand it as a command, but merely as a suggestion, and they were not sent. On learning this at early light, I immediately sent forward a scout of 10 men, supported by two companies of the Thirteenth Regiment, but the report from these men of the retreat of the rebels did not come in till after 4 p. m., on receiving which I immediately gave the orders for marching to overtake them. For this I felt the more prepared as I had ordered and expected down to join me the force that were at Cassidy's Mill, having authorized the aide who was sent there to order them direct to Fayette road if the enemy were proven to be retreating, and it would be surely safe to do so. But this last order was also misunderstood, and although a portion of this command of mine had occupied Fayetteville from 11 a. m. without finding they had the means to communicate with me, they were recalled, and unfortunately made the circuit around to this place again. At length, by 5 p. m., we moved forward from the Union school-house to the Dickerson farm, which we reached before 7, finding the evidences of a most hasty retreat in the remains of large quantities of tents and camp equipage destroyed by fire. At a short distance beyond this farm the command was closed up, halted, and rested for about four hours, and the detachment of the Forty-fourth and Seventh joined me, making my moving strength about 2,700 men. With this force at 11 p. m. I pushed forward, arriving about 4 a. m. of the 14th at Hawkins' farm, about 5 miles beyond Fayetteville, being delayed much by scouting the roads in advance. On the route further evidences of the hasty retreat were shown in the tents, wagons, and large quantities of ammunition left behind.

At 7 we again moved forward, with the belief, which proved to be the fact, that part at least of their train was encamped 5 miles from Hawkins'. The advance was led by Colonel Smith, of the Thirteenth, to whose presence and caution during that day we owe it that not a single man of ours was killed or wounded, and scouting most cautiously though of course slowly forward, we met the advanced posts of the enemy after 4 miles' march at 9.30 a. m., where a sharp contest with our advance continued for nearly half an hour, when, besides several other losses, the rebels had mortally wounded the colonel of Floyd's cavalry, Col. St. George Croghan (son of the late Inspector-General Croghan). These outposts being driven in, we advanced carefully about one mile farther, where the enemy were found posted in considerable force behind a ridge covering McCoy's Mill. A regiment of cavalry and different regiments of infantry are reported as distinctly seen. After an interchange of fire between these and our advance for twenty minutes Captain Schneider's rifled artillery was brought up with good effect, the officers reporting that they saw many fall at their fire. As however I soon discovered a ridge that made out from our rear to our right, that commanded at close range the left of the enemy, I sent my aide to direct Lieutenant-Colonel Creighton, with the Seventh and half of the Thirty-seventh Regiments, under Major Ankele, to pass down this ridge to attack their left. This movement, I regret to say, was delayed fully half an hour by the resistance of Colonel Siber to this order, he at first neglecting or refusing to send the number of men required and demanding the right to command it, as reported by my aides. When at length this attack was made it was entirely successful, and with the first concentrated volleys of this command of about 750 men, uniting with the fire of the Thirteenth Regiment, the whole of the enemy retreated in confusion, with the last of their wagon train. Their position was soon, though cautiously, taken possession of, when it was found thickly strewn with blankets, clothing, camp equipage, &c., as evidence of a precipitous flight. A short time for rest was now given, and we then moved forward, with the usual scouting parties in advance, through an escarped road upon a steep mountain side, in a defile, continuing for about 4 miles between two mountains up the Big Loop Creek, finding about midway of the defile a bridge of some size broken down, which delayed us nearly an hour to repair. Yet still, as the guides informed us that there was a long and difficult hill for the passage of wagons about 2 miles in advance of the bridge, I decided to push forward, in the hopes of overtaking it, although the men had been marching nearly all the night previous, as well as during most of that day, in for a greater part of the time a drenching storm and over roads in many places to a great extent of tenacious mud, and many of them by the failure of expected trains with less than half their rations. On reaching at 4 p. m. the outlet of this defile at Keton's farm, about 15 miles from Fayetteville and 20 miles from our previous bivouac near Cotton Hill, we found the expected steep hill some 2 miles distant, and their wagons over it or not in sight, and therefore I concluded to bivouac the men there with such food as we could best obtain and report the case, as I did, to General Schenck at Fayetteville, who had assumed the direction by order of General Rosecrans, and suggesting to him to join me with his force (about one-half of mine), that we might attack or drive the enemy in Raleigh the next day.

The first dispatch of General Schenck informed me that he had sent the Twenty-sixth Regiment and some mounted men to re-enforce me. A second note, received at 10 p. m., informed me that the Twenty-sixth Regiment was ordered to return, while it directed me also to return as soon as practicable to this place. As the men were still for more than nine-tenths of them without any shelter in a most drenching rain or succession of violent thunder showers, many without their blankets even, which had been thrown off in the ardor of the chase, and as they were still standing around their fires unable to sleep in the rain upon the open ground, the greater part of the command, though most unwilling to give up the pursuit, felt that if it was so ordered it must be best for themselves, after their few hours' halt (it could not be called rest), to retrace their steps that very night rather than remain standing in the cold and wet till morning with only the prospect before them of their return. We accordingly commenced our return soon after 1 o'clock, and reaching McCoy's about 4, we rested till after 6 a. m. of the 15th, or to-day, when we moved onward, and with a single rest about midway the command reached this place soon after noon, being still in excellent spirits, their main disappointment being in not having been permitted to continue the pursuit of the rebels. We are at this hour partly in houses, but a great number out in the open air in the village, where it is now snowing upon them in their bivouac, which, added to their really great exposure, will, I fear, half annihilate their effective strength.

The main facts and circumstances of the expedition are therefore that after remaining about one week upon Loop Creek awaiting the co-operation of another force, and with my command of about 3,000 men divided in four portions, as ordered by General Rosecrans, I at length moved forward with one-half this force to meet the enemy in front to the farthest point of Cotton Hill. There in the night after our first engagement with his outpost on the afternoon of the 13th the enemy made a most precipitous retreat, leaving portions of his baggage, wagon loads of ammunition, tents, clothing, &c., on the route, besides the evidences of the destruction of a much greater portion; that when from the un-known and difficult nature of the country some twenty hours had elapsed before his retreat was assured, and without which we did not feel it safe to pursue him to his works at Dickerson's farm (since found it to be of the strongest character for field works) with my force, then of less than 2,000, and not one-half of the least of his supposed numbers, he was most vigorously followed up by my command through rain and storm and mud till overtaken at about 18 miles from the camp he left, and the heavy force of his rear guard was there routed and further camp equipage taken after another action, by which his train was still kept in advance of us, and the pursuit was still continued until, from the difficult nature of the defile beyond, the breaking of bridges, &c., our exhausted forces needed to rest for the night, when we were recalled by the orders of General Schenck; and this was accomplished with the loss of 1 man killed and 4 wounded on our part in the fight at Laurel Creek and none at the affair at McCoy's Mill, while it is certain that the loss of the enemy was three times that amount, including that of their chief colonel of cavalry killed, and Floyd was pursued for about 30 miles from his batteries of Gauley Bridge, and driven, as was ascertained, to Raleigh, and for some 9 miles farther than our last bivouac.

I can only add, in conclusion, that had I not been ordered to return, and had the forces which were sent over the river been moved up to Keton's to support me, as I asked by a courier that evening that they should be, we could have moved forward to Raleigh to-day, as I intended, and, as I am well satisfied, captured that place and depot with their train, and certainly routed, if not captured, the whole of Floyd's force.

I have now but to report the noble conduct of the forces during the most toilsome march, where through all their great exposure in the storm upon the route, and in bivouac, without shelter against the rain or snow that fell in each of the last three nights, not a murmur was heard by me, but every duty was performed with the greatest cheerfulness and alacrity. And the principal officers of the command were worthy of the men they led. Of Col. W. S. Smith, commanding the Thirteenth Regi-ment, I have frequently expressed my opinion in my report of the battle of Carnifix Ferry, and all there stated was here more than confirmed. Colonel White, of the Twelfth Regiment, who has recently been pro-moted, and made the most praiseworthy and successful efforts for the discipline of his regiment of fine men, did not behave less nobly than if he had been fully in most successful battle, by yielding as he did to the exigencies of the occasion a desire with much of equity in it, which was shared by himself and his men, to lead the advance of the march. Colonel Woods, of the U. S. Army, at this time acting in command of the Tenth Regiment, led that regiment in advance at a rapid and safe pace at the latter part of the march on the 14th with great good judgment and gallantry, and Captain Schneider, of the rifled artillery of the Thir-teenth Regiment, a very gallant and deserving officer, was most prompt and successful in the management of his guns. Captain McMullin, though his howitzers were not brought into play in action, was prompt and ready at every point on the march, as he is ever at every call of duty, and Lieutenant-Colonel Creighton, of the Seventh, executed the maneuver from our right flank which decided the rout at McCoy's Mill in most gallant style; the Forty-fourth, under its very effective officer, Major Mitchell, not having the opportunity of participating in the action, as well as the Thirty-seventh Regiment, from their position in the rear.

My high acknowledgments are also due to each of my personal staff for the efficiency and gallantry on the field with which every duty was performed. To the brigade surgeon, Dr. Shumard, ever most watchful over both the surgeons and the men for their health and safety, and my aide, Captain Atkinson, of rare ability and efficiency, and to Captain Stanage, acting assistant adjutant-general, of whose excellent conduct I had the pleasure to report at Carnifix, as also to Captain Mallory, the commissary, of whom my expectations in that action were fully borne out, and to the brigade quartermaster, Capt. D. L. Smith, one of the most efficient in his department in the service, although detained by my orders at the camp, the highest praise is due for his care and forethought, not only in forwarding constantly the amplest supplies of provisions, but in having the tents which had been struck at our late position repitched by the time of the return of the men from their toilsome and wearied march and amply provided with all the necessary comforts of the camp.

I am, sir, very respectfully, your obedient servant,

H. W. BENHAM,
Brigadier-General, U. S. Volunteers.

Maj. J. DARR, Jr., *Acting Assistant Adjutant-General.*

[Inclosure.]

HEADQUARTERS DEPARTMENT WESTERN VIRGINIA,
Camp, Gauley Mountain, November 6, 1861.

GENERAL: Inclosed you will find a sketch, marked, showing the west side of Kanawha from Fayette to Paint Creek, with such roads marked as we have information of. You will find smaller sketch, which shows the information we can collect about the country between Loop Creek and the Fayette road. A memoir inclosed explains this. You have received telegraphic orders to cross the Kanawha with effective force, and also, subsequently, to establish yourself solidly and comfortably over there, holding the mouth of Paint by small watch guard, and occupying Loop Creek up to a good point of the main branch, far enough above Taylor's to secure that thoroughly against a movement or regiment or two down from Kincaid's, and then secure the road up the left-hand branch of Loop to the top of the ridge, so that we can use the passage at or near some point X 9 due [?]. Should also secure the heights above the creek by a line of pickets judiciously placed and carefully concealed.

It may become necessary to combine our forces and operate on the left-hand branch at the same time by way of Kincaid's, to cut off their rear, and your object will be to secure to us the use of these routes, at least to the points referred to. The advantages of this will be that should we be unable to cross in their rear above, thus we may still have a chance of operating on their rear in that direction. Whether we shall be able to cross the New River with chances of success will probably be determined when the examination that is going on shall be completed and reported to me. I will then communicate to you any modifications deemed necessary in consequence of the result of the reconnaissance.

I again repeat, make ample provision for the covering and subsistence of your troops in solid position and have convenient communication between your headquarters and the opposite shore and below. Have the road up Loop and above you on the Kanawha examined and repaired so as to make it passable, but avoid exciting observation. Admonish your field officers of the day to do all they can to perfect the

guard and outpost duties, and take every practicable means of increasing the efficiency and certainty with which the troops can act.
Very respectfully, your obedient servant,
W. S. ROSECRANS,
Brigadier-General, U. S. Army.
Brig. Gen. H. W. BENHAM, *Camp Huddleston.*

No. 5.

Report of Col. Carr B. White, Twelfth Ohio Infantry, of skirmish on Laurel Creek, November 12.

CAMP HUDDLESTON, VA., *November* 18, 1861.
SIR : At the skirmish on Laurel Creek at the crossing of the Kanawha and Fayetteville road, Company H, Twelfth Regiment, which was detached from my command in the morning as an advance guard, under command of Col. W. S. Smith, with Company A, Thirteenth, had 3 men wounded severely, 1 of whom has since died, viz : Corporal Samuel Burke, since dead ; Private John S. Kirk and Private George S. Reed. In a scout on the 10th instant, conducted by Lieutenant-Colonel Hines, of the Twelfth, and Captain Atkinson, of your staff, Carey Johnson, Company B, was severely wounded.
C. B. WHITE.
Brig. Gen. H. W. BENHAM.

No. 6.

Report of Col. William S. Smith, Thirteenth Ohio Infantry, of skirmishes (November 12) on Laurel Creek and (November 14) near McCoy's Mill.

HEADQUARTERS THIRTEENTH REGIMENT O. V. I.,
Camp Huddleston, Va., November 18, 1861.
SIR : I have the honor to submit the following report of the part taken by my regiment in the recent rout and pursuit of Floyd's forces :
On the 6th instant, at 4.30 o'clock p. m., we crossed the Kanawha River, together with the remaining portion of the First Provisional Brigade, under command of Brigadier-General Benham, and encamped near the mouth of Loop Creek, where we remained until the morning of the 12th instant. We then marched up the left bank of the Kanawha River to Montgomery's Ferry, and thence by the Fayette road over Cotton Hill to a point near the crossing of Laurel Creek, my regiment leading the column.
While the command was yet upon the eastern declivity of Cotton Hill a halt was ordered by General Benham, and Captain Carey's company of the Twelfth Ohio and Captain Beach's company of the Thirteenth Ohio were ordered to make a reconnaissance of the Laurel Creek ravine just in advance of us and through which our road lay for the distance of about half a mile. These companies had but fairly entered the ravine when they came upon a strong outpost of the enemy lying in ambush. A sharp skirmish ensued, our men instantly taking cover and returning the fire of the enemy, which was poured in upon them at short range. Both officers and men behaved with great coolness

and intrepidity, driving the enemy steadily before them until he was strongly re-enforced, when General Benham, after having ordered a detachment of the Thirty-seventh Regiment forward to support Captain Beach, ordered our skirmishers to retire, and sent my regiment forward to scour the woods and bring off the wounded. In this skirmish John Remley, of Company A, Thirteenth Regiment, was killed, and John Heister, of the same company, was very severely wounded. Several of the enemy were seen to fall, and one of them was found dead upon the field the following day, not carried off, after having been dragged a long distance.

The night of the 12th we bivouacked on Cotton Hill, and on the morning of the 13th moved forward toward Fayette. After proceeding about 2 miles we discovered an intrenchment on a high hill about a mile ahead, and so situated that, although but a few men could be seen, we found it impossible to ascertain for a certainty whether it was held by the enemy in force until we had consumed about six hours in scaling the surrounding heights. It was at last discovered that the work had been entirely abandoned by the enemy, and we again pushed forward and bivouacked about 1 mile beyond the Dickerson farm. Here we rested but four hours, and then marched forward again through Fayette, continuing our march until the moon set, about 3 o'clock a. m., when we halted at a point 5 miles beyond Fayette, in the direction of Raleigh. Here we rested until about 6 a. m. (14th), and then moved forward again, keeping our skirmishers well out on both flanks. We had proceeded but about 4 miles when my skirmishing company, under command of Captain Gardner, came suddenly upon a scouting party of the enemy's cavalry, numbering 40 men. A sharp skirmish ensued, during which Col. St. George Croghan was mortally wounded. Several of his men, as he stated, were also wounded, though they escaped, leaving their horses to the number of five. The colonel was left at a farm house by his men and treated with the utmost kindness by our assistant surgeon, Dr. Chase, up to near the time of his death, which took place at 2 o'clock p. m.

After this skirmish we moved forward and came upon the enemy in force near McCoy's Mill, where the firing became so sharp, that our forces were immediately disposed for battle. Companies A, D, F, and I, of my regiment, were immediately thrown well to the front as skirmishers and put under cover. The remainder of my regiment was thrown behind the crest of a hill to the left of the road. When these dispositions had been made, different regiments of the enemy were seen to be retreating over the distant hills, and a body of cavalry, apparently 400 strong, was seen winding around the base of a hill about 1 mile distant. I immediately put one of my two rifled cannons, under the command of Captain Schneider, in a position from which we had an enfilading fire upon the road, and opened upon the enemy's cavalry, throwing them into the utmost confusion and putting them to flight. At the first discharge from the rifled gun the enemy's skirmishers broke from their cover and ran, taking the fire of the four companies constituting our advance as they went. Here, again, several were seen to fall, and in their precipitate retreat they threw away their guns and equipments, which we found strewn in every direction on the field. The enemy seemed thoroughly demoralized and thoughtful only of a safe retreat.

Our officers and men behaved with the greatest coolness and courage, their obedience to orders and the accuracy of their aim eliciting my highest admiration.* As the enemy ran we pursued, following him as

---

* In separate letters Colonel Smith specially notices the gallantry of Capts. Albert F. Beach and Isaac R. Gardner and Private Robert K. Siez.

far as the Blake farm, which we reached at 4 o'clock p. m. Here a halt was ordered, as our men were exceedingly weary, and it was ascertained that the enemy were so far ahead of us as to render it impossible to overtake him again before nightfall. We were moreover with short rations, and were informed that none could come forward for us that night.

At about 2 o'clock a. m. (15th) we started on our return, and reached Fayette at 3 o'clock p. m. The following day (16th) we returned to this camp, having been exposed to ten days of such hardships as men are rarely called upon to endure, but exultant that it had been our privilege to give the last chase from the valley of the Kanawha to the very troops which first fled before us from Ripley before the advance of our troops up the valley, and having driven General Floyd and his forces nearly 40 miles from his position in sight of the headquarters of this department of our army.

Very respectfully submitted.

WM. S. SMITH,
Colonel, Commanding Thirteenth Regiment O. V. I.
Capt. JAMES O. STANAGE, *Acting Assistant Adjutant-General.*

No. 7.

Reports of Brig. Gen. John B. Floyd, C. S. Army.

HEADQUARTERS ARMY OF KANAWHA,
Camp Dickerson, November 7, 1861.

SIR : I asked instructions from the War Department nearly two weeks since as to the best point to be occupied by this command as winter quarters.* In my previous dispatches I attempted to present such facts and reasons as would possess the Department of my views upon the general policy which might be considered in determining the point. Since that time I have marched to this point, and have driven the enemy entirely across the Kanawha, where, except the very hurried predatory parties, he is now strictly confined. I send you herewith a sketch† of the country immediately around here, which will enable you to see at a glance our position, that of the enemy, and to understand what has been accomplished by the movement to the Kanawha.

When I crossed New River the enemy were in possession of all the country on the south side of Kanawha River as far as Raleigh Court-House. They had laid waste the village of Fayetteville and the country upon their lines of march. They had penetrated within 70 miles of the Virginia and Tennessee Railroad, and had produced the greatest alarm amongst the people of Mercer, Giles, and Monroe, who felt that whilst the enemy could with impunity occupy this region (Fayette and Raleigh Counties), there could be no safety for them even in their homes. The feeling of confidence and security is now fully realized by all the country in the rear of us, and it becomes a question of great importance to select a proper point for winter quarters, that the advantage we have gained may not be lost, and that the people may remain at their homes following their regular pursuits. This point itself presents many advantages. The position is strong. Our right flank is completely protected by the cliffs of New River and the Gorge of Piney for the dis-

---

* See Benjamin to Floyd, November 15, in "Correspondence, etc.," *post.*
† Not found.

tance of 40 miles. Our front can be easily rendered impregnable to five times our number. It is in the immediate vicinity of the enemy, where we annoy him constantly, and holding it, he is unable to advance upon us except with an overwhelming force, or to advance upon Lewisburg, or to leave his position without abandoning the great connecting link between the northwest proper, the railroad at Clarksburg, and the Kanawha Valley, and I think it would be impossible for the enemy to hold his position if we had guns of large caliber.

Fuel here is extremely abundant and the exposure a good one for the mountains. The chief obstacle to this point is the difficulty of transportation. The line is 100 miles long from the railroad, over a mountain road (not macadamized) which becomes very deep and muddy in the winter. Probably most of the advantages pertaining to this position could be realized by falling back to the point at or near Raleigh Court-House, 35 miles nearer the railroad, but to fall back beyond that point, I am very clearly convinced, would prove extremely disastrous to the country and to our cause in this region. Colonel Russell, of Mississippi, takes this communication, and is fully possessed of my views, which he can, if you choose, explain more in detail.

I have the honor to be, very respectfully, your obedient servant,

JOHN B. FLOYD,
Commanding Army of Kanawha.

Hon. J. P. BENJAMIN, *Secretary of War.*

—

HEADQUARTERS ARMY OF KANAWHA,
Camp Piney, November 19, 1861.

SIR: In execution of a general plan, of which you were fully advised in my last dispatch, I succeeded [November 1] in placing my guns in battery on the south side of the Kanawha River, near the junction of the New and Gauley Rivers. This I accomplished after much arduous labor, by transporting by hand the guns over a very abrupt and precipitous locality for the distance of several miles. When they were gotten in position they proved a source of considerable annoyance to the enemy. They not only bore upon the ferry where formerly stood the Gauley Bridge, but commanded for some considerable distance the road by which the enemy transported his provisions. The result was that the plying of his ferry-boats across the Gauley was stopped, one of them sunk, and all transportation over the road by day cut off. The sharpshooters, too, whom I posted on the bank of the river and under cover of my large guns, harassed him very much. The range was too great for the very successful use of small arms; still at certain points on the river many of his horses were killed and not less than 50 men. This blow was inflicted without the loss of a man on our side or the sustaining of a wound. In this juncture of affairs, had a vigorous advance from the direction of Sewell Mountain and the Hawk's Nest been made upon the enemy it would have compelled him either to meet this attack and leave his rear open to my forces, or to cross the river in order to fight me, in the face of my guns and in open boats, pressed by the column advancing from the Hawk's Nest, or to take position at a lower point on the Kanawha. In either of these cases we could have engaged him with many advantages to us, and it is my conviction would have achieved a victory over him. The advance of such a force I hoped for when I left my position on Sewell Mountain, and regretted that the emergency of the service at Cheat Mountain rendered it necessary, in the judgment of General Lee, to send the force to that point which I hoped would co-operate with me.

Such was the position of the two forces for three weeks. During this time there was incessant skirmishing from across the river, resulting from the superiority of our position uniformly in our favor, and during this time, though employed in constant efforts to cross the river, the enemy succeeded in but one instance. He threw over, under cover of night, a force of about 100 men, led by Colonel De Villiers. They attacked the guard of one of the guns, who, commanded by Major Thorburn, gallantly met and repulsed them, after killing several and capturing 6. Colonel De Villiers very narrowly escaped being captured.

On the night of this skirmish the enemy received a re-enforcement of 5,000 from Ohio. They landed at the mouth of Loop Creek, with the view of intercepting my retreat should this become necessary or of falling upon my rear or upon my left flank in case of a general engagement. The better to watch the movements of this column, I fell back 3 miles from Cotton Hill to within a short distance of the intersection of the Loop Creek road and the turnpike upon which my force was. The enemy advanced in force from Cotton Hill. I ordered three regiments to meet them. A warm skirmish followed, which had resulted in a general engagement between these forces had not the enemy, though much superior in numbers and in positions of their own selection, disgracefully retreated. The conduct of our men, who were engaged in this action under my own eye, was gallant and worthy of commendation. The position which I had selected was very strong, so much so that, with my force inferior in numbers to either column of the enemy, I had been willing, in fact desired, to engage him there. I would have done so with strong confidence of success. He, however, declined attacking me, and I, deeming it prudent to have a position beyond the intersections of the many roads leading from the Kanawha River with the turnpike, fell back upon Loop Mountain. The enemy followed, but with great timidity. Near this point [McCoy's Mill, November 14] a skirmish occurred between scouting parties, in which I am grieved to inform the Department Lieut. Col. St. George Croghan was killed. Colonel Croghan was one of the most gallant officers in the service. His bravery and gentlemanly demeanor, which characterized him to his latest breath, rendered him dear to all who knew him. His death has cast a gloom over the spirits of the entire army. In this no one shares more sincerely than I do.

I may be allowed here to state that the column which advanced from the mouth of Loop Creek was piloted along obscure and unused paths by two men recently discharged from confinement in Richmond. I would respectfully but most urgently call the attention of the Department to this matter, and would suggest that under no circumstances should a traitor be let loose upon the country who has been arrested and sent to Richmond by this army, except, upon a careful weighing of all the testimony in his case, he proves himself innocent. In some cases the witnesses are inaccessible at a given time. Of one thing, however, the Department may be well assured, such a character is never arrested by my act or authority unless his liberty is dangerous to the public safety.

In my position on Loop Mountain the enemy declined attacking me, but retreated from that to Gauley in a very disorderly manner. It was, however, one of no strategic value. I thought it best to fall back to this position on Piney Creek. Here I have been for two days. The position is impregnable. Here I hoped to winter my forces, but I find the country so stripped of its means of subsistence, in the first place by the militia and then by the forces under my command, that I have been forced to surrender this hope. In addition to this, the road for 12 or 15 miles east of this point is at present almost impassable. Under these circumstances I deem it best to take position on New River, where subsistence for the men and beasts may be had in abundance.

I take occasion here to state that some two weeks since I ordered Colonel Clarkson, in command of my cavalry, to proceed in the direction of the Ohio River, and to strike the enemy a blow whenever and wherever he thought it prudent to do so. He went as far as the town of Guyandotte, attacked a force of the enemy about 300 strong stationed there [November 10], and, to use his own language, annihilated them. He took 95 prisoners, killed or drowned the remainder, and captured about 300 Enfield rifles. The prisoners I have the honor to send to Richmond. Colonel Clarkson executed his mission in the most satisfactory and gallant manner, and merits the highest commendation.

Hoping that the several movements above detailed of the army which I have the honor to command may meet with the approbation of the Department, I have the honor to be, very respectfully, your obedient servant,   JOHN B. FLOYD,
              Brigadier-General, Commanding Army of Kanawha.

Hon. J. P. BENJAMIN, *Secretary of War.*

OCTOBER 20, 1861.—Reconnaissance to Hunter's Mill and Thornton Station, Virginia.

Report of Maj. Amiel W. Whipple, U. S. Corps of Engineers.

ARLINGTON, VA., *October 22*, 1861.

SIR: I have the honor to report that on Sunday last, in compliance with the orders of Major-General McCall, I made a reconnaissance from Dranesville to Hunter's Mill and Thornton Station, on the Loudoun and Hampshire Railway. I left Dranesville with 10 mounted men under the command of a lieutenant, and near Hunter's Mill met Lieutenant-Colonel Kane with a battalion of the Tiger-tail Rangers, who had a skirmish with a detachment of secessionists at that place, and routed them. This position is one of some military importance, and can be defended by us against a superior force approaching by the Fairfax road. Thence we ascended by a road upon the north side of the railway. Entered the road leading from Lewinsville to Fryingpan. Left it at the crossing of the railroad, and took a less traveled road through woods north of railway. Crossed headwaters of Colville Run, and came to Thornton's Station. Here were a few secession cavalry, who, after showing a disposition to make a stand, fled. Thence, by a road which seemed at night pretty level and smooth, we returned in a direction nearly north to Dranesville. The road by Hunter's Mill is the main road from that region to Fairfax Court-House, and is moderately good. Colonel Kane afforded every facility for the reconnaissance in his power, and kindly gave me the odometer distances taken under his direction.

*   *   *   *   *   *   *

Very respectfully, your obedient servant,
                                              A. W. WHIPPLE,
                                                    Major of Engineers.
Lieut. Col. J. N. MACOMB, A. D. C., *Corps of Engineers.*

OCTOBER 21-24, 1861.—Operations on the Potomac near Leesburg, Va., including engagement at Ball's Bluff* (21st) and action (22d) near Edwards Ferry.

REPORTS, ETC.†

No. 1.—Maj. Gen. George B. McClellan, U. S. Army, with orders.
No. 2.—Brig. Gen. Charles P. Stone, U. S. Army.
No. 3.—Return of casualties in the Union forces.
No. 4.—Col. Charles Devens, Fifteenth Massachusetts Infantry.
No. 5.—Col. Edward W. Hinks, Nineteenth Massachusetts Infantry.
No. 6.—Lieut. Col. Francis W. Palfrey, Twentieth Massachusetts Infantry.
No. 7.—Capt. William F. Bartlett, Twentieth Massachusetts Infantry.
No. 8.—Col. Milton Cogswell, Forty-second New York Infantry.
No. 9.—Lieut. Col. James J. Mooney, Forty-second New York Infantry.
No. 10.—Lieut. Col. Isaac J. Wistar, Seventy-first Pennsylvania Infantry.
No. 11.—Capt. F. G. Young, U. S. Army, of Colonel Baker's staff.
No. 12.—Brig. Gen. Charles P. Stone, U. S. Army, of operations opposite Edwards Ferry, October 23-24.
No. 13.—Brig. Gen. Willis A. Gorman, U. S. Army, of operations opposite Edwards Ferry, October 21-24.
No. 14.—Maj. John Mix, Third New York Cavalry, of reconnaissance and skirmish, October 21, on Leesburg road.
No. 15.—Brig. Gen. John J. Abercrombie, U. S. Army, of operations opposite Edwards Ferry, October 22-24.
No. 16.—Maj. Gen. Nathaniel P. Banks, U. S. Army, of march to re-enforce Brigadier-General Stone.
No. 17.—Francis L. Buxton, U. S. Secret Service, of Confederate strength at Leesburg, Va.
No. 18.—Brig. Gen. Charles P. Stone, U. S. Army, (letter) to chairman of Joint Committee on Conduct of the War.
No. 19.—Secretary of War (letter) to Speaker of the House of Representatives.
No. 20.—General G. T. Beauregard, C. S. Army, with congratulatory orders.
No. 21.—Brig. Gen. N. G. Evans, C. S. Army, including action October 22, with correspondence.
No. 22.—Return of casualties in the Confederate forces, October 21-22.
No. 23.—Col. William Barksdale, Thirteenth Mississippi Infantry, of operations October 21, 22.
No. 24.—Capt. W. J. Eckford, Thirteenth Mississippi Infantry, of action near Edwards Ferry.
No. 25.—Capt. L. D. Fletcher, Thirteenth Mississippi Infantry.
No. 26.—Col. W. S. Featherston, Seventeenth Mississippi Infantry.
No. 27.—Lieut. Col. John McGuirk, Seventeenth Mississippi Infantry, of events October 20-23.
No. 28.—Capt. W. L. Duff, Seventeenth Mississippi Infantry.
No. 29.—Lieut. Col. Thomas M. Griffin, Eighteenth Mississippi Infantry.
No. 30.—Col. Eppa Hunton, Eighth Virginia Infantry.
No. 31.—Col. Walter H. Jenifer, C. S. Army, commanding cavalry.

---

* This engagement is also known as the battle of Leesburg, Harrison's Island, or Conrad's Ferry.

† Of engagement at Ball's Bluff, when not otherwise indicated.

19 R R—VOL V

No. 1.

Report of Maj. Gen. George B. McClellan, U. S. Army, with orders.*

HEADQUARTERS ARMY OF THE POTOMAC,
Washington, November 1, 1861.

SIR : I have the honor to forward herewith Brigadier-General Stone's report of the engagement near Leesburg on the 21st ultimo. I also transmit a copy of the telegram sent by me to General Stone on the 20th [A], being the same mentioned in the beginning of his report as the basis of his movements. I also inclose a copy of his telegram in reply on same date [B]. My telegram did not contemplate the making an attack upon the enemy or the crossing of the river in force by any portion of General Stone's command, and, not anticipating such movement, I had upon the 20th directed Major-General McCall to return with his division on the morning of the 21st from Dranesville to the camp from which he had advanced, provided the reconnaissances intrusted to him should have been then completed. Being advised by telegrams from General Stone, received during the day and evening of the 21st, of the crossing of the river, the fall of Colonel Baker, the check sustained by our troops, and that nearly all his (Stone's) force had crossed the river, I sent to him at Edwards Ferry the following telegram at 10.30 p. m.: " Intrench yourself on the Virginia side and await re-enforcements if necessary." I immediately telegraphed Major-General Banks to proceed with the three brigades of his division to the support of General Stone, and advising the latter that he would be thus supported, I directed him to hold his position at all hazards. On the 22d I went personally to the scene of operations, and after ascertaining that the enemy were strengthening themselves at Leesburg, and that our means of crossing and recrossing were very insufficient, I withdrew our forces from the Virginia side.

I am, sir, very respectfully, your obedient servant,

GEO. B. McCLELLAN,
Major-General, Commanding U. S. Army.

The Hon. SECRETARY OF WAR.

[Inclosure A.]

CAMP GRIFFIN, *October* 20, 1861.

Brigadier-General STONE, *Poolesville :*

General McClellan desires me to inform you that General McCall occupied Dranesville yesterday and is still there. Will send out heavy reconnaissances to-day in all directions from that point. The general desires that you keep a good lookout upon Leesburg, to see if this movement has the effect to drive them away. Perhaps a slight demonstration on your part would have the effect to move them.

A. V. COLBURN,
Assistant Adjutant-General.

[Inclosure B.]

POOLESVILLE, *October* 20, 1861.

Major-General MCCLELLAN:

Made a feint of crossing at this place this afternoon, and at the same time started a reconnoitering party towards Leesburg from Harrison's

---

*See also McClellan's report, pp. 32-35, and Fry to McDowell, October 24, in " Correspondence, etc.," *post.*

Island. Enemy's pickets retired to intrenchments. Report of reconnoitering party not yet received. I have means of crossing 125 men once in ten minutes at each of two points. River falling slowly.

CHAS. P. STONE,
Brigadier-General.

GENERAL ORDERS, }　　HDQRS. ARMY OF THE POTOMAC,
　No. 31.　　}　　　　*Washington, October* 22, 1861.

The major-general commanding, with sincere sorrow, announces to the Army of the Potomac the death of Col. Edward D. Baker, who fell gloriously in battle on the evening of Monday, the 21st of October, 1861, near Leesburg, Va.

The gallant dead had many titles to honor. At the time of his death he was a member of the United States Senate for Oregon, and it is no injustice to any survivor to say that one of the most eloquent voices in that illustrious body has been silenced by his fall. As a patriot, zealous for the honor and interests of his adopted country, he has been distinguished in two wars, and has now sealed with his blood his devotion to the national flag. Cut off in the fullness of his powers as a statesman, and in the course of a brilliant career as a soldier, while the country mourns his loss, his brothers in arms will envy while they lament his fate. He died as a soldier would wish to die, amid the shock of battle, by voice and example animating his men to brave deeds.

The remains of the deceased will be interred in this city with the honors due to his rank, and the funeral arrangements will be ordered by Brig. Gen. Silas Casey.

As an appropriate mark of respect to the memory of the deceased, the usual badge of military mourning will be worn for the period of thirty days by the officers of the brigade lately under his command.

By command of Major-General McClellan:

S. WILLIAMS,
Assistant Adjutant-General.

GENERAL ORDERS, }　　HDQRS. ARMY OF THE POTOMAC,
　No. 32.　　}　　　　*Washington, October* 25, 1861.

The major-general commanding the Army of the Potomac desires to offer his thanks, and to express his admiration of their conduct, to the officers and men of the detachments of the Fifteenth and Twentieth Massachusetts, First California, and Tammany Regiments, the First U. S. Artillery, and Rhode Island Battery, engaged in the affair of Monday last near Harrison's Island. The gallantry and discipline there displayed deserved a more fortunate result; but situated as these troops were—cut off alike from retreat and re-enforcements, and attacked by an overwhelming force, 5,000 against 1,700—it was not possible that the issue could have been successful. Under happier auspices such devotion will insure victory. The general commanding feels increased confidence in General Stone's division, and is sure that when they next meet the enemy they will fully retrieve this check, for which they are not accountable.

By command of Major-General McClellan:

S. WILLIAMS,
Assistant Adjutant-General.

No. 2.

Reports of Brig. Gen. Charles P. Stone, U. S. Army, with orders.

HEADQUARTERS CORPS OF OBSERVATION,
Poolesville, October 19, 1861.

GENERAL: The following is the substance of information derived from an intelligent mulatto teamster, who deserted from the Thirteenth Mississippi Regiment, near Leesburg, and came in last night; was brought before me to-day.

Was at Manassas last week, Tuesday; went there to get a load of pickled pork, which came by railroad from Mississippi. At Manassas saw a great many fortifications; most of them built of bags of sand, some built of rails, with dirt thrown up in front. Saw a great many guns, all iron, rounded off like at the butt; saw as many as fifty of these guns; great many soldiers drilling them. They were expecting a fight at Fairfax Court-House and at Leesburg. He was at Fairfax Court-House on Tuesday last for a load of flour. They were then expecting an immediate attack there and were sending off large quantities of stores to Manassas. Went into the office with the wagon master to get a pass, and saw in another part of the room two gentlemen, said to be General Beauregard and General Davis. He described Beauregard accurately and Davis' face. He got back to Goose Creek on Wednesday afternoon. On Wednesday night there was an alarm that General Stone was crossing the river and the trains were all brought from Leesburg to Goose Creek; that he heard them say all the heavy baggage was in the trains and that the troops would fight at Leesburg, and then, if defeated, fall back to Widow Carter's Mill, below Goose Creek, where they would make another stand, and if defeated there they would fall back to Manassas; that the wagons were all kept ready to start for Manassas. He says they have near Leesburg four brass cannons, some rifled, drawn by four horses each; the ammunition carried in two-horse wagons. He says the railroad bridge on Goose Creek has not been rebuilt; and that the track is torn up for 3 miles south of the burnt bridge. States that General Evans is in command at Leesburg and Colonel Barksdale is in command of the Thirteenth Mississippi Regiment, to which he was attached as teamster.

I believe the fellow?s story. The evidences of the alarm he mentions were apparent, and it was probably induced by my strengthening the force on Harrison's Island and making use of a large flat-boat there. The place he mentions as the second for a stand (Mrs. Carter's Mill) is a strong position about 1 mile from Aldie, on the road from Leesburg to Gum Spring. The wagon trains rendezvous near that point.

I send herewith the Richmond Dispatch for Tuesday and Wednesday last, which was procured by our pickets on Harrison's Island this afternoon.

I have prepared slight intrenchments on Harrison's Island capable of covering several hundred men; sufficient to cover an advance of a considerable force to the island, and to hold it for an hour or two in spite of any artillery which might be placed on the commanding ground on the Virginia side.

Very respectfully, your obedient servant,

CHAS. P. STONE,
Brigadier-General, Commanding.

Maj. Gen. GEORGE B. MCCLELLAN,
Commanding Army of the Potomac.

HEADQUARTERS CORPS OF OBSERVATION,
Poolesville, October 29, 1861.

As much time must elapse before complete reports can be obtained from the various commanders of regiments, I have the honor to submit the following preliminary report of the operations of my command on the 21st instant.

On the 20th instant, being advised from headquarters of the movement of General McCall to Dranesville and to make a demonstration to draw out the intentions of the enemy at Leesburg,* I proceeded at 1 p. m. to Edwards Ferry with Gorman's brigade, the Seventh Michigan Regiment of Volunteers, two troops of the Van Alen Cavalry, and the Putnam Rangers, sending at the same time to Harrison's Island and vicinity four companies of the Fifteenth Massachusetts Volunteers, under Colonel Devens, who had already one company on the island, and Colonel Lee, with a battalion of the Twentieth Massachusetts Volunteers, and to Conrad's Ferry a section of Vaughan's Rhode Island Battery, and the Tammany Regiment, under Colonel Cogswell. A section of Bunting's New York State Militia battery, under Lieutenant Bramhall, was at the time on duty at Conrad's Ferry, and Ricketts' battery already posted at Edwards Ferry, under Lieutenant Woodruff.

The movement of General McCall on the day previous seemed to have attracted the attention of the enemy, as just before my arrival at Edwards Ferry a regiment of infantry had appeared from the direction of Leesburg, and taken shelter behind a wooded hill near Goose Creek, about 1¾ miles from our position at the ferry.

I ordered General Gorman to display his forces in view of the enemy, which was done without inducing any movement on their part, and then ordered three flat-boats to be passed from the canal into the river, at the same time throwing shells and spherical-case shot into and beyond the wood where the enemy were concealed and into all cover from which fire could be opened on boats crossing the river, to produce an impression that a crossing was to be made.

Orders were also sent to Colonel Devens, at Harrison's Island, 3½ to 4 miles up the river and nearly east of Leesburg, to detach Captain Philbrick, with 20 men, to cross from the island and explore by a path through the woods, little used, in the direction of Leesburg, to see if he could find anything concerning the enemy's position in that direction, but to retire and report on discovering any of the enemy.

The launching of the boats and shelling at Edwards Ferry caused the rapid retiring of the force which had been seen there, and I caused the embarkation of three boat loads of 35 men each from the First Minnesota Volunteers, who, under cover of the shelling, crossed and recrossed the river, the boats consuming in the passage four minutes, six minutes, and seven minutes, respectively. The spirit displayed by officers and men at the thought of passing the river was most cheering, and satisfied me that they could be depended on for most gallant service whenever something more than a demonstration might be required of them.

As darkness came on I ordered Gorman's brigade and the Seventh Michigan Volunteers back to their respective camps, but retained the Tammany Regiment, the companies of the Fifteenth Massachusetts Volunteers, and the artillery near Conrad's Ferry in their positions, awaiting the result of Captain Philbrick's scout, remaining with my staff at Edwards Ferry.

---

*See inclosure A to report No. 1, p. 290.

About 10 o'clock p. m. Lieutenant Howe, regimental quartermaster Fifteenth Massachusetts Volunteers, reported to me that Captain Philbrick had returned to the island after proceeding unmolested to within about a mile of Leesburg, and that he had there discovered, in the edge of a wood, an encampment of about thirty tents, which he had approached to within 25 rods without being challenged, the camp having no pickets out any distance in the direction of the river. I at once sent orders to Colonel Devens to cross four companies of his regiment to the Virginia shore, march silently, under cover of night, to the position of the camp referred to, to attack and destroy it at daybreak, pursue the enemy lodged there as far as would be prudent with his small force, and return rapidly to the island, his return to be covered by a company of the Massachusetts Twentieth, which was directed to be posted on the bluff directly over the landing place.

Colonel Devens was ordered to use this opportunity to observe the approaches to Leesburg and the position and force of any enemy in the vicinity, and in case he found no enemy or found him only weak, and a position where he could observe well and be secure until his party could be strengthened sufficiently to make a valuable reconnaissance which should safely ascertain the position and force of the enemy, to hold on and report.

Orders were dispatched to Colonel Baker to send the First California regiment to Conrad's Ferry, to arrive there at sunrise, and to have the remainder of his brigade in a state of readiness to move after an early breakfast. Also to Lieutenant-Colonel Ward, of the Fifteenth Massachusetts, to move with a battalion of the regiment to the river bank, opposite Harrison's Island, to arrive there by daybreak. Lieutenant French, of Ricketts' battery, was detached with two mountain howitzers, and ordered to the tow-path of the canal opposite Harrison's Island.

Colonel Devens, in pursuance of his orders, crossed the river and proceeded to the point indicated by the scouting party, Colonel Lee remaining on the bluff with 100 men to cover his return.

In order to distract attention from Colonel Devens' movement and at the same time to effect a reconnaissance in the direction of Leesburg from Edwards Ferry, I directed General Gorman to throw across the river at that point two companies of the First Minnesota Volunteers under the cover of a fire of Ricketts' battery, and sent out a party of 31 Van Alen Cavalry, under Major Mix, accompanied by Capt. Charles Stewart, assistant adjutant-general, Captain Murphy, Lieutenants Pierce and Gourand, with orders to advance along the Leesburg road until they should come to the vicinity of a battery which was known to be on that road and then turn to the left, and examine the heights between that and Goose Creek, see if any of the enemy were posted in the vicinity, ascertain as nearly as possible their number and disposition, examine the country with reference to the passage of troops to the Leesburg and Georgetown turnpike, and return rapidly to cover behind the skirmishers of the Minnesota First.

This reconnaissance was most gallantly conducted by all in the party, which proceeded along the Leesburg road nearly or quite 2 miles from the ferry, and when near the position of the hidden battery came suddenly upon a Mississippi regiment, about 35 yards distant, received its fire, and returned it with their pistols. The fire of the enemy killed 1 horse, but Lieutenant Gourand seized the dismounted man, and, drawing him on his horse behind him, carried him unhurt from the field. One private of the Fourth Virginia Cavalry was brought off by the party a prisoner. This prisoner being well mounted and armed, his mount replaced the one lost by the fire of the enemy. Meantime, on the right Colonel Devens having, in pursuance of his orders, arrived at the position indicated by the scouts as the site of the enemy's camp, found that the scouts had been deceived by the uncertain light, and had mistaken openings in the trees for a row of tents. He found, however, a wood, in which he concealed his force from view, and proceeded to examine the space between that and Leesburg, sending back to report that thus far he could see no enemy. Immediately on receipt of this intelligence (brought me by Lieutenant Howe, regimental quartermaster, who had accompanied both the parties), I ordered a non-commissioned officer and 10 cavalry to join Colonel Devens, for the purpose of scouring the country near him while engaged in his reconnaissance and giving due notice of the approach of any force, and that Lieutenant-Colonel Ward, with his battalion of the Fifteenth Massachusetts, should move on to Smart's Mill, half a mile to the right of the crossing place of Colonels Devens and Lee, where, in a strong position, he could watch and protect the flank of Colonel Devens in his return, and secure a second crossing place more favorable than the first, and connected by a good road with Leesburg.

Captain Candy, assistant adjutant-general on General Lander's staff, who did me the honor to serve through the day on mine, accompanied the cavalry, to serve with it.

For some reason never explained to me, neither of these orders was carried out. The cavalry were transferred to the Virginia shore, but were sent back without having left the shore to go inland, and thus Colonel Devens was deprived of the means of obtaining warning of any approach of the enemy. The battalion under Lieutenant-Colonel Ward was detained on the bluff in rear of Colonel Devens, instead of being directed to the right.

Colonel Baker, having arrived at Conrad's Ferry with the First California Regiment at an early hour in the morning, reported in person to me at Edwards Ferry, stating that the regiment was at its assigned post, the remainder of his brigade under arms ready to march, and asking for orders. I decided to send him to Harrison's Island to assume command, and in a full conversation with him explained the position of things as they then stood according to reports received; told him that General McCall had advanced his troops to Dranesville, and that I was extremely desirous of ascertaining the exact position and force of the enemy in our front, and exploring as far as it was safe on the right towards Leesburg and on the left towards the Leesburg and Gum Spring road; that I should continue to re-enforce the troops under General Gorman opposite Edwards Ferry, and try to push them carefully forward to discover the best line from that ferry to the Leesburg and Gum Spring road already mentioned, and pointed out to him the position of the breastworks and hidden battery which barred the movement of troops directly from left to right. I detailed to him the means of transportation across the river, of the sufficiency of which he was to be the judge; authorized him to make use of the guns of a section each of Vaughan's and Bunting's batteries, together with French's mountain howitzers, all the troops of his brigade and Cogswell's Tammany regiment, besides the Nineteenth and part of the Twentieth Regiments Massachusetts Volunteers, and left it to his discretion, after viewing the ground, to retire the troops from the Virginia shore under the cover of his guns and the fire of the large infantry force, or to pass over re-enforcements in case he found it practicable and the position on the other side strong and favorable; that I wished no advance made unless the enemy were in inferior force, and under no circumstances to pass beyond Leesburg, or a strong position between it and Goose Creek, on the Gum Spring (Manassas) road. I cautioned him in reference to passing artillery across the river, and begged him, if he did so, to see it well supported by good infantry. I pointed out to him the positions of some bluffs on this side the river from which artillery could act with effect on the other, and, leaving the matter of crossing more troops or retiring what were already over to his discretion, gave him entire control of operations on the right.

This gallant and energetic officer left me at about 9 or 9.30 a. m. and proceeded rapidly up the river to his charge. Re-enforcements were rapidly thrown to the Virginia side by General Gorman at Edwards Ferry, and his skirmishers and cavalry scouts advanced cautiously and steadily to the front and right, while the infantry lines were formed in such positions as to act rapidly and in concert in case of an advance of the enemy, and shells were thrown by Lieutenant Woodruff's Parrott guns into the woods beyond our lines as they gradually extended, especial care being taken to annoy the vicinity of the battery on the right.

Messengers from Harrison's Island informed me soon after the arrival of Colonel Baker opposite the island that he was crossing his whole force as rapidly as possible, and that he had caused an additional flatboat to be lifted from the canal into the river, and had provided a line by which to cross the boats more rapidly.

During the morning a sharp skirmish took place between two of the advanced companies of the Massachusetts Fifteenth and a body about 100 strong of Mississippi riflemen, during which a body of the enemy's cavalry appeared, causing Colonel Devens to fall back in good order on Colonel Lee's position; after which he again advanced, his officers and men behaving admirably, fighting, retiring, and advancing in perfect order, and exhibiting every proof of high courage and good discipline. Had he at this time had the cavalry scouting party which was sent him in the morning, but which most unfortunately had been turned back without his knowledge, he could doubtless have had timely warning of the approach of the superior force which afterwards overwhelmed his regiment and their brave commander and comrades.

Thinking that Colonel Baker might be able to use more artillery I dispatched to him two additional pieces of Vaughan's battery, supported by two companies of infantry, with directions to its officer to come into position below the place of crossing and report to Colonel Baker. My opinion was justified by his suggesting the same thing later in the day, and only a short time before the guns must have arrived.

After Colonel Devens' second advance Colonel Baker seems to have gone to the field in person, and I am sorry to say he has left no record of what officers and men he charged with the care of the boats and insuring the regular passage of the troops. If any were charged with this duty it was not performed, for it appears that the re-enforcements as they arrived found no system enforced, and the boats delayed most unnecessarily in transporting back, a few at a time, the wounded as they happened to arrive, with their attendants. Had an efficient officer with one company remained at each landing guarding the boats, their full capacity would have been made serviceable, and sufficient men would have passed on to secure the success of his operation. The forwarding of artillery (necessarily a slow process) before its supporting force of infantry also impeded the rapid assembling of an imposing force on the Virginia shore. The infantry, which was waiting with impatience, should have been first transported, and this alone would have made a difference in the infantry line at the time of attack of at least 1,000 men; enough to have turned the scale in our favor.

At about 12.30 or 1 o'clock p. m. the enemy appeared in force in front of Colonel Devens, and a sharp skirmish ensued, which was maintained for a considerable time by the Fifteenth Massachusetts, unsupported, and, finding himself about to be outflanked, Colonel Devens retired a short distance in good order, and took up a position in the edge of a wood about half or three-quarters of a mile in front of the position of Colonel Lee, where he remained until 2 o'clock p. m., when he again fell back, with the approval of Colonel Baker, and took his place in line with those portions of the Twentieth Massachusetts and First California Regiments which had arrived. Colonel Baker immediately formed his line and awaited the attack of the enemy, which came upon him with great vigor about 3 o'clock p. m., and was met with admirable spirit by our troops, who, though evidently struggling against largely superior numbers (nearly if not quite three to one), maintained their ground and a most destructive fire on the enemy. Colonel Cogswell, with a small portion of his regiment, succeeded in reaching the field in the midst of the heaviest fire, and they came gallantly into action with a yell which wavered the enemy's line.

Lieutenant Bramhall, of Bunting's battery, had succeeded, after extraordinary exertion and labor, in bringing up a piece of the Rhode Island Battery, and Lieutenant French, First Artillery, his two mountain howitzers; but while for a short time these maintained a well-directed fire, both officers and nearly all the men were soon borne away wounded, and the pieces were hauled to the rear to prevent their falling into the hands of the enemy.

At about 4 p. m. Colonel Baker, pierced by a number of bullets, fell at the front of his command while cheering his men, and by his own example sustaining the obstinate resistance they were making.

Colonel Lee then took command, and prepared to commence throwing our forces to the rear, but Colonel Cogswell, of the Tammany regiment, being found to be senior in rank, assumed the command, and ordered dispositions to be made immediately for marching to the left and cutting a way through to Edwards Ferry. Unfortunately, just as the first dispositions were being made, an officer of the enemy rode rapidly in front of the Tammany regiment and beckoned them towards the enemy. Whether the Tammany understood this as an order from one of our officers or an invitation to close work, is not known; but the men responded to the gesture with a yell, and charged forward, carrying with them in their advance the rest of the line, which soon received a murderous fire from the enemy at close distance. Our officers rapidly recalled the men, but in the position they had now got into it was impracticable to make the movement designed, and Colonel Cogswell reluctantly gave the order to retire. The enemy pursued our troops to the edge of the bluff over the landing place, and thence poured in a heavy fire on our men, who were endeavoring to cross to the island.

Rapid as the retreat necessarily was, there was no neglect of orders. The men formed near the river, deployed as skirmishers, and maintained for twenty minutes or more the unequal and hopeless contest rather than surrender. The smaller boats had disappeared, no one knew where. The largest boat, rapidly and too heavily loaded, swamped at 15 feet from the shore, and nothing was left to our soldiers but to swim, surrender, or die. With a devotion worthy of the cause they were serving, officers and men, while quarter was being offered to such as would lay down their arms, stripped themselves of their swords and muskets and hurled them out into the river to prevent their falling into the hands of the foe, and saved themselves as they could by swimming, floating on logs and concealing themselves in the bushes and forest to make their way up and down the river bank to a place of crossing.

The instances of personal gallantry of the highest order were so many, that it would be unjust now to detail particular cases. Officers displayed for their men and men for their officers that beautiful devotion which is only to be found among true soldiers.

While these scenes were being enacted on the right, I was preparing on the left for a rapid push forward to the road by which the enemy would retreat if driven, and entirely unsuspicious of the perilous condition of our troops on the right. The additional artillery had already been sent in anticipation, and when I questioned the messenger who left the field about 3 o'clock as to Colonel Baker's position, he informed me that the colonel, when he left, seemed to feel perfectly secure and could doubtless hold his own in case he should not advance. The same statement was made by another messenger half an hour later, and I watched anxiously for a sign of advance on the right, in order to push forward General Gorman. It was, as had been explained to Colonel Baker, impracticable to throw Gorman's brigade directly to the right by reason of the battery in the woods, between which we had never been able to reconnoiter.

At about 4 p. m. I telegraphed to General Banks, requesting him to send a brigade from his division, intending it to occupy the ground on this side the river near Harrison's Island, which would be abandoned in case of a rapid advance, and shortly after, as the fire slackened above, I awaited a messenger on whose tidings I should give orders either for the advance of Gorman to cut off the retreat of the enemy or for dispositions for the night in our present position.

Captain Candy arrived from the field of Colonel Baker a little before 5 p. m. and announced to me the melancholy tidings of Colonel Baker's death, having no news of any further disaster, but stating that re-enforcements were slow. I instantly telegraphed to Major-General Banks and the major-general commanding the fact of Colonel Baker's death, and rode rapidly to the right to assume command.

Before arriving opposite the island the evidences of the disaster began to be met in men who had crossed the river by swimming, and on reaching the boat landing the fact was asserted in such a manner as not to be doubted. The reports brought me of the enemy's force were highly exaggerated, it being stated at 10,000 men. I gave orders for the island to be held for the removal of the wounded, established a patrol on the tow-path from opposite the island to the line of pickets near the Monocacy, and returned to the left to secure the troops there from disaster, preparing means of removing them as rapidly as possible.

Orders arrived from headquarters Army of the Potomac to hold the island and Virginia shore at Edwards Ferry at all hazards, promising re-enforcements, and I caused additional intrenching tools to be forwarded to General Gorman, with instructions to intrench and hold out against whatever force might appear.

I should add, that having learned that General Hamilton, with his brigade, was on the march from Darnestown before I left to go to the right, I caused orders to intercept him, and instructed him to repair to Conrad's Ferry, where I had orders awaiting him to so dispose of his force as to give protection to Harrison's Island and protect the line of the river.

Early in the night the telegraph informed me that Major-General Banks was on his way with his division to re-enforce me, and at about 3 o'clock a. m. the general arrived and assumed command.

A report of my division for the following days will be speedily made out and forwarded.

I cannot conclude this report without bearing testimony to the courage, good discipline, and conduct of all the troops of this division during the day, the events of which have been related in this hurriedly-written report. Those in action behaved like veterans, and those not brought into action showed that alacrity and steadiness in their movements which proved their anxiety to engage the foe in their country's cause.

We mourn the loss of the brave departed dead on the field of honor, if not of success; and we miss the companionship of those of our comrades who have fallen into the hands of our enemies. But all feel that they have earned the title of soldier, and all await with increased confidence another measurement of strength with the foe.

Very respectfully, I am, general, your most obedient servant,

CHAS. P. STONE,
Brigadier-General, Commanding.

Brig. Gen. S. WILLIAMS,
Assistant Adjutant-General, Headquarters Army of the Potomac.

HEADQUARTERS CORPS OF OBSERVATION,
Poolesville, October 20, 1861.

Col. CHARLES DEVENS,
Commanding Fifteenth Regiment Massachusetts Volunteers:

COLONEL: You will please send orders to the canal to have the two new flat-boats now there opposite the island transferred to the river, and will at 3 o'clock p. m. have the island re-enforced by all of your regiment now on duty on the canal and at the New York battery.

The pickets will be replaced by the companies of the Nineteenth Massachusetts there.

Very respectfully, your obedient servant,

CHAS. P. STONE,
Brigadier-General.

SPECIAL ORDERS, } HEADQUARTERS CORPS OF OBSERVATION,
No. —.   } *Poolesville, October* 20, 1861—10.30 p. m.

Colonel Devens will land opposite Harrison's Island with five companies of his regiment, and proceed to surprise the camp of the enemy discovered by Captain Philbrick in the direction of Leesburg. The landing and march will be effected with silence and rapidity.

Colonel Lee, Twentieth Massachusetts Volunteers, will immediately after Colonel Devens' departure occupy Harrison's Island with four companies of his regiment, and will cause the four-oared boat to be taken across the island to the point of departure of Colonel Devens.

One company will be thrown across to occupy the heights on the Virginia shore after Colonel Devens' departure to cover his return.

Two mountain howitzers will be taken silently up the tow-path, and carried to the opposite side of the island under the orders of Colonel Lee.

Colonel Devens will attack the camp of the enemy at daybreak, and, having routed them, will pursue them as far as he deems prudent, and will destroy the camp, if practicable, before returning. He will make all the observations possible on the country; will, under all circumstances, keep his command well in hand, and not sacrifice them to any supposed advantage of rapid pursuit.

Having accomplished this duty, Colonel Devens will return to his present position, unless he shall see one on the Virginia side, near the river, which he can undoubtedly hold until re-enforced, and one which can be successfully held against largely superior numbers. In such case he will hold on and report.

CHAS. P. STONE,
Brigadier-General.

Great care will be used by Colonel Devens to prevent any unnecessary injury of private property, and any officer or soldier straggling from the command for curiosity or plunder will be instantly shot.

CHAS. P. STONE,
Brigadier-General.

—

HEADQUARTERS CORPS OF OBSERVATION,
Poolesville, November 2, 1861.

GENERAL: The persistent attacks made upon me by the friends (so called), of the lamented late Colonel Baker, through the newspaper press, have made it my duty to call the attention of the major-general commanding to distinct violations of my orders and instructions to that officer in the affair of October 21st ultimo, more pointedly than it has been my wish to do in an official report concerning one who is no more. Painful as it may be to censure the acts of one who has gallantly died on the field of battle, justice to myself and to those who served under me requires that the full truth should be made to appear. Up to this time duties more imperative have engrossed my time. I could not, for the purpose of shielding myself from unjust popular censure, neglect the care which I owed to the comfort and well-being of the thousands of men under my command, and especially the measures necessary to the comfort and recovery of the numerous wounded in our hospitals. Meantime I have been fiercely attacked in some newspapers, which have not waited for official reports, but have seized upon every word of any friend of the late colonel who might choose to invent or color a description of the disaster. Every false statement has been pronounced to be true, unless denied by myself, who have had too many and too important duties to permit me to write to the public prints, even were such a course allowable to a soldier.

I will, in anticipation of my final report, which cannot be presented until the subordinate reports shall all come in, relate a few facts which will clearly show who was responsible for the defeat of our troops at Ball's Bluff. At 7 o'clock in the morning there were between Harrison's Island and Leesburg, on the Virginia side, only six companies of our troops, which, under the cover of two guns then on the island, of four guns on the Maryland shore, and the large infantry force there, might easily have been withdrawn even in the face of a largely-superior force, and with the means of transportation which I knew to be there. It was my strongly expressed desire that, if a respectable force should threaten, this one should be withdrawn, and Colonel Baker left me at Edwards Ferry with a full knowledge of my desire and with full power to withdraw it. He knew as well as I that should he attempt to re-enforce them his means of transportation were very limited, and yet before he ever reached the island he stated to Lieutenant Howe, Fifteenth Massachusetts Volunteers, that he should cross over with all the force at his command. At the distance I was from his position I could only judge that he was satisfied of his ability to cross in force in time to meet the enemy, for he then knew, what had not reached my ears and did not for more than half an hour afterwards, that a hostile force had approached Colonel Devens and discovered him and his command.

It has been asserted and published that Colonel Baker received an order from me to attack Leesburg on Sunday, the 20th. It is absurd. Colonel Baker did not receive an order from me of any kind on Sunday, nor any order until about 2 o'clock on Monday morning, when he received one directing him to send one regiment to Conrad's Ferry and to hold the remainder of his brigade in readiness to march. (A copy of this order is herewith forwarded.) He was not in any manner informed of the object of the movement, which was intended solely to insure the safe return of Colonel Devens and his command, until his arrival at Edwards Ferry on Monday morning. The order, stained with blood, found in his hat has been somewhat altered either by the stains or by "friendly" hands, which may easily happen in a pencil order; but even in that as published, and still stronger as it was written, he was to use his discretion about crossing his force or retiring that already over. The "friends" of Colonel Baker state that on his receiving that order he exclaimed, "I will obey General Stone's order, but it is my death-warrant." Shame upon them to put false words in the mouth of the brave dead! Colonel Baker received that order from my own hands on the field and at his own request, that he might "have some written authority for assuming command" (I use his own words), and seemed delighted at receiving it; this after the fullest and freest explanation in person of all that was known up to that time to have transpired—a full statement of the slight means of transportation across the river, and the use that could be made of artillery and infantry from this side and from the island in covering the return of the force then over.

The change of destination of five companies of infantry which I had ordered into a strong mill on the right of Devens' line was sanctioned by Colonel Baker, whose object seems to have been not that of, under any circumstances, withdrawing our small force from the face of a superior one, but the holding of that superior force in check until he could try conclusions with it, and this with a full knowledge of what he knew I must be ignorant of, viz, that the small force had been discovered and engaged. There was plenty of time for withdrawing those troops, and he alone, within reporting distance, had the power to withdraw them. Colonel Devens received notification early in the day that Colonel Baker had assumed command, but received no order or message from him until 2.15 p. m., when he (Devens) had been pressed back to the final line of battle. That Colonel Baker was determined at all hazards to fight a battle is clear from the fact that he never crossed to examine the field, never gave an order to the troops in the advance, and never sent forward to ascertain their position until he had ordered over his force and passed over a considerable portion of it. From the time that he left me for several hours but one message was received by me directly from him, and that one was simply to state that he had decided to cross, and was increasing his means of transportation by a large boat lifted from the canal. I warned him, when I ascertained it, that I believed 4,000 troops would be opposed to him; there was still time to retire, and when he replied, "I shall not retire," I had no doubt, and I have now no doubt, that he felt perfectly able to meet that force.

I must now touch a point that I would gladly leave unnoticed, but which the friends of the late colonel, in their efforts to crush another, force to the light. The troops were most unfortunately posted, whether the intention was to drive the enemy or to hold the position assumed and await re-enforcements. Colonel Baker had on the field between 1,600 and 1,700 bayonets. A short distance in his rear was a steep bluff, and immediately behind that bluff the river Potomac. On his left was a valley, and on the opposite side of that valley (which opened on the river) was a wooded hill. This wooded hill, giving access to the rear of his left flank, might have been expected to be taken advantage of by an active enemy, and from the nature of the position a reserve could be valuable only at the edge of the bluff. Yet Colonel Baker sacrificed from his line four stout companies to form a reserve near the center, which reserve could do nothing in the battle but shoot down his own men in the line, and at the same time they were posted so near the line and so in the open ground as to be exposed to a galling fire from the enemy during the entire action.

A second reserve was posted near the opening of the valley guarding the left flank, the true point of defense of which was far in advance, and only two companies of skirmishers were thrown out to the left flank. The two companies of skirmishers were able to arrest the progress of an entire regiment moving to turn his left flank, and they bravely held that regiment at bay for 20 minutes, but were finally overcome and destroyed. How different the result would have been if his two reserves had been employed in extending his line to cover his weak point it is mournful now to think.

When the determined two companies of the California regiment brought an entire regiment on the charge to a halt, and forced it first to open fire, and then to waver before their well-maintained fire from the wood, had the two reserves been there to charge, instead of standing idle lookers-on and yet exposed to a galling fire, the force which at last turned his left flank would have been thrown in confusion upon the enemy's right, and victory would have been Baker's, instead of defeat and death. As the troops were arranged on the field I feel that increased force would only have given us increased loss. The plain truth is that this brave and impetuous officer was determined at all hazards to bring on an action, and made use of the discretion allowed him to do it. Had his eye for advantage of ground in posting troops equaled his daring courage, he would have been to-day an honored, victorious general of the Republic, instead of a lamented statesman lost too soon to the country.

Very respectfully, I am, general, your most obedient servant,

CHAS. P. STONE,
Brigadier-General, Commanding.

Brig. Gen. S. WILLIAMS,
Assistant Adjutant-General.

[Inclosure.]

HEADQUARTERS CORPS OF OBSERVATION,
Edwards Ferry, October 20, 1861—11 p. m.

COLONEL: You will send the California regiment (less the camp guard) to Conrad's Ferry, to arrive there at sunrise and await orders. The men will take with them blankets and overcoats and forty rounds of ammunition in boxes, and will be followed by one day's rations in wagons. The remainder of the brigade will be held in readiness for marching orders (leaving camp guards) at 7 o'clock a. m. to-morrow, and will all have breakfasted before that hour.

Very respectfully, your most obedient servant,

CHAS. P. STONE,
Brigadier-General, Commanding.

Col. E. D. BAKER, *Commanding Third Brigade.*

[Memorandum.]

The above order was sent by the hands of Captain Candy, assistant adjutant-general, who left Edwards Ferry at about 11.30 o'clock p. m. on the 20th. As the distance to Colonel Baker's camp was between 4 and 5 miles, and as many guards and pickets had to be passed, it is probable that the order was delivered between 1 and 2 o'clock a. m., 21st October. This order was followed by a verbal one, sent by Dr. J. S. Mackie, volunteer aide-de-camp, cautioning Colonel Baker not to allow his troops to march with music, but to have the march silent as possible; and to prevent accidental discharge of fire-arms, he was ordered to see that the men marched with unloaded arms.

CHAS. P. STONE,
Brigadier-General.

———

Copies of orders alluded to in the foregoing report as found in the hat of Col. E. D. Baker after his death.

HEADQUARTERS CORPS OF OBSERVATION,
Edwards Ferry, October 21—11.50.

Col. E. D. BAKER, *Commanding Brigade:*

COLONEL: I am informed that the force of the enemy is about 4,000, all told. If you can push them, you may do so as far as to have a strong position near Leesburg, if you can keep them before you, avoiding their batteries. If they pass Leesburg and take the Gum Spring road you will not follow far, but seize the first good position to cover that road. Their design is to draw us on, if they are obliged to retreat, as far as Goose Creek, where they can be re-enforced from Manassas and have a strong position.

Report frequently, so that when they are pushed Gorman can come in on their flank.

Yours, respectfully and truly,

CHAS. P. STONE,
Brigadier-General, Commanding.

HEADQUARTERS CORPS OF ——— [Torn off],
Edwards Ferry, October 21, 1861.

Col. E. D. BAKER, *Commanding Brigade:*

COLONEL: In case of heavy firing in front of Harrison's Island, you will advance the California regiment of your brigade or retire the regiments under Colonels Lee and Devens upon the Virginia side of the river, at your discretion, assuming command on arrival.

Very respectfully, colonel, your most obedient servant,

CHAS. P. STONE,
Brigadier-General, Commanding.

HEADQUARTERS CORPS OF OBSERVATION,
Poolesville, November 6, 1861.

GENERAL: I have the honor to inclose herewith memoranda of the river transportation which Brigadier-General Gorman and Colonel Baker respectively had at their disposition on the morning of October 21, ultimo.
Very respectfully, I am, general, your obedient servant,

CHAS. P. STONE,
Brigadier-General, Commanding.

[Inclosures.]

River transportation at Edwards' Ferry at the disposition of Brigadier-General Gorman, October 21, 1861.

HEADQUARTERS CORPS OF OBSERVATION,
Poolesville, November 6, 1861.

Three flat-boats, newly constructed, each 25 feet long, 12 feet wide, 2 feet deep; 1 four-oared ship's boat; 1 small flat-boat, new; 2 skiffs. The easy capacity of the above was as follows:
Each of the three large flat-boats, 40; total, 120; four-oared ship's boat, besides oarsmen, 12; small flat, 12; skiffs, 12; total easy capacity, 156 men; the possible capacity, at least one-third greater, 52; total capacity, 208. The longest time occupied in crossing by large flat-boats in calm day trial, 7 minutes; shortest time, 4 minutes, each containing in trial 35 men. On the morning of October 21 General Gorman added to his transportation a large decked flat-boat, taken from the canal; easy capacity, 66 men.

CHAS. P. STONE,
Brigadier-General, Commanding.

River transportation opposite Harrison's Island, October 21, 1861, *at the disposition of Col. E. D. Baker.*

One new flat-boat, 27 feet long, 12 feet wide, 2 feet deep, newly constructed, tested with weight of 65 men, with which it settled but four inches in the water, convenient capacity, say, 45 men; 1 new flat-boat, 25 feet long, 12 feet wide, 2 feet deep, just constructed, convenient capacity, say, 40 men; 1 second-hand ferry-boat, which had been used by the pickets occupying Harrison's Island (had carried 50 men), capacity, say, 50 men; 1 metallic life-boat, four-oared, in perfect order, which had frequently and safely carried 25 men; 2 skiffs, which had carried 8 each, easy capacity 12 men; total capacity of boats in water and ready for use at 6 a. m., 172 men. To this transportation was added during the morning a new ferry-boat lifted from the canal, 48 feet long, 10 feet wide, easy capacity 100 men; total, 272 men.
Of these boats, two-thirds should have been kept running between the Maryland shore and the island; one-third between the island and Virginia shore. Managed with order and regularity, the trips could have been made with ease once in ten minutes, throwing across 180 men each trip, or 1,080 men every hour; allowing one trip in 15 minutes, 720 men every hour.

CHAS. P. STONE,
Brigadier-General, Commanding.

Correspondence relative to the flag of truce sent for the benefit of the wounded at Leesburg.

HEADQUARTERS CORPS OF OBSERVATION,
Poolesville, November 7, 1861.

GENERAL: I have the honor to forward herewith papers marked 1, 2, 3, 4, 5, 6, concerning a flag of truce sent for the recovery of the body of the late Captain Alden, Tammany regiment, and for the benefit of our wounded at Leesburg. The following money and supplies were sent, viz: $100 in coin, 24 blankets, 24 flannel shirts, 24 pairs socks, and a supply of tea, sugar, and salt.

Hoping that the action taken in this matter will meet the approval of the Major-General Commanding-in-Chief, I am, general, very respectfully, your most obedient servant,

CHAS. P. STONE,
Brigadier-General, Commanding.

Brig. Gen. S. WILLIAMS,
A. A. G., Hdqrs. Army Potomac, Washington, D. C.

[Inclosure No. 1.]

HEADQUARTERS,
Poolesville, October 30, 1861.

Brigadier-General Stone presents his compliments to the general commanding the forces in the vicinity of Leesburg, Va., and begs to know if the body of an officer buried on the field of the late action of October 21 can be disinterred and brought away by his friends and whether letters and supplies can be transmitted under flag of truce to the prisoners captured in the same action. Should it meet the views of the general commanding the forces at Leesburg, General Stone would be happy to dispatch an officer of rank to Edwards Ferry, to confer with one who may be designated on the other part.

CHAS. P. STONE,
Brigadier-General, Commanding.

[Inclosure No. 2.]

LEESBURG, VA., *October* 30, 1861.

Brigadier-General Evans presents his regards to General Stone, and reports that the subject-matter of his letter will be forwarded for the consideration of the general commanding the Army of the Potomac. General Evans would, however, assure General Stone that the prisoners of the U. S. Army now here are properly cared for.

N. G. EVANS,
Brigadier-General, C. S. Army.

[Inclosure No. 3.]

EDWARDS FERRY, *November* 4, 1861.

Memorandum made this 4th day of November, 1861, at 4.45 p. m., by the bearer of a flag to the Virginia shore, opposite Edwards Ferry, immediately upon the return of the flag.

The flag was received by Lieutenant-Colonel Jenifer, attended by Captain Rogers, of General Evans' staff, Lieutenant Clark, and an escort of cavalry. Five inclosures for General Stone, or to his care, were delivered to the bearer. The bearer was informed that a party might present itself on the following day at 9 a. m. at Harrison's Island, near the scene of the affair of the 21st, cross and recover the buried body of a captain and probably of any other buried dead. Money and clothes might be sent to the wounded and probably little comforts, though it was alleged they did not need them. Open letters for prisoners would probably be received. Where a positive answer was not returned, it was promised in the morning. Entire courtesy was shown by the party receiving the flag.

FRANCIS WINTHROP PALFREY,
Lieut. Col., Comdg. 20th Regt. Mass. Vols., Bearer of the Flag.

NOTE.—Error of date. The occurrence took place November 5, at the hours stated.

C. P. S.

[Inclosure No. 4.]

HEADQUARTERS CONFEDERATE FORCES,
Leesburg, November 4, 1861.

The compliments of General Evans to General Stone, and informs him that there are but a few of his wounded now at this place, and are as comfortable as their wounds will permit. No objection is entertained, however, to General Stone's sending them such supplies of clothing, money, &c., as he may deem necessary. An officer with the rank of lieutenant-colonel will meet an officer of like grade of the Federal forces at Edwards Ferry to make arrangements for the disinterment and removal of the remains of the officer requested by General Stone.

N. G. EVANS,
Brigadier-General, C. S. Army.

[Inclosure No. 5.]

HEADQUARTERS, POOLESVILLE, MD.,
November 5, 1861.

General Stone presents his compliments to General Evans, and acknowledges the receipt of his communication of the 4th instant, through Lieutenant-Colonel Jenifer. In accordance with the terms of General Evans' appreciated note, the sum of $100 is sent herewith, for the benefit of the wounded of the United States service now at Leesburg, together with some articles of clothing which may add to their comfort, and a few hospital stores. Lieutenant-Colonel Palfrey will, as arranged with Lieutenant-Colonel Jenifer, be at Harrison's Island to-morrow morning at 9 o'clock to attend to the disinterment of the body of the late Captain Alden. General Stone takes this occasion to express his appreciation of General Evans' soldierly courtesy, which the former will be at all times happy to reciprocate.

CHAS. P. STONE,
Brigadier-General.

[Inclosure No. 6.]

Lieutenant-Colonel Palfrey, accompanied by Lieutenant Garland, of the Tammany regiment, Captain Brown, and a lieutenant of the Thirty-fourth New York Volunteers, Mr. Comstock (friend of the late Captain

Alden), and assistants, crossed at Harrison's Island, November 6, at 9 a. m.   Had a courteous interview with Lieutenant-Colonel Jenifer, to whom were delivered the stores and money intended for the wounded of our forces at Leesburg.   The body of Captain Alden was disinterred and removed.   Lieutenant-Colonel Jenifer assured Lieutenant-Colonel Palfrey that the wounded of our troops at Leesburg were as well cared for as their own wounded.   He also stated that six of our wounded had died and that our dead had all been buried; that none of the field and staff of the Twentieth Massachusetts were wounded; that Colonel Cogswell was slightly wounded in the finger, and nowhere else.

(From report of Lieutenant-Colonel Palfrey.)

CHAS. P. STONE,
Brigadier-General, Commanding.

—

POOLESVILLE, *December* 2, 1861.

Lieutenant-Colonel HARDIE, *Aide-de-Camp* :

Stated concisely, the narrative would be this:

General Stone directed Colonel Baker to go to the right and in his discretion to recall the troops then over the river or cross more force. Colonel Baker made up his mind and declared it before he reached the crossing place, to cross with his whole force.

General Stone directed five companies to be thrown into a strong mill on the right of Ball's Bluff.   Colonel Baker allowed these companies to be diverted to the front.

General Stone sent cavalry scouts to be thrown out in advance of the infantry on the right.   Colonel Baker allowed this cavalry to return without scouting and did not replace it, although he had plenty at his disposition.

Colonel Baker assumed command on the right about 10 a. m., but never sent an order or messenger to the advanced infantry until it was pressed back to the bluff about 2.15 p. m.

Colonel Baker spent more than an hour in personally superintending the lifting of a boat from the canal to the river, when a junior officer or sergeant would have done as well, the mean time neglecting to visit or give orders to the advanced force in the face of the enemy.

No order of passage was arranged for the boats; no guards were established at the landing; no boats' crews detailed.

Lastly, the troops were so arranged on the field as to expose them all to fire, while but few could fire on the enemy.   His troops occupied all the cleared ground in the neighborhood, while the enemy had the woods and the commanding wooded height, which last he might easily have occupied before the enemy came up.

The within narrative will be sent to-morrow, unless, as to-day, important duties prevent its being finished.

CHAS. P. STONE.

No. 3.

*Return of casualties in the Union forces in the engagement at Ball's Bluff, Virginia,
October 21, 1861.**

Command.	Killed.		Wounded.		Missing.		Aggregate.
	Officers.	Enlisted men.	Officers.	Enlisted men.	Officers.	Enlisted men.	
Fifteenth Massachusetts	2	12	4	57	8	219	302
Twentieth Massachusetts	†2	13	6	38	6	129	194
Forty-second New York	3	4		6	6	114	133
Sixth New York Battery			1				1
Seventy-first Pennsylvania	3	10	3	37	6	222	281
First Rhode Island Artillery, Battery B				5		4	9
First United States Artillery, Battery I			1				1
Total	10	39	15	143	26	688	921

No. 4.

Report of Col. Charles Devens, Fifteenth Massachusetts Infantry.

HDQRS. FIFTEENTH REGIMENT MASS. VOLUNTEERS,
Poolesville, Md., October 23, 1861.

GENERAL: I respectfully report that about 12 o'clock Sunday night, October 20, I crossed the Potomac by your order from Harrison's Island to the Virginia shore with five companies, numbering about 300 men, of my regiment, with the intention of taking a rebel camp, reported by scouts to be situated at the distance of about a mile from the river, of destroying the same, of observing the country around, and of returning to the river, or of waiting and reporting if I thought myself able to remain for re-enforcements, or if I found a position capable of being defended against a largely superior force. Having only three boats, which together conveyed about 30 men, it was nearly 4 o'clock when all the force was transferred to the opposite shore. We passed down the river about 60 rods by a path discovered by the scouts, and then up the bluff known as Ball's Bluff, where we found an open field surrounded by woods. At this point we halted until daybreak, being joined here by a company of 100 men from the Twentieth Massachusetts, accompanied by Colonel Lee, who were to protect our return.

At daybreak we pushed forward our reconnaissance towards Leesburg to the distance of about a mile from the river, to a spot supposed to be the site of the rebel encampment, but found on passing through the woods that the scouts had been deceived by a line of trees on the brow of the slope, the opening through which presented, in an uncertain light, somewhat the appearance of a line of tents. Leaving the detachment in the woods, I proceeded with Captain Philbrick and two or three scouts across the slope and along the other line of it, observing Leesburg, which was in full view, and the country about it, as carefully as possible, and seeing but four tents of the enemy. My force being

* Compiled from records in Adjutant-General's Office.
† Including one drowned.

well concealed by the woods, and having no reason to believe my presence was discovered, and no large number of the enemy's tents being in sight, I determined not to return at once, but to report to yourself, which I did, by directing Quartermaster Howe to repair at once to Edwards Ferry to state these facts, and to say that in my opinion I could remain until I was re-enforced.

The means of transportation between the island and the Virginia shore had been strengthened, I knew, at daybreak, by a large boat, which would convey 60 or 70 men at once, and as the boat could cross and recross every ten minutes, I had no reason to suppose there would be any difficulty in sending over 500 men in an hour, as it was known there were two large boats between the island and the Maryland shore, which would convey to the island all the troops that could be conveyed from it to the Virginia shore.

Mr. Howe left me with his instructions at about 6.30 a. m., and during his absence, at about 7 o'clock, a company of riflemen, who had probably discovered us, were reported on our right upon the road from Conrad's Ferry. I directed Captain Philbrick, Company H, to pass up over the slope and attack them, while Captain Rockwood, Company A, was ordered to proceed to the right and cut off their retreat in the direction of Conrad's Ferry, and accompany Captain Philbrick as he proceeded to execute the order. Captain Philbrick's command proceeded over the slope of the hill, and the enemy retreated down on the other side, taking the direction of a corn field in which the corn had lately been cut and stood in the shocks. The first volley was fired by them from a ditch or trench, into which they retreated. It was immediately returned by our men, and the skirmish continued hotly for some minutes. I had ordered Captain Forehand, Company G, to re-enforce Captain Philbrick, but a body of rebel cavalry being reported on our left, I directed Captain Philbrick to return to the wood, lest he might be cut off from the main body of the detachment. This he did in good order.

In the skirmish 9 men of Company H were wounded, 1 killed, and 2 were missing at its close, although the field was carefully examined by Captain Philbrick and myself before we left it. They probably were wounded and crawled into the bush, which was growing in portions of it.

On returning to the wood I remained waiting for an attack for perhaps half an hour. At the end of this time, as my messenger did not return, I deemed it prudent to join Colonel Lee, which I did; but after remaining with him upon the bluff a short time, and having thoroughly scouted the woods, I returned to my first position.

I was rejoined at 8 a. m. by Quartermaster Howe, who reported to me that I was to remain where I was, and would be re-enforced, and that Lieutenant-Colonel Ward would proceed to Smart's Mill with the remainder of the regiment, that a communication should be kept up between us, and that 10 cavalry would report to me for the purpose of reconnoitering. For some reason they never appeared or reported to me, but I have since learned they came as far as the bluff. If they had reported to me, they could have rendered excellent service. I directed Quartermaster Howe to return at once and report the skirmish that had taken place, and threw out a company of skirmishers to the brow of the hill, and also to my right and left, to await the arrival of more troops.

At about 10 o'clock Quartermaster Howe returned and stated that he had reported the skirmish of the morning, and that Colonel Baker would shortly arrive with his brigade and take command. Between 9

and 11 o'clock I was joined by Lieutenant-Colonel Ward with the remainder of my regiment, making, in all, a force of 625 men, with 28
officers, from my regiment, as reported to me by the adjutant, many of
the men of the regiment being at this time on other duty.

About 12 o'clock it was reported to me a force was gathering on my
left, and about 12.30 o'clock a strong attack was made on my left by a
body of infantry concealed in the woods and upon the skirmishers in
front by a body of cavalry. The fire of the enemy was resolutely
returned by the regiment, which maintained its ground with entire
determination. Re-enforcements not yet having arrived, and the attempts of the enemy to outflank us being very vigorous, I directed
the regiment to retire about 60 paces into an open space in the wood,
and prepare to receive any attack that might be made, while I called
in my skirmishers. When this was done I returned to the bluff, where
Colonel Baker had already arrived. This was at 2.15 p. m. He directed me to form my regiment at the right of the position he proposed
to occupy, which was done by eight companies, the center and left
being composed of a detachment of the Twentieth Massachusetts, numbering about 300 men, under command of Colonel Lee. A battalion of
the California regiment, numbering about 600 men, Lieutenant-Colonel
Wistar commanding; 2 howitzers, commanded by Lieutenant French,
and a 6-pounder, commanded by Lieutenant Bramhall, were planted in
front, supported by Company D, Captain Studley, and Company F, Captain Sloan, of the Fifteenth Massachusetts.

The enemy soon appeared in force, and, after sharp skirmishing on
the right, directed his attack upon our whole line, but more particularly
upon our center and left, where it was gallantly met by the Twentieth
Massachusetts and the California battalion. Skirmishing during all the
action was very severe on the right, but the skirmishers of the enemy
were resolutely repulsed by our own, composed of Companies A and I,
Captains Rockwood and Joslin, of the Fifteenth Massachusetts, and
Company —, of the Twentieth Massachusetts, under the direction of
Major Kimball, of the Fifteenth Massachusetts.

The action commenced about 3 p. m., and at about 4 p. m. I was
ordered to detach two companies from the left of my regiment to the
support of the left of the line, and to draw in proportionately the right
flank, which was done, Companies G and H, Captains Forehand and
Philbrick, being detached for that purpose. By this time it had become
painfully evident, by the volume and rapidity of the enemy's fire and
the persistency of his attacks, that he was in much larger force than we.
The two howitzers were silent and the 6-pounder also. Their commanders came from the field wounded.

Soon after I was called from the right of my regiment, there being at
this time a comparative cessation of the enemy's fire, to the center of
the line, and learned for the first time that Colonel Baker had been
killed, and that Lieutenant-Colonel Ward, of the Fifteenth Massachusetts, had been carried from the field severely wounded. Colonel Lee
supposing it his duty to take command, I reported myself ready to execute his orders. He expressed his opinion that the only thing to be done
was to retreat to the river, and that the battle was utterly lost. It soon
appeared that Colonel Cogswell was entitled to the command, who
expressed his determination to make the attempt to cut our way to
Edwards Ferry, and ordered me, as a preliminary movement, to form the
Fifteenth Regiment in line towards the left. The Fifteenth Regiment
accordingly moved across from the right to the left of the original line.
Two or three companies of the Tammany New York regiment, just then

arrived, formed also on its left. While endeavoring to make the necessary disposition to retreat, confusion was created by the appearance of an officer of the enemy's force in front of the Tammany regiment, who called on them to charge on the enemy, who were now in strong force along the wood occupied formerly by the Fifteenth Massachusetts during the former portion of the action. The detachment of the Tammany regiment, probably mistaking this for an order from their own officers, rushed forward to the charge, and the Fifteenth Massachusetts, supposing that an order had been given for the advance of the whole line, rushed with eagerness, but was promptly recalled by their officers, who had received no such order. The detachment of the Tammany regiment was received with a shower of bullets, and suffered severely. In the disturbance caused by their repulse the line was broken, but was promptly reformed.

After this, however, although several volleys were given and returned and the troops fought vigorously, it seemed impossible to preserve the order necessary for a combined military movement, and Colonel Cogswell reluctantly gave the order to retreat to the river bank. The troops descended the bluff, and reached the bank of the river where there is a narrow plateau between the river and the ascent of the bluff, both the plateau and the bluff being heavily wooded. As I descended upon this plateau, in company with Colonel Cogswell, I saw the large boat, upon which we depended as the means of crossing the river, swamped by the number of men who rushed upon it.

For the purpose of retarding as much as possible the approach of the enemy, by direction of Colonel Cogswell I ordered the Fifteenth Regiment to deploy as skirmishers over the bank of the river, which order was executed, and several volleys were given and returned between them and others of our forces and the enemy, who were now pressing upon us in great numbers and forcing down furious volleys on this plateau and into the river to prevent any escape. It was impossible longer to continue to resist, and I should have had no doubt, if we had been contending with the troops of a foreign nation, in justice to the lives of men, it would have been our duty to surrender; but it was impossible to do this to rebels and traitors, and I had no hesitation in advising men to escape as they could, ordering them in all cases to throw their arms into the river rather than give them up to the enemy. This order was generally obeyed, although several of the men swam the river with their muskets on their backs, and others have returned to camp, bringing with them their muskets, who had remained on the Virginia shore for two nights rather than to part with their weapons in order to facilitate their escape.

Having passed up along the line of that portion of the river occupied by my regiment, I returned to the lower end of it, and at dark myself swam the river by the aid of three of the soldiers of my regiment. On arriving at the island I immediately gathered a force of 30 men, who had reached it with safety, and placed them at the passage of the river to prevent any attempt of the enemy crossing in pursuit, but soon learned that Colonel Hinks had arrived with the Nineteenth Massachusetts Regiment, and would take charge of the island.

Our loss, in proportion to the numbers engaged of the regiment, is large, as will be seen by the list of the killed, missing, and wounded, which I annex.* A large proportion of those reported missing are probably prisoners in the hands of the enemy.

---

* See report No. 3.

Although the result of the day was most unfortunate, it is but justice to the officers and men of the Fifteenth Massachusetts Regiment, as well as to the other troops engaged, to say that they behaved most nobly during the entire day; and that the nation has no occasion to blush for dishonor to its arms. The loss of the regiment in arms, equipments, and clothing is necessarily heavy, the particulars of which I will immediately forward.

In conclusion, it may not be improper for me to say that, notwithstanding the regiment mourns the loss of the brave officers and soldiers whose names are borne on the list I annex, its spirit is entirely unbroken and its organization is in no way demoralized. It will answer any summons from you to another contest with the foe, although with diminished numbers, with as hearty a zest as on the morning of October 21.

I remain, general, respectfully,

CHAS. DEVENS,
Colonel.

No. 5.

Reports of Col. Edward W. Hinks, Nineteenth Massachusetts Infantry.

HDQRS. NINETEENTH MASS. VOLUNTEERS,
Camp Benton, near Poolesville, Md., October 23, 1861.

SIR: Learning that a column of our troops was crossing the Potomac on the 21st instant at a point near the center of Harrison's Island, in which the companies of my regiment, stationed as pickets upon the river, had been ordered to join by General Baker, I hastened thither in anticipation of orders from General Stone.

I arrived there about 1.30 p. m., and found among the troops at the point of crossing great confusion, no competent officer seeming to have been left in charge of the transportation, and the progress made in embarking was very slow. I at once took charge at this point; caused a line to be stretched across the river by which to propel the boats, and forwarded troops in the following order, to wit: Part of California regiment, not already crossed; the Rhode Island and New York Batteries; the Forty-second New York (Tammany) Regiment, and the Nineteenth Massachusetts. With the latter regiment I proceeded to the island. I learned that General Baker had been killed, and found everything in confusion, our column being entirely routed and in precipitate retreat, throwing away their arms, deserting their killed and wounded, and leaving a large number of prisoners in the hands of the enemy. I at once took command, arrested as far as possible the progress of the rout, restored order, and, to check the advance of the enemy, who threatened to occupy the island, I sent the Nineteenth Massachusetts Regiment to the front, and placed one gun of the Rhode Island Battery and two of the New York Battery in position, supported by two companies of the Twentieth Massachusetts and so much of the Tammany regiment as was upon the island and could be induced to remain, which disposition being made, and pickets extended upon the Virginia side of the island, I commenced active measures for the gathering of the wounded and the rescue of straggling parties of our troops upon the Virginia shore by the construction of rafts and the use of small boats, the boats used for crossing to the Virginia shore having been swamped and lost in the precipitate and disorderly retreat. No field officer was on duty upon the island, with the exception of Major Bowe, of the New York Tammany regiment.

After the passage of the Nineteenth Massachusetts Regiment no re-enforcements crossed to the island, although several regiments were upon the tow-path on the Maryland side, but returned to their camps during the night. A considerable number of unarmed fugitives, from various regiments, were passed to the Maryland shore during the night, and the transportation of the wounded was continued until noon of the 22d.

On the morning of the 22d I dispatched Lieutenant Dodge, of the Nineteenth Massachusetts, with a flag of truce, to request of the Con-federate commander permission to remove our wounded, of which num-bers lay in view, uncared for, on the Virginia shore. This request was denied, except in the case of a few, apparently mortally wounded. The remainder were taken prisoners. Permission for my surgeon to cross and treat the wounded was also refused, except upon condition that he should remain a prisoner in their hands. Subsequently I dispatched Captain Vaughan, of the Rhode Island Battery, with another flag of truce, to obtain permission to bury the dead, which was acceded to, with the stipulation that no movement of troops should be made from the island to the Maryland shore in retreat while the burying party was employed, and I dispatched Captain Vaughan, with a party of 10 men, for that purpose, who remained until after dark, and succeeded in burying 47 bodies, which he reported to be about two-thirds of the num-ber lying upon the ground; but night coming on, he was unable to bury the remainder.

During the afternoon factious complaint was made by the rebel com-mander that I had violated the stipulations under which the flag of truce was protected,* accompanied by a threat to retain Captain Vaughan and his party as prisoners of war.. I at once addressed a note to the rebel commander denying the accusation; threw up new entrenchments, and made disposition of troops, with a view of renewing hostilities if the threat was carried into execution. Subsequently, how-ever, Captain Vaughan returned with his party, and informed me that my explanation was deemed satisfactory by the rebel commander.

Immediately after Captain Vaughan's return, under cover of the night, I commenced a retreat, in pursuance of orders previously received from General Hamilton, and transported three pieces of artillery, with caissons and ammunition, thirty-six horses, and the eleven companies of infantry under my command, numbering some 700 men, in good order, to the Maryland shore, without any casualties or loss whatever, and, completing the retreat at 12 o'clock, I immediately passed my compli-ment to the rebel commander in the form of four shells from Captain Vaughan's guns, which had been placed in battery upon the high ground overlooking the canal and river.

During the retreat I was re-enforced by five companies of the Second Massachusetts, under the command of Captain Tucker, who remained upon this side of the river, where I stationed him, with his command, in support of the battery, and ordered to camp the companies of the Nineteenth and Twentieth, who were greatly exhausted, having been constantly employed in the intrenchments, burying the dead, removing the wounded, and transporting the artillery to and from the island. The enemy known to have been engaged consisted of the Eighth Vir-

---

*See note at close of report.

ginia Regiment, under command of Colonel Jenifer, and the Seventeenth and Eighteenth Mississippi Regiments, with a squadron of horse and battery, the whole under command of General Evans.

Our loss in killed, wounded, and missing cannot be determined, as large numbers of wounded and unwounded were drowned when the boats were swamped as well as in attempts to swim the river during the night, and no reports as yet have been sent to me. The Fifteenth and Twentieth Massachusetts Regiments, Baker's California regiment, and a part of the Tammany regiment lost a large number of men, who were made prisoners. Colonel Lee and Major Revere, of the Twentieth, and Colonel Cogswell, of the Tammany regiment, are reported missing. Lieutenant-Colonel Ward, of the Fifteenth Massachusetts, was severely wounded. We have lost two howitzers and one rifled gun belonging to Captain Vaughan's Rhode Island Battery, and a considerable number of small arms (say 1,500), with equipments. I shall make a further report of the killed that were identified before burial.

I have to report that the remnant of the Tammany regiment, under command of Major Bowe, deserted its post in the intrenchments on the island at an early hour in the forenoon of the 22d, and passed to the Maryland shore in disobedience of orders, while I was engaged in arranging for the removal of the wounded and the burial of the dead.

I cannot close this report with justice to our troops, who fought valiantly, without commenting upon the causes which led to their defeat and complete rout. The means of transportation for advance in support or for a retreat were criminally deficient, especially when we consider the facility for creating proper means for such purposes at our disposal. The place for landing upon the Virginia shore was most unfortunately selected, being at a point where the shore rose with great abruptness for a distance of some 150 yards, at an angle in many places of at least 25 degrees, and was studded with trees, being entirely impassable to artillery or infantry in line. At the summit the surface is undulating, where the enemy were placed in force, out of view, and cut down our troops with a murderous fire, which we could not return with any effect. The entire island was also commanded by the enemy's artillery and rifles. In fact, no more unfortunate position could have been forced upon us by the enemy for making an attack, much less selected by ourselves. Within a half mile upon either side of the points selected a landing could have been effected where we could have been placed upon equal terms with the enemy, if it were necessary to effect a landing from the island. My judgment, however, cannot approve of that policy which multiplies the number of river crossings without any compensation in securing commanding positions thereby.

Respectfully submitted.

EDWARD W. HINKS,
Colonel Nineteenth Mass. Vols., Commanding Brigade.

Brig. Gen. F. W. LANDER.

NOTE.—The fact that the remaining fragment of the Tammany regiment had left the island without orders was construed by the Confederate commandant as a violation of the stipulation that no movement of troops should be made from the island to the Maryland shore while the burying party was employed.

—

HEADQUARTERS FIRST BRIGADE,
Camp Benton, Md., November 4, 1861.

SIR: General Orders, No. 24, this day received and promulgated to this brigade,* though not refuting the statement alluded to, is one of implied censure to myself for stating a matter of unquestioned fact in the performance of the disagreeable duty that devolved upon me to report "that the remnant of the Tammany regiment, under the command of Major Bowe, deserted its post at the intrenchment on the island at an early hour in the forenoon of the 22d and passed to the Maryland shore in disobedience of orders."

I therefore request to state that at about 9 o'clock on the evening of the 21st ultimo I was informed by Lieutenant-Colonel Devereux, of the Nineteenth Massachusetts, whom I dispatched to apprise you of the condition of affairs at Harrison's Island, that your directions were to hold the island at all hazards, and as the enemy was in considerable force, apparently threatening to occupy the island, I availed myself of all the forces there, consisting of nine companies of the Nineteenth Massachusetts, two companies of the Twentieth Massachusetts, and about three companies of the New York Tammany regiment, together with the three pieces of artillery, commanded by Captain Vaughan, to enable me, at whatever cost, to hold the island, in accordance with your directions.

Just at daybreak on the morning of the 22d I changed the disposition of the troops, with a view of defending the island against any attempt of the enemy to occupy it, either from the vicinity of Ball's Bluff or from the crossing near Smart's Mill. In making the disposition, I directed Major Bowe to place the companies under his command behind the breastworks, in the rear of the ditch from the corner of the old tobacco mill to the water at the Maryland side of the island, which ditch and breastwork were made under your personal direction, with a view, as I supposed, of defending the position against any advance of the enemy from the direction of Smart's Mill. I received no orders for the relief of these companies, neither were they relieved by any other troops, neither were any other troops at my disposal to relieve them.

Between 8 and 9 o'clock on the morning of the 22d, while upon the opposite side of the island, in conversation with the rebel officers, relating to a flag of truce, I was informed by Lieutenant Merritt, of the Nineteenth Massachusetts, that the companies of the Tammany regiment had taken possession of the boats and were passing to the Maryland shore. I hastened thither, and found that a portion of them had already crossed; others were preparing to cross. I addressed them, and inquired by whose authority they left the island. Several voices replied that no orders had been given for them to do so, of which fact I, as commander of the forces upon the island, had no need to be informed. I at once replaced them with companies G and F of the Nineteenth Massachusetts, which I moved from another part of the island for the purpose.

At 5 o'clock on the evening of the 22d an order stating that troops would be sent for my re-enforcement, a copy of which I here inclose (A), was received from General Hamilton, and four hours later the re-enforcements alluded to arrived upon the tow-path and reported to Lieutenant-Colonel Devereux.

A summary of the matter may be presented, as follows: A remnant of the Tammany regiment was upon the island subject to my command. In accordance with your directions for the holding of the island this detachment was placed in position at the intrenchments. This position was deserted. The remnant did pass to the Maryland shore in disobedience of orders given by myself to maintain the position. Twelve

*Attached hereto as inclosure B.

hours after it had deserted its post fresh troops arrived upon the towpath, by which it might have been relieved had it remained at its post.

Consequently it became my duty, however disagreeable, to report the fact in precisely the terms that I used. For this report of facts, which as yet remain undisputed, I have been censured in orders. I therefore respectfully request a court of inquiry, as provided in the ninety-second article of war. I beg further to state that I had and now have no desire to cast any aspersion upon any regiment or body of men in the service of the country, much less upon the gallant spirits who rallied to the call of Cogswell, or dashed upon the foe with O'Meara; but truth compels me to state that had the men of the Tammany regiment upon the island put forth but a single response to my directions to bring a boat from the Maryland to the Virginia side of the island, many, if not all, of O'Meara's men now in imprisonment would have been rescued from their perilous position on the Virginia shore to engage again in their country's battles. And the act of desertion by this remnant of the Tammany regiment seemed to me to be the more reprehensible, from the fact that they were fresher troops than any others there stationed, and were called upon to do less of duty and encounter less danger than any others upon the island, and all other troops vied with each other in kind offices to the wounded and ready response to calls for laborious duty in the burial of the dead, the erection of additional field works, and the digging of rifle-pits to render our position more secure. Upon the men of my own regiment, as well as the Twentieth Massachusetts and Captain Vaughan's Rhode Island Battery, I hesitated not to impose any task, and had but to speak to be obeyed; but to intimate, and the work was done, notwithstanding nearly all of them had been for two successive days and nights subjected to constant and fatiguing duty.

I am, very respectfully, yours,

EDWARD W. HINKS,
Colonel Nineteenth Mass. Vols., Comdg. First Brigade.

Brigadier-General STONE,
Commanding Corps of Observation, Poolesville, Md.

[Inclosure A.]

COLONEL: Three companies of the Second Massachusetts Regiment, Colonel Gordon, have been ordered to your assistance, and will report to you after supper. They will take post on this side of the river, and will not cross to the island unless you shall deem it necessary. After dark you will withdraw your artillery and public stores from the island and then proceed to evacuate it, taking post with your regiment on the Poolesville road, out of the range of shot. The Second Massachusetts will remain doing picket duty until further orders.

By order of Brigadier-General Hamilton:

L. H. D. CRANE,
Major Third Wisconsin, Acting Assistant Adjutant-General.

Colonel HINKS, *Nineteenth Massachusetts.*

[Inclosure B.]

GENERAL ORDERS, }   HDQRS. CORPS OF OBSERVATION,
      No. 24.   }   *Poolesville, Md., November 4*, 1861.

The general commanding has, with deep regret, observed in a report rendered to Brigadier-General Lander by Col. E. W. Hinks, commanding Nineteenth Regiment Massachusetts Volunteers, of what he (Colonel

Hinks) saw from Harrison's Island of the engagement on the Virginia shore on the 21st ultimo and of his own regiment's part in guarding the island and securing and caring for the wounded as they were brought from the field, a statement reflecting severely on the conduct of the gallant Tammany regiment. Colonel Hinks reports that a portion of the Tammany regiment deserted the island on the morning of October 22d in disobedience of orders.

The commanding general deems it proper to give publicity to the fact that he himself requested Major-General Banks to relieve the companies of the Tammany early on that morning, and that the order was given immediately that they should be relieved and replaced by fresh troops from General Hamilton's brigade.

Commanding officers are cautioned against making unnecessary and rash statements in their reports, especially in cases where the honor and reputation of other regiments may be involved; as from such statements not only great injustice may be done, but ill-will, most prejudicial to the good of the service, is certain to be engendered.

By order of Brigadier-General Stone:

C. STEWART,
Assistant Adjutant-General.

No. 6.

Report of Lieut. Col. Francis W. Palfrey, Twentieth Massachusetts Infantry.

HDQRS. TWENTIETH REGIMENT MASS. VOLUNTEERS,
Camp Benton, Poolesville, Md., October 24, 1861.

GOVERNOR: It is my painful duty to make the following report:

On the morning of the 21st Colonel Lee, with Major Revere and Adjutant Pierson, conducted the whole or the greater part of Companies A, C, D, E, G, H, and I, of the above regiment, to a point on the Virginia shore opposite Sullivan's [Harrison's] Island, a little below Conrad's Ferry. The command numbered something over 300 men. They were accompanied or followed by other troops, the Fifteenth Massachusetts, Colonel Devens, among them. They were soon attacked by the enemy, who outnumbered them greatly. The attack continued to be made at intervals, and most of the fighting was in the afternoon.

They were very severely treated, and the following is the result, as nearly as I can state it: Missing: Colonel Lee, Major Revere, Adjutant Pierson, Assistant Surgeon Revere, and First Lieut. George B. Perry, believed to be prisoners; First Lieutenant Babo and Second Lieutenant Wesselhoeft, believed to be drowned.

Wounded in this camp: Captain Dreher, shot through the head from cheek to cheek, recovery possible; Capt. J. C. Putnam, right arm taken off at socket, doing well; First Lieut. O. W. Holmes shot through chest from side to side, doing well; Captain Schmitt, shot three times through leg and through small of the back from side to side, doing well; First Lieut. J. J. Lowell, shot in leg, not serious, and Second Lieutenant Putnam was shot in the bowels, and died in this camp yesterday. His body was sent on to Boston this morning.

Our loss in killed, wounded, and missing of non-commissioned officers and privates is reported at 147, of whom 45 are at this camp, and most of them will recover. The other wounded are believed to be prisoners.

At about 3 o'clock on Tuesday morning I was ordered to march with all my remaining troops, including even the camp guard, to the river, and cross and join the advance. I did so, and we returned this morning. We were under fire for a few moments, and in a position of great peril all the time. I have had to go through such fatigue and anxiety for the past four days, and had so much to do in arranging what is left of this gallant and unfortunate regiment, that I can only write briefly, and at a late hour, to state the principal facts of the sad story.

All the accounts agree that the conduct of officers and men was gallant in the extreme. The enemy paid them the highest tribute when they permitted our burying party to land the following day.

You will see from the following table that our loss was about 50 per cent.:

Officers engaged 22
Officers safe 9
Killed 1
Missing 7
Wounded 5
Rank and file engaged 318
Killed, wounded, and missing * 147

I may add that I was ordered to remain in charge of the camp, and that I was called from attendance on the wounded, who were arriving all night, to form my men for the advance to the other side. I brought all my men back in safety. I shall endeavor to write at greater length by the next mail.

Very respectfully, your obedient servant,
FRANCIS WINTHROP PALFREY,
Lieutenant-Colonel, Comdg. Twentieth Regiment Mass. Vols.

To His Excellency Governor ANDREW.

No. 7.

Report of Capt. William F. Bartlett, Twentieth Massachusetts Infantry.

CAMP BENTON, *October* 23, 1861.

GENERAL : I have to report that 100 men of the Twentieth Regiment crossed from Swan's (or Harrison's) Island at 3.30 a. m. on Monday morning, October 21, to support the detachment of the Massachusetts Fifteenth and cover its retreat. We climbed the steep bank, 150 feet high, with difficulty, and took post on the right of the open space above, sending out scouts in all directions. The detachment of the Twentieth consisted of two companies, I and D, in all 102 men, under command of Colonel Lee. A little after daylight First Sergeant Riddle, of company I, was brought in, shot through the arm by some pickets of the enemy on the right. At 8 a. m. a splendid volley was heard from the direction of the Fifteenth, who had advanced half a mile up the road leading from the river, and soon wounded men were brought back towards the river. We were then deployed by Colonel Lee as skirmishers on each side of the road mentioned, leaving an opening for the Fifteenth to pass through in retreat. They fell back in good order at about 10 a. m. At 11 the other companies of the Fifteenth arrived from the island, and Colonel

* See repot No. 3.

Devens, with his command, moved inland again. At this time the remaining men of the Twentieth, under Major Revere, joined us.

Major Revere had during the morning brought round from the other side of the island a small scow, the only means of transportation excepting the whale-boat, holding 16, and the two skiffs, holding 4 and 5, respectively, with which we crossed in the morning. At 2 o'clock the detachment of Baker's brigade and the Tammany regiment had arrived, and Colonel Baker, who disposed the troops under his command. The 318 men of the Twentieth were in the open space, the right up the river. The Fifteenth were in the edge of the woods on the right; a part of the California (Baker's) regiment on their left, touching at right angles our right.

One company of the Twentieth, under Captain Putnam, was deployed as skirmishers on the right in the woods; one under Captain Crowninshield on the left. Captain Putnam lost an arm in the beginning of the engagement and was carried to the rear. His company kept their ground well, under Lieutenant Hallowell. The Fifteenth had before this, after the arrival of General Baker, fallen back the second time in good order, and had been placed by General Baker as above mentioned.

The enemy now opened on us from the woods in front with a heavy fire of musketry, which was very effective. They fired low, the balls all going within from 1 to 4 feet of the ground. Three companies of the Twentieth were kept in reserve, but on the open ground, exposed to a destructive fire. It was a continual fire now, with occasional pauses of one or two minutes, until the last. The rifled cannon was on the left in the open ground, in front of a part of Baker's regiment, exposed to a hot fire. It was not discharged more than eight times. The gunners were shot down in the first of the engagement, and I saw Colonel Lee carry a charge to the gun with his own hands. The last time that it was fired the recoil carried it down the rise to the edge of the bank. The men of the Twentieth Regiment behaved admirably, and all that were left of them were on the field after the battle was declared lost by General Baker. They acted, at least all under my command, with great coolness and bravery, and obeyed every order implicity; and even after the intimation had been given that we must surrender in order to save the men that were left, they cheerfully rallied, and delivered a well-directed fire upon two companies which we came upon which had just advanced out of the woods. We were slowly driven back by their fire in return, and covered ourselves with the slight rise mentioned above.

We now tried to induce the colonel to attempt an escape, and got him down the bank unhurt. I turned to collect the remnant of my company, and when I returned to the bank they told me that the colonel (Lee), major, and adjutant had got into a small boat, and were by this time safely across. Feeling at ease then about them, I collected all that I found of the Twentieth, and gave permission to all those who could swim, and wished to, to take the water, and sent over reports and messages by them. I then ordered those of the regiment who could not swim to follow up the river, in order to get them out of the murderous volleys which the enemy were pouring down on to us from the top of the bank. About 20 of the Twentieth Regiment, 20 of the Fifteenth, and 40 of the Tammany and California regiments followed us. We went up as far as the large mill, where I found, by means of a negro there, a small sunken skiff in the mill-way, and induced him to get it out of water and down to the river. It was capable of holding 5 men, and I began to send them over, expecting every minute to be discovered by the enemy. In an hour they were all over, and I crossed with Lieutenant Abbott, of my company, and Captain Tremlett, of Company A, Twentieth. I reported with the men at the hospital on the island. They got across to this side during the night. They were obliged to stop at the ferry, and sleep out, many without overcoats or blankets, until morning.

Out of 22 officers that were with us in the engagement 13 are killed, wounded, or missing. Of 318 men, 146 are killed, wounded, or missing.* The colonel (Lee) I learned at the island had not crossed, but I have since learned that he and his companions went farther up the river, found the boat which I afterwards used, thought it impracticable, and went on. They were, by the report of one or two men who have since come in, taken prisoners. Colonel Lee, Major Revere, Adjutant Pierson, Dr. Revere, and Lieutenant Perry are supposed to have been together.

I supposed it was my duty to make this report of that part of the regiment engaged, as senior officer of those saved.

Very respectfully,

WM. F. BARTLETT,
Captain Company I, Twentieth Regiment.

General STONE,
Commanding Corps of Observation.

No. 8.

Report of Col. Milton Cogswell, Forty-second New York Infantry.

NEW YORK, *September* 22, 1862.

GENERAL: I have the honor to submit the following report of the action at Ball's Bluff:

On Sunday, the 20th October, 1861, at about noon, I received verbal orders at the camp of the Tammany regiment from your headquarters to march with my regiment to the vicinity of Conrad's Ferry, and there await further orders. At this time four companies of my regiment were on picket duty along the Potomac between Conrad's Ferry and the Monocacy. With the six companies then in camp I moved to the point directed, and with four companies re-enforced the pickets, retaining two companies with me in bivouac through the night. At about 2 o'clock p. m. on the following day (21st October) I received orders to cross the Potomac at Harrison's Island, taking with me the battery of artillery, which was posted at the same point with myself. Arrived at the landing opposite Harrison's Island, I found the greatest confusion existing. No one seemed to be in charge, nor any one superintending the passage of the troops, and no order was maintained in their crossing. The eight companies of my regiment on picket were rapidly concentrated at the crossing, and I moved with one company of my regiment and two pieces of artillery, belonging to the Sixth New York Battery, to the island, leaving verbal orders with Major Bowe, who remained in charge, to push the remainder of my regiment on as soon as possible. I immediately crossed the island to make the passage of the second branch of the river, and there found still greater confusion existing than at the first landing. The California regiment had already gained the Virginia shore, and just as I arrived Lieutenant-Colonel Wistar, its com-

---

* See report No. 3.

mander, was moving from the island landing in the life-boat. I then crossed in a scow, taking with me Company C, Captain McPherson, of my regiment, and one piece of artillery, with its horses, under Lieutenant Bramhall, Sixth New York Battery. At this time the enemy was maintaining a fire of musketry on the boats from a wooded hill on our right, and to disperse them I ordered Captain McPherson to move with his company to the right and front and brush them away; which order was handsomely executed, and thus the passage of the second branch was made safe from that quarter.

Ordering Lieutenant Bramhall to move his piece by a path to the left and report to Colonel Baker on the field, I ascended the bluff (about 70 feet high) and reported myself to the same commander. I found Colonel Baker near the bluff, on the edge of an open field of about eight or ten acres' extent, trapezoidal in form, the acute angle being on the left front, the shortest parallel side near the edge of the bluff, and along this line was the First California Regiment, while the Fifteenth Massachusetts Regiment was formed in line in the open woods, forming the right-hand boundary of the field, its line being nearly perpendicular to that of the California regiment. Two mountain howitzers, under Lieutenant French, of the U. S. artillery, were posted in front of the angle formed by these two regiments. A deep ravine, having its mouth on the left of the point where we landed, extended along the left of the open field and wound around in front of it, forming nearly a semicircle, bounded by wooded hills commanding the whole open space. Some companies of the Twentieth Massachusetts Regiment were posted in reserve behind the line of the California regiment.

Colonel Baker welcomed me on the field, seemed in good spirits, and very confident of a successful day. He requested me to look at his line of battle, and with him I passed along the whole front. He asked my opinion of his disposition of troops, and I told him frankly that I deemed them very defective, as the wooded hills beyond the ravine commanded the whole so perfectly, that should they be occupied by the enemy he would be destroyed, and I advised an immediate advance of the whole force to occupy the hills, which were not then occupied by the enemy. I told him that the whole action must be on our left, and that we must occupy those hills. No attention was apparently paid to this advice, and Colonel Baker ordered me to take charge of the artillery, but without any definite instructions as to its service. About twenty minutes afterwards the hills on the left front to which I had called attention were occupied by the enemy's skirmishers, who immediately opened a sharp fire on our left. I immediately directed the artillery to open fire on those skirmishers, but soon perceived that the fire was ineffectual, as the enemy was under cover of the trees, shooting down the artillerists at easy musket range. Soon Lieutenant Bramhall and nearly all the artillerymen had been shot down, and the pieces were worked for a time by Colonel Baker in person, his assistant adjutant-general (Captain Harvey), Captain Stewart, assistant adjutant-general of the division, a few other officers, and myself.

Leaving the pieces, as I saw the whole strength of the enemy was being thrown on the left, I proceeded to the extreme left, where I found Lieutenant-Colonel Wistar had been badly wounded, and that the left wing, without a commander, was becoming disorganized. I then ordered Captain Markoe, of the First California Regiment, to move his company to the left, and hold the hill at all hazards. Captain Markoe moved as directed, engaged the enemy's skirmishers, and held his ground for some time, but could gain no advantage over the enemy. About half an hour afterwards Colonel Baker came from the right of the line and passed in front of the line of skirmishers, when he was instantly killed by the fire of the enemy's sharpshooters.

By this time the hills on the left front were fully occupied by the enemy. Two companies of my regiment, under Captain Alden, arrived on the field, cheering most heartily, and with this fresh force we pushed the enemy some 50 yards back, but they had now obtained too strong possession of the hills to be dislodged. An unequal contest was maintained for about half an hour, when Captain Harvey, assistant adjutant-general, reported to me that, Colonel Baker having been killed, I was in command of the field, and that a council of war was being held by the remaining colonels. I repaired to the point occupied by Colonels Lee and Devens, and found that they had decided on making a retreat. I informed them I was in command of the field; that a retreat across the river was impossible, and the only movement to be made was to cut our way through to Edwards Ferry, and that a column of attack must be at once formed for that purpose. At the same time I directed Captain Harvey, assistant adjutant-general, to form the whole force into column of attack, faced to the left.

Having given these orders, I proceeded to the front, and finding our lines pressed severely, I ordered an advance of the whole force on the right of the enemy's line. I was followed by the remnants of my two companies and a portion of the California regiment, but, for some reasons unknown to me, was not joined by either the Fifteenth or the Twentieth Massachusetts Regiments. We were overpowered and forced back to our original position, and again driven from that position to the river bank by overwhelming numbers. On the river bank I found the whole force in a state of great disorder. As I arrived, two companies of my own regiment, under Captains Gerety and O'Meara, landed from the large boat. I ordered these fresh companies up the bluff, and they instantly ascended and deployed as skirmishers to cover the passage to the island, while I took about a dozen men and moved to the left to check a heavy fire of the enemy which had opened on us from the mouth of the ravine near. We were almost immediately surrounded and captured. This took place shortly after dark, and my personal knowledge of the transactions of the day ended here.

I feel it my duty to annex to this report my high sense of the merit of certain officers whose actions during the day deserve grateful recompense and grateful memory from the nation.

Captain Harvey, assistant adjutant-general of Baker's brigade, served both before and after the fall of Colonel Baker with distinguished courage, coolness, and ability. He came upon the field almost disabled, but filled his place wherever its duties carried him. In him a brave and valuable officer was lost to the country.

Captain Stewart, assistant adjutant-general of the division, came upon the field during the action, and displayed that distinguished bravery and coolness in danger for which he is known.

Lieutenant Bramhall, Sixth New York Battery, served the gun which he had brought to the field with great gallantry, and was most severely wounded.

Lieutenant-Colonel Wistar, First California Regiment, after displaying great gallantry, was severely wounded and carried from the field, and his regiment did gallant service before and after his loss. In that regiment I would particularly mention Captain Markoe, Lieutenant Kerns, and the color bearer. The latter, whose name I regret not to have learned, boldly held fast to his colors, waved them in front of the line, cheering the men to the defense of their flag.

Of the Fifteenth Massachusetts Regiment I would particularly mention Captain Bowman, who, in addition to gallantry on the field, volunteered to assist the last companies which formed on the bluffs to cover the passage of the river.

Reports of the Fifteenth Massachusetts and the First California Regiments have, I understand, been made direct to your headquarters. No report has been received by me from the Twentieth Massachusetts Regiment.

Of my own regiment, the Tammany, I cannot speak too highly, and would mention the conduct of Captain Alden, who brought two companies into action, drove the enemy back, checked them, and fell nobly doing his duty. Captains Gerety and O'Meara brought their companies in good order to the field after the repulse, and with their brave men held the bluff until long after nightfall, thus saving the command a long time from a murderous fire. In this duty Captain Gerety lost his life and the regiment a most valuable officer. Lieutenant Gillies, who acted as my adjutant and aide-de-camp during the day, performed his duty most gallantly, and fell after the final repulse.

Before closing my report I deem it my duty as commander of the field during the last part of the action to state my convictions as to the principal causes of the untoward results of the day: First. The transportation of troops across the two branches of the river was in no way guarded or organized. There were no guards at any of the landings. No boats' crews had been detailed, and each command as it arrived was obliged to organize its own. No guns were placed in position either on the Maryland side or on the island to protect the passage, although several pieces were disposable on the Maryland shore near the landing. Had the full capacity of the boats been employed, more than twice as many men might have crossed in time to take part in the action. Second. The dispositions on the field were faulty, according to my judgment. Had the hills on our left front been occupied half an hour after I came on the field, as they might have been without loss, it would have been impossible to dislodge us, and we might have been indefinitely reenforced. As the lines were formed it was impossible ever to bring more than 300 or 400 men into action at a time, and yet from the choice of ground those men not in action were still exposed to fire. The whole brunt of the action fell, as had been pointed out to the commander, on the left and the right, and the reserve could render no service or assistance to their brave comrades, whilst they were themselves being shot down at their separate posts.

I have the honor to be, general, your most obedient servant,

M. COGSWELL,
Colonel Forty-second New York Volunteers, Commanding.

Brig. Gen. CHARLES P. STONE.

No. 9.

Report of Lieut. Col. James J. Mooney, Forty-second New York Infantry.

HEADQUARTERS TAMMANY REGIMENT,
Camp Lyon, near Poolesville, Md., November 4, 1861.

SIR: I herewith transmit to you a complete report of an engagement with the rebels at a point on the Potomac River, in the State of Virginia, known as Ball's Bluff, in which the Tammany regiment from New York were active participants.

On the morning of the 21st ultimo Colonel Cogswell received orders from Brigadier-General Stone to hold the regiment in readiness to march on a moment's warning to a point 2 miles below Conrad's Ferry, in the State of Maryland. On arriving at the point the whole regiment was transported in good order and without accident to Harrison's Island, about midway between the Maryland and Virginia shores, in the Potomac River.

Here, in accordance with the orders of the general in command, the regiment commenced crossing to the Virginia shore to a steep acclivity, some 50 feet in height. The passage across was slow and tedious, owing to the inadequate means of transit provided, only about a single company being able to cross at a time. Company A, Captain Harrington; Company C, Lieutenant McPherson; Company E, Capt. T. H. O'Meara; Company H, Capt. H. H. Alden, and Company K, Capt. M. Gerety, had succeeded in crossing to the Virginia shore, and were hotly engaged in a sanguinary and uneven conflict with the rebels, when the boat used for the transportation of troops to the battle-field was swamped on a return trip, laden with wounded and dead soldiers who had just fallen on the field of battle. How many of our bleeding soldiers were thus buried beneath the waters of the Potomac it was impossible in the confusion that followed to ascertain. No inconsiderable number were rescued by their comrades in arms on the island, and others, not seriously injured, escaped by their own exertions, but there is no doubt but some were drowned by this unfortunate occurrence. As this was the only boat at command, Companies B, Lieut. J. McGrath; D, Capt. Isaac Gotthold; F, Capt. J. W. Tobin; G, Captain Quinn; and I, Capt. D. Hogg, were thus prevented from crossing to Virginia to assist their compatriots already in conflict with a largely superior force of the enemy. The men evinced the deepest anxiety to go to the rescue of their brother soldiers, and manifested the most unmistakable sorrow on learning the impossibility of engaging with the enemy.

The detachment of the Tammany which succeeded in crossing to the Virginia shore was marched up the steep acclivity, and immediately entered into the conflict, already progressing, with a spirit and intrepidity that would have done credit to older and more experienced soldiers, but the contest was too uneven, and, notwithstanding the valor and steadfastness of the men, the battle went against us, though twice the troops of the Tammany impetuously and with great effect charged on the enemy after the order for the retreat had been given. The retreat was conducted with the most perfect order to the river, our soldiers contesting every inch of the ground in retiring. On arriving at the river and finding no means of conveyance to the island, our troops were ordered to throw their arms into the river and such of them who could swim to do so, as this was their only alternative from being taken prisoners.

Below I transmit to you a list of those killed, wounded, and missing. Having no means of ascertaining the actual facts in the case, of course there are many unavoidable inaccuracies in the list, and it is but reasonable to suppose that at least a large proportion of those reported as wounded and missing are among the dead.*

On the death of Col. E. D. Baker, acting brigadier-general, Col.

---

* The nominal lists omitted above show casualties to have been 9 killed, 10 wounded, and 135 missing; but see report No. 3.

Milton Cogswell, of the Tammany regiment, assumed command of the brigade. Though the fortunes of the Union forces had already commenced to wane, Colonel Cogswell rallied them with consummate skill, and when retreat became inevitable, drew off the men in the best possible style, ordering them to cast their muskets and accouterments into the river rather than leave them as trophies for the rebels. He was wounded in the hand, though it is supposed not seriously, sufficiently so, however, to prevent him from swimming to the island, in consequence of which he was doubtless taken prisoner.

Captain Harrington [Company A] conducted himself both on the battle-field and in the retreat with great coolness and discretion. On seeing that he must either be killed or taken prisoner, he threw his sword in the river, divested himself of his wearing apparel, and swam to the island.

Too much praise cannot be awarded to Captain O'Meara [Company E] and those under his command. They fought with undaunted bravery and great efficiency, and when vanquished at last, Captain O'Meara swam to the island and implored Colonel Hinks, then in command there, for the use of a boat to rescue his brave men from the hands of the enemy, and failing in this, he recrossed the river to Virginia in order to assist his men in person with the best means he could devise to escape. As he did not return it is presumed that he is now a prisoner in the hands of the enemy. His persistent efforts in behalf of the safety and welfare of those under his command are worthy of the highest encomiums.

Captain Alden [Company H] fell at almost the first volley from the enemy. His remains were afterward recognized by Captain Vaughan, of the Third Rhode Island Battery, who crossed to the Virginia shore with a flag of truce on the 23d instant and buried a portion of the dead. Though deprived of their commander thus early in the action, the company still continued to fight with commendable ardor.

The supposition that Captain Gerety [Company K] is among the killed is well founded, though not fully authenticated. He shouldered a musket and was seen to be engaged in the conflict in person. It is credited that he was killed pierced with several balls, and that his body was afterward terribly mutilated by passing cavalry of the enemy. Sergt. Thomas Wright, of Company G, who was detailed on the island to assist in the transportation of troops, is missing.

The detachment of the Tammany regiment that remained on the island in consequence of the accident heretofore mentioned—consisting of Companies B, Lieut. James McGrath commanding; D, Capt. Isaac Gotthold commanding; F, Capt. J. W. Tobin commanding; G, Capt. John Quinn commanding; and I, Capt. David Hogg commanding—were on active and arduous service from the moment of their arrival on the island until 2 p. m. of the succeeding day in taking care of and conveying the wounded to the hospital, and in standing in the intrenchments as a guard under a heavy and incessant fire from the enemy. Notwithstanding the inclement wind and storm that prevailed during the night, the men performed the disagreeable task assigned them without a murmur.

During the forenoon of the 22d the Tammany regiment was relieved by the Twenty-seventh Indiana Regiment, of General Hamilton's brigade.

The regiment was then marched back to Camp Lyon, and though grieved and disappointed at the result of the engagement with the enemy, their zeal and ardor are unabated. The inauspicious result, which was entirely beyond the control of those engaged, and for which they cannot in the slightest be held responsible, has had the effect of inspiring the men with renewed determination, instead of producing discontent and disorganization, which too often follow upon the heels of such lamentable disasters.

It would be unjust to close this report without paying tribute to the exertions of Maj. Peter Bowe and Lieut. Thomas Abbott in superintending the transportation of troops to the Virginia shore and bringing back to the island the dead, dying, wounded, and discomfited soldiers. The task was a severe one, but they performed it with fidelity and promptitude. Their assiduous attention to the duties devolving upon them deserves the highest and most honorable mention.

Respectfully,

JAMES J. MOONEY,
Lieutenant-Colonel, Comdg. Tammany Regiment N. Y. S. V.
His Excellency EDWIN D. MORGAN,
Governor of the State of New York.

No. 10.

Report of Lieut. Col. Isaac J. Wistar, Seventy-first Pennsylvania Infantry.

HEADQUARTERS FIRST CALIFORNIA REGIMENT,
Near Poolesville, Md., October 22, 1861.

SIR: I have the honor to send for the examination of the general commanding a rebel officer captured yesterday by Capt. John Markoe in one of the enemy's charges upon our position at Conrad's Ferry. Captain Markoe was afterward captured himself by the enemy.

Having been severely wounded myself near the close of the action, I am unable to make a detailed report of my losses on the occasion, further than my killed, wounded, and missing amount to more than one-half those engaged. Most of those who escaped swam the river, consequently my loss in muskets is very great; but comparatively few fell into the hands of the enemy, they mostly having been destroyed in the river to prevent it.

I went into action with about 600 men, being the first battalion of my regiment, yesterday afternoon about 2 p. m.

The action continued until dark, with a heavy loss on both sides, the firing on both sides being very spirited and effective.

Out of the whole force I can parade this afternoon about 270 men, the officers having suffered disproportionally great.

My own wounds are severe and painful but not fatal, with ordinary good fortune, as I understand, and I hope to make a detailed report shortly.

I have the honor to be, captain, your obedient servant,

ISAAC J. WISTAR,
Lieutenant-Colonel, Commanding California Regiment,
Per JNO. L. WINKHON,
(Colonel Wistar being unable to write.)
Captain STEWART,
Assistant Adjutant-General.

No. 11.

Report of Capt. Francis G. Young, of Colonel Baker's staff.

SIR: At the request of the relatives and many friends of Colonel Baker I have the honor to submit a statement of the facts of the engagement on last Monday, the 21st instant, fought opposite Harrison's Island, on the Virginia shore.

In obedience to an order of General Stone, the first battalion of the California regiment, Baker's brigade, under the command of Lieutenant-Colonel Wistar, left Camp Observation, near the mouth of the Monocacy, at 4 a. m. Monday, and reached Conrad's Ferry at sunrise. The battalion stacked arms, and I proceeded to Edwards Ferry, distant 5 miles, and reported to General Stone for orders. Lieutenant Howe, of the Fifteenth Massachusetts, arrived there at the same time, and reported that he had crossed the river at Harrison's Island during the night, and with some others of his regiment had scouted the country in the direction of Leesburg and found no enemy. General Stone thereupon directed me to return to Lieutenant-Colonel Wistar, with an order for the battalion to stand fast until perchance he should hear heavy firing in front, and in that event to cross to the Virginia shore at Harrison's Island. At this time the summit of the bluff opposite the island on the Virginia side was occupied by six companies of the Fifteenth Massachusetts, Colonel Devens, a detachment of the Twentieth Massachusetts, Colonel Lee, and two companies of the Tammany regiment; also, two small howitzers of the Rhode Island Battery on the island. These forces had crossed during the night preceding, and on my return to Colonel Wistar irregular firing of musketry was heard from the bluff opposite the island. Shortly afterwards Colonel Baker arrived with the other officers of his staff, and in a little while General Stone dispatched to him from Edwards Ferry an order in writing that in the event of heavy firing in direction of Harrison's Island he should advance the California regiment or retire the Union forces from the Virginia side of the river at his discretion, and to assume the command on reaching the Virginia side. Colonel Baker immediately sent for three regiments and a squadron of cavalry from his brigade and for Colonel Cogswell and the rest of his Tammany regiment.

Proceeding to the crossing at Harrison's Island, we found the means of transportation to consist of two flat-boats of the capacity of 25 to 40 men, and a small skiff, which would carry but 3 or 4 men. The river was swollen and the current rapid, and there was much labor and delay in making use of the boats. Another flat-boat was found in the canal 1 mile distant, and being towed down to the crossing, was with much difficulty got into the Potomac. Colonel Baker immediately crossed with me and as many men as could be got into the boats to the island, and reaching the opposite side of the island found one flat-boat and a small metallic boat. He crossed to the Virginia shore without delay with Adjutant-General Harvey, sending me back with an order for Colonel Cogswell to bring over the artillery.

It was now 2 o'clock p. m., and Colonel Cogswell coming over from the Maryland side with two pieces of artillery, horses and men, we carried with us the two howitzers of the Rhode Island Battery and crossed to the Virginia side. The bank is of miry clay, and the heights almost precipitous, with fallen trees and rocks, making it very difficult to get up the artillery. Arriving by circuitous routes on the summit, we found an open field of six acres, covered with wild grass, scrub oak,

and locust trees, and forming a segment of a circle, the arc of which
was surrounded with trees. Colonel Baker apprised Colonel Devens
that he had been placed in command, and learned that the Fifteenth
Massachusetts, after having advanced for a mile in the direction of
Leesburg, had been attacked and fallen back to the position which they
then occupied, just in the edge of the woods on the right. The other
forces were lying under the brow of the hill, and with the exception of
an occasional rifle shot all was quiet, and no sight of an enemy. The
two howitzers and one piece of artillery were drawn by the men out
into the open field, pointing to the woods in front, the artillery horses
not being brought up the steep.

After a quarter of an hour had passed, the enemy making no sign,
two companies of the California battalion, A and D, were sent out from
the left as skirmishers through the wood. They had advanced but a
few rods, when with a yell a tremendous volley of rifle shot from the
concealed enemy drove them back, and from that moment up to the
fall of Colonel Baker there was no cessation of heavy firing from the
enemy in the woods. The re-enforcements from the island came up very
slowly, and it was evident to all that unless aid in force reached us
from the left we should be driven into the river, as the increasing
yells and firing of the enemy indicated their larger number and nearer
approach. The two howitzers were of no service, and the 12-pounder,
being manned by Colonel Baker, Lieutenant-Colonel Wistar, Adjutant-
General Harvey, Captain Bieral, and a few privates of his company
(G), was fired not more than five or six times, and, excepting the last
time, with doubtful effect, as the enemy was at no time visible. We
simply fired at the woods.

Colonel Baker was at all times in the open field, walking in front of
the men lying on the ground, exhibiting the greatest coolness and courage. The fire of the enemy was constant, and the bullets fell like hail-
stones, but it was evident that the enemy was firing into the open field
without direct aim. Colonel Baker fell about 5 o'clock. He was standing near the left of the woods, and it is believed he was shot with a
cavalry revolver by a private of the enemy, who, after Colonel Baker
fell, crawled on his hands and knees to the body and was attempting
to take his sword, when Captain Bieral with 10 of his men rushed up
and shot him through the head and rescued the body. At the time
Colonel Baker was shot he was looking at a mounted officer, who rode
down a few rods into the field from the woods, who, being shot at by one
of our men, returned to the woods and appeared to be falling from his
horse. Colonel Baker, turning about, said, " See, he falls," and immediately fell, receiving four balls, each of which would be fatal. I had but
a moment before, standing by his side, been ordered by Colonel Baker
to go with all possible dispatch to General Stone for re-enforcements
on the left, as there was no transportation across the river for the wants
of the hour. There was some confusion on the field, and the officers of
the companies of the Fifteenth Massachusetts Regiment ordered their
men to retreat. The enemy then for the first time came out of the wood
at double-quick, and receiving a double charge of grape-shot from the
12-pounder, broke in disorder and returned to the woods. There were
but few of the Federal forces now on the field, having returned to the
river side down the steep, but finding no means of escape, some 200
charged up the hill and poured in a volley, the enemy at this time
occupying the field. It was getting dark, and some one tied a white
handkerchief to a sword and went forward. Many were taken prisoners
at the moment, and some fled into the woods on either side, and many

others ran down to the crossing. I got the body of Colonel Baker on the flat-boat, at this time partly filled with water, the dead and wounded, and safely reached the island. Throwing away their arms the men swam the river, the enemy firing upon them from the heights. The boat returning to the Virginia side was overcrowded, and, being leaky, sank in the middle of the river, and many drowned at that time.

Lieutenant-Colonel Wistar, an hour before, having received four shots in various parts of his body, had been carried from the field, and Colonel Cogswell being wounded in the arm, there was no officer in command. Adjutant-General Harvey had a shot in his cheek, but remained on the field and was taken prisoner. Colonel Devens safely reached the shore; but I can give no information concerning Colonel Lee. He with Colonel Cogswell are probably prisoners.

When Colonel Cogswell crossed the river he brought a second order in writing with him from General Stone, to the effect that Colonel Baker should, if he could, advance in the direction of Leesburg, and that he might count upon meeting the enemy in force of about 4,000. These orders I found in Colonel Baker's hat, after he had fallen, stained with his blood.

During the engagement our forces to the number of 5,000, with many pieces of artillery, were in plain view on the Maryland side, but having no means of transportation, were of no service. The position occupied by our forces was but a few rods from the river side, and there were no houses or roads in view. I have no means of stating accurately the number of our loss but that of the California battalion, which is about 260 out of 689. Colonel Baker and all the officers were on foot throughout the engagement, leaving their horses tied to the trees, and they all fell into the hands of the enemy. There was an ineffectual effort to throw the 12-pounder and howitzers down the steep into the river, but being obstructed by fallen trees, they did not reach the water, and the next day were drawn by the enemy up on the hill.

A first lieutenant of the Eighth Regiment Virginia Infantry, named J. Owen Berry, by mistake rode into our lines, having been left behind by his company, and was taken prisoner in the early part of the engagement and sent to our camp. He states that the rebels are abundantly supplied with arms, ammunition, and rations, but are sadly in want of clothing. A few privates also fell into our hands, but not being able to carry them away, they escaped from us.

The depth of the river at the crossing ranges from 3 to 10 feet, and the width of the first crossing is about 100 yards, and of the second 60 yards; it may be more. There was no regularity or order in the movement of the boats.

I have the honor to be, your obedient servant,

FRANCIS G. YOUNG,
Captain, of General Baker's Staff.

Col. E. D. TOWNSEND.

[Indorsements.]

HEADQUARTERS OF THE ARMY,
Washington, October 28, 1861.

Respectfully referred to General Stone, by whom it should be forwarded in due course. It is proper to state that Captain Young stated in person that he had wished to prepare an account of the battle in which Colonel Baker was killed, having been one of his staff. He was told to submit it in writing, which he did.

E. D. TOWNSEND,
Assistant Adjutant-General.

Received headquarters Corps of Observation, Poolesville, October 31, 1861.

This extraordinary production of a fertile imagination is respectfully forwarded. I have no time to notice its misstatements, but would simply call attention to the last clause in the communication, which I am informed is true: "There was no regularity or order in the movement of the boats." Had there been, there would have been no disaster, and Mr. Young, the author of the within, was Colonel Baker's quartermaster.

CHAS. P. STONE,
Brigadier-General, Commanding.

No. 12.

Report of Brig. Gen. Charles P. Stone, U. S. Army, of operations opposite Edwards Ferry, Maryland.

HEADQUARTERS CORPS OF OBSERVATION,
Poolesville, November 2, 1861.

GENERAL: On the 23d October, at about 10.30 o'clock a. m., I received the special order of which the inclosed is a copy at the hands of Col. A. V. Colburn, assistant adjutant-general. In obedience thereto I immediately crossed the river at Edwards Ferry and assumed command of the troops then on the Virginia side, which I found to be as follows, viz: General Abercrombie's brigade, of General Banks' division; General Gorman's brigade, of my division; 130 Van Alen Cavalry [Third New York], under Majors Mix and Lewis; 7 companies Seventh Michigan Volunteers, Colonel Grosvenor; 2 companies Twelfth Regiment Massachusetts Volunteers, under Lieutenant-Colonel Palfrey; the Andrew Sharpshooters;* the rifle company of Boston Tiger Zouaves, Captain Wass, and a section of Ricketts' battery (howitzers), under Sergt. Hart.

I immediately placed General Gorman in charge of the operations at the ferry, the Seventh Michigan Volunteers being detailed to guard the landing and man the boats.

Having seen the landing place properly guarded, I dispatched Lieutenant Pierce, Van Alen Cavalry, with a small party, to scout up Goose Creek to the bridge and across that along the Georgetown road to the vicinity of Frankville, causing him to be cautiously followed by a party of 15 marksmen from the picket at the bridge, and while awaiting his report made a rapid visit to each separate command, and to the right, front, and left of the positions held by our troops. I caused the right of the line, the Monroe house, to be strengthened by 2 companies, and pointed out to the commanding officer (Captain Wass) the best method of quickly strengthening his position by slight intrenchments, extended the line of pickets to the river bank, and then proceeded far enough to the left and front to get a view of Leesburg from the Tuscarora Valley, without seeing anything of the enemy.

While engaged in this examination I was suddenly informed that the enemy were advancing in force on the right. Although this information was delivered in a confused manner, I deemed it but prudent to prepare for action, and immediately ordered the troops to form, having the artil-

---

* Or first company Massachusetts Sharpshooters, attached to Fifteenth Massachusetts Infantry.

lery in the center, in front of the first bluff from the river, with the detachment of the Twentieth Massachusetts and a company of First Minnesota in support; the cavalry and Sixteenth Indiana Volunteers on the right, with the Thirtieth Pennsylvania in reserve; and the Thirty-fourth New York Volunteers, Second New York State Militia, and First Minnesota on the left. The Andrew Sharpshooters were placed along a fence running from the Monroe house on the right to the wooded hill near the bridge on the left, which wooded hill was strengthened to 12 companies of infantry from the various regiments, all under the command of Lieutenant Colonel Lucas. These arrangements were rapidly made, but on sifting the information I was satisfied no advance had been made by the enemy, and allowed the troops to leave the lines, holding themselves in readiness to resume them at a moment's notice.

The scouting party towards Frankville returned, Lieutenant Pierce reporting that he had proceeded to a point near that village without meeting any of the enemy, but that from the first house of it a cavalry picket was seen. I immediately ordered a strong infantry picket to be stationed in the wood on the Frankville road at an advantageous point described by Lieutenant Pierce, with a cavalry patrol beyond it to watch that road, and on the right sent out infantry pickets to occupy the woods in front of the Monroe house, watch the Leesburg road, and indicate by their firing any approach of the enemy in that direction. I at the same time reported to the major-general commanding the amount of re-enforcements which I deemed sufficient for holding the position.

At this time a new report was brought to me that the enemy were advancing in two heavy columns, one on the right and the other on the left. This report, although indistinct, came through official channels, and the line was again formed and report made to the major-general commanding, in order that re-enforcements might be in readiness to move over promptly to our support in case of attack. As it was impossible to ascertain to what extent the enemy had been re-enforced, and Colonel Woodbury, Engineer Corps, having just then arrived and reported for duty, I sent him with an escort of cavalry to the left front to reconnoiter, while I proceeded to the right to see that all was secure there.

Orders were sent to Lieutenant-Colonel Lucas to hold the wood and bridge on the left until the last moment, and if driven by overwhelming numbers from that position, to fall back along the left bank of Goose Creek and take up a position in rear of the Thirty-fourth New York Volunteers. Colonel Lucas was also directed to follow the advice of Colonel Woodbury in rapidly strengthening his position by means of his axes.

The reconnaissance proved there was no near approach of the enemy, and all arrangements were made for holding the position for the night and receiving and posting re-enforcements, when I received from the major-general commanding, shortly after dark, orders to retire the whole force to the Maryland side of the river. Previously to the receipt of this order I had sent General Gorman to the Maryland side to facilitate the passage of the re-enforcements, and he was now charged with the duty of superintending the debarkation of our troops there and forwarding the empty boats with regularity and dispatch. The holding of the right of the line during the embarkation was intrusted to Brigadier-General Abercrombie; the holding of the left to Colonel Dana, First Minnesota Volunteers. The advanced pickets and cavalry scouts were kept out and additional fires lighted, and while the Indiana Sixteenth, under the orders of General Abercrombie, held the line of the bluff on the right, and the First Minnesota Volunteers, under Colonel Dana, the same line on the left, the regiments between the bluff and the river were silently withdrawn and transferred to the boats as they arrived. Next, the regiments outside the line of the bluff were withdrawn, the artillery with its support, the Andrew Sharpshooters, and (as fast as flat-boats could be secured) the cavalry with their horses. Finally, when none remained excepting the outlying pickets and the two regiments, sufficient boats were secured along the bank to receive at once all that remained, and the pickets were rapidly withdrawn by the left and right and marched to the boats. The delicate and responsible duty of calling in these pickets was admirably performed by Capt. Charles Stewart, assistant adjutant-general, and Lieutenant Gourand, Van Alen Cavalry. I should also mention in this connection Brigade-Surgeon Bryant, of Lander's brigade, who accompanied me through the day, making all necessary arrangements for his department, and at night performed most valuable service in transmitting with rapidity and exactitude many of my orders.

The pickets having been recalled and placed on the boats, the Sixteenth Indiana and First Minnesota were withdrawn from the bluff, formed on the river bank, and embarked, and at about 4 o'clock a. m. on the 24th the last boat containing troops pushed from the Virginia shore, not an accident having occurred in the entire operation. Having seen what appeared to be the last of the command safely afloat, I was pulled in a row-boat, under charge of Captain Williams, Seventh Michigan Regiment, up and down the river to inspect the shore opposite the lines which we had occupied, and being satisfied that not a man or horse had been left behind, I crossed the river and reported at headquarters near Edwards Ferry.

I beg leave to record my high sense of the bearing of the troops, and especially of the First Minnesota Volunteers and the Sixteenth Indiana, whose steadiness and coolness could not have been greater had they been the first instead of the last to leave the ground. General Abercrombie and Colonel Dana were indefatigable in their labors, and displayed the same coolness and self-possession which they have long since shown in other campaigns, and which here insured the quiet and successful embarkation of all. Colonel Grosvenor, Seventh Michigan Volunteers, remained long after his regiment had passed over, aiding in the embarkation. Colonel Patrick, Thirtieth Pennsylvania, crossed with the main body of his regiment, and returned to await the calling in of the pickets, because one of his companies was on that duty, and he would not leave the Virginia shore until the last of his men had crossed. Dr. James S. Mackie, of the State Department, who had rendered me most valuable service as volunteer aide-de-camp for several days previous, placed me under renewed obligations by his active and intelligent services on this night. Maj. John Mix, Van Alen Cavalry, again proved himself a most valuable officer. Although he had been almost continually in the saddle for the preceding forty-eight hours, his labors were through the night incessant and effective. General Gorman speaks highly of the services of Lieutenant Foote, quartermaster Second New York State Militia, in managing the boats; and I am informed that Quartermaster Goff, of the Van Alen Cavalry, was peculiarly active and useful in the same service.

I have the honor to be, general, respectfully, your obedient servant,

CHAS. P. STONE,
Brigadier-General, Commanding.

Brig. Gen. S. WILLIAMS,
Asst. Adjt. Gen., Hdqrs. Army of the Potomac.

No. 13.

Report of Brig. Gen. Willis A. Gorman, U. S. Army, of operations opposite Edwards Ferry, Maryland.

BRIGADE HEADQUARTERS, NEAR EDWARDS FERRY,
October 26, 1861.

I have the honor to communicate to the general commanding the division the facts and events connected with my brigade in the advance across the Potomac, made under his orders. On the 20th instant I received orders to detach two companies of the First Minnesota Regiment to cover a reconnaissance on the Virginia side of the Potomac, whereupon Colonel Dana sent forward Companies E and K, who crossed the river, but were soon recalled. On the morning of the 21st two other companies of the same regiment crossed and covered the advance of a cavalry party under Major Mix, at the same time driving in the enemy's pickets.* Orders were received by me to have the Second New York State Militia and First Minnesota Volunteers at Edwards Ferry on Monday, the 21st instant, at daylight, or as near that hour as possible. These two regiments arrived there at the time specified. I also ordered the Thirty-fourth New York Volunteers to proceed to the same point at as early an hour as possible from Seneca Mills, 8 miles distant. They arrived with great promptitude at 11 o'clock. During that day and night (the 21st) the entire brigade crossed the river, numbering about 2,250 men.

Just about the time I got the first regiment across a severe battle commenced near Conrad's Ferry, distant 5 or 6 miles. Before the brigade got over news of a repulse of our troops at Conrad's Ferry reached the general commanding, who sent me an order in writing to "commence intrenchments immediately" on the Virginia side. With the utmost dispatch intrenching tools were placed in the hands of the Seventh Michigan Regiment (whose guns were almost worthless), who did good service, and very soon rifle-pits were dug and other intrenchments begun. From the commencement of the crossing on Monday I was ordered in command of the troops at the Ferry and in charge of the means and manner of disposing of them as the re-enforcements arrived; also of crossing them over the river. On the arrival of Major-General Banks on the 22d I received the same order from him. I seized all the canal-boats within 2 miles of the Ferry—above and below—and all the flat, scow, and row boats to be found, and put seven canal-boats and two scow-boats into the Potomac from the canal, placing them in charge of Captain Foote, quartermaster of the Second New York State Militia, who managed the crossing with great energy, so that by Tuesday, 22d instant, at 10 o'clock a. m., we had crossed 4,500 men, 110 or more of Van Alen's Cavalry, and two 12-pounder howitzers of Ricketts' battery, immediately under the charge of Lieutenants Kirby and Woodruff.

About 4 o'clock on the 22d instant the enemy was seen advancing upon us in force. They immediately, and with great spirit and determination, attacked our outposts near the woods adjacent to Goose Creek, to the left and in front of our lines, and about 3 miles from Leesburg. They numbered over 3,000 infantry, with some cavalry in

---

* Reference to this skirmish is in General Stone's report (October 29) of Ball's Bluff, No. 2, p. 293.

reserve. Our forces met the attack with equal firmness, and for a short time the firing was rapid, when the two pieces of artillery opened upon the enemy a well-directed fire, doing fearful execution, causing them to give way in confusion and make a hasty return within their breast-works near Leesburg, suffering a loss of 60 killed and wounded, as ascertained from their wounded and from citizens in the vicinity. The loss in my brigade is one killed and one severely wounded, both belonging to Company I, First Minnesota Volunteers.

On the 23d, by the general's orders, I directed further intrenchments around the White house near the enemy's works. I also had the fences, yard, and lane barricaded, and strengthened with logs, rails, old plows, wagons, and lumber. On the night of the 23d, about 7 o'clock, the general ordered me again to proceed to the Maryland side, and take charge of the crossing of artillery and more troops. On arriving I started across four more pieces of artillery. A storm of wind which had been prevailing nearly all day seemed to forbid the possibility of further re-enforcements from this side. Provisions were getting short; the artillery on the Virginia shore were short of ammunition; the wind was setting strongly from the Virginia shore; the means of transportation were heavy scows and clumsy canal-boats, managed by poles, when at 8 o'clock p. m. I received notice from Major-General Banks that General McClellan had ordered the withdrawal of the whole force from the Virginia to the Maryland side, and orders to proceed quietly, but with all energy, to make the arrangements necessary on the Maryland side, and directed me to call to this work the boatmen and lumbermen of the First Minnesota Volunteers, as it was evident that everything depended on the energy, courage, and muscles of the boatmen to contend against the adverse wind-storm. This detail was made, to which was added 100 men from Colonel Kenly's Maryland regiment, 100 more from the Thirty-fourth New York Volunteers, and 150 from the Seventh Michigan Regiment. The plan being matured, the seemingly impossible enterprise was entered upon with a spirit and energy that knew "no such word as fail," and between 9 o'clock p. m. of the 23d and 5 o'clock a. m. of the 24th every man, horse, and piece of artillery was safely withdrawn from the Virginia shore, and landed on this side again without an accident or the loss of a man or a horse, except the casualty of the fight. The fortitude, endurance, and energy displayed by the men detailed to perform this work deserve the highest commendation. The Minnesota lumbermen performed their part with such skill as to merit special notice. The courage and coolness of the officers and men of my brigade, in most part, as exhibited in their crossing the river, engaging the enemy, and their orderly withdrawal across again, give reliable assurance of their efficiency.

It may not be improper here to state that the result of this movement as a reconnaissance must prove highly beneficial to any future movement in that direction. Each order was strictly followed, and the desired result accomplished.

Trusting that I have performed satisfactorily the somewhat difficult and responsible duty to which General Stone and General Banks assigned me, I am, very respectfully, your obedient servant,

W. A. GORMAN,
Brigadier-General.

Capt. CHARLES STEWART,
Asst. Adjt. Gen., Brig. Gen. Stone's Division.

No. 14.

*Report of Maj. John Mix, Third New York Cavalry, of reconnaissance
and skirmish on Leesburg road, Virginia.*

CAMP BATES, NEAR POOLESVILLE, MD.,
November 4, 1861.

SIR: I have the honor to submit the following report of my reconnaissance on the 21st ultimo:

In compliance with the instructions of Brigadier-General Stone, I
crossed the Potomac at Edwards Ferry about 7 o'clock a. m., with a
party of 3 officers and 31 rank and file, Capt. Charles Stewart, assistant
adjutant-general, accompanying the party. A line of skirmishers, consisting of two companies of the First Minnesota, commanded the line of
the hill to the right and front. After carefully examining our arms
and equipments, we moved quickly forward on the Leesburg road. The
house to the right, about 2 miles from the landing, known as Monroe's,
was found vacant, and appeared to have been left in great haste, most
probably during the cannonading of the 20th. At this passing the
road enters a thick wood, with a great growth of underbrush, impene-
trable to our flanking at the gait we were moving. They were consequently drawn up the road and ordered to proceed at a slow gallop. The
road was here so narrow and crooked that they could not keep over 40
paces in the front. Three hundred yards from the house a road crosses
the one we were upon, running to the bridge over Goose Creek on the left
and to Leesburg on the right. I, however, kept straight on, as the road
presented little opportunity for observation, and would sooner reach the
high and open country around the enemy's breastworks to the left and
front. Soon after reaching this point we drove in a vedette of the
enemy, who took the alarm too soon to allow a reasonable chance of our
capturing him, and I did not wish to fatigue our horses by useless pursuit.

A negro whom we had met reported that a regiment of infantry and
a body of cavalry had left the immediate neighborhood that morning at
daylight, and taken the Leesburg road. With this intelligence we proceeded on our way, and when about 1,200 yards farther in the woods
our advance suddenly halted and signalized the enemy in sight. Pushing rapidly forward, we saw the bayonets glistening above the brush; but
for the thick undergrowth but few of the enemy could be seen. In an
instant the head of the columns "by fours" came upon the road within
35 yards of us, and 5 yards of one of our men (Sergeant Brown), who
held his position when he discovered them. At the same moment a
rise in the ground disclosed to me a long line of bayonets pushing
rapidly forward with the evident intention of flanking the road on our
left. I immediately directed a fire on them from our revolvers, which
took effect on at least 2 of them, one an officer who was leading the
column, probably a lieutenant; we wheeled quickly about, when instantly their first platoon opened fire upon us from a distance of not
over 30 yards. We retired at a smart gallop about 100 yards, when a
turn in the road protected us from their fire, which was now very rapid,
but ineffective. Within 30 yards of their column a horse was shot,
another stumbled and fell, leaving 2 men almost in the ranks of the
enemy. These men were rescued and brought back in a most gallant
manner by Capt. Charles Stewart and Lieut. George E. Gourand, and
were quickly mounted, when we formed for a charge, but the enemy
had deployed to the right and left of the road and again compelled us

to retire, which we did leisurely, examining the ground to the right and left and leaving vedettes at the most commanding positions.

The enemy did not follow us beyond the edge of the woods in the front of Monroe's house. Lieutenant Pierce and Sergeant Chesbrough were left here to observe his movements, while the remainder of the party proceeded to the left. A scout belonging to the Fourth Virginia Cavalry, Ball's company, was then captured. He had been reconnoitering and had fallen in with our party unexpectedly. Having examined the country to the left and front without discovering anything of further importance, we fell back on our line of skirmishers, leaving the open country and the Monroe house occupied by our vedettes.

Thus closed our movements as a reconnoitering party, but at their own request Captain Murphy, Lieutenant Pierce, and Sergeant Chesbrough remained and gathered much important information during the day and chased several parties who ventured out of the woods back into them. Upon one of these occasions they captured a wooden canteen and saddle-bags which a scout dropped in his hurried retreat.

In conclusion, sir, I cannot but commend in the highest terms the conduct of both officers and men under my command. Their coolness and prompt obedience speak well for their future reputation.

I am, sir, very respectfully, your obedient servant,

J. MIX,
Major, Commanding.

Capt. CHARLES STEWART,
Asst. Adjt. Gen., Headquarters Corps of Observation.

No. 15.

Report of Brig. Gen. John J. Abercrombie, U. S. Army, of operations opposite Edwards Ferry, Md.

HEADQUARTERS FIRST BRIGADE, VOLUNTEERS,
Seneca Mills, Md., ———, 1861.

GENERAL: I have the honor to report: In obedience to your order of the 21st instant a portion of my brigade, consisting of the Sixteenth Indiana and Thirtieth Pennsylvania Regiments, marched from Dawsonville at 8 p. m. on that day to Seneca Mills, when further orders were received from you to continue the march to Edwards Ferry, where the brigade arrived, after a fatiguing night's march, about 4 a. m. of the 22d.

Immediately on our arrival further instructions were received to cross to the Virginia side of the Potomac. Accordingly, hungry and wet as the troops were, they proceeded, and without a murmur, commenced crossing, the Sixteenth Indiana leading, as fast as the limited means of transportation at hand would admit; the Thirtieth Pennsylvania followed, and, by great exertions, effected a landing about 2 p. m. Encamped near the ferry I found the First Minnesota Regiment, Colonel Dana; Second New York, Colonel Tompkins; the Thirty-fourth New York, Colonel La Dew, and Seventh Michigan, on the crest of the hill, running nearly parallel to the course of the river, and perhaps some 400 or 500 yards beyond it; one company of the Nineteenth Massachusetts Tiger Zouaves, Captain Wass, occupying a farm house to the right; a company of telescopic rifle sharpshooters, Captain ———, in rifle pits on their left, extending along the ridge nearly to Goose Creek, which enters the Potomac at the ferry and nearly at right angles to it, between the zouaves and sharpshooters, and on the same line a section of a light battery in charge of a sergeant.

Not being aware that any officer of superior rank to myself was present on duty with the troops on the Virginia side, I assumed the command, and commenced my arrangements for resisting an attack by posting the Thirtieth Pennsylvania Regiment on the extreme right of our position to guard against a flank movement between the heights in front and the river. The Sixteenth Indiana was posted about the center of the plain, fifty or sixty paces from the river; the New York and Minnesota regiments on its left, in the direction of the ferry and resting on Goose Creek; the Seventh Michigan being in advance immediately at the foot of the hill, on which were the sharpshooters and the cavalry, about 30 in number, under Major Mix, of the Van Alen Regiment, to their right, and similarly posted.

About 4 p. m. on the 22d the enemy were seen in the distance, cavalry and infantry, advancing cautiously. The Indiana and Minnesota regiments were ordered to advance and support the sharpshooters and artillery, which was done with great promptness. The remaining force was held in reserve, to act as circumstances might require. Previous, however, to this disposition an advance picket from the New York and Minnesota regiments had been thrown forward to prevent the enemy from crossing a bridge about a mile and a half above the ferry and across Goose Creek, and to hold the wooded hill adjacent to it.

As the enemy approached, the artillery opened a fire of shell; the sharpshooters also delivered a well-directed fire, while the pickets at and near the bridge did the same, which caused the rebels to retrace their steps in the direction of Leesburg. The troops remained in position as long as there was the least probability of a renewal of the attack, when the Indiana and Minnesota regiments were withdrawn to resume their respective stations near the bank of the river, and the outposts at the bridge and on the hill near by were re-enforced by three companies of the Indiana and two of the Pennsylvania regiments. During the night everything was quiet.

On the following day several alarms of the approach of the enemy were given, which, however, proved to be nothing more than small parties of cavalry endeavoring to make a reconnaissance. General Stone, in the mean time having arrived and assumed the command, ordered the Indiana and Minnesota regiments to return to the hill, where they remained until dark, when they returned to camp.

About 9 p. m. I was informed by General Stone that instructions had been received to recross the river. The Indiana and Minnesota regiments were again sent forward to occupy their previous positions on the hill, and to remain there until all the outposts had been withdrawn and embarked, including the cavalry and artillery, and were the last to leave the Virginia side.

Much credit is due to the chaplain of the Twelfth Massachusetts, who acted for the time as one of my aides, and superintended the embarkation of the troops, which was done in a masterly manner, and by his activity and admirable management enabled the whole company to cross before the dawn of day.

Throughout the time we occupied the Virginia side the troops conducted themselves with great propriety and coolness, and responded with alacrity to every call to meet the enemy. I regret to say there were a few instances where the officers exhibited less zeal than their men; some of whom having absented themselves and were found on the Maryland side when their regiments were recalled. As it is possible they may be able to justify their conduct, I forbear to mention their names.

As far as I have been enabled to learn, 1 man was killed by the enemy, 1 shot by mistake, and 1 of the enemy wounded and taken prisoner.

General Lander, whom I presume came as a volunteer on the occasion, received a flesh wound in the leg. These are all the casualties I know of.

It is much to be regretted that circumstances, over which the commanding general could have no control, prevented the troops assembled on the Maryland side from crossing in time to re-enforce those already over, as I am fully impressed with the belief, from information received through various sources, and where there could be no collusion, the enemy's forces at the time my brigade crossed did not exceed 4,400 at or near Leesburg. If so, in six hours after we reached Virginia the division under your command might have been in possession of it.

J. J. ABERCROMBIE,
Brigadier-General, Commanding First Brigade Volunteers.
Major-General BANKS, *Commanding Division.*

No. 16.

Report of Maj. Gen. Nathaniel P. Banks, U. S. Army, of march to re-enforce General Stone.

HEADQUARTERS,
Edwards Ferry, October 22, 1861.

SIR: I received the order of the commanding general to send General Hamilton's brigade to Poolesville at 4 o'clock yesterday evening, and at 5.30 an order to march to Seneca Mills with the remaining brigades of my division. At 8 o'clock all the troops were in motion except the sick and those left in charge of the camps. General Hamilton reached Poolesville at 10 o'clock, and was placed in position to cover Harrison's Island by General Stone, which position he still holds with his brigade. Harrison's Island is nearly opposite Poolesville, and is important chiefly as it facilitates the passage of the river from either side. The Virginia shore opposite the island is abrupt and rocky, in possession of the enemy, who seem to possess it in some force. The deficiency of materials for forcing a passage has rendered it impossible to do more than protect the troops who occupied it, and who brought to the island the wounded and dead of yesterday. It is, however, less tenable than I represented in my dispatch of this morning. The enemy can shell it from the prominent shore they occupy, and dislodge our men, unless it be strongly fortified and defended. This may be done.

The two brigades *en route* for Seneca Mills reached their destination at 10 o'clock. At 12 o'clock midnight they received an order from the commanding general to march at once to Poolesville, and taking the river road the head of the column reached Edwards Ferry between 3 and 4 o'clock. marching during the night about 18 miles. The exigency which first required their presence here was probably over before they had received the order to march. The morning presented a different state of affairs. The point of land made by the intersection of Goose Creek with the Potomac was occupied by some 2,000 of our troops, no demonstration having been made by either side during the night or thus far in the day to disturb the quiet which existed, except to threaten by the enemy the possession of Harrison's Island. It was impossible to execute our order by immediately crossing the river. There were but three boats—one canal-boat and two flats. It would have occupied more than the entire day to have set one division over. General Abercrombie commenced moving his brigade over, and completed it by 12 o'clock. General Williams will follow, but it may be deferred on account of an order received to-day. There are now 4,400 troops on the Virginia shore, a statement of which in detail I inclose.

The suggestion by the commanding general as to the occupation of the ground I think the best that could be made. We can obtain in a day or two boats enough to make the passage of the river perfectly secure and to bridge Goose Creek also. Strong intrenchments can be made, and the occupied point can be defended from the Maryland side as well as on the ground itself. We have about twenty pieces of artillery, and shall have a force of nearly 16,000 men.

Everything is in perfect quiet across the river up to this hour.

I am unable to give an account of the affair of yesterday or its results, which I suppose you have already learned.

With great respect, I am, your obedient servant,

N. P. BANKS,
Major-General, Commanding Division.

Brigadier-General WILLIAMS,
Asst. Adjt. Gen., &c., Army of the Potomac.

No. 17.

Reports of Francis L. Buxton, U. S. Secret Service, of the Confederate forces at Leesburg, &c.

POINT OF ROCKS, MARYLAND,
October 25, 1861.

COLONEL: I have just arrived here, and to begin at the end of my journey I will first say to you that there are no troops north of Leesburg except Home Guards and pickets. The Mississippi regiment which was at Winchester joined the force at Leesburg on the very morning of the day on which the engagement took place between Leesburg and the Potomac. The force at Leesburg remains at the numbers I last stated to you, viz, 11,000, with the addition of the Mississippi regiment just attached, 750 strong, and two regiments which were out on picket duty—one Mississippi and one Virginia. Each numbers about 600 men. The numbers are therefore now:

Sixteen regiments	11,000
One regiment	750
Two regiments	1,200
Total force now at Leesburg (on Sunday, yesterday)	12,950

I have been thus particular on account of rumors in the neighborhood that there were 50,000 men at Leesburg. This I pledge you my life is not the case. I was distressed beyond measure in coming through Virginia to hear the jubilant tone of the Army. They have the most exaggerated reports; people really believe that 10,000 Union men were opposed to 4,000 rebels, and that the latter almost massacred them. I am very glad to learn that it is not so bad as was at first supposed. Poor Baker must have been very rash to rush with his small force into the jaws of 7,000 men.

I wish to inform you, colonel, of what I know from an undoubted source, that signals were made from the Maryland shore when the first boat crossed, which enabled the rascals to be ready for just what they are waiting for, to entrap a small force at a disadvantage. This is their only object and policy at Leesburg. Had 20,000 men been quickly transported across the river and made a simultaneous advance, they would not have fought there. I dare not disguise from you the fact that their generals have made great capital out of this engagement, and have to some extent succeeded in creating enthusiasm among the men. They are erecting earthworks about a mile and a half south of Leesburg near the railway, and another in the woods about a mile to the west of it, but at present there are no guns there. I think they are to cover a retreat if one is necessary.

The army at Manassas and forward to Centreville is neither diminished nor augmented, except that two regiments have been removed from Fredericksburg to Gainesville. They say they have invincible batteries on the lower Potomac, but evidently do not believe it themselves, as they continually fear an attack from that direction. Two batteries have recently been erected on James River; one is at a point commanding the river and a creek near Williamsburg, the other I cannot find out, but free negroes have been compelled to go from Richmond to work on them, and some guns have been sent there. Some free negroes who pleaded other employment were told that they would be sold and sent farther South if they did not go.

I meant to have said, in connection with Leesburg, that they give the list of 60 officers as having been killed there.

The general belief in Richmond is that the fleet at Old Point Comfort is bound for Galveston, and some information has reached Mr. Davis that there is no doubt of it. What action he has taken I am unable to say; but no troops have left Manassas, and, except some stray companies, there are none in Richmond to send.

There are preparations making at Norfolk to run the blockade as soon as the fleet leaves there. A large ship, the name of which I forget, is said to be ready for sea. I know not whether the information is of any value, but I can assure you beyond a doubt that there is no force above the hill about a mile north of Leesburg, and will reiterate that I am quite certain that the numbers stated at Leesburg are, strictly speaking, correct.

I shall return to-morrow morning to Leesburg; hope to get away before daylight. I have drawn upon General Banks for some money ($125), having none, which you will please refund. If I get any important information within two or three days I shall return here and come to Washington. I do not believe the rebels have any plan of attack whatever, but are simply waiting (Micawber-like) for something to turn up. They are certainly in better spirits than they were two weeks ago and better off for provisions. It is openly boasted at Manassas that they have Confederates in the United States Army, but in such a way as would lead one to suppose that it is mere braggadocio.

With great respect, I am, colonel, your obedient servant,

BUXTON.

Colonel MARCY, *Headquarters Army of the Potomac.*

POINT OF ROCKS, *October* 28, 1861.

GENERAL: I beg you to send this report to Colonel Marcy. I am deeply grieved at General Stone's disaster. It was only ten days ago, a day or two before it happened, that General McClellan had positive information from me, via Fort Monroe, that there were 11,000 men still at Leesburg. It would therefore seem he (Stone) must have acted without proper information.

They have been waiting there for no other purpose than to catch a small party at a disadvantage.

I am, general, your most obedient servant,

FRANCIS L. BUXTON.

Major-General BANKS.

No. 18.

Brig. Gen. Charles P. Stone's letter to Hon. Benjamin F. Wade, chairman of Joint Committee on the Conduct of the War.

WASHINGTON, D. C., *March* 6, 1863.

SIR: During my recent examination (27th ultimo) you asked me the question, " Who arrested you?" My answer was long, and referred to a number of papers which I had not with me. As my answer indicated, I am yet in doubt as to whom the responsibility of the arrest attaches; but I inclose copies of such papers (ten in number) as are now in my possession, and respectfully place them at the disposition of the honorable the committee.

Very respectfully, I am, sir, your most obedient servant,

CHAS. P. STONE,
Brigadier-General.

[Inclosures.]

ORDER, }   WAR DEPARTMENT,
No. —. }   *Washington City, D. C., January* 28, 1862.

Ordered, That the general commanding be, and is hereby, directed to relieve Brig. Gen. C. P. Stone from command of his division in the Army of the Potomac forthwith, and that he be placed in arrest and kept in close custody until further orders.

EDWIN M. STANTON,
Secretary of War.

HEADQUARTERS OF THE ARMY,
Washington, February 8, 1862.

GENERAL: You will please at once arrest Brig. Gen. Charles P. Stone, U. S. volunteers, and retain him in close custody, sending him under suitable escort by the first train to Fort Lafayette, where he will be placed in charge of the commanding officer. See that he has no communication with any one from the time of his arrest.

Very respectfully, yours,

GEO. B. McCLELLAN,
Major-General.

Brig. Gen. ANDREW PORTER, *Provost-Marshal.*

HEADQUARTERS OF THE ARMY,
Washington, February 8, 1862.

SIR: This will be handed to you by the officer sent in charge of Brig. Gen. Charles P. Stone, who is under close arrest.

You will please confine General Stone in Fort Lafayette, allowing him the comforts due his rank, and allowing him no communication with any one by letter or otherwise, except under the usual supervision.

GEO. B. McCLELLAN,
Major-General.

COMMANDING OFFICER FORT LAFAYETTE.

WASHINGTON, D. C., *February* 9, 1862.

GENERAL: This morning about 1 o'clock I was arrested by Brigadier-General Sykes, commanding city guard, and made a close prisoner by order, as I was informed, of the Major-General Commanding-in-Chief.

Conscious of being and having been at all times a faithful soldier of the United States, I most respectfully request that I may be furnished, at as early a moment as practicable, with a copy of whatever charges may have been preferred against me and the opportunity of promptly meeting them.

Very respectfully, I am, general, your most obedient servant,

CHAS. P. STONE,
Brigadier-General.

Brig. Gen. S. WILLIAMS,
Assistant Adjutant-General, Hdqrs. Army of the Potomac.

FORT HAMILTON, BAY OF NEW YORK,
April 5, 1862.

COLONEL: I respectfully request of you a copy of the order by authority of which, on the 10th of February last, I was confined in Fort Lafayette.

Very respectfully, I am, colonel, your most obedient servant,

CHAS. P. STONE,
Brigadier-General.

Lieut. Col. MARTIN BURKE, *Fort Hamilton.*

P. S.—I would also request copies of any letters which have passed between any authority in Washington and yourself relating to the nature and place of my confinement since that date.

HEADQUARTERS ARMY OF THE POTOMAC,
September 7, 1862.

SIR: I have been applied to by General Stone for permission to serve with the Army during the impending movements, even if only as a spectator.

I have no doubt as to the loyalty and devotion of General Stone, but am unwilling to use his services unless I know that it meets the approval of Government.

I not only have no objection to his employment in this army, but, more than that, would be glad to avail myself of his services as soon as circumstances permit.

Very truly, yours,

GEO. B. McCLELLAN,
Major-General.

Hon. E. M. STANTON, *Secretary of War.*

WASHINGTON, D. C., *September* 25, 1862.

GENERAL: I have the honor to submit the following for the consideration of the General-in-Chief:

On the 8th February, 1862, about the hour of midnight, I was arrested by an armed guard, commanded by Brig. Gen. George Sykes, and placed in close confinement, under guard, in the quarters of the officers of the provost-marshal's guard.

At the time of the arrest I asked of General Sykes the cause, but was informed that he was perfectly ignorant of it.

Early on the morning of the 9th February I addressed the following letter to the headquarters of the Army of the Potomac, viz:

WASHINGTON, D. C., *February* 9, 1862.

GENERAL: This morning, about 1 o'clock, I was arrested by Brigadier-General Sykes, commanding City Guard, and made a close prisoner, by order, as I was informed, of the Major-General Commanding-in-Chief.

Conscious of being and having been at all times a faithful soldier of the United States, I most respectfully request that I may be furnished, at as early a moment as practicable, with a copy of whatever charges may have been preferred against me, and the opportunity of promptly meeting them.

Very respectfully, I am, general, your most obedient servant,

CHAS. P. STONE,
Brigadier-General Volunteers.

Brig. Gen. S. WILLIAMS,
Assistant Adjutant-General, Headquarters Army of the Potomac.

The above letter was carried by General Sykes to General Williams early in the morning of the 9th February. No answer has ever been received by me.

During the night of February 9 I was conveyed, in charge of a lieutenant and two police officers, to Fort Hamilton, New York Harbor, and turned over to the custody of Lieut. Col. Martin Burke, Third Artillery, who immediately sent me in charge of a guard to Fort Lafayette, where I was delivered to Lieutenant Wood, Ninth Infantry.

At Fort Lafayette the money was taken from my pockets, and I was placed in solitary confinement in a room ordinarily used as enlisted-men's quarters, where I was kept forty-nine days, no letter being allowed to reach or to leave me without inspection.

During this confinement I applied at different times, through the proper channels, for speedy trial, for charges, for change of locality, and access to the records of my office and headquarters to enable me to prepare for trial, &c., but never received any response to any of my communications.

After forty-nine days I was transferred to Fort Hamilton, and allowed opportunities of obtaining air and exercise, but the same restrictions were continued on my correspondence.

I applied for a copy of the order placing me in confinement, but could not obtain it.

I applied to my custodian to learn what crime was alleged against me, and he informed me that he knew nothing of it.

After thus awaiting charges more than two months, I applied for suspension of arrest and opportunity to serve before Yorktown, but received no reply.

Again, on the occasion of the retreat of our forces from the Shenandoah Valley, I applied for suspension of arrest and opportunity to serve, but received no reply.

On the 4th of July I again applied, but received no reply.

I applied for an extension of limits, but received only the reply that the Secretary of War was absent, and no extension could be given until his return.

Finally, on the 16th August, 1862, after one hundred and eighty-nine days of confinement, I was fully released from arrest, without any order what to do.

I immediately reported myself for duty.

I would respectfully represent that the law requires, peremptorily, that when an officer is placed in arrest, it shall be the duty of the officer who orders the arrest to see that the officer arrested is furnished within eight days with a copy of the charges against him.

Two hundred and twenty-eight days have now elapsed since my arrest, and not only have no charges been furnished me, but no allegation of crime to justify arrest has been made to me or to those who had me in custody.

I now respectfully apply again to the General-in-Chief for a copy of any charges or allegations which may have been made against me and the opportunity of promptly meeting them, and in case trial cannot be had, I would respectfully ask that at least the charges may be furnished, so that I may know what falsehoods require refutation and witnesses I shall require to accomplish the refutation.

It is perhaps superfluous for me to call attention to the fact that those who have served under my orders, and therefore must be the witnesses of my conduct in service, have been falling in battle and by disease by hundreds and thousands since the date of my arrest. So great have been the casualties, that the command from which I was taken is now reduced more than one-half.

Very respectfully, I am, general, your most obedient servant,

CHAS. P. STONE,
Brigadier-General.

Brig. Gen. L. THOMAS, *Adjutant-General U. S. Army.*

HEADQUARTERS OF THE ARMY,
Washington, September 30, 1862.

GENERAL: Your letter of the 25th to the Adjutant-General of the Army has been referred to me for reply.

I learn from the Secretary of War that the order releasing you from Fort Hamilton also released you from arrest. You therefore are no longer under arrest, but as you have not been assigned to me for duty, I can give you no orders.

I have no official information of the cause of your arrest, but I understood that it was made by the orders of the President. No charges or specifications are, so far as I can ascertain, on file against you.

The matter, I learn, is to be immediately investigated, and copies of charges, when preferred, will be furnished you by the Judge-Advocate-General.

Very respectfully, your obedient servant,

H. W. HALLECK,
General-in-Chief.

Brig. Gen. CHARLES P. STONE, *Washington.*

WASHINGTON, D. C., *December 1, 1862.*

GENERAL: At the time of my arrest and imprisonment, in February last, the officer who effected it (Brigadier-General Sykes) claimed to act under your order, although he exhibited no other authority than an armed force.

Under the eleventh section of the act of Congress approved July 17, 1862, it is made the duty of any officer who shall order the arrest of another to see that a copy of the charges be furnished to the arrested officer within eight days of the date of the arrest; and by proviso the requirements of the section were made applicable to all officers under arrest at the date of the passage of the act.

Under this law I respectfully request that you will cause me to be furnished with a copy of the charges which led to my arrest, and which I have repeatedly asked for, through the ordinary channels of official communication, without success.

I have the honor to remain, general, with much respect, your most obedient servant,

CHAS. P. STONE,
Brigadier-General.

Maj. Gen. GEORGE B. McCLELLAN, <i>U. S. Army, New York.</i>

NEW YORK, December 5, 1862.

GENERAL: I have the honor to acknowledge the receipt of your letter of the 1st instant.

The order for your arrest in February last was given by the Secretary of War. I had the order in his handwriting several days before it was finally carried into effect.

When the order was first given by the Secretary, he informed me that it was at the solicitation of the Congressional Committee on the Conduct of the War and based upon testimony taken by them.

On the evening when you were arrested I submitted to the Secretary the written result of the examination of a refugee from Leesburg. This information, to a certain extent, agreed with the evidence stated to have been taken by the committee, and upon its being imparted to the Secretary he again instructed me to cause you to be arrested, which I at once did.

At the time I stated to the Secretary that I could not from the information in my possession understand how charges could be framed against you; that the case was too indefinite.

On several occasions after your arrest I called the attention of the Secretary to the propriety of giving you a prompt trial, but the reply always was either that there was no time to attend to the case or that the Congressional committee were still engaged in collecting additional evidence in your case, and were not yet fully prepared to frame the charges.

I am, general, very respectfully, your obedient servant,

GEO. B. McCLELLAN,
Major-General, U. S. Army.

Brig. Gen. CHARLES P. STONE,
    U. S. Volunteers, Washington, D. C.

[NOTE.]—On the receipt of General McClellan's letter of December 5, 1862, General Stone addressed a letter to him, asking that he might be furnished with the name of the Leesburg refugee referred to and a copy of his statement. The following reply was received:

WILLARD'S HOTEL,
Washington, D. C., December 10, 1862.

GENERAL: I am directed by General McClellan to acknowledge the receipt of your note of December 8, 1862.

The name of the refugee he does not recollect, and the last time he recollects seeing the statement was at the War Department, immediately previous to your arrest.   If he has a copy, it is among his official papers, which papers are *en route* for New York, and will be examined on his return, and if the paper referred to be found among them, he will furnish you with a copy.

I am, general, very respectfully, your obedient servant,

N. B. SWEITZER,
Lieutenant-Colonel and Aide-de-Camp.

Brig. Gen. CHARLES P. STONE, *U. S. Volunteers.*

[NOTE.]—The statement referred to within has not up to this date been furnished me.

CHAS. P. STONE,
Brigadier-General.

MARCH 6, 1863.

No. 19.

Reply of the Secretary of War to resolution of House of Representatives.

WAR DEPARTMENT,
Washington, December 12, 1861.

SIR: I have the honor to acknowledge the receipt of a resolution of the House of Representatives calling for certain information with regard to the disastrous movement of our troops at Ball's Bluff, and to transmit to you a report of the Adjutant-General of the U. S. Army, from which you will perceive that a compliance with the resolution at this time would, in the opinion of the General-in-Chief, be injurious to the public service.

Very respectfully,

SIMON CAMERON,
Secretary of War.

Hon. G. A. GROW, *Speaker House of Representatives.*

[Inclosure.]

HEADQUARTERS OF THE ARMY,
ADJUTANT-GENERAL'S OFFICE,
Washington, December 11, 1861.

SIR : In compliance with your instructions I have the honor to report, in reference to the resolution of the honorable the House of Representatives, received the 3d instant, " That the Secretary of War be requested, if not incompatible with the public interest, to report to this House whether any, and if any, what measures have been taken to ascertain who is responsible for the disastrous movement of our troops at Ball's Bluff," that the General-in-Chief of the Army is of opinion an inquiry on the subject of the resolution would at this time be injurious to the public service.

The resolution is herewith respectfully returned.

Respectfully submitted.

L. THOMAS,
Adjutant-General.

Hon. SECRETARY OF WAR, *Washington.*

No. 20.

Report of General G. T. Beauregard, C. S. Army, with congratulatory orders.

HDQRS. FIRST CORPS, ARMY OF THE POTOMAC,
Near Centreville, December 6, 1861.

GENERAL : I have the honor to transmit with this the report of Brig-adier-General Evans of the battle fought by the troops of his command, near Leesburg, Va., on the 21st of October, 1861. I shall also inclose herewith lists of the killed and wounded * and the reports of the separate regimental and battalion commanders.

I have also to forward for the information of the War Department, and as a part of the history of the operations resulting in that battle, my letter of instructions to Brigadier-General Evans, dated October 17, 1861. A map prepared by General Evans will be forwarded by hand.

Respectfully, your obedient servant,

G. T. BEAUREGARD,
General, Commanding.

General S. COOPER,
Adjutant and Inspector General, Richmond, Va.

[Inclosure.]

HDQRS. FIRST CORPS, ARMY OF THE POTOMAC,
Near Centreville, October 17, 1861.

COLONEL : Your note of this date has been laid before the general, who wishes to be informed of the reasons that influenced you to take up your present position, as you omit to inform him. The point you occupy is understood to be very strong, and the general hopes you will be able to maintain it against odds should the enemy press across the river and move in this direction. To prevent such a movement and junction of Banks' forces with McClellan's is of the utmost military importance, and you will be expected to make a desperate stand, falling back only in the face of an overwhelming enemy. In case, unfortunately, you should be obliged to retire, march on this point and effect a junction with his corps.

If you still deem it best to remain at Carter's Mill, the general desires you to maintain possession of Leesburg as an outpost by a regiment without baggage or tents, and to be relieved every three or four days.

As you may be aware, this army has taken up a line of triangular shape, with Centreville as the salient, one side running to Union Mills, the other to Stone Bridge, with outposts of regiments 3 or 4 miles in advance in all directions and cavalry pickets yet in advance as far as Fairfax Court-House.

Respectfully, your obedient servant,

THOMAS JORDAN,
Assistant Adjutant-General.

Col. N. G. EVANS, *Commanding at Leesburg, Va.*

---

* A tabular statement, compiled from those lists, appears as report No. 22, p. 353.

GENERAL ORDERS, }   HDQRS. ARMY OF THE POTOMAC,
    No. 47.   }   October 22, 1861.

The commanding general announces to the Army with satisfaction a brilliant success, achieved yesterday, near Leesburg, by Colonel Evans and his brigade. After a contest lasting from early morning until dark this brigade routed and drove back to the river a very large force of the enemy, capturing six cannons and 200 prisoners, and killing and wounding a large number. The skill and courage with which this victory has been achieved entitles Colonel Evans and the Seventh Brigade of the First Corps to the thanks of the Army.

By command of General Johnston:

THOS. G. RHETT,
Assistant Adjutant-General.

—

GENERAL ORDERS, }   HDQRS. 1ST CORPS, ARMY OF POTOMAC,
    No. 64.   }   *Near Centreville, October 23, 1861.*

The general commanding, in communicating to his army corps General Orders, No. 47, dated October 22, from the headquarters of the Army of the Potomac, must avail himself of the occasion to express his confident hope that all of his command, officers and men, by the brilliant achievement of their comrades in arms of the Seventh Brigade, on the 21st instant, will be assured of our ability to cope successfully with the foe arrayed against us, in whatsoever force he may offer battle. Under the inspirations of a just cause, defending all we hold dear on earth or worth living for, and with the manifest aid of the God of Battles, we can and must drive our invaders from the soil of Virginia, despite their numbers and their long accumulating war equipage.

Soldiers of the First Corps! your enemy is demoralized by these defeats. His numbers give but temporary confidence, which at all times you can dissipate in an instant, when animated by the resolution to conquer or die facing him.

After the success of the Seventh Brigade in the conflict of the 21st of October no odds must discourage or make you doubtful of victory when you are called upon by your general to engage in battle.

By command of General Beauregard:

THOMAS JORDAN,
Assistant Adjutant General.

———

No. 21.

Reports of Brig. Gen. N. G. Evans, C. S. Army, with correspondence.

HEADQUARTERS SEVENTH BRIGADE,
Leesburg, Va., October 31, 1861.

COLONEL: I beg leave to submit the following report of the action of the troops of the Seventh Brigade in the battle of the 21st and 22d instant with the enemy at Leesburg, Va.:

On Saturday night, the 19th instant, about 7 o'clock p. m., the enemy commenced a heavy cannonading from three batteries, one playing on my intrenchment (known as Fort Evans), one on the Leesburg turnpike, and one on Edwards Ferry. Heavy firing was also heard in the direction of Dranesville.

At 12 o'clock at night I ordered my entire brigade to the Burnt Bridge, on the turnpike. The enemy had been reported as approaching from Dranesville in large force. Taking a strong position on the north side of Goose Creek, I awaited his approach. Reconnoitering the turnpike on Sunday morning, the courier of General McCall was captured, bearing dispatches to General Meade to examine the roads leading to Leesburg. From this prisoner I learned the position of the enemy near Dranesville. During Sunday the enemy kept a deliberate fire without any effect.

Early on Monday morning, the 21st instant, I heard the firing of my pickets at Big Spring, who had discovered that at an unguarded point the enemy had effected a crossing in force of five companies and were advancing on Leesburg. Captain [Wm. L.] Duff, of the Seventeenth Regiment, immediately attacked him, driving him back, with several killed and wounded.

On observing the movements of the enemy from Fort Evans at 6 o'clock a. m., I found he had effected a crossing both at Edwards Ferry and Ball's Bluff, and I made preparations to meet him in both positions, and immediately ordered four companies of infantry (two of the Eighteenth, one of the Seventeenth, and one of the Thirteenth) and a cavalry force to relieve Captain Duff; the whole force, under the immediate command of Lieut. Col. W. H. Jenifer, who was directed to hold his position till the enemy made further demonstration of his design of attack. This force soon became warmly engaged with the enemy, and drove them back for some distance in the woods.

At about 10 o'clock I became convinced that the main point of attack would be at Ball's Bluff, and ordered Colonel Hunton, with his regiment, the Eighth Virginia Volunteers, to repair immediately to the support of Colonel Jenifer. I directed Colonel Hunton to form line of battle immediately in the rear of Colonel Jenifer's command and to drive the enemy to the river; that I would support his right with artillery. About 12.20 o'clock p. m. Colonel Hunton united his command with that of Colonel Jenifer, and both commands soon became hotly engaged with the enemy in their strong position in the woods.

Watching carefully the action, I saw the enemy were constantly being re-enforced, and at 2.30 o'clock p. m. ordered Colonel Burt to march his regiment, the Eighteenth Mississippi, and attack the left flank of the enemy, while Colonels Hunton and Jenifer attacked him in front. On arriving at his position Colonel Burt was received with a tremendous fire from the enemy concealed in a ravine, and was compelled to divide his regiment to stop the flank movement of the enemy.

At this time, about 3 o'clock, finding the enemy were in large force, I ordered Colonel Featherston, with his regiment, the Seventeenth Mississippi, to repair at double-quick to the support of Colonel Burt, where he arrived in twenty minutes, and the action became general along my whole line, and was very hot and brisk for more than two hours, the enemy keeping up a constant fire with his batteries on both sides of the river. At about 6 o'clock p. m. I saw that my command had driven the enemy near the banks of the Potomac. I ordered my entire force to charge and to drive him into the river. The charge was immediately made by the whole command, and the forces of the enemy were completely routed, and cried out for quarter along his whole line.

In this charge the enemy were driven back at the point of the bayonet, and many killed and wounded by this formidable weapon. In the precipitate retreat of the enemy on the bluffs of the river many of his troops rushed into the water and were drowned, while many others, in overloading the boats, sunk them, and shared the same fate. The rout now, about 7 o'clock, became complete, and the enemy commenced throwing his arms into the river. During this action I held Col. William Barksdale, with nine companies of his regiment, the Thirteenth Mississippi, and six pieces of artillery, as a reserve, as well as to keep up a demonstration against the force of the enemy at Edwards Ferry.

At 8 o'clock p. m. the enemy surrendered his forces at Ball's Bluff, and the prisoners were marched to Leesburg. I then ordered my brigade (with the exception of the Thirteenth Regiment Mississippi, which remained in front of Edwards Ferry) to retire to the town of Leesburg, and rest for the night.

On Tuesday morning I was informed by Colonel Barksdale that the enemy were still in considerable force at Edwards Ferry. I directed him to make a thorough reconnaissance of the position and strength of the enemy and attack him. At 2 o'clock p. m. he gallantly attacked a much superior force in their intrenchments, driving them to the bank of the river, killing 30 or 40, and wounding a considerable number. About sundown, the enemy being strongly re-enforced and stationed in rifle-pits, Colonel Barksdale wisely retired with his regiment to Fort Evans, leaving a guard of two companies to watch the movements of the enemy, who, evidently expecting a renewed attack, retired during the night and recrossed the river at Edwards Ferry.

On Wednesday morning, finding my brigade very much exhausted, I left Colonel Barksdale, with his regiment, with two pieces of artillery and a cavalry force, as a grand guard, and I ordered the other three regiments to fall back towards Carter's Mill to rest and to be collected in order. Colonel Hunton, with his regiment and two pieces of artillery, were halted at a strong position on the south bank of the Sycolin, about 3 miles south of Leesburg.

I would here state that in an interview on Monday night with the commissioned officers of the Federal Army taken prisoners I was convinced that they expected to be recaptured either during the night or the next day, and as the captured officers refused their parole not to take up arms against the Southern Confederacy till duly exchanged, I ordered the whole number to be immediately marched to Manassas. This parole was only offered to give them the liberty of the town, as I did not wish to confine them with the privates.

In the engagement on the 21st of October, which lasted nearly thirteen hours, our loss, from a force of 1,709 aggregate, was as follows : *

*   *   *   *   *   *   *

The force of the enemy, as far as I have been able to ascertain, was five regiments and three pieces of artillery at Ball's Bluff, and four regiments, two batteries, and a squadron of cavalry at Edwards Ferry, numbering in all about 8,000 troops. In addition to this force three batteries of long range were constantly firing on my troops from the Maryland side of the river.

The loss of the enemy, so far as known, is as follows: 1,300 killed, wounded, and drowned; captured 710 prisoners, 1,500 stand of arms, three pieces of cannon, one stand of colors, a large number of cartridge-boxes, bayonet scabbards, and a quantity of camp furniture. Among the killed of the enemy was General Baker, formerly Senator from Oregon, and several other commissioned officers. Among the prisoners

---

* Statement omitted is tabulated in report No. 22, p. 353.

taken were 22 commissioned officers, the names of whom have already been furnished.

General C. P. Stone commanded the Federal forces until 3 o'clock on the morning of the 22d, when he was superseded by Maj. Gen. N. P. Banks.

The engagement on our side was fought entirely with the musket. The artillery was in position to do effective service should the enemy have advanced from their cover. The enemy were armed with the Minie musket, the Belgian gun, and Springfield musket; a telescopic target rifle was also among the arms found.

In closing my report I would call the attention of the general commanding to the heroism and gallantry displayed by the officers and men of the Seventh Brigade in the actions of the 21st and 22d of October. The promptness with which every commander obeyed and the spirit with which their men executed my orders to attack the enemy in much superior force and in a position where he had great advantages entitles them to the thanks of the Southern Confederacy. Without food or rest for more than twelve hours previous to the commencement of the battle, they drove an enemy four times their number from the soil of Virginia, killing and taking prisoners a greater number than our whole force engaged. To witness the patience, enthusiasm, and devotion of the troops to our cause during an action of thirteen hours excited my warmest admiration.

As my entire brigade exceeded my most sanguine expectations in their intrepidity and endurance, I am unable to individualize any particular command, as the tenacity with which each regiment held their positions was equaled only by their undaunted courage and firm determination to conquer.

To my general staff I am much indebted. Maj. John D. Rogers, brigade quartermaster, was directed to conduct the baggage train beyond Goose Creek, which difficult duty was performed in the night with great regularity. Captain Orr, brigade commissary, was actively engaged in securing commissary stores and in providing cooked rations for the brigade. To my acting aide-de-camp, Lieut. Charles B. Wildman, of the Seventeenth Regiment Virginia Volunteers, and my volunteer aide, Mr. William H. Rogers, I am particularly indebted for services on the field of battle. Lieutenant Wildman conducted the Eighteenth Regiment and Mr. Rogers the Seventeenth Regiment of Mississippi Volunteers to their respective positions in the action, and both repeatedly bore my orders under heavy fire. Capt. A. L. Evans, assistant adjutant-general, though detained by other duty till 2 o'clock p. m., rendered valuable service. The medical staff, both brigade and regimental, were all actively engaged during the day in removing the dead and wounded and in patriotically administering relief to the dying on the field.

I am pained to report the fall of the gallant Col. E. R. Burt, of the Eighteenth Regiment Mississippi Volunteers. He was mortally wounded about 4 o'clock p. m., while gallantly leading his regiment under a tremendous fire. His loss is truly severe to his regiment and to our common cause.

At about 2 o'clock p. m. on the 21st I sent a message to Gen. R. L. Wright to bring his militia force to my assistance at Fort Evans. He reported to me in person that he was unable to get his men to turn out, though there were a great number in town and arms and ammunition were offered them.

The prisoners taken were sent to Manassas under charge of Capt. O. R. Singleton, of the Eighteenth Regiment Mississippi Volunteers, with his company, and Capt. W. A. P. Jones, of the Seventeenth Regiment Mississippi Volunteers, and a detachment of cavalry, the whole under the command of Captain Singleton, who conducted 529 prisoners nearly 25 miles after the great fatigue of the battle.

Accompanying this report I inclose an accurate map of the field of battle,* and the reports of the immediate commanders; to the latter I would respectfully refer for individual acts of gallantry and patriotism. I also forward the report of the field officer of the day, Lieutenant-Colonel McGuirk, of the Seventeenth Regiment Mississippi Volunteers, to whom I am much indebted for information of the flank movements of the enemy. Lieut. Sheffield Duval, here on duty as Topographical Engineer, and Sergt. William R. Chambliss, of the Eighteenth Regiment Mississippi Volunteers, my private secretary, rendered material service, the former by fighting on foot with his musket as a private, the latter by conveying my orders on the field of battle under heavy fire.

Very respectfully, your obedient servant,

N. G. EVANS,
Brigadier-General, Commanding Seventh Brigade.

Lieut. Col. THOMAS JORDAN,
A. A. G., 1st Corps, Army of the Potomac, near Centreville.

—

HEADQUARTERS THIRD MILITARY DISTRICT, S. C.,
Adams Run, S. C., March 7, 1862.

SIR: As I see by the newspapers that a resolution has passed the Confederate Congress calling for the report of Col. W. H. Jenifer's cavalry force of the battle of Leesburg, I deem it but justice to the troops under my command at Leesburg, on October 21st and 22d, to state that Colonel Jenifer was never placed in command of any other troops but the five companies first engaged. I sent for Colonel Jenifer and placed him in command of these companies and of none others; neither was Colonel Jenifer acquainted with the plan of attack, as is shown by the reports of the regimental commanders engaged. I would also state that I sent for Colonel Jenifer and called his attention to the contradictory statements in his report. I also communicated the facts of his report to Colonels Barksdale, Featherston, Hunton, and Griffin, who expressed their surprise, as they received no orders from Colonel Jenifer.

I make this statement to explain the contradictory reports. By reference to the reports of the colonels commanding a true history of the battle will be found.

Should Col. W. H. Jenifer's report be published, I respectfully request that this statement be also published.

Very respectfully, your obedient servant,

N. G. EVANS,
Brigadier-General, C. S. Army.

Hon. SECRETARY OF WAR, *Richmond, Va.*

[Indorsements.]

MARCH 12, 1862.

If Colonel Jenifer's report was transmitted through General Evans, he had then the opportunity to make the proper indorsement on it and cannot now add other remarks, and thus irregularly change the record after the parties have separated. If the report was not transmitted by General Evans, he has now the right to annex to it the within statement.

* Not found.

The Secretary may receive an additional report from the commanding officer, and as such may of course submit it for transmission to Congress, but this should be in cases where further information was to be communicated.

JEFFERSON DAVIS.

MARCH 15, 1862.

General Evans' report of the battle of Leesburg, together with the reports of the officers who were under him (Colonel Jenifer included) were forwarded by him through General Beauregard, and were received at this office December 3, 1861.

Copies of the whole of these papers were furnished Congress December 10, 1861.

JNO. WITHERS,
Assistant Adjutant-General.

—

HEADQUARTERS THIRD MILITARY DISTRICT, S. C.,
Adams' Run, S. C., March 25, 1862.

SIR: I have the honor to acknowledge the receipt of your communication of the 18th instant in reply to my letter of the 7th of March, and beg leave to state that it was not my intention to alter the records of the War Department, but to make a supplementary report (which is not unusual) to my report of the battle of Leesburg. As to the separation of the parties, whom I suppose to be General Beauregard and myself, as we are the only persons concerned in the indorsements and forwarding of the reports, my letter can be readily forwarded for the indorsement of General Beauregard. I would therefore respectfully request that my letter be considered as a supplementary report and forwarded for the indorsement of General Beauregard.*

Very respectfully, your obedient servant,

N. G. EVANS,
Brigadier-General.

Hon. SECRETARY OF WAR, *Richmond, Va.*

—

No. 22.

Return of casualties in the Seventh Brigade, First Corps, Army of the Potomac, at the battle of Leesburg, Va., October 21, 22, 1861.

Command.	Killed.		Wounded.		Missing.		Aggregate.	Remarks.
	Officers.	Enlisted men.	Officers.	Enlisted men.	Officers.	Enlisted men.		
Thirteenth Mississippi	1	3	.....	2	......	1	7	
Seventeenth Mississippi	2	......	1	8	......	......	11	
Eighteenth Mississippi	......	22	7	56	......	......	85	Colonel Burt, since dead.
Eighth Virginia	......	8	4	39	1	......	52	Three privates, since dead, one lieutenant captured.
Total	3	33	12	105	1	1	155	

* A copy so forwarded, under date of April 2, 1862, was returned April 12, by General Beauregard, indorsed "Respectfully forwarded, having no remarks to make."

No. 23.

Report of Col. William Barksdale, Thirteenth Mississippi Infantry.

REGIMENTAL HEADQUARTERS,
Fort Evans, near Leesburg, October 28, 1861.

GENERAL: I have the honor to report that in obedience to your orders I left my encampment near Ball's Mill, on Goose Creek, with my regiment, on Sunday morning, the 20th instant, at 5 o'clock, and encamped the following night on the Alexandria turnpike road, near the Burnt Bridge over Goose Creek, about 4 miles east from Leesburg, with the Eighth Virginia Regiment, Colonel Hunton, on my right, and the Seventeenth Mississippi Regiment, Colonel Featherston, on my left.

Early on Monday morning the guns of the enemy opened upon us from their batteries on the Maryland side of the Potomac River, but without effect. At 8 o'clock I proceeded with my regiment to Fort Evans, and forthwith took position in the woods to the right of the fort, where I could observe the movements of the enemy.

About 12 o'clock I dispatched Capt. L. D. Fletcher's company (D) to report to you at Fort Evans. I herewith inclose his report of the company's movements that day. During the whole of the engagement it was in the thickest of the fight, rendering efficient service, and bearing itself with undaunted courage.

About 1.30 o'clock I was ordered by you to advance in the direction of Edwards Ferry, and to ascertain the position and number of the enemy. I marched at once in that direction, and halted in a skirt of woods near the Daily house, at the same time directing Captain McIntosh to skirmish in the woods and near the river on the left, and Captain Eckford, with a platoon of his company, to skirmish on the right of that house, and report without delay the result of their observation. Both reported that the enemy were in force in large numbers on this side of the river and just beyond the Daily house. I immediately ordered the regiment to advance, and when near the house a number of shots were fired by the advance guard on both sides, killing 1 man of my regiment. The loss of the enemy not ascertained.

Perceiving that the object of the enemy was to outflank me on the right, and learning that Colonels Burt and Featherston, with their respective commands, had been ordered in another direction, I formed my regiment on the right of the Edwards Ferry road, intending to commence the attack from the woods stretching along the Daily plantation and to the right of the house, at the same time directing Captain Bradley to skirmish on the left and Captain [Wm. H.] Worthington on the right.

At this moment I was ordered by you to hasten to the support of the Eighth Virginia Regiment and the Seventeenth and Eighteenth Mississippi Regiments, which were engaged with the enemy 2 miles from Edwards Ferry and near Conrad's Ferry. I at once, and in double-quick time, started to their relief, leaving Captain Worthington's company to observe the movements of the enemy at Edwards Ferry, but before reaching the scene of action I received two peremptory orders from you to return to the vicinity of Fort Evans, which was accordingly done, directing the companies of Captains [Saml. J.] Randell, [D. R.] McIntosh, and Worthington to remain in the rear, to prevent the advance of the enemy that night from Edwards Ferry.

I am satisfied that the presence of my command in position at Edwards Ferry prevented the advance of a large column of the enemy, which was intended to re-enforce General Baker's command near Conrad's Ferry, then engaged in battle with our forces.

On Tuesday morning I was ordered by you to reconnoiter the enemy at Edwards Ferry, and attack him if in my judgment his numbers and position would warrant me in doing so. Reaching the ground I occupied the day before, I ordered Captain Randell to skirmish on my left and Captain Eckford on my right. They reported that the enemy in very large numbers were stationed, as on the preceding day, near the banks of the river. From their movements, which could be easily seen from my position, I supposed they were planting a battery at the point of woods jutting out into the field to the right of the Daily house. I determined to make the attack at that point, and accordingly ordered Captain Eckford to advance with his and Captain McElroy's companies, to commence the engagement, and to charge and take the battery, if one should be found there.

Taking the road leading to Kephart's Mill, I halted the regiment in the woods to the right of the Daily plantation, and in a few minutes Captain Eckford commenced the attack upon several companies of pickets which were stationed along the field, charging upon and driving them in great disorder and confusion before his fire. I ordered the regiment at once to advance, and the engagement in a moment became general. Under a heavy fire from the enemy's batteries on both sides of the river and an incessant fire from his lines on this side the regiment continued to advance some 400 yards, firing as it advanced, driving the enemy before it back to the river, and killing, so far as I have been able to learn, 35 or 40 of their number. The enemy having been driven back behind his field works, and greatly outnumbering my command, having also artillery on both sides of the river, I did not deem it proper further to continue the assault, and hence withdrew the regiment to its position near Fort Evans, which I reached some time after dark.

I herewith inclose Captain Eckford's report.

Every order I gave during both days was obeyed with promptness and alacrity, and the engagement on Tuesday was marked by the greatest possible zeal, courage, and enthusiasm on the part of both officers and men.*

* * * * * * *

WILLIAM BARKSDALE,
Colonel, Comdg. Thirteenth Regiment Mississippi Volunteers.

General N. G. EVANS, *Headquarters, Leesburg.*

No. 24.

Report of Capt. William J. Eckford, Thirteenth Mississippi Infantry, of action near Edwards Ferry.

CAMP NEAR FORT EVANS, *October 26, 1861.*

SIR: I have the honor to report that on the evening of the 22d inst., obedient to orders, I proceeded with my company and Captain [K.] McElroy's company (G) to open the engagement with the enemy posted about Edwards Ferry, by attacking a battery supposed to be planted in a point of woods on a ridge which made out from Goose Creek to Daily's field, and in front of the left of the enemy's line. Advancing

---

* For statement of casualties omitted see report No. 22, p. 353.

with the division by a narrow road which led through dense thickets to the corner of Daily's field, I examined the ground, and found it necessary to move some hundred yards to the right of the road, in order to avoid being observed by the enemy's pickets, who were posted in large numbers along a cross fence running from Daily's house to the point of the ridge on which we were advancing. I accordingly filed the division by the right about 150 yards, crossed a small ravine, and filed by the left to the top of the ridge, where the line was formed, about 75 paces to the rear of the supposed position of the enemy's battery.

At the signal to advance the division moved in excellent order, and with as much silence as practicable, through the dense undergrowth of pine which separated us from the point of attack to within 30 paces of the enemy's pickets. Here the firing commenced on either side, when I ordered the charge, which was obeyed with the greatest enthusiasm and gallantry. The enemy fled in great confusion, and were pursued into the open field, when I ordered the division to fall back and load under cover of the woods. The enemy's battery had been removed from the position taken in the morning, and their batteries stationed in the open field several hundred yards from the front of the division opened upon us with shell, when I gave the order to advance and form on the right of the regiment, which was done. During the charge of the regiment and division upon the enemy in the open field Lieut. H. C. Fluker and Private Asa Simmons, of Captain McElroy's company (G), were mortally wounded. In the charge of the enemy some 30 are supposed to have been killed.

Very respectfully, your obedient servant,

W. J. ECKFORD,
Captain Company C, Thirteenth Regiment Miss. Vols.

Col. WILLIAM BARKSDALE,
Thirteenth Regiment Mississippi Volunteers.

No. 25.

Report of Capt. L. D. Fletcher, Thirteenth Mississippi Infantry.

LEESBURG, *October* 22, 1861.

SIR : I beg leave to submit the following report of the part my company took in the engagement on yesterday, the 21st, near this place :

In obedience to an order received from you I reported my company, numbering about 90 men, to General Evans at Fort Evans, who ordered me to advance and skirmish a skirt of woods opposite and near to a small house, said to be Mrs. Jackson's. Upon my arrival there I encountered the pickets of the enemy, who held a position along a line of fence. They opened a fire upon my company, which was returned, the pickets of the enemy falling back into the field and some of them occupying positions in and around the house of Mrs. Jackson. My company continued to advance until we reached the fence just left by the enemy, who continued to fire upon us from the field and house, the fire being constantly returned by my men.

Finding that the enemy were so concealed that they could fire upon me with effect without my being able to reach them, I ordered my men to go over into the field and drive them from it and the house. My order was promptly obeyed by every man except two, who had been wounded. In a very short time we succeeded in driving them from their hiding place and put them to flight, killing and wounding 7 or 8 of their number. Having succeeded in clearing that locality of the enemy, I had done all that I had been ordered to do. After a few moments' delay I advanced my company across the field in the direction the enemy had taken, but found none of them.

Here I received an order to place my company on the left of the Eighth Virginia Regiment, which was said to be passing through the woods in the direction of the main body of the enemy to give them battle. This I attempted to do, but failed to find the Eighth Virginia, but soon a general engagement commenced between the Virginians and the enemy on my right. As soon as I could procure a reliable guide who knew the positions occupied by the contending forces I started to the Eighth Virginia Regiment to assist them. Upon my arrival my company was thrown forward into the field side by side with the Eighth Virginia Regiment and a part of the Eighteenth Mississippi Regiment, who had come up also, under command of Maj. E. G. Henry. Then it was that quite a spirited and hot contest ensued, in which my company acted a conspicuous part. The enemy having a position near a battery of howitzers, an order was given to charge the battery, which was responded to instantly by my company and the Virginians, and I think a portion of the Eighteenth Mississippi. The charge was successful, the guns were taken, several of my men being among the first to reach the guns and take part in their removal. In this charge I suffered no loss except one man (James E. Ballon), who fell mortally wounded, having been shot through the breast while making his way to the guns. At the time he fell he was among those farthest in advance.

Notwithstanding my line had become broken and my men, as well as all others who were here engaged, had become scattered, still none were seen to falter. I continued in the engagement until its close, when I returned with my company to the regiment near Fort Evans.

My loss during the day was 1 killed, 4 wounded; 2 very slightly by pieces of bombs while on our way to join the Eighth Virginia; the other 2 are not seriously hurt.

It affords me pleasure to be able truly to state that every man in my company, both officers and privates, did his whole duty nobly, willingly, and gallantly.

Very respectfully, your obedient servant,

L. D. FLETCHER,
Captain Co. D, Minute-men of Attala, Thirteenth Miss. Reg't.

Col. WILLIAM BARKSDALE,
Colonel Commanding Thirteenth Mississippi Regiment.

No. 26.

Report of Col. W. S. Featherston, Seventeenth Mississippi Infantry.

HDQRS. SEVENTEENTH REGIMENT MISS. VOLS.,
Camp near Leesburg, October 25, 1861.

SIR: In obedience to your order I beg leave to submit the following report of the action of this regiment in the battle of the 21st instant upon the banks of the Potomac, near Leesburg:

On the morning of the 21st, intelligence having been received that the enemy had crossed the river at Edwards Ferry in large force, and it being expected that they would advance upon Leesburg by the road from that point, this regiment was ordered to move from its position at the Burnt Bridge upon Goose Creek, where we had been bivouacked during the preceding day and night, and to take a position upon the right of the road in order to meet and repel him.

The Eighteenth Regiment Mississippi Volunteers was posted on the left of the same road, and Colonel Barksdale, with the Thirteenth Regiment Mississippi Volunteers, was ordered to advance through the woods lying between the road on which we were posted and that leading from Leesburg to Kephart's Mill, where it was expected that he would be the first to meet and engage the enemy. We remained in this position from about 7 o'clock a. m. until between 2 and 3 o'clock p. m., when the Eighteenth Mississippi Regiment was ordered to move up the river in quick time to a point opposite Harrison's Island, where the enemy had crossed in large numbers and made an attack upon the Eighth Virginia Regiment and some detached companies from this and the other Mississippi regiments which were stationed at that point.

About 3 o'clock p. m. I was ordered to advance rapidly to the support of these regiments, which were then engaged with a greatly superior force of the enemy, and accordingly we moved at a double-quick a distance of more than 2 miles to the field, when, perceiving that there was an interval of about 200 yards between the two other regiments, I immediately occupied it with my regiment. Learning that Colonel Burt had been dangerously wounded and borne from the field, I conferred with Lieut. Col. T. M. Griffin, commanding the Eighteenth Mississippi Regiment, and formed my regiment on the center of our line, in the edge of the woods, and immediately in front of the enemy, who were drawn up in the woods upon the opposite side of a small field, at the same time requesting Colonel Griffin to form the Eighteenth Regiment upon my right, which he did promptly. One company of the Eighteenth Regiment which was on our left fell into our line and continued to act with us in that position.

While we were forming our line, the Eighth Virginia Regiment, which, together with a detached company from this and one from the Eighteenth Regiment, was engaged with the enemy upon our left, made a gallant charge upon their right wing. At the same time Colonel Hunton, commanding that regiment, informed me that his ammunition was exhausted.

I then ordered the Seventeenth and Eighteenth Mississippi Regiments to advance without firing until they were close to the enemy, and then to fire and charge. This order was gallantly obeyed. The two regiments moved forward slowly and steadily under a heavy fire, but without returning it, until we had crossed the field and penetrated the woods in which the enemy were posted, and to within 40 or 50 yards of their line, when we poured in a close and deadly fire, which drove them back, and continued to advance, loading and firing until the enemy were driven to seek shelter beneath a high bluff immediately upon the brink of the river, and some of them in the river itself.

A few shots were fired into them while in this position, when they begged for quarter and asked to surrender. I ordered our men to cease, and told the enemy that if they desired to surrender they must send up one of their superior officers, to which they replied they had no such officer, and all of them had been killed. I then told them to send up their captain, when one captain came up, bearing a white flag, and surrendered to me. I then ordered their men to lay down their arms and march into our lines in small squads, which they did. Afterwards they were marched into town in charge of a company from this and one from the Eighteenth Regiment. The number of prisoners surrendered at that time in a body was about 300, among whom were two colonels and about twenty commissioned officers.

In all of the movements of which I have spoken the Seventeenth and Eighteenth Mississippi Regiments acted together, the Eighth Virginia Regiment not being engaged after the charge which I have mentioned. I cannot refrain from expressing my admiration for the gallantry displayed by the officers and men of the Eighteenth Regiment while under my observation, and particularly of Lieutenant-Colonel Griffin and Major Henry, their commanding officers.

All resistance on the part of the enemy having ceased, and night rendering further movements impracticable, the main body of the Seventeenth and Eighteenth Regiments was withdrawn to an open field near the town, where they bivouacked for the night, leaving two companies upon the field under the command of Lieutenant-Colonel McGuirk, of this regiment, to secure stragglers from the enemy. About 11 o'clock p. m. I sent another detachment of 90 men from my regiment to the field, to gather up and remove our dead and wounded. These detachments, together with one from the Eighth Virginia Regiment, secured about 200 additional prisoners during the night and about the same number during the next morning.

I have neglected to mention that in our advance upon the enemy we captured one 12-pounder rifled cannon near the banks of the river. The other gun captured was taken in the same movement a little in advance and to the left of the rifled cannon. Lieutenant-Colonel McGuirk having been ordered on detached service by you as field officer of the day was not able to act with the regiment till late in the day. As soon, however, as it was possible, and before the battle had closed, he joined the regiment, and entered at once upon the discharge of the duties of his position with courage and skill. During his absence I requested Major Lyle to act as lieutenant-colonel and Capt. W. D. Holder to act as major. Both of these gentlemen discharged the responsible duties of their respective positions in a manner entirely satisfactory and worthy of all commendation.

Capt. E. W. Upshaw, of this regiment, who had been ordered to the left to re-enforce the Eighth Virginia Regiment, joined that regiment in their last charge, in which they drove back the right wing of the enemy, forcing them to abandon a piece of artillery which was afterwards brought off by our troops.

For two months previous to the battle Captain Duff, of this regiment, had been stationed with his company on picket duty at Big Spring, between Leesburg and the river. Their position was a dangerous and trying one, being constantly exposed to sudden attacks from the enemy, and its duties were at all times arduous, but I am only the more gratified to say that they were uniformly discharged in the most satisfactory manner. Early on the morning of the 21st Captain Duff was attacked near Big Spring by a body of the enemy outnumbering his own command at least four to one, but after a sharp skirmish he repulsed them with considerable loss. Later in the forenoon of the day, he, in connection with two companies of the Eighteenth Regiment and Captain Ball's troop of cavalry, who had been sent to his support, engaged the enemy twice, in both of which affairs they were successfully met and repulsed. I submit herewith the report made to me by Captain Duff, giving a detailed account of his movements during the day.

It gives me much pleasure to express my entire satisfaction with the conduct of the officers and men of my regiment during the entire day. Indeed too much praise cannot be given to our troops for the coolness and courage with which they met and repulsed the enemy at every point. In the last charge, which crowned our success and completed the discomfiture of the enemy, no troops could have behaved better. The whole line moved forward in the most admirable order upon a vastly superior force, reserving their fire until within the most effective range; then pouring it in with deadly effect, and rushing forward over ground broken into abrupt hills and ravines and covered with thick woods, without a single halt or waver, until the enemy were literally driven into the river; and this, too, under a heavy fire, and after having been under arms almost without intermission for more than thirty-six hours, and while wearied with several long and rapid movements made during the preceding day and night. While such a spirit animates our soldiers we can never know defeat.

In all our movements during the battle, as well as those preceding and following it, I was much indebted to the officers of my staff for their active and cheerful exertions and co-operations. Adjutant Fiser, in particular, rendered most important and effective service upon the left of our regiment during the battle, and also in carrying communications between myself and other commanders, in which he was often exposed to great danger.

When all the troops engaged, both officers and men, behaved with so much gallantry, it would be unnecessary and invidious to attempt to particularize any of the numerous instances of individual heroism which have come to my notice.

In conclusion I would state, with much pleasure and thankfulness, that notwithstanding the heavy fire to which we were exposed our loss is remarkably small, being only 2 killed and 9 wounded. I can attribute this under Providence only to the fact that throughout the entire engagement my regiment preserved the most perfect order in their alignments and obedience to orders.

I am, very respectfully, your obedient servant,

W. S. FEATHERSTON,
Colonel Seventeenth Regiment Mississippi Volunteers.

General N. G. EVANS,
Comdg. Seventh Brigade, First Corps, Army of the Potomac.

No. 27.

Report of Lieut. Col. John McGuirk, Seventeenth Mississippi Infantry, of events October 20–23.

HDQRS. SEVENTEENTH REGIMENT MISS. VOLS.,
In Camp near Carter's Mill, October 25, 1861.

GENERAL: I beg leave to report that, in accordance with your instructions, issued to me as field officer of the day at the burnt bridge, on the Alexandria and Leesburg turnpike, October 20, at 5 o'clock p. m., I proceeded in the direction of Edwards Ferry. I found Colonel

Burt, with his regiment, in the road between Kephart's Mill and Daily's house. By your directions I told the colonel to move his command forward to Daily's house, and send forward two companies with me to the ferry. When I arrived at the road leading to the ferry I met the cavalry picket, who stated positively that the enemy had driven him in, leveling their guns at him, they having crossed two regiments before he left. I instructed this picket to report to you at once; took 10 picked men and a lieutenant, together with your Mr. Alexander. I went to the mouth of Goose Creek, and found no enemy. There were signs of a boat having touched the bank. I reported the fact to you about 11 o'clock on the night of the 20th October. I also told you that I left a picket of our men at the burnt warehouse, and that I informed Lieutenant-Colonel Jenifer of the fact. You then instructed me to inform the colonel that he might, with his command, go to bed; and you ordered me to go at once to White's Ford, visiting Captain Duff's pickets up the river to the head of Mason's Island, and report after daybreak. I reached the pickets at White's Ford, and shortly after I was on the heights above Mrs. Orrison's house, watching a brigade (four regiments) drawn up in line of battle, apparently awaiting marching orders. As this was the only demonstration I witnessed in my travels, I watched the movements of this brigade, and as I waited one of the pickets at White's Ford came up and told me he heard firing of small-arms down the river. I left him to watch, and started as the brigade filed down the river towards the point at which the firing was reported.

When I reached White's Ford I was informed that there was fighting towards Leesburg, in the direction of Conrad's Ferry. I hastened on and met a courier near Henry Ball's house, who informed me that I was cut off, as the enemy was between me and the town engaging our forces. I hastened forward and arrived at the intrenchments a little after 4 p. m., and informed you of the approaching forces to sustain the enemy, and asked permission to join my regiment, which you granted. I found on my entrance upon the battle-field a detachment of the brave Eighth Virginia Regiment resting upon their arms, being forced to retire (as I learned) from exhaustion and the want of ammunition. I also found a company of the Eighteenth Mississippi Regiment, which I put in line upon the left of my regiment (the Seventeenth Mississippi). I then reported to Col. W. S. Featherston, who assigned me my position upon the right of my regiment, and informed me that Col. E. R. Burt, Eighteenth Mississippi Regiment, had been carried from the field wounded. I found the Eighteenth Regiment, under command of Lieutenant-Colonel Griffin, formed on the right of the Seventeenth Mississippi Regiment. These forces were under command of Col. W. S. Featherston, who had drawn them into line and was advancing firing. He ordered the right and left wings up, thus forming a crescent line, which enabled us with raking fire to cut down the advancing enemy. The men manifested confidence under the coolness of their officers. They seemed fighting a sham battle, when above the roar of musketry was heard the command of Colonel Featherston, "Charge, Mississippians, charge! Drive them into the Potomac or into eternity!" The sound of his voice seemed to echo from the vales of Maryland. The line arose as one man from a kneeling posture, discharged a deadly volley, advanced the crescent line, and thus encircled the invaders, who in terror called for quarter and surrendered.

Upon the surrender of Colonel Cogswell (to whom, being wounded, I loaned my horse) I was left with two companies of the Eighteenth Regiment to secure and bring forward the balance of the prisoners. On leaving the field with a strong detachment of prisoners I was met by Colonel Hunton, of the Eighth Virginia Volunteers, who requested me to return with 15 men to act as picket guard. I went forward, reported the prisoners to you, and by you was ordered back to the battle-field and to remain until relieved. I took from my regiment a detachment of 90 men. When I reached the field I found a small picket under charge of a lieutenant. Shortly after I arrived Mr. E. White (of Ashby's cavalry) entered the field with two companies of the Eighth Virginia Volunteers. I joined my force to his, and leaving a small detachment above to fire on the enemy if they attempted to escape by boats across to the island, with the remainder of the detachment we went forward under the cliffs and took many prisoners; in fact the greatest number taken at any one time. To do this we were compelled from the Red Shale Cliffs to fire upon them as they attempted to cross in the scows to Harrison's Island. Many who had reached half way across turned back.

I rendered the prisoners to Mr. White (whose gallant action during the day deserves commendation), who conducted them to headquarters. According to your orders I remained at that point during the night, superintending the collecting of arms and the sending forward of captured arms, ammunition, accouterments, and other captured property found on the battle-field. On the next day Captain Vaughan, of the Federal Army, asked permission, under flag of truce, to come to the river bank and bury the dead. This was granted, by the enemy remaining upon the island without attempting to add to or diminish their forces. During the time Captain Vaughan was on this side I discovered the enemy moving off the island and towards Edwards Ferry. I notified Captain Vaughan of the fact, and told him if the two boats loaded were not brought back I would hold him as prisoner of war on account of violating the treaty. He had them brought back. I did this from the fact that there was a large force on the island, which I could hold in check with my small force and prevent the troops from re-enforcing the enemy who had landed at Edwards Ferry.

About 3 or 4 o'clock you came on the field and ordered me to the rear of Colonel Barksdale's regiment, on the Edwards Ferry road, to estimate the number of the enemy, who were reported as advancing towards Fort Evans, up the Edwards Ferry road. I placed Major Henry, of Eighteenth Mississippi Regiment, in command of the field, and immediately proceeded to discharge the duty assigned me. I found Colonel Barksdale slowly retreating in the direction of Fort Evans. I went to the rear of the retreating force. In the direction of the ferry, near Daily's house, I discovered about one company of the enemy's infantry. I could see none other. I endeavored to draw their fire by firing upon them, but could not, although I was in range of ordinary muskets. Not deeming it prudent to advance farther I returned to the breastworks, and was there met by your orderly, with instructions to proceed to the town of Leesburg and collect all stragglers. While in the discharge of this duty I was thrown from my horse, about 9 o'clock p. m. October 22. My horse fell upon me, and gave me such a shock that I was unable unassisted to get into the saddle. At the hotel I was taken from my horse and assisted to my room, where I remained until early light. Hearing you contemplated a retreat, I proceeded under your directions, on the morning of the 23d, to collect the artillery, ammunition, and small-arms captured from the enemy, and sent them forward in advance. I regret that owing to the want of transportation many small-arms were necessarily left behind when you ordered us forward.

I was fifty-three hours in the saddle before I met with the accident. I broke down one horse, and Captain Jayne presented me with a captured horse secured while we were taking prisoners. The gift from him is held by me subject to your approval or your order.

I make this report thus full for two reasons: 1st. That you may know the manner in which I executed your order. 2d. That my regiment may know officially that in their trials on marching and on their entrance into the fight I was not willingly absent from them. You, who know, can do justice to my actions. I desire you to do so, and oblige one who rejoices that through your exertions great glory has been reflected upon Mississippi arms.

Respectfully submitted.

JNO. McGUIRK,
Lieut. Col. and Field Officer of the Day.

General N. G. EVANS,
Comdg. Seventh Brigade, First Corps, Army of the Potomac.

No. 28.

Report of Capt. W. L. Duff, Seventeenth Mississippi Infantry.

CAMP AT CARTER'S MILL, VA., *October 25, 1861.*

COLONEL: I have the honor to submit the following report of the action near Big Spring on the morning of the 21st instant: We had, as you are aware, been on detached service since August 24, having pickets at Stuart's Mill, Conrad's Ferry, Ball's Mill, and Mrs. Mason's Island. Early on the morning of the 21st our pickets were fired upon and driven in by the enemy. They reported the enemy crossing opposite Harrison's Island at the Big Bluff. On receiving this intelligence I ordered Lieutenant Harten to report these facts to General Evans, and immediately formed my company and marched in the direction of Stuart's Mill, where my pickets had been driven in. On reaching the mouth of the lane leading to the river, some 500 or 600 yards from the mill, I threw forward twelve skirmishers to scour out a clump of woods to the front and right, ordered one of my men to bring in the rest of my pickets, filed my company to the right up a long hollow in an old field, leaving the clump of woods on my left. When we reached the top of the hill near Mrs. Stephens' house we saw the skirmishers of the enemy on the left, and in large force in Mrs. Jackson's yard, some 150 yards in front. I filed to the right, for the purpose of getting between them and Leesburgh, and formed a line of battle.

The enemy threw forward a strong force in line of battle. I having but 40 men in line thought it best to draw him as far as possible from his reserve. I accordingly fell back on the foot of the hill, some 300 yards from his reserve, and in the direction of Leesburg. He advanced in line of battle in good order at a "make ready," his force amounting to at least five or six companies. I halted my company and ordered the enemy to halt five or six times. He responded each time, "Friends," but continued to advance within 60 yards, when I ordered my men to kneel and fire, which they did with deadly effect, completely breaking his line. The second time he fell back, but getting re-enforcements from the reserve he rallied, and maintained his position about twenty minutes, when the whole force fled in confusion to a thicket of woods to the right of Mrs. Jackson's house, carrying with them most of the killed and wounded.

Not knowing where our forces were, and having but few men, I thought it best to fall back about 300 yards, so as to command the main road from Big Spring to Leesburg, thinking the enemy might throw a force in that direction and cut me off; but learning that some of our troops were on my right in the fortifications, I resumed my former position.

I captured 3 wounded prisoners and 14 or 15 stands of arms. I maintained my position in front and about 600 yards from the enemy under a scattering fire from their long-range guns. I had 1 man seriously wounded and 2 slightly wounded in the engagement.

About 10 o'clock a. m. Capt. J. W. Welborn, who had command of two companies on my right, sent to me to know if I would support him in an attack on the enemy in his position. I sent him word that I would. He accordingly moved on the enemy from the right. I filed to the left, and under cover of his file charged the enemy, who fled in the utmost confusion to a thicket of woods near the Potomac.

I had one man wounded in this charge—a man who had fallen in with my company in this charge, and who belonged to the Thirteenth Regiment Mississippi Volunteers.

At 12 o'clock m. the Eighth Virginia Regiment came to our support. I was ordered by Colonel Jenifer to occupy the extreme left wing and throw forward 20 skirmishers and advance with my company in the direction of Stuart's Mill. On reaching a point about 100 yards from the river I halted. Two of my skirmishers on my right advanced to the river, came back, and reported that they saw the enemy crossing artillery on to this side the river, some 500 or 600 yards below the mill. Colonel Jenifer ordered me to move in double-quick time to the point indicated and prevent their crossing. When we reached the above point we were unable to see the enemy crossing. I threw forward skirmishers, with the intention of moving lower down to get a better view of the river. This was in a dense thicket on the banks of a deep ravine. One of the skirmishers was halted within ten steps of my line by a man who proved to be an officer in the Tammany regiment of New York. He burst a cap at the skirmisher, but Lieutenant Stephens saw him and shot him down before he could fire.

The fire now became general, but the bushes were so thick that we could but with difficulty see the enemy, notwithstanding they were within 20 yards of us. After we had been engaged some time Captain Ball's company of dismounted cavalry came to our assistance and occupied the left, a short time after which we received an order to join our regiment in the intrenchments. We were engaged in this contest about one-half an hour. Owing to the peculiar position of the ground which we occupied, it affording cover for my men while loading, we did not lose a single man. We started in the direction of the intrenchments, and had proceeded as far as an old field, just back of where the Eighth Virginia Regiment was engaged, when the order to join our regiment was countermanded. I then halted my men, rested, and refreshed them with food and water, the first they had in twenty-eight hours, and held myself in readiness to go to the support of the Virginians if necessary. At dark I was ordered to my former position at Big Spring.

The officers and men under my command all acted nobly, gallantly driving back more than ten times their number; ever ready to move in any direction or discharge any duty, however perilous; fighting all day without food or water, and that, too, without a murmur.   My lieutenants all shouldered their guns and fought all day long, and were all the time at their posts, cheering the men and placing themselves in the most exposed position.

I have the honor to be, your obedient servant,

W. L. DUFF,
Captain Co. K, Seventeenth Regiment Mississippi Volunteers.

Col. W. S. FEATHERSTON,
Commanding Seventeenth Regiment Mississippi Volunteers.

No. 29.

Report of Lieut. Col. Thomas M. Griffin, Eighteenth Mississippi Infantry.

HDQRS. EIGHTEENTH REGIMENT MISS. VOLS.,
Camp near Oakland, Va., October 25, 1861.

GENERAL: I have the honor to report the part taken by the Eighteenth Regiment Mississippi Volunteers in the battle near Leesburg on the 21st instant.

The enemy, having landed a large number of troops on the west bank of the Potomac at Harrison's Island during the night of the 20th instant, commenced their march on Leesburg about 7 o'clock in the morning, when they were met by Captain Duff, of the Seventeenth Regiment Mississippi Volunteers, about 1 mile from town, and after a sharp conflict driven back to the woods.

Soon after this Captains Welborn and J. C. Campbell, of the Eighteenth Regiment, were ordered to the support of Captain Duff, with some cavalry, all under the command of Colonel Jenifer, who kept the enemy in check until near 12 o'clock.   The enemy having received large re-enforcements, the Eighth Virginia was ordered to the support of Colonel Jenifer and went into action between 1 and 2 p. m. and fought the enemy for more than an hour, when the Eighteenth, which with the Seventeenth and Thirteenth had been holding in check a large force of the enemy at Edwards Ferry, was ordered up, and reached the field about 2.30 o'clock, and were soon warmly engaged.   Taking position on the right of the Eighth Virginia Regiment, the line of battle was formed and a heavy fire opened on the enemy's line.   The Federalists were strongly posted, with artillery—one 12-pounder rifled gun and two mountain howitzers—on an eminence with an open field in front, their right protected by woods, their left by woods and a deep ravine.

Colonel Burt fell mortally wounded while gallantly leading the regiment at the commencement of the charge on the enemy's battery, when the command of the regiment devolved upon me.

Finding that the enemy were making some demonstrations on my right flank, I ordered Captain Hann's company to the right, who soon cleared the wood of their skirmishers.   The line was advanced to within a short distance of their guns, when several heavy volleys were fired, forcing them to fall back into the ravine for shelter.   At 3.30 o'clock Colonel Featherston, with the Seventeenth Regiment, arrived on the ground, when the two regiments were formed in line of battle, and charged the enemy until they were driven into the Potomac or captured.

I cannot speak in too high terms of the officers and men of the Eighteenth Regiment. They did their whole duty. Captains Jayne, Hann, Singleton, Browne, Hill, and Lieutenant Day, in command of the Mc-Cluney Rifles, who composed the right wing, behaved most gallantly. Adjt. S. T. Nicholson and Sergt. Maj. O. E. Stuart were active in the performance of their duties. Lieutenant Bostwick,* of Hann Rifles, was seriously wounded while charging with his company on the enemy's battery. Captain A. P. Hill received a wound while gallantly leading his company in the charge. Captains Welborn and Campbell were detached in the morning to assist Captain Duff, and acted with the Eighth Virginia Regiment. Captain Welborn received a wound in the neck. Lieutenant Fearn, of the Burt Rifles, was seriously wounded. Captains Luse and Kearney were deployed to the left of the enemy's battery, under the command of Major Henry. This detachment was joined by the companies of Captains Welborn and Campbell and Captain Fletcher's company of the Thirteenth Regiment, who rendered most efficient service. Captain Kearney's company was afterward sent to re-enforce the right, and ably assisted to bring about the rout and capture of the enemy. Major Henry, who commanded on the left, displayed the utmost coolness in handling the men under his charge. Captain Jayne and Lieutenant Day, of the McCluney Rifles, were thrown forward on the right flank during the last charge, with their companies, and contributed much to the capture of the enemy at the river bank. There were many instances of individual heroism, which I have not space to particularize.

The Federal force fought well. A number were killed with the bayonet by my men. The battle lasted until 6 o'clock p. m., when the enemy surrendered. Our victory was most complete. The enemy had at least 3,000 men in the fight, besides a still heavier force at Edwards Ferry. Our whole force did not exceed 1,500 men. The enemy's loss could not have been less than 1,500 killed, wounded, and prisoners, with a loss of three pieces of artillery and nearly 2,000 stand of arms.

I cannot close my report without mentioning the noble and gallant conduct of Colonel Featherston and Major Lyle, of the Seventeenth Regiment. The Eighth Virginia Regiment behaved most gallantly, and contributed their full share in winning the victory. Inclosed you will find a list of the casualties of the day.†

   *   *   *   *   *   *   *

I have the honor to be, very respectfully,

THOMAS M. GRIFFIN,
Lieutenant-Colonel, Comdg. Eighteenth Mississippi Volunteers.

Brig. Gen. N. G. EVANS,
Commanding Seventh Brigade, Army of the Potomac.

No. 30.

Report of Col. Eppa Hunton, Eighth Virginia Infantry.

HEADQUARTERS EIGHTH VIRGINIA REGIMENT,
Camp Burt, October 29, 1861.

GENERAL: In obedience to your orders, on Monday, the 21st instant, leaving Captain Wampler's company at the burnt bridge on the turnpike, I marched the rest of my command by the fort to a woods about

---

* Probably F. Bostick, killed on that date.
† Embodied in return of casualties on p. 353.

1½ miles northeast of the town of Leesburg, and about 12 o'clock m., forming a line of battle, charged through the woods some 700 yards, and met the enemy strongly posted in the edge of the woods with two howitzers and one rifled cannon. The regiment, weakened by the detachment of the gallant Wampler's company, and by sickness, with less than 400 men, with but little aid, fought the enemy in large force strongly posted for about four hours, and drove them back to cover in the woods. At the first fire from my regiment nearly every man at the enemy's cannon was shot down, and so incessant and galling was the fire we kept up, that there were only three discharges of cannon after the first fire from the Eighth.

At this period our ammunition was nearly exhausted, a large portion of the men having none at all, although they were supplied with forty rounds in the beginning. The enemy had retired under cover of the woods, and the Seventeenth and Eighteenth Misssissippi Regiments had arrived on the ground. I gave the order to cease firing for a moment, distributed the few cartridges remaining so as to give all a round of ammunition, and ordered a charge upon the enemy. This charge was made in the most gallant and impetuous manner. Nothing could exceed or scarcely equal the intrepid daring and gallantry displayed by my officers and men in making this charge. Relying almost solely upon the bayonet, they rushed upon and drove back a heavy column of the enemy just landed and captured the two howitzers. In this charge I was assisted by Captain Upshaw, of the Seventeenth Mississippi, Captain Kearney and Captain Welborn, of the Eighteenth Mississippi Regiments, who displayed great gallantry in the charge.

After I had driven the enemy into the woods on my right, my men entirely exhausted by the fatigue of the fight, the Seventeenth Mississippi and I understand a portion of the Eighteenth, charged and gallantly pursued the enemy through the woods on my right until a little after dusk, when they sent in a flag of truce and surrendered. My command captured many prisoners during the fight.

Some time after nightfall I marched my command to the fort, leaving a picket of 12 men, under Lieut. Charles Berkeley, who volunteered for the service. I also requested Elijah White, of Colonel Ashby's regiment, who was with me during the fight, to remain during the night with this picket. He did so, and by his intimate knowledge of the country and daring courage rendered great service. Lieutenant Berkeley and White reported during the night that there was still a large number of Yankees on the river, and a volunteer expedition was immediately started, under command of Capt. William N. Berkeley, consisting of about 40 men, many of them officers. This small force, guided by Mr. White, marched to the river and captured 325 prisoners, mostly with arms in their hands. They also took a quantity of military equipments. I would like to mention the names of this heroic band, and will if their names can be procured. Officers volunteered and went into the ranks as privates.

I cannot speak too highly of the daring gallantry of the officers and soldiers under my command. With rare exceptions they fought like heroes, bore the great exertions of the day and night with cheerfulness, and responded to every order with alacrity. I would like to enumerate the various and numerous instances of individual heroism by officers and soldiers on that day, but in truth nearly every one who stood by me in the fight acted the hero. I was very efficiently aided during the battle by Lieut. Col. C. B. Tebbs and Maj. N. Berkeley, to each of whom I am much indebted for the successful fight of the Eighth Virginia Regiment on that day. Adjutant Bowie and Sergeant-Major Hutchison and my courier, George W. F. Hammer, also acted very gallantly and rendered me valuable service. While rejoicing over our brilliant victory, I stop to drop a tear to the memory of the gallant dead who gloriously fell on that day in defense of all that is dear to freemen.

Below is a list of the killed and wounded,* which is smaller than might have been expected, owing in part to the fact that I fought my command a portion of the time under the cover of the crest of a hill.

Respectfully submitted.

EPPA HUNTON,
Colonel Eighth Virginia Regiment.

Brig. Gen. N. G. EVANS.

No. 31.

Report of Col. W. H. Jenifer, C. S. Army, commanding cavalry.

HEADQUARTERS CAVALRY CAMP,
Near Leesburg, Va., October 28, 1861.

GENERAL: I have the honor to submit my report of a battle with the enemy which took place near Leesburg on the 21st instant.

At 8 o'clock a. m. it was reported to me that the enemy was crossing the Potomac River below Smart's Mill, and about 2 miles distant from Leesburg. Their skirmishers of two companies were advancing rapidly on the town, when they were attacked and driven back by Captain Duff's company, of the Seventeenth Mississippi Regiment. The loss of the enemy in this engagement was 2 killed and 3 wounded. Soon after the enemy was driven back I arrived on the ground with four companies of cavalry, and assisted Captain Duff in securing the wounded of the enemy.

At 9 o'clock I received an order to report with my cavalry to you at Fort Evans. After obeying this order you gave me permission to take my cavalry near the enemy's position in order to make an attack should he again advance. I concealed the cavalry in a ravine near Mr. Trundle's house, ready to make a charge should an opportunity offer. The enemy at this time was under cover of the thick woods between the river and Leesburg, and reported by the prisoners just taken to be six full companies of 100 men each.

At 11 o'clock I determined to attack the enemy, and, if possible, drive him from his strong position, and sent you a dispatch to that effect. Captain Campbell, of the Eighteenth Mississippi Regiment, with two companies of infantry, placed himself under my command. I then sent an order to Captain Duff, who had taken his position about three-quarters of a mile on my left, to hold himself in readiness to attack the enemy's right flank. So soon as sufficient time had elapsed for Captain Duff to receive the order I advanced towards the enemy's position, and when within a few hundred yards of him two more companies of infantry joined me by your order. My whole command then consisted of three companies of cavalry, commanded respectively by Capt. W. B. Ball, Capt. W. W. Mead, and Lieutenant Moorehead (Captain Adams' company), and five companies of infantry, commanded

----

respectively by Captains Campbell and Welborn, Eighteenth Mississippi Regiment; Captain Duff, Seventeenth Mississippi Regiment; Captain Fletcher, Thirteenth Mississippi Regiment, and one other captain, whose name I do not remember; numbering in all about 320 men.

Captain Campbell was ordered to deploy one of his companies, Captain Welborn's, as skirmishers, and to feel the enemy's position. The other companies were directed to advance in the following order: Captain Campbell on the right, Captain Duff on the extreme left, Captain Fletcher and the cavalry on the center. Capt. William B. Ball was placed in command of the cavalry.

Upon a nearer approach to the enemy it was found to be impossible to charge with cavalry, owing to a high and strong fence between the enemy and my command. I therefore ordered Captain Ball, at his request, to dismount his company and fight on foot. The attack was then made, and a brisk fire kept up through the fence. Finding the enemy was not disposed to fall back, I ordered a charge over the fence, which order was promptly obeyed, and so soon as a portion of the fence could be torn down I leaped my horse over, followed by Captain Ball, Lieutenant Woolridge, Lieutenant Clarke, and Lieutenant Weisiger, of Captain Ball's cavalry, and Lieutenant Baxter, Loudoun Cavalry, and Mr. R. L. Hendrick, of Mecklenburg, Va., who kindly volunteered his services. The enemy was soon driven from his first position, but a heavy fire was kept up from the thick woods to which he had retreated. Fearing my small command would be led into an ambuscade, I ordered it to fall back and take position in rear of the fence it had just passed, and sent to you for re-enforcements.

Some twenty or thirty minutes elapsing before re-enforcements came, I had time to gather up the enemy's wounded and 2 prisoners, including 1 captain, and send them to Leesburg.

In this charge on the enemy I would respectfully call the attention of the general commanding to the officers who were with me. Captain Ball deserves particular notice for his coolness whilst carrying orders under a heavy fire, as well as for his words of encouragement to his own men and the infantry. Captain Campbell and the officers of the infantry companies also deserve much praise for their coolness in the charge. Lieutenants Wooldridge, Clarke, and Weisiger, Messrs. Hendrick and Peters, civilians, were among the first in the fight, and did good service. Lieutenant Weisiger, my acting adjutant, had his horse shot in the head whilst obeying an order just before the engagement commenced. These officers I particularly mention, having witnessed their individual coolness and courage.

At 12 o'clock you sent the Eighth Virginia Regiment, commanded by Col. Eppa Hunton, to my support, and it was reported to me that you would send artillery, but none came. I again advanced upon the enemy in the following order: Captains Campbell's, Welborn's, and Fletcher's companies in front, with skirmishers in advance and on their right. These companies were supported by the Eighth Virginia Regiment. Owing to thick woods and roughness of ground they were lost sight of for a few minutes, and the Eighth Virginia Regiment took its position in front, with the four companies first named on its right. Captain Duff's company advanced on the left, throwing out skirmishers, supported by Captain Ball's cavalry, dismounted. After marching several hundred yards through dense woods our troops were fired upon by the enemy's skirmishers, who were concealed behind trees and in deep ravines. At the same time a constant fire was kept up by artillery, which had previously been landed on this side of the river, throwing shell and round shot. Their artillery was also playing upon us from the opposite side of the river.

At 1.30 o'clock I left my position on the left and rode through the thick woods to where Colonel Hunton's regiment (Eighth Virginia) was stationed, and requested him to throw out his skirmishers to the right and left, to prevent the enemy from flanking us and getting to our rear. Colonel Hunton, like a true gentleman and soldier, granted my request, notwithstanding I was his junior in rank. I also suggested to him to make his men crawl on their hands and knees to the brow of the hill just in front, in order to make a more successful attack on the enemy, who was in the open field beyond, and not more than 50 or 60 yards distant; but before the colonel had time to place his men in this position the enemy opened a terrific fire on his command with musketry, grape, and shell. To this fire Colonel Hunton gallantly replied, and soon drove the enemy back to his strong position behind the bluff at the river, killing all the cannoneers at the guns.

At this time (3 o'clock) you sent me a message that you would re-enforce me with another regiment. The Eighteenth Mississippi Regiment, Colonel Burt, then came up and took position in the woods, and in advance of the right of the Eighth Virginia. The heavy fire of the enemy was still kept up, and was replied to with telling effect by the Eighth Virginia and Eighteenth Mississippi Regiments. Here the gallant Colonel Burt fell mortally wounded about 4 o'clock. The command of the Eighteenth Mississippi then devolved upon Lieutenant-Colonel Griffin.

About 4.30 or 5 o'clock you sent the Seventeenth Mississippi, which I sent forward to support Colonel Hunton, whose men had been fighting for more than four hours. You also sent word by my adjutant (Lieutenant Weisiger) that "you would re-enforce me as long as I desired it." At the same hour the Thirteenth Mississippi, Colonel Barksdale, was ordered up to me, but as the enemy was driven back to the bluff and our forces holding their position, I sent an order to Colonel Barksdale to resume his position, which he held most of the day, keeping the enemy's extreme left flank in check. This regiment, though not in the engagement on the 21st, held one of the most important positions, and prevented the enemy from flanking us.

About 5.30 o'clock Colonel Hunton's Eighth Virginia Regiment charged and captured two of the enemy's 6-pounder howitzers. The regiment was without ammunition at the time. Between 5 and 6 o'clock I rode up to Colonel Hunton and asked if I could render him any assistance, observing that his men were completely exhausted and lying flat on the ground within 125 yards of the enemy, but under cover of a small hill. The colonel replied that he was without ammunition, and that his men were broken down from fatigue and hunger. It was at this time I sent my adjutant to you for ammunition and provisions, and if provisions could not be had at once, to send a barrel of whisky to refresh the men. I told the colonel I would send to you for what he required, and advised him to let his men rest until they could be refreshed.

During this conversation between Colonel Hunton and myself, a part of the Seventeenth Mississippi and Eighteeenth Mississippi, about 50 yards in advance of Colonel Hunton's right, were engaging the enemy, and receiving his heavy fire like regular soldiers. These were the last volleys fired, and I left the battle-field to collect my scattered cavalry, which had been watching the enemy's flanks during the day. At 8 o'clock p. m. I reported to you at your headquarters in Leesburg. The forces engaged on the 21st were composed of the following regiments and detachments: Detachments of three companies Virginia cavalry, numbering about 70; the Eighth Virginia Regiment, 375; the Eighteenth Mississippi Regiment, 500; the Seventeenth Mississippi Regiment, 600; one company Thirteenth Mississippi, 60. Total, 1,605. Our loss in killed, 35; wounded, 115. No officer was killed in the action. Colonel Burt mortally wounded.

The enemy's force engaged in the action was, as near as I can estimate it, about four or five regiments, with three pieces of artillery on the Virginia shore, and several pieces on the opposite side of the river. From the report of prisoners taken in the battle the enemy numbered 4,000. Independent of this force engaged there were three or four regiments of infantry and one or two squadrons of cavalry on his extreme left, about 2 miles distant, at Edwards Ferry. This command was, as I have previously stated, held in check by Colonel Barksdale, Thirteenth Mississippi Regiment. I think I can safely estimate the force of the enemy's infantry and cavalry on this side of the river at seven or eight regiments of infantry and one or two squadrons of cavalry. The number of pieces of artillery, except those captured, is not known. The prisoners taken in the action reported the companies of infantry to average 100 men.

The following regiments were represented in the battle, prisoners having been taken from all of them: First California Regiment, Forty-Second New York (Tammany) Regiment, Fourth, Fifteenth, Nineteenth, and Twentieth Massachusetts Regiments, New York Zouaves, and artillery. Two or three regiments of infantry, with cavalry and artillery, at Edwards Ferry, as previously mentioned.

The following is the loss of the enemy, as near as can be ascertained, including two colonels and one major prisoners, and General Baker killed: In killed, 200; wounded, 500; drowned, 300; prisoners—privates, 692; officers, 24. Total, 1,716. The number of killed is from a report of a Federal officer, and is no doubt greater than stated. The number of arms taken from the enemy about 1,500, besides a large number of cartridge boxes and clothing of different kinds. The number of prisoners taken by each regiment will be stated in the regimental reports. The cavalry captured about 85 prisoners on the 22d, and brought them into Leesburg.

Before closing my report I would respectfully call the attention of the commanding general to the gallant conduct of the officers, non-commissioned officers, privates, and citizens who were with me during the day. Too much praise cannot be given to Colonel Hunton and Captain Ball for the manner in which they managed their respective commands. Lieutenant Baxter, of Loudoun Cavalry, deserves praise for the gallant manner in which he made a charge with 10 men on two companies of the enemy's infantry early in the morning. While assisting Captain Duff, Mr. White, of Colonel Ashby's cavalry, volunteered his services during the day. I never witnessed more coolness and courage than this young gentleman displayed, being exposed to the heaviest fire of the enemy. He rode in front of a part of the Seventeenth Mississippi, cheering and encouraging the men. Lieut. Charles B. Wildman deserves particular notice for his courage and gallant conduct during the day. Sergeant Strother, Madison Cavalry, Acting Sergeant-Major Baugh, Chesterfield Cavalry, and Private Toler, of Loudoun Cavalry, rendered good service in carrying orders. I have also to report that on the evening of the 22d, after I had executed your order to receive the enemy's flag of truce for permission to bury their dead, some of my cavalry pickets who were stationed near the river were fired into several times by the enemy from the opposite side. This disgraceful act was committed by some of the troops under the command of Colonel Hinks, of the Federal Army, who was perfectly aware that some of his officers and men were on the Virginia side burying their dead.

In submitting this report to you I have only stated what came under my personal observation, except in some cases where I have taken the reports from officers and men captured by us.

Feeling the position I held during the day a responsible one, and not at all coveted by me, I sent an officer to you at dark, with the request that you would send your orders to Colonel Hunton, as he ranked me. Up to this time you had been sending all your orders to me, which compliment I highly appreciated, but preferred your paying it to Colonel Hunton.

I am, sir, very respectfully, your obedient servant,

W. H. JENIFER,
Colonel, Commanding Cavalry, Seventh Brigade.

Brig. Gen. N. G. EVANS, *Commanding Seventh Brigade.*

OCTOBER 22, 1861.—Affairs around Budd's Ferry, Maryland.

REPORTS.

No. 1.—Col. Nelson Taylor, Seventy-second New York Infantry.
No. 2.—Capt. Robert S. Williamson, U. S. Topographical Engineers.

No. 1.

Report of Col. Nelson Taylor, Seventy-second New York Infantry.

HEADQUARTERS THIRD REGIMENT,
Budd's Ferry, October 22, 1861.

GENERAL: I arrived here at 12 m., and encamped about 1 mile south of Mr. Posey's house. This morning before leaving camp a man came to me, representing himself as Charles Bentrick, ranking as master in the Navy, and commanding one of the small steamers in the Government service, called E. H. Herbert. He stated that having an intimation of my detachment being in that vicinity, Commodore Craven had sent him on shore to inquire the strength of the force. He also stated that the commodore desired me to arrest Messrs. Posey, Mason, and Runyea, but for no other reason that I could understand than that they were suspected of entertaining secession sentiments. This I of course disregarded. I should very much like to have the inquiry made at the Navy Department to know if Charles Bentrick has the position he represents himself to hold.

Captain Williamson commenced work on the shore this afternoon immediately in front of the battery at Shipping Point. During the afternoon five or six shots were fired at passing vessels, but without effect. The batteries appeared to be confined to a space of about 1 mile on the river fronting Budd's Ferry and ranging up and down the river. The batteries are situated between Chopawamsic and Quantico Creeks. The battery at Freestone Point has been discontinued since the opening of the lower ones. I cannot learn that there has ever been a battery at Cockpit Point. A ball was thrown to the rear of Mr. Posey's house, which was supposed to have been thrown from a battery of a single gun planted at an elevation of 150 feet. The place where the gun is supposed to be is quite visible with a glass, but not the gun, or at least not plainly. With a good glass six guns in the upper and five in the lower battery can be counted. It is quite certain that there are more guns in position, as one of those fired yesterday was out of sight. Its location was made known by the smoke.

Heavy firing was heard from below last evening, which from the direction was supposed to have taken place at Mathias Point. Field batteries have been seen on the opposite shore, but are out of sight now. The supports of the batteries appeared to be at least a mile in the rear. Judging from the great quantity of smoke constantly rising above the timber, which it is supposed comes from camp fires, their force must be very considerable.

Very respectfully,

NELSON TAYLOR,
Colonel, Commanding Detachment.

Brig. Gen. D. E. SICKLES, *Commanding.*

No. 2.

Reports of Capt. Robert S. Williamson, U. S. Topographical Engineers.

CAMP NEAR BUDD'S FERRY,
Tuesday Morning, October 22, 1861.

GENERAL: I have the honor to report that I arrived at this point, about 40 miles distant from Sickles' camp, yesterday about 1 p. m., and shortly afterwards visited that part of the river shore opposite three of the enemy's batteries. There is one on the southern bank of Quantico Creek, at its mouth, at what I suppose to be Evansport. Five guns are plainly visible with my glass, and there is doubtless at least one more, which, being directed down the river, is hidden by an embankment. The plan of the work is a crescent or curved line, the northernmost guns pointing across the river, while two others point down it. Another battery is at a short distance (probably about a mile) below, at Shipping Point. Here three guns only can be seen, but the earthwork extends sufficiently below the last visible gun to afford room for from three to five guns more.

North of the mouth of the Quantico, on a hill, is another battery of probably but one gun. I suppose it to be at least 100 feet, and probably as much as 150 feet, above the river, and so distant that I am not sure what I saw is a gun; but the bare spot on the timbered hill-side and the report of the inhabitants that a heavy gun is there leaves no doubt in my mind that it is so. These are all the batteries I can see in this vicinity. Report says field artillery are stationed near there. I have no evidence to show there are guns at Cockpit Point.

Four guns were fired from these batteries last evening, one from the lower battery and three from the one at Evansport. They were fired at small schooners which were passing close to this shore. They did no damage. An elongated heavy shell from the Evansport battery lodged in a bank near the water's edge without exploding, and was carried to this camp.   It was estimated to weigh about 60 pounds, and was measured—6 inches in diameter and 14 inches long.   Heavy cannonading was heard about 5 p. m. last evening in a direction about 20 degrees south of east, which is the direction of Mathias Point.   Twenty-five or thirty shots were heard.

On this bank, opposite the battery, for several miles the ground is low, never exceeding 20 feet in altitude.   For a mile from the river the ground is lower than on the immediate bank; afterwards it rises about 50 feet.   The two rebel batteries on the river are on ground about 20 feet high.   There is a commanding point on this side, opposite the line of batteries and near the house of Mr. Posey, where a battery might be erected, but as the distance from it to Evansport is about 3 miles, it would be of little value to oppose those of the rebels.   Mr. Posey informs me a ball from the gun on the hill passed over and beyond his house.   The river here is about 2 miles wide, and small river craft pass close to the land, but I am told ships must pass within a mile of the batteries.

The estimates I give are not instrumental, but simply from my own judgment.   A few hours only will be required to measure the width of the river, but it has rained so heavily last night and this morning, with little prospect of clearing up, that I cannot use a triangulating instrument at present, but will do so as soon as possible.   I selected yesterday a base line about a mile long, which I will chain this morning.   There are now seven days' provisions in this camp.   You will please remember that my original instructions contemplated the reconnaissance to be made in six days, but subsequently I was directed to remain until further orders; hence I brought with me only some small surveying instruments.   Should the erection of any work be contemplated in this vicinity, I respectfully request that a spirit-level and two leveling staffs may be sent to me.

I have the honor to be, very respectfully, your obedient servant,

R. S. WILLIAMSON,
Captain, U. S. Topographical Engineers.

Brig. Gen. S. WILLIAMS,
Assistant Adjutant-General, Department of the Potomac.

—

CAMP NEAR BUDD'S FERRY, *October* 22, 1861—Noon.

GENERAL: Your letter of October 21 is just received.   I sent to General Williams this morning a report which I believe covers all the ground you speak of, but I will be more positive in my opinions.   The river I am confident is nearly or quite 2 miles opposite the batteries. The ground for a mile back on this side is low, but there are points 20 feet above the river bank on the immediate bank where batteries can be erected.   You can judge of the effect of shot or shell at such a distance.   The rebels have large guns.   Their works appear to be nothing but earthworks.   The high ground 50 or 60 feet above the river on this side is suitable for batteries, but too distant.   Shot will easily reach across, but can you destroy the enemy's works from such a distance?   My information on the route led me to suppose Shipping Point and vicinity the principal locality for their batteries.

I can gain no information to induce me to suppose there are batteries at Cockpit Point; hence I went here first.   The infantry travel slowly, but I made many side trips with small cavalry escort to learn the nature of the country, hence I did not arrive here before the infantry. I have no information as to the rebel force here except what I see. Some men seen on the route say the rebels in very small parties are in the habit of visiting this side every night. Others say (and those here) that they have been here but once, when they destroyed a vessel in the creek near by. People here are said to be generally secessionists, but they say nothing.

As soon as I make the measurement of the river and gain any other information I will report.

I have the honor to be, very respectfully, your obedient servant,

R. S. WILLIAMSON,
Captain, U. S. Topographical Engineers.

Brig. Gen. R. B. MARCY,
　Chief of Staff of General McClellan, Washington, D. C.

—

CAMP NEAR MATTAWOMAN CREEK,
Five miles north of Budd's Ferry, October 25, 1861.

GENERAL: I have the honor to report that I started early yesterday morning from a camp near this place, and with a small escort returned to Budd's Ferry, and succeeded in completing the measurement of a base line and triangulating across the river. The line measured was 7,800 feet long, and no part of it distant from the river more than 150 yards.

I find that the batteries at Evansport, at the mouth of Quantico Creek, are nearer to this shore than the one at Shipping Point by 100 yards, and that the former are 7,800 feet from the nearest point of this shore, or a short 1½ miles (1.48 miles). The two batteries are 1,400 feet apart. I find also that directly opposite the nearest battery there is a point which slightly projects farther than the general line of the shore, and there the ground is a little higher than above or below, being about 15 feet above the water. If a battery is to be placed opposite those of the rebels, this point should be selected. There is a thin line of trees at that point, but not enough to produce an efficient cover.

I mentioned in a former letter that the general character of the shore for 1½ miles opposite the rebel batteries is a slightly elevated bank, about 10 feet above the water, and lower ground behind it. This bottom extends from three-quarters of a mile to a mile from the river, where there is a bluff from 50 to 100 feet high, affording good sites for mortar batteries. They can be constructed in timber to afford shelter, and the timber subsequently cleared away.

The two batteries opposite Budd's Ferry are said to be the most important ones on the river, but there are many others. There is a battery at the mouth of Chopawamsic Creek, the size of which I could not ascertain with my glass, but I saw a flag flying there yesterday, and about 100 men in its vicinity.

I have found a man by the name of Anderson, who knows every road and lane about here, and the name and character of each inhabitant, and I have engaged him as a guide, at $1.50 per day. I hope this will be approved of. He says the rebels knew of our arrival near Budd's Ferry on the day we reached there. He says also it is the intention of the rebels to go from Richmond to the mouth of Aquia Creek by railroad, and then cross over to Smith's Point. This is to be done in a week or two. Mr. Anderson learned this yesterday from a friend who lives 3 miles below Budd's Ferry, and who has a brother in the rebel camp opposite. The two brothers are in constant communication.

I have the honor to be, very respectfully, your obedient servant,

R. S. WILLIAMSON,
Captain, U. S. Topographical Engineers.

Brig. Gen. S. WILLIAMS,
Asst. Adjt. Gen., Div. of the Potomac, Washington, D. C.

—

CAMP, FIVE MILES ABOVE BUDD'S FERRY,
October 29, 1861.

GENERAL : General Hooker has informed me that he has had a conference with the commanding officer of the naval forces on the Potomac, and that it has been deemed expedient to throw up some earthworks in the vicinity of Indian Head to prevent the rebels from erecting batteries on the opposite shore. I was directed to examine the locality by General Hooker, which I did yesterday. I found that at the mouth of Mattawoman Creek the land is low and swampy, but that at some little distance above it rises, forming a bluff some 2 miles in length and from 60 to 120 feet high. The bluff or cliff has very steep sides, and abuts directly upon the water. The land on the opposite side of the river is much lower, being, according to my estimate, from 20 to 40 feet high. The Coast Survey map makes the river in this vicinity 2½ miles wide, but I can scarcely believe it to be more than 1½ miles, and this is the estimate of the commodore.

At the first high land above Mattawoman Creek a battery can be erected, some of the guns from which will give a fire down the river, while others will fire across it. Just above this the bluff is broken by a ravine, and a road now runs through it to the river. Above the ravine the bluff continues as described (but with increased altitude) without interruption for 1½ or 2 miles, when it terminates, and where there are two wharves within 100 yards of each other, where vessels drawing 10 feet of water can land. This is about the place marked Glymont on the Coast Survey map of the river. The deep water is near the left or this bank of the river. The land is higher above the ravine than below it, and at about a quarter of a mile above it the edge of the bluff is higher than farther inland, forming a gentle slope in that direction. There is there space enough on good ground for the camp of a regiment of infantry, with water from the ravine near by. At this place I would break ground. If the works to be erected do not require protection from the rear, a simple parapet can be built along the edge of the cliff, where as many guns can be placed as may be required. The fire from them will be across the river, though, as some parts of the cliff are higher than others, it will be possible at some few points to command a fire up or down the stream. Subsequently a detached work can be erected below the ravine. This description will, I hope, give you the general character of the ground, and enable you to decide upon the nature of the erection. There is no known rebel battery near.

This letter is submitted to General Hooker before forwarding it.

I have the honor to be, very respectfully, your obedient servant,

R. S. WILLIAMSON,
Captain, U. S. Topographical Engineers.

Brig. Gen. S. WILLIAMS,
Asst. Adjt. Gen., Division of the Potomac, Washington, D. C.

Camp near Headquarters Hooker's Division,
November 13, 1861.

General: I have the honor to report that on the day before yesterday I commenced an embankment for a battery of four heavy guns at the river bank, about one-third of a mile below the ferry-house, at Budd's Ferry. The point selected is about 20 feet above the water, and directly opposite to the two rebel batteries at Evansport and Shipping Point. The soil is loose sand, and the interior slope will be revetted with poles about 4 inches in diameter. The work will require from six to eight working days. I respectfully request you will inform me what kind of guns are intended for this work—whether it is to be for mortars or guns, and if the latter, whether I shall place them in barbette or embrasure. If the latter, the fire will be directed only upon the two batteries aforesaid, but the same work can be continued at an angle of 37° with this, making a wide-mouthed redan, the second face giving a fire with four more guns upon the battery at the mouth of Chopawamsic Creek, a mile and half below, where the rebels have a few heavy guns. If the guns are to be in barbette, they can be directed upon both the two upper and the lower batteries.

I have the honor to be, very respectfully, your obedient servant,

R. S. WILLIAMSON,
Captain, U. S. Topographical Engineers.

Brig. Gen. R. B. Marcy,
Chief of Staff, Army of the Potomac, Washington, D. C.

OCTOBER 23–27, 1861.—Confederate reconnaissance in the Kanawha Valley West Virginia.

Report of Col. J. N. Clarkson, C. S. Army.

In obedience to your orders I have reconnoitered the valley of the Kanawha on the southwest side of the river from the mouth of Loop Creek to Lens' Creek, a point 26 miles below the falls. I entered the valley with a part of my command on the evening of the 23d, as soon as it was dark enough to avoid observation, and proceeded as far as Montgomery's house, opposite Cannelton, without meeting any of the enemy or attracting their attention. About a quarter of a mile above Cannelton, at the mouth of Smithers' Creek, the enemy have one regiment infantry stationed, and one or two companies at Slater's Run, just below Cannelton. In passing this point we were discovered by the enemy on the opposite side of the river, and before we left we heard their drums beating the alarm and their boats crossing over to our side. From this place we pushed on down the river, stopping wherever we would be likely to gain information, without meeting with any obstruction until we got to Lens' Creek. I had originally intended to move on rapidly to Malden or Charleston, cross the river, surprise the small force of the enemy stationed there, recross the river, and return up Lens' Creek by the way of Peytona, on Coal River, but learning that there would be a large attendance on Paint and Cabin Creeks on the election to be held the next day, I determined to return and go up those creeks. Near Lens' Creek we hailed a steamboat ascending the river and fired into her several rounds. After the first fire she made three attempts to land, but owing to the length of my line along the river bank I could not prevent my men from continuing their fire to permit her to land until she finally got as far from us in the stream as she could and escaped us. But for this I have no doubt that she would have come to after our first fire and been captured. From the confusion and cries on board the boat we must have done considerable execution. On my return I divided my command, sent part of them up Cabin Creek, and brought the remainder up Paint Creek. We succeeded in breaking up the election on both of these creeks, taking and bringing away the poll-books. We also captured a large number of disloyal citizens on both streams, including their ringleaders, and a number of horses, that we took from the Union men; brought away prisoners, including 3 Yankee soldiers, who were caught prowling on the creeks, and encamped for the night, between 8 and 9 o'clock, after having been twenty-six hours in the saddle, and having traveled a distance of 90 or 100 miles without food or rest. I gained much valuable information in the Kanawha Valley about the strength and position of the enemy, which I think can be relied on. From the falls down they have about 2,500 men in the valley, districted as follows: 800 at Smithers' Creek and Station's Run, 800 at McConchay's, opposite Lens' Creek, 500 divided between Malden and Charleston, and 400 at Winfield, the county seat of Putnam County. I feel satisfied, also, that it would require a large force of the enemy (at least 10,000 men) to guard the different approaches to the Kanawha Valley so as to prevent incursions by small bodies of cavalry into the valley. I think the expedition under my command will be productive of great good, in its moral effects, both upon our own people and upon the enemy. It will encourage our loyal citizens who are compelled to remain at home, and intimidate the traitors to feel that we are near the valley, and that we will enter it at every practicable point, and that we will avail ourselves of every opportunity to visit them. I cannot omit the occasion to testify to the loyalty and zeal of many of the people on whom we called, who received us with a cordiality and warmth that proved them to be reliable and true, and who bestowed their best wishes on us and our cause when we left them. The effect upon the enemy by this and similar expeditions will be to annoy and harass him; he will feel that his strength, his positions, and to some extent his plans can be discovered by parties penetrating his lines and following in his rear. It will also cause him to divide his forces and dissipate his strength, so as to guard, if possible, the approaches to the valley.

I have the honor to be, your obedient servant,

JNO. N. CLARKSON,
Colonel, Commanding Cavalry.

Gen. JOHN B. FLOYD.

OCTOBER 26, 1861.—Action at Romney, West Virginia.

Report of Brig. Gen. Benjamin F. Kelley, U. S. Army, and congratulatory message from General Scott.

CAMP KEYS, ROMNEY, VA., *October* 28, 1861.

GENERAL: In obedience to your order by telegram of the 24th instant, I proceeded without delay to concentrate the available forces of my command on the line of the Baltimore and Ohio Railroad at New Creek Station, 25 miles west of Cumberland, and distant from this point

26 miles. This force consisted of a portion of the Seventh, one company each of the Third and Fourth Virginia Infantry, nine companies of the Eighth Ohio, and Ordnance Sergeant Nixon and 10 men, who had gallantly volunteered for the occasion, with a 6-pounder gun. These troops left New Creek Station at 12 o'clock at night of Friday, the 25th instant, and were joined by nine companies of the Fourth Ohio Infantry, from Camp Pendleton, Md., with a detachment of infantry who had volunteered to man two guns—one a 12, the other a 6-pounder. The whole force was concentrated near the junction of the New Creek and North-western roads on the morning of Saturday, the 26th, and moved forward over the Northwestern road towards this point in the following order, viz: The Ringgold Cavalry, under Captain Keys, preceded the column, for the purpose of watching the movements of the enemy. The Fourth Ohio Infantry, under command of Colonel Mason, Lieutenant-Colonel Cantwell, and Major Godman, took the right of the column. Lieutenant-Colonel Cantwell, having a day or two before resigned his commission, gallantly volunteered to accompany the expedition.

The Seventh and two companies of the Third and Fourth Virginia Infantry followed the Fourth Ohio, under command of Lieut. Col. J. G. Kelley and Maj. C. E. Swearingen. The Eighth Ohio, under command of Colonel Depuy and my assistant adjutant-general, Benjamin F. Hawkes. Then followed the artillery, under command of Lieutenant Jenks and Ordnance Sergeant Nixon, Captain McGee's cavalry bringing up the rear.

Colonel Johns' regiment, of the Maryland Brigade, was ordered to move from the mouth of Patterson's Creek, on the Baltimore and Ohio Railroad, at 12 o'clock at night, by way of Frankfort and Springfield, and enter the town on its eastern border, and occupy the Winchester road at 3 o'clock p. m., the hour at which I was to attack them in front. The object of this movement was to prevent their retreat on Winchester. I am sorry to say that this portion of my plan was, unfortunately, not carried out, Colonel Johns having been repulsed at the Wire Bridge, 7 miles below this point, and was therefore unable to get into position.

At Patterson's Creek, 14 miles west of this point, the troops were halted, took dinner, and rested. At 12 o'clock m. we resumed our march in the same order. At 2.15 p. m., when within 6 miles of Romney, the enemy opened fire upon the head of our column, when our artillery was ordered forward and replied. We then continued our march, with the artillery in front, to the mouth of Mechanicsburg Gap, distant 3 miles from Romney, a position the natural strength of which is unsurpassed by any other in the country. Skirmishers having been thrown out on the right and left, the column was moved through the gap, without, however, receiving a shot. When the head of the column emerged from the pass, it was found that the artillery of the enemy was strongly posted on the east side of the river, in a cemetery lot, on an eminence commanding the entire western approaches to the town, and the infantry and dismounted cavalry occupied intrenchments on the heights, commanding the bridge and the ford. Our artillery was then ordered to open fire upon them, which was promptly replied to by the rebels, and for about an hour a severe cannonade took place between the artillery. Lieutenant Jenks, of Daum's battery, commanding, displayed commendable courage and gallantry, and evinced consummate skill in the handling of his guns.

Finding we could not silence their guns, the order was given for the whole column of infantry to move forward and charge through the bridge and to attack the enemy in their intrenchments. At the same time the cavalry, under Captains Keys and McGee, were ordered to charge through the ford and under the bridge, which was most gallantly executed. The enemy, after firing a few rounds, now gave way and fled from their works; the infantry throwing down their arms and fleeing to the woods and mountains and dispersing. The cavalry and artillery retreated through the town towards Winchester, pursued by our cavalry. They attempted to rally and make a stand at the east end of the town, but the impetuous charge of the cavalry and the approach of the infantry on "double-quick" caused them to retreat, without firing a gun up the Winchester road and through a mountain gap similar to the one west of town, where they were pursued by the cavalry, and all their artillery and baggage trains captured. The enemy were so hard pressed that they had not time to discharge or spike their pieces, which fell into our hands all loaded. About 300 stand of small arms, a large quantity of ammunition, their camp equipage, entire baggage train, with about 100 horses and mules, fell into our hands.

The officers and men of my command all displayed great coolness and courage under fire. Where all behaved so well it would seem invidious to make particular mention of individual cases. I must be pardoned, however, in calling the attention of the country to the brilliant charges of the cavalry under Captains Keys and McGee. I venture to say they are unsurpassed by any other in the annals of American warfare. As a compliment to Captain Keys, the senior officer, for his gallant conduct, I have named my camp at this point Camp Keys.

The staff officers all discharged their duty with bravery and coolness; and I return my sincere thanks to my assistant adjutant-general, Benjamin F. Hawkes, for his untiring energy and watchfulness during the march, and for his gallant conduct in the action. Our loss was only 1 killed and about 20 wounded. It seems to be almost a miracle that our loss should be so small, considering that we had to advance across a causeway and over a bridge in the face of the enemy's intrenchments. Among the wounded was Dr. Benjamin Tappan, surgeon of the Eighth Ohio, who was struck by a piece of a shell.

Respectfully, your obedient servant,

B. F. KELLEY,
Brigadier-General, Commanding.

Lieut. Gen. WINFIELD SCOTT, *Washington. D. C.*

HEADQUARTERS ARMY,
Washington, October 30, 1861.

Brigadier-General KELLEY, U. S. A., *Romney, Va.:*

Your late movement upon and signal victory at Romney do you great honor in the opinion of the President and of Lieutenant-General Scott. You shall be re-enforced as soon as practicable. In the mean time, if necessary, call for any troops at Cumberland or New Creek.

By command:

E. D. TOWNSEND,
Assistant Adjutant-General.

OCTOBER 26, 1861.—Skirmish at South Branch Bridge, West Virginia.

REPORTS.

No. 1.—Brig. Gen. C. M. Thruston, U. S. Army.
No. 2.—Col. Thomas Johns, Second Maryland Infantry, Potomac Home Brigade.
No. 3.—Col. A. Monroe, One hundred and fourteenth Virginia Militia.

No. 1.

Report of Brig. Gen. C. M. Thruston, U. S. Army.

CUMBERLAND, *October* 27, 1861.

COLONEL: I have the honor to forward a report from Col. T. Johns, Second Regiment Potomac Home Brigade. Though his expedition did not attain its entire object, yet it served to test the character of his troops. They behaved, to a man, with perfect obedience and entire steadiness. Mr. I. I. Grehan (whom I desire to appoint my aide-de-camp) volunteered on the expedition, and confirms Colonel Johns' report of Captain Shaw's gallantry and of the eagerness of all for the contest. Brigadier-General Kelley entered Romney about 4 o'clock yesterday afternoon.

With great respect, your obedient servant,
C. M. THRUSTON,
Brigadier-General.

Col. E. D. TOWNSEND, *Assistant Adjutant-General.*

No. 2.

Report of Col. Thomas Johns, Second Maryland Infantry, Potomac Home Brigade.

HDQRS. SECOND REGIMENT POTOMAC HOME BRIGADE,
Camp Thomas, Cumberland, October 27, 1861.

GENERAL: In compliance with verbal orders, received after consultation between General Kelley and yourself, on the night of the 25th instant I concentrated 700 of my regiment at the North Branch Bridge, and on the following morning at 5 o'clock marched in the direction of Romney, passing through Frankfort. Upon arriving at a point one and a half miles from Springfield, the rear of my column was fired into by the enemy from the heights of the road, severely wounding 2 men, detaining the column about one hour, which was occupied in clearing the woods of the enemy and dressing the wounded. We marched thence through Springfield, seeing frequent signs of the enemy's horsemen in retreat towards the bridge over the South Branch of the Potomac. Upon arriving within half a mile of the bridge my flankers and skirmishers on the left and front discovered the enemy on the opposite side of the river, when a brisk fire at once commenced.

About this time the guns of General Kelley's column in the vicinity of Romney were heard. After skirmishing with the enemy across the river about half an hour I determined to force a way over the bridge. The enemy, numbering, by the best information we could get, from 400 to 600, including cavalry, having beforehand prepared to defend its passage, had arranged covers for his riflemen on an eminence immediately fronting the bridge. Capt. Alexander Shaw, of Company A, who led the advance of the column to this point, was with his company directed to lead the way across the bridge at a double-quick step, supported by the remainder of the regiment. Captain Shaw promptly moved his company as directed, and when about half way across the bridge discovered that a portion of the plank flooring on the farther side had been removed. The enemy, on discovering the movement, opened fire by volley, killing 1 and wounding 6 of my men, causing the company to seek shelter behind the parapets of the bridge.

After skirmishing some time from the parapets of the bridge and an eminence on our left, and not hearing the firing of General Kelley's column for the previous hour, I concluded he had carried Romney, and the object of my march—to create a diversion in his favor—being accomplished, I determined to retire, which we did in good order, to Old Town, in Maryland, arriving there about 9 o'clock p. m., after a march of 25 miles.

It is with pleasure I speak of the good behavior of all my officers and men, and would call your attention particularly to the gallant charge led by Capt. Alexander Shaw. Captain Firey, of dragoons, with his company rendered very efficient service by drawing the fire of the enemy from my regiment at the bridge. I was much gratified at and indebted to Mr. Grehan, who volunteered to march with me, for his prompt and cheerful assistance. Mr. Grehan was frequently exposed to severe fire of the enemy.

I am, with great respect, your obedient servant,

THOMAS JOHNS,
Colonel Second Regiment, Potomac Home Brigade.

Brig. Gen. C. M. THRUSTON.

No. 3.

Report of Col. A. Monroe, One hundred and fourteenth Virginia Militia.

HDQRS. ONE HUNDRED AND FOURTEENTH REG'T VA. M.,
Hanging Rock, November 22, 1861.

SIR: After a delay which I hope under existing circumstances you will pardon I beg leave to submit the following report, to wit:

On Saturday, the 26th day of October last, at 1 o'clock p. m., information was brought to me at my camp that a large force of the enemy had advanced in the direction of Romney as far as Springfield, a small village 9 miles north of the former place. My camp was on the Old Ferry road, about three-eighths of a mile from the main road, three-quarters of a mile from the suspension bridge, which is 1½ miles from Springfield on the main road to Romney.

On receiving the above intelligence I ordered all the men there under my command to repair to the bridge as fast as possible, all our way being through fields, with the exception of a skirt of wood-land surrounding our camp about 20 poles in width.

When we had reached the cleared land I saw that the advance of the enemy had reached Cain's Hill, south of Springfield, and deeming it best to send a part of my command to the ford, which is below the bridge some 300 yards, I accordingly ordered Company F, commanded by Lieut. Jacob Baker, and Company K, commanded by Lieutenant Wilbert, consisting in all of about 40 men, to take position there, directing them on their way to deploy in single file, exposing themselves to the full view of the enemy, which was then about a mile off. Companies A, B, and E, consisting of about 80 men, commanded respectively by Captain Hardy, Lieutenant Pownell, and Captain Higby, I led in person on foot down a small hollow, concealed from the observation of the enemy. This I did hoping to make the enemy believe that our entire force was at the ford, and in this I am happy to inform you that I completely succeeded.

In order that you may the better understand our position I will give you a brief description of the ground. At this point the South Branch, which is a little more than 100 yards wide, cuts a ridge at right angles, which bears about north 40° east. On the north side there is a perpendicular wall of rock about 150 feet high. On the south side, which points down more gradually, we had erected a breastwork directly opposite the south end of the bridge, about 150 yards from it, and at an elevation of about 20°. The gap from our breastwork to the top of the rocks on the opposite side is from 250 to 300 yards wide.

The enemy first appeared on the top of the rocks, and opened a fire on my men at the ford, which was kept up by both parties for 30 minutes. The three companies with me kept close behind our fortification, unobserved by the enemy. After becoming fully satisfied that our whole force was at the ford the enemy left the rocks and fell in line, four deep, and started at double-quick across the bridge. When they had advanced to a point on the bridge I had marked out I fired my rifle at them, which by previous arrangement was the signal for my men to fire, which they did with the utmost regularity. As soon as we fired they retreated from off the bridge, leaving 30 muskets, 3 Mississippi rifles, 40 hats, and one big Yankee they could not drag off. A portion returned again to the rocks and opened a most terrific fire upon us, which we returned, with considerable effect, whenever a good opportunity offered. They kept up a continual fire for about two and a half hours, but I am happy to inform you that not one of my men received as much as a scratch from them. They then commenced a general retreat, and did not stop till they reached Maryland, a distance of some 12 miles. They advanced in two columns—one from Cumberland, via Frankfort, consisting of one company of cavalry, and infantry, amounting in all to 600 men; the other from Old Town, via Green Spring, consisting of 600 infantry. I am not prepared to say with certainty how many we killed, but from the most reliable information I have, by the time they had reached Cumberland their loss in killed was 60, besides a great many wounded.

I had forgotten to remark that I had taken the precaution to place Lieutenant-Colonel Lupton and Adjt. J. Monroe on an eminence to give me timely information in the event of the enemy attempting to place cannon on the rocks. I will further add that the enemy left a very good sword on the bridge, which we got. The guns are now in the hands of my men, and are greatly superior to the ones they had.

On hearing that the enemy had completely routed Colonel McDonald and taken possession of Romney I fell back to North River Mills, a distance of 16 miles. I have subsequently, in obedience to the order of General Jackson, encamped at Hanging Rock, 15 miles east of Romney.

Respectfully submitted.

A. MONROE,
Colonel One hundred and fourteenth Reg't Virginia Militia.

The SECRETARY OF WAR, *Confederate States of America.*

OCTOBER 28, 1861.—Skirmish near Budd's Ferry, Maryland.

Report of Brig. Gen. Joseph Hooker, U. S. Army.

HEADQUARTERS HOOKER'S DIVISION,
Six Miles from Budd's Ferry, Md., October 28, 1861.

GENERAL: The most important event of this day was the attempt of a steamer to ascend the river, when three new batteries from the rebel side opened to dispute her passage, numbering not less than fourteen or fifteen guns. These batteries are located from a quarter to half of a mile below the batteries of which you are already advised, and which had hitherto escaped our attention. These guns, as well as those of the batteries before known to us, appear to be field guns, though it is reported that there is one large gun among them. The steamer was so remote we could not determine whether or not she was struck, nor is it known what vessel she is. I am informed that she delivered the first fire. I shall probably know to-morrow.

This occurrence took place about 3 o'clock p. m. I was not present, but when reported to me I sent instructions for the light batteries to be put in readiness to open on the rebel steamer Page, in case the steamer had been disabled and an attempt made to make a prize of her. While the firing was going on, masses of infantry in the woods behind the batteries were descried from the glittering bayonets—in what numbers I have no means of determining. In this regard the opposite side of the river remains a sealed book to me. I have not been able to find any one able or willing to furnish me with any satisfactory information as to the number of the rebel force opposed to me. Of one fact, however, I am almost confident, and it is this: that they expect an assault more than they do of delivering one. Up to this time I have not been able to make a personal inspection of the opposite bank of the river, but will do so as soon as my arrangements are a little better perfected in my own command, which will be either to-morrow or next day.

Another event requires mention. About 10 o'clock a. m. to-day a boat bearing a white flag was seen making for our shore, and a party of 10 or 12 men proceeded to the bank of the river to receive it. The boat stood on her course until within about one-third of the width of the river of our shore, when they threw overboard a barrel and retired as rapidly as they could pull. The boat was near enough to have been emptied with my sharpshooters in case they had delivered their fire. The barrel remains apparently anchored. Whether it was thrown over to mark out the channel, or is one of their infernal machines, as my men call it, is still an enigma. I only recur to it to inform you to what base uses the most sacred emblem of all Christian countries is applied by the rebels.

My pickets continue to patrol the shore to my satisfaction. The enemy appear to be as busy with their hammers night and day as ever. It is now 10 o'clock p. m. Captain Williamson has just come in from an examination of Indian Point. His report will reach me in season to forward to-morrow morning. He had an interview with Captain Craven, who stated among other matters that the enemy had three depots of boats in this vicinity, containing not less than 100 in each. He has had a much better opportunity to be informed on this subject than myself, but if it be a fact, the enemy doubtless intends to slip up the river with them instead of crossing it. Such is my opinion. The examination of the Posey case is not yet concluded, therefore I cannot furnish you at this time the evidence elicited. I have been notified by

Lieutenant-Colonel Wells, who is charged with the management of this case, that it is advisable to have Mr. Linton, formerly engaged as a foreman painter at the Capitol and now in Washington, arrested at once. He is a son-in-law of Posey.

I have subsistence for my command to include Thursday next.

By the mail to-day I received several communications addressed to the First Regiment Michigan Volunteers. If that regiment is still regarded as belonging to my command, be pleased to have me advised of the fact.

Very respectfully, your obedient servant,

JOSEPH HOOKER,
Brigadier-General, Commanding.

Brig. Gen. S. WILLIAMS,
Assistant Adjutant-General, Army of the Potomac.

NOVEMBER 3-11, 1861.—Expedition into Lower Maryland.

REPORTS.

No. 1.—Brig. Gen. Oliver O. Howard, U. S. Army.
No. 2.—Brig. Gen. George Sykes, U. S. Army.

No. 1.

Report of Brig. Gen. Oliver O. Howard, U. S. Army.

HDQRS. FIRST BRIGADE, CASEY'S DIVISION,
Bladensburg, November 9, 1861.

CAPTAIN: In accordance with General Casey's instructions, I have the honor to submit the following report of my expedition to the lower counties of Maryland:

After leaving your office I proceeded to General Marcy's, and received from him such verbal instructions as would facilitate the execution of my orders already received. General Marcy advised me to make my headquarters at Lower Marlborough instead of Upper Marlborough, and also to communicate with General Sykes, who had been assigned to the second brigade of your division. I then proceeded to my camp at Bladensburg, and issued the necessary orders to move four regiments of the brigade and the squadron of cavalry at 9 a. m. on the following day (Sunday, November 3, 1861). I gave a special order to Colonel Miller, Thirty-sixth Pennsylvania Regiment, at Good Hope, to move in time to join the rest of the brigade at Upper Marlborough. All day Saturday it rained hard, so that Sunday morning it was impossible to ford the Eastern Branch in time. I took a circuitous route across the railroad bridge, and passed back into Bladensburg by a narrow plank pathway, only allowing the men to march by file. I found it to be nearly 12 m. when the three regiments—the Fourth Rhode Island, Fifth New Hampshire, and Forty-fifth Pennsylvania—and the cavalry had cleared Bladensburg and closed up. I then continued the march till sunset under the direction of a guide, halted and bivouacked near Centreville, Md. General Sykes was at the same place. Colonel Miller, with the Thirty-sixth Pennsylvania, joined us here. The next day I detached Colonel Miller, adding to his command two companies of the Fifth New Hampshire and 30 of Major Wetherell's cavalry, with instructions to make his headquarters at Upper Marlborough; to send two companies to Nottingham and vicinity, one to Piscataway, and one to Queen Anne, with permission to make such other distribution of his force as he should deem necessary to carry out the instructions I gave him (a copy of which is marked A).* With the rest of the command I proceeded Monday, the 4th instant, to the vicinity of Lower Marlborough, making a march of 27 miles.

The next day (Tuesday, the 5th) I detached Major Wetherell, of the cavalry, with 100 of his own command and 50 picked men from the Forty-fifth Pennsylvania, and sent him to Saint Leonard's. I sent Colonel Welch, with the balance of the Forty-fifth Pennsylvania, to Prince Frederick. I also sent the Fourth Rhode Island to encamp close by the village of Lower Marlborough, retaining the eight companies of the New Hampshire men at my headquarters, at the Hon. Mr. T. J. Graham's farm, some 2½ miles from the town. The instructions given to Colonel Miller, of the Thirty-sixth Pennsylvania, were in substance given to each detached commander. (See copy marked A.)* Colonel Miller, of the Thirty-sixth Pennsylvania, was the only one who departed from the letter of his instructions. I told him to consult with gentlemen in the district as to the best distribution of his force, and as to the best means of preventing an obstruction of the polls by badly-disposed men. This he did, and, as will be seen by his report, he caused the oath of allegiance to be administered at two of his precincts. He assures me that at one precinct the deputy marshal sent by Major General Dix's authority caused the same oath to be administered to every voter.

Throughout Calvert County I found very warm receptions from Union men and others. At Prince Frederick alone was there any open attempt of violence directed towards Union men. The following persons were arrested: Hon. Augustus R. Sollers, Ex-M. C. He used the most violent and treasonable language, drew a large knife, and cut to the right and left. He was secured and brought in by Colonel Welch to Lower Marlborough, where he was taken so ill with gout that I could not bring him, but left him on his parole to report at Washington as soon as he is able to move. Mervin B. Hance, Walter Hellen, William D. Williams, and John Broome were arrested, charged with treasonable language and with carrying weapons. They also were brought to Lower Marlborough. I released them under oath of fealty and that they had not borne arms against our forces.

At Lower Marlborough Colonel Rodman made several arrests, but subsequently released the individuals. They had been disorderly while under the influence of strong drink.

At Saint Leonard's all went off very quietly without any arrest. (See report marked E.)*

Thursday morning all the detached forces were drawn in, and last night all were in this camp except the Forty-fifth Pennsylvania, which had one day's march more than the rest. This regiment is now here.

I must speak with special praise of the conduct of every colonel and of the commander of the cavalry. Our troops were new, the roads bad, without an experienced quartermaster or commissary. I think we have been particularly fortunate in the march. We were the hardest pushed to get forage, as there is scarcely any hay after crossing the Patuxent.

The different reports of the detached commanders are annexed, and

---

* Not found.

will give in detail the operations at each separate precinct in Prince George's and Calvert Counties.

Colonel Cross makes no report, because he was with me at Lower Marlborough. He, too, did his duty well in marching and disciplining his command.

Colonel Welch reports that the brigade quartermaster neglected to turn over to him oats that I had ordered purchased at Upper Marlborough, and that his horses suffered badly in consequence.

Very respectfully, your obedient servant,

O. O. HOWARD,
Brigadier-General, Commanding.

Capt. H. W. SMITH, *Assistant Adjutant-General.*

[Indorsement.]

Respectfully submitted to the commanding general. The energy displayed by General Howard in placing his brigade in position is, in my opinion, commendable. The conduct of the officers and men was satisfactory.

SILAS CASEY,
Brigadier-General, Commanding Division.

No. 2.

Report of Brig. Gen. George Sykes, U. S. Army.

HEADQUARTERS SECOND BRIGADE, CASEY'S DIVISION,
Washington, D. C., November 11, 1861.

SIR: Pursuant to General Orders, No. 4, from the headquarters of this division, I left Washington on the 3d instant, with two squadrons of horse and the Fifth, Sixth, Seventh, and Eighth Regiments of New Jersey Volunteers, my destination being Charlotte Hall, Md. I reached that village at 7 a. m. on the 5th instant, and established my camp with the regiments of Colonels Starr and Hatfield. At the same time, I detached Colonel Revere, Seventh New Jersey Volunteers, to Chaptico, on an inlet of the Potomac, 10 miles distant; the cavalry, under Captain Harrison, U. S. Army, and Major Beaumont, Halsted's regiment, to Oakville, near the Patuxent, 12 miles distant, and the Eighth New Jersey Regiment, under Colonel Johnson, to Bryantown, 8 miles north of Charlotte Hall. Leonardtown, the county seat, was not occupied, because my supplies of subsistence would not permit it.

The villages in possession of the troops were election precincts, and on the following day (6th) the polls were opened and the elections held without trouble or disturbance. The troops were not permitted to interfere, and the votes registered differed by a very small fraction from the number usually cast. It is believed that not a single inhabitant of that region, soldier or citizen, returned from the Virginia side of the river on the day of the election.

Before the arrival of the command exaggerated rumors as to its mission had been circulated, and the inhabitants were in a state of great alarm. This was happily quieted, and kindness and a general desire to supply our wants continued during our stay. By many the vouchers of the Quartermaster's Department were received in lieu of immediate payment. I was informed by various gentlemen of standing that had my troops been the first among them the feeling towards the Union would have been greatly strengthened, but that the carrying away of slaves and horses and the destruction of private property by a command under a Colonel Dwight, of Sickles' brigade, had alienated many and driven others across the Potomac, who otherwise would have remained at home. Complaints of this command were universal. This brigade behaved better than I expected, and marched exceedingly well. In their biv- ouacks they were exposed to a great deal of rain, and for infantry the roads were worse than I have ever seen. General Howard communi- cated with me from Lower Marlborough.

Not deeming it important, I gave General Hooker no notice of my position in his rear.

I am, sir, respectfully, your obedient servant,

GEO. SYKES,
Brigadier-General Volunteers, Commanding Brigade.

Capt. H. W. SMITH,
Volunteer Service, Assistant Adjutant-General.

[Indorsement.]

Respectfully submitted to the Commanding General. The endeavor of Brigadier-General Sykes to conciliate the feelings of the inhabitants is commended by me. Officers and men of the brigade conducted them- selves with propriety.

SILAS CASEY,
Brigadier-General, Commanding Division.

NOVEMBER 4, 1861–FEBRUARY 21, 1862.—Operations in the Valley Dis- trict, Virginia, and West Virginia.

SUMMARY OF THE PRINCIPAL EVENTS.

Nov.   4, 1861.—Maj. Gen. Thomas J. Jackson, C. S. Army, assumes command of
               the Valley District.
Dec.   8, 1861.—Skirmish at Dam No. 5, Chesapeake and Ohio Canal.
      17–21, 1861.—Operations against Dam No. 5.
Jan. 3– 4, 1862.—Skirmishes at Bath, W. Va.
           4, 1862.—Skirmishes at Slane's Cross-Roads, Great Cacapon Bridge, Sir John's
               Run, and Alpine Depot, W. Va.
           5, 1862.—Bombardment of Hancock, Md.
           7, 1862.—Skirmish at Hanging Rock Pass (Blue's Gap), W. Va.
          10, 1862.—Romney, W. Va., evacuated by Union forces.
Feb.   7, 1862.—Union forces reoccupy Romney, W. Va.
          12, 1862.—Skirmish at Moorefield, W. Va.
          14, 1862.—Affair at Bloomery Gap, W. Va.

REPORTS, ETC.

No. 1.—Maj. Gen. Thomas J. Jackson, C. S. Army, of operations November 4, 1861–
           February 21, 1862.
No. 2.—Maj. Gen. Nathaniel P. Banks, U. S. Army, of skirmish at Dam No. 5.
No. 3.—Maj. Gen. Nathaniel P. Banks, U. S. Army, of operations against Dam No.
           5, from December 17–21, with orders.

No. 4.—Capt. Samuel S. Linton, Thirty-ninth Illinois Infantry, of skirmish near
    Bath, W. Va.
No. 5.—Capt. James H. Hooker, Thirty-ninth Illinois Infantry, of skirmish at Sir
    John's Run, W. Va.
No. 6.—Brig. Gen. Benjamin F. Kelley, U. S. Army, of skirmish at Hanging Rock
    Pass, W. Va.
No. 7.—Col. Samuel H. Dunning, Fifth Ohio Infantry, of skirmish at Hanging Rock
    Pass, W. Va.
No. 8.—Brig. Gen. Frederick W. Lander, U. S. Army, of affair at Bloomery Gap,
    W. Va.
No. 9.—Col. J. Sencendiver, Virginia Militia, of affair at Bloomery Gap, W. Va.

No. 1.

*Reports of Maj. Gen. Thomas J. Jackson, C. S. Army, of operations
from November 4, 1861, to February 21, 1862.**

HEADQUARTERS VALLEY DISTRICT,
Winchester, Va., February 21, 1862.

MAJOR : In obedience to orders from the War Department, I arrived
here on November 4 last and assumed command of the Valley District.
As Romney had but recently fallen into the hands of the enemy, and
Federal forces were at various points north of the Potomac, and might
at any time move upon Winchester by good roads from Romney, Williamsport, and Harper's Ferry, and the only forces in the field at my disposal consisted of parts of Generals Boggs', Carson's, and Meem's brigades
of militia, McDonald's cavalry, and Captain Henderson's mounted company, I at once issued an order calling out the remaining parts of the
brigades above named. The call was responded to with a promptness
that reflects credit upon the militia of the district.

Near the middle of November McLaughlin's battery and Colonel J.
F. Preston's (now Brig. Gen. R. B. Garnett's) brigade, composed of the
Second, Fourth, Fifth, Twenty-seventh, and Thirty-third Regiments
Virginia Volunteers, arrived here.

Early in December Col. William B. Taliaferro's brigade, consisting of
the First Georgia, Third Arkansas, Twenty-third and Thirty-seventh
Virginia Volunteers, of the Army of the Northwest, reached Winchester.

Near the close of December the last re-enforcements arrived here
from the same army under Brig. Gen. W. W. Loring, consisting of the
brigades of Col. William Gilham and Brig. Gen. S. R. Anderson, with
Shumaker's and Marye's batteries. The former of these two brigades
comprised the Twenty-first, Forty-second, and Forty-eighth Regiments
Virginia Volunteers, and the First Battalion Virginia Regulars, and
Captain Marye's battery; the latter, the First, Seventh, and Fourteenth
Tennessee Volunteers and Captain Shumaker's battery. The quartermaster's, commissary, and medical departments, under their respective
chiefs—Majors John A. Harman and W. J. Hawks, and Dr. Hunter
H. McGuire, officers admirably qualified for their duties—were being rapidly organized for active service. Maj. D. Truehart, jr., chief of artillery, was alike successful in the work assigned to him.

The governor of Virginia, alive to the importance of driving the
enemy from the district, not only sent 1,550 percussion muskets to
replace the flint locks then in the hands of the militia, but also fur-

---

*See also "Correspondence, etc.," for this period, *post*.

nished a field battery of five pieces, with equipments and harness complete.

The Chesapeake and Ohio Canal having been repaired to such an extent as to render it boatable and of great service to the Federal Army at Washington, I determined, if practicable, to cut off western supplies by breaking Dam No. 5. For this purpose an expedition was undertaken in the early part of December, but, in consequence of the enemy's resistance and for want of adequate means, the object was not accomplished. A few days subsequently Capt. R. T. Colston, Company E, Second Regiment Virginia Volunteers, who was well acquainted with the locality of the dam and its structure, volunteered to take charge of the working party to accomplish the desired object. As there was reason to believe that General Banks could soon concentrate a large force there, I moved, with Garnett's brigade, part of the cavalry under Lieutenant-Colonel Ashby, and part of Carson's brigade, to the neighborhood of the dam. General Carson made a demonstration towards Falling Waters and Williamsport, while the remaining troops took such a position as to support the working party.

The work was commenced on the night of December 17, and by the morning of the 21st a breach, supposed to be sufficiently large for the object in view, was effected. Though Federal re-enforcements of artillery and infantry were ordered up and opened their fire upon us, our loss was only 1 man killed.

On the 1st day of the present year Garnett's brigade, with McLaughlin's, Carpenter's, and Waters' batteries, Loring's command, consisting of Anderson's, Gilham's, and Taliaferro's brigades, Shumaker's and Marye's batteries, and Meem's command, moved from their various encampments near Winchester in the direction of Bath.

On the evening of the second day's march General Carson, with part of his brigade and parts of two companies of cavalry, under Captain Harper, joined the main body, thus swelling the command to about 8,500 in the aggregate.

On January 3 the march was resumed, and when within about 10 miles of Bath the militia, under Generals Carson and Meem, inclined to the left and crossed the Warm Springs Mountain for the purpose of attacking Bath from the west, while the main body, General Loring's command leading, continued to advance via the Frederick and Morgan turnpike. When nearly 3 miles from Bath we were met by a party of the enemy, consisting of probably 30 infantry and as many horse.

After some skirmishing the enemy were driven back, 8 of them being taken prisoners. Another of the party was captured on the following morning.

Our loss was 4 wounded, 1 lieutenant and 3 privates.

Darkness coming on, the command encamped for the night. The militia on the west of the mountain also drove in the enemy's advance and encamped a few miles from the town.

The next morning (January 4) the march was resumed, General Loring still in front, and continued without further interruption until within a mile or two of the town, when General Loring, without sufficient cause, permitted the head of the column repeatedly to halt, and thus lost so much time as to make me apprehensive that unless I threw forward other troops I would have to remain out of Bath another night. Accordingly he was directed to order a regiment to advance on our left along the mountain which commanded the town. He directed Colonel Maney to execute the order, and it was undertaken with a patriotic enthusiasm which entitles the First Tennessee Regiment and its commander to special praise. Subsequently Colonel Hatton's regiment, and a section of Shumaker's battery, under Lieutenant Lanier, were instructed to co-operate with the advance on the left. Colonel Campbell's regiment advanced along the hill on our right. The forces on the right and left had not advanced far before the enemy fled, leaving their baggage and stores in our possession. The cavalry, under Lieut. Col. William S. H. Baylor, of my staff, rushed into the town, where it encountered and routed the enemy's cavalry, which fled precipitately towards Hancock, and was rapidly pursued by ours, but could not be overtaken.

So prematurely and repeatedly had General Loring permitted the head of the column to halt, that even his skirmishers were not kept within continuous sight of the enemy. Though I followed after the cavalry and entered the town in advance of the skirmishers, yet both the enemy's artillery and infantry were out of sight. I moved on towards Sir John's Run Depot, the direction in which there was reason to believe that they had retreated, until I had advanced sufficiently far to prevent Colonel Gilham from missing the way to the depot. Immediately afterwards I returned to the road leading to the railroad bridge over the Big Cacapon River, and directed Colonel Rust to move to the bridge and destroy it. I then returned towards Bath, for the purpose of following in person the road taken by the fugitive cavalry, and which was the only remaining one by which the enemy could have escaped, and on the way directed Colonel Maney to continue scouring the hill that he was then moving upon, and afterwards to join me.

On my way I met the cavalry returning from the pursuit of the enemy's, which they had been unable to overtake; but as it was important, if practicable, to enter Hancock that night, the pursuit was renewed and continued until we arrived within sight of the town, when part of the cavalry was ordered to dismount and scour the woods to our right and front. Soon after some of the Federal cavalry was seen, and orders were given to charge upon them, but the fire from an ambuscade rendered it imprudent to proceed far in this charge.

Lieutenant Launtz and 2 privates were wounded.

Captain Harper and his command in this charge deserve special mention.

Shortly afterwards General Loring came up with infantry and artillery, but as it was now dark, instructions were given to clear the woods of the enemy by a few rounds of artillery. As the U. S. troops had repeatedly shelled Shepherdstown, and had even done so while there were no troops in the place and it was not used as a means of defense, I determined to intimate to the enemy that such outrages must not be repeated, and directed a few rounds from McLaughlin's battery to be fired at Hancock.

Colonel Gilham, while moving with his brigade in the direction of Sir John's Run Depot, came up with the enemy, but as he neither attacked them nor notified me of the cause of not doing so, nor even of his having overtaken the Federal forces, their artillery and infantry were permitted to escape.

Colonel Rust, in command of his own and Colonel Fulkerson's regiment and one section of Shumaker's battery, when near the railroad bridge over the Big Cacapon, became engaged with the enemy and sustained some loss, but there is reason to believe that the loss of the enemy was still greater. Colonel Rust and his command merit special praise for their conduct in this affair.

At this point Captain [Geo. D.] Alexander, a meritorious officer of the Third Arkansas, lost his left arm.

Darkness rendered it necessary for Colonel Rust to postpone until morning the full execution of his instructions, and he prudently withdrew to a better position for spending the night.

The next morning (January 5) General Loring was directed to proceed with Colonel Rust's command, and Colonel Gilham's, if necessary, and complete the work that had been intrusted to Colonel Rust, if he should find that it had not been already executed. General Loring, having with his artillery driven off the enemy who were defending the bridge, destroyed the structure and railroad buildings, and also the telegraph for some distance, and rejoined me at Hancock.

On the evening of the 4th Lieutenant-Colonel Ashby, who, in command of a detachment composed of some cavalry and an infantry force under Maj. E. F. Paxton, and a working party under Capt. R. T. Colston, had been enlarging the break in Dam No. 5, joined me at Bath. From the most reliable information received the force of the enemy at Bath was 1,500 cavalry and infantry, with two pieces of artillery. The next morning I demanded the surrender of Hancock, stating that if the demand was not acceded to the place would be cannonaded. The commanding officer refused to comply with my demand, and I cannonaded the place for a short time, and proceeded to construct a bridge for crossing the Potomac about 2 miles above the town. This work was intrusted to Col. W. A. Forbes, who commanded and progressed with it in a manner highly creditable to himself and his command. Colonel Forbes was assisted in this work by Captain Briscoe, assistant quartermaster, an enterprising and valuable officer.

On the 6th the enemy was re-enforced to such an extent as to induce me to believe that my object could not be accomplished without a sacrifice of life, which I felt unwilling to make, as Romney, the great object of the expedition, might require for its recovery, and especially for the capture of the troops in and near there, all the force at my disposal.

The invader having been defeated and driven across the Potomac, the telegraph line broken at several points, and the railroad bridge across Big Cacapon destroyed, thus throwing material obstacles in the way not only of transmitting intelligence from Romney to Hancock, but also of receiving re-enforcements from the east, arrangements were made for moving on Romney.

The next day, the 7th, the command was put in motion; Lieutenant-Colonel Ashby, with his cavalry, brought up the rear; but before leaving Alpine Depot, opposite Hancock, destroyed a large amount of public stores that had fallen into our hands and could not be removed for want of means.

Before night a dispatch reached me giving intelligence of our disaster that morning at Hanging Rock, where the enemy not only defeated our militia under Colonel Monroe, but captured two guns.

On arriving at Unger's Store I halted the command for several days, for the purpose of resting the men and ice-calking the horses.

The day that the command left Winchester the weather was mild, but soon after it suddenly changed to very severe, and the snow and sleet made the roads almost impassable for loaded wagons, unless the teams were specially shod for the purpose.

The enemy evacuated Romney on the 10th. The town was soon occupied by Sheetz's and Shand's companies of cavalry, which were subsequently followed by other troops. The Federal forces, abandoning a large number of tents and other public property which fell into our possession, retreated to between the railroad bridges across Patterson's Creek and the Northwestern Branch of the Potomac, which was as far as they could retire without endangering the safety of the two bridges.

Our loss in the expedition in killed was 4, in wounded 28. The Federal loss in killed and wounded not ascertained. Sixteen of them were captured.

After the arrival in Romney of General Loring's leading brigade, under Colonel Taliaferro, I designed moving with it Garnett's brigade and other forces on an important expedition against the enemy, but such was the extent of demoralization in the first-named brigade as to render the abandonment of that enterprise necessary.

Believing it imprudent to attempt further movements with General Loring's command against the Federals, I determined to put into winter quarters in the vicinity of Romney, and accordingly gave directions to Lieut. Col. S. M. Barton to select suitable locations for the several brigades, and steps were taken for putting the troops into huts as rapidly as practicable; and having made a suitable disposition of the militia force of that section of the district, for the purpose of not only holding the country and preventing the surprise of General Loring, but also of acting offensively against the enemy as occasion might offer, the regiments of Cols. A. Monroe, E. H. McDonald, and W. H. Harness were each assigned to the region of their homes, thereby securing all the advantages resulting from knowledge of localities and their inhabitants. Colonel Johnson's regiment was with Colonel Harness in Hardy. In addition to the distribution of militia, three companies of cavalry were left with General Loring, and one of these was the daring company of Captain George F. Sheetz, which was familiar with all that section of country.

To Captain Sheetz I am indebted not only for most reliable information respecting the enemy, for the prisoners from time to time captured, but for the extent to which he has armed and equipped his company at the expense of the enemy.

These forces, in addition to General Loring's three brigades and thirteen pieces of artillery in the vicinity of Romney, and a defensible mountain in his rear, which commanded the town, should, with care, have rendered safe the right of the Army of the Northwest. This disposition of General Loring's forces enabled me to avoid dividing his command, which was thus stretched along the South Branch of the Potomac, his right, under his immediate command, extending towards the Potomac; his left, under Brig. Gen. Edward Johnson, resting upon the Alleghanies with the intervening Moorefield Valley (which is one of the most fertile portions of the Confederacy), three graded roads extending to the rear, and thus connecting his line with the great valley of Virginia, from which ample supplies, if necessary, could be drawn.

I have dwelt thus much on General Loring's position at Romney in consequence of the Secretary of War having regarded the position of the troops there so unsafe as to require me to order them to Winchester, and in consequence of the general having favored an application made by some of his officers to the War Department for the removal of his troops from the position which I had assigned them.

After thus posting the troops in the western part of the district, and having previously sent General Carson to Bath, General Meem to Martinsburg, and distributing the cavalry along the frontier, I directed General Garnett to return to Winchester, in the vicinity of which his brigade proceeded to construct its winter quarters. The position assigned to this brigade as a reserve would enable it promptly to move towards any threatened point as circumstances might require, and I am well assured that had an order been issued for its march, even through the depth of winter and in any direction, it would have sustained its reputation, well earned during the past campaign; for, though it was not under fire during the recent expedition, yet the alacrity with which it responded to the call of duty and overcame obstacles showed that it was still animated by the same spirit that characterized it at Manassas. Thus far all had been accomplished that I could reasonably have expected.

On January 2 there was not, from the information I could gather, a single loyal man of Morgan County who could remain at home with safety. Within less than four days the enemy had been defeated, their baggage captured, and, by teaching the Federal authorities a lesson that a town claiming allegiance to the United States lay under our guns, Shepherdstown protected, which had repeatedly before, though not since, been shelled; the railroad communication of Hancock with the west broken; all that portion of the country east of the Big Cacapon recovered; Romney and a large portion of Hampshire County evacuated by the enemy without the firing of a gun; the enemy had fled from the western part of Hardy; had been forced from the offensive to the defensive—under these circumstances, judge what must have been my astonishment at receiving from the Secretary of War the following dispatch:

Our news indicates that a movement is being made to cut off General Loring's command. Order him back to Winchester immediately.

I promptly complied with the order, but in doing so forwarded to the Secretary of War my conditional resignation. Up to that time God, who has so wonderfully blessed us during this war, had given great success to the efforts for protecting loyal citizens in their rights and recovering and holding territory in this district which had been overrun by the enemy. It is true that our success caused much exposure and suffering to the command. Several nights the troops had to bivouac, notwithstanding the inclemency of the weather, their tents not coming up on account of the bad condition of the roads, yet every command, except part of General Loring's, bore up under these hardships with the fortitude becoming patriotic soldiers.

Lieut. Col. J. T. L. Preston, assistant adjutant-general, rendered very valuable service, not only during the expedition, but preparatory to it.

Lieut. Col. William S. H. Baylor, inspector-general, in addition to his duties as a staff officer, gallantly led the cavalry charge at Bath.

Maj. John A. Harman, chief quartermaster, was, much to my regret, unable on account of a serious attack of sickness to accompany the expedition. His duties devolved successively upon Capt. T. R. Sharp and Lieut. Col. M. G. Harman, both of whom discharged their duties faithfully and efficiently.

Dr. Hunter H. McGuire, medical director, and Maj. W. J. Hawks, chief commissary, were untiring in the zealous discharge of their respective duties.

Lieut. Col. S. M. Barton, acting chief engineer of this district, deserves special mention.

Maj. A. H. Jackson, assistant adjutant-general; First Lieut. George G. Junkin, aide-de-camp; First Lieut. A. S. Pendleton, aide-de-camp, and Lieut. J. M. Garnett, chief of ordnance, rendered valuable service.

General Loring's evacuation of Romney and returning to the vicinity of Winchester was the beginning of disasters. The enemy, who up to that time had been acting on the defensive, suddenly changed to the offensive and advanced on Romney; next drove our troops out of Moore-field on the 12th of this month; two days after forced our militia from Bloomery Pass, thus coming to within 21 miles of Winchester and cap-turing a number of prisoners.

Soon after the intelligence reached me of the enemy's being in pos-session of Bloomery Pass I directed Lieutenant-Colonel Ashby, of the cavalry, to move in that direction with all his available force, which he did with his accustomed promptness, and on the morning of the 16th, after a short skirmish, recovered the position. I am under many obli-gations to this valuable officer for his untiring zeal and successful efforts in defending this district.

I do not feel at liberty to close this report without alluding to the reprobate Federal commanders, who in Hampshire County have not only burnt valuable mill property, but also many private houses. Their track from Romney to Hanging Rock, a distance of 15 miles, was one of desolation. The number of dead animals lying along the road-side, where they had been shot by the enemy, exemplified the spirit of that part of the Northern Army. As Col. G. W. Lay, inspector-general of this department, has recently, by your order, visited Winchester on a tour of inspection, it may be unnecessary for me to say more respecting the condition of this district.

I would respectfully call attention to the report of General Loring, an official copy of which is forwarded herewith.*

Respectfully, your obedient servant,

T. J. JACKSON,
Major-General, Commanding.

Maj. THOMAS G. RHETT,
Assistant Adjutant-General, Department of Northern Virginia.

—

HEADQUARTERS VALLEY DISTRICT,
Winchester, Va., December 14, 1861.

GENERAL: Yours of the 12th instant is at hand.* I have made two attempts to prevent navigation on the canal, but have not thus far suc-ceeded. The only good results that I am aware of having been effected was the capture of 1 captain, 2 corporals, and 5 privates of the Twelfth Indiana Regiment, and damaging this end of Dam No. 5, and killing 1 of the enemy. On our part 2 men are supposed to be mortally wounded. The injury done to Dam No. 5 is not sufficient to admit the passage of water on the Virginia side.

In consequence of the importance of economizing ammunition and keeping the batteries and other troops that would be required for sup-ports at drill, I do not think that it would be advisable to attempt with artillery anything more than the protection of our working parties en-gaged in turning the water around one of the dams, or making a break in the canal. I have had some small boats made for the purpose of crossing a party to the Maryland side if necessary. I hope in this way to stop the navigation for a while, but my desire is to complete the work commenced on the dam, and for this purpose have made arrangements for marching with Garnett's brigade at 6 a. m. on Monday.

During the greater part of next month I expect to have my head-quarters near Martinsburg. If this plan succeeds—as through the

---

* Not found.

blessing of Providence it will—Washington will hardly get any further supply of coal during the war from Cumberland; but should General Kelley advance on me, I may have to content myself with trying to make a break in the canal.

I have not received any additional force except Colonel Taliaferro's brigade, which is well encamped and giving its time to drilling.

The enemy are, from last information, near 9,000 strong in Hampshire, principally at Romney. Their present principal damage to us is the demoralization of our people in Hampshire. They picket near 6 miles this side of Romney. I should not be surprised any day to hear of his (General Kelley) advancing. He says that he does not design going into winter quarters in Romney; that as soon as the weather becomes cold enough to require such protection, if not before, he expects to receive orders to advance. I hope that I will be in a condition to move before he does.

Respectfully, your obedient servant,

T. J. JACKSON,
Major-General, Commanding Valley District.

Gen. J. E. JOHNSTON,
Commanding Department of Northern Virginia.

———

HEADQUARTERS VALLEY DISTRICT,
Unger's Store, Morgan County, Virginia, January 11, 1862.

MAJOR: Though on the 4th instant Bath and all that part of Morgan County east of the Big Cacapon River was recovered from the enemy, and their stores at Bath and at the mouth of the Big Cacapon River, as well as those opposite Hancock, fell into our hands, and the railroad bridge across Big Cacapon River was destroyed by our troops, yet on the 7th the enemy surprised our militia at Hanging Rock Pass, distant 15 miles from Romney, drove back our troops from their fortifications, burned their huts, captured 2 pieces of artillery (one a 4-pounder rifled, the other a 4-pounder smooth bore); the limber of the rifled piece was saved, but both caissons lost. So soon as they had accomplished this and burned the buildings of Col. Charles Blue, near by, killed his live stock, leaving it on the ground, they returned to Romney.

The Federal forces in and about Romney have for the last month been apparently acting upon the principle of burning every house in which they ascertain that any of our troops have been.

Respectfully, your obedient servant,

T. J. JACKSON,
Major-General, Provisional Army Confederate States.

THOMAS G. RHETT, *Assistant Adjutant-General.*

———

No. 2.

Report of Maj. Gen. Nathaniel P. Banks, U. S. Army, of skirmish at Dam No. 5.

FREDERICK, MD., *December 9, 1861—11 o'clock.*

The force referred to in my dispatch last night proves to be cavalry, and does not indicate occupation. The firing Saturday was at Dam No. 5, near Clear Spring. No damage done. Rebels driven back with loss of some men. They had 6 Parrott guns. No rebels between Hancock and Romney, and General Kelley in no danger of attack. Have ordered Colonel Leonard to support him, if necessary.

N. P. BANKS.

Major-General McCLELLAN, *Commander-in-Chief.*

No. 3.

Reports of Maj. Gen. Nathaniel P. Banks, U. S. Army, of operations against Dam No. 5, from December 17–21, with orders.

FREDERICK, MD., *December* 18, 1861.

Colonel Leonard reports, at 12 m., rebels still in position at Falling Waters. Thinks they intend to cover attack on Dam No. 5, where, under cover of guns, they began to cut away, but were driven back with loss of life. Now skirmishing across river. Jackson in command.

N. P. BANKS.

Brig. Gen. S. WILLIAMS, *Assistant Adjutant-General.*

FREDERICK, MD., *December* 18, 1861.

SIR: Information is received from various sources, believed to be reliable, that the enemy contemplates an attach upon Dam No. 4 or No. 5, with a view to the destruction of the canal. You will march your regiment with all expedition to one or the other of these localities, as necessity may require or as the movements of the enemy may dictate, and resist at all hazards the destruction of the dam or any efforts to cross the river. Your long service at these posts will render you familiar with the duties required of you. If the presence of the enemy at Sharpsburg or at Dam No. 4 demands your attention, you will take your post there, assuming command of the forces at that point. If the enemy is above, co-operate earnestly with Colonel Leonard to defeat all his plans. Much must be left to your discretion, your energy, and vigilance. Report progress of affairs constantly. If re-enforcements are wanted, they will be sent.

I am, respectfully, your obedient servant,

N. P. BANKS,
Major-General, Commanding Division.

Colonel KENLY,
Commanding First Maryland Volunteer Regiment.

FREDERICK, MD., *December* 18, 1861—11 o'clock.

Your dispatch of 6.30 duly received. Do you need more men? Let us hear from you often.

Do not allow your attention to be drawn altogether from General Kelley by the movement in your front. It may be a feint.

N. P. BANKS,
Major-General, Commanding Division.

Colonel LEONARD, *Williamsport.*

FREDERICK, MD., *December* 18, 1861—12 m.

Colonel Leonard reported last night and again this morning at 6.30 a threatened attack on Dam No. 5 by Jackson in force with boats. He thinks he is strong enough to protect it.

Have cautioned him not to withdraw attention from position by General Kelley, as this may be cover to other movements. [I] do not leave Frederick on this account.

N. P. BANKS.

Brig. Gen. S. WILLIAMS.

—

FREDERICK, *December* 18, [1861]—10 p. m.

Colonel Leonard reports enemy in position at Falling Waters.

Firing all day, but no loss on our side. Four regiments on the river between Hancock and Shepherdstown, with eight guns. Two regiments and two guns *en route* to-night. Citizen of Baltimore from Richmond reports that Richmond paper Saturday stated that orders had been given for destruction of canal, thinking it essential to Washington. Perfect quiet at all other points.

N. P. BANKS.

Brigadier-General WILLIAMS.

—

FREDERICK, *December* 19, 1861—10 o'clock.

Enemy began cannonading Dam No. 5 this morning. No damage. They have not appeared at Dam No. 4. They commenced shelling our camp at Point of Rocks this morning, but were driven back at once. Force probably from Leesburg. Nothing important occurred during the night.

N. P. BANKS.

General WILLIAMS.

—

FREDERICK, MD., *December* 19—6 p. m.

Heavy firing most of the day at Dam No. 5. Enemy driven from the dam. Several killed. Skirmishing at Falling Waters, opposite Williamsport. No loss reported on our side. No serious impression made upon the dam.

Thirty-ninth Illinois guarding the river at Hancock, under Kelley; all quiet, and at Romney at last advices. Captain Best went up to-day for direction of artillery.

N. P. BANKS.

General WILLIAMS.

—

FREDERICK, MD., *December* 20, [1861.]

Three o'clock p. m. enemy withdrawn from Dam No. 5. All quiet there. Mill burnt by our men, who crossed over and returned with lot blankets, intrenching tools, &c.; dam but little injured; will be repaired at once. At Falling Waters enemy's camp shelled last night, but few seen this morning; it is believed they have retired.

N. P. BANKS,
Major-General, Commanding Division.

General WILLIAMS.

FREDERICK, *December* 20, 1861—8.30 p. m.

All quiet on the line of the river at Harper's Ferry, and also at Williamsport and above. Slight skirmishing at Little Georgetown. No artillery to-day. Six guns concentrated at Williamsport; ample protection for the dams. Fifth Connecticut at Hancock. No news there from General Kelley. One prisoner taken last night. Two deserters from rebels are in custody; they report Jackson's force 15,000. Enemy appears to have withdrawn.

'General Hamilton goes up to-morrow.

N. P. BANKS,
Major-General, Commanding Division.

General WILLIAMS.

—

HEADQUARTERS DIVISION,
Frederick, Md., December 20, 1861.

SIR: I received to-night your dispatch of 5 p. m. and the several telegrams and reports* made since the enemy appeared on the river, and am very much gratified with all that has been done and the results thus far accomplished. So far as I know of events transpiring under your command, your course has entire approval. With reference to possible ulterior movements I have directed General Hamilton to visit Williamsport and other points on the river. He will consult with you, and, if necessary to his purpose, assume command while on the river. You will please aid him in his movements as far as in your power, and oblige, yours, very truly,

N. P. BANKS,
Major-General, Commanding Division.

Col. S. H. LEONARD,
Commanding at Williamsport and Upper Potomac.

—

HEADQUARTERS BANKS' DIVISION,
December 22, 1861.

SIR: Telegram from Colonel Leonard states as follows:

WILLIAMSPORT, 21ST.

Canal-boats running to-day both ways. Two guns were brought to Little Georgetown and some infantry appeared this morning. A few shots been exchanged. The Twenty-ninth Pennsylvania have moved to Dam 4. I hear no rebels have been there yet. From Falling Waters the rebels have moved up towards Dam 5, but a few pickets left there (F. W.). Captain Best has gone to Dam 5.

Respectfully submitted.

N. P. BANKS,
Major-General, Commanding.

Brig. Gen. R. B. MARCY.

—

Extract from "Record of Events" return of Banks' Division, Army of the Potomac, for December, 1861.

*   *   *   *   *   *   *

On the 18th, having received information that General Jackson threatened Williamsport, the Fifth Connecticut Volunteers, Lieutenant-Colonel Kingsbury commanding; the Twenty-ninth Pennsylvania Vol-

———
* Not found.

unteers, Colonel Murphy commanding; the First Maryland Volunteers, Colonel Kenly commanding; Company F, Fourth Artillery, Capt. C. L. Best commanding, and two companies of Maryland cavalry, were ordered to march [from Frederick, Md.] to Williamsport, to report to Colonel Leonard, commanding there. These troops made a quick march to that place, and were engaged in defending Dams Nos. 4 and 5 for some days. There was some sharp-shooting, but with little loss on either side, the enemy at last falling back. During the continuance of the contest the Fifth Connecticut Volunteers and a portion of Best's battery, together with the Thirty-ninth Illinois Volunteers, were sent to Hancock. The Twenty-ninth Pennsylvania Volunteers and the Fifth Connecticut Volunteers were, after the danger had subsided, recalled to their former quarters near this city, and Captain Matthews' Pennsylvania battery was ordered to Hancock to relieve Best's battery, which then returned to their camp, near the Second Brigade. During the continuance of the enemy's attack all the companies of Lamon's brigade were ordered by the commanding general to join General Kelley, which order was issued anew from these headquarters to Colonel Leonard at Williamsport, and the troops sent on to Hancock.

*   *   *   *   *   *   *

No. 4.

Report of Capt. Samuel S. Linton, Thirty-ninth Illinois Infantry, of skirmish near Bath, W. Va.

HDQRS. CO. D, THIRTY-NINTH REG'T ILL. VOLS.,
January 8, 1862.

SIR: In accordance with your orders I make the following report of the doings of my company on Friday and Saturday of last week:

On Friday morning [3d instant] we were occupying the same position at Bath, Morgan County, Virginia, that we had held since our first entry into that place on December 22 last. During the day indefinite reports had reached us to the effect that the enemy in force were marching upon the place.

About 3 p. m. I was ordered by Maj. O. L. Mann, commanding, to divide my company into several squads and scout in the direction of the enemy until I had ascertained with some degree of accuracy their position and strength. I immediately dispatched Lieutenant Towner, with 10 men, up on the west side of Warm Springs Mountain, that he might discover any attempt of the rebels to get in our rear, and with the remainder proceeded up the center of Bath Valley along the Winchester grade. The reports throughout the day had all indicated that they were approaching us by way of this road. We had marched but 1½ miles from town when we came suddenly upon their advance guard, consisting of 8 mounted men. They fled without returning our fire. I at once detached Lieutenant Linton to the right and Sergeant Snowden to the left, each with 5 men, to discover any ambuscade and guard against my being suddenly flanked by the enemy, while I continued up the grade. After getting beyond our range some distance the enemy's guard that we had put to flight halted and fired three signal shots. Just at that time Maj. O. L. Mann, accompanied by Lieutenant Belcher and 6 cavalrymen, of Captain Russell's company, came up and passed my men on the road and ordered them to follow close upon their heels, which order they obeyed, thus leaving my flanks entirely in the rear. The road just there making a turn to the right, Lieutenant Linton took advantage of it to go in his proper position, while Sergeant Snowden and his squad were thrown still farther in the rear. After passing this turn in the road a short distance a large party of the enemy's infantry, with scattering horsemen on their right and left, showed themselves in the edge of a small piece of timber, but about 150 yards in our advance, and opened fire upon us. The lieutenant's squad and mine immediately took cover behind a fence that ran from the grade up over a bare hill on the right (the only available shelter), along which we deployed, and opened fire upon them so briskly that they were obliged to retire full 100 yards into the timber. As we fired we gradually worked our way towards the summit of the hill. While behind this fence the enemy's balls rattled against it like hail, still not one of my men exhibited the least symptom of fear or excitement, but loaded their pieces with promptness and fired as coolly as though practicing at a target. By thus keeping up a steady and well-directed fire we forced the enemy to remain in the woods until we had reached the summit of the hill.

By this time Sergeant Snowden and his squad, who had been laboriously making their way along the left side of the road, suddenly came upon a battalion of the enemy that lay concealed in a ravine to our rear, and drew the fire of every one of them. By falling flat upon the ground he and his men escaped uninjured. This volley discovered to us that our direct retreat was cut off. The cavalry party of our side made good their escape when the firing first commenced. We continued the firing from the summit of the hill until we had collected all of our men that were engaged along the fence, and then retreated towards Warm Springs Mountain, which we reached without difficulty, and by mountain paths made our way to Bath, where we arrived about 12 o'clock at night without further adventure. Sergeant Snowden became entirely surrounded, and only escaped by taking advantage of the darkness of the night to pass close by the enemy and being mistaken by them for a party of their own men. Lieutenant Towner, with his squad, proceeded up the west side of Warm Springs Mountain, and when 2 miles from town came in collision with a large party of the enemy's infantry, apparently a whole regiment. He and his men exchanged a few shots with them and then retired. He reached town about 11 p. m.

I have no means of knowing the number of the enemy that were killed and wounded in these skirmishes, but have reasons for believing that it was quite large.

After refreshing my men with three hours' rest and their supper, I took position, in accordance with an order from the commanding officer, on the summit of Warm Springs Mountain, where we remained until ordered to march with the other forces to Sir John's Run. We then crossed the river in boats and marched to Hancock, where we arrived about 9 o'clock of Saturday evening without incident. My company is now posted in the east end of this town, as by you ordered.

During the skirmish of Friday afternoon and night I had 3 men slightly wounded, lost 8 as prisoners to the enemy, and 1 that I cannot satisfactorily account for, though I have good reasons for believing that he has neither been killed nor taken prisoner.*

*   *   *   *   *   *   *

The order for our march from Warm Springs Mountain to Sir John's Run and thence to Hancock forced us to desert one of our men, named Clark Spinnings, who was too sick in bed at Bath to be moved. We

---

* Nominal list of prisoners omitted.

have since learned that the rebels placed a guard over his room and forbid his being disturbed; also that a rebel physician, more solicitous than ever our own surgeons had been for his welfare, visited and prescribed for him without compulsion. Any assistance that you may render in securing the return of the above members of my company to their comrades by way of exchange or otherwise will cause you to be ever remembered with the warmest feelings of gratitude by all the members of my command.

Your obedient servant,

SAMUEL S. LINTON,
Captain Company D, Thirty-ninth Regiment Illinois Volunteers.
Lieut. Col. T. O. OSBORN.

No. 5.

Report of Capt. James H. Hooker, Thirty-ninth Illinois Infantry, of skirmish at Sir John's Run, W. Va.

———, —, 1862.

The night before the attack on Bath First Lieutenant Whipple, with 25 men from Company E, was detailed to go to Great Cacapon to assist Captain Slaughter. The balance of the company were left at Sir John's Run to guard the Baltimore and Ohio Railroad at that point.

The attack on Bath was expected, and in the morning, January 4, we set ourselves at work on a commanding hill to prepare a good position in case of emergency, and kept out a strong picket during the day. The rebels, some 10,000 in number, attacked Bath about noon. Company D, Captain Linton, Company K, Captain Woodruff, and Company I, Captain Phillips, under command of Major Mann, of the Thirty-ninth Regiment Illinois Volunteers, had a sharp skirmish with the rebels, doing good execution, but the rebels kept constantly advancing upon them, taking some twelve prisoners from Companies D and K. The Eighty-fourth Pennsylvania, Colonel Murray, came to support them, but having just received their arms, found they were in no condition for service, and Colonel Murray ordered a retreat. Meanwhile we were overjoyed at Sir John's Run by seeing the Thirteenth Indiana unload from the cars and falling in in good order, and start for Bath with their band playing and in good spirits. Not knowing that our forces were retreating they made for Bath, but on nearing the place were obliged to fall back without getting sight of the enemy.

Meanwhile we busied ourselves getting a flat-boat out of the ice to provide against the worst, as there was considerable of value to save in case of a retreat. While thus engaged our forces came into Sir John's Run in good order. I went immediately to find out what the order was; they replied a retreat. The Eighty-fourth Pennsylvania Regiment kept on down the railroad to Hancock. I, being acquainted with the positions, prevailed on the three companies of the Thirty-ninth Illinois Regiment and the Thirteenth Indiana to try taking positions, one on the right and the other on the left hill, both having command of all the accessible roads and paths from Bath. On the hill with the Thirty-ninth Lieutenant Muhlenberg would have an opportunity to plant his artillery and take a range on Bath, and enable all to do good execution, and no chance for the enemy to cut off our retreat. After getting this move fairly under way and the forces partly up the hill, the order, "Halt; let's go to Bath," was given, and a consultation was had, which resulted in ordering a second retreat across the river. I have since learned this very move—going up the hill—proved a providential saving of our forces, as the enemy, had they not seen us taking those positions, would have followed and occupied the same, cutting the companies of the Thirty-ninth to pieces as they waded the river.

The Thirteenth Indiana loaded into the train which was standing on the railroad track and started for Great Cacapon. Sergt. John L. Ripple, John Harvath, and myself, with the assistance of a few citizens, kept at work getting over the sick and company baggage till the rebel skir-mishers came into Sir John's Run, which was after dusk. Sergeant Ripple then came to me and said, "Captain, we will have to leave now; they are upon us." We loaded the things into the boat and pushed off, John Harvath having been taken prisoner. When we reached the Maryland shore we found all our regiment had gone to Hancock with Major Mann, except 12 men. I then said to them my company was stationed there to guard the railroad, and with their assistance would perform that duty still. The first move was to station a guard at the river to prevent their stealing the march on us, and then we moved our baggage to a safe place.

It was about 8 o'clock in the evening before the main body came into Sir John's Run. The guard then came to me and said they were breaking the ice. I went down to the water's edge and found, instead of breaking the ice, they were at work at the railroad track. We leveled our pieces and blazed away as though we had thousands of backing. They dropped their bars and picks, returned the fire with a volley which made the hill look like lightning-bugs, and rained the balls around us in showers. Our guards exchanged shots with them for several rounds, whereupon they left the railroad, which they did not venture to disturb again, being on the bank of the river in good range of our excellent guns. We then proceeded to stop the culvert under the canal to prevent their crossing with cavalry and select posi-tions for our men, stationing them in the rifle-pits built of stone, so as to be ready for an attack in the morning.

As the day broke we, conscious of being few in numbers, rather with-held firing, but finally opened fire, keeping it up all day on every man that made their appearance, killing 8 of them and preventing their doing any damage to the railroad, losing but 1 man, John Harvath, who was taken prisoner.

All of the men acted nobly, especially Sergt. John L. Ripple, who staid with me on the other side helping over the sick till all had crossed, and securing everything of value to the company.

J. H. HOOKER,
Captain Company E, Thirty-ninth Regiment Illinois Volunteers.

No. 6.

Report of Brig. Gen. Benjamin F. Kelley, U. S. Army, of skirmish at Hanging Rock Pass, West Virginia.

HEADQUARTERS,
Cumberland, Md., January 17, 1862.

GENERAL: I herewith inclose you Colonel Dunning's report of the expedition to Blue's Gap on the 8th [7th] instant.

I am happy to say that the expedition was an entire success. The effect was, as I intended, to divert the attention of General Jackson from Hancock, he supposing that I was moving on Winchester with my whole force, and therefore beat a precipitous retreat from Hancock and fell back on Winchester.

I am happy to say that the troops under my late command evinced on that occasion the same energy and gallantry that have characterized them ever since they have been under my command.

Respectfully, your obedient servant,

B. F. KELLEY,
Brigadier-General.

General L. THOMAS,
Adjutant-General U. S. Army, Washington, D. C.

No. 7.

Report of Col. Samuel H. Dunning, Fifth Ohio Infantry, of skirmish at Hanging Rock Pass, W. Va.

ROMNEY, VA., *January 9,* 1862.

GENERAL : In obedience to your orders by telegraph, received at these headquarters January 7 [6], directing me to make a detail of six companies from each of the following regiments : Fifth Ohio, Fourth Ohio, Seventh Ohio, First West Virginia, Fourteenth Indiana, and, by special request of Colonel Carroll, six companies of the Eighth Ohio, with one section of Baker's Parrott guns, Daum's battery, the Ringgold Cavalry, the Washington Cavalry, and three companies of the First West Virginia Cavalry. Owing to sickness and large numbers on picket duty, the response was small, and the whole force did not exceed 2,000 men.

The command assembled about 11 p. m., and by 12.30 o'clock the column was in motion for its destination at Blue's Gap. The fall of snow, with the disagreeable and cold night, rendered it difficult for the troops to march, but by 7 o'clock in the morning we reached a hill within about a mile of the gap. On this hill the Parrott guns were planted, and from it the enemy could be seen preparing to fire the bridge. I then ordered the Fifth Ohio to advance by double-quick. The order was responded to by a shout, and in a few minutes the advance of the regiment was on a bluff near the bridge, and with a few shots compelled the rebel forces to retire from the bridge to the gap. The column was then ordered to advance rapidly on and over the bridge, and the Fifth Ohio was deployed up the mountain to the left and the Fourth Ohio to the right. A sharp action then ensued, first on the left of the gap and then on the right. Our forces pressed on, driving the enemy from the rocks and trees, behind which they had taken position, and to the top of the mountain to the left they were found in rifle-pits. A charge was ordered, but before bayonets could be fixed the rebels had left their pits and were fleeing down the mountain in haste to the back of the gap. At this time the remaining detachments of infantry pressed through the gap, and the victory was complete. The cavalry was then ordered to charge, which was done promptly, but the enemy had by this time scattered in the mountain, rendering the charge of little avail.

The enemy left behind them two pieces of artillery (6-pounders, one a rifled gun), their caisson, ammunition, wagons, and ten horses; also their tents, camp equipage, provisions, and correspondence. Seven prisoners were taken and 7 dead bodies were found on the field. Not one of my men were either killed or wounded.

I take pleasure in stating to you that our officers and men seemed to vie with each other in the promptness with which they obeyed orders, and all advanced with the bravery of veteran soldiers.

I desire to return my sincere thanks to Lieut. C. W. Smith, acting adjutant Fifth Ohio, and Adjutant Green, of the Fourth Ohio, for the assistance rendered me on the occasion; also to Lieut. William B. Kelley and Assistant Adjutant-General Hawkes, of General Kelley's staff, for the efficient manner in which they discharged their duties as volunteer aids in this enterprise.

Finding the mill and hotel in the gap were used for soldiers' quarters, I ordered them to be burned, which was done; but I am sorry to say that some straggling soldiers burned other unoccupied houses on their return march.

The force of the rebels was stated by negroes and citizens at from 800 to 1,000, but their papers show that rations were drawn for 1,800 men.

We marched to the gap, fought the battle, and returned to camp within 15 hours, bringing with us prisoners, cannon, and other captured articles.

Respectfully submitted.

　　　　　　　　　　　　　　　S. H. DUNNING,
　　Colonel Fifth Ohio Volunteer Infantry, Comdg. Post of Romney.
Brigadier-General KELLEY.

No. 8.

Report of Brig. Gen. Frederick W. Lander, U. S. Army, of affair at Bloomery Gap, West Virginia.

　　　　　　　　　　PAW PAW, *February* 14, 1862—8 p. m.

The railroad was opened to Hancock this morning. Telegraph the same. Had an important forced reconnaissance last night completed to-day. Broke up the rebel nest at Bloomery Gap. Ran down and caught 17 commissioned officers, among them colonels, lieutenant-colonels, captains, &c. Will forward a descriptive list. Engaged them with 400 cavalry. Infantry not near enough to support, and enemy retiring. In all, 65 prisoners; killed 13. Lost 2 men and 6 horses at their first fire. Led the charge in person. It was a complete surprise. Colonel Carroll, commanding Fifth or Eighth Ohio, made a very daring and successful reconnaissance immediately afterwards to Unger's Store.

Major Frothingham is entitled to credit for building, under my direction, in 4 hours, in the dead of night, a complete bridge of wagons across the Great Cacapon, at an unfrequented road. Two columns of 2,000 men each marched 32, one column 43, miles since 4 p. m. yesterday, besides bridging the river. Papers taken and my own reconnaissance south prove the country clear and Jackson and Loring in Winchester. Made the move and occupied Bloomery Gap and Point's Mill east on belief by deserters that General Carson's brigade was there.

General Dunning has just arrived at New Creek from Moorefield, 40 miles south of Romney. Captured 225 beef cattle and broke up the guerrilla haunt there. Two of his men badly wounded. Killed several of the rebels.

As the work intrusted to me may be regarded done and the enemy out of this department, I most earnestly request to be relieved. If not relieved, must resign. My health is too much broken to do any severe work.

F. W. LANDER,
Brigadier-General.

Major-General McCLELLAN.

NOTE.—General Williams can move over the river without risk. I respectfully commend Colonel Carroll to your notice. He is a most efficient and gallant officer. Lieut. H. G. Armstrong, acting assistant adjutant-general, and Fitz-James O'Brien joined me in a charge by which rebel officers were captured and confidence restored after cavalry had been checked.

No. 9.

Report of Col. J. Sencendiver, Virginia Militia, of affair at Bloomery Gap, West Virginia.

HDQRS. SIXTEENTH BRIGADE, VIRGINIA MILITIA,
Pughtown, February 17, 1862.

SIR: I have the honor to submit the following report of the engagement into which we were surprised on the morning of the 14th instant:

Our advanced pickets came in about daylight and reported the enemy advancing upon us in large force. I gave orders to have the baggage packed immediately and the men prepared to meet the enemy and repulse him if possible. The Thirty-first Regiment, Colonel Baldwin, being quartered nearer the point from where the enemy was advancing than the balance of the command, rushed hurriedly to meet him. The Fifty-first, Major Wotring, and a portion of the Eighty-ninth, commanded by Major Davidson, hastened to his aid, but before they reached him the enemy's cavalry dashed through his ranks and inclosed him between them and their infantry and captured himself and nearly all his command. Majors Wotring and Davidson then took position on [a] hillside near the road and commenced a brisk fire on the cavalry, who advanced about 400 strong in full speed in pursuit of our wagons. While they were engaged with cavalry the infantry flanked them on the right and captured a number of their men and officers. As the cavalry neared our teams they were met by the Sixty-seventh Regiment and Company A, of the Eighty-ninth Regiment, who took a position on the hill-side near the road and poured a heavy volley into them and checked them for a short time, but they again dashed forward, overtook our wagons, captured several of them, and turned them back towards Bloomery. At this juncture the Sixty-seventh and Company A, Eighty-ninth Regiment, advanced rapidly on either side of the road and commenced a brisk fire on them, and finally drove them back and recaptured the wagons. This was effected without the loss of a man. The enemy lost several men and horses killed at this point.

We then continued on after our wagons. The enemy followed us from this point about 2 miles, but at respectful distance. He picked up 1 or 2 stragglers and then retired.

We reached this place at sundown, and, as before reported, I sent yesterday morning a party with a flag of truce to bring off our dead and

wounded.   After a diligent search they did not find any killed and but
two wounded, neither of them mortally.

They learned that the enemy was from 7,000 to 10,000 strong, commanded by General Lander.   He returned the same evening towards
Paw Paw, but threatened to return in two days.   His loss was 11 killed
and several wounded.

Our loss, I regret to say, is over 50 officers and privates missing.

Annexed is a list of officers captured: Col. R. F. Baldwin, Thirty-first
Regiment; Capts. William Baird, acting assistant adjutant-general, and
G. M. Stewart, Eighty-ninth Regiment; Capts. Thomas McIntyre, Will-
iam Lodge, and Byron Lovett, Thirty-first Regiment; Capt. James
Willis, Fifty-first Regiment; Lieut. Charles H. Brown, Thirty-first Regi-
ment; First Lieut. William Wilson, Eighty-ninth Regiment; Lieuts.
William A. Holland, Thomas Steele, R. L. Gray, A. L. White, H. R.
Hottel, Isaac Rewner, and Joseph Seibert, Fifty-first Regiment.

All the officers and men engaged behaved themselves with commendable bravery, and I think they deserve great credit for having saved
our stores and baggage.

Very respectfully reported.

> J. SENCENDIVER,
> *Colonel, Commanding Brigade.*

Major-General JACKSON.

NOVEMBER 9, 1861.—Expedition to Mathias Point, Virginia.

REPORTS.

No. 1.—Brig. Gen. Joseph Hooker, U. S. Army.
No. 2.—Brig. Gen. Daniel E. Sickles, U. S. Army.
No. 3.—Col. Charles K. Graham, Seventy-fourth New York Infantry.

No. 1.

Report of Brig. Gen. Joseph Hooker, U. S. Army.

HEADQUARTERS HOOKER'S DIVISION,
Camp Baker, Lower Potomac, Md., November 12, 1861.

GENERAL: It was reported to me that the rebels were planting a
battery at Boyd's Hole, which threatened to be of some annoyance to the
portion of the flotilla under Captain Harrell, at present lying off Smith's
Point. Accordingly I proceeded to that point for the purpose of making an examination of that vicinity, with a view, if deemed expedient,
of attacking and destroying it.   The battery in question is a field one,
perfectly harmless as it is, and probably displayed for no other purpose
than to have an effect upon the flotilla.   They appear to be the guns of
a single company, without supports.   I could have embarked a regiment
3 miles below Port Tobacco and landed them a short distance above the
batteries without the use of lighters.   The supply steamer Baltimore,
now with the flotilla, is well adapted for this service.   I have abandoned
the idea of attacking it, for the reason that the battery can be moved to
the rear faster than infantry can follow it.

I inclose herewith the report of Colonel Graham [No. 3] of his descent
on Mathias Point, as it contains reliable information of the condition of
that much-talked-of point.   The expedition was projected without my

authority or even knowledge. As it appears to have had no unfortunate sequence so far as I have learned I shall not censure him, but in future no operations will be projected without my sanction; otherwise my command may be dishonored before I know it.

The operator informs me that the wires are in good working condition.

The balloon made several ascensions to-day, but so far removed from the enemy's works as to be of little or no service to us. It will be transferred to a point near Budd's Ferry to-morrow, and then probably to a locality still farther south.

The rebels in considerable force appeared to be busily at work during the day nearly across from Sandy Point in the establishment of new batteries.

On board of what is called the ice-boat of the flotilla is a rifled gun of the largest class, perhaps a 60-pounder. Its weight is five tons, and is of no use, I learn, where she is, the steamer being unserviceable. I think it might be dumped overboard and hauled ashore at some suitable landing, and thence, by the truck used for that purpose, delivered at the work which Captain Williamson is constructing. I am informed that it is a good weapon. Its range is enormous, but for some cause up to this time its shells have not exploded. If guns are to be mounted in the work Captain Williamson is engaged on, in my opinion this should be one of them.

The houses burned by Colonel Graham had been made use of by the rebels for military purposes.

Prisoner Dent requires especial attention.

Very respectfully, your obedient servant,

JOSEPH HOOKER,
Brigadier-General, Commanding Division.

Brig. Gen. S. WILLIAMS,
Adjutant-General, Army of the Potomac.

No. 2.

Report of Brig. Gen. Daniel E. Sickles, U. S. Army.

HEADQUARTERS EXCELSIOR BRIGADE,
Second Brigade, Hooker's Division, November 12, 1861.

CAPTAIN : Herewith I have the honor to inclose Col. Charles K. Graham's report of a reconnaissance of Mathias Point and the peninsula of which it is the terminus [No. 3]. Colonel Graham was effectively assisted by Lieut. Commander Samuel Magaw, of the U. S. steamer Freeborn; Acting Master Arnold Harris, of the U. S. steamer Island Belle, and Acting Master W. T. Street, of the U. S. cutter Dana.

The party, which consisted of 400 men of the Fifth Regiment, under the command of Colonel Graham, embarked on Sunday evening last at Chapel Point, in Port Tobacco Creek, on board the Island Belle and Dana, and proceeded, the Dana towed by the Island Belle to Mathias Point. The embarkation and the landing were effected in admirable order, under the immediate direction of Acting Master Harris, who was the first to land. One of the enemy's pickets, while about to fire upon Master Harris, was killed by that officer. Several others were wounded. The pickets were mounted, which enabled them to retreat rapidly and escape. Colonel Graham suffered no loss. The enemy was reported to be in some force, with three pieces of artillery, at Hampstead, 9 miles from the place of landing, inland, but it was not consistent with Colonel Graham's instructions to advance so far, or to seek an encounter with any force which he had reason to believe superior in numbers to his own detachment.

It is satisfactorily ascertained from this examination of Mathias Point and the contiguous territory for some 4 miles inland, that no guns are in position there, although it seems, in corroboration of previous accounts, that the enemy has made preparations to mask a battery on the point. A few rifle-pits were also noticed.

Between 30 and 40 negroes, some of whom returned with the troops and others making their way over in boats obtained on the Virginia shore, are now in Colonel Graham's camp. I will thank you to favor me with instructions as to the disposition to be made of these persons. I presume much reliable information may be gathered from them.

This expedition, and the examination recently made of the Occoquan River by a party from the Fourth Regiment [Seventy-third New York Infantry], confirm the opinion heretofore expressed of the facility with which enterprises may be executed on the Virginia shore at almost any point which may be indicated. If I am honored with particular instructions as to any place on the shore to be visited, either in small parties or in force, the duty will be promptly, and I believe successfully, performed; or, if left to the exercise of my own judgment as to the place of landing and the force to be employed, there is little doubt that, with the able and enthusiastic co-operation we are sure to receive, if permitted, from the gallant officers of the flotilla, some useful results may be confidently promised. It is reported to me that in one of the creeks below the point about 30 boats are now collected. These can be cut out and captured or destroyed. I learn from a report verbally made to me by Captain Morey (Fifth Regiment) that, from information since obtained, Colonel Graham's detachment was within 2½ miles and in the rear of the battery recently disclosed some 5 miles above Mathias Point, which on Monday fired upon the Freeborn and arrested her farther progress up the Potomac. There is little doubt that if the existence of this battery had been known to Colonel Graham he could have taken it without difficulty, as it is said to be feebly supported by infantry.*

*   *   *   *   *   *   *

I am, captain, very respectfully, your obedient servant,

D. E. SICKLES,
Brigadier-General.

Capt. WILLIAM H. LAWRENCE,
Aide-de-Camp, and Acting Assistant Adjutant General.

No. 3.

Report of Col. Charles K. Graham, Seventy-fourth New York Infantry.

HEADQUARTERS FIFTH REGIMENT EXCELSIOR BRIGADE,
Camp Fenton, near Port Tobacco, Md., November 11, 1861.

GENERAL: Shortly after my arrival at this point Captain Wilkinson, of Company I of this regiment, by my orders seized several small boats and manned them with crews of sailors picked from his company.

---

* Some matters of detail omitted.

They were employed in reconnoitering the Potomac shore and neighboring creeks and in keeping a general surveillance over the movements and actions of the secession sympathizers on this shore. In the numerous expeditions he made, Captain Wilkinson was frequently materially assisted by Lieut. Commander Samuel Magaw, of the U. S. steamer Freeborn, and Acting Master Arnold Harris, of the U. S. steamer Island Belle. I was on board these steamers in several of their reconnaissances, and from information gleaned from reliable sources I became convinced that there were no batteries at Mathias Point sufficient to oppose the landing of troops. The commanders of the gunboats above named agreed with me in this opinion, and also as to the desirability of a thorough inspection of this point. They very kindly placed their vessels at my disposal for such a purpose.

Sunday evening was the time agreed upon for this service, but Lieutenant Magaw was unfortunately prevented, by orders from his superior officer, from carrying out his intentions in this particular, but Acting Master Wm. T. Street, of the U. S. cutter Dana, volunteered the service of himself and vessel. The Island Belle, with the Dana in tow, ran up Port Tobacco Creek to Chapel Point, and on them I embarked about 400 picked men of my regiment. The embarkation was conducted silently and in good order. Arrived at Mathias Point, the force was landed under the admirable direction of Masters Harris and Street, and made a thorough reconnaissance of the point for several miles around. Master Harris, of the Island Belle, was the first to land, and, accompanied by a squad of skirmishers, pushed forward and took possession of Grimes' house. About a quarter of a mile from shore he came suddenly upon 3 of the enemy's pickets, 1 of whom raised his musket and was about to fire, when Master Harris shot him dead in his tracks with his revolver. The other 2 pickets took to their heels. We secured a musket of 1 and the horses of all. The main body of the command, under my own guidance, then made a thorough inspection of the point for some 4 miles inland. We met 2 of the enemy's pickets, and endeavored to capture them, but they escaped; 1 of them, however, wounded by a musket-ball. We discovered a few rifle-pits and a battery partially masked, but upon which no guns had been mounted. Several rebel houses and barns were burned. Beyond this there were no batteries or troops to be found, except a party of perhaps 20 cavalry, who retreated as we advanced. We were informed that there was a rebel camp at Hampstead, consisting in part of three pieces of artillery. Captain Street offered his howitzer and crew, but I decided not to expose my command to too great risk, and concluded not to attack the enemy in his camp, some 9 miles from the landing. A large amount of forage and grain was burned and several horses belonging to the enemy were captured.

I was also fortunate enough to secure Mr. George Dent and son, and brought them as prisoners to this camp. We found them armed, and under circumstances which leave no doubt of their complicity with treason. I shall transmit them to you, with the papers found in their possession, as soon as possible. Several attempts were made to burn the woods on the Point, but owing to their non-inflammable nature at this season, with but qualified success. By this means, however, the only earthworks on the Point were unmasked.

After having completed my reconnaissance the force was withdrawn in good order to the beach and re-embarked on the gunboats, and reached camp about 1 p. m. without injury of any kind. A large number of negroes followed, some on board the gunboats, but a majority in a large launch, which by some means they had obtained.

I cannot close this report without again referring to the valuable and important services rendered by Master Harris, of the Island Belle, and Master Street, of the Dana. Both gentlemen exerted themselves to the utmost to render the expedition a complete success, and all that their vessels afforded, whether in men or arms, was cheerfully placed at my disposal. The bravery of Master Harris in boldly advancing as he did upon the rebel pickets cannot be too highly spoken of. Master Street personally supervised the embarkation and landing, and the orderly manner in which it was accomplished is chiefly due to him.

Of the officers and men of my regiment concerned I cannot speak in too high terms. Not the slightest trepidation was evinced by any, and all vied with each other in striving for the posts of danger. Had we met the enemy in force, the coolness and bravery of the little force with me would, I doubt not, have been still more manifest. I need not particularize the officers when all did so well. It might, however, be stated that to Capt. A. Wilkinson, Company I, much of the credit of arranging the general plans of the expedition is due. Quartermaster O'Kell and Lieut. Charles W. Squier accompanied me as aides, also Mr. John McMillan, master's mate of the Island Belle.

The successful expedition by so small a force, and upon so important a point, cannot fail to have inspired the enemy with fear for the large portion of unprotected coast along the Potomac, and will not fail, I think, to cause them to scatter their forces along the exposed points, and thus prevent them concentrating a large force at any one position.

I have the honor to remain, your obedient servant,

CHARLES K. GRAHAM,
Colonel.

Brig. Gen. DANIEL E. SICKLES,
Headquarters Excelsior Brigade.

NOVEMBER 10, 1861.—Affair at Guyandotte, W. Va.

Report of Adjt. J. C. Wheeler, Ninth Virginia Infantry, U. S. Army.

COMMONWEALTH OF VIRGINIA,
Adjutant-General's Office, Wheeling, November 13, 1861.

The undersigned, adjutant of the Ninth Virginia Regiment, a new regiment just forming at Guyandotte, Va., would beg leave respectfully to report that on Sunday evening, the 10th instant, just after 7 o'clock, the said regiment, consisting of only 150 men yet in camp, was completely surprised by 700 cavalry, under command of Jenkins, [Clarkson], the guerrilla chief, and cut to pieces and captured, with the loss also of about 30 horses, a small stock of Government stores, and 200 Enfield rifles. The dead and wounded on either side could not be clearly ascertained, but supposed to be 10 or 12 killed and 20 or 30 wounded. The enemy captured 70 prisoners and their loss in killed and wounded was equal to if not greater than ours. They left one of their captains dead on the street. His name was Hubbell, or a name similar in sound. Three other dead bodies were found in the street, and they were seen to throw several from the Suspension Bridge into the Guyandotte River, killed by our men while they were crossing the bridge; besides, a wagon load was hauled off in the night. Three of our dead were found. One was known to have been shot 1 mile above town, on the bank of the Ohio River, and 4 in crossing. Several others are missing and supposed to be killed. Among the number is Capt. G. B. Bailey, of Portsmouth, Ohio, who commanded a company under Colonel McCook at Vienna and Bull Run, and was to have been the lieutenant-colonel of this regiment. I have since learned that his body was found in the river near the mouth of the Guyandotte.

Among those taken prisoner are the Hon. K. V. Whaley, member of Congress, who was in command of the post; T. J. Hayslys, esq., quartermaster-sergeant; Capt. Uriah Payne, of Ohio, who was one of the first three to plant the American flag on the walls of Monterey, in Mexico, and Captain Ross, of Ironton, an intelligent Scotchman. Captain Thomas, of Higginsport, Ohio, is supposed to be taken, and also Dr. Morris, of Ironton, the first surgeon.

The enemy also arrested and carried off the following Union citizens, after having first taken and destroyed their property: William Dowthit, merchant, and his son; Dr. Rouse, druggist, who was also a commissioner of the Federal court; Albert White, and perhaps others. At Barboursville, the county seat of the same county, they captured John W. Alford, a candidate for the legislature; Matthew Thompson, a merchant, whom they stripped of all his goods; old Mr. Kyle, a gunsmith, and Mr. Morey, a tanner.

The attack was so sudden and unexpected that not more than 40 of our men got into line to resist them. Others, however, fought them singly, and all who got into the fight at all exhibited commendable courage and contended against the overwhelming force with which we were surrounded for more than one hour, and those only escaped who were satisfied at the beginning of the overwhelming number of the enemy and fled immediately, except in a few instances, where they hid under houses and log piles, and were not discovered. Some 50 or 60 are known to have got away, and perhaps others will yet come in.

The rebels held the place until about 8 o'clock the next morning, when the steamboat Boston came up with about 200 of the Fifth Virginia Regiment, under Colonel Zeigler. They were joined by a number of the Home Guards of Lawrence County, Ohio, who had assembled at Proctorsville, opposite, to prevent the rebels from landing in Ohio, which they had threatened to do. On the arrival of the Boston some shots were fired from a small cannon aboard, sending a ball through a rebel's brick house. The rebels immediately left on double-quick time, and the hypocritical secession citizens, who had been instrumental in getting up the attack, came on the bank of the Ohio with a great number of white flags, which they waived with great apparent earnestness. Our troops passed over, fired a few shots at the retreating rebels, whose rear was still in sight, and the armed citizens from Ohio set fire to the town, and a large portion of it in value was burned up.

All our papers, books, rolls, &c., were captured.

Respectfully submitted.

J. O. WHEELER,
Adjutant Ninth Virginia Regiment of Vols., U. S. Army.

General W. S. ROSECRANS.

NOVEMBER 12, 1861.—Reconnaissance to Pohick Church and the Occoquan River, Virginia.

REPORTS.

No. 1.—Brig. Gen. Samuel P. Heintzelman, U. S. Army, commanding division.
No. 2.—Brig. Gen. Israel B. Richardson, U. S. Army, commanding brigade.
No. 3.—Col. Henry D. Terry, Fifth Michigan Infantry.
No. 4.—Col. Samuel B. Hayman, Thirty-seventh New York Infantry.
No. 5.—Capt. Frederick Hendrich, First New York Cavalry.
No. 6.—Col. Hiram G. Berry, Fourth Maine Infantry.
No. 7.—Capt. Henry B. Todd, First New York Cavalry.
No. 8.—Lieut. John Ennis, First New York Cavalry.

No. 1.

Report of Brig. Gen. Samuel P. Heintzelman, U. S. Army, commanding division.

HEADQUARTERS OF DIVISION,
Fort Lyon, November 13, 1861.

GENERAL: The enemy having made a demonstration against our pickets on the 11th instant, I sent out two small parties of cavalry to reconnoiter. On their return I received a report that the rebels, with 400 cavalry and two regiments of infantry, were encamped near Pohick Church. Believing I could disperse them, I telegraphed to the commanding general, and was authorized to prepare an expedition.

On the 12th instant, at 3 a. m., General Richardson's brigade, with Company G of the Lincoln Cavalry [First New York], and Captain Thompson's and Captain Randolph's batteries of artillery, advanced upon Pohick Church by the Telegraph road, followed an hour later by General Jameson's brigade, and Company E, Lincoln Cavalry. The instructions I gave were for General Richardson to divide his brigade at Potter's house, just beyond Piney Run, he to follow the Telegraph road, and the other two regiments, with a battery and company of cavalry, to cross to Accotink, and reach Pohick Church by the Accotink and Pohick continuation of the Alexandria turnpike, so to time his march as to have both columns reach the church at the same moment. General Jameson's brigade followed an hour later on the Telegraph road, as a reserve.

I left headquarters at daylight, and overtook the advance where they were halted, a short distance this side the church. We soon ascertained that the rebel cavalry had left, having encamped at the church the night before. We advanced and occupied the ground, and sent out parties on the different roads. The regiments under Colonel Hayman took the road to Colchester. There were no signs of the enemy having been recently in that vicinity, nor were there any indications of their occupying the opposite bank of the Occoquan at that point. Colonel Terry, who commanded the troops which followed the Telegraph road to Mrs. Violet's, learned that the enemy's pickets had left there two hours before. On the opposite side of the Occoquan there was seen a small force of cavalry and infantry, evidently apprised of our advance. The cavalry pickets on the road towards Elzey's had also retreated very recently. Having ascertained these facts, the troops returned to their camp.

I am much gratified with the spirit, zeal, and activity displayed by the troops. We were five hours at Pohick Church. The main body marched 22 miles, and the regiments which were pushed forward to the Occoquan about 30. All were back to their camps by 9 p. m.

Colonel Berry's regiment of General Sedgwick's brigade, with Captain Todd's company of Lincoln Cavalry, marched at 4 a. m. on the Old Fairfax road to halt at the Accotink, and push forward a reconnaissance as far as the Pohick. (Colonel Berry, I think, has mistaken Fairfax Station for either Springfield or Burke's Station; the latter is the more probable. On the second page of his report he says he took the road towards Pohick Church. He should have followed the Old Fairfax road as far as the Pohick.)

By taking the road towards Pohick Church his scouts came in sight of our troops in advance of the church, and mistook them for the enemy drilling. Our skirmishers saw them, and reported the rebel cavalry and infantry on that road. I advanced a force to meet them, but after sending forward no one could be discovered, and the troops were withdrawn.

Of the Lincoln Cavalry, Sergeant O'Brien is killed; Bugler Denton mortally wounded, since dead; Private Miller wounded, missing; Private Mitchell wounded, slightly; Captain Todd missing; Private Johnson missing, and 7 horses missing.

This loss was sustained from the negligence of the officers of this cavalry in permitting their men to straggle in the presence of the enemy and to plunder.

The rebels evidently occupy several points on the railroad in force; have a cavalry station at or near Elzey's and Sangster's Cross-Roads, and a force at Wolf Run Shoals.

I was accompanied and assisted by Captain Moses and Lieutenant Hunt of my staff, and Lieutenant-Colonel Schickfuss and Captain Otto, of the Lincoln Cavalry.

The reports of the different commanders are inclosed.

I have the honor to be, general, your very obedient servant,

S. P. HEINTZELMAN,
Brigadier-General, Commanding Division.

General S. WILLIAMS,
Assistant Adjutant-General, Washington.

No. 2.

Report of Brig. Gen. Israel B. Richardson, U. S. Army, commanding brigade.

HEADQUARTERS RICHARDSON'S BRIGADE,
Camp near Fort Lyon, November 13, 1861.

GENERAL: I have the honor to report that in pursuance of your orders I left this camp at 3 o'clock a. m. yesterday, the 12th of November, with my brigade, consisting of the Second, Third, and Fifth Michigan Regiments, and the Thirty-seventh New York Regiment, for the purpose of advancing to Pohick Church, and of dislodging the enemy, who were reported to be at that place in force. The brigade was accompanied by two batteries of field artillery, commanded by Captain Thompson, U. S. Army; also a squadron of the Lincoln Cavalry.

On arriving at Potter's, on the Telegraph road to Richmond, distant from Pohick Church 3 miles, I detached Colonel Hayman, of the Thirty-seventh New York Regiment, in command of that regiment, and the Third Michigan Regiment, and one battery, ordering him to take the road to Accotink village, and, crossing the stream, to proceed towards Pohick Church, I myself moving on with the two remaining regiments and Captain Thompson's battery and a company of cavalry on the Telegraph road to Accotink Creek, distant 1 mile from Pohick Church, and there halted, sending forward my aide, Captain Norvell, with a cavalry company, to reconnoiter. That officer proceeded towards the church, and in a short time reported to me that there was no enemy at that place. I moved the command into the village and occupied it. General Heintzelman came up about the same time, and directed me as soon as Colonel Hayman's command arrived to send forward a reconnaissance on the Colchester road, and also on the Telegraph road as far as the Occoquan, unless we fell in with the enemy's pickets.

General Jameson's brigade, which had been ordered up as a reserve, arrived soon after the general. Colonel Hayman arrived at about 11 o'clock a. m., some two hours after I had occupied the village, and I directed him to make the reconnaissance to Colchester with his regiment and a company of cavalry, and also directed Colonel Terry, of the Fifth Michigan Regiment, to make the reconnaissance to Occoquan with his regiment, four pieces of Captain Thompson's battery, and a company of cavalry. Both those commands returned at about 3 o'clock p. m. without having fallen in with the enemy, Colonel Terry reconnoitering as far as the Occoquan River.

Having followed out your instructions I returned to camp with my brigade, which arrived at about 9 o'clock p. m., after a march of 35 miles.

I have the honor to be, very respectfully, your obedient servant,

I. B. RICHARDSON,
Brigadier-General, Commanding Richardson's Brigade.

Brig. Gen. S. P. Heintzelman.

P. S.—Please find herewith inclosed the reports of Colonels Terry and Hayman.

No. 3.

Report of Col. Henry D. Terry, Fifth Michigan Infantry.

HDQRS. FIFTH REGIMENT MICHIGAN INFANTRY,
Camp Lyon, near Alexandria, Va., November 12, 1861.

GENERAL: In pursuance of your orders, received this morning through Captain Norvell, at Pohick Church, I at once proceeded with the Fifth Michigan Regiment, four pieces of Captain Thompson's battery, and a squadron of cavalry, upon the Richmond Telegraph road towards Occoquan. After advancing half a mile I detached Companies E and K of the infantry as skirmishers, and sent them forward half a mile in advance, when the column moved on to within 1½ miles of Occoquan, to a point where a road puts off from the Telegraph road to Sangster's Station, and near the residence of Mrs. Violet. I then ascertained the fact that four cavalry pickets stationed there had left about two hours before on the Sangster's Station road. Not deeming it prudent to advance the column farther, I threw out skirmishers towards Occoquan and Sangster's Station, and ascertained as the result that at Occoquan village there was a small cavalry force, probably less than a company, and a battalion of infantry, not exceeding, I should judge, five companies.

About half a mile west of Mrs. Violet's, on the Sangster's Station road, a cavalry picket post was discovered, apparently just deserted, with the camp-fires still burning, showing that they had retired westward. From information received from various sources, the enemy has a cavalry camp at Sangster's Cross-Roads, about 3 miles to the eastward of the station.

Having ascertained these facts, I returned with the command to Pohick Church.

All of which is respectfully submitted.

I have the honor to be, &c.,

H. D. TERRY,
Colonel Fifth Michigan Infantry, Commanding Reconnaissance.

Brigadier-General RICHARDSON.

No. 4.

Report of Col. Samuel B. Hayman, Thirty-seventh New York Infantry.

HDQRS. THIRTY-SEVENTH NEW YORK VOLUNTEERS,
Richardson's Brigade, November 13, 1861.

CAPTAIN: In compliance with the general's direction, I have the honor to report that I left this camp on the morning of the 12th instant at 3 o'clock, and followed the brigade in rear of the Fifth Michigan Volunteers until reaching the cross-road leading to Accotink Village. Here I was assigned the command of the Third Michigan, under the immediate command of Lieutenant-Colonel Stevens; a battery of Rhode Island artillery, under command of Captain Randolph, and a squad of cavalry, in addition to my own regiment, and instructed to proceed to the rear of Pohick Church. I directed Lieutenant-Colonel Burke, of the Thirty-seventh New York, to deploy skirmishers to his front and right and to march in advance. The Rhode Island Battery followed the Thirty-seventh and the Third Michigan. My command followed the cross-road to Accotink Village, where I procured a guide, who conducted it within half a mile of its destination, when, becoming suspicious of his good faith, I ordered Lieutenant O'Beirne, of the Thirty-seventh New York, to reconnoiter the road. Just as he rendered his report an order reached me from the general to join him by the road leading to the front of the church. On reaching the church I was ordered to proceed with my own regiment and a few cavalry on the Colchester road, in the direction of Occoquan River, "to feel the enemy's pickets; if fired upon, to return and not to cross the stream." I followed the road to Occoquan without finding an enemy, and then returned to Pohick Church and thence to my camp.

Very respectfully, your obedient servant,

S. B. HAYMAN,
Colonel Thirty-seventh Regiment, Commanding.

Capt. J. M. NORVELL,
Assistant Adjutant-General, Richardson's Brigade.

No. 5

Report of Capt. Frederick Hendrich, First New York Cavalry.

By order of Lieutenant-Colonel Von Schickfuss, I left our camp at 2.30 o'clock a. m. to join the reconnoitering party under the command of Brigadier-General Richardson. My command consisted of Companies G and E, Lincoln Cavalry, all together 112 men, with 5 commissioned officers and 117 horses.

On reaching the brigade of General Richardson, I was ordered to march in the rear of the brigade. Half way to Pohick Church a detachment, under Lieutenant Kryniski, was detailed to join Colonel Hayman's column, marching to our left flank. One mile this side Pohick Church General Richardson ordered me by his adjutant as advance guard through the wood, which I did, 20 men as skirmishers ahead. Skirmishers of infantry were, after my opinion, absolutely necessary for that purpose, but by inquiring of the general I could not procure them.

After reaching Pohick Church I sent some pickets out to three different directions, and joined afterwards, not meeting the enemy there, the column marching in the center. That column returned at 3 o'clock, and I was dismissed by the colonel commanding. On the way home I found the whole road scattered with soldiers from different regiments, hallooing and shooting, and so the balls came over our heads and reached just our camp, where one horse of my company was wounded.

At 6 o'clock p. m. we were at home safe, without missing a man or horse.

FREDERICK HENDRICH,
Captain Company G, Lincoln Cavalry.

No. 6.

Report of Col. Hiram G. Berry, Fourth Maine Infantry.

HDQRS. FOURTH REGIMENT MAINE VOLUNTEERS,
November 12, 1861.

SIR: In conformity to your orders [following], I left camp with my regiment at precisely 4 o'clock this morning, and proceeded on the road to the Accotink Creek. At 4.30 o'clock I was joined by Captain Todd and some 40-odd men of the Lincoln Cavalry. We passed our outer line of pickets, halted, loaded the guns, and hove out a full company of skirmishers in advance and on the flanks. In this manner we proceeded carefully along the Old Fairfax road, examining all cross-roads minutely. We found no signs of the rebels having been on this side of the Accotink in force for some four or five weeks. Large bush tent accommodations were discovered on the road leading from Fairfax Station to Accotink, sufficient to accommodate at least 10 full regiments; these tents bore the appearance of having been deserted some four or five weeks since.

We arrived at Accotink about 9 o'clock and halted. After making a careful reconnaissance of the creek and hills surrounding, I ordered my skirmishers across, followed by 2 more companies of riflemen. I ordered my main body to remain on this side of the creek, in conformity with your instructions. I crossed with the cavalry in this manner. We proceeded carefully along for 2 miles to the road leading from Burke's

Station to Pohick. This road bore the marks of recent extensive travel. I halted, and whilst making a careful survey, my skirmishers sent in 3 men, evidently farmers. On questioning them minutely I learned that a large force of infantry was encamped on this road, and about 2 miles on my right, estimated by them to be fully 5,000. They also informed me that that was the main traveled road for the rebels between Burke's Station and the Pohick. I therefore placed a small body of men here at the junction in the woods. Retaining the prisoners, I proceeded on some three-fourths of a mile, halted my men, and instructed Captain Todd to take his cavalry and make a personal reconnaissance towards Pohick Church. He did so, and reported that the enemy were drilling a cavalry and infantry force some three-fourths of a mile in advance. Not hearing anything from the force sent down by the other road, and as it was evident that we were in the vicinity of a large force of the enemy, who controlled roads in my rear, I deemed it best under the instructions I received to return to the Accotink and halt and give my men their dinner. I therefore ordered the cavalry in, and also faced about my skirmishers and the column, and came back to Accotink.

Captain Todd informed me a few minutes after that some of his company were still out, and that he would go out and bring them in. I said to him I should take a position near the top of the hill controlling a cross-road and await his arrival. I moved my regiment into a proper position, hove out sentries, and awaited the captain's arrival. After waiting an hour or more we heard the reports of some three or four guns. In a few minutes 3 of the absent men came in, 2 wounded and 1 unhurt, all 3 having plunder strapped on their horses, consisting of a side-saddle, bedclothes, &c. On questioning them I found they had been wandering in all directions and plundering the inhabitants. I therefore concluded that the persons robbed had fired upon them. Knowing the enemy to be near in force, and thinking it most likely that they had been made aware of our presence through the indiscretions of these wandering men, I concluded, as the object of my reconnaissance had been accomplished, to return to camp. The lieutenant commanding the cavalry company informs me that the captain is absent and 4 men.

Respectfully, your obedient servant,

H. G. BERRY,
Colonel Fourth Maine Volunteers.

WILLIAM D. SEDGWICK,
Assistant Adjutant-General, Eighth Brigade.

—

HEADQUARTERS SEDGWICK'S BRIGADE,
Camp Sacket, November 11, 1861.

COLONEL: In pursuance of orders from the general commanding the division, you will take your entire regiment, leaving only a sufficient number to take care of the tents, and, omitting to send the detail heretofore ordered for work on the fort, make a reconnaissance on the Old Fairfax road as far as the Accotink, there to halt, and push forward a detachment to reconnoiter as far as the Pohick, if it is found safe, taking care to observe well the roads on the right flank, it having been reported that 400 rebel cavalry were to-day at Accotink and that two regiments were about to encamp at Pohick Church. General Heintzelman will send out a force upon the roads on our left leading to Pohick Church. You will take a day's rations in the haversacks of the men, and will return in the evening, and upon your return make your report to these headquarters. You will be accompanied or followed by a company of the Lincoln Cavalry.

By order of Brigadier-General Sedgwick:

WM. D. SEDGWICK,
Assistant Adjutant-General.

Colonel BERRY, *Fourth Maine.*

No. 7.

Report of Capt. Henry B. Todd, First New York Cavalry.

RICHMOND, VA., *November 21, 1861.*

DEAR SIR : Noticing in a Richmond paper of this date an extract from a Washington paper, in which the reconnaissance made by the troops under your command of November 12 is mentioned, and feeling that injustice is done me in said report, I wish to state to you the facts, so that I may be exonerated from blame or want of proper caution. I with my company of cavalry accompanied Colonel Berry's command. After crossing Accotink Run, at Colonel Berry's request I threw out my company as vedettes, 100 feet apart, in advance of the infantry. I soon joined the advanced vedettes, and proceeded cautiously until we came in sight of a body of cavalry and infantry about 1 mile in advance and a little on our left. I then halted my men, who were hid from observation by some woods, and ordered them to remain as they were, under a lieutenant, until I communicated with Colonel Berry. I proceeded immediately to him and reported, when we both started to make a more thorough reconnaissance, but before reaching the spot where I had left my advance we met the lieutenant and men galloping in, and saying that the skirmishers of the enemy were close upon them, but had not yet seen them. Colonel Berry then showed me his written instructions, and I coincided with him that we should fully carry them out by retiring, which we immediately did, across Accotink Run, where we rested. When forming to start for camp I found 7 of my men absent (my advanced vedettes), who had not received notice to come in from the lieutenant. Humanity forbade me to go and leave them, and with Colonel Berry's consent I returned for them, and in returning with them we were fired on from an ambush nearer camp than the place from which I parted with Colonel Berry. I earnestly request you will consult Colonel Berry, and I am confident he will confirm my statement as far as it relates to him.. My men had not straggled at all, and were perfectly obedient to orders. Please to do me justice in this matter, and my imprisonment, &c., will be much lightened. Sergeant O'Brien is not dead, but a prisoner, as are also Privates Miller, Johnson, and Trowbridge.

With great respect, I am, sir, your obedient servant,

HENRY B. TODD,
Captain Company B, Lincoln Cavalry.

General HEINTZELMAN.

[Indorsement.]

HEADQUARTERS DIVISION,
Fort Lyon, December 9, 1861.

I have seen Colonel Berry, Fourth Maine Regiment. On the return of the troops to the Accotink 7 of the cavalry were absent. Captain

Todd then started to bring them in; after waiting more than an hour 3 of the missing men came in, 1 mortally wounded, and all with plunder on their horses. All the evidence goes to show that these men were fired upon by the persons whom they had plundered, as the country had been thoroughly examined and no enemy seen. The 4 men taken prisoners make up the 7 that were missing.

Respectfully forwarded.

S. P. HEINTZELMAN,
Brigadier-General, Commanding.

No. 8.

Report of Lieut. John Ennis, First New York Cavalry.

CAMP SCHICKFUSS, VA., *November* 13, 1861.

Yesterday a reconnaissance was made in the vicinity of Occoquan Creek. Captain Todd's company (B), of the Second Division, Lincoln Cavalry, was detached to accompany Colonel Berry, of the Fourth Regiment Maine Volunteers, being under instructions from General Heintzelman's command, the extent of which only was to ascertain the proximity and position of the Confederate forces, to avoid a collision with them if possible, and yet not allow themselves to be cut off. The troops formed early in the morning, and proceeded in the direction of the creek and Burke's Station, the infantry at the same time making vigilant skirmish the whole way. On reaching the creek the column halted to reconnoiter, and having satisfied themselves of the absence of rebels, crossed the creek and marched 3 miles, when Captain Todd obtained permission to lead with a detachment from his company of 14 men to skirmish, leaving the remainder in command of First Lieutenant Ennis, who followed up with his men in single file, each at some distance apart, the infantry meanwhile skirmishing through the woods.

On attaining an open space at what appeared to be the extremity of the woods the column was signaled to halt, in consequence of a body of cavalry being seen on the adjacent fields and about a mile and a half from us. These appeared to number about 400 men. Captain Todd, having taken as much observation as was necessary to know their being rebels, hastened to report to the colonel commanding, leaving his detachment there to watch their movements, Lieutenant Ennis taking his place at the head of the company in the absence of the captain while reporting. On going forward he met the guide, reporting to have seen 24 infantrymen crossing the fields below, they evidently moving in a direction to cut our troops off, and having assured himself on observation such to be the case, hastened to consult the colonel and Captain Todd, when it was decided to retreat to the creek, then make a stand. The captain meanwhile left his detachment on their guard until further orders, while the remainder of his company retreated with the infantry to the creek, when they halted, reconnoitered a while, until it was satisfactory that there were no rebels this side in that neighborhood, and therefore the column was ordered to march home. Captain Todd in the mean time having sent a man to relieve those left behind, but neither of them returning, repaired thither himself. The colonel commanding, finding that the captain and his men had not returned, halted to await him for an hour and a half, placing the cavalry on the several turns of the road so as to communicate in case the enemy should approach, when in a short time some cavalrymen were seen riding at full speed, a volley being heard previously very distinctly from where they stood, which is supposed to be about 1 mile from the Occoquan Creek. Two of the men were severely wounded, 1 of whom has since died. The colonel, not wishing to exceed the general's command, ordered the column forward. Since then 5 of Captain Todd's skirmishers have returned to their quarters; the captain and the others are still missing.

JOHN ENNIS,
First Lieutenant, Acting Captain Company B.

NOVEMBER 14, 1861.—Affair at the mouth of Mattawoman Creek, Maryland.

REPORTS.

No. 1.—Brig. Gen. Joseph Hooker, U. S. Army.
No. 2.—Lieut. Col. George D. Wells, First Massachusetts Infantry.
No. 3.—Lieut. Adelbert Ames, Fifth U. S. Artillery.

No. 1.

Report of Brig. Gen. Joseph Hooker, U. S. Army.

HEADQUARTERS HOOKER'S DIVISION,
Camp Baker, Lower Potomac, Md., November 14, 1861.

GENERAL: The right of my camp was enlivened to-day by a spirited contest for a prize in the shape of a schooner freighted with wood. She had attempted to ascend the river under easy sail, when the wind failed her opposite the mouth of Mattawoman Creek. Her condition was soon remarked by the rebels, and at once a light battery was drawn up at Cockpit Point and opened a brisk fire on her. This alarmed the crew, and they doused anchor and made for our shore. As soon as this was communicated to me I directed Lieutenant-Colonel Wells to proceed to the point of interest with a battalion of the First Regiment Massachusetts Volunteers, and for Lieutenant-Colonel Getty to dispatch a section of his battery to prevent any effort on the part of the rebels to capture the vessel. Both of these commands literally flew to their positions, but did not reach them until after the rebels had boarded the schooner and set fire to her. A few of the infantry immediately manned a small boat at hand, boarded the schooner, extinguished the fire, and then up anchor and towed her beyond the reach of danger.

I am informed by those who witnessed this exploit—and there were many spectators on both shores of the Potomac—that it was executed with an air of true heroism. Those engaged with the battery are no less deserving of my commendation. Of itself it is an affair of no importance; as an expression of the feeling animating our troops it is full of significance.

I inclose herewith the reports of the officers most interested, as they will furnish details which I cannot transcribe.

Not anticipating that we would be able to remove the schooner from her perilous situation, I dispatched a messenger to the officer commanding the flotilla, in whose presence almost this event happened, requesting that a tug might be dispatched to her relief; but the schooner was removed before the dispatch could have been delivered.

In view of Liverpool Point becoming the landing point of my supplies, I have given directions for some scows lying at Maryland Point to be seized, and have requested the commanding officer of the Second Division of the flotilla to have them taken in tow and delivered to my pickets at Liverpool Point. I have experienced some difficulty and more delay in discharging freight, from my omission to take this precaution in Mattawoman Creek. I request that six wagons may be sent to Lieutenant-Colonel Getty for the use of his three batteries. It is impossible for the teams now with him to haul his forage and provisions. I also request that a box of signal rockets may be forwarded for the pickets at Sandy Point, that I may, in case the Page should attempt to escape at night, convey the information to the flotilla below.

The enemy appear to be increasing in numbers immediately in my front. It may be the affair of the schooner caused more of them to show themselves.

The weather is unfavorable for the ascension of the balloon. It is now in the vicinity of the Posey house.

Very respectfully, your obedient servant,

JOSEPH HOOKER,
Brigadier-General, Commanding Division.

Brig. Gen. S. WILLIAMS,
Adjutant-General Army of the Potomac.

No. 2.

Report of Lieut. Col. George D. Wells, First Massachusetts Infantry.

HDQRS. FIRST REG'T MASSACHUSETTS VOLUNTEERS,
Camp Hooker, Maryland, November 14, 1861.

SIR: This morning, at 8 o'clock, three guns opened from the other shore, about a mile above Shipping Point, on a schooner lying off Stump Neck, apparently becalmed or at anchor. At his own suggestion, Lieutenant Candler, with 2 men, was sent by me to ascertain the result of the firing and the position of the batteries. He found the schooner, deserted by her crew, at anchor within full range of the batteries and without any protection against capture from the other shore. She had been hit three times, but was not damaged. He sent a report of these facts to me, and I directed Lieutenant Roberts, of Company H, to cross the creek with 20 men and proceed by land for her protection. He had hardly embarked when word was brought from the lookout on the hill that a small boat with 12 men had left the opposite shore and a large barge full of men was preparing to start. Uncertain by which route she could be reached first, I sent Captain Smith, with Company B, over the neck, and Captain Baldwin, with Company E, and Captain Wild, with a part of Company A, with directions to cross the creek and then divide, one to land at the point and hurry to the vessel, the other to go around the point by water. I also notified Colonel Getty, who immediately dispatched two 10-pounder Parrotts to the scene. The small boat reached the schooner, boarded her, set fire to her, and left. Lieutenant Roberts came up and met Lieutenant Candler just as the enemy were boarding.

They were soon joined by Captain Baldwin and Captain Adams with a party of Company F, doing guard duty at Posey's house. A brisk fire was opened from the shore, but the distance was great and the enemy well protected by the schooner. Only 2 were seen to fall. The flames were under full headway, pouring out of the hatchways, and the rebel boat nearly to the other shore before Captain Wild came round the point in the First Regiment barge, with detachments from Companies A and E. He pulled direct for the schooner, boarded her, threw off her deck load of wood, cut through the deck, and extinguished the fire; then weighed anchor, set the jib and flying-jib to catch the little breeze stirring, and, towing in his boat, took her up the river some distance and gave her in charge of one of the flotilla. Just as the schooner was getting under headway our artillery came up and opened upon the enemy, silencing their batteries at the first fire. Until their arrival a continuous cannnonade was kept up from the opposite shore, and our men have brought away many specimens of their shot.

After Captain Wild's boat came in sight their attention was directed from the men on shore to her. Eighty-five shots were fired between this time and the cessation of fire. The shot aimed at the boat went over, striking the water between it and the shore. The range on the schooner was very good and the shots were very close. While our men were on board four shots went through the sails, one cut the main-stay, and a percussion shell, striking the main-sail, exploded, scattering the fragments on both sides of the vessel. Providentially no one was injured. In all the enemy have wasted at least 250 rounds in this attempt to destroy the vessel. The only damage done on our side of the river was one pig killed and one mule wounded, belonging to Mr. Milstrad. His buildings also have some shot holes.

It is hardly necessary to remark to you upon the daring and gallantry of the officers and men, who, under heavy fire, boarded the schooner and conducted the subsequent operations for her relief with such courage and judgment. The men on land were equally eager, pressing to the shore, regardless of the shot, and chafing because there were no boats with which to reach the schooner. Their guns were two 12 and one 6 pounder rifled pieces. One regiment of infantry and one of cavalry were in sight near the guns. I should judge there were three regiments encamped above Quantico Creek. They also appear to have slightly fortified Bald Hill to resist land attack.

Very respectfully, your obedient servant,

GEO. D. WELLS,
Lieutenant-Colonel, Commanding.

Col. ROBERT COWDIN.

No. 3.

Report of Lieut. Adelbert Ames, Fifth U. S. Artillery.

CAMP HOOKER, CHARLES COUNTY, MD.,
November 14, 1861.

SIR: In accordance with your orders, I submit the following report of the action of a section of Battery A, Fifth Artillery, on this afternoon:

Immediately on the notification that the rebels were crossing the river to a schooner becalmed at the mouth of Mattawoman Creek, I moved a section of the battery in that direction, to render all assistance possible. The distance being some 5 or 6 miles and the roads heavy, the rebels, after setting fire to the vessel, had time to escape to near the opposite shore by the time of our arrival. The fire was soon extinguished by members of a Massachusetts regiment, and the vessel towed into the creek. We came into battery at once, and opened fire. The first shot aimed at the boat struck the water near her. It was a line shot, but owing to the mist and rain that began to fall I could not tell with certainty on which side of her it fell; I thought the near, others who were present the farther side. The next shot aimed at the rebel battery struck in the ground in their midst. They were seen to run in opposite directions, and the battery which had been firing up to this time ceased firing at once, and was not again heard from. Other shots were fired at a house near the battery, but their effect could not be ascertained, the increasing rain rendering the opposite shore indistinct. It is my opinion that the last, like the first, went directly to the point intended.

It was calculated that the rebels fired over a hundred shots at the schooner above referred to, two or three only striking her, and those doing little or no damage. The projectiles used by them were cylindrical, with ovoidal points covered with soft metal, and were thrown from rifled guns. One of the two kinds of projectiles weighed about twelve or fifteen pounds, the other about six, and were used in guns with eight grooves. No injury was done by their firing, which was far from being accurate.

It is my opinion that the rebels have no permanent works at the place where their guns were located while firing at the vessel. In fact, an officer observing them with a glass says he distinctly saw them limber up their pieces and retire after the fall of our shot among them. We saw no signs of works of any kind near them.

The guns used by us were the 10-pounder Parrott.

I am, sir, your obedient servant,

ADELBERT AMES,
First Lieutenant, Fifth Artillery, Commanding Battery A.

Lieut. Col. GEORGE W. GETTY,
Commanding Artillery Division.

NOVEMBER 14–22, 1861.—Expedition through Accomac and Northampton Counties, Virginia.

REPORTS, ETC.

No. 1.—Instructions to Brig. Gen. Henry H. Lockwood, U. S. Army.
No. 2.—Reports of Maj. Gen. John A. Dix, U. S. Army.
No. 3.—Reports of Brig. Gen. Henry H. Lockwood, U. S. Army.

No. 1.

Instructions to Brig. Gen. Henry H. Lockwood, U. S. Army.

BALTIMORE, *November* 11, 1861.

GENERAL: You will proceed with the forces under your command into the counties of Accomac and Northampton, Virginia, and carry out the assurances given in the proclamation to be issued by me on the 13th instant. One of the objects in view, though not stated in the proclamation, is to bring these counties back to their allegiance to the United States and reunite them to the Union on the footing of West Virginia. The first step in the accomplishment of this object is to disarm and disperse the military corps encamped within them. If these corps are in the service of the Confederates, they should be made prisoners and sent to this city. A conciliatory course should be pursued in regard to those who are not under arms and have not been in the pay of the Confederate Government. It will require great discretion and prudence in bringing about the desired result; but if the people of these counties can be induced to declare their independence of the Confederates, the strongest assurance may be given to them of an efficient protection by the Government.

It will be advisable to have a free and frank conference with the leading Union men as soon as you think the time has come for disclosing the wishes of the Government. In advancing into the interior great care will be necessary to guard against surprises. It is understood that the intention is to carry on a guerrilla warfare against you, and that the character of the country favors it. Against this you will take the requisite precaution by carefully feeling your way. You will, if possible, send me a brief note of your progress every day. As soon as you reach Drummondtown your supplies will be sent to Pungoteague Inlet, and it will not be necessary to keep up your line of communication for supplies with the rear. You will nevertheless consider it advisable, should you be able to dispense with any part of your force, to leave detachments at particular points. The best disciplined troops should be kept with you, as you will have no hostile force in your rear. The imperfectly trained can be left in detachments of not less than a company where they are needed.

The battery at Pungoteague Inlet must be carried before our transports can enter the harbor, and this should be done as soon as possible after you reach Drummondtown. In this, as in all other matters, I rely on your prudence and discretion, to which much of the detail of the movements is left.

You will take with the expedition Captain Tyler, who is now with you, as assistant quartermaster. I have requested that funds should be placed in his hands to purchase the forage, fuel, and animals to replace any which you may lose.

The utmost vigilance is required to preserve discipline among your troops and to prevent any outrage upon persons or property. If any man violates your orders in this respect, you will put him in irons and send him to these headquarters. No distinction should be made between the citizens of those counties in regard to the past. All who submit peaceably to the authority of the Government are to be regarded as loyal. If any persist in acts of hostility, it is for you, as commander of the expedition, to decide what measures shall be taken in regard to their persons or their property, and with this prerogative no subordinates can be permitted to interfere. The notion has been far too prevalent that the persons and property of secessionists may be unceremoniously dealt with by commanders of regiments or corps, and the sooner it is corrected the better.

I am, general, very respectfully, your obedient servant,

JOHN A. DIX,
Major-General, Commanding.

——

HEADQUARTERS,
Baltimore, November 14, 1861.

GENERAL : I send you 500 of the Seventeenth Massachusetts Volunteers, under Colonel Amory, which will make your command a very formidable one. I will send some ammunition for 6-pounders immediately.

You will want a few days to organize, and nothing will be lost, as the people will be considering the subject of my proclamation. Thinking it very desirable to get it out, that no time might be lost, I authorized Colonel Warren, in case you should not have reached Newtown, to distribute it. You are at a distance, and if some deviation from certain details of my instructions becomes necessary, you will exercise a reasonable discretion. If you do not want the bridge over the Swan's Gut Creek, you need not replace it unless you choose, though I think it will do us no discredit with the people of Accomac if we repair the damage of their own madcaps. Let me know what you want, and it shall be promptly furnished. I have the peaceful settlement of this difficulty with the Eastern Shore of Virginia much at heart, and know you will spare no effort to accomplish it. I intend all your troops shall have 100 rounds of ammunition. Let me know of any deficiency.

I am, very respectfully, yours,

JOHN A. DIX,
Major-General, Commanding.

—

HEADQUARTERS,
Baltimore, November 18, 1861.

GENERAL: Lieutenant Dix arrived this morning with your dispatch, communicating the gratifying intelligence that the rebel organizations in your neighborhood had dissolved. You are right in supposing that I wish you to go to Eastville, leaving such portions of your force as you may deem proper at points in your rear. The entrance to the Pocomoke River is so bad that I am desirous of exchanging it for Pungoteague Inlet as soon as you reach Drummondtown.

Please bear in mind the ulterior object of the expedition—to bring these counties by their own voluntary action back into the Union—and with this view see their leading men as you advance.

You must try and make your transportation do. I learn that the thirty wagons were at Salisbury on Sunday morning, and I suppose they must be with you now. Dispose of the State prisoners of whom you write to me as you think proper.

I am, general, respectfully, yours,

JOHN A. DIX,
Major-General.

—

HEADQUARTERS,
Baltimore, November 20, 1861.

GENERAL: Lieutenant Coffin, of the Hercules, arrived with his vessel to-day, just missing the sloop with coal. He has some repairs to make, and will not be able to leave until the day after to-morrow. I wish you would advise me when you are to receive your supplies. I thought the Pungoteague the best place on account of the water, but Lieutenant Coffin thinks a better may be found near Onancock. Let me know when you will need provisions. If I do not hear from you by the 23d I shall send you a further supply, but it is very important to know where they are to be sent. I send you some more hay by the Star. Send her back as soon as possible. I must have her or the Balloon.

You must not fail to secure the ten or twelve cannon in the two counties. Your very gratifying dispatches, with Captain Knight's report from Drummondtown, are received. I will write to you on the subject of reorganization as soon as Northampton is secured. I will attend to the postal, light-house, and other matters.

I wrote to Commodore Goldsborough a week ago, and have his answer. He will watch the lower part of the peninsula at all points, and prevent the escape of the rebel force.

Officers who have been in the pay of the Confederates should be arrested and held as prisoners until the order of the Government is announced. Rank and file, if they have laid down their arms, need not be disturbed.

In regard to correspondence, I see no objection to the free circulation of letters to all portions of the two counties in which the authority of the Government is re-established.

You are right in your opinion that no act of a rebel convention or legislature can be recognized. In all these respects the two counties must, when they come back, be in the *statu quo* before the rebellion. Until some principles of reorganization can be agreed upon, either as a part of Maryland or of Western Virginia, their corporate powers as counties will be sufficient to meet all their exigencies. I speak without having examined the statutes of Virginia, but on all these points I will write you hereafter.

NOVEMBER 21.

The captain of the Star was directed to call here for dispatches at 7 p. m. yesterday. He failed to do so, and this letter has in consequence been kept over. I send it by way of Salisbury.

I am, very respectfully, yours,

JOHN A. DIX,
Major-General.

HEADQUARTERS,
Baltimore, November 21, 1861.

GENERAL: Lieutenant Coffin, commanding the Hercules, will leave to-morrow for Pungoteague Inlet. I sent letters to you to-day by mail, via Salisbury, with my last instructions. You will please send a small force south of Eastville, to take Cape Charles light-house, and to make such reconnaissances as to assure yourself that the rebel organizations are entirely broken up. Please give Lieutenant Coffin such instructions as may be necessary for the protection of your supplies and transports, and for preventing the escape of persons connected with the rebel corps in Accomac and Northampton Counties.

I am, very respectfully, your obedient servant,

JOHN A. DIX,
Major-General.

HEADQUARTERS,
Baltimore, November 21, 1861.

GENERAL: Ascertain, if possible, the parties who committed the depredations referred to in your letter and order, and send them back, as directed, in irons. If you have any thieves with you, get rid of them as soon as possible. I wish the troops to be sent back here as soon as they can be spared. I think if, as you suppose, there is to be no fighting in Northampton, and you get possession of the cannon in the two counties, you can send back the Fourth Wisconsin, the Fifth New York, the Sixth Michigan, the Seventeenth Massachusetts, the Twenty-first Indiana, Nims' light battery, and Richards' cavalry, reserving only the Delaware and Maryland troops. Captain Knight thought two companies would be sufficient to hold the two counties. I would be glad to have your views on the subject. My impression was that it would be advisable to have 500 men in each county. The force in Accomac might winter in Drummondtown, and the force in Northampton at Eastville, with a detachment of a few men from each to take care of the light at Cape Charles and Pungoteague. Early arrangements should be made to cover these troops for the winter, and as soon as you see what may be needed please advise me.

I am, very respectfully, your obedient servant,

JOHN A. DIX,
Major-General, Commanding.

—

HEADQUARTERS,
Baltimore, Md., November 25, 1861.

GENERAL: I have received your three dispatches of the 22d instant, dated at Drummondtown, and am much gratified with the judicious and efficient manner in which you are carrying out my instructions, and with the readiness with which the people of Accomac are disposed to accede to the friendly overtures made to them in my proclamation.* All that has been promised should be fully executed, and the most liberal interpretation should be given to its declarations. Orders have already been given by the Government at my solicitation to restore the mail service from Snow Hill to Eastville and to re-establish the light at Cape Charles. The Light-House Board are now making the necessary arrangements, and an agent of the Post-Office Department is, I believe, already on his way to Snow Hill. I have written to the Secretary of the Treasury in regard to the reopening of trade with the loyal States, and have telegraphed Major-General McClellan, soliciting his interposition to insure the prompt action of the Government.

There are two or three matters on which you ask my directions:

1. As to the officers of the volunteer force who have been arrested: They were not found in arms, as I understand. In that case I think they may justly claim the immunities pledged by my proclamation, but in order to become entitled to them, they must recognize the authority of the United States. The test we have a right to prescribe, and I know of no other than the oath of allegiance required by section 1 of the act of Congress of August 6, 1861, chap. 64, of the first session of the Thirty-seventh Congress. I inclose you the form, marked A.† Should they decline to take this oath, they cannot be considered as belonging to the classes of persons to whom the benefits of the proclamation are promised. In that case you will, if they were not found in arms, release them on their parole of honor to abstain from all acts of hostility to the United States, &c. I inclose a form for the purpose, marked B. If they decline giving their parole in the form prescribed, you will send them to Fort McHenry.

2. As to civil officers: It is desirable that the administration of the civil and municipal concerns of the two counties should go on if possible without any interruption whatever. If any of the civil officers now in the execution of their trusts have taken an oath of allegiance to the

---

* See p. 431.   † Omitted as unimportant.

Confederate Government, they should be required to take the oath inclosed, marked A.* It is especially desirable that the courts should hold their sessions as usual, so that justice may be administered without adding to the law's delay.

3. If the people return to their allegiance to the United States, they should make such temporary provision for their own government, not inconsistent with the Constitution of the United States, as they may think best. For the time being it seems to me that it would be well for them to act with Western Virginia, and hold elections by proclamation of the governor, as you suggest. Before taking any action on the subject myself, I should like to know the views of their discreet men, and see what is done in the meetings about to be held. I think it very important on their own account that they should be represented in the next Congress, and I have very little doubt that a member duly elected will be received if they act in concurrence with Western Virginia. As preliminary to this, it seems to me very desirable, if not necessary, that they should send a member to the legislature of Western Virginia.

I intended to have stated, in connection with what I have said in regard to the officers you have secured, that I suppose them to belong to a volunteer force raised in the two counties, although you call them officers of the Confederate Army. My information was different, but if I am mistaken in this particular, you will hold them till I can obtain the direction of the Government as to the disposition to be made of them.

I am, very respectfully, your obedient servant,

JOHN A. DIX,
Major-General.

[Inclosure B.]

I, ——— ———, do give my parole of honor that I will do no act in hostility to the Government of the United States; that I will not go beyond the limits of the county of ——— without permission of the commanding officer of the United States forces in said county; that I will report myself in person to the said commanding officer once in seven days; that I will surrender myself to him whenever required to do so, and that in the mean time I will hold no correspondence or conversation with any person on political subjects, and have no communication, direct or indirect, with the States in insurrection against the United States, or with any person within the said insurrectionary States.

No. 2.

Reports of Maj. Gen. John A. Dix, U. S. Army.

HEADQUARTERS,
Baltimore, Md., November 8, 1861.

GENERAL: I informed you by telegraph that I had sent Col. H. E. Paine's Fourth Regiment Wisconsin Volunteers, with Nims' light battery and Captain Richards' company of cavalry, to Worcester County, Maryland, adjoining Accomac, Virginia, about 20 miles below Salisbury. I heard from them the second day after they left. They landed on Tuesday morning and marched through Princess Anne, the county town of Somerset, into Worcester the same day. General Lockwood is here, and I am arranging the details of the expedition with him. There are

---

* Omitted as unimportant.

about 1,000 men under arms in the different encampments in Accomac and Northampton, and from 1,500 to 2,000 militia, which they may call out. In the former county there are many Union men; in the latter very few. The camps can be easily broken up, and by judicious management with little if any bloodshed. The information sent to me by General McClellan through Captain Allen will be very useful. It accords with all I have gathered, and gives many valuable details which I had not. The people are (if what Governor Wise is reported to have said of them be true) as a general rule very ignorant, and are under the grossest misapprehensions in regard to the intentions of the Government. They think if we go among them it will be to steal and emancipate their negroes. When these apprehensions are corrected the reaction in our favor must be very great. It has occurred to me that we might avail ourselves of this feeling and other influences to effect a political as well as a military revolution in this part of Virginia, which was Governor Wise's Congressional district. Trade is almost entirely cut off with Baltimore, on which the people have always depended for supplies. They have an unusually abundant crop of oats, which can be purchased at 20 cents a bushel, besides other agricultural products. The reopening of trade with Maryland and the expenditure of some money for the purchase of forage, which we need, might, with a correction of prevailing errors in regard to our intentions, change the whole political character of this district and give us a loyal member of Congress, placing it on the footing of Western Virginia. I am not yet at all acquainted with the *personnel* of this district, and in order to effect such a revolution there must be one or two strong and fearless men to lead off.

The population of these two counties is curiously mixed. There are 13,659 whites, 5,469 slaves, and 7,290 free colored; or 13,659 whites and 12,759 blacks; total, 26,418. The proportion in which these elements combine is favorable to the object in view. The importance of controlling this district of country, and of changing its political character if possible, arises from its locality and its geographical relation to the Eastern Shore of Maryland and the State of Delaware. As long as it is in the hands of a disloyal population, it will be a medium of illicit trade and correspondence with the Confederate Government and Army in Virginia, and contribute to disturb and demoralize the adjoining counties in Maryland.

In order to overawe opposition, I propose to send a force of 3,500 men. The troops sent from here on Monday and General Lockwood's command will amount to about that number. If I find the latter too raw, I can send 500 of the Zouave Regiment from Federal Hill and an equal number from some other regiment here, so as to have a well-trained force of 2,500 men with the expedition. They can be spared for ten days or a fortnight, and as they have been in camp several months, a little service in the field will be useful to them.

Another very important public object to be accomplished by the expedition is to re-establish the light on Cape Charles, the extinction of which has been very disastrous to the commercial community.

It was General Lockwood's intention to put his command at Snow Hill for the winter. I think that it would be better that it should winter at Drummondtown and Eastville, if the expedition is successful.

I am, very respectfully, your obedient servant,

JOHN A. DIX,
Major-General, Commanding.

Brig. Gen. R. B. MARCY, *Chief of Staff.*

BALTIMORE, *November* 15, 1861.

MY DEAR SIR: I inclose a proclamation which I have issued to the people of Accomac and Northampton Counties, Virginia. Its purpose, as will be apparent to you from its tone, is to bring about a peaceable submission on their part. If they resist, they are advised that they may expect severe chastisement. The case of these counties is peculiar. They have not engaged in any active hostility to the United States. Their people have never crossed the Maryland line. Their greatest offenses are sympathizing with the Richmond leaders and carrying on an illicit trade with the Eastern Shore of Virginia. One of their captains fired on a barge belonging to one of our revenue steamers, but the act was disapproved by their leading men. If they can be reclaimed and induced to throw off their connection with the Confederates it will be a great point gained, especially as the residence of Governor Wise, their former Representative, is in Accomac; and I thought it worth while to make the effort by quieting their fears in the first place, for they have got it into their heads that we want to steal and emancipate their negroes; and by giving them the strongest assurances of kind treatment and protection if they do not resist the authority of the Government, I trust—I ought to say I hope rather than trust—that they may be gained over without bloodshed. As their case is peculiar, I have endeavored to meet it with a remedial treatment adapted to the special phase of the malady of secessionism with which they are afflicted.

I have sent an additional force since my return from Washington. The whole number will be 4,500—among them about 3,500 as well disciplined troops as any in the service. In my instructions to General Lockwood, who commands the expedition, I have directed him to disarm and make prisoners of all persons found with arms in their hands. I have also inclosed him a copy of the act of Congress of the 6th August last, entitled "An act to confiscate property used for insurrectionary purposes," the last section of which concerns persons held to labor and service, and I have instructed him to enforce its provisions as far as practicable.

In all I have done in this matter I have had the best interest of the Government in view, and I shall be much gratified if it meets your approbation.

I have the honor to be, very respectfully, your obedient servant,

JOHN A. DIX,
Major-General.

His Excellency A. LINCOLN.

[Inclosure.]

PROCLAMATION.

To the People of Accomac and Northampton Counties, Virginia:

The military forces of the United States are about to enter your counties as a part of the Union. They will go among you as friends, and with the earnest hope that they may not by your own acts be forced to become your enemies. They will invade no rights of person or property; on the contrary, your laws, your institutions, your usages will be scrupulously respected. There need be no fear that the quietude of any fireside will be disturbed, unless the disturbance is caused by yourselves. Special directions have been given not to interfere with the conditions of any persons held to domestic service; and in order that there may be no ground for mistake or pretext for misrepresentation, commanders of regiments and corps have been instructed not to permit any such persons to come within their lines. The command of the expedition is intrusted to Brig. Gen. Henry H. Lockwood, of Delaware, a State identical in some of the distinctive features of its social organization with your own. Portions of his force come from counties in Maryland bordering on one of yours. From him and from them you may be assured of the sympathy of near neighbors as well as friends, if you do not repel it by hostile resistance or attack. Their mission is to assert the authority of the United States; to re-open your intercourse with the loyal States, and especially with Maryland, which has just' proclaimed her devotion to the Union by the most triumphant vote in her political annals; to restore to commerce its accustomed guides, by re-establishing the lights on your coast; to afford you a free export for the products of your labor, and a free ingress for the necessaries and comforts of life which you require in exchange; and, in a word, to put an end to the embarrassments and restrictions brought upon you by a causeless and unjustifiable rebellion.

If the calamities of intestine war, which are desolating other districts of Virginia and have already crimsoned her fields with fraternal blood, fall also upon you, it will not be the fault of the Government. It asks only that its authority may be recognized. It sends among you a force too strong to be successfully opposed—a force which cannot be resisted in any other spirit than that of wantonness and malignity. If there are any among you who, rejecting all overtures of friendship, thus provoke retaliation and draw down upon themselves consequences which the Government is most anxious to avert, to their account must be laid the blood which may be shed and the desolation which may be brought upon peaceful homes. On all who are thus reckless of the obligations of humanity and duty, and on all who are found in arms, the severest punishment warranted by the laws of war will be visited. To those who remain in the quiet pursuit of their domestic occupations the public authorities assure all they can give—peace, freedom from annoyance, protection from foreign and internal enemies, a guaranty of all constitutional and legal rights, and the blessings of a just and parental Government.

JOHN A. DIX,
Major-General, Commanding.

HEADQUARTERS, BALTIMORE, MD.,
November 13, 1861.

—

HEADQUARTERS,
Baltimore, November 15, 1861.

DEAR GENERAL: I inclose a copy of a proclamation I sent down to General Lockwood.* It was sent into Virginia to-day. I have given him instructions to make prisoners of all persons taken with arms in their hands, and I have instructed him also to withhold from all who disregard the friendly overtures contained in the proclamation and persist in acts of hostility the promised immunity from punishment. The tone of the proclamation is intended to effect the object set forth in my letter of the 8th, to General Marcy.

General Lockwood will have 4,500 men to-morrow. He has the flower

<hr>

* See p. 431.

of my command. The detachments of 500 men from four of my regiments are each organized into six companies, and two are commanded by their colonels, who are regular officers, Amory and Warren. No effort has been spared to make the movement effective.

I am, dear General, truly, yours,

JOHN A. DIX,
Major-General.

Major-General McClellan.

—

HEADQUARTERS,
Baltimore, November 18, 1861.

General: I have the honor to inclose copies of a dispatch from Brig. Gen. H. H. Lockwood, in command of the expedition to the Eastern Shore, and of a letter to him from Captain Knight, his assistant adjutant-general, communicating the gratifying intelligence that the rebel organizations nearest to the Virginia line in Accomac are broken up [No. 3]. They may rally in Northampton, but I hope not. No effort will be spared to bring those counties back into the Union without bloodshed.

I am, very respectfully, your obedient servant,

JOHN A. DIX,
Major-General.

Maj. Gen. George B. McClellan, *Commanding the Army.*

———

No. 3.

Reports of Brig. Gen. Henry H. Lockwood, U. S. A.

HEADQUARTERS,
Newtown, Md., November 16, 1861.

General: I this morning sent Captain Knight with a flag of truce to the headquarters of the rebel force below. I inclose his letter from Temperanceville, a place 10 miles below the line. From this you will see that the enemy has probably dispersed, certainly fallen back to Eastville. I am the more confirmed in the former opinion from the statement of a Mr. Dickinson, whom I sent down yesterday to distribute proclamations, and who returned an hour ago from the battery 4 miles below New Church. He is vouched for by Dr. McMartins, who also vouches for those in Virginia whom he gives as authority. He says that all agree in saying that the military has all dispersed and gone home, and that the general sentiment is to return to the Union. I deem the news of sufficient importance to justify the expense of an extra train. I have therefore requested Lieutenant Dix to go to Baltimore as bearer of this gratifying intelligence, which I have no doubt will make glad your heart, as it must that of every true patriot.

I shall send two regiments and the battery and cavalry as far as New Church to-morrow at an early hour. I would move down at once with the whole command if the wagons had arrived. New Church is 8 or 10 miles below. If Captain Knight's news is confirmed, on his return I will move them as far as Drummondtown. I am decidedly of the opinion that this dispersion of the enemy should not deter or prevent us from marching our whole force through the territory as far as Eastville.

I, however, await your orders in this respect. Troops may be sent to Baltimore more conveniently from Drummondtown than from this place.

I am, general, very truly, your obedient servant,

HENRY H. LOCKWOOD,
Brigadier-General.

Major-General DIX,
Commanding Department of Pennsylvania, Baltimore, Md.

[Inclosure.]

TEMPERANCEVILLE, VA., *November* 16, 1861.

GENERAL: We have thus far had a triumphant welcome and uninterrupted march. Having passed our pickets and gone about 1½ miles, I came to the place (Beaver Dam Bridge) where the enemy's pickets had been stationed for the past two or three weeks; so the owner of the farm on which their principal outpost was stationed [informed me]. There we saw the foot-prints of a great many horses, being the cavalry of Virginians, as I learned afterwards, but we met none of their forces. I inquired of a farmer who lived on the farm above mentioned what had become of their pickets, and he told me they had all fallen back last night some time in the night. We went on with our white flag flying, and soon we were stopped short by felled trees in the road. We then took a road through the woods, and going by that, guided by the farmer above referred to for about 10 miles, we again struck the main road, and galloped along without meeting with any of their forces until we came to New Church, where we met several men and boys, who told us that the forces had all fallen back, but they knew not when, and could not tell me where I could find Colonel Smith. I moved on about a mile, and their large breastwork presented itself a quarter of a mile ahead, on a slight elevation we were on, and found that it was intended to mount three guns. The breastwork, if it had been thrown up all around, would have been pentagonal. As it was, it gave three sides of a pentagon, and looking north. We inquired there where the forces were, but none knew. All said that they went away some time in the night, but did not know where. We went on and soon began to meet horsemen, whom we halted, and inquired for Colonel Smith. They told us they had been in the cavalry force of the Confederates, but last night they were all disbanded, and were returning to their homes. I commended the act. After asking them many questions about their forces, arms, &c., they told me that about 3,500 of them were disbanded last night. I inquired for their cannon, but could get no clew to their whereabouts.

I went on, and met numbers of horsemen and footmen with and without arms. Many took to the woods and others threw away their arms, while others moved on with them. The militia cavalry had shot-guns, and I learned most had swords, old sabers, and pistols. I met one boy with a flint-lock rifle and a Confederate uniform. He acknowledged to have been in the Confederate service, but that last night they all dispersed. I could see them running in every direction, hiding their arms, &c. I took the liberty when I got to this place to distribute some of those proclamations, as I found that Colonel Smith was at Eastville.

The people here all—and I have seen many—express entire satisfaction at the proclamation of General Dix, and have concluded to submit. I shall go on to Drummondtown, the headquarters of the Confederates, immediately, and inquire for Colonel Smith. If I fail to find him there, I shall get all the information I can and return in haste. I do not want this to be considered a report.

I am, very respectfully, your obedient servant,

JOHN H. KNIGHT,
Assistant Adjutant-General.

Brigadier-General LOCKWOOD.

———

No. 1.]   HEADQUARTERS PENINSULAR BRIGADE,
Drummondtown, Va., November 22, 1861.

GENERAL: I beg leave to inform you that the major portion of this command is now in camp at this place, and that an advance party, consisting of the Fifth New York, Twenty-first Indiana, one section of Nims' battery, and 70 troop of horse, are now well on their way to Eastville. Purnell's Legion was left at Oak Hall, 20 miles north of this. Early next week I purpose joining the advance party at Eastville, with the remainder of my forces, the Legion and Second Delaware excepted.

Finding the landing on the Chesconessex and the access to the same extremely bad, I have caused all the vessels containing commissary and quartermaster's stores to be brought around to the head of the Onancock, which is 4 or 5 miles from this place. I shall establish a coal depot on the Pungoteague, which is more accessible than any other inlet on the coast, the Cherrystone, perhaps, excepted.

I have ascertained that an inlet from the Atlantic side will bring vessels of 15 feet within 2 or 3 miles of this place. If this be as I am informed it is, the stores for winter supplies of our troops should come by sea from New York, rather than from Baltimore.

I am happy to inform you that I have succeeded in securing and bringing to this place seven 6-pounder iron guns, mounted, together with their limbers and a small supply of ammunition. They are now in park opposite my headquarters. This artillery is entirely new, and of its kind may be regarded as first class. Two iron guns, without carriages, were taken near Oak Hall, as I informed you in a previous letter. I have likewise secured a limited number of small-arms, which are, however, of little value. I have secured the persons of two captains and one lieutenant of the Confederate Army, and am using active efforts to find Smith, Winder, Finney, and other leading spirits of the late rebel forces on this peninsula. I take it for granted that these will be sent to Fort McHenry, but as they claim the benefit of your proclamation I have thought best to consult you before doing so. Please advise me in this regard at your earliest convenience.

I am happy to inform you that the discipline of the troops now here, under the rigid system of police established by me, is now good. None of those disorders which marked their first entrance into Virginia, and which both annoyed and surprised me, have occurred.

I am, sir, very respectfully, your obedient servant,

HENRY H. LOCKWOOD,
Brigadier-General, Commanding.

Major-General DIX,
Commanding Department of Pennsylvania.

No. 2.] HEADQUARTERS PENINSULAR BRIGADE,
Drummondtown, Va., November 22, 1861.

GENERAL: I find myself somewhat embarrassed by the present aspect of affairs in regard to those holding certain civil offices in these counties who received commissions for the same from the Virginia State authorities previous to the ordinance of secession and who continued to hold them after that time on taking the oath of allegiance to the Confederate Government. Regarding this oath as corrupting their tenure under the legal government of Virginia, I have hitherto ignored all such officials; but as Judge Pitts, the leading gentleman of this section of the country, thinks that it would be politic to allow the magistrates to hold their monthly courts for the transaction of certain business that cannot be well delayed, it occurs to me that perhaps this might be allowed as a temporary expedient, provided these functionaries took the oath of allegiance to the Federal Government. I should be glad to have your views on this subject at your earliest convenience.

I am happy to inform you that a readiness is manifested to declare the allegiance of these two counties to the Federal Government, and that measures are already in progress for holding county meetings for this purpose. The basis of the system in Western Virginia will be adopted as a temporary measure. All with whom I have conversed look to an annexation with Maryland as an event much to be desired whenever it can constitutionally be accomplished. This they think can be done by regarding themselves, together with Western Virginia, as the true State of Virginia, and inducing the State thus constituted and the State of Maryland to pass the necessary laws. I think it would be well for you to write to the governor of Western Virginia, asking him as soon as this people shall have declared their allegiance to the Federal Government and their position in the State to issue his proclamation ordering an election for the civil officers and a Representative to the Congress of the United States. It is extremely fortunate in this connection that the legislatures of Virginia and Maryland as well as the Congress of the United States all hold their sessions within the next month. I hope that by their joint action this interesting people may be relieved from their present position, and brought into that association with the State of Maryland to which their geographical position naturally points.

I am, sir, very respectfully, your obedient servant,

HENRY H. LOCKWOOD,
Brigadier-General, Commanding.

Major-General DIX,
Commanding Department of Pennsylvania.

No. 3.] HEADQUARTERS,
Drummondtown, Va., November 22, 1861.

GENERAL: The people here to all appearances have entirely submitted to the power which has been brought among them, and they are now asking for the protection and advantages which you promise them in your proclamation. They desire that trade may be reopened with the loyal States and that officers of customs may be appointed; that the lights on their coasts may be re-established and their postal arrangements restored. Really I can scarcely perceive any traces of disloyalty among them, and they appear to receive the power of the Government as their deliverance from misery and great suffering; and I would most respectfully beg that all the advantages in the power of the Government may be speedily given them, that this once-deluded people may be again happy under our beneficent Government. On Monday a meeting of the citizens is to be held to advise together in regard to the means of restoration of civil authority. I hope you will give them the advantage of your better judgment and large experience.

I am, general, very respectfully, your obedient servant,

HENRY H. LOCKWOOD,
Brigadier-General.

Major-General DIX, *Commanding, Baltimore, Md.*

NOVEMBER 16, 1861.—Capture of Union foraging party at Doolan's Farm, Virginia.

REPORTS.

No. 1.—Brig. Gen. James S. Wadsworth, U. S. Army.
No. 2.—Col. Timothy Sullivan, Twenty-fourth New York Infantry.
No. 3.—Capt. John Murray, Assistant Adjutant-General, U. S. Army.
No. 4.—General Joseph E. Johnston, C. S. Army.
No. 5.—Maj. William T. Martin, Second Mississippi Cavalry.

No. 1.

Report of Brig. Gen. James S. Wadsworth, U. S. Army.

UPTON'S, *November* 16, 1861.

You will have heard that a company of the enemy's cavalry captured a captain, lieutenant, and 35 privates of the Thirtieth, and five teams loaded with corn. It was the result of gross carelessness on the part of our men. This party was sent out contrary to my advice and without my knowledge.

JAS. S. WADSWORTH.

General MCCLELLAN.

No. 2.

Report of Col. Timothy Sullivan, Twenty-fourth New York Infantry.

HEADQUARTERS GENERAL KEYES' BRIGADE,
Upton's Hill, Va., November 16, 1861.

It has just been reported that a foraging party sent out from this brigade this morning has been cut off. The facts are as follows: This morning about 7 o'clock a train of six wagons, with teamsters and 18 extra men for loading wagons, under an escort of 50 men and 1 lieutenant, commanded by Captain Laning, of Company B, all of the Thirtieth Regiment New York Volunteers, proceeded to the front towards and past Birch's house, taking the road leading to the southwest from a point between Taylor's Corner and Falls Church. Passing Birch's house about a mile and a half the party arrived at Doolan's farm and commenced loading wagons. A guard of outposts and scouts were posted round and through the woods, but the main road appears to have been left unguarded by the officer commanding. They arrived at Doolan's about 10 a. m., and by about 12 m. the wagons were loaded, and while the men were at dinner an alarm was given, and before they could more than gain their arms they were charged upon by a body of cavalry, supposed to be about 100 strong. Captain Laning ordered his men to retreat to the woods, which they did, but were intercepted on the other side by another body of cavalry, the result of which was that the most of the party and five teams were cut off, including Captain Laning and Lieutenant Andrews. Up to this hour (4.15 p. m.) 16 men and 5 teamsters only have returned, reporting as above, and that three of their comrades, including Lieutenant Andrews, were seen to fall, and the rest surrendered. A 4-horse ambulance, under an escort of five companies from the Twenty-fourth Regiment, commanded by a field officer, have been ordered out to bring in the dead and wounded. The body will move immediately.

T. SULLIVAN,
Commanding Brigade,
Per JOHN MURRAY,
Assistant Adjutant-General.

General McDowell.

[Indorsement.]

HEADQUARTERS DIVISION,
Arlington, November 16, 1861—7.20 p. m.

This report relates to an affair not creditable to the officer commanding the escort. He is not here to justify himself, but from the within he would seem to have merited his fate of being captured. He might have taken warning from the capture on the 8th instant at a place 1½ miles this side of the scene of his own disaster of two men engaged, as was his own party, in eating their dinner, when they should have been on the watch. I purpose commenting on the case in orders, with the view of drawing some profit from it for the troops in the future. Respectfully forwarded.

IRVIN McDOWELL,
Brigadier-General.

P. S.—The foregoing just came into my hands on my return from Bailey's Cross-Roads, making preparations for the review of the Army this side of the river.

No. 3.

Report of Capt. John Murray, Assistant Adjutant-General, U. S. Army.

UPTON'S, *November* 16, 1861.

At 7 a. m. this morning a foraging train of six wagons, with 3 men each, started from brigade headquarters, under escort of 50 men and Lieutenant Andrews, of the Thirtieth New York Volunteers, the whole commanded by Captain Laning, of the same regiment. They proceeded along the Annandale road to Doolan's farm, where they arrived about 10 o'clock, and immediately commenced loading the wagons with corn, having previously posted guards and scouts in the woods and surrounding fields, but neglected to place guards over the road. The wagons were loaded by about 12 m., and started on their return and reached camp in safety. The others remained with the escort, who were then allowed to get dinner, and while dining it appears that a company of the White Horse Cavalry dashed in before most of the men could reach their arms, and cut them off from retreat. Two or 3 men are reported hit, and 1 of the rebels was seen to fall from his horse. Some 20 men have since come in, being those posted in the woods and fields, and report as above. Five companies were immediately dispatched by Colonel Sullivan, commanding the brigade, to the scene, but have returned without accomplishing anything.

By command of Colonel Sullivan I have been to the front and visited all the pickets and outposts guarded by this brigade. I have this moment returned, and report all quiet. In regard to the loss of the forage train and party I have nothing new to report, except that I learned from some negroes near Doolan's house that his relative and neighbor, Birch, had the rebel cavalry concealed until our party had loaded their wagons and had all gone to dinner. They then dashed in and surprised the party. I have directed Doolan and Birch to be detained until further orders, and meantime instituted a search for evidence of their complicity.

JOHN MURRAY,
Assistant Adjutant-General.

S. WILLIAMS.

P. S.—I should add that I found guards on Porter's and Blenker's fronts careless and in many instances without the countersign.

No. 4.

Report of General Joseph E. Johnston, C. S. Army.

HEADQUARTERS,
Centreville, November 28, 1861.

SIR: I have the pleasure to transmit herewith the reports of three successful skirmishes by parties of our cavalry,* and respectfully invite the attention of the Government to the good conduct of Colonel Ransom, Lieutenant-Colonel Lee, and Major Martin, as well as that of their men.

Most respectfully, your obedient servant,

J. E. JOHNSTON,
General.

General COOPER, Adjutant and Inspector General.

No. 5.

Report of Maj. William T. Martin, Second Mississippi Cavalry.

CAMP COOPER, November 16, 1861.

GENERAL: I have to report that I have to-day made the reconnaissance ordered by you this morning in the neighborhood of Doolan's, southeast of Falls Church. Guided by Major Ball, brigade quartermas-

---

*See No. 5, p. 439; also Lee's report (No. 2) of skirmish, November 18, between Falls Church and Fairfax Court-House, p. 442; and Ransom's report (No. 2) of skirmish, November 26, near Vienna, p. 446.

ter, and Mr. J. C. Chichester I was enabled to approach, unperceived by the enemy, to within 150 yards of Doolan's house with my command, consisting of 58 non-commissioned officers and privates, and Lieutenant Henderson, of Captain Gordon's company. In an orchard near the house a vedette was discovered, and having reason to believe a company of infantry was at or near the house, I immediately ordered a charge. My men dashed over the fence through the orchard, part turning to the left, with the lieutenant, towards the house, part under my immediate command passed on to a corn field to the right and beyond the house. Several shots were fired at us in the orchard and quite a number from the house. Leaving the lieutenant to attack those near the house, I, with the greater portion of my command, pushed on to a corn field, where we discovered 40 or 50 men, with some wagons. The enemy dispersed on our approach, and endeavored to escape through a marsh meadow into thick woods near by. We pursued them, and succeeded in capturing 17—1 captain, 1 lieutenant, 1 sergeant, 3 corporals, and 11 privates. Lieutenant Henderson, with his party, captured near the house 13 privates.

We have taken 30 prisoners of the Thirtieth New York Regiment of Volunteers, 33 muskets, 23 cartridge boxes, and 31 belts, 5 new army wagons and 20 valuable horses, with the harness, and about 120 bushels of excellent corn, ready shucked and in the wagons.

My command escaped unhurt. Of the enemy, 4 were killed and several wounded. The latter escaped in the thick brush.

The force of the enemy was between 50 and 75. All my men, though most of them were for the first time under fire, behaved with great gallantry. I would especially call to your notice the fearless conduct of Lieutenant Henderson and Sergeants Carroll and Sherman, and Private McGraw, of Captain Gordon's company, and Private Jesse Sparkman, of Captain Perrin's company.

To Major Ball, brigade quartermaster, and J. C. Chichester I was greatly indebted, not only for their guidance, but for their valuable assistance and boldness during the brief contest.

My force was composed of details from the companies of Captains Gordon, Perrin, Stone, and Tayloe. Captain Conner's company was on picket, and did not participate in the affair.

In obedience to your orders I have delivered the prisoners into the custody of the provost-marshal at Centerville, and will to-morrow turn over to the proper officer the muskets and cartridge boxes. I have General Johnston's permission to retain the wagons and horses for the use of my command.

I have the honor to be, your obedient servant,

WM. T. MARTIN,
Major, Second Mississippi Cavalry.

Brig. Gen. J. E. B. STUART,
Commanding Cavalry Brigade, Army of the Potomac.

[Indorsement.]

HEADQUARTERS CAVALRY BRIGADE,
Camp Qui Vive, November 17, 1861.

Respectfully forwarded.

I highly commend Major Martin, his officers and men, for this highly creditable affair. Major Ball, of my staff, a participator, speaks in high terms of Major Martin's personal gallantry and prowess, and I respectfully submit that he has on this as on every other occasion vindicated his claim for the post of lieutenant-colonel, which is a legitimate promotion, as he now commands five companies of excellent cavalry.

J. E. B. STUART,
Brigadier-General, Commanding.

NOVEMBER 18, 1861.—Skirmish on the road from Falls Church to Fairfax Court-House, Va.

REPORTS.

No. 1.—Lieut. Col. Edward B. Fowler, Eighty-fourth New York Infantry.
No. 2.—Lieut. Col. Fitzhugh Lee, First Virginia Cavalry.

No. 1.

Report of Lieut. Col. Edward B. Fowler, Eighty-fourth New York Infantry.

CAMP MARION, UPTON'S HILL, VA.,
Fourteenth Regiment N. Y. State Militia, November 19, 1861.

SIR: I have to report a skirmish with the enemy's cavalry by our picket outpost yesterday. At about 3 p. m. a body of cavalry, numbering about 300, appeared in front of our outpost on the road leading from Falls Church to Fairfax Court-House. When first discovered they were deployed, occupying a front of at least one-quarter of a mile, with a column by platoon in rear of their center on the road. They dashed up to our outpost, driving our pickets in the woods, some of whom they surrounded. They then advanced within our lines about 300 or 400 yards, when, after halting for a short time (about ten minutes) and taking a cart from Benz's house to carry off their dead and wounded, they retired rapidly in several directions. I was at the village when the firing was heard, and on riding up the road I received intelligence from a scout (Sherman) that the cavalry were upon us, numbering 500 or more. I immediately marched up the reserve, consisting of three small companies of infantry, to check their advance down the road. After advancing about a mile, thinking this might be only a feint to cover a more important movement, I halted and deployed a company as skirmishers on the right flank, which I knew to be wholly unprotected, and deployed skirmishers on both sides of the road. I then sent to the rear to give information of the attack at headquarters and also to notify General Porter's pickets. I then advanced under Major Jourdan a body of skirmishers to the outpost that our pickets were driven from, and followed with the main body, picketing the road as I advanced.

On our arrival at the outposts the enemy were not in sight. Shortly after arriving at the outpost General Wadsworth and Colonel Frisby came up and gave directions that the pickets should occupy the same position for the night, and they were so posted. My impression is that the enemy had an object in view besides the cutting off of a small outpost and losing more than they gained, and that they found us in stronger force than they expected. They were seen to carry away 3 dead men (1 an officer) in a cart, and several wounded men were conveyed to their rear on horseback by their comrades. One valuable horse is lying dead near the scene of action and several horses were seen galloping through the fields without riders. Our list of casualties is as follows: 2 killed, 1 wounded, and 10 missing—all of Company H, which was the only company engaged. During the skirmish none of the pickets fell back except on the point attacked.

Respectfully, your obedient servant,

E. B. FOWLER,
Lieutenant-Colonel, Comdg. Fourteenth Regiment N. Y. S. M.

Colonel SULLIVAN, *Commanding Brigade.*

No. 2.

Report of Lieut. Col. Fitzhugh Lee, First Virginia Cavalry.

CAMP COOPER, VA., *November* 19, 1861.

SIR: I have the honor to report the result of a scout of a detachment of the First Virginia Cavalry, under my command, which left this camp yesterday, in pursuance to orders from cavalry brigade headquarters, for the purpose of obtaining certain valuable information in the vicinity of Falls Church.

Learning that a picket of the enemy obstructed my route, I resolved, if possible, to capture them, and prevent my presence being discovered and allowing them to advance in numbers upon me while gaining the desired knowledge. Accordingly, getting as near as possible, I charged them, they retiring rapidly toward the woods and pines, while we quickly lessened the distance, driving one picket upon another, and both upon the reserve, which retreated toward a thicket upon the side of the road and poured in quite a destructive fire upon us from their sheltered position. Followed by a portion of my command, I got in between them and some tents visible and completely surrounded them, another detachment having been ordered up on the other side.

Thus hemmed in, the enemy still fought with bravery and desperation, and made it necessary to dismount some of my men and dislodge them.

Our loss was 1 private killed and 2 slightly wounded. I also report with deep regret that Mr. John C. Chichester, my brave, gallant guide, was dangerously wounded, and has since died. I lost one horse, ridden by Sergt. Jasper N. Jones, of Company L, having run off after the sergeant had dismounted to fight. The horse of Lieut. James S. Larrick, Company A, was severely wounded, and my own horse killed under me during the action. The loss of the enemy, as far as I could ascertain, was 7 killed and 1 left mortally wounded, being shot through the body. Ten were made prisoners, including the lieutenant commanding and the first sergeant, 3 being wounded; 2 severely and 1 slightly (shot in the arm). I brought away my dead (1) and Mr. Chichester, together with two of the enemy, badly wounded, in vehicles taken for the occasion, the enemy appearing in considerable force from the direction of Falls Church, but not venturing an attack. The loss of Mr. Chichester must be deeply deplored, and in Private Thomas Tucker, of Company A, the regiment has lost one of its bravest and most efficient members. Asst. Surg. Talcot Eliason accompanied me, and was as conspicuous with his pistol making wounds as he was afterwards with other instruments healing them.

Of the detachment engaged the highest compliment I can pay is to say that they acted as the First Cavalry always have done, obeyed orders, coolly riding up and shooting the deluded men with their pistols, regard only being paid to carrying out instructions and not to their own lives.

The enemy were a portion of the Fourteenth New York State Militia, of Brooklyn, and fought with much more bravery than the Federal troops usually exhibit. It is the same regiment that so thickly dotted the field of Manassas upon the 21st with red.

When the action ceased it was so late in the day I deemed it inexpedient to carry out the object first in view, encumbered as I was with prisoners and wounded men, and returned slowly to camp. The fight took place a little over a mile this side of Falls Church, upon the road leading to Fairfax Court-House.

Very respectfully, your obedient servant,

FITZ. LEE,
Lieutenant-Colonel First Virginia Cavalry, Commanding.

Capt. L. S. BRIEN, *Assistant Adjutant-General.*

[Indorsement.]

HEADQUARTERS CAVALRY BRIGADE,
Camp Qui Vive, November 20, 1861.

Respectfully forwarded for the information of the commanding general Army of the Potomac. This gallant and successful affair of Lieutenant-Colonel Lee and his detachment of First Virginia Cavalry against the enemy's best troops in chosen position receives my unqualified praise and commendation.* The loss of the gallant Chichester is a severe one to me, as his services were invaluable.

J. E. B. STUART,
Brigadier-General, Commanding.

NOVEMBER 26, 1861.—Skirmish near Vienna, Va.

REPORTS.

No. 1.—Capt. Charles A. Bell, Third Pennsylvania Cavalry.
No. 2.—Col. Robert Ransom, jr., First North Carolina Cavalry.

No. 1.

Report of Capt. Charles A. Bell, Third Pennsylvania Cavalry.

HDQRS. COMPANY F, THIRD PENNSYLVANIA CAVALRY,
Camp Marcy, November 26, 1861.

SIR: I have the honor to submit to you the following report in full detail of the tour made by Companies F and M (strength 4 officers and 109 enlisted men; taking out 15 men, orderlies and pickets, left 94) of the above regiment, composing the squadron under my command, together with the incidents and occurrences of the day:

After having received your orders and left Camp Marcy this morning at or near 9 o'clock, I proceeded with my command to General Porter's headquarters to report and receive further orders. I saw General Porter, and he gave me orders to the effect that I would march via Vienna

---

* See report No. 4, under "Capture of Union foraging party," &c., November 16, p. 439.

to·Hunter's-Mill, provided that when I approached Vienna I deemed it safe to do so. The object of the march was to ascertain, if possible, the location of the enemy's pickets, together with that of a force of their cavalry which was supposed to be lurking near the road from Vienna to Hunter's Mill. After leaving the orderlies detailed by Adjutant Douglass at General Porter's headquarters I proceeded to Minor's Hill (General Morell), and after having procured a guide started to Vienna via Falls Church. After marching about 2 miles I placed a guard of 12 men and 1 non-commissioned officer in advance of the squadron about 600 yards to act as advance guard. I also placed at equal distances apart, 2 in each place, 4 men between the advance guard and the main body. With all possible precaution we slowly approached Vienna, stopping at nearly every house on the road and making inquiries of all whom we met relative to the position and proceedings of the enemy. Just before entering Vienna, in accordance with a suggestion from the guide, I placed in the rear a guard the same as in front.

Upon arriving at Vienna I halted the squadron and went several rods forward to make observations. I saw the road leading from Vienna to Hunter's Mill and conversed with the guide upon the subject of following it. Everything being quiet in and seemingly so around Vienna, we thought it but little dangerous to proceed to Hunter's Mill. After cautioning my men to be vigilant, keeping a watchful eye on both sides of the road and preparing ourselves, we started.

Before proceeding farther, I will state that the position of the officers was as follows: Captain Bell, Company F, in position as captain commanding squadron; Lieutenant Lane, Company M, center of squadron on right flank; Lieutenant Lodge, Company F, with advance guard; Lieutenant Ford, Company M, commanding fourth platoon.

I think we had proceeded about 1 mile on that road when I heard a report from a loaded piece, the report being repeated in quick succession five times. The alarm was at once given, the attack being made in the rear, and ran from left to right like an electric shock. Immediately after a volley was fired by the enemy, and some one in the rear cried out, "Run for your lives; they're on us!"

Every one seemed seized with a panic, and a rush was at once made by the rear guard on the left of the squadron, and commencing on the left the horses started at a trot. I looked around (my horse being at a walk) and gave the command "Halt!" just previous to a second volley being fired on us. The enemy was then just behind us, and there was a general cry from the rear, "Go forward," at which every one started at a full gallop. It was then utterly impossible to halt the men, so much confusion existing. We were marching in column of twos, the road being very narrow, and hemmed in on both sides with trees, we could only move forward, the enemy following us at full speed. We advanced about 1 mile, when the guide, by a right turn, led us in a new direction. I was then about the center of the fourth platoon, and after turning the corner stopped my horse, all in front running at full speed. I again gave the command "Halt!" and after a few efforts was successful in rallying about 20 men. I was just on the eve of giving instructions, when upon glancing around I observed a much larger body than the other coming from the direction in which we had previously been moving forward, and seeing that an attempt to defend ourselves would prove fruitless, I gave the command to retreat. We did so, the distance between us and the enemy remaining about the same. Firing at will on both sides was very heavy for several minutes. The road on which we were retreating was in miserable condition, and stumbling among the horses was frequent, some falling and throwing their riders, and then running away at full speed, leaving their riders to retreat the best they could on foot.

Lieutenants Lodge, Lane, and Ford were near the head of the column endeavoring to persuade the men to halt, but they (the men) would listen to no commands until we had retreated about 2 miles, when I again rallied a number of them; but our number being small, and the enemy approaching us closely, we started through the woods towards the main road, the guide, of course, being in front. Upon reaching a place of safety, I spoke to the squad about going back to look for those who were missing and probably hurt by a fall from their horses, but our horses would not stand much longer, so we approached slowly our pickets. Upon arriving at our pickets on the Leesburg turnpike I found 7 of our men on horses awaiting us. We rested our horses for a few moments and then started for camp. When just inside the lines a few rods I met General Porter, who ordered us to return with him, and obeying his orders, marched towards the lines a short distance, when his next order was to return to camp. We did so, passing on our road a squadron under your command, and arriving at camp about 8 p. m. this evening.

With the above account, I am, colonel, very respectfully, yours,
CHAS. A. BELL,
Captain, Commanding Sixth Squadron.
Col. WILLIAM W. AVERELL.

[Indorsements.]

HEADQUARTERS SECOND CAVALRY BRIGADE.
Camp Marcy, November 27, 1861.

Respectfully forwarded. It is presumed that many of the men reported missing will find their way back to this camp, and that some of the property may be recovered.

It is hoped that the general commanding will take into consideration the fact that this squadron was never under fire before, and that from want of an infantry support, knowledge of the country, and the critical position of the force, it is a wonder that the panic did not prove more disastrous.

I would add to the report of the captain that he captured two horses and equipments, one of them with blood upon the saddle and evidently belonging to an officer, so that the enemy must have been seen, and in sufficient force to have been commanded by an officer.
WM. W. AVERELL,
Colonel, Commanding.

HEADQUARTERS PORTER'S DIVISION,
Hall's Hill, Va., November 27, 1861.

From the best information I can get, and listening to the statement of those who were dismounted at the first alarm, and who came in today, I infer that the force which made the attack was small, but the panic of the rear guard spread to main body, and in the anxiety to escape confusion reigned, and the men knocked down and ran over each other. The party was not on the road which they were directed to take and were negligent.

The party which made the attack is located beyond Vienna, in a pine forest, about 3 miles from depot, and is composed of the North Carolina

Cavalry. The exact location I shall know to-night, and if they can be struck or enticed out without bringing on a general action I will make a proposition to-night.

F. J. PORTER,
Brigadier-General, Commanding.

No. 2.

Report of Col. Robert Ransom, jr., First North Carolina Cavalry.

HDQRS. FIRST N. C. CAVALRY, NINTH REG'T VOLS.,
Camp William T. Ashe, November 27, 1861.

DEAR SIR: I have the honor to make the following more detailed report of a scout made by a portion of my regiment on yesterday:

With 20 men from each of Companies B, D, E, G, H, and K, we left camp at 9 o'clock a. m., myself, Major Gordon, Adjutant Henry, and Dr. O'Hagan, of the field and staff, and Captains Whitaker, Folk, and Wood, Lieutenants Shaw, Andrews, Bryan, Roane, Gaines, and Ellis. Lieutenant-Colonel Baker was left in charge of the camp.

At a point some half mile to the left of Hockhurst's Mill we were joined by Captains Crumpler, Barringer, Lieutenants Cowles, Greer, and Foard, and about 20 men (a part of those who had been on picket duty and were just relieved).

From this point we moved by a small path through thick pines and oak woods to near where the Dranesville road crosses the railroad, then followed said road to a lane nearly opposite and to the right of the dwelling of Lewis Johnston. This new direction was traveled until we reached an old brick mill. Upon this road were tracks of quite a numerous body of cavalry, but some day or two old. At the mill we turned about to the right, and at the house of Edward Johnston were informed that a body of about 150 cavalry had passed about an hour or two before. We here saw the tracks, and followed them for about a mile. They then turned directly to the left, and in a direction of where we were told the enemy was in force of from 5,000 to 10,000. Their camp is supposed to be not far from a place known as the Old Court-House. Supposing that they had gone to their camp, I deemed it best to proceed in direction of Vienna, and it was fortunate that we did. A few hundred yards from Vienna a road entering the one we were on indicated that the enemy had just passed, and that we were immediately in his rear. A moment after my advance guard reported him in sight.

The column was marching by twos. I at once formed fours, expecting to be upon him almost instantly. We passed Vienna at the trot. The enemy soon turned about to the right upon the narrow road leading in the direction of my pickets and to Hockhurst's Mill. The head of the column soon came in sight of the enemy's rear guard in a deep cut in the road. He had not seen us. The advance guard of 6 or 8 men was ordered to fire, with a view to disconcert him, and I at once charged his column with 120 men. Those of the six companies first enumerated, Captains Crumpler's and Barringer's companies, were held in reserve.

Upon the discharge of the advance guard the enemy fled, and in an instant or two, notwithstanding the narrowness of the road and the start he had, my men, most gallantly led by Major Gordon, came upon his heels. Within 300 yards 1 man was killed, 2 or 3 wounded, and several taken prisoners. The enemy kept the road upon which we found him for about a mile or little more, and then turned short to the right, through a lane leading in the direction of his camp. We pursued him for a mile or two upon the new road, when the rally was sounded.

Just after taking the first prisoners I received a message from the front, saying the enemy was in force of some 200 and about to make a stand. The reserve was at once brought up, but before it came in sight the enemy had again taken to his heels and was out of reach. My men were soon assembled, and I am happy to state that not one was hurt by the enemy. One man received a slight injury from the fall of his horse.

The enemy lost 1 man killed (said to be a Lieutenant Lane), 6 wounded, and 26 taken prisoners. One of the wounded was so badly injured that we were compelled to leave him at a farm house. We captured 17 horses and equipments, 26 sabers, 25 pistols (revolvers), and 15 Sharp's carbines. The prisoners threw away in the woods some of their arms.

From the prisoners we learn that the enemy attacked consisted of two companies of the Third Pennsylvania Cavalry, numbering about 120. The companies named by them were F and M. Some of the prisoners, while unreservedly talking, said there were three companies of 60 each. One or more of those taken had the letter K upon their caps.

I am proud to bear testimony to the admirable conduct of my men upon this their first meeting the enemy. All behaved well, but I do no injustice in mentioning particularly Major Gordon, whom I directed to lead the charge; Captain Wood, who joined him before reaching the enemy; Captain Whitaker, who saw the enemy to the last point, and Captain Folk, who, though in rear, found his way with a portion of his men to the front before the enemy was driven beyond hope of capture. Private Primrose, of Company H, was of the advance guard, and behaved with marked coolness, discretion, and presence of mind.

Dr. O'Hagan was prompt to relieve, as far as practicable, the wounded prisoners, and gave the best guarantee of his efficiency whenever it may be tested on a wider field.

This report is much more lengthy than I considered the importance of the pursuit demanded, but it is made with pleasure, in conformity with the wishes and commands of the generals commanding the brigade.

Very respectfully, your obedient servant,

R. RANSOM, JR.,
Colonel, Commanding First N. C. Cav. (Ninth N. C. Vols.)

Capt. L. S. BRIEN, *A. A. G., Cavalry Brigade.*

[Indorsement.]

HEADQUARTERS CAVALRY BRIGADE,
Camp Qui Vive, November 29, 1861.

Respectfully forwarded. Colonel Ransom's report speaks well and deservedly of the gallantry of his officers and men in this their first meeting with the enemy. It remains for me to call attention to the admirable management of Colonel Ransom himself, to whose untiring zeal and unceasing efforts this regiment owes that efficiency and discipline which will always insure it success. The result of this our first engagement with the enemy's cavalry is, I doubt not, highly satisfactory to the General-in-Chief.*

J. E. B. STUART,
Brigadier-General, Commanding.

---

* See report No. 4, under "Capture of Union foraging party," &c., November 16, p. 439.

NOVEMBER 26–27, 1861.—Expedition to Dranesville, Va., and skirmish.

REPORTS.

No. 1.—Brig. Gen. George A. McCall, U. S. Army.
No. 2.—Col. George D. Bayard, First Pennsylvania Cavalry.

No. 1.

Report of Brig. Gen. George A. McCall, U. S. Army.

HEADQUARTERS McCALL'S DIVISION,
November 27, 1861.

GENERAL: I have the honor to transmit herewith the report of Col.
G. D. Bayard, First Regiment Cavalry, Pennsylvania Reserves, of a
very successful expedition made during the last twenty-four hours in
the direction of Dranesville, where I had ascertained that a picket force
of the enemy was stationed. The men who were sent by the colonel
for ambulances reported to me a strong force opposed to the colonel,
whereupon I put the First Brigade of my division under arms, and with
Kerns' battery was marching to his support, when we met the colonel's
command returning. The troops all evinced praiseworthy alacrity on
the occasion.

I am, very respectfully, your obedient servant,
GEO. A. McCALL,
Brigadier-General, Commanding Division.
General S. WILLIAMS, *Assistant Adjutant-General.*

———

No. 2.

Report of Col. George D. Bayard, First Pennsylvania Cavalry.

CAMP PEIRPOINT, VA., *November* 27, 1861.

SIR: In obedience to orders I started from this camp yesterday with
my regiment at 9 o'clock in the evening, for the purpose of marching
on Dranesville. We reached positions above and behind Dranesville
shortly after 5 in the morning, after a very tedious and toilsome march.
Major Barrows advanced on the town by the northern pike which leads
to it, with two companies of the regiment, whilst I, with the other eight,
gained the rear of the town, and advanced by the Leesburg pike. There
were but two picketmen in the town. These were cavalrymen, belonging to Col. J. E. B. Stuart's regiment of Virginia Horse, and were captured, with their horses and arms, by Captain Stadelman's Company B.
I arrested 6 of the citizens of Dranesville who are known to be secessionists of the bitterest stamp. The names of the citizens taken are as
follows: John T. Day, M. D., Dranesville; R. H. Gannel, Great Falls,
Va.; John T. D. Bell, C. W. Coleman, Dranesville; W. B. Day, M. D.,
Dranesville; J. B. Farr. Upon my return, some miles from Dranesville
a fire was opened upon the head of the column from a thick pine wood.
Assistant Surgeon Alexander was seriously wounded, and Private Joel
Houghtaling was badly wounded, and I had my horse killed. Surgeon
Stanton received a ball in his overcoat and his horse was shot twice.
The woods were instantly surrounded, and the carbineers dismounted
and sent into the woods. We killed 2 and captured 4, one of whom is

shot twice and is not expected to live.   Private Houghtaling is, I fear, mortally wounded.   I captured 2 good horses, 5 shot-guns, 1 Hall's rifle, and 2 pistols.   The names of the prisoners are as follows: W. D. Farley, first lieutenant, South Carolina Volunteers, captain, on General Bonham's staff; F. De Caradene, lieutenant, Seventh South Carolina Volunteers; P. W. Casper, Seventh South Carolina Volunteers; Thos. Coleman, citizen, of Dranesville, is dangerously wounded; F. Hildebrand and A. M. Whitten, privates, Thirtieth Virginia Cavalry, taken at Dranesville on picket.   We killed or captured all we saw.

I cannot close this report without speaking of the splendid manner in which both men and officers behaved.   The fine manner in which Majors Jones, Byrnes (second lieutenant, Fifth Cavalry), and Barrows acted cannot be too highly commended or appreciated.   All acted well, and I cannot but thus publicly express my admiration for their truly admirable behavior.

I am, sir, very respectfully, your obedient servant,

GEO. D. BAYARD,
Colonel First Pennsylvania Regiment Cavalry.

Capt. H. J. BIDDLE, *A. A. G., McCall's Division.*

NOVEMBER 27, 1861.—Skirmish near Fairfax Court-House, Va.

Report of Capt. William H. Boyd, First New York Cavalry, with congratulatory orders.

CAMP KEARNY, NEAR ALEXANDRIA, VA.,
November 27, 1861.

SIR : A reconnoitering party of a squadron of cavalry (consisting of my company and Captain Bennett's) was ordered out this day under my command.

The command proceeded along the Little River turnpike to within a short distance of Annandale, where we passed the last of our pickets. Here we halted, and I ordered the arms to be loaded, and sent forward an advance guard, consisting of a dozen good men armed with Sharp's rifled carbines, under the command of Lieutenant Stevenson, of my company.   I also detached a rear guard and flank patrols under the direction of Lieutenants Woodruff and Thomas, Captain Bennett and myself remaining with the main body.   In this order we proceeded to within 1¼ miles of Fairfax Court-House, where we learned that about a dozen of the enemy's cavalry had been there early in the morning for corn.   From here we marched forward to within about 1,000 yards of the Court-House, when our advance guard were suddenly fired upon by the enemy's infantry from behind a large rifle-pit running diagonally across the turnpike, covering the approach to the village.   The direction of the pit was from right to left.   The advance guard immediately deployed to the right and left, some of them sheltering themselves behind a house on the left of the pit, from which they kept up a lively fire upon the enemy's cavalry, who showed themselves in scattering groups at various points, evidently for the purpose of drawing us out.   On the first shot being fired I rode forward to reconnoiter, having halted the main body and leaving them under command of Captain Bennett, where they remained concealed from the enemy's view during the whole affair, none but the advance guard being engaged.   As one of my men, who was dismounted behind the house raised his carbine to his shoulder he remarked, " I wish I had my old rifle here," and simultaneously with the remark he fired, and one of the cavalry was seen to drop from his horse. During all this time the enemy kept up a desultory fire from the rifle-pits, and fearing that the enemy might be maneuvering to out-flank us, I ordered the men to cease firing, and we started on our way home.

It gives me great pleasure to be able to state here that during the whole affair the officers and men under my command behaved with the most admirable coolness, standing where the enemy's bullets whistled all around them and aiming their pieces in a calm and determined manner, and it was with great reluctance that they left the field. On our return the enemy followed us up at a respectful distance, firing on our rear guard as they advanced. Our men returned the fire, and the enemy soon abandoned the pursuit.

We returned on the Little River turnpike as far as Hayne's house, when we took the left-hand road leading to Mills' Cross-Roads, and from thence on the Fairfax road to Falls Church. When on this road about a mile from Mills' Cross-Roads we were challenged by the advance guard of the Twentieth [Thirty-first] New York Volunteers (Colonel Pratt), who mistook us for rebel cavalry, as a lot of cavalry had been seen on the hills reconnoitering in the neighborhood all day. The officers of this regiment showed they understood their duty, and it would be well for our service if all our outposts exercised the same vigilance. We met no further obstructions, and reached camp about 5 o'clock p. m., having been in the saddle from 9 o'clock a. m.

There ought to be signals adopted, so that outposts and patrols may be enabled to recognize each other, and thus avoid very unpleasant suspicions and more frequent accidents.

It is my opinion that if a squadron of cavalry were allowed to bivouac out overnight some prisoners might be captured, as the enemy's cavalry, in squads of about a dozen, are in the habit of patrolling along the road early in the morning and late in the evening. A few companies of infantry, a section of artillery, and a squadron of cavalry might dislodge the enemy from Fairfax Court-House. The roads from here to Fairfax Court-House are excellent for all arms of the service.

I have the honor to be, sir, your obedient servant,

WM. H. BOYD,
Captain, First N. Y. Volunteer Cavalry, late Lincoln Cavalry.

Capt. E. SPARROW PURDY,
Assistant Adjutant-General, Alexandria Division.

[Indorsement.]

HEADQUARTERS CAMP, *November* 28, 1861.

Respectfully forwarded for the information of the Commanding General. In my opinion the actions of Captain Boyd were characterized by coolness and discretion. The regiment to which he belongs has nothing to show that it belongs to the United States—no guidons or colors of any kind—although the proper requisitions have been made over and over again.

W. B. FRANKLIN,
Brigadier-General, Commanding Division.

SPECIAL ORDERS, ⎫　　　　HDQRS. ARMY OF THE POTOMAC,
　　No. 170.　　⎭　　　　　　*Washington, December* 5, 1861.

*　　　　*　　　　*　　　　*　　　　*　　　　*　　　　*

7. The Major-General Commanding has read attentively and with much satisfaction the report of Capt. William H. Boyd, First New York Cavalry, of the reconnaissance made on the 27th ultimo by the squadron under his command, consisting of Boyd's and Bennett's companies of that regiment. The coolness and discretion displayed on that occasion by Captain Boyd and the officers and men of his command deserve the highest praise, and have won for them the confidence of the Commanding General.

*　　　　*　　　　*　　　　*　　　　*　　　　*　　　　*

By command of Major-General McClellan:

　　　　　　　　　　　　　　　S. WILLIAMS,
　　　　　　　　　　　　　　Assistant Adjutant General.

NOVEMBER 30, 1861.—Skirmish near mouth of Little Cacapon River, West Virginia.

Report of Brig. Gen. B. F. Kelley, U. S. Army.

　　　　　　　　　ROMNEY, VA., *November* 30, 1861—11 p. m.

Nothing new to-night except bushwhackers captured 6 of our horses and wounded 3 men to-day. Teams were out on river road south of town after hay. But to offset that, Captain Dyche's met party of secesh near mouth of Little Cacapon and captured 4 horses, saddles and bridles, one a field officer's. Little Cacapon Bridge will be done to-morrow morning.

　　　　　　　　　　　　　　B. F. KELLEY,
　　　　　　　　　　　　　　　Brigadier-General.

Maj. Gen. GEORGE B. McCLELLAN.

DECEMBER 2, 1861.—Skirmish at Annandale, Va.

REPORTS.

No. 1.—Brig. Gen. Louis Blenker, U. S. Army.
No. 2.—Maj. Alonzo W. Adams, First New York Cavalry.
No. 3.—Brig. Gen. William B. Franklin, U. S. Army.
No. 4.—Brig. Gen. John Newton, U. S. Army.

No. 1.

Report of Brig. Gen. Louis Blenker, U. S. Army.

HDQRS. BRIGADIER-GENERAL BLENKER'S DIVISION,
　　　　　　　　　　Hunter's Chapel, December 4, 1861.

SIR: I respectfully lay before you a detailed report of the skirmish which took place in the afternoon of the 2d instant between our pickets and part of the rebel cavalry. The following are the particulars of this affair:

At about 1 o'clock p. m. the vedettes at Annandale Station discovered some cavalry in front and gave due notice to the grand guard, but at the same instant a force of about 200 cavalry came in full gallop, and thus attacked the several pickets belonging to Company A, Forty-fifth Regiment New York Volunteers, on the left wing, between Annandale Station and the turnpike which leads from Alexandria to Fairfax Court-House. The vedettes were at first under the impression that it was our own cavalry, which made their daily round about this time, and it thus happened that they were overpowered and had to fall back into the woods, where, under the command of Captain Weller, they made a stand, firing on the enemy. The drummer, Feuerstein, gave the sign in time, and it was by his commendable zeal that the two companies at Cox's farm, under Captain Doebke, and a small squad of Mounted Rifles, under command of First Lieut. William R. Parnell, were immediately dispatched on the battle-ground, and at once charged on the enemy and drove him back. First Lieutenant Parnell showed great bravery. The enemy fled towards Centreville. The detail of the Mounted Rifles and four companies of the Forty-fifth New York Volunteers pursued them for two miles; then they formed, as it was necessary, for immediate action.

Patrols were sent out towards Centreville and Fairfax Court-House, who on their return reported " All quiet." After having received the report at these headquarters, I ordered one squadron of cavalry, as well as a battery of light artillery, as re-enforcement, who immediately, under my special command, departed to the scene of action. Two companies of the Mounted Rifles stand till now in readiness upon Mason's Hill, as likewise three companies of the Twenty-seventh Regiment Pennsylvania Volunteers stand as reserve at Rose Hill. The pickets are posted again as before.

The loss of the enemy is 2 prisoners, 2 killed lying outside of the lines, and 7 or 8 wounded. Our loss, as far as ascertained, is 1 killed—Carsten Huhnenberg, private of Company A, Forty-fifth Regiment New York Volunteers—and 12 men missing, also of Company A. There is 1 horse of the enemy killed in the woods and 1 horse captured.

I have further to report that Brevet Second Lieutenant Von Haythausen, of the Forty-fifth New York Volunteers, is missing since Sunday night, and is supposed to have gone over to the enemy. He took along with him a horse belonging to the orderly of the New York Mounted Rifles at Rose Hill. This attack of the enemy's cavalry was caused by a detachment that had been sent out foraging, by statement of the prisoners, although they seemed to be well informed of our position.

There have been arrested and sent to these headquarters the owner of Cox's farm, his son, and two laborers, as by report of officers and men they are suspected to be hot secessionists; but as it is contrary to general orders to arrest persons on suspicion, I ordered them to be set free, notwithstanding at several times in the night signal lights from their farm house have been seen. To avoid similar occurrences as just now reported, strict orders have been issued to the pickets to fire upon any cavalry nearing the same, unless they ride at a slow pace.

According to last night's report from the commander of the outposts there is nothing new to add.

Very respectfully, yours,

LOUIS BLENKER,
Brigadier-General.

Gen. R. B. Marcy,
   Chief of Staff of Maj. Gen. McClellan, Comdg. U. S. Army.

No. 2.

Report of Maj. Alonzo W. Adams, First New York Cavalry.

HDQRS. FIRST REGIMENT NEW YORK CAVALRY,
Camp Kearny, Va., December 2, 1861.

SIR: For the information of the Commanding General I have the honor to report that, in accordance with General Orders, No. 37, and in obedience to instructions from General Franklin, I this day proceeded with a small squadron of cavalry (79 rank and file) up the Little River turnpike to the town of Annandale, and about 1 mile south of the outer line of our pickets. At Annandale I learned that a body of rebel cavalry had been seen yesterday morning in that vicinity. Having an advance and rear guard deployed as flankers and skirmishers, I moved up the turnpike in the direction of Fairfax Court-House about 3½ or 4 miles, without opposition and without discovering the enemy's pickets. I returned to Annandale about 2 o'clock p. m., where I met with Lieutenant-Colonel Pinto, of the Thirty-second New York Regiment, commander of our picket guard, who was accompanied by two officers—lieutenants—and 22 men of the New York Mounted Rifles, by whom I was informed that we were probably surrounded by the enemy, as a battalion of rebel cavalry, more than 200 strong, had, not fifteen minutes before my arrival, dashed through that place, killing one of our pickets and taking with them several more as prisoners. Having thrown out skirmishers and posted vedettes, I disposed my command, including that of the Mounted Rifles, in order of battle, and waited an attack from the enemy.

In the mean time I sent Captain Hendrich, of my squadron, to the lieutenant-colonel of the Forty-fifth Regiment New York Volunteers, who was about half a mile distant, in command of 3 companies of his regiment, with a request that in case of attack, which was momentarily expected, he should support me with his infantry. Captain Hendrich returned with a message from the lieutenant-colonel acceding to my request and promising to move up his command nearer to Annandale. Confidently relying upon this pledge, I held possession of the place until about 5 o'clock p. m., when to my surprise I ascertained that the three companies of the Forty-fifth, instead of coming to my support, had retired in the direction of Falls Church, and probably to their encampment.

About 6 o'clock a messenger whom I had dispatched to General Franklin for orders returned with a message from Brigadier-General Kearny, advising me that General Franklin was in Washington; that I must not attempt to hold Annandale over night, but return with my command to camp; and also that he (General Kearny) had dispatched two squadrons of cavalry to my support. My skirmishers brought in a prisoner, who was arrested by Corporal Lowry, of Company G, while attempting to make his escape, and who, after making various contradictory statements—at first claiming to be a Union soldier, but not being able to give the names of his immediate officers in command—finally admitted that he was a rebel soldier on picket duty; that his name is Williams, and that he belongs to the Fourteenth South Carolina Regiment. After being assured of his personal safety, and that the rebel accounts of cruelty on our side towards prisoners were false, he gave a great deal of information respecting the position and movements of the enemy, which statements, some of them quite improbable, were received by me for what they were worth, and himself forwarded a prisoner to headquarters.

On my return from Annandale, and about 2 miles from that place, I met the two squadrons ordered to my support, under command of Lieutenant-Colonel Schickfuss, and accompanied by Brigadier-Generals Kearny and Newton. By order of General Kearny we all returned to camp, which we reached about 9 o'clock.

All of which is respectfully submitted.

With high regard, I have the honor to be, sir, your obedient servant,

A. W. ADAMS,
Major Second Battalion First New York Cavalry.

Capt. E. SPARROW PURDY, *Assistant Adjutant-General.*

No. 3.

Report of Brig. Gen. William B. Franklin, U. S. Army.

HEADQUARTERS,
Camp Williams, December 6, 1861.

GENERAL: I transmit with this a report of Brigadier-General Newton on the attack made upon our pickets on Monday last. The statements in it show bad behavior on the part of pickets of the division on my right, which I regretfully bring to the notice of the Commanding General. There is a rumor that a sergeant who was acting as lieutenant deserted from these pickets on Sunday, the 1st instant. If this be the case, it may account for the accurate manner in which the dash was made by the enemy's cavalry.

Very respectfully, your obedient servant,

W. B. FRANKLIN,
Brigadier-General, Commanding Division.

Brig. Gen. S. WILLIAMS,
Adjutant-General Army of Potomac, Washington, D. C.

No. 4.

Report of Brig. Gen. John Newton, U. S. Army.

HEADQUARTERS BRIGADE,
Camp Williams, December 6, 1861.

SIR: I have the honor to submit, for the information of the division commander, a brief synopsis of the report of Lieutenant-Colonel Pinto, field officer of the day, in command of the pickets of this brigade on the Little River turnpike, between the 30th of November and the 4th of December, 1861. The case of Lieut. T. Hamilton Haire, found sleeping on picket guard with his whole guards, has already been reported and acted upon.

On Monday, the 2d instant, at about 1 p. m., the enemy's cavalry, reported by Lieutenant-Colonel Pinto at nearly 200 men, burst through the German pickets of Blenker's division (Forty-fifth New York Volunteers), which adjoined and sustained the extreme right flank of my pickets, in three detachments, the first detachment taking the Little River turnpike, leaping and otherwise passing through the barricade about one-quarter mile beyond Padgett's tavern, at the junction of the Little

River and Columbia turnpikes; the second taking the line of the unfinished railroad, and turning the barricade; the third evading the barricade by taking the fields to the north of the Little River turnpike. The pickets of the Forty-fifth New York Volunteers stationed at the barricade and on the unfinished railroad and elsewhere in the neighborhood are positively alleged not to have fired a shot, in consequence of which the rebel cavalry, having penetrated beyond the barricade, made prisoners of 2 men of the Thirty-second New York Volunteers, belonging to my brigade, posted on the Little River turnpike, who were thus taken by surprise and captured; not, however, before they had discharged their pieces at the enemy. The rebel cavalry turned immediately and retreated at full speed, passing the barricade, &c., and I regret to report the pickets of the Forty-fifth again omitted to fire.

Lieutenant Colonel Pinto, knowing that a patrol of 79 men of the Lincoln Cavalry had passed that morning towards Fairfax Court-House, led a company from his pickets to their support, finding them at Annandale shortly after his arrival there. The enemy in their retreat had passed through Annandale before our cavalry arrived there on their return, and thus a meeting of the hostile cavalry forces did not take place.

Lieutenant Colonel Pinto, after due inquiry, places our loss as follows: Two privates of the Thirty-second New York Volunteers, belonging to my brigade, captured 300 yards this side of the barricade; several men of the Forty-fifth New York Volunteers, of General Blenker's division, taken at the barricade, and additional losses along the line of Blenker's pickets; the total being 14 prisoners and 1 killed. The enemy's loss he puts at 3 killed and 2 prisoners.

Colonel Pinto reports a very free use of liquor in the pickets of the Forty-fifth New York Volunteers.

I have only to add that Colonel Pinto seems to have behaved with great coolness, decision, and prudence in the emergency, and that his conduct merits my approbation.

I am, sir, very respectfully,

JOHN NEWTON,
Brigadier-General, Commanding.

Capt. E. SPARROW PURDY,
Assistant Adjutant-General, Division Headquarters.

DECEMBER 6, 1861.—Expedition to Gunnell's Farm, near Dranesville, Va.

Report of Brig. Gen. George A. McCall, U. S. Army.

HEADQUARTERS MCCALL'S DIVISION,
Camp Peirpoint, Va., December 6, 1861.

GENERAL: I have the honor to report that I ordered General Meade's brigade, with Kerns' battery and a squadron of cavalry under Major Jones, to march at 6 o'clock this morning to Gunnell's farm, 2½ miles northeast of Dranesville, with instructions to capture two nephews of Gunnell's and to bring in the forage on his farm. For this latter purpose I put under his charge a train of 57 wagons. General Ord's brigade, with Easton's battery, followed, and halted within supporting distance. Gunnell is a bitter secessionist, and his nephews (Colmans) are bad men. The former is now in the Confederate Army; the latter, formerly of that Army, have more recently been in the habit of watching the Potomac between Great Falls and Seneca and firing on our pickets. They are reported to me by my guide to have shot two stragglers of General Banks' division, and left them for the hogs to devour. On arriving on the ground some time after Meade, I found that he had captured the Colmans and 3 sons of Poole, rank secessionists, and after making the necessary dispositions to resist an attack, commenced loading the train, which work was soon completed, and the command returned, arriving here at 6 p. m.

Nothing of the enemy was seen or heard by the scouts sent out in advance and on the flanks.

I have the honor to be, very respectfully, your obedient servant,

GEO. A. McCALL,
Brigadier-General, Commanding Division.

Brig. Gen. R. B. MARCY, *Chief of Staff.*

P. S.—It is with pleasure that I refer to the very exemplary conduct of all the troops on this occasion, and can commend from personal observation the good discipline maintained. There was no straggling or lagging behind during the march out or returning.

DECEMBER 13, 1861.—Engagement at Camp Alleghany, West Virginia.

REPORTS, ETC.

No. 1.—Brig. Gen. Robert H. Milroy, U. S. Army.
No. 2.—Col. James A. Jones, Twenty-fifth Ohio Infantry.
No. 3.—Hon. J. P. Benjamin, Confederate Secretary of War.
No. 4.—Brig. Gen. William W. Loring, C. S. Army, commanding Army of Northwestern Virginia.
No. 5.—Col. Edward Johnson, Twelfth Georgia Infantry, and response of the Secretary of War.
No. 6.—Lieut. Col. Z. T. Conner, Twelfth Georgia Infantry.
No. 7.—Lieut. Col. G. W. Hansbrough, C. S. Army.
No. 8.—Maj. A. G. Reger, Twenty-fifth Virginia Infantry.
No. 9.—Lieut. C. E. Dabney, C. S. Cavalry.
No. 10.—Return of casualties in the Confederate forces.

No. 1.

Reports of Brig. Gen. Robert H. Milroy, U. S. Army, commanding District of Cheat Mountain, with return of casualties.

CLEVELAND, *December 14, 1861.*

Stevens sends me the following :

General Milroy, with 700 men, met General Johnson, of Georgia, with 2,000, at Alleghany Camp, West Virginia, yesterday, and after 3 hours' hard fighting defeated Johnson, with loss 200 killed, including many officers, and 30 prisoners. Johnson burned his camp and retreated to Staunton. Federal loss about 30.

A. STAGER,
Superintendent.

T. T. ECKERT,
Chief of U. S. Military Telegraph Line, War Department.

Extract from the "Record of Events," return of General Milroy's command, for December, 1861.

Upon December 13 an expedition was sent out and attacked a camp of the enemy, generally known as Camp Baldwin, Alleghany Mountains, in Pocahontas County, Virginia. The expedition consisted of 650 of the Ninth Indiana Regiment, 400 of the Twenty-fifth Ohio Volunteers, 250 of the Second Virginia Volunteers, 300 of the Thirteenth Indiana Volunteers, 130 of the Thirty-second Ohio Volunteers, and 30 of Bracken's cavalry. The result of the expedition is detailed in the official report of General Milroy, now on file in the Department.*

*　　　*　　　*　　　*　　　*　　　*　　　*

The number of prisoners captured by our forces was 26.

Return of casualties in the Union forces in the engagement at Camp Alleghany, W. Va., December 13, 1861.

Command.	Killed.	Wounded.	Missing.	Aggregate.
Ninth Indiana	8	13	......	21
Thirteenth Indiana	2	23	4	29
Twenty-fifth Ohio	6	54	6	66
Thirty-second Ohio	2	10	......	12
Second West Virginia	2	7	......	9
Total	20	107	10	137

No. 2.

Report of Col. James A. Jones, Twenty-fifth Ohio Infantry.

HDQRS. TWENTY-FIFTH REGIMENT OHIO VOLUNTEERS,
Huttonsville, Va., December 13, 1861.

SIR: In compliance with your orders, I have the honor to inform you of the movements and conduct of my regiment and a portion of the Thirteenth Indiana and Thirty-second Ohio, which were temporarily attached to my command, on the 13th instant, at Camp Baldwin, on the summit of the Alleghany Mountains:

After leaving the pike we advanced up the mountain, which was very steep and rocky, for about one mile to the summit on the right and rear of the enemy's camp, to await the attack of the Ninth Indiana and Second Virginia, as you directed; but as we approached the top of the hill we discovered the enemy's pickets, who immediately retreated on our approach. I gave the order to pursue them in double-quick, as the enemy would be informed of our advance. One company of the Thirteenth Indiana, being in advance, was conducted by Lieutenant McDonald, of General Reynolds' staff, until we arrived at the edge of the wood, in full view of the enemy's camp. Finding them already formed, and advancing with a large force to attack us, Lieutenant McDonald halted the company of the Thirteenth Indiana, and ordered it deployed into line. I immediately formed the Twenty-fifth Ohio on his right and the

---

* Not found.

other two companies of the Thirteenth Indiana on our left, and a detachment of the Thirty-second Ohio formed on their left. The fire was already opened on the right, and was carried through the line. After a few rounds the enemy retreated in great confusion, with great slaughter, leaving their dead and wounded. They now again rallied and commenced to advance, returning our fire with great vigor. Some of the men commenced falling to the rear all along the lines. Captains Charlesworth and Crowell, of the Twenty-fifth Ohio; Lieutenant McDonald, Captains Myers and Newland, of the Thirteenth Indiana; and Captain Hamilton, of the Thirty-second Ohio, rallied them and brought them up into line. In a few moments the enemy fell back, and attempted to turn our right flank, but were immediately met and repulsed. Our men by this time had become broken, but were again rallied by the officers of the different commands, who conducted themselves nobly. The enemy again attempted to advance upon us, but shared the same fate as before.

After making several attempts to drive us from the wood, they deployed to the left, to turn our left flank and get in our rear. I ordered a portion of the command to advance and attack them, which was done in a gallant manner, the enemy retreating to their cabins, but soon appeared again. Our men finding that they were not receiving support by the Ninth Indiana and the Second Virginia, quite a number commenced retreating, and it was with great difficulty that they were rallied. Some did not return, but disgracefully left the field, but the remainder of the command fought like veteran soldiers, driving the rebels again to their cabins; but, being soon rallied by their officers, they again renewed the attack with a large re-enforcement, and poured a galling fire into our thinned ranks, our men holding their position and returning the fire with great energy and slaughter, the officers of the different detachments urging and cheering them on. Many of the men had left the field with the wounded, and some without cause, which had much reduced our number, and our ammunition was almost exhausted. The artillery was turned upon us with shot and shell, but without any effect, and the enemy was again compelled to retire to their cabins with great slaughter, as usual. Our ammunition being exhausted, I thought it prudent to fall back to the headquarters of the commanding general, which was done in good order.

I am sorry to be compelled to say some of the men behaved very badly, but it was not confined to any one regiment. I cannot close this report without expressing my entire approbation of the conduct of the officers of the different detachments. Captains Charlesworth, Crowell, Johnson, Askew; Lieutenants Dirlam, Bowlus, Merryman, Wood, and Haughton, of the Twenty-fifth Ohio; Lieutenant McDonald, of General Reynolds' staff, while there; Major Dobbs, Captains Myers and Newland, and Lieutenants Kirkpatrick, Bailey, [?] Harrington, [?] and Jones (who was killed), of the Thirteenth Indiana; Captain Hamilton and other officers of the Thirty-second Ohio, whose names I did not learn, rendered me efficient service by their cool and gallant bearing throughout the engagement, which lasted about three hours. The enemy's force, as near as I could ascertain, was about 2,500, with nine pieces of artillery. The force under my command was about 700. Lieutenant-Colonel Richardson and Major Webster were absent. Captain Brown received an injury on the evening before, and was not able to be in the engagement.

Very respectfully, your obedient servant,

J. A. JONES,
Colonel Twenty-fifth Regiment Ohio Volunteer Infantry, U. S. Army.

Brigadier-General MILROY.

No. 3.

Report of Hon. J. P. Benjamin, Confederate Secretary of War.

WAR DEPARTMENT, C. S. A.,
Richmond, Va., January 3, 1862.

To the PRESIDENT :

SIR : I have the honor to submit herewith for communication to Congress the official reports of the battle of Alleghany Mountain, in which our troops, 1,200 in number, successfully withstood the assault of more than fourfold their number, and drove the enemy from the field after a combat as obstinate and as hard fought as any that has occurred during the war.

Your appreciation of the conduct of Colonel Johnson has already been testified by his promotion to the grade of brigadier-general, and I have taken pleasure in conveying to the gallant troops under his command the expression of approval and admiration that they so fully deserve.

I doubt not that Congress, on the reading of this report, will cordially concur with the Executive in the opinion that in this brilliant combat officers and men have alike deserved well of their country and merit its thanks.

I am, very respectfully,

J. P. BENJAMIN,
Secretary of War.

No. 4.

Reports of Brig. Gen. William W. Loring, commanding Army of Northwestern Virginia.

STAUNTON, *December* 13, 1861.

GENERAL : I inclose the report of Colonel Johnson, which I received to-day. The enemy was informed of our movement, it seems, through deserters, but, as expected, the troops on Alleghany checked and repulsed them with loss. The weather has been so good that they were enabled to attack with their entire force, and will no doubt, as stated by Colonel Johnson, endeavor to possess the pass now occupied by us when it is evacuated. In consequence of their formidable appearance, and not being assured of their intention, I have for the time ordered Colonel Johnson to remain where he is, and given directions for the command to halt upon this road about 20 miles distant, where it will strike it en route to Strasburg. I expect it there in two or three days. I have arranged the march in case we could not, which was highly desirable, get the use of the rail from here to Strasburg, to march through with our own transportation. It will, of course, delay us. Should the weather shortly take an inclement turn, the enemy may be forced to return to Cheat, and enable us to follow up the design contemplated.

With respect, I have the honor to be, your obedient servant,

W. W. LORING,
Brigadier-General, Commanding.

Col. S. COOPER, *Adjutant-General, Richmond, Va.*

STAUNTON, VA., *December* 17, 1861.

SIR : I inclose herewith a copy of the letter [of 15th instant] this day received from Col. E. Johnson, commanding at Alleghany.* In consequence of the necessity of meeting the enemy at Alleghany, and the uncertainty of their movement, I have determined to keep the command of Colonel Johnson where it is for the present, holding it in readiness to move at any time in the direction of Moorefield should it be thought best. I do this for the reason that it would be some days before that command could move, and that it is undoubtedly the determination of the enemy to occupy Alleghany Pass, if possible, and to re-enforce General Kelley by crossing the Alleghany and forming a junction with him via Moorefield. I have, besides the command of Colonel Taliaferro (four regiments), advanced some days ago, the whole of the troops from the Huntersville line, composed of the three Tennessee, two Virginia regiments, and the Hampden and Danville batteries of artillery, in all, about 6,000 men.

Two of the regiments, the Seventh Tennessee and the Twenty-first Virginia, left here on yesterday, via the Valley road, and the remainder are now at Ryan's, about 20 miles distant, on the Monterey road. I shall order to move to-morrow morning, via Harrisonburg, the whole, to form a junction with General Jackson at the earliest possible moment.

I am, very respectfully, your obedient servant,

W. W. LORING,
Brigadier-General.

General SAMUEL COOPER,
Adjutant and Inspector General C. S. Army, Richmond, Va.

No. 5.

Reports of Col. Edward Johnson, Twelfth Georgia Infantry, and response of the Secretary of War.

CAMP ALLEGHANY, *December* 13, 1861.

COLONEL: Yesterday I sent out a scout, who fell in with a column of the enemy, killing some 8 or 10. This morning our pickets were driven in about 4 a. m. I made preparations to meet the enemy. They appeared in force—not less than 5,000 men; attacked my right and left. On the right there are no defensive works. On the hill to the left we have hastily thrown up a trench. I have only about 1,200 effective men. Four hundred of my men met the enemy on the right flank, and after a severe contest defeated them. On the left the enemy attacked our intrenchments, but failed to carry them. They were met on both points with the most determined heroism, and, after a contest lasting from 7 a. m. until near 2 p. m., repulsed with great loss. Our victory has been complete, but dearly bought. We have lost several gallant officers killed and many wounded. Among the killed are Capt. P. B. Anderson, Lee Battery ; Captain Mollohan, Hansborough's battalion. Wounded, Captain Deshler, my acting assistant adjutant-general; Lieutenant-Colonel Hansborough, Lieut. George T. Thompson, Thirty-first Virginia Regiment, and others—Lieutenant Thompson fatally, I fear.

The enemy were led into my camp by a Virginia traitor. Since the battle the Forty-fourth have come up, and the Fifty-eighth, I am informed, is *en route* to this place. The enemy left a large number killed

---

*Reports No. 5, p. 461.

and wounded on the field. They carried off a large number, some ten or twelve ambulance loads of wounded.

I trust immediate action will be taken relative to this position. Under recent orders, I have sent to the rear a large quantity of ordnance and ordnance stores. I have all along contended that this place would be occupied if we abandoned it. I feel confident that they have planned this attack upon information furnished by deserters from this camp, and that they will occupy it if we leave it. The position is one which could with sufficient force be made quite strong, but the extent of ground to be occupied is too large for a small one. My first letter to you will show that I thought the force left here was too small.

Prisoners taken to-day state that the enemy had 5,000 men drawn from Huttonsville, Cheat Mountain, and other places in rear of Cheat Mountain. I will forward you a more detailed report at my earliest convenience. I am making preparations for the enemy in the event, which I do not think probable, of his renewing the attack to-morrow or at any time before we evacuate this position. •

In the event of remaining here, stores must be immediately sent back. If we leave, we should do so as soon as the public property is sent back.

I am, sir, very respectfully,

E. JOHNSON,
Colonel, Commanding.

Col. C. L. STEVENSON,
    Assistant Adjutant-General, Army Northwest.

CAMP ALLEGHANY, December 15, 1861.

COLONEL: I have nothing to report concerning the enemy since the battle except what I hear from prisoners. From a sergeant captured I learn that Generals Reynolds and Milroy commanded, and that the expedition was based upon information furnished them by five deserters from Hansborough's battalion, who left here about a week since. Troops were drawn from Beverly, Huttonsville, and Cheat Mountain. All that they could collect were brought up. The right was guided to our position by a traitor from Northwestern Virginia named Shipman, who is quite familiar with this country. The left was guided by a noted guide and traitor, who lived within 3 miles of this place, named Slater. We had timely warning of their approach, but could not ascertain their numbers before they made the attack. Our works had been suspended in consequence of recent orders. None had been erected before we got here.

The enemy were totally routed. I hear from citizens on the line of their retreat that they carried numbers of dead and wounded by the houses, and acknowledged that they had been badly whipped. They were heard to accuse their officers of deceiving them, insisting that our numbers were largely superior to their own. They were much demoralized, and I hope they have received a good lesson. Four additional dead bodies of the enemy were found this morning. We have 12 or 14 of their wounded, most of whom will die. Our loss has been severe, but with our small number against such odds it was not singular. The Forty-fourth Virginia came up soon after the fight. It is still here.

Immediately after the fight I ordered the transportation of stores from this place to stop, and no more trains to be sent to this place until further orders. I am strengthening my works, and I trust that something decisive will be determined upon, so that I may know what to do. The ordnance ammunition had nearly all been sent back when we were attacked, but most of the fighting was with infantry.

I am, sir, very respectfully, your obedient servant,

E. JOHNSON,
Colonel, Commanding.

Col. C. L. STEVENSON, *Assistant Adjutant-General.*

HEADQUARTERS MONTEREY LINE,
Camp Alleghany, December 19, 1861.

COLONEL : I have the honor to submit the following report of the engagement with the enemy which occurred at this place on the 13th instant :

On the 12th I sent out a scouting party of 106 men, commanded by Major [John D. H.] Ross, of the Fifty-second Virginia Volunteers, with instructions to ambuscade a point on the pike beyond Camp Baxter, on Greenbrier. On the afternoon of that day the advance guard of the enemy approached, were fired into by Major Ross's command, and many of them killed or wounded. Immediately the main body of the enemy approached in force, deployed, and advanced upon our scouting party, who retired and came into camp that night.

On the morning of the 13th, about 4 a. m., I was aroused by the officer of the day, who reported firing at the advance pickets on the pike in the direction of the enemy. I immediately turned out the whole of my command, and prepared to meet them. I ordered Hansbrough's battalion, the Thirty-first Virginia, commanded by Major Boykin, and Reger's battalion to occupy the crest of the mountain on the right, to guard against approach from that quarter. On this hill there were no defenses. There were some fields and felled timber beyond, which reached the crest of the mountain. The enemy advanced to our front, and, conducted by a guide, a Union man from Western Virginia, who was familiar with the roads and trails in the vicinity, turned off from the turnpike about a mile from our position, near the base of the mountain, and reached our right by a trail which led into a road coming into the field slightly in our rear. As they approached this position pickets thrown out from Hansbrough's battalion discovered them, and reported them as advancing in strong force.

About 7.15 o'clock a. m. the enemy advanced, and a terrific fire commenced. The enemy on this flank numbered fully 2,000. They were gallantly met by our troops, who did not exceed 300 at this time. As soon as I heard the firing I ordered two companies of the Twelfth Georgia (Hawkins' and Blandford's), who had at the first alarm been posted on the pike about a quarter of a mile in front down the mountain, to move up immediately to the support of our forces on the right. Three other companies of the Twelfth (Davis', Hardeman's, and Patterson's), Lieut. U. E. Moore commanding, were also ordered to the support of those on the right, who were making a gallant defense and holding the position against immense odds. Gallantly did the Georgians move up, and, taking position on the left, received a terrible fire from the enemy.

By this time the extreme right had been forced back, but seeing the Georgians, who came on with a shout, they joined them, and moved upon the enemy, who, taking advantage of some fallen trees, brush, and timber, poured upon them a terrific fire. Our men were checked, but not driven back. They did not yield an inch, but steadily advanced, cheered and led by their officers. Many of the officers fought by the side of their men and led them on to the conflict. I never witnessed harder fighting. The enemy, behind trees, with their long-range arms, at first had decidedly the advantage, but our men soon came up to them and drove them from their cover. I cannot speak in terms too exaggerated of the unflinching courage and dashing gallantry of those 500 men who contended from 7.15 a. m. until 1.45 p. m. against an immensely superior force of the enemy, and finally drove them from their positions and pursued them a mile or more down the mountain.

I cannot name all who deserve particular mention for this gallantry and good conduct. Colonel Hansbrough, whilst gallantly leading his battalion, was wounded by a pistol-shot and carried from the field. Soon after the fight became general the brave Lieut. G. T. Thompson, of the Thirty-first Virginia, fell severely wounded. His good conduct had attracted my attention, and he fell within a few feet of me. Captain Mollohan, while cheering and leading his men in pursuit of the enemy, fell mortally wounded. Lieutenant Moore, Twelfth Georgia Volunteers, whilst gallantly leading a charge, fell mortally wounded. This gallant officer was ever ready for any expedition involving danger; he was truly brave. Captains Davis, Blandford, Hardeman, and Hawkins, their officers and men, behaved admirably. Captain Davis and his company were conspicuous for their gallantry and good conduct throughout the fight. Adjutant Willis, Lieutenants McCoy, Etheridge, Marshall, and Turpin, Twelfth Georgia Regiment, deserve particular mention for their good conduct. Major F. M. Boykin, jr., commanding Thirty-first Virginia Volunteers, his officers and men, deserve my thanks for their unflinching courage throughout the struggle. This regiment suffered severely. Lieutenants Toothman, J. Johnson, McNewmar, J. R. Philips, all wounded, deserve honorable mention. Captain Thompson, Thirty-first Virginia, deserves special notice. Adjutant Morgan, Lieutenants Robinson, Haymond, Sergeants Jarvis, Roder, Privates Collins, Musgrave, and Green, Hansbrough's battalion, are favorably mentioned by their commanders.

My command consisted of the Twelfth Georgia Regiment, under the immediate command of Lieut. Col. Z. T. Conner; Fifty-second Virginia, Major Ross', Hansbrough's, and Reger's battalions; Thirty-first Virginia, Major Boykin; Lee Battery of artillery, four pieces, Capt. P. B. Anderson; Captain Miller's battery, four pieces, and a detachment of Pittsylvania cavalry, Lieutenant Dabney. The artillery was posted on the hill to the left of my position, which had been intrenched. Immediately after the troops were turned out the Twelfth Georgia and Fifty-second Virginia were ordered into the trenches. The Pittsylvania cavalry, dismounted, under Lieutenant Dabney, also went into the trenches, armed with carbines. A large column of the enemy, led by one Slater, a traitor, well acquainted with the country, approached the left of this position by a road running along a leading ridge.

About half an hour after the attack was made on the right this column came up on the left to our trenches. They were evidently surprised to find us intrenched. Here the brave Anderson, by a fatal mistake, lost his life. As the enemy advanced he rode to the trenches and invited them in, thinking they were our returning pickets, at the same time telling our men not to fire. He was instantly shot down by the advanced body of the enemy's force. Our men then opened a galling fire upon them, and they fell back into the fallen timber and brush, from which they kept up a constant fire at our men in the trenches and upon our artillerists.

My acting assistant adjutant-general, Capt. James Deshler, of the artillery, whilst behaving most gallantly, was shot down in the trenches by a wound through both thighs. He refused to leave the field, and remained in the trenches until the day was over. Captain Miller opened upon the enemy with his guns and behaved with great gallantry, exposing himself at his guns to the fire of the enemy's sharpshooters. After the enemy's force on the right had been repulsed and driven from the field, I ordered all of our men who had been engaged in that quarter to join the troops in the trenches on the left. They took post with the other troops, and opened fire on the enemy as occasion offered. The enemy, under the fire of artillery and infantry, soon retreated from the left, leaving their dead and wounded.

The enemy's force on the left was larger, if anything, than the force on the right. They numbered in all about 5,000 men, who had been drawn from Belington, Beverly, Huttonsville, Elk Water, and Cheat Mountain. My force did not exceed 1,200 effective men of all arms. General Reynolds, U. S. Army, commanded the whole of the enemy's forces, and General Milroy the attack on our right. General Milroy is reported by prisoners captured to have been wounded. The enemy left upon the field 35 dead and 13 wounded. They carried from the field large numbers of dead and wounded. This I get from citizens who reside upon the roads along which they retreated. Ten or twelve ambulances were seen conveying their wounded. We captured 3 prisoners and about 100 stand of arms, which the enemy had thrown away in his flight.

Although we have reason to be thankful to God for the victory achieved over our enemies on this occasion, we can but lament the loss of many valuable lives. Our casualties amount to 20 killed, 96 wounded, and 28 missing. Many of the missing have returned since the day of the battle. I am much indebted to Surgs. H. R. Green, of the Twelfth Georgia Regiment, and W. T. Blanc, of the Thirty-first Virginia Volunteers, for their attention to our own wounded as well as those of the enemy. They have been untiring in their efforts to alleviate their sufferings. Dr. Green was slightly wounded in the hand by a spent ball while attending to the wounded.

Herewith I submit a list of casualties; also the reports of commanders of regiments and corps.

I am, sir, very respectfully, your obedient servant,

E. JOHNSON,
Colonel Twelfth Georgia Regiment, Comdg. Monterey Line.

Col. C. L. STEVENSON,
Assistant Adjutant-General, Army Northwest, Staunton.

———

WAR DEPARTMENT, C. S. A.,
Richmond, December 23, 1861.

SIR: The report of the engagement of the 13th instant, in which your gallant command met and repulsed a vastly superior force with a steady valor worthy of the highest admiration, has been communicated by me to the President, and I rejoice to be made the medium of communicating to you and to your officers and men the expression of his thanks and of the great gratification he has experienced at your success.

I am happy to add that the President readily and cheerfully assented to my suggestion that you should be promoted to the rank of brigadier-general, as a mark of his approval of your conduct, and your nomination will accordingly be this day sent in to the Congress, and take date from the day of the battle.

I am, your obedient servant,

J. P. BENJAMIN,
Secretary of War.

Brig. Gen. EDWARD JOHNSON, *Camp Alleghany.*

No. 6.

Report of Lieut. Col. Z. T. Conner, Twelfth Georgia Infantry.

CAMP ALLEGHANY, *December 17, 1861.*

SIR: I have the honor of submitting this brief and hastily-drawn-up report of the battle of 13th instant:

About 4.30 o'clock in the morning, in obedience to your orders, I proceeded with seven companies of the Twelfth Georgia Regiment to occupy the rude and hastily-drawn-up intrenchments. At 6.30 the enemy were reported in strength upon our right flank, and about sunrise the firing commenced, and was continued without intermission for over two hours, the enemy from their greatly-superior force disputing most obstinately every inch of ground. The contest was so closely waged for some time that I was induced to dispatch two companies from Twelfth Georgia Regiment, Company B, Captain Hardeman, and Company I, the lamented Lieutenant Moore commanding, to re-enforce our little band and aid in driving the enemy back.

About this time the attack was commenced upon our left, the enemy having covered himself by the heavily fallen timber until within 50 paces of our temporary earthworks. The firing had little effect except in exposed positions, which resulted in some deeply-to-be-deplored casualties. The death of those gallant officers, Captain Anderson and Lieutenant Reger, and badly wounding that most efficient, indefatigable, and brave officer Captain Deshler, who, though shot down, utterly refused to be sent from the field until the enemy were repulsed with great loss.

The conduct of the officers and men of the entire left wing was exceedingly creditable. For list of casualties I beg leave to refer you to accompanying tabular statement of Lieutenant Whitesides, acting adjutant Twelfth Georgia Regiment.

I am, very respectfully, your obedient servant,

Z. T. CONNER,
Lieutenant-Colonel Twelfth Georgia Regiment.

Col. EDWARD JOHNSON, *Commanding Alleghany Line.*

No. 7.

Report of Lieut. Col. G. W. Hansbrough, C. S. Army.

CAMP ALLEGHANY, *December 16, 1861.*

COLONEL: After the alarm about 4.30 a. m. on the 13th instant, pursuant to your orders my battalion was stationed in the woods on the hill above and to the right of our encampment. Scouts were sent out by me to the turnpike road below us and towards Varner's on the right. The Thirty-first Virginia, under command of Major Boykin, ordered to co-operate with us, did not come up, owing, I believe, to the impassableness of the blockade in the dark, and were several hundred yards to our left.

Soon after the dawn of day the scouts reported the approach of the enemy in strong force on the extreme right. Determining to feel the enemy with a view to test his strength and temper, I immediately advanced the battalion to meet him, and approached within 150 yards of where he was forming in line of battle a force at least ten times as numerous as mine. I sent a messenger to hurry up the Thirty-first, which was then not in sight, and then ordered the battalion to fire and fall back to meet the Thirty-first. The fire was delivered with coolness, and it is thought with considerable effect. Upon us falling back the enemy poured a volley of Minie balls, which, however, flew harmlessly over our heads.

Meeting the gallant Thirty-first advancing in fine spirits, my men rallied and returned vigorously to the charge. Their advance was retarded, not hindered, by the logs and brush of the blockade. The fight here was almost hand to hand, the roar of musketry was incessant and deafening, but above the roar rang the shouts of officers and men. It must be admitted that not much order was observed. The men fought on their own hook, each loading and firing as fast as possible. The Thirty-first and my battalion were mingled almost indiscriminately. No praise applied to the conduct of officers or men here engaged in battle can be justly deemed excessive. Where all behaved so well it may appear invidious to name any, but I cannot forbear to mention that the calm, the ardent courage and soldierly demeanor of Adjt. C. S. Morgan and the dauntless conduct of the noble Capt. William H. Mollohan commanded the applause of every beholder. Lieutenants Robinson and Haymond, Sergeants Jarvis and Roder, and Privates Collins, Musgrave, Green, and scores of others deserve honorable mention.

Of my own personal knowledge I can say but little more, for here in this first charge, whilst descending from a log on which I had been standing for a moment urging the men forward to the charge, I was prostrated by a pistol ball, which entered my right thigh. In this condition I was borne off the field. The enemy was then recoiling before our fire. Their final discomfiture and retreat, after various vicissitudes, are known to you. Victory has once more been awarded to the defenders of the right, but we have to mourn many casualties. That gallant patriot and soldier Captain Mollohan sealed his devotion to the cause with his life's blood. Lieutenant Haymond was severely wounded. Our entire loss was 4 killed, 13 wounded (1 mortally and several severely), and 5 missing.

Respectfully,

G. W. HANSBROUGH,
Lieutenant-Colonel, Commanding Battalion.

Col. EDWARD JOHNSON, *Commanding, &c.*

No. 8.

Report of Maj. A. G. Reger, Twenty-fifth Virginia Infantry.

HEADQUARTERS TWENTY-FIFTH VIRGINIA REGIMENT,
Camp Alleghany, December 16, 1861.

SIR: I have the honor to report to you that on the morning of the 13th instant orders came to me that the enemy were approaching in force on the Greenbrier road, and to report the men under my command at once to you at the blacksmith shop, near the forks of the road, which was done in the shortest possible time, and after remaining there some time we were ordered to proceed down the Greenbrier road, which was done in good order in double-quick time. When some 200 yards down the road we were ordered up the hill by the right flank through a thick blockade. The hill being very steep and difficult to ascend, the men became very much scattered. When near the top of the hill I received directions as coming from you to occupy the point of the hill on the south side of the turnpike road, as the enemy were reported advancing up the turnpike, which I did with a portion of the men, whilst a portion of the Augusta Lee Rifles, under command of Capt. R. D. Lilley; a portion of the Rockbridge Guards, under command of Lieut. J. J. Whitmore; a portion of the Franklin Guards, under command of Sergt. E. W. Boggs, and a portion of the Upshur Greys, numbering in all about 60 men, went to the support of our forces on the right flank, out of which number 1 was killed and 11 wounded—none supposed to be very dangerous.

The officers and men who went to the right flank are reported to have acted bravely. Dr. Thomas Opie, assistant surgeon of my regiment, has been unremitting in his care and attention to our wounded soldiers, not only of this regiment, but in Colonel Hansbrough's battalion and others.

Respectfully, your obedient servant,

A. G. REGER,
Major, Comdg. Twenty-fifth Regiment Virginia Volunteers.

Col. EDWARD JOHNSON,
Commanding Forces on the Summit of Alleghany.

No. 9.

Report of Lieut. C. E. Dabney, C. S. Cavalry.

HEADQUARTERS CAVALRY CAMP,
Alleghany Summit, December 15, 1861.

SIR: I beg leave to report that on the morning of the 13th instant I caused my command to turn out immediately I received intelligence of the enemy's having driven in our pickets and held it in readiness for orders.

After remaining in this position for nearly two hours the enemy suddenly appeared on the crest of the hill on which the Thirty-first Virginia Regiment was encamped, and commenced a rapid fire of musketry. My position was in full range and my men very much exposed to the fire. I immediately rode to headquarters to get orders, but found Colonel Johnson absent, and was unable to ascertain in what part of the field he was. Under these circumstances I considered it my duty to carry my command where it could render some service, and would not be compelled to stand exposed to a heavy fire from the enemy without a chance of returning it. I accordingly marched it up to the intrenchments on the hill to the left of the turnpike, and made the men dismount and stand to their horses.

After the lapse of some time the enemy appeared in force on our left flank and commenced a heavy fire, which raked the hill. Not being able to find who was in command on the hill, and finding my men very much exposed and in a position in which they could render no service, I took the responsibility of ordering them to secure their horses behind the cabins and to go into the ditches. Directly I met with Colonel Johnson. I informed him of the steps which I had taken and my reason therefor. He approved of them.

The trenches were so much crowded on the left flank that I was not able to get more than 12 or 15 of my carbineers in a position where they could shoot at the enemy with any effect. This detachment, however, kept up a regular and effective fire until the close of the engagement.

I take pleasure in stating that all of my men, and especially those posted where they could fire on the enemy, behaved with coolness and bravery and obeyed my orders promptly.

None of my command sustained any injury except Private John Nuckols, who was slightly wounded in both hands and in the left arm by a musket ball. Only two of my horses were wounded.

Very respectfully, your obedient servant,

C. E. DABNEY,
Second Lieutenant, Commanding Pittsylvania Cavalry.

Lieutenant WILLIS, *Acting Assistant Adjutant-General.*

No. 10.

Return of casualties in Colonel Edward Johnson's command in the engagement at Camp Alleghany, December 13, 1861.[*]

Command.	Killed.		Wounded.		Missing.		Aggregate.
	Officers.	Enlisted men.	Officers.	Enlisted men.	Officers.	Enlisted men.	
Brigade staff			2				2
Twelfth Georgia	1	5	1	36		4	47
Twenty-fifth Virginia	1	1		11		5	18
Thirty-first Virginia	1	5	4	27			37
Fifty-second Virginia				2		6	8
Hansbrough's battalion	1	3	1	10		13	28
Lee Battery	1						1
Miller's battery		1	1	3			5
Totals	5	15	9	89		28	146

DECEMBER 15, 1861.—Affair in Roane County, West Virginia.

Extract from "Record of Events," return of Department of Western Virginia, for the month of December, 1861.

December 15, Captain Baggs, with a company of scouts, pursued the bushwhackers into Roane County, on the Little Kanawha, attacked and routed them, killing 5, wounding several, and taking 9 prisoners, 6 horses, a yoke of oxen, and burned down the houses in which they were quartered. Lowerburn, a noted guerrilla, was killed.

---

[*] Compiled from nominal list made by Lieutenant Willis, acting assistant adjutant-general.

DECEMBER 15, 1861.—Capture of the sloop Victory.

Report of Brig. Gen. Joseph Hooker, U. S. Army.

HEADQUARTERS HOOKER'S DIVISION,
Camp Baker, Lower Potomac, Maryland, December 17, 1861.

GENERAL: I have this moment received a communication from Maj. George H. Chapman, Third Indiana Cavalry, dated Millstone Landing, December 15, 1861, informing me that his pickets had captured a sloop engaged in the rebel trade, and is now awaiting instructions concerning her. She is now at the mouth of the Patuxent. His letter relating to this subject is as follows:

A party of my men captured a sloop, the Victory, of Baltimore, of about 40 tons burden, with a small lot of contraband goods on board. Those on board deserted her on the appearance of my men, and succeeded in making their escape. She was taken near Spencer's Landing, about 7 miles above here. I found on board 86,250 percussion caps, 43 pounds flax thread, 87 dozen fancy brass buttons, 2 boxes of needles, 1 sack of gum shellac, a box of carpenter's tools, 1 carpet-sack and contents, consisting of wearing apparel and some silver forks, spoons, &c., marked J. C. M. and McC., a trunk and its contents, mainly clothing, and $25,328.17 in promissory notes, payable to Hamilton Easter & Co., of Baltimore, on parties throughout the Southern States, directed to Mr. James H. Weedon, 9 Pearl street, Richmond, Va., care Messrs. J. B. Ferguson & Co., with letters of instruction accompanying. I have brought the sloop to this landing. I very much regret that my men did not catch those on board. I will make such disposition of the sloop and things on board as you may direct. The caps are suitable for Colt's revolvers, I believe. I regret that my men are not so armed.

In my opinion the best disposition to be made of her will be to have her, with the property, brought up the Potomac to Liverpool Point with her freight, and shall request the officer in command of the lower flotilla to have a crew placed on board for that purpose. On her arrival the freight can be forwarded directly to Washington, and the sloop, if found suitable, I should like to have retained here for service in the quartermaster's department. This disposition will be made of this prize unless I should be otherwise instructed.

I have now three companies of cavalry operating between Port Tobacco and the mouth of the Patuxent, and it will be much more convenient for them to draw their forage and subsistence from Baltimore than from this point. They should be landed at Millstone Landing, which is in direct steamboat communication with Baltimore. This arrangement will save 60 miles land transportation over horrible roads. I have given directions for Major Chapman to make his requisitions on the heads of those departments in Baltimore, and request that those officers may be directed to honor them.

Very respectfully, your obedient servant,

JOSEPH HOOKER,
Brigadier-General, Commanding Division.

Brig. Gen. S. WILLIAMS, *Adjt. Gen., Army of the Potomac.*

DECEMBER 15-17, 1861.—Operations on the Lower Potomac.

Report of Brig. Gen. S. G. French, C. S. Army.

HEADQUARTERS,
Evansport, December 17, 1861.

SIR: I have not deemed it necessary to report to you the actions of the enemy in front of us. For the last three weeks they have daily opened more or less fire on us from small rifled guns in position on the Maryland shore.

On Sunday last 2 men were severely wounded by a shell, and to-day 2 more were slightly wounded. Eighty-three shells were thrown at the battery to-day. Under this fire teams cannot safely cross the plain to the batteries, and much labor has to be done at night. We could easily silence their fire, but have not ammunition to spare. A battery of light rifled pieces could be advantageously used in replying to them, if necessary. One charge of a heavy gun would make ten or twelve for the latter, and spare powder to a great extent. I am nearly destitute of transportation.

Very respectfully, your obedient servant,

S. G. FRENCH,
Brigadier-General, Commanding.

General S. COOPER,
Adjutant and Inspector General, Richmond, Va.

DECEMBER 15-21, 1861.—Expedition to Meadow Bluff, West Virginia.

Extract from "Record of Events," return of the Department of Western Virginia, for the month of December, 1861.

On the 15th, Col. George Crook, Thirty-sixth Ohio, detached Maj. E. B. Andrews, same regiment, who, with 150 men, proceeded by the Wilderness road to Meadow Bluff; found the rebel encampment there deserted; burned 110 well-built log huts, some tents, &c.; captured two noted guerrillas, 21 rifles and guns, and 21 mules and horses, 95 cattle, and 200 sheep, and returned on the 21st, having had a brush with some rebel cavalry, which fled, in which 2 of our privates were wounded. Major Andrews deserves credit for the conduct of the expedition and the map of the route.

DECEMBER 18, 1861.—Reconnaissance to Pohick Church, Virginia.

REPORTS.

No. 1.—Col. Amor A. McKnight, One hundred and fifth Pennsylvania Infantry.
No. 2.—Capt. John P. Fowler, First New Jersey Cavalry.

No. 1.

Report of Col. Amor A. McKnight, One hundred and fifth Pennsylvania Infantry.

HEADQUARTERS ONE HUNDRED AND FIFTH PA. VOLS,
Camp Jameson, Va., December 19, 1861.

SIR : In obedience to your orders I left this camp at 9 p. m. of the 18th instant with a force consisting of the regiment under my command, a squadron of the New Jersey Cavalry, under Captain Jones, and two sections of artillery, under Lieutenant Monroe, New Jersey Volunteers, and arrived at Potter's house within half a mile of the extreme outposts of our pickets on the right near 11.30 p. m. I found that the pickets had been undisturbed, and immediately proceeded to distribute my force as would best support the pickets and preserve the force itself, should we be attacked. No demonstration was made by the enemy during the night. I left Potter's house for Pohick Church about three-quarters of an hour after daybreak, having been detained that long in developing a movement to capture some of the enemy, but which proved abortive.

We arrived at Pohick about 9 a. m.; was informed that the previous day the enemy had there a force of 200 cavalry, and also a regiment of infantry concealed in the woods to the west of the village. Remained at Pohick about two hours; sent a party down the Telegraph road and discovered, about a mile distant, a rebel picket 6 or 8 strong; fired at them and they fled, but did not pursue, as my instructions did not allow me to proceed beyond this point. Left Pohick Church between 11 and 12 a. m. and returned to camp at 3.30 p. m. Came by the village of Accotink, and was there informed that no rebel forces had been in the village for over a month.

Respectfully submitted.

A. A. McKNIGHT,
Colonel One hundred and fifth Regiment Pa. Vols.

General S. P. HEINTZELMAN.

DECEMBER 20, 1861—9 a. m.

I have at this moment learned from one of my command, who penetrated about a mile and a half beyond Pohick Church along the Colchester road, that he was informed by Mrs. Murray (a farmer's wife residing on the road) that about 10 o'clock a. m. of the 18th instant a force of the enemy numbering near 500 cavalry and a regiment of infantry had passed along the road towards Pohick Church, and that about 6 p. m. of the same day another force of the rebel cavalry, 200 strong, had passed forward in the same direction. She did not see the party return, and the information I have from other sources induces me to believe they went back on the Telegraph road. The advanced enemy's pickets on this road are stationed on a run (name unknown) a few rods west of Mr. Lee's house and about one and three-fourths miles from Pohick Church.

Very respectfully, &c.,

A. A. McKNIGHT,
Colonel One hundred and fifth Regiment Pa. Vols.

[Indorsement.]

HEADQUARTERS DIVISION,
Fort Lyon, December 20, 1861.

This expedition was conducted by Colonel McKnight with much judgment.

Respectfully forwarded.

S. P. HEINTZELMAN,
Brigadier-General, Commanding.

———

No. 2.

Report of Capt. John P. Fowler, First New Jersey Cavalry.

CAMP CUSTIS, VA., *December* 18, 1861.

SIR: I have the honor to report, according to instructions I left with my squadron this morning on a reconnaissance in the neighborhood of the Bone Mill, but finding everything quiet in that direction I proceeded to unite my squadron in the neighborhood of Pohick Church (on my way thither meeting and dispersing some rebel infantry), where Lieutenant Sackett with my second company, consisting of 51 men, was in command, who on arriving there found a number of rebel vedettes, whom he succeeded in driving from their posts after the first fire. On following up their retreat the advance guard of the rebels was discovered. They immediately opened fire on us, but with no result. We returned fire and emptied 4 of their saddles. They retreated on their main body, and with little delay on their part they returned towards us with a large body both of infantry and cavalry and again fired on us. On again returning their fire we succeeded in emptying a few more saddles of their riders. Their large force coming up at this moment compelled us to retire some three-quarters of a mile, where we formed in line of battle. At this time I sent forward the advance guard of both companies, who again met the rebel guard. The rebels immediately turned and fled, we firing on them in their retreat. Their superior force compelled me to act cautiously, and I succeeded in bringing back in safety my entire squadron.

I have the honor, sir, to subscribe myself yours, very respectfully,

JOHN P. FOWLER,
Commanding Squadron.

Brigadier-General HEINTZELMAN, *Commanding Division.*

[Indorsement.]

HEADQUARTERS DIVISION,
Fort Lyon, December 20, 1861.

This detachment of the New Jersey cavalry behaved very well in this attack upon them. The officer is, however, mistaken as to the injury done the enemy. He severely wounded 1 man and disabled 1 horse.

Respectfully forwarded.

S. P. HEINTZELMAN,
Brigadier-General, Commanding.

DECEMBER 19, 1861.—Skirmish at Point of Rocks, Maryland.

Report of Lieut. Col. Gabriel De Korponay, Twenty-eighth Pennsylvania Infantry.

HDQRS. TWENTY-EIGHTH REGIMENT PA. VOLS.,
Point of Rocks, Md., December 19, 1861.

GENERAL: At 10 o'clock this morning the rebels opened a battery of two pieces (guns, brass mounted) from a point near summit of Catoctin Mountain, opposite here, upon our encampment. They were supported with from 150 to 200 infantry. They threw about 20 fuse and percussion shells and solid shot into our midst with great precision in rapidly succeeding shots. The six companies of my command in camp were deployed in places of security, and the section of our battery stationed here opened upon the enemy from an elevation on the margin of the camp with great accuracy of aim. The first shot disabled one of their guns, and the succeeding ones fell so rapidly in their midst that they ceased firing in twenty minutes and retreated precipitately under our fast-continued fire to the reverse side of the mountain out of view. After firing about twelve shots from the first position our guns were advanced to a point back of the village, where they poured successive shots into the enemy's ranks. The whole engagement lasted over half an hour. A third gun advancing by a side road on the mountain to strengthen them was driven back.

Finding that about 150 rebels were secreted in a number of old huts near the "Furnace," their intention being to concert with forces above, our guns were directed from the river bank towards them, driving them out and forcing them to retire.

I have not ascertained how many of the attacking party were killed or wounded, nor of the loss sustained by those in the houses, but I am satisfied it is considerable. Our men behaved with admirable coolness and bravery, and the guns were well served. None of our men were injured, although many narrow escapes were made. The majority of the enemy's shells imbedded themselves in the ground without exploding, and were afterwards dug out. Everything is now quiet, and no enemy are in view.

I have the honor to be, very respectfully, your obedient servant,

GABRIEL DE KORPONAY,
Lieutenant-Colonel, Comdg. Twenty-eighth Regiment Pa. Vols.

The ADJUTANT-GENERAL U. S. A., *Washington, D. C.*

DECEMBER 20, 1861.—Engagement at Dranesville, Va.

REPORTS, ETC.

No. 1.—Brig. Gen. George A. McCall, U. S. Army, with congratulatory response and orders.
No. 2.—Brig. Gen. E. O. C. Ord, U. S. Army.
No. 3.—Col. Thomas L. Kane, First Pennsylvania Reserve Rifles.
No. 4.—Lieut. Col. William M. Penrose, Sixth Pennsylvania Reserve Infantry.
No. 5.—Col. Conrad F. Jackson, Ninth Pennsylvania Reserve Infantry.
No. 6.—Col. John S McCalmont, Tenth Pennsylvania Reserve Infantry.
No. 7.—Capt. Thomas McConnell, Tenth Pennsylvania Reserve Infantry.
No. 8.—Col. John H. Taggart, Twelfth Pennsylvania Reserve Infantry.
No. 9.—Capt. Hezekiah Easton, First Pennsylvania Reserve Artillery.
No. 10.—Return of casualties in Union forces.
No. 11.—Brig. Gen. J. E. B. Stuart, C. S. Army.

No. 1.

Reports of Brig. Gen. George A. McCall, U. S. Army, with congratulatory response and orders.

DRANESVILLE, *December 20, 1861.*

Ord's brigade, with the First Rifles and Easton's battery, had a brisk affair with four regiments and a battery of the rebels at 12 m. to-day. I arrived during the action, and sent for Reynolds, who was left at Difficult Creek. The enemy was defeated, and fled before Reynolds arrived. We have found 40 killed of the enemy and 10 wounded on the field. Our loss, 2 killed and 3 wounded.* We have taken two caissons,

---

*See report No. 10, p. 489.

with the harness, the horses having been killed, The Rifles behaved finely. Lieutenant-Colonel Kane very slightly wounded, but still in the field. I have collected the dead and wounded, and am about to move back to camp.

GEO. A. McCALL,
Brigadier-General, Commanding.

General McCLELLAN.

—

HEADQUARTERS McCALL'S DIVISION,
Camp Peirpoint, December 22, 1861.

GENERAL: I have the honor to present for the information of the General-in-Chief a more detailed account of the affair at Dranesville on the 20th instant, together with the reports of Brig. Gen. E. O. C. Ord, commanding Third Brigade of my division, and the commanders of the Sixth Infantry, Lieut. Col. W. M. Penrose; of the Ninth Infantry, Col. C. F. Jackson; of the Tenth Infantry, Col. J. S. McCalmont; of the Twelfth Infantry, Col. J. H. Taggart; of the First Rifles, Lieut. Col. T. L. Kane; of two squadrons of the First Cavalry, Lieut. Col. J. Higgins; and Easton's battery, Capt. H. Easton, Pennsylvania Reserves.

On the evening of the 19th, having learned that the enemy's pickets had advanced to within 4 or 5 miles of our lines and carried off two good Union men and plundered and threatened others and that their reserve was in the neighborhood of Dranesville, I gave written instructions to Brigadier-General Ord to move with his brigade at 6 a. m. on the 20th to surround and capture this party, and at the same time to collect a supply of forage from the farms of some of the rank secessionists in that vicinity.

Brig. Gen J. F. Reynolds, with the First Brigade, was directed to move on to Difficult Creek, to be ready to support Ord in the event of his meeting a force stronger than his own.

At 10.30 a. m. on the 20th I received a dispatch from General Ord, written on the march, informing me that the guide had learned on the way that there was a full brigade, but without artillery, at Herndon's Station, 500 infantry and cavalry at Hunter's Mill, and 200 infantry between Dranesville and the Potomac. I immediately mounted my horse, and with my staff and an escort of cavalry moved rapidly forward to overtake, if possible, Ord's brigade. I stopped for a few moments with Brigadier-General Reynolds at Difficult Creek, and having directed him to be in readiness to move forward rapidly in case he should be required to support Ord, I rode on. When within about 2 miles of Dranesville I heard the first gun fired by the enemy. It was soon answered by Easton's battery, which imparted to me the fact that the enemy had artillery with them.

A rapid ride soon brought me to the field, where Ord was hotly engaged. I found Easton's battery judiciously placed, and in full blast upon the enemy's battery, about 500 yards in front, on the Centreville road. Here I stopped to observe the practice of our battery, while one of my staff rode off to ascertain where General Ord was. While here, admiring the beautiful accuracy of the shot and shell thrown by this battery upon the battery of the enemy, a force of infantry and cavalry made their appearance from cover on the enemy's right, moving in a direction to turn our left. Colonel McCalmont, whose regiment was on the left, was notified of this movement, but a few shell from our battery skillfully thrown into their midst checked their advance and drove them back ignominiously to cover.

Not hearing anything of General Ord, I sent out in search of him on our right, where brisk firing was at the time going on. Here was the Ninth Infantry, Colonel Jackson, who had gallantly met the enemy at close quarters and nobly sustained the credit of his State.

By this time Captain Scheetz, of my staff, reported that he had found General Ord near the center front. Proceeding there, I found the Rifles and a part of the Sixth Infantry Pennsylvania Reserves engaged under a brisk fire with the enemy. Having met General Ord, we moved forward, and the position where the enemy's battery had been placed was soon gained, and here we had evidence of the fine artillery practice of Easton's battery. The road was strewed with men and horses; two caissons, one of them blown up; a limber; a gun-carriage wheel; a quantity of artillery ammunition, small-arms, and an immense quantity of heavy clothing, blankets, &c.

The battle was now over and the victory won. With my consent General Ord made an advance of about half a mile, but nothing further was to be done, as the enemy in full flight had passed beyond our reach. I then recalled Ord, and prepared for the return of my command. I ordered the harness to be taken off the enemy's horses which lay dead in the road and to be put upon horses of my escort, and brought away the perfect caissons and the limber.

Early in the day, not knowing what force might be thrown forward from Centreville to support the troops we had encountered, I had called forward Brigadier-General Reynolds, First Brigade, and Brigadier-General Meade, Second Brigade, from Camp Peirpoint, to the support of the Third Brigade. Both these distinguished officers promptly brought forward their commands, and I only regretted that the fine disposition of the regiments and battery of Ord's command, together with the gallantry of Colonels Jackson, McCalmont, and Taggart, and Lieutenant-Colonels Kane, Higgins, and Penrose, and Captain Easton, had left nothing for Reynolds and Meade to do. The rout of the enemy was complete; but as I did not consider it justifiable to bivouac at Dranesville when my ammunition was much exhausted and the enemy might easily throw 10,000 or 20,000 men between me and my camp during the night, I ordered every arrangement to be promptly made for the return march. Some time was required to prepare our wounded (60 officers and men) to be transported to camp, and it was very nearly dark before I got the column in motion. Our killed and wounded, as well as so many of the rebel wounded as could be moved, were brought away.

The troops we had engaged and defeated were the First Kentucky Regiment, Col. Tom Taylor, about 800 strong on the field; the Tenth Alabama, Colonel Forney, 900 strong; a South Carolina regiment, whose colonel was not known to the prisoners in our possession, who informed me that no intercourse between different regiments was ever allowed, and a Virginia regiment. The Kentucky prisoners informed me they believed a fifth regiment was present, as two or three regiments had left Centreville at 3 a. m., and they, the Kentucky and Alabama regiments, together with Captain Cutts' Georgia battery and Stuart's Virginia regiment of cavalry, left at 5 a. m. The whole were under command of Brigadier-General Stuart.

General Ord reports as worthy of notice his personal staff, and also Colonels McCalmont and Jackson, Lieutenant-Colonel Kane, Captains Easton, First Pennsylvania Artillery; Niles, First Rifles; Bradbury, Sixth Infantry Pennsylvania Reserves; and Dick and Galway, Ninth Infantry Pennsylvania Reserves.

The number of killed found in front of the position occupied by the

Ninth Infantry, Colonel Jackson, is in my estimation proof enough of the gallantry and discipline of that fine regiment; but where all behaved nobly it is difficult to discriminate. I must, however, call your attention more particularly to Brig. Gen. E. O. C. Ord, commanding Third Brigade, for whose able disposition of his regiments and battery and personal exertions to encourage and urge on his men too much credit cannot be accorded him.

To Capt. H. J. Biddle, assistant adjutant-general, of my staff; Lieut. H. A. Scheetz, aide-de-camp; Captain Clow, brigade commissary, acting aide-de-camp; and Lieut. E. Beatty, ordnance officer, acting aide-de-camp, my thanks are due for their gallantry in carrying orders under fire and for encouraging and urging on the men, and also to Captain Chandler Hall, brigade quartermaster, who was energetically employed in collecting forage. It is proper to mention that deeming it necessary to leave one of my staff at headquarters to superintend the telegraph and to order forward the reserve, viz, the Second Brigade and three squadrons of cavalry, if required, the lot fell upon my aide-de-camp Lieut. Elbridge Meconkey, who discharged this responsible duty entirely to my satisfaction.

Seven prisoners were taken.*

*   *   *   *   *   *   *

The want of ambulances was felt on this occasion, and I would respectfully suggest that a few more be ordered to each regiment of my division, as I was unable for want of transport to bring from the field all the wounded prisoners taken in the affair. Those left I had placed in comfortable quarters in Dranesville, where they can be well attended to, but owing to this deficiency of transportation for the wounded I was compelled to leave in the hands of the enemy some of my prisoners. Last, not least, I brought in sixteen wagon loads of excellent hay and twenty-two of corn.

The following list of killed and wounded on our side is, I regret, greater than I at first reported, viz, 7 killed and 61 wounded, including 1 lieutenant-colonel and 4 captains, and 3 missing.†

From what I have gathered from various reliable sources I am satisfied that the loss of the enemy was, at the very least, 90 killed left on the field, besides those carried off, among whom was certainly Col. Tom Taylor, commanding the First Kentucky Regiment, whom the Kentucky prisoners in my custody state they saw fall from his horse. Colonel Forney is also said to have been killed. This, however, is not so satisfactorily ascertained. General Stuart is reported by one of the prisoners to have been killed or wounded.

I have the honor to be, very respectfully, your obedient servant,

GEO. A. McCALL,
Brigadier-General, Commanding Division.

Brig. Gen. S. WILLIAMS, *Assistant Adjutant-General.*

WAR DEPARTMENT,
Washington, December 28, 1861.

Brig. Gen. GEORGE A. McCALL,
Commanding Division, Camp Peirpoint, Va.:

GENERAL: I have read your report of the battle of Dranesville, and although no reply is necessary on my part, yet as a citizen of the same

---

*Names omitted.   † See report No. 10, p. 489.

Commonwealth as yourself and the troops engaged in that brilliant affair, I cannot refrain from expressing to you my admiration of the gallant conduct displayed by both officers and men in this their first contest with the enemy. Nearly all of your command upon that occasion are either my personal friends or sons of those with whom for long years I have been more or less intimately associated. I feel that I have just cause to be proud that, animated by no other motive than patriotism, they are among the first to revive the glory shed upon our country by the men of the Revolution and the soldiers of the war of 1812. It is one of the bright spots that give assurance of the success of coming events, and its effect must be to inspire confidence in the belief that hereafter, as heretofore, the cause of our country will triumph. I am especially gratified that a Pennsylvania artillery corps, commanded by officers who have necessarily had but limited systematic instruction, have won not only the commendation of their friends, but an unwilling compliment from the enemy for the wonderful rapidity and accuracy of their fire. I wish I could designate all the men who, nobly discharging their duty to the country, have added to the glory of our great Commonwealth. Other portions of the Army will be stimulated by their brave deeds, and men will be proud to say that at Dranesville they served under McCall and Ord.

I am, general, very respectfully, your obedient servant,
SIMON CAMERON,
Secretary of War.

—

GENERAL ORDERS, }   HDQRS. ARMY OF THE POTOMAC,
No. 63.   }   *Washington, December* 28, 1861.

The Commanding General expresses his thanks to Brigadier-General Ord and the brave troops of his brigade, who so gallantly repelled an attack of an equal force of the enemy on the 20th instant. The General takes pleasure in observing the readiness of the remaining troops of McCall's division, and the able dispositions of their commander to repel the enemy in case of the advance of re-enforcements.

The General would also acknowledge the distinguished services of Colonel McCalmont, Tenth Infantry Pennsylvania Volunteer Reserve Corps; Colonel Jackson, Ninth Infantry Pennsylvania Volunteer Reserve Corps; Lieutenant-Colonel Kane, Rifle Regiment Pennsylvania Volunteer Reserve Corps; and Captain Easton, of Easton's battery, which contributed in a large degree to the success of the day.

By command of Major-General McClellan:

S. WILLIAMS,
Assistant Adjutant-General.

———

No. 2.

Report of Brig. Gen. E. O. C. Ord, U. S. Army.

CAMP PEIRPOINT, VA., *December* 21, 1861.

SIR : I have to report that, in obedience to the inclosed order, I at 6 a. m. yesterday started towards Dickey's and Henderson's, about 3 miles this side of Dranesville, on the Leesburg pike, with my brigade, the First Rifles, Lieutenant-Colonel Kane; Easton's battery, and two squadrons of cavalry. I likewise heard that it was probable there was a respectable picket of cavalry at Dranesville, and that the picket supposed by you to be near the river behind Dickey's had left. I then determined to send three companies of the Tenth and 20 cavalry with the foraging party to Gunnell's, between the pike and the river, and with the remainder of the force proceed to Dranesville, satisfied that, though I might be exceeding the letter of my instructions, should I find the enemy and pick up a few you would not object. This I did, though Colonel McCalmont, hearing that there was a large force on our left, remained with his part of a regiment, and that detained the two regiments behind him. I had sent for them, but was obliged to enter Dranesville with my artillery and cavalry and a small advance guard only on the road, the First Rifles and Colonel Jackson's regiment flanking this column in the woods on the right and left.. The cavalry picket in town fled and scattered and remained in small squads watching.

While waiting in Dranesville for the regiments in the rear to come up, I posted my artillery and cavalry and Jackson's regiment of infantry and a couple of companies of the First Rifles so as to cover the approaches, and sent for Colonel Kane's regiment to occupy the road in our then rear, my front being towards Centreville. This I did because from the occasional appearance of a few mounted men on a slope behind some woods in a hollow to my left and front, and a broad mass of smoke in that neighborhood, I felt pretty sure there was a force there preparing some mischief. As soon as Colonel McCalmont came up with his regiment (the Tenth), followed by Lieutenant-Colonel Penrose (the Sixth), and Colonel Taggart with the Twelfth, and while preparing to resist any attack and to cover my foraging party, I learned that the enemy in force had approached on the south side of the Leesburg pike with field pieces and infantry, and had driven in my pickets, wounding 2 men. Thinking they would attack on both sides of the turnpike as I returned eastward, I ordered (to meet this expected attack) Colonel McCalmont's regiment on the left or river side of the road in the woods, left in front, and if the enemy showed himself on that side to bring his regiment forward into line; Colonel Jackson's regiment (of which and its gallant colonel I cannot speak in too high terms) I ordered to flank the road in the same way on the right of the road in the woods, and do the same if the enemy showed on that side. Between these flanking regiments I ordered the Kane Rifles to meet the enemy behind us in the road, the cavalry to follow, and the artillery I took with me to post them and answer the enemy's artillery, which had opened fire on our then right (the south), directing the rear guard to cover the column of the Sixth and and Twelfth Regiments of Infantry in the road from cavalry.

The artillery went at a run past the station I selected for them, capsizing one of their pieces. I brought them back, told the captain where to post his guns, and then went to remove the cavalry, then exposed in the road swept by the enemy, whose attack was from a thickly-wooded hill on our right flank (the south). Their force I saw was a very bold one, very well posted, and the artillery was only about 500 yards off, with a large force of infantry on both its flanks and in front, covered and surrounded by woods and thickets. Moving east with the cavalry, which was of no use here, I came to a place in the road covered towards the enemy by a high bluff and dense thicket, which thicket I intended to occupy with infantry. Here I left the cavalry surrounded by dense forests, wherein they could neither fight nor be hurt. The accompanying sketch will show the ground.*

As I had at first thought the enemy would attack on both sides the

---

* Not found.

road and moved my infantry to meet such an attack, and as their attack was confined to the right, it became necessary for me to change my front. As neither McCalmont nor Jackson had had time to come into line under first orders when I discovered this, and were moving by the flank, and as before I placed the artillery and cavalry I had seen the Rifles closely engaging the enemy by a flank movement, covering themselves by some houses and fences, my right in meeting the attack thus became the village of Dranesville, my left the gorge and woods occupied by my cavalry on the Leesburg pike.

After securing the cavalry, I found by carefully observing the enemy's fire and battery that their guns were in a road which could be enfiladed. I ordered Captain Easton to right the capsized gun and bring it to the spot from which this road could be raked, removed two other guns to this spot, gave the gunners the distance and elevation, observed the result, and finding after a round or two that the enemy's fire slackened and the gunners were raking the road beautifully without being discomposed by the enemy's fire, I told them "to keep at that," and determined to push the infantry forward. I found them (except the Kane Rifles, the Ninth (Jackson's), and the Tenth (McCalmont's), Regiments, which were, as above stated), in the ditches, under fences, and covering themselves as best they could. I started them forward, Kane at the head of his regiment leading. His and Jackson's regiments required no urging. McCalmont's regiment was kept in excellent order by its colonel—than whom a better officer is not found in my brigade—and acted as a reserve. I put them in the woods, pushed and exhorted them up the hill, having directed the battery to cease firing, and proceeding with my infantry with the bayonet.

About this time, between 3 and 4 o'clock (the action began at 2.30), General McCall, I was informed, arrived on the field. As I was very busy urging the men forward, and they required all my attention to keep them to their work, I did not at once report, but when we reached the ground occupied by the enemy's battery I reported to him. He was so kind as to direct me to continue the pursuit in the same order and to continue my dispositions, which I did. The enemy were pursued fully half a mile farther, but they had left the neighborhood in great haste, leaving their arms, a portion of their dead and wounded, clothing, 10 horses, and a quantity of artillery equipments, with 2 caissons and a limber, scattered along the road towards Centreville and in the woods on both sides.

I beg to mention the coolness and courage of my aides, Captain Painter, assistant quartermaster; First Lieut. S. B. Smith, Tenth Regiment Pennsylvania Reserve Corps; First Lieut. S. S. Seward, New York Artillery, and Second Lieut. A. B. Sharpe. They not only carried orders promptly, but in instances requiring it exacted obedience. They deserve a more exalted rank than that they now hold.

The medical officers (especially the brigade surgeon, Dr. Lowman) were prompt and cool, leaving none unattended. The enemy left 21 of their most desperately wounded on the field, who were taken up, carried to houses, and their wounds dressed by our surgeons; but they will nearly all die. Their dead left on the field is variously estimated from 50 to 75.

Our artillery did terrible havoc, exploding one ammunition wagon, and some of their men whom we brought in say the slaughter was terrible. Several dead lay around the exploded caisson, 3 of whose blackened corpses were headless. The prisoners further state that Colonel Taylor was doubtless killed. Two of their officers were left on the ground, and how many were carried off it is difficult to say. After the affair we built our bivouac fires in Dranesville.

Thus, sir, we, on returning to camp, had marched 24 miles, beaten the enemy, loaded our wagons with forage, bringing in (12 miles) our killed (7) and wounded (60), among whom are 4 captains. .Some of our wounded had to be brought the whole distance on stretchers, while I am informed the Pennsylvania ambulances for this division are lying empty at Washington. Lists of killed and wounded and reports of regimental commanders are herewith inclosed.

It is impossible to remember all who were conspicuous, especially as the fighting occurred in thickets and was scattered over much ground. Captain Easton was very efficient and his battery well served.

The wounded officers, Lieutenant-Colonel Kane and Captain Niles, of the Kane Rifles; Captain Bradbury, of the Sixth, and Captains Dick and Galway, of the Ninth, Pennsylvania Reserve Volunteer Corps, were conspicuous, leading their men when wounded. Others there were, as you can well imagine, equally brave, but it would be invidious to attempt to select them.

The prisoners report that the brigade engaged against us was composed of the Kentucky Rifles, an Alabama, a South Carolina, and a Virginia regiment, with a 6-gun battery, all under the command of General Stuart.

I must not forget the prompt manner in which General Reynolds came up from Difficult Creek, some 4 miles off, as soon as he heard the cannonading. He arrived too late, it is true, to take part in the affair, but the certainty that he would come with his brigade insured a victory, and stimulated our men to earn it.

With respect, sir, your obedient servant,

E. O. C. ORD,
Brigadier-General Volunteers.

Capt. H. J. BIDDLE,
Assistant Adjutant-General, McCall's Division.

[Inclosure.]

HEADQUARTERS McCALL'S DIVISION,
Camp Peirpoint, Va., December 19, 1861.

GENERAL: You will please move in command of your brigade at 6 a. m. to-morrow, on the Leesburg pike, in the direction of Dranesville. The First Rifles, Pennsylvania Reserves, Lieutenant-Colonel Kane, have been ordered to form right in front on the pike near Commodore Jones' house and await your arrival, when the commanding officer will report to you for further orders.

Captain Easton's battery has been directed to form on the left of the Rifles. The captain will report to you for orders.

Two squadrons of cavalry will also be placed under your command. The senior officer will report to you this evening for orders. Sherman, the guide, will likewise report to you for duty.

The object of this expedition is twofold: In the first place, to drive back the enemy's pickets, which have recently advanced within 4 or 5 miles of our lines (leaving a force of about 70 cavalry at Henderson's), and carried off two good Union men, and threatened others; and, secondly, to procure a supply of forage.

It has to-day been reported to me that there is a force of about 100 cavalry lying between Dranesville and the river. This force might be captured or routed by sending a regiment of infantry up the pike beyond their position, to strike their rear by a flank movement to the right, while your disposable cavalry, after picketing the cross-roads near Dickey's, might move near the river, and attack them in front or on the left. Should you not arrive at Dickey's in time to make this movement and leave the ground on you return before nightfall, it must not be undertaken, as I do not wish any part of your command to remain out over night.

The forage will be procured at Gunnell's or at some other rank secessionist's in the neighborhood of Dickey's. Direct your quartermaster to confine the selection of forage to corn and hay. Captain Hall will have charge of the wagon train. The regiment intended to move forward from Dickey's (if you think proper, Jackson's) might ride in the wagons as far as Dickey's, and then be fresh for the forward movement.

I am, very respectfully, your obedient servant,

GEO. A. McCALL,
Brigadier-General, Commanding Division.

Brig. Gen. E. O. C. ORD,
Commanding Third Brigade.

No. 3.

Report of Col. Thomas L. Kane, First Pennsylvania Reserve Rifles.

HDQRS. KANE RIFLE REGT., FIRST PA. RES. RIFLES,
Camp Peirpoint, December 21, 1861.

GENERAL: Acknowledging the honor of your orders of December 21, I think I may limit my report to an explanation of my conduct at the commencement of the action before your own welcome appearance upon the scene to push on the fight and inspirit and direct the brave by your personal example and exertions.

We were not quite through with scouring the woods south of Crepplin's, under your first orders, when your aide-de-camp brought the order to return to Dranesville. A party who sought me privately in the absence of the guide (Mr. Hanna) had informed me of suspicious circumstances, which I desired to report to you. I therefore marched to Dranesville very rapidly. It was from the first high ground north of the turnpike fork that I first saw men in motion south and southeast of the village, where there seemed to be no reason to look for the presence of our own forces. Soon after a Confederate flag was displayed, and as we opened in sight a few shots were fired. Others of the enemy also at the same time appeared in view from the edge of the woods on our extreme left. Being fortunately familiar with the ground, I saw at once the importance of occupying the hill on which the brick house stands, which was occupied in October as the headquarters of General McCall, and reaching it before the enemy. My men, obeying the double-quick with spirit, were formed there in line of battle by the time the enemy's guns opened from the road. As soon as I conveniently could I sent my adjutant to you and our brave commander. I believe, sir, you were both good enough to approve of my course in taking this position. The enemy's opinion of its value was shown by the effort to turn it afterwards. You saw the rest. The Bucktails will not forget you.

Of my own officers and the men I love I am too proud to say more than that they all, without an exception, did their duty; but it is my place to mention the courage of Captain Ent during the brief period when you were good enough to place the Sixth under my command. I cannot consider it out of place, either, for me to bear my own testimony to the admirable conduct of Captain Easton and the brave artillerists with him, who served the guns of Battery A, from the regiment of the gallant Charles T. Campbell.

I inclose a copy of the report of Dr. S. D. Freeman, regimental surgeon, showing a list of 3 killed and 27 wounded.* I trust the life of Captain Niles will be spared to his friends and his country. He led the flankers on the left yesterday, and though his tall figure made him a conspicuous mark for the enemy's rifles, he did not cease exposing himself to cheer on his men until he fell. This was but little before the enemy retired.

Very respectfully, your obedient servant,

THOMAS L. KANE.

Brig. Gen. E. O. C. Ord.

No. 4.

Report of Lieut. Col. William M. Penrose, Sixth Pennsylvania Reserve Infantry.

HDQRS. SIXTH REGIMENT INFANTRY, PA. R. V. C.,
Camp Peirpoint, December 21, 1861.

SIR: I herewith transmit you list of the killed and wounded of my command at the battle of Dranesville yesterday, December 20.* The conduct of the troops under my command was all that could be desired, officers and men generally behaving with great coolness and bravery. I would particularly mention as deserving of much praise Lieutenant Bonawitz, of Company K, and Adjutant McKean, for their gallant and soldierly bearing; also Surgeon Bower, who was in the first fire of the enemy, and provided efficient means for bringing in the wounded, not only of our own but other regiments, and rendering them timely assistance.

Very respectfully,

W. M. PENROSE,
Lieutenant-Colonel.

Brig. Gen. E. O. C. Ord.

No. 5.

Report of Col. Conrad F. Jackson, Ninth Pennsylvania Reserve Infantry.

HDQRS. NINTH REG'T PENNSYLVANIA RESERVE CORPS,
December 21, 1861.

SIR: In accordance with your order of this date, to make out an official report of the conduct of my command in the engagement at Dranesville, I would respectfully state that in obedience to orders I marched my regiment into the wood or copse, formed in line of battle, and advanced as directed, with difficulty restraining the men from

---

* See report No. 10, p. 489.

double-quick. As there was nothing to indicate the position of friend or foe, I advanced until we saw and heard the movements of troops in advance of the right of our line. I halted, and formed my right within 60 or 70 paces of the left of the troops referred to. My men showed a great anxiety to fire. At this time an officer of my regiment reported that the troops opposite were the Bucktails. Determined to avoid falling into the fatal error of killing our own men, I at once used all my energy to prevent firing, nor did we fire until after we had received a volley from the enemy, as they proved to be. We received their first fire as Captain Galway was in the act of reporting that he had obtained a view of them, and assured me in the most emphatic manner they were rebels. The order to fire was then given and promptly obeyed, but I found there still existed a doubt on the part of the men as to the true character of the troops we were engaged with, which caused considerable confusion in the ranks, which was overcome to a great extent with some difficulty. I feel perfectly convinced, had the men been assured at the onset that the troops before us were rebels, we might have driven them from their position before they could have fired on us, as we could hear them distinctly load their pieces.

I afterwards learned that the impression that the Bucktails were forming in front was strengthened by the following occurrence: One of the enemy called out, "Don't fire on us." One of my men imprudently asked, "Are you the Bucktails?" The answer was, "Yes, we are the Bucktails; don't fire."

I inclose surgeon's report of killed and wounded.*

Your obedient servant,

C. FEGER JACKSON,
Colonel, Comdg. Ninth Regiment Pennsylvania Reserve Corps.

General E. O. C. ORD.

No. 6.

Report of Col. John S. McCalmont, Tenth Pennsylvania Reserve Infantry.

HDQRS. TENTH REGIMENT PENNSYLVANIA RESERVES,
THIRD BRIGADE, MCCALL'S DIVISION,
Camp Peirpoint, December 21, 1861.

SIR: I have the honor to report the part that the Tenth took in the engagement of Dranesville yesterday.

Two of my companies were on outer picket, and ordered to remain; three were detailed to cover and furnish fatigue party for the division quartermaster, under command of Lieutenant-Colonel Kirk. A platoon of skirmishers remained by mistake with the foraging party. With the remaining four companies and a platoon I marched in advance of the Sixth and Twelfth to Dranesville, where we had been preceded by the advance of the brigade. At Dranesville, after a short halt, we received orders to return, as the object of the reconnaissance was accomplished. Immediately thereafter the general of brigade informed us that the pickets of the Ninth had been driven in on our right. At the same time there was firing on the left of the line. The general having moved the battery to the left, ordered me to flank the column

---
* Embodied in No. 10, p. 489.

and take position on the left of the battery, under cover. In marching we passed through the field directly in rear of our battery, which
had commenced unlimbering under a smart and direct fire from the
enemy's guns. We took our position near the battery in a growth of
cedars on its left.

Being so posted, under orders from the general, I detached Captain
McConnell, with his platoon, as skirmishers, to approach the cannoneers
of the enemy, and see if the enemy was endeavoring to turn our left.
I believe this order was in all respects coolly, gallantly, and effectively obeyed. I inclose herewith the captain's report. He soon sent
me word that the enemy had broken under the fire of artillery and musketry on the right, mostly in a southerly direction. The affair was soon
over.

The general then gave me orders to flank and support the Bucktails
and Twelfth, which were in pursuit. While doing so we observed some
of the enemy's wounded, whom I directed the attendants to remove to
the brick house close by. A number of the enemy's rifles, muskets, caps,
overcoats, &c., were picked up by the hospital attendants and servants.
After this we were ordered to take position south of Dranesville. It
was reported to me by an officer of the Ninth that they had observed
from the hill where they were posted after their gallant conflict a white
flag south of us at a house. Major Allen led a small party to ascertain,
but found none but female inmates, one of whom had appeared with a
white head-dress, which occasioned the mistake.

Our skirmishers observed wagon and horse and foot tracks through
the fields leading south of Dranesville, and on all the by-roads, of which
there are quite a number in that vicinity. They reported that one horse
had leaped quite a high fence, but I did not inquire in which direction,
as such incidents merely afford the men amusement after the fatigue of
the day. We were recalled to take our position in line on the road, preparatory to marching back to camp.

Under circumstances new to nearly if not quite all of this regiment,
it behaved well, and I believe obeyed with spirit every order. I have
occasion to be thankful that I have the honor to report none killed,
wounded, or missing. The men doubtless wished to seal their devotion to the Union and their confidence in their generals with their
wounds. If the rebellion continues, they will likely have other opportunities.

I have the honor to be, sir, respectfully, your obedient servant,

JOHN S. McCALMONT,
Colonel, Commanding Regiment.

Lieut. S. B. SMITH,
A. A. A. G., *Hdqrs. Third Brigade, McCall's Division.*

No. 7.

Reports of Capt. Thomas McConnell, Tenth Pennsylvania Reserve Infantry.

CAMP PEIRPOINT, *December* 21, 1861.

SIR: I have the honor to make the following report:

Shortly after the regiment was placed in the woods by the direction
of General Ord, near Easton's battery, I received your orders to take

the first platoon of my company (the second platoon, under Lieutenant Pattee, having been placed with Lieutenant-Colonel Kirk as a portion of the foraging party) out some distance to the left flank of our line and pick off the artillerymen of the enemy. I immediately marched forward, and when we came to the edge of the woods I found that the enemy's artillery was being removed farther back, but discovered a number of infantry on the extreme right of their line advancing toward us as though they intended flanking us. I then ordered my men to secrete themselves in some deep gullies and fire upon them, which they immediately did so well as to force them back. They then advanced again, and again were forced to retreat. I then moved still farther to our left, so as to defeat any flank movement. Any of the enemy found to the right of their artillery I believe were killed by my men, there being no other troops firing upon the right of their line. I observed a mounted officer of the enemy fall, and believe they carried him off the field. None of my command dead, wounded, or missing.

I have the honor to be, very respectfully,

THOS. McCONNELL,
Captain Company B.

Col. J. S. McCALMONT.

—

CAMP PEIRPOINT, VA., *January* 3, 1862.

SIR: I have the honor to submit the following statement of the battle of Dranesville, which occurred on the 20th December, 1861, my first report being rather brief on account of the haste in which it was prepared.

When the attack was made upon the skirmishers of the Ninth Regiment and Kane's regiment, our battalion was just outside of Dranesville, the artillery and cavalry being in front of us, the Sixth and Twelfth Regiments just in our rear. You then ordered the men to load, and immediately thereafter to give way on the right and left, so that the battery might assume a position in our rear, our troops being in column of platoon, and thus occupying almost the entire road. You then ordered us by the left flank through the fields on the northern side of the road, the fences soon being removed by the pioneers, and at the same time cheered the men by encouraging remarks and by boldly leading the way. When we came opposite Easton's battery, against which the heavy fire of the enemy was almost constantly directed, the balls from their guns flew thick and fast, but fortunately for our gunners and our battalion their aim was too high, all their shells and balls passing over us. Here we moved out to the turnpike, marching by the right flank, and when near Easton's battery you marched us by the left flank and filed right into the woods, our right resting near the turnpike, the entire battalion half-facing towards our battery.

Being on the left of the battalion, you directed me to throw out my platoon to the outer edge of the woods, just by the Alexandria and Leesburg turnpike, with instructions to pick off, if possible, the gunners of the enemy, and at the same time to keep a good lookout that we were not flanked by the enemy on the left. (Here allow me to state that Lieutenant Pattee, with my second platoon, had attached himself to Lieutenant-Colonel Kirk's foraging party, and was not present until after the engagement was over.) When I marched to the opening of the woods I observed one gun of their battery retiring, the others having already disappeared, but at the same time saw a body of infantry on their right, approaching no doubt for the purpose of flanking us and thus succeeding in taking our battery.

We had then to advance 10 or 15 paces for the purpose of secreting ourselves in some deep gullies or trenches, natural rifle pits, or to fall back and in the thick woods protect ourselves. Choosing the former, I ordered my men forward double-quick, and in a moment they were all well secreted. The number under me was then greatly increased by the sergeant of pioneers bringing his men out and stationing them just by mine, placing them under my command. I then ordered all to fire, which order was so well obeyed that the enemy were instantly thrown into confusion, and after another fire retreated to the woods from which they had just advanced. With the exception of a few adventurers who came outside the woods we saw no more of them for some minutes, but soon they rallied in considerable numbers and engaged us warmly during the remainder of the battle, their balls falling thick around, but no one, I am happy to state, receiving any injury therefrom; our men, in the mean time, under my direction, keeping close under cover and reserving their fire until sure of their mark.

Being cautioned by you to look well to the left, in order to prevent a flank movement by the enemy upon the battery after the charge was made by the other regiments of our forces, I ordered my men, the pioneers, and all others who had joined us during the engagement, to march some distance down the Alexandria turnpike, and there remained until I was satisfied that the enemy had retreated, and then marched back and joined our battalion.

I cannot speak too highly of the coolness and courage of the men whilst under fire, and also of the manner in which Sergt. John Gundy, of the pioneers, and the pioneer corps, performed their duty.

I beg leave to state that some three of my men (Sergeant Gundy, of the pioneers, being one, and Sergeant Gilleland another) went over the field after the action and counted 27 men killed (2 being officers) and 2 wounded of the enemy, all by rifle balls, which, from the position of the forces, could not have been reached by any of the infantry engaged in the action except by those under me.

All behaved well and gallantly, but it becomes my duty, under your instruction, to select a limited number to commend to your special notice for recommendation to the State and National Governments. This is not a pleasing duty, but it must be performed.

For coolness, gallantry, and activity in firing and in obeying orders, I therefore mention: First Sergeant David Farrell, Company B, of battalion; Third Sergeant David Gilleland, Company B, left general guide; Sergeant John Gundy, of Company D, commanding pioneers; Corporal Irvine Miller, Company B; Privates Samuel B. Clawges, W. J. McGinn, John McCann, W. B. Gibson, George Wareham, of Company B, and Pioneers Walter D. Byers and George Kelso, Company B; John W. Waterhouse, Company F; Hugh Barnes, Company K, and Eli J. Ague, and John H. Walker, Company B.

I have the honor to be, your obedient servant,

THOS. McCONNELL,
Captain Company B, Tenth Regiment Pennsylvania Reserves.

Col. J. S. McCalmont.

No. 8.

Report of Col. John H. Taggart, Twelfth Pennsylvania Reserve Infantry.

HEADQUARTERS TWELFTH REGIMENT, THIRD BRIGADE,
McCALL'S DIVISION, PENNSYLVANIA RESERVE CORPS,
Camp Peirpoint, December 21, 1861.

GENERAL: Pursuant to orders from brigade headquarters, the regiment under my command, numbering 575 officers and men, marched out upon the Dranesville pike yesterday morning between 6 and 7 o'clock, took position on the left of the brigade, and advanced towards Dranesville. Nothing of special importance occurred until about 1 mile west of Difficult Creek, when the scouting parties reported that a considerable force of the enemy, numbering about four regiments, were drawn up on a field about 1 mile to the left of our line, apparently watching our movements. I immediately halted my regiment upon receiving this information and formed line of battle facing the enemy, but as they showed no disposition to engage, after waiting some time the regiment was again put in march towards Dranesville.

On approaching the village our flanking parties were driven in by a large force of the enemy who were posted in the woods, a dense thicket of pines, on our left. Our scouts reported that they had been fired on by troops concealed in the woods. The fire was returned, when the enemy in large numbers showed themselves and pursed our scouts for some distance towards the left of my regiment, which was instantly halted and formed into line to receive the attack on the turnpike road. My right rested on the hill leading into Dranesville, and the left opposite a brick house on the left of the pike, and behind which the enemy appeared to be in force.

At this juncture Adjt. S. B. Smith was dispatched to you on the right of the brigade, informing you of the state of affairs. Your immediate presence at the scene of attack, and the timely support of the other regiments of the brigade, the Kane Rifle Regiment, the cavalry force, and Easton's battery, are facts which came under your own notice, and therefore need no further mention from me.

Before the regiments had got fairly into position the enemy opened with a heavy fire of shot and shell, which fell thick and fast in the vicinity of the left of my regiment. The shells at first exploded in our rear, tearing up the ground and splintering the fences in every direction, but fortunately did no damage to the men under my command. After firing about fifteen minutes the enemy succeeded in getting a better range, and the shells burst over our heads, but without injury, the men on the left, the most exposed portion of the regiment, being ordered to lie flat on the ground.

Easton's battery now opened upon the enemy from our left with such effect that the firing from the enemy ceased for a time, and we were relieved from the most annoying situation in which a soldier can be placed, that of receiving a fire from the enemy without returning it, which we could not do, as the enemy were entirely hidden from view. The conduct of the men during the time they were under fire, nearly all of them for the first time, was most commendable. There was no flinching, and the line was preserved unbroken.

At this time, by your orders, I dismounted, leaving my horse in the road, and on foot conducted the charge of my regiment into a dense woods opposite the right wing for the purpose of capturing the enemy's battery. We advanced into the woods as rapidly as the nature of the ground and the dense growth of timber would permit, without finding the enemy. We then advanced with a full battalion front to the left, where a heavy firing of musketry was going on. Before we emerged from the woods the firing ceased. We soon gained an open field, in the direction of the enemy, where we halted and awaited orders, which were received from you, to charge into a wood in our front and take the enemy's battery, which was believed to be only a short distance from us. This order was instantly obeyed, and the Twelfth Regiment dashed into the woods. We scoured the thickets in every direction without finding the battery, but discovered dead bodies of the rebel troops lying in every direction, besides a number of wounded, who were properly taken care of and sent to the rear. We continued the pursuit for a considerable distance without meeting the enemy, but on every side there were evidences of a precipitate flight—arms, ammunition, clothing, and provisions being strewed around in every direction.

By your orders we were recalled, and returned by way of a road we had crossed before charging into the woods. Here we discovered the location of the enemy's battery by the piles of cannon balls, shells, and munitions of war. There was one gun-carriage destroyed by the pioneers of my regiment, which was found damaged from the effects of our shot and shell.

The conduct of the officers and men, under the difficult circumstances in which they were placed, in searching a dense forest for a hidden foe, was eminently satisfactory. I desire to mention particularly the services rendered by Quartermaster E. D. Reid, who acted as my adjutant on the occasion. None of the field officers were on duty except myself, and but three captains out of nine. Notwithstanding these disadvantages, the subaltern officers and the men conducted themselves with spirit and bravery, and obeyed with alacrity the orders given them.

I am gratified to have only one casualty to report. Private William R. Fox, of Company K, was shot in the right thigh during the first part of our advance into the woods. The wound is not serious. He made a narrow escape. A porte-monnaie in his pocket was bored through, and a $2.50 gold piece in it was bent nearly double.

I have the honor to be, general, your obedient servant,

JOHN H. TAGGART,
Colonel, Commanding Twelfth Regiment P. R. C.

Brig. Gen. E O. C. ORD,
Commanding Third Brigade, McCall's Division, P. R. C.

No. 9.

Report of Capt. Hezekiah Easton, Battery A, First Pennsylvania Reserve Artillery.

ČAMP PEIRPOINT, *December* 21, 1861.

GENERAL: I have the honor to report that, in obedience to orders from Brigadier-General McCall, commanding this division, I reported to you on the morning of the 20th of this month, at 6 o'clock a. m., and from thence proceeded with my battery, Company A, First Pennsylvania Artillery, in connection with your brigade, to a point on the Leesburg turnpike near Dranesville. No appearance of the enemy was visible until we reached Thornton's house, near the junction of the Alexandria and Leesburg turnpike, when a heavy fire of artillery and musketry was suddenly opened from a thick woods on our left, the enemy evidently lying in large force in ambuscade, while their artillery was posted on the Centreville road, leading through the wood and coming into the Alexandria turnpike between Thornton's and Coleman's houses. My guns were immediately put into battery and opened fire. Having nothing to indicate the position of the enemy but the smoke of their guns, I opened a brisk discharge of shells into the woods occupied by the enemy, which was kept up until your order to cease firing. The examination of the ground afterward showed the successful and destructive effects of our artillery fire. The rebel battery, in my opinion, was unmanned by our third fire. They succeeded in drawing off their guns, but I captured one caisson and one limber, and one other was exploded and the horses fatally injured. The woods in which the enemy were concealed were found thickly strewn with dead and wounded. The mangled bodies of the dead showed the terrible execution of our fire. Besides the ordnance captured, a large quantity of clothing, blankets, knapsacks, haversacks, &c., was found, which the enemy had cast off in their hasty and thorough rout.

I have the satisfaction to state that, although the injury and loss of the enemy was so severe, in my battery there was not a man or horse lost and no injury done my guns. Our only casualty was the slight wounding of one of my men (Charles Osborn), who was struck in the knee by a spent ball, which slightly lamed him.

I have only to add that I was firmly supported by a detachment of the Tenth Regiment (Colonel McCalmont's), and that my whole company, officers, non-commissioned officers, and men, acted with skill and energy and courage worthy the highest praise.

Respectfully submitted.

H. EASTON,
Captain, Commanding Battery A, First Reg't Pa. Art.

Brig. Gen. E. O. C. ORD,
Third Brigade, P. R. C.

No. 10.

*Return of casualties in the Union forces in the engagement at Dranesville, Va., December 20, 1861.**

Command.	Killed.		Wounded.		Missing.		Aggregate.	Remarks.
	Officers.	Enlisted men.	Officers.	Enlisted men.	Officers.	Enlisted men.		
First Pennsylvania Reserve Rifles		3	2	24			29	
Sixth Pennsylvania Reserve Infantry		2	1	12			15	
Ninth Pennsylvania Reserve Infantry		2	2	18			22	
Tenth Pennsylvania Reserve Infantry								No casualties.
Twelfth Pennsylvania Reserve Infantry				1			1	
First Pennsylvania Reserve Artillery, Battery A.				1			1	
First Pennsylvania Reserve Cavalry								No casualties.
Total		7	5	56			68	

*Compiled from records in the Adjutant-General's Office.

No. 11.

Reports of Brig. Gen. J. E. B. Stuart, C. S. Army.

DRANESVILLE, VA., *December* 21, 1861.

We had a hard-fought battle here yesterday. I had four pieces and four regiments, say 1,200 strong. The enemy had from five to ten regiments, six or seven pieces artillery. They said 3,100. Finding heavy re-enforcements arriving, I withdrew my command in perfect order from the field, carrying off nearly all the wounded. The enemy's loss was over 50 killed; our killed 27. They evacuated at dark. I will return to Centreville to-day.

In haste.

J. E. B. STUART,
Brigadier-General.

Gen. D. H. HILL.

—

HEADQUARTERS OUTPOSTS ARMY OF THE POTOMAC,
December 23, 1861.

MAJOR: I have the honor to report that on the 20th instant I was placed in command of four regiments of infantry, 150 cavalry, and a battery of four pieces of artillery, viz, Eleventh Virginia Volunteers, Col. S. Garland, jr.; Sixth South Carolina Volunteers, Lieutenant-Colonel Secrest; Tenth Alabama Volunteers, Col. J. H. Forney, and First Kentucky Volunteers, Col. Thomas H. Taylor, making an aggregate force of 1,600 infantry; Sumter Flying Artillery (four pieces), Capt. A. S. Cutts; One hundredth [?] North Carolina Cavalry, Major Gordon, and Fifty-second [?] Virginia Cavalry, Captain Pitzer, for the purpose of covering an expedition of all the wagons of our army that could be spared (after hay) to the left of Dranesville.

I proceeded at once by the nearest route at daylight towards Dranesville, and the accompanying sketch* will show the route as well as the relative situation of other objects of interest in what I am about to narrate.

Knowing the situation of the enemy's advance posts, I sent the cavalry forward far in advance of the infantry, to take possession of the two turnpikes to the right of Drainesville, leading directly to the enemy's advanced posts, so as to prevent any communication of our movements reaching them, and with the main body I followed on to take a position with two regiments and a section of artillery on each turnpike, also to the right of Dranesville, and close enough to their intersection to form a continuous line.

Such a position I knew I could hold against almost any odds, but as my cavalry came in sight of the turnpike, Captain Pitzer discovered the enemy at the point (A) on the ridge and sent me word immediately. I galloped forward at once, and, reconnoitering for myself, found that a portion of the enemy was in possession of the ridge, and I could hear distinctly artillery carriages passing up the Georgetown turnpike in considerable numbers, and presently saw the cannons mounted on limber-boxes passing up towards Dranesville, about 200 yards from the intersection (A). I knew, too, that the enemy's infantry were in advance, and I at once suspected that he was either marching upon Leesburg or had received intelligence through a spy of our intended forage expedition and was marching upon it. In either case our wagons would have

---
* Not found.

fallen an easy prey to him, and I saw at once that my only way to save them was to make a vigorous attack upon his rear and left flank and to compel him to desist from such a purpose.

I sent back for the infantry to hurry forward, and sent Captain Pitzer with his detachment of cavalry to gain the roads towards Leesburg, give notice to our wagons to return at once to camp, and keep between them and the enemy, threatening his front and flank; and I will state here, parenthetically, that this duty was performed by Captain Pitzer and his gallant little detachment in the most creditable manner; all our wagons reaching camp safely.

In the mean time the enemy's skirmishers took possession of the dense pine in our front, and as our infantry was met by my messenger three-fourths of a mile back, it was some time coming up. Colonel Garland's regiment, leading, was directed to deploy two companies on each side of the road to clear the ground of the enemy's skirmishers. One of these companies, having mistaken its direction, went too far to the right, and Colonel Garland had to replace it with another. The pines were cleared at double-quick, and the battery was ordered in position at (B), and fired very effectively during the whole of the engagement to the front.

The infantry were placed in position as follows: Garland's regiment on the right of the road, a little in advance of the artillery; Secrest's (South Carolina) on the left of the road. Forney's regiment, arriving later, replaced Garland's, which moved by the flank to the right, and the First Kentucky, Colonel Taylor, at first intended as a reserve, was ordered to take position on the left of the Sixth South Carolina.

As our infantry was well secured from the enemy's view, their artillery fire, which opened about fifteen minutes after ours began, had little effect upon the infantry, but played with telling effect along the road, as from its position (C) and the straightness of the road in our rear it raked the latter with shell and round shot completely. Their caissons and limbers were behind in a brick house completely protected from our shot, while our limbers and caissons were necessarily crowded and exposed. There was no outlet to right or left for a mile back by which the artillery could change its position. When our forces took their position the fire of the artillery caused great commotion in the enemy's lines and a part evidently took to their heels.

The right wing was ordered forward, and the Tenth Alabama rushed with a shout in a shower of bullets, under the gallant lead of their colonel (Forney) and Lieutenant-Colonel Martin, the latter falling in the charge. A part of this regiment crossed the road and took position along a fence, from which the enemy felt the trueness of their aim at short range. The colonel was here severely wounded and had to retire. In his absence the command devolved upon Major Woodward.

The Eleventh Virginia, holding position on the right of the Tenth Alabama, were not so much exposed to the fire of the enemy, and consequently suffered less. The Sixth South Carolina gradually gained ground also to the front, and being, together with the Tenth Alabama, exposed to the fire of the enemy's sharpshooters from a two-story brick house, suffered most.

My orders to Colonel Taylor, First Kentucky, were given through Colonel Forney, and I soon knew by the commotion on my left that it was in place. The thicket where the Sixth South Carolina and First Kentucky operated was so dense that it was impossible to see either [their] exact position or their progress in the fight, and I regret to say that the First Kentucky and the Sixth South Carolina mistook each other for the enemy, and a few casualties occurred in consequence, but with that exception the whole force acted with admirable unison, and advanced upon the enemy with the steadiness of veterans, driving him several times from his position with heavy loss.

When the action had lasted about two hours I found that the enemy, being already in force larger than my own, was recovering from his disorder and receiving heavy re-enforcements. I could not, with my small numbers, being beyond the reach of re-enforcements, force his position without fearful sacrifice, and seeing that his artillery, superior to ours in numbers and position only, was pouring a very destructive fire into Cutts' battery, I decided to withdraw the latter at once, preparatory to retiring from the field, judging, too, that I had given our wagons ample time to get out of reach of the enemy.

The battery suffered greatly. Its position was necessarily such that it could fire only to the front, and the caissons and limbers had no cover whatever from such a fire. Three or four cannoneers had been shot at their posts and several wounded, and every shot of the enemy was dealing destruction on either man, limber, or horse.

The conduct of the brave, true, and heroic Cutts attracted my admiration frequently during the action—now acting No. 1, and now as gunner, and still directing and disposing the whole with perfect self-command and a devotion to his duty that was, I believe, scarcely ever equaled. He executed my orders to withdraw his battery under a ricochet fire of great accuracy.

One piece I found it necessary to detail some infantry (Eleventh Virginia) to assist in conducting to the rear, which was done by them under great personal exposure.

Having secured the artillery, I sent orders to the four regimental commanders to disengage themselves from the enemy and retire slowly and in perfect order to the railroad, where a stand would be made. This delicate duty was performed admirably, and our troops marched back leisurely, bringing with them all the wounded that could be found.

The men gathered up their blankets as they passed the points where they had been deposited before the fight. I regret to say, however, that one of the regiments reached the road this side of their blankets and knapsacks, thus missing them entirely; a circumstance which the enemy will construe into precipitate flight. The enemy was evidently too much crippled to follow in pursuit, and after a short halt at the railroad I proceeded to Fryingpan Church, where the wounded were cared for.

Early next morning, with the two fresh regiments furnished me (the Ninth Georgia and Eighteenth Virginia), and a detachment of cavalry, under Lieutenant-Colonel Baker, I proceeded towards the scene of action of the previous day, the cavalry being sent in advance. Learning that the enemy had evacuated Dranesville and had left some of our wounded there, I pushed on to that place to recover them and to take care of the dead. I found our dead on the field, and proceeded at once to remove them all to Centreville for interment. The wounded (about 10) were left by the enemy at a house at Dranesville, who intended to send for them the next day. They had been cared for with the utmost devotion by several of the ladies of the place. They were also removed to Centreville, except two, who were not able to survive the removal, who at their own desire and at the surgeon's advice were left in charge of the ladies.

As to the strength of the enemy, if the concurrent statements of the citizens residing on his route of march can be credited, he had fifteen regiments of infantry, several batteries, and seven companies of cavalry. The latter had started in the direction of our wagons just before the action began, but were then recalled.

Our wounded, who were for the time prisoners, say that the enemy's loss was acknowledged by them to be very heavy, and among the officers killed or mortally wounded was Colonel Kane, of Utah notoriety ; and citizens living below declared that they carried off twenty wagon loads of killed and wounded, besides many dead before them on their horses, and that as soon as their dead and wounded were removed they left the field precipitately, leaving behind much of the material which we left on the field, but which we recovered next day.

I cannot speak in too high terms of Colonel Forney, that gallant son of Alabama, whose conspicuous bravery, leading his men in a galling fire, was the admiration of all ; nor of his lieutenant colonel (Martin), who, with the battle-cry of forward on his lips, fell, bravely encouraging his men. Nor can I do more than simple justice to the officers and men of that regiment, who seemed determined to follow their colonel wherever he would lead.

Colonel Garland and Major Langhorne, of the Eleventh Virginia, behaved with great coolness under fire, and the men of that regiment, though deprived by locality from sharing as much of the danger of the engagement as the Tenth Alabama Regiment, yet acquitted themselves to my entire satisfaction.

The Sixth South Carolina and First Kentucky were, I regret to say, too much screened from my view to afford me the privilege of bearing witness, by personal observation, of individual prowess, but that the Sixth South Carolina, under the fearless Secrest, did its whole duty; let the list of killed and wounded and her battle-flag, bathed in blood, with its staff shivered in the hand of the bearer, be silent but eloquent witnesses. Their major (Woodward) was painfully wounded, but bore himself heroically notwithstanding; while the telling report I could distinctly hear from the left assured me that the First Kentucky, under the gallant Taylor, the intrepid Major Crossland, and daring Desha, was all right.

Our battery's loss in killed and wounded was great, and the men deserve great credit for their devotion to their pieces under such perilous circumstances.

The detachment of North Carolina cavalry, under Major Gordon, was of great service in watching the approaches to our flanks, though the ground was extremely unfavorable for cavalry.

The attention of the general commanding is respectfully called to the detailed reports of commanders of regiments and corps, and to the special mention made by them of individual prowess.

Colonel Taylor became separated from his regiment in passing from its left to its right and found himself beyond the enemy's lines, but by great coolness and presence of mind he extricated himself and joined his regiment that night.

My thanks are due to my adjutant-general, Captain Brien; my aide, Chiswell Dabney, jr.; Lieutenants Throckmorton and Johnson, of the Fairfax Cavalry, and Lieutenant Jackson (aide to General Jones), volunteers for the occasion, for valuable services on the field. Lieutenant Throckmorton accompanied Captain Pitzer and was conspicuously useful during the day, and Lieutenant Johnson was of great service to me.

Corporal Henry Hagan, of [the] First Virginia Cavalry, was of great service in showing the First Kentucky its position in line, and proved himself on this as on every other occasion worthy of a commission.

Redmond Burke, Chief Bugler Steele, Privates Lewis, Barnes, Harris, Barton, Landstreet, Routh, Brigman, Thompson, and Carroll, of my escort, deserve my thanks for their promptness and accuracy in conveying orders and instructions.

Had we effected the safety of our wagons—constituting the greater part of the available means of transportation of this army—with great loss to ourselves, without inflicting much on the enemy, alone would have been a triumph of which the brave men of the four regiments under my command could be proud; but when it is considered what overwhelming odds were against us, notwithstanding which we saved the transportation, inflicted upon the enemy a loss severer than our own, rendering him unequal to the task of pursuit, retired in perfect order, and bringing with us nearly all our wounded, we may rightly call it a glorious success.

Our entire loss is as follows:

	Killed.	Wounded.	Missing.
Eleventh Virginia Volunteers	6	15	
Sixth South Carolina Volunteers	18	45	
Tenth Alabama Volunteers	15	45	6
First Kentucky Volunteers	1	23	2
Cutts' battery	3	15	
Cavalry			
Total	43	143	8

The list of killed has been materially increased by deaths which have occurred since the battle, as the number found dead on the field was only 27.

I have the honor to be, major, respectfully, your obedient servant,

J. E. B. STUART,
Brigadier-General, Commanding.

Maj. THOMAS A. PRATT, *Assistant Adjutant-General.*

DECEMBER 24-25, 1861.—Scout towards Fairfax Court-House, Va.

Report of Lieut. Henry Schickhardt, Thirty-first New York Infantry.

CAMP THIRTY-FIRST NEW YORK VOLUNTEERS,
December 26, 1861.

SIR: In obedience to orders received I started on a scout towards Fairfax Court-House on the 24th instant, accompanied by Lieutenant Frossard, of this regiment, and 2 men of my company. Between the hours of 3 and 11 p. m. on that day we traversed the whole section of country lying between Accotink Creek and the Little River turnpike, but without going farther north than the Falls Church and Fairfax Court-House road, without seeing an enemy, although their many tracks gave evidence of their frequent passage in almost every direction. During the entire night we heard heavy firing in a southwesterly, also in a northeasterly direction. We also heard noises which evidently came from a scouting party of the enemy on the railroad grading which runs from Annandale to Fairfax Court-House.

On the 25th, about 5 a. m., we advanced cautiously through the woods on the north side of the Little River turnpike, when just beyond the trees felled near the road we discovered the enemy's advanced pickets seemingly extended in a line running from north to south about 1¾ miles this side of Fairfax Court-House. There were no fires to be seen along this line, and the line appeared strong and well guarded, as we saw parties of 25 or 30 men stationed at single points. Not being able to advance any farther we retraced our steps, arriving at our advanced posts at about 11 a. m.

According to the statements of some farmers professing loyalty, it appears that the scouting parties of the enemy consist mostly of cavalry, which is used almost exclusively for outpost duty. Whenever the rebels expect an attack on their line they draw their pickets within about half a mile of Fairfax Court-House, and from what I saw and learned I have reason to believe that they would not make a stand this side of their barricades. I would state that from what I learned I am convinced that at the recent advance, on the 18th instant, of the enemy, their entire force consisted of only three companies of infantry, two of cavalry, and one piece of artillery. This movement was executed with great rapidity.

Finally, I would call your attention to the imprudence of some of our advanced posts. In returning from our scouting expedition, when near the bridge beyond Annandale, we met a party of some 15 men belonging to the Thirty-fifth Pennsylvania, who were out without a commissioned or other responsible officer, and whose carelessness was such, that had a party of the enemy come down the road they could have easily killed or captured them all. This party was also engaged in burning a barn situated on the Little River turnpike, about 1 mile beyond Annandale. The carelessness of the outposts of Blenker's division in giving and receiving the countersign signals is in my opinion highly reprehensible.

I am, sir, very respectfully, your obedient servant,

H. SCHICKHARDT,
Lieutenant, Co. E, Thirty-first New York Volunteers.

Capt. E. SPARROW PURDY,
Assistant Adjutant-General, Alexandria Division.

DECEMBER 28, 1861.—Beckley (Raleigh Court-House), W. Va., occupied by Union forces.

Extract from "Record of Events," return of the Department of Western Virginia, for the month of December, 1861.

On the 28th, Colonel Scammon, Twenty-third Ohio, commanding Schenck's brigade, occupied Beckley, the capital of Raleigh County, a key point, where the route from Lewisburg to Kentucky crosses the turnpike from Great Falls to Wytheville, with four companies of infantry and one of cavalry. The move is one of great importance, stopping communication between the rebels in the central and western portions of the State.

DECEMBER 29, 30, 1861.—Capture of Suttonville (Braxton Court-House), and skirmishes in Clay, Braxton, and Webster Counties, West Virginia.

Extract from " Record of Events," return of the Department of Western Virginia, for the month of December, 1861.

On the 29th, Suttonville, garrisoned by one company (Rowand's) First Virginia Cavalry, was attacked by 135 rebel guerrillas. The company retreated to Weston, and the guerrillas burned the town and what commissary stores were there. Colonel Crook, with four companies, went in search of the same gang from Summersville, encountered the flying rascals in Clay and Braxton, killed 6, and chased and scattered them into the mountain towards the Glades.

On the 30th, Colonel Anisansel, with three companies of the First Virginia Cavalry and three of the Third Virginia Infantry, marched to punish the marauders, and pursued them into the Glades in Webster County, killed 22 and burned 26 houses, thus breaking up their nest.

JANUARY 3, 1862.—Descent upon, and skirmish at, Huntersville, W. Va.

REPORTS.

No. 1.—Maj. George Webster, Twenty-fifth Ohio Infantry.
No. 2.—Brig. Gen. William W. Loring, C. S. Army.
No. 3.—Brig. Gen. Edward Johnson, C. S. Army.
No. 4.—Col. George W. Hull, C. S. Army.
No. 5.—Capt. H. M. Bell, Assistant Quartermaster, C. S. Army.

No. 1.

Report of Maj. George Webster, Twenty-fifth Ohio Infantry.

HUTTONSVILLE, W. VA., *January 6*, 1862.

SIR : I have the honor to report that, in obedience to your orders, on December 31, 1861, at 1 p. m., I left this place with a detachment of 400 men of the Twenty-fifth Regiment Ohio Volunteers for Huntersville, Pocahontas County, West Virginia. At Camp Elk Water I was joined by a detachment of 300 men from the Second West Virginia Regiment, under Major Owens, and at Big Spring by a detachment of 38 cavalry, of the Bracken Cavalry, under First Lieutenant Delzell. I appointed First Lieut. Charles B. Jones, of the Twenty-fifth Ohio, acting adjutant.

On the morning of January 3, finding the road at the base of Elk Mountain, and for a distance of 1 mile, so obstructed by felled trees as to render the farther progress of teams impossible, I left my wagons and detached Captain Johnson, of the Twenty-fifth Ohio, with 50 of the most disabled men, to guard them. Avoiding the obstructions by a detour to the left, I pushed forward to Greenbrier River, and ascertained that a considerable number of militia were gathered at the bridge, 1 mile below, on their way to Huntersville. I directed Lieutenant Delzell with his detachment of cavalry to ford the river, and by a rapid movement across the river bottom to gain possession of the road in rear of the bridge. This he did in most gallant style, and cut off from Huntersville the entire militia force at the bridge, except a few mounted scouts. The balance fled back into the country, evidently in great confusion and dismay. Hastily detaching Captain Williams, of the Twenty-fifth Ohio, with 50 men, to hold the bridge, I pushed forward, and when 2 miles from town the enemy's pickets fired upon my advanced guard—Companies E and G, of the Twenty-fifth Ohio—but after a few shots retired.

The column moved forward, and 1 mile from town I discovered the enemy's cavalry at the extreme of a level bottom field, dismounted and posted over the brow of a hilly spur which jutted out into the field from their right, with Nap's Creek on their left. I immediately deployed a part of the Twenty-fifth Ohio up the hill to our left to turn the enemy's right, and with the balance of our force moved up in front. The enemy at once opened upon us and their fire became general, which was vigorously responded to by our men. They soon discovered my flank movement, however, and falling back to their horses hastily mounted and retreated.

I again moved the column forward, crossed Nap's Creek, and found the enemy posted upon a second bottom, extending from our right nearly across the valley and half a mile in front of town. I promptly deployed Companies A and B, of the Twenty-fifth Ohio, into line to our right, at the base of the hill, to attack the enemy's left, and directed Major Owens, with the Second West Virginia and Bracken Cavalry, to make a considerable detour, turn the enemy's right, and take him in rear. The balance of the Twenty-fifth Ohio I formed to attack in front. This disposition made and in the way of rapid execution under the enemy's fire, and Companies A and B having opened upon his left, the enemy again retired, mounted, and retreated into town. After a few minutes' rest I formed my command into two columns, the Twenty-fifth Ohio to move upon the right and the Second West Virginia and cavalry upon the left of the town. In this order the troops rushed forward, cheering, into town as the enemy, after a few inefficient shots, fled from the rear.

We found the place deserted, the houses broken open, and goods scattered, the cause of which was soon stated by a returned citizen. The rebel commander had ordered the citizens to remove all their valuable property, as he intended, if beaten, to burn the town. We found large quantities of rebel stores, consisting in part of 350 barrels of flour, 300 salted beeves, (about 150,000 pounds), 30,000 pounds of salt, and large amounts of sugar, coffee, rice, bacon, clothing, &c, all of which I caused to be destroyed by burning the building in which they were stored, having no means to bring them off. The value of the property thus destroyed I estimated at $30,000. Our forces captured and brought home a large number of Sharp's carbines, sabers, horse-pistols, and some army clothing.

The enemy had in the action 400 regular cavalry armed with Sharp's carbines, and several hundred mounted militia assembled from Pocahontas County the night before. There were also two companies of infantry quartered in town, but fled without making a stand. The enemy's loss is believed to have been considerable. It was reported by a citizen who returned at 1 killed and 7 wounded. Private Oliver P. Hershee, of Company E, Twenty-fifth Ohio, was seriously wounded in the arm. No other casualties occurred on our side. I nailed the Stars and Stripes to the top of the court-house and left them flying.

After remaining in town two hours I marched back to Edray through a drenching rain and sleet, having made 25 miles that day.

To-day I returned to Huttonsville with the detachment from the Twenty-fifth Ohio, having made a winter march of 102 miles in a little less than six days, and penetrated into the enemy's country 30 miles farther than any body of our troops had before gone. The men are in good condition, considering the march, and are in excellent spirits.

To my second in command, Major Owens, of the Second West Virginia; Captains Washburn, Williams, Johnson, Crowell, Green, and Askew; Lieutenants Higgins, Bowlus, Haughton, Blandy, and Ball, and Acting-Adjutant Jones, of the Twenty-fifth Ohio; to Captains Planky, Gibson, and McNally; Lieutenants West, Ecker, Day, Hunter, Smyth, Huggins, and Weaver, of the Second West Virginia, and to Lieutenants Delzell and Bassett, of the Bracken Cavalry, I desire to tender my acknowledgments for the prompt, efficient, and gallant manner in which they performed their respective duties on the march and in the action.

To the men composing my command generally too much praise cannot be awarded. During the lo g and weary march their spirits never flagged. They at all times cheerfully submitted to necessary discipline. For one hour and a half in which they were engaged in driving the enemy from cover to cover, a distance of 2 miles, not a man flinched.

I cannot close this report without expressing the deep obligations of myself and comrades of the Twenty-fifth Ohio to the officers and men of the Second West Virginia for the very hospitable manner in which we were entertained at Camp Elk Water last night, and thereby saved a night's exposure to a storm of rain, hail, and snow.

I have the honor to be, very respectfully, yours, &c.,
GEO. WEBSTER,
Maj. 25th Reg't Ohio Vols., Comdg. Huntersville Expedition.

Brig. Gen. R. H. MILROY.

No. 2.

Report of Brig. Gen. William W. Loring, C. S. Army.

HEADQUARTERS ARMY OF THE NORTHWEST,
January 6, 1862.

SIR: I have the honor to inclose a letter received from General Johnson, commanding the army on the Alleghany, and also one from Colonel Harman, at Staunton, informing me that the enemy were moving against Alleghany. I think re-enforcements ought to be sent him, but it will be impossible for me to do so from this portion of the army, now before the town of Hancock, too great a distance from his position, and he will have to be re-enforced from elsewhere.

I am, respectfully, your obedient servant,
W. W. LORING,
Brigadier-General, Commanding, &c.

Adjutant-General COOPER.

[Inclosure No. 1.]

CAMP ALLEGHANY, *January 2, 1862.*

Colonel HARMAN:

The enemy are at Greenbrier in considerable force. I think it likely I shall be attacked in the morning. We are able to hold our position. I received intelligence a day since from the commanding officer at Huntersville that he expected to be attacked by a large force. Our position may be turned. If the enemy get in our rear intelligence from us may be cut off; so you must look to your own expresses for intelligence from us. The enemy may attack here and at Huntersville. Should we be besieged, re-enforcements may be hurried out. You must keep yourself advised in this matter. I have sent for Scott and Goode to come up.

Respectfully, &c.,

E. JOHNSON,
Brigadier-General, Commanding.

[Inclosure No. 2.]

WINCHESTER, VA., *January* 4, 1862.

General W. W. LORING, *Commanding Army of the Northwest:*

GENERAL: I inclose you a letter from Gen. Edward Johnson, which I received just as I was leaving Staunton. I immediately telegraphed General Cooper, advising that two regiments be sent up to re-enforce him, if it was possible to do so, as the enemy might get to his rear by the Huntersville road and cut off his supplies. I write by this express to General Jackson, inclosing a copy of General Johnson's letter, thinking you might not be near him.

I am, very respectfully, your obedient servant,

M. G. HARMAN,
Lieutenant-Colonel, &c.

No. 3.

Report of Brig. Gen. Edward Johnson, C. S. Army.

HEADQUARTERS MONTEREY LINE,
Camp Alleghany, Va., January 4, 1862.

SIR: Intelligence has just been received that the enemy have entered Huntersville, and that the small force left there by General Loring, some 250 men, had fallen back towards Monterey. I have no authentic information as to the number of the enemy, but it is reported at from 4,000 to 5,000.

I received a communication a day or two since from the commanding officer at Huntersville, stating that he apprehended an attack from the direction of Elk Water. Since the withdrawal of troops from that line it has been at the mercy of the enemy. Colonel Goode, with his regiment, heretofore stationed at Forks of Waters, I ordered to Monterey; Colonel Scott, with his regiment, the Forty-fourth, is at Crab Bottom, some 6 miles from Monterey, in this direction. Both of these regiments are weak—together not exceeding 600 or 700 men. Here I have not in all 1,200 effective men. If it is intended to hold this line it is important that troops should be sent on the Huntersville line or to Monterey. The troops at Monterey, permanently stationed there, are some two or three companies of cavalry. I have sent scouts to ascertain the strength of the enemy at Huntersville. The stores there fell into the hands of the enemy. I got my intelligence from the commanding officer at Monterey, whose report I herewith transmit.

I have directed the commanding officer at Monterey to report directly to Richmond any additional intelligence he may receive. If the enemy advance towards Monterey in force, re-enforcements are imperatively required.

I am, sir, very respectfully, your obedient,

E. JOHNSON,
Brigadier-General, Commanding Monterey Line.

General S. COOPER,
Adjutant and Inspector General, Richmond, Va.

No. 4.

Report of Col. George W. Hull, C. S. Army.

POST MONTEREY, VA., *January* 4, 1862.

GENERAL; I am unofficially informed that a dispatch was sent to you last night from the commanding officer at Huntersville, informing you of the fall of that place, but do not know that it reached you, or was sent, as I was not informed of it until a few moments ago, when the scouts sent out on that road returned with the intelligence. The place, as I hear, was attacked by some 4,000 or 5,000 men yesterday at 1 a. m. Our troops offered but little or no resistance, being overpowered in numbers. They fell back, and are on their road to this post.

I have scouts out on the road to Huntersville some distance, and will keep you fully advised of any movement of the enemy that I may learn. Most, if not all, our stores fell into the hands of the enemy. Fire was set to the buildings, but it is not believed to have consumed them.

Very respectfully, your servant,

GEO. W. HULL,
Colonel Commanding Post.

General EDWARD JOHNSON, *Camp Alleghany, Va.*

No. 5.

Report of Capt. H. M. Bell, assistant quartermaster, C. S. Army.

STAUNTON, VA.,
Sunday Morning, January 5, 1862—5 a. m.

GENERAL: I send you inclosed copies of dispatches just received from Monterey by special express from Whitely. It appears that the enemy in considerable force have advanced upon and taken possession of Huntersville, our small force retiring before them and offering but small resistance. I have no further information upon the subject, but suppose Monterey will be their point of destination, as I suppose they will hardly risk an advance upon the Central road at Millborough with that force, although the movement would be entirely practicable.

I will hold the force of wagon trains here to carry up any re-enforcements that you may send until I hear from you. I want corn.

In haste, yours, respectfully,

H. M. BELL,
Captain and Assistant Quartermaster, Commanding Post.

General S. COOPER, *Adjutant-General.*

P. S.—I ascertained from expressmen that the occupation took place at 1 a. m. yesterday. The force that appeared in General Johnson's front had disappeared at daylight Friday morning, and had not been reported up to dark that night, and is doubtless the same force that is at Huntersville.

[Inclosure No. 1.]

POST MONTEREY, VA., *January* 4, 1862.

COLONEL: Yesterday about 1 o'clock the enemy advanced and took possession of Huntersville. Our forces offered but little resistance, their numbers, as I understand from a member of the Tennessee cavalry, being only about some 200 men, while that of the enemy could not be correctly estimated, but supposed to be about 4,500.

Our command at Huntersville is now on its road to this place and will be in to-night. I cannot give you an account of the fight, but sure it is that the town and all our stores are in the hands of the enemy, unless it be that a barn, in which some of the commissary stores were placed, was burned, as fire was communicated to it; but it might have been extinguished by the enemy, who were near at the time of setting fire to it. Nothing new from Alleghany.

Very respectfully, yours,

GEO. W. HULL,
Colonel, Commanding Post.

Col. JOHN B. BALDWIN, *Commanding Post, Staunton, Va.*

P. S.—We lost no men, and suppose the loss on the side of the enemy to be about 4.

[Inclosure No. 2.]

QUARTERMASTER'S OFFICE,
Monterey, Va., January 4, 1862.

CAPTAIN: I write to say that the Yankees, some 4,000 or 5,000 strong, have taken possession of Huntersville, and our forces, some 250 in number, have retreated to this place. What will happen next I cannot tell, but would not be surprised if their next move would be upon this place. I will keep you fully advised as to what may occur.

Very truly,

P. B. HOGE,
Captain and Assistant Quartermaster.

Capt. H. M. BELL.

JANUARY 12–23, 1862.—Expedition to Logan Court-House and the Guyandotte Valley, West Virginia.

Report of Col. Edward Siber, Thirty-seventh Ohio Infantry.

HDQRS. THIRTY-SEVENTH REGIMENT OHIO VOLUNTEERS,
Camp Clifton, January 23, 1862.

SIR: The high stand of the waters in Coal River did impede me from sending you particular reports concerning the expedition to Logan and the Guyandotte Valley. It was not before the evening of January 11 that I could get real information about the enemy I have been sent to pursue. On this evening some Union men opposite the side of Boone-town informed me that from Little Coal River to Guyandotte a great number of the inhabitants formed a company, which they called "Black Striped Company," and which may number about 60 or 70 men, for the most part of the poorest class, who never did act in any greater force than 10 or 15 men, but which such band did overrun the country between Guyandotte, Mud, and Coal Rivers. In consequence of this information I forded the Little Coal River on the morning of the 12th of January, and moved the same day four companies, under command of Major Ankele, to Chapmanville and on to Guyandotte, whilst one company, under Captain Messner, advanced by Turtle Creek towards the head of Mud River. One company remained with me at Ballard's, on Spruce Fork. All these detachments met with no resistance, because all male inhabitants of this part of the country had fled previous to their arrival to the other side of the Guyandotte. But the next morning, when Major Ankele moved up the right bank of the Guyandotte from Chapmanville, his column was fired at from every house on the opposite side of the river, which by this time was nowhere fordable. By this fire was mortally wounded Captain Goecke, of Company B, which exasperated the men of the regiment so much, that a number of them threw themselves in the river and reached by swimming the opposite bank, destroyed the houses from where they had been fired at, took away some rifles, and made some prisoners.

Having received the report of these unexpected hostilities, I hastened with the companies from Turtle Creek to join those in the Guyandotte Valley, which I reached in the morning of January 14. Marching with the whole detachment under my orders immediately and on both banks of the Guyandotte to Logan, I found this place completely evacuated by the whole male population, which, armed with rifles, had retreated to a steep mountain on the other side of the Guyandotte, where at the same time appeared a number of horsemen, and where had been assembled a number of bushwhackers. By all these was opened a sharp skirmishing fire upon my advanced scouts on the other bank of the Guyandotte and upon pickets which occupied the town. Corporal John Behm, of Company C, was killed on this occasion. The enemy, however, were driven back with loss of men on the road to Sandy. I remained during the night in the court-house at Logan, having occupied the position around it. Seeing, however, that this position was completely commanded by the mentioned mountain on the other side of the Guyandotte, the waters of which began by the heavy rain suddenly to rise, I ordered for the next morning at 4 o'clock the evacuation of the place, which under these circumstances could not be held without more sacrifice of life; and as the inhabitants of this town had acted with so much animosity and treachery, as besides the court-house of Logan and other public buildings of this place had been long ago converted into barracks, used as a principal point of refuge for the rebel cavalry, I thought it to be my duty to deprive the enemy of such position, only valuable to him and useless to us, and ordered to set fire to these buildings before my departure. I retreated through Crooked Creek, Hewitt Creek, and Spruce Fork to Boone, and succeeded in crossing Little Coal River before it became completely unfordable, but was stopped for some days at Peytona by the high waters of Big Coal River.

I have to report that, with the exception of a Union settlement in Hewitt and Spruce Fork, the whole population between Little Coal and Guyandotte are in the highest degree hostile to the Union; that especially at Big Creek, Mill Creek, Upper Hewitt, and on both sides of

Guyandotte those men lived who composed the so-called Black Striped Company. As these men had fled to the other side of the Guyandotte I could not take them up in their houses, and it appears to me that this can only be done by a small detachment of light cavalry who arrive before the news of their march has reached the country. I have sent a list of those men who are reported most dangerous to Brig. Gen. J. D. Cox; also some prisoners.

I am, most respectfully, your obedient servant,

E. SIBER,
Colonel Thirty-seventh Regiment Ohio Volunteers.

L. THOMAS,
Adjutant-General U. S. Army, Washington, D. C.

FEBRUARY 3, 1862.—Reconnaissance to Occoquan Village, Va.

Report of Col. Stephen G. Champlin, Third Michigan Infantry.

HEADQUARTERS PICKET GUARD, *February* 4, 1862.

SIR: I have the honor to report that the reconnoitering party sent out early yesterday morning returned about 3 p. m. The party was commanded by Captain Lowing, and consisted of Lieutenant Brennan and 34 men from Company I, and Lieutenant Ryan and 44 men from Company H. They took the road leading by Millstead and went as far as Barker's, intending to push up as far as Burke's Station and then pass over to Brimstone Hill, returning by way of old Ox road; but the storm was so severe that the captain did not think it advisable to continue farther, so turned off to the left, and passing the house of Williamson, went down to the river side opposite Occoquan Village. The river side was reached through a ravine through which the road passes. Arriving on the shore of the river, the road turns sharply to the north, while a precipitous rocky bluff of near 100 feet high rises immediately behind, leaving only room for the roadway. Upon nearing the river Lieutenant Brennan and 10 men were thrown forward to reconnoiter. He saw but few men in the streets of the village on his arrival, and those seen appeared to be squads of unarmed recruits drilling. The scouting party was soon discovered by the enemy and the alarm given, when armed men rushed out of the houses and opened a fire upon the party. Captain Lowing then came up and ordered the fire to be returned. Three rounds were fired, when the men, being too much exposed and having accomplished the object of their mission, were ordered to retire, and returned by way of Pohick Church.

The falling snow prevented objects from being distinctly seen. Four of the enemy were seen to fall, however, and were carried off by their comrades. Great confusion seemed to prevail. The enemy were evidently taken by surprise. Owing to the difficulty of getting the men under cover Captain Lowing did not deploy his men, but brought them through the ravine in sections of eight men abreast, delivered his fire in this order, retiring from the right and left to the rear, thus exposing the head of the column, the balance being hid in the ravine through which they approached the river. The men delivered their fire deliberately and filed to the rear without confusion, acting with coolness and courage throughout.

A camp of the enemy was seen below Occoquan and on the south side of the river. No fortifications were seen. The range of vision was limited, however, by the falling snow. At the corner near Mrs. Violet's house a cavalry picket post was discovered, but the pickets had fled up the old Ox road. They found a good common tent there, in which the pickets had sheltered themselves. They destroyed the tent, as they were too much exhausted to bring it away with them. With the exception of this, no picket post was seen.

Captain Lowing was informed at Barker's that the enemy kept a picket post at the saw-mill between Barker's and Burke's Station. I am inclined to believe that the old Ox road is picketed by cavalry from Fairfax Station to Mrs. Violet's, though 1 have no certain information of the fact.

On the return, four of Captain Lowing's men becoming so exhausted that they could travel no farther, he directed search to be made for horses on which to mount them. He found two horses in a barn near a deserted house. The owner of the horses could not be ascertained, so he took these horses and mounted the exhausted men on them, and they rode them in. He now inquires as to what disposition he shall make of the horses—whether to hand them over to the brigade quartermaster or to return them to the place from whence taken.

Just before Captain Lowing returned, and when he was in the neighborhood of Pohick Church, heavy firing of musketry was distinctly heard in the direction of Parker's, on the Pohick road. The firing lasted several minutes. I am inclined to think that it was between two detachments of the enemy, and who met at the cross-roads, probably mistaking each other for Captain Lowing's party. I shall request the officer who relieves me to ascertain if possible the cause of this firing.

I strongly second the views of Captain Moses in relation to pushing the right of our line of pickets out to the Springfield road. The advantages are, it gives a stronger line of posts, is more easily and more securely picketed, while in the rear, along the whole line nearly, is strong ground for the pickets to fall back upon if forced from their position. It will take fewer men, thus giving stronger reserves at the threatened points.

I have the honor to be, your obedient servant,

S. G. CHAMPLIN,
Colonel, Commanding Third Michigan Volunteers.

ISAAC MOSES, *Assistant Adjutant-General.*

FEBRUARY 7, 1862.—Expedition to Flint Hill and Hunter's Mill, Va.

REPORTS.

No. 1.—Capt. L. D. H. Currie, assistant adjutant-general, U. S. Army.
No. 2.—Maj. Joseph L. Moss, Fifth Pennsylvania Cavalry.
No. 3.—Capt. John O'Farrell, Fifth Pennsylvania Cavalry.

No. 1.

Report of Capt. L. D. H. Currie, Assistant Adjutant-General, U. S. A.

HEADQUARTERS SMITH'S DIVISION,
Camp Griffin, Va., February 8, 1862.

GENERAL: In pursuance of your orders I proceeded yesterday morning with the cavalry, consisting of five squadrons, under command of

Major Moss, at 4 a. m., to Freedom Hill, and in conjunction with him made the following dispositions : One squadron, under Captain Wilson, to Flint Hill, with myself; one squadron, under Captain Heuser, along the Sawyer's road towards Mrs. Brooks' house, with Lieutenant Scrymser, aide-de-camp; one squadron, under Major Moss, via Johnson's Hill, to Hunter's Mill, with Lieutenant Carey, aide-de-camp; one squadron, under Major Boteler, at Vienna, in support; the remaining squadron, under Captain Hagemeister, to remain at Freedom Hill, also in support.

The object being to clear the road from Flint Hill to Hunter's Mill and capture the rebel picket at Peck's house, it was essential in the first place to drive in the rebels at Flint Hill, on approaching which a vedette on our right gave the alarm and ran into Flint Hill, whereupon I immediately ordered Captain Wilson to charge with his company, taking Capt. J. O'Farrell, with his company, in support. The rebels ran before Captain Wilson's company, which went in pursuit, Captain O'Farrell's company following. I then ordered Captain O'Farrell to bear away with his company to the right of a wood and join Captain Wilson in pursuit. After hunting the rebels across the country for a couple of miles in the direction of Germantown, leaving Fairfax Court-House on our left, the company was halted. I then ordered the company (Captain Wilson's) back to the barn at Mrs. Shaley's, which according to your instructions was fired and burned. As soon as the company was collected, after waiting a few moments to see if Captain O'Farrell's company returned, I ordered the company along the road to Hunter's Mill, and feeling that time was an object I ordered Captain Wilson to trot, and we proceeded quickly along. After passing Vibart's Mill about a mile the advance guard came across the rebel vedette. At the same time we saw a horse picketed at the house, for which Captain Wilson, Capt. Robert D'Orleans, and myself immediately made. The advance guard fired at the vedette we saw, who ran. We tried to cut him off, when the other men of the rebel picket rushed into the house and began firing at us. The company in the mean time surrounded the house. Captain Wilson was shot through the head. I ordered the men immediately to dismount and assault the house, which they did, and brought 4 prisoners out. One rebel was killed in the house. Some of the rebels were still firing at us from the woods, and being anxious to get the captain to a place of safety and the prisoners with their arms and horses secured, I ordered the company on to Mrs. Brooks' house and then on to Vienna, when I met Captain Heuser's squadron, which I ordered to remain where it was until further orders. On arriving at Vienna I found by some misconception of orders that Major Boteler had left with his squadron. I therefore at once sent for Captain Hagemeister's squadron from Freedom Hill to support Captain O'Farrell in the direction of Flint Hill, by which means I was enabled to send an ambulance to Flint Hill to bring in Sergeant Moore, of Company I, who was reported as dangerously wounded. Captain Heuser's squadron I then ordered back in support at Vienna. I then ascertained from a message from Major Moss that he had advanced towards Flint Hill.

In about two hours Captain Hagemeister returned, reporting the junction of the squadrons commanded by Majors Moss and Boteler and Captain O'Farrell's company, and that they had gone in the direction of Fairfax Court-House; upon which I collected the command at Freedom Hill, leaving a company at Vienna, and sending out scouts to Johnson's Hill and Hunter's Mill and Peacock's Hill.

It is difficult to particularize where all performed their duty with coolness and courage, but I should be doing an injustice to a gallant soldier if I did not say that I consider our success due chiefly to the example of daring set by Captain Wilson, and I shall not soon forget the manner in which Corporals Daley and Grier, of his company, led the assault on Peck's house.

I may add that after Captain Wilson was shot, Lieutenant Morris, who succeeded to the company, rendered me valuable assistance.

I would also wish to thank Capt. Robert D'Orleans, aide-de-camp to the Major-General Commanding the Army, for his coolness, assistance, and advice on this somewhat trying occasion.

I have the honor to be, general, your obedient servant,

L. D. H. CURRIE,
Assistant Adjutant-General.

Brig. Gen. W. F. SMITH, *Commanding Division.*

No. 2.

Report of Maj. Joseph L. Moss, Fifth Pennsylvania Cavalry.

HEADQUARTERS,
Camp Griffin, Va., February 8, 1862.

SIR: I have the honor to submit for the consideration of the commanding general of the division the following report of the operations of the Cameron Dragoons on the 7th instant:

At 4 o'clock on the morning of the 7th the Cameron Dragoons left their camp in pursuance of Special Orders, No. 147, of that date, and proceeded as far as Freedom Hill, when our regiment was divided off in the following manner:

Captain Wilson, commanding Company F, and Capt. J. O'Farrell, commanding Company I, forming one squadron, under the command of Captain Currie, assistant adjutant-general, proceeded on the road through Vienna towards Flint Hill for the purpose of driving in the enemy's pickets. When arriving there the squadron was divided, Captain Wilson's company being ordered to charge to the left and Captain O'Farrell to the right, for the purpose of getting in the rear of the enemy's pickets; but before they succeeded in doing this they were discovered by the pickets, who immediately fled in the direction of Germantown, hotly pursued by Captain Wilson's company to within 1½ miles of the town. Not overtaking them they returned to Flint Hill, and, pursuant to orders, set fire to an old barn which has for a long time afforded the pickets protection, and then taking the road to the left, leading to Hunter's Mill, they soon discovered a portion of the enemy's reserve secreted in Mrs. Peck's house. The order was then immediately given by Captain Currie to charge upon the house and surround it, but when within 50 yards of it the enemy opened a brisk fire from within with Colt's repeating rifles as well as from the neighboring hills and woods. Notwithstanding this the men boldly charged to the doors and windows of the house, Captain Wilson at their head (who in doing this received a serious and very painful wound from a rifle-ball, which entered the ear, glanced around the skull bone, and came out at the back of the head), dismounted, entered the house, killing 1 man and succeeded in capturing 4 prisoners (of the First North Carolina Cavalry), 3 horses, and 5 revolving rifles. A number of the company, with their prisoners, were then ordered to fall back to Freedom Hill.

In the mean time Capt. J. O'Farrell, having discovered another portion of the reserve in an old log house, immediately charged upon and surrounded it, the enemy, as before, opening a brisk fire upon them from within, which lasted for several minutes. On reaching the house Capt. J. O'Farrell with a few men immediately dismounted and captured 6 prisoners, with horse equipments and arms. The prisoners were then sent back to Freedom Hill under charge of a guard. In doing this Sergeant Moore, who acted through the whole affair in the most determined and courageous manner, received a fatal wound, which terminated his life at 10.30 in the evening.

Major Boteler, in command of the fifth squadron, was ordered to proceed to Vienna, with instructions that in case he heard firing to immediately advance in the direction of it. Upon hearing the firing he immediately started in the direction of Flint Hill, but when reaching this point the pickets had been driven in and the prisoners captured. He then with his command, together with the balance of Capt. J. O'Farrell's company, proceeded on the road to the right, leading to Hunter's Mill, for the purpose of joining my command, which consisted of Companies D and C and H and a small detachment of Company A. This command left Freedom Hill simultaneously with that of Captain Currie and took the road to the right, leading directly to Hunter's Mill. Here we succeeded in driving back the enemy's pickets some 2 or 3 miles, but in consequence of the ruggedness of the country in this direction and the pickets having discovered us whilst approaching we did not succeed in capturing them. We then halted at Mrs. Brooks', pursuant to previous arrangements, until Major Boteler with his command had joined us; after which the whole command returned to Flint Hill, and from there started in the direction of Fairfax Court-House. When within a mile of this place the pickets to the number of 15 or 20 again made their appearance about a half mile in our advance. Immediately upon seeing them I ordered Captain Brown with 10 or 15 men in one direction, and Lieutenant Cromelien with the same number of men in another, to capture them if possible. They pursued them to within a mile of Germantown, wounding 2 and capturing 3 of them, together with a valuable four-horse team, which was used for hauling forage to the rebel troops.

In the mean time I ordered Lieutenant Hart with 20 men to make a charge through Fairfax Court-House, having first reconnoitered to the right and left of the village and satisfied myself that there were but few, if any, troops there. I then advanced with the whole force into the village; remained there about half an hour, and took the road to the left, leading through Falls Church, thinking I might still get in the rear of their pickets; but they had all fled, leaving their fires burning, leading me to suppose they had left in hot haste for parts unknown.

The village of Fairfax appears to have been (with one or two exceptions) entirely deserted, and has a very dilapidated look. I did not think it expedient to have the houses searched, as the enemy could in a very short time get a strong force down the pike from the neighborhood of Centreville. The enemy have dug 3 or 4 extensive rifle-pits to the right of the road leading from Flint Hill to the Court-House and immediately in front of the same.

I take much pleasure in expressing my general satisfaction at the good conduct of the officers, non-commissioned officers, and men during the day. It is impossible to particularize any one, as they all conducted themselves in a most creditable manner.

I am, sir, with respect, your obedient servant,

J. L. MOSS,
Major, Commanding Cameron Dragoons.

Capt. L. D. H. CURRIE, *Assistant Adjutant-General.*

No. 3.

Report of Capt. John O'Farrell, Fifth Pennsylvania Cavalry.

CAMP GRIFFIN, *February* 7, 1862.

SIR: I have the honor to report that, according to orders received from you at Freedom Hill, I left the main body of the regiment and proceeded with my company, together with Company F, through Vienna in the direction of Fairfax Court-House until we were close to Flint Hill, where I received instructions from Major Currie (then in command of the squadron) to make a charge to the right and get in rear of the rebel pickets, capturing as many as I could, while Company F charged to the left for the same purpose. At the first dash we made the nearest pickets discovering us managed to escape. I then, pursuant to instructions, took through the fields for about 2 miles in the direction of Hunter's Mill, making a dash on the rear of a log hut, where I discovered that a portion of their reserve guard was stationed. When about 50 yards from it and coming towards their rear they opened upon us a brisk fire, which lasted for several minutes before we managed to dislodge them, although we promptly surrounded the hut and returned their fire with vigor. The firing of the enemy was rapid but mostly at random, which accounts for the few casualties on our side. Sergeant Moore, of my company, received a rifle-ball through his leg, fracturing the bone. He has since died. Of the enemy one was killed and another slightly wounded. They being under shelter, where our balls could not penetrate, had every advantage. We took 6 prisoners, with their arms, horses, and equipments, some of which we lost in returning on account of the difficulty we had in bringing in our prisoners, as their pickets, who were now alarmed, kept firing on us from different directions as we returned, having gone some distance inside their lines. This fire we also returned, killing and wounding, as far as we know, two of their horses, and bringing with us all our prisoners and the wounded sergeant, which made our progress slow. The arms taken consisted of Colt's revolving rifles, old-fashioned horse-pistols, and sabers. Having reached our reserves in safety I sent back the prisoners and wounded man with a proper guard, and returned with the remaining portion of my company, and in connection with the main body of the regiment, under Major Moss, passed through Fairfax Court-House, and returned with them to the camp by the way of Falls Church without further casualty. My non-commissioned officers and men behaved remarkably well. I can also speak highly of my first lieutenant, J. W. Pierce, and second lieutenant, Matthew Berry, for their prompt support when I attacked the enemy's pickets.

I remain, sir, your obedient servant,

JOHN O'FARRELL,
Captain, Commanding Company.

Maj. J. L. MOSS, *Commanding Cameron Dragoons.*

FEBRUARY 8, 1862.—Skirmish at the mouth of the Blue Stone, West Virginia.

Report of Lieut. Col. William E. Peters, Forty-fifth Virginia Infantry.

HEADQUARTERS FORTY-FIFTH VIRGINIA REGIMENT,
CAMP AT MOUTH OF BLUE STONE,
Mercer County, West Virginia, February 10, 1862.

DEAR SIR: As instructed by Colonel Jenifer, I took three companies of my regiment to the Jumping Branches day before yesterday (8th). I reached that point at 6 p. m. At 10 p. m. of the same date the cavalry pickets were driven in, stating that the enemy were advancing in some force. I sent out Lieutenant Samuels, of the Border Rangers, to ascertain the truthfulness of the alarm. He confirmed the report, and stated that they were advancing in superior force and with several pieces of artillery. Under the circumstances I concluded to fall back to this point, 5 miles distant from the Jumping Branches, a point that could not be defended against a superior force of any kind, and entirely indefensible against artillery when the opposing force had none. I fell back to this point and selected a point upon which to fight them should they advance. They did advance, attacked us with 450 men and three pieces of artillery (two portable howitzers and one 6-pounder rifle piece), and were signally repulsed. I selected such a position that they could not use their artillery against us with effect. I had not more than 225 men, cavalry included. I did not lose a man. How many of the enemy were killed I am not able to say. My men were in no condition to pursue them. They had worked the day and night before. I hope it may be in the power of the Government to send re enforcements to this portion of the State. The people—a large number of them—are true, and ready to fight if assisted. There is not force enough here to meet the enemy at all of his approaches.

Very respectfully, your obedient servant,
WILLIAM E. PETERS,
Lieutenant-Colonel, Commanding Forty-fifth Virginia Regiment.
General S. COOPER,
Adjutant and Inspector General C. S. Army.

FEBRUARY 22, 1862.—Expedition to Vienna and Flint Hill, Va.

Report of Col. Max Friedman, Fifth Pennsylvania Cavalry.

HEADQUARTERS CAMERON DRAGOONS,
Camp Griffin, Va., February 22, 1862.

SIR: I have the honor to report that in accordance with your orders I left camp at 3.30 o'clock this morning, and proceeded with the whole of my regiment, in company with the Forty-third New York Infantry (Colonel Vinton), as far as Vienna. We left said regiment at that place and proceeded to Flint Hill on double-quick time. I detailed the first squadron, commanded by Captain Rosenthal, as the advance to Flint Hill, at the same time having kept a close chain of communication with the main body (about 300 yards apart). On arriving at Flint Hill the advance took two of the enemy's pickets (mounted), one of whom we wounded, but not seriously. I then detailed the same squadron as the advance on the road to the right, leading to Fox's Mill, I remaining a few moments at Flint Hill. Just about daylight I noticed some 40 of the enemy's cavalry forming on a field about half a mile to my right. I at once intended to charge upon them, but perceiving to my left some artillery of the enemy, I thought it prudent to desist, and left one squadron at Flint Hill to cover my rear and keep the chain of communication open with headquarters. I then followed with the balance of the regiment the advance, and on reaching Fox's Mill learned from a negro that about half a mile on the road in our advance, at one Jacob Fox's, there were some of the enemy's mounted pickets. We proceeded on double-quick time and reached them, and succeeded in capturing 5 of them, with horses, equipments, and arms; also two citizens, one by the name of Jacob Fox and one other in their company. From there we scoured the country to Hawkhurst's Mill and to Hunter's Mill, but no more of the enemy were to be seen. I have noticed on that road some picket fires, but deserted, and part of their breakfast had been left. At Hunter's Mill I met the Sixth Maine Regiment of Infantry (Colonel Burnham), as my reserve. We then took the Johnson's Hill road back to Freedom Hill, Colonel Burnham's infantry regiment following us in our rear. Before starting from Hunter's Mill I detailed an orderly to bring in the squadron left at Flint Hill.

I take great pleasure in informing you that the officers and men under my command behaved in a very soldierly and courageous manner. I am also much indebted to the assistant adjutant-general (Capt. L. D. H. Currie) for his valuable services rendered, who was most of the time in the advance. It is impossible for me to particularize any one, but if I should do so I should award it to Captain Rosenthal for his conduct. The reconnaissance was carried out in every particular according to instructions received, without any mishap on our side.

I remain, sir, very respectfully, your obedient servant,

M. FRIEDMAN,
Colonel, Commanding Cameron Dragoons.

General W. F. SMITH, *Commanding Division.*

[Indorsement.]

Forwarded for the information of the Commanding General, with a decided difference of opinion with reference to artillery being seen near Fairfax Court-House. Captain Read, assistant adjutant-general to General Brooks, took a prisoner; Lieutenant Crane, acting ordnance officer, took one in a personal conflict; and Lieutenant Carey, my aide, took two by himself. Captain Currie, as usual, was everywhere to direct and make successful the expedition.

WM. F. SMITH,
Brigadier-General.

FEBRUARY 24, 1862.—Affair at Lewis' Chapel, near Pohick Church, Virginia.

Report of Brig. Gen. Samuel P. Heintzelman, U. S. Army.

HEADQUARTERS DIVISION,
Camp Lyon, February 24, 1862—2 p. m.

GENERAL: This morning an attack was made on our pickets about a mile beyond Pohick Church, at Lewis' Chapel, with what force not stated, but the enemy's drums were heard all along the line. There are two regiments, about 1,200 men, on outpost duty. Two regiments from General Richardson's brigade have advanced to their support, and a battery of artillery is now on its way to his headquarters, to be within reach should it be required. General Richardson has gone out to take command if necessary. I don't believe that the attack amounts to much.

The telegraph lines around us are all down.

I am, general, very respectfully, your obedient servant,

S. P. HEINTZELMAN,
Brigadier-General.

General S. WILLIAMS,
Assistant Adjutant-General, Washington.

FEBRUARY 25–MAY 6, 1862.—Operations in Loudoun County, Virginia.

Report of Col. John W. Geary, Twenty-eighth Pennsylvania Infantry, including operations of his command to May 6, 1862.

HEADQUARTERS DETACHED BRIGADE,
May 14, 1862.

GENERAL: I have the honor to submit the following report of the movements of my command, both personal and temporarily enlarged, from the moment of the reception of orders from you to cross into Virginia up to May 6, the date of my reception of orders from the War Department to report to Major-General McDowell:

In obedience to orders from you to cross the Potomac at Harper's Ferry, on the evening of February 23 I got my command in readiness for that purpose, leaving detachments of companies on picket at Noland's Ferry, Point of Rocks, Knoxville, Berlin, and intermediately posted. The cars conveyed the seven companies and two guns posted at Point of Rocks to Sandy Hook, which we reached before daylight, where we were joined by the other two guns and the seven companies which had been stationed up the river. Arriving at Harper's Ferry we rigged a rope ferry in the course of a few hours, losing 6 men by the upsetting of the skiffs early sent across. The weather, at first slightly perverse, became so exceedingly violent, and the river rose so rapidly, that it became dangerous to attempt to throw troops across. The storm raged all night of the 24th. Rebel cavalry scouts had been seen in the evening upon the hills beyond Bolivar, and as it was impossible to re-enforce the pioneers, consisting of 2 commissioned officers and 6 privates, we guarded their position by artillery and infantry on the Maryland side.

In the morning a calm ensued, and eight companies and a section of artillery were at once thrown over, and pickets were posted for a circuit of several miles, extending beyond Bolivar. The rope breaking and river running rapidly compelled me to transport two more companies in boats.

Establishing communication over the Shenandoah, we crossed five companies, and ascended Loudoun Heights on the 25th, and found rebel cavalry near, who at once fled. The oath of allegiance was administered to four persons found there. Two guns were placed in position there during the day, and the five companies under Lieutenant-Colonel De Korponay were detached as garrisons in the three fortifications from which we had driven a body of the enemy. He was assailed on the 27th by a squadron of the First Michigan Cavalry, who scouted at desirable points in the neighborhood.

Under verbal orders from Major-General McClellan and yourself I crossed nine companies of my regiment with the four guns of the battery and a battalion of the First Michigan Cavalry over the Shenandoah, and late in the afternoon marched through Pleasant Valley, and about dark proceeded along the banks of the river to reconnoiter, as the trains on the Baltimore and Ohio Railroad were threatened; but our progress being impeded by an unfordable creek, which had risen several feet, we bivouacked for the night.

On the following morning we marched to Lovettsville, and along the route were greeted with enthusiastic demonstrations of joy and manifestations of Union feeling. Before reaching Lovettsville, which we did at noon, the enemy, after a sharp skirmish, fled towards Waterford and subsequently to Leesburg.

We captured 6 prisoners, including the mail-carrier, with his mail. The others were of the Bedford and Loudoun cavalry.

The majority of the inhabitants and many from the surrounding country hailed our presence with gladness, and willingly took the oath of allegiance and claimed the protection of our Government. I learned that the party who had shelled the train on the day previous consisted of about 300 Mississippians with 2 guns.

Finding that the enemy intended making demonstrations against us, I sent a detachment of infantry and one gun to take position on Short Mountain to protect our flank, and also ordered Lieutenant-Colonel De Korponay from his position on Loudoun Heights with the remaining companies of the Twenty-eighth Regiment Pennsylvania Volunteers, under privilege of relief granted by yourself. My scouts daily drove in the enemy's pickets and encountered parties of the rebels, invariably putting them to flight. Collisions with the outposts of the enemy were frequent, in some of which several of our adversaries were killed. We were keeping in check a force of 4,000 rebels, who threatened us from Leesburg, and it became necessary that we should hold the place determinedly, as they had expressed a determination to attempt a repetition of their attacks upon the cars on the Baltimore and Ohio Railroad, and by a bold dash cross the river in boats to destroy a portion of the road and several viaducts, to cripple thereby the main line of our operations. Our presence here materially intercepted the supply communications of the enemy.

On March 3 a strong rebel force advanced upon us with the intention of attacking and outflanking us. To their surprise they found us in line of battle. They changed their original intentions and retired to Hillsborough.

On the 4th our scouts reported about 1,000 of the enemy with artillery and 200 or 300 cavalry at Coatesford, 6 miles from us, and General Smith's brigade, 3,000 strong, at Gum Spring. Active reconnaissances were prosecuted, and the enemy had not the temerity to give us battle.

Two deserters from the Eighteenth Mississippi came into our lines on March 5. A general expression of loyalty had transpired in the county, and the majority of the people were desirous of being protected from the dominion of rebel soldiery.

On the morning of the 7th I learned that there were about 1,000 infantry, some artillery, and between 200 and 300 cavalry at Waterford, who had determined to make an attempt to destroy the railroad during the day, then burn Wheatland and Waterford. Afterwards they, together with General Hill's command, would fall back, thinking re-enforcements would arrive, which, in conjunction with my command, would move on Leesburg. In full expectation of our advance General Hill sent his stores and baggage to Middleburg, and commenced burning hay and grain stacks to prevent them falling into our hands.

About noon I put my main body, with cavalry and artillery, in motion, leaving instructions for the balance to follow during the night. We entered Wheatland in time to prevent the incendiary designs of White's cavalry, who would have burnt it. This created a panic among the troops at Waterford, who fled to Leesburg without applying the torch.

We entered Waterford about 11 o'clock at night, where the command rested 3 hours. By a forced march we reached Leesburg shortly after sunrise, and took possession of Fort Johnston, where we planted the Stars and Stripes, and then entered the city. The rear of General Hill's retreating forces could be seen in the distance. They retired to Middleburg. General Hill and staff retreated at full gallop. My other detachments joined me during the day. We at once took possession of the court-house, bank, and all other public buildings, and Forts Beauregard and Evans. We found considerable secession feeling, and established a rigid provost-marshalship, and enforced strict order and decorum. We garrisoned Fort Johnston and made every preparation to resist attack. We took a number of prisoners of note, whom we dispatched to the division provost-marshal. The day of our occupation was announced for a general impressment of citizens into the army. Many persons came forward and took the oath of allegiance, and paroles of honor were administered to many rank secessionists. Hon. John Janney, Major Scott, and other distinguished Virginians gave their parole.

On the 9th we ascertained that the rebel troops were falling back to the Rappahannock near Gordonsville, and that their artillery was moving southward. We scouted upon the trail of the retreat of the enemy as far as Carter's Mill, and found their path blackened with devastations hurriedly committed, and that they had burned the bridge over Goose Creek, impeding our farther progress, as it was unfordable.

On the 12th, in obedience to orders, we marched to Snickersville, a distance of 16 miles, leaving a garrison at Fort Johnston consisting of three companies of infantry and one gun, Twenty-eighth Pennsylvania Volunteers, under command of Lieutenant-Colonel De Korponay. Prior to our leaving Leesburg the inhabitants of that city unanimously expressed their intention of preserving order and abnegating any local government opposed to that of the United States, soliciting protection against guerrilla parties of the enemy who might return. We effectually reconnoitered Snicker's Gap and vicinity of Blue Mountains to Front Royal, resulting in my decision to push on to Upperville, 10 miles distant, after a stay of forty-eight hours.

The order preserved and respect for property maintained (unexpected, through misrepresentations made with regard to the Federal Army) left a favorable impression on the people, and friends to the Union came forward in every town and village and proclaimed their allegiance to the Government.

We reached Upperville March 15, at 4 p. m. We scouted that section, and took prisoners an officer and a number of privates of the Sixth Virginia Cavalry and a private of Ashby's cavalry. The rear guard of the enemy was only 4 or 5 miles south of us, and upon the first evening 125 cavalry retreated from our scouts. We had effectually driven the enemy out of Loudoun County.

Deeming Leesburg and its vicinity now perfectly safe without a garrison (from the pledges given by the inhabitants), I ordered Lieutenant-Colonel De Korponay to join me with his detachment, that I might concentrate my forces against any attempt made upon the left of the column on this line, and prevent destruction intended to impede the progress of our troops. It was necessary to keep these mountains clear, as they afforded great natural advantages of defense. We reconnoitered some distance along the railroad and found the country very rugged and mountainous. Three or four bridges had been burned, one of them over Goose Creek at Piedmont. We extended it also into the mountain region towards the river through Paris. About 125 cavalry fled as we approached Piedmont on the 19th. We took prisoners of the Eighth Virginia Infantry and the Sixth Virginia Cavalry.

As a portion of our supply train was absent at Harper's Ferry, a short delay was occasioned in obeying Special Orders, No. 2, dated March 23, ordering the command to proceed to Aldie. We were without sufficient transportation for subsistence and quartermaster's stores. In conformity with said orders the detachment at Leesburg, under De Korponay, Twenty-eighth Pennsylvania Volunteers, was ordered to proceed to Aldie and rejoin this command there, leaving Leesburg without a garrison.

On the 21st large bodies of rebels were reported in and around Warrenton and Salem.

On the 24th, in obedience to orders from General Williams, we marched to Aldie and encamped, and on the following morning, under orders from General Abercrombie to march to Winchester to support the division, we returned to Snickersville, where we were joined by our Leesburg detachment and encamped.

Receiving *contra* orders on the following morning from yourself, through General Abercrombie, to push forward to White Plains and commence repairs on the railroad towards Strasburg, we took up the line of march at noon, encamped at Philomont at sunset, and on the following morning marched to Middleburg, where we repulsed a body of about 300 of the enemy's cavalry with a reserve of infantry, who had approached from the direction of Upperville. We opened a well-directed fire upon them, when they retreated in disorder to the mountains. Owing to the violent secession feeling manifested in this town, we remained here a day and a half and enlisted some of the leading men of the place in our wishes to preserve order. Among others who gave their parole were Generals Rogers and Wright, and Colonel Chancellor, the latter of the One hundred and thirty-second Virginia Militia.

A revulsion of feeling took place, and we left on the morning of the 29th, and reached White Plains at 2 o'clock of the same afternoon. We found no troops here. We encamped in the strongest position on the road. We proceeded to examine the line of railroad to Salem and also to Thoroughfare, and found it in good running order to Salem, and the only break in the direction of Thoroughfare was a burned bridge about 1½ miles from the town. The bridge was 40 feet long, in two spans, resting on a stone pier in the center, which remained undisturbed. Immediately after our occupation of the place the rebels evacuated Warrenton.

Late in the afternoon of April 1 I received an order from General McClellan, through General Abercrombie, dated March 29, to proceed at once to Warrenton Junction and report for temporary duty to General Sumner. At the same moment I was in receipt of instructions from yourself, dated March 30, to proceed with the repairing of the railroad. Accompanying the orders from General McClellan was a communication from General Abercrombie from his headquarters, 5 miles from Warrenton Junction, expressing his expectations to see me at the junction, in consonance with General McClellan's orders, as soon as I could get through. The same day Adjutant Phelps, First Michigan Cavalry, was shot and killed by the accidental discharge of his revolver. A party of 10 cavalry and 1 citizen, who went to Salem to obtain a coffin for deceased, was surrounded by a superior number of enemy's cavalry. Seven were captured; the citizen (John Downey), a guide from Lovettsville, was mortally wounded, 1 man only escaping. Three of the enemy were afterwards taken prisoners by a reconnoitering party in a skirmish with the same body.

At night the command marched to Thoroughfare Gap, 5 miles distant, over very rough roads, for the purpose of effectually avoiding a large force of the enemy who were endeavoring to surround and capture the command. This force was supposed to have been re-enforcements sent to Jackson, and who had not been able to cross the river at Front Royal, and turned their attention towards my command.

We took up a strong position in the gap and prepared for attack, but during the day were informed that the enemy, baffled, had retired across the Rappahannock, and on April 3 we marched to Greenwich, a distance of 13 miles, and encamped, resuming our march on the following morning towards Warrenton Junction, and arriving at Catlett's Station, where we encamped, about noon.

Late on the 5th I received a telegram from you to join the column by the shortest and safest road, and at sunrise on the 6th left Catlett's Station in obedience thereto, and at noon reached Warrenton, compelling a force of about 800 rebel cavalry to retreat across the Rappahannock, a similar force having retired early the same morning. We took formal possession of the town and encamped near it. We captured here the flag of the Forty-ninth Virginia Regiment, formerly commanded by Ex-Governor William Smith. We were joined by Companies H and I, First Michigan Cavalry, ordered to report to me.

On the morning of the 7th we took up the line of march, but being overtaken by a violent snow-storm, we pitched tents about 6 miles from Warrenton. The storm continued with unabated violence for four days, compelling us to remain where we were encamped.

On the 10th your body guard, Zouaves d'Afrique, joined our command.

On the 11th I received orders from you to move to White Plains and report to Colonel McCallum to assist in repairing the road. We immediately marched to that place and encamped on the same day. We here learned that a large force of the enemy was concentrated near Waterloo, threatening to attack us. We put the road in good running order to Rectortown, and had men actively engaged on a bridge of 120 feet span over Goose Creek. I dispatched a train to Alexandria for the requisite timbers, which were furnished promptly, together with materials and force of workmen sent by Colonel McCallum. In order to push the work actively forward the building of the bridge over Cedar Run was temporarily delayed.

On the 14th we marched to Rectortown, Va., where we encamped in an elevated position, and a reconnoitering party was attacked by and had a skirmish with rebel cavalry near Piedmont, in which 2 of our advance guard were killed. We immediately repaired the telegraph line to Front Royal. Munford's regiment of cavalry was scouting daily in the vicinity of the road at various points, threatening to obstruct and destroy it.

At noon on the 16th the train crossed over the bridge at Goose Creek and the workmen at once engaged themselves on two bridges at Piedmont, each of 60 feet span, which were completed on the evening of the 18th, the timbers for some of the work being cut in the vicinity of the bridges. The four bridges between Piedmont and Markham now occupied our attention, and the work was rapidly pushed forward. At Linden the road required the attention of the engineers. The mountains were infested with forces of cavalry, in bodies of between 200 and 300, having designs against the bridges already constructed, making it necessary to strictly guard the entire road. The rebels made several unsuccessful attempts to force our pickets to accomplish their designs.

A continuous storm from April 18 to 22 materially retarded progress on the road. The creeks all became swollen; the bridge over Bull Run was carried away, and the whole force of workmen was recalled to rebuild it. The bridge over Goose Creek at Rectortown was partly washed away, and three others above it were somewhat injured. The persistence of the rebel cavalry in their attempts to obstruct the road became a daily annoyance. Scouting parties of my command were in frequent pursuit of them in every direction.

Two of White's cavalry were taken prisoners while creeping up to my pickets in the darkness with the intention of murdering them—a nightly occurrence. Other prisoners—noted enemies to our Government and abettors of the enemy—were taken in various sections of the surrounding country.

I had detachments posted from Salem to Linden guarding the road. The Eleventh Pennsylvania Regiment, Colonel Coulter, was guarding from Manassas to White Plains, leaving 30 miles of the most important section in my hands. The work progressed under persevering effort and almost unremitting labor, and no exertion was spared to expedite the completion of the road.

On the 27th I pushed forward detachments to Front Royal, establishing stations at all the important intermediate points. The railroad to Front Royal was in complete running order on the afternoon of the 29th, and five trains laden with subsistence, forage, &c., passed over to that point, and my command was then guarding 32 miles of the road, disposed as follows: Four companies of cavalry, taking charge of road from White Plains to Rectortown, patrolling it, viz, one company of cavalry at Salem and three at Rectortown; my headquarters, 1½ miles west of Rectortown, near large bridge over Goose Creek, where I had seven companies of infantry and one company of artillery; two companies of infantry and one company of cavalry were located at Piedmont; two companies of infantry at Markham, and four companies of infantry and one company of cavalry posted from Linden to the Shenandoah, the latter companies guarding the workmen engaged upon the bridge over that river and the stores of forage and subsistence which had been deposited at that place. Owing to our line of advance and various positions held being detached from all direct facilities of transportation from any central depot of stores, we were compelled to procure our forage and subsistence through our quartermaster from citizens throughout the country, and many local places were so impoverished that numerous difficulties were attendant upon getting our necessities.

I take pleasure in being able to represent to you the indomitable, persevering, and uncomplaining spirit of the men of my command under trying circumstances and in the endurance of hardships necessarily attendant upon some of our movements; also their unflinching determination and zeal in moments when danger was imminent.

In obedience to orders from the Secretary of War, on May 2 I established a line of mounted couriers between Front Royal and Strasburg, with relays at intervals, until repairs to the telegraph were made. I was informed by a telegram from Major-General McDowell, bearing date May 5, that I should from that date report to him; and upon May 8 I received the following dispatch:

WAR DEPARTMENT, —— —, 1862.

Col. JOHN W. GEARY:

Report daily to this Department; also to General McDowell, from whom you must take your instructions.

P. H. WATSON,
Assistant Secretary of War.

In closing this report, which I respectfully submit to you, permit me to express my high appreciation of the many great favors you have bestowed upon my command, as well as myself, while in your division, our connection with which we have always had occasion to be proud of. We have been recipients of many high honors at your hands, and in your selection of us to fill posts in which we could serve the cause of our country most effectually and susceptible of credit to ourselves. Your orders, which have always been replete with urbanity, we have taken pride in executing to the best of our ability, and our severance from your command, with which we have been assimilated since our earliest appearance in the field (a period of ten months) is not without its many regrets to one and all.

I have the honor to be,

JNO. W. GEARY.

Major-General BANKS,
　　Commanding Department of the Shenandoah.

MARCH 5, 1862.—Skirmish at Bunker Hill, Va.

Report of Brig. Gen. Alpheus S. Williams, U. S. Army.

HEADQUARTERS THIRD BRIGADE, BUNKER HILL, VA.,
March 6, 1862—10 a. m.

MAJOR: I reported yesterday afternoon my arrival here. We found a small picket of cavalry and a few infantry, several of whom were taken—furloughed men—who probably preferred being captured. I send them forward this morning to Provost-Marshal Andrews.

The information I get from Winchester is that Jackson is being considerably re-enforced, some say very strongly; that the slopes of the hills west of Winchester are strongly intrenched with rifle-pits and several earthworks with heavy guns. The works near the railroad southeast of Winchester you are probably well advised of. Jackson, Loring, and Kirby Smith are said to be at or near Winchester, but it does not seem possible to get any reliable information of number of troops. A good many of the Virginia militia are home on furlough. One man recently in Winchester reports Jackson as saying that he left Winchester once to whip us at Manassas, and now he is going to do the same for us here unless these intrenchments are very strong. I trust he will prove a false prophet. General Shields I knew was at Martinsburg after I left yesterday. I could get nothing reliable about the position of his command. I doubt if it has left Paw Paw. I should like some written action of future movements, especially with reference to my supply trains.

It takes over an hour to pass four wagons over the river, including getting in and off boats. I may appear over-anxious on this point, but its importance I regard as paramount. I find the Twelfth Massachusetts and Twelfth Indiana and First Maryland without tents. They are pretty comfortably placed in barns and public buildings here.

I am, very respectfully, your obedient servant,

A. S. WILLIAMS,
Brigadier-General.

Major COPELAND, *Assistant Adjutant-General, Charlestown.*

MARCH 5, 1862.—Skirmish near Pohick Church, Va.

REPORTS.

No. 1.—Col. Alexander Hays, Sixty-third Pennsylvania Infantry.
No. 2.—Lieut. Col. A. S. M. Morgan, Sixty-third Pennsylvania Infantry.

No. 1.

Report of Col. Alexander Hays, Sixty-third Pennsylvania Infantry.

CAMP JOHNSTON, NEAR FORT LYON, VA.,
March 8, 1862.

GENERAL: In obedience to instructions from you I have the honor to transmit the following statement of circumstances connected with the skirmish which occurred on the 4th [5th] instant near Pohick Church between a party of the Sixty-third Pennsylvania Volunteers and a scouting party of the rebels:

Having reason to believe that the scouts of the enemy were in the habit of approaching our line of pickets, I directed Lieutenant-Colonel Morgan to take a sufficient force and advance a short distance beyond our lines. He left my quarters at 3 o'clock a. m. with a force of 50 men and three commissioned officers. Two hours afterwards I was aroused by volleys of musketry and cheers. I at once hurried forward a company which I had in reserve at Pohick Church. When I arrived at our picket line I found Colonel Morgan's party retiring, with the loss of 1 captain, 1 first lieutenant, and 1 private, killed, and 1 private wounded. I herewith transmit a statement, made by Lieutenant-Colonel Morgan, which will explain the affair in detail.

Lamentable as the result has been—most to me, as the commanding officer of the regiment—I have the satisfaction of knowing that the rank and file of my regiment stood nobly to their work. The surprise was sudden, and after the first volley the enemy retreated, covered by darkness and a knowledge of the country, which enabled them to get beyond the bayonets of our men. The death of the two officers reported is more attributable to their own want of caution, in direct violation of my orders, than to any fault of their commanding officer.

Respectfully submitted.

ALEXANDER HAYS,
Colonel Sixty-third Regiment Pennsylvania Volunteers.

Brigadier-General HEINTZELMAN,
Commanding Third Brigade, Army of the Potomac.

No. 2.

Report of Lieut. Col. A. S. M. Morgan, Sixty-third Pennsylvania Infantry.

CAMP JOHNSTON, *March* 7, 1862.

SIR: I left the line of our pickets about 3.30 o'clock in the morning of March 5, in command of a detachment of about 50 men, including three commissioned officers, going out the Telegraph road, to carry out the plan arranged after consultation with yourself and the guide Williamson, that I should take possession of the road, leading from Violet's to Colchester, by which the parties of rebels were believed to come who had been seen on the hills opposite the left of our line. On reaching the point where the road alluded to leaves the Telegraph road, and finding that there was no opportunity to keep the men concealed beyond the fork of the road, I took them into the Colchester road, and placed them in ambush along that road in the bushes which are between them. Captains Chapman and McHenry were lying near me in a narrow cleared piece of ground, which runs from one road to the other, and just at the head of my command, the head being towards the forks of the road.

A little before day I heard the footsteps of one man approaching us. I thought at first that it was the guide Williamson, who had disappeared, moving down the open space towards the lower road immediately after we took the position, and when he had been inquired after no one of the officers knew where he was, but in a few seconds heard a body of men coming, and soon saw that they were passing down the Telegraph road, which is considerably lower in level than the Colchester road. It was too late to change my position, which had been taken in order to see the upper road, and I could just see the outline of men, not sufficiently to see whether or not they were armed. I could not have said that they were not men of our own regiment, though I believed them to be rebels. The uncertainty as to their character, and the fear that I could not swing my left around in time so that I could have any advantage in the attack, caused me to think that I had better avoid the risk of an attack when I found they were passing by without observing us.

As soon as it commenced to get somewhat light we started to return by the road we went, as I did not think it prudent to risk an attack with another body which might pass along when a body of the enemy was now known to be between us and our lines. The guide Williamson, who appeared just after they were past, reported them rebels, and that he estimated them to be 30 in number. In returning I sent a sergeant and 4 men in advance to see that the road was entirely clear of any enemy, Captain Chapman, Quartermaster Lysle, Williamson, and myself walking a little in front of the main body. The advance guard proceeded very cautiously, several times motioning us to stop and then to come on. Captain Chapman and Lieutenant Lysle gradually moved forward until they got half way between the two parties. When the guard reached a run a mile from the lines they stopped, motioning to us to stop. The two officers above named went on and joined them. They all soon moved in together. We crossed the run, and soon after again stopped on seeing them appear to suspect something wrong, in a dense thicket, which runs close up to the road and commencing about 125 yards from the run.

The advance guard stopped just before they got opposite the thicket. The two officers who were with it moved slowly in. Captain Chapman stopped once and turned back, then turned and went forward, he going close to the bushes and evidently looking into them, but no signal of any kind was made to me by any one of them. The officers were fairly in front of the thicket when a volley was fired from it by the concealed enemy, when both officers fell and one of the advance party was shot through the elbow. The main body at once, and without any order, fired into the thicket, and then left the road and took shelter behind a house opposite to which they were standing. As soon as they had re-treated I ordered Captain McHenry to deploy across the road so as to enter the thicket in the flank and to the rear of the enemy, which was at once done, the men charging forward with a shout as they reached the edge of the woods, the enemy running and escaping back through the woods. One private of my command was shot and killed as he entered the woods. After the enemy was fairly driven some distance I had the bodies of Captain Chapman, Quartermaster Lysle, and Private Moore, Company G, carried into the lines. Besides these who were killed the only other casualty was that Private Ferguson was shot through the elbow.

Respectfully submitted.

A. S. M. MORGAN,
Lieutenant-Colonel Sixty-third Pennsylvania Volunteers.

Col. ALEXANDER HAYS,
Commanding Sixty-third Regiment Pennsylvania Volunteers.

[Indorsement.]

HEADQUARTERS DIVISION,
Fort Lyon, March 14, 1862.

The report of Lieutenant-Colonel Morgan is unsatisfactory. I saw the guide Williamson, who says there was sufficient light to distinguish, and that there was no doubt of the men passing belonging to the enemy. It would have been very easy to have halted them and thus determined the fact. It shows a gross neglect of duty on the part of the commander then and afterwards when he was returning to his lines. I am clearly of the opinion that the case demands a court of inquiry.

Respectfully forwarded.

S. P. HEINTZELMAN,
Brigadier-General, Commanding.

MARCH 7, 1862.—Skirmish near Winchester, Va.

REPORTS.

No. 1.—Brig. Gen. Alpheus S. Williams, U. S. Army.
No. 2.—Capt. William D. Wilkins, Assistant Adjutant-General, U. S. Army.
No. 3.—Lieut. Col. Turner Ashby, C. S. Army.

No. 1.

Report of Brig. Gen. Alpheus S. Williams, U. S. Army.

HEADQUARTERS THIRD BRIGADE,
Bunker Hill, Va., March 8, 1862.

MAJOR: Frequent reports having come to me that the rebel cavalry in small squads were scouting the numerous cross roads west of this, seizing the property and persons of Union people, and that they had a considerable cavalry camp some miles above, on the Winchester pike, I determined to send out a reconnoitering party on that road with a force of infantry to return on two parallel roads west and beat up the hiding places of these marauding patrols. I sent forward Captain Cole's cavalry company, accompanied by Captain Wilkins and Captain Beman, of my staff, the latter to make a sketch of the country southwest of this with a reference to the cross-roads. I ordered one section of the artillery, under Captain Matthews, and the Fifth Connecticut and Forty-sixth Pennsylvania (encamped on that road) to follow, the two infantry regiments to turn to the left and return to camp by the middle road and the ridge road, both running nearly parallel to the pike within a distance of 3 miles west. The cavalry and artillery were to return on the pike when the infantry turned off.

The cavalry came in sight of the advanced vedettes of the rebels soon after leaving the outer posts of our own pickets (say 3 miles above), which, however, retired some miles up, where they joined the main body, deployed on both sides of the pike in the woods. Here they made a stand, and being in much superior force to our cavalry, were able to hold their advantageous position until they observed that detachments of our infantry were getting towards their rear, when they fled up the pike without again halting. Captain Matthews tried his new guns on them as they fled with very satisfactory results, as he reports to me. He could have punished them earlier, but it was reported that our infantry would be able to reach their rear and cut off the retreat of the whole command.

I regret to report that we had 3 privates of the cavalry wounded. The horse of Captain Cole was killed under him, and that of Captain Wilkins, assistant adjutant-general, so badly wounded as to be permanently disabled.

The officers and men behaved very gallantly while under fire of men sheltered for the most part by the trees.

My staff officers speak with high praise of the cool and daring conduct of Captain Cole and Lieutenant Vernon, of the cavalry.

My two staff officers (Captain Wilkins and Captain Beman) exposed themselves, I fear, almost to rashness.

I inclose a report of Captain Wilkins of this reconnaissance.

If the results were not important, the effect has been to stir up the blood of the men and put them in good spirits for any work ahead.

I hear the cavalry have shown themselves again this morning 3 or 4 miles west of this, seizing horses and committing depredations on all citizens supposed to be loyal. I have but one company of cavalry, and cannot pursue and punish these marauders as I could wish. I propose, however, to send out a pretty large guard of infantry to occupy those cross-roads, and, if possible, get possession of some of these rebel robbers.

I have the honor to be, very respectfully, your obedient servant,
A. S WILLIAMS,
Brigadier-General.

Major COPELAND, *Assistant Adjutant-General.*

P. S.—I get nothing but the same contradictory reports from W——— [Winchester]; by some that the rebels are going off, by others that they are thought re-enforced. Citizens from the vicinity of the skirmish yesterday report that the rebels had 6 killed and 7 wounded. I think the report very probable, as we had several amateur officers with their rifles present who had very deliberate aim upon the rebel troops. Major

Cook, of Twenty-eighth New York, and Lieutenant Skeels, regimental quartermaster Twenty-eighth New York, were especially active with their fine rifles. I inclose report of Captain Cole.* I have nothing from General Shields' command.

No. 2.

Report of Capt. William D. Wilkins, Assistant Adjutant-General.

HDQRS. THIRD BRIGADE, GENERAL BANKS' DIVISION,
Bunker Hill, Va., March 8, 1862.

GENERAL: I have the honor to report the result of a reconnaissance made by your orders yesterday afternoon on the Winchester turnpike, for the purpose of ascertaining the position and strength of a camp of the enemy's cavalry, reported upon apparently reliable authority to be situated 4 miles from this place, and also to ascertain whether any defensive works existed on the road for any distance outside the town. The force consisted of Cole's company of mounted cavalry, a section of Matthews' battery, and the Forty-sixth Pennsylvania and Fifth Connecticut Regiments of Infantry. We met the enemy's pickets of cavalry about 3 miles from this place and drove them before us with our cavalry about 5 miles farther, when, ascertaining at a farm house that they had been strongly re-enforced and that Colonel Ashby was in command, I deemed it prudent to wait for the artillery, and gave the order to halt. At this moment a heavy fire was poured in upon us from a large force (apparently two companies) of cavalry, dismounted, and firing behind stone fences and from a brick house on our left. Hoping to keep them in play until on the arrival of the artillery they might be shelled to advantage, we continued to exchange shots with them for about twenty minutes, the cavalry advancing by sections, firing, and retiring to reload, with great coolness. Here we lost 2 men slightly and 1 dangerously wounded and 2 horses shot. We observed two of the enemy to drop from their saddles, and several of their horses were seen running loose. The artillery, arriving, opened with shell upon the enemy, and about this time our infantry skirmishers appeared on his flanks. We then charged with the cavalry, and, driving the enemy from behind his fences, pursued him about half a mile farther, when, deeming the object of the reconnaissance to be accomplished (having advanced to within 3 miles of Winchester), I directed the cavalry to retire, and the troops arrived at camp in good order. We found no defenses on the road of any kind for the distance we advanced, but found the turnpike to be very much broken up.

I beg leave to call your attention to the gallant conduct of Captain Cole, who was very conspicuous in leading and cheering on his men and who had his horse killed under him; and to Captain Beman, commissary of subsistence of your staff, who rendered valuable service in bringing up our artillery and infantry supports and in leading our cavalry skirmishers across the field to the left under a heavy fire.

I am, general, very respectfully, your obedient servant,
WM. D. WILKINS,
Captain and Assistant Adjutant-General.

Brig. Gen. ALPHEUS S. WILLIAMS,
Commanding Third Brigade and other troops at Bunker Hill.

---

* Not found.

No. 3.

Report of Lieut. Col. Turner Ashby, C. S. Army.

CAVALRY CAMP,
On Martinsburg Turnpike, Va., March 8, 1862.

I have the honor to report the result of a skirmish between Capts. S. B. Myers' and Koontz's companies with the advancing column of the enemy coming out from Bunker Hill on yesterday, brought on by his advance, while Captains Myers and Koontz and myself were visiting the outposts of pickets.

Upon learning that he was advancing in force, I ordered these two companies up from their rendezvous (1 mile in our rear), ordering the pickets, under charge of Lieutenant Neff, to keep him in check as long as possible, which he did most gallantly until these companies arrived, only amounting to 45, as many of them were still on duty as pickets. Having ordered them to form behind a skirt of timber, which reached across the turnpike, under charge of Captain Myers, Captain Koontz and myself moved forward to make an observation, when I became sat-isfied, from movements made by the enemy's officers, that he had a co-operating force upon each flank and was quite strong, which afterwards proved true, as I saw two regiments in column on our left, one-half mile from the turnpike, and had reports from scouts of another column on the right. Being, however, confident of being able to elude them at the proper time, I determined to check the column advancing upon the turnpike as long as prudent to remain, which I did for more than one hour, as upon every advance he made my men give him such a galling fire as to drive him back out of sight under the hill, at one time driving him for one-fourth of a mile. I did not allow my men to pursue, as I had a position of my choice, and feared, in the excitement, they might charge to the supporting column of infantry. After the column of in-fantry upon my left made its appearance, double-quicking, and had passed beyond me about 300 yards, I ordered my men to fall back slowly, which they did in a walk, turning every time the enemy made a demonstration to charge and driving them back.

In the stand made behind the timber the enemy had 3 men wounded that I know of and 2 horses left on the ground; 1 wounded (that of an officer). I had 1 man dangerously wounded.

I skirmished before the advancing column for 3 miles, he throwing shot and shell from two pieces which he had on the turnpike. Upon meeting three companies of cavalry, which I had ordered to re-enforce me, I again formed across the road, when the enemy halted, and after a little time returned towards Bunker Hill, near to which place I fol-lowed them, they having their encampment three-fourths of a mile this side, their pickets 1 mile, into which I fired.

I am pleased to express my highest commendation and appreciation of the conduct of Capts. S. B. Myers and Koontz, as well as Lieutenants Neff, Clarke, and Myers, and also of the privates of their companies, who gave evidence of much hope of success to our cause when the strug-gle for the valley comes.

Respectfully,

TURNER ASHBY,
Lieutenant-Colonel, Commanding Cavalry.
GEORGE G. JUNKIN, *Acting Assistant Adjutant-General.*

MARCH 7–9, 1862. Withdrawal of the Confederate forces from Evansport, Dumfries, Manassas, and Occoquan, Va.

REPORTS, ETC.

No. 1.—Brig. Gen. Joseph Hooker, U. S. Army, with correspondence and orders.
No. 2.—Lieut. Robert H. Wyman, U. S. Navy.
No. 3.—General Joseph E. Johnston, C. S. Army.
No. 4.—Letters from President Davis to General Johnston.
No. 5.—Brig. Gen. W. H. C. Whiting, C. S. Army, with congratulatory order from General T. H. Holmes.
No. 6.—Col. Wade Hampton, C. S. Army.
No. 7.—Col. J. J. Archer, Fifth Texas Infantry.
No. 8.—Maj. Stephen D. Lee, C. S. Army.
No. 9.—Capt. D. F. Summey, C. S. Army.

No. 1.

Reports of Brig. Gen. Joseph Hooker, U. S. Army, with correspondence and orders.

MARCH 9, 1862—10.30 a. m.

I have dispatched the statements of the contrabands to Captain Wyman, with the request that he will forward them to you at once. Whiting's command, consisting of five regiments and one battery of six pieces, expects to reach Fredericksburg to-night. They left in great haste, leaving their supplies of clothing and provisions behind them.

JOSEPH HOOKER,
Brigadier-General, Commanding Division.

Brig. Gen. R. B. MARCY.

—

WASHINGTON, D. C., *March 9, 1862.*

Your dispatch regarding Whiting's movement to Fredericksburg received.

The General Commanding desires you and Captain Wyman to keep a sharp lookout upon the batteries opposite you, and if you find they are abandoned or so feebly manned that you can destroy them without running any great risk, do so. Please communicate with Captain Wyman at once and hold yourself ready to seize the first favorable moment that presents itself.

Send back your spies as soon as possible and keep the general commanding informed of everything that occurs.

R. B. MARCY,
Chief of Staff.

General JOSEPH HOOKER, *Camp Baker.*

—

HEADQUARTERS HOOKER'S DIVISION,
Camp Baker, Lower Potomac, Md., March 9, 1862.

I am directed by the brigadier-general commanding the division to request that you will detach 500 men, with instructions for them to proceed to the opposite side of the Potomac River to examine and bring off all ammunition and stores of any value left by the enemy in their sudden evacuation of the camps and batteries at Cockpit Point and Evansport. A portion of the detachment should be provided with axes, spades, and picks, to cut away the parapet if necessary, in order tha'; hawsers may be attached to the guns, for the purpose of hauling them off the banks on which they stand, that they may be secured by vessels of the flotilla. Some of these pieces are represented to be of great value. The detachment should be commanded by a discreet officer, with instructions to keep his men well together, with pickets well thrown out to prevent surprise, should rebel parties be found lurking in that vicinity. The detachment will be directed to be on board one of the barges now lying at Rum Point as early as sunrise to-morrow morning, as one of the vessels of the flotilla will be in readiness to tow them across the river at that hour. As soon as the work assigned them is completed. the command will return to camp. The officer in command will be directed to collect all possible information of the movements of the rebels and report it as early as practicable.

Very respectfully, &c.,

JOS. DICKINSON,
Assistant Adjutant-General.

Col. S. H. STARR, *Commanding Third Brigade.*

—

HEADQUARTERS HOOKER'S DIVISION,
Camp Baker, Lower Potomac, Md., March 10, 1862.

GENERAL: I have nothing important to add to the advices sent you yesterday concerning the abandonment by the enemy of their positions in my front along the shores of the river. Everything left behind indicates that they left hastily and in great confusion. All the guns in the Cockpit Point battery were left mounted on their carriages and in good condition, except the guns being spiked. An effort was made to burn the carriages of most of the guns at Shipping Point, which the rebels succeeded in accomplishing in the majority of cases. The large English rifled piece, 98-pounder, remains on its carriage, uninjured. Most of the magazines were blown up and great quantities of clothing and subsistence stores destroyed. I have sent 1,000 men across the river to tumble the ordnance over the bluff banks on which the greater part of their batteries stand, in order that they may be more easily removed to such points as may hereafter be determined on. It is reported that the rebels took little or nothing with them in their retreat. Their roads appear to have been worse than ours, and their teams utterly worthless, from overwork and little or no feed.

I feel very confident that the Merrimac wears no armor the bolts of the Whitworth will not penetrate. Evidences of their accuracy, length of range, and effect are to be seen all over the deserted camps of the enemy. Two shots were fired at a house standing nearly half a mile in rear of the Shipping Point battery and in the center of one of their camps, both of which struck it about 4 feet from the ground and within 2 or 3 feet of each other. One of these shot was found on the mantel-piece, labeled "Fired by the Yankees February 27, 1862."

Very respectfully, your obedient servant,

JOSEPH HOOKER,
Brigadier-General, Commanding Division.

Brig. Gen. S. WILLIAMS,
Adjutant-General, Army of the Potomac.

HEADQUARTERS HOOKER'S DIVISION,
Camp Baker, Lower Potomac, Md., March 11, 1862.

GENERAL: I have the honor to report that the rebel batteries at Cockpit Point were entirely destroyed yesterday. The valuable guns of these batteries were tumbled over the bank on which they stood, and are now where the vessels of the flotilla can remove them at their leisure. An effort was also made to demolish the batteries at Shipping Point and vicinity, but in consequence of their remoteness from the bank, the great weight of the pieces, and the absence of all aid from the vessels of the flotilla, the work was not completed. My men have been waiting on board of one of the barges for a tug to come for them to return to that duty to-day. It is now 11 o'clock a. m., and no tug has come. I regret this, as large quantities of powder and shell still remain on the rebel shore. Several loads were brought over yesterday. I will report more particularly when the reports of those in charge with that duty reach here. The rebels burned 800 barrels of flour before quitting Dumfries. I send to the provost-marshal by the steamer 3 prisoners, captured yesterday, whose testimony it may be interesting, if not valuable, to learn.

Very respectfully, your obedient servant,
JOSEPH HOOKER,
Brigadier-General, Commanding Division.

Brig. Gen. S. WILLIAMS,
Adjutant-General, Army of the Potomac.

No. 2.

Report of Lieut. Robert H. Wyman, U. S. Navy.

WASHINGTON NAVY-YARD, *March* 9, 1862.

Hon. E. M. STANTON, *Secretary of War:*

I have just received the following message to Secretary of the Navy:

SIR: The Cockpit Point and Shipping Point batteries are abandoned. They have been shelled for an hour without a reply from them. Large fires at Shipping Point and Evansport make it apparent that they are destroying their material there. The Page also I believe to have been burned and blown up. Many explosions have occurred.

Very respectfully,
R. H. WYMAN,
Lieutenant, Commanding.

JNO. A. DAHLGREN.

No. 3.

Report of General Joseph E. Johnston, C. S. Army.

HEADQUARTERS, RAPPAHANNOCK BRIDGE,
March 12, 1862.

GENERAL: The troops left Manassas and its vicinity on the evening of the 9th. The chief quartermaster having reported that the public property of value would be removed before Friday, I had ordered the troops to march on Saturday morning, their baggage wagons leading. So much was found remaining on Saturday, however, that the troops were kept until Sunday evening. The miserable performance of the railroad rendered this measure almost useless. A good deal of property, public and regimental, was destroyed.

Smith's and Longstreet's divisions followed the Warrenton turnpike; Ewell's and Early's the railroad and a route through Brentsville. The first named is now near Culpeper Court-House. The two last have this morning completed the passage of the river here. Our pickets are on a line a little beyond Warrenton and the Warrenton Junction.

A reserve depot was established at Culpeper Court-House, the stores in which I have ordered to be removed to Gordonsville. I will remain here to cover that operation unless otherwise ordered. The management of this railroad is so wretched that it may require a week or 10 days.

My post-office for the present is Culpeper Court-House, 10 miles off.

A. P. Mason, for whom I have asked a commission on my staff, is very useful to me. I hope that the commission can be given.

Most respectfully, your obedient servant,

J. E. JOHNSTON,
General.

General S. COOPER, *Adjutant and Inspector General.*

No. 4.

Letters from President Davis to General Johnston.

RICHMOND, *March* 15, 1862.

Your letter of 13th received this day,* being the first information of your retrograde movement. Have no report of your reconnaissance and can suggest nothing as to the position you should take, except it should be as far in advance as consistent with your safety.

JEFFERSON DAVIS.

JOSEPH E. JOHNSTON, *Culpeper Court-House.*

RICHMOND, VA., *March* 15, 1862.

GENERAL: I have received your letter of the 13th instant,* giving the first official account I have received of the retrograde movement of your army. Your letter would lead me to infer that others had been sent to apprize me of your plans and movements. If so, they have not reached me; and before the receipt of yours of the 13th I was as much in the dark as to your purposes, condition, and necessities as at the time of our conversation on the subject about a month since.

'Tis true I have had many and alarming reports of great destruction of ammunition, camp equipage, and provisions, indicating precipitate retreat; but, having heard of no cause for such a sudden movement, I was at a loss to believe it. I have not the requisite topographical knowledge for the selection of your new position. I had intended that you should determine that question; and for this purpose a corps of engineers was furnished to make a careful examination of the country to aid you in your decision.

---

* Not found, but see report No. 3, p. 526.

The question of throwing troops into Richmond is contingent upon reverses in the West and Southeast. The immediate necessity for such a movement is not anticipated.

Very respectfully,

JEFFERSON DAVIS.

General JOSEPH E. JOHNSTON,
    Headquarters Army of the Potomac.

No. 5.

Reports of Brig. Gen. W. H. C. Whiting, C. S. Army, with congratulatory order from General T. H. Holmes.

HEADQUARTERS, CAMP BARTOW, VA.,
March 22, 1862.

SIR: In obedience to the orders of the President, conveyed through you to Major-General Holmes, on account of certain unofficial reports which had reached his excellency about the destruction of tents, ammunition, public property, &c., in my division, I have made a detailed report to Major-General Holmes.

I trust that it will completely satisfy his excellency that I have been maliciously slandered. Something is due to me, and I most respectfully demand from the justice of the President the source of his information. I also respectfully request that my report may be referred, *in extenso*, to General J. E. Johnston, under whose orders I acted entirely. I also respectfully request to be informed whether my division alone is the subject of such reports. If it is taken as the exemplar in this matter, in justice to the officers and men I may say, without offense, that the country and the cause have reason to congratulate itself on the army.

Very respectfully,

W. H. C. WHITING,
Brigadier-General.

Hon. J. P. BENJAMIN, *Secretary of War, Richmond, Va.*

HEADQUARTERS, CAMP BARTOW, VA,
March 21, 1862.

GENERAL: I have received from you to-day the following copy of a letter addressed to you by the Secretary of War:

WAR DEPARTMENT,
Richmond, Va., March 20, 1862.

GENERAL: The President requests that I should inform you that unofficial reports have reached him of great destruction of property—burning tents, destruction of ammunition, &c.—in the division commanded by General Whiting in the recent retrograde movement of the army, and he desires that you will require of General Whiting a detailed report on the subject.

I am, your obedient servant,

J. P. BENJAMIN,
Acting Secretary of War.

I submit, accordingly, the following report upon the subject of these unofficial imputations:

The distribution of my division for the defense of the Occoquan and support of the Evansport battery (the right of General Johnston's position) was as follows: Hampton's brigade in advance, consisting of four regiments and three batteries. Of this, two regiments and two batteries were at Wolf Run Shoals and Davis' Ford, on the Occoquan; the Legion, with one battery, at Colchester, and one regiment near the village of Occoquan, at the forks of the Telegraph and Brentsville roads. This line was 10 miles in extent. In support the Texas brigade, Colonel Archer; three regiments of this were posted on the Telegraph road, between and upon Neabsco and Powell's Runs, with one battery. The First Texas at Talbot's Hill, on the Quantico, to cover the left of the Evansport battery. In support the Third Brigade; Fifth Alabama battalion and one company of the First Tennessee at Cockpit battery; one regiment and one battery at Dumfries; and four regiments and one battery on Powell's Run, 3 miles above Dumfries, equidistant from Evansport, Wolf Run Shoals, and Colchester. One squadron of cavalry and the legion of cavalry picketed the Potomac from Evansport to Colchester and the Occoquan in front.

To maintain this force provisions and forage had to be hauled over the worst kind of roads in no case less than 16 miles, and to many of the regiments a distance of 30 to 40. Regimental and brigade teams had during the whole winter been in constant requisition to maintain even the daily supply, which exhausting labor had greatly weakened them. I had finally to resort to pack-mules, and often to half rations, on account of the roads.

I mention this and the distribution to show the difficulties of the country and the position from which I had to withdraw my command. The enemy was in force in front and on the river, and daily skirmishes took place. Such was the condition when General Johnston gave me confidential orders to prepare to move on Fredericksburg whenever he should give the signal. I was to be ready at any moment, and yet was in the embarrassing position of being obliged to subsist my men from day to day. The trip for supplies, if successful, occupied three days, and I might have, while the wagons are off, to move without them, abandoning everything.

In a district full of disaffection great caution was necessary. I communicated my orders to Colonels Hampton and Archer, and commenced sending off sick, baggage, &c., preparing teams, &c.

At midday on the 7th I received orders to move at daylight on the 8th. A copy of the order (herewith, marked A) was sent to every regiment in the command. I had twenty-eight field guns, with their caissons and ammunition, the extra ammunition in hand, that of the sick and furloughed men and their arms, and the camp equipage and baggage of 11,200 men to move.

1st. As to the Third Brigade, under my immediate supervision, not a cartridge was abandoned or destroyed, nor any public property whatever, except a few worn-out tents and 8 condemned wagons, without animals to haul them. It should be observed that the tents of the Third Brigade, their own property, brought with them to Harper's Ferry and in use from there to Dumfries, had been condemned as entirely worn-out some months before, on the troops getting hutted, and no requisition for new ones had been made on the Quartermaster's Department. A few of the best were brought, together with the entire quartermaster's stores, tools, &c. Most of the regiments also succeeded in getting off a large amount of private baggage. A portion was distributed and concealed, with a view to recovery, at farms in the rear, and a portion given to poor and loyal people in the vicinity.

2d. Cockpit battery, commanded by Captain Frobel. By his energy and activity all the tents and baggage of the Fifth Alabama, cooking utensils, together with all the ammunition, material, and equipments of the battery, even to the powder emptied from the loaded shells, were brought safely off and are now here. The shell and shot were buried in secure concealment. The only ammunition expended was 25 cartridges, which the rear guard had so stationed to fire on the enemy in case he attempted to cross during the movement. Captain Frobel conveyed his property in a scow on the river into Chopawamsic.

3d. The cavalry. Tents and camp equipage brought off complete; some private property destroyed or concealed.

4th. Imboden's battery. Nothing left behind; tents, ammunition, camp equipage, and battery complete, though the guns and caissons had to be brought out of Dumfries one at a time, twelve horses being required to each.

5th. Reilly's battery complete and in as perfect order as when first equipped. Fifteen barrels of breadstuff were reported by the First Tennessee Regiment as left, not possible to carry them. Most of this was taken by the men of the other regiments in their haversacks. The entire ammunition, stores, and property were brought off. So much for the Third Brigade.

The report of Colonel Archer, commanding the Texas brigade, is herewith submitted [No. 7]. It is due to Colonel Archer to state that the route by which he had to retire was the worst of all—the old stage road. Teams in first-rate condition could barely haul 1,000 pounds over it, and all transportation had been very much weakened by the exhausting labor of the winter and the want of long forage.

It must be stated also, in justice to the entire command, that immediately after the furloughs were granted orders were issued from headquarters Army of the Potomac making each company commander responsible for the arms of the furloughed men, and requiring them to be kept with the regiments. I had applied, then, to be allowed to send them to Richmond until the expiration of the furloughs, on the very ground that, if required to move in any direction, I could not carry them—my camp equipage and the ammunition—but for satisfactory reasons the permission was denied.

The report of Colonel Hampton, commanding the advance brigade, is herewith submitted [No. 6], together with that of Maj. Stephen D. Lee, commanding battalion of artillery [No. 8]. Colonel Hampton being in general charge of an extended line, and having no officer available of rank to whom I could intrust the delicate maneuver of withdrawing from Wolf Run Shoals, the key of our position, in the face of the enemy, I had to assign Major Lee, as chief of the brigade staff, with the immediate direction of the movement. He executed it in a masterly manner.

The difficulties surrounding Colonel Hampton were indeed great. An extended line, insufficient transportation, an active and superior enemy in his front, incessant skirmishing all along his outposts; his army was watched and shelled from the enemy's fleet. Balloons had been up every day for some days previous on both sides of the Potomac, and from the activity of the enemy and the fact that the country people and negroes had got suspicion of the move it was considered certain that the enemy would attack at once.

It is due to that distinguished, active, and vigilant officer to say that here, as everywhere, he conducted his brigade with consummate judgment, precision, and skill. His loss of property, except private, amounts to nothing.

The twenty-four wagons of which he speaks were a train-loaded with forage, which arrived at my headquarters at 9 p. m. on the night of the 7th, having been three days on the route from Manassas, and which I had to send even then to Colonel Hampton. They only reached him at 4.30 o'clock on the morning of the 8th—8 miles. This may illustrate Prince William County and its roads.

Although ready in the Third Brigade and the Texas Brigade to march at sunrise and our trains already off, I kept them both under arms in position until 1.30 p. m., until General French had been two hours clear of Evansport and Colonel Hampton's rear guard had passed Greenwood Church or Neabsco.

The whole division marched over the Rappahannock by brigades, on Monday and Tuesday following the 8th, in perfect order.

I call attention to the foregoing general orders of Major-General Holmes, so far as it refers to my division.*

I hope this report will be satisfactory to the President. I respectfully demand that it be referred to my commanding general (General Joseph E. Johnston), under whose special orders I acted, and who has honored me with special confidence.

I also respectfully demand, with regard to the use of public property in my division and vigilance over the expenditure of public money and stores, that reference be made to General Johnston's inspector, Col. A. Cole, who inspected a few days before the move.

Very respectfully,
W. H. C. WHITING,
Brigadier-General, Commanding Division, Occoquan, Va.
Major-General HOLMES,
Commanding Aquia District, Virginia.

—

HEADQUARTERS CAMP BARTOW, VA.,
March 22, 1862.

GENERAL: Since I dispatched my report to you Colonel Archer has informed me (and this is the first that I have ever heard of it) that General Wigfall had accumulated at Dumfries an extra supply of ammunition for his brigade. It had not been issued to regiments nor reported to division headquarters, probably owing to General Wigfall's absence in Congress. The wagons were loaded with as much of it as could be possibly taken; but thirty rounds had to be sacrificed. This is the first information as to that (or even as to there being any supply other than that required by my general orders) I have ever had, and I cannot consider myself at all responsible either for its accumulation or its loss.

Very respectfully,
W. H. C. WHITING,
Brigadier-General.
Major-General HOLMES,
Commanding Aquia District, Virginia.

[Inclosure A.]

HEADQUARTERS CAMP FISHER, VIRGINIA,
March 7, 1862.

The wagons will be hauled into the company parade grounds and the teams taken to the stables and fed.

----

* See inclosure B.

Packing will be commenced at once. Commissioned officers will see that the wagons are not overloaded, and they will be held responsible for this.

If there is any forage to be had, each team will carry a small supply. Quartermasters and wagon-masters will see to this. Quartermasters and wagon-masters will also see that wagons are not overloaded, and report all violations of this order to the colonel.

During the night two or three days' provisions will be cooked and distributed to the men, after which such of the cooking utensils as are to be carried will be put on the wagons.

During the night guards are required to maintain perfect order, silence, and discipline. Commanding officers of regiments will be held responsible for their own commands.

At daylight in the morning the trains will start, the brigade train leading, all accompanied by the train guards, and the sick, if there are any, under charge of a commissioned or non-commissioned officer.

Ammunition wagons will accompany their respective regiments and remain with them.

On march all officers are emphatically ordered to preserve the formation of rank and prevent the men from straggling. Colonels will frequently allow their regiments to file past them, to see that they are well closed, and will direct the field and staff to give their whole attention to the march. Brigade commanders will direct the halts. Troops will move left in front. They will remain in position until notified. The colors will be carried displayed.

W. H. C. WHITING,
Brigadier-General, Commanding Division.

Colonel HAMPTON.

[Inclosure B.]

GENERAL ORDERS, }   HEADQUARTERS AQUIA DISTRICT, VA.,
    No. 27.   }   *March* 17, 1862.

The major-general commanding the Aquia District desires to congratulate his own and the division of General Whiting on the admirable discipline and zeal for the service they have ever shown. The regularity and order of their march from Occoquan, Dumfries, and Evansport, made under circumstances of much difficulty, and their perfect subordination in this city, are speaking acts in evidence that have given him greatest satisfaction. Let us all remember that we are now at the threshold of those great events which must decide the fate of our beloved country. Each soldier in such a cause should be a hero. Let every man now in arms for the glory and independence of his home resolve to continue in that obedience and patience which equally with courage constitute the true soldier. Thus shall we be prepared to meet, and with God's blessing to defeat, the advancing columns of our enemies.

By command of Maj. Gen. T. H. Holmes:

ARCHER ANDERSON,
Assistant Adjutant-General.

No. 6.

Report of Col. Wade Hampton, C. S. Army.

CAMP BARTOW, VA., *March* 21, 1862.

GENERAL: On my arrival here I had the honor to make to you a report of my movement from the Occoquan, and I now beg to lay before you a more detailed statement, showing the quantity of public stores removed from my different camps on the line I occupied, as well as the amount of property destroyed.

Before doing this, I must, in justice to my command, state the positions occupied by me and give the amount of transportation at my disposal. The brigade store-house was at Bacon Race Church, 9 miles from Manassas by the nearest road, and by the only one we could use 12 miles. Here a very large amount of public and private property was accumulated. Three miles in front of the church I had two regiments posted, one at Wolf Run Shoals and the other at the lower Davis' Ford. Three batteries were also stationed near the church, one regiment (the Nineteenth Georgia) was placed near Occoquan Village, 7 miles from Bacon Race, and the Legion was opposite Colchester, 2 miles lower down. My brigade thus occupied a line on the river 12 miles long, and had to be supplied with forage and subsistence from Manassas altogether. Knowing the difficulties of my position, Major Barbour frequently sent trains from Manassas to the church to bring my supplies so far. The Sixteenth North Carolina Regiment, at Wolf Run, had ten wagons; the Fourteenth Georgia, at Davis' Ford, had nine; the Nineteenth Georgia had four, and the Legion seven. The teams, with the exception of those with the Legion, were in wretched order, and the roads were almost impassable.

At 3.30 p. m., while I was on my return from Bacon Race, on Friday, the 7th instant, I received your order to march at daylight the next morning. Couriers were at once sent to the different regiments, and in spite of the short notice and our very limited transportation the trains began to move at the hour appointed. My own movement was delayed by an attack of the enemy on my pickets at Colchester. I marched the Legion down to repel this attack, and as soon as I thought it safe to do so they were withdrawn and put in motion.

All the guns of my sick men and all the ammunition were first placed in the wagons, and all were brought to this point except a small quantity of ammunition, which had to be destroyed on the road because the teams were unable to haul it. From the same cause I was forced to leave on the road fifty-nine of my tents. They were not destroyed until all the private baggage of the men had met the same fate. With the wagons you sent to me, and which did not reach me until 4.30 a. m. on the 8th, I moved all the public stores I possibly could. Besides this, I sent back to Manassas 130 sick. Twelve wagons were loaded with public stores, and nine with those of the commissary department. Forage had also to be brought with us a great part of the march.

With the means at my disposal I moved, literally in face of the enemy, four regiments of infantry, three batteries, containing 31 guns and gun-carriages, and 120 cavalry, bringing all to this point safely, over roads that were scarcely passable, a distance of 50 miles. There was no straggling, no confusion, and after the first day's march no loss of any property. If ample transportation had been placed at my command, not one particle of property, public or private, would have been destroyed. As it was,

I think the loss of public property was remarkably small. My greatest regret is that I cannot say the same as to private property, for it seems to be a hard case to make the soldier bear a loss which was caused by no fault of his own.

The report of Major Lee [No. 8], which is inclosed, will show what was done at Bacon Race. That of Captain Summey, quartermaster Sixteenth North Carolina, will tell what was brought and what left by that regiment, which contains twelve companies, and is a very large one. The reports from the other regiments, with that of the brigade commissary, will be sent to you as soon as they are handed in.

My letters to you and to the Quartermaster's Department will show that I foresaw the consequences of our weak transportation, and that I constantly and earnestly called attention to this branch of the service. It was not, doubtless, in the power of the Department to afford the assistance needed, but it is unquestionably due alone to the condition of our transportation that anything was lost, and I cannot feel that any blame should attach to the division you command, especially when the only foundation upon which such blame is based is a vague and unofficial report.

As to the brigade which I have had the honor to command for some months, and which has during that time held the advanced position in face of an enemy greatly its superior, I can only say that in the recent retrograde movement it brought with it all the public property that it possibly could. That any should have been lost is a source of regret to me; but my regret is entirely free from the slightest feeling of self-reproach.

I am, general, very respectfully, your obedient servant,

WADE HAMPTON,
Colonel, Commanding Brigade.

General WHITING, *Commanding Division.*

No. 7.

Report of Col. J. J. Archer, Fifth Texas Infantry.

HEADQUARTERS FIFTH REGIMENT TEXAS VOLUNTEERS,
Camp Wigfall, Va., March 21, 1862.

MAJOR: I have the honor to report that from the time of receiving your order to put my brigade in complete marching order the whole of my brigade train was constantly engaged in carrying the sick to the rear, and one-half of each regimental train in carrying the most valuable of the camping property, including a large quantity of spare arms. As it was contemplated that the enemy might attack during the movement, it was not deemed prudent to send any of the ammunition in advance; and when the final order came every wagon at my disposal was loaded under the immediate supervision of the regimental commanders and the brigade quartermaster and commissary, and every article which, with my limited means of transportation in the existing state of the roads, could possibly be carried was brought away.

Respectfully, your obedient servant,

J. J. ARCHER,
Colonel Fifth Texas Regiment.

Maj. JAMES H. HILL, *Assistant Adjutant-General.*

No. 8.

Report of Maj. Stephen D. Lee, C. S. Army.

CAMP BARTOW,
Near Fredericksburg, Va., March 21, 1862.

SIR: In compliance with instructions in circular of this date I have the honor to submit the following report with reference to the amount of transportation, baggage brought, and baggage destroyed in the recent retrograde movement from the Occoquan to this point:

First, under my immediate command I had three batteries of artillery, leaving out two pieces with the Legion at Colchester (twelve guns and carriages). These guns were at Bacon Race Church, Wolf Run, and Davis' Fords, on the Occoquan. There were seven transportation and two ammunition wagons. With these wagons all the tents and equipage were brought to this point, excepting five tents belonging to one company, and six boxes of 12-pounder ammunition (seventy-two rounds), which I ordered destroyed on the road, it being impossible, with the indifferent teams, to transport them.

Several days before the retrograde movement I was appointed chief of staff to the brigade, and charged by Colonel Hampton with the withdrawal of the two regiments at Wolf Run Shoals and Davis' Ford, on the Occoquan (Sixteenth North Carolina Regiment, Lieutenant-Colonel Love, and Fourteenth Georgia Regiment, Colonel Price), as also with the disposition of the public stores at Bacon Race Church, which was the depot for the troops on the Occoquan. The North Carolina regiment had about ten wagons, and brought all their tents and equipage which was of any value. The Fourteenth Georgia had nine wagons, and brought only their cooking utensils. Colonel Price reported he had to destroy his tents for want of transportation. He was instructed to load his wagons only with equipage. The tents he destroyed were of little value.

At Bacon Race Church, at the time I took charge, several days before the movement, I found about 100 stands of arms, a quantity of ammunition, medical and quartermaster's stores; also about fifteen old wagons and harness (unserviceable). I succeeded in sending to Manassas, and in transporting to this point with twelve wagons, which were put at my disposal the night before the movement and in the return transportation trains to Manassas, all the arms, ammunition, and stores of value. All that was destroyed were the old wagons and harness (which were unserviceable), a quantity of loose cartridges, amounting to several boxes, and a quantity of private baggage. I should also state that a small amount of commissary stores were issued to the poor people in the vicinity by my order, there being no transportation for them.

I regret not being able to be more explicit; but being placed in charge but a few days before the movement I could not give a correct inventory, but can state generally that nothing of any value was destroyed, all the valuable stores being sent to Manassas or brought in the twelve wagons to this point. Considering the dreadful state of the roads, I consider that all the property that was of any value was saved.

Respectfully submitted.

STEPHEN D. LEE,
Major, Provisional Army Confederate States,
Commanding Artillery Battalion, Occoquan, Va.

Lieut. T. G. BARKER,
Acting Assistant Adjutant-General of Brigade, Occoquan, Va.

No. 9.

Report of Capt. D. F. Summey, C. S. Army.

INVENTORY OF THE TRANSPORTATION OF THE SIXTEENTH NORTH
CAROLINA REGIMENT, MARCH 8, 1862.

Ten wagons and teams complete; 7 horses and mules that had been
sent to Manassas for inspection came to camp first night on march at
Cole's Store, one of the wagons loaded with the sick.

Public property destroyed at camp was—

    2 ambulances, that had been useless for some weeks.
    4 sets of ambulance harness.
    2 wagons, old and broken.
    8 sets of wagon harness (old and broken; no new harness).
    1 keg of nails.
    1 grindstone, nearly worn-out.
    24 axes, most of them broken, being in use for some time.
    20 axes, good.
    24 picks (about), spades, and shovels, much worn.
    100 tents, 35 of them condemned.

Sent to Manassas and whereabouts unknown—

    6 hospital tents.
    1 Sibley tent.
    4 wagons and harness.
    12 pack-saddles.
    50 pairs of shoes (about), a few flannel shirts and cotton drawers,
        quantity not known.

Public property brought away—

    Wagon harness, above enumerated.
    40 tents.
    Nearly all the cooking utensils in the regiment.

D. F. SUMMEY,
Acting Quartermaster Sixteenth North Carolina Regiment.

MARCH 7–11, 1862.—Union advance to Centreville and Manassas, Va.

REPORTS, ETC.

No. 1.—Brig. Gen. Philip Kearny, U. S. Army.
No. 2.—Col. Alfred T. A. Torbert, First New Jersey Infantry.
No. 3.—Lieut. Col. Robert McAllister, First New Jersey Infantry.
No. 4.—Maj. David Hatfield, First New Jersey Infantry.
No. 5.—Capt. Sylvester Van Sickell, First New Jersey Infantry.
No. 6.—Col. Isaac M. Tucker, Second New Jersey Infantry.
No. 7.—Col. George W. Taylor, Third New Jersey Infantry.
No. 8.—Col. James H. Simpson, Fourth New Jersey Infantry.
No. 9.—Capt. Joseph K. Stearns, First New York Cavalry.
No. 10.—Lieut. William Alexander, First New York Cavalry.
No. 11.—Letter from Col. David McM. Gregg, Eighth Pennsylvania Cavalry.

No. 1.

Reports of Brig. Gen. Philip Kearny, U. S. Army.

HEADQUARTERS FIRST BRIGADE,
Three miles from Bull Run, March 9, 1862—2.30 p. m.

SIR : On information of my scouts, &c., I felt justified in making this day a reconnaissance to Sangster's Station. We have done this with caution and forced in the enemy's pickets, which were in some force at Sangster's.

Colonel Taylor commanded the advance. Colonel Simpson, with uncommon judgment, echeloned our supports and guarded us from attacks from our right.

A cavalry charge, unrivaled in brilliancy, headed by Lieutenant Hidden, Lincoln Horse, broke, captured, and annihilated them, but was paid for by his life. A lieutenant and many foot-men are in our hands.

The Lincoln Horse has distinguished itself also in our patrols, which report the Ox road and farther country safe. The Third Regiment New Jersey Volunteers has been so far in the advance, the Second supporting it; Colonel Simpson holding Fairfax Station, and intermediate company (First Regiment) at Burke's. The country has been safely covered at all points. The enemy evidently is disheartened and retiring. Their cars are continually running to Manassas.

I await further orders, my original ones being to remain at Burke's.

Respectfully, your obedient servant,

P. KEARNY,
Brigadier-General.

Captain PURDY, *Assistant Adjutant-General.*

P. S.—The lieutenant taken was Lieutenant Stewart, late of West Point. The general has sent Colonel Simpson on to Fairfax Court-House.

———

FIRST BRIGADE, FRANKLIN'S DIVISION,
Centreville, March 10, 1862—10.30 p. m.

SIR : As I informed you yesterday, I was led to drive back the enemy's pickets from information that seemed somewhat reliable. At night I occupied Burke's Station carefully, and Fairfax Court-House, Fairfax Station, and the intermediate line, as well as Sangster's Station, with regiments or strong detachments. This morning I occupied, at 12.30 p. m., Centreville with a detachment of the First Infantry, the regiment following, entering Centreville by the old Braddock road.

The last detachment of the enemy left late last night, blowing up the bridge on Cub and Bull Run.

I have also this day occupied Sangster's Station with the Third New Jersey Volunteers, pushing heavy detachments to the front. I was without orders, but necessarily found myself occupying the country in advance of all the columns as a necessary precaution for my own flanks, even securing Burke's Station and all that railroad most perfectly.

Very respectfully, your obedient servant,

P. KEARNY,
Brigadier-General, Commanding.

Captain PURDY, *Assistant Adjutant-General.*

P. S.—I have to state that at Fairfax Court-House, as at Centreville, the column found my troops previously in occupation.

No. 2.

Report of Col. Alfred T. A. Torbert, First New Jersey Infantry.

HDQRS. FIRST REG'T, FIRST BRIG., FRANKLIN'S DIV.,
Camp Seminary, Va., March 17, 1862.

SIR: I have the honor to forward the inclosed reports concerning the
First Regiment, First Brigade, Franklin's division, under the immediate
command of Lieutenant-Colonel McAllister, being myself at the time
unable to ride on horseback on account of rheumatism, but was in the
field during the time, making myself as useful as possible under the circumstances.

Very respectfully, your obedient servant,
A. T. A. TORBERT,
Colonel First Regiment New Jersey Volunteers.

Capt. JAMES M. WILSON,
Assistant Adjutant-General, First Brigade.

No. 3.

Report of Lieut. Col. Robert McAllister, First New Jersey Infantry.

FIRST REGIMENT NEW JERSEY VOLUNTEERS,
Camp Seminary, Va., March 17, 1862.

SIR: In accordance with your request I herewith transmit to you a
report of the movements of our regiment.

After leaving this place for Burke's Station, on Friday, March 7, we
left our brigade drill ground and marched across to the Little River
turnpike. On this side of Annandale I was ordered to send forward
our two flank companies, leaving us seven companies (one company being on picket). We reached Burke's Station at about 1 o'clock a. m. on
the 8th. Our regiment was then stationed along the edge of the woods
near Burke's house.

After General Howard's brigade left we were ordered to take a position along the woods north of the railroad, which order I executed immediately. I then examined all the roads leading to the camp grounds,
placed pickets, and rested for the night. On the morning of the 9th I
received an order to send three companies to Burke's house. We started
at once. Then came another order to send two companies, under the
command of Major Hatfield, to the old Braddock road. I detailed Companies B and E. They started without delay, leaving me but two companies. After 2 p. m. I received an order to bring in the three companies at Burke's house, and march up the railroad to support Colonel
Simpson at the church near Fairfax Station. On reaching that I did
not see Colonel Simpson, but met General Kearny, who ordered me to
march up to Farr's Cross-Roads, leaving one company (Company K) at
Payne's Church. With the remaining four companies I arrived at Farr's
Cross-Roads about 5 p. m., and formed line of battle, and remained in that
position until our general arrived from Fairfax Court-House, when he
told me to encamp there for the night; to be on the alert; that it was an
important point; that the enemy were in the neighborhood, and if attacked to hold it until re-enforcements came to my aid. I put out

pickets up the Centreville road 1½ miles, also down the Fairfax road towards Payne's Church, and also towards Fairfax. We were vigilant that night, but were unmolested.

About 8 o'clock next morning received a verbal order from General Kearny, by his aide-de-camp, Lieutenant Barnard, to throw forward scouts in rear of Centreville, and am happy to say that I soon found a corporal and 3 men ready and willing to undertake this apparently dangerous enterprise. In about an hour afterwards I received an order to send forward towards Centreville one company. I immediately ordered Company B, Captain Van Sickell, to push forward, and in accordance with our general's instructions had a communication kept up with me, and through me with General Kearny, by Captain Van Sickell sending back a man every three-fourths of a mile that he advanced. Between 12 and 1 o'clock the general ordered me to advance with our regiment to Centreville, which I did, Captain Van Sickell and Lieutenant Tantum, with Company B, having reached that place before we did, and some hours ahead of any other troops. Permit me to say here that our regiment was the last to leave Centreville at the Bull Run retreat, and a part of it the first to enter it on the retreat of the enemy. We staid all night, and the next morning were ordered to return to Fairfax Court-House.

In conclusion, permit me to say that General Kearny deserves a great deal of credit by this bold push towards the enemy's lines, and by the energy and bravery thus displayed caused the enemy to leave in great haste, leaving many valuables behind them.

Respectfully, your obedient servant,

R. McALLISTER,
Lieutenant-Colonel First Regiment New Jersey Volunteers.
A. T. A. TORBERT, *Colonel First New Jersey Volunteers.*

No. 4.

Report of Maj. David Hatfield, First New Jersey Infantry.

FIRST REGIMENT NEW JERSEY VOLUNTEERS,
Camp Seminary, Va., March 17, 1862.

SIR: On Sunday morning, March 9, I was ordered by General Kearny to take two companies and proceed to Farr's Cross-Roads by the old Braddock road, and there wait for re-enforcements from Fairfax Station. I arrived at the Cross-Roads about noon. My command consisted of Companies B and E. At the cross-roads we discerned the enemy's cavalry on a hill near the court-house, but having positive orders to remain at the Cross-Roads, I did not feel at liberty to pursue them. However, I sent out a small detachment, under command of Lieutenant Tantum, in order to get as near the enemy as possible under cover of the pines, so as to watch their movements. By so doing we found that the enemy was moving back and forth from the Court-House to the old Braddock road, a distance of about 1 mile.

At 4 o'clock the Fourth New Jersey, under Colonel Simpson, came up, when we marched to the Court-House. The two companies under my command were deployed as skirmishers. When near the Court-House, by order of General Kearny, we marched on at double-quick, and I may also add that the enemy did the same, only in an opposite direction. I then received orders from General Kearny to march back to the Cross-Roads and join my regiment, and there bivouacked for the night.

Very respectfully, your obedient servant,

DAVID HATFIELD,
Major First Regiment New Jersey Volunteers.

A. T. A. TORBERT, *Colonel First New Jersey Volunteers.*

No. 5.

Report of Capt. Sylvester Van Sickell, First New Jersey Infantry.

FIRST REGIMENT NEW JERSEY VOLUNTEERS,
Camp Seminary, Va., March 17, 1862.

SIR : I have the honor to report that I was ordered by Lieutenant-Colonel McAllister, on Monday morning, 10th instant, at 8.30 o'clock a. m., while stationed a Farr's Cross-Roads, to take my command and proceed cautiously up the Braddock road towards Centreville, and after passing our pickets to send out an advance guard, which I did, sending Lieut. William H. Tantum on with 14 men. I was also furnished with 4 cavalrymen to act as a patrol, and to report to him at intervals as we proceeded. I received the first communication from Lieutenant Tantum when at Cub Run, which I forwarded to Lieutenant-Colonel McAllister, saying that he had possession of five contrabands, and had caught up with the four scouts sent in advance. Lieutenant Tantum halted with his guard until I brought up my reserve. He then advanced about a mile, when I received word that appearances were favorable—to come on with all possible dispatch, as he would be in Centreville in an hour. The message I immediately sent to Lieutenant-Colonel McAllister, and proceeded on. Lieutenant Tantum arrived at Centreville about 11.30 a. m., where he immediately posted four sentries in different places in the village, one at each of three forts. I arrived there at fifteen minutes after 12 o'clock noon, and took possession of General Johnston's headquarters, and there awaited the arrival of the First Regiment, which came in about 4 p. m. The New York Forty-fourth Regiment arrived at about 3.30 o'clock p. m.

Very respectfully, your obedient servant,

S. VAN SICKELL,
Captain Company B, First Regiment New Jersey Volunteers.

A. T. A. TORBERT, *Colonel First New Jersey Volunteers.*

No. 6.

Report of Col. Isaac M. Tucker, Second New Jersey Infantry.

HDQRS. SECOND REGIMENT NEW JERSEY VOLUNTEERS,
Camp Seminary, Va., March 16, 1862.

SIR : I proceed to furnish to the headquarters of the First Brigade (General Franklin's division) a detailed account of the movements of this regiment during the past week, while upon its march towards Manassas and vicinity.

Pursuant to brigade orders, the regiment, excepting Captain Tay's company, doing picket duty at the time, repaired to the brigade parade on Friday, the 7th instant, at 1 o'clock p. m., where General Kearny's command was formed. The regiment was provided with the shelter tents, six days' rations, forty rounds of ball cartridges issued to each man and in the cartridge-boxes, together with thirty extra rounds to each man transported by the quartermaster. With the knapsacks packed and thus provided the regiment, in company with the rest of the brigade, proceeded on its march to Burke's Station, on the Orange and Alexandria Railroad, by way of the Little River turnpike and the old Braddock road, reaching its destination about midnight, after a long and tedious march, the road after leaving the turnpike being considerably obstructed with mud.

On the march the flank companies, commanded by Captains Close and Wildrick, were detached and placed under the command of Lieutenant Colonel Brown, of the Third Regiment, constituting, with similar companies from other regiments, a light battalion, in advance of the brigade. The remaining seven companies under my command encamped at the Station that night, and remained there until the morning of Sunday, the 9th instant, when, by order of General Kearny, we proceeded up the railroad to Fairfax Station, leaving two companies, under Captains Wiebecke and Stoll, at the rifle-pits constructed by the enemy in rear of the Station. From this point a scout of 20 men, under Lieutenant Vreeland, accompanied by 2 mounted dragoons, proceeded in the direction of Fairfax Court-House, while the balance of Lieutenant Vreeland's company, under Lieutenant Blewett, skirted the dense woods adjoining the Station on the north. Communication was at once opened with Colonel Taylor, in command of the Third Regiment, in advance, at Sangster's Station, and with Colonel Simpson, in command of the Fourth Regiment, in the rear. While occupying this position two companies (Captains Bishop and Hopwood), under command of Major Ryerson, were sent forward to act as flankers for Colonel Taylor's command.

About 11 o'clock a. m. I received information that the enemy's pickets had been driven back by a detachment of cavalry just in front of Colonel Taylor's regiment, and at the same time was ordered to withdraw the companies acting as flankers, also Lieutenant Blewett's command, skirting the adjoining wood, and proceed with my battalion to the support of Colonel Taylor, which order was promptly executed. About 2 p. m. I was ordered with my command, consisting of five companies, to take position in line of battle on a commanding hill just in advance of Colonel Taylor's regiment, and hold it until the darkness of the evening would enable me to withdraw without being observed. This hill was the picket station occupied by the enemy and from which our cavalry had just driven them, and was but little more than 5 miles from Manassas Junction.

About 7 p. m. I left this position (the companies retiring behind the hill separately) and proceeded back to Fairfax Station, where we encamped, in company with the Third Regiment, and where we remained until the morning of Tuesday, the 11th instant, when, pursuant to orders (the flank companies and the picket company having now joined us), we took up our line of march to Fairfax Court-House, and entered the town with band playing. Here we encamped upon the ground selected by Colonel Simpson for this regiment, and remained in camp there until Friday, the 14th instant, when, in company with the whole brigade, at 7 p. m., we struck our tents and took up our line of march back to this camp, arriving here about midnight. The men returned in good health and full of enthusiasm, created by the movements of this brigade during its absence from camp.

A single casualty occurred during our absence. Captain Duffy's company was detailed by Colonel Taylor, commanding the post at Fairfax Station, on Monday, the 10th instant, as a guard for the erection of the telegraph from the Station to the Court-House. A private of this company (Thomas W. Spriggs) was accidentally shot through the head while removing his musket from the stack, and expired in a few moments.

Your obedient servant,

I. M. TUCKER,
Colonel Second Regiment New Jersey Volunteers.

Capt. JAMES M. WILSON, *Assistant Adjutant-General.*

No. 7.

Report of Col. George W. Taylor, Third New Jersey Infantry.

CAMP NEAR FORT WORTH, VA., *March* 16, 1862.

SIR: In pursuance of order, this moment received, I have the honor to report the following as an account of the movements of the Third Regiment New Jersey Volunteers during the march of the last week towards Manassas:

Left Camp Fort Worth Friday, March 7, 1862, about 4 p. m., with the First Brigade (General Kearny's). That night marched to Burke's, 12 miles, and bivouacked. On the 8th the Third Regiment marched to camp near the railroad, one mile east of Fairfax Station, and relieved the picket of the Sixty-fourth New York State Volunteers. Left camp the 9th on a reconnaissance, with 20 cavalry of the First New York Regiment, towards Occoquan. Returned to Fairfax Station about noon. Soon after received orders from yourself in person to take some five companies, or parts thereof (the balance of our regiment being picketed to guard our left flank and Fairfax), and proceed by railroad and march upon Sangster's Station, 3 miles east of Bull Run. About half a mile this side of Sangster's the enemy appeared in reconnoitering parties of cavalry and some infantry on the right and left of the railroad.' They fell back as our flankers advanced. The regiment marched steadily until the advance reached Sangster's. There, in your presence and by your orders, they occupied a commanding position in line of battle on the crest of a hill to the right of railroad. I had under my orders of the First New York Cavalry 16 men and one corporal, under First Lieutenant Hidden. Just before leaving the railroad I ordered this officer to advance in the open fields and reconnoiter, and if the force was not greatly superior to his own he might charge them. He went off at a brisk trot, nor did he check his horses until he charged into the midst of their pickets, the enemy being greatly superior in numbers, and having the advantage of cover of pines. He lost his life in the gallant charge, but drove the enemy into a rapid retreat, leaving arms and many knapsacks and blankets. Thirteen prisoners were taken, with a lieutenant and non-commissioned officer. They proved to be the First Maryland Regiment.

Very soon after the Second Regiment of Kearny's brigade came up and joined us. They occupied the ground of the enemy's picketing regiment until night, when a small company was left to guard Sangster's

Station until next day. That day, the 10th instant, by your orders, eight companies of the Third Regiment marched upon Union Mills late in the day and bivouacked the same night beyond Sangster's Station. At 4 a. m., 11th instant, continued the march, arrived at Bull Run, and found the bridge partially burned. It took about one hour to repair it. Crossed, and continued a rapid march to Manassas Junction. Arrived at 9.30 a. m., previously having deployed into line of battle, and sent Captain Gibson, with a flank company of skirmishers, into the place. We found it deserted except by a few citizens with two or three wagons, loading the spoils left by the rebels. The flag of the Union was instantly hoisted upon the flag-staff of one of the enemy's works, about which time you joined our regiment, upon which, by your order, had been conferred the honor and great satisfaction of hoisting the American ensign upon the notorious hold of the rebels. The regiment, by your orders, marched the same day to Centreville, where they arrived at sunset. The following morning, the 12th instant, returned to Fairfax Station and the same day to Fairfax Court-House. Remained at Fairfax Court-House until the 14th instant at 6 o'clock p. m., at which time the regiment marched with the brigade, under your orders, to our present camp at Fort Worth, arriving at 1.30 a. m., 15th instant, having been detained nearly one hour in crossing Cameron Run. The regiment stood the march remarkably well.

I have the honor to be, very respectfully,

GEO. W. TAYLOR,
Colonel Third New Jersey Volunteers.

Brig. Gen. PHILIP KEARNY,
Commanding First Brigade, Franklin's Division.

No. 8.

Report of Col. James H. Simpson, Fourth New Jersey Infantry.

HEADQUARTERS FOURTH NEW JERSEY VOLUNTEERS,
Camp Seminary, Va., March 16, 1862.

GENERAL: I have the honor to make the following report of the movements of the Fourth Regiment New Jersey Volunteers since the 7th instant:

On that day it received orders to march with the other regiments of the brigade to Burke's Station, on the Alexandria and Orange Railroad, 14 miles from this camp. The regiment left at 3 p. m., and in consequence of its being the rear guard of the whole brigade, including the wagons, and the very bad state of the cross road from Annandale, it did not reach its destination till 4 o'clock the next morning, everything, however, having been brought up in good order. The regiment was immediately put in position by your orders as a movable force to attack the enemy at any point he might present himself, the three other regiments occupying eligible positions on the approaches to the Station from the south, west, and north.

In the afternoon, by your direction, I accompanied you in a reconnaissance of the country about the place for several miles, the object being to become thoroughly acquainted with the roads, so as to be ready to meet the enemy at any point, and in parting with me you gave me my orders for the night.

The next morning about sunrise eight contraband slaves came in from Manassas, and reported to you that the rebels were sending away their guns and other property, and were about leaving their fortifications. You thought their representations such as to cause a more thorough questioning, and directed me to conduct it. I did so, putting down the result in a letter to you, which you dispatched immediately to General Franklin. Directly after this you ordered the brigade to move forward towards Sangster's Station, 7 miles up the railroad, and within 3 miles of Bull Run. The Third New Jersey was directed to take the advance along the railroad, the Second New Jersey en echelon at proper distance to support the Third, the Fourth New Jersey similarly disposed to support the Second, two companies of the First New Jersey to flank the railroad by the Braddock road to the north, and the remaining companies of the First to hold Burke's Station. In this way the advance was cautiously made as far as Fairfax Station, a distance of 4 miles.

Reaching this place, the brigade, by your direction, was again advanced farther forward cautiously, the different regiments occupied the same relative position, but the Third moving more directly on Sangster's Station; the Second taking position on the right of the railroad about a mile beyond Fairfax Station, at the lead-colored house, on an eminence; the Fourth at the little church at Fairfax Station to guard the road leading to Fairfax; the First Regiment remaining as before at Burke's Station and the Braddock Corners. At this time the rebel cavalry could be very plainly seen with my glass about 1½ miles off to the northwest, posted behind a fence in front of a woods.

Up to this period I had by your direction accompanied you in the field. Leaving me to go forward to join the Third in the advance, you directed me to take command of the Second and Fourth and give orders according to the exigencies as they might occur. Soon after I heard the advance engaged with the enemy, and receiving an order from you through Assistant Adjutant-General Wilson to push forward the Second to the burned railroad bridge to sustain the Third, the Fourth to take the place of the Second, and the First that of the Fourth, the two companies of the First still remaining at the Braddock Corners. I made the changes accordingly, and then rode forward to report to you at Sangster's Station. Here I found you writing a dispatch to General Franklin, informing him of the brilliant charge which had just been made by a small detachment of Captain Stearns' company of Lincoln Cavalry, which formed your escort, against a large body of the rebels, said to be 150 strong, by which they were totally routed and 14 made prisoners, among them a Lieutenant Stewart, late from West Point. You immediately ordered me to join my regiment, and with it two companies of the First New Jersey under Major Hatfield, which had been posted at the Braddock road, midway between Fairfax Station and Fairfax Court-House, and a company of the Lincoln Cavalry, under Captain Stearns, to take Fairfax Court-House. I promptly returned to my command, found it eager for the work, and ordering at the Braddock road Major Hatfield and command of two companies of the First and Captain Stearns to join me I dispatched Lieutenant-Colonel Hatch, Fourth New Jersey Volunteers, with two companies of the Fourth New Jersey and Captain Stearns' company of cavalry, to make a detour to the left, to cut off the enemy in his retreat from Fairfax Court-House by the Centreville road. The enemy's pickets were seen between us and the town, and it was supposed they were backed up by a large force in the neighborhood.

Waiting till the proper time to make the dispositions come out simultaneously at Fairfax Court-House, I took immediate command of the balance of my forces, and had the pleasure of seeing Lieutenant-Colonel Hatch just in position to cut off the retreat of the enemy while I was ready to press him in front. Skirmishers were thrown out to the front and on either flank in our advance, and just before entering the town, when the opportunity admitted, the main body was deployed into line of battle. Unfortunately for the real test of our troops we found, to our surprise, no enemy, the great body having left, as I learned from the inhabitants, some time in October, and only the scouts and pickets who had been seen in the morning having occupied it since. This fact, however, does not at all militate against the spirit and determination of my command, which was all that might be expected from the inheritors of the military fame of Jerseymen, and who only await a standing foe to show their real metal. I would be derelict did I not also report that you joined me before entering the place, and with your usual spirit and good judgment led the troops into the town, which we entered at about 5 p. m.

By your direction I immediately wrote a dispatch to General Franklin, reporting our occupation of Fairfax Court-House, and you then left me with instructions to hold possession of the town with the Fourth New Jersey. This I did till the next morning, March 10, when, the Federal troops pouring in, the advance under Colonel Averell, and receiving an order to march to the Braddock Corners to support the advance of the First Regiment by that road to Centreville, I left the town with my regiment, took position at the Corners, remained there all night, and next morning returned by your direction to the vicinity of Fairfax Court-House, where I selected the camping ground for the brigade. Here we remained till the afternoon of the 14th instant, when, receiving an order at 5 o'clock from general headquarters to return to this post, the whole brigade moved at 6, and reached our destination after midnight.

I think it proper to state that when at Fairfax Court-House, on the 13th instant, with Assistant Adjutant-General Purdy and Assistant Adjutant-General Wilson and other officers and a squadron of dragoons, I visited the battle ground at Manassas of 21st July last, and at the recent headquarters of the Confederate Army of the Potomac, a building said to belong to a Mr. Weir, I found a large number of official documents, among them the original order of General Beauregard, dated July 20, promulgating, "confidentially," to the commanders of brigades his plan of battle for the next day. Accompanying this was the order of General Joseph E. Johnston, approving the plan, and directing it to be carried into execution. I also found the original reports of Lieutenant Alexander, Engineer Corps, general staff, giving a statement of the prisoners and wounded and of the property found after the battle. The leaving of these important documents, like the other property which I saw scattered around, shows with what haste the rebels must have retreated before our forces; but what discovers the perfect panic which must have ensued is the fact, which I witnessed, of their having left four dead bodies laid out in their hospital dead-house ready for interment, but which they had forgotten or neglected to bury.

Very respectfully submitted.

J. H. SIMPSON,
Colonel Fourth New Jersey Volunteers.

Brig. Gen. PHILIP KEARNY,
   Comdg. First Brigade, Franklin's Division, Army of Potomac.

No. 9.

Report of Capt. Joseph K. Stearns, First New York Cavalry.

CAMP KEARNY, VA., *March* 15, 1862.

SIR: I hasten to lay before you a report of the movements of the squadron (Companies A and H) of the First New York (Lincoln) Cavalry while attached to your brigade during your advance to Centreville and Manassas. Leaving our camp at 3 p. m. Thursday, the 6th instant, I joined your column on the Little River turnpike, furnishing the advance guard, commanded by myself, and the rear guard in charge of Lieutenant Thomson. On the march that day and evening my command was constantly employed in scouting, bearing orders, &c. At 4 o'clock a. m. of Friday I reached Burke's Station, and was assigned my camping ground. Shortly after daylight my entire squadron was drafted away in squads of from five to twenty men each to act as vedettes and scouts in the vicinity of Burke's Station, and to operate with the various infantry regiments of your brigade, being subject to the orders of their several colonels.

On Saturday Captain Jones, with 15 men, accompanied yourself on an extended visit to all the pickets and sentries of your command. This detachment, accompanied by yourself, also made an extended reconnaissance along the line of railroad towards Fairfax Station. The remainder of my command, in charge of myself, Lieutenants Hidden, Alexander, and Thomson, was detached in small parties reconnoitering and acting with the different regiments of your brigade. On Sunday morning the usual number of pickets and orderlies was furnished by me and duly posted. At 10 o'clock Lieutenant Alexander with 20 men was dispatched on scouting service towards the Occoquan. His report is forwarded herewith. At the same time Captain Jones, myself, Lieutenants Hidden and Thomson reported with 20 men to yourself. Lieutenants Hidden and Thomson were dispatched to the different picket stations to obtain more mounted men, and shortly after reported to you at Fairfax Station with an additional force of 30 men.

At this point Lieutenant Alexander also reported from his scouting expedition, thus increasing my command to 70 men. While awaiting the arrival of the infantry my young officers were dispatched with men in every direction to look for the enemy, who was known to be near us. When the infantry came up, myself, Captain Jones, and Lieutenant Thomson were sent with 25 men to scour the woods around Payne's Church as far as the old Braddock road. Lieutenants Hidden and Alexander accompanied you to Sangster's Station, as detailed in Lieutenant Alexander's report. From Payne's Church I dispatched Lieutenant Thomson to you with a report of my movements. I subsequently received orders from you to advance to Fairfax Court-House, in company with a detachment of infantry, and soon arrived at that place, approaching it cautiously, to find that it had been evacuated by the enemy but a short time before. Shortly afterward I returned to Fairfax Station, arriving there at dark, and received orders to occupy Payne's Church for the night. I was here joined by Lieutenants Alexander and Thomson and their detachments. I here learned of the glorious death of Lieutenant Hidden, of my company. He was a splendid officer and a courteous gentleman, whose loss is deeply regretted by all who knew him, but by none more than myself.

On Monday morning I was forced to return to Burke's Station with my entire command, for the purpose of obtaining forage for my jaded horses. In the afternoon I was dispatched to headquarters with orders. Lieutenant Alexander, with 15 men, was ordered to accompany you to Centreville, which he did, entering that strongly-fortified place with you in advance of any other Union troops. Subsequently Captain Jones received orders to follow you with the remainder of the squadron, and did so without loss of time. An extended reconnaissance was then made towards Bull Run by Lieutenant Alexander, who learned that the rebel forces were but a few hours in advance. That night the squadron returned to Payne's Church to await further orders.

On Tuesday morning I received orders from you to take a position beyond Sangster's Station, for the purpose of holding the railroad to that point. At 4 p. m. I returned to Payne's Church, and before my men could dismount was ordered to march to Manassas and occupy that point, relieving the Third New Jersey Regiment. After a tedious march of five hours, without forage for the tired and hungry horses, I arrived at Manassas at 9 p. m., to find myself with 100 men far in advance of the army occupying the rebel stronghold, while on every side was found evidence showing that the enemy had taken a hasty departure but a few hours previously. Our camp was alarmed once during the night by the approach of several horsemen, who fled at the fire of the sentry. We were surprised shortly after daylight on Wednesday by the arrival within our lines of several contrabands, and when we left at 4 p. m. to return 30 negroes had sought our protection, some of them having walked 25 miles the previous night.

On Wednesday afternoon I reported to you at Fairfax Court-House, and was again quartered at Payne's Church. On Thursday you kindly permitted my command to rest, a relaxation from duty being absolutely required by the horses in the squadron. On Friday I was ordered to report with my squadron to my regiment at Fairfax Court-House, and was thus relieved from duty with your brigade.

In concluding this report I beg to return you my sincere thanks for the kindness and attention which my command universally received at your hands, and I beg to assure you that it is a matter of deep regret with both officers and men of the squadron that they were not permitted to serve longer under your immediate command. In conclusion, I take this opportunity to return my thanks to the officers and men of the squadron for the energy and alacrity displayed in performing the arduous duties required of them. I also forward herewith at your request the names of the men who so nobly sustained Lieutenant Hidden in his brilliant charge at Sangster's Station on the 9th instant: Corporal E. Lewis, Company H, since promoted to be sergeant; Privates Charles P. Ives, Company H; Robert C. Clark, Company H; Albert H. Van Saun, Company A; Michael O'Neil, Company H; James Lynch, Company H; Cornelius Riley, Company H; Hugh McSauley, Company H; Herman Cameron, Company H; John Cameron, Company H; Martin Murry, Company H; John Bogert, Company H; William Simonson, Company A; Chester C. Clark, Company A; John Nugent, Company A; John R. Wilson, Company A; Henry Higgins, Company A.

Private Wilson alone captured three prisoners, compelling them to lay down their arms and accompany him from the field.

I have the honor to be, sir, your obedient servant,

J. K. STEARNS,
Captain, Commanding Squadron.

Brigadier-General KEARNY.

No. 10.

Report of Lieut. William Alexander, First New York Cavalry.

HEADQUARTERS FIRST NEW YORK CAVALRY,
Camp Kearny, March 17, 1862.

SIR: I have the honor to report that, in obedience to orders received from Brigadier-General Kearny, I marched from Burke's Station on the morning of the 9th instant with 20 men. My orders were to proceed to the Pohick road and scour the country right and left, which I did as far as Brimstone Hill. I then returned to Elzey's, where I learned from the officer commanding the pickets of the Third New Jersey Regiment that a squad of rebel cavalry had just driven in two of his pickets. I immediately started in pursuit, and having followed them about 3 miles, returned to Fairfax Station and reported the circumstances to the commanding general.

I was then ordered by the general to accompany him to Sangster's Station, and on arriving there to occupy a road leading to the right, going into a large wood, my orders being to intercept a body of rebel infantry from getting in there. It was about this time that the brilliant charge was made by Lieutenant Hidden, of our regiment. General Kearny then rode up and informed me that Lieutenant Hidden had fallen and was perhaps only wounded, and ordered me to charge with my party and drive the enemy into the woods, and procure the body if possible. We did so, Lieutenant Thomson and myself, and recovered the body. I then returned to Fairfax Station and reported to you.

I am, sir, very respectfully, your obedient servant,
WM. ALEXANDER,
Lieutenant and Adjutant, First Battalion.

Capt. JOSEPH K. STEARNS,
Commanding Company H and Squadron.

No. 11.

Letter from Col. David McM. Gregg, Eighth Pennsylvania Cavalry.

CAMP NEAR HAMPTON, VA., *April 21, 1862.*

DEAR COLBURN: A few days ago I saw published a letter from the General-in-Chief to General Kearny concerning the first occupation of Manassas by our troops. The first troops at Manassas were the Third and Eighth Pennsylvania Cavalry. These being there before other regiments was the simple performance of a designated duty, and as such not deserving a public recognition. The reply of the General-in-Chief, however, acknowledges that the Third Pennsylvania Cavalry was, in fact, the first regiment at Manassas, and the object of the correspondence being evidently to secure to one or the body of troops the credit of the first occupation, I write you thus to ascertain if it is known at the headquarters of the Army that the Eighth Pennsylvania Cavalry entered Manassas with the Third Regiment.

An official recognition of the service is not asked for my regiment; but since I was personally instructed by the Commander-in-Chief to perform a certain duty, it would be gratifying to myself and regiment to know that he was informed that the duty had been successfully performed.

I am, your friend,

D. McM. GREGG,
Colonel Eighth Pennsylvania Cavalry.

MARCH 8, 1862.—Occupation of Leesburg, Va., by Union forces.

Report of Col. John W. Geary, Twenty-eighth Pennsylvania Infantry.

HEADQUARTERS ADVANCE BRIGADE,
Leesburg, Va., March 9, 1862.

SIR : On the morning of the 7th I learned there were about 1,000 infantry, some artillery, and between 200 and 300 cavalry at Waterford, who had determined to make an attempt to destroy the railroad during the day, then burn Wheatland and Waterford, after which they, with General Hill's command, would fall back, thinking that re-enforcements would arrive, which, in conjunction with my command, would move on Leesburg. In full expectation of our advance, General Hill sent his stores and baggage to Middleburg, and commenced burning hay and grain stacks, to prevent their falling into our hands.

To intercept their various works of destruction, about noon I put my main body, with cavalry and artillery, in motion, leaving instructions for the balance to follow during the night. I entered Wheatland in time to prevent the incendiary designs of White's cavalry, who would have burned it. The rebels who left there upon my approach created a panic among the troops at Waterford, who fled precipitately to Leesburg, without applying the torch. We entered Waterford at 11 o'clock at night, where I rested the command three hours. We found some Union feeling existing there, and proclaimed our intention of protecting the people from the enemy. By a forced march we reached Leesburg shortly after sunrise and took possession of Fort Johnston, where we planted the Stars and Stripes and then entered the city. The rear of General Hill's retreating forces could be seen in the distance. They retired to Middleburg, where the bulk of their baggage and stores is concentrated. General Hill and staff retired at full gallop. My other detachment joined me during the day.

I at once took possession of the court-house, post-office, bank, and all public buildings, and Forts Beauregard and Evans. I find considerable secession proclivity here, but we have made an impression upon them by a respect for property and proper exhibition of decorum, which they have been educated to suppose was foreign to us, as we were designated as ruthless pillagers. Fort Johnston is occupied by a portion of my troops, with two guns commanding the city. I have declared martial law and have an active provost-marshalship in operation. Middleburg is now the last link in Loudoun County. When that place is rid of the presence of the enemy, Loudoun County is free of rebel rule and the presence of rebel soldiery.

The prisoners whom I have sent you are of note. I have administered the oath of allegiance to many willing residents.

Very respectfully, your obedient servant,

JNO. W. GEARY,
Colonel Twenty-eighth Reg't Pa. Vols., Commanding Brigade.

Maj. R. MORRIS COPELAND, *Assistant Adjutant-General.*

MARCH 14–16, 1862.—Reconnaissance to Cedar Run, Virginia.

REPORTS.

No. 1.—Brig. Gen. George Stoneman, U. S. Army.
No. 2.—Col. Samuel K. Zook, Fifty-seventh New York Infantry.

No. 1.

Report of Brig. Gen. George Stoneman, U. S. Army.

HEADQUARTERS ARMY OF THE POTOMAC,
Washington, March 16, 1862.

SIR: I inclose copy of a report just received from General Stoneman. I am confident that the force seen near Warrenton Junction did not come from Aquia, but that it is the rear guard of the troops who left Manassas. Captain D'Orleans reports the roads very bad on their return march, and that they had great difficulty in getting back. Bridges on the railroad all burned up to Cedar Run, inclusive.

In haste, very respectfully,

GEO. B. McCLELLAN,
Major-General, U. S. Army.

Hon. E. M. STANTON, *Secretary of War.*

[Inclosure.]

HEADQUARTERS CAVALRY FORCE,
Union Mills, Va., March 16, 1862.

We arrived here last evening about dark. We got corn for horses; no provisions for men. Bull Run too high to cross. Had we staid an hour longer we should not have got here to-day, owing to high water in the streams. Felt the enemy cautiously, and found him in force at Warrenton Station. Saw two regiments of cavalry and three bodies of infantry on the other side of Cedar Run. Had we crossed, should not have been able to get back for high water. Had three men of Fifth Cavalry hit driving in enemy's pickets, one slightly wounded in the head; two men of Pennsylvania cavalry shot through the foot by their own carbines; one man (infantry) wounded by his own bayonet. Enemy acted confidently, and followed us some way back on the road, but did not molest us in any way.

Enemy's force consisted of Stuart's and Ewell's cavalry, a battery of artillery, and some infantry. Railroad bridges all burned down up to Warrenton Junction; still entire beyond, but all in readiness to burn at a moment's warning, having dry wood piled upon them. Heard cars running during night before last; probably bringing up troops from Rappahannock. Heard of two regiments of infantry at Warrenton engaged in impressing the militia and securing forage. Heard of a large force of infantry this side of Rappahannock River, having come up to Warrenton Junction from Aquia Creek day before yesterday. Bridges all destroyed this side of Broad Run. The Duke and Count, who take this, will give you further particulars.

Very respectfully, &c.,

GEO. STONEMAN,
Brigadier-General, Commanding.

Colonel COLBURN.

No. 2.

Report of Col. Samuel K. Zook, Fifty-seventh New York Infantry.

HDQRS. FIFTY-SEVENTH NEW YORK VOLUNTEERS,
Manassas Junction, March 18, 1862.

SIR: On the 14th instant, about 9.30 a. m., this regiment marched with a brigade of cavalry, all under the command of Brig. Gen. George Stoneman, via the Orange and Alexandria Railroad, to Cedar Run. The march was rendered somewhat tedious and difficult by having nothing better than the ruins of burned railroad bridges upon which to cross at Broad and Kettle Runs.

At 6.30 p. m. we arrived at a point about a mile and a half east of Cedar Run, where the enemy had driven back a small force of the Sixth Cavalry. General Stoneman here ordered me to send two companies to drive in their pickets. I ordered out Companies A, Captain Chapman, on the south side of the road, and H, Captain Horner, on the north, under the command of Major Parisen. Advancing as skirmishers, they drove the enemy before them in the dark to the west side of the run. Here a portion of Captain Chapman's company, becoming exposed by the light of some burning cars on the road, received a few shots from the enemy, which were promptly returned, but with what effect is not known further than that the enemy retreated beyond the hills.

About midnight Lieutenant Reid, of Company F, with 20 men, returned to the regiment. He had been sent forward with Lieutenant Bowen from the vicinity of Bristoe Station in the morning. He reported having seen the enemy's scouts at a distance several times during the day. In the morning General Stoneman ordered the whole regiment forward to Catlett's Station. Two companies, B and I, under Captain Throop and Lieutenant Mott, being deployed in advance as skirmishers, continued their march to the run. Shortly after Major Parisen was sent to assume command of them. They had arrived but a short time when small parties of the enemy appeared on the opposite bank. The orders of the general prohibited firing except in reply to fire. But little time, however, was lost in consequence, for they soon commenced firing upon both companies. Their fire was promptly and effectually returned, two or three of their saddles being emptied.

The general's object having been accomplished, the regiment retired. The skirmishers were drawn in as a rear guard, and the whole command commenced the march to this place. The return march was severe on account of the incessant rain and the bad condition of the roads. The difficulty of recrossing Broad and Kettle Runs was increased by the rapid rise of the water. At the former the ruins were swept away whilst two men yet remained to cross. There was no alternative but to leave them behind, but both have since come in.

Very respectfully, your obedient servant,

S. K. ZOOK,
Colonel Fifty-seventh New York Volunteers.

Lieut. J. M. FAVILLE, *Acting Assistant Adjutant-General.*

CORRESPONDENCE, ORDERS, AND RETURNS RELATING SPECIALLY TO OPERATIONS IN MARYLAND, NORTHERN VIRGINIA, AND WEST VIRGINIA FROM AUGUST 1, 1861, TO MARCH 17, 1862.

UNION CORRESPONDENCE, ETC.

GENERAL ORDERS, }   HEADQUARTERS A. O. W. V.,
No. 7.   }   *Clarksburg, Va., August* 3, 1861.

The line of the Baltimore and Ohio Railroad from Cumberland to Wheeling, and the Northwestern Virginia Railroad from Grafton, with the military posts, stations, and depots thereon, will, until further orders, constitute a special military district, to be called the District of Grafton.

Brig. Gen. B. F. Kelley, U. S. Volunteers, is assigned to the District of Grafton.

*   *   *   *   *   *   *

By order Brigadier-General Rosecrans:

[No signature.]

HDQRS. ARMY OF OCCUPATION OF WESTERN VIRGINIA,
Clarksburg, Va., August 4, 1861.
Col. E. D. TOWNSEND,
Assistant Adjutant-General, Washington, D. C.:

COLONEL: Lower Cheat River region appears to be entirely free of rebel forces as far as Winchester. Eight thousand militia reported at Harrisonburg, 2,000 between Monterey and Cheat Mountain Pass. I think the rebel forces in Western Virginia are mostly about Lewisburg.

I have directed the building of small field works below Gauley Bridge, and Cox to open communication with Tyler at Summersville. Two Ohio regiments sent to Kanawha; Twenty-first Ohio (three-months' men) ordered out; Twenty-second Ohio at Parkersburg, on its way out; Seventeenth Ohio, the last, at Weston to-night, on its way home. One of the Ohio regiments coming up will move to Elk River by Bulltown and scour that country. A detachment from Glenville also scours a region now infested with guerrillas. Ten days will probably complete all this work, and, were we prepared to hold it, enable me to seize Lewisburg, which is but five days' march from head of steamboat navigation on the Kanawha; propose a provision depot of ample size, properly fortified, there. In twenty days I shall have a packed train for 5,000 men—ten days' rations.

As soon as the new Ohio regiments begin to come in, so that we can secure this front here, I shall begin to dispose matters for the movement on Wytheville and East Tennessee. I propose to seize that place, and take possession of the railroad as far down as Abingdon; break the railroad bridges down east of Wytheville, so as to prevent the enemy from coming in that direction; make a fortified depot of it and a good road from thence to the Great Falls of the Kanawha, and there concentrate all the troops we can spare on that line. In the interim shall make every effort towards the restoration of peace, law, and order in Western Virginia.

I am, very respectfully, your obedient servant,
W. S. ROSECRANS,
Brigadier-General, U. S. Army.

HEADQUARTERS DEPARTMENT OF THE SHENANDOAH,
Near Harper's Ferry, Va., August 4, 1861.
Colonel LEONARD,
Thirteenth Regiment Massachusetts Volunteers:

SIR: The general commanding directs that you proceed to Sharpsburg, Md., near the Potomac River, and there take post until further orders. You will detach from your regiment the following number of companies, to take post as follows:

Two companies at Antietam Ford; two companies at the ford a short distance below Shepherdstown; one company at the ford at Shepherd's Island, some distance above Shepherdstown; one company at the ford a short distance below Dam No. 4.

You will instruct the commanders of these detachments to be particularly on the alert, in order to put a stop to all contraband trade in the vicinity of their posts; to put a stop to all treasonable correspondence, without interfering with the United States mail, should there be one, and to arrest all persons engaged in treasonable acts, against whom sufficient proof can be obtained. It is the general's wish that travel between Maryland and Virginia be stopped, except with persons of proved loyalty to the United States Government. He relies freely upon the discretion, energy, and good judgment of yourself and your subordinates for carrying out the above instructions.

The detachment of U. S. cavalry now at Antietam Ford will be relieved from duty at that post upon the arrival of your detachment.

I am, very respectfully, your obedient servant,
ROBT. WILLIAMS,
Assistant Adjutant-General.

HEADQUARTERS DIVISION OF THE POTOMAC,
Washington, D. C., August 6, 1861.
Brig. Gen. I. McDOWELL,
Comdg. Department of Northeastern Virginia, Arlington, Va.:

Information I have received induces me to caution you to be carefully on your guard to-night and to-morrow morning against an attack by the enemy. Let Hunt hold at least two batteries ready to move to this side, if necessary, at the shortest notice. Communicate this to Franklin, Kearny, Blenker, and Sherman.

GEO. B. McCLELLAN,
Major-General, Commanding.

CAMP TENNALLY, *August 6, 1861.*
Maj. S. WILLIAMS, *Assistant Adjutant-General:*

MAJOR: I made this morning a reconnaissance of the country reported last evening to be occupied by the enemy, by an officer I had sent to examine the country in front of the point at which my pickets communicate with those of Colonel Smith, of the Vermont regiment. I discovered that what he had supposed to be camps of the insurgents proved to be, under the scrutiny of the glass, only clusters of whitewashed houses, negro cabins, and fences on the opposite side of the Potomac.

I afterwards prosecuted the examination of both banks of the river as far as the head of the aqueduct, but discovered no signs of the presence of the enemy on that section of the river lands. I was told by a man who lives about 5 miles from this camp that he had heard the drum the night before on the hills opposite. No camp was visible.

I have the honor to be, very respectfully, your obedient servant,

GEO. A. McCALL,
Brigadier-General, Commanding.

AUGUST 7, 1861—6.45 a. m.

P. S.—I received at 3 a. m. a dispatch from Colonel [W. F.] Smith, saying he had received your dispatch directing him to be " particularly cautious about an attack to-night." My brigade was immediately under arms and is still in order of battle, but I have no intelligence of the advance of the enemy yet.

GEO. A. McCALL.

HEADQUARTERS, SANDY HOOK,
Near Harper's Ferry, Va., August 6, 1861.

Col. E. D. TOWNSEND, *Assistant Adjutant-General:*

SIR: I was much gratified to receive the order authorizing the transfer of stores, &c., to Frederick. Immediate measures will be taken to carry it into effect and to bring the war regiments here. The telegram advising the withdrawal of stores from Hagerstown to Sandy Hook was duly received, and orders were given to the quartermaster to hold them in readiness for removal; but there were no buildings at Sandy Hook, and the camp covers were exhausted in protecting our own stores. We were preparing buildings at Knoxville when the order of yesterday was received. Prisoners taken from the Virginia side of the river speak to those they think prisoners of their expectations that Johnston will enter Leesburg shortly with a large force. The general tenor of our intelligence is of an advance in that direction, if any is made. We have now nearly 12,000 men, and the regiments are rapidly improving in discipline and drill.

I am, sir, with great respect, your obedient servant,

N. P. BANKS,
Major-General, Commanding.

HEADQUARTERS OF THE ARMY,
August 6, 1861.

Brig. Gen. ROSECRANS, U. S. A.,
Commanding, &c., Clarksburg, Va.:

It is said that Lee intends attacking Cheat Mountain Pass. It is advisable for you to push forward rapidly the fortifications ordered by General McClellan on that mountain and near Huttonsville. No intelgence of any move on Red House via Romney.

WINFIELD SCOTT.

CLARKSBURG, VA., *August 6, 1861.*

Col. E. D. TOWNSEND, *Assistant Adjutant-General:*

Every day's experience with volunteer troops convinces me of the absolute necessity of having some officers of military education among them. Whole regiments are mustered into the service and sent upon active duty without a single officer who knows thoroughly company drill, much less the organization or drill of a regiment. I am convinced that the detail of a second lieutenant from the Military Academy to act as major even would in six weeks increase the military power of a regiment at least one-third. If, then, the volunteers will this year cost the Government $300,000,000, this would produce the same amount of military at $100,000,000 less. This seems enormous, but I have no doubt of the truth of it. Can nothing be done? Appears there will be no difficulty in effecting this arrangement with all the regiments now forming. Are there not plenty officers in California that could be brought here? Please present this matter to General Scott.

W. S. ROSECRANS,
Brigadier-General.

CLARKSBURG, VA., *August* 6, 1861.

Col. E. D. TOWNSEND, *Assistant Adjutant-General, Washington:*

Tell General Scott his dispatch is received. I have ordered the Seventeenth Indiana to Beverly, seven of the Fourth and nine of the Tenth to Buckhannon, [and] a vigorous prosecution of the work in Cheat Mountain, on the Huntersville road. Cox moved a body of his forces to Summersville to join Tyler and from thence to threaten Huntersville. Sent Lieutenant Wagner to fortify at mouth of Gauley. Appointed Benham acting inspector-general. Sent him also to thoroughly examine troops of the Kanawha Brigade, supervise the defenses, and select a provision depot for 30,000 to 40,000 men, to be stationed near the head of steamboat navigation on the Kanawha. Will have a packing train ready in twenty days for 4,000 men—ten days' rations. Ask the General, for Heaven's sake, to make some such provision as I have suggested for the military instruction of the reorganized and new regiments, which by this means may soon be put to service. Could not the Academy term be made to open, say, in November, and the cadets detailed, one for each regiment, as instructors of tactics or drill-masters? But my choice is to have at least majors from the young officers of the Army.

Please let me know also whether I am to have a brigade of regulars and a major-general over me.

W. S. ROSECRANS,
Brigadier-General, U. S. Army.

HEADQUARTERS DIVISION OF THE POTOMAC,
Washington, August 7, 1861.

Brig. Gen. W. S. ROSECRANS,
Commanding Department of the Ohio, Clarksburg, Va.:

General Dix telegraphs that he is reliably informed that Lee and Johnston are actually on their march to crush you in Western Virginia. It is probable that they will move either on Huttonsville or Gauley. Complete as rapidly as possible the intrenchments near those places. Get your artillery in position, drawing, if necessary, on Allegheny Arsenal for heavy guns. These intrenchments must be as strong as the locality and the means at your hands will permit. They cannot be too strong. Place eight regiments near the Gauley Pass, one at Summersville, one at Bulltown, eight near Huttonsville, two at Beverly, one at Parkersburg and vicinity, perhaps one at Clarksburg, one at Grafton, five at Red House. If you have more than this number of regiments available, post them in preference at Beverly, or Leadsville, and the Gauley. Establish your own headquarters at Buckhannon for the present, and at once establish a telegraphic communication thence to the Gauley. In no event permit the enemy to re-enter Western Virginia. Carry out these instructions immediately. What progress is being made in the organization of Virginia troops? Report frequently. Push your patrols and pickets well to the front. No more regular officers can at present be sent to you. The pack-train movement does not seem advisable under present circumstances. The desired object can be better effected by a different arrangement, for which, probably, orders will soon be given.

By order of Lieutenant-General Scott:

GEO. B. McCLELLAN,
Major-General.

HEADQUARTERS DEPARTMENT OF PENNSYLVANIA,
Fort McHenry, Md., August 7, 1861.

Col. E. D. TOWNSEND,
Assistant Adjutant-General, Headquarters of the Army:

COLONEL: I received the telegraphic dispatch of the General-in-Chief, to send General King and two Wisconsin regiments to Washington, this afternoon, at 5.15 p. m. The orders have been issued and the regiments will leave the moment transportation can be provided. General King returned to Washington this afternoon. When the dispatch was received my force in this State had been disposed as follows: First Regiment Pennsylvania Volunteers, at Annapolis and Annapolis Junction; Fourth Regiment Wisconsin Volunteers, at Relay House; Fourth Regiment Pennsylvania Volunteers, at West Baltimore street; Fifth Regiment Wisconsin Volunteers, at McKim's mansion; Sixth Regiment Wisconsin Volunteers, at Patterson's Park; Twentieth Regiment Indiana Volunteers, on Northern Central Railroad; Third Regiment New York Volunteers, at Fort McHenry; Twenty-first Regiment Indiana Volunteers, near Fort McHenry; Fifth Regiment New York Volunteers, at Federal Hill; Fourth Regiment New York Volunteers, six companies on Baltimore and Philadelphia Railroad; Fourth Regiment New York Volunteers, four companies at Mount Clare; Second Regiment Maryland Volunteers, five companies at Mount Clare; Second Regiment Delaware Volunteers, five companies at Havre de Grace. The time of these five last-named companies is about to expire, and they are to be replaced by the four companies of the New York Fourth at Mount Clare.

I had occupied all the important eminences nearest to Baltimore. The removal of the Fifth and Sixth Wisconsin compels me to abandon two of them. It is very desirable that they should be occupied as soon as possible. Two companies of cavalry have arrived; both are without arms, and one without horses. I must request that the General-in-Chief will order sabers and pistols to be sent to me from Washington. There is nothing here but Hall's carbines, and they are without slings. The Third and Fourth New York Volunteers came here from Fort Monroe in a state of disorganization. I am doing all I can to restore order among them. They were recruited in cities, and this is a bad place for them.

One has been shut up in the fort and the other is to be scattered as a guard to the railroad bridges between Baltimore and Havre de Grace.
Very respectfully, yours, &c.,

JOHN A. DIX,
Major-General, Commanding.

WAR DEPARTMENT,
Washington, August 8, 1861.
Brigadier-General ROSECRANS,
Commanding Western Virginia Department, Grafton, Va.:

SIR: The governor of Virginia having applied to the Department for the arms, ammunition, and camp equipage recently captured in the operations in Western Virginia, for the purpose of arming and equipping the Union men in that section of the country, you will, if it can be done without injury or inconvenience to the public interest, please cause the property referred to to be delivered to Governor Peirpoint, at Wheeling, Va., and take his receipt therefor.

I am, sir, very respectfully, your obedient servant,

THOMAS A. SCOTT,
Assistant Secretary of War.

Memorandum.

WASHINGTON, *August 9,* 1861.

At Potomac Creek, just below Aquia, they have a camp with four field pieces below the creek, and above the creek there is every appearance of a heavy battery, although it has not been fired to our knowledge. At Aquia Creek it has been reported that they have taken over flat-boats and scows from the Rappahannock. The steamer Page is there ready for service when she can get out.

For the past few days there have been very few persons seen about there. The flags on the batteries have been hauled down. From these circumstances, and from the apparent quiet on the river, I have augured that some operation is going on.

At Mathias Point, from the best information I can obtain, which is through the blacks, there are 300 or 400 men about 2 miles back from the point. A picket is said to be kept on this point, although they have never been seen in the daytime, but have several times been heard talking and laughing. It is said that they are throwing up breastworks on the point, though as yet they have no batteries.

There are several other points on the river where their troops are stationed, and, in my opinion, in all the inlets and creeks the enemy are collecting flat-boats and several boats of all kinds, which should be destroyed.

R. H. WYMAN,
Lieutenant-Commander, Commanding Steamer Yankee.

HEADQUARTERS DIVISION OF THE POTOMAC,
Washington, August 11, 1861.
Brig. Gen. CHARLES P. STONE, *U. S. Volunteers, Commanding, &c.:*

GENERAL: I have to request that you will proceed with the force placed under your command to the vicinity of Poolesville, and there observe the Potomac River from the Point of Rocks to Seneca Mills. You will keep the main body of your force united in a strong position near Poolesville, and observe the dangerous fords with strong pickets, that can dispute the passage until re-enforced. Keep up a constant communication with General Banks' pickets near Point of Rocks, as well as with those of General McCall and Colonel Smith, until the telegraphic communication is established. Make such arrangements as will enable you, in the event of an attack in force, to fall back on General McCall, or to enable him to move up to your support at some strong position which we can hold with the force at our disposal. Should you see the opportunity of capturing or dispersing any small party by crossing the river, you are at liberty to do so, though great discretion is recommended in making such a movement. The general object of your command is to observe and dispute the passage of the river and the advance of the enemy until time is gained to concentrate the reserves of the main force. I leave your operations much to your own discretion, in which I have the fullest confidence.

I am, sir, very respectfully, your obedient servant,

GEO. B. McCLELLAN,
Major-General, Commanding.

HEADQUARTERS, *August* 12, 1861.

Major-General BANKS, U. S. A.,
Commanding, &c., Sandy Hook, Md.:

Brigadier-General Stone has been assigned, with six regiments, a battery, and a company of cavalry, to watch the ferries and fords between Great Falls of the Potomac and Point of Rocks. His headquarters will be at Poolesville. He will communicate with you on his arrival.

WINFIELD SCOTT.

HEADQUARTERS DEPARTMENT OF PENNSYLVANIA,
Baltimore, Md., August 12, 1861.

Col. E. D. TOWNSEND,
Assistant Adjutant-General, Headquarters of the Army:

COLONEL: The importance of this city, not only in its relations to the State of Maryland, but to the capital of the country, suggested to me at an early day after assuming the command of this department the necessity of a better system of defense than we have now. The few regiments in position here are scattered over too large a surface to support each other, and, with the exception of one within the public grounds which surround Fort McHenry, none of them are covered by defensive works. They occupy eminences, not one of which could be held against a superior force. The hostile feeling which exists in the city, and which does not even seek to disguise itself, indicates the absolute necessity of occupying and fortifying a commanding position nearer than Fort McHenry. The latter may reduce the city to ashes, but it is too distant to assail particular localities without injury to others. I do not underrate the value of this fort. It controls the commerce of the city, and I think it needs to be protected from a possible bombardment from a height about 200 feet more elevated, and about 2 miles distant, in a northerly direction. Of this I shall speak hereafter.

But I desire first to call the attention of the General-in-Chief to the propriety of intrenching Federal Hill. He is no doubt familiar with the locality. It is about 80 feet above the basin, overlooks it throughout its whole extent, and is about 800 yards from the wharves and the railroad running through Pratt street. About a fortnight ago I requested Major Brewerton to survey it, and ascertain its capacities for defense by a strong intrenchment—one which could be held against a large force on the land side and covered on the water side with a heavy battery, overawing the city, and capable, from its proximity, to single out and assail particular localities in case of an outbreak. When I requested Major Brewerton to make the examination the place was occupied by the Eighteenth Regiment of Pennsylvania Militia. It is now occupied by Colonel Duryea's Fifth Regiment of New York Volunteers, or the National Zouaves. They have a rifled cannon, three howitzers, and some field pieces, belonging to Fort McHenry. They are becoming well drilled as artillerists, but have no breastworks. I propose, then—

1. That Federal Hill should be strongly intrenched. The Zouaves will do the greater part of the work.

2. That the height before referred to should also be strongly intrenched. It not only commands Fort McHenry, which should be rendered secure from bombardment, but it commands every other eminence from which the fort can be assailed and overlooks a part of the city which is rank with secession. This work should be at least as extensive as Fort Corcoran, and should be furnished with a battery of heavy cannon and mortars. This work can be chiefly done by the volunteer regiments, if I can have the force, which in my letter of the 24th of July I considered necessary for the security of the city and State.

I am not quite satisfied with Fort McHenry. It is very strong on the water side, but, like most of our harbor fortifications, was constructed with no special reference to attack by land. The approach from Baltimore is faced by a curtain, which was only designed for infantry. Major Morris, who has done all for the work it is capable of, has placed some mortars behind it, but there is no room for cannon. I suggested to Major Brewerton the construction of an outwork between the two bastions which this curtain connects. It should be a permanent work, and, with the prevailing indications, it would be wise to make preparations for a long-continued contest. If the suggestions I have made are carried out, I think the city of Baltimore can be controlled under any circumstances. I have thought proper to make them before asking the engineer for plans, for the reason that a gentlemen for whose judgment I have a great respect thought such indications of a determination to overawe the city would increase the bad feeling existing there. I do not agree with him. I do not think the secessionists could be more intemperate than they are now, and the Union men would be encouraged and strengthened by such a demonstration.

I am, respectfully, yours,

JOHN A. DIX,
Major-General, Commanding.

GENERAL ORDERS, }　　　HDQRS. CORPS OF OBSERVATION,
　　No. 1.　　 }　　　　　*Rockville, August* 12, 1861.

By virtue of orders from Headquarters Division of Potomac, dated August 10, 1861, the undersigned assumes command of the forces of the United States along the line of the Potomac between Point of Rocks and Seneca Falls, including the forces at both places.

CHAS. P. STONE,
Brigadier-General.

HEADQUARTERS OF THE ARMY,
August 13, 1861.

Major-General BANKS, U. S. A.,
  Commanding, &c., Sandy Hook, Md.:

You are authorized to withdraw your batteries and troops from Maryland Heights and Harper's Ferry, leaving a guard to observe the enemy, and to take such position with your army as you deem best, between Frederick and the Potomac and on either side the Monocacy, to observe the enemy across the Potomac and protect the canal. If involved in or threatened with active operations you may absorb the upper part of Stone's command or, in an extreme case, the whole of it within your reach.

WINFIELD SCOTT.

HEADQUARTERS CORPS OF OBSERVATION,
Rockville, August 13, 1861.

Maj. S. WILLIAMS,
  Assistant Adjutant-General, Headquarters Division of Potomac:

MAJOR: I have the honor to report that I arrived here yesterday morning with Battery I, First U. S. Artillery. Found here the Tammany [Forty-second New York] Regiment and Second New York State Militia [Eighty-second New York Volunteers].

The streams are swollen by the heavy rains and the roads are heavy and badly cut up.

Inexperienced management of the trains has caused delay in the arrival of a large portion of the wagons of the Tammany Regiment, and it cannot advance until some of the delayed wagons arrive.

I go to-day to Seneca, and shall, if practicable, move the artillery and one regiment of infantry to Darnestown.

The Second New York Regiment is weak in numbers and greatly disorganized. No dependence can be placed in it for some time to come.

Very respectfully, I am, major, your obedient servant,
CHAS. P. STONE,
Brigadier-General, Commanding.

WAR DEPARTMENT,
Washington, August 14, 1861.

Maj. ALBERT J. MYER, *Signal Officer:*

SIR: You will at once and with the utmost expedition establish a system of signals along the line of the Potomac through Maryland, connecting the column under Major-General Banks with those under Brigadier-Generals Stone and McCall and the forces in and about this city. Should you find it necessary, you are authorized to purchase a small telegraphic train, to aid you to communicate with those points which cannot be reached by signals, to be paid for out of the telegraphic fund. Major-General McClellan will be directed to give you the necessary aid by details of officers and men from the respective columns and also Major-General Banks.

I am, sir, very respectfully, your obedient servant,
THOMAS A. SCOTT,
Assistant Secretary of War.

HEADQUARTERS DIVISION OF THE POTOMAC,
Washington, August 14, 1861.

Lieut. Gen. WINFIELD SCOTT, *Commanding U. S. Army:*

GENERAL: I am informed by Brigadier-General McDowell that 62 non-commissioned officers and privates of the Second Regiment of Maine Volunteers have formally and positively, and in the presence of their regiment, refused to do any further duty whatever, falsely alleging that they are no longer in the service of the United States. I concur in the suggestion of General McDowell that this combined insubordination, if not open mutiny, should be immediately repressed; and I approve of his recommendation that the insubordinate soldiers should be immediately transferred in arrest and without arms to the Dry Tortugas, there to perform such fatigue service as the commanding officer there may assign to them, until they shall by their future conduct show themselves worthy to bear arms.

Very respectfully, your obedient servant,

GEO. B. McCLELLAN,
Major-General, Commanding.

HEADQUARTERS DIVISION OF THE POTOMAC,
Washington, D. C., August 14, 1861.

Brig. Gen. ANDREW PORTER,
Provost-Marshal, &c., Washington, D. C.:

GENERAL: The brigade commander of the Seventy-ninth Regiment New York Volunteers having reported that the regiment is in a state of open mutiny, Major-General McClellan directs that you proceed with a battery, the two companies of the Second Cavalry, at the Park Hotel, and as many companies of regular infantry as you may deem proper, to the encampment of that regiment. On your arrival there you will order such as are willing to move to march out of the camp, leaving the disaffected portion of the regiment by themselves. You will then order the latter portion to lay down their arms, and will put them under a strong guard. The ringleaders you will put in double irons.

You are authorized, if necessary, to use force to accomplish the object. Report the result as soon as possible.*

I am, sir, very respectfully, your obedient servant,

A. V. COLBURN,
Assistant Adjutant-General.

WHEELING, VA., *August* 15, 1861.

Hon. SIMON CAMERON, *Secretary of War:*

Lee has one body of 8,000 men near Monterey, in Highland; another force of equal if not greater strength is this side of Huntersville. Still another body of considerable size is marching by the way of Mingo Flats on to Huttonsville. We have no force guarding the Mingo Flats road. Rosecrans is at Clarksburg, a respectful distance. For God's sake send us more troops and a general to command, or else we are whipped in less than ten days.

---

* See report No. 1, of reconnaissance September 11, 1861, to Lewinsville, &c., p. 168.

The Huntersville force and Wise and Floyd's force are all moving on us by the way of Mingo Flats, and we are without any guard or fortifications to that pass.

JOHN S. CARLILE.

HEADQUARTERS DEPARTMENT OF THE SHENANDOAH,
August 15, 1861.

Col. E. D. TOWNSEND, *Assistant Adjutant-General:*

SIR : In obedience to instructions by telegram of the 13th and by order of the 14th instant, both of which were duly received, I have made preparations to change the position of this column to a point between Frederick and the Potomac River, leaving at this post a corps of observation, and providing for the protection of the canal and river as directed. A portion of our force (Colonel Geary's regiment) was sent to Point of Rocks on Tuesday evening. The movement of the main part of the column will be speedily completed. Everything is quiet at that point now. A few rebels have shown themselves opposite Sharpsburg, where a regiment (Thirteenth Massachusetts, Colonel Leonard) is stationed. I send an intercepted letter from Richmond,* which represents the opinion of a portion of the people there.

I have the honor to be, with great respect, your obedient servant,

N. P. BANKS,
Major-General, Commanding.

HEADQUARTERS, *August* 16, 1861.

Major-General BANKS, *Commanding, &c., Sandy Hook, Md.:*

In approximating your forces to those lower down the Potomac, I think it best to cross the Monocacy, in order to have that river as a line of defense.

WINFIELD SCOTT.

WASHINGTON, *August* 16, 1861.

General BANKS, *Commanding, Sandy Hook:*

From information received this evening it is deemed important that the change of position ordered by General-in-Chief should be made without delay. What part of your command has been moved?

SIMON CAMERON,
Secretary of War.

HEADQUARTERS DEPARTMENT OF PENNSYLVANIA,
Baltimore, Md., August 16, 1861.

EDWARD McK. HUDSON, *Aide-de-Camp:*

SIR: I am directed by Major-General Dix to acknowledge the receipt of your communication of the 15th instant, addressed to Brigadier-General Dix, commanding Department of Baltimore, and inclosing paragraphs from newspapers published in this city.*

He requests me to say that he is the major-general commanding the Department of Pennsylvania, composed of the States of Pennsylvania,

---

* Not found.

Delaware, and all of Maryland except the counties of Alleghany and Washington, which belong to the Department of the Shenandoah, and the counties of Frederick, Montgomery, and Prince George's, which belong to the Department of Washington. If any changes have been made in his command he has no information, official or unofficial, in respect to them. He received last evening a dispatch, signed Lawrence A. Williams, aide-de-camp, in the name of the commanding general of the division, and though it contained nothing more definite in regard to the authority from which it emanated, he assumed that it came to him by direction of the Government, and immediately sent for the agent of the Sun newspaper, the proprietor being absent, and he thinks the result of the interview will be to cause a discontinuance of exceptionable articles like those which have recently appeared in that paper.

Major-General Dix requests me to say to Major-General McClellan that his attention, since he assumed the command of this department, has been so engaged by official duties that the course of the secessionist papers in Baltimore was not noticed by him until the early part of this week. He has been considering whether the emergency would not warrant a suppression of the papers referred to, if, after warning them of the consequences of a persistence in their hostility to the Union, they should refuse to abstain from misrepresentations of the conduct and motives of the Government and the publication of intelligence calculated to aid and encourage the public enemy. It was his intention in a matter of so much gravity—one affecting so deeply the established opinions of the country in regard to the freedom of the press—to ask the direction of the Government as soon as he should feel prepared to recommend a definite course of action. In the mean time it will give him pleasure to do all in his power to suppress the publication of information in regard to the movements, position, and number of our troops, as Major-General McClellan requests, as it is possible that orders may have been issued affecting his command and by accident not have reached him.

Major-General Dix will be glad to receive any information you may have in regard to the modification, if any has been made, of General Orders, No. 47.*

I am, very respectfully, yours,

WM. D. WHIPPLE,
Assistant Adjutant-General.

HEADQUARTERS DIVISION OF THE POTOMAC,
Washington, August 16, 1861.

Brig. Gen. W. S. ROSECRANS, U. S. A.,
Commanding Department of the Ohio, Clarksburg, Va.:

Telegram of the 16th received. Do not abandon the Gauley. Hold Bulltown, Huttonsville, and the works in front of it. One regiment, or at most two, should now suffice for Red House and Grafton. Clarksburg and the line of railroad may be temporarily weakened or abandoned. Attack the enemy on Cranberry or wherever he debouches, always having intrenchments in your rear. You have the advantage of a central position within the mountains. Must use your intrenchments to check the enemy with small forces, while by rapid movement you attack his columns in succession with overwhelming forces. Never

_____

* Of July 25, 1861. See p. 763, Vol. II, of this series.

wait for him to attack your main column, but crush the enemy nearest to you and then go after the next. Take no tents in your movements, and march with the utmost rapidity. You have a most brilliant opportunity. Two regiments have been ordered from Ohio to Fremont; all the rest are at your disposal as they are organized. I need here for the defense of the capital every regiment that can be spared, and ought to take all that Ohio can furnish. It would be better to use in person the regiments you now have before asking for any more.

GEO. B. McCLELLAN,
Major-General, U. S. Army, Commanding.

HEADQUARTERS DIVISION OF THE POTOMAC,
Washington, August 16, 1861.

Brig. Gen. W. S. ROSECRANS, U. S. A.,
Commanding Department of the Ohio, Clarksburg, Va.:

The reason of my communication was that I have learned from the most reliable authority that Cheat Mountain Pass was not fortified as I directed, but only in a temporary way. This is confirmed by date of August 15. Carry out my previous instructions to the fullest extent. Leave at the Red House the minimum force necessary to hold the works near there. Occupy Kanawha Valley with the minimum force necessary to hold the Gauley Pass. Secure Grafton and the railroad line thence to Benwood by the smallest possible force. Disregard, for the present, the interior of Western Virginia, or else hold it with your worst troops, who are not fit to take the field. Concentrate the remainder of your available force in the vicinity of Huttonsville, placing a strong reserve at that point, and occupying the works on the Cheat Mountain and the Huntersville road with a force sufficient to hold them until support can arrive. Strengthen both of these fortifications as rapidly as possible, and take there all your available artillery. Make a strong reconnaissance in the direction of the enemy's works towards Huntersville, and if possible drive them out before their works are completed and their force concentrated. Communicate this at once by telegraph to Reynolds.

GEO. B. McCLELLAN,
Major-General, U. S. Army, Commanding.

GENERAL ORDERS, }   HDQRS. DIVISION OF THE POTOMAC,
No. 4.   }   *Washington, August 16, 1861.*

All passes, safe-conducts, and permits, heretofore given, to enter or go beyond the lines of the U. S. Army on the Virginia side of the Potomac are to be deemed revoked, and all such papers will hereafter emanate only from the War Department, the headquarters of the U. S. Army, or of this division, or from the provost-marshal at Washington. Similar passes will be required to cross the river, by bridge or boat, into Virginia.

Strict military surveillance will be exercised within the lines of the Army on the northern side of the Potomac, and upon all the avenues of every kind, by land and water, leading to and from the city of Washington, as well over persons holding passes as all others. Passes will not be required at or within the lines of the Army north of the

Potomac, but disloyal or suspected persons will be liable to arrest and detention until discharged by competent authority, and contraband articles will be seized.

Officers and soldiers of the Army will obtain passes as heretofore ordered.

All complaints of improper arrests, seizures, or searches, made or purporting to be made under military authority, will be received by the proper brigade commanders or provost-marshals, who will at once investigate the same, and in each instance make report to these head-quarters.

By command of Major-General McClellan:

S. WILLIAMS,
Assistant Adjutant-General.

SANDY HOOK, NEAR HARPER'S FERRY,
August 17, 1861.

Col. E. D. TOWNSEND, *Assistant Adjutant-General:*

SIR: We greatly need more artillery. Major Doubleday's battery is very heavy for field service. Excluding that, we have but fourteen pieces. This is wholly insufficient for active service in the new position we are to occupy. Captain Tompkins has recruited a company in Rhode Island, which arrived here last night. The battery is in Washington; the company here. Either the battery should be sent to us or the company ordered to Washington. We wait instructions upon this subject. I most earnestly press upon the Commander-in-Chief our necessities for an increase of artillery, and hope that a liberal supply will be ordered to us for service in the new position we are to occupy.

We leave one regiment at Harper's Ferry, the Second Massachusetts, Colonel Gordon; one at Sharpsburg, Colonel Leonard, Thirteenth Massachusetts; one at Berlin, Colonel Donnelly, Twenty-eighth New York. Colonel Geary is at Point of Rocks since Wednesday night. The rest of our column is *en route* for a position between Frederick and the Potomac east of the Monocacy, according to the orders of the Commander-in-Chief. The country is quiet in this section. No more than the usual cavalry scouts are seen, though they are more bold and active. Some miles south of Point of Rocks Colonel Geary observed a force moving in the direction of the Potomac. It is the same probably that has been seen at Lovettsville, Morrisonville, and towns in that neighborhood, and is from 1,500 to 2,000 strong. The river is rising and rain falls lightly this morning.

I have the honor to be, sir, your most obedient servant,

N. P. BANKS,
Major-General, Commanding.

HEADQUARTERS DEPARTMENT OF PENNSYLVANIA,
Baltimore, Md., August 17, 1861.

Col. G. W. CULLUM,
Aide-de-Camp, Headquarters of the Army:

COLONEL: I inclose a map of the city of Baltimore, on which I have marked the eminences we examined in our hasty reconnaissance of yesterday. I have numbered them in the order in which we visited them, and I have added the ascertained elevation of each. A few memoranda may fix more firmly in your mind what you wished to remember:

1. *Federal Hill, 83 feet 6 inches above mean high tide.*—It is to be imme-diately intrenched by order of the General-in-Chief in accordance with the suggestions in my letter of the 12th instant. Next to Fort Mc-Henry it is the most important position in the harbor of Baltimore. It commands the railroad through Pratt street to the President-street depot, the entire basin, the whole lower part of the city, and in the hands of an enemy might be dangerous to Fort McHenry, from which it is 2 miles distant. The distance to Pratt street at the head of the basin is about 800 yards.

2. *Patterson's Park, 124 feet 9 inches above mean high tide.*—A com-manding position, 2 miles from Fort McHenry, and would be very important if No. 3 (Potter's Race Course) were not to be fortified. It is surrounded by a loyal population, and its present occupation is not as necessary as that of No. 4 (the McKim mansion). A regiment has been encamped there until recently. It has been unoccupied since the 7th instant, when the Sixth Wisconsin Regiment was ordered to Wash-ington.

3. *Potter's Race Course, 180 feet above mean high tide.*—A strong work on this height is indispensable to the safety of Fort McHenry, which it commands, and from which it is less than 2 miles distant. It also com-mands Patterson's Park, and is the only point, with the exception of the latter and No. 4, from which the eighth ward, one of the most disloyal in the city, can be assailed. It is to be immediately fortified by order of the General-in-Chief.

4. *McKim's Mansion, 119 feet 9 inches above mean high tide.*—It is in the eighth ward, and commands that portion of the city as effectually as Federal Hill commands the lower portion and the basin. For con-trolling the population of the city and suppressing outbreaks this posi-tion is second only to the latter. It was occupied by the Fifth Wiscon-sin Regiment until the 7th instant, when that regiment was ordered to Washington. If I had a regiment to spare I should place it here in preference to Patterson's Park. It has excellent and ample ground for battalion drill.

5. *Steuart's Mansion, Mount Clare, 184 feet 7 inches above mean high tide.*—This position is important from its vicinity to the Baltimore and Ohio Railroad and the Mount Clare depot on that road, as well as from the relation it holds to the direction from which the city is most likely to be assailed from without. It is occupied by the Fourth Pennsyl-vania Volunteers, numbering 823 men, and Nims' Boston Light Artil-lery, numbering 156. The Second Maryland Regiment (six companies) is encamped on the line of the same railroad and in the same neighbor-hood with 579 men. I have therefore in this locality 1,558 men.

My force is disposed as follows:

Fort McHenry, inside: Regulars, 194; outside: Third New York Vol-unteers, 795; Twenty-first Indiana Volunteers, 845. Total, 1,834.

Federal Hill: Fifth New York Volunteers, Colonel Duryea, 1,028.

Mount Clare: Fourth Pennsylvania, 823; Second Maryland, 579; Nims' Light Artillery, 156. Total, 1,558.

Agricultural Ground, north of the city: Two companies of Pennsyl-vania Cavalry, unequipped, 213. Grand total, 4,633.

My effective force is under 4,000. I need three regiments more. The first I shall place at No. 3 (Potter's Race Course) to work on the pro-posed intrenchments; the second at No. 4 (McKim's mansion) to take care of the eighth ward, and the third at No. 2 (Patterson's Park) until No. 3 is fortified. The home guard is in course of organizing in the city, and I think can be armed next week. It will number 850 men.

We have nothing for them but flint-lock muskets or Hall's breech-loading rifles, also with flint locks. With this force I should feel safe except from external attack. In case of an advance from the Potomac we should need to be strengthened in some proportion to the number of our assailants.

I am, very respectfully, yours,

JOHN A. DIX,
Major-General, Commanding.

POOLESVILLE, MD., *August* 17, 1861.

Maj. S. WILLIAMS, *Assistant Adjutant-General:*

MAJOR: I have the honor to report that this command arrived here the day before yesterday. The main body is encamped around the village, while Edwards Ferry, Conrad's Ferry, and the Monocacy are occupied by strong pickets.

Small bodies of the enemy appeared yesterday opposite Edwards Ferry and fired on a canal-boat passing down. The fire was returned by the pickets of the Minnesota regiment, without result, I think, on either side.

The Thirty-fourth New York Regiment remains at Seneca. Pickets are thrown out to connect with those of General McCall at Great Falls.

The weather remains most unfavorable for any movements, and the river has risen considerably in consequence of the rains. Fording is now rendered difficult and dangerous.

I have been unable as yet to discover the presence of any large force opposite.

Very respectfully, I am, major, your most obedient servant,

CHAS. P. STONE,
Brigadier-General, Commanding.

GENERAL ORDERS, }   HEADQUARTERS OF THE ARMY,
No. 15.   }   *Washington, August* 17, 1861.

The Departments of Washington and Northeastern Virginia will be united into one, to which will be annexed the Valley of the Shenandoah, the whole of Maryland and of Delaware, to be denominated the Department of the Potomac, under Major-General McClellan—headquarters Washington—who will proceed to organize the troops under him into divisions and independent brigades.

By command of Lieutenant-General Scott:

E. D. TOWNSEND,
Assistant Adjutant-General.

DIVISION OF THE POTOMAC,
Washington, August 18, 1861.

Brig. Gen. CHARLES P. STONE, U. S. A.:

GENERAL: Your letter of August 17, 10 p. m., has been received. Information received from General Banks to-day confirms the belief that the enemy intends crossing the Potomac in your vicinity and moving on Baltimore or Washington. There are also strong indications of their intention of attempting the passage of the Potomac south of this city, near Aquia Creek, where they are erecting strong batteries, or at some other point. I will recommend to you the utmost vigilance, and that you continually bear in mind the necessity of securing your retreat towards Rockville should you be unable to prevent the passage of the enemy.

General Banks will be instructed to move up to your support in case of necessity, and will also be instructed to effect his retreat in the same direction in conjunction with you should it become necessary. It is still my wish that the enemy's passage and subsequent advance should be opposed and retarded to the utmost of your ability, to give me time to make my arrangements and come up to your assistance.

A general order has been issued merging the Departments of Northeastern Virginia, the Shenandoah, and Baltimore into the Department of the Potomac, under my immediate command.

Steps have been taken which will secure us a large re-enforcement during the coming week.

*   *   *   *   *   *   *

Very respectfully, your obedient servant,
GEO. B. McCLELLAN,
Major-General, U. S. Army, Commanding Department.

HEADQUARTERS CORPS OF OBSERVATION,
Poolesville, August 19, 1861—1 p. m.

Maj. Gen. GEORGE B. McCLELLAN,
Commanding Division Potomac, Washington, D. C.:

GENERAL: Your letter No. 1, of yesterday's date, is just received. I have made and caused to be made the most careful examinations practicable of the opposite side of the Potomac in front of my position, and believe that the only force in the immediate vicinity is a regiment of Mississippi troops at Leesburg and one of Mississippi or South Carolina troops on Goose Creek. The enemy appear to be throwing up additional intrenchments about 3½ miles back from Edwards Ferry, on the Leesburg road, in an excellent position for guarding the approach to Leesburg, but good for nothing for offensive operations. These works were commenced previous to the battle at Bull Run, and are now being extended, according to report. These works might be reached by shot from a rifled gun planted on the heights above Edwards Ferry.

The troops of this command are now posted as follows, commencing on the right: Three companies of the Second New York Militia [Eighty-second Volunteers] are stationed at the mouth of the Monocacy, with pickets thrown out 2 miles above and the same distance below, connecting above with pickets of the Twenty-eighth Pennsylvania, of General Banks' command. This outpost is supported by the remainder of the Second Regiment, 300 strong only, stationed one-half mile from Poolesville, on the Monocacy road. A picket of cavalry patrols the vicinity of the Monocacy. The Tammany [Forty-second New York] regiment (Cogswell's) is stationed 1 mile from Poolesville, on the road to Conrad's Ferry, and has four companies detached to watch that ferry. The strength of this regiment is 531 in camp, besides the four companies on outpost. The outpost at Conrad's throws out pickets to meet those from the Monocacy above and those from Edwards Ferry below. The Minnesota regiment (Gorman's), 788 strong, is stationed 2½ miles from

Poolesville, on the road to Edwards Ferry, furnishing an outpost of four companies to that ferry. This outpost throws out pickets to meet those from Conrad's on the right and those from Seneca on the left. Seneca being 8 miles from this point, I have left an entire regiment there at the crossing of the river road and the road from Rockville. An outpost is kept on the river bank, throwing out pickets to meet Gorman's above and General McCall's below. One section of Hascall's battery is stationed on the heights above Edwards Ferry. The road from Edwards Ferry to Seneca is very hilly and rough, almost impracticable for artillery or wagons.

The constant rains for the past week must have made the roads very bad on the low grounds on the opposite side of the river and have made the fords at least a foot deeper. If there exists reliable information that a crossing is intended here, I would respectfully recommend that two additional regiments be sent here and a few long-range guns. If I might be permitted to express a preference, I would ask for the Fifteenth Massachusetts Regiment, now in Washington, and the Ninth New York State Militia [Eighty-third Volunteers] now with General Banks. There was a rumor here yesterday that 5,000 men of General Banks' command had arrived near the Monocacy, but I was at the outpost there about sunset, and could see nothing of troops, camps, or smokes.

A negro, who crossed yesterday from near the Monocacy, informed me that two regiments of Southern troops were said to have passed up from Leesburg towards Hillsborough, Waterford, and Lovettsville on Wednesday and Thursday last, and this story was confirmed by a civilian belonging to Washington, who came yesterday from the Virginia side near the Point of Rocks.

Very respectfully, I am, general, your obedient servant,

CHAS. P. STONE,
Brigadier-General.

The enemy keep small pickets near Edwards and Conrad's Ferries, but apparently none near the Monocacy. Their pickets fire on ours and on canal boats passing occasionally.

HEADQUARTERS DEPARTMENT OF PENNSYLVANIA,
Baltimore, Md., August 19, 1861.
Maj. Gen. GEORGE B. MCCLELLAN,
Commanding Division of the Potomac:

GENERAL: In obedience to the direction contained in your dispatch by telegraph of last evening, I have the honor to inclose a return of the troops in this department. They are scattered not only by regiments, but by companies, over a large surface, and I am unable to furnish a complete return of all up to a later date than the 1st instant. All but one are up to the 16th instant.

I also inclose copies of two letters—one of the 12th, and the other of the 17th instant—to the General-in-Chief, concerning the defense of this city.* The latter, intended as a memorandum or memoir, shows the disposition of my force in this immediate neighborhood and the aggregate of each regiment and corps from the morning reports of the 16th instant. Accompanying these letters is a map of the city, illustrating the proposed plan of defense.

---

* See, under these dates, pp. 558, 565.

ANNAPOLIS.

The First Regiment Pennsylvania Volunteers, headquarters at Annapolis, has six companies there and four at Annapolis Junction, with detachments from both stations guarding the intermediate bridges and cross roads.

Contraband goods are carried across this line to the lower counties on the Western Shore of Maryland bordering on the Potomac, and sent into Virginia at Mathias Point and other places.

To watch it effectively five more companies are needed; a regiment would be better.

THE RELAY HOUSE.

The Fourth Regiment Wisconsin Volunteers is stationed at the Relay House, 9 miles from Baltimore, at the junction of the Baltimore and Ohio Railroad and the Washington Branch. It has one company between the Relay House and the Annapolis Junction, and has detachments on both roads, all within the range of 9 miles from the headquarters of the regiment.

PHILADELPHIA, WILMINGTON AND BALTIMORE RAILROAD.

The Fourth Regiment New York Volunteers, with its headquarters at Havre de Grace, is guarding the Baltimore, Wilmington and Philadelphia Railroad. It is disposed as follows:

At Perryville, on the east side of Susquehanna, one company.

At Havre de Grace, on the west side of Susquehanna, three companies.

At Perrymansville, 9 miles from Susquehanna, one company.

At Bush River, 12 miles from Susquehanna, two companies.

At Gunpowder River, 24 miles from Susquehanna, two companies.

At Back River, 7 miles from Baltimore, one company.

NORTHERN CENTRAL RAILROAD.

The Twentieth Regiment Indiana Volunteers is guarding the Northern Central Railroad and the Pikesville Arsenal. Its headquarters are near Cockeysville, 15 miles from Baltimore, where there are three companies. There is one company at the Pikesville Arsenal, 8 miles from Baltimore, and the other six are scattered along the line of the railroad in detachments, guarding some 65 bridges and culverts in Maryland and a few across the Pennsylvania line. The position and strength of all the other regiments and corps in Maryland are shown by the inclosed copy of my letter of the 17th instant to Colonel Cullum, aide-de-camp, intended as a memoir for the information of the General-in-Chief.* They are all in and around Baltimore. The New York Third and the Indiana Twenty-first, outside of Fort McHenry, are subject to heavy details for detached service. One company of the former is guarding a powder-house three-quarters of a mile from the fort. Two companies of the latter are under instruction in the fort as artillerists, and two others are guarding steamers engaged in the transportation of supplies between Baltimore and Washington. The charters of these steamers are about to expire.

There are less than 200 artillerists in Fort McHenry to man 72 guns.

---

* See p. 565.

To supply this deficiency two companies of the Twenty-first Indiana Volunteers are in training.

The only two regiments intact are the Fifth New York Volunteers and the Fourth Pennsylvania Volunteers.

Fort Delaware has a garrison of less than 50 artillerists. It ought to be immediately re-enforced by another company.

The Fifth New York Volunteers is well drilled in the schools of the soldier, the company, and the battalion. The Third and Fourth New York Volunteers are tolerably well trained. The residue of the regiments under my command are new levies, and have been so much cut up by detached service that they have had no opportunity of being instructed, except in the school of the soldier and the company.

In regard to this city I feel safe for the moment, even with my present inadequate force; but if the Confederates should cross the Potomac into Maryland, it would need to be doubled in order to secure us against an outbreak on the part of the disloyal population. I have never put my estimate of the troops required in and around Baltimore at less than 7,000.

I am sorry to say that the Third and Fourth Regiments New York Volunteers are greatly demoralized. I had serious difficulty with the former a few days ago; but by prompt and rigorous measures the insubordination was quelled.

I am, general, very respectfully, your obedient servant,

JOHN A. DIX,
Major-General, Commanding.

P. S.—It has been nearly impossible to get correct returns from the volunteer regiments which arrived here the last of July, those particularly which were immediately broken up and put on detached service. Those around the city, and thus within our reach, make their morning reports regularly, but with the others we have great trouble. Our arrangements are now made to get reports from them every Monday morning, and I hope to be able, within the next two or three days, to send you a full return up to this morning.

Since finishing my letter the Sixteenth Regiment Massachusetts Volunteers has arrived, and, by order of the General-in-Chief, goes into camp here.

HEADQUARTERS DEPARTMENT OF THE SHENANDOAH,
August 19, 1861.

Colonel KENLY, *First Maryland Regiment:*

SIR: The general commanding directs that upon receipt of this communication you at once detach from your regiment as follows:

Two companies at Antietam Ford, to relieve the detachment of the Thirteenth Massachusetts Regiment at that place.

Two companies at Shepherdstown Ford, to relieve the detachment of the Thirteenth Massachusetts Regiment at that place.

One company in vicinity of locks and ford at Shepherd's Island, also to relieve a detachment of the Thirteenth Massachusetts Regiment.

One company at Dam No. 4, to relieve a detachment of the Thirteenth Massachusetts Regiment.

Headquarters of the regiment with the remaining companies to be at Williamsport.

The Thirteenth Massachusetts Regiment, on being relieved, will be governed by orders from these headquarters.

In view of the recent proclamation of the President, the general directs that, as far as is in your power, you put a stop to all intercourse whatever with the State of Virginia in the vicinity of your posts.

It is not thought probable that any serious attack will for the present be made upon any of your posts. Should you be forced to call them in and retreat, you will retire upon Frederick. The headquarters will after to-day be for the present in the vicinity of Hyattstown.

Very respectfully, your obedient servant,

ROBT. WILLIAMS,
Assistant Adjutant-General.

HEADQUARTERS DIVISION OF THE POTOMAC,
Washington, August 20, 1861.

Maj. Gen. JOHN A. DIX, *Commanding, &c., Baltimore, Md.:*

GENERAL: Inclosed I send you an order for Captain De Russy's company (K), Fourth Artillery, to proceed without delay to this city to be mounted. The services of that company are indispensably necessary at this place with a light battery. I desire that you replace the company at Fort McHenry by one or more of the best volunteer companies under your command. The First and Fourth Regiments of Pennsylvania Volunteers, now under your command, are required here, to complete General McCall's division. I wish you to forward them to this city as soon as they are relieved by other troops, and in place of them you are authorized to detain in Baltimore and its vicinity any three regiments that are there, except Colonel Black's Pennsylvania regiment and the Rhode Island regiment.

This, together with the Sixteenth Massachusetts, will give you two additional regiments. As soon as there are troops enough here to make the capital perfectly secure, I propose to increase your command; but for the present I think the safety of Baltimore can better be secured by concentrating troops in this vicinity than by leaving them there.

I am, sir, very respectfully, your obedient servant,

GEO. B. McCLELLAN,
Major-General, Commanding.

HEADQUARTERS DEPARTMENT OF PENNSYLVANIA,
Baltimore, Md., August 20, 1861.

His Excellency THOMAS H. HICKS, *Governor of Maryland:*

SIR: I should be glad to know your opinion in regard to the measures which should be adopted to break up the active communication manifestly going on between the Eastern Shore of Maryland and the Western Shore of Virginia. There have been rumors for some time that there is a rebel camp in Northampton County, on the Eastern Shore of Virginia. If this be so, it appears to me that it should be broken up. Whatever we do should be well considered, and then carried out with promptness and vigor.

I am, very respectfully, your obedient servant,

JOHN A. DIX,
Major-General, Commanding.

NAVY DEPARTMENT, *August* 20, 1861.

Hon. SIMON CAMERON, *Secretary of War:*

SIR: The importance of keeping open the navigation of the Potomac is so obvious that no argument is necessary on the subject. So far as is possible this Department has and will continue to discharge its duty in this matter by an armed flotilla; but there are one or two points where shore batteries can be made to interrupt communication, and, in view of that danger and recent information, I would most urgently request that immediate measures be taken by the War Department to fortify and intrench Mathias Point. A single regiment, aided by two of our steamers, could heretofore, and perhaps may still, take possession of and secure it. But if more than a regiment is required, it appears to be indispensable that the requisite number should be furnished. Attention on repeated occasions has been called to the particular necessity of holding that place as absolutely essential to the unobstructed navigation of the Potomac. The Navy will at any moment contribute its efforts towards seizing and holding that place, and I apprehend there should not be any delay. Cannot a sufficient force be sent down forthwith to seize and, in connection with such armed vessels as we can order for that purpose, hold Mathias Point, and thus keep open the navigation of the Potomac? I understand that troops will be sent to the Lower Maryland counties, to keep the peace and prevent batteries from being erected on the left bank. This is a timely and wise precaution, but it is equally necessary that we should take possession of Mathias Point. Should the insurgents get possession of that point, it will require a very large force to dispossess them.

I remain, sir, very respectfully, &c.,

GIDEON WELLES.

[Indorsement.]

Respectfully referred to the immediate attention of the Lieutenant-General.

SIMON CAMERON,
Secretary of War.

HEADQUARTERS CORPS OF OBSERVATION,
Poolesville, August 20, 1861.

Maj. S. WILLIAMS, *Headquarters Division of the Potomac:*

MAJOR: The condition of this command remains good, and to all appearances the positions of the enemy have not changed opposite us since my letter of yesterday's date to the General Commanding.

I am still under the impression that there is no very large force in my immediate front, but of course it could be held within one day's march of either of the ferries and yet be out of view.

The river is not deemed fordable here to-day in consequence of the recent rains; but should the rain cease, the water will probably fall in forty-eight hours so as to render three fords passable.

I have received no news from General Banks' command directly; shall send up the river to learn something of his position this evening.

If there is any reasonable chance of an attempt to cross here, I would respectfully ask for at least two more regiments and additional artillery.

My cavalry force is so weak, that I cannot make the use I desire to of that arm without breaking down both horses and men.

Very respectfully, I am, major, your obedient servant,

CHAS. P. STONE,
Brigadier-General, Commanding.

HEADQUARTERS DEPARTMENT OF THE SHENANDOAH,
Near Buckeystown, Md., August 20, 1861.

General GEORGE B. MCCLELLAN, *Washington, D. C.:*

I have near here 10,860 infantry, 549 artillerymen, 333 cavalry, and fourteen pieces light artillery. At Frederick the First Maryland Regiment, nearly 750, and the Fourth Connecticut Regiment, nearly 750. At Sharpsburg nearly 1,000. Detailed report will be sent by mail. No news here this evening.

N. P. BANKS,
Major-General, Commanding.

HEADQUARTERS DEPARTMENT OF THE SHENANDOAH,
August 20, 1861.

Colonel GEARY, *Twenty-eighth Pennsylvania Regiment:*

SIR: The General Commanding directs that you station detachments from your regiment at the different fords on the Potomac River from Harper's Ferry to the Monocacy Aqueduct. These will relieve Colonels Donnelly's and Gordon's regiments. You will at once send the four pieces of the Rhode Island Battery, now at Point of Rocks, to rejoin its brigade at this place. On being relieved by your detachments, Colonels Donnelly's and Gordon's regiments, with the two guns of the Rhode Island Battery, now at Berlin, will rejoin their respective brigades.

The General wishes you as far as possible to put a stop to all intercourse with the State of Virginia in the vicinity of your posts. Should you be forced to retire by largely superior forces of the enemy, you will endeavor to concentrate your regiment as much as you can in retreating and retire upon Hyattstown, where your brigade will be for the present. You will at once send off all your baggage, except that which is absolutely necessary. In case you are forced to retreat, you will destroy the railroad and telegraph as far as possible.

Very respectfully, your obedient servant,

ROBT. WILLIAMS,
Assistant Adjutant-General.

HEADQUARTERS DIVISION OF THE POTOMAC,
August 20, 1861.

Brig. Gen. ANDREW PORTER, U. S. A.,
Provost-Marshal, Washington, D. C.:

GENERAL: Major-General McClellan directs that throughout the day to-morrow you hold in readiness to march at a minute's warning a light battery, two companies of cavalry, and as many companies of infantry as you may deem necessary, to put down a mutiny in Colonel Baker's California Regiment.

Should any portion of that regiment mutiny (and there is now some reason to suppose that they will), you are authorized to use force if necessary to quell it. If they refuse to obey, you are authorized to fire on them.

I am, sir, very respectfully, your obedient servant,

A. V. COLBURN,
Assistant Adjutant-General.

GENERAL ORDERS, }   HDQRS. ARMY OF THE POTOMAC,
       No. 1.   }   *Washington, August* 20, 1861.

In accordance with General Orders, No. 15, of August 17, 1861, from the headquarters of the Army, I hereby assume command of the Army of the Potomac, comprising the troops serving in the former Departments of Washington and Northeastern Virginia, in the valley of the Shenandoah, and in the States of Maryland and Delaware.

The organization of the command into divisions and brigades will be announced hereafter.

The following-named officers are attached to the staff of the Army of the Potomac:

Maj. S. Williams, assistant adjutant-general.
Capt. A. V. Colburn, assistant adjutant-general.
Col. R. B. Marcy, inspector-general.
Col. T. M. Key, aide-de-camp.
Capt. N. B. Sweitzer, First Cavalry, aide-de-camp.
Capt. Edward McK. Hudson, Fourteenth Infantry, aide-de-camp.
Capt. Lawrence A. Williams, Tenth Infantry, aide-de-camp.
Maj. A. J. Myer, signal officer.
Maj. Stewart Van Vliet, chief quartermaster.
Maj. H. F. Clarke, chief commissary.
Surg. C. S. Tripler, medical director.
Maj. J. G. Barnard, chief engineer.
Maj. J. N. Macomb, chief topographical engineer.
Capt. C. P. Kingsbury, chief of ordnance.
Brig. Gen. George Stoneman, volunteer service, chief of cavalry.
Brig. Gen. W. F. Barry, volunteer service, chief of artillery.

GEO. B. McCLELLAN,
Major-General, U. S. Army.

HEADQUARTERS ARMY OF OCCUPATION,
Clarksburg, W. Va., August 20, 1861.

To the Loyal Citizens of Western Virginia:

You are the vast majority of the people. If the principle of self-government is to be respected, you have a right to stand in the position you have assumed, faithful to the constitution and laws of Virginia as they were before the ordinance of secession.

The Confederates have determined at all hazards to destroy the Government which for eighty years has defended our rights and given us a name among the nations. Contrary to your interests and your wishes they have brought war on your soil. Their tools and dupes told you you must vote for secession as the only means to insure peace; that unless you did so, hordes of abolitionists would overrun you, plunder your property, steal your slaves, abuse your wives and daughters, seize upon your lands, and hang all those who opposed them.

By these and other atrocious falsehoods they alarmed you and led many honest and unsuspecting citizens to vote for secession. Neither threats, nor fabrications, nor intimidations sufficed to carry Western Virginia against the interests and wishes of its people into the arms of secession.

Enraged that you dared to disobey their behests, Eastern Virginians who had been accustomed to rule you and to court your votes and ambitious recreants from among yourselves, disappointed that you would not make good their promises, have conspired to tie you to the desperate fortunes of the Confederacy or drive you from your homes.

Between submission to them and subjugation or expulsion they leave you no alternative. You say you do not wish to destroy the old Government under which you have lived so long and peacefully; they say you shall break it up. You say you wish to remain citizens of the United States; they reply you shall join the Southern Confederacy to which the Richmond junta has transferred you, and to carry their will there, Jenkins, Wise, Jackson and other conspirators proclaim upon your soil a relentless and neighborhood war. Their misguided or unprincipled followers re-echo their cry, threatening fire and sword, hanging and exile, to all who oppose their arbitrary designs. They have set neighbor against neighbor and friend against friend; they have introduced a warfare only known among savages. In violation of the laws of nations and humanity, they have proclaimed that private citizens may and ought to make war.

Under this bloody code peaceful citizens, unarmed travelers, and single soldiers have been shot down, and even the wounded and defenseless have been killed; scalping their victims is all that is wanting to make their warfare like that which seventy or eighty years ago was waged by the Indians against the white race on this very ground.

You have no other alternative left you but to unite as one man in the defense of your homes, for the restoration of law and order, or be subjugated or driven from the State.

I therefore earnestly exhort you to take the most prompt and vigorous measures to put a stop to neighborhood and private wars. You must remember that the laws are suspended in Eastern Virginia, which has transferred itself to the Southern Confederacy. The old constitution and laws of Virginia are only in force in Western Virginia. These laws you must maintain.

Let every citizen, without reference to past political opinions, unite with his neighbors to keep these laws in operation, and thus prevent the country from being desolated by plunder and violence, whether committed in the name of secessionism or Unionism.

I conjure all those who have hitherto advocated the doctrine of secessionism as a political opinion to consider that now its advocacy means war against the peace and interests of Western Virginia. It is an invitation to the Southern confederates to come in and subdue you, and proclaims that there can be no law or right until this is done.

My mission among you is that of a fellow-citizen, charged by the Government to expel the arbitrary force which domineered over you, to restore that law and order of which you have been robbed, and to maintain your right to govern yourselves under the Constitution and laws of the United States.

To put an end to the savage war waged by individuals, who without warrant of military authority lurk in the bushes and waylay messengers or shoot sentries, I shall be obliged to hold the neighborhood in which these outrages are committed responsible; and unless they raise the hue and cry and pursue the offenders, deal with them as accessaries to the crime.

Unarmed and peaceful citizens shall be protected, the rights of private property respected, and only those who are found enemies of the Government of the United States and peace of Western Virginia will be disturbed. Of those I shall require absolute certainty that they will do no mischief.

Put a stop to needless arrests and the spread of malicious reports. Let each town and district choose five of its most reliable and energetic citizens a committee of public safety, to act in concert with the civic and military authorities and be responsible for the preservation of peace and good order.

Citizens of Western Virginia, your fate is mainly in your own hands. If you allow yourselves to be trampled under foot by hordes of disturbers, plunderers, and murderers, your land will become a desolation. If you stand firm for law and order and maintain your rights, you may dwell together peacefully and happily as in former days.

W. S. ROSECRANS,
Brigadier-General, U. S. Army, Commanding.

HEADQUARTERS DEPARTMENT OF PENNSYLVANIA,
Baltimore, Md., August 21, 1861.

Capt. EDWARD McK. HUDSON, *Aide-de-Camp:*

SIR: The Secretary of the Navy is in error in supposing that I have the means of effectually blockading the Patuxent. I have but two revenue cutters at my disposal, both sailing vessels, the Forward and the Hope. The former belongs to the revenue service, but is in bad order and ought to be hauled up for repairs. The latter is a yacht, which her owner, who commands her, offered for gratuitous service. She lies opposite Fort McHenry, and has been very useful and efficient. She is entirely unsuited to the service which would be required of her in the lower part of the bay. Armed steamers are indispensable. The Secretary of the Treasury promised me four steamers of from three to four hundred tons. With these I thought the whole commerce of the Chesapeake north of the Potomac could be effectually controlled. I inclose a copy of a letter to him of the 8th instant,* explaining the necessity for such a force. My opinion still is that nothing short of it will suffice to break up the illicit commercial intercourse carried on between the Eastern Shore of Maryland with Virginia through the Patuxent and Potomac.

I have twice called the attention of the Government to the fact that there is a rebel camp in Northampton County, on the Eastern Shore of Virginia, which is a nucleus of disaffection for Accomac and the counties on the Eastern Shore of Maryland up to the Delaware line. It is very important that it should be broken up. Two regiments, with a discreet commander, could march through this important district and put down all opposition.

I am, respectfully, yours,

JOHN A. DIX,
Major-General, Commanding.

---

* Printed in Series III, Vol. I.

HEADQUARTERS DEPARTMENT OF THE SHENANDOAH,
Near Hyattstown, Md., August 21, 1861.

Colonel LEONARD, *Thirteenth Massachusetts Regiment:*

SIR: In view of instructions, received this day from headquarters of the Army in Washington, it becomes necessary for you to take post in the vicinity of Harper's Ferry. The Commanding General directs that you proceed with your regiment to Sandy Hook, and to take post on the Maryland side of the Potomac, so as to prevent an enemy from crossing at the ford or ferry, and to hold the Maryland Heights.

Very respectfully,

ROBT. WILLIAMS,
Assistant Adjutant-General.

HEADQUARTERS OF THE ARMY,
Washington, August 22, 1861.

Major-General McCLELLAN, U. S. A.,
Commanding Department of the Potomac:

SIR: The General-in-Chief directs me to say that, on information considered by the War Department as important and reliable, orders were given to Major-General Dix, commanding in Baltimore, to stop, until further orders, all boats between Baltimore and Saint Mary's or the neighboring counties of Maryland and Virginia. This order was given the 15th instant. Permission was given the 18th for a steamboat to make one trip to bring away families left behind.

The Hon. Reverdy Johnson, of Baltimore, proposes that the boats shall be permitted to renew their trips for the purpose of carrying freight only, without the privilege of taking passengers, under such guard or regulations as may be necessary for the public safety. The object of this arrangement would be to enable the loyal people of Maryland to send their produce to the Baltimore market, as they have been in the habit of doing. The General-in-Chief wishes you to refer this proposition to Major-General Dix, and if he thinks well of it, to have it carried into effect.

I am, sir, very respectfully, your obedient servant,

E. D. TOWNSEND,
Assistant Adjutant-General.

SENECA, *August* 22, 1861.

Maj. S. WILLIAMS,
Asst. Adjt. Gen., Hdqrs. Division of the Potomac:

MAJOR: I have the honor to report, for the information of the Major-General Commanding, that all is quiet throughout my lines; no change opposite.

This morning there was cannon firing near Leesburg, either two salutes or practicing; more probably the latter.

General Banks is at Hyattstown, some 9½ or 10 miles northeast of Poolesville, connecting with my position by a reasonably good road, and with Rockville by an excellent one.

I fear there is too much nervousness on my right—that is, in the command of Colonel Geary, at Point of Rocks. His ambulances came hastily into my camp this morning, having been sent off at 10 p. m. last night. The river is not fordable for wagons or artillery at this time.

I am unable to discover any signs of raft or boat preparation, and the only signs of the enemy on the bank are small pickets, while there are no signs of large camps except at Leesburg and on Goose Creek. Those two do not appear very extensive, say for one or two regiments each. With a long-range rifle cannon I could stir up the intrenchments erected for the defense of Leesburg, and perhaps make them betray the power of their guns, if they have any in position, which I doubt.

Major Myer, signal officer, arrived at Poolesville this morning, and will make trials to-night between my left and General Banks' position.

I would respectfully request that General McCall's force at Big Falls may be instructed to throw out pickets, say 4½ miles above that position, to meet the pickets of the Thirty-fourth New York Volunteers.

Five negroes crossed the river yesterday, running away, as they say, from being sent to Manassas to work on the fortifications. I respectfully ask instructions as to the disposition to be made of them. They say there is no large camp opposite this place for 3 miles back.

Very respectfully, I am, major, your most obedient servant,

CHAS. P. STONE,
Brigadier-General, Commanding Corps of Observation.

HEADQUARTERS ARMY OF THE POTOMAC,
Washington. D. C., August 23, 1861.

Brig. Gen. CHARLES P. STONE, *Commanding Brigade:*

GENERAL: Major-General McClellan directs me to inform you that it is a very well authenticated fact that the enemy are suffering severely with the small-pox, measles, and camp fevers. They have fallen back from Vienna to Flint Hill, taking all their sick with them. They moved even those who were so very sick that one or more died on the march. The pickets have been drawn back throughout the whole length of the line. They will probably change their plan of operation, as they see that we had divined their original plans and had made preparations to frustrate them. This is written simply to keep you posted. The general does not wish you to be the less watchful because appearances indicate a retrograde movement on the part of the enemy.

I am, sir, very respectfully, your obedient servant,

A. V. COLBURN,
Assistant Adjutant-General.

OFFICE CHIEF OF ARTILLERY, ARMY OF THE POTOMAC,
Washington, August 23, 1861.

Major-General McCLELLAN, *Commanding Army of the Potomac:*

GENERAL: In obedience to your directions I have the honor to submit the following:

To insure success, it is of vital importance that the Army of the Potomac should have an overwhelming force of field artillery. To render this artillery the most effective, the field batteries should as far as possible consist of regular troops. At present, of the twenty-five batteries of your army thirteen are regulars and twelve are volunteers. With every disposition to do their best, the volunteer artillery do not possess the knowledge or experience requisite for thoroughly efficient service. I would therefore recommend that companies of regular artillery be withdrawn from many of the forts on the Atlantic and Pacific sea-boards and ordered to this point at as early a date as possible, to be mounted as field artillery. For this purpose I am of the opinion that four of the seven companies at Fort Monroe, one of the two companies at Fort McHenry, and seven of the eleven companies on the Pacific coast—in all twelve companies—can very well be spared. Their places in the forts might be very well filled by companies or battalions of volunteer artillery. For this latter purpose I would recommend that corps of volunteer artillery be raised for this special service exclusively. In many of our cities and large towns in the immediate vicinity of the sea-board forts, portions of the militia have been drilled at or have otherwise become familiar with the sea-coast guns. It is believed that many such persons, who would not enlist under ordinary circumstances, would readily enroll themselves for the sole purpose of garrisoning works in the immediate vicinity, and intended for the defense of their homes and places of business.

I am, general, very respectfully, your obedient servant,

WILLIAM F. BARRY,
Brigadier-General, Chief of Artillery.

OFFICE CHIEF OF ARTILLERY, ARMY OF THE POTOMAC,
Washington, August 23, 1861.

Maj. Gen. GEORGE B. MCCLELLAN, *Commanding:*

GENERAL: I have the honor to submit a proposed organization of the artillery for the Army of the Potomac. This organization is based upon an establishment of 100,000 men, and as it is presumed a large majority of the troops will not be over-well disciplined or instructed, the artillery, to give them confidence and steadiness, is arranged upon the basis of three pieces to 1,000 men: Three pieces to 1,000 men—two-thirds guns of which one-fourth are 12-pounders, three-fourths are 6-pounders, and of each of which one-half are rifled; one-third howitzers, of which one-eighth are 32-pounders, one-eighth are 24-pounders, and three-fourths are 12-pounders, the whole distributed as follows:

For the infantry, two pieces to 1,000 men—light 12-pounders, Parrott 10-pounders, James 13-pounders, or 6-pounder guns and 12-pounder howitzers, assembled in mounted batteries.

For the cavalry, two pieces to 1,000 men—6-pounder guns and 12-pounder howitzers mixed, and 12-pounder howitzers alone, assembled in horse artillery batteries.

For the reserve, one piece to 1,000 men—one-half 6-pounder horse artillery and mounted batteries and one-half 12-pounder mounted batteries.

As the troops improve in discipline and become veterans by experience and continued service the ratio of guns to men might be reduced one-half, and thus a force of three hundred guns would amply suffice for an army of 200,000 men. Seven thousand five hundred men and 5,000 horses will be required to equip an artillery force of the above organization.

With regard to the artillery of the field works erected and erecting for the defense of Washington, I have the honor to state the defensive works at present completed mount seventy-eight guns. Of these, thirty are shell guns, five are rifle guns, and thirty-four are 24 and 32 pounders, the remainder being field-guns for flank defense. The new defensive works in process of construction will mount about fifty guns. One thousand one hundred men will be required for the service of these guns.

These men can be readily furnished by details from the volunteer foot regiments assigned as garrisons for the works.

I am, general, very respectfully, your obedient servant,

WILLIAM F. BARRY,
Brigadier-General, Chief of Artillery.

HEADQUARTERS DEPARTMENT OF PENNSYLVANIA,
Baltimore, Md., August 23, 1861.

Maj. Gen. GEORGE B. McCLELLAN:

GENERAL: The inclosed letter, which I think of sufficient importance to be submitted to you, only conveys intelligence which I am every day receiving from numerous sources. The secessionists are active and confident throughout the counties on the Eastern Shore of Maryland and Virginia, and the friends of the Government discontented and to some extent depressed. They ask for arms, and in some cases for the presence of Federal troops. I am satisfied there are from 1,000 to 1,500 rebels embodied at Eastville, Northampton County, Virginia, and at other points. Two regiments marched from Salisbury, the terminus of the railroad from Wilmington, down to the southern extremity of the Eastern Shore would break up an immense traffic in contraband, disperse the rebels, and give courage to the friends of the Union.

I am, very respectfully, your obedient servant,

JOHN A. DIX,
Major-General, Commanding.

[Inclosure.]

NEWTOWN, *August 12, 1861.*

Gen. JOHN A. DIX, *Commanding Department of Annapolis:*

DEAR SIR: I have given my friend C. C. Adreon, esq., a complete statement of affairs in this region. I have endeavored to show to him the necessity for troops to protect our citizens in their persons and rights. They have become most insulting and threatening towards us, and are actually driving men suspected of holding Union sentiments from the State, Virginia, and some of them, a Dr. Stickney and family, are here in Newtown now for protection. There is a secession flag at this time waving in sight of me whilst I write. I have been informed that some of our Union men here doubt the practicability of sending troops to the line at and below this place, but I know these men to have personal considerations at the bottom of their prudence. Mr. Sharpe passed through here last week, having in his possession several rifles; was showing them at the hotel of Mr. Dryden, where he amused his disunion friends by showing them the facility by which they were loaded and discharged. They were Sharp's and Merrill's patents, and numbered eight or ten. Mr. Adreon can give you his experience among the Virginians and all other particulars you may require. They have at their command about eight good, serviceable cannon, and about 800 men in a camp, armed with good muskets and rifles. The balance of the men in the camp (about 1,500) are armed with shot-guns and fowling pieces without bayonets. They have also several other pieces of cannon they can mount in battery. Those eight pieces are nice brass guns and mounted. They are beginning to throw up earthen fortifications along the shore of their different rivers, and the sooner troops are sent, in my judgment, the better it will be. For further information I refer you to Mr. Adreon.

Your humble servant,

GEO. S. MERRILL.

HEADQUARTERS,
Alexandria, Va., August 24, 1861.

Maj. S. WILLIAMS, *Assistant Adjutant-General:*

MAJOR: I received information a few days ago which led me to believe that a correspondence between the Maryland and Virginia sides of the river was kept up by means of small boats, which were kept hidden when not in use in marshes near the mouth of Hunting Creek. I sent to the commanding officer of the Perry, the vessel of war which lies off the town, and asked him to send a boat with a guide, whom I would furnish, to look after these small boats, and if possible catch the men engaged in this business. Yesterday he called to see me, and informed me that he could not make the search without direct orders from the Secretary of the Navy. I then asked him if he would search such boats as might be caught in the act of passing and he declined, on the ground that officers of the Navy must be very careful in making searches of boats, &c. I report these facts because the matter in question is important, and in case of emergency it might be necessary to get an order from the Secretary of the Navy to fire on the enemy on the same principle.

Very respectfully,

W. B. FRANKLIN,
Brigadier-General, Commanding Alexandria.

HEADQUARTERS CORPS OF OBSERVATION,
Poolesville, August 25, 1861.

Maj. S. WILLIAMS,
Assistant Adjutant-General, Hdqrs. Army of the Potomac:

MAJOR: There is nothing of importance to report since my report of last night. The enemy have fired a few cannon-shot this morning from Conrad's Ferry. In all, they have fired at that point about eighty shot and shells, causing damage to the ferry houses, but only two very slight wounds to our men.

Very respectfully, I am, major, your most obedient servant,

CHAS. P. STONE,
Brigadier-General, Commanding.

HEADQUARTERS CORPS OF OBSERVATION,
Poolesville, August 28, 1861.

Maj. S. WILLIAMS, *Headquarters Army of the Potomac:*

MAJOR: I have the honor to report that in the recent firing across the river on my outposts the enemy are reported to have lost by our riflemen 3 killed and 7 wounded, while on our side 3 men were contused; none wounded or killed.

I can see no indication of an increased force opposite, but have information that there are two regiments of Mississippi troops at Leesburg and one of South Carolina and one of Virginia troops at Lovettsville and Waterford respectively, while a corps of irregular cavalry, three or four companies, move up and down the river from Goose Creek to Point of Rocks.

Major-General Banks informs me that he has ordered General Hamilton's brigade to this point for temporary service.

I caused a few rounds to be fired yesterday from the Rhode Island section rifled 6-pounders, and find that with guns of that class we can reach the outworks of Leesburg.

The Fifteenth Massachusetts Regiment joined this command yesterday morning.

Very respectfully, I am, major, your most obedient servant,

CHAS. P. STONE,
Brigadier-General, Commanding.

HEADQUARTERS GENERAL BANKS' DIVISION,
Near Darnestown, Md., August 31, 1861.

General STONE:

SIR: Major-General Banks directs me to inform you that he arrived at this place day before yesterday. He requests that you will at your earliest convenience send him, by some responsible agent, some information as to your pickets, their posts, the position of your main body, &c., and that you will communicate to him any information in your possession concerning the positions, numbers, &c., of any troops which may be between Darnestown and Washington. He requests that you will order the section of the Rhode Island Battery now with you to join him at your earliest convenience.

Very respectfully, your obedient servant,

ROBT. WILLIAMS,
Assistant Adjutant-General.

HEADQUARTERS CORPS OF OBSERVATION,
Poolesville, September 2, 1861.

Maj. S. WILLIAMS,
Assistant Adjutant-General, Hdqrs. Army of the Potomac:

MAJOR: I have the honor to report that two or three regiments broke up their camp near Leesburg this forenoon, and marched nearer the river, the bulk of two regiments approaching Conrad's Ferry. They strengthened all their pickets throughout the line. There is no appearance of re-enforcement.

My impression is that the movement was caused by a feeling of alarm lest we should attempt a crossing in force, as one of the advanced pickets of the Tammany regiment crossed the river last night and cut out and brought over a large ferry-boat.

I have caused the outposts to be strengthened by infantry and artillery, but do not anticipate any advance of the enemy.

Very respectfully, I am, your obedient servant,

CHAS. P. STONE,
Brigadier-General, Commanding.

CAMP NEAR DARNESTOWN, *September* 4, 1861.

Hon. SIMON CAMERON, *Secretary of War, &c.:*

SIR: I visited the Potomac at Edwards Ferry, opposite Poolesville, last evening. There are no indications of movement more than for a month past. Their force at Leesburg appears to be about three or four regiments. Two or 3 miles from the river they have thrown up a slight breastwork and the pickets have been increased, but this is perhaps on account of some encroachments by our troops on the Virginia side. Above Point of Rocks there is no increase of rebel forces. The cavalry seems to be chiefly of local character. Last night we were informed that the troops at Leesburg were moving westward, which would take them towards Lovettsville, but this is not well authenticated.

Our force is about 14,000 men. Of this Geary's regiment is at Point of Rocks; Leonard's (Thirteenth) at Harper's Ferry; Kenly's (First Maryland) at Williamsport. They guard the river from the mouth of the Monocacy to the country above Williamsport.

We are much in want of clothing, shoes, &c. We have now but eight pieces of artillery, and are deficient in staff officers, upon which I have addressed you a note.

The news of the capture of the forts in North Carolina has given to our troops the greatest satisfaction and spirit. I congratulate you upon this evidence of a turning tide in the affairs of the country.

Nearly all our insurgent men are returning to duty. The division is in excellent health.

I have the honor to be, respectfully, your obedient servant,

N. P. BANKS.

HEADQUARTERS ARMY OF THE POTOMAC,
Washington, D. C., September 4, 1861.

Col. EDWARD D. BAKER:

You will march with your brigade immediately and report to General Smith at his position, in advance of the Chain Bridge. You will bring with you two days' cooked rations. You will have the men bring their overcoats or blankets, leaving as small a guard as necessary to guard your camp and baggage left at your present position.

GEO. B. McCLELLAN,
Major-General, Commanding.

HEADQUARTERS ARMY OF THE POTOMAC,
Washington, D. C., September 4, 1861.

Brig. Gen. CHARLES P. STONE, *Commanding, &c., Poolesville, Md.:*

SIR: I have the honor to acknowledge the receipt of your communication of the 1st instant. The Commanding General directs me to invite your particular attention to the importance of keeping a careful watch upon the Potomac in front of your position. It is believed, from recent information derived from sources deemed reliable, that the enemy still entertains the design of crossing the river in force at some point above Washington.

There being now no separate military department within the district of country occupied by the Army of the Potomac, the Commanding General is the only person who, under the sixty-fifth article of war, is competent to appoint general courts-martial for this army. Should you find it necessary to make application for a general court-martial, you are requested to furnish at the same time a suitable detail for the court, including the judge-advocate.

The commanding general will at an early day request the War Department to appoint a board to examine into the qualifications of officers.

I am, sir, very respectfully, your obedient servant,

A. V. COLBURN,
Assistant Adjutant-General.

WASHINGTON, D. C., *September* 4, 1861.

Maj. Gen. N. P. BANKS, *Commanding, &c., Darnestown, Md.*:

SIR: The Commanding General directs me to invite your particular attention to the importance of keeping a careful watch upon the Potomac in front of your position. It is believed, from recent information derived from sources deemed reliable, that the enemy still entertains the design of crossing the river in force at some point above Washington.

I am, sir, very respectfully, your obedient servant,

A. V. COLBURN,
Assistant Adjutant-General.

HEADQUARTERS CORPS OF OBSERVATION,
Poolesville, Md., September 4, 1861.

Maj. Gen. GEORGE B. MCCLELLAN,
Commanding Army of the Potomac:

GENERAL: Your telegram of this date I have had the honor to receive, and its requirements have been complied with, so far as making preparations for marching promptly, with two days' provisions cooked.

There are three camps in the immediate vicinity of Leesburg, one apparently large enough for two regiments, the others for one each.

Movements of troops were believed to be heard last night opposite Conrad's Ferry, going west, but I cannot satisfy myself from the reports of the pickets that any considerable body moved.

The Eighth Virginia Regiment now furnishes the pickets opposite ours at Edwards Ferry, while Mississippi troops are posted opposite Conrad's.

The troops of this command are in good spirits, and, with the exception of the First Minnesota, in good health. In the latter the measles is increasing the sick report.

Very respectfully, your obedient servant,

CHAS. P. STONE,
Brigadier-General, Commanding.

HEADQUARTERS ARMY OF THE POTOMAC,
Washington, September 5, 1861.

Hon. S. CAMERON, *Secretary of War:*

SIR: I have most urgently to request that the following-named companies of regular artillery be ordered to report to me with the least possible delay, viz:

Seven of the nine companies of the Third Regiment of Artillery, now stationed on the Pacific coast.

Four of the eight companies now stationed at Fortress Monroe, Va.

The necessity for an increase of the regular artillery force under my command is most pressing.

I have also to request that all the officers belonging to Companies E and H, First Regiment U. S. Artillery, be ordered to join their respective companies without delay. These companies, now mounted as light artillery, have but one officer each on duty with them. In this condition they are not and cannot be efficient.

I am, sir, very respectfully, your obedient servant,

GEO. B. MCCLELLAN,
Major-General, U. S. Army.

SPECIAL ORDERS, }   HDQRS. ARMY OF OCCUPATION, W. VA.,
    No. 89.   }   *Sutton, Va., September* 6, 1861.

The command will move to-morrow morning in the direction of Summersville at — o'clock and in the following order, viz:

1. General Benham's brigade in the order named : Tenth Ohio Volunteers, McMullin's battery, Thirteenth and Twelfth Ohio Volunteers.
Cavalry as the general may direct.

2. Colonel [R. L.] McCook's brigade, Ninth, Twenty-eighth, and Forty-
seventh Ohio Volunteers. Cavalry under direction of the colonel.

3. Colonel [E. P.] Scammon's brigade (with the exceptions hereafter
named), Mack's battery, Twenty-third Ohio Volunteers.

*   *   *   *   *   *   *

The colonel commanding Third Brigade will detach four companies
of the Thirtieth as a guard for this depot. The remaining six will accompany and guard the train.

*   *   *   *   *   *   *

By order of General Rosecrans :

                                    GEO. L. HARTSUFF,
                                    Assistant Adjutant-General.

HEADQUARTERS ARMY OF THE POTOMAC,
                    Washington City, September 6, 1861.

Hon. SIMON CAMERON, *Secretary of War :*

SIR : I have the honor to suggest the following proposition, with the
request that the necessary authority be at once given me to carry it out.
To organize a force of two brigades of five regiments each of New England men for the general service, but particularly adapted to coast
service. The officers and men to be sufficiently conversant with boat
service to manage steamers, sailing vessels, launches, barges, surf-boats,
floating batteries, &c. To charter or buy for the command a sufficient
number of propellers or tug-boats for transportation of men and supplies,
the machinery of which should be amply protected by timber, the vessels to have permanent experienced officers from the merchant service,
but to be manned by details from the command. A naval officer to be
attached to the staff of the commanding officer. The flank companies
of each regiment to be armed with Dahlgren boat guns and carbines
with water-proof cartridges; the other companies to have such arms as
I may hereafter designate, to be uniformed and equipped as the Rhode
Island regiments are. Launches and floating batteries, with timber
parapets, of sufficient capacity to land or bring into action the entire
force. The entire management and organization of the force to be under
my control and to form an integral part of the Army of the Potomac.

The immediate object of this force is for operations in the inlets of
Chesapeake Bay and the Potomac, by enabling me to transport and
land troops at points where they are needed. This force can also be
used in conjunction with a naval force operating against points on the
sea-coast. This coast division to be commanded by a general officer of
my selection. The regiments to be organized as other land forces. The
disbursements for vessels, &c., to be made by the proper departments
of the Army, upon the requisition of the general commanding the division, with my approval.

I think the entire force can be organized in thirty days, and by no
means the least of the advantages of this proposition is the fact that it

will call into the service a class of men who would not otherwise enter the Army.

You will readily perceive that the object of this force is to follow up, along the coast and up the inlets and rivers, the movements of the main army when it advances.

I am, sir, very respectfully, your obedient servant,

GEO. B. McCLELLAN,
Major-General, U. S. Army, Commanding.

WASHINGTON, *September* 7, 1861.

General McCLELLAN:

DEAR SIR: A dispatch from our master of transportation, Mr. William P. Smith, received last evening, says:

Have just heard that Confederates have taken up about 9 miles of the iron on our track above Martinsburg for repairs of their roads toward Richmond, and have also removed a considerable portion of our telegraph wires for transfer in the same direction. All this is in addition to five locomotives and some $40,000 worth of valuable machinists' tools and materials for railroad repairs, &c., lately taken from our Martinsburg shops, and of which they stated they were greatly in need at the South. The engines were hauled by turnpike through Winchester to Strasburg or some other point on Manassas road. They will require heavy repairs, however, before use.

With the wear and tear upon the Southern roads, caused to an extraordinary extent by military transportation, and with the blockade preventing their obtainment of materials and machinery for repairs, it will not require much calculation to determine the to them almost inestimable value of this property of which they have just robbed our company. Thus the great capabilities of our road to aid the Government in the suppression of the rebellion, if our line were connected through, are used in part to facilitate the operations of the rebels. I know that you will appreciate the bearings of this late outrage more readily than probably any other person, and that as soon as you have the means placed in your hands you will remedy the matter, or rather prevent its repetition.

It may be desirable for you to know that at Piedmont we have about as much of a stock of materials and machinists' tools as was taken from Martinsburg, and probably half as much at Cumberland also. The great value of such things to the Confederates at this time, irrespective of other considerations, may tempt them to make raids in that direction also.

Very respectfully, your obedient servant,

J. H. SULLIVAN,
General Transportation Agent Baltimore and Ohio Railroad.

HEADQUARTERS ARMY OF THE POTOMAC,
Washington, September 8, 1861.

Hon. SIMON CAMERON, *Secretary of War:*

SIR: Your note of yesterday* is received. I concur in your views as to the exigency of the present occasion. I appreciate and cordially thank you for your offers of support, and will avail myself of them to the fullest extent demanded by the interests of the country. The force

---

* Not found.

of all our arms within the immediate vicinity of Washington in nearly
85,000 men. The effective portion of this force is more than sufficient to
resist with certain success any attack on our works upon the other side
of the river. By calling in the commands of Generals Banks and Stone
it will probably be sufficient to defend the city of Washington from
whatever direction it may be assailed.

It is well understood that, although the ultimate design of the enemy
is to possess himself of the city of Washington, his first efforts will probably be directed towards Baltimore, with the intention of cutting our lines
of communication and supplies, as well as to arouse an insurrection in
Maryland. To accomplish this he will no doubt show a certain portion
of his force in front of our positions on the other side of the Potomac,
in order to engage our attention there and induce us to leave a large
portion of our force for the defense of those positions. He will probably
also make demonstrations in the vicinity of Aquia Creek, Mathias Point,
and Occoquan, in order still further to induce us still further to dissemi-
nate our forces. His main and real movement will doubtless be to cross
the Potomac between Washington and Point of Rocks, probably not
far from Seneca Falls, and most likely at more points than one. His
hope will be so to engage our attention by the diversions already named
as to enable him to move with a large force direct and unopposed on
Baltimore. I see no reason to doubt the possibility of his attempting
this with a column of at least 100,000 effective troops. If he has only
130,000 under arms, he can make all the diversions I have mentioned
with his raw and badly-armed troops, leaving 100,000 effective men for
his real movement. As I am now situated, I can by no possibility bring
to bear against this column more than 70,000, and probably not over
60,000, effective troops.

In regard to the composition of our active army, it must be borne
in mind that the very important arms of cavalry and artillery had been
almost entirely neglected till I assumed command of this army, and
that consequently the troops of these arms, although greatly increased
in numbers, are comparatively raw and inexperienced, most of the cavalry not being yet armed and equipped.

In making the foregoing estimate of numbers I have reduced the
enemy's force below what is regarded by the War Department and other
official circles as its real strength, and have taken the reverse course as
to our own. Our situation, then, is simply this: If the commander-in-
chief of the enemy follows the simplest dictates of the military art we
must meet him with greatly inferior forces. To render success possible,
the divisions of our army must be more ably led and commanded than
those of the enemy. The fate of the nation and the success of the
cause in which we are engaged must be mainly decided by the issue of
the next battle to be fought by the army now under my command. I
therefore feel that the interests of the nation demand that the ablest
soldiers in the service should be on duty with the Army of the Potomac, and that, contenting ourselves with remaining on the defensive
for the present at all other points, this army should be re-enforced at
once by all the disposable troops that the East and West and North
can furnish.

To insure present success the portion of this army available for
active operations should be at least equal to any force which it may be
called to encounter. To accomplish this, it is necessary that it should
be at once and very largely re-enforced. For ulterior results and to
bring this war to a speedy close, it will be necessary that our active
army shall be much superior to the enemy in numbers, so as to make

it reasonably certain that we shall win every battle which we fight, and at the same time be able to cover our communications as we advance.

I would also urgently recommend that the whole of the Regular Army, old and new, be at once ordered to report here, excepting the mounted batteries actually serving in other departments and the minimum numbers of companies of artillery actually necessary to form the nucleus of the garrisons of our most important permanent works. There should be no delay in carrying out this measure. Scattered as the regulars now are, they are nowhere strong enough to produce a marked effect. United in one body, they will insure the success of this army.

In organizing the Army of the Potomac I have selected general and staff officers with distinct reference to their fitness for the important duties that may devolve upon them. Any change or disposition of such officers without consulting the Commanding General may fatally impair the efficiency of this army and the success of its operations. I therefore earnestly request that in future every general officer appointed upon my recommendation shall be assigned to this army; that I shall have full control of the officers and troops in this department, and that no orders shall be given respecting my command without my being first consulted. It is evident that I cannot otherwise be responsible for the success of our arms. In this connection I respectfully insist that Brig. Gens. Don Carlos Buell and J. F. Reynolds, both appointed upon my recommendation and for the purpose of serving with me, be at once so assigned. In obedience to your request I have thus frankly stated in what manner you can at present aid me in the performance of the great duty committed to my charge, and I shall continue to communicate with you in the same spirit.

Very respectfully, your obedient servant.

GEO. B. McCLELLAN,
Major-General, Commanding.

HEADQUARTERS HOOKER'S BRIGADE,
Camp Union, September 8, 1861.

Colonel COWDIN,
Commanding First Regiment Massachusetts Volunteers:

The major-general commanding the Army of the Potomac is informed that two companies of rebel troops and other small portions were seen this morning in the direction of Upper Marlborough and extending down the Patuxent towards Lower Marlborough. For this and other reasons the brigadier-general commanding the brigade directs that you proceed with your regiment to Upper Marlborough by the most direct route, and from that point send out scouting parties in direction of Alexandria and Lower Marlborough. For this service two companies of cavalry will be ordered to report to you, and the whole of your command will march, provided with five days' rations and forty rounds of ammunition and with a dozen axes and spades. Your men will take their overcoats and blankets, and you may require five or six wagons. Let their loads be light, so as not to embarrass your progress. You will watch the enemy and report at once anything of importance that may occur. It is possible that the parties seen were local troops, which should be captured; also, all supplies intended for their use or that of the rebel forces. You will use your cavalry freely, and collect all the information possible about the enemy's movements, and will also hold your force in hand and not permit them to commit depredations upon the citizens.

As General Sickles will send the same amount of force to Patuxent as your own, it is desirable that your parties should connect between that and Upper Marlborough. You will exercise great care to prevent your scouts firing on those of Sickles' brigade. You will report to me regularly twice a day, and will make special reports of anything of consequence that occurs.

Very respectfully, your obedient servant,
JOS. DICKINSON,
Assistant Adjutant-General.

WHEELING, VA., *September* 9, 1861.
THOMAS A. SCOTT:

We are suffering greatly for the want of arms. There are 4,000 musket, at Bellaire, in charge of Crispin. They would answer for our Home Guards, and are useless for any other service. Can't you let us have them? I am informed by the field officer in the Second Virginia Regiment that out of 250 altered muskets in that regiment 50 of them are useless. Can they not be furnished with a good gun immediately?
F. H. PEIRPOINT,
Governor.

UPPER MARLBOROUGH, MD., *September* 10, 1861.
Brig. Gen. JOSEPH HOOKER:

SIR: In accordance with orders received from your headquarters* we proceeded from Bladensburg to this place, arriving here at 6.30 p. m., and are now encamped in the wood upon the outskirts of the village. There are also here five companies of Sickles' brigade, under command of the lieutenant-colonel. They are located in the village, in the rear of the court-house.

From my own convictions, upon investgiation, and from consultation with Lieutenant-Colonel Potter, of the other detachment, I am satisfied that no companies of rebel troops are in this vicinity or have been for some time. There is no doubt but that troops have been raised here for the rebel army, and that the sympathies of the people are with the Confederates. The commanding officer of the Sickles detachment has sent out scouting parties in the direction of Alexandria Ferry and Lower Marlborough, and has seen nothing to warrant the belief that any bodies of armed men exist in this country, if at all on this side the river.

The cavalry that was to join us has not arrived, and there are but 9 attached to the Sickles detachment. I await your further instructions by return of messenger.

I am, sir, very respectfully, your obedient servant,
ROBERT COWDIN,
Colonel, Commanding First Regiment Massachusetts Volunteers.

---

* Dickinson to Cowdin, September 8, p. 589.

UPPER MARLBOROUGH, MD., *September* 10, 1861.
Brig. Gen. JOSEPH HOOKER:

SIR: I have to inform you that the cavalry, under command of Captain Hamblin, arrived here at 1 this p. m. Lieutenant-Colonel Potter, having received definite instructions, leaves immediately for Butler and Queen Anne, and shall proceed to-morrow morning towards Lower Marlborough, covering the ground that has not already been explored by Lieutenant-Colonel Potter's command, and, if found expedient, shall go still farther down the country.

During the day I have been trying to gain such information as may aid me in future operations. I find by conversation with leading men of the town that Federal troops have been expected here for some time past, and they therefore were not disappointed in seeing us come.

ROBERT COWDIN,
Colonel, Commanding First Regiment Massachusetts Volunteers.

HEADQUARTERS CORPS OF OBSERVATION,
Poolesville, September 10, 1861.
Maj. S. WILLIAMS, *Headquarters Army of the Potomac:*

MAJOR: I have the honor to report for the information of the major-general commanding that while there seems to be no increase of force on the opposite side of the river, there was considerable activity to be noticed in improving the defensive works on the road from Edwards Ferry to Leesburg. The same works cover the approaches to Leesburg from the Chain Bridge and Alexandria turnpike. The pickets have many of them been withdrawn from opposite Conrad's Ferry and patrols are less frequent.

The work on the intrenchment above noticed is carried on so ostentatiously, that it may be a stratagem to deceive us as to their real intentions, but I am inclined to think not.

Two colored teamsters deserted from Waterford on the 7th instant and reached our lines yesterday. One of them is quite intelligent. They report that the Eighth Virginia Volunteers is at Waterford and a corps of cavalry 300 strong have headquarters at Lovettsville; that two Mississippi and one South Carolina regiment occupy the vicinity of Leesburg. They also state that the rebel forces have sufficient beef, corn meal, coffee, and sugar, but are short of salt; that until within a few days they had no coffee or sugar, but received a supply from Manassas Gap; that the people in Loudoun County are destitute of coffee, sugar, and salt, none being offered for sale in any of the village groceries.

They report that the Eighth Regiment Virginia Volunteers had plenty of ammunition, one of the teamsters stating that he drove an ammunition wagon loaded with forty boxes, while the men carried their cartridge-boxes full. One of these men brought off the diary of a cavalry officer, in which I find that the force which recently passed from Leesburg to Lovettsville, &c., consisted of two regiments infantry, 200 cavalry, and two pieces of cannon. One of these regiments has since returned to Leesburg.

The health of this command is good, and its discipline constantly improving.

Very respectfully, I am, your obedient servant,

CHAS. P. STONE,
Brigadier-General, Commanding.

HEADQUARTERS ARMY OF OCCUPATION, W. VA.,
Camp Scott, near Cross-Lanes, Va., September 11, 1861.

Brig. Gen. J. D. COX, *Gauley Bridge, Va.:*

GENERAL: Yesterday we reached the Cross-Lanes at 2 o'clock; drove in the rebel pickets; followed them closely up to their intrenched camp, which was situated in a dense forest. Reconnoitered so closely that our reconnaissance was about to change into an assault, when, night coming on, we drew our weary and exhausted troops out of the woods and bivouacked on our arms about three-quarters of a mile from the intrenched camp. At 5 o'clock in the morning our pickets found their camp was evacuated, and was taken possession of by one of our companies. It was found to contain a large quantity of plunder, commissary stores, quartermaster's stores, &c. A few prisoners were taken, and about 30 of Lytle's men sick in hospital on the other side of Gauley, and their ferry-boats destroyed.

We heard your cannonading yesterday, and presume you proved another tough nut to crack. We have not been able to follow them into the defile of Meadow River for want of a ferry or means of making one, and our provision train being behindhand. We are encamped advantageously, and will hurry our preparations to unite the two forces as soon as possible. You will probably have discovered our movements and have sent up a strong force on the New River road to watch and follow Wise's retreating column. If you have not, do so at once on the receipt of this, starting your men with three days' cooked rations in their haversacks, their blankets, and forty rounds in cartridge-boxes, and let the provision train follow your column. Your adversary Wise begins to respect you.

Very respectfully, your obedient servant,

W. S. ROSECRANS.

HEADQUARTERS CORPS OF OBSERVATION,
Poolesville, September 12, 1861.

Col. R. B. MARCY, *Chief of Staff, Army of the Potomac:*

COLONEL: I would respectfully call the attention of the major-general commanding to the condition of this command as it is to be when existing orders shall be executed.

It now consists of five regiments of volunteer infantry, one troop Fifth Cavalry, one company regular field artillery, one company (half full) volunteer artillery.

By Special Orders, No. 43, the cavalry company is now detached from the command and two companies of volunteer cavalry ordered to replace it.

From our position, guarding 22 miles of river and canal, embracing three fords, well-instructed cavalry vedettes are peculiarly necessary to prevent surprise on the one hand and needless alarms on the other.

My labors will be vastly increased by having uninstructed cavalry, and the proper training of this arm of volunteers more than any other requires the contact of regular troops of the same arm. I hope that it may be found consistent with the interests of the service to have one regular cavalry company here.

Colonel Gorman, commanding First Regiment Minnesota Volunteers, has been appointed by the President brigadier-general and ordered to report in person at Washington. If practicable, I deem it important that he should be near this regiment, which requires his experience and military knowledge.

I understood from the major-general commanding that eight regiments were to be ordered here as soon as that number of troops could be spared, and in such case General Gorman might perhaps have command of a brigade within this command. This I throw out merely as a suggestion, should there be no more important pressing duty for him. I shall be somewhat uneasy about the condition of the First Minnesota Regiment should General Gorman be immediately detached.

Very respectfully, I am, colonel, your most obedient servant,

CHAS. P. STONE,
Brigadier-General, Commanding.

HEADQUARTERS GENERAL BANKS' DIVISION,
Near Darnestown, Md., September 12, 1861.

Colonel GEARY,
Twenty-eighth Regiment Pa. Vols., Point of Rocks, Md.:

SIR: I have the honor to acknowledge the receipt of your letter of this date.* I have submitted it to Major-General Banks, who instructs me to say that he has requested General Stone to send you two pieces of cannon, if they can be spared.

I send you 10,000 caps for Major Gould. The general instructs me to say that you will at once send to these headquarters the reasons why you have kept Major Gould's command this long without reporting the deficiency.

The general instructs me to say that, having selected you to fill a very difficult and exceedingly important position, on account of qualities he believed you possessed, he is surprised at the feeling you evince at the first approach of an enemy in any force. He directs me to say that, in case you are attacked by a greatly superior force, you will defend the crossings over which you have command as long as it is possible for you to do so without endangering the safety of your whole command. In case you are forced to retreat, you will, if possible, fall back upon General Stone, at Poolesville, and for this purpose will keep yourself in daily communication with him. Should you be unable to unite with General Stone by the intervention of an enemy in sufficient numbers to oppose your progress, you will retire upon Monocacy Junction, breaking up the railroads and cutting the telegraph wires as you retire.

The general instructs me to say that he expects you to make good your position along the line of your pickets against any force not exceeding 3,000 men. Your wagons will be sent you as soon as arrangements can be made for them to leave. He instructs me to say that you will communicate with these headquarters daily the state of your command along the river, and for this reason are authorized to employ two reliable messengers.

Very respectfully, your obedient servant,

ROBT. WILLIAMS,
Assistant Adjutant-General.

POINT OF ROCKS, MD., *September* 12, 1861.

Capt. ROBERT WILLIAMS, *Assistant Adjutant-General:*

SIR: I have to report that the enemy still continues to threaten my lines at Harper's Ferry and above and below that place for 2 or 3 miles

---

* Not found.

each way. I have just received a report from Major Gould, in which he says:

> The attack on us is not made, but there is a jubilant force near. There was a skirmish yesterday at Shepherdstown between the rebels and our troops. A canal-boat was passing at the time and 1 boatman was mortally wounded. The Confederates seem to know our weakness in numbers, and are becoming saucy.
>
> I am credibly informed that there are now about 6,000 troops in Jefferson County ready to push, and intend to do so, on our lines.
>
> I received your note, and thank you for your activity in my behalf. I hope General Banks will look favorably on my petition for a field piece, for, in obedience to your orders, I do not wish to be driven from this place.

Since I wrote last night, I furnished caps to him, which I have received from Washington City, and will also furnish him those you sent me to-day.

I am making preparations to resist any attack at all hazards and have given orders at every point of the line to that effect.

Since I commenced writing I received your communication of to-day and have carefully noted its contents. I sincerely thank General Banks for his promptness in ordering up a couple of pieces of artillery, and the caps you sent are already on the way to the major.

In obedience to General Banks' orders, I will state that when Colonel Leonard passed this place *en route* to join your command on or about the 3d instant, upon my inquiry whether he had mustered and inspected his regiment on the 31st of August, he informed me he had done so. I asked him if his regiment was sufficiently supplied with ammunition. He informed me it was.

Upon assuming the command of the detachment under Major Gould, I directed him to keep me promptly advised of all his wants, either as to provisions or ammunition. The letter which I forwarded you this morning from him was the first intimation that he wanted caps. If I have been derelict in this matter, it certainly has been most unintentionally so, and I trust that by future attention and watchfulness to continue to merit the general's confidence, which it has been my greatest pleasure to enjoy. As to any feeling I may have expressed in my letter of last night, I was not aware that I had expressed any, for the note was a hurried one, written when just aroused from sleep, and I trust the general will overlook the whole matter.

My command is in good order and is ready and anxious to meet the enemy, and I most confidently assure you it will give a good account of itself if an opportunity is afforded. All the orders of the Major-General will be carried out to the letter. Your last order to communicate daily will be strictly obeyed.

I am pushing the general's instructions with regard to Wilson as rapidly as I can.

With assurances of high regard, I am, your obedient servant,

JNO. W. GEARY,
Colonel Twenty-eighth Regiment Pa. Vols., Comdg. Post.

HEADQUARTERS GENERAL BANKS' DIVISION,
Near Darnestown, Md., September 12, 1861.

Brig. Gen. R. B. MARCY,
Chief of Staff to General McClellan, Washington, D. C.:

SIR: Major-General Banks directs me to ask if there is any possibility of his obtaining any more artillery and cavalry for his division. He instructs me to say that he has now but eight effective pieces of artillery.

Captain Best has six pieces, but two of them are non-effective, for want of men. His pieces are smooth bore, and, therefore, not so good for preventing a passage over a river of such width as the Potomac. Besides, the guns of the enemy are rifled, and by their long range our smooth-bore guns could be easily driven from the banks of the river or their vicinity. After to-day we shall have but two companies of cavalry, and they irregular. It is not possible for this command, called upon to prevent an enemy from crossing the Potomac for a distance of over 50 miles, to do so in its present condition. The enemy can easily cross, and even have time to erect breastworks and batteries to cover his passage in any force he may wish, before we could even fire a gun against him from the main body of the division. The nearest point of the Potomac from this position is about 4 miles. It would take us at least an hour and a half to reach that point in force sufficient to oppose a passage with any hopes of success. Should we immediately send our artillery and cavalry, from the nature of the country, wooded and hilly, it would only be to lose them. The fords and ferries in our vicinity are from 8 to 15 miles distant, and the same reasons would hold with much more force.

Very respectfully, your obedient servant,

ROBT. WILLIAMS,
Assistant Adjutant-General.

LOWER MARLBOROUGH, MD., *September* 12, 1861.

General HOOKER, *Commanding, &c.:*

GENERAL: Yesterday we proceeded down the river towards Lower Marlborough. After proceeding 5 or 6 miles and finding everything quiet I had determined to return to Upper Marlborough. I was met by a lieutenant belonging to Colonel Dwight's regiment, of Sickles' brigade. He showed me his instructions, which were from Colonel Dwight, directing the lieutenant to find the regiment belonging to Hooker's brigade, and to inform the colonel commanding that regiment that he, with his command, was expected to form a junction with Colonel Dwight at Lower Marlborough. I accordingly proceeded to a spot near Lower Marlborough and encamped for the night. This morning, subsequent to sending my courier to you, I received from Colonel Dwight a dispatch, of which the following is a copy:

SEPTEMBER 12—4 p. m.

Colonel COWDIN:

COLONEL: I shall proceed towards Benedict by an easy march. I shall reach there to-morrow. At Prince Fredericktown there is a company of cavalry, and each house known to contain a member will have to be searched. I hope to see you in my vicinity, near Port Tobacco, by Saturday noon.

Very respectfully,

WM. DWIGHT,
Commanding.

I addressed him a communication, of which the following is a copy, directing it to Col. William Dwight, jr., commanding on west side of Patuxent River:

HEADQUARTERS FIRST REGIMENT MASSACHUSETTS VOLUNTEERS,
Lower Marlborough, Md., September 12, 1861.

Col. WILLIAM DWIGHT:

COLONEL: I propose to proceed back from this place to a point which will enable me to march either north or south, where I shall await instructions from General

Hooker. My present instructions will allow me to advance no farther than Lower Marlborough.

I have the honor to be, yours, respectfully,

ROBERT COWDIN,
Colonel.

I intrusted this communication to Lieutenant Candler, of Company A. Lieutenant Candler reported to me that he saw Colonel Dwight and had a long interview with him, in the course of which Colonel Dwight showed him all his instructions from General Sickles. Extracts from these instructions I herewith submit.

First order, early Monday morning, between 2 and 3; received between 4 and 5 a. m. :

> After effecting a junction with the detachment from Hooker's brigade, you will proceed along the Patuxent and make a thorough reconnaissance of the country, moving with circumspection and with the utmost vigilance to detect the presence, in whatever force he may be, and destroying, dispersing, and capturing such of the enemy as you may be able to encounter successfully. You will lose no precaution to keep open a line of communication with the base of operations and with the detachment from Hooker's brigade.

Subsequent order, written September 11, at 8 p. m.; received September 12 (this morning):

> I have received express instructions from headquarters to extend this expedition to Port Tobacco, with a view to its capture and occupation. The whole force afloat might co-operate with you. I would then take 1,500 picked troops with you. Be sure and visit Frederick. I was informed of the operation of the force sent from General Hooker's brigade. It was to move down the Patuxent in conjunction with your force, which will move in the same direction.

Lieutenant Candler also reports that Colonel Dwight intends to move to Port Tobacco, remaining upon the west side of the river, and that he had marked out for us to take the following route: From Lower Marlborough to Huntingtown, from Huntingtown to Fredericktown, from Fredericktown to Mackall's Ferry; thence to cross the river, and form a junction at Benedict with Colonel Dwight's force, which will proceed to that point direct; thence, by different routes, to Port Tobacco. Lieutenant Candler further said that Colonel Dwight would call on me at 2 p. m. and talk the matter over.

At 2 o'clock a messenger from Colonel Dwight handed me the following communication, together with the message that Colonel Dwight was waiting on the other side of the river, and would receive me or any other person I might wish to send:

SEPTEMBER 11, 1861.

COLONEL COMMANDING FORCES FROM GENERAL HOOKER'S BRIGADE:

> COLONEL: Your courier arrived here last night, as did the lieutenant I had sent out to communicate with you. As their statements did not entirely agree with each other, or with my instructions from headquarters, I detained your courier until I should have heard once more from headquarters. In order to cross your force to this side it will be necessary to use some of the larger river crafts. It seems that that means can be used as well below here as at this point; therefore I think my instructions will be best carried out by your moving down the river to Prince Fredericktown, on your side of the river, while I move to Benedict, on my side. There is a schooner here, which I shall have dropped down the river as we march. I shall send couriers to her four times a day with any intelligence I may have for you, and you will please to keep me notified by couriers sent often to her. If you meet any considerable force of the enemy I can easily throw you re-enforcements, and you can cross to me at any moment I deem it necessary, if it should be necessary before you reach Prince Fredericktown. I move very slowly and carefully, and, as I hear there are cavalry of the enemy on your side, it will be necessary that you should do the same. I am not able to say certainly whom I am addressing, as your courier does not know the name of the colonel. I take it to be Colonel Cowdin, of the First Massachusetts, and I shall be happy to meet him.

I have the honor to be, colonel, your obedient servant,

WM. DWIGHT,
Colonel, Commanding Expedition.

I returned to Colonel Dwight a communication, of which the following is a copy:

HEADQUARTERS FIRST REGIMENT MASSACHUSETTS VOLUNTEERS,
Smithville, Md., September 12, 1861.

Colonel DWIGHT:

SIR: My instructions from headquarters do not contemplate any movement below Lower Marlborough. If you have received any orders applicable to this command, please forward to me copies thereof, in order that my movements may be governed thereby. My present intention is to move down to Lower Marlborough, and, unless I receive through you or otherwise some different instructions, then, in compliance with my original orders from General McClellan, I shall return towards Upper Marlborough to-day, and shall reach that place some time to-morrow. It will give me great pleasure to meet you, if possible, and exchange compliments, and consult upon the state of affairs in this section of the country.

I am, sir, yours, very respectfully,

ROBERT COWDIN,
Colonel First Massachusetts Volunteers.

As I cannot gather from my instructions that the regiment is to be detached from your brigade to occupy Port Tobacco, under the command of Colonel Dwight, I shall proceed to a point from which I can move easily in either direction, and await further orders from you. If I move at all, it will be towards Upper Marlborough. I can find no indications of any enemy in this neighborhood, except that negroes report that some thirty or forty of the residents here meet occasionally for cavalry drill, and that they seem to keep up partially their old militia organization.

While preparing this dispatch Captain Wild has come in from a scouting party and I inclose his report.*

As our stores have run low, I shall be obliged to make requisitions upon the country for supplies. In relation to the lamented death of Lieutenant Hogg, I learn that the accident was caused by the unseaworthy condition of the boat, which gave way under the weight of the men and horses on board. I should be glad to be instructed by you whether I shall cause the houses to be searched in which I am informed there are single cavalry sabers and uniforms.

ROBERT COWDIN,
Colonel.

P. S.—Later—4 p. m. I am now on my way towards Upper Marlborough.

HEADQUARTERS HOOKER'S BRIGADE,
Camp Union, September 13, 1861.

Col. ROBERT COWDIN, *Commanding Detachment, &c.:*

SIR: The report of your operations, dated 2 p. m. on the 12th instant, reached here this morning. Prior to its receipt I had advised you of the views of the brigadier-general commanding in regard to your future movements, and also informed you that additional rations for your command would be forwarded to you this morning. They have left, and will reach you to-day, even if you should still be at Lower Marlborough.

From the spirit of the general's instructions from headquarters of the Army of the Potomac, he is of the opinion that it was not contemplated that you should extend your reconnaissance farther to the south than

_____
* Not found.

Lower Marlborough; nor can it be at this time, unless you should be in possession of information which you have failed to communicate, which I presume is not the case.

It is impossible to make your instructions any other than general, where the extent and character of your operations must depend mainly on information which it is your object to acquire from observation and intercourse with the people around you. If I may form an opinion from the extracts you have furnished me from Colonel Dwight's instructions, I conclude that his instructions warrant him in covering a much larger field of operations than was intended for your command, and unless you have reliable information that the rebels are in force at Port Tobacco, or that an extensive trade in contraband goods was going on from that point, which it will require your assistance to destroy, I would not advise you to take part in the operations of Colonel Dwight in that direction. If this movement was suggested at headquarters, and it was designed that you should participate in it, it is quite probable that I would have been so advised. Be that as it may, I desire that you will keep open your communication with Colonel Dwight, and hold yourself in readiness to support him in all times of need.

The general requests that you will keep a good lookout in the direction of the Potomac while Colonel Dwight is operating in the direction of Port Tobacco; but at all times observe and be governed by your own instructions, rather than the alleged ones of others. The general is gratified with your adherence to them, so far as he is informed. It is not advisable to direct houses to be searched for individual arms, and in no case unless you have good reasons to suppose that they are used by the rebels as places of deposit for arms and contraband stores.

Be pleased to have the wagons and escort sent you to-day returned without delay.

Very respectfully, your obedient servant,

JOS. DICKINSON,
Assistant Adjutant-General.

HEADQUARTERS ARMY OF THE POTOMAC,
Washington, September 13, 1861.

Hon. SIMON CAMERON, *Secretary of War:*

SIR: I have the honor to inclose herewith the report of the Sanitary Commission.*

Proper arrangement in field and hospital for the sick and wounded of an army is one of the most imperative, and has always been found one of the most difficult, duties of a government. From its very nature it should be under the immediate direction of the commanding general, and the whole organization intrusted to him, free from the tedious delays, inconvenient formalities, and inefficient action incident to every bureau system, however ably administered.

The Medical Bureau of the United States, like every other branch of the military service, was organized in reference to a very small army, operating generally in small divisions, and in time of peace, and hence it could not fail to be inadequate to the sudden and enormous exigencies of the present war, while its failure affords no ground of imputation or reproach against the distinguished medical officers intrusted with its administration. By no administrative talent can a system

----
* Not found.

devised for the purposes of small divisions of an army (not exceeding in the whole 12,000 men) be adapted to the necessities of an army of 100,000, actively operating upon a great theater of war. To meet their wants, there must be a medical system commensurate with the army, and the nature of its operations so organized as to be in harmonious action with every other branch of service and under the same military command. The humane and disinterested services of the Sanitary Commission have enabled them to make several judicious suggestions, and their labors entitle them to the gratitude of the Army and of the country.

The following suggestions by them are worthy of approval and immediate adoption:

1st. The appointment of a medical director of the Army of the Potomac by its commanding general, with such powers as he may deem proper from time to time to commit to such director.

2d. The immediate organization of an ambulance corps, to act under the medical director's command.

3d. The employment of an adequate corps of male and female nurses by the medical director, to act under his supervision.

4th. That "the relations of the Sanitary Commission and the Medical Bureau be placed on a basis of entire confidence and co-operation; that their disinterested counsel be received without jealousy."

These suggestions of the Commission merit and receive the cordial sanction of the Commanding General. He concurs with them in their judgment "that they have earned the right to the confidence of the Department which originally, with generous reliance, called them into being, and does not doubt that they still enjoy this confidence"; and he agrees with them in the wish "to see it extended fully from the Medical Bureau."

Very respectfully, your obedient servant,

GEO. B. McCLELLAN,
Major-General.

HDQRS. ARMY OF OCCUPATION OF WESTERN VIRGINIA,
Camp Scott, near Cross-Lanes, Va., September 14, 1861.

Brigadier-General Cox:

SIR: Colonel McCook, commanding a provisional brigade to cross the Gauley this morning and open communications with your forces, reported to be on the Lewisburg road, and at the same time to reconnoiter Wise's position, reported at Dogwood Gap. Should he be found there we shall prepare to attack him as soon as we have thoroughly reconnoitered; sooner, if there be signs of retreat. Dispose your command to follow up the movement if we deem it advisable. To this end have your provision and ammunition trains inspected and numbered, arranging for the ammunition to give, with what they have in cartridge-boxes, 100 rounds to each man.

Leave a regiment to hold the mouth of the Gauley and protect the provision and ammunition trains below. Report your opinion and the facts on which it is based with respect to the present rebel force west of the Kanawha. We shall start our provision trains to draw supplies from your lines of transportation. Send Wagner forward to reconnoiter and report on the topographical and military features of the road to Lewisburg, the report to be sent through to me if possible.

I am, sir, very respectfully, your obedient servant,

W. S. ROSECRANS.

SANDY HOOK, *September* 14, 1861—4 p. m.

Capt. ROBERT WILLIAMS, *Assistant Adjutant-General:*

SIR: The threatening attitude of the rebels upon this portion of my line has induced me to remain here to-day.

The report now is that 3,000 infantry and Captain Ashby's command of cavalry will visit Harper's Ferry this evening. I do not place much confidence in the story; it comes from the town itself.

A messenger from Capt. John W. Wilson, commanding near Sharpsburg, stating that his camp is being attacked by a large force, consisting of infantry, cavalry, and artillery, supposed to be about 600, asking aid from me. The cannonading is still going on from the rebel side, but thus far has produced no casualties on our side. As soon as scouts now out return I will decide upon the matter of his request.

For sake of prompt communication along my extended front, I have agreed to permit Mr. Smith, master of transportation on the Baltimore and Ohio Railroad, to reconstruct that portion of the telegraph line which was destroyed by Colonel Donnelly's order at Berlin, and to place an office here, under the supervision of Major Gould, with the understanding that if we are at any time attacked by an overwhelming force the line and office should be destroyed. As a consideration for this permission, Mr. Smith proposes to keep a train of cars and an engine to transport my troops without delay to any point to defend against sudden attack. This seems to me to be [an] admirable arrangement, and I trust it will meet the approbation of General Banks.

Lieutenant-Colonel De Korponay is in command of my camp at Point of Rocks, and he informs me that everything is quiet upon all parts of my command below.

Major Burbank, of the Twelfth Massachusetts Regiment, was here to-day. He informed me that he was ordered to Monocacy Aqueduct with two companies, and wanted to know where he should be provisioned from. I told him if he had orders to report to me I would furnish him from Point of Rocks, but if he was to be under General Stone's command, he would be furnished from that quarter. He requested me to communicate my general instructions to him, which I did, and stated to him if he was ordered to report to me I would give them to him in writing.

Another excellent 6-pounder (iron cannon) has been brought over from Virginia to-day, and will be mounted here for the defense of this point.

The Massachusetts men captured three mules from the secessionists to-day.

Considerable skirmishing is occasionally going on across the river between our pickets, 1 or 2 miles above, and several of the enemy have been killed and wounded; some horses also killed.

Rest assured a perfect defense of the line will be made.

With high regard,

JNO. W. GEARY,
Colonel Twenty-eighth Regiment Pa. Vols., Comdg. Post.

HEADQUARTERS HOOKER'S BRIGADE,
Camp Union, Md., September 14, 1861—7 a. m.

Col. ROBERT COWDIN, *Commanding, &c., near Patuxent:*

COLONEL: I am directed by the brigadier-general commanding to inform you that he received late last evening from the headquarters of the Army of the Potomac instructions for you to proceed to Frederick-town and Saint Leonard's, and gain all the information possible regarding the designs and movements of the enemy, capturing such organized parties as you may meet with, and taking all the arms and munitions of war you may fall in with; but you will not allow your men to depredate upon citizens who attend to their own legitimate business and do not afford aid to the enemy, even if they are secessionists. When this is executed, you will return to Lower Marlborough and await further orders.

The general is also informed that Colonel Dwight is ordered to Port Tobacco. The necessary supplies will be forwarded to you; but in order to do this it is necessary for you to report the strength of your command and the most direct route over which they should be forwarded to Lower Marlborough. This you can determine from your own observation. Stores forwarded to you yesterday were dispatched in season to reach you at Lower Marlborough that day, and it was expected that on the receipt of this information you would have halted your command if on the march, if you did not return to that point. If, on inquiry, you should find that you have not on hand rations for your whole command for the time necessary for you to execute the foregoing instructions, you will divide it, and send forward as large a party as you are able to find. If the teamsters return in season, additional supplies will be sent from here to-morrow, and should be able to reach Lower Marlborough the same night.

It is presumed that you are senior officer to Colonel Dwight.

Very respectfully, your obedient servant,

JOS. DICKINSON,
Assistant Adjutant-General.

HEADQUARTERS ARMY OF THE POTOMAC,
September 15, 1861.

General W. B. FRANKLIN, *Fort Williams:*

For important reasons, I desire you to push forward to completion the defensive works around your position as rapidly as possible (especially that work on the south side of Hunting Creek), with all your available force.

GEO. B. McCLELLAN,
Major-General, Commanding.

LOWER MARLBOROUGH, MD., *September* 16, 1861.

Brigadier-General HOOKER, *Commanding Hooker's Brigade:*

GENERAL: We are now quartered near Lower Marlborough, on the road to Prince Fredericktown. In regard to the number of the cavalrymen, we were informed by the commanders that there were 130 men, but since find that they have only 90, and have not been reenforced. Some of their men who have been sent as messengers have not reported themselves back, and the conduct of the whole force during their connection with me has been anything but satisfactory. I shall march with my whole force to Fredericktown to-day.

In answer to the inquiry as to how long it will take to perform the expedition, I would say that we can probably return to Lower Marlborough by Friday night. You will please forward rations for five days, complete, to Lower Marlborough, and three boxes of ammunition, as some of ours got wet.

ROBERT COWDIN,
Colonel, Commanding First Regiment.

PRINCE FREDERICKTOWN, MD., *September* 16, 1861.

Brig. Gen. JOSEPH HOOKER:

GENERAL: I arrived at this place this evening. I find that there have been organized in this town two companies—one of cavalry and one of infantry. I have sent out scouting parties to-day and shall send more to-night. I shall remain here to-morrow, and shall send forward a detachment of cavalry to Saint Leonard's, if nothing occurs to change my plans.

The majority of the citizens are opposed to the Government, and many fled the town at my approach, as has been the case in many other secession places. The professed object of the two companies organized is home protection, in case of negro insurrection. I shall thoroughly investigate the matter, with the view of ascertaining the true state of affairs.

I received a dispatch from Colonel Dwight to-day and replied. He was at a short distance from Benedict, moving on towards Port Tobacco.

ROBERT COWDIN,
Commanding First Massachusetts Volunteers.

LOWER MARLBOROUGH, MD., *September* 16, 1861.

Col. WILLIAM DWIGHT:

COLONEL: Your message is just received. My instructions contemplate a visit to Prince Fredericktown and Saint Leonard's and a return to this place. I am also instructed to keep open a communication with yourself. I cannot, upon my own responsibility, exceed these instructions, unless you should be attacked or are in danger of being cut off, neither of which contingencies seem to me probable. In case either should occur, however, I will take every means in my power to render you immediate assistance. I feel very much indebted to you for the use of the steamer yesterday, which saved my men a very fatiguing march.

I am, sir,

ROBERT COWDIN,
Colonel First Regiment Massachusetts Volunteers.

HDQRS. ARMY OF OCCUPATION, WESTERN VIRGINIA,
Camp Cross-Lanes, Va., September 16, 1861.

Brig. Gen. J. D. COX, *Camp at Spy Rock, Va.:*

GENERAL: The Commanding General directs that you advance with the main body of your column only far enough to occupy a good camping ground in a strongly defensible position, and wait for your tent and baggage trains to come up. Send forward a strong advance guard, if practicable, to the top of Big Sewell. If that cannot be done, send one as far forward as practicable without endangering its safety, and push your outposts well to the front, ordering the most advanced ones to ambush and capture all scouts from the rebels. Bring everything into the most perfect order, and have daily drills until we can get our ammunition and provision trains up, when we will cross over also. Keep up daily line of couriers to end of telegraph and to Gauley. As soon as Tyler gets down call up all your available force, and order Tyler to prepare for the construction of Gauley Bridge for the crossing of our trains.

W. S. ROSECRANS,
Brigadier-General, U. S. Army.

HDQRS. ARMY OF OCCUPATION, WESTERN VIRGINIA,
Camp Cross-Lanes, Va., September 17, 1861.

Brig. Gen. J. J. REYNOLDS, Elk Water:

A pressure of occupations prevented me from announcing to you, as I should have done, that after a march of 18 miles on the 10th we attacked Floyd's intrenched camp at 3 o'clock p. m., but were prevented from carrying the intrenchments by coming on of night and the exhaustion of our troops. We withdrew from the woods which covered his front into the fields, three-fourths of a mile distant, where we lay overnight in order of battle. The next morning we took possession of his camp, which he had evacuated during the night. Having destroyed the ferry and all means of passing, we were unable to pursue. The rebels had five or six regiments, at least eight pieces of artillery, and three companies of cavalry. Wise's force consisted of three or four regiments, and they were met by one from Carolina and one from Georgia, 15 miles from here, on the Lewisburg pike, making from ten to twelve regiments. As soon as we could send word General Cox advanced. We have added a brigade to him. Both forces are now on the Lewisburg road. We are preparing to join them. The rebels have retreated over Big Sewell, if not to Meadow Mountain. They may join forces and try to crush us with their augmented strength. They cannot crush you. I will dispatch you again this evening.

W. S. ROSECRANS,
Brigadier-General, U. S. Army.

HDQRS. ARMY OF OCCUPATION, WESTERN VIRGINIA,
Camp Cross-Lanes, Va., September 17, 1861.

Brig. Gen. J. J. REYNOLDS, Elk Water, Va.:

In my dispatch of this evening you have the result of our first battle at Carnifix Ferry. The information of following up the movement; the importance of the Kanawha Valley to the rebels; the immense length and dangerous direction of our line of communication with the depots; taking immense trains over bad roads, and requiring guards at so many points; the necessity of adding a portion of the moving column to Cox's brigade, and the fact that it takes six days to reach you, and other considerations, have induced me to throw this column on the Lewisburg and Kanawha pike, adding to it the Kanawha Brigade, confiding in your ability to hold the forces in your front. Watch them, therefore, with all care; open well the road to your front;

keep it clear; hold your position securely, and the moment you see any signs of an opportunity, fall on them, and worry and harass them, if you can do no more. If your troops move lightly, carrying the necessary provisions to go and return, you can so harass them that you may prevent their leaving their position and stop any force they can bring against you. Hasten up your troops, and when your column is re-enforced we may have the opportunity to strike a decisive blow. Keep well advised.

Yours,

W. S. ROSECRANS,
Brigadier-General, U. S. Army.

HEADQUARTERS DEPARTMENT OF PENNSYLVANIA,
Baltimore, Md., September 19, 1861.

Maj. Gen. G. B. McCLELLAN,
Commanding Army of the Potomac:

GENERAL: There are several companies in Caroline, Queen Anne, and Carroll Counties under arms once or twice a week drilling. They are composed exclusively of secessionists, and are armed with rifled muskets. I have not been able to ascertain whether they are organized in every instance under the laws of this State, but it makes no difference. If they are, they are acting in violation of the order of the governor, who called on them some months ago to give up their arms. If they are unauthorized organizations, they ought to be broken up. If you approve of the suggestion, I will send a few policemen, with a competent military force, from 50 to 100 men in each case, and take their arms from them. I know the governor approves the measure, and I propose to consult him in each case before I act. We can get a few hundred arms of the best quality, and take them out of the hands of men of the worst character.

I am, very respectfully, your obedient servant,

JOHN A. DIX,
Major-General, Commanding.

GENERAL ORDERS, ⎰   WAR DEPT., ADJ'T GEN.'S OFFICE,
    No. 80.   ⎱   *Washington, September 19, 1861.*

I. The Military Department of Ohio will in future consist of the State of that name, Indiana, and so much of Kentucky as lies within 15 miles of Cincinnati, under the command of Brigadier-General Mitchel, of the U. S. Volunteers; headquarters, Cincinnati.

So much of Virginia as lies west of the Blue Ridge Mountains will constitute in future a separate command, to be called the Department of Western Virginia, under Brigadier-General Rosecrans. Headquarters in the field. The latter will continue to draw re-enforcements by requisitions upon the governor of Ohio as heretofore, or by order addressed direct to the U. S. commander in that State, as often as may be necessary.

*   *   *   *   *   *   *

By order:

L. THOMAS,
Adjutant-General.

LOWER MARLBOROUGH, MD.,
September 20, 1861.

Brig. Gen. JOSEPH HOOKER, *Commanding Hooker's Brigade:*

GENERAL: Your communications of the 18th and 19th are received.* I took up my line of march at 6 o'clock last evening and arrived here this morning at 1 o'clock, after having visited, by detachments, among others, the following places: Plum Point, Huntingtown, Parker's Creek, Mackall's Ferry, Buzzard's Creek, Battle Creek, Saint Leonard's, Drum Point, Cove Point, Fishing Creek, Port Republic, Buena Vista, and Point Patience, which is at the extreme end of the Peninsula. There is no doubt that the march of the regiment through this part of the country has had a good effect, and has broken up or paralyzed all military organizations in this vicinity, and I am of the opinion that there will be no new organizations created, the leaders having fled and a large majority of the members having expressed their determination not to oppose the Government.

In your communication of the 18th instant you say rumors have reached you of irregularities committed by my command. I am aware that such complaints have been made, but have no doubt that the accounts of them have been much exaggerated. All cases brought to my notice have been investigated and the parties punished. I believe that some of the cavalry, while on detached duty, have been chiefly the cause of these complaints, it being almost impossible to control them. Numbers of them have been intoxicated and unfit to perform their duty. I have hesitated to make this report, it having been my endeavor, since their connection with my command, to make them conduct themselves as soldiers.

I have been unable to find any trace of contraband trade, and think that if it exists on this side of the Patuxent it must be on a very small scale. I am also of the opinion that the object of the expedition has been accomplished as far as lies in my power, and that there is no further necessity of a large body of troops remaining in this vicinity.

I have the honor to be, your obedient servant,

ROBERT COWDIN,
Colonel First Regiment Massachusetts Volunteers.

HEADQUARTERS OF THE ARMY,
Washington, September 25, 1861.

General ROSECRANS, U. S. A., *Cross-Lanes, Va.:*

No blow has been struck at you. That phrase objectionable.† Draw re-enforcements and supplies as before. According to your means, clear as much of Western Virginia of the enemy as practicable. No precise instruction can be safely given from this distance, either for attack, pursuit, or falling back. You are a soldier, a scientific general, and confidence is reposed in your judgment and discretion, as well as in your zeal and valor; consequently good results are expected from you. There are two Illinois regiments at Camp Dennison subject to your call, through the governor, or, preferably, Brigadier-General Mitchel. Captain Gilbert's company is serving in the Western Department, and cannot be withdrawn. The captain was ordered to report to you for

---

* Not found.
† The dispatch thus answered not found.

such light duty as he could do, as judge-advocate, and while suffering from his wound. Your staff—McLean, Burns, Dickerson, and Dr. Wright—are not to be taken from your orders.

WINFIELD SCOTT.

CAMP TYNDALE, POINT OF ROCKS,
September 28, 1861.

General CHARLES P. STONE, *Commanding Corps of Observation:*

DEAR GENERAL: I have reliable information, and such as should be believed, that there are about 27,000 men in the neighborhood of Leesburg, General Johnston commanding in person. Their intention is to attack my lines in several places and to make a crossing in the neighborhood of Noland's Ferry, or at Mason's Island, about one mile and a half above that point. My informant is Mr. Buxton, who is now here, and left Leesburg this morning.

Now, if all this be true, it behooves us to be up and doing. With some more troops and a couple more pieces of artillery I feel very confident I can make a successful resistance. I hope therefore, that you will lend me your aid when the trying hour comes, for, without counting numbers, I will stoutly resist.

Yours, truly,

JNO. W. GEARY,
Colonel.

DARNESTOWN, MD., *September 28,* 1861.

General STONE:

SIR: I received your letter of this morning at 7 o'clock. We have sent the Twelfth Indiana, a good regiment, with a section of Captain Best's artillery, to the relief of Colonel Geary. They start at once, and will reach Noland's Ferry by nightfall.

Very truly, yours,

N. P. BANKS.

WASHINGTON, *September 28,* 1861.

Maj-Gen. GEORGE B. MCCLELLAN:

GENERAL: I have the honor to report that in compliance with your instructions I went down the Potomac yesterday as far as Mathias Point. In company with me were Lieutenant Wyman, U. S. Navy, of the Potomac flotilla, and ——— Sherburne, late of the rebel army. Lieutenant Wyman's knowledge of the river was of great service in pointing out the different localities. The first point available to the enemy for the erection of batteries to obstruct navigation is Whitestone. The lower part of this point is a bluff about 100 feet high, the face of which may have an extent of five or six hundred yards. From this bluff batteries would rake the channel below as far as shot or shell would reach. It is thickly wooded up to its very edge, and through a portion of the extent the woods extend down the face of the bluff to the water's edge. The river opposite Whitestone Point is but slightly over a mile wide. The next location requiring notice is Hallowing Point. This point is mostly level and cleared; elevation only from 20 to 30 feet. Batteries on this point would be very effective, but it is so low and open to observation that we can prevent their construction or make it very difficult to hold them if constructed. High Point comes next. The river is full 2 miles wide here. In the military sense of the term the channel could not be "obstructed" by a battery so distant. Commercial vessels would, however, be reluctant to pass under its fire. The point I should not judge to be more than 30 or 40 feet high. It is wooded, too, within a few yards of the crest of the bluff. The water is so shoal for a mile or more in front of it that our own vessels of war cannot efficiently shell it. I think we may soon look for a battery here. Freestone Point comes next, and a battery exists there, supposed to have five guns, one of which (perhaps two) is said to be a rifled 30-pounder. In passing down the ship channel I found it impossible to distinguish this battery—the weather was not clear—but I can readily judge of its position. Its elevation is probably 50 or 60 feet, the gun rising still higher behind it, and, though its front was concealed by a skirt of wood, a corn field extends behind it one or two hundred yards, and then woods again clothing the elevation behind. To the left and southward are open slopes extending down to the water. Probably, therefore, the rear of the battery would be quite accessible, so far as physical obstacles are concerned, to an attack. Why has a battery been placed here so far from the ship channel of the Potomac? Not unlikely it is for defensive purposes, as I presumed those at Aquia Creek five weeks ago to be.

Cockpit Point is 40 or 50 feet high, with a very low spit projecting a few hundred feet into the river. The height is wooded, if I recollect rightly. From this point to the Quantico the river bank rises in irregular hills, partly wooded, partly open, offering numerous points where batteries could be established to bear by cross-fire on the channel. Even here, however, the narrowest part of the river after passing Hallowing Point until Mathias Point is reached, vessels can keep themselves from one and a half to two miles from the batteries. Shipping Point (Evansport) lies between the Quantico and Chopawamsic. A plateau, generally cleared, forms the termination of this peninsula, very near behind which the hills rise, and are generally wooded. The point next the Quantico is the most favorable for a battery, but it is level, open, and not more than 20 or 30 feet high, and easily accessible to our vessels. After passing the Chopawamsic the river widens, and the shores recede too much from the channel to offer favorable locations for batteries. The batteries of Aquia and Potomac Creeks need no special allusion in this brief communication. They are evidently defensive. Mathias Point is the one of the whole river (except perhaps Whitestone) where the navigation could be most effectually closed. The favorable location for batteries is the northern extremity, comprising an area of no great extent, and thickly covered with young pines. Why has not this point been before this occupied by hostile batteries? Simply, I believe, because it would require a good many guns and a good many men to protect those guns at a remote point, where the men and guns would be lost for any other purpose than this subordinate one of interrupting our navigation. The enemy would not risk a battery here without either a strong field work for 1,000 men or a large field force in the vicinity. Such a field work we are perfectly sure has not been built, and the evidence is in favor of the opinion that there are no batteries there. The best way to prevent their construction seems to me to cut or burn off the pine wood. A regiment, I think, would cut it off in a few hours if protected by our vessels. It the timber will burn standing, an operation on a smaller scale will do the business. In the same manner the construction of batteries on Whitestone Point may be prevented.

Batteries at High Point, at Cockpit Point, and thence down to the Chopawamsic, cannot be prevented. We may, indeed, prevent their construction on certain points, but along here somewhere the enemy can establish, in spite of us, as many batteries as he chooses. What is the remedy? Favorable circumstances, not to be certainly anticipated nor made the basis of any calculations, might justify and render successful the attack and capture of a particular battery. To suppose that we can capture all, and by new attacks of this kind prevent the navigation being molested, is very much the same as to suppose that the hostile army in our own front can prevent us building and maintaining field works to protect Arlington and Alexandria by capturing them one and all as fast as they are built. As long as the enemy is master of the other shore he can build and maintain as many batteries as he chooses. If we cannot take his batteries, we can counter-batter them—that is, we can on Stump Neck and Budd's Ferry Point establish superior batteries to his, and it is probable we can so molest him on all points where his batteries could be effectually treated as to cause him to abandon his effort. It must be considered, however, that this is an operation costly in men and munitions. We must have numerous and powerful guns; we must have several strong field works, the location of which may have to be changed by some unexpected change in the disposition of an antagonist's batteries. I should estimate that we should require ten to twenty heavy guns on Indian Head and fifty established on the shore from opposite Cockpit Point to opposite Evansport. In the same manner, should the enemy actually succeed in establishing batteries on Whitestone Point and Mathias Point, we could counter-batter them from the opposite shores. At Mathias the shore just north of Upper Cedar Point and the bluff north of Pope's Creek furnish, at 2 miles' distance, good employment for batteries. My apprehension that the enemy will actually occupy those points is not sufficient to induce me to recommend (particularly should the timber be cut off) the construction of the necessary batteries and the inclosing field works as a preventive measure. As to counter-batteries for the portion of the river between High Point and Evansport, I would wait until the disposition and ability of the enemy seriously to molest the navigation is more fully developed before commencing.

I am, very respectfully, your most obedient,

J. G. BARNARD,
Brigadier-General and Chief Engineer.

UNITED STATES STEAMER POCAHONTAS,
September 29, 1861.

Major-General McCLELLAN:

SIR: Since making the excursion down the Potomac with General Barnard I have been trying to come to some conclusion regarding the reason why the enemy should have selected Freestone Point as a site for a battery. It commands nothing; is merely an annoyance on the river and no more. It does not even prevent landing should such be desired at Occoquan Mills or below the point. I feel confident that it is merely a ruse, a blind, to draw our attention from the other points to that until they are prepared at their more important points, such as High Point, Cockpit Point, and the bluff just above Evansport, on the south side of the Quantico Creek. I consider these three points as meriting the first attention. There is one circumstance that strikes me with regard to Freestone Point, viz, that their workmen there were not so carefully concealed as usual, and to me it appears that they were intentionally exposed to view, as there was no necessity for bringing them at all outside the thick growth of trees until ready, and then they would have cut the trees at night and opened their battery at daylight. Besides this, a week or so before about 20 men were seen going up towards this bluff from the northward. This exposure is not in keeping with their usual maneuvers, and besides the road direct lies on the south side of the bluff.

I called yesterday morning to speak to yourself or General Barnard in regard to this matter, but not finding you in, my duties did not permit me to wait, and I trusted that I might have found an opportunity to call before going down the river. As I shall go probably by 10 to 11 a. m. to-morrow, I take the liberty of writing, in accordance with the permission given by yourself.

I am, sir, very respectfully, your obedient servant,

R. H. WYMAN,
Lieutenant-Commander, U. S. Steamer Pocahontas.

HEADQUARTERS DEPARTMENT OF PENNSYLVANIA,
September 30, 1861.

Brigadier-General LOCKWOOD, *Cambridge:*

SIR: I am authorized by Major-General McClellan to disarm any companies on the Eastern Shore of Maryland which are training with supposed hostile intentions toward the Government. There is a company at Riall's Landing, on the Nanticoke River, commanded by Captain Moore, and called the Tyaskin Guards, which ought to be disarmed. Will you please see that is done?

I am, your obedient servant,

JOHN A. DIX,
Major-General, Commanding.

HEADQUARTERS EXCELSIOR BRIGADE,
Good Hope, September 30, 1861.

Brig. Gen. S. WILLIAMS,
Assistant Adjutant-General, Army of the Potomac:

GENERAL: I have the honor to report my return to camp last night. The order of yesterday, to hold my command in readiness to march at short notice, reached me at Piscataway, where the force detached under the command of Colonel Dwight was encamped. Regarding this order as superseding the instructions heretofore received (to halt the detachment at Piscataway until further orders), I directed Colonel Dwight at noon to break camp and move to Good Hope, where the column arrived at 6 p. m.; a march of 15 miles. A rumor prevailed among the men that an action would take place to-day, so they prevailed upon their officers not to halt, and they did not.

On Friday I examined the position of the battery at Freestone Point. It seems not well placed to impede the navigation of the Potomac. Observing how close to the shore the channel runs at Cockpit and Hallowing Points and other places on the Virginia side, and where as yet no batteries have been disclosed, the inference is suggested that the works now on the river have for their main object a river line of defense, and that they are not seriously thought of by the enemy as menacing the navigation of the Potomac. The considerable bodies of troops encamped near the batteries at Aquia Creek, Occoquan, Freestone and Mathias Points corroborate this suggestion.

The shores on each bank of the Potomac abound in excellent places for the embarkation and landing of troops, from some of which commanding positions are easily and quickly accessible. Between Dumfries and the mouth of Powell River, on the Virginia side, there is a good shore for disembarkation, while from Budd's Ferry or Chapman's Point, on the west bank, a very large force could be conveniently and secretly put on board transports. If it were thought advisable to effect a landing lower down the river, menacing Fredericksburg and the enemy's line of communications, Pope's Creek and Lower Cedar Point, on the Maryland side, and the line from Roder's Creek to Monroe Creek, on the opposite shore, would deserve consideration, in view of the facilities afforded by an accessible open country for an advance.

The general commanding having directed my particular attention to Hilltop, in Charles County, I have to observe that it is a commanding position, overlooking an extensive valley to the left (southeast), unbroken almost to the bank of the Potomac. The valley is about a thousand yards in width, and proceeding east of north towards Budd's Ferry and the Chicamaxen River there is another range of hills nearly as high as Hilltop, which slopes gradually towards the river. The country is generally wooded, with occasional openings of cultivated land. The roads are bad, often passing through defiles. An advancing force could be impeded and harassed at every step, and for artillery the roads would present many serious inconveniences.

There are other facts and observations which I might add with reference to the topographical and military aspects of the country, but these are omitted, lest this communication might be found tedious. If a more particular report be desired, it will be promptly transmitted.

Several scouts were sent out by Colonel Dwight, but they were in every instance stopped while crossing the river by vessels of our flotilla. On Friday, after communicating with the commander of the Island Belle, from whom I have to acknowledge many courtesies and much valuable co-operation, F was enabled to land on the other side, near Mathias Point, several intelligent scouts, from whom a report may be expected at an early day.

One company, Captain Burgess' (Fifth Regiment), which was sent to Leonardtown, has not yet reported; it will probably reach camp to-morrow.

Inclosed herewith you will please find Colonel Dwight's summary of the several daily reports heretofore made, to which I respectfully invite attention.*

The population on his line of march were generally in communication with the enemy. He has, however, made but few arrests or seizures, in view of the very limited authority given to him by my instructions. One of the most important is that of one Jones, the manager of a ferry at Pope's Creek, who has been actively engaged in conveying men, arms, ammunition, and correspondence for the enemy. He will be sent to headquarters with several others as soon as Colonel Dwight's report of prisoners arrested and property taken is received.

I have the honor to be, general, your most obedient servant,

D. E. SICKLES,
Brigadier-General.

---

* Not found.

GENERAL ORDERS, }   HDQRS. ARMY OF THE POTOMAC,
    No. 18.   }   *Washington, September* 30, 1861.

*   *   *   *   *   *   *

XI. The works in the vicinity of Washington are named as follows:
The work south of Hunting Creek, Fort Lyon.
That on Shooter's Hill, Fort Ellsworth.
That to the left of the Seminary, Fort Worth.
That in front of Blenker's brigade, Fort Blenker.
That in front of Lee's house, Fort Ward.
That near the mouth of Four Mile Creek, Fort Scott.
That on Richardson's Hill, Fort Richardson.
That now known as Fort Albany, Fort Albany.
That near the end of Long Bridge, Fort Runyon.
The work next on the right of Fort Albany, Fort Craig.
The next on the right of Fort Craig, Fort Tillinghast.
The next on the right of Fort Tillinghast, Fort Ramsay.
The work next on the right of Fort Ramsay, Fort Woodbury.
That next on the right of Fort Woodbury, Fort De Kalb.
The work in rear of Fort Corcoran and near canal, Fort Haggerty.
That now known as Fort Corcoran, Fort Corcoran.
That to the north of Fort Corcoran, Fort Bennett.
That south of Chain Bridge, on height, Fort Ethan Allen.
That near the Chain Bridge, on Leesburg road, Fort Marcy.
That on the cliff north of Chain Bridge, Battery Martin Scott.
That on height near reservoir, Battery Vermont.
That near Georgetown, Battery Cameron.
That on the left of Tennallytown, Fort Gaines.
That at Tennallytown, Fort Pennsylvania.
That at Emory's Chapel, Fort Massachusetts.
That near camp of Second Rhode Island Regiment, Fort Slocum.
That on Prospect Hill, near Bladensburg, Fort Lincoln.
That next on the left of Fort Lincoln, Fort Saratoga.
That next on the left of Fort Saratoga, Fort Bunker Hill.
That on the right of General Sickles' camp, Fort Stanton.
That on the right of Fort Stanton, Fort Carroll.
That on the left towards Bladensburg, Fort Greble.
By command of Major-General McClellan:

                                S. WILLIAMS,
                                Assistant Adjutant-General.

———

GENERAL ORDERS, }   HDQRS. ARMY OF THE POTOMAC,
    No. 19.   }   *Washington, October* 1, 1861.

The attention of the General Commanding has recently been directed to depredations of an atrocious character that have been committed upon the persons and property of citizens in Virginia by the troops under his command. The property of inoffensive people has been lawlessly and violently taken from them; their houses broken open, and in some instances burned to the ground.

The General is perfectly aware of the fact that these outrages are perpetrated by a few bad men, and do not receive the sanction of the mass of the army. He feels confident, therefore, that all officers and soldiers who have the interest of the service at heart will cordially unite their efforts with his in endeavoring to suppress practices which disgrace the name of a soldier.

The General Commanding directs that in future all persons connected with this army who are detected in depredating upon the property of citizens shall be arrested and brought to trial; and he assures all concerned that crimes of such enormity will admit of no remission of the death penalty which the military law attaches to offenses of this nature.

When depredations are committed on property in charge of a guard, the commander, as well as the other members of the guard, will be held responsible for the same as principals and punished accordingly.

By command of Major-General McClellan:

S. WILLIAMS,
Assistant Adjutant-General.

HEADQUARTERS ARMY OF THE POTOMAC,
Washington, October 5, 1861.

Brigadier-General LOCKWOOD, *Comdg., &c., Cambridge, Md.:*

GENERAL: I am directed by the General Commanding to reply to your letter of the 23d as follows:

With regard to the employment of detectives, the General is unable to place any funds for their employment at present at your disposal. It would be very desirable to destroy any detachment of the enemy on the Eastern Shore of Virginia, and the general hopes you may be able to effect that object, but he is not able to furnish you any troops of artillery or cavalry, nor can he supply, it is feared, field guns or artillery or cavalry equipments for any troops of those arms should you raise them. Whatever can be done in this connection, however, the General is disposed to do. For the dispersing of meetings for drill and other purposes hostile to the Government in localities accessible by water the General has directed General Dix to furnish you a steamer from Baltimore, if one can be spared.

With regard to the long-range arms for the Delaware troops, it has been found impossible to arm the troops of this army with the most desirable arms. Every effort has been made, however, to furnish the best that can possibly be obtained under the circumstances. With these the troops for the present must be content. You are authorized to remove your camp to wherever you may find it to the interests of the public service to fix it. General Van Vliet, chief quartermaster, has been ordered to furnish the transportation for the marches which you may find it necessary to make.

Very respectfully, your obedient servant,

S. WILLIAMS,
Assistant Adjutant-General.

HEADQUARTERS ARMY,
Washington, October 6, 1861.

Brigadier-General ROSECRANS, U. S. A.,
Commanding Cross-Lanes, Western Virginia:

By Tuesday next [8th instant], at the latest, 3,000 men will leave Pittsburgh to join you by boats up the Kanawha to Gauley, or as high up as they can go. Your staff at Cincinnati is ordered through General Mitchel to forward them supplies. It is intended to send you six regiments in all as soon as possible.

E. D. TOWNSEND,
Assistant Adjutant General.

POINT OF ROCKS, *Sunday, October* 6, 1861.

Colonel MARCY:

I arrived this morning at this post, traveling all night from Williamsport. It is my duty to inform you that the Potomac is not properly guarded there, as I came across myself, a little below, in a small boat piloted by a negro, unchallenged.

The movements of troops in Virginia are numerous and uncertain. They are expecting an attack and scarcely know where to look for it. They have been strengthening a place called Brentsville, which is approached from Occoquan Creek and also Dumfries.

The arrangements of Beauregard have been materially interfered with by Johnston and also by the authorities in Richmond. By the orders of the latter, four regiments since last Tuesday have left by rail for Tennessee, and the cars up to last night had not returned; and by Johnston's [order] four regiments (about 2,500 men) have been stationed in the neighborhood of Newtown and Berryville, in the neighborhood of Winchester. Strong pickets are out north and east of these places. I discovered the sole object of this expedition. It has been represented to Johnston that as soon as the river is low enough 1,200 men could cross at Williamsport, take the First Maryland Regiment prisoners, and obtain supplies of salt and other necessaries for which they are in distress. I feel sure this will be attempted unless provided against.

A council of war was held at Manassas on Thursday and immediately afterwards two general officers left for Richmond. The feeling is prevalent among the troops, and it is said to be shared in by Beauregard, that the present rebel army of the Potomac is not large enough to cope with General McClellan's forces, whilst Johnston prates of their "invincibility." The forces at Leesburg have been kept up to nearly 27,000. The troops sent north were taken from positions near Middleburg and Falls Church.

I believe there is no intention to cross the river except on the Upper Potomac, where they make sure they could recross, before being interrupted. There is very little ammunition at Leesburg. A messenger was sent there for some for the troops near Winchester; he was told to go farther south, as they had only 24 rounds for each man.

Pardon my suggesting that if the national army advance shortly, and Occoquan Creek could be threatened at the same moment, there would be a general falling back upon Manassas, and that by a prompt movement via Falls Church, and a simultaneous one on the part of General Stone, the whole force at Leesburg might be captured.

While the rebels are less hopeful about Washington, they are very jubilant at the state of things in Missouri. I was in Richmond one whole day, and whilst there was informed that a message had been received by President Davis from General Price, stating that if 6,000 disciplined troops could be sent immediately, he would establish his headquarters in Saint Louis within ten days.

At my request Colonel Geary telegraphed to you immediately upon my arrival to have a man named Larmour, at Baltimore, arrested. He is expected at Manassas again in a week. He has several times taken letters and information, and took letters there with important information just previous to McDowell's advance.

There are two men now in Baltimore or Washington who have left Manassas on "spying" expeditions; one is named Maddox; he belongs to Loudoun County; was once a medical student at Jefferson College, Philadelphia; said to be a very smart fellow. I should have come to Washington, but these men may have seen me when there ten days ago;

and as I hope to be of some good service in the future, I had better not be spotted.

The troops are getting impatient; many of the Georgians openly expressing their desire to go home. They have not been paid and their clothes are getting very shabby.

The batteries at Leesburg I ascertained have not been touched. Should anything occur you will have information. At Martinsburg yesterday morning I found two Eastern men, carpenters, who lodge at the house of Mrs. Cushwa, a good Union woman; they both evinced a strong desire to risk their lives for their country; one of them has gone to Leesburg under the pretense of getting employment, and will communicate with the other every movement.

I propose, after I hear from you, to go quickly, which I can easily do, to Richmond, via Winchester, Strasburg, and Manassas, and report at Louisville, to you through General Anderson. I think you will see the importance of this in view of recent movements. I also fear to lie about there too long at a time. I have a splendid foothold, if I can only maintain it till something of importance occurs; and if you desire it, I will remain about the neighborhood of Manassas. I shall await your orders by telegraph.

The expected attack upon the coast is exciting a great deal of feeling, and should it come in Georgia or Louisiana, I believe hundreds of the army here, under pretense of going to the rescue, would go to swear allegiance to the United States.

Will you please authorize Major-General Banks to pay me what you think I am entitled to for sixteen days' services and risk.*

Should I think of any other point I will send it on.

With great respect, I am, your obedient servant,

BUXTON.

HEADQUARTERS DEPARTMENT OF PENNSYLVANIA,
Baltimore, Md., October 7, 1861.

Maj. Gen. GEORGE B. McCLELLAN,
Commanding Army of the Potomac :

GENERAL: In reply to the letter of your assistant adjutant-general, Major Williams, of the 5th instant, inclosing an extract of a letter from General H. H. Lockwood, of the 23d of September, I desire to say that there is not a steamboat or tug at my disposal here, and I do not think there is a single one among those recently purchased fit for the service for which General Lockwood requires one. They all draw too much water. I have not seen one that draws less than 10 feet. Two months ago, about a fortnight after I assumed command here, I asked for four steamers, with suitable armaments, of not more than four hundred tons burden. They ought not to draw over 5 feet of water. With such a vessel one could go up the rivers and enter the numberless inlets and bays on the Eastern Shore of Maryland, breaking up the illicit trade now carried on with Virginia and the meetings which are held at various points in hostility to the Government. Some steamboats have been fitted up here, but they are poor things, heavy, inconvenient, and cramped, with scanty accommodations even for the crews, and utterly incapable of carrying a company of soldiers. I was on board of one, the Hercules, a few days ago. She is a clumsy craft, with one gun, and draws over 10 feet of water. None of these vessels have

----

* Some matters of detail omitted.

been placed under my control. The only two vessels I have here are the Hope and the Jackson, both revenue cutters, sailing craft, and drawing over 10 feet. If there is a different class of vessels at Washington it would be very well, in case they can be spared, to order two or three of them here. I can send one to General Lockwood and employ the others to a very great advantage. If there are none, it is very important to secure a few by purchase or otherwise.

I am, very respectfully, your obedient servant,

JOHN A. DIX,
Major-General, Commanding,

POOLESVILLE, *October* 8, 1861—10 p. m.

Major-General McCLELLAN, *Commanding Army of Potomac:*

The enemy have evidently been excited by our occupation of Seldon's Island, and some of the troops which marched from Leesburg yesterday afternoon have appeared in front of it. I think they re-enforced that point by about a regiment.

The island is commanded by the Virginia shore, and the channel between that and the island is only 60 to 80 feet wide and knee-deep. It is hardly safe to occupy so long a space unless in very large force and with considerable intrenching, as well as artillery protection of good proportions. I had a party of 20 on it, all our boats could carry at once, but they are off to-night, as they could be easily captured. The river on this side is from 250 to 300 feet wide and breast-deep. The enemy cannot cross there.

CHAS. P. STONE,
Brigadier-General.

MOUNTAIN COVE, VA., *October* 8, 1861.

Col. E. D. TOWNSEND:

Withdrawn our forces, 5,200 men, from top of Big Sewell on Sunday. Came to Camp Lookout, 20 miles above Gauley and 14 in rear of Camp Sewell, without accident. We failed to draw the rebels out. Our reasons for this movement were want of transportation, want of force, roads almost impassable. We can reoccupy this ground whenever we require. Our troops will fall back nearer to the Gauley and get their pay and clothing. Hold a threatening position, and cut off all assault. The troops you send me will be brigaded, and ready as soon as arrived.

W. S. ROSECRANS,
Brigadier-General.

WHEELING, *October* 8, [1861].

General ROSECRANS:

I learn that the rebels in Calhoun and Wirt have assembled 200 strong, and have killed 7 Union men last week, and are burning property daily. They call for help. Colonel Lightburn's regiment is full; has four companies at Roane Court-House. He was at Point Pleasant. Can you not order his whole regiment in that direction? They are armed and equipped. Let them quarter and feed on the enemy.

F. H. PEIRPOINT.

HEADQUARTERS DEPARTMENT OF PENNSYLVANIA,
Baltimore, Md., October 9, 1861.

Brig. Gen. HENRY H. LOCKWOOD,
Commanding at Cambridge, Md. :

GENERAL: All the disunion companies in Queen Anne County should be disarmed. I much prefer that you should do the work with your Delaware troops. Arms and prisoners should be sent here. I am trying to get a steamer to put at your disposal. If I do not succeed, I must send you our tug at Annapolis. We can spare her two or three days in a week.

If you can get any legitimate authority, executive or military, in Delaware to direct the disbandment or disarming of companies in that State it should be done. In that case I think the arms had better be deposited at Fort Delaware. I have been urging the Government for two months to send a force into Accomac and Northampton Counties, Va., and break up the rebel camps there. General McClellan encouraged me to believe that it would be done, and I trust it will not be delayed much longer.

I am, general, very respectfully, yours,

JOHN A. DIX,
Major-General, Commanding.

GENERAL ORDERS, }   HDQRS. DEPARTMENT OF WESTERN VA.,
No. 1.   }   Camp at Mountain Cove, Va, October 11, 1861.

I. In accordance with General Orders, No. 80, from the War Depart-ment [September 19], this department will hereafter be called the Department of Western Virginia, and will comprise so much of the State of Virginia as lies west of the Blue Ridge Mountains.

*   *   *   *   *   *   *

By command of Brigadier-General Rosecrans:

GEO. L. HARTSUFF,
Assistant Adjutant-General.

HEADQUARTERS ARMY OF THE POTOMAC,
Washington, October 12, 1861.

Hon. SIMON CAMERON, Secretary of War:

SIR: Lieut. Col. B. S. Alexander, of the Corps of Engineers, has been detailed to take charge of the construction of bridge and engineer trains for the use of the Army of the Potomac in its forward movement. I respectfully request authority to have constructed under his superin-tendence from ten to fifteen of the Birago combined trestle and pontoon equipages. The work should be commenced at once, but I cannot at present determine the exact length of each train or the precise number required. I would be glad to have full authority to arrange these mat-ters as more mature consideration may determine. I learn that the Engineer Department has no funds at its disposal for this purpose, and I would therefore suggest that the expense be defrayed by the Quar-termaster's Department until a special appropriation can be obtained from Congress. General Barnard is favorably impressed with Murphy's suspension bridge for field purposes. I would ask authority to expend $3,000 in experimenting upon this bridge, should further examination render it probable that it would be successful.

I learn that Company A, Engineers, has arrived at West Point, and request that it may be at once ordered to report to me here with all the serviceable tools and wagons in its possession, and that the recruits ready for it be directed to join it here. I would also request that volunteers may be transferred to this company and the three others recently authorized by Congress without the consent of their commanders. The vital importance of this class of troops renders the course I have suggested absolutely necessary.

Requesting your early attention to this letter, I remain, very respectfully, your obedient servant,

GEO. B. McCLELLAN,
Major-General, U. S. Army.

WASHINGTON, D. C., *October* 13, 1861.

Brig. Gen. J. G. BARNARD,
Chief Engineer Army of the Potomac, Washington:

SIR: In compliance with your request of yesterday, I proceed to state such views as strike me to be important, after one day's study, in relation to bridge and engineer trains and the organization of engineer troops.

If this army moves from here or from any other point into the territory of seceded States, the war becomes a war of invasion; and considering the numerous rivers that must be crossed, the natural and artificial obstructions of various kinds that must be overcome, the fortifications that may have to be invested and reduced before the war can be terminated successfully, to move forward without bridge equipage, without engineer troops and engineer trains, would be to invite defeat. As well might the army move without its artillery, and rely entirely on its infantry and cavalry, as to go forward without its engineers. Such a course, against such an enemy as we have to meet, we know would result in disgrace and disaster, in whatever numbers we may move.

But we have as yet no bridge equipage, no engineer trains, and no instructed engineer troops. It is true we have one untried pontoon bridge, and one organized company of engineer soldiers, but these are as a drop in a bucket when we contemplate our future wants.

What, then, are we to do? This becomes a grave question, and I could wish that it had been committed to wiser heads than mine.

The answer must be, however, we must make them. Our country is full of practical bridge-builders. We must secure their services. It is full of instructed labor of a kind so nearly akin to that which we require in engineer troops, that we must, if possible, embark it in that channel.

If time permitted, and we had authority from Congress to raise and equip a brigade of engineers, the pay being such as to command the services of the best mechanics in the country, and if we had a year in which to prepare to build our bridges, and learn how to use them under all circumstances, to organize and equip our trains, and to instruct our engineer troops, the problem would become comparatively simple. But we have not the time, nor have we the authority to do these things, as they ought to be done, unless the President shall so order it. We are here in the face of the enemy, and, as I understand the matter, something must be done speedily.

If I were the general commanding, and possessed no more light on the subject than I do at present, I would in the first place direct that the four companies of engineer soldiers now authorized by law be filled up to the maximum. This, I believe, may be done by transfers from the volunteer force now assembled near this city.

Let us limit the force here to one hundred regiments, and say we want 500 men. This will call for 5 men from each regiment on an average. If the order inviting or authorizing such transfers should limit the number to be taken from each regiment, without the consent of the colonel, to 10, I believe the four engineer companies may at once be filled, and after an explanation of the absolute necessity for such troops all opposition on the part of regimental commanders would be silenced, or could at least be met by silence. These men should not be taken at random. Only such as are qualified by previous pursuits to make engineer soldiers should be transferred.

This would soon give us a small body of men, but by no means the number that the emergency requires. Without the authority of law to raise such troops, and without the power to raise the pay so as to command the services of good mechanics, I see no other way to supply them than by taking two or three of our best volunteer regiments, detaching them from the line of the Army, and instructing them as best we may with the limited number of officers who have made this a specialty in the duties of engineer troops. I understand that there have been several volunteer regiments organized with a view of being converted into engineer troops. These will probably be the regiments to be selected.

We shall have roads and railroads to build and repair; telegraph lines to put up; bridges to construct and destroy; and fortifications to build, to defend, and reduce. Except in the construction of military bridges, and the investment and reduction of fortified places, it may be hoped with some degree of confidence that after a little experience our engineer troops so obtained would soon become proficient. These two subjects require study. Each of them is a specialty, and I confess that my ideas are not sufficiently matured to enable me to give clear and distinct views on the subject—to direct your attention to something that is fixed and will not require alteration hereafter.

As to bridges, we shall want several equipages. We can therefore afford to begin at the beginning. The India-rubber pontoon bridge that we have ought to be tried, and, if necessary, perfected. Our engineer troops, if a proper proportion of them are sailors, will soon learn to use it. A few trestle bridges may be made, using, say, for one bridge, the common trestle; for another, the Birago trestle; and for another, the Birago trestle and pontoon combined. I made the canvas boats that Lieutenant Ives, of the Topographical Engineers, used in his expedition on the Colorado River. Before letting them go out of my hands I used them on several occasions. I was much pleased with them, and Lieutenant Ives afterwards informed me that they answered his purpose admirably. I confess myself favorably impressed with this boat. A bridge train with these boats for pontoons could be very rapidly made.

We have 100 corrugated-iron wagon bodies now here in the Quartermaster's Department. This gives us the foundation for still another bridge, which can be readily made. These wagon bodies, if they are as good as the testimonials in relation to them seem to imply, will become very useful. By themselves each one of them is a large boat, and, if properly made, they ought together to be easily converted into a bridge.

I am very favorably impressed with Murphy's suspension bridge, a drawing of which you have in your office. For deep and narrow streams, for torrents, or where ice may be encountered, I have not a doubt but that the suspension principle is the correct one. Three or four spans of this bridge might be ordered, and I should suppose could soon be made. It appears to me, however, that manila rope ought to replace the wire rope for all running rigging, and in all cases, except for the suspension cables. It is easier repaired, and our troops will more readily understand it. We can go to New York and get 10,000 men to splice or put a thimble in a manila rope. By going to Mr. Roebling's establishment in Trenton it is possible that we might find 20 men who could do the same thing with a wire rope.

These would give us half a dozen complete bridges, adapted to different circumstances. The experience acquired in their construction would lead to improvements and perhaps to the adoption of other bridges. It should not be forgotten that in any advance of our army we ought to avail ourselves of the mechanical skill of our soldiers and the timber of the country to replace all such bridges, where it is possible, by more permanent structures. In many cases ferry-boats may be made to take the place of bridges if we carry the necessary tools with which to construct them and the necessary rigging with which to maneuver them in the engineer trains.

After we shall have obtained the necessary engineer troops, and provided bridge equipages, intrenching and siege tools, we will be prepared to commence the instruction of our troops in the operations of a siege—in making fascines, gabions, and sap-rollers, and in the method of laying out and constructing approaches.

But, as I did not propose to enter into any discussion of this subject at present, I will close with only this allusion to it, which will serve to remind us how much we have to do and how much we have to learn before we can place ourselves in a condition to commence the siege of any fortified place.

Very respectfully, your obedient servant,

B. S. ALEXANDER,
Lieutenant-Colonel Engineers.

HEADQUARTERS ARMY OF THE POTOMAC,
Washington, October 14, 1861.

Hon. THOMAS A. SCOTT, *Assistant Secretary of War:*

SIR: On Friday last [October 12] I had the honor to address to the War Department a communication, in which I requested authority to cause the construction of from ten to fifteen of the Birago bridge trains, referring also to other matters pertaining to the engineer service. A more full consideration of the subject has convinced me that we may not have time enough to construct the necessary number of bridge trains of that peculiar pattern, although it is the best now in use in Europe. As the exigency of the case admits of no delay, I would respectfully suggest to be immediately empowered to have bridge trains constructed in such numbers and of such kinds as may prove to be best adapted to our wants. It is necessary to avail ourselves at once of all the resources which the mechanical skill and ingenuity of the country can furnish in this matter. As much time is necessary to prepare these trains, I would respectfully request an immediate answer to this communication, as well as to the other requests embodied in my letter of Friday.

As the four regular companies of engineer troops authorized by the late law of Congress are not yet organized, and when filled will prove totally insufficient for our purposes, I respectfully request authority to detail for this service such regiments of volunteers or such portions of regiments as may prove best adapted to the duty.

Although I have the full authority to detail them on that service, it would be well to have the special authority of the War Department as an additional security for their obtaining from Congress at its next session some increase of pay commensurate with the arduous and difficult nature of their duties.

Very respectfully, your obedient servant,
GEO. B. McCLELLAN,
Major-General, U. S. Army.

———

HEADQUARTERS DEPARTMENT OF PENNSYLVANIA,
Baltimore, Md., October 14, 1861.

Brig. Gen. HENRY H. LOCKWOOD, Cambridge, Md.:

GENERAL: I send you the steamer Balloon, Captain Kirwin, which is placed at your disposal for the purpose of aiding you in breaking up the commercial intercourse with the Confederate States of which the Eastern Shore of Maryland furnishes the material. You have, as I suppose, ere this taken measures to seize all merchandise brought from Delaware to Salisbury by rail and destined to Virginia. With the aid of the Balloon you may intercept much of that which finds its way down the Chesapeake by water, and I trust be able to confine this illicit traffic to very narrow limits. It is believed that the Balloon will also be of essential use in sending to different points the force necessary to disarm such companies of militia or such unauthorized military bodies as are training with intentions notoriously hostile to the Government. The duty is one of the greatest delicacy, and requires the utmost prudence and discretion. It is not doubted that numbers of individuals on the Eastern Shore of Maryland have been led into the support of disloyal measures by gross misrepresentations of the views and intentions of the Government. While the purpose you have in view should be steadily maintained and carried out with inflexible firmness, those who have been deceived and misled, instead of being confirmed in their prejudices and driven hopelessly off by harshness on our part, should, if possible, be reclaimed by kind treatment, and convinced of their error by correcting the misapprehensions under which they labor. If, in spite of all efforts to induce them to discontinue their acts of hostility to the Government, they persist in carrying on correspondence with the enemy and in giving him aid and comfort, they should be arrested and sent to Fort McHenry; but unless a case of extraordinary urgency should occur, I trust it may not be necessary to make an arrest without first consulting me. I have full authority from General McClellan to act in all cases.

You will bear in mind that we are on the eve of an election in Maryland of vital importance. The preservation of this State is indispensable to the safety of the capital. It is not doubted that all your measures will be so tempered with discretion as to give strength to the cause of the Union; but while all the just rights even of those who are disloyal should be respected, they should be made to feel that no act of open hostility to the Government will be tolerated for a moment.

I inclose copies of letters which have passed between Major-General McClellan, Governor Hicks, and myself in regard to the disarming of military companies.* The one at Westminster has been already disarmed by a force sent from this city. All those on the Eastern Shore of Maryland are left to you, and I consider any company drilling in avowed hostility to the Government as coming within the authority given to me by Major-General McClellan and sanctioned by Governor Hicks, though not specifically named in the letter of the latter. The authority conferred on me is hereby delegated to you, not doubting that it will be firmly and discreetly exercised. It will be advisable to consult with our leading friends in the counties in which you adopt these stringent and delicate measures.

You will please report to me the result of every such movement with all convenient dispatch. Should you deem the co-operation of a police force advisable in any case, please notify me, and it shall be provided.

I am, general, very respectfully, yours,

JOHN A. DIX,
Major-General, Commanding.

WAR DEPARTMENT,
Washington, October 15, 1861.

Major-General McCLELLAN, *Commanding Army of the Potomac:*

SIR: Yours of the 14th instant, relative to the construction of bridge trains, has been duly received. Upon inquiry at the Engineer Office I find that one train is now ready for use, and you will consider yourself authorized to give directions to the Engineer Department for the construction of such others as the wants of the service may require. You have full authority to detail the whole or parts of volunteer regiments for engineer service, and will exercise your own discretion in relation thereto. For such service the Department will recommend that Congress give such increased pay as you may determine to be right and proper.

Respectfully,   THOMAS A. SCOTT,
Assistant Secretary of War.

WAR DEPARTMENT, *October* 16, 1861.

Brigadier-General NEGLEY, *Pittsburgh, Pa.:*

Embark your regiments for the Kanawha to-day. Do not delay for artillery and cavalry; they can follow. We are much disappointed that you did not move on Monday, as expected.

THOMAS A. SCOTT.

POOLESVILLE, *October* 17, 1861—8.20 p. m.

Major-General McCLELLAN, *Commanding Army of Potomac:*

A large body of the enemy seems to have suddenly left the vicinity of Leesburg. They took advantage of the thick weather this morning, and their absence was not perceived until this evening.

My impression is that they have marched in the direction of Fairfax, but they may have got off by the Waterford and Hillsborough road.

CHAS. P. STONE,
Brigadier-General.

---

* No inclosures found.

HEADQUARTERS OF THE ARMY,
October 17, 1861.

General ROSECRANS, *Big Sewell, W. Va.*:

The troops heretofore promised you from Western Pennsylvania have been just ordered to Kentucky instead.

E. D. TOWNSEND,
Assistant Adjutant-General.

HEADQUARTERS ARMY OF THE POTOMAC,
Washington, October 18, 1861.

Brig. Gen. J. G. BARNARD,
Chief Engineer, Army of the Potomac:

GENERAL: Major-General McClellan directs that yourself and General Barry proceed as soon as practicable to determine the minimum strength of garrisons—artillery and infantry—required for the various works in and about Washington to satisfy the conditions of a good defense. A report is desired as soon as you shall have concluded your deliberations.*

Very respectfully, your obedient servant,
S. WILLIAMS,
Assistant Adjutant-General.

Sketch of a plan to cut the communications of the rebel army now at Manassas Junction.

DIVISION HEADQUARTERS,
Fort Lyon, October 18, 1861.

Advance from Lewinsville, Falls Church, Little River turnpike, and on the left towards Elzey's and Occoquan, when the enemy will fall back beyond Bull Run, if he has not already done so.

The force on the left would by this movement reach the Occoquan and be in position to co-operate with another force to be landed between Occoquan and Dumfries. This force would advance and take possession of the railroad in front of Brentsville or at Bristoe.

To prevent the large force said to be at Aquia Creek from interrupting this movement, have some of the larger men-of-war and transports, with some troops, to ascend the Potomac, attack the batteries, and threaten to land troops to attack them in the rear, thus preventing any force from being detached towards Dumfries.

The smaller vessels and gunboats and transports could ascend the Potomac to cover the crossing between Occoquan and Dumfries. A portion or all the troops preparing for the expedition at Annapolis can be brought here, as well as a portion of those above on the Potomac. This would only delay this secret expedition a few days.

As the transports could not carry a sufficient force at one time, a portion can march down on the Maryland side.

S. P. HEINTZELMAN,
Brigadier-General.

---

* See joint reports of Barry and Barnard, October 22 and 24, pp. 624, 626.

HEADQUARTERS OF THE ARMY,
Washington, D. C., October 20, 1861.
Brig. Gen. C. M. THRUSTON, U. S. A.,
Cumberland, Md., via Grafton, Va.:

Organize and dispatch a detachment of troops from those nearest at hand to protect the North and South Branch Bridges, with other parts of the Baltimore and Ohio road within easy reach of Cumberland. Brigadier-General Lander will be sent to take general direction of the service in that quarter, with other instructions and troops for the same object. The greatest expedition is required in this first movement from Cumberland. The agent of the road will be instructed to give you all advice and assistance in his power. If time permit, call for any necessary detachment of troops from New Creek, or even Grafton, to save the bridges of the road.

WINFIELD SCOTT.

HEADQUARTERS DEPARTMENT OF PENNSYLVANIA,
Baltimore, Md., October 21, 1861.
Maj. Gen. GEORGE B. McCLELLAN,
Commanding Army of Potomac:

GENERAL: I have received the letter of Mr. James Hubbard, of Laurel, Del., in regard to the rebel force at Jenkins' Bridge, on the Eastern Shore of Virginia. I think he estimates the rebel force in Accomac County too high. I think it nearer 2,500 than 4,500. In the two counties (Accomac and Northampton) there may be from 4,000 to 5,000 in the different camps. I think two infantry regiments, a battery of light artillery, and two companies of cavalry would break up and disperse the entire force. They have received some arms lately, from what quarter it is very difficult to say. It is extremely desirable to have a decided demonstration of force in that direction by the 1st of November. The election in this State comes off on the 6th, and our Union friends in the lower counties are disheartened and in danger of being overawed by the influence of these rebel organizations on the secessionists in those counties.

I am, very respectfully, your obedient servant,

JOHN A. DIX,
Major-General, Commanding.

HEADQUARTERS DEPARTMENT OF PENNSYLVANIA,
Baltimore, Md., October 21, 1861.
Col. R. B. MARCY, *Inspector-General, Army of the Potomac:*

COLONEL: It has occurred to me that it might be interesting to you to know the system adopted in Baltimore to secure the inhabitants from annoyance by the bad conduct of our soldiers and to keep our men within their encampments.

A few days after I took command, the latter part of July, some 300 of our men had escaped from their regiments, and were disgracing the service by their drunkenness and disorderly conduct in the city, where most of them were secreted. I immediately issued an order to the police to arrest all soldiers found in Baltimore without passes signed by the captains of the companies and the colonels of the regiments to which they belonged, and I adopted very stringent rules in regard to permits to soldiers to leave their camps. In about ten days the absentees were all hunted up in the streets and in their hiding places and brought back to their regiments. Since that time there has been no repetition of these disorderly scenes. All soldiers arrested in the city are taken to the exterior stations of the police, and guards are sent for them every morning and evening. During the month of September, of about 7,000 men in and around the city, only 140 were taken in custody by the police, and of this number 59 belonged to the Second Regiment Maryland Volunteers, which was recruited in Baltimore.

The city has never been so free from disorder, disturbance, and crime as it has been during the last sixty days, and during the whole time not a single soldier has been employed in aid of the police. Much is no doubt due to the presence of a military force, and it is due to the regiments under my command to say that the orderly conduct both of officers and men has produced an improved feeling among large numbers of citizens who have been exceedingly hostile to the Government. I may say this most emphatically of the Sixth Regiment Michigan Volunteers and the eighth ward, the most disloyal in the city, within which the regiment is stationed, at the McKim mansion.

I am, very respectfully, your obedient servant,

JOHN A. DIX,
Major-General, Commanding.

WASHINGTON, D. C., *October* 22, 1861.

General S. WILLIAMS, *Assistant Adjutant-General:*

GENERAL: Circumstances preventing a circumstantial report* to-day of the number of men required for the garrisons of the defenses of Washington, we respectfully present the following summary, with the intention of giving another report to-morrow or as soon as practicable:

For full garrisons of works of exterior line south side of Potomac....	5,952
For three reliefs of gunners for Forts Ellsworth and Scott............	363
For one relief of gunners for Forts Runyon, Jackson, Corcoran, Bennett, and Haggerty..	230
Total garrisons south of Potomac.................................	6,545
Garrisons of works at Chain Bridge...............................	1,500
Total..	8,045
For three reliefs of gunners for all the works south of the Potomac.........	3,000
Total garrisons considered necessary for all the works.............	11,045
For reserves south of Potomac from Fort Lyon to Fort Corcoran.........	12,000
Reserve at Chain Bridge...	750
Reserves in city...	10,000
Total..	33,795

The full garrisons of the works north of Potomac would amount to 9,000 men. The above estimate is based on the supposition that in all ordinary circumstances it would be only necessary to supply them with men enough to man the guns.

Respectfully submitted.

WILLIAM F. BARRY,
Brigadier-General, Chief of Artillery.
J. G. BARNARD,
Brigadier-General, and Chief Engineer.

---

* See Williams to Barnard, October 18, p. 622, and supplementary report, October 24, p. 626.

HEADQUARTERS OF THE ARMY,
Washington, October 22, 1861.

Brig. Gen. B. F. KELLEY, *Grafton, W. Va.:*

Proceed with your command to Romney and assume command of the Department of Harper's Ferry and Cumberland until the arrival of Brigadier-General Lander.

WINFIELD SCOTT.

WASHINGTON, *October 23, 1861.*

Brigadier-General ROSECRANS, U. S. A.,
Camp Tompkins, W. Va.:

Your telegram of 18th received and is satisfactory.* Report of Carnifix also received. All your operations meet entire approval of the General. Subject of Ohio not yet decided. General Kelley's command has been ordered to Romney, in a new department.

E. D. TOWNSEND,
Assistant Adjutant-General.

CAMP NEAR BUDD'S FERRY,
October 23, 1861.

Brig. Gen. S. WILLIAMS,
Assistant Adjutant-General:

GENERAL: I have the honor to transmit to you a few lines this evening. I went this morning to Stump Neck (directly opposite Cockpit Point), from which point I could see Freestone Point, Shipping Point, and intermediate places.

At Freestone and Cockpit Points are embankments on side hills, the former perhaps 100 and the other 50 feet above the water, but there are no guns or men visible. Midway between Cockpit and Shipping Points is a heavy mortar, mounted on a side hill. The three batteries mentioned in a former report are farther down the river than the mortar. From that point of view I could see guns pointing up the river from Eastport, which were hidden from my view when at Budd's Ferry.

While at Stump Neck there arrived a steamer with a rebel flag flying, and known to be the Geo. Page, which was kept at the mouth of Aquia Creek by the vessels of our fleet. The arrival of this vessel affords the rebels the means of landing troops and artillery across the river to this or a higher point. If large forces are sent across above Mattawoman Creek, or even to Stump Neck, this detachment may be entirely cut off. Colonel commanding the troops here has thus decided to move to near Mattawoman, where the road crosses it. In the mean time a strong cavalry outpost is to remain here to watch the rebels, and I shall prosecute my work of ascertaining the width of the river, &c., as if the command were to remain here, unless interrupted by the enemy crossing.

I have the honor to be, very respectfully, your obedient servant,

R. S. WILLIAMSON,
Captain, U. S. Topographical Engineers.

---

* Not found.

SPECIAL ORDERS, ⎰   HDQRS. ARMY OF THE POTOMAC,
    No. 115.   ⎱   *Washington, October* 23, 1861.

*   *   *   *   *   *   *

10. Brig. Gen. Ambrose E. Burnside, volunteer service, will establish his headquarters, for the present, at Annapolis, Md., and will assemble at that point the troops under his command.

*   *   *   *   *   *   *

By command of Major-General McClellan:

S. WILLIAMS,
Assistant Adjutant-General.

ARLINGTON, *October* 24, 1861.

General McDOWELL, *Eighteenth and Q Streets:*

The following just received from General McClellan:

The affair in front of Leesburg, on Monday last, resulted in serious loss to us, but was a most gallant fight on the part of our men, who displayed the utmost coolness and courage. It has given the utmost confidence in them. The disaster was caused by errors committed by the immediate commander, not General Stone.

I have withdrawn all the troops from the other side, since they went without my orders and nothing was to be gained by retaining them there.

JAMES B. FRY,
Assistant Adjutant-General.

WASHINGTON, D. C., *October* 24, 1861.

General S. WILLIAMS, *Assistant Adjutant-General:*

GENERAL: In our report of the 22d instant we stated the number of men we deemed necessary for garrisons and reserves " for the various works in and about Washington to satisfy the conditions of a good defense." It seems proper to exhibit more clearly the grounds on which our estimate is founded. We have adopted the rule, which experience showed to be satisfactory for the lines of Torres Vedras, in computing the garrison of the various works, viz: Two men per running yard of front covering line and one man per running yard of rear line, deducting spaces occupied by guns. Computed in this manner, the total of the full garrisons of all the works would amount to 19,789 men, of which 6,581 should be gunners, in order to furnish three reliefs to each gun. Of these works, however, the following on the south side of the Potomac are on interior lines, and do not require full garrisons, while the exterior line is intact, viz: Forts Ellsworth, Scott, Runyon, Jackson, Corcoran, Bennett, and Haggerty.

Fort Albany might, perhaps, have been included in the above list in our estimate of the 22d. However, we have considered it as fully garrisoned.

As Fort Ellsworth and Fort Scott have commanding views of the valleys of Hunting Creek and Four-mile Run, we have considered it necessary to provide for the efficient service of all their guns by three reliefs of gunners; to the others we have assigned but one relief. With regard to the assignment of garrisons to works of the exterior lines, we remark that if Washington were thrown upon its own defenses, without external aid, and the enemy were so far in the ascendant in the field as to be able to act on either shore, it is evident that all the works should be fully garrisoned.

We do not consider this extreme supposition the proper basis for garrisoning the works, and it is evidently desirable to shut up in them as few men as possible. The more probable supposition is that the army moves from here in force, fully occupying the bulk of the enemy's forces by its own movement, leaving the capital so strengthened by its defensive lines as to prevent danger of sudden seizure by a strategical movement of the enemy, and enable it to be held a reasonable time in case of serious reverses to our own arms in the field.

On this basis we have estimated for full garrisons of all the works of the exterior line south of the Potomac, for three reliefs of gunners for Forts Ellsworth and Scott, and for one relief for the other interior works, and for three reliefs of gunners only for all the works north of the Potomac, giving a total, as stated in our report of October 22, of 11,045 men. As without reserves a line of detached field works possesses little or no strength, we have considered as included in our instructions to provide for these. We are of opinion that two brigades should be distributed along the lines from Hunting Creek to Four Mile Run and two between Four Mile Run and Fort Corcoran, making, say, 12,000 men; one regiment in reserve at Chain Bridge of 750 men, and stationed in the city a reserve of 10,000 men; making a total of reserves of 22,750 men. As the total of full garrisons of all the works north of the Potomac is 7,343 men, it will be seen that in case of necessity part of these works or all might be full garrisoned from the reserves, still leaving over 15,000 men.

We herewith inclose two tabular statements, giving the names of works, perimeters, full garrisons, number of gunners, of works north and south of the Potomac. We would add that the system is not entirely completed, and that three or four more works than are mentioned in these statements may yet be found necessary.

RECAPITULATION.

For full garrisons of all works of exterior line south of the Potomac, except the Chain Bridge	5,952
Full garrisons of Forts Ethan Allen and Marcy	1,500
Three reliefs of gunners at Forts Ellsworth and Scott	363
One relief of gunners for other interior works	230
For three reliefs of gunners for all works north of Potomac	3,000
Total	11,045
Total garrisons	11,045
Reserves	22,750
Total	33,795

We have the honor to be, general, very respectfully, your obedient servants,

WILLIAM F. BARRY,
Brigadier-General, Chief of Artillery.
J. G. BARNARD,
Brigadier-General, and Chief Engineer.

[Inclosure.]

Names.	Perimeter.	Guns.	Men to man guns.	Total garrison.	Names.	Perimeter.	Guns.	Men to man guns.	Total garrison.
North of the Potomac.	*Yards*				*South of the Potomac.*	*Yards*			
Battery Cameron	......	2	......	......	Fort Lyon	937	41	570	1,200
Battery Martin Scott.	......	2	......	......	Fort Worth..	463	14	210	630
Battery Vermont	......	3	45	......	Fort Ward	576	17	255	780
Fort	.....	5	75	400	Fort Ellsworth	618	17	255	843
Fort (north of reservoir).	......	5	75	300	Fort Blenker	360	10	150	510
Fort	......	5	75	300	Fort	172	6	105	225
Fort Gaines..........	105	4	75	250	Fort Scott	226	6	108	487
Fort Pennsylvania...	440	12	180	600	Fort Albany.......	429	13	183	585
Fort (Schwartz's house).	190	7	105	250	Fort Runyon	1,484	21	315	2,120
Fort Massachusetts..	168	10	150	200	Fort Jackson	......	4	60	200
Fort Slocum	250	13	195	300	Fort Richardson ..	316	8	120	444
Fort Totten..........	272	14	180	350	Fort Craig.........	......	7	105	400
Fort Bunker Hill	205	8	120	270	Fort Tillinghast ...	......	7	105	300
Fort Saratoga........	109	6	120	220	Fort Ramsay	......	5	75	300
Fort	......	4	60	200	Fort Woodbury....	161	5	75	300
Fort Lincoln........	446	16	140	600	Fort De Kalb	196	9	135	450
Fort (Benning's Bridge).	354	10	150	500	Fort Corcoran	576	12	183	800
Fort	......	8	120	300	Fort Bennett	146	5	75	200
Fort	......	8	120	300	Fort Haggerty.....	128	4	60	172
Fort	......	8	120	300	Fort Ethan Allen ..	736	21	375	1,000
Fort Stanton	322	18	270	483	Fort Marcy	338	7	105	500
Fort	......	10	150	400					
Fort Carroll	......	12	180	400	Total south of the Potomac.	......	239	3,621	12,446
Fort Greble..........	327	15	255	420					
					Grand total......	......	444	6,581	19,789
Total north of the Potomac.	......	205	2,960	7,343					

WILLIAM F. BARRY,
Brigadier-General, Chief of Artillery.
J. G. BARNARD,
Brigadier-General, and Chief Engineer.

HEADQUARTERS DEPARTMENT OF PENNSYLVANIA,
Baltimore, Md., October 25, 1861.

Maj. Gen. GEORGE B. McCLELLAN,
Commanding Army of Potomac:

GENERAL: A great deal of anxiety is felt in this State in regard to the voters in the Maryland regiments. I have had several delegations from the Union men and to-day a communication from the State Central Committee on the subject. There are some 6,000 men now embodied in regiments and corps raised in this State. About half the number are in this city, and it was expected they would remain until after the election. I saw an order in Quartermaster Belger's office last evening ordering five companies of Colonel Purnell's regiment to Salisbury, Md., although it has not been sent to me. This order has produced a good deal of solicitude among the Union men in Baltimore. They wish to show their whole strength. Some even apprehend that there may be danger of losing the State if the votes in the military service are not secured. I do not think there is just ground for this apprehension. At the same time I think it very important for our future quietude that the Union ticket should not merely be carried, but that it should have an overwhelming majority. I earnestly hope, therefore, that the Government will make all practicable arrangements to enable the voters in the Maryland corps to attend the polls in the districts in which they reside on the 6th of November next.

I am, very respectfully, general, your obedient servant,

JOHN A. DIX,
Major-General, Commanding.

———

CAMP ABOVE BUDD'S FERRY,
October 27, 1861.

Brig. Gen. R. B. MARCY,
Chief of Staff, Department of Potomac, Washington, D. C.:

SIR : In reply to your communication marked "Confidential,"* I will state that if the only object were to sink the Geo. Page, it would be an easy matter, if she remains opposite Budd's Ferry. I have before informed you that the river bank at the ferry is elevated some 10 feet at least. About 150 or 200 yards back from the river is a depression. Heavy guns can be carried to within a mile of the ferry without being seen, and at night they can be carried this 1 mile to the inner edge of the elevated part of the bank, so that they can not only be screened from view, but be protected by the bluff bank, which forms a natural parapet. The guns must of course be put on top of this bluff and earthworks thrown up to protect them, but the guns can be put near the desired position without the enemy's knowing it, unless informed of it by rebel spies, of which there are many. If the Geo. Page remains opposite the ferry and in the river (Potomac), the distance from her to the proposed battery will be a little more or less than $1\frac{1}{2}$ miles, according to her position on the river. But this proposed work must be constructed under the fire of at least a dozen guns opposite, and we know that some of them throw a shell $6\frac{1}{2}$ inches in diameter and 14 inches long. A line of batteries as long and as formidable as may be required can be constructed on this side, but they must be made in sight of and subject to the enemy's fire.

Lieutenant Harrell, of the Navy, attached to the United States steamer Union, informed an officer of cavalry yesterday that there was on board his vessel a rifle cannon, probably a 64-pound gun, and one of the best in the Potomac flotilla, which is too heavy for the Union, and if the Army will transport it to its proper position, the Navy will land it at a suitable point. The cavalry officer said the information can be considered official, and he reported it to me. But there is no heavy truck here by means of which such a gun [can] be transported.

But the results to be obtained from the destruction of the Page are not in my opinion commensurate with the danger and probable loss of life attending the construction of this battery, when it is considered that as soon as such a battery is constructed the Page will withdraw out of its range, and the attempt to destroy her by this means will probably be futile. If any batteries are to be established, they should be with a view to opening and keeping open the river; to do which from this side there should be a long line of the most formidable guns, with mortar batteries on the hills in the rear, which when completed will be able to destroy those of the enemy. Our Army occupying this part of Maryland, there is little chance of the enemy attempting to cross the river.

———

* Not found.

The Page is not of much importance to either party. The river is effectually closed by batteries from Mathias Point to where our fleet lies. The object of batteries must be to open the river and destroy the enemy's works, and the work is a formidable one, and cannot be done in a night.

My examinations of the river have given me all the general information required, and there are several reasons why I should be allowed to go to Washington for a day or two. If I am to construct batteries I should like to have a personal interview with you and arrange plans, &c. I left Washington, expecting to return in six days. The bureau has estimated for money for my use, and doubtless it is ready for me now. I want instruments, and have now nothing but a little goniometer and a prismatic compass. I want to provide myself with camp equipage, that I may be independent of the messes of line officers. I have not brought with me clothes for an extended stay in camp, and I want to buy another horse. For these and other reasons I request you will send me an order to repair to headquarters at such time as you think my services can be dispensed with in this vicinity. In the mean time I will endeavor to accumulate more matter for your information. I can go to the city on horseback or by water and return in the same manner; distance, 40 miles.

I have the honor to be, very respectfully, your obedient servant,

R. S. WILLIAMSON,
Captain, U. S. Topographical Engineers.

P. S.—Mr. Posey's house is on a hill about a mile back from the ferry, and his windows are in full view of the rebel batteries. He is undoubtedly in concert with the rebels, but tangible proof is wanting. It is believed, however, he communicates intelligence to the enemy by means of mirrors and candles from his windows, the women of the house taking an active part in these proceedings. It is very certain the rebels know all that we are doing. If heavy guns are to be brought to the ferry, that house should be closed or the inmates sent away. The field artillery is now camped back of his house.

I have answered the word confidential in its literal sense. Do you wish me to consult with General Hooker and converse with him on the subject?

WASHINGTON CITY, *October* 28, 1861.

Lieut. Gen. WINFIELD SCOTT, *Commanding U. S. Army:*

GENERAL: I have the honor to introduce my acting aide-de-camp, Simon F. Barstow, esq., a gentleman whom you will find worthy of your favorable consideration; also the following views to offer, begging you to consider that the urgency of the case must be my excuse for these suggestions:

It is very clear to me that Kelley must be supported at once; his success is a blow in the very face of the rebels, and they will hardly remain quiet under it. He is brave to audacity, and, although exactly the right man in the right place, should be strengthened with a class of experience, and the very little caution required, which he does not possess.

For these reasons, referring you confidentially to the accompanying letters, I especially advise the calling up of Brigadier-General Benham, the Tenth and Thirteenth Ohio Volunteers, now in General Rosecrans' column, to support him. Benham being an excellent engineer officer, such a course will relieve the necessity of detaching one from the Army of the Potomac; and as he is on the best personal terms with Kelley, and not apparently on good terms with Rosecrans, I think the efficiency of the public service would also be promoted by the change. The troops to be detached from Rosecrans are of a peculiar class, adapted to the service in hand. I need them, and they can be readily replaced from Ohio; and as the rebels will undoubtedly, for the sake of carrying on their drafting and recruiting, endeavor to repossess themselves of Romney, I think no time should be lost in making these changes if they meet with your approval. Supported, as I have stated, by using a small corps of mounted men, and by free disbursement of secret-service money, Kelley can certainly keep himself apprised of any movements of the enemy, whether from the South, Lee's column, or the direction of Winchester. In the present state of the public mind in Upper Virginia and Western Maryland, growing out of our late defeat at Ball's Bluff, any reverse which might happen to Kelley would have a very bad effect on the success of our proposed recruitments.

Again, as the Government is now fairly committed, by the taking of Romney, either to a retreat or the reconstruction of the Baltimore and Ohio Railroad, can we fail as strategists to call our forces within supporting distance while our recruitments are going on? As the troops gather the reconstruction of the road takes place, and suddenly, and much before our enemies expect it, this important avenue of supplies will not only be opened, but the Army of the Potomac, connected by rapid transportation with those of the West, re-enforced and strengthened.

Mr. Barstow will present to you my personal views on the subject of the letters to which I refer.

With the utmost regard, General, I have the honor to be, most respectfully, your obedient servant,

F. W. LANDER,
Brigadier-General, U. S. Volunteers.

HEADQUARTERS HOOKER'S DIVISION,
Six miles from Budd's Ferry, Md., October 29, 1861.

Brig. Gen. S. WILLIAMS,
Adjutant-General Army of the Potomac:

GENERAL: At 8 o'clock this evening I received your communication dated the 28th instant,* directing me to throw up, during the night, if practicable, earthworks to protect the two 20-pounder Parrott guns while opening fire upon the rebel steamer Page. After consultation with Captain Williamson, I informed Captain Craven that the steamer had not been visible from this side of the river since the arrival of our batteries except for a few hours directly on their reaching here. She is up the river, and owing to a bend in it and the high banks make her perfectly safe from any fire we may deliver either on land or water. Indeed, the tops of the smoke pipes cannot be seen from an elevated position behind this bank. The tops of most of the schooners lying with her are scarcely perceptible.

---

* Not found.

I shall to-morrow morning throw up the earth works at the point named. As it is sheltered by trees, it can be done as safely and with as much secrecy by day as night. I am to inform Captain Craven when the Page shows herself.

The enemy have been busy in establishing new batteries to-day, which in part confirms me in the opinion that they are still acting on the defensive. They have thrown a few shot to-day from the battery directly opposite to Budd's Ferry. To-morrow I intend to make an examination of the rebel works myself, and shall be able to make a more satisfactory report concerning them. I had hoped that ere this my information respecting the rebel force would have enabled me to suggest the expediency of having my command transferred across the river, either above or below these batteries. With my guns in position, I think the Page will not venture down the creek except at night.

I inclose the report of Captain Williamson's examination of the bank of the river at or near Indian Point.

The Posey trial is not yet concluded; more arrests have been made.

Very respectfully,

JOSEPH HOOKER,
Brigadier-General, Commanding Division.

HEADQUARTERS DEPARTMENT OF PENNSYLVANIA,
Baltimore, Md., October 29, 1861.

J. CRAWFORD NEILSON,
Glenville, Harford County, Maryland :

SIR : I have just received your letter of the 28th. We have no Merrill rifles, and, as I said to you, the Government prefers to rely for the safety of Maryland on the military corps regularly enlisted into the service of the United States. There are some 6,000 Maryland troops now organized, and there will be an addition of at least 2,000 to this number before the 1st of December. They are ready to uphold the Government against all adversaries. Could we rely on the gentlemen in whose hands you propose to place arms for support under all circumstances ? Suppose a Confederate army should succeed in crossing the Potomac into this State, would they not be as likely to go over to it as to co-operate in repelling it as a hostile invasion? In other words, would they not be disposed to welcome the invaders as friends rather than to resist them as enemies ? Would the gentlemen referred to be willing to take the oath of allegiance prescribed by Congress, a copy of which I annex ? Would you take the oath yourself? You will not understand me as desiring to inquire into your political opinions, but as you have asked the Government to furnish you and your neighbors with arms, I am naturally anxious to be assured that the conditions on which such applications are granted under any circumstances would be complied with. I should be very sorry to have it supposed that the inquiries I have made imply any doubt of the patriotism of yourself or your neighbors. They are not, I assure you, so intended. But in this most unnatural conflict I have found among those for whom I have always had the sincerest respect opinions which seemed to me utterly irreconcilable with what I regard as the clearest obligations of duty as citizens.

It would be a most happy thing for Maryland and for the whole Union if the 5,000 cavalry which you say can be furnished could be rallied now in defense of the Government. The appearance of such a body of men on the north bank of the Potomac—the property-holders, I may say the *élite* of the State—ready to sacrifice their lives in defense of her soil and to aid in putting down rebellion, would, I have no doubt, have a moral influence on both sides of the present line of conflict which would do much to bring the war to a speedy conclusion. In this result no one would rejoice more than myself. But when I witness the active movements at this moment to embarrass the Government, misrepresent its motives, and compel it to disarm, in order that the enemy at its door may the more effectually overthrow it, I confess I must come back to the conclusion that, until a better feeling prevails, the preservation of Maryland to the Union (and without her the Union could not exist) cannot be safely left to herself. I trust the time is not far distant when it may, and when my occupation will be gone.

I am, very respectfully, yours,

JOHN A. DIX,
Major-General.

HEADQUARTERS HOOKER'S DIVISION,
Six miles from Budd's Ferry, Md., October 30, 1861.

Brig. Gen. S. WILLIAMS,
Adjutant-General Army of the Potomac:

GENERAL: I have just returned from Budd's Ferry, where I have been to examine the enemy's defenses, and also, in company with Captain Williamson, to determine on the best point to throw up the earthwork which I was directed to do last night. Instead of establishing it on the line A, as was indicated, we are of opinion that it should be on the bank of the river, and about 70 yards north of Budd's house. The ground is favorable; it can be approached by the batteries under cover, and is on an angle of the enemy's main work, between the guns which are planted to range upstream and those to fire downstream. Some of their guns, however, are not confined by embrasures, but they are fewer in number. Another advantage in this location, it is three-fourths of a mile nearer to the object in view. It is directly across the river from the steamer Page. We could see about three-fourths of the length of her smoke-pipe and the greater part of her walking-beam. Her hull is entirely concealed from view; near to her, but higher up the stream, are two schooners, indicating that the stream is not navigable much above that point. The steamer may be able to move a little higher up or down the river, but in neither case will it improve her anchorage, as from the nature of the ground she is as much concealed as she can be. She presents a small object to strike at our distance, but it is practicable, and I have given directions for the work to be done to-night. Captain Williamson is on the ground to commence work soon after dark. It is to be merely a shelter for the men and guns. Even if it should not be wanted against the Page at her present anchorage, it may some time be of service when she leaves it, if she ever does. I omitted to state in my report of yesterday that I have no 20-pounder Parrott guns, the largest caliber being 10-pounders, of which I have eight. Lieutenant-Colonel Getty informs me that the rebels have one 30-pounder rifle piece and three of smaller caliber; the former is supposed to be the one captured at Bull Run.

The rebels are engaged in establishing new batteries, and are busy all night long in hammering, chopping, sawing, and driving on heavy timber. From my examination to-day, I am satisfied that it will require an immense expenditure of time, labor, and material to silence the batteries now erected by the rebels to dispute the navigation of the Potomac at this point, and, if my opinion was asked, would not advise it. Directly above the main work of the enemy, that at Quantico, is high ground on the edge of the river, which could be readily taken possession of, and in one night, with the necessary supply of intrenching tools, could be put in condition of defense against three times my number which commands their batteries, and with field artillery would compel them to abandon their guns the first day we opened fire on them. With these means at our disposal, the Navy, and a plenty of scows, my command can be transferred to that side of the river very quietly any night. I can see no other speedy and successful mode of opening the navigation of the Potomac and keeping it open. I am aware of the presence of large bodies of troops in the neighborhood, but they need not know it until the next morning, when it will be too late. If my command is insufficient, which I do not believe, sufficient force is close at hand, with water communication, to place the result beyond peradventure. I write of this with great confidence, for the reason that I feel no doubt of its absolute and complete success.

The enemy were discharging their guns more or less almost every hour during the day without any apparent object—certainly with no effect. The steamer arrived to-day, and will be discharged so as to return to-morrow. I inclose my morning report of yesterday, which is the first one I have been able to prepare since my arrival.

I have dispatched a messenger to the telegraph people, to inform them of the direction to run the wires to my camp.

I have continued to address all my communications to Brig. Gen. S. Williams. If this is incorrect, please inform me.

Very respectfully,

JOSEPH HOOKER,
Brigadier-General, Commanding Division.

HEADQUARTERS ARMY, *October* 30, 1861.
General ROSECRANS, U. S. A., *Camp Tompkins, W. Va.:*

General Scott says detach Brigadier-General Benham and his brigade to Romney, to report to General Kelley, as soon as possible.

E. D. TOWNSEND,
Assistant Adjutant-General.

WASHINGTON, *October* 31, 1861.
General ROSECRANS, *Camp Tompkins, W. Va.:*

Telegram [of] T. T. Eckert was right, but is countermanded, as you desire. Object is to re-enforce Kelley at Romney as soon as possible. If you can spare troops to do it, send them.

E. D. TOWNSEND,
Assistant Adjutant-General.

HEADQUARTERS HOOKER'S DIVISION,
Camp Baker, Lower Potomac, Maryland, October 31, 1861.

Brig. Gen. S. WILLIAMS,
  Adjutant-General, Army of the Potomac:

GENERAL: This afternoon Lieutenant-Colonel Getty introduced himself through two of his 10-pounder Parrott guns to the rebel steamer Page. She lay at her moorings, as reported by me on yesterday. Apparently the enemy were not apprised of the presence of our battery until we commenced fire. The first shot seemed to inform them of our object, for the steamer instantly fired up and moved about 100 yards higher up the river, without improving her anchorage. She kept up steam until after we had ceased firing. She must have been nearly 2 miles distant, for our guns could only reach her at an angle of 8° or 9°. For line shooting the practice was excellent, and I think established this fact, that it would be extremely hazardous for her to venture out of the river by daylight while our guns are in their present position, for in so doing, in order to pass into the channel of the Potomac, she would have to approach us from one-half to three-fourths of a mile.

The enemy was at work at two of their batteries while our firing was kept up, but with no effect. As it was intended by the major-general commanding that vessels of the fleet should be in the vicinity at the time, I sent word to Commodore Craven of my intention, and he promptly responded by dispatching three or four vessels to co-operate in case an opportunity presented itself. I had previously informed him that with the caliber of my guns I looked for no important result from the experiment.

I have directed one company of the Indiana cavalry to be in readiness to move at daylight to-morrow morning, under the guidance of Capt. P. S. Dennis, for the concealed arms. They will probably be absent three days.

I desire to call the attention of the major-general commanding to the mode in which rations are forwarded to my command. They are incomplete. Of the 60,000 rations forwarded by steamer, I find by an examination of the invoices no beans or potatoes included. These are of the regular issues; of the extra issues, no molasses. These omissions were of frequent occurrence while I was at Camp Union.

Very respectfully, &c.,

JOSEPH HOOKER,
Brigadier-General, Commanding Division.

HEADQUARTERS ARMY OF THE POTOMAC,
Washington, October 31, 1861.

Brig. Gen. J. HOOKER, *Commanding Division:*

GENERAL: The major-general commanding has received your letter of yesterday. He desires that I should communicate to you his approval of the change of location suggested for the earthworks.

The general will take into serious consideration your proposition as to the occupancy of the high ground above the main works of the enemy at Quantico. The scheme will involve considerable additions to your force, and before coming to a final determination upon the subject the general would be glad to have full information as to the ground, the approaches, the character of landing; in fine, upon every material point relating to the matter.

Very respectfully, your obedient servant,

S. WILLIAMS,
Assistant Adjutant-General.

Abstract from return of the Department of Western Virginia, Brigadier-General Rosecrans, U. S. Army, commanding, for October, 1861.

Stations.	Commands.	Present for duty.		Aggregate present and absent.	Pieces of field artillery.
		Officers.	Men.		
Cheat Mountain, Elk Water, and Beverly.	Reynolds' brigade	377	10,421	12,382	26
Grafton, and Baltimore and Ohio Railroad.	District of Grafton (Kelley)	109	2,804	3,715	6
Kanawha Valley	Cox's (Kanawha Brigade)	123	2,842	3,970	5
Camp McNeil, near Gauley Bridge.	Benham's brigade.	72	2,021	2,929	*4
Camp Anderson	McCook's brigade.	75	1,676	2,447	.....
Camp Ewing	Schenck's brigade	72	2,005	2,548	.....
Summersville	Crook's command	16	447	1,129	.....
Buckhannon	Fifth Ohio Infantry (Dunning)	25	520	771	.....
Sutton	Thirtieth Ohio Infantry (Jones)	.....	.....	444	.....
Red House	Thirty-fourth Ohio Infantry (Piatt)	28	734	977	.....
Camp Montgomery	Thirty-seventh Ohio Infantry (Siber)	31	624	824	.....
Near Charleston	Forty-fourth Ohio Infantry (Gilbert)	32	728	994	.....
Cross-Lanes	Forty-seventh Ohio Infantry (Elliott)	.....	.....	432	.....
Camp Carlile	First [West] Virginia Infantry	.....	.....	†880	.....
Ceredo	Zeigler's command‡ (six regiments)	.....	.....	†2,810	.....
Clarksburg	Garrison	3	139	179	*4
Do	First [West] Virginia Cavalry	.....	.....	†600	.....
Parkersburg	Second [West] Virginia Cavalry	27	520	†640	.....
	Totals	990	25,481	38,671	45

* Mountain howitzers.
† Not fully organized.
‡ Fifth, Eighth, Ninth, Tenth, Eleventh, and Twelfth [West] Virginia Regiments.

HEADQUARTERS HOOKER'S DIVISION,
Camp Baker, Lower Potomac, Maryland, November 1, 1861.

Brig. Gen. S. WILLIAMS,
Adjutant-General, Army of the Potomac:

GENERAL: I very much regret to find myself involved in a correspondence on the subject of ambulances, and I regret still more that the complaint of the commander of the Second Brigade and of his brigade surgeon was not transmitted through the channel prescribed by the Regulations of the Army, or, if that was sanctioned, that it was not referred to me for explanation before the major-general commanding and the medical director had deemed it proper to give it their action; and, waiving all considerations of courtesy, I regret more than all to find two officers of my command, holding high and responsible positions, showing so little concern for the efficiency and welfare of the command to which they are assigned as to seek by artifice and unfairness to destroy one and disregard the other. In the mode and substance of their correspondence they have practiced both.

My order requiring all ambulances except one to a regiment to be placed in depot has been before you. The reasons for its issuance I have stated in the presence of both of those officers, and I will now state them again.

During the march from Good Hope I found them overloaded with lazy soldiers, officers, and women's trunks and knapsacks to such an extent as to lead me to fear that if they reached camp at all, it would be with crippled horses and broken-down ambulances, and in consequence I repeatedly ordered the men out of them, some of whom would heed me and others would not. With such an undisciplined crowd, with no assistance from a single officer of the command, I abandoned my purpose and passed on to camp. When the troops reached their destination I directed the ambulances to be put in depot, with instructions to Surgeon Bell to receive them and to report to me their condition, which is herewith respectfully inclosed. The First Brigade had but one ambulance to a regiment to accompany them, and those they retain.

When you reflect that the Second Brigade had but 28 miles to march, you will be able to form a just appreciation of the perils to which the ambulance train was exposed. Had the march been double that distance, I question if I should have had one serviceable ambulance among them remaining.

Among new troops, as you doubtless know, there is a feeling of destructiveness towards everything belonging to the Government, and I must say that I never saw it more fully expressed than during my late march. This is one of the outrages committed by some portions of my command, as you will be informed in due time. In some regiments there appears to be a total absence of anything like authority. The officers are on the same footing with the men, and I have yet to receive the first report from any officer of the outrages and depredations committed by their men.

For these reasons I have felt it to be my duty as well as interest to protect and preserve the public property necessary to the wants of my command. I have placed the ambulance train where I can see it, and given directions for ambulances to be furnished when they are required for the sick, and for no other purpose. If they cannot be cared for on the march, they will not be in camp. On the slightest pretext a line of them will be established on the road between here and Washington, and that will be the end of them. If a regiment marches, of course they will be provided, for the most remote camp is not more than one and a half hours' drive from where they are collected. General Sickles calls this "field service"; so was his camp at Good Hope just as much. But I have no inclination to reply to any portion of his letter. I return it with a trace of the camp, and the general will be able to form his own opinion of its fairness or unfairness.

In my official intercourse with veteran politicians suddenly raised to high military rank, I have found it necessary to observe their correspondence with especial circumspection.

If with these facts before the major-general commanding it is his wish that the ambulances should be put in the hands of the Second Brigade, I request that you will inform me.

Very respectfully,

JOSEPH HOOKER,
Brigadier-General, Commanding Division.

HEADQUARTERS HOOKER'S DIVISION,
Camp Baker, Lower Potomac, Maryland, November 1, 1861.

Brig. Gen. S. WILLIAMS,
Adjutant-General, Army of the Potomac:

GENERAL: Of the events of to-day the most deserving of mention are the exercises of the battery. Seven shots were fired from a section of Battery A, at an elevation of 13° and 14°. The fourth shot is supposed to have taken effect on the steamer. With our small pieces I think it advisable to discontinue the practice, and only permitted it to enable some of the young officers with the batteries to have a little practice.

Firing was kept up at long intervals during the day from the rebel batteries. Oyster boats continue to pass up and down in safety. The random shooting of the enemy renders it an adventure of comparative safety. My observation is that they are as likely to be struck by lightning as by the rebel shot.

The company dispatched to search for the concealed arms left at daylight.

Very respectfully,

JOSEPH HOOKER,
Brigadier-General, Commanding Division.

HDQRS. DEPT. OF HARPER'S FERRY AND CUMBERLAND,
Camp Keys, Romney, Va., November 1, 1861.

Lieut. Gen. WINFIELD SCOTT,
Commanding Army of the United States, Washington, D. C.:

DEAR SIR: Inclosed you will find proclamation of the general to the people of Hampshire County and the Upper Potomac. I am happy to inform you that it is effecting great good among the people. The Union sentiment of this county is rapidly developing itself, and many of the citizens are coming in and availing themselves of the terms of the proclamation. The general being a Virginian himself, and a personal acquaintance of many of the inhabitants, is enabled to exercise a salutary influence over them. The general arrived from New Creek this evening, and I am sorry to say is not very well. I hope he will be better in a day or two.

And am, with great respect, yours, &c.,

BENJ. F. HAWKES,
Captain, and Assistant Adjutant-General.

[Inclosure.]

To the People of Hampshire County and the Upper Potomac:

My object in addressing you is to give you assurance that I come among you, not for the purpose of destroying you, but for your protection in all your rights—civil, social, and political. I am here, backed by the forces of the United States, to protect you in the rights of property as well as person, so long as you are peaceful citizens and loyal to the Government of the United States, the flag of which has so long and so well protected you, and under the folds of which you have lived long, happily, and prosperously. But if you attempt to carry on a guerrilla warfare against my troops, by attacking my wagon trains or messengers, or shooting my guards or pickets, you will be considered as enemies of your country, and treated accordingly. I shall put as few restrictions upon the ordinary business of the people as possible, and will give as free ingress and egress to and from Romney as the safety of my troops will admit. Citizens who have fled, under an erroneous belief that they will be imprisoned or killed, are invited to return to their homes and families, assured that they shall be protected whenever they give evidence that they will be loyal, peaceful, and quiet citizens. Every reasonable facility will be given the people to seek a market on the railroad for their surplus produce, and to obtain supplies of merchandise, groceries, &c. All persons who have taken up arms against the Government are hereby required to lay them down, return to their homes, and take an oath of allegiance to support the Government of the United States. By so doing they will receive all the protection due to an American citizen.

B. F. KELLEY, *Brigadier-General.*
ROMNEY, VA., *October* 28, 1861.

WHEELING, *November* 1, 1861.
General ROSECRANS:

Can't you spare General Benham's brigade to assist General Kelley in holding his position at Romney and enable him to advance? It is of great importance at this time. A quick movement in the direction at this time might enable them, with Reynolds, to bag all the rebels on Cheat Mountain.

F. H. PEIRPOINT.

GENERAL ORDERS, }   WAR DEP'T, ADJT. GEN.'S OFFICE,
No. 94.   }   *Washington, November* 1, 1861.

The following order from the President of the United States, announcing the retirement from active command of the honored veteran Lieut. Gen. Winfield Scott will be read by the Army with profound regret:

EXECUTIVE MANSION,
Washington, November 1, 1861.

On the 1st day of November, A. D. 1861, upon his own application to the President of the United States, Brevet Lieut. Gen. Winfield Scott is ordered to be placed, and hereby is placed, upon the list of retired officers of the Army of the United States, without reduction in his current pay, subsistence, or allowances.

The American people will hear with sadness and deep emotion that General Scott has withdrawn from the active control of the Army, while the President and a unanimous Cabinet express their own and the nation's sympathy in his personal affliction, and their profound sense of the important public services rendered by him to his country during his long and brilliant career, among which will ever be gratefully distinguished his faithful devotion to the Constitution, the Union, and the Flag, when assailed by parricidal rebellion.

ABRAHAM LINCOLN.

The President is pleased to direct that Maj. Gen. George B. McClellan assume the command of the Army of the United States. The headquarters of the Army will be established in the city of Washington. All communications intended for the Commanding General will hereafter be addressed direct to the Adjutant-General. The duplicate returns, orders, and other papers, heretofore sent to the assistant adjutant-general, headquarters of the Army, will be discontinued.

By order of the Secretary of War:
L. THOMAS, *Adjutant-General.*

HEADQUARTERS HOOKER'S DIVISION,
Camp Baker, Lower Potomac, Maryland, November 3, 1861.
Brig. Gen. S. WILLIAMS, *Asst. Adjt. Gen. of the Army:*

GENERAL: I have to acknowledge three communications from the headquarters of the Army of the 2d instant.* I had previously given directions for four companies of the Indiana cavalry to hold themselves in readiness to march to various points in the Peninsula at which the polls will be opened on the 6th instant, in order to preserve quiet and good order, and to suppress any attempt at coercion or intimidation on the part of the secession leaders. I had considered this force, in connection with the regiments stationed at Pomonkey, Hilltop, and Port Tobacco, sufficient to accomplish this object throughout the length and breadth of Lower Maryland. A solitary troop of cavalry can march without molestation and execute any order with which it may be charged through Southern Maryland. The population is sparse at best, but at the present time no doubt but that a majority of the young men of the country are with the rebel troops and those remaining are filled with terror. They have no arms and no heart for resistance, however much they may desire it.

The vote polled will be a very small one in the whole district lying south of Bladensburg. Perhaps I am at fault in not having communicated this information earlier. Of parties who have returned from Virginia to influence the election I have heard of but one, and he a rebel officer. I heard of him at Pomonkey, and sent for him at once, and my scouts are still in his pursuit. By my last advices he was concealed in the neighborhood of Good Hope.

The most noisy resident rebel is Perry Davis, a tavern-keeper at Port Tobacco, and the secession candidate for the legislature. I learn he has been stumping the district and filling the heads of his listeners with his secession heresies. I shall give directions for him to be arrested to-day and forwarded to me.

I am informed that a secession barbecue will be given at what is called White Horse Tavern on election day, at which I shall take the liberty to invite a full company of Indiana cavalry.

Lieutenant-Colonel Getty informs me by report to-day that a schooner passed down under sail without injury, although thirty-two shots were fired at her from seven batteries. These batteries are established along the bank of the river, commencing at Quantico and extending to Sandy Point. Most of the guns are planted to throw shot diagonally across the river.

Your instructions in regard to the telegraphic people had been anticipated. I am informed that the line will be completed to-morrow or next day, should the weather continue favorable.

Very respectfully, your obedient servant,

JOSEPH HOOKER,
Brigadier-General, Commanding Division.

HEADQUARTERS HOOKER'S DIVISION,
Camp Baker, Lower Potomac, Maryland, November 3, 1861.
Brig. Gen. S. WILLIAMS, *Adjt. Gen., Army of the Potomac:*

I have this moment received your communication of the 30th ultimo.* In answer, I know of no other mode by which the steamer Page can be

---

* Not found.

destroyed from this shore except by the use of mortars. If the Major-General Commanding should determine on having mortars forwarded, be pleased to advise me as early as convenient, that the beds may be in readiness to receive them on their arrival.

The work at Indian Head will be prosecuted at once.

Very respectfully,

JOSEPH HOOKER,
Brigadier-General, Commanding Division.

HEADQUARTERS DEPARTMENT OF PENNSYLVANIA,
Baltimore, Md., November 4, 1861.

Col. H. E. PAINE,
Commanding Fourth Regiment Wisconsin Volunteers:

COLONEL: You will embark this afternoon with your regiment, Captain Nims' company Massachusetts light artillery, and Captain Richards' company of cavalry, with rations for fifteen days, proceed to the Wicomico River, on the Eastern Shore of Maryland, and land at White Haven, in Somerset County, as early as possible on Tuesday morning. You will immediately take up your line of march to Princess Anne, in the same county, and thence to Snow Hill, in Worcester County, so as to reach there by Tuesday night and encamp. Should it be deemed advisable, on consulting with the principal Union men of Princess Anne and Snow Hill, you will march at the earliest hour possible on Wednesday morning to Newtown, on the south side of Pocomoke River, if you can reach there by 11 o'clock, or if on consultation with the leading Union men at Princess Anne it is thought advisable that you should march to Shelltown or Newtown on Tuesday in preference to Snow Hill, you may do so; but you will in either case have your whole force at Snow Hill on Thursday, and there await my further orders.

The object of the expedition is to give protection to the Union men of Somerset and Worcester Counties, and to prevent the migration or importation of voters from Accomac and Northampton Counties, in Virginia, or elsewhere, with a view to carry the election of the 6th instant by spurious votes. A further object is to aid the United States marshal and his deputies in putting down any open demonstration of hostility to the Government or resistance to its authority. While you will in every proper mode employ the force under your command in effecting these objects, you will see that loyal and peaceable citizens are not molested or interfered with in any manner whatever. Your force is intended for their protection. You will see that it is not perverted by the misconduct of any one under your command to their annoyance. By the fifty-second article of the rules and articles of war any officer or soldier who quits his post to plunder or pillage subjects himself to the penalty of death. If any man under your command so far forgets what is due to himself, his comrades, or his country as to commit any outrage on the person or property of any citizen, you will put him in irons and send him back to these headquarters, that he may be punished, and no longer dishonor his associates and the profession of arms by his presence among you.

In your intercourse with the inhabitants you will do all in your power to correct misapprehension in regard to the intentions of the Government in the war which has been forced on it. Multitudes are laboring under delusions, the fruit of misrepresentations and falsehood, which you may do much to dispel. Our mission is to uphold the Government against treasonable attempts to subvert it. We wage no war with individuals who are pursuing their peaceable occupations, but with those who are in arms against the United States and those who encourage or aid them in their treason. If any such persons come within your reach you will take them into custody, and send them by the earliest opportunity to Fort McHenry. You will also take into custody in like manner any person who may have come from Virginia or elsewhere beyond the limits of Maryland, and who may be shown to you to have voted or attempted to vote in Somerset or Worcester Counties.

You will take especial care not to interfere in any manner with persons held to servitude, and in order that there may be no cause for misrepresentation or cavil, you will not receive or allow any negro to come within your lines.

Very respectfully, your obedient servant,

JOHN A. DIX,
Major-General, Commanding.

HEADQUARTERS HOOKER'S DIVISION,
Camp Baker, Lower Potomac, Maryland, November 4, 1861.

Brig. Gen. S. WILLIAMS,
Assistant Adjutant-General, Army of the Potomac:

The rebels have been busy at work to-day on the steamer Page. From this circumstance it is inferred that she suffered some injury from our shot, though that is not conclusive. Additional troops are constantly arriving, so that now in point of numbers they exceed my own. I can see no indications that warrant me in supposing that they will attempt to cross the Potomac. I regret their policy, for I shall be in much better condition to engage them on my own ground than on theirs. Up to this time I have not been able to discover their batteries south of Sandy Point. All is quiet on both sides of the river.

I have concluded to move to a point nearer to the shore of the Potomac, where my presence is most required, which will render it necessary to run the telegraph wire about 5 miles farther than I had at first proposed. It will probably be completed to-morrow.

Very respectfully,

JOSEPH HOOKER,
Brigadier-General, Commanding Division.

HEADQUARTERS HOOKER'S DIVISION,
Camp Baker, Lower Potomac, Maryland, November 5, 1861.

Brig. Gen. S. WILLIAMS,
Adjutant-General, Army of the Potomac:

GENERAL: Intelligence has been received by me that the force sent out to search for concealed arms in the vicinity of Charlotte Hall, under the guidance of Captain Dennis, has been unsuccessful. They extended their search far beyond my instructions, and to-night are at Port Tobacco on their return. As no available cavalry remained in camp for that purpose, I have directed the company to proceed to Allen Fresh, a precinct of some importance, and to remain there until after the polls are closed to-morrow, and then to return to camp. Previous to this I had dispatched four companies of the Indiana cavalry as follows: One to White Horse Tavern and Piscataway, one to Leonardtown, one to Trappe, and one to Pleasant Hill. They will return the day after election.

We have no news to report in our front. A few shots were fired by the rebels in the course of the day, but for what object is not apparent.

I must call the attention of the Major-General Commanding to the condition of our land communication with the city. It was reported to me to-day that not less than twenty of my teams are on the road struggling to work their way through the mud, some of the wagons broken and the teams worried and exhausted. How they came there is more than I know; certainly without my authority or knowledge. If this should be continued, I shall not have a serviceable team in my train, nor will the depot quartermaster in Washington if he permits his teams to be put on the road.

To-morrow orders will be issued forbidding all land communication with the city and vicinity except on horseback, and I request that the Quartermaster's Department may be informed of this circumstance, in order that proper facilities may be extended to my command by means of steamer. Is it not advisable to have regular days appointed for her to make her trips?

We have now nearly if not quite exhausted this district for 30 miles around of all supplies except the new crop of corn, which cannot be fed to animals safely at present, and it will therefore be an easy problem to determine what amount of transportation will be required for our supplies. I trust that the proper Departments may speedily give this subject their attention.

I have discovered that the transportation with which the Second Brigade moved to this point is not regularly assigned to it, but that the greater part of the wagons belong to the general train. I have directed them to be returned, and for requisitions to be sent in at once to provide each regiment with fourteen wagons, one to each company, one to the field and staff, and three to transport and shelter the 60,000 rounds of ammunition required to be kept on hand for each regiment. This I learn is in conformity with the rules of the Department. I hope that orders may be given for them to be provided without delay. As soon as they are received, and understanding from my instructions that it is the design of the Major-General, I propose to post my brigades in the order of battle along the shore of the Potomac and just beyond the reach of the rebel batteries, with the exception of one regiment, which is to locate in the vicinity of the landing on Mattawoman Creek. This will require less hauling for the supply of the division than posted as it now is. This arrangement will remove the regiment and battery from Hill-top and also from Port Tobacco, which, now that the election is over and the supplies nearly exhausted, are not needed there. The flotilla above and below protects the landing points on our wings.

The line of telegraph will be completed to-morrow, but from some cause the person in charge informs me that it is not in working order. Whether the wires have been cut or trees fallen across it will soon be determined, as the party will follow the line on their return. Up to the time of writing I have heard nothing from Brigadier-General Sykes.

Very respectfully, your obedient servant,

JOSEPH HOOKER,
Brigadier-General, Commanding Division.

HDQRS. DEPT. OF HARPER'S FERRY AND CUMBERLAND,
Camp Keys, Romney, Va., November 6, 1861.
Maj. Gen. GEORGE B. MCCLELLAN,
Commanding the Armies of the United States, Washington, D. C.:

GENERAL: I reported to you by telegram my strength, position, &c. By reference to the map you will see at a glance the importance of holding this place. It is the key to the valley of the upper branches of the Potomac, and commands the counties of Hampshire, Hardy, Pendleton, and Highland, all of which would have been Union counties long since if the Federal troops could have been near them to protect them. The Baltimore and Ohio Railroad forms almost a semicircle around this place, it being from 16 to 28 miles from this place to the two extreme points of the arc, comprising a distance of about 60 miles of the line of the road. From here to Winchester it is 40 miles, by the Northwestern turnpike, a very fine road. From here to Monterey, up the valley of South Branch, is about 70 miles, also a good road. Now, in order to afford protection to the Union population in this valley, as well as to protect the Baltimore and Ohio road, a force equal to that which I now have should be wintered here; and should you desire to strike an offensive blow either on Winchester or Monterey, this is the position to concentrate the force. If I had 8,000 or 10,000 men I could go up this valley and fall on the rear of the rebel forces at Monterey and Greenbrier, and cut off their supplies, and utterly destroy their whole force now in the mountains in front of General Reynolds.

The Baltimore and Ohio Railroad Company are now reconstructing their bridges that the rebels have destroyed over the North Branch and over Patterson's Creek, east of Cumberland, so that in a few days the company will be enabled to run their trains to Green Spring, and distant from here only 16 miles, and to which point I have commenced to-day to construct a telegraph line, which will be done in three or four days. From that point east to a point opposite Hancock, Md., the road can be protected with a small force, if vigilant. So you will see that the Baltimore and Ohio Railroad can be opened for trade, travel, and the use of the Government within a few days if there can be a sufficient force at Harper's Ferry and Martinsburg to force the rebels back from its line.

Respectfully, General, your obedient servant,
B. F. KELLEY,
Brigadier-General, Commanding.

CUMBERLAND, *November 7, 1861—10 a. m.*
A. V. COLBURN, *Assistant Adjutant-General:*

My force consists of Second Virginia, Sixth Ohio, Third Ohio, and Seventh Indiana, and dismounted battery at Elk Water, under General Dumont; Ninth Indiana, Twenty-fourth Ohio, Twenty-fifth Ohio, Thirty-second Ohio, and dismounted battery on Cheat Mountain, under General Milroy; Howe's battery, Fourth Artillery, one company cavalry, and one company infantry at Beverly, under Colonel Bosley; Thirteenth, Fourteenth, Fifteenth, and Seventeenth Indiana, with Loomis' battery, at Huttonsville, my headquarters; Robinson's Ohio cavalry, distributed; Bracken's Indiana cavalry, resting. Eight regiments, the two dismounted batteries, one company cavalry, and one mounted battery are amply sufficient to hold these posts this winter.

J. J. REYNOLDS,
Brigadier-General.

HEADQUARTERS HOOKER'S DIVISION,
Camp Baker, Lower Potomac, Maryland, November 7, 1861.

Brig. Gen. S. WILLIAMS,
Assistant Adjutant-General, Army of the Potomac:

My pickets report to me that the rebel steamer Page made her escape at 3 o'clock this morning. The wind was blowing fiercely when she left, and it was so dark that any effort to check her with our battery would have been ineffectual. She passed to the southward, probably to Aquia Creek. Of the whereabouts of the flotilla during this time I am not informed. It is also reported to me that the troops on the opposite side of the river are withdrawing, and that the movement commenced on yesterday. They are moving to the south likewise.

I have received reports from several of the precincts at which the election was held yesterday. So far as heard from it passed off quietly, and a much larger Union vote was polled than anticipated. One arrest was made at Port Tobacco, but after an examination of the case I found that he had been arrested on suspicion only. Finding no evidence against him, he was discharged.

I have directed all the ambulances and wagons belonging to the general depot to be returned, including those which I had temporarily retained for the use of Lieutenant-Colonel Getty's command. Several regiments of the Second Brigade have remaining but three wagons, and it is out of question for that number to do the necessary hauling for the regiment. Lieutenant-Colonel Getty also informs me that he requires six additional wagons, and I concur with him. It is an ill-advised economy to require two or three teams to do the work of six or eight.

I have given directions for the brigade surgeons to select some central point for the establishment of brigade hospitals, and if they should not be able to find suitable structures for their accommodation, I propose to put up log houses for that purpose. It requires but little time to do it, and it is better for the men to have employment than to be idle. The only difficulty I apprehend in their construction will be to find suitable timber for the roofing. The experience of the last week has satisfied me that the sick require something more than canvas to shelter them from the storms. As soon as the brigade hospitals are established I intend to break up those at Camp Union and Good Hope, and have the invalids transferred to them. I also propose to arrest the practice of sending them from here to Washington. I know of no reason why the sick cannot be as well cared for here as elsewhere, and in that opinion I am sustained by the senior medical officer of the division. Hereafter I intend to locate my encampments in the edge of the forests, when it can be done without the sacrifice of position, as they will afford shelter and protection to the tents, and will enable my command to supply themselves with wood without purchase. I can see no good reason for not supplying ourselves with fuel when we can help ourselves to it. Some regiments have made no purchase of this article since their arrival here.

I wish to call the attention of the Major-General Commanding that I have twice made a requisition for the work on Bayonet Exercises—once while at Camp Union, and again since I reached this camp. Two of the regiments in my old brigade are proficient in that drill, and I desire to have them all; not that battles are often decided by the use of that weapon, but it inspires men with confidence in the use of their pieces in all service they may be called on to render. It is estimated that one man who is skilled in this exercise is equal to seven who are not. I deem it of great importance to impress on our soldiers this feeling of superiority at all times, and particularly when the remembrance of our reverses at Bull Run and Ball's Bluff are so vividly before them. They only consider the result, without reflecting whether those unfortunate fields proceeded from the absence of generalship on the field or the character and conduct of those engaged. The answer returned to my requests has been that the work would be furnished me as soon as printed. This was eight weeks since.

The steamer arrived at noon to-day, and will be discharged as soon as possible.

Who will be assigned as operator at this end of the wires?

Have received your communication of the 5th instant, authorizing me to employ a person conditionally to collect information.

Very respectfully,

JOSEPH HOOKER,
Brigadier-General, Commanding Division.

P. S.—I am just informed that my pickets were in error in regard to the departure of the steamer Page. She is still at her moorings in Quantico Creek.

HEADQUARTERS HOOKER'S DIVISION,
Camp Baker, Lower Potomac, Maryland, November 8, 1861.
Brig. Gen. S. WILLIAMS,
Assistant Adjutant-General, Army of the Potomac:

This has been another day of uninterrupted quiet on both sides of the river. All appearances indicate that the rebel force has been considerably reduced within the last few days. They appear to be apprehensive of our crossing the river. For two nights in succession we have heard the long-roll about midnight. Last night it was occasioned by the seizure of some boats along the shore of the Potomac by the First Regiment Massachusetts Volunteers, and the removal of them to the Mattawoman Creek, where they could be used in discharging the steamer.

I have not been able to complete my arrangements to ascertain in what force the rebels are, but hope to be able to accomplish it soon.

All my cavalry have returned from the posts to which they were assigned on election day, and complied with their instructions to my satisfaction. The company ordered to Leonardtown did not reach their destination in time to be present while the polls were open, in consequence of having been lost, but did good service in making rapid and orderly marches through the settled districts of the Peninsula. This cavalry corps, with good arms and a little training, might be of great service, for it is filled with excellent men. I felt a little apprehension in dispatching them in troops, beyond supporting distance, with no arms of any account but their sabers, and they not skilled in the use of those. They had no disturbance with any one, and their presence at the polls seemed to have given satisfaction to the citizens everywhere.

Perry Davis, the secession candidate for the legislature, was arrested at Port Tobacco and brought in to me for making treasonable speeches during the canvass, but on his assuring me that he made them while running for office in a secession district, and that in case of election, which was probable, he should vote against the ordinance for secession if an opportunity presented itself, I deemed it politic to give him his liberty. Besides, the election was over.

The First Brigade has established its hospitals, which will be able to accommodate all of our sick; and I have given directions for the hospital at Camp Union to be broken up. It has been a source of some annoyance to have my command so much scattered. Shall expect to be able to make a like disposition of Good Hope in a day or two. These remote establishments are alleged as a reason for unusual absence of both my officers and men.

Captain Williamson has returned.

The Second Brigade are gradually concentrating in the vicinity of Sandy Point. In addition to the reason assigned for this disposition yesterday, I may state that discipline is so lax in some of the regiments of that brigade that it is necessary for me to see them oftener than I have heretofore been able to do, and, further, the roads are becoming so muddy that it is necessary for me to reduce the hauling as much as practicable to spare the teams.

Very respectfully,

JOSEPH HOOKER,
Brigadier-General, Commanding Division.

CAMP GAULEY MOUNT, *November* 8, 1861.

Brig. Gen. H. W. BENHAM:

The following came to me in cipher to-day:

WASHINGTON, *November* 7, 1861.

Brigadier-General ROSECRANS, for BENHAM:

It was order of Scott for you to join Kelley at Romney with the two regiments named by you. Shumard not ordered. I think I was then to be put in charge of opening the Baltimore and Ohio Railroad. Am now wounded, and have no idea of my future destination. The report as to my promotion was a sand shell. Probably resign soon. The order is on its way.

F. W. LANDER.

W. S. ROSECRANS,
Brigadier-General, U. S. Army.

GENERAL ORDERS,   }   HEADQUARTERS OF THE ARMY,
No. 97.   }   *Adjt. Gen.'s Office, Washington, November* 9, 1861.

The following departments are formed from the present Departments of the West, Cumberland, and Ohio:

*   *   *   *   *   *   *

5. The Department of Western Virginia, to consist of that portion of Virginia included in the old Department of the Ohio,* to be commanded by Brig. Gen. W. S. Rosecrans, U. S. Army.

By order:

JULIUS P. GARESCHÉ,
Assistant Adjutant-General.

---

* Which was so much of the State as lay north of the Great Kanawha, north and west of the Greenbrier, and west of a line thence northward to the southwest corner of Maryland, &c. G. O. No. 19, War Department, May 9, 1861. See Vol. II, p. 633, of this series, and G. O. No. 80, p. 604, this volume.

HDQRS. FIRST REG'T MASSACHUSETTS VOLUNTEERS,
November 10, 1861—9 p. m.

GEORGE H. JOHNSTON, *Acting Assistant Adjutant-General:*

SIR: I make a report of the present condition of things on the other bank, mostly gained from the report of Lieutenant Candler, who has been down the river in a boat to-day. The upper battery, on the bluff above the anchorage of the Page, is growing each day, and men are seen constantly at work upon it. No guns are mounted. On the creeks near the water's edge are small breastworks, some apparently of sand bags. The siege guns of the point battery have been apparently removed. The two guns mounted *en barbette*, looking up the river, are still there. One of them is very heavy. It has been fired but once, and from the report and its general appearance it is judged to be a 10-inch columbiad. The battery is strongly palisaded in the rear and on the flanks. The middle battery is fast approaching completion, and is a formidable work. It mounts five guns at present. It is being finished with sand bags. The lower battery seems not to be intrenched. Four very heavy guns are there mounted *en barbette*.

Ten distinct lines of camp fires were seen to-night between Quantico Creek and Chopawamsic Creek. The plateau stretching out into the Potomac between the two points seems to be their main position, and their camps lie back from it in the wood between the two creeks.

Below the Chopawamsic, in a distance of 3 miles, are two regiments. Lieutenant Candler went near enough to-day to hail the lowest of them, and learned that it was the Fourth Alabama. He describes the colonel as being a fine-looking man, handsomely uniformed, and mounted on a large, black horse. He saw many cattle on the other shore opposite our position. Just about Quantico Creek is a camp on the other side of the hill, probably of light artillery or cavalry, judging from the number of horses which feed over the hill and the appearance of the men who watch them. Day before yesterday I saw there both gray and blue uniforms. We find many boats on the shore, some of them quite large. My orders are to bring away all that can easily be made serviceable and destroy the remainder. I would also mention that all along the front of the plateau between the two creeks the earth is freshly broken in several places—perhaps for rifle-pits, to resist an attempted landing. Upon the hill back of the lower battery is an earthwork for one gun. No gun mounted.

Yours, respectfully,

GEO. D. WELLS,
Lieutenant-Colonel, Commanding.

HEADQUARTERS HOOKER'S DIVISION,
Camp Baker, Lower Potomac, Maryland, November 11, 1861.

Brig. Gen. S. WILLIAMS,
Assistant Adjutant-General, Army of the Potomac:

Between 9 and 11 o'clock a. m. some of the rebel batteries were in active operation. Three schooners passed up the river under a six-knot breeze without the slightest injury, although thirty-seven heavy guns were discharged to dispute their passage. The crews seemed to entertain a just appreciation of the batteries, for they sailed along with as much unconcern as they would to enter New York Harbor. They do fire wretchedly. Whether it is owing to the projectiles or to the guns I am not informed. Several of the pieces are rifled, but they seem to throw more wildly, if possible, than the smooth bores. From what was witnessed to-day and on previous occasions, I am forced to the conclusion that the rebel batteries in this vicinity should not be a terror to any one.

The balloon was inflated about 8 o'clock p. m.; but whether an ascension was made or not I am not advised. If the elements should favor, she will to-morrow.

In the morning I propose to visit the flotilla lying off Smith's Point. I received information that the rebels have constructed a battery on the opposite shore in that vicinity.

It will be advisable on the return of the supply steamer for her to take in tow a scow or two of large size to assist in discharging her freight. The boats here are mere wrecks, and though I have men at work repairing them, I question if they can be put in condition for good service.

　　　Very respectfully,
　　　　　　　　　　JOSEPH HOOKER,
　　　　　　　　Brigadier-General, Commanding Division.

HDQRS. DIVISION, NEAR SENECA CREEK, MARYLAND,
　　　　　　　　　　　　　　November 11, 1861.

Brig. Gen. S. WILLIAMS, *Assistant Adjutant-General, &c.:*

SIR: I regret to be obliged to report to the Commanding General increasing sickness among the troops of this division. The diseases are not of a serious character so far as they have appeared. Purging, vomiting, intermittent fever, camp fevers, approaching somewhat the typhoid in character, are among the principal diseases. They are undoubtedly caused by the cold rains we have had since our return and on our march to Edwards Ferry and the wet grounds upon which we are encamped, where the clay soils hold all the water that falls, and the autumn sun—what little we have of it—does not seem to dry the camp grounds at all. The men have done all possible in the way of building furnaces and huts to make their camps comfortable. It is chiefly when on duty they suffer.

I do not make these suggestions with a view to broach in any way the subject of permanent quarters, but to say that [if] we were to remain in this part of the State for two or three weeks it might be well to remove our general camp to some other position. If it did not improve the health of the division, it would relieve the minds of the men, who attribute their suffering in a great degree to the locality. If we are to remain here but a few days, of course a change would be unadvisable.

In reference to locality, I should say the neighborhood of Rockville would be most conducive to the health of the division. It has extensive grounds, which the people would be glad to have us occupy, and in the event of a removal towards the capital, a paved road the whole distance would transport our trains and troops without difficulty in any weather. I ought to say, however, that at Rockville we should be chiefly dependent upon Washington for supplies and forage.

In the event of a more permanent camp, Frederick County offers greater advantages. It is a healthy location; the country about would support the division entirely. It would be connected by railroad with Baltimore and Washington; by canal and railroad also with Washington and Cumberland, and, with an interval of 5 miles only, with Hagerstown and the Middle and Western States. We should there obtain abundant supplies, and be ready for immediate movement in any direction. In either case the river could be guarded as now.

The inhabitants here inform us that there is a chance that the roads here may become absolutely impassable at any time from the middle of this month to the close of December. An unfavorable season may so close us in here that we could move only with great delay, labor, and difficulty.

I regret to call attention to this subject, but increasing sickness, continually threatening rain, and a possibility of being bound in by impassable roads seems to make it necessary.

I am, sir, with great respect, your obedient servant,

N. P. BANKS,
Major-General, Commanding Division.

P. S.—The forage we now obtain is brought from Frederick, this neighborhood being exhausted as to forage and other supplies. Captain Bingham has addressed a letter to General Van Vliet upon this subject.

Abstract from consolidated morning report of the Army of the Potomac, Maj. Gen. George B. McClellan, U. S. Army, commanding, for November 12, 1861.

Stations.	Commands.	Aggregate present for duty, equipped.			Aggregate present.	Pieces of artillery.
		Infantry.	Artillery.	Cavalry.		
Near Muddy Branch....	Banks' division.	14, 355	374	375	14, 882	18
Hunter's Chapel........	Blenker's division	7, 738	302	75	8, 354	13
Washington	Casey's division	6, 969	340	152	13, 240	......
Do...................	City Guard (A. Porter.)	1, 078	....	123	1, 418	6
Seminary	Franklin's division. ..	9, 411	446	447	11, 440	18
Fort Lyon	Heintzelman's division.	6, 929	251	417	10, 896	12
Near Bladensburg.......	Hooker's division	6, 775	....	519	8, 342	16
Near Washington.	Keyes' division	9, 902	249	92	11, 062	12
Camp Peirpoint, Va.....	McCall's division.	9, 377	395	763	12, 391	17
Arlington................	McDowell's division ..	9, 615	381	750	11, 471	18
Hall's Hill..............	Porter's (F. J.) division.	11, 208	406	879	13, 948	18
Camp Griffin............	Smith's (W. F.) division.	* 9, 964	....	* 946	13, 184	......
Poolesville, Md.........	Stone's division	9, 346	360	471	11, 639	18
Camp Duncan...........	Artillery reserve (H. J. Hunt).	....	996	....	1, 068	42
Washington and Ball's Cross-Roads.........	Cavalry (Stoneman)...	....	....	4, 755	8, 125	......
Annapolis, Md..........	Burnside's command -	....	....	....	†5, 746	......
Cambridge, Md........	Camp of Instruction, (Lockwood).	....	....	....	1, 228	......
Fort Ellsworth	Garrison..............	....	....	....	‡401	......
	Naval Battery........	....	....	....	‡143	......
	Miscellaneous	* 2, 075	* 2, 359	....	4, 847	§ 115
	Miscellaneous	....	....	....	‡5, 469	......
	Totals	114, 742	6, 859	10, 764	169, 294	323

* "Present for duty."   † No returns ; estimated as above on original report.
‡ "Aggregate strength."   § Forty-eight of these armament of Fort Washington, Md.

HEADQUARTERS DIVISION, NEAR SENECA,
November 13, 1861.

Brig. Gen. WILLIAMS, *Assistant Adjutant-General:*

SIR : I have the honor to inclose a report from Colonel Leonard, commanding at Williamsport, Md., giving information of the force of the enemy in that part of Virginia opposite to his post. According to the information given him the aggregate would reach the number of 66,000. I cannot but regard it as a most exaggerated estimate of their forces. Yet I thought it proper to forward it as one of the reports of the day. If correct, it would imply an intention towards aggressive movements, as we have no corresponding forces in that locality. The other suggestion may be of importance.

A few days' fine weather and a change in the location of a few regimental camps has greatly improved the condition of this division as to health, as the morning report will show.

I have the honor to be, with much respect, your obedient servant,

N. P. BANKS,
Major-General, Commanding Division.

[Inclosure.]

HDQRS. THIRTEENTH MASSACHUSETTS VOLUNTEERS,
Williamsport, November 8, 1861.

Major-General BANKS, U. S. A., *Commanding Division:*

SIR: I have the honor to report that since my letter inclosed I received the following information:

At Martinsburg there is 350 militia, and 30 of them mounted. Ashby's command is at Jefferson, 800 strong, some of which are at Duffield's Depot and some at a place called Flowing Spring, this side of Charlestown. There is a large force in the vicinity of Winchester, reported to be five full brigades, of 5,000 men each, under command of General Jackson. General Johnston's command is in their rear, and said to number 40,000. A reported conversation between two rebel officers at Martinsburg is as follows: To draw General Kelley from Romney over a bridge on the South Branch of the Potomac, and then destroy the bridge and attack him and his forces in the rear. The latter information was conveyed to me by a loyal lady, in a direct manner, from Martinsburg.

I have the honor to be, your obedient servant,

S. H. LEONARD,
Colonel.

———

HDQRS. DIVISION, NEAR SENECA CREEK, MARYLAND,
November 14, 1861.

Brigadier-General WILLIAMS,
Headquarters Army of the Potomac:

GENERAL: Referring to my orders from the Secretary of War and the Commanding General in reference to the protection of Union men at the polls during the late election, I have the honor to report that I sent detachments of troops, cavalry or infantry, to the following places in Maryland: From Colonel Leonard's command at Williamsport, to Hagerstown and Funkstown; from Colonel Geary's regiment to Sandy Hook, Petersville, Jefferson, Urbana, New Market, Buckeystown, and Frederick City; and from the division here, under direction of Major Stone, provost-marshal, to Woodsborough, Myersville, Wolfsville, Emmittsburg, Mechanicstown, Wolf's Tavern, Rockville, and a few other election precincts. No armed [men] went near the polls, and no serious disturbance occurred in this part of the State. At three or four places preparations had been undoubtedly made by disloyal men for an interference with the polls, but they failed to make the attempt in the presence of troops. Some arrests were made, but the men were released and allowed to vote. The people generally express their satisfaction with the conduct of the troops and the result of the election. The men who were furloughed for the exercise of the elective franchise have returned, with few exceptions, where detained by sickness, or arrest, or not having passes. The average majority will reach 30,000 votes for the Union; a more favorable result than was anticipated. Ten thousand would have satisfied the Union men very well.

Both branches of the legislature are for the Union, which will enable the State to contribute its quota of men and money for the war.

I have the honor to be, with respect, your obedient servant,

N. P. BANKS,
Major-General, Commanding Division.

HEADQUARTERS DIVISION, NEAR SENECA CREEK,
November 14, 1861.

Brigadier-General WILLIAMS, *Assistant Adjutant-General:*

SIR: I have the honor to acknowledge the receipt of your letter of the 12th instant in answer to my note of the 11th instant upon the subject of the location of the division. While I would approve the measure suggested for a "sanitary inspection of the present location of the division and of the sites suggested," I desire the Commanding General not to forget the possible, not to say probable, condition of the roads in this neighborhood. The soil is a pure clay to the depth of 5 or 6 feet, and one week's rain, which must be expected at this season, would make all the roads here absolutely impassable for the troops or division trains.

The health of the division would suffer from such a state of weather; yet should a sanitary inspection, looking to the question of health alone, result in the conclusion that the present location was sufficiently favorable in that regard, as it might well happen at this time, nevertheless we might in one week after, by the state of the roads, be completely cut off from supplies, except by the canal, and prevented from moving in any direction. We must preserve our communications as well as the health of the division. We are in danger in this respect at any time from the middle of November to the last of December.

I have the honor to be, with much respect, your obedient servant,

N. P. BANKS,
Major-General, Commanding Division.

HEADQUARTERS HOOKER'S DIVISION,
Camp Baker, Lower Potomac, Maryland, November 15, 1861.

Brig. Gen. S. WILLIAMS,
Assistant Adjutant-General, Army of the Potomac:

This afternoon the rebels have discharged no less than seventy or eighty guns at a solitary steamer passing down the river without effect. The batteries used were those in the immediate vicinity of Evansport. It cannot be possible that they will persevere much longer in their fruitless efforts to close the navigation of the river. The result of their labors to-day confirms me in the opinion I have entertained for ten days past that it is not in their power to present any formidable barrier to the almost uninterrupted passage of vessels up and down the Potomac. I am aware that a different opinion prevails among those whose experience should entitle their opinion to more consideration than my own, and for that reason it is with some reluctance that I advance it; nevertheless it is my conviction. For instance, to-day the vessel descended the river soon after midday with a three or four knot breeze and was not struck. Of all the rebel firing since I have been on the river, and it has been immense, but two of their shot have taken effect, and that was the wood schooner anchored in the middle of the river. She was hit twice, once in her hull and once in her main-sail, if that may be called hit. With a light breeze or a favorable current, a seventy-four line-of-battle-ship can ascend or descend the river at night with impunity.

I desire that 500 blank morning reports may be forwarded to me.

Herewith I inclose the report of Lieutenant-Colonel Wells, First Massachusetts Regiment, which was not received in season to send with the communication of the 14th instant.*

Very respectfully,

JOSEPH HOOKER,
Brigadier-General, Commanding Division.

HEADQUARTERS HOOKER'S DIVISION,
Camp Baker, Lower Potomac, Maryland, November 16, 1861.

Brig. Gen. S. WILLIAMS,
Assistant Adjutant-General, Army of the Potomac:

For several days past my leisure hours have been passed in endeavoring to ascertain, with as much accuracy as circumstances will permit, the position and number of the rebel forces in my immediate vicinity. And of this it has been necessary to form my opinion almost wholly from their camp fires, for, strange to say, I have not, during my three weeks' sojourn, fallen in with any one able or willing to enlighten me on this subject. If the citizens of this district are not secessionists, they might as well be, so far as it regards their services to our cause. Nor have I been more fortunate in my endeavor to acquire reliable information through agents in my own employment. Perhaps I may, but I am wearied of the delay.

The main body of the enemy's forces visible are stationed in rear of the batteries between Quantico and Chopawamsic Creeks. Two regiments appear to be posted near each other on the bank of the Quantico, and one regiment about one-third of a mile to the south of them. In rear of the former, in the valley extending towards Dumfries, are a long line of encampments, and a valley making off from that at Quantico at nearly right angles in a southerly direction is also occupied with camps. To the observer on this side of the Potomac all hills covered with forests but conceal a line of smoke rising above them. Farther to the south other camps can be seen at intervals of a mile or more. On the north of Quantico Creek, and behind a bold hill, is another camp of infantry, cavalry, and a field battery; all of these showed themselves the day we had the contest for the schooner.

This bold hill commands all the batteries in the vicinity of Evansport, and is the one I proposed to occupy soon after reaching here. It is

* See p. 422.

within a week that the rebels have established the camp at its base farthest from the Potomac.

Nearly in rear of Cockpit Point is another infantry encampment. The enemy, I presume, are encamped by regiments, and if the troops resemble other Southern regiments with which I have served, they are small in comparison with our own.

On a reconnaissance from the balloon no doubt I shall be able to furnish you with more specific and satisfactory information.

Nothing has occurred deserving of mention since my report of yesterday.

Lieutenant-Colonel Getty has submitted to me a requisition for lumber to shelter his horses, which I have approved, for the reason that I am in ignorance of the intentions of the Major-General Commanding as it regards the disposition to be made of this command. If it is to remain here any length of time I would advise the issue, for if this weather continues the loss in horses in a few nights will exceed the cost of the lumber.

In view of Liverpool Point being made the landing place of our supplies, I have seized fourteen boats to serve as lighters, and they are now in charge of the picket at that point.

Very respectfully, your obedient servant,

JOSEPH HOOKER,
Brigadier-General, Commanding Division.

GENERAL ORDERS, }   HEADQUARTERS ARMY OF THE POTOMAC,
No. 45.   *Washington, November* 16, 1861.

I. No change will be made in the armament established by the chief engineer and chief of artillery for the field works occupied by this army, or any diversion permitted from the original location of the implements, equipments, or ammunition pertaining to the guns of the field works, without the express sanction of the Commanding General.

II. The fort on Upton's Hill will hereafter be known as Fort Ramsay, and that heretofore called Fort Ramsay as Fort Cass.

By command of Major-General McClellan:

S. WILLIAMS,
Assistant Adjutant-General.

HEADQUARTERS,
Baltimore, Md., November 19, 1861.

General S. WILLIAMS, *Assistant Adjutant-General:*

GENERAL: The letter of Major Van Buren, my assistant adjutant-general, of the 11th instant,* has explained the reason why your communication of the 6th,* in regard to the absorption of the Department of Pennsylvania into others, has not been sooner answered. A brief reference to the orders concerning its organization and limits will show why I considered it in existence until your communications were received. Since they came to hand my orders and letters have been dated at headquarters, Baltimore, omitting Department of Pennsylvania. The department was created by General Orders, No. 47, from the War Department, on the 25th of July last. It was composed of a

---

* Not found.

portion of Maryland, all of Pennsylvania, and all of Delaware. As thus constituted, it has never been dissolved by general orders, either from the War Department or the headquarters of the Army.

General Orders, No. 15, from the headquarters of the Army, dated 17th of August last, created the Department of the Potomac, and absorbed Maryland and Delaware, but still left me in command of Pennsylvania, over which I continued to exercise military jurisdiction until the receipt of the communications referred to, and for this reason I continued to date my orders and communications at headquarters Department of Pennsylvania.

On the 20th of August last Major-General McClellan, by General Orders, No. 1, assumed command of the Army of the Potomac, comprising the troops serving in the former Department of Washington and Northeastern Virginia, in the valley of the Shenandoah, and in the States of Maryland and Delaware. The State of Pennsylvania was left untouched, and the Department of Pennsylvania was not dissolved either in terms or by designating the geographical boundaries of the command of Major-General McClellan. By the Army Register, dated September 10, 1861, page 72, the State of Pennsylvania is assigned to the Department of the East. The Register was not sent to me until about six weeks after its date, and I did not notice until a late day the new arrangement of Departments. In the mean time my communications to the War Department, the headquarters of the Army, and the Army of the Potomac were all dated headquarters Department of Pennsylvania, without any intimation that I was acting under a misapprehension.

Communications also came to me from the Adjutant-General's Office, addressed to me as commanding the Department of Pennsylvania. I inclose four envelopes, three of them post-marked as late as November, with the same address. The communications which they contained were directed in the same manner. During the whole of this period I continued to exercise military jurisdiction over the State of Pennsylvania, ordering troops from thence from time to time and receiving muster rolls from the mustering officer, Lieutenant-Colonel Ruff.

I have not gone into this detail for the purpose of contending against the views of the subject presented in your communication of the 6th instant, but to explain that, as the Department of Pennsylvania had not been dissolved, but only a portion of it, as originally organized, taken away by general orders, I assumed that it still existed. The only public considerations connected with the subject are those which concern the sentences in course of execution pronounced by the court-martial of which Colonel Curtenius was president. Only one of the commissioned officers tried was dismissed, the others were acquitted; but a number of privates sentenced for very grave offenses escaped punishment, and two have been dishonorably discharged from the service. But if, as I suppose, it involves the question of double rations, there are personal considerations of some importance to myself, as I have received my pay and emoluments for September, and may be called on to refund the double rations. In that case I shall, without intending any disrespect, contend before the proper authority, first, that the Department of Pennsylvania was never dissolved by general orders; second, that I performed the duties of commanding general thereof until November 6; and, third, that I was entitled to notice of its absorption with others.

I desire to suggest to the Commanding General that the general in command of Baltimore is in great need of the powers incidental to a

geographical department. A day rarely passes without an urgent necessity for giving orders, signing requisitions, &c., beyond the limits
of the regiments and corps composing my division. A very convenient
department might be formed of Delaware, the Eastern Shore of Maryland and Virginia, and so much of Maryland on the Western Shore as
includes Baltimore and the counties of the east. If there are no public
considerations which conflict with such an arrangement, it would relieve
the General-in-Chief of a good deal of detail, and I think would greatly
promote the convenience and efficiency of the service in this quarter.
I do not ask it on personal grounds, although, as the senior major-general of volunteers, I might perhaps not unreasonably do so.

I am, very respectfully, your obedient servant,

JOHN A. DIX,
Major-General.

HDQRS. OF THE ARMY, ADJUTANT-GENERAL'S OFFICE,
Washington, November 19, 1861.

Brigadier-General ROSECRANS,
Comdg. Dept. of Western Virginia, Camp Gauley Mountain:

Copies of telegrams to Generals Cox and Reynolds of the 16th instant
have been sent you by mail; to the former, to send three Ohio and
the latter one Indiana regiment to Kentucky. Eight regiments in all
will go from your command; six Ohio and two Indiana.

L. THOMAS,
Adjutant-General.

HDQRS. DEPARTMENT OF WESTERN VIRGINIA,
Camp Gauley Mountain, Western Virginia, November 19, 1861.

Maj. Gen. GEORGE B. McCLELLAN,
Commanding U. S. Army, Washington, D. C.:

GENERAL: My last written dispatch was dated the 16th. I beg you
will excuse the omission of two days. Unavoidable pressure of business prevented compliance with your order for daily letters.

My telegraphic dispatches have advised you of events in my command to this date. I have only to add that a flag of truce we sent to
Meadow Bluff came within one mile of their position. They report the
roads horribly bad, and dead horses strewn along the way between Sewell and Meadow Bluff. The rebels they saw were illy clad and armed.
They were very much disconcerted by our visit, and Gibbs (Maj. C. F.
S.) actually slept between the two captains of our escort the night they
remained there.

I have sent Capt. W. F. Raynolds with a flag of truce to Floyd, proposing that he should put a stop to the abhorrent practice of kidnap-
ing unarmed citizens, and promising on that condition to release certain hostages now in our possession. He will be able to report where
the rebels are to be found.

Reynolds reports Gilham not nearer than Greenbrier Bridge, 12 miles
from Huntersville, on the Monterey road; the rebels are preparing
arbor cantonments.

The rebels at Piketon were not so desperately annihilated as I had
hoped. They will give some trouble on the river below Point Pleasant,
but I feel very willing to have them eat out the "secesh" inhabitants of
Logan. When they find their corn and cattle gone, without a *quid pro*

quo, they will be better prepared to appreciate the friends who have done it.

General Thomas ordered General Cox to send the three Ohio regiments longest in Western Virginia to Covington, Ky., and General Reynolds to send five regiments from his line, without even notice to me of it. When I telegraphed, asking his meaning, he replied it was a mistake. Now I have a telegram saying copies of those were forwarded to me by mail, and that eight regiments will go from my command. I have telegraphed to know if I am to have the selection. When I receive the reply I will be able to say how many troops are to be brigaded.

As to plans, they are to hold Kanawha Valley and the Gauley Pass, with its outlets towards Raleigh and Sewell; to hold Cheat Mountain Pass on both roads; to hold Romney and the Red-House Pass; guard the railroads; put the Mud River and Guyandotte Valleys in order, and recruit and discipline the regiments that have been worn down and thinned out by casualties and discharges for disability. The first necessity will be to apply the examination provided for by law, and get rid of the lazy, cowardly, slothful, and worthless officers who infest our army. This will require you to send me a few more regular officers. Should any opportunity offer, my intention was to take all my spare regiments on the Baltimore and Ohio Railroad for winter quarters, but if they are to be required elsewhere, well.

My dear general, this is addressed directly to you, because I thought it possible such might have been your intention for a short time. You will assist me very greatly in preparing my troops for the coming season if you will let me know what brigadiers you can assign me.

You must observe that Colonel McCook does not want to be acting. General Benham will never do when there is any great or dangerous enterprise. I have tried him sufficiently, and will never trust him more. General Schenck has gone home dangerously ill. General Cox is the only reliable man here, and General Reynolds and General Kelley are in the eastern end of the department. There should be one more brigadier-general here and one on the other line. The portion of Ohio contiguous to Virginia ought to belong to this department. Please let me know what troops are to be taken from the command and who is to select them.

Send me one or two brigadiers, an aide-de-camp, and an order giving so much of Ohio to this department as may enable me to have such points as Cincinnati for hospital and headquarters of staff; Gallipolis, Marietta, and Bellaire for the use of depots, hospitals, &c. I did not know but you might wish to give me Kentucky, but see you have a better man.

Very truly and respectfully, your obedient servant,

W. S. ROSECRANS,
Brigadier-General, U. S. Army.

HEADQUARTERS ARMY OF THE POTOMAC,
MEDICAL DIRECTOR'S OFFICE,
November 20, 1861.

General S. WILLIAMS,
Assistant Adjutant-General, Army of the Potomac:

GENERAL: I have the honor to report that, in obedience to your instructions of November 12, I directed Surg. C. C. Keeney to repair to the headquarters of Major-General Banks, and in concert with Surg. W. S. King, U. S. Army, to examine into and report upon the sanitary characteristics of the ground now occupied by the troops and the positions suggested by General Banks in the neighborhood of Rockville and in Frederick County. Surgeon Keeney has performed this duty, and his report is herewith submitted.

The present position of the troops under General Banks is decidedly objectionable, for the reasons set forth in the report. Moreover, any severe rains would render the camps almost inapproachable as well as uninhabitable. I cannot therefore too strongly recommend their immediate removal.

The sanitary condition of this division is now excellent; and to preserve it in this condition a location with better drainage will be indispensable.

The choice seems to be between Rockville and Frederick. The hygienic reasons, in my opinion, are in favor of Frederick. I know this position to be eligible from personal observation. I had once before selected it for the general hospital of General Banks' division, and I consider the country about it as offering superior advantages for the location of camps and for the comfort of the troops. Rockville, from the nature of the soil, being less easily drained, and from being less protected against the prevailing winds in winter, will be likely to furnish a greater number of typhoid-fever cases and of diseases of the respiratory organs. Frederick promises greater immunity from these. Whether strategic reasons in favor of Rockville may decide that some greater risk of health should be incurred I am unable to say; if they do not, I would advise the removal of the division to Frederick, but either location will be far preferable to the present.

Very respectfully, your obedient servant,

CHAS. S. TRIPLER,
Surgeon and Medical Director, Army of Potomac.

[Inclosure.]

ARLINGTON, VA., *November* 18, 1861.

Surgeon TRIPLER, *Medical Director, Army of the Potomac :*

SIR: In obedience to your instructions to proceed to the headquarters of Major-General Banks, and in concert with Surgeon King, medical director, to examine into the medical topography of the camps of that division, I have the honor to state, we have made the examinations of those grounds as well as others, and submit to you the following observations:

The face of the country in the neighborhood of Rockville is rolling, and sparsely covered with timber.

The soil is of clay, is moist and cold. The grounds are ample for a camp of 15,000 or 20,000 men, but would be cold and bleak from the northwesterly winds.

In a sanitary point of view, these grounds offer but few objections as regards fevers and other ailments arising from local causes.

The town of Rockville is distant 15 miles from Georgetown. The houses are few and of poor quality, affording limited accommodations for the sick and wounded of this division.

After the examination of these grounds I proceeded to the headquarters of General Banks, and in company with Surgeon King went over the camping grounds of the division.

We found most of the regiments encamped on Muddy Branch, a small tributary of the Potomac. The country in this vicinity is exceedingly abrupt, and its small ravines are filled with marshes and stagnant pools. The soil consists of a tenacious clay, is cold, and, in consequence of retaining moisture a long time, the camps are most always in an impassable condition, on account of the tenacious mud produced by the slightest agitation of the soil. Anywhere on these camping grounds a tent pin when driven in the ground brings water. In a sanitary point of view we cannot but regard these camping grounds as exceedingly unhealthy, owing, no doubt, to their close proximity to the river, to the low marshy grounds around about the camps, and to the peculiar nature of the soil.

The division has occupied these grounds but ten or fifteen days, not long enough to affect the health of the command as yet materially; but it is our opinion that if the command occupies these grounds for any length of time the sick report will be increased twofold from local causes alone.

There is another very serious objection to occupying these grounds; as there are approaching indications of increasing sickness in the division, there will be no hospital accommodations for the sick short of Washington, and as the roads are now nearly impassable from the deep mud, it will be impracticable to transport the sick either to Frederick or to Washington without much suffering.

At present the health of the division is remarkably good, and the immunity from disease which the whole division has enjoyed for the last two months is without parallel in our armies. During the month of September the mean strength of the division was little less than 16,000, and the number of deaths from disease alone was 16. As far as the regimental sick reports for the month of October have been received, they go to show that the command was equally as healthy.

The prevalent diseases now in camp are measles (a few cases), mild forms of intermittent and other fevers, and catarrhal affections. But typhoid pneumonia may be expected to prevail to a great extent soon, if the troops occupy these same camping grounds much longer.

We next proceeded to examine the medical topography of the country in Frederick County, in the vicinity of Frederick. On the eastern slope of the Blue Ridge, some 4 miles northwest of the town of Frederick, we found the face of the country presenting a more favorable aspect for a large encampment. For several miles along the base of the Blue Ridge the country is gently undulating, affording beautiful slopes for camps, and being well protected from the prevalent cold northwesterly winds by the Blue Ridge range. These grounds are well timbered, with oak openings, and abundantly supplied with numerous streams of good water.

The soil of these grounds differs materially from that of Rockville or the grounds occupied by General Banks' division. It is composed of sand and clay (argillo-arenaceous) and is covered with flint, indicating the soil to be hard, dry, and warm.

The prevailing winds, as above stated, are from the northwest, but being so well sheltered by the high ridge in the rear and receiving the morning sun, these grounds cannot but be well adapted to the health of troops.

The town of Frederick contains between 7,000 and 8,000 inhabitants. There are in the city many fine buildings suitable for hospital purposes, and if occupied for these purposes would obviate the necessity of sending the sick and wounded to Baltimore and Washington, although if necessary they could easily be conveyed to the above cities in a few hours by railway.

As above seen, these grounds present superior advantages over all others. First, in a sanitary point of view, their locality would present a smaller sick report; would add more to the comforts of the sick, as all bad cases could be treated in the city of Frederick, and, if need be, could easily be conveyed to Baltimore or Washington by railway; and all supplies can be easily, quickly, and at all times procured from the cities of Baltimore and Washington.

CHAS. C. KEENEY,
Surgeon, U. S. Army.

HEADQUARTERS,
Baltimore, Md., November 20, 1861.

Hon. S. P. CHASE, *Secretary of the Treasury:*

SIR: The people of Accomac County have submitted to the authority of the United States. The people of Northampton will, I am confident, follow the good example of their neighbors, and I hope to see a loyal member of Congress from this part of Wise's district in his seat next winter. Our troops have been thus far well received. In Northampton there may be a rally on the part of the Confederates, but I think not. I look for a peaceable submission.

Will you give orders to the Light-House Board to re-establish the light on Cape Charles? Our troops will be there this week. There are two other lights which have been extinguished. Your immediate attention to this matter is earnestly requested, as I am anxious to see the old order of things restored as soon as possible.

I am, very respectfully, your obedient servant,

JOHN A. DIX,
Major-General.

HEADQUARTERS,
Baltimore, November 20, 1861.

Hon. M. BLAIR, *Postmaster-General:*

SIR: The people of Accomac County have submitted to the authority of the United States. I have no doubt the people of Northampton County will do likewise. Can you not authorize the mail to be carried from Snow Hill to Eastville? Our troops are in all probability in the latter place to-day. I am anxious that the old order of things should be promptly re-established, and that a loyal member of Congress from this part of Wise's district should be returned in December. The postmasters of Salisbury and Snow Hill can easily arrange the matter of the mail if authorized by you.

I am, very respectfully, your obedient servant,

JOHN A. DIX,
Major-General.

SENECA CREEK, MD., *November* 21, 1861.

Brig. Gen. S. WILLIAMS, *Army of the Potomac:*

SIR: In communicating to you, for the information of the Commanding General, Colonel Leonard's report of the rebel forces in Northern

Virginia, near Winchester, I remarked that I had sent Mr. Strother, in the employ of the Topographical Department, to make further inquiries. His report I have the honor to inclose. It gives a correct view of affairs there I think, and nothing would delight this division more than to make the expedition to Winchester which is suggested by him and which I believe to be entirely feasible.

I have the honor to be, with much respect, your obedient servant,

N. P. BANKS,
Major-General, Commanding Division.

[Inclosure.]

HANCOCK, MD., *November* 18, 1861.

Maj. Gen. N. P. BANKS:

SIR : I have received the following intelligence from Virginia, which I believe to be entirely reliable. It is the statement of an intelligent and loyal gentleman who has returned from Richmond through Winchester, where he was in pursuance of some private business.

When Romney was taken the citizens of Winchester, apprehending the occupation of their town, sent to General Johnston for a force to protect them. He positively declined sending any. Influential citizens of Winchester then applied to the Secretary of War at Richmond, who granted their request to the extent of ordering Jackson with his brigade to their assistance.

My informant said the brigade near Winchester numbered, according to his estimate, 4,000 men. This is the highest estimate that I have heard of this force, and it is probably overstated.

On arriving at Winchester, General Jackson immediately called out the militia *en masse;* all were between the ages of sixteen and sixty. This call has been very feebly responded to, and the force thus collected is thought to be utterly worthless except for show. In face of an enemy it would be rather a disadvantage than an assistance. With this force Jackson is making a demonstration in the direction of Romney, probably as far as Hanging Rock, on the Cacapon River.

General Jackson is reported to have said that the militia of the district ought to be able to defend it. This with Johnston's refusal to send the regular troops from Manassas seems to indicate that there would be no effort to hold, much less to retake, Winchester if assailed or occupied by any considerable force of United States troops.

My father is confident that the advance of 5,000 men, with cavalry and artillery, from Harper's Ferry would sweep the valley, occupy Winchester, and, if made with secrecy and celerity, might cut off Jackson's whole force.

My informant also says the Union sentiment, hitherto suppressed in and about Winchester, is again becoming clamorous and restive.

The officer in command here tells me that he has had a letter from General Kelley, at Romney, stating his force at 11,000 men.

The conduct of the militia at Harper's Ferry and at Romney justify fully the opinion above expressed of their unreliable character. At Romney, I am credibly informed that a force of 1,500 or 2,000 fled before Kelley's advance of 130 cavalry, firing only a few scattering shots and making no serious resistance, leaving everything—arms, baggage, and artillery— in the hands of the Union troops.

It is supposed here that Kelley will take Winchester within ten days. This of course is mere supposition. He is advancing his outposts 15 or 20 miles on the line of the river and railroad, repairing the railway as he advances. He has also, according to reports, advanced on the Winchester road the same distance.

I have heard nothing further of the force reported to have moved from Leesburg toward Winchester, but suppose it may occupy some strategic point, ready to act on either point (Leesburg or Winchester) that circumstances might indicate—Snickersville, possibly.

I have no doubt myself that if a strong demonstration was made on Winchester Jackson would either retire or be taken, and the position remain in our hands without further dispute.

This intelligence of the Confederate forces in the valley is the most recent, and I have full reliance on its general accuracy.

I submit the above with respect.

Yours, &c.,

DAVID H. STROTHER,
Assistant Topographical Engineer, U. S. Army.

HEADQUARTERS,
Baltimore, November 21, 1861.

Hon. S. P. CHASE, *Secretary of the Treasury:*

SIR: I wrote to you yesterday in regard to the re-establishment of the light on Cape Charles. I write now to ask whether vessels may not go from this city under the usual custom-house restrictions to Accomac County and to Northampton as soon as the authority of the Government is re-established there. The inhabitants are in want of many of the necessaries of life, and by bringing about open intercourse with Maryland and other loyal States the object we have in view will be promoted.

Asking an early reply, I am, very respectfully, your obedient servant,

JOHN A. DIX,
Major-General.

CAMP GAULEY MOUNTAIN, VA.,
November 21, 1861.

Major-General McCLELLAN:

Since No. 14 Captain Raynolds in with flag of truce. Found rebels on Piney, 5 miles south of Raleigh. Union man from Richmond by Meadow Bluff reports only 600 effective there. Defenses 4 miles nearer Lewisburg. Greatest defense impassable roads. The pack-mule train would be extremely serviceable for enterprise. I could put some afoot very soon. The two wants for this region are the shelter-knapsacks and pack-mule train. If nothing prevents will have them.

W. S. ROSECRANS,
Brigadier-General.

NOVEMBER 22; 1861.

Brig. Gen. J. J. REYNOLDS, *Huttonsville, W. Va.:*

The order you received from General Thomas has been superseded by an apology and an order directing six Ohio and two Indiana regiments to be taken from this department, effective, at my discretion. Designate the two Indiana and one Ohio you would recommend being sent from your command, and say how soon you can conveniently spare them. I learn you stampeded the rebels at the Greenbrier Bridge last week. We have chased Floyd, and with good conduct on the part of

Benham might have caught him. He is probably at Newbern, on the Southwestern Virginia Railroad. Let us keep ready to harass. Have your troops the shelter-tents or India-rubber blankets?

W. S. ROSECRANS.

———

HEADQUARTERS HOOKER'S DIVISION,
Camp Baker, Lower Potomac, Maryland, November 22, 1861.
Brig. Gen. S. WILLIAMS,
Assistant Adjutant-General, Army of the Potomac:

GENERAL: An animated fire was kept up from the rebel batteries on two or three schooners descending the river this afternoon with no better success than heretofore. The rebels will certainly abandon their purpose of claiming the navigation of the Potomac by means of the batteries now in position ere long. They must see that it is labor in vain. Of late a large number of vessels have passed and repassed at night, and no effort has been made to check them. Thus far their labor has been equally fruitless during the day.

Professor Lowe has not returned from his mission to Washington. I see no effort making to inflate the balloon on shore, as was intended by him at the time of leaving.

The two companies of cavalry dispatched to the lower part of the Peninsula have not returned.

Very respectfully, your obedient servant,

JOSEPH HOOKER,
Brigadier-General, Commanding Division.

———

NOVEMBER 23, 1861.
Brig. Gen. J. J. REYNOLDS, *Huttonsville, W. Va.:*

The commanding general [Rosecrans] directs that you send to Covington, Ky., in accordance with the orders of Brig. Gen. L. Thomas, Adjutant-General, the following regiments: Third, Sixth, and Twenty-fourth Ohio, and Fifteenth and Seventeenth Indiana Regiments.

[No signature.]

———

NOVEMBER 24, 1861.
Col. W. B. HAZEN, *Gallipolis, Ohio:*

Zeigler's detached companies return to Ceredo; the Thirty-fourth Ohio occupies Barboursville. Either of them can strike Front Hill and catch that cavalry. The only road known of here from Ceredo to Logan Court-House is by Louisa and Sandy. It is not less than 60 miles from Front Hill to Logan, through a mountainous country, traversed by streams, now swollen, and over roads that cannot be good. The expedition you propose with a regiment, in such weather and by such a route, seems to be likely to break down your troops and be unsuccessful. You will observe the distance from Front Hill is such that it would take you nearly three days, as the roads are, to Logan. You speak of returning by Barboursville. The Commanding General has ridden that road on horseback about this season of the year, and it took two full days to ride it. The road is utterly impassable for wheels, and nearly so for horses, the nearest mountain paths in many places twice or thrice fording the Guyandotte belly-deep to a horse, besides crossing several of its tributaries that have no bridges. As for sustenance along that route, he found it difficult to get feed for self and horse. You can now judge from this of the practicability of the march, and then all the cavalry have to do to escape is to get on their horses and ride back to Raleigh.

W. S. ROSECRANS.

HEADQUARTERS ARMY OF THE POTOMAC,
OFFICE MEDICAL DIRECTOR,
Washington, November 25, 1861.

General R. B. MARCY, U. S. A.,
    Chief of Staff Army of the Potomac:

GENERAL: The necessity for a better protection for the men than the common tent affords, without going into the construction of extensive huts, which would give the appearance of going into permanent winter quarters, has been for some time engaging my attention. The severity of the winters in this climate renders some protection absolutely necessary, or we must expect a vast increase of disease of the respiratory organs, and unless by our system we can secure a tolerable ventilation, as well as protection against the rains, snow, and cold, we have reason to fear a prevalence of typhus and typhoid fevers among the troops.

To guard against these, so far as practicable, I have the honor to suggest that in the first place, in addition to the ordinary trench about the tents, the *tracé* of every regimental camp shall be provided with a ditch not less than 12 inches wide and deep, to secure a more perfect drainage.

Secondly. That an inclosure equal to the base of each tent shall be constructed of small logs or poles about 3 feet in height, over the top of which the tent shall be secured to serve as a roof. Such constructions have already been made in some of the camps; they can readily be put up by the men themselves.

Upon some of the camp grounds the timber that has been felled will furnish the poles or logs. Where these are not to be had, clapboards or any cheap material will answer the purpose.

For warming the tents and drying the ground a modification of the Crimean oven, which has been devised and put in operation by Dr. McRuer, the surgeon of General Sedgwick's brigade, appears to me to be the cheapest and most effective. Dr. McRuer has submitted to me a report on this subject. General Heintzelman, who has inspected his arrangement, informs me that it appears to be perfect in all its details; that it is at the same time efficient and economical. Dr. McRuer thus describes his plan:

A trench 1 foot wide and 20 inches deep to be dug through the center and length of each tent, to be continued for 3 or 4 feet farther, terminating at one end in a covered oven fire-place and at the other in a chimney. By this arrangement the fire-place and chimney are both on the outside of the tent; the fire-place is made about 2 feet wide and arching; its area gradually lessening until it terminates in a throat at the commencement of the straight trench. This part is covered with brick or stone, laid in mortar or cement; the long trench to be covered with sheet-iron in the same manner. The opposite end to the fire-place terminates in a chimney 6 or 8 feet high; the front of the fire-place to be fitted with a tight movable sheet-iron cover, in which an opening is to be made, with a sliding cover to act as a blower. By this contrivance a perfect draught may be obtained, and no more cold air admitted within the furnace than just sufficient to consume the wood and generate the amount of heat required, which not only radiates from the exposed surface of the iron plates, but is conducted throughout the ground floor of the tent so as to keep it both warm and dry, making a board floor entirely unnecessary, thereby avoiding the dampness and filth, which unavoidably accumulates in such places. All noise, smoke, and dust, attendant upon building the fires within the tent are avoided; there are no currents of cold air, and the heat is so equally diffused, that no difference can be perceived between the temperature of each end or side of the tent. Indeed, the advantages of this mode of warming the hospital tents are so obvious, that it needs only to be seen in operation to convince any observer that it fulfills everything required as regards the warming of hospital tents, and I respectfully ask you to appoint a commissioner to examine the hospital tents of the Eighth Brigade, and ascertain by observation the justness of this report.

The whole cost to the Government of constructing the above apparatus for the four hospitals of the Eighth Brigade is the cost of 112 feet, 1 foot wide, of sheet-iron, one barrel of lime, and four sheet-iron doors, the stone and brick were picked up by the men, who likewise did all the labor.

By this plan floors to the tent are rendered unnecessary; the ground within the tent is kept perfectly dry, and the temperature can be regulated by increasing or diminishing the fires; all smoke, dust, and noise within the tent are obviated; the flues may be carried through a range of five or six tents, making one fire all that is necessary for each set. If the description of this furnace cannot be understood, and it is deemed expedient to put them in general operation, Dr. McRuer might be temporarily detached from his brigade to construct a model in each division in the Army.

I have further to recommend that the men should be required to make daily use of desiccated vegetables in their soups. Where fresh vegetables are to be had, this is not necessary, but in the winter season a sufficient supply of fresh vegetables cannot be depended upon. Soup should form a daily part of a soldier's dinner, and a liberal portion of desiccated vegetables should enter into its composition. Soup requires three and one-half hours for its proper preparation; volunteers will not take so much trouble unless it is enjoined upon them by a positive order, and also made the duty of the company officers to see that it is done. Cold weather and the want of vegetable food are almost sure to engender scurvy. If it is possible to supply an additional allowance of blankets, it would contribute essentially to the preservation of the health of the men.

Very respectfully, your obedient servant,

CHAS. S. TRIPLER,
Surgeon and Medical Director, Army of the Potomac.

HEADQUARTERS DIVISION,
Baltimore, Md., November 28, 1861.

Brig. Gen. H. H. LOCKWOOD, *Commanding Eastern Shore:*

GENERAL: Your dispatches of the 26th instant,* by Captain Knight, are received. It is natural that our Union friends in Accomac County should feel nervous and desire to get rid of their late oppressors. While we look calmly and dispassionately to important and more remote results, we must do all we can, consistently with our public pledges to the people of Accomac and Northampton, to give courage to those who desire to place the affairs of the counties on their former footing. In the language of the proclamation, the Government asks that its authority may be recognized. In pursuance of this purpose we have a right to require, as you have done, that those who are in the execution of public trusts should take the oath of allegiance. If they refuse, they decline to recognize the authority of the Government, and can claim none of the benefits or immunities promised by the proclamation. On the contrary, by seeking to defeat the very object for

---

* Not found.

which the expedition was sent into these counties, they array themselves against the Government, and cannot expect to be treated as friends. If the county clerk, as is alleged, has openly exerted his influence to dissuade the magistrates from taking the oath of allegiance, he should be arrested for an overt act of hostility to the Government.

The rules by which you should be governed may be stated briefly as follows:

1. No arrests should be made for acts done before the proclamation was published.

2. No man should be disturbed who acquiesces in the authority of the Government, no matter how cold, or reluctant, or sullen his submission.

3. Any person who exerts his influence to dissuade individuals from attending the meetings of the people called to declare their allegiance to the United States cannot for the reasons assigned be considered as entitled to the benefits and immunities promised by the proclamation. On the contrary, he is to be regarded as an enemy, to be dealt with at your discretion.

4. Any person who at any such meeting resists a proposition to declare the allegiance of the two counties to the United States can only be regarded as an adherent of the rebel Government and coming within the category of No. 3.

5. The twenty persons who have been named to you as deserving arrest should be watched, and at the very first indication of hostility to the Government they should be taken into custody. But if they have submitted in good faith, they are entitled to the protection pledged by the proclamation. It must, however, be a real and not a pretended submission. It must be exemplified by an abstinence in fact from all attempts to dissuade others from au open and public declaration of their allegiance to the United States. And if you have good reasons to believe that any one of them is exerting a secret influence against the Government, you may with perfect propriety send for him, and require him to take the oath.

Now, let me say one word to our Union friends. I understand their feelings perfectly. I have gone through the same process here which you are passing through in Accomac County. I have succeeded with the aid of a very judicious police in re-establishing order and bringing back the State to its true allegiance; but I have been constrained to differ frequently from our Union friends. They ask too much. They looked more to forcible measures than to a quiet, firm, and steady adherence to fixed principles. Our Union friends in Accomac must not be unreasonable. They must act boldly and decisively, and they will beat their adversaries without difficulty. With all we have done and are doing to support them; with the certainty that they will be sustained under all circumstances, they will have no excuse if they do not come out fearlessly, no matter what the course of secret traitors may be. As men of sense they cannot fail to see that treachery cannot long be kept secret, and that their game is a sure one. I trust, therefore, they will come out promptly and strongly, and set the authors of the past mischief at defiance. If these mischief-makers continue their operations, you will soon detect and bring them to punishment.

I send $2,000 in specie per Captain Tyler. The Kent will wait till Monday, if necessary, for the Seventeenth Massachusetts.

I am, very respectfully, your obedient servant,

JOHN A. DIX,
Major-General.

[Received Headquarters Army of Potomac, November 28, 1861.]

Memorandum concerning transportation by water.

General Burnside reports vessels belonging to his command of capacities as follows:

One side-wheel steamer (900 bunks), will carry for short distance	1,200
One stern-wheel, 18 draught (bunks), will carry for short distance	500
Five propellers (bunks, 500 each), will carry for short distance 700 each	3,500
Four propellers (bunks), will carry for short distance 600 each	2,400
Seven sailing-vessels (700 each)	4,900
Five floating batteries (i. e., canal-boats), fitted up with shot-proof bulwarks, (280 each)	1,400
Twenty-five surf-boats (40 each)	1,000
Six launches (75 each)	450
	15,350

The above vessels will tow—

Two vessels, carrying 500 each	1,000	
Eleven vessels, carrying	5,500	
		6,500
		21,850

N. B.—The eleven vessels to be towed would have to be furnished. This could be done in the river here, from canal-boats or schooners.

It will be seen, therefore, that if Burnside's fleet is to be counted on, it is only necessary to add to it a dozen or so canal-boats or schooners, to be found readily at any time, to have transportation for 1,000 men.

MEANS OF TRANSPORTATION TO BE DERIVED FROM THE NAVY-YARD AND POTOMAC FLOTILLA.

The Navy has four side-wheel passenger boats, two of which are, however, now at Hampton Roads, which will carry each, say, 500 men; in all, 2,000. Also the ferry-boat Stepping Stones, which will carry 1,500. Also about eight gunboats, belonging to flotilla, and tugs, which would tow barges enough to carry 20,000 men.

It would only be necessary, therefore, with the means the Navy Department could furnish, to provide barges to be towed.

QUARTERMASTER'S DEPARTMENT.

The quartermaster has now in his service the following vessels:

One steamboat, which will carry	1,000
One steamboat, which will carry	800
Three steamboats, which will carry 500 each	1,500
Two now at Annapolis, which will carry 1,500 and 800	2,300
Besides which he has usually four or five Schuylkill barges employed, which will carry, say, 400 each	2,000
	7,600

Colonel Rucker gives me the following names of steamers in his employment:

City of Richmond, large sea-going vessel.
Columbia, large sea-going vessel.
Philadelphia, small vessel, propeller.
Ann Eliza, small vessel, propeller.
Sophia, small vessel, propeller.
Ermin, small vessel, propeller.

MEANS OF WATER TRANSPORTATION OBSERVED AT THE WHARVES, IN THE CANAL, ETC.

An agent employed by me reports nine steamers, four of which, however, are identical with the last four just named, which are generally small propellers or tugs, but which he thinks would tow barges enough to carry 15,000 men. He finds nine Schuylkill barges, each of which will carry 400 or 500 men, and eighteen coal boats, capable of carrying 200 men each. He thinks that in a week he could collect, not counting the Navy Department vessels, means to transport down the Potomac 20,000 men.

From the foregoing statements it will be seen:

1st. That if Burnside's fleet is counted as available for our purposes, nothing additional is requisite except ten or twelve Schuylkill barges, most of which can be found here and the balance made up from coal and wood barges.

2d. That by use of what the Navy and quartermaster could furnish, and by collection of barges and schooners usually to be found, transportation for 20,000 men could be had at short notice.

It would seem that with the number of steamers usually available and other craft to be found there was no actual necessity for further collections. With a view, however, to being independent of hasty collections, and having on hand a cheap class of vessels, admirably calculated either for carrying men or freight, and which will make existing steam power capable of doing an indefinite amount of work, it would be a good step to purchase from the Pennsylvania canals twenty of their large barges, which can be arranged, on a draught of 5 feet water or 6 at utmost, to carry 500 or 1,000 men; also to collect 50 landing boats, capable of carrying 40 men each.

To carry out these views, or whatever views the Commanding General may adopt, a special agent should be appointed, who should be either a member of the Quartermaster's Department or a Navy officer. Such an officer as Lieutenant Phelps, U. S. Navy, who assisted me in establishing ferries, &c., would be admirably calculated. Lieutenant Wyman, lately of the Potomac flotilla, expressed a desire to serve with the Army.

Mr. Cathcart, a clerk in the Treasury Department, is a nautical man, full of expedients and resources, and very familiar with the Potomac River and Chesapeake and Ohio Canal; he would be a very proper man for this service.

Respectfully submitted.

J. G. BARNARD,
Brigadier-General, Chief Engineer, Army of Potomac.

SPECIAL ORDERS, }   HEADQUARTERS ARMY OF THE POTOMAC,
No. 161.   }   *Washington, November 28, 1861.*

*   *   *   *   *   *   *

6. Brig. Gen. P. St. Geo. Cooke, U. S. Army, having reported to these headquarters, in compliance with instructions from the headquarters of the Army, is assigned to the command of the regular cavalry serving in the Army of the Potomac.

*   *   *   *   *   *   *

16. The division of Major-General Banks will take up a position at or in the vicinity of Frederick City, to be selected by the division com-

mander, who is also assigned to the command of the Maryland Home Guards raised in that quarter. General Banks will protect the portion of the Chesapeake and Ohio Canal lying between Cumberland and the Monocacy River.

17. The Fifth, Sixth, Seventh, and Eighth New Jersey Volunteers will constitute a brigade, to be commanded for the present by the senior colonel, and will form part of the division of Brigadier-General Hooker, which they will join with as little delay as practicable. Brigadier-General Casey will arrange with Brigadier-General Van Vliet, chief quartermaster, as to the route and means of transportation.

*   *   *   *   *   *   *

By command of Major-General McClellan:

S. WILLIAMS,
Assistant Adjutant-General.

[NOVEMBER 29, 1861.]

Brig. Gen. CHARLES P. STONE, *Commanding at Poolesville:*

Please inform General Hill that I have no wish to protect robbers, and that I will cordially unite in any proper effort to repress marauding. If he will turn these men over to me, with the evidence necessary to convict them before a commission, they shall be tried and punished in good faith. Say to him that I have no plea to interpose for men who have disobeyed my orders by stealing, except to recommend the utmost care and reflection in the infliction of a punishment which, although just, may lead to reprisals beyond my power to control, and may lend to this contest a degree of ferocity which I desire to avoid.

GEO. B. McCLELLAN,
Major-General, Commanding U. S. Army.

HEADQUARTERS DEPARTMENT OF WESTERN VIRGINIA,
Camp Gauley Mountain, Virginia, November 29, 1861.

Brig. Gen. L. THOMAS, *Washington, D. C.:*

SIR: I have the honor to say, for the information of the Commanding General, that I am so far convalescent as to be able to attend to business.

On the 26th instant I found it necessary to arrest Brig. Gen. H. W. Benham for unofficer-like neglect of duty. He applied for a leave of absence on a medical certificate, with permission to visit a city, and has gone to New York.

The Tenth and Ninth Ohio are probably at Covington, or farther, on their way to join the command of General Buell. The Thirteenth, detained by the state of the roads, will probably go down to-day or to-morrow. No pen can describe the desperate condition of the roads; they are next to impassable. They are the military obstacle of the remainder of the season.

Presuming the Commanding General has no special directions to give about matters I have been presenting for his consideration relative to this department and the contiguous part of the State of Ohio, I have made the following dispositions of the forces in this valley, and shall proceed to Wheeling as soon as practicable:

First. At Fayetteville, Schenck's brigade, cantoned in secession houses, deserted by their inhabitants, to be intrenched.

Second. At this point, intrenched post, Forty-seventh Ohio, under Poschner; one 20-pounder Parrott and two howitzers.

Third. At Gauley Bridge, Twenty-eighth [Ohio], Colonel Moor, intrenched.

Fourth. At Summersville and Cross-Lanes, Thirty-sixth [Ohio], Colonel Crook.

Fifth. At Cannelton and west side of Kanawha, Thirty-seventh [Ohio], Colonel Siber, in barns and houses, made in cantonments; supervision of country from Loop to Cabin Creek.

Sixth. At Camp Piatt, opposite the Boone and Kanawha turnpike and head of ordinary steamboat navigation, Forty-fourth [Ohio], Colonel Gilbert.

Seventh. At Charleston and Kanawha River, with supervision of the defenses of the valley, to Brigadier-General Cox, whose brigade will be quartered in the vicinity of Charleston; Eighth Virginia at Buffalo.

Eighth. At Point Pleasant, Fourth Virginia, Colonel Lightburn.

Ninth. At Barboursville and Mud River, Thirty-fourth Ohio, Colonel Piatt.

Tenth. At Guyandotte, Second Virginia Cavalry, Colonel Bolles.

Eleventh. At Ceredo, Fifth Virginia at present.

On the other line, Brigadier-General Reynolds at Beverly, one regiment by detail and in turn at Cheat, one at Elk Water, one at Huttonsville, two at Beverly, and one at Philippi. At Romney, Kelley re-enforced by two Indiana regiments and a battery. The points for enterprises appear to be Wytheville, Logan Court-House, and Kelley's front.

I urgently beg for a few regular officers to form an examining commission. Major Slemmer is near the point of death from typhoid fever. He is at a private house, 5 miles from Beverly. His wife is with him. If he recovers, it will be two months at least before he can do any duty.

Very respectfully, your obedient servant,

W. S. ROSECRANS,
Brigadier-General, U. S. Army.

ADJUTANT-GENERAL'S OFFICE,
Washington, D. C., November 30, 1861.

Brig. Gen. W. S. ROSECRANS,
Commanding Dep't W. Va., Camp Gauley Mountain:

SIR: Your several communications have been considered by the General-in-Chief, and the following are his instructions and remarks:

In the orders heretofore sent you the Kentucky regiments were not included, but only Ohio and Indiana regiments, in the detachments to be made by you to Kentucky.

At present it is impracticable to designate any other brigadier-generals for your department, but it will be done as soon as possible. Please suggest the names of any colonels of your command who may be suitable for that appointment.

You will please detach from your command the following troops: The regular battery of artillery, commanded by Captain Howard, Fourth Artillery, to report to Brigadier-General Kelley at Romney. Order the regular battery commanded by Captain Mack, Loomis' volunteer battery (Michigan), and four more infantry regiments to Kentucky, making in all twelve regiments to Kentucky, to report to Brigadier-General Buell.

Order Howe's battery, Fourth Artillery, to Washington, to join the Army of the Potomac.

The two Virginia regiments will be furnished with guns by the Ordnance Department. Orders will be given here for five regiments to report to Brigadier-General Kelley at Romney. Instruct General Kelley, on their arrival, to order the eight Ohio regiments to Camp Chase, to be reorganized and then sent to Kentucky.

The general staff officers at Cincinnati will be no longer under your command. The affairs of the depot there will be regulated by the bureau here. Your requisitions for supplies will be made on that depot as usual. Captain McLean, assistant adjutant-general, has been ordered. The recruiting service for volunteers will be conducted according to General Orders, No. 69. There are mustering officers at Cincinnati, Columbus, and Cleveland.

As far as possible you will avoid sending your sick beyond your department limits. A general hospital may be established at Wheeling. If the regimental surgeons give proper attention to sanitary precautions in the camp the sick list may be reduced.

You can continue the depots at Bellaire and Marietta, or move them within the limits of your department, as you deem best.

I am, sir, &c.,

L. THOMAS,
Adjutant-General.

Memorandum for General McClellan.

[Made on or about December 1, 1861.]

The idea of shifting the theater of operations to the James, York, or Rappahannock has often occurred. The great difficulty I have found in the matter is that of moving a body as large as necessary rapidly, and of making the necessary preparations for such a movement, so that they should not in themselves give indications of the whereabouts of the intended operations in time to meet them.

The first thing to be considered is the old danger attending all similar operations. In cutting the enemy's line of operations you expose yourself, and a bold and desperate enemy, seeing himself anticipated at Richmond, might attempt to retrieve the disaster by a desperate effort upon Washington.

Leaving, then, as we should do, the great mass of the enemy in front of Washington, it would not be safe to leave it guarded by less than 100,000 men; that is, until we became certain that he had withdrawn from our front so far as to render his return upon it impracticable. It seems to me, too, that the full garrisoning of the works up to the standard fixed upon should be completed without delay. These works will but imperfectly serve their purpose if they are not defended by troops who have some familiarity with their positions and duties. (Lieutenant McAlester asks urgently for the regiment of Colonel Poe, Heintzelman's division, to be added to the 600 men under Colonel Christian at Fort Lyon; in the first place to give an adequate and efficient garrison to that important work; in the second, to enable him to get fatigue parties large enough to finish it off.)

The works between Potomac Eastern Branch [?] are finished and armed (with exception of the three small works above Chain Bridge, not quite done). Of those over Eastern Branch, Forts Greble, Carroll, Stanton, and work near Benning's Bridge are nearly or quite done, and garrisons may be assigned. The gap between Benning's Bridge work and Fort Stanton is being filled up by three or four works now under construction.

I dwell on this matter somewhat, since, if the army moves, particularly if it makes a flank movement, leaving the enemy in front, the measures for defense of the city cannot be too carefully taken.

Now as to the expedition: Considering the great difficulty of transporting at one time large numbers, the confusion which will attend the landing, and consequent difficulty of getting the columns into prompt marching order after landing, with our new troops, if the numbers are great, I should be disposed to make the first descent with a comparatively small but select corps, not over 20,000—at outside 30,000 men.

Let it be supposed the latter number is adopted. How shall the movement be made so as to attract least attention in its preparations and to deceive the enemy as to their object?

General Burnside's force I suppose to be about 10,000 men. His flotilla, including his seven sailing vessels and five floating batteries, will carry that number. (In my former memorandum I estimated 15,350, but I now exclude the surf-boats and launches and diminish the numbers, as I then estimated for a short voyage, not leaving the Potomac.)

I suppose there would be three batteries and, say, 1,000 cavalry accompanying this division.

I suppose that, among the large steamers about Baltimore, the additional transportation for this artillery and cavalry could be found. If so, we have a force of 10,000 or 11,000, with artillery and cavalry, provided for.

For a second column, I think I would embark it from the Port Tobacco River. The concentration of troops under Hooker would cover a movement that way, and it would threaten the Potomac batteries.

The Navy will furnish four side-wheel steamers and the Stepping Stones, which will carry 3,500.

The Quartermaster's Department has seven steamers, which will carry 5,000, and, collecting the eight or nine Schuylkill barges to be found here and schooners and tugboats, so doubtless transportation could be commanded for 10,000 men, with three batteries of artillery and 1,000 cavalry. You will observe my estimates are much lower than before, for then I was considering an operation restricted to the Potomac and of not more than 50 or 60 miles.

Now for additional numbers: I am inclined to think it is easier to carry troops to New York (twelve hours), embark them there, and make but one thing of it, than to bring the shipping to Annapolis or the Potomac. However that may be, if it is determined that the additional number shall be 10,000 men or 20,000 men, or more, I would command the transportation at once in New York, the place where everything can be had in unstinted quantities and of the most suitable kind. All sea steamers (not otherwise chartered), the large sound steamers, the large North River, sound, and coasting propellers, can be had there; and there all the appliances to fit them for troops, horses, &c., can be quickest made.

Perhaps the best way, therefore, would be to commence at once and send the troops, artillery and cavalry, to Fort Monroe, to hold themselves ready for shipment at a moment's notice; to order the transportation necessary in New York.

According to the foregoing propositions, there would be three columns ready for a simultaneous movement: 10,000 at Annapolis, 10,000 at Port

Tobacco River, and 10,000 or 20,000 at Fort Monroe. The times of starting could be arranged so that the times of arrival should be as desired.

Probably it would be better to have more than one point of debarkation. As soon as the first column was landed the transports could go immediately to Annapolis or Baltimore for more.

The arrangements give no indications of the intended point of attack. They threaten the Potomac, or Norfolk, or the Southern coast, as much as or more than the Rappahannock.

I presume there would be no difficulty in sending our steamers down to Port Tobacco; whether there would be in towing the barges there, I do not know. This Potomac column does not satisfy me as well as the others, for the collection of troops at Port Tobacco, in connection with collecting at Fort Monroe and Annapolis, would rather indicate an operation in the Lower Chesapeake.

Distance of points mentioned: Urbana to Annapolis, 120 miles; Port Tobacco, 90 miles; Fort Monroe, 60 miles.

Respectfully submitted.

> J. G. BARNARD,
> *Chief Engineer, Army of the Potomac.*

HEADQUARTERS OF THE ARMY,
Washington, D. C., December 2, 1861.

Maj. Gen. N. P. BANKS, *U. S. Service, Commanding, &c.:*

SIR: The General-in-Chief desires you to order Lander's brigade, as soon as it receives arms, to re-enforce General Kelley at Romney, Va.

I am, sir, &c.,

> L. THOMAS,
> *Adjutant-General.*

HEADQUARTERS HOOKER'S DIVISION,
Camp Baker, Lower Potomac, Maryland, December 2, 1861.

Brig. Gen. S. WILLIAMS,
Assistant Adjutant-General, Army of the Potomac:

GENERAL: The rebels within the last day or two appear to be more active than they have been for some weeks past. New encampments have been formed and additional earthworks have been thrown up above and below me. I am informed that a regiment has within this time encamped opposite Indian Head, and that lines of new intrenchments are visible in that vicinity. Additional encampments have also been formed below, and about Cockpit Point they are also unusually active. We have not heard from the batteries to-day.

The New Jersey Regiments will be encamped in close proximity and along the ridge of high ground making up from the Chicamaxen.

Bunting's battery, ordered to my command by Special Orders, No. 154, dated Headquarters Army of the Potomac, November 23, 1861, and which I was informed by the chief of artillery would leave Washington on Thursday last, has not yet joined.

Very respectfully, your obedient servant,

> JOSEPH HOOKER,
> *Brigadier-General, Commanding Division.*

EXECUTIVE DEPARTMENT,
Wheeling, Va., December 3, 1861..

His Excellency ABRAHAM LINCOLN:

At the instance of Governor Peirpoint I have drawn up the inclosed petition, and, concurring heartily in the measure, I submit the following in support of the same, outside of what the petition contains. It will, if granted, inspire the people with confidence, where all is now doubt and terror.

That a river, populous on either bank, is not a proper boundary of departments (military) when war exists. That concert of action in the conterminous counties of Kentucky and Virginia are absolutely necessary to a complete success in the prosecution of the war in that region. That no additional expense will be incurred, as the regiments are now in the service. That the commanders of the departments from which the proposed one is to be made will have ample fields remaining in which to act, nor feel the excision of the new one. That the Virginians will lose their sectional prejudices when mingling with their Kentucky neighbors, and carry home to them that they are fighting their friends and associates and those allied to them by similar habits and feelings. That we can erect the civil government of West Virginia, when it is impossible to do so under existing state of things.

Very respectfully, your obedient servant,
H. I. SAMUELS,
Adjutant-General of Virginia.

[Inclosure.]

To His Excellency ABRAHAM LINCOLN,
President of the United States:

Please take the map of Virginia, Kentucky, and Ohio. You will find the most southern portion of Ohio near the junction of these three States, at which point the Big Sandy River, a river navigable for steamers at this season for 60 miles, almost due south, in the direction of the Great Southwestern Railroad and East Tennessee, enters the Ohio River, and which forms the common boundary of Virginia and Kentucky for a hundred miles.

Running parallel with the Big Sandy River is the Guyandotte on the east, and Little Sandy River and Tygart's Creek on the west, all emptying into the Ohio, and all traversing an exceedingly mountainous region of country.

That part of the territory of Virginia watered by the Guyandotte and the Sandy Rivers is in a state of perfect anarchy, no one claiming to hold a civil office, and a perfect terrorism paralyzes every effort to restore law and order in that region; and such will be the state of the country as long as the rebel chiefs (Jenkins and Clarkson) are permitted to remain in that region and make their periodic raids through the same at pleasure. The people are divided in sentiment, but would flock to that power that would inspire confidence that they would be protected.

The people of Kentucky, on the waters of the Sandy, Little Sandy, and Tygart's Creek are mostly loyal, and have raised two entire regiments of men, now ready for service; and the people, in their manners, customs, habits, feelings, and prejudices much like the people in the region of Virginia referred to, and the same similarity in the geographical features of the country exists.

This region of country has been neglected by the Federal generals, because of its being the dividing line between the Departments of Kentucky and Western Virginia, and because the character of the warfare required too much detail and division of troops to occupy the time and attention of the commanders of departments, and we are satisfied that a general who would avail himself of the peculiar characteristics of the inhabitants would do more to clear that region of rebellion than large armies directed by military science and skill.

The valleys of the Sandy and the Guyandotte have been highways through which the rebels have introduced arms and munitions of war ever since the rebellion started to their armies menacing the camps at Gauley and Sewell Mountain.

We believe a brigadier, with latitudinous powers, if possessed of shrewdness, a capacity to seize and avail himself of the occurrences passing, with the mental constitution and mannerism to inspire the people with respect and confidence, not hampered or thwarted by officers near him, would, with the military material now there and which he could gather, clear the country of roving banditti now infesting it, and restore civil government, law, and order.

We therefore pray your excellency to erect a new military department, to be called the Department of Big Sandy; commit it to the charge of a brigadier-general, to take command of the Fourth and Fifth Virginia Volunteer Infantry; the First Virginia Volunteer Cavalry; the volunteers in Kentucky, in the region described—being the regiments commanded by Hon. L. T. Moore and Colonel Wilson—and that the region of country named, together with such adjacent counties in Ohio, be the bounds of such new department.

And as in duty bound will ever pray, &c.

F. H. PEIRPOINT,
Governor of Virginia,
By H. I. SAMUELS,
Adjutant-General of Virginia.
H. I. SAMUELS,
Adjutant-General of Virginia.
RALPH LUTE,
Of Ohio.

HEADQUARTERS HOOKER'S DIVISION,
Camp Baker, Lower Potomac, Maryland, December 6, 1861.
Brig. Gen. S. WILLIAMS,
Adjutant-General, Army of the Potomac:

GENERAL: I have to-day dispatched a squadron of the Third Indiana Cavalry to take post at Millstone Landing, with instructions to radiate from that point in all directions and at all times, and to visit all places deserving of notice lying near the coast between Port Tobacco and Lookout. The command is under Major Chapman, of that regiment. They will intercept all contraband trade and correspondence, and arrest persons concerned in it, and all traitors, and send them under guard to camp. For this service I prefer cavalry to infantry, for they move with more celerity, and can do more service than three times the number on foot. They can encounter no resistance in this part of Maryland they cannot overcome, and by moving rapidly they inspire more fear than can a column of infantry.

With the roads in their present condition it is of great consequence to detach the smallest possible force necessary, from the difficulty in supplying them. I have a cavalry company also doing picket duty from Smith's Point to Port Tobacco. This makes a continuous line of pickets along the shores of the Potomac from Mattawoman Creek to Cape Lookout. They may not be able to cut off all intercourse across the Potomac; this I cannot expect; but they will arrest some, and defeat the plans of many.

I have nothing new to report of my command or of the enemy.

Very respectfully, your obedient servant,

JOSEPH HOOKER,
Brigadier-General, Commanding Division.

WASHINGTON, *December* 6, 1861.

Maj. Gen. GEORGE B. MCCLELLAN,
Commanding Army of the Potomac, &c.:

GENERAL: It appears probable that our available appropriations will not suffice to complete entirely the defensive works about Washington. Forty-eight different works, some of which, like Forts Ethan Allen, Runyon, and Lyon, are of very large size, extensive abatis, &c., have been constructed, and many of them, besides the usual magazines, are provided with extensive bomb-proofs for quarters. For these constructions the sum of $344,053.46 has been available. It is probable that this sum will not entirely suffice, and that it will be more than exhausted by the close of the present month. I therefore request that an application be made to Congress for the immediate appropriation of the sum of $150,000 for completing the defenses of Washington.

You are aware that while hired labor has been extensively employed south of the Potomac, the works north of the river have been almost exclusively constructed by it.

I am, very respectfully, your obedient servant,

J. G. BARNARD,
Brigadier-General and Chief Engineer, Army of Potomac.

HEADQUARTERS, DIVISION AT FREDERICK,
December 7, 1861.

Brig. Gen. R. B. MARCY, *Chief of Staff:*

DEAR SIR: The division is well camped in the vicinity of Frederick, in good position, and with plenty supplies of all kinds. We are on the different lines of railway and turnpike, and can move in any direction in full force at a moment's notice.

I returned last evening from a visit to Sandy Hook and Harper's Ferry. The town is a picture of desolation. In the interior the rebels are active and their scouts on the move constantly. They are now endeavoring to put the railway from Winchester to Harper's Ferry in working condition if possible.

General Jackson is fortifying Winchester as far as he is able and calling in the militia to strengthen his forces, which do not now exceed 5,000 or 6,000. General Carson is said to be at or near Berkeley Springs, with about 1,500 men. They are sensitive to the chances of an attack by our forces, and I do not think that they are likely to disturb General Kelley at present. Colonel Leonard is in connection with General Kelley before this, but we have not heard from him yet. Reports in

Loudoun County, Virginia, represent that 9,000 or 10,000 men have been drawn south from Manassas.

The canal is now open to navigation. We were told that boats with coal were near Harper's Ferry yesterday on the way to Georgetown, and that 1,000 tons daily would soon be sent to the town for public and private use.

The opening of the railway is a feasible project, but it will require the whole force of our division to protect the work.

I am, sir, with great respect, your obedient servant,

N. P. BANKS,
Major-General, Commanding Division.

WASHINGTON, D. C., *December* 7, 1861.

Brigadier-General MARCY:

SIR: I have the honor to submit the following report concerning the facilities for passing troops across the Potomac at Harper's Ferry, Williamsport, &c. At Harper's Ferry the river is about 600 feet wide. The Maryland shore is of difficult access, owing to the canal bank, being nearly 20 feet high and supported by masonry. The Virginia shore is in like manner difficult, owing to the embankments of the arsenal yard, which are supported by masonry.

There is a lock leading from the canal into the Potomac a short distance below the remains of the railroad bridge; at low water usually from 4 to 6 feet, but rises very rapidly on sudden rains to a height of 26 feet. The difficulties of a bridge at this point are the approaches. Passing up the river about 1 mile to the Government dam the river widens a little, but the Virginia shore is of a much easier access, and the country road leading from Harper's Ferry to Charlestown can be reached by passing one-half mile over a country road. The Maryland shore at this point must be reached by passing a short distance upon the tow-path of the canal, which is sufficiently wide for one track but difficult for two. There is also a lock leading into the Potomac at this place.

As directed, I consulted Captain Duane (Colonel Alexander being ill), and learn that the pontoon bridge at the Eastern Branch is serviceable, and can be sent to any point you may direct. The bridge, being of India rubber, is not very stable and is easily damaged.

I would respectfully suggest a bridge supported by canal-boats instead. There is a sufficient number of boats in the canal, and lumber of suitable size can be procured at Baltimore or Cumberland on very short notice. The bridge-builders of the Baltimore and Ohio Railroad can without doubt be procured to do the work. The boats can be locked into the river and anchored in their places immediately.

At Williamsport the river is of nearly the same width as at Harper's Ferry; current not rapid; approaches on either shore of easy access. A small ferry-boat of a few tons burden plies by means of a wire cable from shore to shore. A bridge supported by two flat-boats, such as are found in nearly every level of the canal, would enable from 300 to 500 men to cross at once. There being no lock between Dams Nos. 4 and 5, the boats must be moved from the canal by means of a derrick or like machinery. Plank can be procured at different points on the canal—at

Williamsport, Point of Rocks, &c. I have never been at Hancock or Sir John's Run.

I have the honor to be, general, respectfully, your obedient servant,
O. E. BABCOCK,
Corps of Engineers.

HEADQUARTERS DIVISION,
Frederick, Md., December 8, 1861.
Colonel LEONARD, *Commanding at Williamsport:*

MY DEAR SIR: Reports by way of Philadelphia represent that heavy and close cannonading was heard at Chambersburg all the afternoon in the direction of Hancock. You will ascertain, if possible, what was the occasion of the firing, and, so far as you can, the purpose of the rebels in regard to General Kelley. Do not hesitate, if he is threatened, to send him aid at once—if need be, all your force—and I will supply your place on the river upon notice of your movement. Keep us well informed of the movements in his locality, as in your own. Obtain all the information you can concerning Martinsburg, its forces, defenses, &c., and especially the lay of the land about the town.

Very truly, yours,
N. P. BANKS,
Major-General, Commanding Division.

P. S.—Lander's brigade will be sent to re-enforce General Kelley as soon as it arrives.

[DECEMBER 10, 1861.—For McClellan to Lincoln, in reference to forward movement, found too late for publication here, see Series I, Vol. XI, Part III.]

OFFICE CHIEF ENGINEER ARMY OF POTOMAC,
Washington, D. C., December 10, 1861.
General J. G. TOTTEN, *Chief of Engineers, &c.:*

SIR: The resolution of the House of Representatives of July 8, of which the following is the tenor—

Resolved, That the Secretary of War be requested to furnish this House, as soon as practicable, plans and estimates, to be prepared by the Engineer Department, for completing the defensive works on the south side of the Potomac, near this city ; and also to report upon the expediency of constructing similar works of defense on the northern side of this city, with estimates for the same, so as to reduce to a minimum the number of troops required for the protection and defense of the capital—

having been submitted to me in July last, I now make the following statement :

At the time when the resolution was referred to me I was attached to the headquarters of Brigadier-General McDowell as chief engineer, and a few days thereafter I was in the field engaged in the campaign of Bull Run. Previous to this movement the army of Washington, yet weak in numbers and imperfectly organized. under General Mansfield, had crossed the Potomac and occupied the south bank from opposite Georgetown to Alexandria.

The first operations of field engineering were, necessarily, the securing of our debouches to the other shore and establishing of a strong point to strengthen our hold of Alexandria. The works required for these limited objects (though being really little towards constructing a defensive line) were nevertheless, considering the small number of troops available, arduous undertakings. Fort Corcoran, with its auxiliary works, Forts Bennett and Haggerty, and the block-houses and infantry parapets around the head of the Aqueduct, Forts Runyon, Jackson, and Albany (covering our debouches from the Long Bridge), and Fort Ellsworth, on Shooter's Hill, Alexandria, were mostly works of large dimensions. During the seven weeks which elapsed between the crossing of the Potomac and the advance of General McDowell's army the engineer officers under my command were so exclusively occupied with these works (all of which were nearly completed at the latter date), as to make impracticable the more general reconnaissances and studies necessary for locating a line of defensive works around the city and preparing plans and estimates of the same.

The works just mentioned on the south of the Potomac, necessary for the operations of an army on that shore, were far from constituting a defensive system which would enable an inferior force to hold the long line from Alexandria to Georgetown or even to secure the heights of Arlington.

On the retreat of our army such was our situation. Upon an inferior and demoralized force, in presence of a victorious and superior enemy, was imposed the duty of holding this line and defending the city of Washington against attacks from columns of the enemy who might cross the Potomac (as was then deemed probable) above or below.

Undecided before as to the necessity, or at least the policy, of surrounding Washington by a chain of fortifications, the situation left no longer room to doubt. With our army too demoralized and too weak in numbers to act effectually in the open field against the invading enemy, nothing but the protection of defensive works could give any degree of security. Indeed, it is probable that we owe our exemption from the real disaster which might have flowed from the defeat of Bull Run—the loss to the enemy of the real fruits of his victory—to the works previously built (already mentioned), and an exaggerated idea on his part of their efficiency as a defensive line.

The situation was such as to admit of no elaborate plans nor previously-prepared estimates. Defensive arrangements were improvised and works commenced as speedily as possible where most needed. A belt of woods was felled through the forest in front of Arlington and half-sunk batteries prepared along the ridge in front of Fort Corcoran and at suitable points near Fort Albany, and a battery of two rifled 42-pounders (Battery Cameron) was established on the heights near the distributing reservoir above Georgetown to sweep the approaches to Fort Corcoran.

Simultaneously a chain of lunettes (Forts De Kalb, Woodbury, Cass, Tillinghast, and Craig) was commenced, connecting Fort Corcoran and the Potomac on the right with Fort Albany on the left, and forming a continuous defensive line in advance of the heights of Arlington. The wooded ridge which lies north of and parallel to the lower course of Four Mile Run offered a position from which the city, the Long Bridge, and the plateau in advance of it could be overlooked and cannonaded. While our external line was so incomplete, it was important to exclude the enemy from its possession. Access to it was made difficult by felling the forest which covered it (about 200 acres), and the large lunette (Fort Scott) was commenced as soon as the site could be fixed (about the middle of August). The subsequent establishment of our defensive line in advance throws this work into the same category with Forts Corcoran, Albany, Runyon, &c., as an interior work, or second line, but it is nevertheless an important work, as, taken in connection with Forts Richardson, Craig, &c., it completes a defensive line for Washington independent of the extension to Alexandria.

The defense of Alexandria and its connection with that of Washington was a subject of anxious study. The exigency demanding immediate measures, the first idea was naturally to make use of Fort Ellsworth as one point of our line, and to connect it with Fort Scott by an intermediate work on Mount Ida. An extended study of the topography for several miles in advance showed that such a line would be almost indefensible. Not only would the works themselves be commanded by surrounding heights, but the troops which should support them would be restricted to a narrow space, in which they would be overlooked and harassed by the enemy's distant fire. The occupation of the heights a mile in advance of Fort Ellsworth, upon which the Episcopal Seminary is situated, seemed absolutely necessary. The topography proved admirably adapted to the formation of such a line, and Forts Worth and Ward were commenced about the 1st of September, and the line continued simultaneously by Forts Blenker and Richardson to connect with Forts Albany and Craig. Somewhat later the work intermediate between Blenker and Richardson—filling up the gap and having an important bearing upon the approaches to Forts Ward and Blenker and the valley of Four Mile Run—was commenced.

The heights south of Hunting Creek, overlooking Alexandria and commanding Fort Ellsworth, had been always a subject of anxiety. The securing to our own possession the Seminary Heights, which commanded them, diminished materially the danger. As soon, however, as a sufficient force could be detached to occupy those heights and protect the construction of the work it was undertaken, and the large work (Fort Lyon) laid out and commenced about the middle of September.

Previous to the movement of the army defensive measures had been taken at the Chain Bridge, consisting of a barricade (bullet proof, and so arranged as to be thrown down at will) across the bridge, immediately over the first pier from the Virginia side, with a movable staircase to the flats below, by which the defenders could retreat, leaving the bridge open to the fire of a battery of two field guns immediately at its Maryland end, and a battery on the bluff above (Battery Martin Scott) of one 8-inch sea-coast howitzer and two 32-pounders. As even this last battery was commanded by heights on the Virginia side, it was deemed proper, after the return of the army, to erect another battery (Battery Vermont) at a higher point, which should command the Virginia Heights and at the same time sweep the approaches of the enemy along the Maryland shore of the Potomac.

During the months of May and June the country between the Potomac and the Anacostia had been examined mainly with the view of obtaining knowledge of the roads and defensive character of the ground, not in reference to locating field defenses. At the period now in question there was apprehension that the enemy might cross the Potomac and attack on this side. Of course what could be done to meet the emergency could only be done without that deliberate study by which a complete defensive line would best be established. The first directions given to our labors were to secure the roads, not merely as the beaten highways of travel from the country to the city, but also as in general occupying the best ground for an enemy's approach.

Thus the sites of Forts Pennsylvania, Massachusetts, Slocum, Totten, Bunker Hill, Saratoga, and Lincoln were rapidly chosen, and works commenced simultaneously at the first, second, third, and sixth of these points early in August. The others were taken up as speedily as the clearing of the woods and the means at our disposal would admit, and the gaps in the line afterwards partially filled up by construction of Fort Gaines, Forts De Russy, Slemmer, and Thayer. The works mentioned are at this date essentially completed and armed, though there is still considerable to do in auxiliary arrangements. Our first ideas as to defensive works beyond the Anacostia contemplated only the fortification of the debouches from the bridges (Navy-Yard Bridge and Benning's Bridge), and the occupation of the heights overlooking the Navy-Yard Bridge. With that object Fort Stanton was commenced early in September. A further examination of the remarkable ridge between the Anacostia and Oxen Run showed clearly that, to protect the navy-yard and arsenal from bombardment, it was necessary to occupy an extent of 6 miles from Berry's place (Fort Greble) to the intersection of the road from Benning's Bridge (Fort Meigs).

Forts Greble and Carroll were commenced in the latter part of September, and Fort Mahan, near Benning's Bridge, about the same time. Forts Greble and Stanton are completed and armed; Forts Mahan and Carroll very nearly so. To fill up intervals or to sweep ravines not seen by the principal works, Forts Meigs, Dupont, Davis, Baker, Good Hope, Battery Ricketts, and Fort Snyder have been commenced, and it is hoped may be so far advanced before the winter sets in as to get them into a defensible condition. The occupation of the Virginia shore at the Chain Bridge was essential to the operations of our army in Virginia. It was only delayed until our force was sufficient to authorize it. General Smith's division crossed the bridge September —, and Forts Ethan Allen and Marcy were immediately commenced and speedily finished.

A few weeks later (September 28) the positions of Upton's and Munson's Hills and Taylor's Tavern were occupied and Fort Ramsay commenced on Upton's Hill. The enemy's works on Munson's and the adjacent hill were strengthened and a lunette built near Taylor's Tavern.

Comprised in the foregoing categories there are twenty-three field forts south of the Potomac, fourteen field forts and three batteries between the Potomac and Anacostia, and eleven field forts beyond the Anacostia, making forty-eight field forts in all. These vary in size from Forts Runyon, Lyon, and Marcy, of which the perimeters are 1,500, 937, and 736 yards, down to Forts Bennett, Haggerty, and Saratoga, &c., with perimeters of 146, 128, and 154 yards. The greater portion of them are inclosed works of earth, though many—as Forts Craig, Tillinghast, Scott, &c., south of the Potomac, and Forts Saratoga, Gaines, &c., on the north—are lunettes with stockaded gorges. The armament is mainly made up of 24 and 32 pounders on sea-coast carriages, with a limited proportion of 24-pounder siege guns, rifled Parrott guns, and guns on field carriages of lighter caliber. The larger of the works are flanked, but the greater number are not, the sites and dimensions not permitting. Magazines are provided for one hundred rounds of ammunition, and many of the works have a considerable extent of bomb-proof shelter, as Forts Lyon, Worth, and Ward, in the bomb-proofs of which probably one-third of the garrison might comfortably sleep and nearly all take temporary shelter. In nearly all the works there are either bomb-proofs like the above, or log barracks, or block-houses of some kind.

It would be impossible to go into any details about these constructions. I am in hopes ultimately to be able to deposit in the Engineer Office drawings of each work with sufficient detail for most purposes.

The accompanying sheets, Nos. 1 and 2, will exhibit the general location and bearings of the works.* The tabular statement herewith will show the perimeters, number of guns, amount of garrison, &c.†

It should be observed that most of the works south of the Potomac, having been thrown up almost in the face of the enemy, have very light profiles, the object having been to get cover and a defensive work as speedily as possible. The counterscarps of all the works, with few exceptions, are surrounded by abatis.

It is impossible, at present, to indicate the exact extent of forest cut down. (The drawings herewith represent the forest as it existed before the works were commenced.)‡ The woods in advance of Forts Worth, Ward, and Blenker have been felled; all surrounding and between the next work on the right and Fort Richardson; all the wood on the ridge on which is Fort Scott—a square mile probably—in advance of and surrounding Forts Craig, Tillinghast, and Woodbury, besides large areas north of the Potomac, &c. This fallen timber (most of which still lies on the ground) rendered an enemy's approach to the lines difficult. The sites of Forts Totten, Slocum, Bunker Hill, Meigs, Stanton, and others were entirely wooded, which, in conjunction with the broken character of the ground, has made the selection of sites frequently very embarrassing and the labor of preparing them very great.

The only case in which forts are connected by earthworks is that of Forts Woodbury and De Kalb, between which an infantry parapet is thrown up, with emplacements for field guns. The construction here was suggested by the fact that this was on one of the most practicable and probable routes of approach for the enemy. Infantry trenches have, however, been constructed around or in advance of other works, either to cover the construction (as at Fort Lyon), or to see ground not seen by the work (as at Forts Totten, Lincoln, Mahan, &c.).

The works I have now described do not constitute a complete defensive system.

We have been obliged to neglect much and even to throw out of consideration important matters. We have been too much hurried to devise a perfect system, and even now are unable to say precisely what and how many additional points should be occupied and what auxiliary arrangements should be made.

It is safe to say that at least two additional works are required to connect Fort Ethan Allen with Fort De Kalb.

The necessity of protecting the Chain Bridge compelled us to throw the left of our northern line several miles in advance of its natural position, as indicated by the topography to the sites of Forts Ripley, Alexander, and Franklin. Between these and Forts Gaines or Pennsylvania one or two intervening works are necessary.

Between Forts Pennsylvania and De Russy at least one additional work is necessary.

Fort Massachusetts is entirely too small for its important position. Auxiliary works are necessary in connection with it.

Small *têtes de-pont* are required around the heads of Benning's and the Navy-Yard Bridges.

Between Forts Mahan and Meigs one or more intervening works and between Forts Du Pont and Davis another work of some magnitude are required, the ground along this line not being yet sufficiently known. A

---

* To appear in Atlas.

† No tabular statement found as an inclosure to this report, but see Barnard and Barry to Williams, October 24, pp. 626–628.

‡ Omitted.

glance at the map will show it to be almost a continuous forest. It is not deemed necessary to connect the works by a continuous line of parapet, but the intervening woods should be abatised and open ground traversed by a line of artificial abatis, and infantry parapets, half-sunk batteries, &c., placed so as to protect these obstructions and to see all the irregularities of the ground not now seen from the works. Considerable work is also required in the way of roads, the amount of which I cannot state with any precision. Several miles of roads have actually been made. The works themselves would be very much strengthened by caponieres in the ditches, additional internal block-houses, or defensive barracks, &c.

The aggregate perimeter of all the works is about 15,500 yards, or nearly 9 miles, including the stockaded gorges, which, however, form a small proportion of the whole, requiring, computed according to the rule adopted for the lines of Torres Vedras, 22,674 men (about) for garrisons.

The number of guns, most of which are actually mounted, is about four hundred and eighty, requiring about 7,200 men to furnish three reliefs of gunners. The permanent garrisons need consist of only these gunners, and even in case of attack it will seldom be necessary to keep full garrisons in all the works.

The total garrisons for all the works (one hundred and fifty-two in number) of the lines of Torres Vedras amounted to 34,125 men; and as the total perimeters are nearly proportional to the total garrisons, it appears that the lines about Washington involve a magnitude of work of about two-thirds of that in the three lines of Torres Vedras.

The works themselves, fewer in number, are generally much larger than those of Torres Vedras, and involve, I believe, when the amount of bomb-proof shelter in ours is considered, more labor per yard of perimeter; but the latter lines involved a greater amount of auxiliary work, such as the scraping of mountain slopes, palisading, abatis, roads, &c., than we have had occasion to make.

The lines of Torres Vedras were armed with five hundred and thirty-four pieces of ordnance (12, 9, or 6 pounders, with a few field howitzers); ours with four hundred and eighty pieces, of which the greater number are 32-pounders on barbette carriages, the rest being 24-pounders on the same carriages, 24-pounder siege guns, 10, 20, and 30 pounder rifled guns (Parrott), with a few field pieces and howitzers. As to number of guns, therefore, our armament approaches to equality with that of the famous lines mentioned; in weight of metal more than doubles it.

The above applies to our works as now nearly completed, and has no reference to the additional works I have elsewhere mentioned as hereafter necessary. It is impossible to give any other statement of actual cost of the works than the total amount expended thus far. The work has been done partly by troops and partly by hired laborers, the works north of the Potomac being mostly done by the latter. The large amount of carpentry in magazine frames and doors and blindages, barrier gates, stockades, block-houses, defensive barracks, &c., has kept a large gang of carpenters all the time at work, and caused a large expenditure for lumber. The entire amount made available by the Department for these works has been $344,053.46, and this will all have been expended (or more) by the end of the present month. This would give an average of a little over $7,000 for each of the forty-eight works; but of course the real cost of them has been very unequal.

The importance of perfect security to the capital of the United States in the present state of affairs can scarcely be overestimated, and these works give a security which mere numbers cannot give, and at not a tithe the expense of defense by troops alone.

It is impossible to make anything like a reliable estimate of what additional amount of funds will be required. In a letter to the General-in-Chief commanding Army of the Potomac, of December 6, I urged an immediate appropriation of $150,000, and this appropriation has been asked for of Congress by the Secretary of War.

Should the auxiliary works which I have suggested be undertaken and the scarps be revetted, I believe a larger sum than this may be judiciously expended. I therefore recommend that an additional $100,000, or $250,000 in all, be provided for the continuation and completion of the defenses of Washington. These works acquire new importance if the probability of a foreign war is taken into consideration. In view of this new importance, of the semi-permanent or possibly permanent necessity for such works, it is proper to suggest that early in the spring the scarps be protected by a timber or thin brick revetment, and the exterior and other slopes, where not already done, be sodded, and that wooden caponieres, or counterscarp galleries, be arranged to flank all unflanked ditches—at least of important works. The strengthening of the profiles where necessary has already been mentioned as important.

It remains with me to express my sense of the zeal and efficiency with which the officers of engineers serving with me since April have discharged their duties. To their energy and skill I am mainly indebted for the successful accomplishment of this really great work, and I feel that I have a right to say that for the safety of the capital in the hour of its greatest danger; for saving the cause of established government and the Constitution from the most serious blow the rebels could have inflicted, the country owes much to the labors of the engineers. From their great experience and constant association with me since April the services of Colonels Woodbury and Alexander have been particularly important in the laborious reconnaissances and in directing the execution of extensive lines of works.

General Wright laid out and superintended the construction of Fort Ellsworth, and General Newton, who since the 1st of September until recently had charge of the works below Four Mile Run, laid out and directed the construction of Fort Lyon.

Captains Blunt and Prime, Lieutenants Comstock, Houston, McAlester, Robert, Paine, Cross, Babcock, and Dutton have served with efficiency during the whole or part of these constructions, and the lamented Snyder lost his life from over-zealousness in discharge of his duties while in impaired health from his services at Charleston Harbor and Fort Sumter. Since the relief of Captain Prime, Lieut. H. L. Abbot, of the Topographical Engineers, has taken his place, proved himself a most energetic and valuable assistant, having completed Fort Scott and built Forts Richardson and Barnard. In carrying out so many works at the same time, and for organizing and managing the large bodies of hired laborers employed, it has been found necessary to call in the aid of civil engineers, not only because the engineer officers were too few to keep proper supervision, but because a large portion of those under my orders have been called off to other duties, such as the organization of bridge trains, the instruction of engineer troops, &c. Civil Engineers Gunnel, Frost, Faber, Childs, and Stone have rendered valuable services; also Mr. (now major of the Fifteenth New York Volunteer Regiment) Magruder. I should also express my warmest acknowledgment to Mr. James Eveleth, of your office, who, as disbursing agent and paymaster of the large bodies of hired laborers, has performed an amount of duty I should hardly have expected from one individual. I could wish that the law under which he serves the Engineer Department, might be so modified in his case as to enable him to receive some adequate compensation for the extra duties he has voluntarily assumed. I should have mentioned, in connection with my statement of the amount actually expended, that the Treasury Department has advanced over $20,000 on account of the defenses of Washington, which should be refunded. I feel it my duty in this place to urge that Congress should take immediate measures to assess the land and other damages arising from these works and from the occupation of troops. In most cases the owners are ill able to bear temporarily the losses to which they have been subjected.

In conclusion, I would add that to the great importance attached to these works by the commanding general (now Commander-in-Chief), to his valuable suggestions and prompt and cordial co-operation, the present state of efficiency of the defenses of Washington is in no small degree due.

I am, very respectfully, your obedient servant,

J. G. BARNARD,
Maj. of Eng., Brig. Gen., and Chief Eng. Army of Potomac.

GENERAL ORDERS, ╲　　　HDQRS. CORPS OF OBSERVATION,
　No. 33.　　　╱　　　　*Poolesville, December 10,* 1861.

In compliance with Special Orders, No. 322, of December 6, 1861, headquarters of the Army, received this day, the undersigned assumes military supervision of the Chesapeake and Ohio Canal.

All officers commanding lines of pickets between Great Falls and the Monocacy River are commanded, and all officers commanding pickets and lines of pickets along other portions of the canal are requested, to give all aid and assistance in their power, consistent with the good of the service, to the Canal Company authorities in the preservation and improvement of the canal.

CHAS. P. STONE,
Brigadier-General, Commanding.

GENERAL ORDERS, ╲　　　HDQRS. DEPT. WESTERN VIRGINIA,
　No. 16.　　　╱　　　　*Wheeling, Va., December 11,* 1861.

I. The headquarters of the Department of Western Virginia will until further orders be Wheeling, Va.

*　　　*　　　*　　　*　　　*　　　*　　　*

By command of Brigadier-General Rosecrans:

GEO. L. HARTSUFF,
Assistant Adjutant-General.

HEADQUARTERS,
Baltimore, December 12, 1861.

Hon. S. P. CHASE, *Secretary of the Treasury:*

SIR: In a letter to you of the 5th instant I mentioned, in connection with a recommendation of two persons in Accomac and Northampton

Counties, Virginia, for the offices of collector and surveyor, that all my information from these counties was very satisfactory. I have to-day received a letter from General Lockwood, in which he says that he summoned all the magistrates of Accomac County before him; that they all took the oath of allegiance, as well as the sheriff and his deputies and clerks. He adds: "After this there was quite a rush of smaller officers to do likewise." He was to go in a day or two after to Northampton and pursue the same course. He has made but a single arrest for disloyalty.

I consider the restoration of these counties to the Union complete, and if our troops were to be entirely withdrawn I am satisfied that there would be no movement against the Government. Of the 3,200 men sent from here I have brought back 3,100. There are about 1,000 left in the two counties. As soon as convenient I trust you will appoint a collector and surveyor.

I am, very respectfully, your obedient servant,

JOHN A. DIX,
Major-General.

HEADQUARTERS HOOKER'S DIVISION,
Camp Baker, Lower Potomac, Maryland, December 13, 1861.

Brig. Gen. S. WILLIAMS,
Assistant Adjutant-General, Army of the Potomac:

The commander of the Second Brigade reported to me this morning that the rebels had established a battery opposite to Maryland Point, where the channel makes in close to the Virginia shore, which promised to give our transports and other vessels some little annoyance in ascending the river. Not being able to give it a personal inspection, I made application to the officer commanding the second division of the flotilla for information concerning it. In reply I learn that it is a field battery, and the one to which I have before alluded. It is a light field battery of six rifled pieces, planted on the bank of the river during the day and removed at night. It has a regiment or two, as supports, in its vicinity.

I am further informed that vessels, in order to pass up and down the river, have to pass within three-quarters of a mile of the Virginia shore, and in case it is required of them, in my opinion, some of the guns of the flotilla can with advantage exchange shots with this battery, as it is entirely exposed; they have longer range, and are not more exposed than the enemy. But for the broad river I might possibly surprise them, but to do that with steamboats is almost an absurdity; I have more confidence in being able to whip them than I have in being able to surprise them or even of capturing their battery.

About 2 o'clock a. m. two steamers passed from the upper to the lower flotilla, when they were saluted with two discharges from the enemy's heavy rifled gun. It fairly shook the earth on this side of the river. This was the only effect of it. Our vessels fired a few shots in answer and passed on.

I can remark no changes either in location or number of the rebel encampments.

Very respectfully, &c.,

JOSEPH HOOKER,
Brigadier-General, Commanding Division.

HEADQUARTERS HOOKER'S DIVISION,
Camp Baker, Lower Potomac, Maryland, December 15, 1861.
Brig. Gen. S. WILLIAMS,
Adjutant-General, Army of the Potomac :

To-day the enemy have exposed a battery of two pieces on a bluff bank, nearly midway between Cockpit and Shipping Points. It is directly across the river from the head of Stump Neck. The battery is concealed from view by the forest in which it is planted, but from the reports of the pieces and the accuracy of fire it is the opinion that the guns were taken from what is called the Maryland field battery of 12-pounders, which is encamped in the vicinity. We will know more of this in a day or two. The river is narrower at this point by a quarter of a mile than at Shipping Point, but as the channel hugs our shore a little closer than at Budd's Ferry, the difference of range cannot be material. I am not yet prepared to say that it will add to the annoyance of vessels navigating the river.

I desire to call the attention of the Major-General Commanding to the hazards of my position from the closing of the river by ice. From the present time until the 1st of March the navigation is liable to be interrupted from this cause, and in 1855 it was continuously suspended for a period of six weeks. It is not an unusual occurrence for the Potomac to be frozen over to its mouth. This will prevent supplies reaching us either from Washington or Baltimore.

I have not visited Liverpool Point for several days, but learn that our mechanics are making good progress with our store-house.

Very respectfully, &c.,
JOSEPH HOOKER,
Brigadier-General, Commanding Division.

[WHEELING,] *December* 15, 1861.
Brig. Gen. L. THOMAS, *Washington, D. C. :*

I have the honor to report, for the information of the Commanding General, my return to this place. The general orders of the 30th have been executed, except as to the four more regiments to Kentucky. The state of affairs now existing should be brought to the General's attention, as it may require his orders for a delay. There is a strong force reported on the headwaters of Sandy, not in my department. There is a direct turnpike road from Charleston to Sandy and from Sandy to Raleigh. Our stores are ordered up to Fayette, Gauley, Charleston, &c. Would it not be well not to thin still more the scattered forces until we see if an expedition cannot be arranged to cut off this rebel force? Sandy region ought, it seems to me, to belong to this department. Will the Commanding General allow me to come to Washington and see him in reference to these and many other details relating to the good of our service?

W. S. ROSECRANS.

ADJUTANT-GENERAL'S OFFICE,
Washington, D. C., December 16, 1861.
Brig. Gen. B. F. KELLEY, *U. S. Service, Romney, Va. :*

The news from Virginia is that you are to be attacked by some 7,000 or 8,000 men, probably from Winchester. It is supposed troops enough to repel them have been ordered to join you.

L. THOMAS, *Adjutant-General.*

FREDERICK, MD., *December* 16, 1861—9 o'clock.
Colonel LEONARD, *Williamsport:*
Let the Illinois regiment go at once. Be ready to move yourself.
Messenger on the road.

N. P. BANKS,
Major-General, Commanding Division.

FREDERICK, MD., *December* 16, 1861—10 p. m.
Colonel LEONARD, *Commanding at Williamsport:*
SIR: We have report to-night at 9 o'clock that General Kelley may be attacked to-night—perhaps from Winchester. Be ready to assist him with all your disposable force. The Fifth Connecticut Regiment will leave at daybreak for your post, with a section of artillery. You can order them on to Romney, if necessary, and call upon us for more troops, if they are wanted. Do not fail to be ready to move at the first call. Send messengers towards Kelley for news and telegraph us often. The Adjutant-General telegraphs to-night that you should dispose of the arms sent to Williamsport as follows.: Three thousand for the Lamon brigade; two thousand to be sent to Romney, by the way of Hancock, for the Pennsylvania regiments. This was the first order, and it is repeated again to-night by telegraph. Be on the alert, and keep us posted. We had a verbal report from Colonel Link, Twelfth Indiana, that rebels threatened to cross the river to-night at or near Sharpsburg. Do you know that danger of that kind exists? The messenger said he had lost his dispatches, but gave us the substance.
Very truly, yours,

N. P. BANKS,
Major-General, Commanding Division.

ADJUTANT-GENERAL'S OFFICE,
Washington, December 18, 1861.
Brig. Gen. W. S. ROSECRANS, U. S. A., *Wheeling, Va.:*
The General-in-Chief says it is not necessary for you to come to Washington. General Buell has made dispositions for the Big Sandy Valley. Co-operate with him if necessary, and also look to valley of Guyandotte, especially Logan Court-House.

L. THOMAS,
Adjutant-General.

GENERAL ORDERS, }   HDQRS. ARMY OF THE POTOMAC,
No. 56.   }   *Washington, December* 19, 1861.
I. Inasmuch as some misunderstanding appears to prevail on the subject of passes within the limits of this army, the existing regulations on the subject are republished for the benefit of all concerned.
1. No civilian can cross the Potomac into Virginia without a pass signed by the provost-marshal of Washington, or given at these headquarters, or at the headquarters of the army.
Civilians not suspected of disloyalty do not need a pass to enable them to travel within the section of country north of the Potomac.

2. No civilian needs a pass to cross the Potomac from Virginia into Washington.

3. Division and brigade commanders and provost-marshals (except the provost-marshal of Washington) have no authority to grant passes to civilians to cross the Potomac at all, unless the civilians be employed in connection with the army, in which case that fact will be stated on the pass.

4. Division and regimental commanders, the military governor and commander at Alexandria, and the commanders of bodies of troops not brigaded south of the Potomac may give passes to officers and soldiers and to civilians connected with the army to cross and recross the bridges and ferries.

Commanders of troops not brigaded will state on the pass the fact of their exercising such command. If the individual passed over be on official business, the pass should so state. A soldier's furlough or an officer's order of leave of absence, issued from the proper source, are sufficient evidences of authority to cross the Potomac going on leave.

5. No wine, beer, or ardent spirits, unless they be for hospital or subsistence stores, or the private stores of an officer, for his own use, (when they should be so marked,) shall pass the guards at any bridge or ferry on the Potomac or the guards of any camp or barracks, without a pass from the provost-marshal of Washington to cover the stores, or from these headquarters.

6. Loyal citizens, residents within our lines south of the Potomac, after having visited Washington, must have, to return to their homes, passes signed by the provost-marshal of Washington. Certificates as to their loyalty, from brigade or division commanders within the limits of whose command they reside, would have the effect to enable the provost-marshal to decide promptly upon the propriety of furnishing them with passes.

7. Commanders of the troops about Washington north of the Potomac can give no passes to any description of person to cross the river.

II. All fast riding or driving by officers and soldiers in the streets of Washington is prohibited.

The provost-marshal is directed to enforce this order.

Officers dispatching mounted messengers conveying papers will state upon the envelope of the dispatches the gait the messenger is to take—whether a walk, a trot, or a gallop.

The same directions may be indicated by the seals on an envelope—one seal for the walk, two for the trot, and three for the gallop. Officers will be held responsible for the instructions they give to mounted orderlies as to the gait of the messenger.

III. Quartermasters will instruct their wagon-masters and teamsters that trains passing through the streets of Washington shall leave an interval equal to the width of the street between every 10 wagons. Unnecessary locking of wheels is prohibited.

IV. Neither division nor brigade commanders can give leaves of absence to officers or furloughs to soldiers to leave this army at all. Neither officer nor soldier can pass beyond the limits of this army without permission from these headquarters. Leaves of absence for forty-eight hours and furloughs for the same period, not to go beyond the limits of this army, may be given by the division and brigade commanders.

The commanding generals at Baltimore, Frederick, and Poolesville are excepted from the above restrictions, in so far that they may approve furloughs for soldiers, restricting them to cases of urgent necessity and for short periods of time, and may grant leaves of absence to officers for forty-eight hours to pass beyond the limits of this army.

There are frequent cases of commanding officers ordering individuals to proceed beyond the limits of their superiors' commands without their consent or authority. This practice must be discontinued. The rights of command can only be exercised within the proper sphere of command.

By command of Major-General McClellan:

S. WILLIAMS,
Assistant Adjutant-General.

CAMP BAKER, LOWER POTOMAC, MARYLAND,
December 20, 1861.

Brig. Gen. S. WILLIAMS,
Adjutant-General, Army of the Potomac:

GENERAL: In compliance with instructions received from your office this evening, instructions have been given for requisitions to be prepared for forage and subsistence stores for this division for six weeks, They will be forwarded to the proper officers by to-morrow morning's steamer.

A small schooner passing down the river under gentle sail drew the fire this forenoon of all the rebel batteries. She presented so fair an object, and was gliding along so leisurely, that the enemy were tempted to expend some eighty or ninety shots on her, but she passed them all unharmed. If ever they should succeed in crippling one of our vessels, and attempt to take it, you must not be surprised to hear of a conflict on the water. It will be necessary to rescue her, whether of any value or not, for the effect it will produce on my troops. If I cannot control their irritation at these frequent exhibitions of power, it appears to me to be my duty to prevent their witnessing any of its triumphs.

I have received this evening another report from Major Chapman, dated the 18th instant, of the operations of his command in the southern extremity of the State. Inclosed you will receive such extracts from it as will be of interest or value to you.* The prisoner James B. Loker will be forwarded to the provost-marshal in Washington to-morrow morning. Directions will be given for the captured mail and money to be delivered with this report. The property reported as having been taken will be forwarded as soon as received.

The intelligence, energy, and good conduct displayed by Major Chapman and his command in the service in which they are engaged merit and will receive my commendation.

The Third Indiana Cavalry have been on the wing almost all the time since they joined me, singly and in bodies, and I have yet to learn of the first irregularity. The conduct of the enlisted men is as exemplary in the absence of authority as it is when present. It seems that no example, no temptation, can lead them astray.

Very respectfully, your obedient servant,

JOSEPH HOOKER,
Brigadier-General, Commanding Division.

---

* Not found.

GENERAL ORDERS, }   HDQRS. DEPT. OF WESTERN VIRGINIA,
    No. 20.   }   Wheeling, W. Va., December 20, 1861.

I. Both banks of the Gauley and Kanawha Rivers and all that portion of this department lying south of them will, until further orders, constitute a district, to be called the District of the Kanawha, and will be commanded by Brig. Gen. J. D. Cox. * * * The order creating the Kanawha Brigade is hereby revoked.

II. That portion of the department lying south of the railroad, west of Cheat Mountain, including it, and extending southward to the District of the Kanawha, will constitute a district, to be called the Cheat Mountain District, to be commanded by Brigadier-General Milroy. * * *

III. The railroads in the department, with the posts on them, will constitute the Railroad District, to be commanded by Brigadier-General Kelley.

* * * * * * *

By command of Brigadier-General Rosecrans:
                                    GEO. L. HARTSUFF,
                                        Assistant Adjutant-General.

                    HEADQUARTERS ARTILLERY RESERVE,
                                        December 22, 1861.
General S. WILLIAMS,
    Assistant Adjutant-General, Army of the Potomac:

GENERAL: I have respectfully to call attention to the want of men in the batteries of the reserve. The number of companies present is seventeen; total strength required for seventeen batteries, 2,550. There are but thirteen batteries, two companies being united in four cases in the same battery. The number of men required for thirteen batteries is 1,950. The total number of enlisted men reported this morning as belonging to the companies, (including) 69 reported absent, is 1,435.

To complete fully the thirteen batteries would therefore require 500 men; to complete the seventeen batteries 1,100 are required; from 400 to 1,000 men would probably answer.

I respectfully urge that some means be taken to furnish recruits to these batteries. They are commanded many of them by experienced officers, and are supplied with old non-commissioned officers, whose services it is important to make available to the fullest extent. If special recruiting rendezvous cannot be established, recruits may possibly be obtained from the regiment of volunteers by discharging from the service those who are willing to re-enlist from the batteries, with a promise that they shall be discharged at the end of the war if they desire it.

I am, sir, very respectfully, your obedient servant,
                                    HENRY J. HUNT,
                                        Colonel, Commanding.

                        EXECUTIVE DEPARTMENT,
                        Wheeling, Va., December 24, 1861.
Hon. SIMON CAMERON, Secretary of War, Washington, D. C.:

SIR: For some time past I have felt the necessity of altering the Military Department of Western Virginia at the dividing line between Virginia and Kentucky. There ought to be a separate division, embracing the waters of the Guyandotte River and all that part of Kentucky drained by the waters of the Big Sandy, or all of that part of Kentucky drained by the waters of the Big Sandy should be added to the Western Virginia Department—perhaps the latter would be the best—and assign a brigadier to that section, which has suffered somewhat for the want of a brigadier in the valley of the Sandy and Guyandotte, who would enforce better the administrative discipline of the army.

For the efficiency of the army I think there ought to be two, if not three more brigadiers in Western Virginia, and there should be a major-general in command of the division.

Upon the subject of brigadiers, if it is the policy to appoint merely politicians, without reference to their military experience, I desire to claim the rights of Virginia in the appointments. If, however, the administration should decide to appoint from the Regular Army men of military education fit for the position, without reference to locality, I shall be satisfied, and would decidedly recommend that course. It is military knowledge and discipline that are going to make the army effective.

With this view I would call your attention to Major Crawford and Captain Hartsuff, of the Regular Army. From a personal acquaintance with these men I am favorably impressed with them as men of large views and worthy of the consideration of the country. They have been in Western Virginia from the commencement of the war and are identified with us. They understand the wants and the necessities of the division.

I have tried to inform myself of General Rosecrans' operations in Western Virginia, and I think the people are well satisfied with his management of the campaign. I have been unable to see where it could have been bettered, and would respectfully ask that he be appointed major-general of this division, and the whole western part of the State, with that part of Kentucky drained by the waters of the Big Sandy, be put in his division.

Excuse me, sir, for making these suggestions. It is only my deep interest in the cause that urges me to this liberty.

I am, yours, &c.,

F. H. PEIRPOINT.

WASHINGTON, D. C., *December 26*, 1861.

Brigadier-General MARCY, *Chief of Staff:*

SIR: I have the honor to submit the following report upon the facilities for passing troops across the Potomac at Harper's Ferry and Williamsport.

I proceeded to Baltimore, had an interview with the president of the Baltimore and Ohio Railroad Company, who says the employés and such lumber as they have suitable for bridge building is at the service of the Government. The company has all the lumber necessary, and of suitable size for building.

From Baltimore I proceeded to Sandy Hook, via Frederick City. I found the water low, now fordable, and upon careful inquiry find the river is not usually subject to rise at this season. It is my opinion that a serviceable flying bridge cannot be put in at this point, nor can sufficiently extensive ferries be established upon short notice. I would respectfully recommend a bridge supported upon canal-boats. Such a bridge can be best placed about 100 yards above the remains of the railroad bridge, to enter the arsenal yard through an opening in the arsenal wall.

The bridge at this place will be about 800 feet long, requiring between twenty-five and thirty boats, depending upon the length of the timbers used. The Baltimore and Ohio Railroad Company have in their service 60 canal boats, and will have upon short notice the number required for a bridge at and near Sandy Hook.

The lift-lock of the canal at Sandy Hook is in good order. The president of the railroad informed me that a sufficient number of ships' anchors to anchor the bridge can be procured in Baltimore. Such bridge can be constructed in a short time, be made very stable and serviceable for all purposes.

A good ferry, supported upon flat-boats (a great many flat-boats can be found on the canal) across the Shenandoah, will be sufficient, as but a small number of men need be placed upon Loudoun Heights.

I visited Williamsport also. There is now a ferry there capable of carrying the four-horse country wagons heavily loaded. A piece of light artillery or 125 men can be taken at once, and in about three minutes. It is held by a wire cable six-eighths or seven-eighths of an inch in size. An extensive ferry might be quietly established there by using flat-boats. Plank and light lumber can be found in sufficient quantity at Williamsport. This ferry can be worked by a cable or with poles. The river is now fordable at this place.

I was also requested to give my opinion of the number of men sufficient to occupy Martinsburg. If Loudoun Heights are occupied by 400 or 500 infantry, Keys' Ferry (across the Shenandoah), with a like number of men and one or two pieces of artillery, I think a division sufficient to occupy Martinsburg, or if overwhelmed to make a safe retreat to Harper's Ferry. I would suggest that a strong detachment should be left at Charlestown to secure the rear. While such move is being made Winchester could be threatened by forces from Romney, and when Martinsburg is occupied a junction can be made with the troops at Hancock via Springfield. Harper's Ferry need be occupied by a garrison only. As it would be necessary to leave the artillery in position on the Maryland Heights, I think General Banks should be re-enforced by at least one or two batteries before making such move.

I have the honor, general, to be your obedient servant,

O. E. BABCOCK,
Corps of Engineers.

FREDERICK, *December* 27, 1861—7.30 p. m.

Brig. Gen. S. WILLIAMS,
Assistant Adjutant-General, Washington, D. C.:

All is quiet. A scout from Virginia states that the enemy have retired to Winchester; 400 infantry at Martinsburg; 500 cavalry scouting the river; seven guns (34-pounders) in position at Winchester; one 54-pounder.

General Jackson has about 7,000 men—4,000 volunteers, rest militia; twelve light guns, one rifled. Railroad iron of Baltimore and Ohio Railroad piled up at Charlestown and Halltown.

Respectfully submitted.

R. MORRIS COPELAND,
Assistant Adjutant-General.

SPECIAL ORDERS, }   HDQRS. GENERAL BANKS' DIVISION,
     No. 3.   }   *Frederick City, Md., January 5, 1862.*

1. The Forty-sixth Regiment Pennsylvania Volunteers will march as early as practicable to-morrow morning, January 6, for Williamsport, Md., carrying with it all its camp and garrison equipage, with two days' rations in haversacks.

*   *   *   *   *   *   *

2. The Third Brigade, Col. D. Donnelly commanding, will march immediately for Hancock, and report to Brigadier-General Lander at that place as soon as possible.

*   *   *   *   *   *   *

By command of Major-General Banks:
                    R. MORRIS COPELAND,
                         Assistant Adjutant-General.

HEADQUARTERS OF DIVISION,
Frederick, Md., January 7, 1862.

Brig. Gen. R. B. MARCY, *Chief of Staff, &c.:*

SIR : It would not have occurred to me to have transmitted *in extenso* all the dispatches of General Lander from Hancock had he not requested it, nor should I have suggested to the Commanding General the idea of writing upon affairs at Hancock had I anticipated the instructions which passed through the office to-day.

I have not thought it my duty to encourage General Lander's views in regard to our crossing the river. Had the event indicated in my instructions occurred, to wit, the passage of the Potomac by the enemy, the call would have been more imperative and reasonable; but we have thought from the first that he had no such purpose. All the features of the affair at Hancock resemble closely that at Williamsport when the attempt was made to destroy the dam, and seemed to be a cover for an attack upon the railway between Cumberland and Hancock.

Unless the enemy had crossed the river, any attempt to intercept and cut him by our crossing would have been unsuccessful. From Bath to Winchester is but 30 miles, directly south, while the distance from our camp to any possible point of interception via Harper's Ferry or Shepherdstown would have been more than double the distance, with a difficult river to cross and recross, for which we had no adequate material. It would have resulted in almost certain failure to cut off the enemy, and brought an exhausted force into his presence to fight him in his strongholds at Winchester. In either case it promised no positive prospect of success, nor did it exclude large chances of disaster. Every intelligent officer here familiar with the plans of the enemy and the features of the country confirmed this view of his ultimate purpose and the probable results of a forced passage of the river as suggested.

I beg the Commanding General to believe that my division will face any possible danger cheerfully and manfully which our position demands, but I hesitate to put my command, without orders, upon a forced march for one purpose, without any certainty of success, when I know that without any agency of our own, and by the natural course of events, it may be changed to another fruitful disaster. Such was the course of events at Ball's Bluff. It began in a reconnaissance and ended in a battle, for which our friends were not prepared. And such I feared might be the case should we suddenly cross the river to cut off the retreat of the enemy, and find ourselves unexpectedly obliged to flee before him or fight him in his intrenchments.

In view of the harassing policy adopted by the enemy, it seems to be necessary to keep a stronger force than hitherto on the important points of the river. The forced marches we are obliged to make, without any real service, discourage and demoralize the troops, and greatly weaken the division for any sudden emergency. We have now but four smooth-bore 6-pounder guns with the division. The others are at different points of the river, where they seemed to absolutely required on account of threatened movements of the enemy. I should be glad to know if, by any combination of events we should be compelled to move suddenly, I might be permitted to call on General Dix or General Stone for assistance in artillery.

I beg permission to suggest, in addition to the observations contained in a former letter upon the reconstruction of the road, that until we hold so much of the country through which it passes as to enable us to protect the whole, it will avail but little to attempt the reconstruction of any part of it.

I can only add to the suggestions then made my belief, formed upon recent events, that the enemy will resist with all its power the reopening of the road. This does not change my opinion as to its practicability. It demands, however, that we should undertake the work at our own time and with full preparation, and especially that we should avoid being drawn into this country by adventitious circumstances, promising no certain good, and having no connection and offering no support to the great work in contemplation.

I hope for the full and speedy recovery of the Commanding General. That he may soon regain his strength, and not allow the impatience of Congress or of the people to move him from the development of his material plans for one moment, is the earnest wish of one who wishes well to his country and the commander of its forces.

With much respect, I am, your obedient servant,

N. P. BANKS,
Major-General, Commanding Division.

HEADQUARTERS HOOKER'S DIVISION,
Camp Baker, Lower Potomac, Maryland, January 8, 1862.
Brig. Gen. S. WILLIAMS,
Adjutant-General, Army of the Potomac:

I have reason to believe that the rebel force in my front has been considerably reduced within the last two days. At the time the last deserters came in to my camp (January 3), there were six encampments visible from this side of the river; now I can see but two. Not knowing but the smoke of their camps might be concealed from their new mode of encamping, which is that of excavating tenements on the side of the hills, directions were given to my pickets to observe their reveille and tattoo calls, and they report to me that they can hear but those of two regiments. I therefore conclude that some of the regiments have been removed.

Long before daylight this morning a heavy cannonade was heard to the south, which turns out to have proceeded from two or three vessels of the second division of the flotilla off Aquia Creek. I am informed that they were engaged in shelling a rebel camp, but as it was done in the night, I conclude that no great damage was done. The vessels withdrew at daylight. Their fire was not returned.

*   *   *   *   *   *   *

Very respectfully, &c.,

JOSEPH HOOKER,
Brigadier-General, Commanding Division.

FAYETTEVILLE, VA., *January* 9, 1862.

Capt. GEORGE L. HARTSUFF,
Asst. Adjt. Gen., U. S. Army, Hdqrs. Dept. of W. Va.:

SIR: I regret to say that the railroad expedition has for the present been prevented by the absolutely impassable condition of the roads. At the time appointed for the march a heavy fall of snow made it improper to commence so long a march as was contemplated, and Dr. Hayes, the brigade surgeon, was of opinion that only the last necessity would justify it. Since then we have had rain; the snow has disappeared, but the rain is unceasing, and the roads mud.

My efforts to obtain information have been unceasing. I have now scouts trying to get to the railroad. I think they will succeed. Major Comly, at Raleigh, is untiring in making reconnaissances, sending out scouts, and swearing Union men. The Twenty-sixth leaves as soon as possible and within the time for which I was permitted to keep them. Notwithstanding their departure, I will go to Princeton as soon as the roads permit.

The militia are called out in the adjacent counties south, but I fancy that the result of the call will not be dangerous, although it necessitates more watchfulness on our part. I think that the people here are under the impression that rebellion is not a success. Even the disloyal in Southwestern Virginia think so, and the entering upon successive points of the road south as if we meant to stay there without fear, though prepared for serious opposition, indicates something stronger than bushwhacking. The condition of this command is in most respects good. The efforts to keep up efficient guards is attended with more difficulty than anything else.

We have not yet succeeded in finding the arms left near Dickerson's. There are there, I think, some 200 or 300 muskets. Intrenching tools in considerable numbers have been found buried, and the search for arms still continues.*

Very respectfully, your obedient servant,

E. P. SCAMMON,
Colonel, Commanding Third Provisional Brigade.

FREDERICK, *January* 10, 1862—8.30 p. m.

Maj. Gen. GEORGE B. McCLELLAN, *Commanding:*

Dispatch received.† General Williams telegraphs from General Kelley, 7.30 p. m., that Loring was 18 miles from Romney, Winchester road. Lander falling back on Cumberland. Three regiments, one section artillery, marched this morning for Romney. Two cavalry companies move

---

*Some matters of detail omitted.
† Not found.

to-night. Have ordered him to put so much of his brigade in readiness to march as can be spared. He has five regiments and four guns. Fears to part with more artillery. Can spare infantry. I think enemy reported at Bath again moving on Hancock; not believed by General Williams.

N. P. BANKS,
Major General, Commanding Division.

JANUARY 10, 1862.

Hon. SIMON CAMERON, *Secretary of War :*

Mr. David, the person in charge of the telegraph at General Kelley's headquarters, Cumberland, sends me the following this p. m. :

General Lander has information which leads him to believe that Jackson is advancing on Springfield. If true, he will have to fall back on New Creek. Telegram to General Kelley from Big Cacapon says a country clerk from Bath reports Jackson's force 16,000, made up of militia from Morgan, Frederick, Berkeley, and Hampshire Counties, and regulars from Georgia, Arkansas, Tennessee, and Virginia. Thinks militia numbers 3,000. He counted twenty-four pieces of artillery, two of them 32-pounders.

Very respectfully, yours,

ANSON STAGER.

HEADQUARTERS HOOKER'S DIVISION,
Camp Baker, Lower Potomac, Maryland, January 11, 1862.

Brig. Gen. S. WILLIAMS :

Since my interview with the Major-General Commanding on Friday last it has suggested itself to me that it might not be unimportant for him to be informed of the facilities at Port Tobacco for embarking troops. The wharf at the town is 50 feet long, with 9 feet water at high tide. Three miles below, on the bay, troops can step from the shore on to vessels drawing not over 5 or 6 feet water. This town is 32 miles distant from Washington, with better roads than those leading to my camp.

The piles for my wharf are nearly all driven and many of them capped. It will be 300 feet long, of the form of an **L**, and wide enough for a four-horse wagon to turn on it without difficulty at the outer extremity. There I will have 6 feet water. (This is at Rum Point.)

To-morrow I propose to send the pile-driver to Liverpool Point, where I shall require it a couple of days. A wharf there of 60 feet in length will give me 6 feet water. These two wharves are indispensable.

Since my return from Washington I have learned that a negro on the steamer Freeborn visited the neighborhood of Aquia and brought away his wife and children. He reports the number of troops in that vicinity to be that already communicated. He is ready and willing to visit that district any night. Brooke's Station is on the north side of the Potomac River, where the railroad bridge crosses that river, and 6 miles from Aquia bridge, about 300 feet in length. From Brooke's Station to Fredericksburg is 7 miles. Three bridges cross Rappahannock at this town. The railroad bridge stands on stone piers, and is about 600 feet in length. The others are wooden bridges, one about one-third of a mile, the other about one mile from the railroad bridge. I can learn of the presence of but few troops in the vicinity of Fredericksburg. They are to be found in small bodies and at long intervals along the shores of the Potomac. A prisoner sent to Washington yesterday informed me of about 1,800 stationed around Nomini Bay. My belief is that the great majority of the rebel forces are encamped well in the advance, in anticipation of their inability to move promptly at this season of the year.

I have no changes to report in my immediate front.

Very respectfully, &c.,

JOSEPH HOOKER,
General, Commanding Division.

HEADQUARTERS HOOKER'S DIVISION,
Camp Baker, Lower Potomac, Maryland, January 12, 1862.

Brig. Gen. S. WILLIAMS,
Adjutant-General, Army of the Potomac:

GENERAL: The Pensacola passed the batteries about 5 o'clock this morning unharmed. Fifteen or twenty shots were fired by the rebels as she descended the river, when she must have been lost sight of from that shore. From the Maryland shore an indefinable dark object was all that my pickets could see of her:

Later in the day the rebels were very active with their heavy guns, and blazed away at almost every object that presented itself, whether within the range of their guns or not. To me it seemed like an ebullition of anger on the escape of the Pensacola, for they had evidently made unusual preparation to receive her. Their accumulation of ammunition was afterwards expended on objects of little or no importance and without result.

It is deserving of remark in the history of these heavy batteries, that during my sojourn here the enemy have discharged them not less than 5,000 times, and, with the exception of the single shot which struck one of the vessels of the flotilla a few days since, while she was engaged in exchanging shots with them, not a vessel has been damaged in navigating the river nor the skin of a person broken on our shore.

I regret to learn that one of our barges was sunk two or three days since, off Alexandria, while on her way with stores for this camp. She is now at Rum Point. I am informed that she has on board stores from all of the departments, and I hope with care that no great loss will be suffered.

Very respectfully, your obedient servant,

JOSEPH HOOKER,
Brigadier-General, Commanding Division.

OFFICE OF CHIEF ENGINEER, ARMY OF THE POTOMAC,
January 13, 1862.

General S. WILLIAMS, *Assistant Adjutant-General:*

GENERAL: I deem it my imperative duty, after many representations to headquarters and to the chief of artillery on the subject of garrisoning the fortifications and preserving them from dilapidation, to call the attention of the Commanding General again to the subject, and to say that unless more effective measures are taken, these works, with their armament, must fall into ruin.

General Barry informed me on Saturday that General Wadsworth had written to him that much of the board revetment of Fort Ramsay had been stripped off by the men, and asked for permission to use the rest. Colonel Alexander reports to me that he found Fort Corcoran on Saturday in a shocking condition from neglect; that the guns are not used at all, and some appeared to require adjustment of platforms to be capable of use.

The whole line of works from the Potomac to the Eastern Branch and thence along its eastern shore to the Potomac again—twenty-eight works —are without garrisons; the small guards placed at them are changed daily (I believe). Of course they have no idea of what is required to keep the armament or earthwork in condition (which indeed is not much a part of their duty), and, as represented to me, perform even their duties as guard very inefficiently.

These ungarrisoned works have now 200 guns mounted, for which no ammunition can be supplied until there are garrisons, or at least ordnance sergeants to care for it. (At the present time I am obliged to keep hired men at most of the finished works to look after public property.)

I need scarcely say that if circumstances called for the action of these works against an enemy, it would require much time for the Ordnance Department to supply them all with ammunition. I look upon the garrisoning of these works—that is, with artillerymen—as under all circumstances indispensable, and an absolutely necessary preliminary to any offensive operations of the Army. Such offensive operations, if made against distant points, may throw the defense of Washington, against the bulk of the enemy's forces, upon these works (assisted by reserves); or, as at Bull Run, it is in the range of possibilities that a disaster in the field may paralyze our active army, or throw it back disorganized, to rally under protection of these works. Not only that they should fulfill such purposes, but be preserved from dilapidation, requires efficient garrisoning, and some more efficient system of supervision or command than has yet been established.

In some cases (as of the works in charge of the Fourteenth Massachusetts and Fourth Connecticut) the commanding officers and subordinates feel pride in preserving their works in perfect order. Such is not always the case, as the use and importance of the works are not appreciated, and where it is not, we may expect to see the timber work and abatis converted into tent floors and fire-wood. The uses and services expected from this enormous work we have made at an expense of a half million of dollars (armament not included) will not be rendered without careful preservation and efficient garrisons; and that these last should be efficient, a number of regular artillery officers of rank are required to visit such work every day, attend to and enforce the drill, and see that the work and armament are properly cared for.

Very respectfully,

J. G. BARNARD,
Chief Engineer.

WHEELING, *January* 13, 1862.
Adjutant-General THOMAS:

I transmit the following for the information of the General-in-Chief, whom I have this morning informed of the available force in the department this side of Kanawha Valley:

HUTTONSVILLE, *January* 13.
At the four posts of Beverly, Huttonsville, Elk Water, and Cheat Mountain there is about a million dollars' worth of Government property. Rebels know this and our

weakness, and, rumor says, are concentrating a large force at Monterey to retaliate the Huttonsville blow. I desire force enough to give me some chance. Can I have them? Plenty of provisions here.

R. H. MILROY,
Brigadier-General.

General, I wait instructions thereon.

W. S. ROSECRANS,
Brigadier-General.

DEPARTMENT OF STATE,
Washington, January 14, 1862.

To the SECRETARY OF WAR:

SIR: I inclose and invite your attention to the accompanying communication from Brigadier General Shields to Major-General McClellan, offering suggestions upon the conduct of the war.

I have the honor to be, your obedient servant,

WM. H. SEWARD.

[Inclosure.]

WASHINGTON, *January* 10, 1862.

Maj. Gen. GEORGE B. McCLELLAN,
Commander-in-Chief, U. S. Army:

GENERAL: Profiting by your kind and instructive suggestions the other day, I have taken the liberty of throwing out a few hints in relation to the general mode of prosecuting this war, and respectfully present them for your consideration.

Richmond in the East and Memphis at the West are the two dominating objective points of the Southern Confederacy in this war. The possession of these points will break the power of that Confederacy. Every military effort should be directed to the attainment of this object. Every employment of force in Missouri, Western Virginia, or around the coast (except in support of the blockade), which does not directly or indirectly bear upon the capture of these points, is a waste of force. The movement against Richmond is the principal one, and the other must be subordinate to it. Richmond can be reached by some one of the following routes, without encountering very serious military obstacles: James River, York River, or the Rappahannock. There is doubtless abundant information in the possession of the Department to determine this point with certainty. In the absence of this information I will assume that the route by Yorktown is the most eligible.

The capture of Yorktown would be the first important operation of the campaign. With such assistance as the Navy may be able to lend, an army of 20,000 men of all arms, embracing as many regulars as possible, in addition to the force already at Fort Monroe, would make the result certain.

In the operations against Yorktown nothing should be left to accident. Nothing in the nature of an assault upon their works ought to be attempted in the first stages of the campaign. The place should be carried by regular and systematic approaches, if only to instruct the men and accustom them to work under fire and work and move and operate together. Six weeks will suffice for the reduction of Yorktown, and six weeks before that place will give the men an amount of steadiness and practical discipline which they cannot get in six months around Washington. The better to insure the success of this movement, the army may be assembled outside of Fort Monroe, and strong and threatening demonstrations and even substantial preparations may be made for a movement on Norfolk. This may be made in such a way as to deceive them as to our first purpose, and, if so, a sudden spring on Yorktown may make its capture an easy matter, or at all events certain. Once in our hands, it can be strengthened into an excellent base for further operations, communicating with the ocean. Twenty or thirty thousand men in position at that place will make all the formidable works around Manassas useless. Twenty thousand additional troops can be thrown to Fort Monroe, the ostensible object of course a march upon Richmond; but I repeat, as nothing is to be left to chance in this campaign, I urgently recommend the reduction of Norfolk and the sweeping away of all the defenses around the bays and·lower waters of James River as the first great step in the campaign.

The minor posts will all fall with Yorktown and Norfolk. In the siege of Norfolk the Navy will be able to give efficient aid.

I will venture the prediction, and my reasons for it are more than military, that Virginia will compel the whole force of the Confederate Army to be turned to the relief of Norfolk. The administration will do it reluctantly, but Virginia regards Norfolk as her only naval station, the solitary door by which she communicates with the world, and she dare not and will never give it up without a struggle.

In view of this, let us throw up strong covering works at the outset. The effect of this movement will be to reverse the advantages of position. They will have to seek us in our own works, as we sought them at Manassas, and this alone will decide the campaign. Driven back and followed rapidly to Richmond, the Army and the Government may be hurled South without even a general battle. In case a serious attempt is not made to relieve Norfolk, it is bound to fall by regular approaches within the space of three months. This done, the whole Army, in improved working order and confident in spirits, can then be concentrated for a move on Richmond by Yorktown.

Until the capture of Yorktown and the fall of Norfolk the Army of the West should not hazard a serious engagement. A reverse there would have a discouraging influence upon the principal campaign. This must be avoided by all means. That army should be held in hand and kept in complete readiness to move rapidly on Memphis, flanked by the Mississippi River and supported by a fleet of gunboats. These two great movements, if well combined and well timed, will influence each other.

The advance on Richmond ought to be conducted with such caution and steadiness as to preclude the possibility of any casualty, however insignificant, so that the whole Army should arrive before that place in heart and spirit. There the enemy will have to deliver his great and to him his decisive engagement. The works around Richmond will be found, and cannot be made, sufficiently strong to resist for any considerable time an army that will have achieved so much, been so often under fire, and accustomed to deal with intrenched positions. The struggle there may be bloody, but cannot be doubtful. Richmond will fall. The Government will not abide the shock in that place. It will fly South on the approach of the Northern Army. This will have a disheartening effect upon their cause. Whether the operation then ought to be conducted by slow and certain approaches, or by a rapid, dashing, and irresistible assault, must be determined on the ground and at the time in view of all the circumstances. But in either case the wreck of the Southern Army can be hurled after the Government. The fall of

Memphis is likely to precede the fall of Richmond, and, if so, it will have a decisive effect upon that result.

The Southern Government is a military oligarchy. The head of this oligarchy is in Richmond, and when the head falls a Union sentiment will be found to burst forth in the South, which will soon entomb the body of this foul conspiracy.

These considerations are very general, and from want of accurate information of the position and strength of the enemy and of the exact nature of the country are necessarily defective; but as a sketch of a general plan I beg leave most respectfully to submit it to your practiced judgment. It is substantially your own plan, as I understood you the other day; and permit me to add, respectfully, that if you intrust me with a prominent part in the execution of this plan and take upon yourself the direction and superintendence of the combined movements in the field, I will pledge my poor reputation, past and present, for its successful issue.

With sentiments of personal regard and most profound respect, I have the honor to be, your obedient servant,

JAS. SHIELDS.

PATTERSON'S CREEK, *January* 16, 1862.

General MCCLELLAN:

GENERAL: I have the honor to reply to your inquiries.[*]

When by request, October 25, I gave my views to General Scott on the subject of protecting the Baltimore and Ohio Railroad, I recommended the occupation of Romney by Kelley, he to be immediately re-enforced, but beyond holding the point to break up guerrilla parties I did not propose a strong demonstration here. A column was to cross at Harper's Ferry and occupy Loudoun Heights; thence a force to move on Martinsburg and Bath, or farther south, if circumstances justified even the holding the country west of the Shenandoah; Kelley then to advance, leaving a guard on the railroad as he came on. A strong demonstration was to be from the east, with the intent to cut off Shenandoah Valley from the rebel army by interposing a heavy column along the Blue Mountains and holding the passes. Matters having been postponed, the enemy now hold the Blue Mountain passes, and have a railroad from Winchester to Strasburg, with Jackson's command at Bloomery Gap and near Romney, for the rebel force at Romney now numbers 2,500 men. It is evident that scattered guards along railroad will not protect all troops brought out from the west.

Strengthen the Army of the Potomac, and troops brought up from the west can be placed along railroad here as it is open, perhaps prior to being so placed to be massed and a blow given to Jackson; in short, an attack made to take Shenandoah Valley from the enemy. My camp here is so placed that while I hold a peninsula, resting each flank on unfordable rivers, the whole line can be raised and take cars at short notice. I have half Jackson's forces, and cannot do much as to guarding the road unless re-enforced. When able to leave road guarded in my rear, I propose to advance to Big Cacapon, on the Virginia side, and cover General Williams' crossing. I am having boats built for him in Cumberland, and if I am strongly re-enforced from Ohio at once I have no doubt of effecting a junction with Banks south of Potomac. He need not cross till the Virginia side is secured by me. The presence of

----

* Not found.

Jackson's large force changes the aspect of matters along the Baltimore and Ohio Railroad. I regard Milroy at Cheat Mountain in measure isolated, and in view of an advance of Loring via Moorefield and Philippi, perhaps too much so. With the aid of General Kelley, now in Cumberland, whose advice and knowledge of this country will prove highly useful, Milroy might secure this road in my rear to Big Cacapon necessarily re-enforced.

Should I advance, I can cross 4,000 infantry at Little Cacapon Bridge, fall on Romney, via Winchester turnpike by a mountain road, and retake at any time. I have hesitated to do so only that I am not massed and ready for sudden emergency with my whole force, and the enemy would break to the mountains and have nothing there worth capturing. Should a merely defensive course be adopted, my successor here should be a soldier and disciplinarian. This command is more like an armed mob than an army.

Resolved to a brief statement, this force can join Williams along the railroad at some risk of encountering a much larger one. If the railroad be guarded at once by re-enforcements from Ohio it can take Bath, and a portion of Banks' column then threatens Martinsburg. It can take Martinsburg should Banks cross; it can take Winchester and hold the Blue Mountain Pass, or fall on Leesburg and join McCall. In the latter case the enemy's left would endeavor to cut it off at Leesburg, but only by exposing himself by a flank march to your right.

Colonel Dunning, of the Fifth Ohio, is ranking officer here; an able and competent man. If Colonel Grover, of Utah celebrity, were appointed brigadier-general he might relieve me.

Trusting that I have not exceeded the terms of your instructions, I am, respectfully,

F. W. LANDER,
Brigadier-General.

HEADQUARTERS DIVISION, AT FREDERICK, MD.,
January 18, 1862.

Major-General McCLELLAN, *Commander-in-Chief U. S. A.:*

GENERAL: It gives me pleasure to acknowledge the receipt of your letter of the 16th instant,* proposing certain inquiries in regard to the number and disposition of forces necessary to guard the Potomac and the reconstruction of the Baltimore and Ohio Railway.

I. In regard to the disposition and number of forces necessary to guard the Potomac in the event of an advance of the main army:

It is not practicable in my judgment to substitute cavalry altogether for the infantry now guarding the river, but to a large extent it will make a more available and effective defense than now exists, as it will enable us to keep a more perfect observation of the enemy's movements; to concentrate suddenly upon points threatened, and to avoid the unhappy effects of forced marches that infantry will be compelled to make, usually without any satisfactory service or results. The exceptions to an exclusively cavalry guard will occur at those points where villages lie on the bank of the river, or at the dams which support the canal, or the most practicable fords, the defense of which demands the long range and effective fire of the rifled cannon and musket. With such exceptions cavalry can replace infantry with advantage.

---

* Not found.

There are now upon our line between Point of Rocks and Hancock nine regiments and twelve guns devoted to this duty. The substitution of effective cavalry for a part of this force would allow it to be reduced, if necessary, to two regiments and six guns, with such a reserved force at a central point, say Hagerstown, as the strength and movements of the enemy should require. Inclosed you will please observe a schedule of troops, with their dispositions, cavalry and infantry, based upon the view I have presented. The infantry could not well be diminished except as to the reserve, which could be strengthened or reduced as circumstances should require; the cavalry might be increased at pleasure. Posted in small numbers, at convenient distances, some of the burdens of the service would be lessened, such as quarters, supplies, forage, &c., as they would make available the resources of neighborhoods, and the activity of their duties would preserve discipline and increase their strength, which in infantry is sometimes seriously impaired by similar service.

II. In regard to the dispositions of troops near Patterson's Creek:

It appears to me that a line upon what is called the South Branch of the Potomac, running parallel with Patterson's Creek, about 5 miles farther westward, is in all respects preferable to General Lander's position at the mouth of the creek. This offers little advantage except the protection of the road at that precise point, and places him at the disadvantage of having the river in his rear. If he follows the creek southward towards Burlington he puts the creek in his rear, as the road passes principally on the enemy's side. But upon the line of the river between Paddytown and Cumberland he has communication in both directions by railway, highway, and river, which last is always between him and the enemy. In case of necessity communication is open to Piedmont, 4 miles westward, which is an impregnable position, taking advantage of the mountain pass, and connects by railroad, common road, and river with Cumberland, and westward with Wheeling by railway. This seems to be a stronger and more expansive position than any which Patterson's Creek affords, and equally effective for the protection of the road. I do not believe, however, that that wing of the road can be protected so long as the enemy holds undisputed possession of Winchester and surrounding country. The reconstruction of the road, I think, should commence on the other wing, and follow our occupation of that country.

III. I am clearly of opinion that it is impracticable to reconstruct the Baltimore and Ohio Railroad while the enemy holds possession of all the country south of its line. He must be expelled either by a decisive contest on this line or on that in front of Washington. More recent events have led me to believe that he will resist the reconstruction with all his power.

I have the honor to be, with great respect, your obedient servant,

N. P. BANKS,
Major-General, Commanding Division.

[Inclosure.]

Dispositions of troops on the Potomac between the mouth of the Monocacy and Sir John's Run, above Hancock.

UPPER DEPARTMENT.

Sir John's Run, one company cavalry.
Hancock, two companies cavalry, two companies infantry.

Sleepy Creek, one company cavalry.
Back Creek, two companies cavalry.
Cherry Run, one company cavalry; Clear Spring, six companies infantry, two guns.
Dam No. 5, one company cavalry.
Four Locks, one company cavalry.
Williamsport, two companies cavalry, two companies infantry.
Shaefersville, one company cavalry.
Total, twelve companies (one regiment) cavalry; ten companies infantry (one regiment).
Hagerstown, one brigade (?) and two guns.

LOWER DEPARTMENT.

Dam No. 4, one company cavalry.
Shepherd's Island, two companies cavalry.
Antietam, one company cavalry, two companies infantry.
Two Locks, one company cavalry.
Sandy Hook, two companies cavalry, six companies infantry, two guns.
Berlin, one company cavalry.
Point of Rocks, two companies cavalry, two companies infantry.
Monocacy Village, one company cavalry.
Monocacy mouth, one company cavalry.
Total, twelve companies (one regiment) cavalry; ten companies infantry (one regiment).

HEADQUARTERS DIVISION,
Frederick, January 21, 1862.
Major-General McCLELLAN,
Commander-in-Chief U. S. Army :

GENERAL : Major Perkins, Captain Abert, and Colonel Geary yesterday made an examination of the river at Harper's Ferry, to ascertain definitely the practicability of crossing at that point. They agree that in the present condition of the river it is impracticable there, and in this conclusion I concur. They also present at my request a report upon the subject and a plan for bridges, to which I would ask serious attention. There are many difficulties attending the use of canal-boats, and in the end they will cost the Government more than proper material easy of transportation, that will be safe and available at any point and any hour. Captain Abert will present the report to you at your convenience.

I am, sir, with much respect, your obedient servant,
N. P. BANKS,
Major-General, Commanding Division.

[Inclosure.]

DIVISION HEADQUARTERS,
Frederick, Md., January 20, 1862.
Maj. Gen. N. P. BANKS,
Commanding Division of Army of Potomac, Frederick, Md.:

GENERAL : In obedience to your verbal orders of yesterday evening, the undersigned proceeded to Harper's Ferry to-day, and made examination of the Potomac at that point with reference to the crossing of troops in sufficient number for offensive operations on the Virginia side.

We found the river swollen by recent rains some 10 feet above its ordinary height, and observation of this condition, which is certain to occur many times between this date and the 1st of May next, convinced us of the impracticability of using to advantage clumsy canal-boats for the purpose of bridging. Their employment would of necessity restrict your crossing both as to time and place, either of which would retard, if not render utterly impossible, your movement at the decisive moment. It will be unnecessary to give reasons in detail.

Flying bridges, rafts, and rope and pulley ferries are but inadequate and but tardy means of transport under favorable circumstances, but to the last degree uncertain and dangerous in cases of disaster or even of emergency.

We are of the opinion that not a moment should be lost in procuring bateaux, say 31 feet in length and 4 feet in width, made of white pine, and well calked, to serve as floating supports for string pieces and plank flooring, all according to the dimensions furnished by Captain Abert, topographical engineer, of your staff.

This arrangement will possess the advantage of being made away from observation of the enemy and brought to the place of employment complete. The bateaux are easily placed and anchored; they offer but little exposure to injury from a strong current or swollen stream, and the flooring is easily and quickly laid.

It is not known at what particular point within your lines you may desire to cross, and the bridge we propose will enable you to vary your line of operations at pleasure, for all the parts can be transported easily with the troops in all seasons, and put together at any point where a crossing might be desirable.

We are aware that you deem some safe and sure means of crossing the Potomac within your lines indispensably necessary, and if the Government cannot furnish you a pontoon train, we believe the arrangement we suggest is the nearest approach to it in economy, efficiency, and certainty of good result.

We have the honor to be, general, your obedient servant,

D. D. PERKINS,
Major and Aide-de-Camp, Chief of Staff.
JAMES W. ABERT,
Captain, U. S. Army, Topographical Engineers.

GENERAL ORDERS, }   HDQRS. OF THE ARMY, A. G. O.,
No. 6.   }   *Washington, January* 23, 1862.

I. The boundaries of the Department of Western Virginia are incorrectly defined in the Army Register for 1862, page 90. They should be as follows: So much of Virginia as lies between its entire boundary on the west, the western slope of the Alleghany Mountains on the east, the boundaries of Pennsylvania and Maryland on the north and northeast, and of Tennessee on the south.

*   *   *   *   *   *   *

By command of Major-General McClellan:

L. THOMAS,
Adjutant-General.

POTOMAC FLOTILLA, *January* 24, 1862.

Brigadier-General HOOKER, U. S. A.,
  Commanding Division, U. S. Army, Lower Potomac:

SIR: In answer to your inquiries of yesterday, I have the honor to inform you that the force at present under my command consists of eleven steamers, scattered from Hallowing Point to Point Lookout. The force of these vessels in battery is four 9-inch shell guns, four 8-inch shell guns, four 32-pounders of 33 hundred-weight; two Parrott rifled 30-pounders, one rifled 50-pounder, three 24-pounder howitzers, and six 12-pounder rifled howitzers. These are all light and extremely vulnerable boats. Their draught of water is from 7 to 9 feet. Two of them are ferry-boats, one drawing 8 feet, the other 4½ feet of water. I judge that they would not carry conveniently more than 1,000 men above the number of their crews; the ferry-boats taking about 600 of this number. I am of opinion that were it desired to cross the river the vessels, with the exception of the ferry-boats, could render better service in towing launches, barges, &c., loaded with troops, than by taking them on their decks.

From Otterback's farm, above High Point, to within range of the Cockpit battery, below Freestone Point, these vessels can approach the beach within about 200 yards—perhaps somewhat nearer on the north side of Freestone Point, where a landing could be effected on the beach below the bluff. Under Cockpit Point the water is quite deep well up to the shore, and this continues to the Evansport batteries, from below which it runs off shoal again near the Virginia shore. Just above Mathias Point the water is again quite deep, allowing a steamer to go close in.

The enemy appear to be in considerable force in the neighborhood of Occoquan Mill, and have constructed a fort on the southern side of the Occoquan River. A few weeks since they had a full field battery at this point of about 9 to 12 pounders, rifled. Back of Freestone Point, on the road leading to Dumfries, I think that there is not more than one regiment. Lately their camp fires have not been so distinct or numerous at these points. About two weeks since two vessels shelled the railroad depot at Aquia Creek. Their batteries did not reply. The next day troops were marched to Aquia, and now I have reason to believe that three regiments are there, and an additional rifled gun placed in their battery at that point, with which they have practiced, without effect, on one of the vessels. There has been an encampment at Hook's Landing, and a field battery drawn occasionally to Boyd's Hole, but lately the battery has disappeared. The camp has been shelled, but I think without effect. It sets too far back for the range of our guns.

This morning I made a reconnaissance of Occoquan Bay. Their main encampment seems to be about 2 miles back from the bay, extending from Occoquan towards Neabsco Creek. Back of Neabsco Creek, near the junction of the roads from Colchester and Occoquan towards Dumfries, there appears to be a considerable breastwork thrown up, but no guns are visible. A body of cavalry was fired upon, but their field battery was not brought down as before.

I am, sir, very respectfully, your obedient servant,
                    R. H. WYMAN,
          Lieutenant, Commanding Potomac Flotilla.

HEADQUARTERS DIVISION,
Arlington, Virginia, January 26, 1862.

Brig. Gen. S. WILLIAMS,
  Asst. Adjt. Gen., Hdqrs. Army of the Potomac, Washington, D. C.:

GENERAL: I have the honor to report as follows in answer to your telegram of the 23d instant, inquiring whether, in the event of a forward movement, there are any regiments in my command unfit either in point of equipments or discipline for the emergencies of the field:

WADSWORTH'S BRIGADE.

Twentieth New York, armed with Austrian rifled muskets.
Twenty-first New York, armed with Springfield rifled muskets.
Twenty-third New York, armed with Enfield rifled muskets.
Twenty-fifth New York, armed with Austrian rifled muskets.
Equipped and well disciplined for volunteers.

KING'S BRIGADE.

Second Wisconsin, Austrian rifled muskets.
Sixth Wisconsin, Belgian rifled muskets.
Seventh Wisconsin, Springfield altered smooth bore.
Nineteenth Indiana, Springfield rifled muskets.
The muskets of the Seventh Wisconsin are reported as bad, and that the men lack confidence in them.

The brigade is equipped, with some slight exceptions, and well disciplined for volunteers. The Nineteenth Indiana the least so. A special report will be made as to this regiment after a special inspection next Monday.

AUGUR'S BRIGADE.

Fourteenth New York (Brooklyn), Springfield rifled.
Twenty-second New York, smooth-bore Springfield.
Twenty-fourth New York, rifled muskets, caliber .58.
Thirtieth New York, Springfield rifled.
Equipped and well disciplined for volunteers. The Twenty-second need other guns.

CAVALRY.

Second New York (Ira Harris). Equipped, save that 100 horses are required. Drill and discipline good for volunteers; above average. One company—a new one—defective in drill, but are armed with carbines, and are said to be good marksmen.

ARTILLERY.

Company B, Fourth Artillery. Manned mostly by volunteers; good.
Rhode Island Battery. Good for volunteers.
New Hampshire Battery. Good for volunteers. Not as good as Rhode Island.
Pennsylvania Battery. Reported by Captain Gibbon as not in a fit condition to take the field. The materials, the officers and men and horses are all good, but the battery is not instructed.
The batteries lack ammunition, and the regular battery, Napoleon guns, need extra caisson to carry sufficient ammunition.
The change of small-arms leaves the division for the moment short of ammunition; a deficiency soon supplied.
The men would suffer much less were they supplied with—
1st. India-rubber ponchos, to answer for shelter tents.
2d. Cowhide boots; two-thirds have them.

3d. Portable camp equipage, such as was determined upon by the Major-General Commanding last summer.

I have the honor to be, very respectfully, your most obedient servant,

IRVIN McDOWELL,
Brigadier-General, Commanding Division.

HEADQUARTERS HOOKER'S DIVISION,
Camp Baker, Lower Potomac, Maryland, January 27, 1862.

Brig. Gen. S. WILLIAMS,
AdjutantGeneral, Army of the Potomac:

GENERAL : I have already acknowledged your communication of the 20th instant.*

From the most reliable information received from others, and from my own personal observation, I am of opinion that the mode to attack the rebels productive of the greatest results will be to commence on the left of my line at Aquia Creek with one brigade, on the following morning to assault their batteries in front with two columns of a regiment each, and the day following with as much of my division as I can cross; land at or near Powell or Neabsco Creek, advance on the Colchester road, attack in rear the rebel batteries planted to dispute the passage of the Occoquan, and open the doors for Heintzelman to cross that river.

My reasons for preferring to commence on the left are that at Liverpool Point I can embark the necessary force without exposing my object, can move to the point of landing without being observed, and can destroy their batteries and depot before it will be in their power to parry the blow, except with the force now in that vicinity. The effect of this on my command will be to inspire confidence. On the enemy, it will deprive a portion of them of their depot of supplies; with the balance it will threaten their communication with Richmond, and if it does not put some of them *en route,* and their roads resemble ours, will compel their regiments to locate nearer their new depots.

The primary object in delivering an attack on my immediate front I consider should be to destroy the batteries, in order to give us the free use of the river, and not to give battle; for there are other fields equally accessible, affording greater advantages. Its proximity to the masses of the enemy is a great objection to our attempting to cross the broad Potomac in any considerable force, for it can be executed with more chances of success lower down the river, and when once there the enemy will be more or less crippled from the condition of the country as it regards the difficulty of moving artillery and trains. They must move, for they must protect their communication to the rear.

It is recommended that the assault be made in two columns, for the reason that Quantico Creek divides the batteries and is not fordable below Dumfries, and to attempt to turn it would force us into an engagement under disadvantageous circumstances. Finally, I consider that the possession of that bank of the river, leaving out of consideration the batteries, affords neither army any particular advantages.

With regard to the movement to relieve Heintzelman and its consequences, it is open to the objection of proximity to the rebels ; but, considering its advantages, as they are presented to one not at all acquainted with the views and intentions of the Major-General Command-

---

* Not found.

ing, I have ventured to recommend it. If resisted, the force necessary can be landed under the guns of the flotilla, and can advance with great hope of success.

The successful execution of all of these movements will call into exercise great secrecy, dispatch, resolution, and, indeed, all the brightest virtues of a soldier, but with the relative position of the two armies, as I understand them, to no greater degree than will be required for an advance anywhere along the whole line. The enemy have the advantage in position—they in the center; we on the circumference, with great natural and artificial obstacles between.

As it regards the details of execution, I inclose herewith a sketch taken by Lieutenant Magaw,* commanding lower flotilla, which represents with great accuracy the position of the depot, the batteries, and number of guns in each. I determined on the lower point of Split Rock to land, as there we have 4 feet water, and can march directly to the rear of the batteries.

From my best information I believe but three regiments are stationed here to work and defend these guns, and those are on the opposite side of the hill from them. No tents are visible about the batteries.

As the vessels of the flotilla have but limited capacity for transporting troops, and the most of them draw too much water, I recommend that canal-boats be used, and have them towed across by one of the tugs. Enough of them should be employed to transport 4,000 men, and should be sent to Liverpool Point at a time not to excite remark. I shall take no horses or baggage. On board the Freeborn are two 12-pounder howitzers with light carriages that I wish to take along, with a few artillerists. The men can haul them.

The batteries at Shipping Point are the same as when the sketch was taken forwarded to you through Colonel Small. They appear to have a company each to work the guns, and one regiment as a support, encamped near the figure 8 on the sketch. These batteries are on what is called an island formed by the waters of the Quantico and Chopawamsic almost uniting. A bridge connects it with the mainland on the south, recently built. Both the streams run through deep and miry channels; in fact, impassable except by the bridge. This can easily be destroyed. For this reason it may be deemed expedient to land directly on the island in the vicinity of the saw-mill. Here the water is shoal, and will require boats of light draught. To land by the aid of lighters would greatly hazard the success of the movement. After the guns are spiked the flotilla can take position to render great assistance.

The battery at Possum Nose has been established recently. It has four guns, two pointing up and two down the river. It is midway between Cockpit Point battery and what is called Newport Town. There appears to be a company to each battery to work the guns, and a regiment almost in rear of Cockpit Point to serve as supports. The steamer Baltimore, of the flotilla, will be a good transport for this service. The assaults on these batteries and those of Shipping Point should be simultaneous, and vessels of the flotilla should take positions to co-operate. At or near Powell's Creek will be a good landing.

To cross my division will require all the transportation named above, the use of the flotilla, and then may have to make two trips for the men. Another division will be required for this service, and should be landing near by at the same time.

---

* Not found.

My balloon having failed me up to this time, I am unable to report the position of the rebel camps in the distance. From the smoke I judge that two or three regiments are encamped behind the high ground in rear of Shipping Point batteries. Camp marked 7 has entirely disappeared. With my glass I can see camps north of Dumfries stretching off in the direction of Colchester. They occupy a position to dispute the passage of the Potomac or Occoquan, as may be needed. By referring to the sketch of Lieutenant Magaw two batteries will be observed at the mouth of Potomac Creek. I learn that they are supported by about 300 men. These appear to invite capture.

Very respectfully, your obedient servant,

JOSEPH HOOKER,
Brigadier-General, Commanding Division.

WAR DEPARTMENT,
Washington City, D. C., January 29, 1862.

Major-General BANKS, *Willard's Hotel:*

GENERAL: You will please report to this Department the state of the force under your command, and whether you are in condition to make an advance movement across the Potomac, if ordered; and, if not, what is needed to place you in that condition.

Yours, &c.,

EDWIN M. STANTON,
Secretary of War.

HEADQUARTERS ARMY OF THE POTOMAC,
January 30, 1862.

Brig. Gen. L. THOMAS, *Adjutant-General:*

GENERAL: In compliance with instructions contained in your letter of the 28th instant, I have the honor to forward to you the inclosed statement of the troops of the different arms of the service now serving in this army, namely:

	Commissioned officers.	Enlisted men.	Total.
Infantry	7, 297	162, 936	170, 233
Cavalry	1, 037	21, 460	22, 497
Artillery	633	15, 173	15, 806
Sharpshooters	60	1, 409	1, 469
Engineer Corps	77	1, 883	1, 960
	9, 104	202, 861	211, 965

Referring to the inclosed table for further details,* I am, general, very respectfully, your obedient servant,

S. WILLIAMS,
Assistant Adjutant-General.

---

*Detailed statement omitted. The stations much the same as indicated on p. 732.

OFFICE OF CHIEF ENGINEER, ARMY OF THE POTOMAC,
Washington, February 1, 1862.

Col. A. V. COLBURN, *Assistant Adjutant-General:*

COLONEL: In compliance with the wishes of the Commander-in-Chief, communicated through you, I, in company with Captain Duane, engineer, had an interview with General Banks in reference to the means of crossing his army over the Upper Potomac. He stated that his orders were to be prepared to cross at short notice, to operate against the heavy columns of the enemy in Winchester Valley and westward, and appeared to be impressed with the idea that a bateau bridge (or, in other words, such a bridge equipage as we have provided for the Army of the Potomac, for it amounts to this) was important and indispensable. I expressed my conviction that to cross a river like the Potomac at this season, to encounter an enemy who has the power to make himself superior, on an ordinary pontoon bridge, which may be swept away in twenty-four hours or less, that for a great many reasons, which I need not introduce here, I considered Harper's Ferry the best place to cross, and whether that was selected as the place or not it must be held, and a bridge communication kept up there; that canal-boats and materials (according to Lieutenant Babcock's statement) could be easily accumulated there, and that a bridge could be established in forty-eight hours; that if other secure crossings were wanted above, they must be established after the passage of our armies; and, finally, that if circumstances should dictate to him a passage at another point, I believe a flying bridge made of two canal-boats could be promptly established, would be comparatively secure, and would possess a capability of carrying over troops nearly equal to a bateau bridge.

Should these reasons not appear satisfactory, and a bateau bridge be decided necessary, and that to be capable of transportation, so that the point of passage may be selected or changed at will, then we can only meet the demand by ordering an equipage of fifty boats, with wagons and teams (100), and with it should be sent one or two companies of engineer troops. To build such an equipage would require three or four weeks, and it could not be supplied in shorter time unless the general chooses to send some of the equipage already provided. General Banks' idea of the economy of resorting to a bateau bridge was founded upon an imperfect idea of what was necessary to constitute one.

The general left me, saying he would consider the subject further.

Captain Duane coincides with me in these views.

I am, very respectfully, &c.,

J. G. BARNARD,
Chief Engineer.

GENERAL ORDERS, }   HDQRS. OF THE ARMY, A. G. O.,
    No. 9.   }   *Washington, February* 1, 1862.

I. The States of Pennsylvania and New Jersey are added to the limits of the Department of the Potomac.

*   *   *   *   *   *   *

By command of Major-General McClellan:

L. THOMAS,
Adjutant-General.

Memorandum accompanying letter of President to General McClellan dated February 3, 1862.

1st. Suppose the enemy should attack us in force *before* we reach the Occoquan, what? In view of the possibility of this, might it not be safest to have our entire force to move together from above the Occoquan?

2d. Suppose the enemy in force shall dispute the crossing of the Occoquan, what? In view of this, might it not be safest for us to cross the Occoquan at Colchester rather than at the village of Occoquan? This would cost the enemy two miles more of travel to meet us, but would, on the contrary, leave us 2 miles farther from our ultimate destination.

3d. Suppose we reach Maple Valley without an attack, will we not be attacked there in force by the enemy marching by the several roads from Manassas; and, if so, what?

HEADQUARTERS ARMY OF THE POTOMAC,
MEDICAL DIRECTOR'S OFFICE,
February 6, 1862.

General S. WILLIAMS,
Assistant Adjutant-General, Army of the Potomac:

GENERAL: In obedience to your instructions, I have the honor to inclose a tabulated report of the sick in the several divisions and brigades of the Army of the Potomac as far as the returns in this office will enable me to do so.

I have to observe that these tables show the whole number of sick in the regiments, whether in quarters or hospital, as reported by the medical officers. Of the men thus reported, more than one-half are affected with trivial complaints, that could scarcely justify their being left behind in case the army should be put in motion.

In the cavalry regiments the sick report is swollen considerably in consequence of injuries to the men received from the horses. A very considerable item in many of the regiments is due to the number of men waiting discharges in consequence of disqualification from old physical infirmities.

Among the regular troops the sick report is seriously increased by the number of venereal cases, some of which were received from California; others contracted here.

Measles, which seems to be scourging the whole Army of the United States, still breaks out from time to time in different regiments. Berdan's Sharpshooters have been and are still severely affected with that disease. It is hoped that hospital and field arrangements already made and in progress will soon abate this evil. It will be perceived that among the Vermont troops in Brooks' brigade there is a wide difference in the ratio of sick between the Second and Third Regiments and the other three. I have already endeavored to give some explanation of this is in a former report. I have now to state that I have sent a large detachment of convalescents to Philadelphia in order to make room for the sick of this brigade in the general hospitals, in hopes some beneficial effect may result to the well from removing the sick from their sight, thus avoiding the depressing influence of the daily observation of so much sickness among their comrades.

---

* See p. 41.

As a general rule it would seem, as is natural, that the ratio of sick is inversely as the military age of the men. When a departure from this rule is perceived, as it will be in certain brigades, one important reason for it will probably be found in the lax and inefficient discipline of the regiment. I called attention to an instance of that sort a few days since, and was told that the regiment was demoralized from the inefficiency of the officers.

I ask attention in this place to a letter I have received from Brigadier-General Peck, a copy of which I inclose to show how much may be done by attention to certain sanitary measures that I have frequently suggested, and which have been more than once directed from your office. If officers could be impressed with the necessity of such measures, and convinced of their certain beneficial results, I feel sure they would all be zealous in enforcing them.

I am gratified to be able to state that typhoid fever, which I feared would seriously increase with the cold weather, has been much decreased in a very great majority of the regiments, and upon the whole I think I am justified in saying that the sanitary condition of this army is very satisfactory.

I take this occasion to say that I have sent an inspector of hospitals to Lander's division, and that as soon as the inspections of Alexander's and Duane's commands are completed, I shall send another to Perryville, Md., where I have just learned that typhoid fever has appeared and is increasing in one of the regular regiments stationed at that point.

Very respectfully, your obedient servant,

CHAS. S. TRIPLER,
Surgeon and Medical Director Army of the Potomac.

[Inclosure No. 1.]

STONE'S DIVISION.

Brigade and regiment.	Mean strength.	Total sick.	Percentage.	Brigade strength.	Brigade sick.	Brigade percentage.	Division strength.	Division sick.	Division percentage.
GORMAN'S BRIGADE.									
First Minnesota	960	32	3.33						
Second New York State Militia	832	30	3.60	1,792	62	3.46			
COLONEL GROSVENOR.									
Seventh Michigan	990	20	2.02						
Twentieth Massachusetts	637	30	4.71						
Andrew Sharpshooters	639	71	11.11	2,266	121	5.34			
BURNS' BRIGADE.									
Sixty-ninth Pennsylvania	952	29	3.41						
Seventy-first Pennsylvania	1,129	26	2.30						
Seventy-second Pennsylvania	1,415	50	3.53						
One hundred and sixth Pennsylvania	1,036	15	1.45						
Light artillery	585	23	3.93	51.17	143	2.79			
Tammany Forty-second New York	803	54	6.72						
Fifteenth Massachusetts	809	68	8.40						
Van Alen Cavalry	860	23	2.67						
Company I, First Artillery	150	6	4.00	2,622	151	5.75	11,797	477	4.04

McCALL'S DIVISION.

Brigade and regiment.	Mean strength.	Total sick.	Percentage.	Brigade strength.	Brigade sick.	Brigade percentage.	Division strength.	Division sick.	Division percentage.
REYNOLDS' BRIGADE.									
Second Pennsylvania Reserves	519	21	4.04						
Eighth Pennsylvania Reserves	885	40	4.52						
Fifth Pennsylvania Reserves	936	45	4.80						
First Pennsylvania Reserves	894	63	7.04	3,234	169	5.22			
MEADE'S BRIGADE.									
Seventh Pennsylvania Reserves	913	51	5.58						
Eleventh Pennsylvania Reserves	968	38	3.92						
Third Pennsylvania Reserves	930	64	6.88						
Fourth Pennsylvania Reserves	809	41	5.06	3,620	194	5.22			
ORD'S BRIGADE.									
Ninth Pennsylvania Reserves	972	44	4.52						
Sixth Pennsylvania Reserves	966	49	5.07						
Tenth Pennsylvania Reserves	965	7	0.72						
Twelfth Pennsylvania Reserves	846	37	4.37	3,749	137	3.65			
First Pennsylvania Rifles	889	67	7.53						
First Pennsylvania Artillery	375	22	5.87						
First Pennsylvania Cavalry	890	96	10.77	2,154	185	8.58	12,757	685	5.37

F. J. PORTER'S DIVISION.

Brigade and regiment.	Mean strength.	Total sick.	Percentage.	Brigade strength.	Brigade sick.	Brigade percentage.	Division strength.	Division sick.	Division percentage.
MARTINDALE'S BRIGADE.									
Twenty-second Massachusetts	1,157	47	4.06						
Second Maine	700	76	10.85						
Eighteenth Massachusetts	973	48	4.93						
Twenty-fifth New York	636	12	1.88						
Thirteenth New York	700	39	5.57	4,166	222	5.32			
MORELL'S BRIGADE.									
Fourteenth New York	950	47	4.94						
Fourth Michigan	1,050	29	2.76						
Ninth Massachusetts	1,017	31	3.04						
Sixty-second Pennsylvania	1,120	55	4.91	4,137	164	3.96			
BUTTERFIELD'S BRIGADE.									
Seventeenth New York	800	33	4.12						
Stockton's Michigan [Sixteenth]	840	39	4.64						
Eighty-third Pennsylvania	1,023	72	7.02						
Forty-fourth New York	1,040	40	3.84	3,703	184	5.35			
CAVALRY BRIGADE.									
Third Pennsylvania Cavalry	1,090	45	4.13						
Eighth Pennsylvania Cavalry	1,110	74	6.66	2,200	119	5.40	14,206	689	4.85

HOOKER'S DIVISION.

Brigade and regiment.	Mean strength.	Total sick.	Percentage.	Brigade strength.	Brigade sick.	Brigade percentage.	Division strength.	Division sick.	Division percentage.
SICKLES' BRIGADE.									
First Excelsior	1,020	30	2.94						
Second Excelsior	900	45	5.00						
Third Excelsior	978	67	6.85						
Fourth Excelsior	799	3	0.38						
Fifth Excelsior	864	48	5.55	4,561	193	4.23			
COWDIN'S BRIGADE.									
First Massachusetts	850	32	3.76						
Eleventh Massachusetts	874	30	3.54						
Twenty-sixth Pennsylvania.	900	42	4.66						
Second New Hampshire	1,000	24	2.4						
Third Indiana Cavalry	550	7	1.27	4,174	136	3.25			
COL. S. H. STARR'S BRIGADE.									
Fifth New Jersey Volunteers	914	57	6.24						
Sixth New Jersey Volunteers	936	43	4.60						
Seventh New Jersey Volunteers	919	51	5.55						
Eighth New Jersey Volunteers	954	47	4.90	3,723	198	5.32	12,458	527	4.22

BLENKER'S DIVISION.

STAHEL'S BRIGADE.									
Forty-fifth New York	896	19	2.12						
Eighth New York	947	55	5.80						
Twenty-seventh Pennsylvania	692	19	2.74						
Thirty-ninth New York	882	15	1.70	3,417	108	3.16			
STEINWEHR'S BRIGADE.									
Fifty-fourth New York	813	51	6.27						
Twenty-ninth New York	672	33	4.91						
Seventy-third Pennsylvania.	503	22	4.37						
Sixty-eighth New York	807	21	2.60	2,795	127	4.54			
BOHLEN'S BRIGADE.									
Fifty-eighth New York	650	58	8.92						
Thirty-fifth Pennsylvania	732	24	3.27						
Fortieth Pennsylvania	868	32	3.68	2,250	114	5.06			
NOT BRIGADED.									
Fourth New York Cavalry	750	38	5.06						
Forty-first New York Volunteers	905	34	3.75	1,655	72	4.35	10,117	421	4.15

SMITH'S DIVISION.

HANCOCK'S BRIGADE.									
Sixth Maine	940	77	8.19						
Forty-third New York	750	69	9.00						
Forty-ninth Pennsylvania	850	149	17.53						
Fifth Wisconsin	998	64	6.41	3,538	359	10.12			

SMITH'S DIVISION—Continued.

Brigade and regiment.	Mean strength.	Total sick.	Percentage.	Brigade strength.	Brigade sick.	Brigade percentage.	Division strength.	Division sick.	Division percentage.
BROOKS' BRIGADE.									
Second Vermont	1,021	87	8.53						
Third Vermont	900	84	9.33						
Fourth Vermont	1,047	244	23.30						
Fifth Vermont	1,000	271	27.10						
Sixth Vermont	970	224	23.00	4,938	910	16.40			
BRANNAN'S BRIGADE.									
Forty-ninth New York	876	73	8.34						
Thirty-third New York	800	41	5.13						
Forty-seventh Pennsylvania	982	44	4.88						
Seventh Maine	808	107	13.24	3,466	265	7.64			
Cameron Cavalry	1,000	96	9.60	1,000	96	9.60	12,942	1,630	12.60

CASEY'S DIVISION.

Brigade and regiment.	Mean strength.	Total sick.	Percentage.	Brigade strength.	Brigade sick.	Brigade percentage.	Division strength.	Division sick.	Division percentage.
FIRST BRIGADE.									
One hundred and fourth Pennsylvania	924	22	2.38						
Fifty-sixth New York	1,480	117	7.90						
Eleventh Maine	920	91	9.89						
Fifty-second Pennsylvania	850	119	14.00	4,174	349	8.38			
SECOND BRIGADE.									
Fifty-ninth New York	849	33	3.94						
Eighty-sixth New York	900	44	4.88						
Eighty-fifth Pennsylvania	849	36	4.24	2,598	113	4.35			
THIRD BRIGADE.									
Ninth New Jersey	1,143	44	3.85						
Eighty-fifth New York	900	67	7.45						
Seventy-seventh New York	900	20	2.22						
Eighty-seventh New York	875	31	3.54	3,818	102	4.24			
PROVISIONAL BRIGADE.									
Sixty-fourth New York	892	161	19.18	892	161	19.18	11,482	785	6.83
GENERAL SYKES' BRIGADE				2,495	136	5.45			
Colonel Hunt's artillery reserve				1,677	125	8.05			
GENERAL COOKE'S BRIGADE.									
First Regiment U. S. Cavalry	424	48							
Second Regiment, seven companies. Fourth Regiment, two companies	506	61							
Fifth Regiment	632	60							
Sixth Regiment	984	101		2,546	260	10.21			
NOT BRIGADED.									
First Berdan Sharpshooters	745	71	9.53						
Second Berdan Sharpshooters	720	132	18.33	1,465	203	13.85			

KEYES' DIVISION.

Brigade and regiment.	Mean strength.	Total sick.	Percentage.	Brigade strength.	Brigade sick.	Brigade percentage.	Division strength.	Division sick.	Division percentage.
COUCH'S BRIGADE.									
Seventh Massachusetts.....	1,005	20	1.99						
Thirty-sixth New York.....	800	17	2.12						
Second Rhode Island.......	877	4	.45						
Tenth Massachusetts.......	1,011	33	3.26	3,693	74	2.00			
PECK'S BRIGADE.									
Fifty-fifth New York.......	600	10	1.66						
Sixty-second New York	902	20	2.21						
Thirteenth Pennsylvania...	1,106	26	2.35						
Ninety-eighth Pennsylvania	824	10	1.21						
Ninety-third Pennsylvania	1,018	35	3.43	4,450	101	2.26			
GRAHAM'S BRIGADE.									
First Long Island	817	12	1.46						
Twenty-third Pennsylvania.	1,460	64	4.38						
Thirty-first Pennsylvania...	880	13	1.47						
Sixty-third Pennsylvania [?]	850	49	5.82						
Batteries of artillery.......	268	63	2.31	4,275	201	4.70	11,400	376	3.29

McDOWELL'S DIVISION.

KING'S BRIGADE.									
Sixth Wisconsin...........	960	76	6.04						
Seventh Wisconsin.........	996	40	4.11						
Second Wisconsin..........	821	57	6.94						
Nineteenth Indiana.......	892	70	7.84	3,669	263	7.17			
WADSWORTH'S BRIGADE.									
Twenty-first New York....	735	23	3.12						
Twenty-third New York....	878	31	3.54						
Thirty-fifth New York.....	976	35	3.59						
Twentieth New York.......	915	37	4.04	3,504	126	3.59			
AUGUR'S BRIGADE.									
Thirtieth New York	800	33	4.12						
Twenty-second New York..	837	24	2.85						
Twenty-fourth New York .	825	53	6.42						
Fourteenth New York (State Militia).............	650	24	3.69	3,112	134	4.30			
Second New York Cavalry..	982	107	10.89						
Batteries of artillery........	563	19	3.37	1,545	126	8.15	11,830	649	5.49

HEINTZELMAN'S DIVISION.

RICHARDSON'S BRIGADE.									
Second Michigan.	1,000	57	5.70						
Third Michigan	935	43	4.60						
Fifth Michigan.	930	42	4.52						
Thirty-seventh New York..	727	55	7.56	3,392	197	5.80			
SEDGWICK'S BRIGADE.									
Third Maine........	800	26	3.25						
Fourth Maine..............	864	36	4.17						
Thirty-eighth New York...	718	41	5.71						
Fortieth New York........	957	60	6.27	3,339	163	4.58			
JAMESON'S BRIGADE.									
Sixty-third Pennsylvania...	1,037	49	4.74						
Ninety-ninth Pennsylvania	620	61	9.84						
Sixty-first Pennsylvania....	579	26	4.49						
One hundred and fifth Pennsylvania	934	88	9.42	3,170	224	7.17			
First New Jersey Cavalry..	1,000	69	6.9						
Three batteries artillery....	411	5	1.23	1,411	74	5.24	11,312	658	5.81

FRANKLIN'S DIVISION.

Brigade and regiment.	Mean strength.	Total sick.	Percentage.	Brigade strength.	Brigade sick.	Brigade percentage.	Division strength.	Division sick.	Division percentage.
KEARNY'S BRIGADE.									
First New Jersey	1,000	34	3.4						
Second New Jersey	1,027	33	3.21						
Third New Jersey	1,040	32	3.07						
Fourth New Jersey	884	28	3.16	3,951	127	3.21			
NEWTON'S BRIGADE.									
Thirty-second New York	775	39	5.03						
Thirty-first New York	850	45	5.29						
Eighteenth New York	779	38	4.87						
Fifty-fourth Pennsylvania	985	36	3.65	3,389	158	4.66			
SLOCUM'S BRIGADE.									
Twenty-seventh New York	840	49	5.83						
Sixteenth New York	900	101	11.22						
Fifth Maine	828	92	11.11						
Ninety-sixth Pennsylvania	927	32	3.45						
Batteries of artillery	434	23	5.30						
Lincoln Cavalry	1,100	111	10.00	5,029	408	8.11	12,369	693	5.60

BANKS' DIVISION.

	Mean strength.	Total sick.	Percentage.	Brigade strength.	Brigade sick.	Brigade percentage.	Division strength.	Division sick.	Division percentage.
Twenty-seventh Indiana	1,005	33	3.28						
Ninth New York State Militia	1,016	29	2.85						
Second Massachusetts Volunteers	990	62	6.26						
Twenty-ninth Pennsylvania Volunteers	916	23	2.51						
Twenty-eighth Pennsylvania Volunteers	1,551	25	1.61						
Forty-sixth Pennsylvania Volunteers	934	51	5.40						
Nineteenth New York Volunteers	664	31	4.67						
Thirteenth Massachusetts Volunteers	1,005	11	1.09						
First Maryland Volunteers	912	14	1.53						
Twelfth Massachusetts Volunteers	1,008	4	0.40						
Fourth Artillery, Company F. First Pennsylvania Artillery, Company A	198	9	4.54						
First Michigan Cavalry	1,121	62	5.53						
Third Wisconsin Volunteers	935	34	3.64						
Thirtieth Pennsylvania Volunteers	651	20	3.07						
Sixteenth Indiana	882	70	7.93						
Seven companies First Virginia Regiment Volunteers Second Home Brigade	725	33	4.55						
Twenty-eighth New York Volunteers	706	36	5.10						
Fifth Connecticut Volunteers	935	20	2.25						
Twelfth Indiana Volunteers	958	15	1.57						
First Regiment Home Brigade	895	90	10.05						
Division Hospital at Frederick City		132					18,007	1,059	5.88

SUMNER'S DIVISION.

Brigade and regiment.	Mean strength.	Total sick.	Percentage.	Brigade strength.	Brigade sick.	Brigade percentage.	Division strength.	Division sick.	Division percentage.
HOWARD'S BRIGADE.									
Fifth New Hampshire	998	102	10. 22						
Fourth Rhode Island									
Sixty-first New York	725	81	11. 17						
Eighty-first Pennsylvania	750	35	4. 67	2,473	218	8. 82			
MEAGHER'S BRIGADE.									
Sixty-third New York	713	33	4. 63						
Sixty-ninth New York	694	33	4. 75						
Eighty-eighth New York	659	35	5. 45	2,066	101	4. 89			
FRENCH'S BRIGADE.									
Fifty-second New York	712	41	5. 75						
Fifty-seventh New York	728	21	2. 88						
Sixty-sixth New York	738	53	7. 18						
Fifty-third Pennsylvania	940	72	7. 66	3,118	187	5. 96			
Eighth Illinois Cavalry	1,123	220	19. 59	1,123	220	19. 59	8,780	726	8. 04

MISCELLANEOUS.

General Hospital, Baltimore		254							
Dix's division—total							13,442	1,129	8. 32

[Inclosure No. 2.]

HEADQUARTERS BRIGADE,
Tennallytown, D. C., February 5, 1862.

Surg. CHARLES S. TRIPLER, *Medical Director Army of the Potomac:*

SIR: When so many statements are flying about touching the health of this army, I desire to invite your attention to the reports from my brigade, which seem to show that its sanitary condition is very excellent. With five regiments, in this rainy season, the number of sick had been as low as 59, and averaging about 70.

This state of things is not accidental, but mainly the results of a well-digested system persistently followed. Camps have been changed frequently. Tents have been often struck; the ground cleaned and aired. Side hills and high ground have been preferred. Much attention has been paid to drainage. Troops were not allowed to go below the surface in their tents. Vaccination has been general.

I am fortunate in having a skillful, intelligent, and faithful brigade surgeon.

Most respectfully, your obedient servant,

JOHN J. PECK,
Brigadier-General.

HEADQUARTERS DEPARTMENT OF WESTERN VIRGINIA,
Wheeling, February 7, 1862.

Brig. Gen. L. THOMAS,
Adjutant-General U. S. Army, Washington, D. C.:

GENERAL: I have the honor to submit for the consideration of the General-in-Chief the following:

1. Up to the present date there is but little force of rebels scattered along the southern and western border of this department and covering the railroad lines adjacent thereto.

2. Two columns organized as secretly as possible, with pack-trains and shelter-tents, instead of wagons and tents, carrying hand-mills for grinding corn for bread, one moving from Big Sandy Valley, the other from Raleigh Court-House, would be able to strike the Southwestern Virginia and Tennessee Railroad at Abingdon on the west and Central on the east, and completely break that road up and hold the valley.

3. The present force in the Big Sandy and Guyandotte Valleys, aided by one or two more regiments and under one commander, would suffice for one column. Five more regiments in Kanawha Valley would give strength enough for the other; that is to say, eight more regiments, including one of cavalry, would answer and hold the Kanawha Valley strongly enough for all probable purposes.

4. There would be required not more than 2,000 animals in addition to those now on hand to carry out these plans.

5. I have now about 100 trained packers, and orders are being executed by which all the teamsters of every regiment in this department will be instructed in packing.

6. There may probably be found forage enough on the routes to subsist the trains through to the valley and certainly enough there.

7. If the General-in-Chief sees great military advantages in carrying out the complete disruption of that rebel railroad route, and will give me directions to prepare the ways and means of doing it on the general plan indicated, or any modification thereof found desirable, and will place the west side of Big Sandy with its present force under my command, I will be answerable for the work.

8. I wish orders in reference [to] General Denver, who informs me he is ordered to report to me.

9. I wish Hartsuff to command the Big Sandy column if I can possibly get him.

Very respectfully, your obedient servant,
W. S. ROSECRANS,
Brigadier-General, U. S. Army.

HEADQUARTERS DIVISION AT FREDERICK,
February 10, 1862.

Brig. Gen. S. WILLIAMS,
Assistant Adjutant-General, Washington, D. C.:

GENERAL: Owing to the discontent existing among the rebel troops, and the oppressive measures adopted to force citizens of Virginia into the service of the Confederate States, the number of deserters and refugees from rebels at Hancock is becoming very large, and the expense of transportation correspondingly great. Cannot we limit the number sent forward to Washington upon some safe principle of discrimination, so as to avoid the otherwise necessary expenditures?

I am, general, most respectfully, your obedient servant,

N. P. BANKS,
Major-General, Commanding Division.

HEADQUARTERS OF THE ARMY,
Washington, February 14, 1862.

Brig. Gen. W. S. ROSECRANS,
Commanding Department of Western Virginia:

GENERAL: Your letter of the 7th is received. The general idea of your proposed march is an excellent one, but allow me to suggest for your consideration a modification.

I have reason to believe that there is a fair pike leading from Prestonburg, Ky., to Abingdon, the usual road followed by drovers, &c., the distance between the two points being about 70 miles in a right line, and the Sandy being navigable to Prestonburg nearly all the year. If this be so, this line would seem to present the most favorable chance, and the operation could be conducted with wagons several weeks earlier than would be practicable by the route you suggest.

I would be glad to have you take this matter into consideration and inform me of the conclusions at which you arrive.

In haste, very truly, yours,

GEO. B. McCLELLAN,
Major-General, Commanding U. S. Army.

HEADQUARTERS ARMY OF THE POTOMAC,
Washington, February 15, 1862.

General LANDER:

From the information received here as to the strength of the enemy at Romney, and from the fact that he is establishing a telegraph line between Winchester and Romney, it is supposed that he is determined to hold that place at all hazards.

Under these circumstances the Commanding General desires me to enjoin the utmost caution upon you in your movements. As you are on the spot you can better see how favorable the occasion may be for a contest with the enemy than the Commanding General, but no desperate risks are to be incurred, no uncertainty of result to be hazarded. The General's designs are not such as to include any unnecessary hazard at this moment.

By command of Major-General McClellan:

JAS. A. HARDIE,
Lieutenant-Colonel, Aide-de-Camp.

FEBRUARY 15, 1862—9.45 p. m.

Brig. Gen. R. B. MARCY, *Chief of Staff:*

It is out of the question to make the attack to-night. It is not yet reported to me that the boats from Baltimore have arrived. In other respects I am not ready. I must point out to two or three of my colonels from this shore my plan of attack, and must have daylight to do it in. I must know if I am to have the co-operation of the flotilla, and to what extent. If so, I must have an interview with the captain commanding, and have an understanding, that we may act in concert. Nor is the night auspicious, for a boat is visible on the water for a greater distance than the width of this river. I have no reasons for preferring the mode of attack already suggested by me except those furnished.

JOSEPH HOOKER,
Brigadier-General, Commanding Division.

DIVISION HEADQUARTERS,
Frederick, Md., February 17, 1862.

Hon. E. M. STANTON, *Secretary of War:*

SIR: On the day I received your instructions to report the condition of my division with reference to advance movements, orders were issued to increase its artillery and effect an immediate exchange of inefficient for efficient arms. So much uncertainty attends the execution of orders issued, that I deemed proper to defer a final answer to your inquiries until the full effect of these orders should be ascertained.

It gives me infinite pleasure now to inform you that my division, so far as my armament is concerned, is in condition for any service. Instead of four 6-pounder smooth-bore guns, I have now with the troops at Frederick three full batteries of 10-pounder Parrotts, and these, with the guns accompanying the different detachments on the river, which we actively guard and defend for more than 100 miles, will constitute an artillery force of five full batteries available for active service. Imperfect muskets are in daily process of exchange for good weapons. The health of the division is not surpassed by any division in the Army, and the men have a very sharp appetite for work.

Altogether I am happy to report my division in excellent condition for hard work.

With great respect, I have the honor to be, your obedient servant,

N. P. BANKS,
Major-General, Commanding Division.

HEADQUARTERS HOOKER'S DIVISION,
Camp Baker, Lower Potomac, Maryland,
February 17, 1862—12 m.

Brig. Gen. S. WILLIAMS,
Adjutant-General, Army of the Potomac:

The steamer Columbia, with four barges, arrived at Liverpool Point at 9 o'clock last night. She reports that the remaining six barges will arrive some time to-day.

When in Washington last the Major-General Commanding reported that an experiment was being made to have these barges bridged to enlarge their capacity for transporting troops, but as no frames have arrived for that purpose, I conclude the project has been abandoned. I request that I may be informed if it has been ascertained by experiment, or only by measurement, that ten barges of the class sent me can transport 4,000 troops. As the experiment here will attract attention, I have been indisposed to make it.

The rain of to-day indicates that a favorable moment for my enterprise is close at hand. I must have a dark'morning, for if the enemy observe my movements early the news can be communicated to Dumfries, and I shall have a larger force thrown on me than I can conveniently handle. The snow and moon together would be fatal to my success.

Be pleased to telegraph me respecting the capacity of the barges.

Very respectfully, &c.,

JOSEPH HOOKER,
Brigadier-General, Commanding Division.

FEBRUARY 18, 1862—8 p. m.

Brig. Gen. S. WILLIAMS:

It has been reported to me, and I credit it, that about 250 rebels have been breaking ground directly across from Liverpool Point to-day. The river is 3½ miles across at that point, and if for the purpose of establishing a battery, it can do no harm. If they cannot strike vessels distant 1 mile, they are not to be apprehended at more than three times that distance. It is estimated that about 250 men are at work there. The balloon was up all the morning, but the observations were unsatisfactory—the atmosphere being thick in the morning and foggy in the evening. The snow also obscures the outlines of the camps.

JOSEPH HOOKER,
Brigadier-General, Commanding Division.

FEBRUARY 18, 1862.

Brig. Gen. S. WILLIAMS:

With the data before me I am of opinion that the invasion of Virginia by Fouke's Landing or Boyd's Hole will be productive of the same results as at Aquia, with this difference: it gives us a better country to campaign in. The effect on the war in Eastern Virginia would depend very much on the strength of the column. If of three divisions, it would compel the enemy in the north to fall back without his railroads, enable us to take Richmond, or, if considered of more importance, capture Magruder's command.

JOSEPH HOOKER,
Brigadier-General, Commanding Division.

HEADQUARTERS HOOKER'S DIVISION,
Camp Baker, Lower Potomac, Maryland, February 20, 1862.

Brig. Gen. S. WILLIAMS,
Adjutant-General, Army of the Potomac:

As Captain Wyman did not call on me on his return, as was expected by the Major-General Commanding in his letter of the 17th instant, and not knowing but that there might be something remaining which that officer had not communicated to me, I visited him this p. m. This was my earliest opportunity of doing so.

I learned nothing of the subject of our meeting which had not already been communicated in his letter of the 18th instant,* and which was answered by my letter to Brig. Gen. S. Williams on the same day.

My observations from the balloon satisfy me that the batteries in my

---

* Not found.

front can be stormed and carried in the manner I have already communicated whenever a suitable night presents itself for that service; or, if that should not be deemed the most satisfactory mode of destroying them, I now have the means, with the aid of the flotilla, of landing three brigades of my division on the rebel shore and of demolishing the batteries regularly.

To do this I would begin the attack on Cockpit Point, and march down the river, crossing the Quantico by boats. With six Dahlgren howitzers from high ground on the north side of the Quantico I can drive the rebels from the batteries at Shipping Point in two hours. These guns, with ammunition, I can procure from the flotilla.

The Whitworth guns have arrived. If these guns possess the virtues assigned them, I believe that the camps of all the supports of the batteries can be broken up. I will know as soon as I can have them put in position.

The steamer Page will also be in danger, if I am not mistaken.

The free navigation of the river will give us immense advantage over the rebels, particularly so long as the roads remain in their present condition, and the destruction of the batteries will in no way expose future intentions of the Major-General in the conduct of the war.

Very respectfully, &c.,

JOSEPH HOOKER,
Brigadier-General, Commanding Division.

FREDERICK, MD., *February* 22, 1862.

General R. B. MARCY, *Chief of Staff, &c.:*

GENERAL : In relation to the subject considered in the interview with General McClellan, I am able to report that the troops of this division are ready for immediate movement. The quartermaster and commissary are completing their arrangements for transportation and supplies. As soon as the additional troops which were spoken of by General McClellan can be designated and put in communication with us, the General can put us on the march.

Colonel Geary is prepared to occupy the Loudoun Heights. Parties to which I referred for destroying the bridge designated by me, and one other westward, if possible, on the same railway, crossing the sources of Goose Creek, which falls into the Potomac at Edwards Ferry, are at work. These are bridges spanning streams as wide as the Potomac at Harper's Ferry, although less rapid and deep, and the opinion is expressed here that once broken they could not be reconstructed in some weeks. The engineers will have explained their views of the most practicable crossing. My own opinion, after such reflection as I could give the subject, is that the pontoon train will serve best for the first crossing; it can be thrown across in a few hours, and we can transport artillery and supply wagons across by hand instead of teams, if necessary. The canal-boat bridge can be constructed immediately after, and the railway company will replace theirs in two weeks' time for permanent use.

The Charlestown road is the best for travel, and carries us to the weakest points of the town. I am entirely satisfied that the outline of movement suggested will be a successful one.

I should be glad to receive the maps of that part of Virginia which exhibits the roads at Romney, Unger's, Bloomery Gap, &c., and the details of information of the field works, &c., at W———, which you were kind enough to say you would send me within a day or two.

All rebel troops, except pickets, have been withdrawn from Martinsburg and fallen back to Winchester. Rumor suggests two objects in this movement: the first is, that they contemplate moving to Richmond; the second is, that Jackson will move again on Romney. My own impression is that they stand at Winchester.

The report of Mr. Faulkner's speech is confirmed by Colonel Leonard, who says it is undoubtedly correct.

The day has been observed by all classes of people here; salutes were fired, and "the address" was read to a very large concourse of soldiers and citizens. The services were impressive, and will produce an excellent effect here.

I have the honor to be, with great respect, your obedient servant,
N. P. BANKS,
Major-General, &c.

HDQS. DIVISION, FREDERICK, MD., *February* 23, 1862.

Brig. Gen. R. B. MARCY, *Chief of Staff, &c.:*

GENERAL: My letter of Saturday missed the messenger by accident. It is forwarded to-day. We shall accomplish all contemplated under the march in my orders received this afternoon. If the pontoon train arrives to-morrow we shall occupy Harper's Ferry to-morrow night, and be on the road to Charlestown in the morning. It is expected Colonel Geary will seize the heights to-night. If the bridge is thrown across by Captain Duane we shall cross at night with 6,000 men, one regiment of cavalry, and 16 pieces of artillery. The cavalry will march the wagon roads, the artillery be divided between cars and road, as the weight is too great for travel at this season; their arrival will be delayed somewhat on this account. Colonel Leonard can cross at Williamsport with 1,900 men; General Williams, if not engaging the enemy with General Lander, will have 3,000 more men; and should it prove that no encounter with the enemy at Bath or in that vicinity will take place, ought we not to put in execution the plan of attack on Winchester, if the anticipated battle does not occur outside? This is a favorable opportunity. The roads to Winchester are turnpikes and in tolerable condition, and the only roads that are passable. The enemy is weak, demoralized, and depressed. The result is sure, if we can compass the force contemplated in the conference with the General Commanding. In co-operation with General Lander and General Burns, with the increase of artillery and a regiment of regular cavalry, we will not ask odds of fortune. Our force alone is not sufficient, but we will gladly risk it.

I have the honor to be, with great respect, yours, &c.,
N. P. BANKS,
Major-General, Commanding Division.

FEBRUARY 23, 1862.

T. T. ECKERT, *Washington:*

I consider a favorable morning for landing of more importance than the presence of the Ericsson. I would not wait for her. If the additional force is sent, will it not be advisable to include Fredericksburg in the programme? The force directed against the batteries will soon be at liberty to re-enforce the column directed against the last-named place. They can be landed at Fouke's, it being nearer than at Aquia Creek. I shall require fourteen landing planks, 4 feet wide and 16 feet long, with strong ropes 15 feet long fastened at each of the four corners. If practicable, I should like two more scows, similar to those now in use, as lighters. These should not be brought here, but left with the flotilla until called for.

Please advise me what post Heintzelman will take. If the plan should embrace Fredericksburg, I should have a regiment of cavalry, in order by a night movement to destroy some of the bridges on the rebels' chief line of communication. Will endeavor to cross over one or two light batteries for the same object.

JOSEPH HOOKER,
Brigadier-General, Commanding Division.

DIVISION HEADQUARTERS,
February 23, 1862—5 p. m.

Colonel LEONARD, *Commanding at Williamsport:*

SIR : Since you left information has been received that the enemy may attack Bath. If so, General Lander will give him battle and General Williams will co-operate with him. You will therefore make preparations to cross with Colonel Link and the Twelfth Indiana at Williamsport to-morrow (Monday) night. You will receive instructions to-morrow as to time. All the rest will proceed as agreed upon to-day. Please report progress to these headquarters and any information you have of enemy's movements.

Very truly and respectfully, your obedient servant,

N. P. BANKS,
Major-General, Commanding.

SANDY HOOK, *February 26*—10.20 p. m.

Hon. E. M. STANTON :

The bridge was splendidly thrown by Captain Duane, assisted by Lieutenants Babcock, Reese, and Cross. It was one of the most difficult operations of the kind ever performed. I recommend Captain Duane to be made a major by brevet for his energy and skill in this matter; also Lieutenants Babcock, Reese, and Cross, all of the Corps of Engineers, to be captains by brevet. We have 8,500 infantry, 18 guns, and two squadrons of cavalry on the Virginia side. I have examined the ground and seen that the troops are in proper positions and are ready to resist any attack. Loudoun and Bolivar Heights, as well as the Maryland Heights, are occupied by us. Burns' brigade will be here in a couple of hours, and will cross at daybreak. Four more squadrons of cavalry and several more guns pass here. Reports that G. W. Smith with 15,000 men is expected at Winchester.

Colonel Geary deserves praise for the manner in which he occupied Virginia and crossed after the construction of the bridge. We will attempt the canal-boat bridge to-morrow. The spirit of the troops is most excellent. They are in the mood to fight anything. It is raining hard, but most of the troops are in houses.

GEO. B. McCLELLAN,
Major-General.

SANDY HOOK, *February* 27—1 p. m.

General R. B. MARCY:

Do not send the regular infantry until further orders. Give Hooker orders not to move until further orders.

GEO. B. McCLELLAN.

———

SANDY HOOK, *February* 27, 1862—3.30 p. m.

R. B. MARCY, *Chief of Staff:*

The difficulties here are so great that the order for Keyes' movement must be countermanded until the railway bridge is finished or some more permanent arrangement made. It is impossible to supply a large force here. Please inform Garrett at once.

GEO. B. McCLELLAN,
Major-General, Commanding.

———

SANDY HOOK, *February* 27, 1862—3.30 p. m.

Hon. E. M. STANTON, *Secretary of War:*

The lift-lock is too small to permit the canal-boats to enter the river, so that it is impossible to construct the permanent bridge, as I intended. I shall probably be obliged to fall back upon the safe and slow plan of merely covering the reconstruction of the railroad. This will be done at once, but will be tedious. I cannot, as things now are, be sure of my supplies for the force necessary to seize Winchester, which is probably re-enforced from Manassas. The wiser plan is to rebuild the railroad bridge as rapidly as possible, and then act according to the state of affairs.

GEO. B. McCLELLAN,
Major-General.

———

General McCLELLAN:

If the lift-lock is not big enough why cannot it be made big enough? Please answer immediately.

EDWIN M. STANTON,
Secretary of War.

———

SANDY HOOK, *February* 27—10.30 p. m.

Hon. E. M. STANTON, *Secretary of War:*

It can be enlarged, but entire masonry must be destroyed and re-built, and new gates made; an operation impossible in the present stage of water and requiring many weeks at any time. The railroad bridge can be rebuilt many weeks before this could be done.

GEO. B. McCLELLAN,
Major-General.

———

SANDY HOOK, *February* 27, 1862.

General MARCY:

Revoke Hooker's authority, in accordance with Barnard's opinion. Immediately on my return we will take the other plan, and push on vigorously.

GEO. B. McCLELLAN,
Major-General.

BALTIMORE, *February* 27, 1862.

General GEORGE B. McCLELLAN, *Headquarters* :

Have this moment received the following dispatch from P. Willard, one of our supervisors of trains at Cumberland : "A man has just arrived here from Patterson's Creek, with the information that the bridge has been fired and was burning when he left." This bridge is within 8 miles of Cumberland, east. We fortunately have timber prepared in the vicinity. As the line is subject to raids, and the maintenance of these structures is most important to military movements as well as to our ability for repairs, pray order military guards on all important bridges west. Notwithstanding the very brief notice, we are much gratified to state that our arrangements are perfecting to accomplish fully your wishes as to movements of batteries, troops, &c. The cars for the service ordered this morning were concentrated through the night at Washington, and we confidently expect these movements to be prompt and effective. We will feel much obliged and relieved if you can telegraph us regarding bridges from Great Cacapon west. Mr. Heskit, who takes charge of reconstructing bridge at Harper's Ferry, has gone up on mail train; timber is also being unloaded. I trust you can grant him an interview soon after his arrival.

J. W. GARRETT,
President Baltimore and Ohio Railroad.

SANDY HOOK, *February* 27.

J. W. GARRETT, Esq.:

Will give orders to secure bridges. Glad to hear that your measures are so effective.

GEO. B. McCLELLAN,
Major-General.

BALTIMORE, *February* 27, 1862.

General R. B. MARCY:

I understand that the General Commanding directs that all the arrangements for transportation of troops from Washington be stopped, and that the movements will not take place until further notice. The General Commanding also telegraphs to send back all the troops that have started, which order I have communicated to Mr. Smith, now at Relay, in charge of transportation at that point. Shall the horses and artillery be ordered back? I have directed the trains held, awaiting your instructions regarding the latter.

J. W. GARRETT,
President.

WAR DEPARTMENT,
Washington, D. C., February 28, 1862—1 p. m.

Maj. Gen. GEORGE B. McCLELLAN:

What do you propose to do with the troops that have crossed the Potomac?

EDWIN M. STANTON,
Secretary of War.

SANDY HOOK, *February* 28, 1862.

Hon. E. M. STANTON:

Your dispatch received. I propose to occupy Charlestown and Bunker Hill, so as to cover the rebuilding of the railway, while I throw over the supplies necessary for an advance in force. I have just men enough to accomplish this. I could not at present supply more.

GEO. B. McCLELLAN,
Major-General.

SANDY HOOK, *February* 28, 1862. (Received 9.30 p. m.)

ABRAHAM LINCOLN, *President:*

It is impossible for many days to do more than supply the troops now here and at Charlestown. We could not supply and move to Winchester for many days, and had I moved more troops here they would have been at a loss for food on the Virginia side. I know that I have acted wisely, and that you will cheerfully agree with me when I explain. I have arranged to establish depots on that side so we can do what we please. I have secured opening of the road.

GEO. B. McCLELLAN,
Major-General, Commanding.

HEADQUARTERS ARMY OF THE POTOMAC,
Washington, February 28, 1862.

Hon. E. M. STANTON, *Secretary of War:*

SIR: I have received the following from General McClellan this morning:

SANDY HOOK, *February* 27, 1862.

General R. B. MARCY:

It being impossible to build a bridge of canal-boats, as well as impossible to unload and take across the river with sufficient promptness the supplies needed by our large force, on account of the very limited space, I have determined on the course I indicated to the President and Secretary of War, viz, to cover the opening of the railway and the rebuilding of its bridges. In the mean time depots can be established, which will make an advance easy. But this requires time. The fact that canal-boats could not be used was ascertained only to-day, and I regarded the other projected operations as too important to be deferred for the time necessary to accomplish this, which can be done at any time hereafter, the railway being meanwhile opened.

GEO. B. McCLELLAN,
Major-General, Commanding.

Very respectfully, your obedient servant,

R. B. MARCY,
Chief of Staff.

CHARLESTOWN, *February* 28, 1862—12.30 p. m.

Hon. E. M. STANTON, *Secretary of War:*

I have decided to occupy this town permanently, and am arranging accordingly. I make other arrangements on the right which render us secure. You will be satisfied when I see you that I have acted wisely and have everything in hand.

GEO. B. McCLELLAN,
Major-General.

BALTIMORE, *February* 28, 1862.

Hon. E. M. STANTON:

I have the pleasure of informing you that the reconstruction of the bridge over Patterson's Creek was completed at 1 this a. m., and the road is again in order to Hancock.

J. W. GARRETT,
President.

CHARLESTOWN, VA., *February* 28, 1862—2 p. m.

General F. W. LANDER :

Move with least possible delay on Martinsburg, whither Williams is also ordered at once. When you hold command in hand occupy Bunker Hill, and open your communication with this place. Cause repairs of railroad to be pushed as rapidly as possible, so as to draw your supplies from the West.

GEO. B. McCLELLAN,
Major-General, Commanding.

HEADQUARTERS HOOKER'S DIVISION,
Camp Baker, Lower Potomac, Maryland, February 28, 1862.

Brig. Gen. S. WILLIAMS,
Adjutant-General, Army of the Potomac :

GENERAL: I received last evening the instructions of the Major-General Commanding to suspend my movement across the river until further orders. Of course it is not for me to know or inquire for influences at work to bring about this suspension.

I am permitted to state that almost every officer returning from Washington during the past week has communicated to me the fact that my command was to cross and attack the batteries, and it was even announced several days since in the Baltimore Clipper. Colonel Dwight returned last evening, and assured me that he was informed of it by Mr. Garett, I think of the Judge-Advocate's Office, at the breakfast table some days previous. For these reasons it ought no longer to be considered as an adventure of strictly a private character.

I have found but one opportunity to experiment with the Whitworth guns. From that I am satisfied that they are unrivaled pieces for accuracy of shooting and length of range. Should have gone out with them again to-day but for the high wind; it blows a gale.

Very respectfully, your obedient servant,

JOSEPH HOOKER,
Brigadier-General, Commanding Division.

Abstract from return of the Army of the Potomac, commanded by Maj. Gen. George B. McClellan, U. S. Army, for the month of February, 1862.

Commands.	Stations.	Present for duty.		Aggregate present and absent.	Pieces of artillery.	
		Officers.	Men.		Heavy.	Field.
General staff		74		74		
Alexandria Division	Camp Williams, Va	497	11,997	14,487		18
Banks' division	Charlestown, Va	565	13,671	16,801		32
Blenker's division	Hunter's Chapel, Va	411	7,985	10,455		18
Casey's division	Washington, D. C	180	4,109	5,325		
Dix's division	Baltimore, Md	500	10,544	13,430		20
Heintzelman's division	Fort Lyon, Va	442	9,877	12,151	29	18
Hooker's division	Lower Potomac, Md	387	10,417	12,845		18
Keyes' division	Washington, D. C	450	10,914	12,800		16
McCall's division	Camp Peirpoint, Va	415	10,701	12,722		16
McDowell's division	Arlington, Va	524	11,230	13,732	34	53
Porter's (F. J.) division	Hall's Hill, Va	553	12,995	15,596		24
Sedgwick's division	Harper's Ferry, Va	367	9,104	11,470		18
Lander's division	Paw Paw Tunnel, Va	482	11,387	15,731		26
Smith's division	Camp Griffin, Va	457	10,138	13,248		18
Sumner's division	Camp California, Va	383	7,520	9,859	6	12
Provisional Brigade	Washington, D. C	73	1,337	1,617		
City Guard and detachments	Washington, D. C	229	4,675	6,124		1
Railway Brigade	Annapolis Junction, Md	135	2,805	3,317		
Engineer Battalion	Sandy Hook, Md	2	197	270		
Engineer Brigade, volunteers	Washington, D. C	52	1,402	1,730		
Cavalry, regular	Near Washington, D. C	79	2,016	2,788		
Cavalry, volunteer	Washington, D. C	288	5,786	7,133		
Reserve artillery	Camp Duncan, D. C	76	1,726	2,233		90
Field works and artillery	About Washington, D. C	237	4,869	5,882		67
Fort Washington	Fort Washington, Md	6	154	198		
Total		7,864	177,556	222,018	69	465

POOLESVILLE, MD., *March 1, 1862.*

Major-General BANKS, *Harper's Ferry :*

The enemy unusually demonstrative on their line of pickets to-day, exhibiting both infantry and cavalry, also six baggage wagons opposite Mason's Island. They shelled us from their position opposite Edwards Ferry and at Ball's Bluff this afternoon, but discontinued as soon as we replied. There were smokes in their camps. These demonstrations may be for a blind, but I am unable to assert it positively.

N. J. T. DANA,
Brigadier-General.

HEADQUARTERS ARMY OF THE POTOMAC,
Washington, March 2, 1862.

S. F. BARSTOW,
Assistant Adjutant-General, Camp Chase, Paw Paw :

During the illness of General Lander let the next officer in rank assume command and move the available troops on Martinsburg via Hedgesville, covering construction of roads as troops advance. General Williams will be in Martinsburg with some 5,000 men. It is desirable to have the troops of General Lander's command in Martinsburg with least possible delay. Sufficient guards must be left to cover the railroad.

GEO. B. McCLELLAN,
Major-General, Commanding.

General Orders, } Headquarters of the Army, A. G. O.,
    No. 23.   }   Washington, March 3, 1862.

I. The eastern limits of the Department of Western Virginia are extended so as to embrace the valleys of the South Branch of the Potomac and of the Cow Pasture Branch of James River, the valley of the James River to the Balcony Falls, the valley of the Roanoke west of the Blue Ridge, and the New River Valley. The eastern boundary of the said department will be then as follows: Commencing at the north, the Flinstone Creek, in Maryland; the South Branch Mountain; Town Hill Mountain; Branch Mountain, or Big Ridge; the North, or Shenandoah Mountain; Purgatory Mountain; Blue Ridge; Alleghany Mountains to the borders of North Carolina.

*   *   *   *   *   *   *

By command of Major-General McClellan:

                                    L. THOMAS,
                                        Adjutant-General.

———

                                    CHARLESTOWN, March 4, 1862.
Brig. Gen. JOHN SEDGWICK:

DEAR SIR: General Williams, commanding third brigade of my division, has probably reached Martinsburg. My belief is that he arrived there with his full force last night; if so, he has at his command 5,000 troops, and will probably to-day move on and occupy Bunker Hill. This by order of General McClellan. As soon as he moves we shall place ourselves in supporting distance and stand ready to advance upon Winchester at any moment. I desire you to place your division within supporting distance of Berryville, to which point we shall direct our force. It will give me pleasure to confer with you and your officers, if you please, either here or at Harper's Ferry as you please, and will do so upon the receipt of your answer.

I am, general, very respectfully, your obedient servant,

                                    N. P. BANKS,
                                Major-General, Commanding Division.

———

            HDQRS. TWENTY-EIGHTH REGIMENT PA. VOLS.,
                                Lovettsville, Va., March 4, 1862.
Maj. R. MORRIS COPELAND,
    Assistant Adjutant-General:

SIR: In pursuance of the original intention of preventing the rebels who had infested this vicinity and that towards Leesburg from carrying out their designs of molesting our troops under transportation in trains on the Maryland side of the river, my command has held a firm and decided position at this point, keeping in check about 4,000 rebels who threatened us from Leesburg. It becomes necessary that I should hold this place a few days longer, as I have reliable information that the enemy has expressed a determination to attempt a repetition of their attacks upon the cars in the employ of our Government daily passing over the Baltimore and Ohio Railroad, and by a bold dash put into execution a plan they have concocted to cross the river in boats and destroy a portion of the road and several viaducts, which would greatly cripple the progress on the main line of our operations. After consummating this their intention was to evacuate Leesburg and go farther south.

A general expression of loyalty has transpired in this county, and joyous manifestations of fealty to the old Government have greeted us, and hundreds of the residents have come forward and claimed our protection from the dominion and obnoxious restrictions placed upon them by the rebel soldiery. So great has been the dependence on our power and willingness to protect them as people of the same Government and of sympathetic feelings, that it would seem almost cruel to abandon them in our withdrawal to the rage of those whom they have in their denunciations avowed as enemies. The remedy I would respectfully suggest is the taking of Leesburg, which I can accomplish with a slightly augmented force. By doing this the whole of this section of Virginia will be free to declare its undoubted Union sentiment without molestation or fear.

The rebels once driven from that point will fall back effectually, and rid a large circuit of this portion of the State of their despotism and rule of terror. I think they can be driven out of the county in a day or two, which would be very essential, as this valley is a golden granary, from which they have gathered many of their stores, and upon which the supplies for the troops in Centreville have been mainly dependent. I have materially intercepted their supply communication.

I very respectfully tender these suggestions for your consideration and await a reply thereon, and would call your attention to their bearing upon my orders to report to the division as soon as possible after the enterprise upon which I am at present engaged has been completed.

Very respectfully, your obedient servant,

JNO. W. GEARY,
Colonel Twenty-eighth Regiment Pa. Vols., Comdg.

CHARLESTOWN, VA., *March 4, 1862.*

General R. B. MARCY, *Chief of Staff:*

General Williams is at Martinsburg, and will move upon Bunker Hill early. Our information is that the railroad will be open to Martinsburg by the middle of the week. We have no knowledge of the position of General Lander's forces. Letters intercepted yesterday from officers at Winchester to their families speak of expected withdrawal towards Strasburg; they are desponding in tone. General Dana observes no change in affairs at Leesburg. Hard storm yesterday; day clear and cold.

N. P. BANKS,
Major-General, Commanding.

HEADQUARTERS DEPARTMENT WESTERN VIRGINIA,
Wheeling, March 4, 1862.

Hon. FRANK P. BLAIR, Jr.,
Chairman Military Committee House of Representatives:

SIR: Owing to the negligence of officers or their inability to control the men under their command, much property has been unnecessarily destroyed by the troops in this department. Fences and houses have been burned, horses seized and appropriated, without authority or warrant of necessity. Claims for property so taken or destroyed are almost daily presented to me. This state of affairs requires some stringent preventive measures. Some legal provision embodying the substance of the printed slips* which I have the honor to inclose would, I think, prove effectual.

Very respectfully, your obedient servant,

W. S. ROSECRANS,
Brigadier-General, U. S. Army.

HDQRS. TWENTY-EIGHTH REGIMENT PA. VOLS.,
Lovettsville, Va., March 5, 1862.

Maj. R. MORRIS COPELAND, *Assistant Adjutant-General:*

SIR: Our scouts report this morning that 1,000 of the enemy, with artillery and 200 or 300 cavalry, have stationed themselves at Waterford, within 6 miles of us.

General Smith's brigade, about 3,000 strong, is at Gum Spring.

Union feeling is developing itself in great magnitude in this county and masses of people come to us daily, placing themselves under our protection. The cause of the rebels is openly reviled by them, and our location here is hailed by the people as the dawning of a new era.

Very respectfully, your obedient servant,

JNO. W. GEARY,
Colonel Twenty-eighth Regiment Pa. Vols., Comdg.

MARCH 5, 1862.

Brig. Gen. S. WILLIAMS:

Have received General Marcy's telegram.* Will make every possible effort to accomplish his wishes. I can find persons to attempt it, but have many doubts as to their being able to get on shore. The enemy's pickets are extremely vigilant. Sickles sends me word that the rebels have been re-enforced by four regiments to-day. Do not know whether it is so or not. Will ascertain early in the morning from the balloon and let you know, if the weather is propitious.

JOSEPH HOOKER,
Brigadier-General, Commanding Division.

SPECIAL ORDERS, }   HDQRS. GENERAL BANKS' DIVISION,
No. 52.   }   NEAR CHARLESTOWN, VA., *March* 5, 1862.

*   *   *   *   *   *   *

6. Brig. Gen. C. S. Hamilton will put his brigade in readiness and march towards Smithfield, with one battery of artillery and a squadron of cavalry, to-morrow morning, March 6, 1862, as early as practicable. General Hamilton will take position in the vicinity of Smithfield wherever in his judgment he will be in supporting distance of Brig. Gen. A. S. Williams, now at Bunker Hill. As soon as he shall have started he will send forward messengers to General Williams announcing his approach and his orders. Should circumstances compel him to advance to the support of General Williams, he will, as senior brigadier, assume command of the brigades.

*   *   *   *   *   *   *

By command of Maj. Gen. N. P. Banks:

R. MORRIS COPELAND,
Assistant Adjutant-General.

---

* Not found.

HEADQUARTERS ARMY OF THE POTOMAC,
Washington, D. C., March 8, 1862.

Maj. Gen. GEORGE B. McCLELLAN,
Commanding Army of the Potomac:

GENERAL: 1 have the honor to report the following information relative to the forces and defenses of the Army of the Potomac obtained to
this date, which has been extracted from current statements made here
by spies, contrabands, deserters, refugees, and rebel prisoners of war, in
the order of time as hereinafter indicated, and which at the time of reception were made the subject of special reports to you. I have also
appended to this report extracts from statements, and have made the
same a part of this report, a varied summary of the rebel forces and defenses of the line of the Army of the Potomac, showing by different
combinations about the probable number of these forces and the locality
and strength of their defenses.

By reference to the summary of this report it will be seen that a medium estimate of the rebel army of the Potomac is 115,500, located as
follows, viz: At Manassas, Centreville, Bull Run, Upper Occoquan, and
vicinities, 80,000; at Brooke's Station, Dumfries, Lower Occoquan, and
vicinities, 18,000; at Leesburg and vicinity, 4,500; in the Shenandoah
Valley, 13,000.

Of the above-mentioned forces information has been received up to
date, as shown by summary in this report, of the following specific organizations, viz: At Manassas, Centreville, Bull Run, Upper Occoquan,
and vicinity, sixty-one regiments and one battalion infantry; eight regiments, one battalion, and seven independent companies cavalry; thirty-
four companies artillery. At Brooke's Station, Dumfries, Lower Occoquan, and vicinities, eighteen regiments and one battalion infantry; one
regiment and six independent companies cavalry, and fifteen companies
artillery. In the Shenandoah Valley, twelve regiments infantry, two
brigades militia, one regiment cavalry, seven companies artillery. At
Leesburg, four regiments infantry, one regiment militia, five independent companies cavalry, and one company artillery.

It is unnecessary for me to say that in the nature of the case, guarded
as the rebels have ever been against the encroachment of spies and
vigilant as they have always been to prevent information of their forces,
movements, and designs from going beyond their lines, it has been impossible, even by the use of every resource at our command, to ascertain
with certainty the specific number and character of their forces. It may,
therefore, safely be assumed that in so large an army as our information
shows them to possess very much of its composition and very many of
its forces have not been specifically ascertained, which, added to those
already known, would largely increase their numbers and considerably
swell its proportions.

The summary of the general estimates shows the forces of the rebel
Army of the Potomac to be 150,000, as claimed by its officers and sanctioned by the public belief, and that over 80,000 were stationed at Centreville, Manassas, and vicinity, the remainder being within easy supporting distance.

The statements of several reliable persons, who derived their information from the Commissary Department, show that in March, 1862, 80,000
daily rations were issued to the army at Manassas and Centreville; and
the evidence is equally positive that each wing of the army, one in the
Shenandoah Valley and the other on the Lower Potomac, had its sepa-

rate commissary department, and derived their supplies from other sources than did the main body at Manassas and Centreville.

All of which, general, is respectfully submitted by your obedient servant,

E. J. ALLEN. [ALLEN PINKERTON.]

[Inclosure.]

JANUARY 27, 1862.

A deserter from the Sixth Louisiana Regiment states that he left Centreville about 25th December, 1861, and Manassas about January 7, 1862; that it was then understood that the rebel forces at Manassas, Centreville, and vicinity were about 60,000, under command of Generals Johnston, Beauregard, and Smith; that he got his information from a clerk in the rebel Commissary Department; that General Taylor's brigade, to which he belonged, was of General Smith's division, composed of Sixth Louisiana Regiment, Colonel Seymour, 840 men; Seventh Louisiana, Col. Harry Hays, 840 men; Eighth Louisiana Regiment, Colonel Kelly, 900 men, and battalion of Louisiana Tigers, five companies, under the command of Major Wheat; that the headquarters of Brigadier-General Van Dorn were near Union Mills, and his cavalry pickets extend to Fairfax Court-House; that General Early's brigade, near Bull Run, west of the railroad bridge, is composed of the Twentieth Georgia, Twenty-fourth Virginia, Thirteenth North Carolina, and two other regiments, with one battery—one of the regiments is commanded by Colonel Hope; that General Bonham's South Carolina brigade is on the new military road from Centreville to Union Mills, composed of five regiments and one battery; that General Cox's brigade is encamped near Centreville, on Manassas road, and includes the celebrated Eighth Virginia; that two brigades are located 2 miles from Centreville, on Stone Bridge road, and in one of them are the First Kentucky and Sixteenth Mississippi; that Stuart's cavalry brigade is near Stone Bridge, two of the regiments under command of Colonels Fields and Radford; that Washington Artillery, four companies, under Major Walton, guns mostly brass and rifled, four mortars, is stationed on east side of New Bull Run Bridge.

Batteries.—That near General Bonham's brigade are four half-moon batteries; several forts on the heights about Centreville, no guns mounted on any of them; that logs shaped like guns, the outer ends painted black, are put into position to appear like guns from the outside, being covered with brush to hide the character of the "guns" and hinder revealment of true state of affairs; that informant knows this to be true, having helped to make and place in position these mock guns; that the log guns are on those forts only nearest this way outside Centreville; that there are no stationary guns east side of Bull Run. Heavy guns have been taken from Manassas batteries for the blockade on the Potomac; that General Rodes' brigade is near to mouth of Bull Run, on the Occoquan; in his brigade are the Fifth and Sixth Alabama Regiments and others not known; also the Black Horse Cavalry.

Recapitulation of forces stated as being in vicinity of Manassas, Centreville, Union Mills, Stone Bridge, and Benson's Ford, to wit: General Taylor's brigade, General Bonham's brigade, General Early's brigade, General Cox's brigade; two brigades 2 miles west-southwest of Centreville; several regiments west side Bull Run; Stuart's cavalry brigade; General Rodes' brigade; Washington Artillery, four companies, 16 guns. No troops known to have lately left for other parts of the country. Mostly in winter quarters. Troops well armed. Roads bad. Railroad from Manassas to Centreville progressing; 300 "miners" at work on it. Provisions plenty.

Conclusion: Informant entitled to credit; his statement believed truthful.

CHARLESTOWN, VA., *March* 8, 1862.

General R. B. MARCY, *Chief of Staff, &c., Washington, D. C.*:

GENERAL: Inclosed you will please find a diagram of our positions on the base of the Smithfield road.* Our line extends from the Shenandoah to North Mountain substantially, and our pickets cover that line for 1½ miles in front. We learn by dispatch from General Williams that General Shields' forces were to arrive at Martinsburg last night. If so, this will make our contemplated strength complete.

Our troops are in good health and spirits, eager for work. I do not yet know General Shields' strength, and therefore cannot state our exact force. We have given out here that our chief object is the opening of the Baltimore and Ohio Railway. Our troops are, however, pressing forward in the direction of Winchester, and will gradually press upon Winchester.

Beyond the point we now occupy I have received no instructions from the Commanding General—whether we are to move on as a force destined to effect a specific object by itself or to perform a part in combined operations. I shall be glad to receive more specific instructions. If left to our own discretion, the general desire will be to move on early.

I am, sir, with great respect, your obedient servant,

N. P. BANKS,
Major-General, Commanding Division.

HEADQUARTERS, *Baltimore, March* 8, 1862.

Hon. E. M. STANTON, *Secretary of War:*

SIR: The police commissioners appointed by the legislature of Maryland under the late act reorganizing the police of this city called on me last evening and announced their readiness to enter on the discharge of their duties. The act fixes the 10th of this month as the day on which their appointment takes effect; but they are not to assume their office until after the Government of the United States shall have notified them of the withdrawal of the provost-marshal and police established under its authority. This may be safely done at once, provided a provost-marshal and not exceeding 20 policemen are appointed to perform special duties, as suggested in my letter of 31st January.

I also mentioned in that letter that an appropriation of $15,000 per annum would be necessary to meet the expenses incident to the maintenance of such a force, including their compensation, which should be paid once a month. Will you please authorize me, if you approve the measure, to appoint such a force and fix their compensation? I ought also to be authorized to notify the police commissioners that the Government withdraws the provost-marshal and policemen appointed by its direction.

---

* Not found.

An early answer is respectfully solicited, as the police commissioners are anxious to commence the performance of their duties, and as the compensation of the police force is in arrears, and measures should be taken to pay them.

I am, very respectfully, yours,

JOHN A. DIX,
Major-General.

HALL'S HILL, VA., *March 9, 1862.*

The SECRETARY OF WAR:

In the arrangements for the advance of to-morrow it is impossible to carry into effect the arrangements for the formation of army corps. I am obliged to take groups as I find them and to move them by divisions. I respectfully ask a suspension of the order directing it till the present movement be over.

GEO. B. McCLELLAN,
Major-General.

WAR DEPARTMENT, *March 9.*

Major-General McCLELLAN:

I think it is the duty of every officer to obey the President's orders, nor can I see any reason why you should not obey them in present instance. I must therefore decline to suspend them.

EDWIN M. STANTON,
Secretary of War.

HEADQUARTERS ARMY OF THE POTOMAC,
March 9, 1862—9.40 p. m.

General N. P. BANKS, *Charlestown, Va.:*

The batteries on the Lower Potomac have been abandoned by the enemy, and it is believed that they either have or are about abandoning Manassas. We have it from four different sources. The General Commanding directs that you push out strong reconnaissances towards Winchester to-morrow morning and feel the enemy. He also directs that you hold your whole command ready to move to-morrow morning.

General Dana has been directed to be ready.

R. B. MARCY,
Chief of Staff.

HEADQUARTERS,
Charlestown, Va., Sunday, March 9—12 p. m.

General C. S. HAMILTON:

GENERAL: Dispatch from headquarters states that batteries on the Lower Potomac are withdrawn, and it is believed that the rebels have abandoned or are about abandoning Manassas.

We are instructed to make a strong reconnaissance towards Winchester early to-morrow. General Williams will move two regiments in that direction at daybreak, with a detachment of cavalry and two sections of artillery. You will follow with your brigade to Bunker Hill, keeping within supporting distance, and in the event of combined action upon Winchester, you will, as senior officer, assume command of the forces on that line and co-operate with the troops of this line under such orders as may be hereafter issued. The column of reconnaissance here will move upon the Berryville road as soon after daybreak as possible.

General Dana is ordered to our support from Poolesville. The advance parties will avoid any general action.

Will communicate again in the early morning.

By order of—

N. P. BANKS,
Major-General, Commanding.

SPECIAL ORDERS, }   HDQRS. GENERAL BANKS' DIVISION,
No. 57.   }   *Near Charlestown, Va., March* 9, 1862—12 p. m.
*   *   *   *   *   *   *

3. Information has been received that the enemy has abandoned the batteries on the Lower Potomac and is preparing to abandon Manassas. General Sedgwick is therefore ordered to put his command in condition to move at 7 a. m. to-morrow, and will order General W. A. Gorman to make a reconnaissance towards Winchester, on the Berryville road, to-morrow morning at daybreak, with one battery of artillery and two squadrons of cavalry.

4. Information has been received that the enemy has abandoned the batteries on the Lower Potomac and is preparing to abandon Manassas. General J. J. Abercrombie is therefore ordered to put his brigade in condition to move at 7 a. m. to-morrow.

5. It is believed that the rebels have withdrawn their batteries on the Lower Potomac and are preparing to abandon Manassas. Pursuant to instructions, we shall make a strong reconnaissance in the direction of Winchester at daybreak to-morrow morning, Monday. You will put your brigade in readiness for immediate movement, and with at least two regiments, a detachment of cavalry, and four pieces of artillery, push forward at daybreak in the direction of Winchester for purposes of reconnaissance, avoiding any general engagement with the enemy until our forces may be combined.

General C. S. Hamilton is instructed to move to Bunker Hill and keep within supporting distance, and in the event of combined operations General Hamilton, as senior officer, will assume command of the forces upon that line, and act under such orders as may be hereafter issued from these headquarters.

By command of Maj. Gen. N. P. Banks:

R. MORRIS COPELAND,
Assistant Adjutant-General.

HALL'S HILL, VA., *March* 10, 1862—1 a. m.

Hon. E. M. STANTON, *Secretary of War:*

You have entirely misunderstood me, and the idea I intended to convey was simply that I could not, under the pressure of the new aspect of affairs, immediately carry out the President's orders as to the formation of army corps. It is absolutely necessary that I should at once move divisions as they stand. If you require me to suspend movements until army corps can be formed I will do so, but I regard it as a military necessity that the divisions should move to the front at once, without waiting for the formation of army corps. If it is your order to wait until the corps can be formed, I will, of course, wait. I will comply with the President's order as soon as possible. I intended to do so to-morrow, but circumstances have changed. If you desire it I will at once countermand all the orders I have given for an advance until the formation of army corps is completed. I have only to add that the orders I have given to-night to advance early in the morning will be dictated solely by the present position of affairs. If the leave to suspend the order be granted, there will be no unreasonable delay in the formation of army corps. I await your reply here. If you so direct that I may countermand my orders at once, please reply at once.

GEO. B. McCLELLAN,
Major-General, Commanding.

WAR DEPARTMENT,
Washington City, D. C., March 10, 1862.

Major-General McCLELLAN, *Hall's Hill:*

GENERAL: I do not understand the President's order as restraining you from any military movement by divisions or otherwise that circumstances in your judgment may render expedient, and I certainly do not wish to delay or change any movement whatever that you have made or desire to make. I only wish to avoid giving my sanction to a suspension of a policy which the President has ordered to be pursued. But if you think that the terms of the order as it stands would operate to retard or in any way restrain movements that circumstances require to be made before the army corps are formed, I will assume the responsibility of suspending the order for that purpose, and authorize you to make any movement by divisions or otherwise, according to your own judgment, without stopping to form the army corps.

My desire is that you should exercise every power that you think present circumstances require to be exercised, without delay; but I want that you and I shall not seem to be desirous of opposing an order of the President without necessity. I say, therefore, move just as you think best now, and let the other matter stand until it can be done without impeding movements.

EDWIN M. STANTON,
Secretary of War.

HALL'S HILL, *March* 10, 1862—2.50 a. m.

Hon. E. M. STANTON, *Secretary of War:*

Your reply received. The troops are in motion. I thank you for your dispatch. It relieves me much, and you will be convinced that I have not asked too much of you.

GEO. B. McCLELLAN,
Major-General.

FAIRFAX COURT-HOUSE, *March* 10—8.20 p. m.

Hon. E. M. STANTON, *Secretary of War:*

I have given all the orders necessary for the movement, and soon start for Washington, merely to spend the night. I want to join my headquarters near Alexandria early in the morning. I could not leave my troops to-night until I had done all in my power to expedite the movement.

GEO. B. McCLELLAN,
Major-General, Commanding.

FAIRFAX COURT-HOUSE, *March* 11, 1862.

General MARCY:

Telegraph to General Banks that the troops have all left Manassas, and probably the whole or the greater part of the troops have left Winchester, and that General McClellan desires that he push forward to that place as soon as possible, and hold himself in readiness to move with the whole or a part of his force on Manassas. In the order for the transportation to come to Washington do not include that for transporting wagons and animals from Perryville and Annapolis. Let them remain where they are, subject to other orders.

GEO. B. McCLELLAN,
Major-General.

FAIRFAX COURT-HOUSE, *March* 11, 1862—8.30 p. m.

Hon. E. M. STANTON, *Secretary of War:*

I have just returned from a ride of more than 40 miles. Have examined Centreville, Union Mills, Blackburn's Ford, &c. The rebels have left all their positions, and from the information obtained during our ride to-day I am satisfied that they have fallen behind the Rapidan, holding Fredericksburg and Gordonsville. Their movement from here was very sudden. They left many wagons, some caissons, clothing, ammunition, personal baggage, &c. Their winter quarters were admirably constructed, many not yet quite finished. The works at Centreville are formidable; more so than Manassas. Except the turnpike, the roads are horrible. The country entirely stripped of forage and provisions. Having fully consulted with General McDowell, I propose occupying Manassas by a portion of Banks' command, and then at once throwing all the forces I can concentrate upon the line agreed upon last week. The Monitor justifies this course. I telegraphed this morning to have the transports brought to Washington, to start from there. I presume you will approve this course. Circumstances may keep me out here some little time longer.

GEO. B. McCLELLAN,
Major-General.

FAIRFAX COURT-HOUSE, *March* 12, 1862—8.30 a. m.

Hon. E. M. STANTON, *Secretary of War:*

Sumner's division occupies Union Mills and Manassas to-day. I could not occupy it from Centreville, as roads thence to Manassas are impassable for artillery and wagons. General Sumner will cover repairs of railway, and obtain his supplies by that. The troops are now well pleased and doing well. The great difficulty is about forage; there is absolutely none in the country. Richmond Whig of 6th contains a reprint from Charleston Mercury violently attacking Jeff. Davis.

GEO. B. McCLELLAN.

FAIRFAX COURT-HOUSE, *March* 12, 1862.

Hon. JOHN TUCKER:

Please be ready to see that the vessels are properly arranged as they arrive and arrangements made for the rapid embarkation of troops and artillery at Alexandria, Georgetown, Fort Corcoran, Washington, &c. Will communicate in detail in very few hours.

GEO. B. McCLELLAN,
Major-General.

SEMINARY, *March* 12, 1862—8 p. m.

Hon. E. M. STANTON, *Secretary of War:*

I have been waiting some time expecting to be able to inform you that Porter's division was under way. When I left town this afternoon his artillery was on board and the infantry rapidly embarking. Everything going on in good order and expeditiously. Still I find capacity of many transports overrated.

GEO. B. McCLELLAN,
Major-General, U. S. Army.

FAIRFAX COURT-HOUSE, *March* 12, 1862.

Hon. E. M. STANTON, *Secretary of War:*

I have sent for commanders of army corps designated by the President to consult with them as to immediate movements. They should be here about 7 p. m. Will at once inform you of decision arrived at and ask your approval. Troops in fine spirits.

GEO. B. McCLELLAN,
Major-General, U. S. Army.

MARCH 12, 1862.

Maj. Gen. N. P. BANKS, *Charlestown, Va.:*

Dispatch received. As soon as possible occupy Bunker Hill and open your communication with it. I congratulate you on the success which has attended our movements.

GEO. B. McCLELLAN,
Major-General, Commanding.

BUDD'S FERRY, *March* 12, 1862.

Brigadier-General MARCY:

The cars were running between Aquia and Fredericksburg all last night, hence the bridge must have been standing at that time. I have no doubt it is still standing, as the rebel sick have been on the road between Dumfries and Aquia to-day, and could not have reached the depot before night. My spies are in that vicinity to-night. Shall know positively on their return. Some contrabands now in my camp passed fifteen or sixteen loads of sick on the road to-day. Another contraband is in from Centreville, who tells me that the enemy in and around Manassas retreated to Gordonsville. This was talked of all over the rebel camp. The portion of the army immediately on the Potomac left to take post at Fredericksburg. This I learn from some contrabands and white people—from the former every hour in the day. Of these, Whiting's, Archer's, and Rodes' brigades number about 12,000; the garrison in Fredericksburg about 3,000, and the force of Aquia and Potomac Creeks about 2,000, which will give the force in or near Fredericksburg 17,000. If they have been re-enforced from the Manassas army, it is that much greater. I have two companies in Dumfries to-night for the purpose of collecting information. It is reported to me that Hampton's Legion, stationed at Occoquan, fell back on Manassas.

JOSEPH HOOKER,
Brigadier-General.

BUDD'S FERRY, March 12, 1862.

Brig. Gen. R. B. MARCY:

Have received your dispatch of to-day. Shall proceed to execute to the best of my ability. From my most reliable information I can learn of but two companies of cavalry nearer me than the center of Stafford County. The report among the citizens of Prince William County is that the rebels have retired, to make the Rappahannock their line of defense. Too much faith should not be put in this. The pickets remain at Aquia Creek. The cars were running all night from that depot.

JOSEPH HOOKER,
Brigadier-General.

HEADQUARTERS DEPARTMENT OF WESTERN VIRGINIA,
Wheeling, March 12, 1862.

Brig. Gen. L. THOMAS,
  Adjutant-General U. S. Army, Washington, D. C.:

GENERAL: The General-in-Chief directed me to examine into the advantages of the Big Sandy route from the Ohio River to the Southwestern and Tennessee Railroad. He also directs me to cause the troops and material thrown into this department by General Orders, No. —, headquarters of the Army, to be thoroughly inspected, and to report their condition, and also what troops I wanted ; and, if so, what, if any more, cavalry. These considerations involving that of the operations advisable to be undertaken within the department, I have thought it better to present the whole matter in a report, which I have the honor herewith to inclose.

Very respectfully, your obedient servant,

W. S. ROSECRANS,
Brigadier-General, U. S. Army.

[Inclosure.]

HEADQUARTERS DEPARTMENT OF WESTERN VIRGINIA,
Wheeling, March 12, 1862.

Brig. Gen. L. THOMAS,
  Adjutant-General U. S. Army, Washington, D. C.:

GENERAL: Since the valley of Virginia, except the valleys of Great and Little Cacapon and of the Shenandoah, has been added to the limits of this department, I beg leave to submit for the consideration of the Secretary of War a project of operations deemed feasible within the limits of this department:

1. The exclusion of Rockbridge and Augusta Counties, containing Lexington and Staunton, leaves nothing to be done on our eastern limits but to expel the slight rebel forces of, say, 3,500 men, from the valley, to occupy the passes on main roads, hold the important points with forces sufficient to guard them, and tranquilize the country. This should be done by a force moving from Cumberland, New Creek, &c., up the valley of the South Branch of the Potomac, via Franklin and Dunwiddie's Gap, to capture if possible the rebel forces at Fort Alleghany, on the Beverly and Staunton turnpike. The main force at Huttonsville should co-operate with this, leaving a sufficient guard against a flank movement by General Heth, who commands at Lewisburg and Huntersville.

The force required for this operation from Cumberland should be four regiments of infantry, one of cavalry, and a good battery of artillery, of which three regiments of infantry and the one of cavalry are still required. The conduct of this column should be such, if possible, as to cut off the retreat of the rebel troops on Staunton, and when the Beverly road is in our hands the troops on Cheat Pass should unite with this column, seize the railroad at Millborough, and act as occasion may require towards the rebel forces in the direction of Staunton and Lexington, while we in sufficient force seize Warm Springs and Jackson River Depot, cutting off the retreat eastward of any rebel troops that may be in Greenbrier.

The general commanding should be charged with the restoration of law, order, and confidence in the Government of the United States, and should the rebels hold their ground east of the Blue Ridge, to guard the great passes from East to West Virginia against unexpected projects or reverses of our arms.

Second objective, by a simultaneous movement, begun with the least practicable delay, should be from Gauley Bridge to seize Lewisburg, White Sulphur, and to strike the Southwestern Virginia and Tennessee Railroad at some point between Bonsack's and Salem, the nearer Bonsack's the better. This column should consist of a force sufficient to expel Heth, hold Greenbrier, protect the depots there, and hold the railroad with 2,000 men, a field battery, and a couple of squadrons of cavalry. They should establish and garrison depots at Lewisburg and Union.

A third objective would be holding Fayette, to establish a depot at Raleigh, and from thence seize the railroad at Wytheville or Newbern, hold it in force against the rebels, and pacify the country there immediately.

Fourth object. The force now on Big Sandy can be supplied with provisions by small steamboat navigation in time of high water to Pikeville, whence it is 88 miles over bad roads to Baker's Station, on the Southwestern Virginia and Tennessee Railroad. This column should move by the Louisa Fork to Buchanan and Jeffersonville, seize the Northwest Virginia Branch Bank there, and thence take possession of the railroad at the Salt Works. Should the rebels be at Pound Gap a demonstration of a movement should be made and watched to keep the attention of them, while the main column, pursuing the route indicated, would seize the railroad and cut off the retreat of these rebel forces.

These forces once in the valley, Wytheville, Abingdon, Newbern, &c., all succumb. Troops purchase what they need for subsistence.

The estimated force requisite for all these purposes, based on the assumption that rebel capacity for local mischief in these regions should be about what it has been during the last two months, in addition to what we now have, would be:

For the Cumberland column—Three regiments of infantry, one regiment of cavalry, and one battery of artillery.

For Cheat Pass—One regiment of infantry.

For Kanawha—One regiment of infantry and one battery of artillery.

For Big Sandy—One regiment of infantry.

Total—Six regiments of infantry, one regiment of cavalry, and two field batteries, the most important of which are the three regiments of infantry and one of cavalry at Cumberland. They should be sent there without delay. Should they be ordered from an adjoining State, time could be gained by sending forward all troops on the railroad except those strictly requisite to guard the railroad line and the depots. Should the rebel forces east of the Blue Ridge fall back towards Lynchburg, retaining their organization and force, as now seems possible, I would advise strengthening the Lewisburg column so as to make an effective force of from 12,000 to 15,000 men, with orders to seize the Southwestern Virginia and Tennessee Railroad, and make a strong demonstration on Lynchburg, seizing it if opportunity offers. On this supposition an additional force of 6,000 or 8,000 men should be thrown into the great valley, to occupy Augusta and Rockbridge and watch the passes through the Blue Ridge there and southward.

Very respectfully, your obedient servant,

W. S. ROSECRANS,
Brigadier-General, U. S. Army.

HEADQUARTERS,
Baltimore, March 12, 1862.

Hon. E. M. STANTON, *Secretary of War:*

SIR: I would suggest that the police force of this city be transferred at once to the police commissioners recently appointed by the Legislature of this State, with the exception of the provost-marshal and some 10 policemen, without waiting for the appropriation asked for, and referred to in your letter of the 10th instant. The city authorities can then provide for the payment of the remaining 440 officers and men, and the United States be relieved from all responsibility in regard to them.

I am, very respectfully, your obedient servant,

JOHN A. DIX,
Major-General.

CHARLESTOWN, *March* 13, 1862.

Brig. Gen. R. B. MARCY, *Chief of Staff:*

General Hamilton occupied Winchester this morning at 7 o'clock. The rebel force left the town at 5 o'clock yesterday. The cavalry of the enemy left but an hour in advance of our forces. The railway and telegraph will be put in immediate operation between Harper's Ferry and Winchester.

N. P. BANKS,
Major-General, Commanding.

GENERAL ORDERS,)   HDQRS. GENERAL BANKS' DIVISION,
No. 26.   )   *Winchester, Va., March* 13, 1862.

The troops of the command now in the vicinity of Winchester, Va., will not be allowed to leave their respective camps without passes approved by commanders of regiments, detachments, or batteries. The provost-marshal is ordered to arrest all soldiers absent from their commands without such written permission.

The troops are cautioned against any injury to private or public property or any interference with the rights of citizens. Every abuse of this character, by whomsoever committed, will be rigidly investigated and punished with severity. The commanding general learns with sincere regret that officers in some cases, from mistaken views, either tolerate or encourage depredations upon property. This is deeply regretted. He calls upon them to reflect upon the destructive influences which attend such practices, and to remember the declaration of the great master of the art of war, that pillage is the most certain method of disorganizing and destroying an army.

All well-disposed persons are invited to pursue their ordinary vocations. Those who enter the town for the purpose of trade or to supply its markets at reasonable prices will be assured of all proper protection by the provost-marshal. It is the object of the military authorities to re-establish the privileges hitherto enjoyed by all classes of the American people, and such intercourse as may be necessary for this purpose between the different towns in the neighborhood will be permitted, under such general regulations as may be published by the provost-marshal, who is directed to facilitate, within proper limits, all branches of trade.

No arrest of persons or seizure of property will be made without orders from headquarters or from the provost-marshal. Every arrest will be forthwith reported to the provost-marshal, and all property taken will be turned over to the officer designated to superintend the collection of supplies for the use of the army. Every article of property taken for this purpose will be receipted for by the officer taking it, and compensation will be hereafter made for the same by the Government. Any person who shall directly or indirectly furnish intoxicating liquors to the troops may expect punishment, without mercy; the liquors and all other goods found with them will be forfeited, and the persons offending subject not only to imprisonment, but will be punished with unrelenting rigor to the last limit of military law. The authorities of the town and its citizens, as well as the officers and soldiers of the command, are earnestly requested by the commanding general to aid in enforcing this order.

By command of Maj. Gen. N. P. Banks:

R. MORRIS COPELAND,
Assistant Adjutant-General.

MARCH 13, 1862—11.15 a. m.

Major-General McCLELLAN:

You need apprehend no trouble on the question of rank with General Wool. Many circumstances require that your movement, whatever it may be, should be prompt. General Meigs reports that transports will be ready as fast as you can use them. I desire you to keep me advised of your progress and movements.

EDWIN M. STANTON,
Secretary of War.

WASHINGTON, *March* 13, 1862.

General BANKS:

The General Commanding directs that General Sedgwick's division move without delay to Harper's Ferry and remain in readiness to leave that place at short notice. He also directs that you at once send one of your divisions to Centreville, by the Little River pike, through Snicker's Gap, Aldie, and Pleasant Valley, taking the road from Saunders' tollgate to Centreville. You will find no supplies on the road, and it will be necessary to transport all you require to last the division to Centreville.

Please inform as soon as possible when General Sedgwick's division will be at Harper's Ferry and when the division will leave for Centreville. General Sedgwick's division to be detached from your command, and will probably be sent by rail to Annapolis.

R. B. MARCY,
Chief of Staff.

FAIRFAX COURT-HOUSE,
March 13, 1862. (Received 2.30 p. m.)

General MARCY:

Prepare to embark Hunt's reserve artillery, together with all the reserve ammunition belonging to it. When will the transportation be ready?

GEO. B. McCLELLAN,
Major-General.

FAIRFAX COURT-HOUSE,
March 13, 1862. (Received 2.40 p. m.)

General MARCY:

Direct the barges at Perryville and Annapolis containing wagons to be ready to move at one hour's notice. Have the teams loaded at same places at once.

GEO. B. McCLELLAN,
Major-General.

FAIRFAX COURT-HOUSE,
March 13, 1862. (Received 3 p. m.)

General S. WILLIAMS, *Assistant Adjutant-General:*

Relieve General Hamilton at once from duty with General Banks, and order him to assume command of General Heintzelman's division. Relieve Kearny from Franklin's division, and order him to take command of Sumner's division; Couch to take command of Keyes' division, and King of McDowell's; to be done as soon as possible.

GEO. B. McCLELLAN,
Major-General, Commanding.

FAIRFAX COURT-HOUSE, *March* 13, 1862.

General R. B. MARCY:

The following is a copy of message to General S. P. Heintzelman, Fort Lyon:

General McClellan directs that you hold General Hamilton's division in readiness to embark to-morrow morning at Alexandria.   General Hamilton has been ordered to report to you with as little delay as possible.

A. V. COLBURN,
Assistant Adjutant-General.

FAIRFAX COURT-HOUSE,
March 13, 1862.   (Received 3.20 p. m.)

Hon. E. M STANTON, *Secretary of War :*

I have sent out a strong cavalry force under General Stoneman, to go as far as the Rappahannock. I have moved a regiment of infantry out to guard the forage train of the cavalry to-night, holding a brigade also at Manassas Station. I have ordered one of Banks' divisions to move down here at once. Your dispatch received, and measures will be taken accordingly.

GEO. B. McCLELLAN,
Major-General.

FORT MONROE, VA., *March* 13, 1862—3.05 p. m.

Hon. E. M. STANTON, *Secretary of War :*

In reply to Major-General McClellan's desire to know what I wanted for defense of my position, I replied, for immediate defense, as follows, viz: Two thousand regular infantry and 8,000 volunteer infantry; five batteries of light artillery (regulars, if possible); 1,100 horses for the five batteries, to complete the batteries I have here and to mount Dodge's cavalry. I have received only three regiments: First Michigan, Fifth Maryland, and Fifty-eighth Pennsylvania. I require several companies of regular artillery in Fort Monroe. I have only about 110 regulars for Fort Monroe and Newport News. Fort Monroe is too important a position to be neglected. I have never failed to so represent, and ask for troops and other means of defense.

JOHN E. WOOL,
Major-General.

WINCHESTER, VA., *March* 13, 1862—3.30 p. m.

Brigadier-General WILLIAMS, *Assistant Adjutant-General :*

I beg leave to report that I was able to bring 7,000 men here yesterday, and have upwards of 4,000 more *en route* for this point. The command is an efficient one, and able to do efficient service. I stand much in need of an able assistant quartermaster for the division. If there be any efficient man off duty, I hope he may be assigned to me. If not efficient and a man of experience, I don't want him. I reported as ordered to Major-General Banks. Rumors among citizens have it that the rebels mean to concentrate all their disposable strength and give us one grand battle between here and Richmond.

JAS. SHIELDS,
Brigadier-General.

FAIRFAX COURT-HOUSE, *March* 13, 1862—4.30 p. m.

General MARCY :

Organize General Casey's division for the field at once.

GEO. B. McCLELLAN,
Major-General.

WAR DEPARTMENT,
Washington City, D. C., March 13, 1862—5.20 p. m.

Major-General MCCLELLAN:

General McDowell has arrived here and presented a paper purporting to be the opinion of the generals commanding army corps, but it contains nothing indicating that it is your plan.* The Department has nothing to show what is your plan of operations. Will you be pleased to state specifically what plan of operations you propose to execute under the present circumstances? Please state at what time this dispatch is received by you and at what hour your answer is transmitted. This rule had better be observed in all our telegraphic communications. There is nothing new from Fortress Monroe.

In respect to General Wool's question of rank, I will remark that he will be relieved from command whenever you desire to assume it at that place, and if you determine to make Fortress Monroe your base of operations, you shall have the control over the forces under General Burnside's command. All the forces and means of the Government will be at your disposal. This dispatch is transmitted at 5.20 p. m.

EDWIN M. STANTON,
Secretary of War.

———

WINCHESTER, *March* 13, 1862—5.45 p. m.

General R. B. MARCY:

Orders have been issued to General Sedgwick to move his division to Harper's Ferry in accordance with instructions; distance, 20 miles. Will be there to-morrow night. Will report later when division can leave for Centreville. All quiet here.

N. P. BANKS,
Major-General.

———

WINCHESTER, VA., *March* 13, 1862—5.45 p. m.

Brig. Gen. JOHN SEDGWICK, *Berryville:*

GENERAL: It is ordered by the Major-General Commanding the Army that you move your division " without delay to Harper's Ferry, and remain in readiness to leave that place at short notice."

You will please execute this order with all dispatch. In answer to inquiry, I have reported that you would probably be at Harper's Ferry Saturday afternoon, 15th instant.

General Dana intended when I left Charlestown to remain there until to-morrow (Friday) morning, and will then move towards you unless otherwise ordered.

I am, general, with much respect, your obedient servant,

N. P. BANKS,
Major-General, Commanding, &c.

———

GENERAL ORDERS, }   HEADQUARTERS, SEDGWICK'S DIVISION,
    No. 30.   }   *Berryville, Va., March* 13, 1862.

The division will move toward Harper's Ferry to-morrow morning.

   *   *   *   *   *   *   *

By order of Brigadier-General Sedgwick, commanding division:

WM. D. SEDGWICK,
Assistant Adjutant-General.

———

* See McClellan's report, pp. 55, 56.

ADJUTANT-GENERAL'S OFFICE,
Washington, March 13, 1862.

Hon. GIDEON WELLES, *Secretary of the Navy:*

SIR: I am directed by the Secretary of War to say that he places at your disposal any transports or coal vessels at Fort Monroe for the purpose of closing the channel of the Elizabeth River to prevent the Merrimac again coming out.

I have the honor, &c.,

L. THOMAS,
Adjutant-General.

FAIRFAX COURT-HOUSE,
March 13, 1862. (Received 8.30 p. m.)

Adjutant-General THOMAS:

In doubtful uncertainty as to General Burnside's position and how far he may now be engaged in his final operation, it is difficult to give him very precise orders at present. I think it would be well that he should not engage himself further inland than at New Berne and should at once reduce Beaufort, leaving there a sufficient garrison in Fort Macon. He should at once return to Roanoke Island, ready to co-operate with all his available force, either by way of Winton or by way of Fort Monroe, as circumstances may render necessary. I advise this on the supposition that Captain Fox is correct in his opinion that Burnside will have New Berne this week. If he has become fairly engaged in the movement, I would not stop him.

GEO. B. McCLELLAN,
Major-General.

FAIRFAX COURT-HOUSE,
March 13, 1862. (Received 9.30 p. m.)

Hon. E. M. STANTON, *Secretary of War:*

Your dispatch of 7.40 just received and will be at once carried into execution. I returned only a short time since from reviewing Smith's division, and found it in admirable condition and spirits.

Contrabands just in report enemy on Rappahannock and Gordonsville in force.

GEO. B. McCLELLAN,
Major-General.

HEADQUARTERS ARMY OF THE POTOMAC,
Fairfax Court-House, March 13, 1862. (Received 9.40 p. m.)

Hon. E. M. STANTON, *Secretary of War:*

I would respectfully suggest that the Secretary of the Navy be requested to order to Fort Monroe whatever force Du Pont can now spare, as well as any available force that Goldsborough can send up, as soon as his present operations are completed.

GEO. B. McCLELLAN,
Major-General.

FAIRFAX COURT-HOUSE,
March 13, 1862, 10.50 p. m.   (Received 11.15 p. m.)
JOHN TUCKER, Esq., *Assistant Secretary of War:*

Has the additional rolling stock for the Orange and Alexandria Railroad and the Loudoun and Hampshire Railroad arrived? If so, how much of it? What transports are certainly on hand at Alexandria and Washington for troops, horses, and guns, and for how many of each kind? I cannot make my arrangements for details of movements until I know exactly what is on hand. It is absolutely necessary that I should be kept constantly informed. I wish to move, so that the men, &c., can be moved direct on board ship.

GEO. B. McCLELLAN,
Major-General.

FAIRFAX COURT-HOUSE, *March* 13, 1862—11 p. m.
Hon. JOHN TUCKER, *Assistant Secretary of War:*

I have made it Colonel Astor's duty to remain and keep recorded all information in regard to transports, so that I may always know the exact condition of the transports and their locality. Will you please send him by express as early to-morrow as practicable a complete list of the transports hired, the capacity of each for the particular purpose for which hired; name of captain; amount of stores on board, including water; whether it has cooking arrangements, &c.; in short, all the information you possess in regard to them, including draught of water? In addition, please keep him constantly informed by telegraph of arrival of vessels.

GEO. B. McCLELLAN,
Major-General.

NAVY DEPARTMENT, *March* 13, 1862.
Hon. E. M. STANTON, *Secretary of War:*

SIR: I have the honor to suggest that this Department can easily obstruct the channel to Norfolk so as to prevent the exit of the Merrimac, provided the Army will carry the Sewell's Point batteries, in which duty the Navy will give great assistance.

Very respectfully,

GIDEON WELLES.

WAR DEPARTMENT, *Washington, March* 13, 1862.
Maj. Gen. GEORGE B. McCLELLAN:

General Patrick was nominated upon your request several days ago. I took the nomination myself to the President, and saw it signed by him, and will go to the Senate to-morrow to urge the confirmation. Any others you may designate will receive the like attention. Nothing you can ask of me or this Department will be spared to aid you in every particular.

EDWIN M. STANTON,
Secretary of War.

NAVY DEPARTMENT, *March* 13, 1862.

Maj. Gen. GEORGE B. MCCLELLAN, *Fairfax Court-House:*

The Monitor is more than a match for the Merrimac, but she might be disabled in the next encounter. I cannot advise so great dependence upon her. Burnside and Goldsborough are very strong for the Chowan River route to Norfolk, and I brought up maps, explanations, &c., to show you. It turns everything, and is only 27 miles to Norfolk by two good roads. Burnside will have New Berne this week. The Monitor may, and I think will, destroy the Merrimac in the next fight, but this is hope, not certainty. The Merrimac must dock for repairs.

G. V. FOX.

FORT MONROE VA., *March* 13, 1862.

Hon. E. M. STANTON, *Secretary of War:*

Major-General McClellan desires by telegraph to know if the channel between Sewell's Point and Craney Island could be blockaded. I reply that it would be impracticable without first taking the battery of thirty guns on Sewell's Point and then sink twenty boats loaded with stone, exposed, however, to a fire of thirty guns on Craney Island. Flag-Officer Goldsborough agrees with me in this opinion. To take the batteries it would require the Monitor. Neither of us think it would do to use the Monitor for that service, lest she should become crippled. She is our only hope against the Merrimac.

JOHN E. WOOL,
Major-General.

MARCH 13, 1862.

Brig. Gen. R. B. MARCY:

General Sickles informs me this morning that the cars were running from Aquia last night. Captain Magaw states that he is informed that the rebels are fortifying Fredericksburg, and that they are evacuating Aquia. The Freeborn was off Aquia yesterday within easy range, and no shots fired.

JOSEPH HOOKER,
Brigadier-General, Commanding Division.

BUDD'S FERRY, *March* 13, 1862.

Brigadier-General MARCY:

Every appearance indicates that the rebels will not retire immediately from Aquia. The bridge across the Potomac is not essential in case a movement should be made on Fredericksburg. Without running stock the railroad would be of no use. In that event our boat landing will be near Fouke's. Of course the rebels will destroy bridges and everything else as they advance.

JOSEPH HOOKER,
Brigadier-General.

BUDD's FERRY, *March* 13, 1862.

Brigadier-General MARCY:

The bridges at Aquia Creek are still standing and guarded. Two Northern men have arrived at Liverpool Point from Fredericksburg yesterday. They represent large numbers of troops in the vicinity of Fredericksburg. They have been using the batteries at Aquia to-day. We can take possession of the bridges, if you desire, between this and morning, with the aid of the Stepping Stones. My negro spies are not in, but this information is reliable.

JOSEPH HOOKER,
Brigadier-General.

WASHINGTON CITY, D. C., *March* 14, 1862—8.45 a. m.

Maj. Gen. JOHN E. WOOL, *Commanding at Fortress Monroe:*

The following dispatch from General McClellan has been received by this Department:

FAIRFAX COURT-HOUSE, *March* 13—11.20 p. m.

Hon. E. M. STANTON, *Secretary of War:*

I would be glad to have instructions given to General Wool that the troops and stores now being sent down to Fort Monroe are of my command and not to be appropriated by him.

GEO. B. McCLELLAN,
Major-General.

The request of General McClellan is approved, and you are instructed to act in accordance with it, and to acknowledge the receipt of this communication.

EDWIN M. STANTON,
Secretary of War.

FAIRFAX COURT-HOUSE, *March* 14, 1862.
(Received 11.45 a. m.)

Hon. E. M. STANTON, *Secretary of War:*

Have placed General Richardson in command of General Sumner's division instead of Kearny, who prefers remaining with his old brigade. Please inform the President.

GEO. B. McCLELLAN,
Major-General.

FAIRFAX COURT-HOUSE, *March* 14, 1862—1.30 p. m.

General R. B. MARCY:

Direct General Banks to leave General Shields' command at Winchester for the present, including all cavalry of the divisions of Banks and Shields—General Banks to come in person here as soon as possible, preceding his old division.

GEO. B. McCLELLAN,
Major-General, Commanding.

FAIRFAX COURT-HOUSE, *March* 14, 1862.
(Received 3 p. m.)

Hon. E. M. STANTON, *Secretary of War:*

For especial reasons, I have changed the organization of the army corps as follows : First Corps, McDowell; divisions, Franklin, McCall, and King. Second Corps, Sumner; divisions, Richardson, Blenker, Sedgwick. Third Corps, Heintzelman; divisions, Hooker, Hamilton, Smith. Fourth Corps, Keyes; divisions, Porter, Couch, Casey. Fifth Corps, Banks; divisions, Williams and Shields.

GEO. B. McCLELLAN,
Major-General.

HEADQUARTERS ARMY OF THE POTOMAC,
March 14, 1862—3 p. m.   (Received 3.30 p. m.)

Hon. E. M. STANTON, *Secretary of War:*

As fast as transportation is ready we shall move to the new line of operations. It is important that the available force at Fort Monroe should be under the control of the commander of the army acting there, and I desire to form another division, under Mansfield, from the troops now in the vicinity of Fort Monroe, and to annex that division to the First Army Corps as soon as McDowell is confirmed as major-general. First Corps leads the movement.

GEO. B. McCLELLAN,
Major-General.

No. 5.]   FAIRFAX COURT-HOUSE,
March 14, 1862.   (Received 4.10 p. m.)

Hon. E. M. STANTON, *Secretary of War:*

I would advise that no change be made now in the organization of divisions. It would be very pernicious at such a moment as this. The division is the real unit of force, and should be intact. The third word is omitted in your dispatch, and I do not know whether you mean Kearny or Richardson; but it makes no difference, as my opinion is based on general principles. I am hard at work.

GEO. B. McCLELLAN,
Major-General.

FAIRFAX COURT-HOUSE,
March 14, 1862—5.30 p. m.   (Received 6 p. m.)

Hon. E. M. STANTON, *Secretary of War:*

*　　*　　*　　*　　*　　*　　*

All goes well. Franklin, McCall, Keyes, and McDowell are *en route;* also the regulars. I will not disappoint you. Porter and Smith start in the morning.

GEO. B. McCLELLAN,
Major-General.

BUDD'S FERRY, *March* 14, 1862—9 a. m.

General S. WILLIAMS:

All of the rebel batteries extending from Cockpit Point to Aquia Creek are now utterly demolished. All the guns that were worth preserving have been tumbled over the bluff banks on which they stood to where they can be picked up by the vessels of the flotilla. Yesterday my men succeeded in moving the Homan's English rifled gun, 95-pounder, to the edge of the river, and it is now, I presume, at the navy-yard. The rebels left everything behind. Some of my regiments have been constantly at work in removing stores of all kinds, and to-day I hope the Sixth New Jersey Volunteers will complete that work. A defeat could not have been more disastrous to the rebels. They left in the utmost consternation. The defensive works of the rebels in and around the batteries were stupendous. I am informed that the rebels still hold to the positions on Aquia Creek.

JOSEPH HOOKER,
Brigadier-General.

———

BUDD'S FERRY, *March* 14, 1862.

Brig. Gen. S. WILLIAMS:

One of my negro spies reports that he went to the Rappahannock; saw large bodies of troops yesterday below Fredericksburg, on the Caroline side of the river. Troops, he says, are concentrating there in good numbers. Intrenchments are being thrown up on the race-course—a place, it is said, artillery commands the approach for a great distance; vicinity a level plain. The bridges about Fredericksburg are standing. The rebels expect a great battle there. The prominent citizens there have their goods packed, ready for a move. This can be relied on.

JOSEPH HOOKER,
Brigadier-General.

———

HEADQUARTERS HOOKER'S DIVISION,
Camp Baker, Lower Potomac, Maryland, March 14, 1862.

Lieut. Col. JOHN P. VAN LEER,
Commanding Sixth Regiment New Jersey Volunteers :

You will land five companies of your command on the north side of the Quantico, and five companies on the south side of the Chopawamsic, and direct both columns to march on Dumfries. You will direct careful search to be made on both for all scows and boats, and send down the river as many as practicable that may be of service. Throughout all your march you will capture and bring off as many of the rebel stores as may be of service to us. Should you meet with resistance, capture and destroy them ; also destroy all rebel stores that can be of no service to us. Let the march be made with great caution. Allow no straggling, and keep your advanced guard and flankers well thrown out. Members of the signal corps will accompany you to communicate any important information you may have to send me. Return to-night.

Very respectfully, &c.,

JOS. DICKINSON,
Assistant Adjutant-General.

———

WAR DEPARTMENT,
Washington, D. C., March 14, 1862.

Maj. Gen. GEORGE B. MCCLELLAN, *Fairfax Court-House:*

About twenty-five steamers to carry troops are here. Others must arrive rapidly. I will directly let you know the carrying capacity of those that are here. At Perryville there are barges for all the wagons and schooners for about one-third of the horses there, and a large fleet was just below Perryville last night. The change from Annapolis to Washington will cause some delay, particularly in the transportation of horses. I send by express to Colonel Astor the detailed information you require. I will telegraph again as soon as I get reports of arrival this morning.

JOHN TUCKER,
Assistant Secretary of War.

HEADQUARTERS MOUNTAIN DEPARTMENT,
Wheeling, March 14, 1862.

Major-General McCLELLAN:

Colonel at Gauley Bridge learns large force for Lewisburg arrived at Jackson River Depot last week, and was turned back by orders. Send it as an item. My report went to Adjutant-General Thomas 12th. Where am I to go?

W. S. ROSECRANS,
Brigadier-General.

Organization of brigades in Banks' division, Winchester, Va., March 14, 1862.*

FIRST BRIGADE.	SECOND BRIGADE.
Brig. Gen. A. S. Williams, commanding.	*Brig. Gen. J. J. Abercrombie, commanding.*
Fifth Connecticut Infantry.	Twelfth Indiana Infantry.
First Maryland Infantry.	Sixteenth Indiana Infantry.
Twenty-eighth New York Infantry.	Twelfth Massachusetts Infantry.
Twenty-eighth Pennsylvania Infantry.	Thirteenth Massachusetts Infantry.
Forty-sixth Pennsylvania Infantry.	Eighty-third New York Infantry.

THIRD BRIGADE.

Col. George H. Gordon, commanding.

Twenty-Seventh Indiana Infantry.	Twenty-Ninth Pennsylvania Infantry.
Second Massachusetts Infantry.	Third Wisconsin Infantry.

WASHINGTON, *March* 15, 1862.

Maj. Gen. GEORGE B. McCLELLAN, *Seminary:*

In reply to your dispatch to this Department of yesterday [13th], which was transmitted to the Secretary of the Navy, he replies as follows:

NAVY DEPARTMENT, *March* 14, 1862.

Hon. E. M. STANTON, *Secretary of War:*

SIR: Yours inclosing the dispatch of Major-General McClellan, suggesting that the Secretary of the Navy be requested "to order to Fort Monroe whatever force Du Pont can now spare, as well as any available force that Goldsborough can send up, as soon as his present operations are completed," has been received. If a movement is to be

---

*Announced in General Orders, No. 27, of that date, from division headquarters.

made upon Norfolk—always a favorite measure of this Department—instant measures will be taken to advise and strengthen Flag-Officer Goldsborough, but unless such be the case, I should be extremely reluctant to take any measure that would even temporarily weaken the efficacy of the blockade, especially at the points under the command of Flag-Officer Du Pont. The importance of capturing Norfolk is, I know, deemed almost indispensable by Flag-Officer Goldsborough, who will be happy to co-operate in a movement in that direction, and will, I need not assure you, have the active and earnest efforts of this Department to aid him with all the force that can be placed at his disposal.

I am, respectfully, your obedient servant,

GIDEON WELLES.

The foregoing letter was received late last night.

EDWIN M. STANTON,
Secretary of War.

WASHINGTON CITY, D. C., *March* 15, 1862.

Maj. Gen. GEORGE B. McCLELLAN, *General, Commanding:*

GENERAL: Application has been made to this Department by representatives from the State of Virginia that the force under General Lockwood, now in Eastern Virginia, is no longer needed there, and it would gratify the inhabitants to have all but a small portion removed.

I beg to direct your attention to the subject, and that you will make such order as you deem proper.

Yours, truly,

EDWIN M. STANTON,
Secretary of War.

HEADQUARTERS ARMY OF THE POTOMAC,
Washington, March 15, 1862.

Maj. Gen. I. McDOWELL, *Commanding First Army Corps:*

GENERAL: The commanding general directs that your corps take with it on its transports six days' subsistence, of which at least three days must be cooked and in haversacks.

Each commissary must provide himself with scales, butchers' tools, and whatever else may be necessary for the efficient performance of his duties. Any property that cannot be taken will be left in charge of an agent, whose name, together with a statement of the property so left, will be reported by the Commissary-General of Subsistence.

I am, general, very respectfully, your obedient servant,

A. V. COLBURN,
Assistant Adjutant-General.

HEADQUARTERS ARMY OF THE POTOMAC,
Near Alexandria, March 15, 1862.

Hon. E. M. STANTON, *Secretary of War:*

I have the honor herewith to return the letter of Mr. Reverdy Johnson, having retained a copy.

I would beg to call your attention to the very indefinite nature of the letter. There were many Massachusetts regiments in and near Montgomery County until within a few days past; unless the locality is specified it would seem to be impossible to carry out your orders, for the guilty parties certainly will not volunteer information against themselves.

About ten days since I was informed that some men from a Massachusetts regiment, in Keyes' division, had committed outrages; I at once directed the matter to be laid before General Keyes, with orders to investigate it and bring the parties to punishment. I can form no idea whether this is the same case or not. If Mr. Johnson will give me some clew to pursue I will gladly have the whole thing examined. The charge is so indefinite that I really do not know how I am to proceed in the matter without more distinct information. May I ask you to request Mr. Johnson to give me the necessary data with the least possible delay, for I wish to punish promptly any outrages committed by troops under my command?

I am, very respectfully, your obedient servant,

GEO. B. McCLELLAN,
Major-General, Commanding.

GENERAL ORDERS, } WAR DEPARTMENT, ADJT. GEN.'S OFFICE,
No. 25.   }   *Washington, March 15, 1862.*

The Provost-Marshal-General of the Army of the Potomac and his subordinates will turn over to Brigadier-General Wadsworth, military governor of the District of Columbia, the buildings and premises occupied in the city of Washington and all the public property belonging thereto; and from and after it being so turned over the provost-marshal's office will be withdrawn from the city of Washington, and all the force employed in the military police of the city will be henceforth under command of Brigadier-General Wadsworth, as military governor of the District. General Wadsworth will establish his headquarters in the building heretofore used and occupied by the provost-marshal in the city of Washington.

The Provost-Marshal-General and his subordinates will also turn over to Brigadier-General Wadsworth, as military governor of the District of Columbia, all the military prisons and prisoners within the District of Columbia and all contrabands now in custody, and the same shall henceforth be under command of the military governor of the District of Columbia. General Wadsworth will forthwith assume command as military governor of the said District.

By order of the Secretary of War:

L. THOMAS,
Adjutant-General.

WASHINGTON NAVY-YARD, *March 16, 1862.*

Hon. E. M. STANTON, *Secretary of War:*

The following was received at 6.30:

POTOMAC FLOTILLA, *March 16.*

Captain DAHLGREN:

The information I forwarded regarding gunboats building on the Rappahannock was obtained from negroes living in that vicinity. They had not, however, seen any of the boats. What they stated was from hearsay. The Nicholas is a light side-wheel steamer, the boat seized by a Colonel Thomas, of Maryland. I have no description of the Virginia, but have judged her the same description of boat. I will strive and obtain further information on these points.

R. H. WYMAN.

J. A. DAHLGREN.

WASHINGTON NAVY-YARD, *March* 16, 1862—8.45 a. m.

Hon. E. M. STANTON, *Secretary of War:*

General Van Vliet has just left, having come to confer in regard to the matter under your consideration to-day. He thinks they will have no difficulty in regard to the pilotage, if I will let him have one or two good pilots to lead and the assistance of one or two vessels of the flotilla to watch the Rappahannock. The chief pilot of the yard, on being called in, stated that such of the vessels as he had spoken to had pilots, and he believed most of them had. He also said that the draught of the transports was generally 10 feet. I requested General Van Vliet to see and state his views to you on the subject. Captain Wyman will be up in the morning and will see you, if you choose.

J. A. DAHLGREN.

WASHINGTON NAVY-YARD, *March* 16, 1862—9 a. m.

Hon. E. M. STANTON, *Secretary of War:*

Captain Wyman has just arrived from below, and says that three vessels of his flotilla have already been ordered to convoy the transports to Hampton Roads, and as the quartermaster-general of the Potomac is satisfied with all the other arrangements, it would appear that all your purposes will be executed without my assistance. Captain Wyman also says in regard to the vessels supposed to be building at Fredericksburg, that they are not reported to be far advanced, and he has no information as to their being cased with iron. The reports are derived from negroes at different times. Captain Wyman further states that there is a young man in General Hooker's brigade who lately ran away from Fredericksburg, and may be able to give information on the subject.

JNO. A. DAHLGREN.

POOLESVILLE, *March* 16, 1862.

Brig. Gen. S. WILLIAMS:

Lieutenant-Colonel De Korponay reports that several small detachments of the enemy's cavalry, in all some 40 or 50, have been seen several times the past two days in the neighborhood, reconnoitering this position. This is confirmed by the pickets below Goose Creek, on this side, who report having seen about the same number last evening. Last night several rocket signals were made about 2 miles west of the town, and the pickets the same distance below Edwards Ferry, on this side, report that two were sent up opposite at a distance from the river. Colonel De Korponay has with him 280 men, including 6 of the First Michigan Cavalry, and one piece of artillery.

EDMUND C. CHARLES,
Colonel Forty-second New York Volunteers, Commanding.

WINCHESTER, *March* 16, 1862.

Maj. Gen. N. P. BANKS:

Your message received. Authentic information received to-day of evacuation of Strasburg yesterday by Jackson's forces taking the road to Staunton, with guns and stores. Railroad bridges over North and

South Branches of the Shenandoah burned Friday night. Turnpike bridges on Front Royal road over Shenandoah and North Branch also destroyed.

D. D. PERKINS,
Chief of Staff.

———

HEADQUARTERS HOOKER'S DIVISION,
Camp Baker, Lower Potomac, Maryland, March 16, 1862.
Brig. Gen. D. E. SICKLES, *Commanding Second Brigade:*

The enemy have a cavalry force of about 180 men stationed nearly opposite you and about 3 miles back from the Potomac. This is their headquarters, and from there are sent out pickets along the river and road in the direction of Dumfries. It is desirable to destroy or capture this force, and the brigadier-general commanding requests that you will have five companies detailed from your command, under an intelligent and discreet officer, to attack and destroy that picket to-night. Let the preparation and execution be made with the utmost secrecy. An excellent guide, a negro, whose house is in that vicinity, can conduct the command to the point without observation. He will be sent to report to you to-day. You will require a light-draught steamer, and I have none to send you. You will have to call on Lieutenant Magaw for a tug, and if that cannot be obtained, the expedition will be deferred. After conferring with that officer you may find it advisable to take over a scow and a barge to facilitate the landing, and should the party capture horses, it will be of great service in embarking them.

Instruct the officer charged with the execution of this to march with his command well in hand, his advance guard and flankers well thrown out, and under no circumstance permit an officer, non-commissioned officer, or private to quit the ranks without authority. They will move out and return with dispatch, bringing away or destroying all the stores of the rebels. Forbid by the most stringent orders the destruction of all private property.

Very respectfully, &c.,

JOS. DICKINSON,
Assistant Adjutant-General.

———

BUDD'S FERRY, *March* 16, 1862.
Maj. Gen. GEORGE B. McCLELLAN:

My latest advices from Aquia are of the 14th. To that time it was not known that the rebels had abandoned any of their batteries or withdrawn any of their supports, nor had any additions been made to the defenses or the force. There were three batteries, numbering seven pieces—three on the water and four on the high ground in the rear. Vessels of the flotilla are down in that vicinity now. I have already sent for later information. Will forward it when it comes in.

JOSEPH HOOKER,
Brigadier-General.

———

BUDD'S FERRY, *March* 16, 1862.
Major-General McCLELLAN:

Have just received the last reports from Aquia. The impression of officers belonging to the flotilla is that some heavy guns at Aquia have been removed. A light battery appeared a little to the south of them to-day. The infantry supports have not been strengthened there. This is all I can learn, and this I consider reliable.

JOSEPH HOOKER,
Brigadier-General.

HEADQUARTERS SUMNER'S ARMY CORPS,
Fairfax Court-House, March 16, 1862.

Colonel COLBURN:

COLONEL: I have the honor to forward the inclosed dispatch* just received from Brigadier-General French, commanding third brigade of Richardson's division. General French was left with his brigade and a battery at Manassas Junction, with orders not to retire until General Stoneman passed on his return.

In order to prevent the possibility of your being insulted by any demonstration which the enemy might make, I have deemed it proper to push forward to Bull Run the *élite* of the two brigades of Richardson's division in bivouac here, under the immediate command of General Richardson. The two brigades are accompanied by Clarke's battery and three squadrons of cavalry. The command is now on the march. Blenker's entire division is on hand ready to march, if it prove necessary. Subsequently, the inclosed dispatch from General Stoneman, addressed to you, arrived, and, under the peculiar circumstances of the case, I deemed it my imperative duty to make myself acquainted with its contents. I do not consider myself as called upon by the dispatch to make any change in the above-mentioned dispositions.

Very respectfully, your obedient servant,

E. V. SUMNER,
Brigadier-General, U. S. Army, Commanding Army Corps.

NOTE.—I do not believe that the enemy can threaten our troops at Bull Run, but I think it better to guard against possibilities.

HEADQUARTERS SUMNER'S ARMY CORPS,
Fairfax Court-House, March 16, 1862.

General R. B. MARCY, *Chief of Staff:*

Your dispatch has been received.* General French's brigade has already been ordered to return to Manassas, and the remainder of Richardson's division put *en route* to support it. Does the General Commanding deem it advisable that the remaining division at this point be advanced to the front of Blenker?

E. V. SUMNER,
Brigadier-General, U. S. Army, Commanding Army Corps.

HEADQUARTERS SUMNER'S ARMY CORPS,
Fairfax Court-House, Va., March 16, 1862.

General RICHARDSON:

The general commanding the corps directs that if from any information you may have received you deem it prudent to advance your com-

---
* Not found.

mand farther to the front than Bull Run as a support to General French, after he has returned to Manassas, you [may] use your own judgment in the matter. Supplies will be forwarded to you as rapidly as possible. Keep these headquarters advised of your movements and the reasons therefor.

Very respectfully, your obedient servant,

J. H. TAYLOR,
Chief of Staff and Adjutant-General.

HEADQUARTERS SUMNER'S ARMY CORPS,
Fairfax Court-House, March 16, 1862.

General RICHARDSON:

The general commanding the corps directs, in compliance with orders from headquarters Army of the Potomac, that French's brigade return to Manassas to await further orders, and he directs that you remain with the residue of your division as a support at Bull Run. Three days' rations will be forwarded to you to-morrow, and the general orders that you make such distributions of them as you may deem proper.

Very respectfully, your obedient servant,

J. H. TAYLOR,
Chief of Staff and Adjutant-General.

HEADQUARTERS ARMY OF THE POTOMAC,
Washington, D. C., March 17, 1862.

Maj. Gen. GEORGE B. McCLELLAN,
Commanding Army of the Potomac:

GENERAL: I have the honor to report the following information relative to the forces and defenses of the Army of the Potomac obtained to this date, which has been extracted from current statements made here by spies, contrabands, deserters, refugees, and prisoners of war, in the order of time as hereinafter stated, and which at the time of reception were made the subjects of special reports to you. I have also appended to this report of extracts from statements, and have made the same a part of this report, a varied summary of the forces and defenses of the rebel Army of the Potomac, showing by different combinations about the probable number of these forces and the locality and strength of their defenses:

By reference to the summary of this report it will be seen that 115,500 men is a medium estimate of the rebel Army of the Potomac, which are stated as being located as follows, viz: At Manassas, Centreville, Bull Run, Upper Occoquan, and vicinities, about 80,000 men; at Brooke's Station, Dumfries, Lower Occoquan, and vicinities, 18,000; at Leesburg and vicinity, 4,500; in the Shenandoah Valley, 13,000.

Of the above-mentioned forces information has been received up to date, as shown by summary in this report, of the following specific organizations, viz: At Manassas, Centreville, Bull Run, Upper Occoquan, and vicinities, sixty-one regiments and one battalion infantry, eight regiments, one battalion, and seven independent companies cavalry, thirty-four companies artillery. At Brooke's Station, Dumfries, Lower Occoquan, and vicinities, eighteen regiments and one battalion infantry, one regiment and six independent companies cavalry, and fifteen companies artillery; in the Shenandoah Valley, twelve regiments infantry, two brigades militia, one regiment cavalry, and seven companies artillery; and at Leesburg four regiments infantry, one regiment militia, five independent companies cavalry, and one company of artillery.

It is unnecessary for me to say that in the nature of the case, guarded as the rebels have ever been against the encroachment of spies, and vigilant as they have always been to prevent information of their designs, movements, or of their forces, going beyond their lines, it has been impossible, even by the use of every resource at our command, to ascertain with certainty the specific number and character of their forces. It may, therefore, safely be assumed that in so large an army as our information shows them to possess very much of its composition and very many of its forces have not been specifically ascertained, which, added to those already known, would largely increase their numbers and considerably swell its proportions.

The summary of the general estimate shows the forces of the rebel Army of the Potomac to be 150,000, as claimed by its officers and as sanctioned by the public belief, over 80,000 of which were stationed up to the time of evacuation at Manassas, Centreville, and vicinity, the remainder being within easy supporting distance. This fact is strongly supported by the statement of several supposed reliable persons, to the effect that 80,000 daily rations were issued to the forces at Manassas, Centreville, and vicinity, and by the well-sustained fact that the portions of the army in the Shenandoah Valley and the Lower Potomac each had their separate commissary department and received their supplies from sources entirely independent of the department at Manassas.

It will be seen by reference to several statements included in this report that the parties were engineers, conductors, &c., on the Manassas Gap Railroad, and that they testify under oath that their chance for information about the forces at Manassas and Centreville was the very best, and that the number stationed there up to about the time of evacuation was from 80,000 to 100,000. It is also shown by the statement of a refugee who resided near Fairfax Court-House that he learned from officers of the rebel army that the numbers of their forces at Manassas and Centreville were 75,000, and that 150,000 rations were drawn by the whole army.

All of which is respectfully submitted by your obedient servant,*

E. J. ALLEN. [ALLEN PINKERTON.]

EASTVILLE, VA., *March* 17, 1862.

A. STAGER:

Steamer just in from Fort Monroe. The line is sufficiently guarded by cavalry, and there is a guard night and day at the end of cable, but there is no field piece at Cape Charles to bring boats to, and being but 12 miles from Cape Henry, the blockade is easily run. When cable failed it was foggy. If not cut, it was damaged by anchors. If weather be calm, it will be underrun from both ends to-morrow (Tuesday). Boyle goes to Fort Monroe and I to Cape Charles. In event of interruption, we must rely principally on Fort Monroe. I will make a suggestion to-night to you in cipher.

W. H. HEISS.

---

* Much the same as report of March 8, p. 736.

POTOMAC FLOTILLA, *March* 17, 1862—4 p. m.
Hon. E. M. STANTON, *Secretary of War :*

SIR: I have just obtained the following information, and forward it immediately to you:

The St. Nicholas and Virginia are not armed. They are running from Fredericksburg to Lowry Point, about 45 miles from Fredericksburg, and a short distance from Tappahannock. Edward Taylor and all the neighbors are hauling timber from Lamb's Creek roads to Arnold's Wharf and Farleyville. There is nothing done yet about the gunboats except getting the timber, but they are working hard. A few hundred troops might land at Taylor's, opposite Maryland Point, and march over to a place called Hop Yard Wharf (a distance of 7 miles), where the steamer Neales stops to land passengers, and surprise her, taking her past the batteries under her own colors. So says my spy, but I am somewhat doubtful of the result of such an expedition.

I am, sir, very respectfully, your obedient servant,
V. R. SPENCER,
Commanding Potomac Flotilla.

HEADQUARTERS, *Wheeling, Va., March* 17, 1862.
Hon. E. M. STANTON, *Secretary of War :*

General McClellan promised me to send 3,000 or 4,000 rifled arms, to use in making changes, getting regiments ready for service. They have not yet arrived. Every day is precious. Please order them by installments.

W. S. ROSECRANS,
Brigadier-General, Commanding.

WHEELING, *March* 17, 1862—11 p. m.
Hon. E. M. STANTON, *Secretary of War :*

If you approve my plans for the movement up the valley of South Branch over Cheat, &c., please telegraph me, and order the forces without delay.* The iron is getting hot.

W. S. ROSECRANS,
Brigadier-General.

HEADQUARTERS, BALTIMORE, *March* 17, 1862.
To the Police Commissioners City of Baltimore :

GENTLEMEN: In behalf of the Government of the United States I give notice that the police force established under its authority will be placed under your control on the 20th instant.

In making this communication to you, I respectfully request the retention of Mr. McPhail, whose great executive ability has been of incalculable service to the Government. There is still, as you are well aware, a suppressed feeling of disloyalty in a portion of the population of this city, and I deem it of the utmost importance to the Government that Mr. McPhail should be retained, on account of his familiar acquaintance with the transactions of the last eight months and the public necessi-

---

* See Rosecrans to Thomas, March 12, p. 744.

ties which have grown out of those transactions, and which still continue to exist.

I am, gentlemen, very respectfully, your obedient servant,
JOHN A. DIX,
Major-General.

CONFEDERATE CORRESPONDENCE, ETC.

CAMP BEE, ALLEGHANY COUNTY, *August* 1, 1861.

His Excellency JEFFERSON DAVIS,
President of the Confederate States:

DEAR SIR: I arrived here to-day, and determined to send Colonel Heth at once to Richmond, for the purpose of giving you full information about the condition of this country, and get your orders as to the line of action to be pursued.

General Wise has retreated and burned the bridge over Gauley, leaving the enemy in undisturbed possession of Kanawha Valley up to the Great Falls. His retreat lays open completely the southwestern part of this State. The road by which I intended to reach Kanawha, through Mercer, Raleigh, and Fayette, is now entirely at the command of the enemy. This is a state of things well understood by the whole country, and produces a great alarm. It emboldens the tories and disspirits our people. If you think these forces now in Kanawha should be driven out at once without reference to the operations about Monterey, I think with a union of my people and General Wise's force it might be speedily done. If this force should prove insufficient, I am sure 10,000 men could be quickly raised for the campaign at no more cost to the Government than their food and transportation. In such an event the Yankees could be immediately driven out, and a foray of 80 or 100 miles into Ohio could be successfully made.

I advance these views with hesitation, but the facts upon which they rest you may not possibly be in possession of, and I venture them for what they are worth. I am just from Wythe, through the country where the men would in part be raised, and I never witnessed a better spirit than seems to be almost universal. Whilst for any long service there is a little hesitation, there is none whatever for a campaign. If a force strong enough to drive out the Yankees was sent promptly to effect it, their march could be then directed towards the rear of the enemy at Beverly, which I think would be better than to concentrate all forces in his front, leaving our rear to be threatened from Gauley or the Virginia and Tennessee Railroad, to be exposed to the damage of an attack.

Colonel Heth will get the arms you were kind and thoughtful enough to order me from Manassas, and for which I most cordially thank you. We will have stirring work in the west before a great while, I think.

With the highest regard and esteem, I am, very truly, your friend,
JOHN B. FLOYD.

RICHMOND, VA., *August* 1, 1861.

General JOSEPH E. JOHNSTON:

MY DEAR GENERAL: Inclosed you will find a letter* which will, I suppose, only assure you of that which was anticipated, as, except among sharpshooters, it is the rule. The troops generally need more of instruc-

---
* Not found.

tion than in the face of an enemy it may be practicable to give. To insure something, it was sought to put at least one instructed officer in each regiment organized here. If a major, well; if a lieutenant-colonel, better; if a colonel, best; and in this connection I suggest to you that the instructed officer, as far as possible, be not detached from regimental headquarters, and be employed in instructing especially the commissioned and non-commissioned officers in tactics and field duties.

A few days since I received a telegram from General Beauregard, stating that some of the regiments were without food. An addendum was appended by Colonel Lee, commissary, that the deficiency was of hard bread and bacon, and that he was offered abundance of beef and flour by the inhabitants of the surrounding country. I returned the telegram to General Beauregard, and called his attention to the inconsistency. If, under such circumstances, the troops have suffered for food, the neglect of the subsistence department demands investigation and the proper correction, not only to remedy the evil, but to afford an example which will deter others from thus offending.

We are anxiously looking for the official reports of the battle of Manassas, and have present need to know what supplies and wagons were captured. I wish you would have prepared a statement of your wants in transportation and supplies of all kinds, to put your army on a proper footing for active operations.

General Lee has gone to Western Virginia, and I hope may be able to strike a decisive blow at the enemy in that quarter; or, failing in that, will be able to organize and post our troops so as to check the enemy, after which he will return to this place.

The movement of Banks will require your attention. It may be a ruse, but, if a real movement, when your army has the requisite strength and mobility, you will probably find an opportunity, by a rapid movement through the passes, to strike him in rear or flank, and thus add another to your many claims upon your country's gratitude.

General Holmes will establish a battery above his present position, near the mouth of the Chopawamsic, where it is reported the channel can be commanded so as to cut off that line of the enemy's communication with their arsenals and main depots of troops. This measure will, no doubt, lead to an attack, and hence the preference for a position between his column and yours, rather than one lower down the river, as that of Mathias Point.

Nothing important from James and York Rivers. The movements at and near Fort Monroe were probably only due to the discharge of the three months' men of the enemy.

We must be prompt to avail ourselves of the weakness resulting from the exchange of the new and less reliable forces of the enemy for those heretofore in service, as well as of the moral effect produced by their late defeat. Let me hear from you as your convenience will permit.[*]

JEFFERSON DAVIS.

RICHMOND, August 1, 1861.

General G. T. BEAUREGARD, Manassas :

Your telegram received and submitted to the President, who instructs me to say that information from other sources renders Banks' movement so doubtful as to require further information. He desires you will seek to obtain full and exact knowledge.

S. COOPER,
Adjutant and Inspector General.

---

[*] Some personal details omitted.

MANASSAS, *August* 2, 1861.

Colonel S. COOPER, *Adjutant-General:*

One thousand of Banks' forces sent eastward July 30, by cars.

G. T. BEAUREGARD,
General, C. S. Army.

RICHMOND, VA., *August* 3, 1861.

General JOSEPH E. JOHNSTON, *Commanding Forces, Manassas:*

SIR: I have the honor to acknowledge the receipt of your letter of August 1, and in reply beg leave to say that prompt steps have been taken to procure wagons and teams and artillery horses for your command.

It is expected wagons and teams in quantity to answer your purposes will reach Manassas on Monday, 5th instant. You will oblige me greatly if you will say what number of artillery horses will be required.

Very respectfully, your obedient servant,

A. C. MYERS,
Acting Quartermaster-General.

HEADQUARTERS,
Huntersville, Va., August 3, 1861.

General HENRY A. WISE,
Commanding Kanawha Army, Lewisburg, Va.:

GENERAL: I have just received your letter of the 1st instant to General Loring. The object of your returning from the Kanawha Valley towards Covington and uniting with General Floyd was for the protection of the Virginia Central Railroad, which, after the disaster that befell the Northwestern Army, was threatened through this place and Monterey. The enemy are now held in check from the two last-named points, and if they can be prevented from reaching Lewisburg they will be cut off from Covington and Newbern, on the Central and Southwestern Railroads. Are there any strong positions in front of Lewisburg that you can hold, re-enforced by General Floyd and the people of the country, that would accomplish this object, and can you get correct information of the force, movements, and apparent object of the enemy? It is necessary to stop his advance on both roads, if possible, and his progress east of the mountains. You must take care of the safety of your column, and if that does not require a further retrograde movement, you are desired to halt at Lewisburg till further notice. If obliged to retire, retard the advance of the enemy. Send back to General Floyd to support you. Inform General Loring of the positions you will take, and be prepared by a concentration of forces to strike a blow at the enemy.

I am, very respectfully, your obedient servant,

R. E. LEE,
General, Commanding.

WHITE SULPHUR SPRINGS, VA.,
August 4, 1861.

General R. E. LEE, *Commanding, &c.:*

GENERAL: I received yours of the 3d this evening at this place, where I have come to encamp, with infantry and artillery, leaving 500 cavalry, under Colonel Davis, to be backed by the militia of Monroe and Greenbrier, guarding the passes from Fayetteville, Gauley, and Summersville.

I was very reliably informed last evening that the enemy in the valley had no orders to proceed farther than Gauley as yet. He will scout in strong force to Fayetteville and Summersville. I have ordered axmen to block his way at Bunger's Ferry and on the Big and Little Sewell Mountains. As soon as I refresh and refit my men here I will return in force to the Meadow Bluff, and go on westward as far as our forage and supplies can be had. The first 30 miles this side of Gauley is very poor, and destitute of both. I am fully informed of all the passes and roads. General Loring will have to look out on the road from Summersville by the Birch Mountain.

To defend the Central Railroad was not the main object of my leaving Kanawha Valley. Had I remained there, I should have been shut in, cut off, or driven down through Berkeley and Princeton to Wytheville. The valley was conquered by the enemy already when I got there from Charleston to Point Pleasant. The treasonable population themselves are worse than the invaders. It was rotten with infection in it and all around it so as awfully to expose a minor force. In the second place, if Lewisburg, or the Warm Springs, or Covington was reached by the enemy, we were isolated and cut off from supplies, ammunition, and re-enforcements. In the third place, I would have been jammed at Gauley or driven to the southwest, where forces are not for the present needed, when if I fell back I could be re-enforced or re-enforce. In the fourth place, most of my men from the east and most of the western men are from Greenbrier, Monroe, Alleghany, Rockingham, &c., who desire to defend their own homes. These considerations governed General Cooper, I presume, as well as myself, in ordering to fall back to Covington. It was well I did so as early as I did, for McClellan's forces are augmenting largely every day at both Gauley and Weston, and they are spurring eastward, converging at Summersville, where now they have large advance parties. Their force at Charleston is at present 1,000 and at Gauley 3,500, with re-enforcements coming up the river from Gallipolis every day. Positions at Lewisburg or Covington will not cut them off from Newbern. If General Floyd moves up this way, he ought at present to tend towards Fayetteville, whence he may unite with me at any time on the Gauley turnpike or Old River road, if the enemy moves towards Summersville.

But to answer your questions. There are several very strong positions in front of Lewisburg, which I can hold against 5,000, without re-enforcements from General Floyd; certainly with them, and especially by his moving towards Fayetteville. The people of the county next to Gauley are against us, and are fully demoralized. I have got pretty correct information of the movements of the enemy. Beauregard's victory and my escape and McClellan's call to Washington have staggered them to a stand-still. But I am sure their next move will be, after strong re-enforcements, from Weston and Gauley, to converge on the Summersville road, to re-enforce Huttonsville very powerfully. He may try, I repeat, to fall on General Loring's rear, and if he does, General Floyd and I may fall on him. I can reach the Huntersville road from here or via Lewisburg. To be sure of the safety of my column, I must be allowed to remain here a week or ten days to organize, to refit, and refresh my very worn men, and to procure for them blankets, shoes, tents, and clothing, and to get arms fit for service. I implore you, sir, to order 1,000 stand of good percussion smooth-bore muskets for my command. We have marched and counter-marched, and scouted and fought to some effect, too, and our old arms are found worn-out already in the service. At least 500 of the State troops have deserted since I left Charleston, and they have carried off many good arms. My cavalry, in strong force, are in good pastures, scouting the enemy to their teeth. Will advise of every movement in time for me to advance in front of Lewisburg. I am anxious to meet them somewhere in Nicholas, on ground which I have had well mapped out by Hutton, an able topographer. I will retire no farther; advance as soon as I refit. Will effectually retard and check the enemy, and call on General Floyd when I cannot do so, and General Loring shall be kept vigilantly advised. A concentration of forces soon will be needed.

With the highest respect,

HENRY A. WISE,
Brigadier-General.

RICHMOND, VA., *August 5,* 1861.

General JOSEPH E. JOHNSTON, *Manassas, Va.:*

Troops have been detained here in order that supplies might be sent by rail. When you are sufficiently supplied with subsistence stores troops will be sent forward on notice from you.

S. COOPER,
Adjutant and Inspector General.

SPECIAL ORDERS, }   HEADQUARTERS,
   No. 239.   }   *Huntersville, W. Va., August 5,* 1861.

I. Brig. Gen. S. R. Anderson, in pursuance of orders from the Adjutant and Inspector General of the C. S. Army, is assigned to the command of the First, Seventh, and Fourteenth Tennessee Regiments, with the Army of the Northwest, under Brig. Gen. W. W. Loring.

*   *   *   *   *   *   *

R. E. LEE,
General, Commanding.

WHITE SULPHUR SPRINGS, VA., *August 5,* 1861.

General R. E. LEE, *Commanding, &c.:*

GENERAL: Mr. Hutton, my chief engineer and explorer, is so accurate and reliable, that I fail not to send you the inclosed, just received from him.* He is getting observations on every point between this and Covington. Lest you may want precise maps of Stroud's Glades, formerly Stroud's Knob, and to show what beautiful flying sketches Mr. Hutton is doing for me, I send you a report and map of the very locality to which the enemy is reported by his informant to have advanced. You can reach the cattle he speaks of nearest from Huntersville by sending runners and drivers through the mountain paths to head of Cranberry Creek and down that creek to Gauley, and thence to Beaver Creek. I will order my cavalry to scout the enemy close from the mouth of the Hommony up to Beaver Creek, and assist in driving

---

* Not found.

off the horses, cattle, and all stock. They are encamped at Meadow Bluff in full force.*

It will take me ten days, at least, to refit here. We have many sick and furloughed, and many naked of everything. Many State troops deserting, and a bevy of Kanawha officers resigning. I am glad to get clear of the latter.

Very respectfully, yours,

HENRY A. WISE,
Brigadier-General.

WHITE SULPHUR SPRINGS, VA., *August* 5, 1861.

General R. E. LEE, *Commanding, &c. :*

GENERAL: The copy of your letter to Col. A. Beckley was handed me this morning, and though I wrote you fully last night by express, I hasten to say that the militia, under Beckley (that of Fayette and Raleigh), is awfully demoralized. Capt. Thomas L. Brown has just arrived from Boone, with 105 out of 175 new volunteers (70 deserting), and he met hundreds of deserters from the State forces in my camp; attempted to arrest some 20, and had to desist from the state of popular feeling. The people demand that the Yankees shall not be fired upon, lest it exasperate them. Such is one of a thousand specimens of the disloyalty in which I have been operating. I have advised General Chapman to call out his regiments, make no *en masse* call, but select only true and loyal men, however few, arm them, and supply them with ammunition—say 750 men, ten rounds, and supply them with pickaxes, log wood axes, and shovels, to obstruct roads, passes, and ferries, and to make breastworks. I will return to Meadow Bluff as early as I can refit, and send ahead of me Captain Hutton, with a company, to select positions, construct works, and cause obstructions. Four-fifths of the militia, *en masse*, cannot be relied on, and if they could be, cannot be armed and supplied with ammunition. We want good arms and powder, and can, when we get them, arm the militia with those we now have. I therefore again urge, supply me, sir, I pray you, with 1,000 good percussion muskets.

With the highest respect,

HENRY A. WISE,
Brigadier-General.

HEADQUARTERS,
Huntersville, Va., August 5, 1861.

General HENRY A. WISE,
Commanding Wise's Brigade, White Sulphur Springs, Va. :

GENERAL: I have had the honor to receive your letter of the 4th instant, and am glad to learn the precautions you have taken to check the advance of the enemy. I hope they may be successful, and that as soon as possible you will advance west of Lewisburg to Meadow Bluff, or such other point as you may deem best, to oppose his eastward progress. As far as I am advised, General Floyd is at the Sweet Springs, unless he is on his march to your support at Lewisburg. If his command was at Wytheville, a movement in sufficient force, as you propose, to Fayette Court-House, would materially lighten the pressure of the enemy on your front. But you will perceive he is not in position for such a move, and I hope will join or precede you to Lewisburg.

---

* Some matters of detail omitted.

From the information I get, perhaps not as reliable as that you receive, the number of the enemy at Summersville is about half that you give. I can only learn of five regiments, about 4,500 men, having left Huttonsville for Summersville, to be increased by about the same number from other points. The advance on this line to Middle Mountain, Valley Mountain, and Cheat Range may bring them back to securely guard the railroads to the Ohio. In that event it will relieve your front, and may permit your advance to the Gauley, if desirable.

I much regret to hear that your arms are so poor. There are no percussion muskets for issue by the State of Virginia, unless some have been altered since my departure from Richmond. The only available guns that I am aware of are the flint-lock muskets. I am very sorry to hear that you have lost so many good arms by the desertion of the State troops. They will probably rejoin you on your advance. General Loring will expect to be kept advised of any movement against his rear by your vigilant and energetic scouts.

I am, with much respect, your obedient servant,

R. E. LEE,
General, Commanding.

HEADQUARTERS FLOYD'S BRIGADE,
Camp Bee, near Sweet Springs, Va., August 5, 1861.

The Forty-fifth and Fiftieth [Va.] Regiments, Floyd's brigade, under command of Cols. Henry Heth and A. W. Reynolds, respectively, will move from Camp Bee to-morrow at 5 a. m., and take up the line of march in the direction of Lewisburg. The quartermaster of each command will furnish the same with all the transportation at hand. The commissary will furnish the same with such rations as he has. No unnecessary baggage will be allowed.

By order of Brigadier-General Floyd, C. S. A.:

H. HETH,
Colonel.

ADJUTANT AND INSPECTOR GENERAL'S OFFICE,
Richmond, Va., August 6, 1861.

General JOSEPH E. JOHNSTON,
Commanding Army of Potomac, Manassas, Va.:

GENERAL: Your letter of 30th ultimo, suggesting that the troops instructed to re-enforce the army under your command be placed by brigades in camps of instruction located in healthy neighborhoods, has been submitted to the President, and I am instructed to suggest that you cause to be selected some position possessing the required advantages on the north bank of the Rappahannock River, or in advance, near the Manassas road, in the direction of the Bull Run Mountain. Having regard to the position occupied by your forces, the President is of opinion that the direction above indicated would afford the best location for the camps referred to.

I am, respectfully, your obedient servant,

S. COOPER,
Adjutant and Inspector General.

ADJUTANT AND INSPECTOR GENERAL'S OFFICE,
Richmond, Va., August 6, 1861.

General JOSEPH E. JOHNSTON,
Commanding, Manassas Junction, Va.:

GENERAL: General Beauregard was authorized under an emergency to retain at Manassas the Eleventh North Carolina Regiment, then *en route* for your command at Winchester, but this retention was not intended to be permanent, and it rests with yourself, as commander of the Army of the Potomac, to make such disposition of the regiment as in your judgment the interests of the service require.

I am, sir, respectfully, your obedient servant,

S. COOPER,
Adjutant and Inspector General.

HEADQUARTERS WISE'S BRIGADE,
White Sulphur Springs, Va., August 6, 1861.

General R. E. LEE, *Commanding, &c.:*

GENERAL: Having an opportunity, by a messenger of General Loring's camp, I report to you that General Floyd is within 2 miles of me, encamped. He will see me here this evening. I have not seen him as yet. He is reported to me by Colonel Tompkins as well equipped. I am not—far from it. All I had is worn out, and we need almost everything, especially tents, clothing, shoes, and means of transportation. To obtain these, I have sent to Staunton, and it will take at least two weeks from this time for me to be anything like prepared for marching. I informed you last evening of reported positions of the enemy. My calvary will scout him from Hommony to Cherry Tree River. I venture to suggest that General Loring's scouts might meet mine at Beaver or Cherry Tree. If General Floyd can be ordered to guard New River and turnpike between Gauley and Lewisburg, I can throw my forces in between Huntersville and Gauley.

Respectfully,   HENRY A. WISE,
Brigadier-General.

WHITE SULPHUR SPRINGS, VA.,
August 7, 1861—7 a. m.

General R. E. LEE, *Commanding, &c.:*

GENERAL: I saw General Floyd yesterday evening. He asked whether I had orders from you. I replied none specific. He then notified me that he would move this morning to Lewisburg, and that it was his intent to proceed immediately to attack the enemy at Gauley, but gave me no orders. I dissented from the policy of this attack, suggesting the better course of allowing me to refit my command with clothing and to obtain wagons. I will require ten days or two weeks to do so, and I ask from you special orders, separating the command of General Floyd from mine. Please assign to each one respective fields of operation. I think it would be best to assign him to the guard of the Fayetteville and Beckley roads, and my command to the guard of the Lewisburg turnpike and the roads leading from Summersville to Huttonsville or Lewisburg.

Respectfully,   HENRY A. WISE,
Brigadier-General.

HEADQUARTERS, VALLEY MOUNTAIN, VA.,
August 8, 1861.

General HENRY A. WISE,
   Commanding Wise's Legion, White Sulphur Springs, Va.:

GENERAL: I have just received your letters of the 6th and 7th instant, and am glad to learn that General Floyd is moving on to Lewisburg. In regard to the request to separate the commands of General Floyd and yourself, and to assign to each respective fields of action, it would, in my opinion, be contrary to the purpose of the President, and destroy the prospect of the success of the campaign in Kanawha District. Our enemy is so strong at all points that we can only hope to give him an effective blow by a concentration of our forces, and, that this may be done surely and rapidly, their movements and actions must be controlled by one head. I hope, therefore, that, as soon as your command can move forward, in the preparation for which I feel assured no time will be lost, you will join General Floyd, and take that part in the campaign which may be assigned your brigade.

I am, very respectfully, your obedient servant,

R. E. LEE,
General, Commanding.

No. 2.*]   HEADQUARTERS, CAMP ARBUCKLE,
                       Near Lewisburg, Va., August 8, 1861.

Brig. Gen. HENRY A. WISE:

SIR: I desire to make a movement towards the valley of the Kanawha as speedily as practicable. To this end I desire to know as soon as possible the exact force upon which to rely. Will you have the goodness to inform me the number of men you can furnish, the different arms and ammunition fit for use, the amount of transportation you can rely upon for the movement, and the supplies you will be able to furnish? An answer in detail to these inquiries will much oblige, yours, very respectfully,

JOHN B. FLOYD,
Brigadier-General, Commanding.

WHITE SULPHUR SPRINGS, VA.,
August 8, 1861—6 p. m.

Brig. Gen. JOHN B. FLOYD:

SIR: I reply immediately to yours of to-day, by saying that I am now endeavoring to complete the returns of the exact force of my command. These returns have been hindered and delayed by various causes, then beyond control. My command has, from the first, been composed of mixed troops—State troops and those of the Provisional Confederate Army. Neither have been organized, and both have been without commissioned officers; they have been necessarily intermingled in active service; have been necessarily distributed at four different posts, in parts far distant from each other, and have been doing hard marching service, keeping guard, scouting, and fighting the enemy, and lately falling

---

*The numbering of this and following dispatches between Floyd and Wise is taken from General Wise's letter-book.

back from the valley of the Kanawha, under orders from Adjutant and Inspector General S. Cooper, and from General Robert E. Lee, commanding forces in the State of Virginia. This has prevented the assembling even of my command up to this time. Now, while organizing my artillery and infantry corps, the cavalry of my command are on active duty in checking the enemy and observing their movements on the New River and on the Gauley. Another cause (obstructing returns) is that a considerable portion of the State volunteers considered that they had engaged to serve the time of their enlistment in the valley of the Kanawha alone and on the march from that valley, under orders to defend the Central Railroad, many of them have deserted, and several leading officers of their command have resigned their commissions, after having given furloughs to some of their men, who are now daily returning from their homes to duty. How many will return cannot be ascertained for several days. Connected with the march from the valley thus embarrassed, several serious cases of arrest have occurred, and courts-martial are now sitting and ordered for their trial. More than all, the state and condition of my troops here caused the difficulty and delay of organization, and will cause the delay of my movement for some reasonable time, for refitting, recruiting, and procuring sufficient arms. My men have not been supplied at any time with half sufficient clothing, camp equipage, arms, or ammunition, and many of them not at all with their tents. Many of them are now destitute of blankets, shoes, tents, and clothing, knapsacks, cartridge and cap boxes, mess-pans, and camp-kettles, and have not half enough of wagons for transportation. My sick list in hospital is upward of 300, and we need medical stores of every kind. I have made large requisitions on the Department, and have sent special agents to Richmond to procure these and all other necessaries.

This will require, for indispensable supplies, at least ten days or two weeks to come. By to-morrow I hope to have consolidated reports, as exact as possible, of my whole force here. They will show the number of men; the different arms to which they are attached; the few arms fit for use; the amount of ammunition, and the want of transportation and supplies. I should mention that at no time as yet have I been furnished with a separate commissary and quartermaster. One officer has had to perform the duties of both departments, and the person nominated for quartermaster is now gone to Richmond to give bonds and obtain necessary orders, devolving the duties of both officers still on my commissary alone.

You shall have, as you request, a detailed answer to your inquiries very soon as to the artillery and infantry of my Legion, and somewhat later a detail of my cavalry and of the State volunteers under my command.

I respectfully suggest that I be allowed ample time for the best preparation I can make, under general orders, which I have received from General R. E. Lee, commanding, &c., and then I will cheerfully cooperate with you, sir, in checking the advance of the enemy. In the short interview I had with you the other evening, I informed you I had no special orders from General Robert E. Lee, but the next morning (yesterday) started to exhibit to you my general orders, received from General Robert E. Lee since I left Lewisburg. They are to check the enemy on both roads to Covington and Newbern, and prevent, if possible, his progress east of the mountains, and to halt at Lewisburg till further notice. If obliged to retire, to retard the advance of the enemy, and to send back to General Floyd to support me; to inform General Loring of the positions I will take, and be prepared, by a concentration of forces, to strike a blow at the enemy.

These orders (dated the 3d instant) I have been and am obeying, and have advised General Lee and General Loring that I propose to advance on the Gauley by the Cherry Tree Bottom road.

I am, very respectfully, your obedient servant,

HENRY A. WISE,
Brigadier-General.

N. B.—I ought to add that new companies are coming in every day, and some of them require everything to be provided for a campaign.

No. 3.]   CAMP ARBUCKLE, *near Lewisburg, Va., August 9*, 1861.
Brig. Gen. HENRY A. WISE:

DEAR SIR: I write this note to ask the favor of you to send me, if you have them, sabers and pistols, such as you may have to spare, for 300 mounted men. I will return them to you punctually in a short time, and see that they are kept in good order. If you could spare me a company and two 6-pounders for a week's service you would greatly oblige me. The horses should be good and the pieces provided with forty rounds of ammunition.

With high regard, I am, your obedient servant,

JOHN B. FLOYD,
Brigadier-General, Commanding.

N. B.—It is important to have the arms and company here to-night, if possible.

WHITE SULPHUR SPRINGS, VA., *August 9*, 1861—5 p. m.
Brig. Gen. JOHN B. FLOYD, *Commanding, &c.:*

DEAR SIR: Your note is just at hand. The only sabers furnished to my command were 260, without scabbards, and all that were scabbarded have been distributed, and 3 or 4 of my troops are now waiting to be furnished. In lieu of the sabers and pistols, of which but fifty-three flint and steel have been furnished to my command, I inclose an order to Colonel Davis, at Meadow Bluff, to co-operate with your cavalry, and be, for the time, at your immediate orders, to-night. A company of artillery I cannot spare you. I have but one that can in any degree serve as artillery, the company of Captain McComas, who is absent from the loss of a child; but I send you a detachment of 24 men, of Colonel Tompkins' regiment of State volunteers, the remnant of the Kanawha Artillery, who fought at Scarey, and are pretty good artillerists. It is too short a notice to get them ready to-night, but they will be got ready at once, and be sent to you early in the morning. This is the best I can do at present, and I assure you, sir, it will always gratify me to do the best I can in co-operation with your command.

Very truly and respectfully, yours,

HENRY A. WISE,
Brigadier-General, &c.

P. S.—Captain Caskie reports to me to-day that some scouts of the enemy advanced on the Fayetteville and turnpike roads. We send you forty rounds of ammunition with the pieces.

HEADQUARTERS, MANASSAS, *August* 10, 1861.

To the PRESIDENT:

Mr. PRESIDENT: I have suggested, through the Adjutant and In-spector-General, the importance of increasing our forces of artillery and cavalry—the first by borrowing guns from the States, or by casting, especially at Richmond. If guns are to be made, or if different kinds are to be obtained from States, I urgently recommend 12-pounder howit-zers to constitute the addition to our present material. We are now deficient in those pieces, even on the principle which regulated the com-position of the United States batteries—four 6-pounders and two howit-zers. The effect of the howitzers on a field of battle is, I think, more than double that of 6-pounders. With fifty of them respectably served (in addition to our present artillery) we will not fear the enemy, what-ever his numbers, in the open field. I beg you, therefore, to aid us by adding what you can to our strength in this arm. I am confident from observation that the Northern troops, like other raw soldiers, fear artil-lery unreasonably, and that we shall gain far more by an addition of these guns than by one of a thousand men. We are now, you know, far below even the proportion fixed by military writers for an army of veteran infantry. Without that proportion of artillery and cavalry, without further addition of infantry, we ought to be able to drive back all the Northern hordes that may cross the Potomac. It is certain to my mind that all of Napoleon's successes in 1813 were due to his large proportion of artillery. His infantry was as new and far from being equal to ours.

May I remind you that I have more than once mentioned our defi-ciency in cavalry? We have not half enough for mere outpost duty. If it had been greater our results on the 21st of July would have been better. For a battle I am sure that 3,000 or 4,000 cavalry in a field would be resisted by no Northern volunteers if they had artillery to open their way. For the last two months I have had one regiment of Vir-ginia cavalry, under Stuart, in the presence of superior forces of regular cavalry, who have never appeared in front of their infantry. Our men, and we can find thousands like them, are good horsemen, well mounted. We can find thousands more like them. Can you not give them to us, and with Stuart to command them? He is a rare man, wonderfully en-dowed by nature with the qualities necessary for an officer of light cavalry. Calm, firm, acute, active, and enterprising, I know no one more competent than he to estimate the occurrences before him at their true value. If you add to this army a real brigade of cavalry, you can find no better brigadier-general to command it. With our present force we shall be obliged to depend much upon the country people for infor-mation of the enemy's movements.

Very truly, your friend and obedient servant,

J. E. JOHNSTON.

WHITE SULPHUR SPRINGS, VA., *August* 10, 1861.

General R. E. LEE, *General, Commanding, &c.* :

GENERAL : Yours, dated the 5th at Huntersville, post-marked the 8th at Staunton, is just received. I am pressing every means to ad-vance as far as will meet the enemy on the Gauley turnpike and Sum-mersville road. This morning I re-enforce General Floyd with a detach-ment of artillery (two 6-pounders, forty rounds), and a corps of cavalry, under Captain Corns, in addition to Colonel Davis' force of about 500 horse. As fast as a battalion or regiment is ready, I will lead it on to wherever General Floyd may have advanced. There is no ammunition sent for my howitzer, and there is none (I mean ball and cartridge) for my 10-pounder brought from Malden. General Floyd, with two regiments of his own, all my cavalry nearly, and this detachment of artillery, advances from Camp Arbuckle this morning. I will follow from day to day, as I can clothe my men and fit them for a march. The militia here are wholly unreliable, though I have ordered Colonel Beckley to pick all true men he can select, and arm and supply them with ammunition. The enemy conceal their forces very adroitly. They left 1,000 at Charleston and came up to Gauley with 3,500 and eight pieces of rifled cannon, with re-enforcements constantly coming up the river to Charleston and advanced to Gauley. From Gauley they radiate, via Fayetteville, the Gauley turnpike, and the Summersville roads, converging towards Meadow Bluff, the forces from Weston (not Huttonsville) coming down from Sutton, being now in advance, about 600, under Colonel Tyler. Thus at Gauley they have probably at present from 4,500 to 5,000, with re-enforcements coming up the Kanawha and down through Braxton in moving columns of unknown numbers. General Floyd's command and mine will number, all told, not more than 5,500 efficient men, badly armed. By the time the enemy gets through the Gauley and Sewell Wilderness he will be found in force—8,000 at least. His advance through that Wilderness shall be effectually checked. The advance to the Gauley is not desirable at present, because we can get no provisions from Kanawha, and for 30 miles from Gauley east there are no provisions or forage to be had. My idea is to stop the enemy on or near the eastern verge of the Wilderness, and keep him there in the Wilderness by fronting him on the turnpike and by detours on the Fayetteville and Summersville roads. I repeat that we are not half armed. May I not beg you to use your influence with Adjutant-General Cooper to give us some of the arms captured at Manassas or those which are surplus from the crop of that victory? We ought not to be so neglected as not to have what our glorious victors reject. Many of our deserters are coming in, and that induces me to detain the State volunteers here for a few days. I will be active to scout for General Loring, and to give him the earliest intelligence obtained by me. But one thing, of which we are destitute, is absolutely necessary—the portable forge. I beg you to send us at least two for my command, and I suppose General Floyd needs as many. He has about 300, and I about 500, cavalry, and they are barefooted, and blacksmiths cannot be got here, nor shoes, nor iron to make them.

With great respect, your obedient servant,

HENRY A. WISE,
Brigadier-General.

N. B.—At 10.30 a. m., since the above was written, I have received intelligence that the enemy has moved up, 3,500 strong, to Summersville.

MANASSAS, VA., *August* 11, 1861.

General JOSEPH E. JOHNSTON,
Commanding, Manassas, Va.:

DEAR GENERAL : In order to prevent a *coup de main* from McClellan, as already communicated to you, I have ordered Longstreet to Fairfax Court-House, Jones to Germantown, and Bonham to fall back on Flint Hill, leaving a strong mounted guard at or about Vienna. Cocke goes to Centreville; Ewell, to Sangster's Cross-Roads; Early and Hampton, to intersection of Occoquan road with Wolf Run Shoals road; Evans has gone to Leesburg. The Louisiana Brigade remains for the present at or about Mitchell's Ford.

Will you permit me to suggest that Elzey should concentrate his brigade at or about Fairfax Station, and Jackson at or about the cross of (Stuart to remain where he is) Braddock's road with the Fairfax Court-House and Station road.

From those advanced positions we could at any time concentrate our forces for offensive or defensive purposes. I think by a bold move we could capture the enemy's advance forces at Annandale, and, should he come out to their support, give him battle, with all the chances in our favor; but for that object we must have all our artillery ready in every respect.

Yours, very truly,

G. T. BEAUREGARD.

WHITE SULPHUR SPRINGS, VA., *August* 11, 1861.

General R. E. LEE, *Commanding, &c.:*

SIR: Colonel Davis, from Meadow Bluff, informs me by last night's dispatch that he is confident Tyler has joined Cox, near Gauley, and that the enemy is now 7,000 strong. Their scouts are within about 20 miles of Colonel Davis. General Floyd is at Camp Arbuckle, 4 miles beyond Lewisburg. I have sent him a detachment of artillery (two pieces, 6-pounders), and will send on every corps I can get ready in the next three to five days. General Chapman has recalled his militia, and General Beckley can raise no force of any efficiency at all. I have ordered both to call out select men, but do not rely upon them. The cavalry are actively vedetting, and report the enemy as having 250 to 300 cavalry at Summersville, threatening Davis' rear by the Wilderness road. Colonel Croghan is upon the Cherry Tree Bottom road, but returns to-day to Colonel Davis. With General Floyd's force and my cavalry, the enemy cannot advance before I am ready to make our joint forces some 5,500 men.

Very respectfully,

HENRY A. WISE,
Brigadier-General.

WHITE SULPHUR SPRINGS, VA., *August* 11, 1861.

General R. E. LEE, *Commanding, &c.:*

SIR: Your dispatch [8th instant], by special messenger, came to hand within the last fifteen minutes. I answer immediately, at 8 p. m., that I will cheerfully and earnestly obey your orders to unite with General Floyd's command. The most intimate co-operation, in separate command, was all I sought. I seek no further now than to obey your orders. I am inspecting and organizing still, making good progress, and am in strength and condition of force daily improving. All we want now are tents, good small-arms, and some clothing. I will move before all are had, and as early as possible, to do justice to my men. The enemy are reported at junction at Gauley and at Summersville and a part occupying Fayette (Cox and Tyler); in all, 7,000 strong. I have written to Beckley and Chapman, urging selection of militia corps, such as are willing and are armed, and will work with axes and spades. Chapman had recalled his men and orders. I have insisted on his renewing his call. Our teams are shoeless, and there are but very few blacksmiths. This delays me as much as any other cause.

Respectfully,   HENRY A. WISE,
                                                Brigadier-General.

WHITE SULPHUR SPRINGS, VA., *August* 11, 1861—6 a. m.
JOHN B. FLOYD, *Brigadier-General, &c.:*

SIR : Your note of yesterday reached me last night at 11 o'clock. A letter from Colonel Davis, of the 9th, from Meadow Bluff, was found unopened on my table with yours, no opened dispatches accompanying them. I have received none intended for you. Lest the letter of Colonel Davis to Adjutant-General Harvie may not have been the one opened and read by you, I inclose a copy to you.*

Please inform him that I have sent to you two 6-pounders and a detachment of artillery. I will re-enforce him with about 90 cavalry as soon as blacksmiths can be got to shoe the horses, nearly all of which are barefooted. In two or three days I may be able to move with my artillery and some companies of infantry. If you advance, sir, to Meadow Bluff and beyond to Little Sewell, I will follow as fast as my corps can be organized and made ready for the field.

I regret to learn from General Beckley that General Chapman has recalled the select militia he ordered out. I have ordered General Beckley to proceed in selecting militiamen to co-operate with Major Bailey and Captain Caskie on the Fayetteville road. The militia had better be provided with pick and log wood axes, shovels, and spades to obstruct the roads, which may admit the enemy to our rear from Summersville and other points east of that place on the Gauley. Colonel McPherson, of Lewisburg, might readily select a corps of that description to operate on the road leading from near May's and Meadow Bluff to the Gauley.

Very respectfully,   HENRY A. WISE,
                                                Brigadier-General.

HEADQUARTERS ARMY OF KANAWHA,
Camp Arbuckle, near Lewisburg, August 11, 1861.
His Excellency JEFFERSON DAVIS,
        President Confederate States of America:

DEAR SIR : After a few days' close observation in this part of the country I am quite sure the enemy's policy now is to hold all the western portion of the State lying on the Ohio River and as far eastward as the Cumberland range of mountains. They have at Gauley between four and five thousand men, and a like number at Summersville. They are 35 miles distant from each other. The interests of all the west imperatively demand that these people shall be driven out across the Ohio, which I think can be done with the proper management of the force to be secured in this region. I am a few miles west of Lewisburg and 14 miles west of General Wise.

I have deemed it proper, all points fully considered, to assume the command of all the troops about here. I accordingly have issued the

---

* Not found.

order, a copy of which I send herewith. One line of policy only should be pursued, and this is the only means by which it can be secured.

There is great disorganization amongst the men under General Wise's command, as he told me himself, and the course I propose will help to remedy the evil. I hope to be speedily able now to make a movement towards the enemy, and I trust the course I have taken will meet your approbation. I think the inspection I have ordered will result in show-ing a force sufficiently large, with the volunteer militia who will join us for the campaign, to enable them to move against them.

When we do move it will require great circumspection, attention, and tact to mollify the temper and feelings of the people west of here, if half be true of what has reached me relative to their present exasperated and excited state of feeling.

If the enemy were attacked and driven from Summersville, Cox, at Gauley Bridge, would be helpless and at our mercy, and the junction between these forces I think can be prevented by a prompt but quiet movement. Two well appointed batteries would be of inestimable value to us now. Can't you send them? The service we will render if we can get into the field will amply repay everything, I think. If we can dis-lodge these people from Kanawha Valley the whole force could be turned against the rear—Rosecrans. But of course you understand all these views perfectly well, and can order what is best to be done.

With the highest regard, I am, truly, your friend,

JOHN B. FLOYD.

[Inclosure.]

GENERAL ORDERS, }   HEADQUARTERS ARMY OF KANAWHA,
   No. 12.   }   *Camp Arbuckle, near Lewisburg, August* 11, 1861.

I. The undersigned hereby assumes the command of the forces in-tended to operate against the enemy now occupying the Kanawha Valley and the country adjacent thereto.

*   *   *   *   *   *   *

JOHN B. FLOYD.

HEADQUARTERS, VALLEY MOUNTAIN, VA., *August* 12, 1861.
General HENRY A. WISE,
   Wise's Legion, White Sulphur Springs, Va.:

GENERAL: I have just received your letter of the 10th and 11th in-stant, and I am glad that you are enabled to re-enforce General Floyd so promptly. Your reasons for our troops not advancing to Gauley at present are conclusive, and your plan of stopping the advance of the enemy on the eastern verge of the Wilderness you describe is concurred in until ready to open and penetrate the Kanawha Valley, whence you may draw your supplies. The line of defense you propose, embracing points of strength, is the best.

I have written to General Cooper in reference to arms and forges for your command and forges for General Floyd. I recommend that you forward to Colonel Deas, assistant adjutant-general, headquarters Rich-mond, a State requisition for such supplies as you may be deficient in. I will direct him to see what can be furnished. As already advised, there are no arms at my disposal, except the State flint-lock muskets; of these you have probably sufficient. I recommend that you also make requisition for ammunition for your howitzer upon Major Gorgas, Chief of Ordnance, C. S. Army. There being no 10-pounders in the service, he has not, probably, any ammunition for it. The information of the enemy being re-enforced in front of this position is repeated. Also that he is fortifying at the bridge over the North Branch of the Potomac at New Creek Depot, and occupies Romney. I think it probable that he is spreading his troops over a line of operations from the Kanawha to the Potomac, with a view of influencing the local elections of the Peirpoint dynasty. I hope we shall be able to cut him up in detail. For this purpose our troops must be kept ready for concentration.

I am, with high respect, your obedient servant,

R. E. LEE,
General, Commanding.

———

No. 5.]   HEADQUARTERS ARMY OF THE KANAWHA,
Camp Arbuckle, near Lewisburg, Va., August 13, 1861.
General WISE:

SIR: As requested to do, I send you the accompanying communication from Colonel Davis. I have reason to doubt the authority of the report. Yet, coming to me with the official sanction of Colonel Davis, I do not feel at liberty to disregard it. I shall therefore move immediately to his relief with 1,000 men, and request that you will send to-morrow one battery of artillery, with such other forces as you can spare. I understand that the enemy is strong in large guns.

Very respectfully, your obedient servant,

JOHN B. FLOYD,
Brigadier-General, Commanding.

[Inclosure.]

CAMP AT MEADOW BLUFF.
General FLOYD:

I have reasons to apprehend an attack from the Federal troops to-morrow—probably to-night. They are probably Tyler's force, from Summersville, who have come into this road by the Sunday road (33 miles from here), re-enforced by a detachment direct from Gauley Bridge. Their number is estimated at 3,000. It is now known that there has been a current of Federal troops passing down the Gauley, which confirms the statement. Mr. Tyree, just taken prisoner by the enemy, has continued to send the news to my scouts, in the neighborhood of his father's. I can stop them with 1,000 men and two pieces of cannon. Please urge on re-enforcements. Send this to General Wise, and ask him also to send all the aid he can spare.

Your obedient servant,

J. LUCIUS DAVIS,
Colonel First Regiment Wise's Legion.

P. S.—If the report is modified as to numbers, &c., I will inform you.

———

WHITE SULPHUR SPRINGS, VA., *August* 13, 1861.
General JOHN B. FLOYD, *General Commanding, &c.*:

SIR: I imagine, from the reports to me, that Colonel Davis must have received exaggerated reports. Your advance will, at all events, only anticipate any probable movement of the enemy. Your request should be promptly complied with, but for the fact that our horses for the artillery have no shoes fit to march with, and it is impossible to find smiths, shoes, or nails. I have sent for iron, and am just setting up a shop. This causes, in part, my delay here. In a short time I will be ready to move some 1,500 men.

Very respectfully,

HENRY A. WISE,
Brigadier-General.

No. 6.]   HEADQUARTERS ARMY OF THE KANAWHA,
Camp Arbuckle, near Lewisburg, Va., August 13, 1861.

Brig. Gen. HENRY A. WISE:

SIR: You will please send the regiment of volunteers from beyond New River, recently commanded by Colonel McCausland, to join me at Meadow Bluff immediately upon receipt of this order.

Very respectfully, your obedient servant,

JOHN B. FLOYD,
Brigadier-General, C. S. Army.

WHITE SULPHUR SPRINGS, VA., *August* 13, 1861.

Brig. Gen. JOHN B. FLOYD, *Commanding, &c.:*

SIR: Your order to "send the regiment of volunteers, from beyond New River, recently commanded by Colonel McCausland, to join you at Meadow Bluff immediately upon the receipt of this order," I respectfully represent cannot possibly be complied with.

The regiment of State volunteers, which you describe, as lately commanded by Colonel McCausland, is in a state of great dilapidation and destitution, from the many resignations of its officers and desertions of its men. It is now being reorganized, under the orders of Colonel Tompkins, who has not yet completed his report, and the men who are left to it are without clothing or equipments fit for a march or any efficient service whatever. Many of them are barefooted, and we have received the first supply of shoes for them this evening, and they are unopened. They are bare of clothing, have not a single tent, and number less than 550 men, many of whom have the measles. Colonel Heth has not inspected them, or his report would show you, sir, how utterly unfit in all respects these men are for any movement against an enemy or to march at all from a place where they are sheltered, and where they are just beginning to receive their supplies and outfits.

Very respectfully, your obedient servant,

HENRY A. WISE,
Brigadier-General.

No. 7.]   MEADOW BLUFF, VA., *August* 13, 1861.

Brig. Gen. HENRY A. WISE:

DEAR SIR: Upon arriving here I found much to confirm the reports concerning the approach of the enemy. Colonel Davis' pickets were driven in this evening by the enemy. We are separated to-night only by the distance of 18 miles, which will be much reduced by morning, as the enemy march at night. I hope you will, with all speed, bring up all your force, and furnish one of my companies with arms. It is a fine one, but unarmed, as their guns are behind, with Colonel Wharton. The enemy are very numerous and strong. No artillery. I hope to see you early.

Very respectfully, your obedient servant,
JOHN B. FLOYD,
Brigadier-General, C. S. Army.

[Indorsement.]

Received by General Wise's messenger at 3.30 a. m., August 14, 1861.

WHITE SULPHUR SPRINGS, VA., *August* 13, 1861.

General R. E. LEE, *General, Commanding, &c.:*

SIR: General Floyd yesterday assumed command of the forces for the defense of the Kanawha Valley, announced an adjutant and inspector general for his entire command, and ordered my Legion to be first inspected. That Legion is now ready for inspection, and will soon be ready for active service, as soon as the horses can be shod, and the men can be got some clothes, shoes, and blankets, which are daily expected. I now ask for two general orders from you, being desirous to promptly obey General Floyd and to preserve the harmony of our respective brigades: First, that no order be passed from him to my brigade except through me. Second, that the separate organization and command of my brigade, subject of course to his priority of rank and orders for service, be not interfered with. I beg leave to inquire, also, whether I am to consider the State volunteers, under Colonel Tompkins, and the militia, under General Beckley, as still attached to my brigade and command, subject to General Floyd's general orders of course, or as immediately subject to his orders alone? The enemy have nine regiments in the Kanawha Valley, about 7,200 men. Colonel Croghan reports about 1,500 at Summersville. I hear about 500 are at Fayetteville, 1,000 at Charleston, and about 4,200 at Gauley.

Respectfully,

HENRY A. WISE,
Brigadier-General.

RICHMOND, VA., *August* 13, 1861.

General JOSEPH E. JOHNSTON:

MY DEAR GENERAL: I have stated to Major Gorgas your wish for a larger proportion of 12-pounder howitzers, and he says he can make, say, six per week, and mount them as made, but there is great difficulty in supplying harness. Please send me a statement of the number and caliber of your guns, distinguishing between smooth-bored and rifled; also the number of howitzers. This information has been needed in the preparation of ammunition. It is well to avoid mixing the ammunition further than necessary; say smooth-bore or rifle to be with howitzers, but not both kinds and howitzers in one battery.

I have ordered cavalry to join you, and hope you will soon have a regiment and one or more separate companies.

Your friend,

JEFFERSON DAVIS.

RICHMOND, *August* 13, 1861.

General JOSEPH E. JOHNSTON, *Commanding, &c., Manassas:*

GENERAL: I have your letter of the 10th instant, and will forward to your command a portion of the shoes here. We have sent to Europe for shoes, and I have officers traveling over all the Confederate States purchasing shoes, making contracts with tanners for leather, and with manufacturers for making leather into shoes. Still, if our force is increased to half a million of men, there must be deficiency. The resources of our country are far too limited for the great demand an immense army creates for supplies of every kind. The demand is double what it would be from the same population in times of peace.

A. C. MYERS,
Acting Quartermaster-General.

HEADQUARTERS, VALLEY MOUNTAIN, VIRGINIA,
August 14, 1861.

General HENRY A. WISE,
Wise's Legion, White Sulphur Springs, Va.:

GENERAL: I have had the honor to receive this morning your letters of the 11th and 13th instant, and am highly gratified at the rapid progress you are making in organizing your forces, and that their strength and condition are daily improving. I hope you will receive your supply of tents, clothing, &c. As to small-arms, I do not know when they will be obtained. There were none in Richmond when I left. I hope I need not assure you that I never entertained the least doubt as to your zealous and cordial co-operation in every effort against the common enemy. Your whole life guarantees the belief that your every thought and act will be devoted to the sacred cause, dearer than life itself, of defending the honor and integrity of the State.

As regards the command of your brigade, the military propriety of communicating through you all orders of its movement is so apparent, that I think no orders on the subject necessary. I have always supposed that it was the intention of the President to give a distinct organization to your Legion, and for it to be under your command, subject of course to do service under the orders of a senior officer. General Floyd, I think, understands this, and I apprehend no embarrassment on the subject. As regards the troops hitherto serving with your Legion, it is within the province of the commanding general to continue them, as hitherto, under your command, to brigade them separately, or detach them, as the good of the service may demand. The incessant rains and constant travel have rendered the roads impassable, and so prevented the transportation of supplies as to paralyze, for the present, operations in this quarter.

Very respectfully, your obedient servant,

R. E. LEE,
General, Commanding.

No. 8.]   HEADQUARTERS, NEAR MEADOW BLUFF, VA.,
August 14, 1861—5 a. m.

General HENRY A. WISE:

SIR: You are peremptorily ordered to march at once, upon the receipt of this order, with your Legion and all the forces under your command, to join me at this point.

Your obedient servant,

JOHN B. FLOYD,
Brigadier-General Commanding.

No. 9.]   HEADQUARTERS, NEAR MEADOW BLUFF, VA.,
August 14, 1861—7 a. m.

General HENRY A. WISE:

SIR: The cavalry company sent me by you at Camp Arbuckle inform me that they are without ammunition. They are, as you will remember, armed with carbines and shot-guns, and number about 45 men. Please send 40 rounds of cartridges for 40 men. For the portion of the company armed with shot-guns I can furnish buck-shot and powder. The bearer of this will take charge of the cartridges.

Your obedient servant,

JOHN B. FLOYD,
Brigadier-General Commanding.

[Indorsement.]
AUGUST 14, 1861.

The adjutant-general will cause this request to be complied with.

HENRY A. WISE,
Brigadier-General.

WHITE SULPHUR SPRINGS, VA.,
August 14, 1861—9.30 a. m.

Brig. Gen. JOHN B. FLOYD, *Commanding, &c.:*

SIR: Your peremptory order, to march at once upon the receipt of it, with my Legion and all the forces under my command, to join you at Meadow Bluff, shall be executed as early as possible and as forces and means of transportation are available.

Respectfully, your obedient servant,

HENRY A. WISE.

No. 10.]   WHITE SULPHUR SPRINGS, VA.,
August 14, 1861—11 a. m.

Brig. Gen. JOHN B. FLOYD, *Commanding, &c.:*

SIR: I am hastening my march by all the means in my power. The quartermaster, by every exertion, has been unable to procure half enough wagons. Will you please send me all the wagons you can spare, to assist the expedition of my march to join you?

Very respectfully, your obedient servant,

HENRY A. WISE,
Brigadier-General.

HEADQUARTERS VIRGINIA VOLUNTEERS,
White Sulphur Springs, Va., August 14, 1861.

Brig. Gen. HENRY A. WISE, *Commanding, &c.:*

SIR: I have the honor to acknowledge your orders of this date, directing the movement of troops from this camp, and I feel impelled, most respectfully, to enter my protest against its immediate application to the vounteer forces under my command. I beg you to remember that these troops are now decimated by disease and casualties incurred by weeks of exposure; that they never have been furnished with tents, or even equipments regarded as essential to the ordinary requirements of service, and, above all, that they are actually destitute of clothing, except such as they bore upon their persons in the hurried march from Kanawha. The Twenty-second Regiment especially may be mentioned as having incurred losses by the destruction of the steamer Maffet, and their inability to communicate with Charleston, which should be remembered by you as worthy of immediate consideration. I cannot, therefore, under the circumstances report any companies of the volunteer regiments as fit for the field, and believe that their removal from quarters at present would be attended with detrimental consequences in every respect.

I am, sir, very respectfully, your obedient servant,

C. Q. TOMPKINS,
Commanding Volunteer Brigade.

[Indorsement.]

AUGUST 14, 1861—12.30.

Colonel Tompkins will move only such of the troops under his command as are fit for marching orders. The rest, or, if all are unfit for service, all will remain with him at this post, under my general order of this morning, until further orders or the command is fit to move.

HENRY A. WISE,
Brigadier-General.

WHITE SULPHUR SPRINGS, VA., *August* 14, 1861.

General R. E. LEE, *Commanding, &c.:*

Dispatches were received last night from Colonel Davis, and this morning from General Floyd, giving intelligence of the enemy approaching in full strength from Summersville, via what is called the Sunday road, leading into the Lewisburg turnpike, reported 6,000 strong. I do not credit the report, but, under the peremptory orders from General Floyd, received within the hour, I shall move my entire available force at once to join the general at Meadow Bluff. If my counsel prevails, I shall advance to the west side of Little Sewell. I shall take eight sixes, one rifled piece of artillery, and General Floyd has two sixes. The howitzer was, and is, without ammunition. General Floyd's whole force, all told, he says, is but 1,200; mine available at once, 2,000. The measles is raging here, and I am reduced nearly half of one regiment of my Legion and the State regiments are nearly wholly unavailable. At most, in two and a half days, I can put forward 1,500 and in five days 2,500 men. General Floyd now has his own force, my whole cavalry (550), a detachment of artillery, with two 6-pounders; in all, say, 1,800 men. In three days he will have 100 more of State cavalry. Thus in four or five days he will have available with him 3,800 men, leaving the sick and unfit for service, say 1,000 men, here. I write in haste, while hurrying on the march of all I can move to-day. There is not half the means necessary for transportation here.

Very respectfully,

HENRY A. WISE,
Brigadier-General.

HEADQUARTERS ARMY OF THE KANAWHA,
Camp Six miles west of Meadow Bluff, Va., August 15, 1861.

Brig. Gen. HENRY A. WISE, *White Sulphur Springs, Va. :*

SIR: Your favor of yesterday, informing me of the inability of your quartermaster to procure wagons, &c., enough for your march, and requesting me to send you all the wagons I can spare, has been received. In reply, I have to say that I would take great pleasure in hastening your march to join me, by sending you the necessary transportation, were I able to do so. I have sent quite a number of wagons to Jackson's River to transport subsistence stores for my men from that point. I have a considerable number of men not able to march and not sick enough for the hospital. These must have transportation. I have left at Camp Arbuckle, near Lewisburg, the tents of my people, because of the appropriation, for the purposes just stated, of the wagons intended for their transportation. These causes, I regret to say, place it out of my power to comply with your request.

Very respectfully, your obedient servant,

JOHN B. FLOYD.

WHITE SULPHUR SPRINGS, VA., *August* 15, 1861.

General R. E. LEE, *Commanding, &c.:*

SIR: I thank you, sir, for your approval of my endeavors to obey your orders to look to the safety of my command and the proper plans of defense; and I am especially thankful for the promise of your influence to aid me in obtaining good small-arms and for instructions as to requisitions, &c. The ammunition for my howitzer came yesterday, and this morning at 4 a. m. I moved a corps of artillery, with eight pieces, a howitzer, and three 6-pounders, with three companies, under Colonel Gibbs, and three regiments of infantry of my Legion (in all about 2,000 men), to join General Floyd at Meadow Bluff this evening. My corps of cavalry, 50 strong, and 50 artillery, with two pieces, of the State volunteers, are already there, and of the State volunteer cavalry two companies will join him to-day or to-morrow, making my re-enforcements to him about 2,600. His whole force I understand to be but 1,200 all told, making the joint force by to-night 3,800 troops. This is enough to check the enemy until I can have the two State volunteer regiments, now reduced to about 1,200, got ready for marching orders. They are without shoes, tents, clothing, and ammunition, and the measles is raging among them, and cases for the hospital multiplying daily. I leave Colonel Tompkins here in my command, who will report to you, by my orders, my instructions to him, and explain their import. I regret to say that there is a manifest disposition to mutilate my command. General Floyd asked me when here to transfer the State volunteers to his brigade. I declined, both for want of authority and inclination. Since then his orders have been almost peremptory to send one of the regiments to him, which is totally unfit for service in every respect. Colonel Tompkins is faithfully trying to have it ready and efficient. They were the men who guarded Tyler's Mountain and fought at Scarey unpaid, unclothed, unattended, and have kept the field among deserters. I am obliged, in duty to them, to fit them for the field before they march again. Certain influences have crept in among their officers, and I fear that secret applications have been entertained to have them transferred. I beg you will protect hearty co-operation against any such attempts, which I shall firmly, but calmly, resist to the utmost of my authority. I rely upon you, sir, to interpose admonition to all in time. I protest that I desire harmony and co-operation in every sense of cheerful, as well as efficient and healthful, service, but I cannot, in honor, submit to have my brigade mutilated without you order it. I refer to Colonel Tompkins for full explanations, and he, too, seeks the maintenance of his just authority and the observance of the respect due to him. I will be ready for co-operation.

Yours, &c.,

HENRY A. WISE,
Brigadier-General.

P. S.—My excellent secretary, Mr. Lucas, has extracted from fragments of a mail thrown out by General Floyd some items which may aid you. Colonel Croghan, of my cavalry, penetrated the Birch Mountain and captured this mail; killed 2 and captured 3—a captain, a corporal, and a private.

WHITE SULPHUR SPRINGS, VA., *August* 15, 1861.

Brig. Gen. JOHN B. FLOYD, *Commanding:*

SIR: I have the honor to acknowledge your order of yesterday, received at 7 p. m., and it shall be promptly and punctually obeyed. I have procured some shoes; enough, I hope, to supply the immediate wants of my command. Those regiments were first supplied which marched this morning to join you at Meadow Bluff, and now the regiments left here will be supplied. Transportation, as soon as it can be obtained, shall be furnished, but it is very difficult to obtain sufficient; and, in addition, what is equally necessary, clothing and tents shall be furnished, if possible, under the order of Colonel Tompkins, who is in command of the State volunteers, forming a part of my brigade. I have ordered him to prepare both regiments under him as speedily as possible to join me under your command; but it is impossible for those regiments to join you without some reasonable and necessary delay. To show this, in respect to both regiments, I send you copies of the reports sent to me yesterday by Colonels Tompkins and McCausland.*

Respectfully, sir, your obedient servant,

HENRY A. WISE,
Brigadier-General.

MANASSAS, *August* 16, 1861.

Mr. PRESIDENT: The subject of supplying this army with provisions gives us here much anxiety.

In this connection it has been suggested to me that the quantities of some articles of the ration, such as salt, coffee, and bacon, in the Southern States are too small for our wants; that we will probably be unable to procure bacon enough for two issues a week until that of the next season is ready for use. It is said further that certain responsible business men are known to be ready to undertake to introduce a large stock of bacon into the Confederacy and at a price far below that now paid in Virginia, the payment to be on delivery, and in Confederate States funds. I would make this arrangement without hesitation were the necessary amount of money at my disposal. Permit me to urge its adoption by you, and an order to the Commissary-General to carry it into effect, or authority to myself to have the proper persons employed, contracts made, and measures taken to insure their fulfillment.

---

* Not found.

I will not apologize for troubling you with any matter which seems to me to demand prompt action.

Very truly, your friend and obedient servant,

J. E. JOHNSTON.

No. 11.]   HEADQUARTERS ARMY OF THE KANAWHA,
On the march, forty miles west of Lewisburg, Va., Aug. 16, 1861.

General HENRY A. WISE:

SIR: I understand that an order has been issued by you, requiring the officers of your Legion to communicate with me through you. Such an order can result in nothing but the most serious embarrassment, as your headquarters are 40 miles from my position and that of some of your officers co-operating with me. You will see, therefore, the necessity of revoking immediately that order, if such a one has been issued.

I hope you will hurry up all your available force to my support. I shall in all human probability stand in great need of them almost immediately. I learned from a source deemed worthy of full credit that a large force of the enemy has crossed Gauley, and are advancing by this road. Two hundred of their wagons have been counted this side of Gauley. There is the utmost need for promptness and speed in sending your forces to my support.

I am, sir, very respectfully, your obedient servant,

JOHN B. FLOYD,
Brig. Gen., Comdg. Forces in the Valley of the Kanawha.

HEADQUARTERS, *Manassas, August* 17, 1861.

To the PRESIDENT:

Mr. PRESIDENT: I took the liberty yesterday to trouble you on the subject of our commissariat, and now beg leave to add a few words to what was then written.

There is rarely in store here a stock of provisions sufficient to make us feel secure—never enough for an expedition either to the Potomac or to the Blue Ridge. The latter may, indeed probably will, be necessary; for it seems to me unlikely that McClellan will follow General Scott's plans. We ought, therefore, to have always here stores for twelve or fifteen days at least. We have now for two—if the flour arrived which was expected to-day.

While in the valley, depending upon a commissary quite new to the service, we had alway ⌣undance of those portions of the ration which are not imported.

I am sure that if bacon could be issued four times a week instead of twice, our Southern troops would be more contented and far healthier. The last consideration is fast increasing in importance. On my last morning report the total present is 18,178; the sick amount to 4,809.

Let me beg you to glance at the inclosed papers.

With high respect, your obedient servant,

J. E. JOHNSTON.

HEADQUARTERS,
Richmond, Va., August 17, 1861.

Brigadier-General CARSON,
Commanding Virginia Militia, Winchester, Va.:

SIR: At the earnest request of several citizens of Hardy County the governor of the State has been induced to recommend that the militia from that section be returned to their homes, as it is believed that their presence there will be of service in preventing the inroads of the Federal troops, which have become frequent of late. You will therefore direct the men from Hardy to return to that county under Colonel Harness, who will make such disposition of them as may best conduce to the public protection.

Very respectfully, &c.,

GEO. DEAS,
Assistant Adjutant-General.

TOP OF BIG SEWELL, VIRGINIA,
August 17, 1861.

Brig. Gen. JOHN B. FLOYD, *Commanding, &c.:*

SIR : Lieutenant-Colonel Croghan sent to me yours to him of the 15th instant, giving orders to him directly (and very properly under the circumstances) of the apprehended approach of the enemy, saying : "These orders will be conveyed to you after this through General Wise." On the 16th, at or near Henning's, while present with my command, at the head of my column, I received yours of that day, remonstrating against my general. orders to my command that orders from you and reports to you to and from my officers should be communicated through me, on the ground of the distance of my headquarters, &c., and calling on me to revoke that order. On the same day, and at the same place, Lieutenant-Colonel Richardson, of the First Infantry Regiment of my Legion, reported to me in person your order to him, immediately on its receipt, to advance with all the force under his command to join you, and "*any orders whatever in any way conflicting with yours you thereby revoke.*" Desiring most cordially and cheerfully to co-operate with your command, and to obey and cause to be obeyed all orders properly communicated by you, I extract from a letter of instructions from General Robert E. Lee, dated Headquarters, Valley Mountain, August 14, 1861, the following :

As regards the command of your brigade, the military propriety of communicating through you all orders for its movement is so apparent that I think no orders on the subject necessary.

Bound to maintain the integrity of my command, and whatever is due to it in military propriety, I respectfully reply to your order to Lieutenant-Colonel Richardson, that my general order that your orders to my command must be communicated through me *is not revoked.*

I await your further orders, and am, very respectfully, your obedient servant,

HENRY A. WISE,
Brigadier-General.

No. 12.]   HEADQUARTERS KANAWHA FORCES,
August 17, 1861.

GENERAL : You will occupy with your command the encampment located by me this morning—the top of the Big Sewell Mountain.

Respectfully, your obedient servant,

JOHN B. FLOYD,
Brigadier-General, Commanding.

P. S.—Remain there until further orders.

HEADQUARTERS ARMY OF THE KANAWHA,
Camp on the Sewell, Virginia, August 18, 1861.

General HENRY A. WISE:

SIR: I learn that your Third Regiment is some distance, probably 12 or 15 miles, in your rear. If this be so, you will please hurry them, as we shall in all probability have need of them to-morrow. I have fallen back to this point from Tyree's on account of the advantage of position which it offers for making a stand. I hope to have to-day minute and accurate information of the movements and numbers of the enemy. For this purpose I have sent out large scouting parties.

Very respectfully, your obedient servant,

JOHN B. FLOYD,
Brigadier-General, Commanding Forces in Kanawha Valley.

TOP OF THE BIG SEWELL, VIRGINIA,
August 18, 1861.

General R. E. LEE, *Commanding, &c. :*

SIR: In yours of the 14th instant you say to me:

As regards the command of your brigade, the military propriety of communicating through you all orders for its movements is so apparent that I think no orders on the subject necessary.

I regret to say that orders on the subject have become necessary by the action of General Floyd, which my letter to you anticipated. You will please understand, sir, that when I marched to the White Sulphur I left my whole cavalry force, some 450, in the rear of Meadow Bluff, to guard and scout against the enemy, checking their advance. General Floyd, with about 1,200 men, passed on to Meadow Bluff, and became interposed between my post at the White Sulphur and my cavalry advanced on this road. Passing Meadow Bluff, he addressed the following very proper note of command to Lieutenant-Colonel Croghan, of my Legion:

HEADQUARTERS ARMY OF THE KANAWHA,
Camp six miles west of Meadow Bluff, Virginia, August 15, 1861.

ST. GEORGE CROGHAN, *Lieutenant-Colonel, First Cavalry :*

DEAR SIR: Your note of this evening, by messenger from Meadow Bluff, has just been handed me. In reply I send you orders for the movement of your own troops and all others belonging to the Wise Legion that may be at and in the vicinity of Meadow Bluff. These orders will be conveyed to you after this through General Wise. At present the position of the enemy will not justify the loss of an hour in the movement of troops at the Bluff. I have reliable information that the enemy is rapidly advancing and are very near here. You will therefore see the urgent necessity for an early movement of the troops at and near Meadow Bluff in the morning. I shall move from this point to-morrow morning at 5 o'clock. I shall send the companies of infantry to-night to the relief of Colonel Davis.

Very respectfully,

JOHN B. FLOYD,
Brigadier-General, Commanding.

Previous to this I had issued an order to my command that all orders to them from General Floyd and all reports to them from him must pass through me. Yet no objection could reasonably be made under the supposed, but usual, necessity of the case and the position of commands to the above to Lieutenant-Colonel Croghan.

Again on the 16th I was on my march with my First and Second

Regiments of infantry and corps of artillery, and on the evening of that day reached the eastern slope of Big Sewell, followed by my Third Regiment of Infantry (expected here to-day), nearly all of my Legion, leaving the State volunteer regiments to come on as early as Colonel Tompkins could refit them, showing every disposition to join General Floyd promptly, even before I was half prepared to do so with justice to worn and destitute troops. At Meadow Bluff, on the way, present with my forces, I received the following note myself, and Lieutenant-Colonel Richardson, of the First Regiment of Infantry, received the one following that:

> HEADQUARTERS ARMY OF THE KANAWHA,
> *On the march, forty miles west of Lewisburg, Va., August* 16, 1861.

General HENRY A. WISE:

SIR: I understand that an order has been issued by you, requiring the officers of your Legion to communicate with me through you. Such an order can result in nothing but the most serious embarrassment, as your headquarters are 40 miles from my position and that of some of your officers co-operating with me. You will see, therefore, the necessity of immediately revoking that order, if such a one has been issued.

I hope you will hurry up all your available forces to my support. I shall in all human probability stand in great need of them almost immediately. I learned from a source deemed worthy of full credit that a large force of the enemy have crossed Gauley and are advancing on this road. Two hundred of their wagons have been counted this side of Gauley. There is the utmost need for promptness and speed in sending your forces to our support.

I am, sir, &c.,

> JOHN B. FLOYD,
> *Brigadier-General of Forces in the Valley of the Kanawha.*

To Lieutenant-Colonel Richardson he says:

> HEADQUARTERS ARMY OF THE KANAWHA,
> *On the march, forty miles west of Lewisburg, Va., August* 16, 1861.

Colonel RICHARDSON:

SIR: You are hereby ordered, immediately upon the receipt of this, to advance with all the force under your command to join me. Any orders whatever in any way conflicting with this I hereby revoke.

Respectfully, &c.,

> JOHN B. FLOYD,
> *Brigadier-General, &c.*

Neither myself nor Colonel Richardson has noticed either of these orders. Yesterday morning General Floyd ordered me to occupy this point, which I am doing until his further orders. He advanced 5 miles; has found no enemy, except some scouts, this side of Gauley, and is now, I am told, returning, his advance just arriving. We are here now together, he with about 1,200, and I soon with about 2,000 of my Legion, with this question of communicating orders unsettled. My officers of the Legion cannot be permitted to disregard my general orders nor to take orders directly from General Floyd, and I shall utterly disregard his attempted revocation of it. I lay the case before you in time to prevent collision. If it comes it shall not be my fault, but I will resist, by lawful and respectful means, all encroachments on my legitimate command and the respect which is due it. I will abide your orders, sir, and await your interposition. If General Floyd desires to attach the command of the State volunteers (two regiments) now under Colonel Tompkins to his brigade, I will gladly consent to it, under your orders. Let it be done immediately, and leave me the independent command of my Legion. I beg for this, and prefer to take orders from you. My men will fare better, and our cause will be better served. The enemy have not crossed Gauley at all in any considerable force,

and have now entirely retired.   I am ignorant of the recent movement.
Three, or two, or one thousand men cannot be subsisted between Little
Sewell and Gauley without great sacrifice.   My regiments are reduced
by measles 50 per cent. and the cavalry are ruined ; nothing but hay,
and no shoes.

    With the highest respect,

HENRY A. WISE,
Brigadier-General.

No. 13.]   HEADQUARTERS KANAWHA FORCES,

August 19, 1861.

General HENRY A. WISE :

    SIR : I received last night yours of the 16th instant, in relation to the
military propriety of transmitting from these headquarters, through you,
orders touching your command.   I have the honor to state that the military propriety of thus communicating orders affecting any part of the
troops composing your Legion immediately under your command has
never been questioned by me.   I was informed that you had issued a general order to the officers of your command not to communicate information of any kind directly to me, but first through you only.   This will
necessarily result in requiring your officers to disobey the orders of your
superior, should an occasion arise which in my opinion rendered it necessary for me to give an order directly or to demand a report to be made
directly to me by any officer of your Legion.   If such an order has been
issued, you must see the necessity of its being immediately countermanded.   Should troops be detached from your command, I am the judge
of the propriety whether my orders should be transmitted through you
or directly to the officer in command.

    Respectfully, your obedient servant,

JOHN B. FLOYD,
Brigadier-General, Commanding.

BIG SEWELL, VIRGINIA., *August* 19, 1861.

Brig. Gen. JOHN B. FLOYD, *Commanding, &c.* :

    SIR: I have received your note of this day, in reply to mine of the
16th instant, and regret that it disclosed some difference of understanding between us as to the relations of our respective commands, and some
misapplication, I apprehend, of the military propriety even about which
we agree.   To make my views clear I will call to your mind the different forces which constituted my command when yours became united
to it, and when, as senior in commission, you became superior.   My
command consisted, first, of my Legion; secondly, of the State volunteer force ; and, thirdly, of the militia, under General Beckley, assigned
by orders of the President and General Lee.   The whole of that force
is, and ever has been since assigned to me, *"immediately under my command."*   I am informed of no order, from any authority whatever, detaching any of these forces from my immediate or other command.   But
without detaching Colonel Richardson from my command, and while I
was marching to join you, you directed an order to him, purporting to
revoke a general order of mine, of which you were incorrectly informed,
and while I was present, leading him, in obedience to your orders, and
was at the head of my column at the time.

You say that you was informed that I had issued a general order to the officers of my command not to communicate information of any kind directly to you, but first through me only. Permit me, respectfully, to say that had you required me to inform you what general orders I had issued, I would have copied and sent to you the following General Orders, No. 82, the only one relating to the matter which I had issued, and which will assure you how erroneous was the information given you of its character, to wit:

GENERAL ORDERS, }   HEADQUARTERS WISE'S BRIGADE,
    No. 82.   }   *White Sulphur Springs, Va., August* 14, 1861.

General John B. Floyd, senior in commission to General Wise, having assumed command of the Department of the Kanawha Valley, will be obeyed and respected accordingly. All orders from him to this brigade, and all reports from this brigade to him, will pass through General Wise, or through the officer at the time commanding.
    By order, &c.

Thus, you see, sir, that my order applied not only to my Legion, but to the entire brigade commanded by me, and that, so far from requiring my officers to disobey the orders of my superior, it expressly enjoins both obedience and respect, and prescribed only the proper formality to secure both to the command of my superior. And now, in respect to detaching portions of my command and removing them from my immediate orders, I refer you again to instructions to me from General Lee. In the same letter, of August 14, 1861 (the day of my general orders), in which he said, "as regards the command of your brigade, the military propriety of communicating through you all orders for its movement is so apparent, that I think no orders on the subject necessary," he adds:

I have always supposed that it was the intention of the President to give a distinct organization to your Legion, and for it to be under your command, subject of course to do service under the orders of a senior officer. General Floyd, I think, understands this, and I apprehend no embarrassment on the subject.

He also adds, in contrast or opposition to this:

As regards the troops hitherto with your Legion (meaning the State volunteers and militia), it is within the province of the commanding general to continue them, as hitherto, under your command, to brigade them separately, or detach them, as the good of the service may require.

Thus, sir, I am instructed to command my Legion as a distinct organization, subject to do service under the orders of a senior officer, communicated through me. It cannot be discontinued from my command except by orders of the President or by due course of military law. It cannot be brigaded separately or detached from my command, in whole or in part, by a senior only, for, if it may be detached in part, it may be in the whole, and a junior brigade might be dissolved by being detached, so as to merge it into the senior. Nor can it be mingled with your command, except to unite in the service, under your orders, passed through me, for it is a distinct organization. But as respects the State volunteer forces and the militia the case is otherwise. As yet there have been no orders from you to discontinue my command of them, but you may so order, or you may brigade them or detach them. In respect to these troops, I will cheerfully accede to either order and obey it promptly. But in respect to my Legion, sir, I must respect my sense of duty to maintain its command as my own, subject to your superior orders to do service. Its entirety will be maintained by me, and I will not consent to the whole or any part of it being detached. If the contrary is claimed as your province, I will judge of the propriety of appealing to the superiors of both you and myself in command. In the mean time, and in the face of the enemy, I trust we may rationally adjust our relative commands, and harmoniously co-operate, by your detaching from my command all the forces except my Legion and leaving that in the category described by General Lee.

Very respectfully, your obedient servant,

HENRY A. WISE,
Brigadier-General.

SPECIAL ORDERS, }
  No. —.   }   CAMP WISE, VA., *August* 19, 1861.

Brig. Gen. Henry A. Wise will take up the line of march to-morrow at 7.30 a. m., and proceed with all the forces under his command in the direction of the Kanawha Valley, by way of the James River and Kanawha turnpike. He will place, for the march, his artillery next to his advanced guard of cavalry, and his horse in the rear of his column.

By order of Brig. Gen. John B. Floyd, commanding, &c.:

WILLIAM E. PETERS,
Assistant Adjutant-General, Floyd's Brigade.

HEADQUARTERS WISE'S DIVISION,
Camp Arbuckle, Va., August 19, 1861.

Brig. Gen. JOHN B. FLOYD, *Commanding Forces, &c.:*

SIR: I have received your note of orders for 7.30 o'clock to-morrow morning. The part relating to the cavalry will require Colonel Davis to be notified to fall back with his command in your advance, in order to comply with your order to proceed with my whole command and to place a portion of my cavalry in front and rear. Colonel Davis and Lieutenant-Colonel Croghan have been stationed, under your orders, where, exactly, I do not know. Will you please have a messenger dispatched to Colonel Davis to fall back and meet me on the march, to form the order of march under your command? A portion of the cavalry of my command are at Meadow Bluff, and I will order them up immediately. Am I to consider the detachment of artillery which you borrowed as included in your order in respect to my whole command? They have not yet been detached from my command, and were to be returned to me in a week. We are deficient in wagons. It will be difficult to take our ammunition or to move with all our baggage and tents. Can you assist us with wagons?

Very respectfully,

HENRY A. WISE,
Brigadier-General.

No. 16.]   CAMP WISE, VA., *August* 19, 1861.

Brig. Gen. HENRY A. WISE:

SIR: General Floyd's order of this date is hereby countermanded in so far as you will take up the line of march to-morrow at 9.30 a. m., instead of at 7.30 a. m., as specified in said order. Colonel Davis had orders from General Floyd yesterday to report to him at these headquarters, for the purpose of taking command of the cavalry here, with a view to its better organization. A copy of said order is herewith sent you. General Floyd was not aware until the receipt of your letter of the absence of Colonel Davis from the command temporarily assigned him here. As requested, Colonel Davis will be ordered to fall back and meet you on your march. General Floyd will detach from your command all the forces not belonging to your Legion, hence the detachment of artillery at these headquarters is not included in his order in respect to your command.

As stated in a former communication to you, General Floyd is deficient in the means of transportation. If, however, he ascertains tomorrow morning that he can spare any wagons, it will afford him very great pleasure to place them at your command.

By order of Brig. Gen. John B. Floyd, commanding forces, &c.:

WILLIAM E. PETERS,
Assistant Adjutant-General, Floyd's Brigade.

MANASSAS, *August* 19, 1861.

To the PRESIDENT:

Mr. PRESIDENT: On the 22d of July, just before Brigadier-General Holmes returned to Fredericksburg, he, General Beauregard, and myself agreed as to the expediency of erecting at Evansport a work capable of resisting a *coup de main.* This work, it was further agreed, General Holmes was to have constructed immediately. He selected for its armament five of the captured guns, the 30-pounder and two small Parrott rifles, and two 12-pounder howitzers, which I had sent to him a day or two after. I was much surprised yesterday to learn that the work had not been commenced. We think it of great importance; that its effect would be to prevent the turning that position on its right by the enemy. It will therefore be begun by us. The guns which General Holmes still has should be sent to the place, however, and for the thorough command of the Potomac three or four of the large rifles, which it is understood have been made in Richmond, should be added, and a detachment from Fredericksburg might, I think, be advantageously employed in conjunction with ours.

While on this subject may I suggest that this frontier of the Potomac would better form one command than two? Colonel Wigfall has reported, and without other field officers. I was glad to find it so, because it gives me a hope that you will believe that my Texan friend, R. A. Howard, is the fittest Texan living for military service. He served with me four years in Texas on Indian service. In that I formed the highest opinion of his military character—an opinion which I shared with his West Point associates of highest standing, such as Whiting, Bee, and E. K. Smith. He accompanied Bee in the recent campaign. In the battle I had an opportunity to observe him, and was delighted with his conduct and enthusiastic courage. Colonel Wigfall says that this appointment would be agreeable to him.

We hear of several officers as in Richmond who would be of great value here, Colonels Van Dorn and Walker among them. We require more brigade commanders. It seems to me that our whole strength is to be put forth. In this connection let me recommend as two of the best officers whose services we can command, G. W. Smith and Lovell. They are as fit to command divisions as any men in our service. Smith is a man of high ability, fit to command in chief. These two have not come forward, because, not belonging to seceded States, they didn't know how officers would be received. Perhaps they have not taken the right course. At any rate they have always wanted to serve us. They are now in Lexington, Ky. I venture to recommend, too, from the importance of his position, that our chief quartermaster have the provisional rank of colonel.

Most respectfully, your friend and obedient servant,

J. E. JOHNSTON.

RICHMOND, VA., *August* 20, 1861.

General JOSEPH E. JOHNSTON:

GENERAL: Frequent complaints have been made to me of improper food for the well and a want of care for the sick. I most respectfully invite your attention to both these subjects, and hope that abuses may be promptly corrected. Is it not practicable to construct bake-ovens at or near Manassas, that good bread may be supplied to the troops? The main complaint is of bad bread and of inattention to the sick. I have repelled grumblers, but the clamor has increased in specifications until I have deemed it proper to obtain the facts from you. Captains and colonels, instead of correcting evils by personal attention, seem to have been the sources of no small part of the impressions received and circulated. I have for some time designed to organize a medical board to examine the appointees, and hope soon to do so.

Your friend,

JEFFERSON DAVIS.

BIG SEWELL, VA., *August* 20, 1861—8.15 a. m.

Capt. WILLIAM E. PETERS,
Assistant Adjutant-General, &c., Floyd's Brigade:

SIR: Please inform General Floyd that, owing to one of my infantry ammunition wagons breaking down, I fear delay in advancing at the hour ordered, but every means of transportation shall be exerted.

Respectfully,

HENRY A. WISE,
Brigadier-General.

CAMP WISE, VA., *August* 20, 1861.

General HENRY A. WISE:

SIR: I am instructed by General Floyd to say to you that he cannot spare you any wagons. He finds that he has not enough, by a good many, for the transportation of the equipments of his own people and their provisions.

By order of Brig. Gen. John B. Floyd:

WILLIAM E. PETERS,
Assistant Adjutant-General, Floyd's Brigade.

No. 17.]   DEET'S, AT FOOT OF SUNDAY ROAD, VA.,
August 20, 1861.

Brig. Gen. JOHN B. FLOYD, *Commanding, &c.:*

I hastened on in person to the front this morning. Found Lieutenant-Colonel Croghan reported in danger of being cut off by the advance on the Sunday and Hopping roads, and sent two companies of cavalry to re-enforce him and cover his retreat. The scouts came in immediately afterwards from the Sunday and Hopping roads, reporting they were fired upon, and I heard three volleys, apparently from the Hopping road. Our scouts killed 2 on the Sunday road, and Lieutenant-Colonel Croghan had two encounters on the turnpike; the first about one and a half miles beyond Piggot's, killing 2 and taking 2 prisoners of the enemy. The second was about 2 p. m., half mile this side of Hawk's Nest, at Hamilton's, losing 1 man of Captain Buchanan's company, and 3 wounded. The latter are in a wagon, sent back to a surgeon. A surgeon, if possible, should be sent to the cavalry in front. Colonel Croghan has been met by about 580 of the enemy at Hawk's Nest, and he was obliged to retire. He will report more in detail to you.

Having executed your special orders, I send him back to bring up the cavalry of my Legion in the rear. Several companies are there, refitting and recruiting men and horses exhausted and worn-out by excessive scouting. Several troops of your brigade are very much shattered, and I have ordered Colonel Croghan to take them to the rear to get horses and some grain. I will order the best of the cavalry to be detailed for an advance guard. I think the enemy will be in force to-night at Hawk's Nest, and we ought to have a strong artillery and infantry force at Dogwood Gap and upon the Sunday and Hopping roads. The advance should be made to-night.

HENRY A. WISE,
Brigadier-General.

HEADQUARTERS,
Valley Mountain, Va., August 21, 1861.

General HENRY A. WISE,
Commanding Wise's Legion, Camp, Sewell Mountain, Va.:

GENERAL: I have received your letter of the 18th instant, and, according to your request, have issued the accompanying special orders, of this date, placing the Twenty-second and Thirty-sixth Regiments of Virginia Volunteers subject to the assignment of the commanding general of the Army of the Kanawha, and confining your immediate command to that of the Wise Legion, as organized, by direction of the War Department.

It is proper, as well as necessary, for the commanding general to organize his troops in the field according to the exigencies of the service. It also becomes necessary to detach troops for special service from their appropriate brigades, and thus place them temporarily under other commanding officers. The rights of officers are not thereby violated, provided they are under their senior in rank, whose orders are always respected and obeyed in well-constituted armies. The necessities of war require the organization of the forces to be adapted to the service to be performed, and sometimes brigades and separate commands have to be remodeled accordingly. This must be done in accordance with the judgment of the commanding officer. The transmission of orders to troops through their immediate commanders is in accordance with usage and propriety. Still, there are occasions when this cannot be conformed to without detriment to the service. Obedience to all legal orders is nevertheless obligatory upon all officers and soldiers.

These remarks are not supposed to be necessary for your information, but to show why I have not considered orders on the subject necessary. Feeling assured of the patriotism and zeal of the officers and men composing the Army of the Kanawha, I have never apprehended any embarrassment or interference in the execution of their respective duties believing they would make everything yield to the welfare of the republic.

I remain, with high esteem, your obedient servant,

R. E. LEE,
General, Commanding.

[Inclosure.]

SPECIAL ORDERS, }   HEADQUARTERS,
No. 243.   }   *Valley Mountain, W. Va., August* 21, 1861.

I. The Twenty-second and Thirty-sixth Regiments Virginia Volunteers, under Colonels Tompkins and McCausland, will be formed into a distinct brigade, or be attached to other brigades of the Army of the Kanawha, as the commanding general of that army may determine.

II. The Wise Legion, as organized, under the directions of the Secretary of War, will be under the immediate command of General H. A. Wise.

III. The militia called into the service of the Confederate States, together with all the troops operating in the Kanawha Valley, will be subject to the orders and under the control of the commanding general of the Army of the Kanawha.

R. E. LEE,
General, Commanding.

———

No. 18.]   CARNIFIX FERRY, W. VA.,
August 22, 1861—10 p. m.

Brig. Gen. JOHN B. FLOYD:

SIR: Yesterday you left two pieces of artillery at Dogwood Gap, which have been ordered to this point this morning. These, added to my eight pieces, make ten under my command. Your verbal orders to me now are to have four pieces of artillery crossed over the Gauley this evening, with one of my regiments of infantry. Permit me to inquire whether you order four of my pieces in addition to your own? And will you please state in written orders the points you wish me to occupy with the remaining portions of my Legion.

Very respectfully, your obedient servant,

HENRY A. WISE,
Brigadier-General.

———

CARNIFIX FERRY, W. VA., *August* 22, 1861.

HENRY A. WISE, *Brigadier-General:*

SIR: You will please send me four pieces of your artillery in addition to my own two; also one of your regiments (the strongest), to have crossed over the Gauley this evening. You will likewise please send me early to-morrow—say 7 a. m.—100 of your most efficient horse. With the remainder of the force under your command you will take such a position as will enable you to watch the movements of the enemy and to check any advance by them. I understand that the regiments commanded respectively by Colonels McCausland and Tompkins are on the march from the White Sulphur and are to-day near you. Should the force of your command, after making the above deductions, be deemed inefficient for the purpose of watching the enemy and checking his advance, you will retain under your command the regiment commanded by Colonel Tompkins, and order the regiment of Colonel McCausland to join me as soon as practicable. I do not think that any serious apprehensions need be entertained of the advance of the enemy from Gauley Bridge. Should you be likewise thus persuaded, you will please send me the regiments of both Colonels McCausland and Tompkins. At all events you will keep a vigilant eye upon the movements of the enemy and keep me informed of the same.

Very respectfully, your obedient servant,

JOHN B. FLOYD,
Brigadier-General, Commanding.

P. S.—Since the above was written I have had a conversation with Colonel Heth, which induces me to recall my request for one of your regiments. I will try and make good my position with my own force and your guns. In lieu of the regiment I must beg of you to send me early to-morrow 100 horse.

ADJUTANT AND INSPECTOR GENERAL'S OFFICE,
Richmond, August 22, 1861.

General JOSEPH E. JOHNSTON,
Commanding Army of Potomac, Manassas, Va.:

GENERAL: In transmitting the inclosed copy of a letter this day sent to General Holmes on the subject of a battery at Evansport, I am instructed by the Secretary of War to state that it is of the first importance that a competent engineer officer should be sent to locate the work and superintend its construction. He therefore desires that you will furnish such officer from your command, and, if practicable, detail Captain Stevens, of the Corps of Engineers, for that duty.

Very respectfully, your obedient servant,

S. COOPER,
Adjutant and Inspector General.

[Inclosure.]

ADJUTANT AND INSPECTOR GENERAL'S OFFICE,
Richmond, August 22, 1861.

General T. H. HOLMES, *Commanding Fredericksburg, Va.:*

GENERAL: In answer to your several communications on the subject of the establishment of a battery at Evansport, I am instructed to inform you that it was intended when you were last here that the erection of a battery at Gray's Point, on the Rappahannock, should be suspended, with the understanding that you would direct your attention to batteries on the Potomac, the point above your position being preferred to that of Mathias Point, if equally effective, because of the advantage it possesses of being in the direction of our forces at Manassas. You will now, therefore, cause to be erected, with as little delay as practicable, the battery at Evansport, as suggested by you. General Johnston, to whom a copy of this communication will be sent, will be instructed to furnish a competent engineer officer from his command for the purpose of locating the work and superintending its construction. General Johnston reports that you had arranged with him when at Manassas to have the work constructed at Evansport immediately on your return, and that you selected for its armament five of the captured guns, viz, the 32-pounder and two small Parrott rifles and two 12-pounder howitzers, which he had sent to you a day or two after your interview with him. Besides these guns, Major Anderson, of the Tredegar Works, has been instructed to send you a rifled columbiad for the same battery. It is presumed these guns will be a sufficient armament for the battery in question. If, however, the rifled columbiad should not be made available at Evansport, it is conceived it might be used with effect at the mouth of Aquia Creek.

Very respectfully, yours, &c.,

S. COOPER,
Adjutant and Inspector General.

CAMP GAULEY, *August* 23, 1861.

Hon. L. P. WALKER, *Secretary of War :*

SIR : I have been enabled, after some days' march, to cross the Gauley River at a point near the village of Summersville, in the county of Nicholas, which we now command. It has been heretofore held by a strong force of the enemy, and constituted an important link in their chain of communications and defenses between the Kanawha River and the forces in the northeast, under Rosecrans. I learned that all the forces from this point had been sent to the mouth of Gauley, with a confident expectation of an attack from us there. Immediately upon hearing this I turned suddenly in the night, and by a forced march, and succeeded in crossing the Gauley River 25 miles above its mouth, and in taking possession of this pass and position, which effectually cuts the enemy's line of communication and enables us, when sufficiently strong, either to attack General Cox in his flank or rear, on the Kanawha River, or to advance against the flank of General Rosecrans, should General Lee so direct.

If three good regiments could be sent to me by way of the Kanawha turnpike to replace the Legion of General Wise, which can be used to better advantage by General Lee, I think the entire valley of Kanawha can be speedily reoccupied and permanently held. I cannot too strongly enforce upon you the importance of this measure, and the sooner it is done the better. Newbern and Dublin Depot, on the Virginia and Tennessee Railroad, would be the best point to start from, and their march to Kanawha Valley would be through Giles, Mercer, Raleigh, and Fayette, by a good turnpike road.

The militia west of Kanawha River are embodied, and I hope in a few days to render General Cox's position untenable.

I have the honor to be, very respectfully, your obedient servant,

JOHN B. FLOYD,
Brigadier-General, C. S. Army.

No. 20.]   HEADQUARTERS ARMY OF THE KANAWHA,
Camp Gauley, Va., August 24, 1861.

Brig. Gen. HENRY A. WISE :

SIR : I have good reason to believe that the enemy have abandoned all idea of crossing the Gauley River in force. If they have any thought of an attack upon us it must be against all at this point, and this I greatly doubt. But I am fully able to defend myself against the combined forces of General Cox and Colonel Tyler both together, and court their assault. I learn that some silly reports are in circulation among the teamsters and camp followers, to the effect that I am in danger of being surrounded and cut up. I hope you will take pains to have this silly and absurd notion exploded, if, indeed, it has made any progress on that side of the river. Such an idea, however absurd, might have a tendency to demoralize the troops. May I ask you to send over the mail, with all dispatches. I have ordered a strong scouting party of my cavalry, still on the left bank of the river, to proceed to Gauley Mountain, and ascertain the position of the enemy, if indeed he is still on that side. I shall be able to cross with the artillery to-morrow.

Very respectfully, your obedient servant,

JOHN B. FLOYD,
Brigadier General, Commanding the Army of the Kanawha.

CAMP AT DOGWOOD GAP, NEAR SUNDAY ROAD,
August 24, 1861—8.30 p. m.

Brig. Gen. JOHN B. FLOYD, *Commanding, &c.:*

SIR: Your messenger met me within the hour, returning from a personal view of the enemy. I could get no reliable information from scouts or citizens, and determined to go in person to the Gauley Mountain and see their camp for myself. I passed our camping ground and rose the gorge on the other side of Liken's Mill, guided by Westlake. He supposed they were encamped in and about a school-house on the hill. I got to the turn of the ascent with a small detachment of cavalry and halted; dismounted, with Colonel Davis and Adjutant Tabb, and went directly up the hill into their camp of the night before, at the school-house. At first it appeared as if evacuated, but going farther and observing ahead more closely, we discovered the smoke of their camp beyond, about 400 yards distant. We returned a short distance to a mound, which failed to command a view, and I then sent Colonel Davis and Adjutant Tabb back, who got a pretty close sight of their sentinels. The camp could not be seen fairly without exposing our party, but the immediate neighbors reported them to be about 700 strong, though but two companies had occupied the school-house last evening. Mrs. Wood, Westlake's daughter, and an intelligent servant, it is said, escaped from their camp last evening, and report that they have moved over to Rich Creek. The latter is the only indication of an intent to attack you. To watch that movement I detailed the returning scouts from Captain Tyree's company, as it passed here to-day. I also detailed Captain Bailey and some 20 men and scouts to cross Bowyer's Ferry and scout that and Miller's Ferry to Fayetteville turnpike down to Montgomery's Ferry, and to report upon the practicability of mounting a 6-pounder on the cliffs on the south side of New River, to give a plunging shot into their camp and barricades at Gauley; and, finally, to descend into their rear on the south side of the valley of the Kanawha, by the Loop, or Paint Creek, or Coal River. This to divert them from an attack upon you. I trust you will approve these orders. I have ordered all my available and shod cavalry to guard as low down as Liken's Mill, and shall move a battalion of infantry to the same point, and gradually step up towards the enemy. To-morrow I will order a daring scout of the Rich Creek road. Colonel Tompkins must before this have reached Carnifix with two regiments, less than 800 men. They have been reduced less than one-half by desertion and measles. I sent Captain Corns' cavalry yesterday and Captain Beckett's to-day and left three pieces of artillery for you, thinking Colonel Tompkins would bring you two pieces besides. The loss of your ferryboat and 4 men was dispatched to me last night by Quartermaster Dunn, very properly, to obtain nails and plank to construct a new and better boat. This was promptly attended to, and the apprehension it caused was doubtless the foundation of the report you name. I do not think these reports will damage your command (if the enemy do not), but I will endeavor to guard you, sir, from both to the utmost of my power. I respectfully submit that an attack from Cotton Hill would have a strong effect upon the enemy. If you will order it, sir, I will try to make it effectual, if artillery can be taken over New River and up its cliffs.

Respectfully, your obedient servant,

HENRY A. WISE,
Brigadier-General.

No. 21.]   HEADQUARTERS ARMY OF THE KANAWHA,
August 24, 1861. (Received August 25—2.30 a. m.)

General HENRY A. WISE:

SIR: I have this evening received information that 500 of the enemy are encamped within 5 miles of this place. This is probably the advance guard of their entire force, who may make an attack upon me to-morrow. To meet this contingency you will send down to the river at once, upon receiving this, one of your regiments—the strongest. The boat will be ready for their conveyance across the river by daylight to-morrow morning. Should subsequent developments prove that no attack upon me is intended, your regiment will be sent back to you. You will also please send me your iron howitzer.

Very respectfully, your obedient servant,

JOHN B. FLOYD,
Brigadier-General, Commanding, &c.

P. S.—You will please issue forty rounds of cartridges to the men and one hundred for the howitzer.

DOGWOOD GAP CAMP, *August* 24, 1861.

General R. E. LEE, *Commanding, &c.*:

SIR: I received your last dispatch this morning, and I confess with a heavy heart. The general instruction is that my command is independent in its organization, and cannot be detached, yet General Floyd may divide and detail it in part, subject to his direct orders, in any proportion of force, so as to deprive me of all opportunity to organize and protect it, and to command the respect from it which I must have, in order to make it efficient or to be myself of any use in the service. To be plain, sir, I am compelled to inform you expressly that every order I have received from General Floyd indicates a purpose to merge my command in his own and to destroy the distinct organization of my Legion. We are now brought into a critical position by the vacillation of orders and confusion of command.

Two days ago I was ordered to proceed down this turnpike to meet the enemy. Everything was put in motion, and the commands were united at the foot of Gauley Mountain, where the foe was found in force. We arrived on the evening of the 21st. That night General

Floyd, for the first time, conferred with me, and I concurred in a plan to attack Carnifix Ferry, on the Gauley, while he should hold the front on the turnpike, and was accordingly ordered to proceed that night at 3 o'clock to take and cross that ferry. He was to check the enemy in front and join me at the ferry, after covering my train and artillery, which he had left at Dogwood Gap. At 3.30 o'clock I marched. Found no enemy on the Sunday road. They had retreated across the ferry, and I arrived there early in the morning. I paused to get breakfast while looking out for boats on which to cross. The enemy had sunk one and sent the other adrift over the falls. I had scarcely paused before General Floyd, with his whole force, arrived by another road, leaving his train and his artillery unprotected on the turnpike. The rain and mud were nearly insufferable the day before yesterday, and the men without tents after a night's march. In the course of the day he changed orders three times, and at last ordered me to divide my batteries, giving him three pieces of artillery, with a detachment for the guns, and 100 horse to follow across the Gauley. The sunken boat having been raised—a single boat of the smallest size for a country ferry—he ordered me, with the remainder of my command, to take position on the road and check the enemy, leaving me four pieces and he taking six—four of mine and two of his own. Under these orders I marched back yesterday to Dogwood, leaving Captain Hart, with my detached artillery, on this side of the ferry, awaiting the opportunity to cross, General Floyd having taken over his own two pieces. Last night his quartermaster dispatched to me the message that their boat sank yesterday and went over the falls, drowning four men, and that all means of communicating with General Floyd are cut off until we can build another ferry-boat. He has with him only about 1,000 men and two pieces of artillery, the enemy having about 4,000 men at Gauley and Rich Creek, and within a few hours' march of him. This unfortunate move may cut him to pieces, but Colonel Tompkins is coming up with about 750 men, and we will do what we can to cover the retreat or to re-enforce his position.

I now ask to be entirely detached from all union with General Floyd's command. I beg you, sir, to present this request to the President and Secretary of War for me. I am willing, anxious, to do and suffer anything for the cause I serve, but I cannot consent to be even subordinately responsible for General Floyd's command, nor can I consent to command in dishonor. I have not been treated with respect by General Floyd, and co-operation with him will be difficult and disagreeable, if not impossible. I earnestly ask that while he is attempting to penetrate Gauley I may be allowed to operate in separate command from him, but aiding his operations, by being ordered to penetrate the Kanawha Valley on the south side, by the Loop or Paint Creek, or by the Coal River; or send me anywhere, so I am from under the orders of General Floyd.

I am, with the highest respect, your obedient servant,

HENRY A. WISE,
Brigadier-General.

HEADQUARTERS WISE'S LEGION,
At Buts', Va., August 25, 1861.

Brig. Gen. JOHN B. FLOYD, *Commanding, &c.:*

SIR: Captain Tabb being absent, I inclose the following memorandum:

AUGUST 25, 1861.

Adjutant Taft will forward a dispatch to General Floyd, stating that the enemy in my front, in large force, have cut the cavalry, under Colonel Jenkins, to pieces, and

I am moving forward two pieces of artillery and a picked corps of infantry, to meet the enemy, and this will delay the regiment to be sent to him.

HENRY A. WISE,
Brigadier-General.

Very respectfully,

DAN'L B. LUCAS.

DOGWOOD, VA., *August* 25, 1861—6 p. m.

Brigadier-General FLOYD, *Commanding, &c.:*

SIR: I wrote to you a hurried note this morning* to excuse my delay in executing orders to send a regiment. Colonel Jenkins' cavalry (the Nelson and Lee Rangers) got into a severe skirmish to-day, in which they were completely ambuscaded by about 700 infantry and suffered much. With untrained horses and men, they broke very badly and left the commander with but few men rallied. None were killed, but some 8 or 10 badly wounded and several horses killed and crippled. The disaster called out my infantry in force and delayed my sending the regiment this morning. It shall be at the Carnifix Ferry early to-morrow morning, and I will have my whole force ready to re-enforce you. Lieutenant-Colonel Croghan is at Meadow Bluff.

Very respectfully,

HENRY A. WISE,
Brigadier-General.

[This note was written at the head of his column by General Wise, leading against the enemy (in the direction of Hawk's Nest). Richardson's regiment was already drawn up and about to start to Carnifix, when the rout of Jenkins' cavalry caused the reverse movement.—D. B. L.]

No. 22.]   HEADQUARTERS ARMY OF THE KANAWHA,
Camp Gauley, Va., August 25, 1861.

Brig. Gen. HENRY A. WISE:

SIR: I am obliged to you for the information you impart to me about the enemy. Although meager, it is all I have been able to gather from that locality since I crossed the river. The enemy no doubt are within a few miles of me, but in what force I have been unable to ascertain up to this time. It may be the whole force of their combined column, for I supposed from the first that their object would be to repossess themselves of all the country this side of Gauley. Hence the probabilities are that the force in our neighborhood is the advance guard of the entire command at Gauley Bridge. Of this I hope to know more before morning. If they come against me with all their people you ought to give me the benefit of your whole force, which would still leave us inferior to them in numbers. In this view, therefore, I think for the present you had better not get your force beyond supporting distance. With one regiment at the river and your others at Dogwood Gap, ready to march at a moment's warning, I would look upon my position here as nearly impregnable. If the enemy do not make a movement against me, which must be determined within twenty-four hours, then no doubt your plan of operations for the left bank of the Kanawha is the correct one, and must result in driving them from the Kanawha Valley. If those operations are properly sustained by energetic measures on this side of the

---

* See Lucas to Floyd, preceding.

Kanawha immediately upon ascertaining certainly the action of the enemy in this direction, I will give orders in conformity to the foregoing views. I am without a field officer for cavalry. Will you oblige me by detailing Colonel Croghan for special service with me for a short time, until I can be supplied? He can be of service to me if you can spare him.

I have the honor to be, very respectfully, your obedient servant,

JOHN B. FLOYD,
Brigadier-General, Commanding Army of the Kanawha.

No. 23.]   HEADQUARTERS ARMY OF THE KANAWHA,
August 25, 1861—3 p. m.

General HENRY A. WISE:

SIR: The enemy are very near us; their advance guard within 3 miles. You will dispatch your strongest regiment to my support and hold your entire command, if you can do this, within supporting distance.

Very respectfully, your obedient servant,

JOHN B. FLOYD,
Commanding Forces, &c.

In the absence of General Floyd I have signed the above order.

WILLIAM E. PETERS,
Assistant Adjutant-General, Floyd's Brigade.

3.30 p. m.—Enemy advancing in battle array.

W. E. P.

SPECIAL ORDERS, }   HDQRS. VALLEY MOUNTAIN, VIRGINIA,
No. —.   }   *August* 25, 1861.

I. Brig. Gen. T. T. Fauntleroy, Provisional Army of Virginia, at his own request, is relieved from the command of the troops in and about Richmond.

*   *   *   *   *   *   *

III. Name the officer to relieve General Fauntleroy or to command the different camps, &c.

By order of General Lee:

————.

HEADQUARTERS, VALLEY MOUNTAIN, VIRGINIA.

Lieut. Col. GEORGE DEAS, *Assistant Adjutant-General:*

COLONEL: Above you have an order relieving General Fauntleroy from duty, in accordance with his request. Before issuing it, please see as to his successor, and append another paragraph, appointing him to the command. If Colonel Dimmock can attend to the duty, appoint him, and, if necessary, see General Cooper on the subject. I have no news. The constant rains and travel have made the roads almost impassable, and the effort is to supply the troops with provisions. Other movements are at a stand. I sent Mayo to Richmond to report to you, on account of his health, which was suffering from the exposure. Sign the above order when completed as usual.

Very truly,

R. E. LEE.

P. S.—Since writing the foregoing I have issued the order from the Adjutant-General's Office, diverting the Fourteenth North Carolina Regiment from this column to General Floyd's. The second paragraph being unnecessary, I have consequently erased it. Re-enforcements are wanted on this line. Can any be had?

RICHMOND, *August* 26, 1861.

General R. E. LEE, *Staunton, Va.:*

GENERAL: The Secretary of War directs that you be informed that your requisitions for clothing are being filled and the articles forwarded. He also wishes you to be informed that Colonel McDonald had previously to your orders to him been directed to proceed with his regiment to Hampshire County, to carry out his original instructions in that quarter, which were highly important.

I am, sir, respectfully, your obedient servant,

R. H. CHILTON,
Assistant Adjutant-General.

RICHMOND, *August* 26, 1861.

Adjutant-General COOPER, *Confederate Army:*

GENERAL: In answer to the petition * of the county court of Shenandoah to Governor Letcher, in relation to that portion of the militia from that county in my brigade now in service at Winchester and by you handed to me for the facts, I have to say:

1st. Governor Letcher and the county court are mistaken as to who ordered the brigade into service. General Johnston made the order, dated June 21, for two regiments, through me, which has been shown to both the Secretary of War and yourself. Under proclamation of the governor of July 19, calling out the militia, the balance of my brigade was condensed into two regiments, making four in my command, and numbering over 3,000 men.

2d. In carrying into effect the several proclamations of the governor every opportunity was given the men to volunteer, and recruiting officers from all sections were permitted to mingle with the men for that purpose. Nearly all the recruits obtained were from the two regiments ordered out by General Johnston. In these two points the county court is mistaken.

3d. That I have never conceived the two regiments ordered into service by General Johnston under the control of Governor Letcher, but the Confederate authorities, and that the two regiments ordered out by his proclamation of July 19, as soon as organized, were under the same control.

It is proper for me to state that four-fifths of the militia now serving at Winchester belong to my brigade, and have been actively engaged in drill, throwing up intrenchments, mounting guns, and for the defense of that place and the valley of Virginia, and that since the battle of Manassas I have received orders from General Johnston to have them drilled and prepared for service wherever needed.

Most respectfully, your obedient servant,

GILBERT S. MEEM,
Brigadier-General, Seventh Brigade Virginia Militia.

---

* See inclosure A to Walker to Johnston, August 29, p. 817.

SPECIAL ORDERS, }   ADJT. AND INSP. GEN.'S OFFICE,
    No. 134.   }   Richmond, August 26, 1861.
    I. Brig. Gen. W. H. T. Walker, Provisional Army, will proceed to Manassas, Va., and report for duty to General J. E. Johnston, commanding.

*   *   *   *   *   *   *

By command of the Secretary of War:
                                          JNO. WITHERS,
                                     Assistant Adjutant-General.

———

RICHMOND, August 27, 1861.
General T. H. HOLMES,
       Brooke's Station, via Fredericksburg:
    GENERAL: Your letter of the 22d instant has been received. The President conceives it important that measures should be taken to occupy with some military force a portion of the Northern Neck against marauding attempts of the enemy, and also for the same purpose a portion of the country south of the Rappahannock River, and it is therefore urged upon you to unite with the Lancaster troop of cavalry, now reported to be in the Northern Neck, Beale's company of horse, and also to send Richardson's regiment to the south side of the Rappahannock, where it is understood some of his companies are serving.
    If this disposition can be made without weakening your command too much in other quarters, it is the President's wish it be done.
    I am, respectfully, your obedient servant,
                                          S. COOPER,
                                          Adjutant-General.

———

HEADQUARTERS ARMY OF KANAWHA,
       Camp Gauley, Nicholas County, August 27, 1861.
Hon. L. P. WALKER, Secretary of War:
    SIR: The force under General Tyler which left this vicinity a few days ago to strengthen General Cox for the expected fight at the mouth of Gauley, upon learning that I had crossed the Gauley and taken position here, returned to this neighborhood night before last. They took up their position 2 miles from my camp, when I attacked them yesterday about sunrise, and defeated them completely after a sharp conflict. Between 45 and 50 of the enemy were killed and wounded, and we have taken over 100 prisoners and some stores. The force of the enemy was completely routed and dispersed in every direction. We are still picking up the stragglers. I hope the result of this fight will enable me to break up entirely all communication between the valley of Kanawha and the forces under General Rosecrans.
    It is a matter of vital importance to the interests of Western Virginia that a strong and controlling force should be sent into this quarter of the country. The undecided and timid portions of the people would at once side against the invaders, and the Union men would diminish to an inconsiderable number. If such should be the policy of the Department, no time is to be lost.
    With great respect, I am, your obedient servant,
                                          JOHN B. FLOYD,
                              Brigadier-General, Commanding Army of Kanawha.

HEADQUARTERS, VALLEY MOUNTAIN, VA., *August* 27, 1861.
General HENRY A. WISE,
        Commanding Wise's Legion, Camp Dogwood Gap, Va.:

GENERAL: I have just received your letter of the 24th instant, and am much concerned at the view you take of your position and its effect upon your Legion. I do not apprehend the consequences you suppose will follow from its being under the general order of the commander of the Army of the Kanawha, or from its forming a part of that army. It will be under your immediate care and control, and, though it may be occasionally detached from your command, it cannot suffer any harm under its regularly-constituted officers. The Army of Kanawha is too small for active and successful operation to be divided at present. I beg, therefore, for the sake of the cause you have so much at heart, you will permit no division of sentiment or action to disturb its harmony or arrest its efficiency. In accordance with your request I will refer your application to be detached from General Floyd's command to the Secretary of War. At present I do not see how it can be done without injury to the service, and hope, therefore, you will not urge it. Your account of General Floyd's position makes me very anxious for his safety, and I would immediately dispatch an infantry force to his support (the only character of troops that could reach him across the mountains), did I not suppose from the time that has already elapsed and the distance they would have to march (about 60 miles) they could not possibly arrive in time to be of any avail. I think, therefore, he will either have retired up the Gauley and recrossed at the ferry, or that you will have built a flat and crossed to his support.

Your obedient servant,

R. E. LEE,
General, Commanding.

WAR DEPARTMENT, C. S. A.,
Richmond, August 28, 1861.
Brig. Gen. GILBERT S. MEEM,
        Commanding Seventh Brigade, Virginia Militia, Winchester:

SIR: In your communication to this Department of the 26th of August you submit for its decision various matters relating to your command at Winchester. Before proceeding to answer your interrogatories it is necessary to inquire into the circumstances under which the forces under your command were called into the Confederate service.

It appears that under the exigencies surrounding General J. E. Johnston he called for a brigade of two regiments from the Third Division Virginia Militia on the 21st of June, 1861, to which call you responded as the brigadier general of this district, and that having raised the two regiments required, you were ordered by General Johnston, on the 2d of July, 1861, to take post at Winchester.

It further appears that on the 19th of July, 1861, Governor Letcher, in obedience to the requisition of the President calling out the militia of Virginia, made a further call upon the militia of the Third Division, under which the other regiments were raised and added to your command at Winchester.

These four regiments thus raised were, in the opinion of General Johnston, necessary to the defense and protection of Winchester, in view of his operations in the direction of Manassas, and they were organized in accordance with the laws of Virginia regulating her militia.

The militia laws of Virginia provide, among other things, "that each major-general, brigadier-general, and colonel shall appoint his own staff," &c. Under this state of facts, the first question arising for the decision of this Department is that propounded by yourself: Whether the staff officers of your brigade appointed by yourself, and the regimental staff officers appointed to each regiment by the colonel thereof, will be recognized and commissioned by the Confederate Government under the provisions of the act of Congress approved March 6, 1861, to provide for the public defense?

This act, in its fifth section, provides that "officers of volunteers below the grade of general shall be appointed in the manner prescribed by law in the several States." But the sixth section of this act provides that "the President shall, if necessary, apportion the staff and general officers among the respective States from which the volunteers shall tender their services as he may deem proper;" and the seventh section of this act reads: "Whenever the militia or volunteers are called and received into the service of the Confederate States under the provisions of this act, they shall have the same organization, and shall have the same pay and allowances, as may be provided for the Regular Army;" and by the ninth section of this act the power is extended to the President, by and with the consent of the Congress, "to appoint one commissary and one quartermaster, with the rank of major, for each brigade of militia or volunteers called into the Confederate service, and one assistant quartermaster and one assistant commissary, with the rank of captain, and one surgeon and one assistant surgeon, to each regiment; the said quartermasters and commissaries and assistant quartermasters and commissaries to give bonds, with good sureties, for the faithful performance of their duties."

The State and Confederate laws in relation to militia staff appointments would seem thus to conflict. Nor does a recurrence to the mere words of the Constitution of the Provisional Government, under which we are acting, serve precisely to settle the difficulty. The sixth section of this instrument provides that Congress, among other things, shall have the power to provide "for calling forth the militia to execute the laws of the Confederacy, suppress insurrections and repel invasions, to provide for organizing, arming, and disciplining the militia, and for governing such part of them as may be employed in the service of the Confederacy, reserving to the States respectively the appointment of the officers," &c.

In this reservation to the States are staff officers as well as commanding officers embraced, or shall it be contended that the Congress, by the act to provide for the public defense, has so far exercised its constitutional power of "organizing and governing" the militia called into the Confederate service as to confer on the President the right to make staff appointments in supercession of State laws? If the first inquiry be answered affirmatively, then your command as at present organized and officered has to be in all respects accepted. If the last position be yielded, the brigade and regimental staff officers of your command will depend upon the discretion of the President, who may or may not accept the appointments made by yourself and your colonels. Whatever appointments are recognized will of course occupy positions under the ninth section of the act to "provide for the public defense," and they will hold the same rank and receive the same pay "allowed to officers of the same grade in the regular service." The act to provide for the public defense evidently regards militia as such and militia as volunteers. In the first light they are subject to draft upon requisition or may be called out *en masse*. In the second light they freely tender their services; and here again a distinction has to be drawn. They may tender their services through State intervention indirectly to the Confederate Government or without State intervention directly to the Confederate Government. If drafted or called out *en masse*, they can only be compelled to serve six months, whereas under a tender of service they may be accepted and compelled to serve for any period specified, according to the necessities of the Government and country. But in whatever light they may stand, the nature of the question as affecting staff appointments demands an interpretation that shall generate unity, consistency, and harmony in the general service of the Army, and which could never be obtained if staff officers were not compelled to give bond and surety to that government whose treasury was at their mercy. It would be a strange anomaly in administration to admit a set of officers into the Treasury of the Confederate Government whose bonds and sureties were given in the line of their commissions to the State authorities, from whose treasuries nothing was to be drawn. How could the Confederate Government exact bond and surety from a State officer? Yet the act "to provide for the public defense" imperatively demands that this Department shall exact "bond and good sureties" from all its agents employed in the Army as "quartermasters and commissaries" and as assistant quartermasters and assistant commissaries. The nature of the case and the reason attendant upon it lead to the conclusion that in every branch of the service staff appointments are with the President, and that he may accept or reject those selected by the officers of your command.

Your second interrogatory is plain. The four regiments under your command, having been called into the Confederate service by proper authority and retained at Winchester, are entitled to the usual pay allowed by law to volunteers and militia for the time they have served and shall continue to serve. Nor is there any difficulty in regard to your third and last inquiry. The militia called into the Confederate service are clothed, subsisted, and paid as other troops.

In conclusion, it may be remarked that this Department has received from the county authorities of Shenandoah and from the Hon. J. Randolph Tucker, the attorney-general of Virginia, earnest petitions for the discharge of all that portion of your command which may be in excess of the 10 per cent. quota demanded by this Government for active service in the field. The question of their discharge will be referred to General Johnston, who will be governed in his decision by the necessities associated with the defense of Winchester and the country comprising the third militia division.

Respectfully,

L. P. WALKER,
Secretary of War.

HEADQUARTERS, CAMP DOGWOOD,
At Dogwood Gap, Va., Monday, August 28, 1861.

General R. E. LEE, *Commanding, &c.:*

SIR: Deeming it proper to keep you fully advised as to movements in this direction, I take occasion to submit the following brief report of the operations of my command during the past few days:

On Monday, the 19th instant, while encamped at Big Sewell Mountain, I was joined by Colonel Henningsen, whom I immediately assigned to the Second Infantry Regiment of this command; also placing him in command of the entire body of my infantry and artillery. General Floyd's brigade was encamped at a little distance westward of me, on the main turnpike leading to Gauley Bridge, and my cavalry, under command of Colonel Davis, was far in advance of the main body of our united forces.

On the evening of the same day I received orders from General Floyd to advance with my command along the turnpike towards Gauley Bridge. This general order was conveyed to me without explanation of the motive or final intent of the movement, nor was I consulted or advised as to any fixed plan of co-operation with General Floyd's forces. I immediately sent orders to Colonel Davis to fall back to a point 15 miles westward of Big Sewell, and on the morning of the next day (Tuesday, the 20th instant) I started early to join Colonel Davis, leaving instructions with Colonel Henningsen to follow on with the rest of my command. Together with the order to move forward General Floyd had sent me an order of march for my command, specifying the hour of 7.30 a. m. as the hour of starting, which, however, by a subsequent order was modified to 9.30 a. m.; but I was not informed whether General Floyd intended the two commands to move together, or, if together, whether my command should move in advance or in rear of his own forces. I was therefore obliged to modify the order of march in such manner as would best adapt itself to my moving separately and in advance. During the day's march I discovered that General Floyd was moving on in advance of Colonel Henningsen, whose command was encamped at Locust Lane, 21 miles from Gauley Bridge and 40 miles from Lewisburg. I learned that General Floyd's command had encamped at the same place on the evening before; that Colonel Henningsen had encamped with him by General Floyd's order, and that shortly before my arrival General Floyd had, without notification to and leaving no order with Colonel Henningsen, broken up his own camp and moved forward. I immediately followed on with Colonel Henningsen's forces, and that afternoon found General Floyd's command encamped at Piggot's Mill. His officers conveyed to me an order to encamp in some meadows which they pointed out. Finding the place thus indicated to me ineligible, I selected another position, where my command would be more securely posted, and where I could better protect General Floyd's camp from the approach of the enemy. On the same evening General Floyd visited me at my quarters, when I expressed to him the desire to be informed, if not consulted, as to his wishes or plans. He replied that he had no idea of operating without the fullest explanation and consultation with me, and proceeded to indicate and discuss several plans of operation. I took occasion to express to General Floyd my regret that my command had been ordered so soon westward from the White Sulphur Springs. Except for his urgent orders I should certainly have remained three weeks longer at that point, at least that time being required for instruction, rest, and refitting. If, however, a move became imperative, I would advise against a direct movement towards Gauley Bridge.

Beyond Piggot's Mill commences a series of defiles continuing to the Hawk's Nest, a naturally strong place, about 6 miles this side of Gauley Bridge, already fortified by the enemy. I suggested that, in view of our inferiority of force, these positions could not be carried except at great loss and dangerous exposure of our rear and flank to the enemy, and that their capture would be barren of result, since, because of the above-named causes, we should be compelled to fall back immediately. General Floyd admitted the justice of these views, and I then called his attention to the fact that Colonel Tyler already occupied, with some

1,800 or 2,000 of the enemy's forces, a position near Summersville. I then suggested that if any move on the enemy was imperative, the most feasible was in this latter direction, and I proposed that General Floyd should remain with his forces at Dogwood Gap to protect the main turnpike from the encroachment of the enemy, while I would march by a cross-road to Carnifix Ferry and dislodge the enemy from and occupy that point. General Floyd heartily approved this proposal, insisting that the movement should be made early, before daybreak, the next morning (Thursday, August 22); arranged that I should leave for him at Dogwood Gap two of my 6-pounders (he having already obtained from me two others); promised himself to occupy Dogwood Gap without delay, to protect my rear from the enemy's forces posted at the Hawk's Nest, and to divert their attention by advancing some militia along the southern bank of New River to a point called Cotton Hill. He also ordered me, in the event of my defeating the enemy either this side of or at Carnifix Ferry, to capture the ferry, cross the Gauley River, hold that position, and report to him, but to proceed no farther. It was past 8 p. m. when I finally received these orders. The roads were very muddy from the incessant rain of several days' duration. My cavalry was worn down by scouting. My infantry had suffered much from the inclemency of the weather and by measles (many only just recovering from that disease), and operations of this nature required that the men should take with them three days' cooked provisions. I had no bread cooked, my beef was on the hoof, and the camp-fires burned out. To relight them would excite the suspicion of the enemy. To slaughter and cook would have deprived my men of all rest during the night previous to their march towards the enemy. The only practical means then was to take three days' provisions of meal, coffee, &c., packed in one wagon for each regiment, and to drive the bullocks along with us. At 1 a. m. the men were quietly awakened, and at 3.30 a. m. the column commenced the march.

On reaching Dogwood Gap we left two pieces of artillery for General Floyd, but here we found only two companies of militia to receive them, who said that they were under orders to march within an hour. Our pieces of artillery required six horses each, and had but four; took, therefore, two horses from each of our caissons (except one) to supply this deficiency. We left behind us five caissons and all our baggage wagons (except one for each regiment). This was done, of course, in the confident anticipation that General Floyd would send a force to take charge of the artillery and protect the position. When half way between the turnpike and Carnifix Ferry we received the intelligence that the militia companies had left Dogwood Gap without being relieved by any other force. I was thus obliged to order all the artillery and baggage left at the latter point to follow in our rear.

On reaching Carnifix Ferry we found that the enemy had precipitately retired, having destroyed one flat and sunk the other The men, who had marched 17 miles ankle-deep in mud and through incessant rain, were ordered to make fires and cook breakfast while preparation was making to cross the river. This had hardly been commenced when General Floyd, with his whole brigade, made his appearance at the junction of the two roads. It was thus evident that soon after my departure from Piggot's Mill General Floyd had started directly for Carnifix Ferry by a shorter route than I had taken, and which we had agreed I should not take, lest the enemy should thereby be apprised of my movement. Doubtless this unexpected move on the part of General Floyd caused the immediate retirement of the enemy's forces from the ferry and the destruction of the boats, besides leaving the main turnpike at the mercy of the enemy, enabling them to cut us off entirely from Lewisburg, and exposing to seizure the baggage and artillery in my rear. The sunken flat-boat having been discovered, General Floyd determined to recross the river.

Late in the afternoon he demanded of me two pieces of artillery and one regiment to accompany him. I prepared to comply with this demand, but determined to accompany the detachment in person (believing that General Floyd would thus expose himself to imminent danger of being cut off), and to send back Colonel Henningsen with the remainder of my command to occupy Dogwood Gap and cover the road to Lewisburg. A few hours afterwards General Floyd changed his mind, and required of me four pieces of artillery and 100 more than all my efficient cavalry. I sent the cavalry and three pieces of artillery, which I placed at his disposal. It was late in the afternoon before General Floyd announced to me his determination.

My troops were kept all day exposed to the rain and mud, their tents not arriving until nightfall. On Friday I marched my remaining force back to Dogwood Gap. On Saturday morning learned that General Floyd had succeeded in transporting his infantry to the other side of the river, but in doing so the flat-boat had been sunk, drowning 4 men, and leaving the cavalry, three pieces of artillery, and all the baggage and provisions on this side. His quartermaster, Captain Dunn, sent to me the same day for assistance to build another flat-boat. On the next day Colonel Tompkins arrived at Dogwood Gap, and at midday marched his two regiments to Carnifix Ferry, to re-enforce General Floyd. On Saturday night General Floyd, being apprehensive of an attack from the enemy, urged me to send another regiment to his relief. My cavalry was then at Piggot's Mill, observing the movements of the enemy and scouting. My infantry and artillery, under Colonel Henningsen's command, were occupying Dogwood Gap, reconnoitering and strengthening the same. Altogether, my whole command was barely sufficient to hold in security the turnpike road, and, in case I should even be driven back to another point on the same road, General Floyd's rear would be left exposed to the enemy. Nevertheless, I determined to march in person, with an infantry regiment and a 12-pounder howitzer, to General Floyd's relief. Shortly before the time fixed (on Sunday morning, the 25th instant) for the marching of the regiment a heavy firing was heard in the direction of Piggot's Mill, and shortly, to our surprise, some fugitives of General Floyd's cavalry rushed in, reporting the advance of the enemy. Within fifteen minutes' time we started eighteen companies of infantry and three pieces of artillery on a double-quick march towards Piggot's Mill, some 5 or 6 miles below. On reaching this point we found that some 150 or 180 of General Floyd's cavalry, under command of Colonel Jenkins and Major Reynolds, had, without any intimation to me, penetrated the defiles beyond Piggot's Mill, and had fallen into an ambuscade of the enemy.

I was exceedingly surprised that General Floyd, after alleging a deficiency of cavalry at Carnifix, and requiring a portion of mine, should without notice to me send his cavalry thus within the lines of my command.

Our scouts (detachments of Captain Brock's and Captain Phelps' companies) were thoroughly acquainted with the ground, and were at the time stationed as vedettes or occupied in scouting the adjacent hills.

They descended at once, and endeavored to warn General Floyd's cavalry. These, however, pushed rapidly on, till, finding a large force of the enemy, they were compelled to retire after exchanging a few shots. But they found the trap closed, several hundred of the enemy's infantry having passed their rear close to the road-side on inaccessible ground. Captain Brock, with 20 men, having come down to warn them, now brought his little force up in good order to their relief. Colonel Jenkins, when caught in the ambuscade, and Captain Brock, who had deliberately come to his assistance, behaved with the greatest gallantry, and ran the gauntlet of the enemy's fire at a few yards' distance, bringing up their forces with very little loss under the circumstances. Captain Brock had 1 man killed and 5 wounded. Colonel Jenkins has made no report to me. He was slightly injured in the arm, lost 1 prisoner, and some 10 or 12 of his wounded were found on the road, besides 3 disabled horses, some 20 hats, and 2 saddles. Many of his men threw away and lost their arms, and, after getting through the defile, were met by us 4 miles from the enemy in an incurable state of panic. Captain Brock's men, with a single exception, were quite cool, kept good order, and were willing to ride in again. The enemy retired immediately to their stronghold in the vicinity of the Hawk's Nest. Since then General Floyd has made an attack on the enemy, caught a regiment at breakfast, and in five minutes put them to flight, with the loss by the enemy of some 100 prisoners, 2 or 3 wagons, and some 20 or 30 killed and wounded, losing himself but 2 or 3 killed (it is said by our own artillery) and a few wounded. The enemy are about 700 strong below the Hawk's Nest, on this side of Gauley, and about 500 on Cotton Hill, the other side of New River, and about 4,000 or 5,000 in a main body, strongly fortified, about the bridge on Gauley River. The militia under Generals Chapman and Beckley (about 1,400), with small detachments of cavalry and infantry from my force (about 75 in all), are moving up the Cotton Hill, whence firing was heard yesterday.

I have the honor to be, most respectfully,

HENRY A. WISE,
Brigadier-General.

RICHMOND, *August* 29, 1861.

General JOSEPH E. JOHNSTON,
     Commanding on the Potomac:

GENERAL: The inclosed petition from the authorities of the county of Shenandoah [A], transmitted to this Department by his excellency Governor Letcher, with his indorsement, in support of the prayer of the petitioners, together with the communication of the Hon. J. Randolph Tucker, the attorney-general of Virginia [B], relating to the same subject, represent that the county of Shenandoah has furnished in volunteers very nearly the full quota of 10 per cent. of the population for service in the Army, without estimating 600 men drafted under your requisition issued to Brigadier-General Meem and 900 men since drafted under the requisition of the President through Governor Letcher, and it is urgently desired that all of these 1,500 men now at Winchester in the brigade of General Meem, over and above the quota of 10 per cent. of the population, may be discharged from further service and be permitted to return to their agricultural pursuits. The case is strongly stated, but the Department must rely upon the judgment of its commanding generals as to the exigencies originally requiring this force to be called into the field, and which may still render it necessary to be retained in service before deciding upon its merits. As it was under your orders and requisition Brigadier-General Meem proceeded to form two out of four regiments now at Winchester under his command, it is deemed the wiser course to refer the entire case, together with the question of discharge, to your better knowledge of the facts and your judgment in the premises.*

I have the honor to be, very respectfully,

L. P. WALKER,

Secretary of War.

[Inclosure A.]

Hon. JOHN LETCHER, *Governor of Virginia:*

The undersigned members of the county court of Shenandoah, at the August term, 1861, sitting, and others, respectfully represent:

1st. That they feel deeply interested in the present struggle for the Southern independence, and that they are willing to yield to none in the sacrifices which they are required to make. Yet they are likewise conscious that unnecessary evil and suffering may arise from circumstances not within their control, but fully within that of the Government. Of this nature they conceive the existing levy of militia to be, not in itself, but from its attendant circumstances, which may be enumerated, as follows:

1st. The population of our county, according to the last census, was 12,829. This, under the terms of your proclamation, would require us to furnish 1,282 volunteers. We have 900 in the field, exclusive of about 100 or 120 teamsters, who have been taken into the service by impressment with their teams or those of others. This would leave us 282 yet to be furnished, provided there were no exempts. These, however, are considerable in number, such as railroad hands, millers, overseers, saddlers, shoemakers, tanners, &c., who would otherwise have been liable to duty. If these were deducted, it is doubtful whether more than 200 would be required to fill out our complement under the proclamation, if, indeed, that number.

2d. What, then, is the fact as to levies already made of the militia, exclusive of the volunteers, teamsters, and exempts?

In the first place, General Johnston, of the Confederate Army, and General Carson, of Frederick County, called out the residue of the militia *en masse.* They were discharged after a few days' service, with instructions to be ready at an hour's notice.

In the next place these generals drafted out of the militia in this county 600 men, out of which, in part, two regiments were formed (two regiments from this brigade being required). Subsequently the residue of the militia of the county was drafted under your last proclamation, although we had already furnished more than the 10 per cent., as will be perceived by the above statement. Under this last call some 900 men have been taken into the service, to the great detriment of their private interests, of their families, and the public. Could we be induced to believe that this is required for the attainment of the great object in view, we would not utter one word of complaint, but we do not so think.

3d. It may be replied that all the needed relief might be secured by making up the difference between the volunteers now in service and the quantum required by the proclamation in volunteers. This might be done, we presume, but for the fact that the militia officers (General Meem, &c.), we understand from good authority, deny the right of any

---

* See Johnston to Walker September 1, p. 826.

of the first two regiments drafted to volunteer, and insist that they have been regularly mustered into the service of the Confederate States. They also insist that those men recently drafted have no right to volunteer, and thus continue them all in service. They likewise insist that they are not subject in anywise to the governor of Virginia. If this be so, they constitute more than our quota, and the whole of the last draft should be permitted to return home, unless there is some overruling necessity requiring their presence in the field. If it is not the fact, then these officers should be imperatively required to adopt some mode by which the quota of our county may be furnished and the residue released.

As you are advised, there are only 443 slaves in this county over twelve years of age of both sexes, and only about 150 working negro men. The labor is performed in a great measure by those who are in the militia, and if they be continued in service at this critical time, when they should be employed in preparing the land for a fall crop, this vast productive agricultural region, instead of being the Egyptian granary whence our armies may be fed in the coming year, will scarcely support our own population in the aggregate, while many must be plunged into the most abject want and thrown upon the hands of the overseers of the poor. This, with the increased taxes called for by the State and Confederate Governments, will render our condition, to say the least, very undesirable.

This matter requires prompt and immediate attention, and we earnestly hope will receive it at your hands if the relief can be afforded by your excellency, and if not, by those who can. In this latter event we desire that you will present this paper to the proper authority, with such suggestions as you may deem proper under the circumstances.

All of which is most respectfully submitted.

JACOB LANTZ, *P. J. P.*

AUGUST 12, 1861.

At a court held for the county of Shenandoah on Monday, the 12th day of August, 1861, a memorial to the President of the Southern Confederacy and to the governor of Virginia respecting the volunteers and militia from this county was approved and ordered to be signed by the court, and copies to be transmitted to President Davis and Governor Letcher.

Test:

S. C. WILLIAMS, *C. S. C.*

The undersigned fully concur in the facts set forth in the foregoing memorial and approve its object, and most respectfully ask for it a favorable consideration.

S. C. WILLIAMS, *Clerk.*
JAS. G. TRAVIT,
Notary Public.
MOSES WALTON,
Attorney at Law.
MARK BIRD,
Attorney for Commonwealth.
WM. SMITH ARTHUR.

[Indorsement.]

EXECUTIVE DEPARTMENT, *August* 17, 1861.

The militia of this county were called into service by Brigadier-General Carson at the instance of General Johnston, and as they have been mustered into service I have no power to relieve them from duty. Under what authority the draft referred to was made I am not informed. The case is one of serious hardship, and I respectfully refer it to your excellency for such relief as you may think it just and proper to grant.

JOHN LETCHER.

[Inclosure B.]

RICHMOND, *August* 27, 1861.

Hon. L. P. WALKER, *Secretary of War:*

DEAR SIR: I am requested by some of the citizens of the valley counties to make a representation to you of the facts bearing upon the call of the militia in that region.

It is the most fertile part of Virginia for wheat and corn growing. It has no other staple of consequence. The call of the militia was at a time when the harvest was scarcely over, and the farmer left his crop standing in the field unhoused. No plow has been put into the ground for the fall seeding of wheat. See, then, the sacrifice which our people in that region are called on to make—to imperil the crop of the past year and to prevent the raising a crop for the coming year.

I know it is supposed the same rule of 10 per cent., being applicable elsewhere, must be applied to the valley, and with no worse results; but one fact will show the contrary: In Shenandoah County there is a white population of 12,800 and a total population of 13,800, showing only 1,000 blacks, free and slave. Ten per cent. of the whites makes a call of 1,280 for militia service drafted from the laborers, the tillers of the soil, and not leaving sufficient slaves at home to work while the master is abroad to fight.

Nansemond County, near Norfolk, has a total population of 13,700, (nearly the same as Shenandoah), of which 5,700 are white and 8,000 black, free and slave. The draft of 10 per cent. draws 570 whites, but leaves the negro to the farm labor.

This is an evil which calls for a remedy, if one can be had. Of the militia at Winchester, numbering, say, 5,000, perhaps one-half are unarmed. Might not furloughs be allowed, or a part be disbanded who are unarmed, upon call to be summoned again if needed, especially since report says the column of General Banks has fallen back from the valley towards Baltimore? If anything can be done for as true and patriotic a people as there are in the South, I appeal to you to do it. When I tell you that in Shenandoah County, which cast 2,500 votes for the secession ordinance and only 5 against it, there are only 700 slaves, I think I may vouch for the integrity of her people upon the great crisis of the South.

I am, with high respect, yours,

J. R. TUCKER.

Shenandoah has furnished about 950 volunteers. Could not enough of her militia be retained to make up her quota and release the residue on furlough? As it is now, she has largely more than her quota in the field, counting her volunteers and her militia.

J. R. TUCKER.

No. 25.] CAMP GAULEY, VA., *August* 29, 1861.

Brig. Gen. HENRY A. WISE:

SIR: Since our signal success over the enemy here and their dispersion and demoralization, I think you might now advantageously move towards Gauley, and take possession of the strong position at and about the Hawk's Nest. In all probability the enemy are likely to retire down the Kanawha, and you should be close at hand to annoy their retiring columns. You send me a report from C. F. Henningsen. Will you be good enough to state whether he is a commissioned officer, and, if so, what commission he holds, and the date of it?

I am, very respectfully, your obedient servant,

JOHN B. FLOYD,
Brigadier-General, Commanding Army of Kanawha.

RICHMOND, *August* 30, 1861.

General JOSEPH E. JOHNSTON,
Commanding Confederate Forces on the Potomac :

GENERAL : Since the communication to you from this Department was closed on yesterday, relating to the discharge of the militia from Shenandoah County on service at Winchester, the inclosed petition from officers of the Seventh Brigade and Third Division, Virginia Militia, in regard to the same subject, has been received from Governor Letcher. You will take it into consideration with the rest in forming your decision upon the case. *

Very respectfully, yours,

L. P. WALKER,
Secretary of War.

[Inclosure.]

WINCHESTER, *August* 25, 1861.

Governor LETCHER:

SIR : The officers of the four regiments from the Seventh Brigade, Virginia Militia, now stationed at this place, have requested me to forward to you the inclosed petition to the President of the Confederate States, and to solicit your aid and influence in its behalf. They have been informed that the power of relief has, in part, been transferred to the President, otherwise the prayer would have been addressed to your excellency; yet, notwithstanding the transfer, we are confident you will lend your aid and influence willingly and cheerfully in procuring the relief asked for, and which is due to a portion of the Confederacy than which none other is more loyal and true to its interests.

Very truly, yours, &c.,

G. W. MURPHY.

[Subinclosure.]

CAMP FAIR GROUNDS,
Near Winchester, Va., August 23, 1861.

Hon. JEFFERSON DAVIS, *President of the Confederate States :*

We, the undersigned, officers of the Seventh Brigade, Virginia Militia, would most respectfully beg leave to represent to you the condition of the men under our commands and the condition in which the great valley of Virginia must be placed unless relief can be rendered.

We desire, first, to say that no portion of Virginia has been more loyal to the South and her interest than the militia of this valley ; that we were among the first to send our volunteers to the field of battle ;

---

* See Walker to Johnston, August 29, p. 816, and Johnston to Walker, September 1, p. 826.

that we have as great a number of volunteers in the field now in proportion to the strength of our militia as any portion of the State; yet, notwithstanding this, the whole of the militia of this brigade have been called into service, and most of them have been here near two months. We fully appreciate the condition of our country, and are willing to make any sacrifice necessary to advance the interest of the South and to secure our independence, yet we would present to you a few facts.

The valley of Virginia is a wheat-growing country, in which slave labor is scarce; consequently the larger proportion of the labor must be performed by white men between the ages of eighteen and forty-five years. The time for seeding the wheat crop has arrived, and unless at least a considerable proportion of the men new here can be returned to their homes to attend to putting that crop in the ground we will be unable to raise supplies sufficient for our own subsistence.

In addition to this, we are here with not more than one-half of our men armed, and they armed with the most inferior guns, so that, if we were to be attacked, we would be compelled to make an inglorious retreat, and bring upon as brave men as can be found in any country the ridicule of the public.

In view of all these facts we regard it as our duty to the men under our commands, and especially to our country, that we should make to you a simple statement, being satisfied that you will render us the relief asked for, if consistent with the interest, prosperity, and happiness of our Confederacy, by permitting us for the present to return to our homes.

MANN SPITLER,
Colonel Second Regiment.
JAS. H. SIBERT,
Colonel Third Regiment.
E. SIPE,
Lieutenant-Colonel First Regiment.
THOMAS BUSWELL,
Lieutenant-Colonel Second Regiment.
J. A. HOTTEL,
Lieutenant-Colonel Third Regiment.
CULLIN W. FINTER,
Major Second Regiment.
JOHN H. NEWELL,
Major Third Regiment.
C. P. HORN,
Major Fourth Regiment, and others.

[Indorsement.]

AUGUST 27, 1861.

His Excellency the PRESIDENT:

Colonel Conn, of Shenandoah, is a most respectable and reliable gentleman, and wields great influence in his section of the State. He desires to consult you in regard to the disposition to be made of the militia now at Winchester. You will recollect that I sent you [August 17] a memorial from the county court of Shenandoah on this subject, with my indorsement thereon.* Any representation Colonel Conn will make to you may be implicitly relied upon for its accuracy.

JOHN LETCHER.

---

* See Walker to Johnston, August 29, p. 816.

No. 26.]   CAMP GAULEY, VA., *August* 31, 1861.
Brig. Gen. HENRY A. WISE:

SIR: The messenger who carries this note to you gives me information, which he will impart to you, to the effect that the enemy have
abandoned Gauley Bridge, and are now advancing upon me at this
point. If this information be correct, you should send me the strongest of your regiments to the top of the hill, near Gauley, with a good
battery, so as to be perfectly in reach of me in case of need, and you
should at once advance with the remainder of your command, and take
possession of the camp at the mouth of the Gauley. I must ask of you
also to send me two companies of efficient cavalry. Mine is in Greenbrier recruiting, and I am measurably without dragoon force. I have
but little doubt of their retreat, although I much doubt of their intention of coming this way. Still, lest it be true, all necessary precautions
should be taken to meet them, and to this end your regiment of infantry and a squadron of horse will probably be essential.

Very respectfully, your obedient servant,

JOHN B. FLOYD,
Brigadier-General, Commanding Army of Kanawha.

HEADQUARTERS OF WISE'S LEGION,
Dogwood Gap Camp, Va., August 31, 1861—10 p. m.
Brig. Gen. JOHN B. FLOYD, *Commanding, &c.:*

SIR: Your messenger, Mr. Carnifix, has just arrived, and is met by
Captain Caskie, just from Cotton Hill. From the latter we learn that
on Wednesday last the enemy were apparently moving up Gauley towards Twenty Mile Creek, but yesterday and to-day they have returned
numerously. Their tents had been struck, and are now erected again.
Certain it is that they have on this side retired from the Hawk's Nest
and Turkey Creek to Big Creek, and have left the heights above Rich
Creek, on the Gauley side of the mountain. I have this day, accordingly, moved up all of my available cavalry, and am preparing to move
up my artillery and infantry to-morrow. My regiments are reduced
one-half by the measles, my cavalry more than one-half in efficiency by
want of forage and horseshoeing and by the detachment of one troop
over New River, and my artillery one-third by the detachment re-enforcing your brigade. My whole available and efficient force here is less
than 1,800 men of all arms. If I send you, then, my best regiment, a
good battery of artillery, and two companies of efficient cavalry, there
will be left, for the defense of this road, or, rather, to execute your order
to take possession of the camp at the mouth of the Gauley, less than
1,100 men and but one piece of artillery. You have three of my pieces
of artillery, and I have but five left. If a good battery is taken away,
and one regiment, the best out of three (now reduced in numbers to
the complement of one and a half regiments), and also nearly all of my
efficient cavalry are detached, I shall not have force enough for defense,
much less to take possession of the camp at the mouth of the Gauley.
Five times my numbers cannot take that camp without any, or with
but one, piece of artillery, well fortified as it is, with nearly double the
number of pieces of our combined commands. The enemy are about
700 strong on this side of the mouth of the Gauley, with artillery in
position. To drive them first across Gauley, in the face of batteries
covering them, from the camp on the opposite side, and then to take

that camp with 1,100 troops (800 infantry only and 300 cavalry, which will be useless in the assault across a rapid river without a bridge and without a ferry for us and without artillery, against double my numbers, intrenched in a stronghold), will be wholly impracticable and desperate in the very attempt.

I therefore submit to you the reconsideration of these orders. My forces are too weak already for the execution of them. I submit this with the less hesitation, as I am informed beyond doubt that another regiment of your own brigade is advancing now, and will join you tomorrow evening probably. I will dispatch a messenger to hurry them on to you, and beg to be allowed to advance upon the enemy with my whole force, throwing one of my regiments across New River, and attacking them from Cotton Hill with a part of my artillery. I venture, respectfully, to submit these suggestions of what I deem the best plan of strengthening your position, by drawing the enemy back from an advance upon it.

In reply to another note received from you this morning, ordering me to advance upon the enemy with my whole force, and asking who Colonel Henningsen is, I have the honor to inform you, sir, that he is a distinguished commander, who is not in his first command, and has accepted, at my request, the colonelcy of one of my regiments; is the senior of infantry in my Legion; is in command of the post at Dogwood Gap, superintending the works for its defense, and is awaiting the commission for the office to which he has been recently appointed and which he has accepted; a gentleman and officer, whose reports are implicitly relied upon by his commanding general.

Very respectfully, your obedient servant,

HENRY A. WISE,
Brigadier-General.

No. 27.]   CAMP GAULEY, VA., *August* 31, 1861—12 noon.
General HENRY A. WISE:

SIR: I have received information, through scouts under command of Captain Corns, that the enemy in full force are advancing from Gauley Bridge in this direction. They are within 12 miles of this point. You will therefore send me without delay, upon receiving this, 1,000 of your infantry, your best battery, and one squadron of your horse.

Your obedient servant,

JOHN B. FLOYD,
Brigadier-General, Commanding, &c.

[Indorsement.]

Received by Brig. Gen. H. A. Wise on September 1, 1861, at 4.40 a. m.

VALLEY MOUNTAIN, VA., *August* 31, 1861.
General HENRY A. WISE,
Comdg. Wise's Legion, Dogwood Gap, West of Lewisburg, Va.:

GENERAL: I have just received and read with much interest your report of the 28th instant. The troops under your command deserve great commendation for the alacrity and cheerfulness they exhibited in the trying march they underwent to Gauley River and the promptitude with which they performed their duty. I regret the loss sustained by

Colonel Jenkins' cavalry, by apparently incautiously advancing into an ambuscade. The behavior of Captain Brock on the occasion was praiseworthy. Danger is so sharp that its frequent presence will inspire coolness and self-possession in the men, and ultimate benefit will result from it. Yet they ought not to be exposed unnecessarily. I am much gratified at General Floyd's success in dispersing and punishing the regiment of the enemy beyond the Gauley, and feel assured that by your united efforts you will be able to drive back to Ohio his whole force. A re-enforcement of two regiments (one from North Carolina and one from Georgia) is on the march to Lewisburg.

I have the honor to be, your obedient servant,

R. E. LEE,
General, Commanding.

Abstract from return of the Department of Fredericksburg, commanded by Brig. Gen. T. H. Holmes, August 31, 1861.

Station.	Present for duty.		Aggregate present and absent.
	Officers.	Men.	
BROOKE'S STATION.			
Camp Bee	25	411	617
Do	40	562	809
Camp Potomac	35	380	666
Camp Howe	31	465	882
Stafford Court-House	34	558	893
Camp Galloway	32	649	869
Mathias Point	11	102	185
Marlborough Point	41	730	1,105
Heathsville	20	315	351
Camp Bee	27	480	711
Camp Clifton	22	236	406
Lancaster County	6	94	101
Tappahannock	27	539	726
Camp Chopawamsic	3	44	72
Do	3	47	65
Dumfries	4	70	99
Camp Bee	3	79	121
Grand total	364	5,761	8,678

Abstract from a field return August 31, 1861, of the First Corps, Army of the Potomac, commanded by General Beauregard, Manassas, Va.

Troops.	Present for duty.		Total present.	Aggregate present.	Total present and absent.	Aggregate present and absent.
	Officers.	Men.				
General staff	15		15	15	15	15
Infantry	1,209	17,990	23,748	25,138	29,177	30,825
Cavalry	90	1,106	1,373	1,470	1,569	1,677
Artillery	48	923	1,044	1,093	1,146	1,200
Grand total	1,362	20,019	26,180	27,716	31,907	33,717

Organization of the First Corps, Army of the Potomac, commanded by General G. T. Beauregard, C. S. Army, headquarters Manassas, August [31 ?] 1861.

FIRST BRIGADE.

Brig. Gen. M. L. Bonham, commanding.

Second South Carolina.
Third South Carolina.
Seventh South Carolina.
Eighth South Carolina.

SECOND BRIGADE.

Brig. Gen. R. S. Ewell, commanding.

Fifth Alabama.
Sixth Alabama.
Eighteenth Alabama.
Twelfth Mississippi.

THIRD BRIGADE.

Brig. Gen. D. R. Jones, commanding.

Fourth South Carolina.
Fifth South Carolina.
Sixth South Carolina.
Ninth South Carolina.

FOURTH BRIGADE.

Brig. Gen. James Longstreet, commanding.

First Virginia.
Seventh Virginia.
Eleventh Virginia.
Seventeenth Virgina.

FIFTH BRIGADE.

Brig. Gen. Ph. St. Geo. Cocke, commanding.

Eighteenth Virginia.
Nineteenth Virginia.
Twenty-eighth Virginia.
Twenty-ninth Virginia.

SIXTH BRIGADE.

Brig. Gen. J. A. Early, commanding.

Fifth North Carolina.
Eleventh North Carolina.
—— North Carolina.
Twenty-fourth Virginia.

SEVENTH BRIGADE.

Col. N. G. Evans, commanding.

Seventh Mississippi.
Thirteenth Mississippi.
Seventeenth Mississippi.
Eighteenth Mississippi.

EIGHTH BRIGADE.

Col. J. G. Seymour, commanding.

First Special Battalion, Louisiana.
Sixth Regiment, Louisiana.
Seventh Regiment, Louisiana.
Eighth Regiment, Louisiana.
Ninth Regiment, Louisiana.

Abstract from return of the Third Division Virginia Militia, commanded by Brig. Gen. James H. Carson, for August, 1861.

Troops.	Present for duty.		Aggregate present.	Aggregate present and absent.
	Officers.	Men.		
SEVENTH BRIGADE.				
First Regiment Infantry	26	367	461	798
Second Regiment Infantry	29	423	661	985
Third Regiment Infantry	21	291	373	644
Fourth Regiment Infantry	31	331	450	770
SIXTEENTH BRIGADE.				
Thirty-first Regiment Infantry	27	115	148	732
Fifty-first Regiment Infantry	20	82	155	251
Eighty-ninth Regiment Infantry	13	67	88	230
One hundred and fourteenth Regiment Infantry	32	415	462	845
One hundred and twenty-second Regiment Infantry	13	38	85	233
Grand total	212	2,129	2,883	5,488

HEADQUARTERS,
Manassas, September 1, 1861.

Hon. L. P. WALKER, *Secretary of War:*

SIR: I have had the honor to receive your letters of the 29th and 30th of August in relation to the militia of the county of Shenandoah now in the service of the Confederate States and the papers inclosed with them.

Two matters are involved : What number of infantry the service requires in and near Winchester and what section should furnish it.

The first question should be answered by me; the second, I suggest, with all respect, should be submitted to the governor of Virginia or answered by the War Department.

While commanding in the valley of Virginia especially, I called into service about 2,500 militia. There were two considerations in fixing the number—the force required and that which the district ought to be called upon to furnish. I still think the force then called out sufficient. But whether it should be furnished by that or some other section of Virginia or of the Confederacy I have no means of forming an opinion. I have no means of ascertaining what percentage of its population any portion of the country may have sent into the field.

Permit me to suggest, therefore, the reduction of the militia force in the valley of the Shenandoah to the number of 2,500, and that the proper authorities of Virginia be requested to select the portion to be disbanded, and to direct such portion to deposit their arms in Winchester and return to their usual avocations.

With high respect, your obedient servant,
J. E. JOHNSTON,
General.

No. 28.]   CAMP GAULEY, VA., *September* 1, 1861.

Brig. Gen. HENRY A. WISE:

SIR: From more recent information I think it doubtful whether the movements of the enemy require at this time the union of your force with mine, as embraced in my last order to you late in the evening. You will therefore retain your forces in camp until further orders. Your explanation about Colonel Henningsen is sufficient, but in future you will require all officers under your command, when making reports to be sent to headquarters, to superadd their rank to their signatures.

I am, sir, very respectfully, your obedient servant,
JOHN B. FLOYD,
Brigadier-General, Commanding Army of the Kanawha.

RICHMOND, *September* 2, 1861.

General JOSEPH E. JOHNSTON,
Commanding Army of the Potomac, Manassas, Va.:

SIR: I am instructed by the President to inquire of you how the regiments of your entire command are organized into brigades, naming in each case the brigade and the regiments of each command ; also such regiments as are associated together but not under a brigadier, and any other regiments which may be serving separately. You are desired to state also the whole force of cavalry, how organized, where posted, and how commanded; also the whole force of artillery, how organized, where posted, and by whom commanded, designating batteries which are associated together, those which are serving separately, and such as form the armament of field works; and, further, designating such batteries or guns as were captured at the battle of Manassas and such as have been sent to your command since that battle.

This report is intended to embrace the whole force of the Army of the Potomac except the command of Brigadier-General Holmes.

Very respectfully, your obedient servant,

S. COOPER,
Adjutant and Inspector General.

RICHMOND, *September* 3, 1861.

General JOSEPH E. JOHNSTON, *Commanding, &c., Manassas, Va.:*

GENERAL : The President desires that you will order Brigadier-General Trimble to Evansport, on the Potomac, to command the battery and troops at that point.

I am, sir, respectfully, &c.,

S. COOPER,
Adjutant and Inspector General.

RICHMOND, *September* 4, 1861.

Hon. L. P. WALKER, *Secretary of War:*

DEAR SIR: According to your suggestion this morning I beg leave to present in writing one or two considerations connected with the military arrests made and being made in the region of the lower valley of Virginia along the Potomac border.

A number of such cases were submitted to my examination by General Johnston while in command at Winchester, and the principle I acted upon was to arrest no one, and to prosecute no one further who had been arrested, when turned over to me, for holding merely in the abstract disloyal opinions, nor even where they expressed them conscientiously and in a general way, but to seize only such as were actively engaged against us in some mode giving aid and comfort to the enemy.

The effect of this policy has been, as I am fully satisfied, to improve greatly the popular sentiment and to strengthen our cause in that part of Virginia where I regret to say it was much needed. Recently, as I have reason to believe, several arrests have been made by the military upon mere general suspicion of the party holding (and perhaps expressing in a general way merely) unsound opinions as to the great issue between us and the North, and I am satisfied evil consequences will result from it. Gentlemen of high character and social position, I understand, are under arrest now at Winchester, without any opportunity or means whatever afforded them of having their cases examined and determined. Others also of like character, I have reason to believe, will soon be taken into custody.

Without troubling you, therefore, further in detail with the reasons which induce me to believe these arrests will be productive of much mischief, I beg leave to suggest that something in the way of a commission, made in part at least of civilians of intelligence and undoubted loyalty, be constituted, to examine into these cases promptly, and make proper disposition of them, by either remitting them to the civil authorities, where prosecutions can be maintained, or turning them over to the proper higher military authorities, or in proper cases discharging them from custody. The law of Virginia is very defective on this subject, and in these border counties, with the enemy around them, it is quite out of the question to pursue the ordinary slow course of prosecuting such cases.

A reply, if addressed to Charlestown, Jefferson County, Virginia, will reach me, though it may not be important that I should have one if proper instructions be given to the military authorities.

Your obedient servant,

ANDREW HUNTER.

HEADQUARTERS DEPARTMENT OF FREDERICKSBURG,
Brooke's Station, September 4, 1861.
General S. COOPER,
Adjutant and Inspector General C. S. Army:

GENERAL : In compliance with the instructions of the Secretary of War I have the honor to report, concerning the fortifications of Grey's Point, that I have no reason to suppose the enemy has or has had any intention of establishing himself there for any purpose, neither do I see any benefit he could derive from so doing.

With regard to the construction of a battery there by ourselves, I think Mr. Montague's calculations are erroneous : first, as to its effect to close the river ; and, second, as to the number of men necessary to defend it. The distance across the channel (1½ miles) is too great for the effective fire of any but rifled guns even in the daytime, while a whole fleet might pass without molestation by night. Should the enemy determine to attack the battery at all, the designated force would be but a tithe of what would be required to defend it, and situated as it is, within four or five hours of Fortress Monroe, with no greater garrison than that suggested, we might soon hear of another Hatteras. If I could detach two regiments from here I would, for the convenience of the people on the river, construct a battery at Grey's Point and another at Cherry Point, opposite ; but I have not now a single soldier more than I think will be required to defend the batteries at Aquia Creek and those which are to be constructed at Evansport.

I am, general, very respectfully, your obedient servant,

TH. H. HOLMES,
Brigadier-General, Commanding Department.

RICHMOND, *September* 4, 1861.
General R. E. LEE, *Staunton, Va.:*

GENERAL : Your several communications were duly submitted to the President, who has read them with much satisfaction and fully approves of all you have done.* He has not ceased to feel an anxious desire for your return to this city to resume your former duties, even while satisfied of the importance of your presence in Western Virginia so long as

---

*No reports found.

might be necessary to carry out the ends set forth in your communications. Whenever, in your judgment, circumstances will justify it, you will consider yourself authorized to return.

I am, sir, respectfully, your obedient servant,

S. COOPER,
Adjutant and Inspector General.

No. 30.]   NEAR HAWK'S NEST, VA., *September* 4, 1861.

Brigadier-General FLOYD, *Commanding, &c.:*

Since writing by Colonel Croghan to-day,* I am urged (by the appearance of the enemy and intelligence of their forces, in order to defend Miller's Ferry and Liken's Mill, which I am determined to hold) to ask that you will re-enforce me by sending to me the whole or a part of Colonel Tompkins' regiment, with him in command, and to return my corps of artillery also. We want two pieces for Cotton Hill, and I can send an additional cavalry force to Loop Creek. I am assured that Colonel Tompkins will not object to this order. Lieutenant Witcher informs me that my attack upon them yesterday drew nearly all their forces from Gauley Bridge.

Respectfully, yours,

HENRY A. WISE,
Brigadier-General.

RICHMOND, VA., *September* 5, 1861.

General JOSEPH E. JOHNSTON:

MY DEAR GENERAL: Yours of the 3d instant† was delivered by Mr. Washington, who promised to call to-day for an answer. I am still weak, and seldom attempt to write; even to you it is necessary to be brief. The view in relation to the number of guns necessary at Evansport was communicated to the Chief of Ordnance, in order that he might, when practicable, furnish them. I do not know whether the movements of troops by the enemy indicates operations from the base, or fear of an attack by us upon that point, or preparation for a movement from Fort Monroe as a base. You have again been deceived as to our forces here. We never have had anything near to 20,000 men, and have now but little over one-fourth of that number. General Walker [who] came here sick, has since gone up to join you. Van Dorn has not been here, and, so far as informed, has not yet left Texas. When relieved he will come here, unless otherwise directed. Magruder applies for 8,000 troops to check projected operations of General Wool in the Peninsula. Wise is dissatisfied with General Floyd, and seeks to be withdrawn. Without his command Floyd cannot hold the valley of Kanawha. We have been disappointed in our efforts to get arms. Had you arms to supply the 10,000 men you want they could soon be had.

Lee is still in the mountains of Virginia. The rains have retarded his march, or I think he would have beaten the enemy in that quarter. Had we the means to move on Beverly from Winchester, it might result in the capture of Rosecrans and the repossession of Western Virginia. To permit the enemy to gain a success over any portion of the

---

*Report of skirmish near Hawk's Nest. See p. 122.
†Not found.

Army of the Potomac would be a sad disaster, and I have done all that was possible to strengthen you since the date of your glorious victory. The enemy has grown weaker in numbers and far weaker in the character of their troops, so that I have felt it remained with us to decide whether another battle should soon be fought or not. Your remark indicates a different opinion.

The organization of the army into divisions would be advantageous if you have junior brigadiers of great merit and senior brigadiers unfit to command. As to a commander-in-chief, it is provided by the rule applying to troops who happen to join and do duty together.

In relation to the command of Brigadier-General Holmes I will only say that it is in easy communication with this place by railroad and telegraph, but has little and tedious connection with Manassas; wherefore it has been kept in direct correspondence with Richmond.

The battery above Aquia Creek was located with reference to width of channel of river and defensibility against attack from Alexandria. The lower side of the Quantico commands the upper. The upper side of the Occoquan is reported to command the lower. The long and circuitous march from Alexandria to Quantico would enable you to strike the column in the flank and reverse. The direct and short march to Occoquan offers no such advantage. If we drive off the vessels from that part of the Potomac, the Marylanders can come safely to us and we may cross to that part of Maryland where our friends are to be found.

Every effort shall be made to furnish the howitzers you want. Colonel Pendleton will give you details. I wish I could send additional force to occupy Loudoun, but my means are short of the wants of each division of the wide frontier I am laboring to protect. One ship load of small-arms would enable me to answer all demands, but vainly have I hoped and waited. I have just heard that General A. S. Johnston is here. May God protect and guide you.

Your friend,

JEFFERSON DAVIS,

WAR DEPARTMENT,
Richmond, September 6, 1861.

General JOSEPH E. JOHNSTON,
Commanding Confederate Forces on the Potomac:

MY DEAR GENERAL: I wish, unofficially, to say that the inclosed copy of a letter of Mr. Vice-President Stephens reveals a case similar to several others that have been brought before me, and which I have been compelled to regard as exceptional to the general rule established by you, that no furlough shall be granted at this time in the Army of the Potomac. You are doubtless aware that every rule, to be perfect, must admit of exceptions, like the case presented, that appeal to the higher and holier principles of humanity, the preservation of which the rule itself acknowledges and is intended to secure. I fully appreciate the necessities of your position regarding the orders you have issued in regard to furloughs and their rigid enforcement; but I respectfully suggest that a case may occasionally arise in itself constituting the essence of the rule.

I have the honor to be, very respectfully, your obedient servant,

L. P. WALKER.

No. 31.]   NEAR HAWK'S NEST, VA., *September* 6, 1861.
Brig. Gen. JOHN B. FLOYD, *Commanding, &c.:*

GENERAL: Last night and this morning my scouts report lights appearing and disappearing, as if shed from dark lanterns, all along the ridges north of my lines, and also blue lights, evidently signaling with those on the side from the Cotton Hill. They have beaten innumerable and indescribable paths in every direction from Shade Creek, just this side of Piggot's Mill, with a view to fall on my rear, and this compels me to extend my posts beyond my effective strength, covering from Dogwood Gap to the Hawk's Nest now, in order to guard my own rear and the approach to Carnifix Ferry. The enemy came up in large re-enforcements the other day from Gauley, with several additional pieces of artillery, and are now at least 1,800 strong. My whole available force here, of all arms, is not over 1,200 men, 300 of whom are cavalry, and not effective, at this point. We are obliged to leave two pieces of artillery at Dogwood, and require at least six pieces here, and we have but three. I beg you to return to me my corps of artillery, with their three pieces, and to re-enforce me with Colonel Tompkins' regiment, less, I believe, than 400 men. I ask this the more unhesitatingly as the Georgia and North Carolina regiments (two full ones) are on the march to you, and will be with you in a few days. And here permit me to add that, by strengthening me here, I can move so as to make your approach down the Gauley towards the enemy perfectly easy. On the 3d instant (when the double attack here and on Cotton Hill was made) he drew a large proportion of his forces from the bridge. I think they will attack me to-night or to-morrow, before they return. I have concerted signals to-day with Generals Chapman and Beckley. Captain Fitzhugh has just left me, on the rumor of a fight at Cotton Hill at 5 o'clock yesterday evening, and the rumor is we have got the cover of Montgomery's Ferry. I will defend Miller's to the last, and can do it certainly if re-enforced. You can draw the enemy back to the bridge if you will move to the mouth of Rich Creek.

Very respectfully,

HENRY A. WISE,
Brigadier-General.

CAMP GAULEY, VA., *September* 6, 1861.
Brig. Gen. HENRY A. WISE:

SIR: I send over this morning, at your request, the Twenty-second Regiment (Colonel Tompkins'), and also that section of your battery heretofore sent me under command of Lieutenant Hart. You will take care not to make any movement which will require the presence for any length of time over a very few days of more troops than your own Legion. I cannot spare any men from this column, and it is very probable your command will be necessarily moved on this line. This will only be done in case of absolute necessity. In the mean time you will with all convenient dispatch send two pieces of artillery across the river to General Chapman, to accompany his column on its march down the left bank of Kanawha. Beyond holding your position at Hawk's Nest, or thereabouts, so as to secure the communication you had already established across New River by the ferries, you had better not attempt anything beyond annoyance against the enemy. That is not the direction from which he can be most successfully attacked. Colonel

Tompkins will not remain longer than until I am ready for a forward movement, which I hope to be very shortly.

Very respectfully, your obedient servant,

JOHN B. FLOYD,
Brigadier-General, Commanding Army of the Kanawha.

No. 32.]   CAMP NEAR HAWK'S NEST, VA., *September* 6, 1861.

Brig. Gen. JOHN B. FLOYD, *Commanding, &c.:*

SIR: I am obliged for the re-enforcements you have sent to me, and especially by the return of the section of my artillery, which is much needed in the position I occupy on this road. Colonel Tompkins' regiment will not be removed at all from this road. Whenever the two pieces of my artillery can be spared from this camp I will order them, under a detachment of my own command, as you direct. The militia of General Chapman are not trained and may lose the pieces. If a piece is required anywhere, it is needed at Cotton Hill.

Very respectfully, your obedient servant,

HENRY A. WISE,
Brigadier-General.

No. 33.]   CAMP NEAR HAWK'S NEST, VA., *September* 6, 1861.

Brig. Gen. JOHN B. FLOYD, *Commanding, &c.:*

SIR: I now send orders to Capt. G. Hart, in command of the men and pieces of artillery you have ordered to be returned to my Legion. I have ordered the pieces belonging to volunteers of the States attached to your command, left at the White Sulphur, to be sent on, and they shall be sent over to you as soon as they arrive. The two you had and these two, with your own battery, will leave no necessity, I hope, for my guns, and if I am to send two of my pieces to co-operate with General Chapman, the Legion will be without guns enough.

Very respectfully,

HENRY A. WISE,
Brigadier-General.

RICHMOND, *September* 7, 1861.

Lieut. Col. J. GORGAS, *Chief of Ordnance:*

SIR: It has come to my knowledge through an official source that the million of cartridges which reached Camp Pickens, at Manassas, a few days since, are lying in piles on the ground, exposed to the rain, and must be damaged. The Quartermaster's Department is responsible for transportation and storage, but I call your attention to the fact stated, and suggest, if it be not your custom, that the ordnance officer at Manassas be notified in advance, so long as there is insufficient storage, of intended transmissions of ammunition for the Army, so that similar casualties and unmerited censure may be avoided as far as possible.*

Respectfully,

L. P. WALKER,
Secretary of War.

---

*Answer, if any, not found.

RICHMOND, *September* 7, 1861.

Lieut. Col. A. C. MYERS,
    Acting Quartermaster-General, C. S. Army:

SIR: I have received from an official source information that the million of cartridges which reached Manassas a few days ago from Richmond are lying in piles on the ground, exposed to the rain, and must be damaged. If sent from Richmond without notice to the quartermaster at Manassas to provide sheds, the blame is in Richmond. If this notice was given, the quartermaster at Manassas is to blame. Every one knows that the deficiency in store-houses at Manassas has existed from the time the army arrived, and this defect should have been remedied long ago. Quartermaster's stores of all kinds lie out in the rain for weeks. I have no patience while powder, &c., is exposed to damage and our plans exposed to failure by want of ordinary management. I do not mean to censure any one, for I know none of the heads of the department; but these facts should be made known in Richmond, and prompt steps taken to remove the evils. I regret to trouble you, and only do so in hopes that some good may be the result. It is only necessary for me to add that the subject demands immediate attention and the evils complained of prompt remedy.*

Respectfully,

L. P. WALKER,
Secretary of War.

RICHMOND, *September* 7, 1861.

Colonel NORTHROP, *Commissary-General Subsistence:*

SIR: In a communication received to-day there appears the following suggestive paragraph in reference to the subsistence of the army at Manassas and on the Potomac:

It is said to be impossible to provide rations ahead for the troops. So it may be if everything comes from Richmond; but if purchases are made in the valley of Virginia, such as flour, corn, oats, bacon, and beef, it is certainly practicable to accumulate any quantity, as two railroads would be in requisition instead of one. Besides, flour can be bought in the valley of Virginia, at the end of Manassas Railroad, one dollar per barrel cheaper than in Richmond, while the cost of transportation would be only one-half that from Richmond.

This communication comes from a source entitling it to consideration.

Respectfully,

L. P. WALKER,
Secretary of War.

RICHMOND, VA., *September* 8, 1861.

General JOSEPH E. JOHNSTON:

MY DEAR GENERAL: I have duly received and considered the letter of General Beauregard of the 6th instant, addressed to you, and your reply of the same date.† The first and controlling point in the case is the occupation of a line in close proximity to the enemy's intrenchments; and on this I am not sufficiently informed to have a decided opinion. If the purpose be to occupy the attention of the enemy by creating alarm of an attack until the battery at Evansport has been completed, the measure can have little permanence and no material effect

---

* Answer, if any, not found.   † Not found.

on your general plan of operations. The purpose not being stated that has occurred to me as the most probable, because I take it for granted that you do not contemplate, with your present means, to attempt regular approaches on the enemy's works; and, from inspection of the map, suppose that, either to prevent a movement by land across the Occoquan and Quantico to attack our position at Evansport or to move your forces to cross the Potomac, you would equally prefer to make your base farther to rear. If, however, you should wait for an attack, still less can it be doubted that you would gain by removing the battle-field as far from the enemy's intrenchment as other considerations may permit. We cannot afford to divide our forces unless and until we have two armies able to contend with the enemy's forces at Washington. Two lines of operation are always hazardous. I repeat that we cannot afford to fight without a reasonable assurance of victory or a necessity so imperious as to overrule our general policy. We have no second line of defense, and cannot now provide one. The cause of the Confederacy is staked upon your army, and the natural impatience of the soldier must be curbed by the devotion of the patriot. I have felt and feel that time brings many advantages to the enemy, and wish we could strike him in his present condition; but it has seemed to me involved in too much probability of failure to render the movement proper with our present means. Had I the requisite arms the argument would soon be changed. Missouri and Kentucky demand our attention, and the Southern coast needs additional defense. It is true that a successful advance across the Potomac would relieve other places; but, if not successful, ruin would befall us.

I had hoped to have seen you before this date. I wish to confer with you and General Beauregard, and, as my health is rapidly improving, expect to be able to do so at no distant day.

General A. S. Johnston will leave very soon for Tennessee and Arkansas, to command on that frontier.

Ever, truly, your friend,

JEFFERSON DAVIS.

———

HEADQUARTERS,
Manassas, September 9, 1861.

Hon. L. P. WALKER, *Secretary of War:*

SIR: I have just had the honor to receive your letter of the 6th instant, inclosed with a note from the Vice-President to you.

After a careful perusal of your letter I am uncertain whether it is intended to explain your motives for granting the leave of absence asked for by the Vice-President for Captain Lamar, or instructions for my guidance, made unofficially out of delicacy to me. May I beg to be informed.

Most respectfully, your obedient servant,

J. E. JOHNSTON,
General.

———

RICHMOND, *September 9, 1861.*

Brig. Gen. T. H. HOLMES,
Commanding, &c., Brooke's Station, Va.:

GENERAL: It was not designed in sending General Trimble to the command of the batteries and troops at Evansport to relieve you from the charge and responsibilities of your command, but rather to assign a competent officer of rank to have the direction there. This will be explained in a communication to General Johnston, lest he may be led into error in respect to the extent of your command. I inclose herewith a letter of General Johnston, and request that you will fill so far as it is possible the requisition contained therein, there being at Norfolk no guns, carriages, or projectiles to meet these wants.

Very respectfully, your obedient servant,

S. COOPER,
Adjutant and Inspector General.

[Inclosure.]

HEADQUARTERS,
Manassas, Va., September 7, 1861.

General HUGER, C. S. A.:

GENERAL: I have just been informed by General Trimble that you have many spare heavy guns, for which there are barbette carriages. Such guns are required for works which have been commenced on the Potomac. I have therefore written to the Secretary of War, asking that you be authorized to send to Evansport, say, twelve 32-pounders (three or four rifled), two 8-inch sea-coast howitzers, two portable furnaces for heating shot, to be sent in the manner suggested by General Trimble.

I have asked you by telegraph to send, if you can, the negroes mentioned in General Trimble's postscript.

Most respectfully, your obedient servant,

J. E. JOHNSTON,
General.

RICHMOND, *September* 9, 1861.

General JOSEPH E. JOHNSTON, *Commanding, &c., Manassas, Va.:*

GENERAL: In reply to yours of 7th instant,* in relation to heavy guns for Evansport, upon inquiry I find there are no heavy rifled guns at Norfolk; no projectiles or carriages. General Holmes has been advised to send up all the guns he can possibly spare to fill the wants of Evansport. Eight guns of heaviest caliber, including the rifled gun taken at Manassas, will have arrived at Evansport this evening, and three 32-pounders, one rifled, will be there within three days. In the assignment of General Trimble to the command at Evansport it was not contemplated to detach this force from General Holmes' command, who has been advised to that effect.

I am, sir, respectfully, &c.,

S. COOPER,
Adjutant and Inspector General.

RICHMOND, *September* 9, 1861.

Hon. L. P. WALKER, *Secretary of War:*

SIR: Your letter of the 7th instant has been received, furnishing me with the following extract:

It is said to be impossible to provide rations ahead for the troops. So it may be if everything comes from Richmond, but if purchases are made in the valley of Virginia, such as flour, corn, oats, bacon, and beef, it is certainly practicable to accumulate any quantity, as two railroads would be in requisition instead of one. Besides, flour can be bought in the valley of Virginia, at the end of the Manassas Railroad, one dollar per barrel cheaper than in Richmond, while the cost of transportation would be only one-half that from Richmond.

---

* Inclosure to Cooper to Holmes, September 9, p 835.

Some weeks ago the President sent to this Department, for me to read and remark on, several reports relating to the subsistence of the Army of the Potomac. The above extract expresses the substance of a part of those reports, and implies similar censure, while it may be only an outside attempt to make me abandon the principles I have fixed upon to supply the army. It evinces the readiness of the writer to criticise the operations of this department without being acquainted with the facts or the plans on which they are based. My replies to the President were placed by him in your hands. They cover all that may be inferred from this paper and explode it. I therefore shall not reply further than to request you to reperuse those papers. I have studied the flour question, and resisted much outside pressure after I arrived here, determining not to buy until the market opened, and then to fix prices on the new crop, as I was the only purchaser in the field. By firmness I held out to the last barrel, and have made ruling contracts in Richmond, Fredericksburg, and Lynchburg.

I will be glad if your correspondent will come forward and accept this proposition, viz: If flour of the same actual (but not inspected) quality can be bought at the end of the Manassas Gap Railroad at $4.25 per barrel, and laid down at Manassas at that price for thirty-three cents freight, which is the substance of the proposition stated in the figures to which my contract in Richmond will bring it, I will take it with pleasure, contracting with the party to furnish the whole Army of the Potomac. No such offer has been made to me from any source. Furthermore, I will contract to receive all the bacon he can deliver to Major Blair for two cents more than that I lately furnished the Army of the Potomac from this city.

I add that Major Blair, who has authority to purchase flour to any extent on the principles of this department, which are admitted by the entire community and the millers to be correct (while objecting to the rule), is now offering to the people of the valley forty-two cents more per barrel than your reliable correspondent says they are willing to take.

I am, very respectfully, your obedient servant,

L. B. NORTHROP,
Commissary-General of Subsistence.

CAMP NEAR HAWK'S NEST, VA.,
September 9, 1861—1.15 p. m.

Brigadier-General FLOYD, *Commanding, &c.:*

SIR : At 8.30 a. m. this morning I received your two notes, the one dated September 8, and the other September 9, 1861, at 1 a. m. The latter date and notation of the hour is obviously a mistake.

I regret exceedingly that any (if it shall be found that any) officer of my Legion should have seized upon a rifled brass 6 pounder or upon anything else belonging to your brigade, at Jackson's River, or anywhere else; and I equally regret that an order was issued for his arrest by you without affording me the opportunity of correcting what may, and, I think will, turn out to be a mistake, upon the one side or the other, of the question to which brigade the gun belongs. For some time past I, too, received notice of a gun for my brigade, forwarded from Richmond, and have been in daily expectation of receiving it, to complete a battery for Captain Roemer's company of artillery, and he had orders to take charge of all artillery pieces which might be sent to my brigade arriving at Jackson's River. He has made no report to me, and I am not informed that he has taken or received any gun, but it is very probable that, finding a gun at Jackson's River, he has brought it on to the White Sulphur, supposing it the one intended for his company. If intended for your brigade, it is obvious that no injury has been done to your command by bringing it on its way to the White Sulphur, especially as you have been anxiously awaiting its arrival at your camp, and I have forwarded orders at once to deliver it up to your officer in charge. It was probably a mere mistake, by which, too, the gun was considerably forwarded on its way to you, and no harm, for the same reason, was done, even if the person made no mistake, and knew the gun was intended for you, and not for the Legion. And, if it is intended for the Legion, then the officer understood the matter correctly, and he did but execute orders in forwarding the gun on its way to me by taking it to the White Sulphur.

In any event, sir, permit me to say that I cannot consent that the order to arrest my officer, issued by you at Carnifix Ferry, shall be executed upon him at the White Sulphur under the circumstances of this case. First, because the White Sulphur is not a place within the bounds of your command, except so far as you may order persons belonging to your brigade. Those belonging to my brigade there are subject only to my orders or those of General Lee. Second, because the complaint for arresting an officer of my immediate and independent command, should have been made to me, and the proper orders should have been passed through me, to have afforded opportunity for inquiry of the officer complained of. Third, because the alleged offense has not been inquired into at all, and is believed to be a mere mistake, doing no harm, at least, if not furthering your wishes, and founded on a zeal to do duty and obey orders. Fourth, because the gun is just as probably intended for the Legion as for your batteries.

If, then, it turns out that my officer has taken a gun to the White Sulphur from Jackson's River, he ought not to be arrested by your orders, both for want of validity and of justice, and the order to that end will be resisted in my command. I therefore (if it shall turn out that this offense has been committed by any officer belonging to my Legion) will, as long as your order for arrest is pending, most respectfully decline to furnish you with a list of my officers and the dates of their commissions, that you may select from among them such names as you would like to be placed upon the court-martial. It will be time enough to do what is legitimate and proper to be done when it is no longer hypothetical whether it will turn out or not that any offense has been committed by anybody, and, if by anybody, whether committed by any officer belonging to my Legion.

I am, very respectfully, your obedient servant,

HENRY A. WISE,
Brigadier-General.

No. 35.]   HEADQUARTERS ARMY OF THE KANAWHA,
Camp Gauley, Va., September 9, 1861—1 a. m.
(Received 8.45 a. m.)

General HENRY A. WISE:

SIR: The enemy are beyond doubt advancing from Sutton. They are reported by the scouts of Colonel McCausland (who, with the regiment, is stationed in Summersville) to be within 12 miles of that place, and in full force, 6,000 strong. My strength, including the regiment of Colonel McCausland, does not exceed 1,600 men. My own scouts returned yesterday with the information, which may be relied on, that there are 1,000 of the enemy at the mouth of Twenty Mile Creek. This would seem to indicate a junction of the forces under Cox with those marching from Sutton. It is highly important that this should be prevented if possible. For me to effect this, it is necessary that I should be strengthened by all the re-enforcements that can be sent me. You will then return me without delay the regiment of Colonel Tompkins, and at the same time send me one of your own regiments. With the remainder of your force you can maintain your position. Should you, however, need any addition to your force, you can draw re-enforcements from the command of General Chapman.

Very respectfully, your obedient servant,

JOHN B. FLOYD,
Brigadier-General, Commanding, &c.

[Indorsement.]

MEMORANDUM.—A verbal message was delivered along with the second dispatch (No. 35) at 2.15 a. m. by J. A. Totten, provost-marshal, as follows: "The enemy are in Webster, about 2,500 strong. Their object seems to be to unite with the column advancing from Braxton. General Floyd wishes to know at what point he can find the re-enforcements he sends for and at what hour he may expect them." Requires immediate return of the messenger. Messenger further reports that at 5 o'clock 4,000 or 5,000 were at the foot of Powell's Mountain, on this side. At the time of messenger's leaving (about 2 at night) they were 4 or 5 miles distant above Summersville; 2,500 were in Webster, about 50 miles distant, advancing.

CAMP NEAR HAWK'S NEST,
September 9, 1861—4 p. m.

General JOHN B. FLOYD, *Commanding, &c.:*

SIR : In obedience to your orders of yesterday, received at 8.30 o'clock a. m. to-day (though dated September 9, 1861, 1 o'clock a. m.), I have passed them to Colonel Tompkins, and he is on his march to join you at Carnifix Ferry. As to sending you one of the regiments of the Legion, I find it impossible to do so without endangering the safety of my command. I am now in front of the enemy, numbering from 2,000 to 3,000 men, and have three regiments, reduced by two companies from each left at Dogwood Gap, necessarily required there, and by measles, to not more than 300 effective men each, and to a corps of artillery, numbering about 150, making in all 1,050 efficient forces, without a breastwork. It is very hazardous to remain where I am with this force, and if one-third of it be called to re-enforce you at Carnifix, I shall have to fall back again to Dogwood Gap, lose all I gained by driving the enemy to Big Creek, and beyond all quick intelligence and easy communication with Generals Chapman and Beckley by Miller's Ferry, and all the advantages of a first-class mill to grind the meal and flour for my men, where both are difficult and costly to be obtained. There is not half force enough now for the defense of this road, and if one-third be taken away, the whole had better be retired. I cannot maintain my position with the remainder of my force, much less annoy the enemy, as you have instructed me. I now need re-enforcement, and cannot draw a man from the command of General Chapman, for he now is calling urgently for re-enforcements from me, and especially to mount artillery on Cotton Hill, and to defend Boone and Cabell Counties, and to penetrate the valley of the Lower Kanawha.

My cavalry, too, is of no use here, for the reason that forage cannot be obtained for more than two companies required for vedettes; and I have been compelled to send five troops, about 250 horse, to Coal River and the Loop for subsistence and better service than they can render here without half enough food.

I beg you, therefore, to relieve me from the order to send you one of my fragments of regiments, and I ask this the more unhesitatingly, because I am reliably informed you have a large re-enforcement advancing on the way to join you, and I am sure that with its aid you can maintain your strong and intrenched position against the odds likely to attack you. For these reasons I feel confident that you will justify me in awaiting further orders and the removal of the immediate pressure of the enemy.

Further, I beg you to order me to attract the enemy from Gauley Bridge, and from advancing against you thence, by promptly proceeding to penetrate the Kanawha Valley down Loop Creek or Coal River with my whole Legion. In this way I am sure, sir, I can re-enforce you without endangering my command; and this consideration alone makes me venture diffidently to ask for the order, without pretending to interfere with the plans of your own judgment.

Very respectfully, your obedient servant,
HENRY A. WISE,
Brigadier-General.

————

CAMP NEAR HAWK'S NEST, VA.,
September 9, 1861—10 a. m.
General R. E. LEE, *Commanding, &c.:*

GENERAL: Again I am harassed with orders which I find it difficult, if not impracticable, to comply with. After attacking the enemy on the 3d instant, he, as well as I, fell back a short distance to better positions. We are now about 3 miles apart, and he is re-enforced to the number of about 3,000 men. I am reduced in effective force to about 1,000 infantry and artillery. My cavalry is useless here among steep hills and for want of forage. In this state I called for re-enforcements from General Floyd. The day before yesterday he sent to me Colonel Tompkins' regiment of the State volunteers. This morning he announces the enemy approaching him from Sutton, as I expected, 6,000 strong, with the apprehensions of 1,000 from the opposite direction at Twenty Mile. This I do not credit; but he orders Colonel Tompkins immediately back, and also one of my regiments to be sent to him. I have issued the order to Colonel Tompkins, but must decline sending one of my regiments, or give up Miller's Ferry and Liken's Mill, and perhaps Dogwood Gap.

Again, some time ago my command had notice of a piece of ordnance forwarded for its service. I left an artillery officer (Captain Roemer) at White Sulphur, to take charge of three pieces there, and to forward on to that place the piece or pieces expected from Richmond. Now, it seems, General Floyd expected four pieces also and several coming to Jackson's River, and my officer, innocently supposing one of them to be the one intended for the Legion, took it to the White Sulphur. Thereupon General Floyd notifies me that he·has sent an officer to arrest him, and calls upon me for the names of commissioned officers of my command to form a court-martial to try him. I shall resist this order, firstly, because the White Sulphur is not a place within the bounds of his command, being subject alone to your orders; secondly, because he (General Floyd) has no right to arrest an officer of my Legion at the White Sulphur by an order issued by him at Carnifix, without passing the order through me and affording opportunity for inquiry into the cause by me; thirdly, because the alleged offense has not been inquired into at all, and is believed to be a mistake, founded on a desire to do duty promptly and to place the guns in service; and, fourthly, because the gun is just as probably belonging to my command as to General Floyd's. For these reasons I shall dispatch counter orders to those of General Floyd as to the arrest. As to the gun, I shall order it to be delivered to General Floyd or his command if his, and to be brought to me if intended for the Legion. I state these matters in order that you may interpose your authority in good season, deeply regretting to be compelled to trouble you with these annoyances of mine so repeatedly.

I am, with the highest respect, your obedient servant,

HENRY A. WISE,
Brigadier-General.

P. S.—Since writing the above Colonel Tompkins has shown to me the inclosed letter, and begs me to add that he could not enter into particulars, for want of time, on the eve of his march; but to say that you may be assured that there is the most disheartening discontent among men and officers with the orders of General Floyd. It extends so far as to threaten both his and my commands, and we concur in the earnest wish and prayer to be separated at once from General Floyd's command, and to have his regiment incorporated into my Legion. By sickness and other causes we are both reduced to one-half our original numbers. General Floyd now has, and has coming very near to him, first, his force with which he arrived at White Sulphur, 1,200; McCausland's State volunteers, 400; another regiment of his brigade, 400; two full regiments, nearly here, from Georgia and North Carolina, 1,600; Generals Chapman's and Beckley's militia, 2,000. In all, besides Tompkins' and mine, 5,600. The Legion has, for present service, effective infantry, 1,200; artillery, 250; cavalry, 350; and Tompkins has about 400. Total, 2,200.

Cavalry is of no use here. Tompkins is now ordered away, and I have but 1,800 men to guard Dogwood Gap and four other principal points, especially the Hawk's Nest, Miller's Ferry, Liken's Mill, and the Saturday road. If I send a regiment to re-enforce Carnifix, I must fall back and lose the quick communication with Chapman and Beckley, while General Floyd is impregnably intrenched with a force of over 4,000 men. This, too, is required when by his falling back this side of Gauley 250 men would defend Carnifix against thousands.

Colonel Tompkins' men are loyal and true, and from the valley, and if we are ordered to cross New River and to penetrate Kanawha Valley below, we can best co-operate with General Floyd and relieve him. He will need relief if he does not enlarge his ferry. I unite, then, in asking that Colonel Tompkins may be incorporated in my Legion, and that we may be ordered to part from General Floyd to the south side of Kanawha. Boone Court-House is just burned, except one stable. We are badly treated, and I protest against the command as it now stands.

HENRY A. WISE,
Brigadier-General.

[Inclosure.]

CAMP NEAR HAWK'S NEST, VA., *September* 9, 1861.

Maj. Gen. R. E. LEE:

SIR: It is with great reluctance that I recur to the subject of two recent letters addressed to you from the White Sulphur. It is very clear to my apprehension that the volunteer forces organized and commanded by me are destined to a disintegration, which, if not in violation of law, is by no means in accordance with the purposes for which they were designed. After joining General Floyd on the 25th ultimo, while our regiments were separated, the Thirty-sixth was sent to Summersville and the Twenty-second sent to this place. I am now under orders to join General Floyd. These demonstrations, superadded to other evidences, warrant the belief that we are the mere appendages of the Legion, without the benefits that may obtain to that arm of service. I respectfully submit that I have not been treated with the consideration due either to past experience or recent service, and, without the most remote wish to promote my own personal interests, I claim your attention to the matter. It is needless to add that I shall most willingly offer the resignation of my commission if it is believed I am incompetent to exercise the command which was specially organized and prepared under my auspices.

I am, General, very respectfully,

C. Q. TOMPKINS,
Colonel Twenty-second Regiment Virginia Volunteers.

P. S.—I return immediately to the camp of General Floyd.

No. 36.]   HEADQUARTERS ARMY OF THE KANAWHA,
Camp Gauley, Va., Sept. 9, 1861. (Rec'd Sept. 10—2.15 p. m.)

Brig. Gen. HENRY A. WISE:

SIR: Within an hour after my dispatch to you this evening one of my most reliable scouts came into camp, with information, which cannot be questioned, that the enemy, at 5 o'clock to-day, were advancing this side of Powell's Mountain. Their force is certainly very large. I am induced to believe that it is not less than 4,000 men. Their object is either to attack me here or to re-enforce General Cox. To defend my position with success against this force, or to prevent their junction with Cox (which is important), I must have re-enforcements. You will therefore hurry up the regiment of Colonel Tompkins, and, in addition, send me at once 1,000 of your own men, with one of your own batteries. With this re-enforcement my own will be inferior in number to the force of the enemy, according to the lowest estimate of their strength.

Your obedient servant,

JOHN B. FLOYD,
Brigadier-General, Commanding.

No. 37.]   CAMP GAULEY, VA., *September* 9, 1861,
(Received September 10—2 p. m.)

Brig. Gen. HENRY A. WISE:

SIR: I have just received intelligence, which is entirely reliable, that the enemy in considerable force is marching through the county of Webster in this direction. This force is certainly a portion of the reserve of Rosecrans, and their object is, I doubt not, to form a junction with the forces at and near Sutton, with a view to a movement upon me or to the re-enforcement of General Cox. Should this junction be effected, their strength will be rendered very formidable. In the present attitude of things you will station your regiment for which I sent last night at Dogwood Gap. There it will be in supporting distance of me, and can be more readily supplied with provisions than here, in consequence of the bad condition of the road between that point and the turnpike. The regiment of Colonel Tompkins will join me here, as ordered in my last dispatch to you.

Your obedient servant,

JOHN B. FLOYD,
Brigadier-General, Commanding Army of the Kanawha.

HEADQUARTERS, VALLEY MOUNTAIN, VIRGINIA,
September 9, 1861.

General HENRY A. WISE,
Commanding Legion, Hawk's Nest, Kanawha Valley, Virginia:

GENERAL; I have just received your report of the 5th instant,* and am very happy to again congratulate you on your success against the enemy. I am very sorry for the necessity under which General Floyd found it necessary to diminish your command, but you know how necessary it is to act upon reports touching the safety of troops, and that even rumors must not be neglected. General Floyd's position is an exposed one and inviting an attack. He is obliged, therefore, to be cautious, and there is no way of being secure against false information. Troops are consequently obliged to be subjected to wearisome marches. But it is not done intentionally. In my opinion it would be highly prejudicial to separate your Legion from General Floyd. It might be ruinous to our cause in the valley. United, the force is not strong enough; it could effect nothing divided. Great efforts have been made to get this force in marching order. Bad weather, impassable roads, and sickness have paralyzed it for some time. There is a prospect now of being able to resume operations.

There must be a union of strength to drive back the invaders, and I beg you will act in concert. I will forward your report to the Secretary of War, that he may be gratified at the account of the bravery of your troops and skill of your officers. But I must tell you, in candor, I cannot recommend the division of the Army of the Kanawha. We must endure everything in the cause we maintain. In pushing your movements against the enemy, I trust you will not allow your troops to hazard themselves unnecessarily or to jeopardize the accomplishment of the general operations.

I am, with great respect, your obedient servant,

R. E. LEE,
General, Commanding.

CAMP NEAR HAWK'S NEST, VA.,
September 10, 1861—6.30 a. m.

Brig. Gen. JOHN B. FLOYD, *Commanding, &c.:*

SIR: Yesterday morning I received your orders to return to you the regiment of Colonel Tompkins and to send you one of my regiments. I dispatched Colonel Tompkins' regiment immediately, and it must have

---

* See p. 124.

reached, if not crossed, Carnifix Ferry yesterday. It will certainly be there this morning, and I prepared dispatches, setting forth the reasons for not sending one of my regiments as ordered. At 2 and 2.30 o'clock last night I received another order, simply to station my regiment at Dogwood Gap, in supporting distance of your forces, and another order to send at once 1,000 of my own men (in addition to the regiment of Colonel Tompkins), with one of my batteries. The messenger who brought the last dispatch said he was instructed (verbally) to say that at 5 p. m. yesterday it was supposed that 4,000 or 5,000 of the enemy had advanced to the foot of Powell's Mountain and on this side of the mountain and 4 or 5 miles north of Summersville, and that 2,500 of the enemy, about 50 miles distant, were supposed to be advancing upon you from Webster.

In addition to this, I inform you that the enemy at Gauley Bridge has advanced 1,000 men up the Gauley, and every indication shows that they intend to advance about 2,500 men up this turnpike and the Saturday road to the rear of your position at Carnifix Ferry. If all these appearances are correct, you will be threatened from three or four points—front, flank, and rear—by not less than 8,000 or 10,000 men, and a disaster will be the loss of this turnpike and of Lewisburg, at least.

The only check upon the enemy's advance upon Carnifix, upon this side of Gauley, is the force under my command. I now have thirty companies of infantry, six of which are at Dogwood Gap, and twenty-four companies here, averaging, reduced as they are by measles, not more than 40 men each, making in all 1,200 effective infantry (960 here and 240 at Dogwood Gap). My artillery, numbering in all about 314 men, is reduced by the same cause, and by one company at White Sulphur, to less than 200 effective men, and six out of eight companies of my cavalry have been sent over New River to Loop Creek and Coal River, there to do more effective duty than they can do here, and to get corn and oats, having been starved here for want of grain. To re-enforce you with 1,000 men and one of my batteries would leave me with only 200 infantry, 100 artillery, and about 120 horse, to meet a force of 2,500. This would render my command wholly inadequate and unsafe. If, then, I am to send 1,000 infantry and a battery, I had better take my whole force, strengthen you the more thereby, and leave none exposed. In either event all the positions for checking the enemy on this turnpike will have to be abandoned (none of them can be held), and we will lose Liken's Mill and Miller's Ferry.

If I am not to cross Carnifix Ferry, it is best to check the enemy before reaching there, and not at the cliffs of Gauley. If I am to cross that ferry, then there will be no force to guard it and your rear. If the enemy advance upon you from the other side of Gauley with 4,000 men, and besiege you in front, while 2,000 of them are allowed to reach Carnifix and command the ferry in your rear on this side, you will be cut off at once from all supplies of food, forage, and ammunition. On this side or the other, then, my command must be endangered at Carnifix (the ferry there is wholly insufficient for your present forces, and would be hardly better than none in case of a retreat in presence of the foe). In any view, then, I submit that the best position to support you at present is to leave my whole command posted on this road. We now can hardly check the enemy or repel him in time for you to recross the Gauley and unite our forces on this side. A few men can on this side, with this turnpike and the roads leading from it to Carnifix guarded, defend that ferry. On the other side our united forces may easily be cut off and starved out by such advance of the enemy as seems to threaten your present position. I respectfully advise that your force shall recross the Gauley, station a permanent guard of a battery (quite sufficient on this side of Carnifix Ferry), the remainder operate here in co-operation with Generals Chapman and Beckley, and that you send my whole Legion over New River to Coal River, to penetrate Kanawha Valley whenever I can strike a blow below the falls, or Charleston, even, and to protect our loyal citizens in Boone, Cabell, and Kanawha Counties. However these suggestions may be received, I feel it to be my duty to protest, respectfully, as I do, against being ordered again to Carnifix, and against crossing that ferry with any portion of my command.

Very respectfully and faithfully, your obedient servant,
HENRY A. WISE,
Brigadier-General.

P. S.—At 10 a. m. I have just received intelligence that the enemy is now advancing upon me, with what force is not exactly ascertained, but three companies are seen on the hills near my advanced post.
HENRY A. WISE,
Brigadier-General.

No. 38.]   CAMP GAULEY, VA., *September* 10, 1861.
Brig. Gen. HENRY A. WISE:

SIR: I am surprised to learn this morning that the men I ordered from your command had not started yesterday. My order was positive, and the reasons for the order were given. The safety of my whole command may, and probably will, depend upon the prompt execution of the orders I have given you. You will immediately, upon the receipt of this order, send to me 1,000 of your infantry and one battery of artillery, if they have not already started, and urge them to advance with all possible speed. Reply, if you please, to this order, and state the hour of its receipt and that of starting your reply.

I am, very respectfully, your obedient servant,
JOHN B. FLOYD,
Brigadier-General, Commanding Army of the Kanawha.

[Indorsement.]

SEPTEMBER 10, 1861.
Message received at 12.05, at Hamilton's, where I am called to meet an advance of the enemy.
HENRY A. WISE.

AT HAMILTON'S, NEXT TO THE HAWK'S NEST, VA.,
September 10, 1861—12.30 p. m.
Brig. Gen. JOHN B. FLOYD, *Commanding, &c.:*

SIR: Mr. Carr has just handed me yours of to-day at 12.05 m. It found me here, called to meet an advance of the enemy, who are reported to threaten my picket at the Hawk's Nest, and all my force of three regiments of infantry, a corps of artillery, and two companies of cavalry are under arms, to prevent, if possible, an obvious attempt to turn our right flank and to pass us at the turnpike, most probably to gain Carnifix Ferry in your rear. Under these circumstances I shall, upon my legitimate responsibility, exercise a sound discretion whether to obey your very peremptory orders of to-day or not. Please excuse my stationery; it is such as I catch on the road, and I have to use your own envelope.

Very respectfully, your obedient servant,
HENRY A. WISE,
Brigadier-General.

No. 39.]   CAMP GAULEY, VA., *September* 10, 1861— 8 p. m.
Brig. Gen. HENRY A. WISE:

DEAR SIR: You are hereby peremptorily ordered to dispatch to me, immediately on the receipt of this, all of your disposable force saving one regiment, with which you will occupy your present position, unless you deem it expedient to fall back to a more eligible one. The enemy has attacked me in strong force, and the battle has been raging from 3.50 till 7 o'clock. I still hold my position, but think the enemy will renew the attack by day in the morning, with perhaps increased force.

Very respectfully, your obedient servant,
JOHN B. FLOYD.

(Signed by the adjutant-general, because General Floyd is disabled in the arm.)

[Indorsement.]

Received from Mr. Carr and Major Glass about 12 or 1 o'clock at night.

H. A. W.

SEPTEMBER 10, 1861.
To His Excellency JEFFERSON DAVIS,
President of the Confederate States of America :

The undersigned, citizens of Hardy County, Virginia, desire to call your attention to the exposed and suffering condition of our county. We have been invaded for the past two months by Northern thieves. Our houses have been forcibly entered and robbed. Our horses, cattle, and sheep in large numbers driven off. Our citizens arrested, carried off, and confined, only because they are loyal citizens of Virginia and the Southern Confederacy. Our cattle, sheep, and horses, to the amount of $30,000, have been forcibly taken from us and appropriated to the support of the Army of the United States.

Our county, unfortunately, is divided, the western portion being disloyal. The Union men, as they call themselves, have called upon Lincoln for protection. He, in answer to their call, has sent amongst us a set of base characters, who not only protect the Union men, but under their guidance are committing acts unheard of in any country claiming civilization. We have been wholly unprotected and unable to protect ourselves. Our enemies have met with no resistance. We do not complain, as it is perhaps impossible to give protection to all who are suffering like depredations; but we would suggest whether the interest of the Confederacy, apart from the large private interest involved, does not require the protection of our beef, our pork, and our corn for the use of the Southern Army. General Lee is now drawing his supply of corn from us. There is perhaps no valley in America of the same extent that produces more fat cattle and hogs than the valley of the South

Branch. Were we protected in the possession of our property we should be able to supply the Army with several thousand cattle and hogs and at the season of the year when the supply from other sources fails; but if no protection should be given us, and the present state of things suffered to go on, we may well despair not only of feeding the army, but of feeding ourselves. Our enemies, not content with driving off our cattle and sheep by hundreds and our horses in numbers, are to-day, we are most reliably informed, engaged in thrashing out the crops of wheat of some of the farmers of Hampshire.

We have been hoping for relief from General Lee's army in Western Virginia; that the necessities of General Rosecrans would compel him to withdraw his forces from us. In this we have been disappointed. We find still a force on our border acting with the Union men sufficient to rob us. The Baltimore and Ohio Railroad at New Creek Station is but about 30 miles from our county seat and so long as that point is suffered to remain in the possession of the enemy we must be insecure. We placed ourselves under the protection of the Confederate States with a full knowledge of our exposed situation, being a border county, yet relying upon the ability and willingness of our more Southern brethren, who are less exposed, to defend us.

We now would most earnestly call upon you, the chosen head of the Confederacy, for relief and continued protection, if not inconsistent with more important interests.

JACOB VAN METER ET AL.

HEADQUARTERS VALLEY MOUNTAIN,
September 10, 1861.

General S. COOPER,
Adjutant and Inspector General, Richmond, Va.:

GENERAL: It has been reported to me that the supplies of provisions for the Army of the Northwest are being exhausted at the depots at Staunton and Millborough, and that no notice has been received of a further supply being ordered from Richmond. I request that directions be given for full supplies to be delivered at those points as soon as possible, if it has not already been done.

I have the honor to be, your obedient servant,

R. E. LEE,
General, Commanding.

P. S.—SEPTEMBER 10. I have just heard that the enemy is withdrawing all his forces from about Romney and along the Baltimore and Ohio Railroad to Huttonsville in our front. The report has been forwarded from Staunton by Major Harman. If true, now is the time for Colonel McDonald to push at the railroad and destroy it. I would write to him, but do not know where he is. I begin to advance to-day.

R. E. L.

RICHMOND, VA., September 11, 1861.

General G. T. BEAUREGARD, *Commanding, Manassas, Va.:*

GENERAL: Your letter of September 6, 1861,* has been submitted to the Secretary of War, who desires that you be informed that at this

---

* Not found.

time it is impossible to spare the two regiments referred to from the particular service for which they are designed. Such unarmed companies as can be sent from this quarter for battery purposes at Fort Pickens and Evansport will be forwarded.

I am, sir, respectfully, your obedient servant,

R. H. CHILTON,
Assistant Adjutant-General.

WAR DEPARTMENT, C. S. A.,
Richmond, September 12, 1861.

General JOSEPH E. JOHNSTON,
Headquarters Army of the Potomac:

GENERAL: I have the honor to acknowledge the receipt of your letter of the 9th instant. In reply I beg leave to assure you that my letter of the 6th instant, to which you refer, was intended wholly as explanatory to yourself personally of my motive and action in the case in question, and not for the purpose of conveying instructions for the guidance of your official conduct.

I have the honor to be, general, very respectfully,

L. P. WALKER,
Secretary of War.

RICHMOND, *September* 12, 1861.

General JOSEPH E. JOHNSTON,
Commanding Army of the Potomac, Manassas, Va.:

GENERAL: Your letter of September 9,* in relation to Colonel McDonald's mounted regiment, has been submitted to the President, who states that he cannot spare at this time Colonel McDonald's regiment from the special and important duties in which that regiment is now engaged; that efforts are being made to send forward cavalry to the Army of the Potomac as rapidly as they can be obtained.

I am, sir, respectfully, &c.,

R. H. CHILTON,
Assistant Adjutant-General.

MANASSAS, *September* 12, 1861.

Brigadier-General WHITING, *C. S. Army:*

MY DEAR GENERAL: General Trimble informs me that there is reason to suspect that the enemy designs the occupation of some point on the Occoquan and fortifying there. He works so fast that we must be able to interrupt him as soon as he lands—that is to say, very soon after.

For this you had better, instead of moving in the direction of Dumfries, take a position somewhere in the vicinity of Bacon Race Church. Colonel Hampton says that the district is a healthy one. Forney's brigade will be a part of your command, should any movement be necessary. After seeing the country, decide as to whether he need move. The position, or location rather, will enable you to help General T. If necessary, act upon the banks of the Occoquan. Colonel H. will give you information, which his cavalry will look for, and be nearer to us than at present, especially our right, by Wolf Run Shoals Ford.

---

* Not found.

My headquarters will be for some time near Fairfax Station. They will be transferred to-morrow; hence the necessity of your commanding Colonel Forney's Brigade in case of emergency.

Colonel Stuart yesterday, with two field pieces, a company of his regiment, and 305 infantry (Virginia), under Major Terrill, put to flight Griffin's battery of eight pieces, three regiments of infantry, and a body of cavalry, strength not given. They left behind 5 dead and 6 prisoners, one mortally wounded.* Stuart is confident that they carried off a good many dead and wounded. A prisoner said that the redoubtable McC. was present. If so, I shall never forgive Stuart for not securing him.

Yours, truly,

J. E. JOHNSTON.

Stuart says our loss was not a scratch to man or horse.

Write to me your opinion of the force necessary for the observation of the Occoquan and succor of Evansport. Would Wigfall's regiment be sufficient for the latter, to be placed somewhere near? I have no objection, in your estimate, to consider Forney's Brigade divisible. Send letters to Cabell for transmittal.

J. E. J.

ADJUTANT AND INSPECTOR GENERAL'S OFFICE,
Richmond, September 12, 1861.

General R. E. LEE, C. S. A.,
Commanding Forces, Staunton, Va.:

GENERAL: I am instructed by the President to say that you have authority to transfer General Wise's Legion proper to any other command than that of General Floyd. You can transfer it to your own immediate command or make any assignment of it which you may deem proper, in order to produce harmony of action, it being clearly evident that the commands of Generals Floyd and Wise cannot co-operate with any advantage to the service. The absence of General Wise's Legion from the future operations of General Floyd will be replaced by orders from here for Colonel Russell's Twentieth Mississippi Volunteers and Colonel Phillips' Georgia Legion, both at Lynchburg, to join General Floyd.

I am, sir, very respectfully, your obedient servant,

S. COOPER,
Adjutant and Inspector General.

No. 40.]   HEADQUARTERS ARMY OF THE KANAWHA,
Camp Walker, Va., September 12, 1861.

Brig. Gen. HENRY A. WISE:

SIR: I understand that a strong column of the enemy is advancing in this direction from Hawk's Nest. I have ordered all my available cavalry to guard Carnifix Ferry. You will, then, send at once a detachment of your cavalry to scout the road upon which it is reported the enemy is advancing, and hold your command in readiness to meet them.

Your obedient servant,

JOHN B. FLOYD,
Brigadier-General, Commanding Army of the Kanawha.

---

* See p. 167.

DOGWOOD CAMP, VA., *September* 12, 1861—10 p. m.
Brig. Gen. JOHN B. FLOYD:

SIR : I have but two companies of cavalry on this side of New River. One is scouting the Sunday road and the other is already beyond Piggot's. The other six companies over New River are ordered back immediately. My scouts have just reported having seen 2 of the enemy's men on the Saturday road, about 4 miles from here. My command will be in readiness to meet the enemy. There is danger from another advance, also, from Carnifix Ferry. My command is not sufficient to guard that as well as Miller's Ferry, near the Hawk's Nest.

Very respectfully,

HENRY A. WISE,
Brigadier-General.

WHITE SULPHUR SPRINGS, VA., *September* 12, 1861.
Brig. Gen. HENRY A. WISE:

GENERAL : According to orders I submit to yourself, in writing, a statement relating to the rifled gun and the subsequent order of Brigadier General Floyd, hoping in a few days to make such a verbal report as will be demanded by you.

On August 29 I met Mr. Hutton (at one time your topographical engineer), who, with orders from General Floyd, was to proceed to Jackson's River Depot in search of such articles as might there be ready for his (General Floyd's) brigade. Expecting some guns for your command, I asked Mr. Hutton to inquire whether or not they had arrived. On his return he told me of five guns at the depot, which might belong to General Wise, and added : "If he had had a better horse he would have ridden into the country for teams, in order to bring General Floyd's ammunition away." He also remarked that, according to General Davis' statement, the rifled gun belonged to General Floyd. I then told Mr. Hutton that I would send teams to the depot for such guns as were destined for General Wise's brigade, promising, as a favor, to bring the rifled gun also, provided the teams sent would not be all employed otherwise. The guns at Jackson's River proved to belong to another artillery company, and the lieutenant (J. W. Watts), whom I sent in charge of the horses and drivers, brought the rifled gun to the White Sulphur Springs. I would not have moved the gun, but for the wish expressed by Mr. Hutton that I should do so; and, secondly, in order to follow up the orders received by me to take charge of the artillery as it arrived at Jackson's River. The rifled gun was not represented to me as *de facto* General Floyd's; consequently, such guns being expected for your command, I directed Lieutenant Watts to bring it, even if the ownership was doubtful, provided the number of horses would allow it. The rifled gun remained at the White Sulphur Springs unclaimed by any one, to my own knowledge, and General Floyd has not experienced any difficulty in obtaining it, but has had the advantage of a start of 30 miles. The order for my arrest was given in plain language, without allowing of any explanation, but the lieutenant bearing it refused to execute it, for reasons obvious to him.

With highest respect for yourself, I remain, sir, your very obedient servant,

B. ROEMER,
Commanding Mountain Artillery.

No. 42.]   HEADQUARTERS ARMY OF THE KANAWHA,
                  Camp Walker, Va., September 12, 1861.

Brig. Gen. HENRY A. WISE:

DEAR SIR: I get information this evening from Carnifix' Ferry (where I stationed this morning a pretty strong guard) that the enemy are attempting to cross the river. It becomes necessary that a prompt and definite line of action should be at once determined upon and executed. May I ask the favor of you to come down this evening, and bring such officers as you choose to join us in council? Thus we may determine what is best to be done and put the plan into execution at once.

Very respectfully, yours, &c.,

JOHN B. FLOYD,
Brigadier-General, Commanding Army of the Kanawha.

[NOTE.—After or at the consultation here spoken of, and as its result, verbal orders were given by General Floyd for the whole command to fall back to the top of Big Sewell, in the direction of Meadow Bluff, which was done on September 13.—D. B. L.]

————

RICHMOND, VA., *September* 13, 1861.

General JOSEPH E. JOHNSTON:

MY DEAR GENERAL: Yours of the 10th instant * is before me, and I can only suppose you have been deceived by some one of that class in whose absence "the strife ceaseth." While you were in the valley of Virginia your army and that of General Beauregard were independent commands; when you marched to Manassas the forces joined and did duty together. I trust the two officers highest in military rank at Richmond were too well informed to have doubted in either case as to your power and duty. Persons have talked here of the command of yourself and Beauregard as separate armies, and complaints have been uttered to the effect that you took the re-enforcements and guns for your own army; but to educated soldiers this could only seem the muttering of the uninstructed, the rivalry of those who did not comprehend that unity was a necessity, a law of existence. Not having heard accusations, I am, like yourself, ignorant of the specifications, and will add that I do not believe any disposition has existed on the part of the gentlemen to whom you refer to criticise, still less to detract, from you. If they believed that you did not exercise command over the whole, it was, I doubt not, ascribed to delicacy.

You are not mistaken in your construction of my letters having been written to you as the commanding general. I have, however, sometimes had to repel the idea that there was a want of co-operation between yourself and the second in command, or a want of recognition of your position as the senior and commanding general of all the forces serving at or near to the field of your late brilliant achievements.

While writing it occurs to me that statements have been made and official applications received in relation to staff officers which suggested a continuance of separation rather than unity in the "Army of the Potomac."

I did not understand your suggestion as to a commander-in-chief for

————

* Not found.

your army. The laws of the Confederacy in relation to generals have provisions which are new and unsettled by decisions. Their position is special, and the attention of Congress was called to what might be regarded as a conflict of laws. Their action was confined to the fixing of dates for the generals of the C. S. Army.

Your friend,

JEFFERSON DAVIS.

SPECIAL ORDERS, }   HDQRS. DEP'T OF FREDERICKSBURG,
No. 129.   }   *September* 13, 1861.

*   *   *   *   *   *   *

II. The First Arkansas, Second Tennessee, and Twelfth North Carolina Volunteers will constitute a brigade, to the command of which Col. J. G. Walker, Provisional Army of the Confederate States, is assigned.

*   *   *   *   *   *   *

IV. General Trimble's command, at Evansport, will consist of Walker's and Andrew's batteries; Swann's and Waller's troops of cavalry; Walker's brigade of infantry, and, in case of attack, the Forty-seventh Virginia Volunteers, now under command of Colonel Richardson, at Clifton Church, are hereby made subject to his orders. He will send daily a courier, by whom he will report all movements of the enemy within his knowledge and the progress of his works, &c., to these headquarters, to which, also, he will make tri-monthly reports of his command on the 10th, 20th, and last days of each month.

*   *   *   *   *   *   *

By order of General T. H. Holmes:

D. H. MAURY,
Assistant Adjutant-General.

HEADQUARTERS VIRGINIA FORCES,
ADJUTANT AND INSPECTOR GENERAL'S OFFICE,
Richmond, Va., September 14, 1861.

General R. E. LEE,
    Commanding, in advance of Valley Mountain, Virginia:

GENERAL: General Cooper having submitted to me your letter of the 10th instant, to make inquiries about your supplies, I have had an interview with the Commissary-General, who informs me that the supplies for the Army of the Northwest are going forward with all the dispatch possible. The commissaries of both Generals Floyd and Wise were here a few days since, and were satisfied with the arrangements which were made for supplying their commands.

Having reference to your remarks in regard to Colonel McDonald's movements, I am directed to inform you that instructions have been already sent to that officer to move in the direction indicated.

I am, very respectfully, your obedient servant,

GEO. DEAS,
Assistant Adjutant-General.

No. 43.]   HEADQUARTERS ARMY OF THE KANAWHA,
                    Camp Sewell, Va., September 14, 1861.

General HENRY A. WISE:

SIR: It is essential that the turnpike west of this point should be watched and scouted to-night, in order that I may be reliably and speedily informed of the advance of the enemy. My cavalry are all on the Wilderness road, under Colonel Croghan. There are of the companies of Captains Corns and Beckett only 10 fit for service. These 10 have been already sent upon the turnpike west of this. This force, it is clear, is entirely inadequate for the purpose of a proper scout. You will therefore detail from your cavalry 20 men, to proceed at once upon the turnpike west of this point, and scout the same as far as practicable.

Very respectfully, your obedient servant,

JOHN B. FLOYD,
Brigadier-General, Commanding, &c.

No. 44.]   HEADQUARTERS ARMY OF THE KANAWHA,
Camp Sewell, Va., September 15, 1861.

Brig. Gen. HENRY A. WISE:

SIR: I learn that your cavalry picket of 12 men, sent out last night to scout the turnpike west of this point, has returned. As the safety of my entire command depends, in a great measure, upon being informed of the advance of the enemy, if they do advance, you will please send, immediately upon receiving this, a strong force of cavalry, with instructions to scout the road between this point and Dogwood Gap, or as far in that direction as possible, and to remain on the road until recalled. As I informed you last night, I have with me only 10 available horsemen. These are scouting this road.

Very respectfully, your obedient servant,

JOHN B. FLOYD,
Brigadier-General, Commanding,
By WILLIAM E. PETERS,
Assistant Adjutant-General.

CAMP AT DIXON'S, *September* 15, 1861.

Brig. Gen. JOHN B. FLOYD, *Commanding, &c.:*

SIR: The detachment of cavalry sent out last night from my camp has returned only to feed their horses. There is no provender in our front, and we have but two companies, which have been on constant service at Dogwood and through the adjacent roads. Owing to the excess of horses and scarcity of forage at and all this side the Hawk's Nest, I sent six of my companies to the Upper Kanawha, at Loop, Paint, and Lens Creeks and Coal River, leaving only their exhausted horses and sick men. My two companies are worn about the same degree as the troops of Captains Corns and Beckett, of your command, a hundred at least of whom are in the rear. They may pick their men, say 25, to unite with as many more from my two companies, and I beg you, sir, so to order them. But permit me, respectfully, to say that the cavalry, worn as they are, are fit only for vedette duty, and they ought to be preceded by at least two of the picked rifle companies, to ambuscade each side of the turnpike, taking the ridges and road-sides, with two days' provisions, using the cavalry to tole the enemy into the ambush.

Yours, respectfully,

HENRY A. WISE,
Brigadier-General.

P. S.—I will order 25 cavalry immediately on duty.

EVANSPORT, NEAR DUMFRIES, VA.,
September 15, 1861.
General B. HUGER, *Commanding, Norfolk, Va.:*

DEAR SIR: I have no reply from you about guns. All we can obtain in Richmond are fourteen; too small a number for our success. You must let us have twelve 32s, six at once and the others if called for. I know you can take six out of the batteries at Norfolk, say four from new batteries at Lambert's and Pinner's Points, and two from intrenched camp. Then mount some of the navy guns in the old batteries at those places on army carriages, in barbette, which will make one gun equal to four in embrasure, by so much increasing the sector of fire. Let 100 rounds of various fixed ammunition come with the guns, and do spare me Lieutenant Taylor, from Lambert's Point, with his artillery company, to work the guns. I want a skillful and vigilant officer here greatly. Our enterprise here is scarcely less important than any now being executed anywhere in the South, and no efforts or risks should be wanted to insure success. I have begun the work, and in a week shall want the guns. I have 3,000 men to support the batteries and hope to erect them unnoticed by the enemy, who keep a daily watch on us from the river, 1½ miles distant from our position.
Yours, truly,

I. R. TRIMBLE.

P. S.—Telegraph me through General Holmes, at Brooke's Station, Aquia Creek, on the receipt of this, and say when we may expect the guns.

No. 45.]   HEADQUARTERS ARMY OF THE KANAWHA,
Camp on Big Sewell, Va., September 16, 1861.
DEAR SIR: I should be pleased to have you in consultation with me, together with such of your officers as you may think proper to have attend you, at my headquarters, at as early an hour this afternoon as possible. Please excuse stationery, as I am out.*
Very respectfully, your obedient servant,
JOHN B. FLOYD,
By WILLIAM E. PETERS,
Assistant Adjutant-General.

HEADQUARTERS ARMY OF THE KANAWHA,
September 16, 1861.
General HENRY A. WISE:

SIR: I am instructed by General Floyd to say to you that it has been determined to fall back to the most defensible point between Meadow Bluff and Lewisburg. He will put his column in motion at once. You will hold your command in readiness to bring up the rear.
By order of Brig. Gen. John B. Floyd:
WILLIAM E. PETERS,
Assistant Adjutant-General.

---

* See General Wise's memorandum of September 18, p. 854.

No. 46.]   HEADQUARTERS ARMY OF THE KANAWHA,
                    Camp at Meadow Bluff, Va., September 18, 1861.

Brig. Gen. HENRY A. WISE:

SIR: I am instructed by General Floyd to inquire of you why his order
of the 16th instant, "to fall back to the most defensible point between
Meadow Bluff and Lewisburg," has not been carried out.

By order of Brig. Gen. John B. Floyd:

                                    WILLIAM E. PETERS,
                            Assistant Adjutant-General, Floyd's Brigade.

[Memorandum on No. 46.]

                    BIG SEWELL, VA., *September* 18, 1861.

On the evening of the 16th instant I received a notice from General
Floyd that he wanted a conference of officers, and a request to take to
his headquarters such officers of my command as could attend. As
early as practicable (about 5 p. m.) I went, accompanied by Major Tyler,
Captain Stanard, Captain Wise, and Colonel Jackson. The interview
lasted from one to two hours. The general wished counsel as to what
movements were best. I urged that his camp on the top of the Big
Sewell was indefensible, and that a position I had taken 1½ miles in
his rear was almost impregnable, if well defended by a small force;
that we ought to occupy that position by my Legion, and he ought to
take ground with his own command on the left, to defend Bowyer's
Ferry and the old State road; that these positions would support each
other easily against largely superior numbers; that Colonel Davis, with
my cavalry, had just won a victory within 12 miles of Charleston, and
ought to be supported by infantry; and that, if he would permit me, I
would take a picked corps from my command and one from his, a regiment or battalion or less, from each, and follow an active movement
down the left bank of the Kanawha. He said he liked the idea, and at
first assented. I told him that upon his retreat from Dogwood I had
ordered my cavalry to fall back to support him on this turnpike, and
asked whether I might countermand that order and renew the one to
descend the Kanawha Valley. Again he assented. I wrote the order,
and sent it from his camp to Colonel Davis, at Raleigh Court-House
or Jumping Branch. After having read it to General Floyd, and after
his approval, I then urged again that he would fall back to my position
and await the enemy. He then said that he would view the position
the next morning, and if he found it strong would wait there for several
days at least, until he could hear from Richmond. This I considered
the concluded arrangement of our movements when I left him. He
inquired whether I knew of any movement by General Lee. I told him
the state of the roads was so bad that General Lee could not move from
his position. Other subjects were mentioned, such as mustering in the
pack company from Mercer into my Legion, as it was raised for it. He
promptly replied that the men should be allowed to elect their own command, and choose the Legion or not, and be mustered in accordingly;
and also that Captain Newman's company, if it so elected, might be
transferred to the Legion from the State volunteers. After this and
other conversations I left.

On returning, Major Tyler remarked the preparations for a movement in General Floyd's camp, and it was thought that a retreat was
intended before I was called to conference. We had hardly ridden to

my headquarters (1½ miles off) when General Floyd's wagons came moving back, and in a short time, while his front column was in motion, he sent me notice that he determined to move to some defensible position between Meadow Bluff and Lewisburg, and would move at once. He was then moving, and he ordered me to hold myself in readiness to bring up his rear. I have held myself in readiness, but have received no orders to move. This morning he addressed me an inquiry why I had not obeyed his order to move. I have replied, stating my reasons in detail, but not in full.

HENRY A. WISE,
Brigadier-General.

CAMP ON BIG SEWELL MOUNTAIN, VIRGINIA,
September 18, 1861—10.30 a. m.

Brig. Gen. JOHN B. FLOYD, *Commanding, &c. :*

SIR : In answer to your inquiry, addressed to me this morning, why your order of the 16th instant, "to fall back to the most defensible point between Meadow Bluff and Lewisburg," has not been carried out, I reply: First, no such order was ever given to me. On the contrary, I was notified late the 16th, after night, that it had been determined to fall back to the most defensible point between Meadow Bluff and Lewisburg, and that you would put your column in motion at once, and that I would hold my command in readiness to bring up the rear. I have obeyed that order, and have received no order to move. It was necessary to remain to bring up some baggage left by your camp. Second, this order to be ready followed immediately after a verbal conference with you, at your request, in which I understood you distinctly as determining to hold, for a time at least, the almost impregnable position which I now occupy. I deem it essential to protect your rear, to prevent the advance of forces from Gauley attempting to form a junction with the enemy's forces from Carnifix. Whatever road they may take, I can effectually check at this position any force from Gauley, and can attack the rear or flank of any enemy from Carnifix when I am obliged to fall back. This will best bring up your rear and prevent the advance of the enemy. Third, your march over the road has rendered it almost impassable, and the rain since has rendered its condition still worse. My camp has many sick, some convalescent, and I deem it inhuman to risk the health of these men in this wet weather. I ask, then, to wait here (in comfortable quarters, at an eligible point) to meet the enemy, until the weather clears up and the roads are passable and I get sufficient wagons to move with facility. Fourth, if I leave this position we will lose the command of Bowyer's Ferry and the old State road. I have a good supply of provisions now here; I cannot leave without risking their loss, and for these reasons submit to your own superior judgment that I am here in best readiness to defend your rear. I can here repulse twice my numbers, and it is only past this point on this road that the enemy can advance their artillery. I can stop them here, and you will, with seven pieces of artillery, have to meet infantry only, advancing upon you at Meadow Bluff, by the Wilderness, or any other road between this and your position. I respectfully and earnestly therefore ask to be permitted to remain in position here until I see whether the enemy will attempt to advance the whole or a part of their forces on this turnpike past this point and until the weather and the roads are better for a march. I pledge myself to defend your rear and to support your command in the most efficient way.

Very respectfully, your obedient servant,

HENRY A. WISE,
Brigadier-General.

P. S.—Inclosed is a report of my quartermaster, to which I beg leave to call your attention.

[Inclosures.]

HEADQUARTERS WISE'S LEGION,
September 18, 1861.

Brig. Gen. HENRY A. WISE, *Commanding Wise's Legion:*

GENERAL: I have been informed by Captain Farrish that two wagons, under my charge, which were sent to Jackson's River Depot for the purpose of bringing stores to this command, were loaded with articles belonging to General Floyd's brigade and sent by Mr. Boyer to him, since which time I have heard nothing of the wagons, and suppose they are still with General Floyd. Two wagons were also sent from the White Sulphur with stores from Colonel Tompkins' regiment, with the express understanding that they would be returned to me immediately; but so far it has not been done. Also one wagon loaded with picks, spades, &c., was sent from White Sulphur to General Floyd, then on the top of Big Sewell, which was also to be returned as soon as unloaded; but as yet I have heard nothing from it, although it should have been received by me yesterday morning. You will see by this that five of our wagons are now in the possession of General Floyd's brigade, and as we are at present much in want of them for the purpose of removing both quartermaster and commissary stores, I would respectfully request you would demand them of General Floyd, as I feel that I can do nothing, as I have already without success requested their return.

Very respectfully, your obedient servant,

F. D. CLEARY,
Captain and Assistant Quartermaster.

CAMP ON BIG SEWELL, VIRGINIA,
September 18, 1861—11.30 a. m.

Brig. Gen. JOHN B. FLOYD, *Commanding, &c.:*

GENERAL: By the foregoing report to me of Captain Cleary, my brigade quartermaster, you will see that five of my wagons were loaned to your brigade and have not been returned. We are short of transportation, and need these wagons very much. On the 16th you very promptly assented to my request to have them returned. There is a large amount of stores, arms, ammunition, baggage, &c., to be moved, and the roads are much worse than when you passed. If my five wagons cannot now be identified, I ask that five others as good shall be sent in their stead, as they are indispensable to my march. And here let me respectfully apprise you that from Dogwood Camp here my wagons and hospitals have been burdened with your sick. They have been left neglected, and several have died on the way. I have attended to them the best I could.

Very respectfully,

HENRY A. WISE,
Brigadier-General.

RICHMOND, VA., *September* 18, 1861.

Maj. M. G. HARMAN, *Quartermaster, Staunton, Va.:*

It is reported that cars are detained at Millborough as store-houses, so as to render it impossible to forward supplies from this place.

JEFFERSON DAVIS.

HEADQUARTERS OF THE VIRGINIA FORCES,
Richmond, September 18, 1861.

Col. ANGUS W. McDONALD, *Winchester, Va.:*

SIR: I am directed by General Cooper to furnish you with the follow-ing. extract from a communication received from General Lee:

SEPTEMBER 10.

I have just heard that the enemy is withdrawing all his forces from about Romney and along the Baltimore and Ohio Railroad to Huttonsville in our front. The report has been forwarded from Staunton by Major Harman. If true, now is the time for Colonel McDonald to push at the railroad and destroy it. I would write him myself, but do not know where he is.

The foregoing is communicated to you for your information and guidance.

I am, very respectfully, your obedient servant,

GEORGE DEAS,
Assistant Adjutant-General.

RICHMOND, VA., *September* 18, 1861.

General JOSEPH E. JOHNSTON,
Care of Major Cabell, Quartermaster, Manassas, Va.:

It is reported that cars are detained at Manassas for storage, so as to render it impossible to forward from this place the supplies required for your command.

JEFFERSON DAVIS.

WAR DEPARTMENT, C. S. A.,
Richmond, September 19, 1861.

General JOSEPH E. JOHNSTON,
Headquarters Army of the Potomac:

SIR: I beg leave respectfully to call your attention to the inclosed correspondence, and to represent to you the necessity of promptly dis-charging and returning the cars of the railroad company as soon as they can be unloaded. This subject is so important, not only to the public interests in general, but also especially to the well-being of your army, that I am sure I need only to call your attention to the complaint in order to insure at once the necessary orders from you for its removal.

I have the honor to be, general, very respectfully,

J. P. BENJAMIN,
Acting Secretary of War.

[Inclosures.]

SUBSISTENCE DEPARTMENT,
Richmond, September 18, 1861.

Hon. J. P. BENJAMIN, *Acting Secretary of War:*

SIR: I received a dispatch from Major Blair, desiring that 1,000 barrels of flour should be sent him from Richmond because of non-arrival of 2,000 barrels ordered from Lynchburg and Fredericksburg. This must be due to some difficulties on the roads, as ample provision has been made at both places. The agent of the Central Railroad writes that it is impossible to transport the flour, and therefore I inclose a copy of the agent's letter, stating the reason.

I am, very respectfully, your obedient servant,

L. B. NORTHROP,
Commissary-General Subsistence.

RICHMOND, *September* 18, 1861.

J. H. CLAIBOURNE, Esq.:

DEAR SIR: The Confederate States have all of our cars at Manassas and Millborough. We cannot get them back. We have only two cars now in Richmond. Our depot is blocked up. If you send the flour to-day we shall be compelled to put it out of doors, and the Confederate States must take the risk.

Respectfully,

S. HUNTER.

———

RICHMOND, *September* 19, 1861.

Lieut. Col. TURNER ASHBY,
C. S. Army, Commanding, Halltown, Jefferson County, Va.:

SIR: In reply to your letter of the —— instant [following], from Halltown, I am instructed to inform you that it has been our object, with the President, for some time past, to destroy the canal at any point where it could not be repaired. If this can be accomplished at the mouth of the Monocacy, the destruction would be irreparable for an indefinite period. The destruction of the canal and the railroad have been cherished objects, and a disappointment at the failure of all past attempts to effect them has been proportionate to the importance attached to their achievement. But while this much is said on the subject, it is intended that any attempt of the kind should be made with the greatest caution, so that the safety of the command may be duly secured. The stores seized by you and sent to Winchester must be regarded as a seizure from the enemy, and may be turned over to the quartermaster and hospital departments for use, receipts being taken for them, as usual.

Very respectfully, &c.,

R. H. CHILTON,
Assistant Adjutant-General.

—

CAMP NEAR HALLTOWN, JEFFERSON COUNTY,
[*September* —, 1861.]

Adjutant-General COOPER:

SIR: Inclosed I send you invoice of goods seized by my order from a store upon the Potomac, in Berkeley County, belonging to A. R. Mc-Qulken, who has fled from the Confederacy. He was a member of the Wheeling Convention. I would be pleased to hear from you as to how to dispose of them. I send them to-day to Winchester to be stored until I hear from you, which directions will find me if directed to Charlestown, Jefferson County. I think it proper to state to you my position. I am in command of a detachment of Colonel McDonald's regiment, together with a force of militia furnished me by General Carson, for the purpose of protecting Mr. Sharpe, Government agent, now removing engines, &c., from Baltimore and Ohio Road to Strasburg. There are now stationed upon the Maryland side of the Potomac, opposite this county, two infantry regiments, guarding the canal, which is transporting coal and other supplies. I am within 1¼ miles of the river, and watch their movements daily for the whole distance which these regiments operate. I am confident, if not inconsistent with the present policy of the Government, that I can move over at some convenient point and break the canal, securing a large amount of salt said to be now in depots opposite this place. The only force above that mentioned by me on the river as far as the Hampshire line is stationed at Williamsport, some 15 miles up the river—about one and a half regiments. I had occasional skirmishes with the enemy in this vicinity, they having crossed twice—once at Harper's Ferry and again at Shepherdstown. I have driven them back each time without loss, having only 1 man wounded, and he doing well. I have killed several of them each time. They fire at every man, woman, child, or horse that passes the river upon this side. I have sometimes allowed my men to return their fire with long-range (small-arms) guns, with some known effect.

I write this to you owing to my peculiar position, acting by order of Colonel McDonald, who is or is to be in a different locality, too far to give his attention to the minutiæ of my movements, and, too, having under my command other forces than from his regiment, with no defined instructions as to policy to be pursued towards the enemy in this locality. Will you give them to me?

Respectfully,

TURNER ASHBY,
Lieutenant-Colonel, Commanding near Harper's Ferry.

HEADQUARTERS ARMY OF THE KANAWHA,
Camp at Meadow Bluff, September 19, 1861.

Brig. Gen. HENRY A. WISE:

SIR: Your favor of yesterday, informing me that five of your wagons were loaned to my brigade, and have not been returned, has been received. Immediately upon receipt of your letter I made such inquiries of the commissary and quartermaster departments of my brigade about the matter, and found that the quartermaster of the Twenty-second regiment, Colonel Tompkins, had in his possession two of the wagons of your legion. The letter of Captain Miller, which accompanies this, will explain to you the circumstances under which the wagons came into his possession, and will inform you that they have been returned to you to-day. They were taken without authority from me, and without my knowledge. I know of no other wagons in my brigade belonging to your Legion.

I supposed that my order to you of the 16th instant was sufficiently explicit, inasmuch as it is therein distinctly stated that I would put at once my column in motion, and that you would hold your command in readiness to bring up the rear, and I have not yet been able to discover how you could bring up the rear of a moving column by remaining stationary after this column had passed. My determination and order to fall back upon the most defensible point between Meadow Bluff and Lewisburg was based upon what I conceived the safety of my command demanded. I felt sure that it was the plan of the enemy to advance upon Lewisburg, and in at least two columns, by the turnpike and the Wilderness road, and to unite their columns at the junction of those roads. In this persuasion I was not mistaken. My scouts on the Wilderness road have just come in, and report that the enemy are advancing upon that road, which in all probability is true. I felt that this junction could be more certainly prevented and, if effected, could be most successfully met by the combined movement of all the forces under my command. If you have not advanced in the direction of my camp on the Sewell I have been misinformed.

Very respectfully, your obedient servant,

JOHN B. FLOYD,
Brigadier-General, Commanding Army of the Kanawha.

[Inclosure.]

CAMP AT MEADOW BLUFF, VA.,
September 18, 1861.

General JOHN B. FLOYD:

GENERAL: As instructed by you, I report the circumstances under which two of General Wise's wagons came into my possession, as assistant quartermaster of the Twenty-second Regiment Virginia Volunteers. Lieutenant Chilton, of this regiment, was sent to White Sulphur Springs recently to bring back some sick soldiers of the regiment, left there when we marched to join your brigade. He was instructed to apply to Captain Adams for transportation. Captain Adams obtained two two-horse wagons for him, and Lieutenant Chilton detailed two of the soldiers to drive them. The wagons arrived at the camp on the Big Sewell Mountain late on the evening of the night we returned to this post. Under the instructions of Colonel Tompkins. they were turned over to me, as assistant quartermaster, and used by me on the march here, and are now in my possession. I had on that day and on the day previous used four of my wagons for bringing into camp forage, provisions, &c., and to convey some sick to the White Sulphur Springs, under the direction of Dr. McDonald, surgeon of the regiment. None of these wagons had returned when we were ordered to march. Without the two wagons I could not have made the march and transported the provisions, baggage, &c., of the regiment. I was compelled, however, to put another horse in one of the wagons, and the other was a very balky, bad team, but which I got to work tolerably well at last. I shall send the two wagons to General Wise's camp to-morrow.

Very respectfully,

S. A. MILLER,
Assistant Quartermaster, Twenty-second Regiment Va. Vols.

CAMP NEAR TOP OF BIG SEWELL, VIRGINIA,
September 19, 1861—11.30 p. m.

Brig. Gen. JOHN B. FLOYD, *Commanding, &c.* :

GENERAL: Your order to me was to be in readiness on the 16th, and no order was given to me to move. I am now intrenched, and cannot move with advantage, and can fight with a confidence of repulsing the enemy. They have about five hundred tents (six men each), and their forces as yet are principally from Gauley, and they may reach 3,500, and cannot re-enforce more from that point, as Colonel Clarkson (just arrived) reports certainly that they sent two regiments from Gauley to meet Colonel Davis' cavalry. What artillery the enemy in front of me may have cannot yet be told, but I can meet them in the trenches with 1,800 infantry and artillery, and by to-morrow will have my eight companies of cavalry (say 350 to 400) in all, 2,200, with nine pieces of artillery. With this force, posted as I am, I can repulse 4,000. I doubt whether the enemy are advancing upon the Wilderness road, and if they are, they cannot take artillery on it. They may be double your force, but without artillery they cannot make a successful attack upon you, your seven regiments and six pieces, numbering at least 3,500, besides your 300 or 400 cavalry. Thus strong, though we may be divided, the enemy are divided too, if your opinion is correct, and the divisions are about proportionately distributed to our respective forces. But if my opinion is correct (that from the Bracken's Creek road the enemy from both Gauley and Carnifix will advance in main force, with artillery, on this turnpike), then I submit that I ought to be re-enforced by one of your regiments, to co-operate with my cavalry. If any or either regiment of your brigade is sent, I ask that you will order Colonel Tompkins' regiment to re-enforce me. I most earnestly protest that I wish in the most efficient way to co-operate with your command, and will not press reasons, otherwise than those already urged, for the course I am pursuing. As to the wagons I sent you, the report of my quartermaster as to the number loaned to your brigade and Mr. Miller's report do not relate to three out of five of them. But, at all events, I beg you to cause my wagons passing Meadow Bluff to hurry on to Frazier's. I regret to urge another matter. Captain Roemer, of my artillery, arrived to-day, and reports that Colonel Croghan has taken some fifty-four of my sabers for your cavalry, which were sent to McLeary, of Lewisburg, to be scabbarded for my artillery. These sabers I sent to Richmond for, expressly for my Legion, and obtained them without scabbards, and myself had them scabbarded and belts made for them. I respectfully ask that Colonel Croghan be ordered to deliver them to me.

Very respectfully, your obedient servant,

HENRY A. WISE,
Brigadier-General.

No. 47.]   CAMP ON BIG SEWELL, VIRGINIA,
September 19, 1861—2 a. m.

Brig. Gen. JOHN B. FLOYD, *Commanding, &c.:*

SIR: Two of my scouts (John T. Amick and Madison Walker) report the enemy approaching on this turnpike, at double-quick, 6 miles off, at Masten's. They left Gauley River, at Carnifix, at 10 a. m., and the enemy were not done crossing the river there then. The Gauley forces, from the bridge, had reached the Sunday road first, and those now advancing are probably some of the latter. The scouts came into the turnpike by the Bracken's Creek road, at Billy Masten's house, at Bracken's Creek, where they came in between two regiments or two companies, they could not see which. They followed the front column up to old Masten's house, about three-fourths of a mile, and found them plundering the house, and then spoke to some of the enemy, and turned back to the Bracken's Creek road, and upon it rode back to Meadow River, and came around into my camp, on the position of my artillery. At Nichol's Mill, at Meadow River, a man told them that 15 of the enemy had been seen there, and at the mouth of the Bracken's road, on the turnpike, they had met another column, in the rear of the first. Thus they saw the rear of one and the front of another column, but cannot describe their numbers. Amick says he was alone when he saw the enemy. Walker joined him at Meadow River, on his way back, and Walker reports hearing their drums at the turnpike, at Sunday road, and at Alderson's all this morning. Amick says there are none across Gauley, on the other side of Meadow River. I shall hold on here and fight the enemy, expecting them to attack me before sunrise this morning.

Please send forward any empty wagons which can be dispatched from Meadow Bluff.

Very respectfully, your obedient servant,

HENRY A. WISE,
Brigadier-General.

No. 48.]   HEADQUARTERS ARMY OF THE KANAWHA,
Camp near Meadow Bluff, Virginia, September 19, 1861.

General HENRY A. WISE:

SIR: I have been aware for several days of the advance of the enemy. Before I left the top of the Big Sewell Mountain I was well assured that his plan was to concentrate all his force at an eligible point (which I thought might possibly be Meadow Bluff) on the Turnpike road and to advance upon Lewisburg. I chose this position to meet him, because I believed it to be the most eligible. I regret exceedingly that you did not think proper to bring up my rear, as directed in my order of the 16th, but on the contrary chose to advance in the direction from which I had come. Disastrous consequences, which may ensue from a divided force, may result from this, unless counteracted by some prompt and decided movement. If you still have time, upon the receipt of this, to join my force and make a stand against the enemy at this point, I hope you will see the necessity of doing so at once. The country has a right, I think, to expect the strongest resistance which all the combined forces under my command can make to the advance of this powerful enemy, and I do not think this just expectation should be disappointed.

I am, sir, very respectfully, your obedient servant,

JOHN B. FLOYD,
Brigadier-General, Commanding Army of the Kanawha.

CAMP NEAR THE TOP OF BIG SEWELL, VIRGINIA.,
September 19, 1861—9.45 a. m.

Brig. Gen. JOHN B. FLOYD, *Commanding, &c.:*

SIR: There are two essential mistakes in your note of this day, just put into my hands. You say that you "regret exceedingly that I did not think proper to bring up your rear, as directed in your order of the 16th." I repeat that I did think proper "to hold my command in readiness to bring up your rear" precisely in the language and sense of your order of the 16th. I justly interpreted your order of that date to mean that I was not to move immediately after your movement. You said in that order that you would move "at once," and ordered me simply to hold myself in readiness to bring up your rear. That order I have obeyed in letter and in spirit better than by moving "at once" after you. I could not move "at once" on the 16th, nor on the 17th, nor on the 18th.

Five of my wagons have been borrowed by your command and not returned, and a number of them had been sent eastward for supplies of corn, and to take on not only my own sick, but many of the sick of your command, whom your surgeons left suffering and dying on the way. And I am informed that your quartermaster has stopped some of my wagons, and that others, containing my supplies, have been turned back. I have a large amount of baggage, ammunition, and stores accumulated here, which I am bound to save, and will save from the enemy, who have approached within 6 miles of me in force.

My position here is strong, and is much stronger than that of Meadow Bluff. I can hold it, repulse the enemy, and thus defend your rear, and fall back in due time without the loss of a single thing of value, and before there can be any junction of the enemy's forces to attack you or any combined forces at Meadow Bluff. I have ascertained this morning that the enemy are not upon the Wilderness road, but they have crossed at Carnifix, and are upon the Bracken's Creek road, leading from Carnifix to Masten's, and upon this turnpike from Gauley. They will, if they form a junction at all, form it at Bracken's Creek, 6 miles west of me.

If they do combine and advance, and our joint forces can repel them at Meadow Bluff, I will repel them here, combined or not combined, and will thus save my stores and supplies, and bring up your rear. You need not re-enforce me here. I will re-enforce you in full time at Meadow Bluff, and, as to the manner of bringing up your rear and saving my command and its baggage and honor, in execution of your order of the 16th, I must, I respectfully urge, be allowed the sound and saving discretion of one trusted with a separate brigade. Further, you not only say that " I did not think proper to bring up your rear, as directed in your order of the 16th, but, on the contrary, chose to advance in the direction from which you had gone." In respect to that, sir, you have been misinformed or are mistaken. I have not chosen to advance in any direction; but, on the contrary, have retired one of my regiments behind my artillery from its advanced position when you left, and have ordered on all my commissary and quartermaster supplies, not necessarily required immediately, towards your camp. I will make a timely move when I can do so safely and without loss to join your force, and make a stand against the enemy at Meadow Bluff. I do not see the necessity of doing so at once, and in the present state of the roads cannot do so " at once," unless my wagons are speedily sent to me from this, eastward, from your command, from Lewisburg, White Sulphur, and Jackson's River. I repeat the request that you will have sent to me the five now held by your quartermaster. I will earnestly endeavor to co-operate in making the strongest resistance, and I am doing so by remaining here for the present at least. I will try hard, on my part, not to disappoint any just expectations of the country in resisting the advance of the enemy, between whom and my command there is now but a very short space. When I fail in meeting such expectations I hope that I may be held to the utmost responsibility of my position as a commander, bound to due obedience, and trusted with sound discretion.

I am, sir, respectfully, your obedient servant,

HENRY A. WISE,
Brigadier-General.

P. S.—As I finish, the enemy appear four miles and a half from my camp. This is certain. I shall await an attack, and leave it to your better judgment to send re-enforcements or not.

RICHMOND, VA., *September* 19, 1861.

Capt. E. T. TUTWILER, *Richmond, Va.*:

SIR: You will proceed without delay to Millborough, and inform your-self of the amount of transportation required for the prompt supply of General Lee's command with every description of stores for the army that we sent to that depot to be forwarded. A supply train has no doubt been already organized on the road from Millborough to Hunters-ville and beyond as far as Valley Mountain. You are authorized to purchase wagons and teams to make the supply train sufficient, and to engage hands to work upon the roads and keep them in order. Major Corley, assistant quartermaster at Huntersville, is the principal officer in the country where General Lee is operating. You will report to him and carry out such instructions as he may give you in furtherance of the duty assigned to you. On your arrival at Millborough you will report to me the amount of supplies on hand to be forwarded to Hun-tersville. * * * You will report yourself to General R. E. Lee when you arrive at his headquarters, and take any orders he may have to give you connected with your special duties.*

A. C. MYERS,
Acting Quartermaster-General.

LEWISBURG, *September* 19, 1861.

His Excellency JEFFERSON DAVIS,
President of the Southern Confederacy;

DEAR SIR: Influenced by no other motive than the promotion of the cause of the Southern Confederacy, I deem it my duty to make to you a statement of a few facts that have come under my own personal observation with regard to the condition of affairs in the western divis-ion of our army, a condition which I think must result in nothing but disaster to the cause unless remedied, and that very soon. I allude to the unfriendly relations existing between the two generals, Floyd and Wise. They are as inimical to each other as men can be, and from their course and actions I am fully satisfied that each of them would be highly gratified to see the other annihilated. I have spent a few days recently in their encampments, and learn that there is great dissatisfac-tion existing among the officers as well as the privates, and am of opin-ion that it would be much better for the service if they were both de-posed, and some military general appointed in their stead to take com-mand of both their divisions. This I am sure would be gratifying to the commandants of the different regiments, and would insure success to our cause, at least in this division of our Army. It would be just as easy to combine oil and water as to expect a union of action between these gentlemen.

I have taken this liberty and responsibility, though a perfect stranger to you, of presenting these facts, in the hope that they may bring about an investigation of the matter, and will refer you to Governor Letcher, Wyndham Robertson, esq., William H. Macfarland, esq., William F. Ritchie, esq., and other prominent individuals of Richmond City.

Believing that you are not aware of this condition of things, and hop-ing that the needful remedy may be applied at once, I am, very respect-fully and truly, your obedient servant,

MASON MATHEWS.

---

* Some matters of detail omitted.

LEWISBURG, *September* 19, 1861.

Mr. Mathews, the author of the foregoing letter, has been and still is our county representative in the legislature—a gentleman of truth and intelligence, whose statements are entitled to the fullest credit. In addition to what he states we have understood from other sources that a great want of harmony exists between Generals Floyd and Wise. The remedy for this dangerous evil we submit to your cooler and better judgment.

Very truly and respectfully,

SAML. PRICE.
M. ARBUCKLE.

LEWISBURG, VA., *September* 19, 1861.

To the PRESIDENT OF THE CONFEDERATE STATES:

Your Excellency will excuse, I hope, the liberty which I have taken of addressing you a few lines relative to the apprehensions which cause much anxiety in our community and the circumstances which have given rise to them. At the time of the battle at Camp Gauley General Wise was at the Hawk's Nest, a short distance this side of Gauley Bridge. Cox's encampment and our militia, 1,500 or 1,800 strong, were at Cotton Hill, opposite to Cox, on the western side of New River, near its confluence with Gauley. In the battle of Camp Gauley our loss was some 5 or 6 wounded, and from all we can learn the slaughter of the enemy was terrific. I have conversed with individuals who were in the engagement, but they could only infer from the exposed condition of the enemy and the quantity of grape, &c., thrown amongst them their probable loss. They suppose it to have been great, but reports from persons in the neighborhood, who got their information from the enemy, represent his loss to have been tremendous. The dead and wounded, they say, amounted to thousands. After the battle General Floyd crossed Gauley and retreated to a point on the James River and Kanawha Turnpike road, about 12 miles south of where the battle was fought—Dogwood Gap. There he was joined by General Wise. Both subsequently retreated to Big Sewell, about 30 miles west of this place, where General Wise yet remains, but General Floyd retreated on Monday night last to Meadow Bluff, 16 miles west of Lewisburg. On yesterday we learned that he was again moving west, but I am unable to say whether by the turnpike or the Wilderness road leading to Summersville, and crossing Gauley at Hughes' Ferry. From the time the battle of Gauley Camp occurred we have been anxiously expecting that General Lee would follow Rosecrans to Summersville, and many reports have reached us that he was doing so, but I fear our hopes in this respect are unfounded. We have no positive knowledge that the enemy in force has yet crossed Gauley, but it is said that his scouts have done so, and I apprehend that he will soon learn that Floyd's and Wise's forces combined are much less than his own. Heretofore I believe he has overestimated our strength. We do not know Rosecrans' strength in the battle of Camp Gauley, or rather the exact number of men with which he marched into Nicholas. It is variously reported at from 7,000 to 12,000. I am disposed to believe the smaller number nearly correct. But a union with Cox will give him probably 10,000 men, unless his reported loss in the battle with Floyd be correct. This force would be too strong for our generals, even if they acted in harmony and concert, which I am very sorry to say I fear they do not from the reports current in the country. Indeed, I have been requested by a gentleman of high standing to write to you upon this subject; but as I know personally nothing of the facts, and am so loath to conclude that two gentlemen so distinguished could permit private feelings of any character to interfere with the discharge of duties so vitally important as those now devolving upon them, I even allude to the matter with extreme reluctance. Inasmuch, however, as the matter is one commonly talked of here, I have concluded to refer to it, confident that a gentleman of your administrative talent and general acquaintance with mankind will know best what weight to attach to it, and whether or not it calls for action on your part. A report has just reached me (3 p. m.) that General Wise has left Sewell and retired several miles nearer to Lewisburg, and is now at Frazier's, 26 miles west of this, and that he has sent for all to join him who can, as he expects an attack from the enemy. Since beginning my letter I learn that General Floyd is to-day at Meadow Bluff. I also learn that a dispatch has been forwarded to Richmond.

I have thus, my dear sir, given you briefly the circumstances which cause us much solicitude. I really fear that our county and town are in great danger of falling into the hands of the enemy, and such an event would indeed be deplorable, not only to our loyal citizens, but to our cause. I hope you will do something for us, and that speedily.

Most respectfully, your obedient servant,

W. H. SYME.

P. S.—Messrs. Price and Mathews some months since, at my instance, addressed you, inclosing a note in pencil from myself. I refer to this fact that you may form some idea of myself, &c.

SPECIAL ORDERS, }   ADJT. AND INSP. GEN.'S OFFICE,
No. 157.   }   *Richmond, Va., September* 19, 1861.
*   *   *   *   *   *   *

6. Maj. Gen. Gustavus W. Smith, Provisional Army, will proceed to Manassas, Va., and report for duty to General J. E. Johnston, commanding the Army of the Potomac.
*   *   *   *   *   *   *

By command of the Secretary of War:

JNO. WITHERS,
Assistant Adjutant-General.

RICHMOND, *September* 20, 1861.

General T. H. HOLMES, *Aquia Creek:*

GENERAL: In the present condition of Maryland the Government feels a deep solicitude in behalf of the unfortunate citizens who are cut off from all hope of escaping from the tyranny exercised over them. I do not desire to make any special order in relation to the mode of securing you against the abuse of such facilities as can be afforded for crossing the Potomac, but it is necessary that some means of passage for our friends be kept open if at all possible. It occurs to me that you might place some one or more confidential officers in command of the point where the boats make their landing on our side, and by proper police regulations guard yourself against spies while affording means of passage for the inhabitants who are seeking refuge with us, as well as for the recruits who desire to join our service. I leave the mode of securing the safety of your command against the intrusion of spies to your discretion, and content myself with requesting that you open the communication at the earliest possible moment in such manner as you may think best.

Your obedient servant,

J. P. BENJAMIN,
Acting Secretary of War.

RICHMOND, *September* 20, 1861.

Lieut. Col. A. C. MYERS, *Acting Quartermaster-General:*

SIR: General Johnston telegraphs the President from Fairfax Station that his chief quartermaster reports that the cars are never unnecessarily detained at Manassas, but unloaded as soon as possible after arriving. The truth on this subject must be ascertained, and the party actually in fault for the detention of the cars and the obstruction in the regular transportation service must be detected. You are therefore instructed to make immediate examination and report to me the facts in the case. The contradictory statements now reported to me officially demand that I should know which of the officers has made a report unfounded in fact.

Your obedient servant,

J. P. BENJAMIN,
Acting Secretary of War.

MILLBOROUGH, VA., *September* 20, 1861.

His Excellency JEFFERSON DAVIS:

I have just received a note from Major Harman, inclosing a dispatch from you stating that you understood that cars were detained here for the purpose of store-houses, and that the cars were wanted, and must be sent down.

The small county of Rockbridge is the only place that I have had to press teams; I have had them in service now for about two months, and, the roads being in such a terrible state, most of them are now broken down, either horses or wagons. I have never been able to get any teams from Staunton, where they have a fine rich country to get teams from.

In consequence of this, provisions have accumulated upon me to such an extent, that I have had to keep some twelve or fifteen cars for several days.

I will immediately have sheds erected to put provisions in, and have them unloaded as soon as possible. We have some ten or fifteen days' provisions ahead with the army.

I would respectfully refer you to General Loring or to Major Corley, the quartermaster of the northwest, for the manner in which provisions have been forwarded from this place heretofore and for the disadvantages under which I have labored.

Very respectfully, your obedient servant,

W. L. POWELL,
Captain, Acting Quartermaster.

CAMP AT MEADOW BLUFF, VIRGINIA,
September 21, 1861.
General HENRY A. WISE,
Wise's Legion, Camp on Big Sewell, Virginia:

I have just arrived at this camp, and regret to find the forces not united. I know nothing of the relative advantages of the points occupied by yourself and General Floyd, but as far as I can judge our united forces are not more than one-half of the strength of the enemy. Together they may not be able to stand his assault. It would be the height of imprudence to submit them separately to his attack. I am told by General Floyd your position is a very strong one. This one I have not examined, but it seems to have the advantage of yours, in commanding the Wilderness road and the approach to Lewisburg, which I think is the aim of General Rosecrans. I beg therefore, if not too late, that the troops be united, and that we conquer or die together. You have spoken to me of want of consultation and concert; let that pass till the enemy is driven back, and then, as far as I can, all shall be arranged. I expect this of your magnanimity. Consult that and the interest of our cause, and all will go well.

With high respect, your obedient servant,

R. E. LEE,
General, Commanding.

FRAZIER'S, *September* 21, 1861—5 p. m.
General R. E. LEE:

GENERAL: I have just returned from feeling the enemy, being out all night and driving in their pickets this morning, and finding their precise position; but, wet, weary, and fatigued as I am, your note reads so like a rebuke, which I do not think I deserve, that I do not dry or warm my person or lose a moment without replying. I am so desirous to deserve and to have your good opinion and approbation, sir, that you must permit me to be plain in saying that I apprehend you have been told something else besides the fact that my position is a very strong one, and regret that I was not heard before inferences were made to which I cannot consent or correct. In the first place, I consider my force united with that of General Floyd as much as it ever has been, and in a way the most effectual for co-operation. General Floyd has about 3,800, and I about 2,200 men, of all arms, and of these at least 5,500 are efficient. The enemy can now spare from Gauley not more than 2,000 men, and has not elsewhere, with which to attack us in any short time, more than from 4,000 to 5,000 men. If he can be driven to attack General Floyd at Meadow Bluff, advancing by the Wilderness road, he must do it without artillery, and 3,000 men can repulse him as long as he is compelled to divide his force in nearly equal parts in order to bring his artillery at all, as he can bring it only by this turnpike. If he brings it by this turnpike he will be repulsed easily by the Legion, if his force on this road does not exceed 3,500 men. Colonel Davis' successful attack on him in the Kanawha Valley, within 12 miles of Charleston, has drawn two of his regiments to the Lower Valley, and the utmost estimate of his force within not less than 6 miles of my camp is 3,000. But 250 tents, of 6 men each, have been counted, and I have driven in his pickets, and killed one of them, to-day, with five companies of infantry only, with impunity.

So much for this road, except that while I am 6 miles from our enemy (who dares not attack me or to advance), my camp is less than

12 miles from General Floyd's, and we can reciprocally support each other against a divided enemy better than we, combined, can defend against him, combined, at Meadow Bluff. With General Floyd's co-operation here the enemy, combined, cannot turn our flanks. He can easily turn either flank at Meadow Bluff. But this is speculation. I know the country well and have scouted the enemy close. He is not yet combined on this turnpike between me and Gauley, and he is not on the Wilderness road at all. He began to advance upon that road and retreated; and if he is to combine on either road, it will be on this turnpike, between me and Gauley. If that be the fact, it will be better to meet him combined on our own part here. It is immeasurably a stronger position than that of Meadow Bluff. But this even aside, I tell you that he is not going to advance on Lewisburg at all by either road against either position. His main object now is to preserve his base line from Gauley to Huttonsville. He dreads you too much, sir, to advance on Lewisburg while your force is in position to advance on Summersville or to strike his rear from Huntersville. I concur in the imprudence of dividing our forces, but submit, most respectfully, that this is the far stronger position in which to combine, notwithstanding Meadow Bluff is said to command the Wilderness road. That position, I hold, commands nothing, by General Floyd's forces and mine, combined, against 7,000 of the enemy well commanded; and this commands all that can be commanded by our joint forces in the defense of Lewisburg. The two roads and the two positions had perhaps better be examined, I respectfully submit, before my judgment is condemned. But, sir, I am ready to join General Floyd wherever you command, and you do not say where. I will join him here or at Meadow Bluff. The enemy, while I am writing, has been firing on my pickets, as just reported, from the other side of Big Sewell. I chased him to-day a half mile beyond Keeny's, his reported position day before yesterday, and he is now feigning to advance as I retire to camp. I laugh him to scorn, and do not stop writing, as I know he wishes to retire more now than I do. Just say, then, where we are to unite and "conquer or die together" against an enemy who dares not to advance upon the rear guard of a retreat, which has sullenly stopped, turned front, and defied all odds of attack. I have been consulted but twice, and then each time all concert was thwarted by every step of action taken in contradiction to my understanding of joint council. I have let that pass. I was obliged to, for want of relief, and turned all my wrath away from my superior upon the common enemy, whom I am now trying successfully to check, if not to drive back. I stop his artillery, and Meadow Bluff cannot stand it. I ask no consideration, no promises of any sort, to do my duty. I will delight to obey you, sir, even when rebuked. Where common justice has been done me, I trust I have never failed, and never will, to be generous, and I challenge contradiction of the honest, earnest claim for myself, that no man consults more the interest of the cause, according to his best ability and means, than I do. I am ready to do, suffer, and die for it, and I trust, sir, that I may cite you triumphantly as a chief witness of the truth and justice of that claim whenever and by whomsoever it may be assailed. Any imputation upon my motives or intentions in that respect by my superior would make me, perhaps, no longer a military subordinate of any man who breathes. I am sure you mean to cast no such imputation, whoever else may dare. I trust all will go well, most confidently, in your hands.

I am, with the highest respect and esteem, your obedient servant,
                                        HENRY A. WISE.

LEWISBURG, VA., *September* 21, 1861.

To the PRESIDENT:

DEAR SIR: I took the liberty of addressing you by the last mail relative to the anxieties of our people; the proximity and strength of the enemy; the positions of our forces and their numerical strength; our generals, &c.

Since writing reports have reached Lewisburg that the enemy have crossed Gauley, and were advancing by the James River and Kanawha Turnpike eastwardly, and on yesterday they were said to be approaching the western base of Big Sewell Mountain, some 34 or 35 miles west of this. It was also said that General Wise, posted just on this side of the top of Big Sewell, was expecting an attack. I understand that Colonel Henningsen regards General Wise's position as a strong one. I have not heard whether General Floyd has gone to the support of General Wise. At last accounts he was at Meadow Bluff, 16 miles west of this.

Our citizens were much pleased at the arrival of General Lee in our town this morning, *en route* for the west. He passed through, and I suppose by this time has reached Meadow Bluff. He had with him only an escort of cavalry, and I have not heard of any re-enforcement to our little army being expected from Cheat Mountain. His presence in our midst has, however, given great satisfaction, as it assures us that, should the reports of want of harmony and concert have been well founded, no ill consequence can now flow from that source.

I observe that the Richmond Dispatch estimates Rosecrans' army, in the neighborhood of Gauley, at 20,000 men. I think, from all I can learn, this estimate too high, but am yet well asssured that our force is entirely too small to accomplish anything of moment upon the Kanawha Valley. Availing himself of our mountain passes, I hope General Lee will be able to prevent the enemy's farther progress eastwardly, but I fear he will be compelled to abandon all offensive operations until strengthened. Could a few regiments be sent down the western side of New River to the mouth of Gauley and 3,000 or 4,000 men be added to General Wise's and General Floyd's forces from Cheat Mountain, we might be able, I think, to cut off Rosecrans' supplies, and probably force him to a surrender. The repossession of the Kanawha Valley is a matter of very great moment to this section of country, and the occupation of Greenbrier by the enemy would, I fear, be deplorably demoralizing in its effect.

A large number of our young men are enlisted in the war, and out of our seven or eight companies two are at Manassas and one with General Loring.

I hope your excellency will do for us all in your power, for should the enemy succeed in his efforts to "hold, occupy, and possess" Greenbrier, I greatly fear that the difficulty of defending Richmond will be materially enhanced.

We started this morning for Richmond some 42 prisoners, taken by Col. J. Lucius Davis, of Wise's brigade, in Boone County. They are a part of the miscreant band which burned Boone Court-House. Through respect to those holy laws which we are not at liberty to disobey, no matter how vile their conduct, we must extend towards our enemies the benefit of Christian charity and forbearance; but truly our people have been sorely tempted, and it is no less a matter of astonishment than of rejoicing that they have so constantly manifested that noble characteristic of the brave—mercy towards the fallen.

We have entire confidence in General Lee, and doubt not he will do all for us that can be done.

With the highest esteem and respect, your most obedient servant,

W. H. SYME.

QUARTERMASTER-GENERAL'S DEPARTMENT,
Richmond, Va., September 21, 1861.

Hon. J. P. BENJAMIN, *Acting Secretary of War:*

SIR: I received your letter of yesterday in regard to the reported detention of cars at Manassas, and, in obedience to your instructions, have the honor to inform you that I received a telegraph yesterday from Major Cabell, chief of the quartermaster's department at Manassas, informing me that the cars of the Central Railroad were never unnecessarily detained at Manassas, and that no cars were now there. His dispatch was in reply to mine ordering the cars immediately to Richmond. I had been informed by a railroad president that some hundred railroad cars were detained at Manassas.

Several of the Central Railroad cars are detained at Millborough, beyond Staunton. As far as I can discover, there is a mistake in the report of the detention at Manassas.

The superintendent of the Central Railroad, in his reply to my questions to him on the subject of the detention of cars at Manassas, concludes with these words: "I have been misinformed."

Very respectfully, your obedient servant,

A. C. MYERS,
Quartermaster-General.

RICHMOND, *September 22, 1861.*

A. C. MYERS, *Quartermaster-General:*

SIR: I have your letter of 21st instant, which exonerates from blame the quartermaster at Manassas, but this is only half the result required in my letter to you of the 20th instant. I desire to know whose is the fault that the transportation on the road was so blocked up by the absence of cars from Richmond that the Commissary-General was unable to get one thousand barrels of flour conveyed to the army in an emergency. We have now a definite issue before us. You have ascertained that the blame was not attributable to the officer at Manassas. Who was the delinquent? I must insist that the investigation be pursued until the question is satisfactorily answered.

Please to report as early as possible.

Your obedient servant,

J. P. BENJAMIN,
Acting Secretary of War.

HEADQUARTERS, BROOKE'S STATION, *September 22, 1861.*

Col. J. P. BENJAMIN, *Secretary of War:*

DEAR SIR: Yours of the 20th instant is received. I do not see how it is possible for me to aid the fugitive patriots in escaping from Maryland.

They excite my liveliest sympathy, and I have given orders that the troops in the neighborhood of Mathias Point shall extend to them every facility should an opportunity occur. All persons coming from Maryland are permitted to land, but very few, and those under the pass of the War Department, are permitted to return or visit Maryland.

I am, sir, very respectfully, your excellency's obedient servant,

TH. H. HOLMES,
Brigadier-General, Commanding.

HEADQUARTERS, NEAR FARR'S CROSS-ROADS,
September 22, 1861.

To the PRESIDENT:

SIR: In confirmation of my telegram to you in relation to the detention of cars at Manassas, I respectfully submit a letter from Major Cabell, chief quartermaster, and a note to him from the agent of the Orange and Alexandria Railroad.

Most respectfully, your obedient servant,

J. E. JOHNSTON,
General.

[Inclosure No. 1.]

CHIEF QUARTERMASTER'S OFFICE, ARMY OF THE POTOMAC,
September 19, 1861.

Maj. THOMAS G. RHETT,
Assistant Adjutant-General, Army of the Potomac:

MAJOR: I have the honor to acknowledge the receipt of a telegram which was received from President Davis by General Johnston, and referred to me.

In reply, I beg leave to state that I received a telegram from Colonel Myers, Quartermaster-General, early this morning, and made the necessary inquiry and issued the necessary orders to have the cars sent down at once. There are no cars detained for storage either at this place or Manassas, nor have I ordered or allowed any cars to be taken for that purpose. No cars of the Central Railroad, from which the complaint originated, I understand from the president of the Orange and Alexandria Railroad, have been detained here. There were, so he informs me, but twelve cars at Manassas Junction, and those belonged there, yesterday evening, and the military superintendent of the road was informed of that from Manassas by the agent of the road. I have given this my personal attention, and have never permitted cars to be detained here a longer time than it was absolutely necessary to unload them, and I cannot understand why the delays are always attributed to this place. From the best information I can obtain, the delay of the cars is on the western terminus of the Central road, at a place called Millborough, and when investigated it will in my opinion prove correct.

It is impossible to unload a train of cars in an hour, but every exertion is made to unload cars promptly, and to insure a speedy unloading when troops arrive the baggage is always taken and placed on the side of the track before the tents are pitched. I feel confident that an investigation of this will show that no cars have been detained for a longer time than absolutely required for unloading.

I am, sir, very respectfully, your obedient servant,

W. L. CABELL,
Chief Quartermaster Army of the Potomac.

P. S.—I inclose a note from the railroad agent at Manassas.

W. L. CABELL,
Major and Quartermaster.

[Inclosure No. 2.]

MANASSAS, *September* 20, 1861.

Maj. W. L. CABELL:

DEAR SIR: In answer to your inquiry I would state that the cars at this place are unloaded with all possible dispatch and returned. There are none in use as store cars.

Yours, very respectfully,

JAMES A. EVANS,
Agent.

HEADQUARTERS, NEAR FAIRFAX STATION,
September 22, 1861.

Hon. J. P. BENJAMIN, *Acting Secretary of War:*

SIR: I had the honor to receive this morning your letter of the 19th instant and the correspondence inclosed with it.

The President had already, by telegraph, given me orders on the same subject. As evidence against the correctness of the charge, I laid before him letters from Major Cabell, chief quartermaster, and Mr. Evans, agent of the railroad company. Copies of the same letters are respectfully submitted to you.* I hope that they may convince you that the negligence with which we are charged does not exist.

I beg leave to suggest that flour could be bought at very moderate prices in the valley of the Shenandoah, and brought to us, with certainty as to time, on the Manassas Gap Railroad.

Very respectfully, your obedient servant,

J. E. JOHNSTON,
General.

CAMP ON SEWELL, VA., *September* 23, 1861.

General R. E. LEE, *Commanding Forces, &c.:*

GENERAL: The enemy are in strong force on the Big Sewell, I believe in full force (of at least 3,000 men), and a scout just in from Nichol's Mill says 7,000 are reported there. I saw the masses crossing the top of Big Sewell, with artillery and cavalry. We could see about four regiments, and now count thirty camp fires. Their advance commenced firing at mine about one-half hour or an hour by sun. I cannot retire my baggage wagons or other present incumbrances. It is now 12 o'clock at night, and we are expecting an attack. My cavalry has crossed New River to this side, and there are none of the enemy on the old State road. Every few hours I get reports from Nichol's Mill, and there have not been seen any but a few stragglers there. The idea of the

---

* See Johnston to President, same date, p. 872.

enemy passing from Sunday road to the Wilderness road by Nichol's Mill is simply absurd. There is hardly a trail there. If one, no army can possibly pass it that would startle a hare. I am compelled to stand here and fight as long as I can endure and ammunition lasts. All is at stake with my command, and it shall be sold dearly.

I am, very respectfully,

HENRY A. WISE,
Brigadier-General.

CAMP, MEADOW BLUFF, VIRGINIA,
September 23, 1861.

General HENRY A. WISE, *Commanding:*

SIR: I have just received your dispatch of this date, saying that the enemy has occupied Sewell Mountain in full force. It is difficult, without knowing more of the facts in the case, to suggest what is your best course. It will depend upon the force against you and your force-power to withstand it. If you cannot resist it, and are able to withdraw your command, you had best do so. At any rate, send to the rear all your incumbrances. It is reported this evening that the enemy is coming from Sunday road, by Nichol's Mill, to the Wilderness road. Should that prove true, General Floyd cannot advance to your aid, but may have to retire. The presence of the enemy before you may be a feint, to keep you in position while they advance by other roads to the rear of General Floyd. If you find that out and cannot disperse them, retire at once. As soon as anything reliable can be ascertained of the reported movements of the enemy on the Wilderness road you will be informed. Colonel Croghan, with his cavalry, has gone on the old State and Chestnutburg roads, to ascertain if there are any movements of the enemy there.

Very respectfully, your obedient servant,

R. E. LEE,
General, Commanding.

SEPTEMBER 23, 1861.

Maj. Gen. R. E. LEE, *Commanding, &c.:*

GENERAL: I am directed by General Wise to say that the enemy in very heavy columns has occupied the top of Sewell Mountain. Infantry, artillery, and cavalry are all plainly visible from our camp, about 1 mile distant. They have not as yet opened fire, and are reported by some of our cavalry as fortifying. When my last letter of to-day was written, I had just returned from the mission of truce, and the enemy came as fast as I did.

With great respect,

NAT. TYLER,
Lieutenant-Colonel, Infantry, C. S. Army.

CAMP ON SEWELL, VA., *September 23, 1861.*

Maj. Gen. R. E. LEE, *Commanding:*

GENERAL: I am directed by General Wise to send you a copy of a letter addressed by me to him, and to say that Captain Magruder reports the number of tents of the enemy now to be seen as much less than before their late retreat; that he is also of the opinion that General Rosecrans is no longer with General Cox, and that the army now threatening Sewell is in command of General Cox only. I will add that Major Bacon and the other officers who accompanied me with the flag of truce concur in the opinion I have expressed in my letter to General Wise. At the same time it is only an opinion, while the circumstances under which it was forwarded are faithfully stated in my letter to General Wise.

Very respectfully, yours,

NAT. TYLER,
Lieutenant-Colonel First Regiment Wise's Legion.

QUARTERMASTER-GENERAL'S DEPARTMENT,
Richmond, September 23, 1861.

Hon. J. P. BENJAMIN, *Acting Secretary of War:*

SIR: I have received your letter of the 22d instant in reply to a report I made you in reference to the detention of railroad cars at Manassas, which I supposed was the main object of your first inquiry on this subject. Your letter to which I now have the honor of replying remarks, "We have now a definite issue before us, to find out the delinquent, and to pursue the investigation until the question is satisfactorily answered." I inclose herewith a letter from the superintendent of the Central Railroad and one from Maj. W. S. Ashe, assistant quartermaster, specially charged with the superintendence of railroad transportation, from which I gather the fact that the road was idle for some time, and sought to transport public stores without receiving them, and that on a sudden a requisition was made for the transportation of 1,000 barrels of flour, which the road had not the capacity to accomplish.

Very respectfully, your obedient servant,

A. C. MYERS,
Acting Quartermaster-General.

[Inclosure No. 1.]

RICHMOND, *September 23,* 1861.

Col. A. C. MYERS, *Quartermaster-General:*

DEAR SIR: Your letter, inclosing one from the Secretary of War, asking information relative to the detention in the transportation of flour, was duly received. Not having heard of this detention, I sent the letter to the superintendent of the Central Railroad for the information desired. His reply to the inquiry I inclose you. I am confident that he is right in stating that a few weeks back he sought transportation of provisions, observing that his cars were going out empty of Government freight, and he would like to have it sent so as to reach him gradually. This fact, if I mistake not, I brought to your attention.

I will, in addition to what he states, remark that it is almost impossible, without previous notice, to transport, on the moment, such a large amount as 1,000 barrels of provisions. It appears from the response of the superintendent that a portion of them went off on the same day the order was given, the balance on the next and the ensuing day. Although this dispatch was not such as was desired, yet I think it was so prompt, that it relieves the company from any charge of dereliction of duty.

I avail myself of this opportunity to call your attention to the absolute necessity of having cars loaded with freight discharged as soon as practicable. Every moment's delay is felt more than any person who is not acquainted with railroad schedules can conceive of. This should not only be done at the various destinations of freight, but also here in Richmond. I am satisfied that a depot situated near the line of the railroad should be established, so that cars so loaded could be discharged without the aid of wagons, &c.

With respect,

W. S. ASHE.

[Inclosure No. 2.]

VIRGINIA CENTRAL RAILROAD,
GENERAL SUPERINTENDENT'S OFFICE,
Richmond, Va., September 23, 1861.

Maj. W. S. ASHE, *Quartermaster, &c.:*

SIR: In answer to the letter from Acting Secretary of War to Col. A. C. Myers, Quartermaster-General, I respectfully submit the following information:

There are three causes why the Government freight has been detained to some extent, as follows:

1st. The want of rolling stock. This road was provided with barely stock enough for the transportation of produce, &c., in ordinary times, and even then we had delays from want of cars at certain seasons. Now we have the armies of the West, the Northwest, and of the Potomac, the population of a considerable city, to supply. I think I am reasonable in saying that 75 per cent. of the supplies for this army is taken over some portion of our road.

2d. The Government freight is irregular. Two weeks since (I write from memory) I applied to you, as you may recollect, for freight to transport, for I feared the very state of affairs which has since occurred, and for want of Government freight we were transporting goods and merchandise for private parties. Then came this rush upon us, to be followed by another leisure spell.

3d. Want of storage room at several of the points where goods are sent from by wagons to the army at Manassas, Fairfax, and Millborough. At these points goods have remained in the cars, because they could not be unloaded for want of storage. It is not long since one of my employés, one who is considered a reliable man, saw thirteen trains at Manassas; eleven of these were loaded. Some of the trains probably came from Lynchburg. But as we have never sent more than two freight trains from Richmond to Manassas, you must see that there has been detention at one time, to say the least. I have no doubt there was good cause for it. I know that the cars have been detained at Millborough. There were probably fifty loaded cars there on Friday last. You have been obliged to issue orders to have them unloaded without a shelter for the goods. In future I suppose this cause of delay will not trouble us.

But with all the delays I can assure you that the detention in Richmond has not been serious. My impression is that it has not exceeded forty-eight hours, except in the case of the flour mentioned. The order for that came the 18th. We sent seventy barrels that day, and the last of the lot was loaded the 21st and went off this morning.

We are taking no private freights without permission from the quartermaster's office.

Very respectfully,

H. D. WHITCOMB,
General Superintendent.

SPECIAL ORDERS, }   ADJT. AND INSP. GEN.'S OFFICE,
   No. 160.   }   Richmond, Va., September 23, 1861.

   *   *   *   *   *   *   *

11. Col. George E. Pickett, Provisional Army, is assigned to temporary command on the Lower Rappahannock, which will include the troops operating on either side of that river. He will repair to Fredericksburg, Va., and report to Brigadier-General Holmes, commanding that department.

   *   *   *   *   *   *   *

By command of the Secretary of War:

JNO. WITHERS,
Assistant Adjutant-General.

RICHMOND, *September* 24, 1861.

General G. T. BEAUREGARD, *Fairfax Court-House:*

MY DEAR GENERAL: I received your message by the Prince of Polignac. You are aware, I presume, that General Van Dorn has been appointed a major-general, and will report to General Johnston. This will give to the army two major-generals, and will somewhat relieve the labors of General Johnston and yourself. I suggest to you that you converse with General Johnston, and determine between yourselves what divisions you would like to have favored, and which of the brigadier-generals you would both recommend for promotion as major-general.

Without, of course, considering your recommendations as conclusive, both the President and myself would consider them as entitled to great weight, and I doubt not we would be able to gratify the wishes of General Johnston and yourself.

Very truly, yours,

J. P. BENJAMIN,
Acting Secretary of War.

RICHMOND, *September* 24, 1861.

General JOSEPH E. JOHNSTON,
Commanding Army of Potomac, Manassas:

SIR: I have just received your letter of 22d instant, in reply to mine of 19th. I was gratified to ascertain before receiving your reply that there was no truth in the assertion that the delay was caused by the detention of the cars at Manassas, and I am resolute to discover who was really to blame, the more especially for making to me an unfounded written statement in relation to the public service. I find that by oversight the original written statements of the parties were inclosed to you in my letter of 19th instant and no copies reserved in the office. Please return them to me at once, retaining copies if you desire them.

Your obedient servant,

J. P. BENJAMIN,
Acting Secretary of War.

RICHMOND, *September* 24, 1861.

Brig. Gen. ROBERT TOOMBS, *Fairfax Court-House:*

MY DEAR SIR: * * * The President says you are mistaken in considering the Army of the Potomac as two distinct *corps d'armée.* It is one army, under command of General Johnston, who commands in chief. He suggests, therefore, that you make your application on the subject to General Johnston.*

Yours, very truly,

J. P. BENJAMIN,
Acting Secretary of War.

MEADOW BLUFF, VIRGINIA, *September* 24, 1861—4 a. m.

General HENRY A. WISE,
Commanding, &c., Camp on Sewell, Virginia:

GENERAL: Your dispatch of the 23d is just received. I am glad to hear that the force of the enemy in your front does not exceed 3,000. No information that is reliable has been received at this camp from Wilderness road or the Chestnutburg road, nor have I any more tidings of the enemy passing from the Sunday road to the Wilderness road than I have already given. It seems from your letter that by the report of one of your scouts, there are 7,000 at Nichol's Mill. In another part of your letter you state that only a few stragglers are there. I am unable, therefore, to form any opinion as to their numbers at that point. I regret to hear that you cannot retire your baggage wagons, &c., and are compelled to remain, as at the distance you are from support it may jeopardize the whole command. Please send word whether you have sufficient ammunition, and any information as to the operations of the enemy that may serve to regulate the movements of General Floyd.

I am, with high respect, your obedient servant,

R. E. LEE,
General, Commanding.

CAMP DEFIANCE, BIG SEWELL, VIRGINIA,
September 24, 1861—7.15 a. m.

General R. E. LEE, *Commanding, &c.:*

GENERAL: Last night in camp, very busy. In pencil I noted what my secretary should communicate to you. I infer from your note of 4 o'clock this morning that he must have reversed everything I noted. The enemy's force in my front is from three to seven thousand. None of them on the old State road, where I have a strong force of cavalry far down below this position, and none even at Nichol's Mill except two stragglers. I sent you no reliable information last night about any road leading from the Sunday to the Wilderness road. There is no such road, or, if any, it is an impassable trail to any but foot, and no enemy yet seen on the Nichol's Mill road in any force. I tell you emphatically, sir, that the enemy are advancing in strong force on this turnpike. They are not advancing on the old State road at all, as yet, and none but two stragglers were seen yesterday at or near Nichol's Mill. Their advance ceased firing at dark last evening, wounding Captain Lewis and 2 privates, neither mortally, though Lewis severely. They were quiet last night, and we are ready this morning. I have a good supply of ammunition and provisions; shall keep them here, and start away my baggage wagons, if I can, this morning. I trust, at least, that their retreat can be protected and guarded by General Floyd's command. If

---

* Personal matter omitted.

you order me to retreat, I ask that my wagons may be emptied of their baggage and the teamsters be forwarded back to me, to take off the ammunition and supplies. I desire to save everything, if compelled to retire.

With the highest respect,

HENRY A. WISE,
Brigadier-General.

CAMP DEFIANCE, VIRGINIA, *September* 24, 1861.
Maj. Gen. R. E. LEE, *Commanding:*

GENERAL: I am directed by General Wise to say to you that the enemy are advancing from their position on Big Sewell towards our lines.

Very respectfully,

NAT. TYLER.

CAMP DEFIANCE, BIG SEWELL, VIRGINIA,
September 25, 1861—5.5 o'clock.
General R. E. LEE:

GENERAL: By your aide (under the approach and fire of the enemy, at a stand, made under my orders, where the struggle will be severe, whatever be the result) I received the within order from the Acting Secretary of War.* It is imperative, requiring "the least delay," but it could not have foreseen these circumstances—the most extremely embarrassing to me. I come to you for counsel, and will abide by it, because I have been under your eye, and you are competent to judge my act and its motive, whatever it may be. I desire to delay my report in person until after the fate of this battle. Dare I do so? On the other hand, can I, in honor, leave you at this moment, though the disobedience of the order may subject me to the severest penalties? Will you please advise and instruct me?

I am, with the highest respect and esteem, your obedient servant,

HENRY A. WISE,
Brigadier-General.

[Answer.]

[No date.]

GENERAL: I will briefly state, in answer to your inquiry, appreciating, as I do, the reluctance and embarrassment you feel at leaving your Legion at this time, what I should feel compelled to do, as a military man, under like circumstances. That is, to obey the President's order. The enemy is in our presence and testing the strength of our position. What may be the result, whether he will determine to attack or whether we may retire, cannot now be foreseen. I can conceive the desire your command would have for your presence, yet they will also do justice to your position.

With highest esteem, your obedient servant,

R. E. LEE,
General, Commanding.

---

* Not found.

STAUNTON, VA., *September* 25, 1861.

General COOPER :

SIR : By an order of General Jackson I have brought the two companies (I and K) of the Twentieth Regiment Virginia Volunteers to this place, to await further orders. From the fact that the two companies have been ordered from active service to this place, I ask leave to submit to you, sir, a report of their condition. They have been engaged in active duties since the 3d of June last.

After our disastrous retreat from Rich Mountain all the companies of the Twentieth Regiment asked to return home for the purpose of recruiting, except Companies I and K. We were ordered to form a separate battalion, and to act as a guard to Captain Shumaker's battery of Danville artillery, which position we have occupied ever since, up to the late order of General Jackson. Shortly after our retreat, before the men could recover from cold contracted from exposure, the measles broke out in our company. In Company I alone there were 50 cases. The men have mostly recovered from the measles, but the debility consequent upon this disease has left them unfit for the hard service of the northwest.

There are at present here now 38 men, rank and file, of Company I. Of this number there are not more than 25 who would be fit for duty. The most of the company were granted furloughs from this place and Richmond, and from last accounts they were, or most of them, convalescent. The same statement is true of Company K. Besides the sickness in Company I at this time 7 have died and 6 were taken prisoners. Company K is under command of first lieutenant in Company I, it being destitute of a commander. Two of their lieutenants were taken prisoners at Rich Mountain. The other has since died. Their captain has been lying in Richmond sick for the last two or three weeks.

In view of all these facts I most respectfully suggest that if it is not the purpose of the Government to muster these companies out of service, they be permitted to visit their homes under a furlough for thirty days, to recruit their health and attend to their business—such as would need their immediate presence to transact. I will further say that, under favorable circumstances, in thirty days each of these companies ought to report at least 60 men, rank and file.

Respectfully submitted.

JOSEPH JONES,
Captain, Comdg. Companies I and K, Twentieth Reg't Va. Vols.

RICHMOND, VA., *September* 25, 1861.

JACOB VAN METER and others,
 Hardy County, Virginia :

GENTLEMEN : In reply to your memorial [of 10th instant] to the President, I have to say that it is hoped the expectations entertained by the citizens of Hardy County with regard to the operation of General Lee's army will be realized, but in any event attention will be given to their exposed condition at the earliest possible moment.

Respectfully,

A. T. BLEDSOE,
Chief of Bureau of War.

HEADQUARTERS ARMY OF KANAWHA,
September 25, 1861.

Maj. ISAAC B. DUNN:

SIR: Your note September 23 is at hand. In reply I am instructed by General Floyd to say that he would urge you to send up his re-enforcements with all possible dispatch. To this end you will use every possible effort to get transportation for them upon arrival at Jackson River Depot. The enemy have concentrated their entire available force in Western and Northwestern Virginia on this road, and it is absolutely necessary to the command of General Floyd and to the cause that he should have re-enforcements, and this speedily. The enemy have already appeared before Wise in large force. General Lee went to his succor with four of General Floyd's regiments, which leaves the latter with a very small force. Hence you see the necessity of rapid re-enforcements.

By order of Brig. Gen. John B. Floyd:

WILLIAM E. PETERS,
Assistant Adjutant-General, Floyd's Brigade.

P. S.—General Wise was fighting yesterday, but with what success I have not learned.

GENERAL ORDERS, }   HDQRS. ARMY OF THE POTOMAC,
No. 31.   }   *September* 25, 1861.

I. Maj. Gen. Gustavus W. Smith, Provisional Army Confederate States, is assigned to the command of the Second Corps of the Army of the Potomac.

II. The Second Corps will consist of the troops of this army not heretofore assigned to the First Corps.

By command of General Johnston:

THOS. G. RHETT,
Assistant Adjutant-General.

HEADQUARTERS ARMY OF THE POTOMAC,
September 26, 1861.

Hon. SECRETARY OF WAR, *Richmond:*

SIR: The troops now under my command occupy a front of about 6 miles from Flint Hill, through Fairfax Court-House and Fairfax Station, to Sangster's Cross-Roads. An advance guard of eleven regiments of infantry and Colonel Stuart's cavalry is stationed at Falls Church, Munson's and Mason's Hills, at Padgett's (where the Columbian turnpike enters that from Alexandria to Fairfax), and at Springfield Station, on the Orange and Alexandria Railroad. Munson's Hill is apparently little more than 3 miles from the enemy's line of works on the heights extending from Georgetown to Alexandria. I assumed this advanced position as soon as the repair of the railroad enabled the Quartermaster's and Commissary Departments to afford us supplies with a twofold object—to remove the troops from the unhealthy atmosphere of the valley of Bull Run and to be ready to turn the enemy's position and advance into Maryland whenever the strength of this army would justify it. By ordering the troops forward, besides securing healthy and comfortable locations, we could keep better watch over the enemy and maintain an attitude in accordance with our recent victory. Thus far the numbers and condition of this army have at no time justified our assuming the offensive. To do so would require more men and munitions.

We are not now in a strong defensive position either to fight a battle or to hold the enemy in check. The position was occupied for a different purpose. It is now necessary to decide definitely whether we are to advance or fall back to a more defensible line. There are very grave and serious objections to the latter course, and the idea even should not be entertained until after it is finally determined to be impracticable to place this army in such condition as would justify its taking at an early day the active offensive. The difficulty of obtaining the means of establishing a battery near Evansport and length of time required for the collection of those means have given me the impression that you cannot at present put this army in condition to assume the offensive. If I am mistaken in this, and you can furnish those means, I think it important that either his excellency the President of the Confederate States, yourself, or some one representing you, should here upon the ground confer with me in regard to this all-important question. I send this by an officer of my staff, who can give you detailed information in regard to the positions now occupied by the troops under my command. I beg you to write an answer by the officer who will deliver this as soon as may be convenient to you.

Most respectfully, your obedient servant,
J. E. JOHNSTON,
General.

DUMFRIES, *September* 27, 1861.
President JEFFERSON DAVIS:

Colonel Hampton's battery, at the mouth of Powell's Run, on my left, opened on several small vessels passing yesterday. The war steamers of Lincoln's hug the Maryland shore and remain silent. The Long Tom is moved this morning farther down the river. My command are looking over into Maryland as the promised land. Major Marshall is with me.
L. T. WIGFALL,
[*Colonel First Texas Infantry.*]

FAIRFAX COURT-HOUSE, *September* 28, 1861.
Hon. J. P. BENJAMIN, *Acting Secretary of War, Richmond, Va.:*

MY DEAR SIR: Your favor of the 24th instant has only this day been received, and in accordance with your suggestion General Johnston and myself have prepared a list of major and brigadier generals which we hope will be approved of by the President and yourself, for they have been selected entirely according to their reputation and merit as officers. They have few equals, and none superior, in any service. What is required is prompt action, for we may at any time be called upon to meet again the "Grand Army of the North," which this time will do its best to wipe out the disgrace of Manassas, and these officers ought to have a few days to organize their divisions and staffs before the battle commences. One or two major-generals only to each corps would not help us materially. General Johnston has seven and I nine brigades of from three to five regiments each of volunteers, so that our orders have to be so multiplied and repeated, that the genius of a Napoleon would get entangled on a day of battle. What we want is a simplification of the whole system, with one head and several co-ordinate branches.

With much respect, I remain, yours, very truly,

G. T. BEAUREGARD.

RICHMOND, *September* 29, 1861.

General JOSEPH E. JOHNSTON,
Headquarters Army of the Potomac:

SIR: Your letter of the 26th instant has been handed to me by Captain Preston, and has received the attention both of the President and myself. It is extremely difficult, even with the aid of such information as Captain Preston has been able to give us orally, as suggested by you, to determine whether or not we can furnish you the further means you may deem necessary to assume the active offensive. We have not in the Department a single return from your army of the quantity of ammunition, artillery, means of transportation, or sick in camp or in hospitals, to enable us to form a judgment of what your necessities may be. Having had charge of the War Department but a few days, my first effort was to master our situation, to understand thoroughly what we had and in what our deficiencies consisted, but I have been completely foiled at all points by the total absence of systematic returns. I beg to call your attention to this, as it will be obvious to you that the Department cannot be administered without a thorough reform in this respect. I have, therefore, earnestly requested the President to visit your headquarters in person, and to learn on conference with you the true position of your army in all respects, and the possibility of a prompt offensive movement. He has consented to this, and I hope will reach your camp within a day or two. Your note relative to Captain Mansfield Lovell will be carefully considered in disposing of the services of that justly-esteemed officer.

I am, respectfully,

J. P. BENJAMIN,
Acting Secretary of War.

DUMFRIES, *September* 29, 1861.

General S. COOPER:

GENERAL: I am happy to inform you that the first of our river batteries at Evansport is finished, and guns mounted ready for service without discovery by the enemy. I write you to-night.

Yours,

I. R. TRIMBLE,
Brigadier-General, Commanding.

Abstract from a field return, September 30, 1861, of the First Corps, Army of the Potomac, commanded by General Beauregard.

Troops.	Present for duty.		Total present.	Aggregate present.	Total present and absent.	Aggregate present and absent.
	Officers.	Men.				
General staff	17	....	17	17	17	17
Infantry	1,286	19,759	25,091	26,549	30,183	31,886
Cavalry	88	1,237	1,411	1,502	1,809	1,925
Artillery	59	1,072	1,223	1,283	1,568	1,645
Total	1,450	22,068	27,742	29,351	33,577	35,478

Abstract from return of the Department of Fredericksburg, commanded by Brig. Gen. T. H. Holmes, for September, 1861.

Station.	Present for duty.		Aggregate present and absent.
	Officers.	Men.	
Evansport and vicinity	124	1,885	3,160
Marlborough Point	3	36	70
Do	36	483	725
Camp Holmes	36	494	855
Camp Bee	38	479	787
Aquia Creek	29	366	869
Cross Roads	3	66	97
King George County	3	44	96
Camp Clifton	25	337	514
Camp Potomac	38	362	646
Mathias Point	9	92	182
Tappahannock	33	416	647
Fort Lowry	3	26	71
Richmond County	26	305	331
Heathsville	19	319	357
Grand total	425	5,710	9,407

Council of war at Centreville.

OCTOBER 1, 1861.*

On the 26th September, 1861, General Joseph E. Johnston addressed a letter to the Secretary of War in regard to the importance of putting this army in condition to assume the offensive, and suggested that his excellency the President, or the Secretary of War, or some one representing them, should at an early day come to the headquarters of the army, then at or near Fairfax Court-House, for the purpose of deciding whether the army could be re-enforced to the extent that the commanding general deemed necessary for an offensive campaign.

His excellency the President arrived at Fairfax Court-House a few days thereafter, late in the afternoon, and proceeded to the quarters of General Beauregard. On the same evening General Johnston and I

* The exact date does not appear in the records. That above is approximately, if not absolutely, correct.

called to pay our respects. No official subjects of importance were alluded to in that interview. At 8 o'clock the next evening, by appointment of the President, a conference was had between himself, General Johnston, General Beauregard, and myself. Various matters of detail were introduced by the President, and talked over between himself and the two senior generals. Having but recently arrived, and not being well acquainted with the special subjects referred to, I took little or no part in this conversation. Finally, with perhaps some abruptness, I said: "Mr. President, is it not possible to put this army in condition to assume the active offensive?" adding that this was a question of vital importance, upon which the success or failure of our cause might depend. This question brought on discussion. The precise conversation which followed I do not propose to give; it was not an argument. There seemed to be little difference of opinion between us in regard to general views and principles. It was clearly stated and agreed to that the military force of the Confederate States was at the highest point it could attain without arms from abroad; that the portion of this particular army present for duty was in the finest fighting condition; that if kept inactive it must retrograde immensely in every respect during the winter, the effect of which was foreseen and dreaded by us all. The enemy were daily increasing in number, arms, discipline, and efficiency. We looked forward to a sad state of things at the opening of a spring campaign.

These and other points being agreed upon without argument, it was again asked: "Mr. President, is it not possible to increase the effective strength of this army, and put us in condition to cross the Potomac and carry the war into the enemy's country? Can you not by stripping other points to the last they will bear, and, even risking defeat at all other places, put us in condition to move forward? Success here at this time saves everything; defeat here loses all." In explanation and as an illustration of this the unqualified opinion was advanced that if for want of adequate strength on our part in Kentucky the Federal forces should take military possession of that whole State, and even enter and occupy a portion of Tennessee, a victory gained by this army beyond the Potomac would, by threatening the heart of the Northern States, compel their armies to fall back, free Kentucky, and give us the line of the Ohio within ten days thereafter. On the other hand, should our forces in Tennessee and Southern Kentucky be strengthened, so as to enable us to take and to hold the Ohio River as a boundary, a disastrous defeat of this army would at once be followed by an overwhelming wave of Northern invaders, that would sweep over Kentucky and Tennessee, extending to the northern part of the cotton States, if not to New Orleans. Similar views were expressed in regard to ultimate results in Northwestern Virginia being dependent upon the success or failure of this army, and various other special illustrations were offered, showing, in short, that success here was success everywhere, defeat here defeat everywhere; and that this was the point upon which all the available forces of the Confederate States should be concentrated.

It seemed to be conceded by all that our force at that time here was not sufficient for assuming the offensive beyond the Potomac, and that even with a much larger force an attack upon their army under the guns of their fortifications on this side of the river was out of the question.

The President asked me what number of men were necessary in my opinion to warrant an offensive campaign, to cross the Potomac, cut off the communications of the enemy with their fortified capital, and

carry the war into their country. I answered, "Fifty thousand effective, *seasoned* soldiers," explaining that by *seasoned* soldiers I meant such
men as we had here present for duty, and added that they would have
to be drawn from the Peninsula, about Yorktown, Norfolk, from Western Virginia, Pensacola, or wherever might be most expedient.

General Johnston and General Beauregard both said that a force of
sixty thousand such men would be necessary, and that this force would
require large additional transportation and munitions of war, the supplies here being entirely inadequate for an active campaign in the enemy's country even with our present force. In this connection there was
some discussion of the difficulties to be overcome and the probabilities
of success, but no one questioned the disastrous results of remaining
inactive throughout the winter. Notwithstanding the belief that many
in the Northern Army were opposed on principle to invading the Southern States, and that they would fight better in defending their own
homes than in attacking ours, it was believed that the best, if not the
only, plan to insure success was to concentrate our forces and attack the
enemy in their own country. The President, I think, gave no definite
opinion in regard to the number of men necessary for that purpose, and
I am sure that no one present considered this a question to be finally decided by any other person than the commanding general of this army.

Returning to the question that had been twice asked, the President
expressed surprise and regret that the number of surplus arms here was
so small, and I thought spoke bitterly of this disappointment. He then
stated that at that time *no re-enforcements could be furnished to this army
of the character asked for*, and that the most that could be done would
be to furnish recruits to take the surplus arms in store here (say 2,500
stand); that the whole country was demanding protection at his hands
and praying for arms and troops for defense. He had long been expecting arms from abroad, but had been disappointed; he still hoped to get
them, but had no positive assurance that they would be received at all.
The manufacture of arms in the Confederate States was as yet undeveloped to any considerable extent. Want of arms was the great difficulty; he could not take any troops from the points named, and without
arms from abroad could not re-enforce this army. He expressed regret,
and seemed to feel deeply, as did every one present.

When the President had thus clearly and positively stated his inability to put this army in the condition deemed by the generals necessary before entering upon an active offensive campaign, it was felt that
it might be better to run the risk of almost certain destruction fighting
upon the other side of the Potomac rather than see the gradual dying
out and deterioration of this army during a winter, at the end of which
the term of enlistment of half the force would expire. The prospect of
a spring campaign to be commenced under such discouraging circumstances was rendered all the more gloomy by the daily increasing
strength of an enemy already much superior in numbers.

On the other hand was the hope and expectation that before the end
of winter arms would be introduced into the country, and all were confident that we could then not only protect our own country, but successfully invade that of the enemy.

General Johnston said that he did not feel at liberty to express an
opinion as to the practicability of reducing the strength of our forces at
points not within the limits of his command, and with but few further
remarks from any one the answer of the President was accepted as final,
and it was felt that there was no other course left but to take a defensive
position and await the enemy. If they did not advance, we had but to
await the winter and its results.

After the main question was dropped, the President proposed that, instead of an active offensive campaign, we should attempt certain partial operations—a sudden blow against Sickles or Banks or to break the bridge over the Monocacy. This, he thought, besides injuring the enemy, would exert a good influence over our troops and encourage the people of the Confederate States generally. In regard to attacking Sickles, it was stated in reply that, as the enemy controlled the river with their ships of war, it would be necessary for us to occupy two points on the river, one above and another below the point of crossing, that we might by our batteries prevent their armed vessels from interfering with the passage of the troops. In any case, the difficulty of crossing large bodies over wide rivers in the vicinity of an enemy and then recrossing made such expeditions hazardous. It was agreed, however, that if any opportunity should occur offering reasonable chances of success, the attempt would be made.

During this conference or council, which lasted perhaps two hours, all was earnest, serious, deliberate. The impression made upon me was deep and lasting; and I am convinced that the foregoing statement is not only correct as far as it goes, but in my opinion it gives a fair idea of all that occurred at that time in regard to the question of our crossing the Potomac.

G. W. SMITH,
Major-General, C. S. Army.

Our recollections of that conference agree fully with this statement of General G. W. Smith.

G. T. BEAUREGARD,
General, C. S. Army.
J. E. JOHNSTON,
General, C. S. Army.

Signed in triplicate.
CENTREVILLE, *January* 31, 1862.

RICHMOND, *October* 1, 1861.

JAMES L. RANSON, Esq., *Charlestown, Jefferson County, Va.:*

SIR: The President requests me to acknowledge the receipt of your letter of 27th instant in regard to border defense, &c., and to express his great gratification with the spirit manifested by you and your fellow-citizens on the border, as expressed in your letter.

I beg leave to call your attention to the act of Congress of August 21, 1861 (No. 229), "To provide for local defense," &c., in explanation of the mode in which volunteers may be enlisted and accepted for such service. It has been the policy of the Department to refer all offers of troops for such special service to the general officer commanding in the district of country for which they are intended, as being best able to judge of the necessities for defense in such locality. So far as may be possible consistently with this policy, every encouragement will be given to the people of the border counties to enlist for the defense of their own homes. All offers of troops should be communicated here, stating manner and time of proposed enlistment, &c.

Volunteer companies elect their own officers.

Respectfully,

J. P. BENJAMIN,
Acting Secretary of War.

RICHMOND, VA., *October* 1, 1861.

Capt. C. R. MASON,
 Assistant Quartermaster, now at Richmond, Va.:

SIR : You are assigned to the special duty of superintending the road from Staunton to Greenbrier River, the headquarters of General H. R. Jackson, and from the Warm Springs to Huntersville; also to the headquarters of General Loring. It will be your especial care to repair the roads and bridges wherever it is required; and to keep them in order for the transportation of supplies from Staunton to the several headquarters named above. You will rebuild the bridges and renew the embankments where required on account of the late freshet. To enable you to perform this work thoroughly you are, with the consent of the governor of Virginia, empowered to use all the appliances for work and labor that have been in use on the State road, and to hire or purchase, as you may regard best, wagons, carts, and teams, and all additional labor you think necessary.*

A. C. MYERS,
 Acting Quartermaster-General.

HEADQUARTERS VIRGINIA FORCES,
ADJUTANT AND INSPECTOR GENERAL'S OFFICE,
 Richmond, Va., October 3, 1861.

Maj. GEORGE S. STEVENS, *Commanding, Nelson Station, Va.:*

SIR : I have the honor to submit to you the following remarks of Governor Letcher relative to your detailed report of the state of the militia in the county of Nelson, dated the 23d ultimo, viz:

EXECUTIVE DEPARTMENT, *September* 28, 1861.

The county of Nelson not having furnished her quota of volunteers, the militia went into camp August 6, 1861. The return of the colonel, one received at the office of the adjutant-general (Richardson), on the 7th of this month, showed that he then had at Camp Mitchell 197. This return shows 163, a reduction of 34. Under the 10 per cent. regulation they were short of their quota upwards of 150 men. While in the camp I proposed, if they would furnish a company of 80 volunteers, I would accept them and disband the balance. These men were to be furnished by a given day, which has long since passed. I still indulged them, and told the officers and others who called upon me that if the number of 80 was not furnished I would order the militia to rendezvous at Staunton, where they would be attached to a regiment being formed at that place. Finding they would do nothing, they were ordered to Staunton. After the order was issued Major Stevens came here to see me, and did not pretend to justify their conduct. Among other things, he said, in the presence of Colonel Dimmock, that they did not think I would order them into service; that I was not in earnest. I told him as the order had been given they could now tell whether I had been jesting on so serious a subject, and that he must return and execute the order without delay.

JOHN LETCHER.

Very respectfully, your obedient servant,

GEO. DEAS,
 Assistant Adjutant-General.

RICHMOND, *October* 4, 1861.

General JOSEPH E. JOHNSTON,
 Fairfax Court-House, Va.:

I have this moment received a dispatch dated at Fredericksburg at 12.30 o'clock, stating that the enemy are landing near Occoquan in

---

*Details omitted.

large numbers, and that General Whiting, at Dumfries, has ordered [*sic*] General Holmes' whole brigade there immediately, and has also notified Captain Kennedy at Aquia Creek to look out.

J. P. BENJAMIN,
Acting Secretary of War.

FAIRFAX COURT-HOUSE, *October* 4, 1861.

Hon. J. P. BENJAMIN, *Secretary of War :*

Your dispatch of to-day received. I have a report from General Whiting, written at 12 m. to-day, that the enemy was advancing toward the Occoquan by the Pohick road. We have no information of such a movement. Our pickets near Pohick were driven early this morning. I have delayed this dispatch for fuller information, but have received none.

J. E. JOHNSTON,
General, Commanding.

SPECIAL ORDERS, }   HEADQUARTERS ARMY OF THE POTOMAC,
No. 401.   }   *October* 4, 1861.

Maj. Gen. Earl Van Dorn is assigned to duty with the First Corps, Army of the Potomac, and will report to General G. T. Beauregard.

By command of General Johnston:

THOS. G. RHETT,
Assistant Adjutant-General.

CHARLESTOWN, *October* 5, 1861.

Hon. J. P. BENJAMIN,
Secretary of War ad interim, &c.:

DEAR SIR : At the instance of a number of the good citizens in this quarter of the State (my own judgment fully concurring) I am induced to call your attention to the condition of things here connected with the operations of the military, and I beg leave to protest that I do so under a full sense of the diffidence and delicacy which should govern a mere civilian in dealing with such subjects. I know of no one connected with the military at Winchester or on this border who is not my personal friend, and as to whom certainly I have none other than the most kindly feelings, and yet I deem it my duty to say broadly that the management of military affairs in this quarter is in utterly incompetent hands.

Ever since General Johnston marched his army from Winchester in July, most absurdly as it seems to me and to hundreds of others here, large bodies of militia have been assembled there and kept there, 30 miles from the border, where the enemy are constantly not only committing depredations, but doing everything in their power to debauch the minds of our people off from their allegiance and loyalty to the South, and recently, at the very time when the enemy are making their boldest inroads upon us, plundering, insulting females, and keeping the whole border for miles into the interior in a state of uneasiness and alarm, the militia from this (Jefferson) county have been marched away to Winchester, and are now held there under the miserable pretext of drilling them.

The feeling is becoming very general among our people that while we have plenty of men ready and willing to protect the border against these incursions of the enemy, yet that we are suffering needlessly for want of competent officers. Without, therefore, entering further into particulars, or preferring complaints of incompetency or inefficiency against any particular officer or officers, I beg leave to submit whether it be not practicable and expedient to send here (that is, on this border of the valley) some competent regular or experienced officer of the army to take charge of and direct the whole military operations in this quarter, or if this can't be done, and we must have the peace establishment militia officers still in command, then that some experienced and intelligent officer be sent here to inquire into the condition of things, and report what is proper to be done.

My friend and colleague Hon. A. R. Boteler I presume is now in Richmond, and he will give you full and minute information about the matters and things referred to in the foregoing.

Very truly, your obedient servant,

ANDREW HUNTER.

HDQRS. FIRST CORPS, ARMY OF THE POTOMAC,
Fairfax Court-House, October 5, 1861.

Maj. Gen. E. VAN DORN, *Commanding Division :*

GENERAL : As active operations are immediately impending, the general directs that you send without delay all heavy baggage of the regiments of your division to Fairfax Station, to be transported thence by rail to Manassas. In charge of this baggage will be sent one commissioned officer from each brigade, one non-commissioned officer from each regiment, and one trusty private from each company.

This party is to remain at Manassas until further orders, and the officer in command will report to Brigadier-General Clark at that post.

Your brigade quartermaster will superintend the forwarding of this baggage from the station, reporting to the chief quartermaster of this corps when he will be ready for a train to receive it.

Respectfully, your obedient servant,

THOMAS JORDAN,
Assistant Adjutant-General.

NEAR CHARLESTOWN, *October* 6, 1861.

Hon. J. P. BENJAMIN,
Acting Secretary of War, Richmond, Va.:

SIR: Your agreeable and most acceptable communication of the 1st instant reached me by yesterday's mail, and all you say upon the subject of our border is encouraging.

The work goes on encouragingly, and the scarcity of horses alone prevents our putting into the field at once a corps of mounted men that would, under a proper leader, render valuable service. Colonel Baylor has a goodly number, and if horses can be had will soon raise one hundred or more. Capt. Jo. Hess has now already mounted one hundred, and both of these patriotic men are scouting the borders of this county night and day, in conjunction with others, Colonel Ashby and Captain Henderson—the last-named gentleman confined at present by a shot by one of his own men ; and in connection with this sad affair I beg leave to say that should the court-martial sitting in Winchester blunder upon an acquittal, or what would be tantamount, fall down to some compromise sentence, it would have a most unfortunate influence throughout this border. There would be great difficulty in future in enforcing subordination. It is reported that a corps of lawyers are engaged, and, as proof, the trial drags, and procrastination is the consequence.

You refer to the law and the policy of the Department. The law we have not, and I fear cannot obtain it short of Richmond, and I dread the control of militia commanders, Letcherized all over, as they generally are, and therefore sought for officers, if to be had, direct from President Davis.

Are there not clever and well qualified officers of the Confederate Army not in the field who have no men ? I remember to have met one or more in the army of the lamented Garnett—Captain Cole and Captain Alexander. The latter, I grieve to learn, died shortly since. The former I should rejoice to meet on our borders—a graduate of West Point and a gallant officer. (Could not Col. Jack Hays be had for this service ? All would acknowledge his pre-eminent qualifications.) But we will do our best. The enemy make daily crossings over the Potomac, and I deem it all important in case of collision that our raw men should be preserved from disaster.

The reference to military commanders—is it militia ? The general of this brigade, a very clever civilian, with no experience in the field, may guide us, and successfully, but I have my fears. The gallant Ashby will do to lead cavalry, but we want a man to lead infantry and artillery.

Hoping the subject of my letter may prove a sufficient apology for this lengthy communication, I am, most respectfully, your obedient servant,

JAMES L. RANSON.

HEADQUARTERS ARMY OF THE POTOMAC,
October 7, 1861.

General S. COOPER, *Adjutant and Inspector General :*

GENERAL : As the cold season of the year is near, it seems to me time to decide whether huts shall be constructed for the troops of this army or they shall continue to lodge in tents.

Should the construction of huts be decided upon, shall the materials be prepared elsewhere and put together on the ground here or shall the troops erect log huts ?

General Beauregard, a skillful engineer, proposes the first method. It would require much time and labor, I think, to collect in this neighborhood timber enough for the second.

I respectfully ask the early decision of these questions by the honorable Secretary of War.

Very respectfully, your obedient servant,

J. E. JOHNSTON,
General.

RICHMOND, *October* 7, 1861.

General JOSEPH E. JOHNSTON,
Headquarters Army of the Potomac:

GENERAL: I have had a conference with the President since his return on the subject of the organization of the Army of the Potomac, as recommended in your letter of the 28th ultimo,* and not received till after his departure for your headquarters.

The President cannot persuade himself that the number of generals of all grades recommended by the joint letter of yourself, General Beauregard, and Major-General Smith can be necessary for the number of troops now forming the Army of the Potomac. The inconvenience of so large an accession of general officers in the service would be felt in more than one way. Not the least of the objections is that it could not be accorded without revolting injustice to the Army of the Potomac alone. Of necessity we should be compelled to make similar appointments in each of the other armies and military departments, and by this vast increase not only cheapen the value of military rank, but augment the expenses of the war at a moment when its hourly increasing proportions admonish us that the most rigid economy is required.

In view of all the facts and circumstances, the President has concluded that an addition to your army of two major-generals and two or three brigadier-generals will afford you as much assistance as could reasonably be required, and he has directed the promotion of Brigadier-Generals Longstreet and Jackson to the rank of majors-general. Your army will then have as general officers two generals; four major-generals of provisional army, namely, Van Dorn, Smith, Longstreet, and Jackson; thirteen brigadier-generals, namely, Bonham, Clark, Walker, Ewell, Jones, Kirby Smith, Toombs, Crittenden, Sam Jones, Whiting, Elzey, Early, and Stuart. Total, nineteen general officers, to whom will be added some two or three other brigadier-generals that it will be necessary to appoint after you shall have made the changes recommended by the President in uniting the troops from each State as far as possible into the same brigades and divisions, so as to gratify the natural State pride of the men, and keep up that healthful and valuable emulation which forms so important an element in military affairs. The whole number of general officers will thus be about twenty-two in an army of —— thousand men. I will not state the number as matter of prudence, but you can make the calculation, and I feel sure you will admit that it is thus as fully officered as armies generally are, and certainly more fully than any army we have in the field.

Please to communicate this answer to Generals Beauregard and Smith, who joined in signing your letter to the Department.

Your obedient servant,

J. P. BENJAMIN,
Acting Secretary of War.

ADJUTANT AND INSPECTOR GENERAL'S OFFICE,
Richmond, October 7, 1861.

Lieut. Col. TURNER ASHBY, *McDonald's Regiment:*

COLONEL: Inclosed herewith you will find copy of a special order increasing your command to four companies of Colonel McDonald's regiment of cavalry and four companies of Colonel Monroe's regiment of

---

* Not found.

Virginia militia (infantry). You are also authorized to muster into service for local defense, in accordance with authority given by inclosed copy of the law, a sufficient number of men to serve the pieces of artillery now with your command, organizing them into a company of artillery. It is desired that you will make out with the cavalry equipments now in the possession of the four cavalry companies, as they cannot be supplied from here.

It is especially desired that you will destroy the Chesapeake and Ohio Canal as quickly as possible wherever found practicable, whether at the Monocacy or other point.

I am, sir, very respectfully,

R. H. CHILTON,
Assistant Adjutant-General.

HEADQUARTERS BROOKE'S STATION,
October 9, 1861.

General S. COOPER, *Adjutant-General C. S. Army:*

GENERAL: I returned from Evansport last night. The two principal batteries could open fire at once, as their guns are mounted; but a letter from General Johnston to General Trimble requests that our fire may be delayed until he has completed certain arrangements of his own, of which he will advise us. I have little doubt the batteries will be abundantly able to block the river, except in dark nights; and if the enemy should attempt to capture them, I have as little doubt that the force there, aided by General Whiting's command near there, will be able to defeat him.

The season is approaching when it will be necessary for us to make our arrangements for winter. Will you do me the favor to advise me whether I shall make preparations in the positions we now occupy, or is it better to wait further developments before acting in the matter?

I am, general, very respectfully, your obedient servant,

TH. H. HOLMES,
Brigadier-General, Commanding.

RICHMOND, VA., *October* 10, 1861.

Maj. Gen. G. W. SMITH, *Army of the Potomac:*

MY DEAR GENERAL: I had the pleasure to receive yours of the 8th* instant last night. The matter of controlling railroad transportation has frequently engaged my attention, but was not presented in the form you offer, that of being under the charge of General Beauregard. He could no doubt do more than any one thought of in that connection; but how can he be spared from his present duties? The plan, as I understood him, which he had contemplated, was to employ an agent. That would be less effective than the one existing, viz, the appointment of a quartermaster, specially selected for the duty, and sustained by direct communications between the Executive and the railroad presidents on all questions which arise. The generals in the field may do much, by giving timely notice of irregularities and by seeing that trains at their depots are not detained improperly or permitted to leave the freight or passengers which the public service requires to be transported.

---

* Not found.

In relation to the list of generals proposed, I will now request you to divide the effective strength of your army by the number of generals you would have if the addition was made. Would not the number more nearly correspond to the command of colonels than generals? For 37,000 men I still think four divisions enough, and am still at a loss to perceive how the change of title would increase the efficiency of a brigadier; but can conceive how a brigadier would lose something of his value by being brought into immediate command and minute supervision of a major-general of a small division, say about equal to an efficient brigade.

Your remarks about the moral effect of repressing the hope of the volunteers for an advance are in accordance with the painful impression made on me, when in our council it was revealed to me that the Army of the Potomac had been reduced to about one-half the legalized strength, and that the arms to restore the number were not in depot. As I then suggested, though you may not be able to advance into Maryland and expel the enemy, it may be possible to keep up the spirits of your troops by expeditions, such as that particularly spoken of against Sickles' brigade, on the Lower Potomac, or Banks', above, by destroying the canal, and making other rapid movements whenever opportunity presents to beat detachments or to destroy lines of communication.

Let me insist that you revive something of your early respect for military grades, as your recommendations evince that you have adopted the militia value for the commission of field officers. I have never regarded one entitled to expect of the Confederacy the same grade he may have held under a State.

How have you progressed in the solution of the problem I left—the organization of the troops, with reference to the States and terms of service? If the volunteers continue their complaints that they are commanded by strangers, and do not get justice, and that they are kept in camp to die when reported for hospital by the surgeon, we shall soon feel a reaction in the matter of volunteering. Already I have been much pressed on both subjects, and have answered by promising that the generals would give due attention and I hope make satisfactory changes.

The authority to organize regiments into brigades and the latter into divisions is by law conferred only on the President, and I must be able to assume responsibility of the action taken by whomsoever acts for me in that regard. By reference to the law you will see that, in surrendering the sole power to appoint general officers, it was nevertheless designed, as far as should be found consistent, to keep up the State relation of troops and generals. Kentucky has a brigadier but not a brigade. She has, however, a regiment. That regiment and brigadier might be associated together. Louisiana has regiments enough to form a brigade, but no brigadier in either corps. All of the regiments were sent to that commanded by a Louisiana general. Georgia has regiments now organized into two brigades. She has on duty with that army two brigadiers, but one of them serves with other troops. Mississippi troops were scattered, as if the State was unknown. Brigadier-General Clark was sent to remove a growing dissatisfaction; but, though the State had nine regiments there, he (C.) was put in command of a post and depot of supplies. These nine regiments should form two brigades. Brigadiers Clark and (as native of Mississippi) Whiting should be placed in command of them, and the regiments for the war put in the army man's brigade. Both brigades should be put in the division commanded by General Van Dorn, of Mississippi. Thus would the spirit and intent of the law be complied with, disagreeable complaint be spared me, and more of content be assured under the trials to which you look forward. It is needless to specify further. I have been able in writing to you to speak freely, and you have no past associations to distrust the judgment to be passed upon the views presented.

I have made and am making inquiries as to the practicability of getting a corps of negroes for laborers, to aid in the construction of an intrenched line in rear of your present position.

Your remarks on the want of efficient staff officers is realized in all their force, and I hope, among the elements which constitute a staff officer for volunteers, you have duly estimated the qualities of forbearance and urbanity. Many of the privates are men of high social position, of scholarship, and fortune. Their pride furnishes the motive for good conduct, and, if wounded, is turned from an instrument of good to one of great power for evil.

General Lovell proposes to leave in the morning for New Orleans.

Nothing has been heard of the armada, which sailed some time since for the subjugation of the Southern sea-port inhabitants.

Bragg made a descent upon Santa Rosa, of which you will see in the journals the telegraphic report.

It will give me pleasure to hear from you frequently and fully.

Very truly, your friend,

JEFFERSON DAVIS.

HEADQUARTERS GREENBRIER RIVER,
October 12, 1861.

General S. COOPER,
Adjutant and Inspector General C. S. Army:

GENERAL: I feel it to be my imperative duty most respectfully to direct the attention of the Department of War to the condition of the staff departments of this division of the Northwestern Army. There is no commissioned quartermaster upon this line. Major Corley, the quartermaster for the Northwestern Army, has not been upon it for upwards of two months. The suffering resulting for the want of transportation, and especially from the want of forage for horses, has been almost incalculable. The public animals have been so reduced as to be at times wholly unfit for active service, and that in a country supposed to abound in grass and grain. I have labored against these difficulties to the best of my ability and to the full extent of my authority, but that authority is limited, and my remoteness from the headquarters of the army renders it impossible, I suppose, for its responsible staff officers to see to the prompt action and systematic movement of their respective departments.

The cold weather is already upon us, and with a winter climate like this, with more than 70 miles between the army and its depot of supplies, with the connecting road becoming daily worse and worse, and with the country immediately adjacent already exhausted, unless new energy be infused into the staff department it is not easy to conceive the amount of loss, embarrassment, and suffering which must in a short time be developed.

I am, sir, very respectfully, your obedient servant,
H. R. JACKSON,
Brigadier-General, &c.

[Indorsement.]

Copy of letter sent to Major Harman, at Staunton, to report upon the condition of the department. It is believed that officers of the Quartermaster's Department have been ordered to General Jackson's command.
Respectfully returned.

A. C. MYERS,
Quartermaster-General.

SPECIAL ORDERS, }   HDQRS. ARMY OF THE POTOMAC,
   No. 419.   }   *October* 12, 1861.

I. Maj. Gen. James Longstreet is assigned to duty with the First Corps, Army of the Potomac, and will report to General G. T. Beauregard, commanding.

II. Maj. Gen. T. J. Jackson is assigned to duty with the Second Corps, Army of the Potomac, and will report to Maj. Gen. G. W. Smith, commanding.

By command of General Johnston:

THOS. G. RHETT,
Assistant Adjutant-General.

WAR DEPARTMENT, *October* 13, 1861.

General JOSEPH E. JOHNSTON,
   Commander-in-Chief of the Army of the Potomac:

SIR: The Adjutant-General has referred to me your letter of 7th in stant in relation to the cantonments required for the troops during the ensuing winter. It is a source of deep regret to the Department to be brought face to face with this necessity. I had hoped almost against hope that the condition of the army would justify you in coming to the conclusion that some forward movement could be made, and that the roofs to shelter the troops during the approaching winter would be found on the other side of the Potomac; but our destitute condition so far as arms are concerned renders it impossible to increase your strength, whilst your recent report to the Adjutant-General develops the painful fact that nearly one-third of your numerical force is still prostrated by sickness.

I have paid earnest attention to the difficult problem now presented to us. The men must not, if it be possible to avoid it, be exposed to the inclemency of the winter under canvas alone. Taking it, then, for granted that the army is to be hutted, the first question that presents itself is, where are these huts to be built? This is a purely military question, which must be decided by yourself as commander-in-chief of the Army of the Potomac. It is evidently impossible that I should undertake to decide for you on the proper locality of your winter quarters, as this is a question dependent on many considerations, such as fuel, water, defensive works, &c., involving a minute knowledge of the topography and resources of the country, familiar to you and unknown to me.

Under the circumstances, and the pressing importance of the subject not admitting of delay, I have availed myself of the able co-operation of the Secretary of State, whose intimate knowledge of the resources of his native State and whose zeal and patriotism have rendered him an invaluable counselor in this emergency. Through his aid I have secured the services of Mr. James Hunter and Dr. John P. Hale, and our joint efforts have devised a scheme—the only practicable one that has suggested itself—by means of which our men can be furnished with comfortable shelter in huts, to be built at a rate which will supply about 800 men per diem, beginning on the 21st instant. At this rate the whole force now under your command would be under cover by 10th December at furthest, and I hope even by the 1st of that month. In order to accomplish this without waste of time I send you this letter by the hands of the two gentlemen above named. They will explain to you the plan proposed, and I know I can rely on your zealous co-operation in furtherance of it. They will require, of course, your countenance and aid as the commander-in-chief, and especially will it be necessary for you to determine (after such consultations, if any, as you may choose to have with the generals under your command) the locality and lines where the huts are to be built. I am also happy to inform you that arrangements are made with Mr. James Hunter for procuring a body of 1,000 laborers for working at intrenchments for the defense of such points as you may indicate as necessary for the protection of your forces. I need not urge on you the absolute necessity of prompt determination of those questions, which are to be decided by you before Mr. Hunter and his associate can commence active work.

Your obedient servant,

J. P. BENJAMIN,
Acting Secretary of War.

————

ADJUTANT AND INSPECTOR GENERAL'S OFFICE,
Richmond, October 13, 1861.

General JOSEPH E. JOHNSTON, *Commanding Army of Potomac:*

SIR: It has been represented to the Secretary of War that there is in the possession of the several regiments and battalions of your command a number of arms over and above those in the hands of the men present, which have been deposited by absentees who have left their commands, either sick, on furlough, or by reason of discharge. The Secretary considers that these surplus arms, as well as the accouterments belonging to them, are liable to loss by reason of the rapid and sudden movements of the troops at any moment, and he therefore desires that you will cause them to be collected and deposited for safe-keeping with the officer in charge of the ordnance department at Manassas (after having them properly labeled with the name and number of the regiment and battalion to which they belong), to be there held for future issue, as the necessities of the service may require.

I am, very respectfully, &c.,

S. COOPER,
Adjutant and Inspector General.

————

SPECIAL ORDERS, }   HEADQUARTERS FIRST CORPS, A. P.,
No. 442.   }   *Fairfax Court-House, October* 14, 1861.

I. Maj. Gen. James Longstreet, having reported for duty with this army corps, is assigned to the command of a division composed of the Fourth and Fifth Brigades. He will at once assume command of his division.

II. Brig. Gen. Charles Clark will turn over the command of the post of Camp Pickens to Col. G. B. Anderson, and report to these headquarters for further orders.

By command of General Beauregard:

THOMAS JORDAN,
Assistant Adjutant-General.

CAMP PICKENS, *October* 15, 1861.

Col. L. B. NORTHROP,
Commissary General C. S. Army, Richmond, Va.:

COLONEL: I have the honor to acknowledge the receipt of your communication of the 12th instant, inclosing complaints of deficiency of supplies from brigade commissary, First Brigade, First Corps, the commissary to Hampton's Legion, and the commissary Ninth S. C. Regiment (one inclosure), and directing me to report "whether or not these regiments were furnished with their due proportion of those articles of the ration of which there was not a full supply." I have to reply that they have been since August 28, 1861, the earliest day after I came upon duty (August 23, 1861) at which I could so systematize the affairs of the subsistence department here as to inaugurate such a system. I am not aware of any failure to receive such proportion by any part of the troops since that time.

Respectfully, your obedient servant,

W. B. BLAIR,
Major, and Commissary of Subsistence.

NEAR CHARLESTOWN, JEFFERSON COUNTY, VA.,
October 15, 1861.

His Excellency President DAVIS, *Richmond, Va.:*

SIR: The enemy crossed the Potomac at Harper's Ferry last week, and in considerable numbers—how many it is not easily ascertained, but sufficient to hold the place—and have been arriving ever since, pillaging and ravaging as they advanced. The farmers below this place are being robbed of slaves, horses, and everything the enemy can use.

Our new recruits are in the field, under Baylor, Glenn, and Hess. Colonel Ashby, with some 300 cavalry and 300 militia from Shenandoah, &c., is also with us. Headquarters near Charlestown, our county seat, and on the Winchester and Potomac Railroad.

The men of this vicinity at last are showing signs of resistance, and I do hope we shall be able to give a good account of the rascals. We do want a military leader in this brigade. General Carson is a most estimable gentleman, but not suited for the time and exigencies of the moment.

The enemy have long been in possession of Harper's Ferry, desecrating our soil, pillaging our defenseless and loyal people, and outraging the sanctity of helpless and loyal families. The widowed mother of Captain Henderson, of a volunteer corps, doing good service all the while until shot by one of his own men, was awfully outraged—three negro men and all valuables that were portable carried off, and her house and farm left desolate. Her sons all at their posts—one, younger than the captain, in General Johnston's army. Other farms are being visited.

Last night a lady swam the Shenandoah to let us know that the enemy were being re-enforced, and the first aim would be to destroy our woolen factories along the Shenandoah; also our large flouring mills. This will be done. The delay heretofore has been caused by the shipping of some 20,000 bushels of wheat seized at Harper's Ferry.

This done, our whole country must be devastated, and, to say nothing of mills, slaves, and other valuable property, all the grain in stack or garner will be burned up.

General Carson's headquarters are at Winchester, distant 30 miles from the enemy, and while all these things are transpiring he has never been in the county or visited our post.

Written in much haste.

With high consideration, your obedient servant,

JAMES L. RANSON.

———

CAMP OF FIFTY-SECOND VIRGINIA REGIMENT,
Top of Alleghany Mountains, October 16, 1861.

Hon. J. P. BENJAMIN, *Acting Secretary of War:*

SIR: Having been stationed at this place with my regiment for two weeks past, I hope it will not be considered a violation of any of the rules of the service if I address to you directly a suggestion or two, involving, as I believe, the safety of my command and of all the Confederate forces on this line.

You are no doubt aware that the army on this line cannot depend upon the surrounding country for supplies of any kind. The country at the best is sparsely populated, and produces no surplus of any kind of provision except live stock, and the troubles of the times have brought upon the people an unusual scarcity of all kinds of supplies. The only points from which any supply of food or forage has been drawn in the past are the Hardy Valley and the region about Staunton, and there is no other promise for the future so far as I know. As to the Hardy Valley, the supply has been much interrupted by incursions of the enemy, who have succeeded in capturing some of our trains and have produced such an alarm among the people that it is almost impossible to induce men to engage in the transportation of supplies to our army. At the best the distance from this point to Petersburg is at least 70 miles, and the road one which in winter would hardly be practicable for loaded wagons. As to the other route, from Staunton, the distance to this point is 60 miles, and to the principal camp at Greenbrier River is 68. The road in summer is good, but in winter may fairly be said to be impassable for wagons, and even now is in such a condition as to require the constant services of a large force to keep it in a tolerable condition. Since I have been stationed at this point the horses of my regiment have repeatedly been reduced to half rations of corn, and for nearly all the time they have been wholly without forage of any kind. They are now subsisting upon the only hay to be procured within 10 miles of the camp, and that supply is only for a very few days.

I by no means seek to obtain information which in the discretion of my superior officers is withheld from me, but if it is the purpose of the Government to retain troops upon this line, it seems to me to be of high, concern to know that a single snow-storm, such as is by no means uncommon in these mountains at this season, would starve every horse in this army, and, unless the other troops are supplied differently from my regiment, would seriously endanger the entire command. Independent of any of these considerations I deem it proper to state that the advance of the season admonishes us of the rapid and near approach of winter. Two weeks from to-day the winter in these mountains may be said to have set in. As yet there is no preparation for the wintering of troops here; no huts or houses have been prepared, nor can any be found in this region already built. I have upon my own responsibility instituted inquiries for the tools necessary to enable my men to build for themselves if required, and to my surprise and alarm I find that we have not in this army enough tools of the most common kind to enable us to use the timber which is so abundant all around us. Already the weather has been such as to freeze the tents of my regiment solid after a soaking rain and to coat the water in vessels with thick ice, and I am satisfied that this is not more than what may be expected at this season in these mountains. If, as I have stated, it is the purpose to retain troops here for the winter, measures cannot be too promptly or energetically taken and pressed for putting them into habitable winter quarters. These facts and my impressions upon them I have felt bound to communicate as a part of my duty to the Government and to the regiment, composed of my neighbors and friends, which has been intrusted to my care.

I hope I shall not be understood as disposed to avoid any fair share of the labors and sacrifices which must fall upon all engaged in our national defense. My men have made no complaint, but are looking forward with calm confidence in the provident care of the Government. I trust their confidence will be fully justified in their future history.

Respectfully, your obedient servant,

JOHN B. BALDWIN,
Colonel Fifty-second Virginia Regiment.

HEADQUARTERS ARMY OF KANAWHA,
Camp on New River, October 16, 1861.

His Excellency the SECRETARY OF WAR:

SIR: In a letter to the President, dated at Meadow Bluff, ———, 1861, I gave some account of the positions then held by the Confederate forces, and of my plans for the occupation of the left bank or southern moiety of the Kanawha Valley.

I preferred to make a stand at Meadow Bluff, because it was a stronger position than Sewell Mountain; because it was nearer the supplies; because it was less exposed to the weather; because there was more probability that the enemy would attack there than on Sewell, and because, should his attack fail, he would not be able to get away from the consequences of that failure. General Lee was constrained by circumstances to hold the ridge near the top of Sewell, and I followed him to that point with all my force. We remained eleven days, and those days cost us more men, sick and dead, than the battle of Manassas Plains. Provisions were hauled up the mountain 16 miles from Meadow Bluff over the worst road in Virginia, and we were exposed to tempests of wind and rain; for the conformation of the ground is such that there are always storms on Sewell Mountain. Finally the enemy retired beyond Gauley. The condition of the main body of our army was such that pursuit was impossible, and General Lee yet remains on Sewell. But he then assented to my plans for the expedition down the left bank of the Kanawha, and I set out without delay with all the force under my command, except the North Carolina regiment and the Fiftieth Virginia, which had been nearly annihilated by sickness, and the Wise Legion, which I found to be in such a state of insubordination and so ill-disciplined as to be for the moment unfit for military purposes. But with the fine regiment from Mississippi, under Colonel Russell, with Phillips' Legion, the Fourteenth Georgia, the Fifty-first, the Forty-fifth, the Thirty-sixth, and Twenty-second Virginia, and 500 cavalry, at least with such portions of those corps that were able to march—in all some 4,000 men—I left Sewell, and after a difficult march over the mountain roads passed New River, which is the name of the upper branch of the Kanawha. From the point where I now am I have one day's march over bad road to the Red Sulphur turnpike, which commands that half of the valley of the Kanawha in which I propose to operate. I hear of several parties of the enemy on this side of the river. The strongest, 800 or 1,000 men, are said to be encamped in the marshes of Cove. If this is so, and if chance favors, I think I shall be able to destroy or capture this body. Their position, if correctly stated, is a great strategic error. They are distant 60 miles from Charleston, with the worst roads in the world, while I shall soon have access to them by one day's march along the Red Sulphur turnpike. If my reports are confirmed, I propose to take 1,500 men under my own command, and fall on them so soon as I get my troops over the hills to the turnpike. But it is now time to consider the proper disposition of the column under my immediate orders in winter quarters. I still adhere to my original purpose of wintering near Logan Court-House, for the following reasons:

1. If you will examine the map of Virginia you will perceive that the Kanawha River divides an immense tract of country, known as the Kanawha Valley, into two nearly equal portions. Charleston is its center, and the northern half partakes of the character of Northwestern Virginia, of which it is properly part. The people on the northern side of the river are generally disloyal to the South. The enemy have 15,000 men to keep at Charleston this whole winter, and the army now under my orders is not sufficient to drive them out during that season. But my presence on the other side of the river will effectually prevent them from extending their dominion to the southern half of the valley. It will also preserve the people of that part of the country in their present temper and opinions, which are excellent; while, on the other hand, if left to the mercy of the enemy, and exposed as they are to marauding detachments, who cross the river and carry off all the grain and cattle of the country, they may by next spring be subdued to the same submission which now characterizes the counties on the northern bank of the river.

2. The pretended new State of Kanawha, for whose existence a regular poll is soon to be taken, comprises the southern as well as the northern half of the valley. The presence of the Confederate troops in its territory will effectually destroy all appearance of legality in the proceedings, and may be useful in preventing embarrassment in future negotiations and treaties which the Confederacy may hereafter have with the United States.

3. The southern half of the Kanawha Valley is that portion of Virginia which touches the State of Kentucky. The presence of my army in that quarter will exercise a good influence on that neighboring country. It may even become very useful to the strategic combinations of General Johnston's forces there. At all events it will be first

in the field of operations next spring, when we may be in condition to contest the possession of Northwestern Virginia with the enemy.

These and other reasons satisfy me that it would be desirable for myself and troops to winter in the Kanawha Valley, if it is possible to subsist them there in a perfectly safe place. Such a position, I think, is to be found near Logan Court-House, at the first fork of the turnpike road. Those who know the topography of the country from the map alone cannot perceive without explanation its complete security. If the enemy have 15,000 troops so near to that place as Charleston, what, they will ask, is to prevent them from marching over there after communications have been cut off with Eastern Virginia by the weather, breaking up my winter quarters, and perhaps capturing my whole command. I answer, the maps do not show that between Charleston and Logan Court-House there are two immense chains of mountains, and that the passes through those mountains are among the most easily-defended localities on the continent. It is ground with which I am perfectly familiar, and with the troops now under me I can safely guarantee my defense against twice the force which the enemy can by any contrivance bring against me.

The question of security may be laid aside. It remains to consider the more difficult matter of supplies at a point so remote from the center of the State. Ammunition and the small commissary stores, such as candles, sugar, coffee, and clothing, would be brought by the Virginia and Tennessee road to a station within 130 miles of my camp. The roads from that point to Logan are of course bad, but I can have them soon put in sufficient repair for my purposes. Forage in sufficient quantities for all my cattle I do not hope to obtain around my proposed camp, and therefore, after establishing myself, I should send away all the horses and mules that I do not absolutely need to Tazewell, where their wants can be fully met. It rests to ascertain whether I can get enough meat and meal in the country for my men. I think I can, but I cannot say so with perfect assurance till I have myself examined the present resources of those counties; but the advantages to be gained by establishing my quarters in that region are so great, that I am determined, unless prevented by your orders, to make the experiment. My plan at present is to try for some weeks what I can do against the enemy's army. Then I will go to Logan, but my troops, stockade my camp, fortify the approaches, repair the roads, and ascertain the capability of the country to support my army. If it is sufficient to carry us through the winter without suffering at all, I shall remain till the spring, unless I should see a good chance for a blow during the winter; but if the country has been too much exhausted by the war and the enemy, I will at least stay there till the end of November, up to which time there can be no difficulty, and then march my men up to the Lynchburg and Tennessee road.

These are my own plans. I wait with anxiety the answer of the Department confirming or altering my views, and will obey with alacrity any instructions it may send; but if the Department would double my force here I can assure them that it is possible to effect great results in this region. If my Government would raise my command without delay to 10,000 men, which it might do in ten days if immediate orders were given, I would seize a point on the Ohio and hold it through the winter in spite of every effort to dislodge me.

I have the honor to be, very respectfully, your obedient servant,

JOHN B. FLOYD,
Brigadier-General, Commanding Army of Kanawha.

BROOKE'S STATION, *October* 16, 1861.

General COOPER:

A messenger from Maryland says McClellan will attack Johnston to-day, to cover an expedition from Annapolis up the Rappahannock. Do you know anything about it?

TH. H. HOLMES,
Major-General.

———

RICHMOND, VA., *October* 17, 1861.

General G. T. BEAUREGARD:

MY DEAR GENERAL: Inclosed you will find a letter and slip referred to in it; also another slip, derived from a different and, as supposed, friendly source. You will be able better than myself to judge of the value or importance of the matters contained in these papers.*

A man has been sent up to confer with General Johnston and yourself in relation to the preparation of winter quarters and the employment of negroes in construction of a line of intrenchment. The Secretary of State commended him as a man of great capacity for such work.

I have thought often upon the questions of reorganization, which were submitted to you, and it has seemed to me that, whether in view of disease or the disappointment and suffering of a winter cantonment on a line of defense, or of a battle to be fought in and near your position, that it was desirable to combine the troops, by a new distribution, with as little delay as practicable. Your army is composed of men of intelligence and future expectations. They will be stimulated by extraordinary efforts, when so organized that the fame of their State will be in their keeping and that each will feel that his immediate commander will desire to exalt rather than diminish his services. You pointed me to the fact that you had observed that rule in the case of the Louisiana and Carolina troops, and you will not fail to perceive that others find in the fact a reason for the like disposal of them. In the hour of sickness and the tedium of waiting for spring, men from the same region will best console and relieve each other.

The maintenance of our cause rests in the sentiment of our people. Letters from the camps, complaining of inequality and harshness in the treatment of the men, have already dulled the enthusiasm which filled our ranks with men who, by birth, fortune, and education, and social position, were the equals of any officers in the land.

The spirit of our military law is manifested in the fact that the State organization was limited to the regiment. The volunteers came in sufficient numbers to have brigadiers, but have only colonels. It was not then intended (is the necessary conclusion) that those troops should be under the immediate command of officers above the grade of colonel. The spirit of the law then indicates that brigades should be larger than customary. The general being the remote commander of the individuals, charged with the care, the direction, the preservation of the men, rather than with the internal police, he has time to visit hospitals, to inquire into supplies, to supervise what others must execute, and the men come to regard him, when so habitually seen, as the friend of the individual; but they also know him in another capacity, and there removed, as it were placed on a pedestal, he seems the power that moves and controls the mass.

———

* Not found.

This is not an ideal, but a sketch of Taylor when general of the little army, many of whom would no sooner have questioned his decisions, or have shrunk from him in the hour of danger than if he had been their father. The other point was the necessity for unity in the Army of the Potomac. The embarrassment was felt and the sentiment of commanders appreciated, but rivalry, running into jealousy, is the unavoidable attendant of difference in the discipline, the usage, and the supplies of camps. How much more so must it be when corps are associated together, with the inevitable diversity resulting from control by different minds, and in which a reference is made to distinct antecedents, which have never disappeared by a visible transition from the existence under independent heads.

I have had applications made to me for transfer from one corps to another, and among the reasons given was that the sick of one were permitted to go to the hospital, when under like circumstances they were in the other confined to their encampments.

Mr. Benjamin informed me that you had expressed the wish, in the event of your corps being made an undivided portion of the army, to be relieved and sent to New Orleans. If I had thought you could be dispensed with, it would have given me pleasure long since to have relieved the solicitude of the people of New Orleans by sending you there; but I cannot anticipate the time when it would seem to me proper to withdraw you from the position with which you are so intimately acquainted, and for which you have shown yourself so eminently qualified. Nor have I felt that to another could be transferred the moral power you have over the troops you have commanded. My appreciation of you as a soldier and my regard for you as a man cannot permit me willingly to wound your sensibility or to diminish your sphere of usefulness.

Very truly, your friend,

JEFFERSON DAVIS.

WAR DEPARTMENT, C. S. A.,
Richmond, October 17, 1861.

General G. T. BEAUREGARD, *Manassas, Va.*:

SIR: I have your letter of the 9th instant,* in which you state that if you are no longer in command of an army corps, you request to be relieved forthwith from your present false position. In reply, I beg to say, in all kindness, that it is not your position which is false, but your idea of the organization of the Army as established by the act of Congress, and I feel confident you cannot have studied the legislation of Congress in relation to the Army. You are second in command of the whole Army of the Potomac, and not first in command of half the army. The position is a very simple one, and if you will take the pains to read the sixth section of the "Act to provide for the public defense," approved the 6th of March, 1861, you will see that the President has no authority to divide an army into two *corps d'armée*, but only into brigades and divisions. Now, your rank being superior to that of a commander of a brigade or a division, and there being no other component parts into which an army can be legally divided, you necessarily command the whole army; but having present with you an officer of equal grade, but older commission, who also commands the whole army, you become second in command.

---

* Not found.

I have entered into these details because in conversation with the President, since his return from your headquarters, he has informed me that he found the same error as to the organization of the army which you seem to entertain very generally prevalent. The error, however, will probably not be productive of any further injurious consequences, as I hope in a few days to communicate to you such general orders in relation to this whole subject as will dissipate all possible conflict of authority, unite the army under one common head, and give to all its leaders appropriate and satisfactory positions. I therefore refrain from making any further allusion to the subject of the Chief of Ordnance, desired by you, as the whole matter will be so arranged as to gratify all your wishes in the general orders above referred to.

I am, your obedient servant,

J. P. BENJAMIN,
Acting Secretary of War.

[Circular letter.]

WAR DEPARTMENT, C. S. A,
Richmond, October 19, 1861.

SIR: On the 8th September the following order was issued to you from this Department, and seems not to have been obeyed:

SPECIAL ORDERS, }   ADJUTANT AND INSPECTOR GENERAL'S OFFICE,
No. 147.   }   *Richmond, September* 8, 1861.

*   *   *   *   *   *   *

II. As it is believed there are many arms in the hands of the troops not required by them, the commander of each army corps will detail a field officer to visit and inspect the various encampments under his control, who will take away and cause to be sent to the ordnance depot in this city all the surplus arms he may find, specifying in his returns the kind and quantity taken from each regiment.

*   *   *   *   *   *   *

By command of the Secretary of War:

JNO. WITHERS,
Assistant Adjutant-General.

The Department requests that you will communicate what obstacles have prevented your compliance with its order; whether those obstacles still exist, and, if so, when you expect to be able to overcome them.

Your obedient servant,

J. P. BENJAMIN,
Acting Secretary of War.

To Generals R. E. LEE, G. T. BEAUREGARD, and JOS. E. JOHNSTON; Maj. Gens. BENJ. HUGER, J. B. MAGRUDER; and Brig. Gen. JOHN B. FLOYD.

ORDERS, }   HDQRS. FIRST DIVISION FIRST CORPS, A. P.,
No. 8. }   *Union Mills, October* 19, 1861.

No private property of citizens of the Confederate States will be taken by any person belonging to this division, except under the authority of the division commander or of the brigadier-generals commanding brigades. When private property is taken under orders for the benefit of the troops of this division, or when taken to prevent it from falling into the hands of the enemy, a statement will be given to the owner thereof, showing forth the kind of property, its value, and the date it was taken. All such property will be taken by or turned over to the quartermaster's department of the division, except cattle taken for the subsistence department. The officers of these departments will bear all such property on their return, and will be held accountable for it.

The attention of the troops of the division is called to the fifty-fourth articles of war. It should be borne in mind that whilst there is nothing more noble and honorable than to fly to arms and offer your lives in the cause of offended liberty and in the defense of your country, there is nothing more disgraceful than to rob or wantonly destroy the private property of your unoffending citizens. The two are entirely incompatible with each other, and any one guilty of the last can never be true to his honor.

The major-general commading regrets having to call the attention of his division to this article of war.

By order of Maj. Gen. Earl Van Dorn:

JOSEPH D. BALFOUR,
Assistant Adjutant-General.

RICHMOND, VA., *October* 20, 1861.

General G. T. BEAUREGARD:

MY DEAR GENERAL: I have the pleasure to acknowledge yours of the 15th and telegram of this date.* To the latter I reply that your rank, being of the highest grade known to our service, is equal to any command. Your inquiry must, therefore, be whether there can be a distinction between an army and a *corps d'armée.* There is none in the law of our army organization. If two corps or armies should happen to join or do duty together, though the senior officer would command the whole, the permanent organization of each army would not properly be disturbed by such accidental junction; but, if two armies should be concentrated into one, indefinitely to remain consolidated, the plainest principles of military organization require that they should be organized as one body, reference being had solely to future efficiency. The junior of the two commanders of the former armies would be second in command of the whole, and would or would not have special charge of a subdivision, according to the circumstances of the case. In your case, it would seem to me better that you should not have special charge of a subdivision, because, in the absence of General Johnston, your succession to the command of the whole would not disturb the relations of the officers and troops, nor involve any changes of positions on the line occupied; and, further, because your acquaintance with the whole body of the army, and the absence of any idea of identification with a part of it, would better qualify [you] for that succession.

The growing importance of the District of Aquia, and the increasing necessity for operations in the valley of Virginia, have suggested to me the propriety of bringing those sections into closer relations to the Army of the Potomac. That, it seems to me, may best be done by sending a general of division to the valley, and by placing the senior general (Johnston) in command of a department, embracing the three armies (of the Potomac, the Aquia, and the Valley). This has, I believe, been already intimated to you by the Secretary of War. Two

---

* Not found.

rules have been applied in the projected reorganization of the Army of the Potomac: First, as far as practicable to keep regiments from the same State together; second, to assign generals to command the troops of their own State. I have not overlooked the objections to each, but the advantages are believed to outweigh the disadvantages of that arrangement. In distributing the regiments of the several States, it would, I think, be better to place the regiments for the war in the same brigade of the State, and assign to those brigades the brigadiers whose services could least easily be dispensed with. For this among other reasons I will mention but one: The commission of a brigadier expires upon the breaking up of his brigade. (See the law for their appointment.) Of couse I would not, for slight cause, change the relation of troops and commanders, especially where it has been long continued and endeared by the trials of battle; but it is to be noted that the regiment was fixed as the unit of organization, and made the connecting link between the soldier and his home; above that all was subject to the discretion of the Confederate authorities, save the pregnant intimation in relation to the distribution of generals among the several States. It was generous and confiding to surrender entirely to the Confederacy the appointment of generals, and it is the more incumbent on me to carry out, as well as may be, the spirit of the "volunteer system." Your military objection to forming a division of the brigades of a particular State is forcible. In your army, however, that is impracticable. Virginia approximates it most nearly, and it might be well, as a defensive measure, when the accession of other troops will justify it, to transfer one Virginia brigade to the Valley District and fill its place in G. W. Smith's division by a brigade from another State. The political objection which you suggest is probably answered by the arrangement which is proposed. You will perceive that of the four divisions, three are commanded by soldiers whose attachment to their profession and good sense will probably exclude ideas of political preferment, and the only major-general who comes immediately from civil life has in his division but one regiment from the State of which he is a native.

I will be happy to receive your views and suggestions on all subjects as fully as your convenience will permit. My sole wish is to secure the independence and peace of the Confederacy; for that I labor assiduously in my present position, and there is none other for which I would not gladly exchange it if there I could better promote the end to which my life is devoted. Others decided against my known desire and placed me where I am. With great distrust the post was accepted, and my best hope has been and is that my colaborers, purified and elevated by the sanctity of the cause they defend, would forget themselves in their zeal for the public welfare.

In a recent letter of General G. W. Smith, he says:

The railroad from Richmond to Manassas does not work efficiently. Let Beauregard try to apply the remedy. This need not interfere with your general agent nor the general plan of the Executive. The subject is of vital importance to this army. Beauregard guarantees to regulate it. Try him.

Inform me what your plan is. You must have an agent, and he, to be useful, must have an appointment. I will gladly accept your aid and give you my support.

Complaints are made to me of shocking neglect of the sick, who are sent down in the trains, such as being put in burden cars which had been used to transport horses or provisions, and into which the sick were thrust without previously cleansing the cars, and there left without water, food, or attention. These representations have been spread among the people, and served to chill the ardor which has filled our ranks with the best men of the land. If such things have occurred, surely others than the railroad companies must share the responsibility.

Your dispatch, I perceive, is dated at Centreville, and otherwise the news has reached me that you had retired from Fairfax Court-House. The enemy may attempt to achieve something before the meeting of Congress. In this view I had contemplated an intrenched line, which would compensate for our want of numbers, and would be glad to have your conclusions upon that point.

General Magruder is anticipating an attack at Yorktown. His force is less than I could wish, but we have little to give him, and I suspect that, though it may become a real attack, it is only designed to be a feint to cover the advance, either by way of the upper or lower flank of your position.

With my best wishes for your welfare, and prayers for your success, I am, as ever, your friend,

JEFFERSON DAVIS.

————

HEADQUARTERS, SEWELL MOUNTAIN,
October 20, 1861.

General JOHN B. FLOYD,
    Commanding Army of Kanawha:

GENERAL: It has been reported to me to-night that General Rosecrans was sending a strong detachment across New River to intercept you. I believe he is aware of you having crossed New River, but if the report I have just stated above is correct, it differs from the report brought me last night by Lieutenant Callison, of Captain Jones' company, Wise's Legion, just from Fayette Court-House. He was aware of no considerable force of the enemy being south of the Kanawha. Predatory excursions had been made across that river. Fayette Court-House was, in the opinion of the citizens, being threatened, but he was not aware of any force being sent towards your route. I consider it, however, sufficiently important to send a special courier to put you on your guard.

I must also inform you that General Loring has received dispatches to-night from Generals Jackson and Donelson confirmatory of several previous reports indicative of attacks on both their lines, and calling earnestly for aid. I have resisted these appeals for some time, and retained General Loring's command here, in the hope of uniting in an attack with your force from the left bank of the Kanawha on General Rosecrans, who still holds his main force on the Gauley. I do not think it proper to retain General Loring any longer, as General Donelson thinks himself unable to maintain his position, and I have not heard what time you expect to make your contemplated movement down the Kanawha.

I shall therefore direct General Loring to commence his return to his line of operations to-morrow, and shall also send the Wise Legion to Meadow Bluff. This latter movement is the more necessary in consequence of the exposed condition of the Wilderness road since the withdrawal of your cavalry from that route and the advance upon it of the enemy's scouts. It would be useless for it, in my opinion, to remain longer here, as it could accomplish no good purpose, and would be liable to be cut off.

It will be necessary for you to keep yourself informed of the enemy's movements on this side of the river, so as to secure this road against his approach. On reaching Meadow Bluff I will inform you of the probable time of my return to Richmond.

Should your descent on the Kanawha cause the enemy to withdraw from the Gauley, as I believe it will, it will tend to the greater security of this section.

I have the honor to be, your obedient servant,

R. E. LEE,
General, Commanding.

RICHMOND, *October* 21, 1861.

Major-General JACKSON, *Manassas:*

SIR: The exposed condition of the Virginia frontier between the Blue Ridge and Alleghany Mountains has excited the deepest solicitude of the Government, and the constant appeals of the inhabitants that we should send a perfectly reliable officer for their protection have induced the Department to form a new military district, which is called the Valley District of the Department of Northern Virginia. In selecting an officer for this command the choice of the Government has fallen on you. This choice has been dictated, not only by a just appreciation of your qualities as a commander, but by other weighty considerations. Your intimate knowledge of the country, of its population and resources, rendered you peculiarly fitted to assume this command. Nor is this all. The people of that district, with one voice, have made constant and urgent appeals that to you, in whom they have confidence, should their defense be assigned. The administration shares the regret which you will no doubt feel at being separated from your command when there is a probability of early engagement between the opposing armies, but it feels confident that you will cheerfully yield your private wishes to your country's service in the sphere where you can be rendered most available.

In assuming the command to which you have been assigned by general orders, although your forces will for the present be small, they will be increased as rapidly as our means will possibly admit, whilst the people will themselves rally eagerly to your standard as soon as it is known that you are to command. In a few days detailed instructions will be sent you through the Adjutant-General, and I will be glad to receive any suggestions you may make to render effectual your measures of defense.

I am, respectfully, your obedient servant,

J. P. BENJAMIN,
Acting Secretary of War.

HEADQUARTERS,
Centreville, October 21, 1861.

General COOPER:

Cannot Ransom's regiment of North Carolina cavalry be ordered to report to me forthwith? The enemy's right was yesterday at Dranesville.

J. E. JOHNSTON.

RICHMOND, *October* 21, 1861.

General JOSEPH E. JOHNSTON, *Centreville, Va.:*

Ransom's regiment leaves here to-morrow morning to join you by route march.

S. COOPER,
Adjutant and Inspector General.

Proceedings of a meeting of the citizens of Lancaster and Northumberland Counties, Virginia.

OCTOBER 21, 1861.

At a meeting of the citizens of Lancaster and Northumberland, held at Lancaster Court-House, on Monday, the 21st day of October, 1861, William T. Jessee was called to the chair, and H. S. Hathaway appointed secretary. Samuel Gresham, esq., stated the object, and submitted for the consideration of the meeting the following resolutions, which were unanimously adopted, viz :

Whereas it is known that in each of the counties of Westmoreland, Richmond, and Northumberland there is a full number of regimental and staff officers of the militia in the service of the State or the Confederate States, and that in the county of Lancaster there is a colonel, surgeon, quartermaster, and commissary, and in all of the said counties a large number of companies with a full quota of company officers;

And whereas it is also well known that, by the volunteering of a large number of the men subject to military duty in the said counties, the regiments and companies in those counties, respectively, are but skeletons, no one of the said regiments containing as many as 400 men, rank and file, as required by the eleventh section of chapter 23 of the Code of Virginia, and it is believed, from information derived from gentlemen of the highest respectability for intelligence and truth in the several counties, that no one of the said regiments contains 300 men, rank and file, which is necessary to prevent a dissolution of the said regiments, according to the same section of the same chapter of the Code ;

And whereas we have been informed by gentlemen of the highest respectability for intelligence and truth, residing in the county of Richmond, that while the said regiment is reported as containing largely over 300 men, that at no time since the militia of that county has been ordered into service have they had over 200 effective men in camp; that many whose names appear upon the muster rolls of the several companies in that county were furloughed when first called into camp and sent home, where they still remain, unable to perform service, and this though they were examined by the surgeon of the regiment and pronounced unfit for military service;

And whereas some of their companies have not more than from 30 to 40 men, with a full force of company officers ;

And whereas we are informed that after the proclamation of the governor, of the — day of July, calling out the militia of the State, and the subsequent proclamation excepting such counties as had furnished their quota, and also such counties as might make up their quota by other volunteer companies, to be then immediately formed and mustered into service, the militia officers of some, if not all, of the said counties did discourage and by all means in their power prevent the formation of other volunteer companies in their counties;

And whereas the militia, as thus organized in the said counties, is costing the State or the Confederate Government a very large sum of money, which we believe to be totally unnecessary for the proper officering the militia;

And whereas we, a part of the tax-payers of the State and of the Confederate States, while we are willing to pay to the last dollar of our means the taxes necessary for the proper defense of our country, and have called upon the proper authorities to spare no expense that is or may be necessary for the efficient prosecution of the war in which we are engaged, yet we are unwilling to pay from three to four times the amount necessary for the proper defense of the country, whether that be as regards the whole expense of the war or the expense to be incurred in any particular locality or section of the country;

And whereas we have unlimited confidence in the Government, that while many abuses may escape their notice and attention, yet, when brought properly to their notice, they will be corrected: Therefore,

Resolved, That in the opinion of this meeting the state of things set forth in this preamble is not known to the proper authorities for correcting the same.

Resolved, That in the four counties above named there are not more effective men belonging to the militia than should constitute one regiment, and that the men now divided into four skeletons of regiments, with a full quota of regimental and staff officers and a much larger number of company officers than necessary, would be much more efficient for the defense of the said counties if thrown into one regiment and placed under the command of one colonel with one field officer in the other counties from which the colonel is not taken, to act as lieutenant-colonel or major, and a proper reduction of the number of companies.

Resolved, That, as at present organized, there is not and cannot be any co-operation between the several regiments in the said counties for the defense of each, but if thrown into one regiment, under one commander, they might and would co-operate with each other by the order of the said commander whenever their services might be required for the defense of either county.

Resolved, That we would not have the militia, by this arrangement we propose, withdrawn from either of the said counties, but would continue them in their counties respectively, under the command of their company officers and one field officer, subject to the order of the commanding officer, unless necessary temporarily to call them from one county to another for immediate defense.

Resolved, That while the proposed arrangement would be more efficient than the present, it would not cost the Government and people of the State who pay the expenses of the war more than one-half of the present organization.

Resolved, That a copy of these proceedings be sent by the secretary of this meeting to his excellency Jefferson Davis, President of the Confederate States, to the governor of the State of Virginia, to Brigadier-General Holmes, and to Col. George E. Pickett, commanding the forces on the Rappahannock River.

On motion, the meeting then adjourned.

WM. T. JESSEE,
Chairman.
H. S. HATHAWAY,
Secretary.

STAUNTON, *October* 21, 1861.

Hon. J. P. BENJAMIN, *Secretary of War :*

DEAR SIR: Inclosed is an urgent letter from General Jackson, and I have done all I could to have the Fifty-eighth to move in accordance with his wishes, but am informed you have allowed them to remain for a short time. If it cannot move, I must ask you to send another regiment up with the least possible delay, to take position on the Hardy line.

With great respect, your obedient servant,

M. G. HARMAN,
Lieutenant-Colonel, Commanding.

[Inclosure.]

GREENBRIER, *October* 20, 1861.

Major HARMAN:

MAJOR: I have good reason to fear that a body of the enemy are making their way, by the direction of the Seneca route, towards Monterey. They may do us vast injury, unless we can meet them. They are plundering and devastating the country as they come.

Is it possible, I would ask, that the Fifty-eighth Virginia Regiment, or any portion of it, will consent, under such circumstances, to remain in Staunton? I am lost in astonishment when I realize it. We are here in the immediate presence of a largely superior force. I cannot spare a man to go back, and yet this command, which could have rendered us so much service, and which I designed for this very duty, and which, had it moved, might have prevented, by its mere presence, this foray of the enemy, lingers in Staunton.

Scarcely a day passes that we are not skirmishing with the enemy here, and our presence here is absolutely necessary at this time to the protection of both lines. For our country's sake, induce this regiment to move, and to move quickly.

I am, very respectfully, your obedient servant,

H. R. JACKSON,
Brigadier-General, &c.

—

STAUNTON, VA., *October* 22, 1861.

His Excellency PRESIDENT DAVIS, *Richmond :*

DEAR SIR: I received on yesterday a pressing letter from General H. R. Jackson, commanding on the Monterey line, to urge the commanding officer of the Fifty-eighth Virginia Regiment to march immediately for Fork of Waters, on the Seneca road. I immediately telegraphed General S. Cooper, and he has ordered the regiment to move without delay. My object in writing to you is to urge the importance of having at least two regiments on the Hardy line to guard the Seneca road. It would be a serious affair indeed if the enemy were to push forward a force on that line and get possession of our supplies at Monterey and come in the rear of our forces on the Alleghany and at Greenbrier River, by which movement, they having a strong force at Cheat Mountain, our forces would be surrounded. The Fifty-eighth Virginia Regiment has a great many men sick in the hospital, and numbers scarcely 400 effective men. I inclose you a copy of General Jackson's letter. I fear that the Seneca road, not being guarded at all, gives an opportunity for pretended friends to pass and give information to the enemy which may induce this movement on their part. I hope you will send a regiment up immediately, if it can possibly be done, if you concur in the importance I attach to guarding this line.

With the highest consideration, I am, very respectfully, your obedient servant,

M. G. HARMAN,
Lieutenant-Colonel, Commanding.

P. S.—I inclosed to the Secretary of War a copy of General Jackson's letter, and also a letter from the commander of the post of Monterey,* which I should like you to see.

CENTREVILLE, *October* 22, 1861.

Hon. J. P. BENJAMIN, *Secretary of War:*

I think that the enemy cannot land near Occoquan without being discovered by our pickets. The report cannot be true. The ordnance officer reports that he can arm 1,000 men with muskets left unmarked, by sick men probably. Please send the men.

J. E. JOHNSTON.

GENERAL ORDERS, }   ADJT. AND INSP. GEN.'S OFFICE,
     No. 15.   }   *Richmond, Va., October* 22, 1861.

1. A department is established, to be known and designated as the Department of Northern Virginia. It will be composed of the three following districts, viz: The Valley District, the Potomac District, and the Aquia District. The Valley District will embrace the section of country between the Blue Ridge and the Alleghany Mountains, the Potomac District between the Blue Ridge Mountains and the left bank of Powell's River, and the Aquia District between Powell's River and the mouth of the Potomac, including the Northern Neck, and embracing the counties on either side of the Rappahannock River from its mouth to Fredericksburg.

2. General J. E. Johnston is assigned to the command of the Department of Northern Virginia, General P. G. T. Beauregard to the command of the Potomac District, Maj. Gen. T. H. Holmes to the command of the Aquia District, and Maj. Gen. T. J. Jackson to the command of the Valley District.

3. The troops serving in the Potomac District will be brigaded and formed into divisions, as follows: First division, under command of Major-General Van Dorn: First Brigade, Brigadier-General Clark, to consist of four Mississippi regiments; Second Brigade, Brigadier-General Whiting, to consist of five Mississippi regiments; Third Brigade, Brigadier-General Stuart, to consist of the cavalry of the army of this district, to be united in one brigade; Fourth Brigade, the Hampton Legion, under Colonel Hampton. Second Division, under command of Maj. Gen. G. W. Smith: First Brigade, Brigadier-General Ewell, to consist of four Virginia regiments; Second Brigade, Brig. Gen. S. Jones, to consist of four Virginia regiments; Third Brigade, Brigadier-General Early, to consist of four Virginia regiments; Fourth Brigade, Brigadier-General Crittenden, to consist of two Virginia regiments, two Tennessee

---

* Not found.

regiments, and one Kentucky regiment. Third Division, under command of Major-General Longstreet: First Brigade, Brig. Gen. D. R. Jones, to consist of four South Carolina regiments; Second Brigade, Brigadier-General Bonham, to consist of four South Carolina regiments; Third Brigade, Brigadier-General Wilcox, to consist of four Alabama regiments; Fourth Brigade, Brigadier-General Rodes, to consist of four Alabama regiments; Fifth Brigade, Brigadier-General Taylor, to consist of five Louisiana regiments. Fourth Division, under the command of Maj. Gen. E. K. Smith: First Brigade, Brigadier-General Walker, to consist of four Georgia regiments; Second Brigade, Brigadier-General Toombs, to consist of four Georgia regiments; Third Brigade, Brigadier-General Elzey, to consist of three Georgia regiments and one Maryland regiment; Fourth Brigade, Brigadier-General Evans, to consist of five North Carolina regiments; Fifth Brigade, Brigadier-General Wigfall, to consist of three Texas regiments and one Louisiana regiment.

The particular regiments for these several brigades will be designated by the commanding general of the Department of Northern Virginia, in conformity to this programme, according to States. The arrangements will be gradually carried into effect as soon as, in the judgment of the commanding general, it can be safely done under present exigencies.*

By command of the Secretary of War:

S. COOPER,
Adjutant and Inspector General.

RICHMOND, *October* 23, 1861.

General JOSEPH E. JOHNSTON, *Centreville:*

I will send you 1,000 unarmed men immediately. Colonel Ransom marches with his regiment of cavalry to-morrow to join you.

J. P. BENJAMIN,
Acting Secretary of War.

LEWISBURG, VA., *Wednesday, October* 23, 1861.

G. W. MUNFORD, Esq., *Secretary of the Commonwealth:*

DEAR SIR : I hope that you will excuse me for troubling you with a line, and if you are not the proper person to write to on such subjects, do, if you please, pass this line to the proper officer. General Loring's command is falling back to this place, which is west of Meadow Bluff, and from here they go northward to Greenbrier River Bridge, where it is said that the Federalists are pressing a regiment left to guard that pass. One regiment passed late last evening, and another regiment is passing while I write. It is cold and raw and showery, and some of the regiment that passed this morning came in last night, and in the dark and wet and mud, poor fellows, could get no place to sleep or anything to eat. A distant relative of mine here of the name of Wetzel provided for six of them. Many lay out in the rain all night; many drank and caroused all night, and I am really fearful that it is this unnecessary exposure that has got so many on the sick list.

For a long time yet Lewisburg must be the base of operations, and there could be, and ought to be, a shed built here, as well to protect [the men] from the weather [and] such military stores as remain here for days

---

* Paragraph 3 modified by G. O., No. 18. See November 16, *post.*

in their transit from Jackson's River Station to the army. A shed, with abundance of straw in it, in which detachments of troops passing to and fro might sleep, is a great desideratum, inasmuch as it would convince our citizen soldiery that all is done that it is possible to do to protect them from exposure, and such a shelter, with such feelings, would do much to exempt them from the great sickness that now desolates these western camps. The expense could not be much of such an erection, and the benefits would be great. The teams are also suffering severely for want of forage. That could be obviated in some degree by a very simple process, not adopted by the Quartermaster's Department, and yet so obvious that any one is surprised at its non-adoption, unless it is purposely omitted. Why could not each wagon that hauls flour or other heavy material for the army from any of the depots take with them from three to five hundred pounds of hay or blades? It would fill the wagon; it would protect the load from the weather; it would sustain the transportation attached to the moving columns of the army; it would prevent the loss of stock, and enable the army to move with more alacrity and facility.

Then there is a very great mistake in hauling flour to the army in the mountains, where they have nothing but flour and meat, and the consequence is indigestible bread, and consequently sickness. A bakery established anywhere in the rear, either at Jackson's River Station or Covington, 9 miles west of that, could bake bread for the army, and the weight would not be greater to haul in bread or crackers than in flour; and if you could not put a load of bread in a wagon, the wagons could be a little altered so that a load could be put on them, or under other circumstances a heavy package of some sort could be put in each bread wagon, so as to give the necessary weight to haul. The expense would be but small, and the gain great in the increased health and efficiency of the men—the fewer hospitals; for, if what I have heard be true, the expense of the hospital at White Sulphur will equal, or nearly equal, the expense of the transportation from Jackson's River Station to the army.

As to vegetables, pounded hominy would be the most convenient, palatable, and healthy that the army could get, winter or summer, and it is the easiest dressed for eating of anything, and could be so easily supplied to each army, and the machines for cracking the corn and hulling it are so abundant and cheap, that it is to me wonderful that some department of the Army had not introduced it. I will venture to say that it is far better than rice, and could be supplied at one-third the cost of that article per pound.

The Tennessee and Georgia troops, with many of whom I have talked, are very averse to serving in the mountains. The climate does not suit them, and toiling up the mountains on marches breaks them down directly. It is strange that they should be sent here to serve while many regiments raised in the mountains, accustomed to the inequalities of the surface of the earth, inured to the rigors of the climate, all having homes or relatives to defend, should be retained in Eastern Virginia and the defense of their homes intrusted to strangers unaccustomed to so rough a country and so bleak a climate. The Twenty-seventh Virginia Regiment, so effective at Manassas, came from Greenbrier, Monroe, and Alleghany Counties, and perhaps a company or two from Rockbridge.

I am no military man. Age has disabled me from bearing the fatigues of a campaign, and if that were not so, blindness has disqualified me from so doing. Amaurosis has wholly obscured one eye, and the other one sympathizes with it. I therefore do not pretend to be a military critic.   But old, blind, feeble, and ignorant as I am, I would have risked a general battle to have got into the valley of the Ohio, to have prevented the vote from being taken to-morrow on the question of the new State of Kanawha, which territory is militarily occupied by the Federal Army, and they really do not seem to care at present about any other portion of Western Virginia.   If that vote shall be overwhelmingly in favor of it, which it is likely to be from the circumstance of the friends of the South being overawed, and Congress shall next winter at Washington pass a law admitting it, you will find that the Federal forces will swarm there this winter; fortifications will be erected, the militia of that region will be called out, and the remainder of Western Virginia will be assailed from each fortress, each one of which will be made a base of operations.   It will be very highly prejudicial to the State in a civil and commercial point of view, and very prejudicial to the Confederacy.   Look at it for one moment.   It is the great coal field of America, from which the South is to obtain the fuel down the Ohio River that will drive their spindles and propel their commerce, both oceanic and river. The timber of that country is indispensable to the South for many purposes—barrels and hogsheads for their molasses and sugar, flooring, and even for building a mercantile marine.   That country would supply the whole Confederacy with salt during the blockade, for my county alone (Mason) can turn out one thousand barrels a day of salt, and Kanawha County could double that.   Some fuel, and flour to almost any amount, would descend the Ohio to the South, to say nothing of butter, lard, and other things of that nature, such as the oils, both natural and artificial, for it is in that region that the cannel coal [is found], out of which they make oil, and in the county of Wirt, northeast from Parkersburg about 30 miles, are the finest wells of natural coal oil in the world.   My county has for years past sent east about one thousand head of stall-fed cattle annually and large quantities of hogs.   These things are articles of prime necessity to the South, which, if not produced in the Southern Confederacy, must be admitted free of duty from the North, and it is no doubt that object in view that induces the attempt to attach that part of Virginia to the Lincoln Government.

Then look at it with reference to the State.   In the first place, great fortunes of many here, friends of the State, are situate there—Judge Allen, Judge Camden, Colonel Jenkins, and hundreds of others, whose property will be confiscated; and if the Governments give up that portion of Virginia a large but just claim will exist against the Governments for compensation—more, perhaps, than the expense of reconquering it.   To leave that portion of Virginia with the Lincoln Government will also very much retard the action of Northern Kentucky, and perhaps also strengthen the Lincolnites in that part of Kentucky; for in my opinion those two sections are acting and reacting on each other, and any decided preponderance of one party or the other in any part of that section in either State will seriously affect the other section.   Besides the command of the Ohio River from near its head—for Northern Virginia reaches within 40 or 50 miles by water of the head of the Ohio, and if Kentucky goes with us, as she will do if not withheld by the State—of that portion of Virginia, it will give the Confederacy such a control of the Ohio River as would enable them to get better terms with reference to the navigation of other rivers not within their boundary—for instance, the Upper Mississippi and Missouri, the upper portion of the Chesapeake Bay, and perhaps other desirable waters.

Leaving these views of the subject, there is another one which ought never to be lost sight of by a Virginia statesman.   If a new State is made, then you may depend upon it that it will be not only a free State, but a bitter abolition one. The very fact of separation will make them bitterly hostile to Virginia and all her institutions, and will carry abolitionism up to the very valley of Virginia. Border quarrels will always occur and reprisals will be made. That will lead to hostile incursions, and that to a border warfare, so that war in fact will exist, though no war be declared.

I could fill a quire of paper with reasons why that country ought not to be allowed to slough off, and while we are engaged in war I think that our true policy would be to hold it, even if in doing so we shall be compelled to stain every square foot of its soil with human blood.

Yours, &c., very respectfully,

HENRY J. FISHER.

[Indorsement.]

EXECUTIVE DEPARTMENT, *October* 26, 1861.

This letter is from a gentleman of great reliability and intelligence, and contains many suggestions, some of which I regard as worthy of consideration. It is therefore respectfully referred to the honorable Secretary of War.

JOHN LETCHER.

HEADQUARTERS ARMY OF KANAWHA,
Camp Dickerson, October 23, 1861.

His Excellency the SECRETARY OF WAR:

SIR: In pursuance of the plan detailed in my late dispatches, I have arrived at a point on the left bank of the Kanawha 5 miles below Fayette Court-House; occupied a strategical point famous for its strength named Cotton Hill, and hold the ferries which lead from it to the other side of the river. I have with me, when all my troops shall have come into camp, some 4,000 men. The enemy occupy the right bank of the river, immediately opposite, with a large force—not less, I have reason to believe, than 13,000 men. Their whole camp is in full view, and we have daily skirmishes. When I arrived in the neighborhood they had 2,000 men on this side, and had made known their intention to occupy and fortify Cotton Hill, which they declared capable of defense, if fortified, against 100,000 men; but on my advance they retreated with precipitation to the other bank. Their present position is admirably selected. It is nothing less than the key to the northwest and the Kanawha Valley. The powerful army which they have assembled there and the fortifications which they have erected around evince their determination to hold it permanently, and I have received some information, though not certain, of re-enforcements on the way to it from the State of Ohio. In this position—the fork of the Gauley and New Rivers—they command the Kanawha River, by which steamboats laden with supplies come within 6 miles of their headquarters, as I witnessed to-day with my own eyes. They command, also, the roads to Clarksburg and the northwest, which they have put in perfect order by employing on them the labor of all their prisoners and all the secessionists in the country which they have overrun. In this position, also, they are always ready to strike Lewisburg whenever the Confederate force at Sewell Mountain and Meadow Bluff is removed. To keep their position is clearly their most important object and purpose in Western Virginia. To dislodge them is equally important to us. I have reconnoitered the country below our two camps with that view, and I find it easy to do so with proper force. I have only to seize the river and roads between them and the Ohio, and the base of their operations is at once destroyed. They would be forced to come and fight me in the positions which I would choose, or retreat by their roads to Clarksburg and the northwest, and abandon the whole of the Kanawha to the Confederates. This is the action which I propose to the War Department and to myself. Had I now in camp the whole force that has been allotted to me and Wise's Legion I would execute my idea without a day's delay, but with the troops already here I cannot think that it would be a prudent course in the face of an enemy so powerful. I hope that the War Department will give the necessary orders for the speedy arrival of re-enforcements. If I can assemble 10,000 men here I shall dislodge the enemy and win the whole Kanawha before the compaign is concluded.

Appended your excellency will please find a dispatch from General Lee, from which it will be seen that the road to Lewisburg will soon be left under the sole protection of Wise's Legion.* This is an additional reason for the immediate re-enforcement of my command at this point, for should the enemy attempt the advance on Lewisburg, while I have a sufficient army to cross the river I can always stop him in full career by cutting his communication and supplies.

I am, sir, your obedient servant,

JOHN B. FLOYD,
Commanding Army of Kanawha.

RICHMOND, VA., *October* 24, 1861.

General G. W. SMITH:

MY DEAR GENERAL: I did not forget your request in relation to Lieutenant Randal. His case has been examined, and it appears that one case, of which he and many others might justly complain, does exist. It was an error, but how can it be remedied? More officers who ranked Lieutenant Randal by former commission are in our service than could be appointed to the grade of captain, so that it is impossible to give him that grade and thus restore his relative position to Childs. The other cases are those of engineers, a corps not having lieutenants, and the members of which were selected for their special qualifications. Before the case was referred back to me he had concluded it by agreement with the Secretary of War, and I hope satisfactorily to him. You ask for his appointment as inspector-general. By reference to the law of organization you will see that no such office is provided for.

My meaning in relation to the revival of your ideas of the value of rank was that you should regard field officers' posts belonging to age or extraordinary merit, and that a soldier, instead of scouting the grade of brigadier-general, might consider it high enough to repay the labor of a life. Your recommendations indicated a disregard of the propriety of passing through the various steps, as they contemplated the long leaps known rather to militia than regular troops.

I will not argue further the question of the number of generals required for an army as small as yours was stated to be, and see no relation to the matter in the following sentence used by you: "Now, because our rank and file have been so much weakened by disease, it is not to be supposed that the reduced force can be more easily made to beat the enemy than when it was at its full, efficient strength." The whole force

---

* See Lee to Floyd, October 20, p. 908.

for duty was a little larger than when the enemy was beaten, the number of generals had been more than proportionately increased, and the only supposition presented was that a further and great augmentation of generals was necessary.   To assume that eight regiments are enough for a major-general's command, without regard being had to the number of men in a regiment, you must have resorted to some other reason than that of the length of the line to be occupied, which was, I thought, the strongest urged in our conversation.   The remedy of recruiting the ranks which you propose when regiments are reduced is more easily proposed than applied to the twelve-months' volunteers, who compose the greater portion of your army.

The recent victory at Leesburg must have a powerful effect, but can hardly change the enemy's plan, though it may postpone its execution. We have reports of the embarkation of a large force at Fortress Monroe.

General Magruder expects an immediate attack at Yorktown.   There is reason to believe a descent will be made on the coast of North Carolina, and I am looking all round to see where the 3,000 troops we have here shall be first and most needed.   Oh, that we had plenty of arms and a short time to raise the men to use them !

Very truly, your friend,

JEFFERSON DAVIS.

CHARLESTOWN, JEFFERSON COUNTY, VIRGINIA,
October 24, 1861.

Hon. R. M. T. HUNTER, *Secretary of State:*

DEAR SIR: In consequence of my absence from home it was only last night that I had the honor to receive your letter, and I exceedingly regret that there is a misconception of our wishes at the War Department in reference to Lieutenant-Colonel Ashby's promotion.   Our main object in asking that he be advanced to a full colonelcy is that we may thereby be enabled to organize under him an additional force of several hundred young men who are anxious to be attached to his command, but will not volunteer under another colonel.   If they organize under Lieutenant-Colonel Ashby now they will constitute a portion of Colonel McDonald's command, and although Lieutenant-Colonel Ashby is at present detached from McDonald's regiment he is under his orders, and the young men I speak of wish to be assured that Ashby alone shall command their regiment.

The condition of our border is becoming more alarming every day. No night passes without some infamous outrage upon our loyal citizens.   Ashby's force is too small to prevent these things, but if he be made a colonel, and those he has with him now be re-enforced by the volunteers ready to rally to his regiment, I promise you that a better state of things will exist up here.   I am reluctant to make suggestions to those who are so much better qualified to conduct affairs, but I trust it will not be deemed presumptuous in me to say that it would also be well to make Ashby provost-marshal for the river counties of Jefferson, Berkeley, and Morgan.   These counties are infested with traitors.   They cannot be controlled or guarded against unless some one be invested with authority to deal with them as they deserve.   They defy all authority now, and are in daily communication with the enemy, as we have reason to believe.   The enemy along the canal has been re-enforced, and yesterday I noticed them busy building a raft or boat at Dam No. 4, and also that coal continues to be sent down the canal.

I have just written a letter to the Secretary of War, and hope that you will favor us with your good offices in securing the full colonelcy for Ashby. A part of his present force is militia, and they are commanded by full colonels, who rank Ashby, which makes some difficulty always, and which was the source of a serious trouble to Ashby in his fight at Harper's Ferry on Wednesday last, which I myself had occasion to notice there.

I am, most respectfully, your obedient servant,

A. R. BOTELER.

RICHMOND, VA., *October* 25, 1861.

General G. T. BEAUREGARD:

MY DEAR GENERAL: Your letters of October 20 and 21 have just been referred to me,* and I hasten to reply, without consulting the Secretary of War. This enables me to say, without connecting his expressions of feeling with the present case, that you have alike his admiration and high personal regard, evinced by so many signs that it cannot be to me a matter of doubt. As the essence of offense is the motive with which words are spoken, I have thus, it is hoped, removed the gravest part of the transaction.

You were unquestionably wrong in the order to recruit a company for the Provisional Army. The Congress, with jealous care, reserved to the men of such companies the power of selecting their own officers. The Executive could not recruit a company except for the Regular Army, and as provided by law; to that extent he could delegate his power to generals in the field, but he could not do more. I presume the objection was not that it was to be a rocket battery, but was to the recruiting of a company for special service, the commander having been selected, not by the men, but the Confederate authority. More than half the controversies between men arise from difference of education and habits of thought. The letter in relation to the law of organization was written like a lawyer, and had it been addressed to one of that profession would not probably have wounded his sensibilities, except in so far as to provoke debate upon the accuracy of his position; but it was addressed to a soldier, sensitive as to the propriety of his motives, and careless about the point which I am sure the Secretary intended alone to present, inattention to, or misconstruction of, the laws governing the case. He desired that your position should be entirely satisfactory to you, and that the freest scope should be given for the exercise of your genius and gallantry in the further maintenance of the cause which amid the smoke and blaze of battle you have three times illustrated. Prompted by that desire, he anticipated my purpose, which had been communicated to him, to place you in the immediate command of the Army of the Potomac, by referring to an order which would soon be issued and which he hoped would be satisfactory to you.

Now, my dear sir, let me entreat you to dismiss this small matter from your mind. In the hostile masses before you, you have a subject more worthy of your contemplation. Your country needs all of your mind and of your heart. You have given cause to expect all which man can do, and your fame and her interests require that your energies should have a single object. My prayers always attend you, and, with confidence, I turn to you in the hour of peril.

Very truly, your friend,

JEFFERSON DAVIS.

P. S.—The Secretary has not seen your letter, and I will not inform him as to this correspondence.

---

* Not found.

HEADQUARTERS FIRST CORPS, ARMY OF THE POTOMAC,
Near Centreville, October 25, 1861.

General S. COOPER,
Adjutant and Inspector General, Richmond, Va.:

GENERAL: I have the honor to acknowledge the receipt of a communication from the War Department, dated 19th instant, which, setting out with the assumption that an order of that Department had not been obeyed, calls for an explanation of the obstacles which have prevented "compliance with its order," and in reply to which I have to state, for the information of the Department, as follows:

Although satisfied that there were no arms in the hands of troops of this corps not required for the ultimate wants of the several regiments to which they had been issued, that is, which would not be needed by the returning sick and recruits, I directed the acting inspector-general of the corps—a field officer—to look after these alleged surplus arms, which he has done, so far as was practicable, and thus far with the result anticipated; that is, no really surplus arms have been found.

The constant shifting of regiments, however, their incessant occupation with outpost duties, and the daily engrossing incidents and engagements of the service of this army corps at this time, in the presence of a powerful enemy, making the execution of the order difficult, have led me not to give as much thought to this investigation as I might otherwise have done, and have perchance unduly diminished its importance in my mind. I shall, however, detail another field officer to take up this investigation, and collect any arms he may find not in hands of men who require them. Meanwhile, in order that I may carry out the wishes of the Department as well as the letter of the orders in question, permit me to ask whether it is designed that arms of the absent sick shall be sent to Richmond or left to me (for my corps), to be disposed of under the existing practice; that is, according to the orders a copy of which I append.

Respectfully, your obedient servant,
G. T. BEAUREGARD,
General, Commanding.

HEADQUARTERS FIRST BRIGADE, SECOND CORPS, A. P.,
Centreville, October 25, 1861.

Hon. J. P. BENJAMIN, *Secretary of War:*

SIR: In reply to your letter [of 21st instant] informing me that I have been assigned to the command of "the Valley District of the Department of Northern Virginia," I have to express my grateful acknowledgment of the honor conferred, and my readiness promptly to comply with the order when received, though it separates me from the brigade which I had hoped to command through the war.

Availing myself of your kind offer to receive suggestions from me respecting the defense of that section of the State, I would, before visiting that region of the State, and ascertaining what troops, stores, and other means of defense are on hand, barely request that, if you have a good and available engineer officer, you would direct him to report to me, and that you will, as far as practicable, send me troops for the war, and keep the supplies, especially of arms, beyond the immediate wants of the forces. Men are more ready to volunteer when told that they can be immediately armed and equipped.

Hoping, through the troops and supplies that you may furnish, soon to see an efficient army in the valley, I remain, most respectfully, your obedient servant,

T. J. JACKSON,
Major-General, P. A. C. S.

CENTREVILLE, *October* 25, 1861.

General S. COOPER,
Adjutant and Inspector General, Richmond :

GENERAL : I have had the honor to receive a copy of General Orders, No. 15 [October 22].

Under that order all the cavalry of this army is to belong to the First Division, Major-General Van Dorn's. I beg this arrangement may be reconsidered by the administration. All the cavalry of the army is now employed on outpost duty. The officer at the head of that service (Brigadier-General Stuart) should be under the immediate orders of the commander of the army, and make his reports to and receive his instructions from him. In like manner, in battle, the commanding general must keep under his own control the largest portion of the cavalry, so that General Van Dorn's division would actually become the weakest in the army, although he is the senior major-general, with high reputation. Should the cavalry be placed with a division of infantry, it must be kept out of position, either for its daily service of observing the enemy or to play its part in battle. Its pickets now cover a front of some 20 miles. To collect its regiments in a division on the right flank of the line would produce great inconvenience, while the loss of time in reporting to the general of division instead of to the commanding general might lead to disaster. For these reasons I respectfully suggest that the cavalry brigade be not included in any division, but left under the immediate orders of the commanding general, and that the First Division be increased by an equal force of infantry.

I regret very much that we have not cavalry enough to give Maj. Gen. E. Van Dorn a division of troops of that arm.

Very respectfully, your obedient servant,

J. E. JOHNSTON,
General.

SPECIAL ORDERS, }   HEADQUARTERS ARMY OF THE POTOMAC,
No. 462.   }   *October* 26, 1861.

Brig. Gen. Cadmus M. Wilcox, P. A. C. S., is assigned to the command of the Fifth Brigade, Second Corps, Army of the Potomac, and will be obeyed accordingly.

By command of General Johnston:

THOS. G. RHETT,
Assistant Adjutant-General.

RICHMOND, *October* 27, 1861.

Governor JOHN LETCHER, *Present :*

DEAR SIR : We are in very urgent straits for powder, which is being required on all sides for the defense of the frontiers of Virginia. During your absence the Secretary of State gave me an order for 500 barrels of rifle powder, to be sent at once to General Joseph E. Johnston, who made a pressing request for its immediate transmission, but I learn that your chief of ordnance has suspended the order. There are also 75 barrels of cannon powder in the Bellona Arsenal, which it would be very important to send to General Magruder for the heavy guns recently sent to Yorktown and Gloucester Point. Could you not do me the favor to put this powder at my disposal? I will settle for it on any reasonable terms, and it shall not be used out of the State.

Yours, very truly,

J. P. BENJAMIN,
Acting Secretary of War.

P. S.—I am told that you have four 12-pounder bronze howitzers not in use. General Johnston is constantly asking for howitzers, and I will send them also to him if you will let me have them.

RICHMOND, *October* 27, 1861.

Maj. Gen. T. H. HOLMES,
Commanding the Department of Aquia:

SIR: Intelligence has reached this Department from various sources that the Federal fleet in Hampton Roads, with 25,000 men, is destined for the Rappahannock River, with the view of executing a flank movement upon your command. I think it proper to give you warning of the reported plan of attack, though the intimation of their intention to make such a movement may have been thrown out to conceal their real purpose.

Colonel [George E.] Pickett, at Tappahannock, has been written to, with orders to call out all the local forces he can muster, armed with their own weapons, do the best he can, and wait your orders.

Your obedient servant,

J. P. BENJAMIN,
Acting Secretary of War.

RICHMOND, VA., *October* 27, 1861.

General JOSEPH E. JOHNSTON,
Commanding Department of Northern Virginia:

SIR: We have received from several quarters information that the enemy intend a movement in force up the Rappahannock, and that he has about 25,000 men in the fleet now concentrated at Fort Monroe for that purpose. This may be a feint, or the information, although coming from friends, may have been allowed to leak out with the view of deceiving us, yet it is of sufficient importance to be sent to you. I send a private note to Colonel Jordan, the adjutant of General Beauregard, by special messenger. The note incloses a communication in cipher, sent to the President from some unknown quarter, and the President has an impression that Colonel Jordan has a key which will decipher it. If so, the contents will no doubt be communicated to you by General Beauregard, if of any importance. We have so many apparently reliable yet contradictory statements about the destination of this great expedition, that we are much at a loss to prepare defense against it. I have ordered up four or five unarmed regiments from Georgia and Alabama, and hope they will be here in a day or two. Let me know by telegraph how many you can arm, and I will send them at once. News from Europe to-day assures us of a very early recognition of our independence and of the breaking of the blockade.

Your obedient servant,

J. P. BENJAMIN,
Acting Secretary of War.

HEADQUARTERS VIRGINIA MILITIA,
Winchester, October 27, 1861.

General S. COOPER, *Adjutant-General:*

The enemy has driven Colonel McDonald's forces from their positions near New Creek and Romney. Many of them are on their retreat to Winchester. Major Funsten is at Blue's Hotel, hurt by a fall. He writes that it may be a general advance on Winchester.

Most respectfully,

J. H. CARSON,
Brigadier General, Commanding.

HEADQUARTERS ARMY OF KANAWHA,
Camp Dickerson, October 27, 1861.

His Excellency the SECRETARY OF WAR:

SIR: The re-enforcements which have been, as I am officially informed, ordered to this command, have not, with the exception of Waddill's battalion of 300, made their appearance or been heard of; and owing to the inevitable hardship and exposures of active operations so late in the season, my force is daily diminished. I have not, it is almost unnecessary to say, attempted the maneuver on the base of the enemy's lines to cut his supplies and communications, for my plans, as detailed in my last dispatch, depended on an addition to my strength, which I now begin to despair of receiving. I am at present busy in harassing and annoying the enemy in front of Cotton Hill, with the hope that he may be provoked to come and fight me in my position. Should he do so, I have no doubt of the result.

On the 24th of the month, after reconnoitering in person the river to Loop Creek, one of its tributaries, I dispatched Colonel Clarkson, with 160 cavalry, farther down, into the counties of Putnam and Fayette, to neighborhoods known to be strongly disaffected, and in which polls had been opened for the first election of the counterfeit State of Kanawha. The expedition was highly successful; the election was broken up; the Unionists fired on and some of them killed, and 40 prisoners, notorious for their hatred of the Confederacy and their robberies and cruelties to their secessionist neighbors, brought prisoners to my camp. Colonel Clarkson reconnoitered the Kanawha River for many miles, discovering several posts of the enemy, and firing into a steamboat laden with supplies on its way up to their camp. The pilot and other persons on it were killed or wounded and the boat visibly damaged, but for want of means to board we were unable to capture it.

I am now preparing batteries on the mountain side which will command the road along the river to the enemy's camp, by which they receive their supplies after they leave the steamboat. I hope to open fire to-morrow morning, and think that they will cause such serious inconvenience and injury, that the enemy will perhaps cross and give me battle under the conditions which I demand for success.   But if the enemy will not do so, and persists in holding on to his present position against all temptations and invitations, his force is so powerful, and mine so small, that I shall be unable to do anything with him unless the Department can prevail on General Lee to make a movement against his front. My march to this point is only part of a larger plan.   By it General Lee, with his large army on Sewell Mountain, should have operated on the front of the enemy, while I made my way through a desert to attack his flank.   I have done my part of this work, but I have not heard of General Lee's movements, and unless he should make them speedily, I fear that this campaign must end without any decisive result, and that all the force lately assembled around Sewell Mountain will be of no profit to the war.

In the mean time I await anxiously the views of the Department as to the proper winter quarters for the troops under my command.   I have already placed the Department in full possession of my own ideas, and pray that it may speedily decide upon them.

I am, sir, your obedient servant,

JOHN B. FLOYD,
Commanding Army of Kanawha.

CENTREVILLE, *October* 28, 1861.

President DAVIS:

Informant in Washington says marine expedition is aimed at Cape Fear River and occupation of Wilmington, Smithville, and Fayetteville Arsenal, North Carolina.

THOMAS JORDAN,
Assistant Adjutant-General

RICHMOND, *October* 28, 1861.

General JOSEPH E. JOHNSTON, *Centreville:*

Just heard from Norfolk that the enemy's great fleet is going to sea, thus indicating that the threat of attack on the Rappahannock was intended to deceive us.

J. P. BENJAMIN,
Acting Secretary of War.

SPECIAL ORDERS, }   ADJT. AND INSP. GEN.'S OFFICE,
No. 192.   }   *Richmond, October* 28, 1861.

*   *   *   *   *   *   *

VII. Maj. Gen. T. J. Jackson, Provisional Army, is assigned to the command of the Valley District in the Department of Northern Virginia, and will proceed to establish his headquarters at Winchester, or such other point as he may select.

*   *   *   *   *   *   *

By command of the Secretary of War:

JNO. WITHERS,
Assistant Adjutant-General.

RICHMOND, *October* 29, 1861.

General JOSEPH E. JOHNSTON, *Centreville:*

Just received a dispatch from General Huger informing me that thirty-six steamers and one transport steamer have gone to sea this morning and two went yesterday. This, I think, removes all probability of an attack on the Lower Potomac or the Rappahannock.

J. P. BENJAMIN,
Acting Secretary of War.

RICHMOND, *October* 29, 1861.

General JOSEPH E. JOHNSTON, *Centreville, Va.:*

MY DEAR SIR: I have just seen General Wigfall, and find from my conversation with him that you cannot have understood my note in relation to Captain Montgomery. I had no funds in the appropriations from which I could pay for recruiting, and not knowing what to do with him, left him subject to your orders, but with no idea of interfering in any way with any arrangement you might make for the command of the battery. I merely suggested (not knowing that there was any charge against him) that it might be well to let him learn how to manage his battery under the command of the officer you had chosen, but even this was a mere suggestion, to be adopted or not at your discretion. Wigfall says that the men won't obey Montgomery, and that he is not fit to command, but that you wish to avoid a court-martial, as they are ineffective and troublesome machines with volunteers. This may all be very true, but what are we to do? I know of no other means of getting rid of an incompetent or unworthy officer. The President has no power to dismiss him. I leave the whole matter to you to do the best you can, and have written these few lines only to remove the impression that I desired at all to interfere with the command of the battery, as ordered by you.

I have explained to Wigfall that the two Texas regiments remaining here have been detained solely to aid in repulsing the enemy in the event of his landing on the Peninsula or on the coast of North Carolina, in the rear of our defenses at Norfolk. By Thursday evening we shall know positively whether they have gone farther south than Hatteras, in which event I will send you up the two regiments immediately. I will also, I hope, have two or three Georgia regiments here about the same time to receive the arms you have on hand.

I have told General Cooper to let you retain General Jackson during the present emergency, but as soon as the battle is fought, or all chance of conflict is at an end, I am anxious to get him into the Valley District, where he enjoys the fullest confidence of the people, and where we hope with his aid to organize a very respectable force.

Yours, &c.,

J. P. BENJAMIN.

RICHMOND, *October* 29, 1861.

Col. ANGUS W. MCDONALD, *Winchester, Va.:*

COLONEL: I am desired to inform you, in answer to your communication of the 20th instant, that Maj. Gen. T. J. Jackson has been ordered to the command of the Valley District, extending from the Blue Ridge to the Alleghany Mountains, with full powers to act in all matters relating to the defense of that district and the military operations therein. General Jackson, as chief in command of the district, will also regulate and direct the subject of winter quarters, to which you refer.

Very respectfully, &c.,

R. H. CHILTON,
Assistant Adjutant-General.

RICHMOND, *October* 29, 1861.

Col. GEORGE E. PICKETT,
Commanding, &c., Fort Lowry:

COLONEL: Yours of the 28th instant, by special messenger, was duly received this morning, and submitted to the Secretary of War, who greatly regrets his inability to send you re-enforcements.* He has, however, directed a supply of percussion arms and ammunition to be forwarded to you with the least practicable delay. It is impossible to furnish you with the rifled cannon mentioned in your communication.

Very respectfully, &c.,

S. COOPER,
Adjutant and Inspector General.

HEADQUARTERS ARMY OF KANAWHA,
Camp Dickerson, October 29, 1861.

Hon. SECRETARY OF WAR:

SIR: I have the honor to request that you will furnish me as speedily as possible two 12-pounder rifled guns and two 24-pounder rifled howitzers. In my present position I feel very seriously the want of heavy artillery, and am quite satisfied that if I had it I could bring the campaign to a successful close. I hold the left bank of New River and am in command of all its ferries. From the river bluffs are plainly seen the several encampments of the enemy at and in the vicinity of the Hawk's Nest. Some of these positions can be reached, from which with such guns as I ask for the enemy could not only be dislodged from his positions, but the navigation of the Kanawha cut off and its ferries commanded. Could this be effected one of two alternatives is left him—either to fight me in my own positions or to retreat out of the valley through the northwest. With 6-pounder guns such as I have I cannot engage with certainty of success the pieces of the enemy, superior in number, range, caliber, and metal. Any position which I can gain, and from which the enemy's can be reached, can be brought within range of his guns. With guns of power equal to or approximating that of his I would attack him with a strong conviction of success.

I earnestly but respectfully call your attention to the matter, with the request that you will inform me at once whether the guns can be furnished.

I am, very respectfully, your obedient servant,

JOHN B. FLOYD,
Commanding Army of Kanawha.

---

* Not found.

BROOKE'S STATION, *October* 29, 1861.

Hon. J. P. BENJAMIN, *Secretary of War:*

An intelligent soldier sent from Evansport across the river reports 15,000 of the enemy there, with eighty pieces of field artillery, to prevent us from crossing, and the batteries are to be attacked as soon as their vessels can be prepared. He heard nothing of the expedition from below, mentioned by Van Camp. He crossed back this morning at Mathias Point.

TH. H. HOLMES,
Major-General.

CENTREVILLE, *October* 29, 1861.

Hon. J. P. BENJAMIN:

MY DEAR SIR: Your note of the 27th instant has been received, with its inclosure. The note in cipher was addressed to me—that is, to Thomas John Rayford, a name I adopted before leaving Washington, for purposes of cipher correspondence with Mrs. Greenhow, by whom the note probably was written. As you will perceive from the translation inclosed, the subject-matter is unimportant. I say Mrs. G. probably wrote the note, but it is quite possible she did not, and that it is a shallow device of the enemy to entice into a correspondence which shall fall into their hands. This is the best light to view it, as a correspondence with her or further use of that cipher is useless. This cipher I arranged last April. Being my first attempt, and hastily devised, it may be deciphered by any expert, as I found after use of it for a time. I accordingly would have discarded it long since had Mrs. G. escaped detection, and had, indeed, arranged a cipher to send her just as she was arrested. The War Department at Washington came into possession of one of her letters in this cipher, and by its aid ought to have worked out the key. That does not matter, as of course I used it with but the lady, and with her it has served our purpose, including the one great service of saving General Bonham from a disastrous surprise on the 17th of July. I hear from another source that a reward is offered for the key. I am inclined to furnish it through a person in Washington, and let the friend get the consideration, for, I repeat, the possession of the key can do them no possible good now, nor can it prejudice any one. My suspicion has been excited by the way the value of the key is dwelt upon in this note and the desire to get at it on part of enemy, for I cannot doubt that an expert could unravel it.

I know not who wrote the letter signed A. M. H. The place of attack he indicates is one that Dr. Van Camp has just come here to inform us has actually been determined on as the place of descent by the Annapolis armada. Callan, clerk of Senate Military Committee, is informant. It is doubted here, however, but the army has been put in order for such an exigency.

Last night I telegraphed information sent me that Cape Fear River, Smithville, &c., were the real points of attack. This came from one (Washington, 24th instant) with capacity and wit to make a most efficient emissary. Circumstances have placed her *en rapport* with me lately, and I expect a good deal of timely, acute observation of useful character from her, but as I cannot be altogether certain of her faith, all will be received with caution, and nothing communicated to her, as was my course, I may also say, with Mrs. G. The person in question communicates the name of an alien just from Portsmouth, Va., one E.

B. Lookins, who is said to have given so much information deemed of value, that he has already been commissioned. This man had drawings of batteries in the Peninsula. He, she says, has a brother-in-law, by name of Ford, now in the works at Sewell's Point, from whom he learned a signal in use by us when our vessels are to run the blockade of York River. If there is such a signal it has been communicated, be assured. Generals Johnston and Beauregard think the matter ought to be examined into.

You rightly say the events of the last six months seem all a dream. The most dreamlike thing in the world's history is the presence here in Fairfax County, in the month of October, 1861, twelve months from the time you were in San Francisco, of two hostile armies, of formidable size, such as now confront each other.

Be assured I shall be pleased to be of the least personal service to you in this quarter.

Yours, truly,

THOMAS JORDAN.

BALTIMORE, *October* 29, 1861.

Hon. J. P. BENJAMIN:

HONORED SIR: The gentleman who will hand you this I have forwarded by our Government route, as he comes on very important business with the Navy Department. He will also give you the Northern papers sent by him up to this day. I have made arrangements to forward them every Wednesday and Saturday. The gentleman who negotiated the purchase of the bonds has been arrested. I will, I think, be able to sell them to other parties, and accomplish our object. Anything that I can do for you here let me know immediately. Any communication directed to Mr. Hermange, Sun office, Baltimore, sent to the river by courier, will reach me safely. Direct inside to me. This is a better arrangement than the one mentioned in my former letter. General Dix has announced his intention of hanging me as a spy if he can find me. That for his intentions.

With every wish for the success of our devoted cause, I remain, very respectfully, yours,

H. A. STEWART.

P. S.—The confusion in Washington is greater than after the battle of Bull Run. An officer of rank says he believes if a decided attack were made on Washington they would capitulate.

HEADQUARTERS FIRST CORPS, ARMY OF THE POTOMAC,
Centreville, Va., October 30, 1861.

Brig. Gen. N. G. EVANS, *Commanding at Leesburg, Va.:*

GENERAL: I send you herewith the copy of letter from General Stuart, giving the positions and probable intentions of the enemy for your information and guidance.* General Johnston says:

It indicates, as far as can be relied on, a movement of Banks eastwardly. Cannot General Evans ascertain the fact? And if the movement has been positively made, then let him join us; that is, by placing himself within striking [distance] of us, to counteract the effect of Banks joining McClellan.

---

* Not found.

Hence you must endeavor to ascertain what the enemy is about on the other side of the Potomac, and should Banks have moved as above stated, you will act as directed by General Johnston, taking up a new position, either to hold in check the enemy's forces you may have in front or to join us at a moment's notice. I suppose in rear of Ball's and Carter's Mills, on Goose Creek, would be the best ones; then Gum Spring or Sudley Spring and Church, according to circumstances and the movements of the enemy.

It would be well for you to dispose of all the heavy baggage of your troops, which can be sent to Manassas in wagons pressed into service for that special object, with a guard of three men from each company and a proper number of non-commissioned and commissioned officers.

You must see to the constant proper supply of provisions, &c., for your whole command, keeping the latter always prepared to move at a moment's notice, without, however, harassing or alarming the officers and men, who must understand that those precautions are necessary for our future strategic operations.

Respectfully, your obedient servant,

G. T. BEAUREGARD,
General, Commanding.

RICHMOND, *October* 31, 1861.

Maj. Gen. EARL VAN DORN, *Army of the Potomac:*

SIR: In the reorganization of the Army of the Potomac your command of the First Division was intended by the President to be composed of all the cavalry, two brigades of Mississippians, and Hampton's Legion. The infantry was attached to the cavalry, because we had not enough cavalry to form for you a division. General Johnston, the commander of the Department of Northern Virginia, has suggested some objections to this disposal of the cavalry which seem to us well founded, and has proposed that additional brigades of infantry be assigned to your division, leaving the cavalry under his immediate separate command. Before, however, making any change the President will receive your views on the matter and consider them. The objections made by General Johnston, and to which the President is disposed to attach great weight, are:

That all the cavalry of the army is now employed on outpost duty. The officer at the head of that service (Brigadier-General Stuart) should be under the immediate orders of the commander of the army, and make his reports to and receive his instructions from him. In like manner, in battle, the commanding general must keep under his own control the largest portion of the cavalry, so that General Van Dorn's division would actually become the weakest in the army, although he is the senior major-general, with high reputation.

In addition to this is the consideration that your rank would entitle you to the right wing, and in any battle that may occur in the neighborhood of the present position of the army the ground to the right is unfavorable for cavalry, which would of necessity be thrown to the center or to the left, thus separating you from either the cavalry or the infantry of your division during actual conflict. The President is therefore inclined to increase your division, by the assignment of other infantry brigades, to its due strength in proportion to your rank, and to leave the cavalry as a separate command.

Be good enough to answer me as promptly as possible.

Your obedient servant,

J. P. BENJAMIN,
Acting Secretary of War.

WINCHESTER, *October* 31, 1861.

General COOPER :

Referring to my letter of the 28th instant you will perceive that personal considerations should restrain me from undertaking to give you a detailed account of the affair at Romney on the 26th instant. Duty, however, compels me to report the present condition of my command. The companies of Captains Jordan, Myers, and Harper have been ordered to post themselves at Cacapon Bridge, 23 miles east of Romney. The companies of Captains Bowen, Sheetz, and Shands have been ordered to post themselves at the Hanging Rock Pass, 16 miles east of Romney, on the Northwestern turnpike. This division of the mounted force of my command has been made owing to the impossibility of obtaining quarters for all of them at any one point.

The artillery sent me has been received, but neither ammunition nor harness accompanied it.

I have delayed in Winchester thus long in order that I might have the better opportunity of again supplying my command with the equipments, arms, ammunition, baggage, &c., now so much needed by them. I shall leave to-morrow for the Hanging Rock Pass above mentioned.

I herewith inclose you a copy of a letter received by me from a reliable source, together with the indorsement upon it.*

I am, sir, very respectfully, your obedient servant,

ANGUS W. McDONALD,
Colonel, Commanding Brigade, C. S. Army.

RICHMOND, *October* 31, 1861.

His Excellency the PRESIDENT OF THE CONFEDERATE STATES :

SIR : I take the liberty of calling your attention to the exposed condition of Hampshire, Hardy, and the neighboring counties of this State, and to submit in the concisest terms some suggestions relative to the subject. I beg to premise by reminding you that the counties referred to, now more or less subjected to the ravages of the enemy, are stocked with every variety of farming product, liable to be destroyed or taken at any moment, which promptness on our part may rescue and secure, and render available for our own purposes. We have, as you are aware, recent accounts, which lead to the apprehension that Romney is now occupied by the enemy in force, about 2,000 strong. If energetic steps are taken before they have time to intrench themselves, they can be easily dislodged and driven beyond the limits of the State. The force already organized under Colonel McDonald and the militia of Hampshire and Hardy, if at once concentrated and led by an active and resolute man, would be fully competent to effect this. Of the large number who have flocked to our standard from Maryland, said to reach from 8,000 to 10,000 men, if but 2,000 could be employed for the purpose they could unquestionably take Cumberland. Holding this point, and co-operating with the forces in the counties spoken of, they could meet the enemy at every point, and effectually protect that portion of Virginia.

The advantages of holding Cumberland, I would respectfully submit, would be very important to the Southern cause. I beg very briefly to refer to some of them. Cumberland is now the eastern terminus of the

---

* Not found.

Baltimore and Ohio Railroad. The enemy use the facilities it furnishes for assembling their forces and making their preparations for their frequent raids into Virginia. To take it would be to break up their stronghold for this purpose. By taking that place we also break up the line of communication between the eastern and western forces of the enemy. We also destroy the trade of Wheeling, the market for whose manufactured and other products is Baltimore. In addition, we would control the navigation of the Ohio and Potomac Canal, and cut off Washington and Alexandria not only from their supply of coal, but also of hay, oats, and fodder for their horses, of which they are now particularly in need since the interruption to the navigation of the Potomac.

Again, the possession of Cumberland might be regarded as the initial step towards obtaining the mastery over the railroad between that point and Wheeling, whether for our own use or for purposes of destruction. I would further suggest that, supposing Cumberland in our hands, it would be the great rallying point of the secession citizens of Maryland, now so harassed and oppressed, and here might be inaugurated the revolution destined to restore that gallant State to liberty. At all events, in this view the moral effects would be most auspicious. Maryland would regard the event as an earnest of future aid, and it would spread hope and encouragement far and wide within her borders.

The troops now in Cumberland amount, I am informed, to a full regiment of the Home Guard and a company of cavalry of 180 men. They are part of the forces raised by the authority of the United States Congress under the auspices of Ex-Governor Frank Thomas. The regiment, I know from personal observation, consists mostly of the very refuse of society, and is badly disciplined and officered. A sudden descent of a force of half their number would scatter them to the winds. Nothing could be easier than the surprise and capture of the place.

I am informed by competent engineers that it could be made defensible by but a small body of men.

Respectfully,

C. H. McBLAIR,
Commander, C. S. Navy.

Abstract from return of the Army of the Potomac, General Joseph E. Johnston, C. S. Army, commanding, for the month of October, 1861.

Troops.	Present for duty.						Effective total present.	Aggregate present.
	Infantry.		Cavalry.		Artillery.			
	Officers.	Men.	Officers.	Men.	Officers.	Men.		
First (Beauregard's) Corps	1,406	19,913	62	911	63	1,273	23,911	28,165
Second (G. W. Smith's) Corps	1,209	16,703			27	480	18,063	21,613
Cavalry brigade (Stuart's)			131	1,487			1,492	1,880
Artillery corps (Pendleton)					39	663	663	777
Total	2,615	36,616	193	2,398	129	2,416	44,131	52,435

Abstract from return of Aquia District, commanded by Maj. Gen. T. H. Holmes, for October, 1861.

Station.	Present for duty: Officers.	Present for duty: Men.	Aggregate present and absent.
Evansport and vicinity	117	1,822	3,422
Hedgeman's farm	22	293	439
Cross-Roads	3	56	96
Camp Clifton	31	307	509
Camp Howe	32	443	863
Fort Lowry	35	453	654
Camp Potomac	34	416	626
Marlborough Point	36	435	717
Heathsville	20	314	352
Mathias Point	4	60	76
Camp Potomac	4	35	70
Lancaster County	14	159	173
Brooke's Station	37	499	757
Camp Potomac	2	45	70
Grand total	391	5,337	8,824

Abstract from return of the Army of the Northwest, Brig. Gen. W. W. Loring, C. S. Army, commanding, for the month of October, 1861.

Troops.	Present for duty. Infantry. Officers.	Present for duty. Infantry. Men.	Present for duty. Cavalry. Officers.	Present for duty. Cavalry. Men.	Present for duty. Artillery. Officers.	Present for duty. Artillery. Men.	Aggregate present.
Anderson's brigade	101	1,831	4	99	2	61	2,237
Donelson's brigade	118	2,005	3	34			2,454
Gilham's brigade	67	969			3	62	1,480
Jackson's brigade	106	1,184			2	72	2,060
Taliaferro's brigade	90	1,172			5	107	1,721
Other commands	93	1,210	11	127			1,748
Total	575	8,371	18	260	12	302	11,700

Abstract from return of the Sixteenth Brigade, Virginia Militia, Army of the Valley, commanded by Brig. Gen. James H. Carson, for October, 1861.

Troops.	Present for duty. Officers.	Present for duty. Men.	Aggregate present.	Aggregate present and absent.
Thirty-first Regiment Virginia Militia, Col. R. F. Baldwin	20	69	126	664
Fifty-first Regiment Virginia Militia, Col. C. E. Shryock	20	69	154	284
Fifty-fifth Regiment Virginia Militia, Col. J. J. Grantham	21	123	171	285
Sixty-seventh Regiment Virginia Militia, Col. J. Sencendiver	11	72	103	266
Eighty-ninth Regiment Virginia Militia, Col. Samuel Johnston	15	37	70	354
One hundred twenty-second Regiment Virginia Militia, Col. W. Dearmont	16	85	159	337
Grand total	103	455	783	2,190

HEADQUARTERS,
Centreville, November 2, 1861.

General S. COOPER, Adjutant and Inspector General:

SIR: About the middle of October I was visited at Fairfax Court-House by a Mr. Hunter, who had entered into an engagement with the War Department to provide materials for and otherwise aid in the construction of huts for winter quarters. He expected, I understood, to have his saw-mills in operation in this vicinity within ten days from that time. I have not heard of him since that interview. As time is very important in the matter of erecting winter quarters, I respectfully ask that Mr. Hunter be requested to commence his operations without delay.

I do not know his address.

Your obedient servant,

J. E. JOHNSTON,
General.

————

HEADQUARTERS,
Centreville, November 2, 1861.

General S. COOPER, Adjutant and Inspector General:

SIR: Brigadier-General Carson, now commanding in the valley of the Shenandoah, reports a force under his command of 900 infantry (militia) and the same number of cavalry, including McDonald's regiment. It appears, therefore, that more than half the militia left in service at Winchester by me have been either discharged or permitted to stay at home. From the latest intelligence from that country I am inclined to think that it may be expedient to send Major-General Jackson to his district. Brigadier-General Carson reports that he has called out three regiments of infantry (militia) from the counties on the southwest of Winchester. I am told by a gentleman just from Winchester that he is sending flint-lock muskets to Richmond to be altered. If he does or has done so, I respectfully ask that they be sent immediately back. I suppose that no other troops than militia can be furnished to General Jackson. If so, I beg that measures may be taken by the War Department to call out several thousand more without delay. I cannot, because without information as to the counties which should be called upon or the arms which can be supplied.

It is reported that the enemy intend to repair the Baltimore and Ohio Railroad and put it in operation. It is of great importance to us to prevent it. For this I will send General Jackson to his district whenever there is prospect of having such a force as will enable him to render service.

General Carson reports the enemy's force in Romney to be from 2,500 to 5,000. It is said also that General Loring has no enemy near him. If so, might he not drive off this party and move into the valley?

Your obedient servant,

J. E. JOHNSTON,
General.

————

HEADQUARTERS FIRST DIVISION, ARMY OF POTOMAC,
Union Mills, Va., November 2, 1861.

Hon. J. P. BENJAMIN, Secretary of War, Richmond, Va.:

SIR: Your letter of the 31st ultimo, in regard to the objections made by General Johnston to the reorganization of my division, has just been received.

In reply I have the honor to say that I consider the objections of General Johnston well founded, and that I shall be glad to have the change made which he proposes. These objections occurred to me after considering the matter and after examining the field of operations in front of us, and I should have suggested the same change, except that I had some hesitation in making propositions so soon after entering a protest against his assignment of me to a command which I considered inadequate to my rank.

If you will allow me to suggest, I would be glad to have the Texas troops assigned to my division in addition to the Mississippians, and such other troops as you may see fit to give me, as I have been identified with the people of that State for several years, and I believe it would be somewhat conducive to the interest of the service if I were placed in command of her troops.

Thanking the President and you, sir, for the consideration you have shown me, I am, very respectfully, your obedient servant,

EARL VAN DORN,
Major-General of Division.

RICHMOND, *November* 2, 1861.

General W. W. LORING, *Huntersville, Va.:*

It is not intended to retain in the mountains for the winter more than the 4,500 men necessary to guard the passes. Instructions will be sent in a day or two for the disposal of the remainder of your forces.*

J. P. BENJAMIN,
Acting Secretary of War.

SPECIAL ORDERS, }   ADJT. AND INSP. GEN.'S OFFICE,
No. 202. }   *Richmond, November* 2, 1861.

*   *   *   *   *   *   *

XII. Brig. Gen. Richard Griffith, Provisional Army, will report to General J. E. Johnston for duty with the brigade lately commanded by Brig. Gen. Charles Clark, Provisional Army.

*   *   *   *   *   *   *

By command of the Secretary of War:

JNO. WITHERS,
Assistant Adjutant-General.

SPECIAL ORDERS, }   HEADQUARTERS FIRST CORPS, A. P.,
No. 480. }   *Near Centreville, November* 2, 1861.

The following disposition of officers and troops will take effect immediately, namely:

I. Brig. Gen. Charles Clark will turn over the command of the Fourth Brigade to the senior colonel; then repair to Leesburg, Va., and assume command of the Seventh Brigade, relieving Brig. Gen. N. G. Evans, who will report in person at these headquarters. Brigadier-General Clark will report in person to the commanding general of the Army of the Potomac for special instructions.

II. Brigadier-General Ewell will turn over the command of the Sec-

---
* See inclosure to Cooper to Floyd, November 5, p. 938.

ond Brigade to Brig. Gen. R. E. Rodes, and will report in person for orders to Maj. Gen. G. W. Smith, commanding Second Corps.

*   *   *   *   *   *   *

By command of General Beauregard:

THOMAS JORDAN,
Assistant Adjutant-General.

SPECIAL ORDERS, }   HEADQUARTERS ARMY OF THE POTOMAC,
No. 486.   }   *November* 4, 1861.

In accordance with Special Orders, No. 18, Adjutant and Inspector General's Office, Richmond, Va., October 22, 1861, Maj. Gen. T. J. Jackson, Provisional Army Confederate States, will proceed to take command of the Valley District of the Department of Northern Virginia.

By command of General Johnston:

THOS. G. RHETT,
Assistant Adjutant-General.

CAMP EVANS, *November* 4, 1861.

SECRETARY OF WAR:

The Potomac is higher than it has been since 1852. It is over the canal bank. The boating is probably over for the season.

TURNER ASHBY.

WINCHESTER, VA., *November* 4, 1861.

General S. COOPER, *Adjutant-General C. S. Army:*

SIR: I have been here two weeks, engaged in paying the militia under General Carson and also Colonel McDonald's regiment of cavalry. I consider it my duty as a disbursing officer of the Government to report the condition of things here. I find brigadier-generals in command of regiments instead of brigades, colonels in command of companies instead of regiments, and captains in command of squads instead of companies. I would therefore respectfully suggest the propriety of consolidating regiments and companies at once and disbanding the supernumerary officers, thereby freeing the Confederacy of all this unnecessary expense.

The Federals are busily engaged at Romney in shucking corn and thrashing grain. They have, it is reported, one hundred teams hauling off all the grain they can lay their hands on.

I have nearly completed my payment to August 31.

I remain, with great respect, your obedient servant.

F. C. HUTTER,
Captain and Assistant Quartermaster, Provisional Army C. S.

SPECIAL ORDERS, }   HEADQUARTERS FIRST CORPS, A. P.,
No. 484.   }   *Near Centreville, Va., November* 4, 1861.

I. Brig. Gen. Richard Taylor, Provisional Army Confederate States, having reported for duty with this army corps, is assigned to the command of the Eighth Brigade.

*   *   *   *   *   *   •

By command of General G. T. Beauregard:

THOMAS JORDAN,
Assistant Adjutant-General.

HEADQUARTERS VALLEY DISTRICT,
Winchester, November 5, 1861.

Hon. J. P. BENJAMIN, *Secretary of War:*

SIR: Yesterday morning I received the order from General J. E. Johnston directing me to assume command of this district, and, leaving Manassas by the first train of cars, arrived here last night.

A prisoner who has escaped from the Federal authorities at Williamsport, Md., states that there are about 1,200 of the enemy ready to cross the Potomac so soon as the river shall be fordable. Lieut. Col. Turner Ashby, of the cavalry, reports that there are near 800 Federal troops opposite Shepherdstown, and that additional troops have been moving up the river recently. The most reliable information received from Romney makes the enemy's strength there near 4,000, and from the last official intelligence they are threatening an advance on this place.

Deeply impressed with the importance of not only holding Winchester, but also of repelling the invaders from this district before they shall secure a firm lodgment, I feel it my duty respectfully to urge upon the Department the necessity of ordering here at once all the troops at Cheat Mountain, and if practicable those also from Valley Mountain, or those near Huntersville. I have frequently traveled over the road from Staunton to Cheat Mountain, and I hope that you will pardon me for saying that if the withdrawal of the Confederate forces from the Cheat Mountain region shall induce the enemy to advance on Staunton it will be his ruin, provided a sufficient available force is kept in this district in marching order. It is very important that disciplined troops of not only infantry, but also of artillery and cavalry be ordered here. It appears to me that there should be at least twenty pieces of field artillery, with their complement of horses, harness, implements, &c., assigned to this command. It will be seen from the accompanying list of ordnance and ammunition that General Carson's command only had three field pieces. General Carson also reports to me that he has in service only 1,461 militia, in addition to 130 mounted militia.

The detailed instructions referred to in your letter announcing my assignment to this command have not yet been received.

The heavy guns here are but imperfectly available for defense, in consequence of not having officers and men acquainted with the method of serving them. If you can order here Lieut. Daniel Truehart, jr., or some other good artillery officer, to take charge of the heavy ordnance, the efficiency of this arm of the service will be greatly increased. A good engineer officer is very desirable. I have ordered Generals Carson, Meem, and Boggs to march their commands here forthwith.

Lieut. Col. J. T. L. Preston, Virginia volunteers, the bearer of this letter, will give you a full statement respecting the defenseless condition of this place.

Very respectfully, your obedient servant,

T. J. JACKSON,
Major-General, P. A. C. S.

———

RICHMOND, *November* 5, 1861.

Brig. Gen. JOHN B. FLOYD:

GENERAL: Inclosed you will receive a copy of a letter to General Loring, directing him to send General Donelson's brigade to re-enforce you. You will perceive that General Donelson is to march to Lewisburg, and thence join you by the best route. If you can send forward to Lewisburg to notify him as to that route and afford him such facilities as may be in your power, it would be advisable to do so. Two Virginia regiments now here are under orders to join you, via Lewisburg, and will probably leave in a day or two. It would be well to have instructions left at Lewisburg as to the route these regiments are to take on leaving there.

Very respectfully, &c.,

S. COOPER,
Adjutant and Inspector General.

[Inclosure.]

RICHMOND, *November* 5, 1861.

General W. W. LORING, *Huntersville, Va.:*

GENERAL: You will send, with the least delay practicable, Brigadier-General Donelson with Colonels Savage's and Fulton's regiments, Tennessee volunteers, to re-enforce General Floyd; and after retaining the 4,500 men for the defense of the Monterey and Huntersville lines, reported by you as necessary to guard the passes, you will send the remainder of the troops of your command to Staunton, there to await orders.

General Donelson's brigade will march to Lewisburg, and thence join General Floyd by the best route.

Very respectfully, &c.,

S. COOPER,
Adjutant and Inspector General.

SPECIAL ORDERS, }   ADJT. AND INSP. GEN.'S OFFICE,
No. 206.   }   *Richmond, November* 5, 1861.

*   *   *   *   *   *   *

II. Maj. Gen. T. J. Jackson, Provisional Army, will immediately proceed to Winchester, Va., and assume command of the Valley District, agreeably to his assignment in General Orders, No. 15, Adjutant and Inspector General's Office, of October 22, 1861. The brigade formerly under his command will with the least practicable delay be attached to the Valley District. The force thus detached from the Potomac District will be replaced by the following troops, viz:

The Fourth and Fifth Texas Regiments to be assigned to Brigadier-General Wigfall's brigade. Colonel Wofford's Eighteenth Regiment Georgia Volunteers, Colonel Judge's Fourteenth Regiment Alabama Volunteers, Colonel Smith's Twenty-seventh Regiment Georgia Volunteers; the last three regiments mentioned to be assigned by General J. E. Johnston.

III. The Fifty-sixth and Fifty-seventh Regiments of Virginia Volunteers, Colonels Stuart and Armistead commanding, will proceed without delay, via Lewisburg, to join Brigadier-General Floyd's command in Western Virginia.

*   *   *   *   *   *   *

By command of the Secretary of War:

JNO. WITHERS,
Assistant Adjutant-General.

RICHMOND, *November* 6, 1861.

General T. J. JACKSON, *Winchester, Va.:*

I have ordered your old brigade to be sent to you at once from Centreville and McLaughlin's company of Rockbridge artillery, and had already ordered a further force of about 6,000 men to be detached from Loring's command and to join you, by way of Staunton, before receiving your letter brought by Colonel Preston. Will send you full instructions by mail.

J. P. BENJAMIN,
Acting Secretary of War.

RICHMOND, *November* 6, 1861.

General W. H. RICHARDSON, *Adjutant-General, Richmond:*

GENERAL: I am instructed by the Adjutant and Inspector General, C. S. Army, to inform you that it is impossible to give you the exact number of Virginia troops in the Confederate service at this time. The exigencies of the service have prevented the commanding generals from furnishing this office with the necessary reports. He hopes to be able to furnish you a complete statement very soon.

There are now in the field: Organized by Virginia, 51 regiments infantry; organized by Confederate States, 8 regiments infantry; organized by Confederate States, 2 regiments cavalry; organized by Virginia, 6 regiments cavalry; organized by Virginia, 1 regiment artillery. Total, 68 regiments volunteers; 1 battalion enlisted men. The regiments will average 750 men each, making 51,000. Added to this is the battalion of enlisted men and very many independent companies, making an aggregate of about 55,000 men. There are in the field several regiments of militia, called out by the proclamation of Governor Letcher, from which no returns have been received.

I am, sir, respectfully, &c.,

N. D. GUNN,
Acting Assistant Adjutant-General.

SPECIAL ORDERS, }   HDQRS. ARMY OF THE POTOMAC,
No. 490.   }   *November* 6, 1861.

Brig. Gen. R. S. Ewell, having been relieved from duty with the First Corps, will report to Maj. Gen. G. W. Smith for duty in the Second.

By command of General Johnston:

THOS. G. RHETT,
Assistant Adjutant-General.

SPECIAL ORDERS, }   HDQRS. ARMY OF THE POTOMAC,
No. 491.   }   *November* 6, 1861.

Maj. Gen. E. K. Smith, P. A. C. S., is assigned to the command of the division to be composed of the following brigades: Brigadier-General Elzey's, Brigadier-General Crittenden's, and Brigadier-General Taylor's.

By command of General Johnston:

THOS. G. RHETT,
Assistant Adjutant-General.

RICHMOND, *November* 7, 1861.

General JOSEPH E. JOHNSTON,
    Comdg. Department of Northern Virginia, Centreville, Va.:

SIR: Your letter of the 4th instant* has been submitted to the Secretary of War, and I am instructed to inform you that the number of troops to be sent to Staunton, Va., under instructions to Brigadier-General Loring, of the 5th inst. (copy herewith),† is estimated at between 6,000 and 7,000 effective men. It is designed by the Secretary of War that this force be sent to your command on its arrival at Staunton, and orders to that effect will be given, unless some unforeseen event should require its presence in a different quarter.

Very respectfully, &c.,

S. COOPER,
Adjutant and Inspector General.

HEADQUARTERS,
Centreville, November 7, 1861.

General S. COOPER, *Adjutant-General:*

I respectfully remonstrate against the sending off the brigade lately commanded by Major-General Jackson to the Valley District. He will be opposed to raw troops, we to the enemy's best. Our force is raw; far too small for the object it is expected to accomplish. I suggest that troops be drawn instead from H. R. Jackson's and Loring's command.

J. E. JOHNSTON,
General.

RICHMOND, *November* 7, 1861.

General JOSEPH E. JOHNSTON, *Centreville:*

The brigade of General Jackson was ordered to join him as a matter of urgent necessity, and on due consideration of your position I send you double the number of men to replace it. The Valley District is entirely defenseless, and will fall into the hands of the enemy unless General Jackson has troops sent to him immediately. You are requested to send him his brigade without delay, as there is imminent danger of the capture of Winchester by enemy. Send with the brigade the battery of Rockbridge artillery, in place of which I have sent you another battery this morning.

J. P. BENJAMIN,
Acting Secretary of War.

RICHMOND, *November* 7, 1861.

General JOSEPH E. JOHNSTON, *Centreville, Va.:*

I have one Alabama and one Georgia regiment here for you, both unarmed, and numbering together over 2,000 men. Shall I send them to Fredericksburg or wait till the railroad can take them to Manassas?

J. P. BENJAMIN,
Acting Secretary of War.

---

* Not found.
† See inclosure to Cooper to Floyd, November 5, p. 938.

WAR DEPARTMENT, C. S. A.,
Richmond, November 7, 1861.

General JOSEPH E. JOHNSTON,
Commanding Department Northern Virginia:

SIR: It is with the greatest surprise and regret that I have read your letter of the 2d instant to the Adjutant-General. I had not the remotest idea that you expected any aid from Mr. Hunter or from this Department in relation to the winter quarters for the troops, nor can I conceive on what basis you entertained such expectation.

On the 13th of last month I wrote you at considerable length on this subject, and in order to avoid delay forwarded my letter by Mr. James Hunter and Dr. John P. Hale.

The arrangements made by me were ample, and orders were given for securing ten portable saw-mills here in Richmond, for the purpose of sawing the lumber necessary for the huts. Aware of the urgency of the case, and unable to act without your co-operation, because of my ignorance of the locality where you proposed to shelter the army, I closed my letter with a distinct statement that the parties could not commence active work till you decided this question. It was plainly necessary that they should have some indication of the place where they were to locate the saw-mills before going to work.

Several days afterwards Mr. Hunter and Dr. Hale returned here and reported verbally:

1st. That you had referred them to General Beauregard for conference on the subject of the winter quarters.

2d. That they had found General Beauregard so much engaged as to be unable to accord to them the time and attention necessary for any concert of action between them and the general.

3d. That Major Cabell, who was present at their conversation with General Beauregard, had observed that it was entirely practicable for each regiment to hut itself in two or three days, as he knew from actual experience in service.

4th. That General Beauregard seemed quite relieved of care on the subject when Major Cabell gave him this assurance.

The two gentlemen returned with the conviction that their services were not desired nor required by the army, and without any information as to the locality where the lumber was to be sawed; and, indeed, Mr. Hunter gave me to understand, what seems probable enough, that you were not willing to leave open any opportunity to the enemy to guess at your plans by putting a number of saw-mills at work in any neighborhood where you expected to establish your winter quarters.

I therefore concluded that you had, in concert with General Beauregard, reached the conclusion that you could dispense with any aid from the Department, and could hut the army on the plan spoken of by Major Cabell. I received no answer from you to my letter. Mr. Hunter represented that you declined his services. The saw-mills previously engaged by him were not purchased, and none are to be had at this time. Mr. Hunter has long since gone home, and I had dismissed all solicitude from my mind on the subject of the cantonment of our troops, when the Adjutant-General submitted to me your letter of the 2d instant, indicating an expectation that Mr. Hunter was to commence operations with his saw-mills.

This is distressing in the extreme, and I am entirely at a loss in what mode to assist you. I will, however, do the best in my power, and can now only make the following suggestions:

Ist. It is now out of the question to build board huts. The lumber cannot be procured in time, and there are no saw-mills now to be had, nor is there now time to carry out the first plan.

2d. It may be possible to procure lumber enough to roof log huts and for forming the openings, but of this I am extremely doubtful, though I will cause instant inquiry to be made here, and beg you will institute similar inquiry in the neighborhood of your intended encampment.

3d. Please send me at once the plan deemed best by you as a substitute for that which I proposed, and which is no longer feasible.

4th. Let me know exactly what is requisite from this place, and the unremitting efforts of the Department shall be directed to furnishing it.

5th. If lumber is required for roofing, and if there is no substitute for it possible, inform me what quantity is required in all, and what proportion of it, if any, can be obtained in your neighborhood.

The importance of affording proper shelter for our troops during the rigors of the coming winter can scarcely be overestimated, and knowing how great your own solicitude on the subject must be, I find it impossible to account for your long delay in noticing my letter of the 13th ultimo, and your failure to exhibit any sign of uneasiness at the non-appearance of the saw-mills or workmen you expected to furnish the lumber. I still entertain the hope, however, that my alarm may be unfounded, and that Major Cabell may be able to suggest some mode of shelter as reported to me, which may enable you to put the troops under cover without the use of lumber, and in time to avoid any great exposure or suffering.

I am, respectfully, your obedient servant,

J. P. BENJAMIN,
Acting Secretary of War.

HEADQUARTERS VALLEY DISTRICT,
Winchester, Va., November 7, 1861.

Maj. THOMAS G. RHETT:
Assistant Adjutant-General, Hdqrs. Army of the Potomac:

MAJOR: I arrived here on the night of the same day that I was relieved from duty at Centreville.

Finding that General Kelley's forces in Romney, a distance of 42 miles, were about 4,000, and that an advance on this place was threatened, I repeated the call previously made by General Carson for the militia in his brigade and in those of Generals Meem and Boggs. The troops are to rendezvous at this place. But as General Carson's brigade and that of General Meem are to a greater or less degree in service, and as General Boggs' command includes the South Branch region, occupied by the enemy, not many men will probably respond to the call.

The militia actually in the field number 1,461, stationed as follows: At Winchester, 442; at Lockhart's, distant 12 miles from here on the Northwestern turnpike, 155; at Cacapon Bridge, about 28 miles on the same road, 304; at Hammock's Gap, 12 miles this side of Romney, 160; at Martinsburg, 200; at Charlestown, 100; at Front Royal, in Warren County, distant 23 miles, 50; at Strasburg, distant 18 miles, 25; and at Mount Jackson, distant 42 miles, 25.

In addition to the foregoing there are 130 mounted militia: At Winchester, 25; at Martinsburg, 75, and at Charlestown, 30.

As Colonel McDonald reports direct to Richmond, and is not, from what I can learn, under my command, his forces are not included in the preceding statement; but they amount to 485, stationed as follows:

Along the Northwestern turnpike, between Cacapon Bridge and Hanging Rock, 285, and at Flowing Spring, 2 miles below Charlestown, on the railroad, 200.

I omitted to mention Captain Henderson's cavalry, at Duffield's Depot, about 8 miles above Harper's Ferry, numbering 60 men, which makes the mounted force 190, thus giving an aggregate of 1,651 under my command.

The enemy are, as reported, about 1,800 strong at Williamsport and near 800 opposite Shepherdstown. General Kelley's command, at and near Romney, number about 4,000.

An official report received states that an advance of near 300 came as far as Blue's, 15 miles this side of Romney, but were repulsed by part of Colonel McDonald's regiment, under Captain Sheetz.

I am now informed officially that if the enemy are not speedily driven from the South Branch, our people, who have heretofore been loyal, may yield and take the oath of allegiance to the United States.

So soon as I can get a report of the ammunition distributed I will forward an ordnance report. There is very little ammunition on hand.

The day after arriving here I sent Lieutenant-Colonel Preston to see the Secretary of War, and wrote a letter urging that the troops on the Cheat Mountain route be ordered here, and also those on the Valley Mountain route, if practicable.

Very respectfully, your obedient servant,

T. J. JACKSON,
Major-General, P. A. C. S., Commanding Valley District.

HEADQUARTERS ARMY OF KANAWHA,
Camp Dickerson, November 8, 1861.

[Hon. J. P. BENJAMIN:]

MY GOOD FRIEND: I write as a duty, resulting from the confidence reposed in me and the kindness with which you treat me at all times.

This army is in confusion, resulting from its disquietude. This disquietude was caused in the first instance by a great horror of Southern troops wintering in what they believe to be a bleak, inhospitable climate, in a country partially desolated by the two opposing armies; but even now Virginia has joined in the cry, back! Those in favor of a retrograde movement raised the cry that the army could not be fed. I made a report demonstrating that I could feed the men certainly. Then I found that, from enjoying more than ordinary popularity with the army, I now feel that the kind courtesy which greeted me on all occasions when I met an officer of rank is no longer extended to me with cordiality. My outside friends following the army inform me that it is in consequence of my sustaining General Floyd's desire to stay here until he gets a fight or can advance. The general impression is that General Floyd's conceptions are too bold—rather rash than considerate. The same men that complain so much and express such fears would bear the ills of which they complain if fighting in the State in which they were raised. A very common complaint uttered every day by Georgians, North Carolinians, Mississippians, Louisianians, and even Eastern Virginians, is, "This country is not worth fighting for." The agitation and anger expressed at General Floyd's determination to winter here will culminate in desertion or rebellion, unless the Secretary of War assumes the responsibility of firmly sustaining General Floyd or of ordering him back to winter elsewhere. Be this as it may, it is my opinion, right or wrong, and it is a conclusion of my mind frankly expressed.

Yours, respectfully,

A. W. G. DAVIS.

SPECIAL ORDERS, }   HDQRS. ARMY OF THE POTOMAC,
No. 500.   }   *November* 8, 1861.

I. The First Brigade, Second Corps, Army of the Potomac, will proceed to Winchester, Va., under the command of the senior colonel, and report to Maj. Gen. T. J. Jackson. This command will be transported by rail, and the quartermaster will furnish the transportation without delay.

II. Brig. Gen. R. S. Ewell, P. A. C. S., will report to General G. T. Beauregard for duty with a Virginia brigade.

*   *   *   *   *   *   *

By command of General Johnston:

THOS. G. RHETT,
Assistant Adjutant-General.

RICHMOND, VA., *November* 9, 1861.

General G. T. BEAUREGARD:

SIR: I have habitually neglected to keep copies of my letters and telegrams addressed to you since you entered on duty with the Army of the Potomac. Desiring now to have them, I request that my friend, C. D. Fontaine, may be permitted to take such copies from the originals in your possession.

Very respectfully, &c.,

JEFFERSON DAVIS.

[Similar letters of same date to Generals J. E. Johnston and Gustavus W. Smith.]

HEADQUARTERS, *Centreville, November* 9, 1861.

General WHITING:

DEAR GENERAL: I received your letter yesterday,* but was too much pressed to answer immediately.

I like your plan much; cannot answer for the guns. I have submitted your letter, with recommendations, to the War Department.

I am mourning over the loss of Jackson's brigade, ordered to Winchester against my remonstrances. The Secretary of War will probably establish his headquarters within this department soon.

Yours, in haste,

J. E. JOHNSTON,
General.

---

* Not found.

SPECIAL ORDERS, }   HEADQUARTERS FIRST CORPS, A. P.,
No. 489.   }   *Near Centreville, Va., November 9, 1861.*

I. The Third Division of this Army Corps is dissolved. The Third Brigade will form part of the Second Division until otherwise ordered, and Brig. Gen. D. R. Jones will report to Major-General Longstreet for orders. The First Brigade is assigned to the First Division, and Brigadier-General Bonham will report to Major-General Van Dorn.

II. Brig. Gen. Richard Griffith is assigned to the command of the Mississippi regiments serving in Loudoun County, Virginia, and will without delay report to Brigadier-General Evans, who for the present will remain in command of all the Confederate troops in that county.

By command of General Beauregard:

THOMAS JORDAN,
Assistant Adjutant-General.

———

RICHMOND, VA., *November* 10, 1861.

General G. T. BEAUREGARD:

SIR: When I addressed you in relation to your complaint, because of the letters written to you by Mr. Benjamin, Acting Secretary of War, it was hoped that you would see that you had misinterpreted his expressions, and would be content. But while in yours of the 5th instant * you accept the assurance given that Mr. Benjamin could not have intended to give you offense, you serve notice that your "motives must not be called into question," and that when your "errors are pointed out, it must be done in a proper tone and style," and express the fear that Mr. Benjamin "will, under all circumstances, view only the *legal* aspect of things, and that insensibly this army and myself (yourself) will be put into the straight-jackets of the law," &c., I do not feel competent to instruct Mr. Benjamin in the matter of style. There are few who the public would probably believe fit for that task. But the other point quoted from your letter presents matter for graver consideration, and it is that which induces me to reply. It cannot be peculiar to Mr. Benjamin to look at every exercise of official power in its legal aspect, and you surely did not intend to inform me that your army and yourself are outside of the limits of the law. It is my duty to see that the laws are faithfully executed, and I cannot recognize the pretension of any one that their restraint is too narrow for him.

The Congress carefully reserved to all volunteers the selection of their company officers and provided various modes for receiving them into service as organized bodies. When you disregarded that right, and the case was brought to the notice of the Secretary of War, it could but create surprise, and the most mild and considerate course which could have been adopted was to check further progress under your order and inform you of the error committed.

Very respectfully, yours, &c.,

JEFFERSON DAVIS.

———

RICHMOND, VA., *November* 10, 1861.

General JOSEPH E. JOHNSTON,
Commanding Department of the Potomac:

SIR: The Secretary of War has this morning laid before me yours of the 8th instant.* I fully sympathize with your anxiety for the Army of

———

* Not found.

the Potomac. If indeed, mine be less than yours, it can only be so because the South, the West, and the East, presenting like cause for solicitude, have in the same manner demanded my care. Our correspondence must have assured you that I fully concur in your view of the necessity for unity in command, and I hope, by a statement of the case, to convince you that there has been no purpose to divide your authority by transferring the troops specified in Order No. 206 [of 5th instant] from the center to the left of your department.

The active campaign in the Greenbrier region was considered as closed for the season. There is reason to believe that the enemy is moving a portion of his forces from that mountain region towards the valley of Virginia, and that he has sent troops and munitions from the east, by the way of the Potomac Canal, towards the same point. The failure to destroy his communications by the Baltimore and Ohio Railroad and by the Potomac Canal has left him in possession of great advantages for that operation.

General Jackson, for reasons known to you, was selected to command the Division of the Valley, but we had only the militia and one mounted regiment within the district assigned to him. The recent activity of the enemy, the capture of Romney, &c., required that he should have for prompt service a body of Confederate troops to co-operate with the militia of the district. You suggest that such force should be drawn from the army on the Greenbrier. This was originally considered and abandoned, because they could not probably reach him in time to anticipate the enemy's concentration, and also because General Jackson was a stranger to them, and time was wanting for the growth of that confidence between the commander and his troops the value of which need not be urged upon you. We could have sent to him from this place an equal number of regiments (being about double the numerical strength of those specified in the order referred to), but they were parts of a brigade now in the Army of the Potomac, or were Southern troops, or were ignorant of the country in which they were to serve, and all of them unknown to General Jackson. The troops sent were his old brigade; had served in the valley, and had acquired a reputation which would give confidence to the people of that region, upon whom the general had to rely for his future success. Though the troops sent to you are, as you say, "raw," they have many able officers, and will, I doubt not, be found reliable in the hour of danger; their greater numbers will to you, I hope, more than compensate for the experience of those transferred; while in the valley the latter, by the moral effect their presence will produce, will more than compensate for the inferiority of their numbers. I have labored to increase the Army of the Potomac, and, so far from proposing a reduction of it, did not intend to rest content with an exchange of equivalents. In addition to the troops recently sent to you, I expected soon to send further re-enforcements by withdrawing a part of the army from the Greenbrier Mountains. I have looked hopefully forward to the time when our army could assume the offensive and select the time and place where battles were to be fought, so that ours should be alternations of activity and repose; theirs, the heavy task of constant watching.

When I last visited your headquarters my surprise was expressed at the little increase of your effective force above that of July 21 last, notwithstanding the heavy re-enforcements which had in the mean time been sent to you. Since that visit I have frequently heard of the improved health of the troops; of the return of many who had been absent sick, and some increase has been made by re-enforcement. You can then imagine my disappointment at the information you give, that on the day before the date of your letter the army at your position "was no stronger than on July 21." I can only repeat what was said to you in our conference at Fairfax Court-House, that we are restricted in our capacity to re-enforce by the want of arms. Troops to bear the few arms you have in store have been ordered forward. Your view of the magnitude of the calamity of defeat of the Army of the Potomac is entirely concurred in, and every advantage which is attainable should be seized to increase the power of your present force. I will do what I can to augment its numbers, but you must remember that our wants greatly exceed our resources.

Banks' brigade, we learn, has left the position occupied when I last saw you. Sickles is said to be yet on the Lower Potomac, and, when your means will enable you to reach him, I still hope he may be crushed.

I will show this reply to the Secretary of War, and hope there will be no misunderstanding between you in future. The success of the army requires harmonious co-operation.

Very respectfully, yours, &c.,

JEFFERSON DAVIS.

HEADQUARTERS ARMY KANAWHA,
Camp Dickerson, November 10, 1861.

Hon. J. P. BENJAMIN, *Secretary of War:*

SIR: As this is a strictly private letter, I write with my own hand. It is now 2 o'clock p. m. I have labored until 2 in the public service, and have taken this afternoon to arrange my papers and make up my cash account. I find leisure while my clerks are at work, not requiring my immediate attention, to write you. This army is utterly demoralized, or, if this term is too strong, it is the most disquieted collection of men I have ever known massed together. They want to go back to some point to winter nearer to provisions for men and horses. I have opposed this, and do now oppose it, for the reason that we will have to conquer territory abandoned in the spring at full as great a sacrifice as it will cost to hold it this winter. The men of this army are dying, it is true, at a fearful rate, but raw men who do duty every other night would die anywhere. We are compelled to have strong pickets, as we are an inferior force in the immediate presence of a vastly superior one. The mutterings that precede a storm are so loud in the army that any one in the army could hear them in the dead hour of the night if not under the influence of some powerful narcotic. Now, sir, you must fully understand, in my position, as I feel and know it to be from the confidence reposed in me (even from the President down I am trusted), I have and do exercise on most occasions an energy that is startling to the sluggish multitude; but kindness, energy, and the performance of duties fail to satisfy an army who resolve upon a purpose which I oppose; and now, from being the most popular man in this army, I am now satisfied, from the requisitions made on me—some legitimate, but many to vex—that I am now not acceptable to the army.

Yours, respectfully,

A. W. G. DAVIS.

P. S.—Inclosed I send you a topographical sketch, which has the merit of being exactly correct.

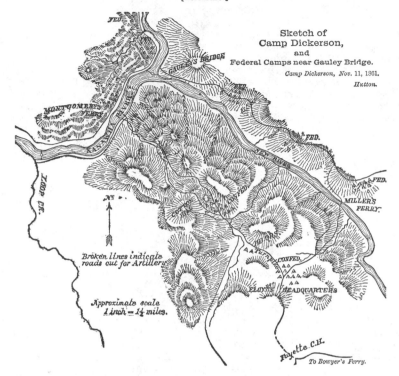

Sketch of
Camp Dickerson,
and
Federal Camps near Gauley Bridge.

Camp Dickerson, Nov. 11, 1861.

Hutton.

Broken lines indicate
roads out for Artillery

Approximate scale
1 inch = 1¼ miles.

To Bowyer's Ferry.

HEADQUARTERS, CENTREVILLE, *November* 11, 1861.
Brig. Gen. W. H. C. WHITING,
    Commanding Troops near Dumfries:

MY DEAR GENERAL: I have sent both your letters on the subject
of a new battery* to the War Department with my concurrence. I look
upon the case as hopeless, however; it is too late to make this additional
preparation against any combined operation against Evansport. Remember that it took our War Department a month to make the mere removal
of guns and a little ammunition to Evansport. If the attack you anticipate is to be made, it must be within that time. Is your position near
enough to Evansport? Will not the distance, 3 or 4 miles, render it
difficult for you to defend both with your force? Consider the whole
question carefully before breaking ground. Would not the masked battery used on a former occasion—I mean the guns and gunners—make a
useful diversion, should the proposed battery not be ready?

Captain Stevens has been very sick and I fear will not be strong
enough for service for some days yet. He is our only engineer, you know.
Before leaving us I shall wish him to plan such additions as may enable
Fort Pickens to be independent of the army for a few days.

I am embarrassed on the subject of winter quarters. I made arrangements a month ago for the beginning of preparations, but was disappointed by the supposed contractor, who gave up the undertaking

_____
* Not found.

without giving me notice. I suppose that, upon occasion, your troops could make themselves log huts in a few days. Here we can't find the logs where the huts will be wanted. ·

Very truly, yours,

J. E. JOHNSTON,
General.

We have just received a report from Stuart that our pickets at Fairfax Court-House have been driven in, and that a large force is gathered at Springfield, on the railroad, 7 miles beyond.

HEADQUARTERS VALLEY DISTRICT,
Winchester, Va., November 12, 1861.

Maj. THOMAS G. RHETT,
Assistant Adjutant-General, Hdqrs. Dept. of Western Virginia :

MAJOR: The enemy at Romney are, from the most reliable information, near 6,000 strong, and are fortifying the town.

Before leaving Centreville I had a conversation with the general commanding the department respecting his ordering Lieut. Col. T. H. Williamson, Corps of Engineers, to this district, and he expressed a willingness to do so when Captain Stevens should recover his health. If Lieutenant-Colonel Williamson can, consistently with the interests of the public service, be ordered here, I respectfully request that it may be done at as early a period as practicable, as his services are much needed.

Please send me all the intrenching tools that you can spare. The Chesapeake and Ohio Canal is so damaged by the late freshets as not to be boatable.

Your most obedient servant,

T. J. JACKSON,
Major-General, Commanding Valley District.

HEADQUARTERS, *Centreville, November* 12, 1861.

Brigadier-General WHITING :

MY DEAR GENERAL: I have received your note of this morning. The location you describe seems to me better than that of Evansport. To a question by telegraph General Cooper replied to-day that the guns you asked for should be sent without delay. This does not encourage me much as to time. In Richmond their ideas of promptitude are very different from ours. By the way, have you seen General Trimble's arrangements for land defense ? If my ideas of the ground, given by a pencil sketch, are at all correct, they amount to nothing. A few of Dahlgren's boat howitzers would knock them to pieces from the hills in rear.

I have very little apprehension of harm from the bombardment of a mere line like those batteries; nothing is necessary but shelter against the fragments of shells, which burst high. At the distance of 2 miles they cannot kill a man a day. I fear landing in force. It is, as you say, that which Holmes and yourself must look out for. I wish the heights in rear of the batteries were converted into an intrenched camp to enable a couple of regiments to hold out for several days. How is your position compared with the other in respect to defensibility on the land side ? If you can prepare for the guns now, why not do it, if it can be done without danger of discovery by the enemy ? We have had another stampede to-day, caused by reports from Pohick again. Stuart made an expedition in that direction on Sunday, and this, I suppose, is retaliation.

You talk of huts for winter; it is rather a trying subject. I am afraid the Northern people are waiting to disturb us as soon as we have become comfortable for the winter. This place is not fit for our winter residence on any account. If I had not been confident that we should have been attacked here before this time, the troops should have been established nearer to you, that material assistance might have been more promptly given. The difficulty of getting our supplies from Manassas is increasing fast; the roads becoming worse and worse fast. The amount of fortification here now is frightful; I fear that it will be harder to reconcile our troops to leaving them than it was to the falling back from Darkesville.

As to the removal of the guns from Evansport to your new position, you and General H. must determine it. I have no means of deciding between the relative merits of the two places. But strength on the land side I hold far more important than exemption from liability to bombardment. How is the comparison in regard to facility of succor? I should suppose the upper position more within our reach than the other.

13th.—Stuart reports from Lieutenant-Colonel Wickham, Sixth Virginia Cavalry, that the expedition of yesterday was of 1,500 infantry, a squadron and five field pieces, which went as far as Mrs. Violet's; a large part of the infantry going as far as Occoquan Creek, on Telegraph road, piloted by Joseph Stiles. Six hundred infantry went to Colchester, piloted by Jonathan Roberts. They are supposed to have bivouacked last night beyond Pohick.

Very truly, yours,

J. E. JOHNSTON.

CENTREVILLE, VA., *November* 13, 1861—10 p. m.

Brig. Gen. W. H. C. WHITING, *near Dumfries, Va.:*

MY DEAR GENERAL: I believe you are nearly correct with regard to your conjecture as to the future movements of the enemy. Those balloon ascensions indicate either offensive or defensive movements, most probably the former. A few days more and we will have this place strong enough to detach a brigade to re-enforce you, *i. e.*, in my opinion, for General J. must decide, and then we could be ready to march a large force to your relief, if you could hold out for one or two days with the assistance of Holmes, who ought to sacrifice, if necessary, some of his minor positions to save Evansport. Have Triplett's and Powhatan Hills been fortified, as had been determined upon; if not, why not? Those and Talbot Hill are the keys of that position; no time ought to be lost in fortifying them, even if it were only for infantry, for if the enemy takes them, how long would the batteries hold out? Not ten minutes! Can you not have it done at once if not already done? I think also the line of the Occoquan to be very important so long as the enemy does not land below it; but where have we the forces to occupy it? We have just lost one of our most important brigades (Jackson's), which has been sent to the valley of Virginia. It would have been worth its weight in gold with you at this moment.

I cannot approve of withdrawing Evans from Leesburg except for a battle. We cannot afford to lose that important point on our left flank so long as we hold this position.

We are going to construct a large bridge on the Occoquan at Bland's Ford; already a small one for infantry is being built there, and will be finished in two or three days. I will discuss the whole subject of your letter with General Johnston as soon as practicable, and he will send you instructions for your guidance.

The above are only my own personal views.

Yours, truly,

G. T. BEAUREGARD.

HEADQUARTERS,
Centreville, November 13, 1861.

Hon. J. P. BENJAMIN, *Acting Secretary of War:*

SIR: I had the honor to-day to receive your letter of the 7th instant, in which you write:

I had not the most remote idea that you expected aid from Mr. Hunter or from this department in relation to winter quarters for the troops, nor can I conceive upon what basis you entertained such expectation, [and] I find it impossible to account for your long delay in noticing my letter of the 13th ultimo and your failure to exhibit any sign of uneasiness at the non-appearance of the saw-mills or workmen you expected to furnish the lumber.

I think that my letter of the 2d instant, to which you refer, shows upon what basis I entertained the expectation in question, and that your letter of the 13th ultimo and my conversation with your agent who delivered it to me account for my failure to exhibit any sign of uneasiness at the non-appearance of the saw-mills or workmen. As to delay in noticing your letter, it merely accredited your agent. It seemed to me to require from one confident in your agent no other notice than assurance to him of such aid, at the proper time, as you required for him.

You informed me in your letter of October 13 that you had employed two gentlemen—one of whom, Mr. Hunter, delivered the letter—to build huts for this army—and that they would explain the plan proposed, for which my co-operation was asked especially. I was to determine the locality and lines where the huts were to be built. Mr. Hunter made the explanation, and was told that the locality could not then be indicated, but that the lumber might be sawed anywhere in rear of Manassas near the railroads, and we parted with the clear understanding on my part that he would have his mills (ten) in operation about the 25th. He was desirous to consult General Beauregard, who had considered the subject, in regard to the plan of the huts, and I saw him no more. But then, as now, believing him to be perfectly reliable, I did not become uneasy until nearly a week after the period fixed upon by Mr. Hunter, and then wrote to the Acting Secretary on the subject.

Most respectfully, your obedient servant,

J. E. JOHNSTON,
General.

P. S.—The laborers promised in your letter of the 13th October have not been heard of.

CAMP, MEADOW BLUFF, *November* 13, 1861.

To the SECRETARY OF WAR, *Confederate States:*

SIR: This position is one of the most important in the State. Here, or in the immediate vicinity, unite the only good roads to the ferries of the New and Gauley Rivers and to the great valley of the Kanawha. It is 15 miles to the west of Lewisburg. The surrounding country abounds in supplies for the commissariat. Wood and coal may be supplied in abundance, and water enough for a large army, by making suitable improvements. With proper attention to drainage and with well-constructed quarters the garrison would be healthy, while a great majority of the people are loyal and true to the Southern Confederacy. The occupation of this post in sufficient force will insure the safety of Lewisburg and the adjacent regions of fertile country and the communications leading thereto, while the enemy would be prevented from making inroads this side of Gauley River, beyond which there is far less loyalty, if sympathy with the North does not actually preponderate. Our forces were, under General Lee, necessarily compelled to fall back to this point by reason of the bad roads. No effective operations can be conducted from this point westward for the reason just stated, transportation except by pack-mules being impossible; while the enemy's communications by land are better than ours, besides his facilities of water transportation.

An advance force of at least 1,500 men would be required to hold this point, in view of the present attitude and number of the enemy. Three or five thousand more should be within supporting distance, for whom a good position can be had a few miles east of this place. To provision 7,000 or 8,000 men in this vicinity would be very difficult in the present condition of the roads—to do so a few miles west of this, during the winter, well-nigh impossible. To make a successful advance towards the Kanawha Valley or Summersville with a sufficient force while the roads are in their present condition is out of the question. It is absolutely necessary to construct good roads. The best material in this region for that purpose is plank. A steam saw-mill suitably located would soon prepare material for putting our communications on a footing nearly equal to those of the enemy. The improvements contemplated would assist materially in establishing the wavering confidence of the community, and I venture to say would not cost as much as the teams, which must be worn out if they are not made. Besides, rapid and successful forward movements of our troops will then soon become possible, and the struggle soon transferred from this region to the banks of the Ohio.

Hoping that this may meet your approbation, I am, very truly, your obedient servant,

J. LUCIUS DAVIS,
Colonel, Commanding at Meadow Bluff.

SPECIAL ORDERS, }   HEADQUARTERS AQUIA DISTRICT,
No. 177.   }   *November* 13, 1861.

I. Brig. Gen. Samuel G. French, having reported for duty in this district, will, in compliance with special orders from the War Department (No. 210), proceed to Evansport and relieve Brig. Gen. I. R. Trimble, in command of the batteries and defenses of that vicinity.

II. After having been relieved by General French, General I. R. Trimble will repair to the station which has been assigned to him by the orders of the War Department.

By order of Maj. Gen. T. H. Holmes:

D. H. MAURY,
Assistant Adjutant-General.

RICHMOND, *November* 13, 1861.

General JOSEPH E. JOHNSTON, *Centreville:*

The road to Manassas is so encumbered with transportation of supplies that in order to prevent further delay I am compelled to order up to your army three or four regiments by way of Fredericksburg. Please send orders to them there. I have ordered two regiments from Staunton to your re-enforcement, and they will leave Staunton to-morrow or day after. General Jackson is urging me to send him an engineer, and I have not one at my command. Have you one that you can possibly spare him?

J. P. BENJAMIN,
Acting Secretary of War.

CENTREVILLE, *November* 14, 1861.

Hon. J. P. BENJAMIN:

Send all the troops you can, and as soon as possible. The Fredericksburg route is good. We have but one engineer officer, who is sick. We require more.

J. E. JOHNSTON,
General.

HEADQUARTERS SECOND CORPS, *November* 14, 1861.

Brig. Gen. W. H. C. WHITING,
Commanding near Dumfries:

DEAR WHITING: We are still waiting the movements of McClellan; but for some time past have been giving more and more attention and thought towards your side than to our front or left flank. Beauregard told me last night that he would suggest to Alexander to practice daily the signal telegraph with you. It is becoming all-important that we have prompt communication. At my suggestion orders have been issued for the making of temporary bridges across the Occoquan. The formation of a reserve for the army has reduced my command here to three brigades. Jackson's went to the valley of Virginia. Elzey's and Crittenden's were put in the reserve; by the way, Crittenden has been appointed major-general, and goes to Cumberland Gap, in Kentucky. I have Sam. Jones, Toombs, and Wilcox here, and your command detached, forming the Second Corps, including Field's cavalry. I am on the wrong flank for prompt movement in your direction, but rely upon it, old fellow, that if they put overpowering numbers against you, I shall give you all the assistance in my power. We are in good condition considering all the drawbacks to which we are constantly subject. My men will move with a will in going to your support.

Allston is here, has taken hold in earnest, and is a great addition to the command. He signed a report yesterday, "Ben. Allston, major, &c., commanding regiment." So you see he is not entirely weaned from you yet.

I sent you the papers the other day and send two this morning. Give my regards to Hill, Wigfall, and other friends. Your brother, Randal, Allston, and others send kind regards to yourself. Write as often as you can.

As ever, your friend,

G. W. [SMITH.]

SPECIAL ORDERS, }   ADJT. AND INSP. GEN.'S OFFICE,
    No. 222.   }   *Richmond, Va., November 14*, 1861.

*   *   *   *   *   *   *

XIV. The Fourteenth Regiment Georgia Volunteers, Colonel [A. V.] Brumly commanding, and the Sixteenth Regiment North Carolina Volunteers, Colonel [S.] Lee commanding, now at Staunton, will proceed by march to Mount Jackson, thence by railroad via Strasburg to Manassas, to report to General J. E. Johnston. The next two regiments arriving at Staunton from General Loring's command will proceed by march to Winchester, and report to Major-General Jackson.

*   *   *   *   *   *   *

By command of the Secretary of War:

JNO. WITHERS,
Assistant Adjutant-General.

WAR DEPARTMENT,
Richmond, November 15, 1861.

General JOSEPH E. JOHNSTON,
    Commanding Department of Northern Virginia:

SIR: I am directed by the President to inform you that after deliberation he has concluded to yield to your suggestions on the subject of assigning the cavalry of the Army of the Potomac to one of the divisions, and that he will accordingly leave the cavalry, like the artillery, to be distributed by you amongst the several divisions or used in such other manner as to you shall seem most effective.

The new organizations into brigades and divisions, rendered necessary in order to assign to General Van Dorn a command suitable to his rank, have also been determined by the President, and will be commuicated to you by the Adjutant-General.

In order to supply the brigadier-generals rendered necessary by recent changes, the President has also made the following provisions:

1st. He has directed that Brigadier-General Trimble be assigned to the command left vacant by the promotion of Brigadier-General Crittenden.

2d. That William M. Gardner be promoted to the grade of brigadier-general, and assigned to the command of Brig. Gen. W. H. T. Walker, resigned.

As General Gardner will be confined for some time to come by his wound, the President has sent to you Brig. Gen. Richard Garnett, to be assigned by you to such duty as you may deem proper until a brigade is formed for him.

3d. In order to supply a brigadier-general to assist Major-General Jackson in the Valley District of your department, the President directs that one of the four brigadier-generals from Virginia, assigned by General Orders, No. 15, of 22d ultimo, to the four Virginia brigades, be selected by you, to be sent to command the brigade of Virginia regiments now in the Valley District.

Your obedient servant,

J. P. BENJAMIN,
Acting Secretary of War.

RICHMOND, *November* 15, 1861.

General JOSEPH E. JOHNSTON, *Centreville:*

The Fourteenth Alabama Regiment, Colonel Judge, left here yesterday for Fredericksburg and Manassas. It will require arms. I telegraphed General Holmes to-day to halt it near Dumfries. A regiment left to-day by Central; another will leave on the 18th by Central road, and one on the 16th and one on the 17th by Fredericksburg, all unarmed. A North Carolina regiment from Loring's command, armed, left Staunton yesterday for Manassas by Central and Orange road.

S. COOPER,
Adjutant and Inspector General.

War Department, C. S. A.,
Richmond, November 15, 1861.

Brig. Gen. John B. Floyd, Commanding Army of Kanawha:

Sir: I have hitherto refrained from replying to your several letters in relation to your proposed movements during the coming winter, because it was necessary first to ascertain what force would be under your command, and whether such force could reasonably be expected to succeed in any offensive operation. I have at last succeeded in sending to your aid three fine regiments, that will be with you before your receipt of this letter, one under Colonel Starke, and two Tennessee regiments under Brigadier-General Donelson. With this force the President is satisfied you ought to be able to hold your position at Cotton Mountain, and he hopes you will not fail to do so, as it is very obvious that on your abandonment of so important a point the enemy, now taught by experience, will not fail to seize it. Hardships and exposure will undoubtedly be suffered by our troops, but this is war, and we cannot hope to conquer our liberties or secure our rights by ease and comfort. We cannot believe that our gallant and determined citizen soldiers will shrink from a campaign the result of which must be to drive the enemy outside of our borders and to secure for us the possession of a valley of such vast importance as that of the Kanawha at the present critical juncture. I therefore hope that you will not feel compelled to abandon Cotton Mountain in order to fall back on Raleigh Court-House, or any other point, until you have forced the enemy to abandon their camp at the junction of the Gauley and Kanawha. I have sent you a rifled twelve-pounder within the last few days, and will send you another in a few days more. I am very sorry we have no 24-pounder howitzers. Do your best to keep your road to Newbern in transitable order, and supplies shall not fail you.

I am, your obedient servant,

J. P. BENJAMIN,
Acting Secretary of War.

Headquarters,
Centreville, November 16, 1861.

Hon. J. P. Benjamin, Acting Secretary of War:

Sir: I respectfully inclose herewith copies of two letters just received from Brigadier-General Whiting. This officer, with his own brigade and three Texan regiments of Wigfall's brigade, is in the neighborhood of Dumfries. I have directed that the three new regiments shall be added to this force—those coming via Fredericksburg.

My object in laying these letters before you is to show the importance of additional re-enforcements to enable Brigadier-General Whiting to defeat such attempts of the enemy as he expects. If you have any disposable troops, I venture to assert that no more important object can be found for their employment. Superior numbers and the control of the river and possession of a great number of vessels, give the United States troops in Maryland opposite to Evansport great advantages over us. Should he (the enemy) establish himself on our shore in force, he will so intrench himself in a few hours as to make it impossible to dislodge him, and we shall soon have a fortified army on our right flank. The condition of the roads is now such from the rains, unusual at this season, that the troops here cannot move with such facility as to be able to guard this position and watch the Lower Occoquan and shore of the Potomac near its mouth. We have great difficulty in transporting our supplies from Manassas even. It is necessary, therefore, in order to prevent the apprehended landing of the enemy, that we should have as nearly as possible a sufficient number of troops to repel the enemy on the Occoquan or the bank of the Potomac. It would be impossible to march from this position in time to aid Brigadier-General Whiting after learning the enemy's designs, which could only be known after his movement should be commenced.

Should the enemy establish a new base on the river below the Occoquan in the manner indicated above, it would be impossible to hold this position. The superiority of numbers against us makes it impracticable to divide this army. This position cannot be given up upon any conjecture of the enemy's designs. I therefore respectfully urge that any disposable troops you may have be ordered to this army for service under General Whiting. Should they be at Richmond, the Fredericksburg road would be most expeditious for a part of the force at least.

The Adjutant-General informed me that 6,000 or 7,000 of General Loring's troops would be near Staunton about this time. They might serve here during the crisis, and afterwards perform the service for which they have been intended.

This will be delivered to you by Lieutenant Lane, son of the late United States Senator from Oregon.

Most respectfully, your obedient servant,
J. E. JOHNSTON,
General.

P. S.—McC. regards the division of this army as his best chance of success.

[Inclosures.]

HEADQUARTERS TROOPS NEAR DUMFRIES,
November 15, 1861.

Private Hanan, of Andrews' battery, has just returned from Maryland, where he has been since October 24. He reports very much the same as all others as to force and intention of the enemy. They will attack by the flotilla above and below, and attempt throwing a very large force across. He landed at Holland Point, and informs me that he learned above Occoquan that they were building a pontoon bridge to cross the Occoquan, and the reconnaissance the other day was to select a place for it. This is important. I have seen French. He pronounces the batteries untenable against fire from the opposite side and the fleets; in fact, expresses himself just as I did, you recollect, when I saw them. He is very much disgusted, and he goes in for my plan of changing to Cockpit. I have written to Richmond for permission. If they cross the Occoquan in heavy force I shall probably fight at the Neabsco crossing.

You must look out on the right. We have tremendous odds against us, and if they cross the run we shall have a heavy fight. It is good that General T. has been relieved, though mighty hard on French. If the re-enforcements come, I will give him two regiments. I have to watch that Occoquan movement. My dear general, the position is difficult and anxious. What wouldn't I give if G. W. [Smith] was in command down here?

As to the change to Cockpit, if it can be executed it will undoubtedly disconcert and delay the enemy. I only fear it may be too late. Where are all the engineer officers of the Army? Hadn't you better show this to Beauregard?

Very truly, yours,

W. H. C. WHITING.

HEADQUARTERS TROOPS NEAR DUMFRIES,
November 16, 1861.

DEAR GENERAL: I sent you yesterday some important intelligence, received from some of our men who have been over in Maryland. Perhaps owing to the swelling of the creeks it did not reach you. The chief point was the certain information that the enemy are preparing a pontoon bridge to cross the Occoquan. They will cross near the town of Occoquan, and I think land at the same time at Deep Hole, where they can put across a very large force. I think you may depend on the grand attack being on our right this time, and we shall catch it here. You must look out for me. There is no time to be lost. The enemy are only waiting for their flotilla organization. The batteries, *per se*, as batteries, will not be tenable against a heavy fleet attack combined with the fire from the other side. They were never constructed so as to protect the guns from being dismounted. I telegraphed for authority to withdraw them and place them at Cockpit. The main question is whether it can now be done in time. If you are fortified up there, and believe as I do in the attack here in heavy force, let a brigade move at once toward Bacon Race. There ought to be a regiment of cavalry here to act, and certainly another battery. I have only Imboden and Hampton, and consequently nothing to act with my brigade, which is and will be the reserve troops, the artillery being posted at certain points for action. Heintzelman's division will I think cross the Occoquan, and Sickles will land in force at Deep Hole. The roads converge at Kankey's farm, on the Neabsco, where I expect Wigfall to meet and hold them in check while I fall on their flank. The Fredericksburg regiments have not arrived spoken of in your note. The sooner they come the better; but order, if you please, your commissariat and quartermaster's department to be energetic. My train has the whole burden of the Texas brigade, which was sent here without transportation from Richmond, &c.

Yours, truly,

WHITING.

———

NOVEMBER 16, 1861.

General JOSEPH E. JOHNSTON:

MY DEAR GENERAL: I believe in all that Whiting says. As to that new battery at Cockpit Point, I fear it is entirely too late. Either we must be prepared to fight them there with some force or withdraw our forces and guns within the line of the Upper Occoquan, and then, should they attempt to move along the Potomac, we must attack them in flank and rear. As to Colonel Anderson, he has received orders to work with his garrison on those new forts around Manassas.

I advise you to send an express to Richmond with a copy of General Whiting's letter to the President, calling his attention to the fact that the intrenched camps and hills in rear of the Evansport batteries have never been constructed, notwithstanding your repeated instructions or advice on the subject.

Yours, truly,

G. T. BEAUREGARD.

HEADQUARTERS,
Centreville, November 16, 1861.

Brigadier-General WHITING:

DEAR GENERAL: A regiment left Richmond on the 14th for Fredericksburg, and another is to do so to-day and another to-morrow, all unarmed. I directed the quartermaster to send you for these new regiments, beginning with the Texans, twenty-four wagons, which will start to-day, should the Occoquan be fordable. They are to take 1,600 muskets (perhaps 1,800) and about 60 boxes of cartridges for the regiments of the 14th and 16th—dates of leaving Richmond. All these new troops are unarmed, and as I said that two could be armed at Manassas, they send five to use the muskets—these people in Richmond.

I requested General Holmes to procure permanent transportation for these troops about Fredericksburg, if possible; I shall therefore wait to hear from him before sending more wagons.

When I hear of the last regiment, arms shall be sent for it, too, if they can be found.

I have had a bridge over the Occoquan begun on the road from Dumfries to Manassas, and am asking for laborers to improve the road.

I have desired General Holmes to have such field works as can now be made begun on the heights at Evansport. Will you advise in the case?

No Staunton regiments are to join Wigfall. His brigade consists of the three Texan regiments belonging to your command. The three regiments to come, also to be under your command, are new, I suppose, being unarmed. Brigade them at your discretion.

Colonel Walker is, I doubt not, a very competent officer. I knew him as an excellent captain.

If the new regiments can serve where there are breastworks it will be well to so place them, by exchanges if necessary. I wish the dividing lines between the districts considered obliterated.

Yours, truly,

J. E. JOHNSTON.

In arming these regiments don't include men not likely to be able to use their muskets soon, for we are to have more men than arms.

————

HDQRS. SECOND CORPS, ARMY OF THE POTOMAC,
Centreville, Va., November 16, 1861.

Brig. Gen. W. H. C. WHITING, *Commanding near Dumfries:*

DEAR WHITING: General Johnston desires me to write you in answer to your letters to him of yesterday and to-day. The position you propose to occupy on the Neabsco and general plan for resisting an advance of the enemy is considered the best that could be adopted. In regard to moving the batteries, he authorizes you to do whatever in your judgment may be best. The only question in his mind is the one suggested by you as to whether there is time. If only part of the guns can be moved, it would perhaps be well to do this; but this and all other points in regard to the disposition of the guns and batteries and their defense are placed under your control. The general expressly directs me to tell you to communicate this fact to General French.

Copies of your letters above alluded to—with certain passages omitted—have been sent by special messenger to the President, with a view to having re-enforcements sent to you by railroad from Staunton or other available sources. A battery will be sent you from here immediately, and a brigade will be kept on the Occoquan in observation. The general suggests that Hampton's Legion, as far as practicable, watch and endeavor to delay and annoy the enemy at the passage of the Occoquan; and above all get definite information in regard to their strength. If they come upon you in large numbers, approaching, say, half of their effective force for field operations, the whole of this army would probably be thrown against them, with a determination to crush them; but if their attack upon you should prove to be only a strong demonstration, or even a real attack with numbers only a little superior to your own, it would not be well further to divide this army.

It is believed here upon the best evidence that McClellan bases his only hope of success in "putting down the rebellion" upon dividing and materially diminishing the strength of this army. The loss of Jackson's brigade was a great disadvantage to us, and was but the beginning of what McClellan is trying to accomplish. I think it will go no further; but that if he ventures from his fortifications on the bank of the Potomac he will have to fight us united. Keep us well advised. A bright eye, clear head, and resolute hand will beat them in spite of their numbers, organization, and equipment. We will do everything we can towards getting information of their movements in your direction from Alexandria, and give you the earliest possible advices.

Major Martin, of the Mississippi squadron of cavalry, attacked a party of 50 men, the escort of a foraging train, about 1½ miles this side of Upton's Hill, this afternoon, killed 4, wounded as many, and took 31 prisoners, among them a captain and lieutenant. He got five wagons—all they had—loaded with corn. On our side "nobody hurt." With best wishes for your complete success over the invaders, I am, as ever, your friend,

G. W. SMITH,
Major-General, Commanding.

RICHMOND, November 16, 1861.

General HOLMES, Brooke's Station, Va.:

General Whiting has been authorized by telegraph to exercise his discretion. So inform him.

S. COOPER,
Adjutant and Inspector General.

EVANSPORT, November 16, 1861.

General JOSEPH E. JOHNSTON, Army of the Potomac:

DEAR GENERAL: I leave for Richmond to-day and hope to be able to rejoin the Army of Potomac under you soon.

One word about Evansport batteries: We have each of these batteries nearly inclosed by separate infantry defenses, and the entire shore is picketed off to effectually prevent a surprise by night. This I have deemed very important, and the inclosure of batteries preliminary to the intrenched camp. On this last point I have changed my opinion, as I think you and General Beauregard would yours if here.

Powhatan Hill and Triplett's are too far from the batteries to protect them by infantry, and we have no heavy guns to put into such a camp; besides this, the enemy can only reach these hills (unless on our shore front) by landing above Quantico and Chopawamsic Creeks and marching 5 miles to the head of those creeks and 5 miles down into this peninsula, opposed all the way by our forces, in a country where scarcely more than a platoon can fight in front. This the enemy doubtless knows, and will never attempt. I have therefore abandoned the intrenched camp on the hills, and propose one down on the river plain to inclose the two upper batteries. This has been laid off but not begun, giving place, as I have remarked, to the pickets on the shore and the closing of the gorge of each battery. I have suggested to General French its rapid completion. But, general, we have too few guns here to resist a combined attack from three or more heavy ships and the batteries on the other side, and we should have more guns, either to put on the hills, or (which I prefer) to plant batteries on Cockpit Point Bluff above us, and thus elude the batteries opposite this point, extending our line of defense farther along the river. The guns, I think, can yet be got up on the George Page at night, if they are ready for use. I shall urge this to General Holmes and also in Richmond. What you have now to meet is a severe bombardment from the other side, combined with heavy ships from above and below our batteries. I do not think the enemy will attempt to land before this, but I believe he will at the same time the attack is made march down on the Occoquan, attempt to cross, and fall on our forces at Dumfries.

With the belief you will again defeat the enemy, I am, truly, yours,

I. R. TRIMBLE.

P. S.—Ask General Beauregard if the intended camp was done, or why not; please give him my views.

We have not the men or tools to do more than we have done; our heavy night pickets and large fatigue working parties have made the duty very severe on the command.

You or General Beauregard or General Smith should come down here and take a look. It is to be the center of the next contest.

CENTREVILLE, *November* 16, 1861.

General S. COOPER:

Please send several naval officers to serve under Captain Sterrett, at the navy batteries at Manassas, as soon as practicable.

J. E. JOHNSTON.

GENERAL ORDERS, }   ADJT. AND INSP. GEN.'S OFFICE,
    No. 18.   }   *Richmond, Va., November* 16, 1861.

Paragraph 3 of General Orders, No. 15 [October 22], current series, is hereby modified, and the several divisions and brigades therein will be arranged as follows, to wit:

First Division, under Major-General Van Dorn:

First Brigade, Brigadier-General Whiting, to consist of five Mississippi regiments.

Second Brigade, Brigadier-General Wilcox, to consist of five Alabama regiments.

Third Brigade, Brigadier-General Rodes, to consist of five Alabama regiments.

Fourth Brigade, Brigadier-General Taylor, to consist of four Louisiana regiments and one Louisiana battalion.

Fifth Brigade, Brigadier-General Griffith, to consist of four Mississippi regiments.

Second Division, under Maj. Gen. G. W. Smith:

First Brigade, Brig. Gen. S. Jones, to consist of four Virginia regiments.

Second Brigade, Brigadier-General Early, to consist of four Virginia regiments.

Third Brigade, Brigadier-General Trimble, to consist of two Virginia, two Tennessee, and one Kentucky regiments.

Fourth Brigade, Brigadier-General Cocke, to consist of four Virginia regiments.

Fifth Brigade, Brigadier-General Garnett, to consist of four Virginia regiments, *en route.*

Third Division, under Major-General Longstreet:

First Brigade, Brig. Gen. D. H. Hill, to consist of five North Carolina regiments.

Second Brigade, Brig. Gen. D. R. Jones, to consist of four South Carolina regiments.

Third Brigade, Brigadier-General Bonham, to consist of four South Carolina regiments.

Fourth Brigade, Brigadier-General Wigfall, to consist of three Texas regiments.

Legion, Colonel Hampton, to consist of the Hampton Legion.

Fourth Division, under Maj. Gen. E. K. Smith:

First Brigade, Brig. Gen. H. R. Jackson, to consist of four Georgia regiments, *en route.*

Second Brigade, Brigadier-General Toombs, to consist of four Georgia regiments.

Third Brigade, Brigadier-General Elzey, to consist of three Georgia and one Maryland regiments.

Fourth Brigade, Brigadier-General Evans, to consist of four Georgia regiments.

By command of the Secretary of War:

S. COOPER,
Adjutant and Inspector General.

DUMFRIES, *November* 16, 1861.

General S. COOPER:

What are they sending me unarmed and new regiments for? Don't want them. They will only be in my way. Can't feed them nor use them. I want re-enforcements, not recruits. Please to put those new regiments somewhere else. They can do no good here, and will only seriously embarrass all operations.

W. H. C. WHITING.

RICHMOND, *November* 17, 1861.
General W. H. C. WHITING, *Dumfries, Va.*:

Communicate with General Johnston, at whose instance the regiments via Fredericksburg were to stop at Evansport, where they were to be armed from the depot at Manassas.

S. COOPER,
Adjutant and Inspector General.

RICHMOND, *November* 17, 1861.
Maj. Gen. T. H. HOLMES, *Brooke's Station:*

The regiment that left here yesterday for Evansport had better remain at Fredericksburg for the present, on account of General Whiting's dispatch. No more unarmed regiments will be sent in that direction.

S. COOPER,
Adjutant and Inspector General.

WAR DEPARTMENT, *Richmond, November* 17, 1861.
General JOSEPH E. JOHNSTON,
Commanding Department of Northern Virginia:

SIR: I have the honor to acknowledge receipt of your letter of 13th instant, received yesterday.

I perceive that your impression of the result of your conversation with Mr. Hunter was entirely different from that which he communicated to me, and this fact is, perhaps, the best proof that it would have been more regular and prudent that you should have communicated to me in writing some reply to my letter of 13th ultimo.

This, however, is a matter of small importance now, as I am gratified to perceive by your omission to call on me for the aid tendered in my letter of 7th instant that you have found means to shelter the army without the assistance of the Department.

Your obedient servant,

J. P. BENJAMIN,
Acting Secretary of War.

P. S.—I am sorry to say that the Hon. R. M. T. Hunter, who tendered his services in procuring the thousand laborers for work on intrenchments mentioned in my letter of 13th ultimo, has been prevented thus far from accomplishing that object by a difficulty in the laws of Virginia. He hoped to get authority from the governor to impress free negroes, but it seems that the power for that purpose does not exist in the governor. The quartermaster is trying to get slaves, in accordance with your recent request, to work on roads in the vicinity of the camp.

RICHMOND, *November* 18, 1861.
General JOSEPH E. JOHNSTON, *Centreville, Va.*:

It is impossible to obtain a naval officer. Every one not otherwise disposed of has been sent South.

S. COOPER,
Adjutant and Inspector General.

RICHMOND, VA., *November* 18, 1861.

General JOSEPH E. JOHNSTON, C. S. A., *Centreville, Va.:*

SIR: Upon representations as to the defective construction of the batteries at and near Evansport and the hazard of bombardment by batteries recently established by the enemy on the Maryland shore, directions have been given to remove the guns to Cockpit, as recommended by General Whiting and others. It will, however, give to the enemy opportunity to make a landing at Ship Point, and thence threaten the position of General Holmes. If a large force should be landed on the Potomac below General Holmes, with a view to turn or to attack him, the value of the position between Dumfries and Fredericksburg will be so great, that I wish you to give to that line your personal inspection. With a sufficient force the enemy may be prevented from leaving his boats, should he be able to cross the river. To make the force available at either of the points which he may select, it will be necessary to improve the roads connecting the advanced posts with the armies of the Potomac and of the Aquia as well as with each other, and to have the requisite teams to move heavy guns with celerity. At Cockpit, if the topography has been correctly reported, our batteries will not be in danger of bombardment from the Maryland shore, but will be more liable to a land attack than when at Evansport; and, being farther removed from support by General Holmes, will need to have a larger garrison in the event supposed.

As I notified you, unarmed troops have been sent to receive the arms in your possession, and three armed regiments have been sent to your department since my last letter to you. (The troops from Staunton may be soon expected.) We must ask of our army that it will perform such service as has distinguished it heretofore, and we hope that our just cause is safe in its keeping, though, if it were possible, I would send to you many more troops.

Very respectfully, yours,

JEFFERSON DAVIS.

BROOKE'S STATION, *November* 18, 1861.

General COOPER:

General Whiting wishes the two other regiments forwarded. He can arm them.

TH. H. HOLMES,
Major-General.

RICHMOND, *November.* 18, 1861.

General T. H. HOLMES, *Brooke's Station:*

There is but one other regiment, which will leave for Fredericksburg day after to-morrow. The other regiments have been sent to Manassas, as General Whiting, by telegraph, declined to receive them.

S. COOPER,
Adjutant and Inspector General.

RICHMOND, *November* 19, 1861.

General JOSEPH E. JOHNSTON,
Commanding Department of Northern Virginia, Centreville:

SIR: Your communications of the 14th, 15th, and 16th instants * were

---

* None of these communications found.

duly received and submitted to the Secretary of War and to such department of the staff to which they related, with instructions. Your inquiries respecting unarmed regiments sent from this city to Manassas and Evansport have been answered by telegraph.

The regiments as they arrive at Staunton from General Loring's command will be pushed forward to Manassas, but it is proper to state that by a letter received to-day from General Loring it is apprehended that the force from that quarter will be considerably reduced, as he remarks that his position immediately in front of the enemy cannot be weakened by the withdrawal of his troops at present.

I am, very respectfully, &c.,

S. COOPER,
Adjutant and Inspector General.

HEADQUARTERS FIRST CORPS, ARMY OF THE POTOMAC,
Centreville, November 19, 1861.

Brig. Gen. N. G. EVANS, *Commanding at Leesburg:*

GENERAL: Your letter of yesterday calling for instructions has been referred to me. None more definite can be given you than those contained in my letters of the 17th* and 30th ultimo. You must be guided by circumstances, as therein referred to. Should you be able to dispute successfully with your present force the passage of the Potomac by the enemy, you are expected necessarily to do so, for which purpose you must have your brigade properly distributed at or about Leesburg, retreating only before a very superior force, which you will endeavor to stop as long as practicable at Carter's and Ball's Mills; from there you will, if overpowered, either join us here or fall back on Manassas via Sudley Spring (according to circumstances), where you will also endeavor to make as long a stand as possible. But you must keep yourself well posted as to the movements and intentions of the enemy, and harass your troops as little as practicable by marches and counter-marches.

You should leave, under proper guard, at or about Carter's Mill all the heavy baggage not already sent back to Manassas and not required by your brigade in a more advanced position.

Very respectfully, your obedient servant,

G. T. BEAUREGARD,
General, Commanding.

HUNTERSVILLE, *November* 19, 1861.

General S. COOPER:

GENERAL: Has my letter of the 9th instant been received, and does Special Orders, No. 222 [November 14], contemplate a further withdrawal from the Huntersville line? Notwithstanding my report therein, at least two regiments will be detached immediately from the Monterey line.

W. W. LORING,
Brigadier-General.

---

* See Beauregard's report of engagement at Ball's Bluff, p. 347.

RICHMOND, *November* 20, 1861.

Brig. Gen. W. W. LORING,
Commanding, &c., Huntersville, Va.:

GENERAL: I have received your telegram of the 19th instant, and, referring to your letter of the 9th,* I have to inform you that Special Orders, No. 222, was not intended to control your discretion in retaining such amount of force as you might find necessary for defensive purposes, &c., but only to make provision for such regiments as you might send from your command to Staunton. It is hoped you may yet be enabled to spare some troops from your command after making all your arrangements; but of this you must judge for yourself. Troops are much wanted both at Manassas and in the Valley District, commanded by Major-General Jackson; but other points must be looked to as well.

Very respectfully, your obedient servant,

S. COOPER,
Adjutant and Inspector General.

HEADQUARTERS VALLEY DISTRICT,
November 20, 1861.

Hon. J. P. BENJAMIN, *Secretary of War:*

SIR: I hope you will pardon me for requesting that at once all the troops under General Loring be ordered to this point.

Deeply impressed with the importance of absolute secrecy respecting military operations, I have made it a point to say but little respecting my proposed movements in the event of sufficient re-enforcements arriving; but since conversing with Lieut. Col. J. T. L. Preston, upon his return from General Loring, and ascertaining the disposition of the general's forces, I venture to respectfully urge that after concentrating all his troops here an attempt should be made to capture the Federal forces at Romney.

The attack on Romney would probably induce McClellan to believe that the Army of the Potomac had been so weakened as to justify him in making an advance on Centreville; but should this not induce him to advance, I do not believe anything will during the present winter. Should the Army of the Potomac be attacked, I would be at once prepared to re-enforce it with my present volunteer force, increased by General Loring's. After repulsing the enemy at Manassas, let the troops that marched on Romney return to the valley, and move rapidly westward to the waters of the Monongahela and Little Kanawha. Should General Kelley be defeated, and especially should he be captured, I believe that by a judicious disposition of the militia, a few cavalry, and a small number of field pieces, no additional forces would be required for some time in this district.

I deem it of very great importance that Northwestern Virginia be occupied by Confederate troops this winter. At present it is to be presumed that the enemy are not expecting an attack there, and the resources of that region necessary for the subsistence of our troops are in greater abundance than in almost any other season of the year. Postpone the occupation of that section until spring, and we may expect to find the enemy prepared for us and the resources to which I have referred greatly exhausted. I know that what I have proposed will be an arduous undertaking and cannot be accomplished without the sacri-

----

* Letter of 9th not found.

fice of much personal comfort; but I feel that the troops will be pre-pared to make this sacrifice when animated by the prospects of impor-tant results to our cause and distinction to themselves.

It may be urged against this plan that ,the enemy will advance on Staunton or Huntersville. I am well satisfied that such a step would but make their destruction more certain. Again, it may be said that General Floyd will be cut off. To avoid this, if necessary the general has only to fall back towards the Virginia and Tennessee Railroad. When Northwestern Virginia is occupied in force, the Kanawha Valley, unless it be the lower part of it, must be evacuated by the Federal forces, or otherwise their safety will be endangered by forcing a column across from the Little Kanawha between them and the Ohio River.

Admitting that the season is too far advanced, or that from other causes all cannot be accomplished that has been named, yet through the blessing of God, who has thus far so wonderfully prospered our cause, much more may be expected from General Loring's troops, ac-cording to this programme, than can be expected from them where they are. If you decide to order them here, I trust that for the purpose of saving time all the infantry, cavalry, and artillery will be directed to move immediately upon the reception of the order.* The enemy, about 5,000 strong, have been for some time slightly fortifying at Romney, and have completed their telegraph from that place to Green Spring Depot. Their forces at and near Williamsport are estimated as high as 5,000, but as yet I have no reliable information of their strength be-yond the Potomac.

Your most obedient servant,

T. J. JACKSON,
Major-General, P. A. C. S.

[Indorsement.]

HEADQUARTERS,
Centreville, November 21, 1861.

Respectfully forwarded. I submit that the troops under General Loring might render valuable services by taking the field with General Jackson, instead of going into winter quarters, as now proposed.

J. E. JOHNSTON,
General.

HEADQUARTERS,
Centreville, November 22, 1861.

General COOPER, *Adjutant and Inspector General:*

SIR: I have received Major-General Jackson's plan of operations† in his district, for which he asks for re-enforcements. It seems to me that he proposes more than can well be accomplished in that high, mount-ainous country at this season. If the means of driving the enemy from Romney (preventing the reconstruction of the Baltimore and Ohio Railroad and incursions by marauders into the counties of Jefferson, Berkeley, and Morgan) can be supplied to General Jackson, and with them those objects accomplished, we shall have reason to be satisfied, so far as the Valley District is concerned.

---

* See Johnston to Cooper, November 22, p. 966, and Benjamin to Loring, November 24, p. 968.
† Jackson to Benjamin, November 20, p. 965.

The wants of other portions of the frontier—Aquia District, for instance—make it inexpedient, in my opinion, to transfer to the Valley District so large a force as that asked for by Major-General Jackson. It seems to me to be now of especial importance to strengthen Major-General Holmes, near Aquia Creek. The force there is very small compared with the importance of the position.

Your obedient servant,

J. E. JOHNSTON,
General.

RICHMOND, *November* 22, 1861.

General W. W. LORING, *Staunton, Va.:*

GENERAL: The Secretary of War is disposed to think, from the great difficulty in obtaining forage and the reported reduced condition of the horses of cavalry companies in the mountains, that you may dispense with a part of the cavalry force with you, retaining that portion of your cavalry which has been raised in Western Virginia, and therefore better able, on the part of both horses and men, to stand the climate. Cavalry is greatly needed in the region of country between the Potomac and Rappahannock, and if you can dispense with the services of Captains Hatchett's and Douglas' companies—the first from Lunenburg, the latter from Kent and King George—and Major Lee's squadron, it is desired that you will at once order them to move down to Major-General Holmes' command, for duty upon the Rappahannock. If you have another company of cavalry (say, Captain Richards') disposable, the Secretary would prefer its being also ordered to that point, three Virginia companies being required to complete a cavalry regiment to be organized, if possible, in the District of the Lower Potomac.

Very respectfully, &c.,

R. H. CHILTON,
Assistant Adjutant-General.

SPECIAL ORDERS, }   HEADQUARTERS ARMY OF THE POTOMAC,
No. 540.   }   *November* 22, 1861.

In compliance with instructions from the Secretary of War, Brig. Gen. I. R. Trimble is assigned to the command of the brigade formerly commanded by General Crittenden, and will report to Maj. Gen E. Kirby Smith.

By command of General Johnston:

THOS. G. RHETT,
Assistant Adjutant-General.

RICHMOND, *November* 23, 1861.

General HOLMES, *Fredericksburg:*

GENERAL: The Secretary of War directs me to say that, having made arrangements for getting newspapers from the United to the Confederate States at stated intervals, he desires that you will instruct Captain Beale to receive the packages on the Maryland shore every Tuesday and Thursday and convey them to the Hague, whence they will be carried to Carter's Wharf, on the Rappahannock, by expressmen, whom you are requested to furnish.   At the latter place the packages will be delivered to Mr. J. J. Grindall or his agents for delivery here.

I am, general, very respectfully, your obedient servant,

JNO. WITHERS,
Assistant Adjutant-General.

RICHMOND, *November* 23, 1861.

[SECRETARY OF WAR?]:

DEAR SIR: I have received letters from home (Greenbrier), express-ing the presence there of great excitement.   General Floyd has fallen back from Cotton Hill to a point some miles south of Raleigh Court-House, and will probably retire to Newbern.   Two regiments from Tennessee, Colonels Hatton's and Savage's, from the Upper Greenbrier country, are now on their way to join General Floyd, whilst a regi-ment or two, lately at Meadow Bluff, have been ordered away either to General Floyd or to some other more eastern or southern point, leav-ing at Meadow Bluff a force of only 500 or 600 men.   Thus, the whole country embraced by the counties of Greenbrier and Monroe are laid open to the ravages of the enemy, in strong force at Gauley Bridge, Hawk's Nest, and Fayette Court-House, with only the small force at Meadow Bluff to resist him.   Hence the excitement in Greenbrier.

If the enemy come into Greenbrier and Monroe, there is nothing to arrest his progress into Botetourt, Rockbridge, and Augusta but dis-tance.   The force at Camp Barton and the Upper Greenbrier Bridge, it is understood, is barely sufficient, if sufficient, to arrest the progress of the enemy from Cheat and Valley Mountains.   Can nothing be done to afford some sort of security to the people of all that large and valuable country?   Can no force be sent there or near enough to that country to be immediately available?   If General Floyd retreats to Newbern, the counties of Raleigh, Mercer, Giles, and Tazewell will also be open to the enemy.   I should be greatly obliged to the Secretary of War for a free personal conference upon this subject.

Very truly and respectfully, yours, &c.,

SAMUEL PRICE.

SPECIAL ORDERS, }   HDQRS. ARMY OF THE NORTHWEST,
No. 56.   }   *Huntersville, Va., November* 23, 1861.

I. Brig. Gen. S. R. Anderson is assigned to command of the forces on the Huntersville line.

*   *   *   *   *   *   *

By order of Brigadier-General Loring:

C. L. STEVENSON,
Adjutant-General.

WAR DEPARTMENT,
Richmond, Va., November 24, 1861.

Brigadier-General LORING, *Greenbrier River:*

SIR: I inclose you herewith a copy of a letter* just received from General Jackson, which explains itself.

I have for several weeks been impressed with the conviction that a sudden and well-concealed movement of your entire command up the valley towards Romney, combined with a movement of General Jack-son from Winchester, would result in the entire destruction, and per-

---

*See Jackson to Benjamin, November 20, p. 965.

haps capture, of the enemy's whole force at Romney, and that a continuation of the movement westward, threatening the Cheat River Bridge and the depot at Grafton, would cause a general retreat of the whole forces of the enemy from the Greenbrier region to avoid being cut off from their supplies; or if the farther movement west was found impracticable, a severe blow might be dealt by the seizure of Cumberland.   The objection to this plan is obvious: It throws open the passes to the enemy in your front, and gives him free access to Monterey and Staunton.   But it is believed, and I share the conviction, that he cannot possibly cross his army at this season and remove so far from his base of supply.   He would starve if dependent on supplies to be drawn from the valley or on supplies to be hauled across the mountains.   It is quite too late in the season for him to move over to Staunton and then go back across the mountain, and it appears to me that General Jackson is right in saying that his crossing to Staunton would render his destruction more certain.

In opposition to all this we have the views of General Lee and yourself, impliedly given in the recommendation to guard the passes through the winter.   We do not desire, under such a state of things, to direct the movement above described without leaving you a discretion, and the President wishes you to exercise that discretion.   If, upon full consideration, you think the proposed movement objectionable and too hazardous, you will decline to make it, and so inform the Department. If, on the contrary, you approve it, then proceed to execute it as promptly and secretly as possible, disguising your purpose as well as you can, and forwarding to me by express an explanation of your proposed action, to be communicated to General Jackson.

The enemy at Romney is not supposed to exceed 4,000 or 5,000, very imperfectly fortified, and wholly unsuspicious of such a movement. General Jackson's forces I suppose to be about 4,500 disciplined troops and 2,000 militia, the latter very good militia.   Of course, if you make the movement, it will be necessary to leave behind you, in charge of a good officer, a few troops of cavalry to protect the country against any mere marauding or foraging parties that might be thrown forward when the enemy ascertain that your army has been withdrawn.

In arriving at a conclusion on the subject you will not, of course, forget the extreme difficulty of keeping open your communications in the coming winter if you adhere to the plan of guarding the passes, and thus wintering some 6,000 or 7,000 men in the severe climate of that mountain region.

I am, your obedient servant,

J. P. BENJAMIN,
Secretary of War.

SPECIAL ORDERS, }   HDQRS. FIRST CORPS, ARMY OF POTOMAC,
No. 505.   }   *Near Centreville, November 24, 1861.*

I. All heavy baggage will be sent forthwith and placed in store at Camp Pickens, where it will be properly secured and guarded; to which end division commanders will issue the necessary orders.

II. In the event of an action with the enemy, the new battle flag recently issued to the regiments of this army corps will alone be carried on the field.   Meantime regimental commanders will accustom their men to the flag, so that they may become thoroughly acquainted with it.

By command of General Beauregard:

THOMAS JORDAN,
Assistant Adjutant-General.

MEMORANDUM.]   HDQRS., CAMP FISHER, *November* 26, 1861.

Premising that the enemy designs to attack the Evansport batteries by a combined land and river movement, let the first be considered. The attacking column can be regarded as crossing the Occoquan at Colchester, and uniting with a force thrown from Indian Head across the Potomac. With the appliances we have seen gathered there this would be matter of no difficulty. Occoquan is 10 or 12 miles from Dumfries, and connected by an excellent road, the old Telegraph road, which crosses in that distance the Neabsco at 6 and Powell's Run at 7 miles from Occoquan. Two miles out of Occoquan the main county road branches out to Brentsville. This from Occoquan to the Neabsco is also an excellent road, and would undoubtedly be used by the enemy as his natural direction for the purpose of turning the left flank of the force supporting Dumfries. It is essential that we shall hold both these roads, especially the latter, by which not only the Evansport batteries but Manassas might be turned. To do this effectually, between the two positions on the Neabsco there is a third, which is vital to both. This is at Stowell's farm. The Third Brigade at Dane's farm, the Texas at Kaube's (and little enough there). We must have at least two regiments to occupy this farm, which is the key-point of the line. A brigade would be better, but perhaps so much is not available. It may reasonably be supposed that the passage of the Occoquan, the march thence to the Neabsco through a strange country, and the forcing of our positions by overwhelming numbers, would occupy more time than daylight at this season. Notice being given of the crossing by the enemy, we ought reasonably to count on twenty-four hours for General Johnston to move by Bacon road (this supposing the main attack to be here). If the enemy had advanced to attack at Dane's farm by that time, Johnston's attack by the route indicated would fall upon his right and rear, and would unquestionably result in his entire annihilation. It is not, however, well to divide General Johnston's army, for at the same time undoubtedly a heavy demonstration, if not a real attack, will be made in front of Centreville. The gain of twenty-four hours, then, is vital. To insure it, I must have more troops. To take them from the batteries will not do. Those are required to watch the river, and few enough they are, since they are threatened both above and below and by the fleet.

Can no aid be given from the well-drilled regiments occupying the Peninsula or from Norfolk? If given, it must be given at once. The enemy has one advantage. The roads from him to us are in capital condition, and pass over a hard, sandy, gravelly soil; ours for supply or for retreat are almost impassable. It should be remembered I have but two field batteries.

                                   W. H. C. WHITING,
                                 Brigadier-General, Commanding.

[Indorsement.]

HEADQUARTERS, CENTREVILLE, *November* 26, 1861.

Respectfully submitted to the War Department. I earnestly recommend that the re-enforcement asked for by Brigadier-General Whiting be sent to him immediately. His force is too small for what it must attempt, and this one is too weak to be further weakened. We must be driven back if the enemy establishes himself near Evansport.

                                       J. E. JOHNSTON,
                                              General.

CENTREVILLE, *November* 27, 1861.
General S. COOPER:
Brigadier-General Whiting requires at least two more regiments. I beg that they be sent to him immediately.

J. E. JOHNSTON.

RICHMOND, *November* 27, 1861.
General JOSEPH E. JOHNSTON, *Centreville, Va.:*
Having already sent all the regiments we have, there can be no objection to your sending two regiments from your command to General Whiting.

S. COOPER,
Adjutant and Inspector-General.

STAUNTON, *November* 28, 1861.
General S. COOPER:
The four regiments will be at Buffalo Gap to-morrow. It is almost impossible to control the men in the town. I suggest that you give Colonel Taliaferro an order to camp at Buffalo Gap, and have transportation ready at that point on the railroad for them to go to Manassas.

M. G. HARMAN.

RICHMOND, *November* 28, 1861.
Lieut. Col. M. G. HARMAN, *Staunton, Va.:*
The superintendent of the Central Railroad reports his inability to send General Jackson's command by that road. You will cause the command to march from their present position to the nearest point of the Manassas Gap road, thence by railroad to Manassas.

S. COOPER,
Adjutant and Inspector General.

CAMP FISHER, NEAR DUMFRIES,
November 28, 1861.
[General JOSEPH E. JOHNSTON:]
MY DEAR GENERAL: I return you your sketch * with some slight corrections. The roads are not correctly laid down. For instance, the county road (Occoquan and Brentsville) should be continued to intersect the Dumfries and Brentsville. It is a broad, good road, and passes by Greenwood Church. The position of my brigade was laid down wrong, as also the fork of the Dumfries and Bacon Run road. In case I should not receive force enough to justify my operating in two bodies on the line of the Neabsco and awaiting the enemy in a pitched battle, and especially in view of Ganysten's [?] resisting the crossing of the Occoquan, I shall block the road from A. to Greenwood Church (you may recollect it passes through very thick and dense pines) at that

---
* Not found.

point, leave my camp, throw my reserves behind Powell's Run, put forward skirmishers to harass and delay the enemy all along the Telegraph road by ambuscade and bush fighting, and place a small force in the breast-works on the south side of Neabsco. This will cause him to halt, reconnoiter, cannonade, deploy, and attack, and I shall cause him to venture into the open country between Kankey's and Powell's crossings, and make my stand along Powell's Run, in the dense woods and heights, which there are in our advantage, as on Neabsco they are his.

From the nature of the country I design to make it an infantry fight, depriving him of the advantage of his artillery, for which the ground is rather favorable to him at Kankey's, while I have but few pieces. If he designs to outflank me, he can only do it by a long and hazardous march by Greenwood Church or, by chance, by the position marked for the Sixth North Carolina. Perhaps I would not do this had I force enough to occupy Greenwood, Stonnel's and Kankey's. Behind Powell's the country is all in my favor and against him, and he cannot make the roundabout march without risking a defeat at Powell's Run, or at any rate a certainty of my knowing his flank movement and meeting it by moving French's lower regiments on the Dumfries and Bacon Run road.

If he comes in very heavy force, say enough to justify you in moving to attack him, I shall not hesitate a moment to sacrifice the blockade of the river—that is, the Evansport batteries—to securing the entire annihilation of his force, which, if he moves as indicated, would be surely accomplished by your coming by Bacon Run and Stafford and cutting off all retreat. All I would have to do would be to hold him, and to do this I should not hesitate to call up French's force, leaving but a few for show on the river. If sufficient re-enforcements arrive, why I may try and make battle on my own hook. Otherwise my course must be as stated, since by that I concentrate on what will be probably his main attack by the Telegraph road and prevent the chance of being cut in two. You gave me no answer about Marshall.

Yours, truly,

W. H. C. WHITING,
Brigadier-General.

CAMP LEE, WESTMORELAND COUNTY,
November 30, 1861.

DEAR COLONEL: * * * I think I discover many slight indications of disaffection to our cause in this section, and full credence to what I hear would render me really very uneasy. The deprivation of salt, sugar, and coffee is severely felt by the poor. Contact with the North in trade had to some extent rendered many very lukewarm, some hostile to slavery, and demagogues if not emissaries represent the war as one for the rich. The obvious importance to the North of securing possession of the south bank of the Potomac, even in the contingency of treating for the acknowledgment of the independence of the Confederate States, would justify strenuous efforts to win over those people, and the almost unrestricted ingress and egress from Maryland affords every facility to tamper with and mislead them. The opinion is expressed that the landing of the enemy would witness the raising of the Union flag now, and an officer in the militia, I hear, thinks over half of his company, if they did not openly take sides with, would at least refuse to fight the Yankees. I do not believe this, yet the knowledge that such belief is entertained by intelligent gentlemen, and the fact that for the defense of the coast we are relying upon those men, often render me sufficiently uneasy to keep me in the saddle all night.

 * * * * * * *

  Very truly, your friend,

            R. L. T. BEALE.

[Indorsements.]

    HEADQUARTERS AQUIA DISTRICT, *December* 2, 1861.

  Major Beale is in command on the Northern Neck. He is a man of cool discrimination, great intelligence, and in every way perfectly reliable. There are only a few companies of volunteers down there, and my great fear is the enemy will attempt in the Northern Neck what they have practiced in Accomac.

  Very respectfully,

           TH. H. HOLMES,

       Major-General, Commanding District.

SPECIAL ORDERS, } HDQRS. FIRST CORPS, ARMY OF POTOMAC,
No. 513.   }   *Near Centreville, Va., November* 30, 1861.

  The following disposition of the troops of this army corps will be made immediately:

  I. Rodes' brigade, of the First Division, will take up a position in rear of Bull Run. One regiment will guard the fords from Union Mills to McLean's Ford, inclusive, and the other three will be encamped as near to the Orange and Alexandria Railroad as the nature of the ground will permit in the direction of Manassas, convenient and central to the fords guarded by the other regiment.

  II. Major-General Van Dorn will select and establish a new line of battle for Bonham's and Early's brigades immediately in rear of Little Rocky Run; Early's right on this new line to rest on Bull Run, in the vicinity of McLean's Ford, and Bonham's left as near to Cocke's present right as practicable from the nature of the ground. For the present these two brigades will not abandon their encampments, however, unless in the event of a seriously-threatened attack by the enemy, when they will immediately remove their encampments to the rear of the new line of battle, under the orders of Major-General Van Dorn.

  III. The ridge commanding McLean's Ford, where Brig. Gen. D. R. Jones had his former headquarters, will be occupied, as an outpost, by a strong detachment from Early's brigade.

  IV. General Van Dorn will complete the bridge at McLean's Ford on trestles, as soon as practicable, and will discontinue work on the one near the railroad—Bull Run Bridge. He will make or open a good road from the rear of the new line of battle, hereinbefore directed, to Blackburn's Ford Bridge, if one does not already exist, and will also shorten, as soon and as much as practicable, the road leading from Camp Walker to Davis' Ford, by cutting off angles, and will make other needful improvements of that road.

  V. Major-General Longstreet will open at once with his division a good and direct road from the right of Cocke's brigade to the left of Bonham's, and will throw a strong bridge across the small run between these two positions.

  By command of General Beauregard:

         THOMAS JORDAN,

           Assistant Adjutant-General.

Abstract from return of the Department of Northern Virginia, commanded by General Joseph E. Johnston, C. S. Army, for month of November, 1861.

Commands.	Present for duty.						Effective total.	Aggregate present.	Aggregate present and absent.	Pieces of artillery.
	Infantry.		Cavalry.		Artillery.					
	Officers.	Men.	Officers.	Men.	Officers.	Men.				
Potomac District:										
First Corps.............	1,137	16,362	32	472	57	1,252	*19,165	23,283	29,885	......
Second Corps..........	838	11,677	....	....	17	374	†12,862	16,440	19,505	24
Reserve Division.....	418	6,290	....	....	14	200	7,000	8,412	10,431	12
Cavalry Brigade......	....	....	177	2,016	....	....	2,204	2,724	3,396	......
Artillery Corps.......	....	....	....	....	30	423	446	563	699	......
Total Potomac District.........	2,393	34,329	209	2,488	118	2,249	41,677	51,422	63,916	36
Valley District.........	332	3,505	34	508	3	114	4,523	5,356	9,813	......
Aquia District‡........	....	....	....	....	....	....	5,743	7,151	8,824	35
Grand total.......	2,725	37,834	243	2,996	121	2,362	51,943	63,929	82,553	71

Notes from original return:
* Effective total (2,680) of forces under Brig. Gen. D. H. Hill to be deducted.
† Effective total (6,781) of forces under Brig. Gen. W. H. C. Whiting to be deducted.
‡ The report of Major-General Holmes does not indicate the "Present for duty."

HEADQUARTERS, *Centreville, December* 1, 1861.

General S. COOPER, *Adjutant and Inspector General:*

SIR: I beg leave to suggest to the War Department the importance of taking immediate measures to keep up our military force during the continuance of the war.

Two occur to me: One to hold out inducements to volunteers for one year to re-engage for the war; leave of absence would be the strongest inducement; the practicability of granting them in this army must depend, however, upon the enemy's course during the winter. The other to form camps in which volunteers for the war shall be instructed (without arms, if arms are not to be had) and accustomed to camp life and go through the course of camp diseases. Such of these men as cannot be armed will be prepared to take the arms of the volunteers who may be discharged in the spring.

Most respectfully, your obedient servant,

J. E. JOHNSTON,
General.

HEADQUARTERS, *Centreville, December* 1, 1861.

Hon. J. P. BENJAMIN, *Secretary of War:*

SIR: Our correspondent in Washington asserts that the United States Government has a spy in the War Office. He does not know the name. He says that an advance is to be made this week in great force; a large force to cross the Potomac below us. The country is in a condition which prevents maneuvering on our part—a great advantage, therefore, to the enemy, who moves on the water.

Most respectfully, your obedient servant,

J. E. JOHNSTON,
General.

STAUNTON, *December* 1, 1861.

Hon. J. P. BENJAMIN, *Secretary of War:*

I have come to Staunton with the view of carrying out the plans proposed in my communication to you.* I have already given every order necessary to do so. Shall I proceed? Four regiments from the Monterey line have been ordered by General Cooper to Manassas. I have directed two other regiments to come here from Millborough. Is it your intention to detach all those regiments from this command? I thought preparatory to the movement I would order them here.

W. W. LORING,
Brigadier-General, Commanding.

———

HEADQUARTERS NORTHWESTERN ARMY,
Staunton, Va., December 1, 1861.

Hon. J. P. BENJAMIN, *Secretary of War, Richmond:*

SIR: I am now pushing the sick and munitions to the rear as rapidly as possible, and have given orders to all trains to go back lightly loaded with grain and return with supplies, a large amount having collected both at Monterey and Huntersville. Since my last letter I have heard of no movement of the enemy, except that they are sending their spare troops near the railroad to Romney. The information comes to me through a reliable spy, sent to Philippi and Laurel Hill. From what he could learn they were not sending any troops from Cheat or Beverly in that direction.

I came here to-day to carry into effect the proposed campaign, and find a telegram sending four regiments to Manassas. It is proper to state that, in consequence of movements made, in which I have been endeavoring to carry out your instructions, officers at a distance from my headquarters have been telegraphing without my authority to Richmond, the result of which has been a conflict of orders.

One of the objects I had in bringing the regiments to Staunton was that they should not only be on the spot for the contemplated movement, but should be in readiness for any emergency.

With respect, I have the honor to be, your obedient servant,

W. W. LORING,
Brigadier-General, Commanding, &c.

———

RICHMOND, *December* 2, 1861.

To QUARTERMASTER AT DUBLIN STATION, VA.:

Send the following instructions, either by telegram or by special express, to General Floyd:

Fall back with your command to Dublin Station, on Virginia and Tennessee Railroad, leaving such portion behind as you may deem necessary to gather up your sick and bring them east.

S. COOPER,
Adjutant and Inspector General.

---

* See Loring to Benjamin, November 29, p. 983.

RICHMOND, *December* 2, 1861.

Col. M. G. HARMAN, *Staunton, Va.:*

Send to their destination without delay, by telegraph or express, the following to General Donelson and Colonel Starke, at Lewisburg:

Retire with your respective commands to the nearest point on the Virginia and Tennessee Railroad, and proceed thence to Bowling Green, Ky., and report to General A. S. Johnston.

S. COOPER,
Adjutant and Inspector General.

RICHMOND, *December* 2, 1861.

General W. W. LORING, *Staunton, Va.:*

Your dispatch to the Secretary of War of yesterday is received, but your communication referred to in that dispatch not yet come to hand. Until the Secretary knows its contents he cannot answer your question. Telegraph so much as will enable him to act. In mean time use your discretion in respect to the two regiments from Millborough.

S. COOPER,
Adjutant and Inspector General.

HEADQUARTERS VALLEY DISTRICT,
Winchester, Va., December 2, 1861.

Maj. THOMAS G. RHETT,
Asst. Adjt. Gen., Hdqrs. Department of Northern Virginia:

MAJOR: The enemy are using the Baltimore and Ohio Railroad as far east as the Little Cacapon, and from official information received last night they commenced working on the Little Cacapon railroad bridge at 3 p. m. on Friday last, and will soon complete the work, as they had all the building material on hand. They are energetically pressing the railroad repairs eastward. With but comparative little exception both tracks have been by our Government taken up from the Furnace Hill, near Harper's Ferry, to Martinsburg, and about 7½ miles of one of the tracks has also been removed west of Martinsburg. One track is as yet preserved for the purpose of hauling away the other to the vicinity of Martinsburg. Captain Sharpe, assistant quartermaster, has repaired a locomotive for the purpose of removing the track more rapidly, and to-day I expect it to commence running, and Captain Sharpe expects to be able with it to remove 1 mile per day of the single track. I have made a detail of 50 men from the militia for the purpose of expediting the work as rapidly as possible.

I have sent General Carson with his brigade into Morgan County. He drove the enemy across the Potomac, took from the railroad at Sir John's Run Depot about 1,000 pounds of lead pipe and some other property. His headquarters are at Bath, and in consequence of the enemy's advance from the west, and the intelligence of his being at Paw Paw Tunnel, I have directed him to fall back, so as to prevent his being cut off.

My old brigade is suffering for want of a brigadier. I respectfully request that, if practicable, the commanding general of the department will send one. Col. James F. Preston is sick, and the command consequently devolves on Colonel Allen. I have near 1,200 militia without arms. Can you forward muskets for them? I have detached Company

A, Twenty-seventh Regiment Virginia Volunteers, commanded by Capt. J. Carpenter, and converted it into a company of mounted artillery. Please inform me if anything more than my order is necessary to entitle it to be mustered and paid as an artillery company.

While the Thirty-third Regiment Virginia Volunteers was *en route* from Manassas to this place one of its companies (Company E) arrived in camp near here without any officer, in consequence of its first lieutenant (T. C. Fitzgerald) having absented himself without leave. In consequence of Colonel Cummings having reported to me that he could not undertake another march with the company, as it was composed of unmanageable Irishmen, and as the company numbered about 30, and as I had two unassigned pieces of field artillery, and also Second Lieut. W. E. Cutshaw, C. S. Army, a graduate of the Virginia Military Institute, was without a command, I assigned him to the command of the company, and ordered the two pieces of artillery to be turned over to him. Yesterday I sent him to Hanging Rock, which is near 15 miles this side of Romney.

Soon after arriving here Maj. W. J. Hawks, chief commissary of this district, purchased 1,000 barrels of flour, at $4.56¼, delivered at this point, but soon Mr. James M. Ranson, of Jefferson County, an agent for Major Blair, offered a higher price, consequently the Government has to make an unnecessary expenditure. If it meets with the views of the commanding general, I hope that purchasing agents, when sent to this district, will be required to conform to the prices given in the same locality by the chief district officer of the department to which the purchases belong.

I have established the telegraph line between this place and Charlestown, and have hired an operator for the Charlestown office, giving him $50 per month. He will be directed to report to the chief of his department.

As yet I have heard nothing of the requisitions for camp and garrison equipage having been received in Richmond. Some days since, when the inquiry was made, they had not arrived. Please let me know whether they received General Johnston's approval and were forwarded.

If you have any spare axes, shovels, picks, or hatchets, please direct them to be forwarded to me.

I have directed Lieut. Col. Turner Ashby, of the cavalry, to establish his headquarters at Martinsburg, so as to be nearer the center of his command.

As yet I have heard nothing from you nor from Richmond respecting the requisite blanks for this district.

Respectfully, your obedient servant,

T. J. JACKSON,
Major-General, P. A. C. S., Commanding Valley District.

RICHMOND, *December 2, 1861.*

Col. M. G. HARMAN, *Staunton, Va.:*

The Central Railroad cannot transport the regiments to Manassas. All its means are required for supplies. The regiments from Millborough must march as already directed for those now on the way to Manassas Gap Junction.

S. COOPER,
Adjutant and Inspector General.

RICHMOND, *December* 3, 1861.

General W. W. LORING, *Staunton, Va :*

Your letter of the 29th ultimo* received this morning. Contents approved. Act as therein indicated. I will send copy of your letter to Winchester.

J. P. BENJAMIN,
Secretary of War.

———

JACKSON'S RIVER, *December* 3, 1861.

General S. COOPER:

Your dispatches to General Donelson and Colonel Starke and Colonel J. Lucius Davis were received last night, and were forwarded by express to their destinations. I have been informed that General Donelson's command is now on the march to General Floyd, at Peterstown.

J. G. PAXTON,
Assistant Quartermaster.

———

HEADQUARTERS, CENTREVILLE, *December* 3, 1861.

Hon. J. P. BENJAMIN, *Secretary of War, Richmond :*

DEAR SIR: Since the letter from the general herewith was sent to my office for transmission, a secret agent was sent to Washington, and a trusty citizen of Maryland has returned with some notes from friends, copies of which I inclose. As you will perceive, our friends insist there will be an advance this season. The Nashville has reached Southampton. Green and Powell are in Washington to take their seats. The returned agent says some ladies of Baltimore say that there is a female spy in Richmond under the assumed name of Mademoiselle Lina, who gives concerts. I have not noticed whether there is such a person, but thought I would mention the matter. This army is in admirable spirit and *morale.* Nothing, indeed, could be better than their mood at present. I will send the message as soon as it reaches me. Shall I telegraph any of its salient positions? If the department needs any books of reference from the North, I can get them without difficulty by our agent.

Respectfully, your obedient servant,

THOMAS JORDAN.

[Inclosures.]

NOVEMBER 25, 1861.

This is from undoubted source—a secret agent of theirs. The plan is to affect to go into winter quarters, but extensive and active preparations are going on, making pontoons, collecting provisions, making preparations for building batteries as they proceed. The army is to be divided into five divisions: Hooker below; McCall, McDowell and McClellan in the center, and Banks above. When all is ready a simultaneous movement is to be made by divisions, and a desperate attack is to be made on the part of Banks and Hooker at each side to outflank and get behind the Confederate Army and fortifications, while the three central push on, fortifying as they go. This move is to be a desperate one, and every effort made to secure success. The expression used was that they would be in Richmond before two weeks.

———

* See inclosure to Benjamin to Jackson, December 6, p. 983.

WASHINGTON, *November* 30, 1861.

I have every reason to believe, from all I can hear, that McClellan will certainly make a bolt at you next week. Watch him on every hand. Every device will be used to deceive you. An impression will be made on every hand that no advance will be made; that the army will go into winter quarters, &c. Pay no attention to such reports. I say, watch by land and by water. I also caution you to look to the several fleets now being fitted out—Butler's and Burnside's; they will make a demonstration soon. Watch Norfolk and York River. A meaner set of devils never lived than Butler and Burnside. They would do anything to succeed—burn cities, murder men, women, and children, and do every other wicked thing they can, if by so doing they can raise themselves a button-hole higher with the Northern Yankee devils. Kill the devils incarnate wherever you find them. Watch your batteries on the Potomac by day and by night. The darkest night may be selected to attack your batteries. I expect to send you a dispatch in a day or two from a lady friend, "Mrs. Argie." You know she received your letter, and was more than delighted to hear from you.

SPECIAL ORDERS, }   ADJT. AND INSP. GEN.'S OFFICE,
No. 252.   }   *Richmond, Va.,* December 3, 1861.

*   *   *   *   *   *   *

20. The regiments from Mississippi now serving in the Potomac District will without delay be organized into brigades, as directed in General Orders, No. 18, from this office, current series, as follows :

First Division, Major-General Van Dorn.
First Brigade, Brigadier-General Whiting.
Second Mississippi Regiment, Colonel [W. C.] Falkner.
Eleventh Mississippi Regiment, Colonel [W. H.] Moore.
Thirteenth Mississippi Regiment, Colonel [William] Barksdale.
Seventeenth Mississippi Regiment, Colonel [W. S.] Featherston.
Eighteenth Mississippi Regiment, Colonel [T. M.] Griffin.
Fifth Brigade, Brigadier-General Griffith.
Twelfth Mississippi Regiment, Colonel [Henry] Hughes.
Sixteenth Mississippi Regiment Colonel [C.] Posey.
Nineteenth Mississippi Regiment, Colonel [C. H.] Mott.
Twenty-first Mississippi Regiment, Colonel [Benjamin G.] Humphreys.
The above regiments will join their respective brigades without delay.
By command of the Secretary of War :

JNO. WITHERS,
Assistant Adjutant-General.

RICHMOND, *December* 4, 1861.

Brigadier-General LORING, *Staunton Va.:*

Your letter of 1st instant received. Use your discretion about all the regiments sent from your command, and countermand, if you think proper, the order sending the four regiments to Manassas.

S. COOPER,
Adjutant and Inspector General.

STAUNTON, *December* 4, 1861.

Maj. R. G. COLE:

Ask whether I can stop the four regiments under Taliaferro now marching to Strasburg. Reply immediately, so that I can do so, as they reach the railroad to-morrow at Mount Jackson.

W. W. LORING.

RICHMOND, *December* 4, 1861.

General LORING, *Staunton, Va.:*

Direct the four regiments under Colonel Taliaferro to proceed to Winchester.

S. COOPER,
Adjutant and Inspector General.

DECEMBER 4, 1861.

Memorandum to Major Blair.

Say to Major Blair that he should at once take steps in case the enemy should get possession of Loudoun County to drive his cattle off as they make their advance. The general understands that the major depends upon that county for his supply of cattle. If the enemy should land in large force about Leesburg, it would be impossible for the army to remain at Centreville. He would then fall back to the Rappahannock, about Brandy Station—in that vicinity. Wants to know where Mr. Buckner is; understands that the major has a packing establishment at Thoroughfare, on the Manassas road; wants him to consider if Brandy Station, Orange and Alexandria Railroad, would not be better. The major should determine this himself. Wants information about the 6,000 cattle mentioned in his letter; should always keep five days' supply on hand; he thinks should be as much beef as bread; says that a large supply of beef, looking to all possible contingencies, should be under the major's control inside of our lines, and with such steps taken as would enable them to be driven off at a moment's notice.

E. J. HARVIE,
Captain, Acting Inspector-General.

SPECIAL ORDERS, }   ADJT. AND INSP. GEN.'S OFFICE,
No. 254.   }   *Richmond, December* 4, 1861.

*   *   *   *   *   *   *

IV. The command under Brigadier-General Floyd will return from its present position and take post near Newbern, on the Virginia and Tennessee Railroad, and there await further orders. A portion of the command will be left to bring up the sick and disabled.

The brigade of General Donelson, to include also the regiment under Colonel Starke, will proceed from their present position to the nearest point on the Virginia and Tennessee Railroad, and thence to Bowling Green, Ky., where they will report for duty to General A. S. Johnston, commanding.

The Wise Legion, under command of Col. J. Lucius Davis, will repair to Richmond, Va., by the nearest railroad route, and report to General Winder, commanding Department of Henrico.

*   *   *   *   *   *   *

By command of the Secretary of War:

JNO. WITHERS,
Assistant Adjutant-General.

SPECIAL ORDERS, } HEADQUARTERS ARMY OF THE POTOMAC,
No. 565.   } *December 4, 1861.*

Brig. Gen. D. H. Hill is assigned to the command of the forces at Leesburg, and will report to General G. T. Beauregard.

By command of General Johnston:

THOS. G. RHETT,
Assistant Adjutant-General.

SPECIAL ORDERS, } HEADQUARTERS ARMY OF THE POTOMAC,
No. 566.   } *December 4, 1861.*

Brig. Gen. Richard B. Garnett will proceed to Winchester, to take command of the First Brigade, and will report to Maj. Gen. T. J. Jackson, commanding the Valley District.

By command of General Johnston:

THOS. G. RHETT,
Assistant Adjutant-General.

ADJUTANT AND INSPECTOR GENERAL'S OFFICE,
Richmond, December 5, 1861.

General HUGER, *Commanding, &c., Norfolk:*

GENERAL: Dispatches (confidential) have been received from the commanders at Manassas conveying important reliable information received by them from different but undoubted sources, and all agreeing in the particulars, the sum of which is that the plan of the enemy is to affect to go into winter quarters, while at the same time extensive and active preparations are going on, making pontoons, collecting provisions, and making preparations for erecting batteries as they proceed. Their army is to be divided into five divisions, Hooker on the Potomac below, McCall, McDowell and McClellan in the center, and Banks above. When all is ready a simultaneous movement is to be made by divisions, and a desperate attack on the part of Banks and Hooker at each side, to outflank and get behind the Confederate Army and fortifications, while the three central divisions push forward and fortify as they go. This movement is to be a desperate one, and every effort made to secure success. The expression used is that they will be in Richmond before two weeks. It is also stated that a simultaneous attack would be made on Norfolk and on James and York Rivers.

This communication is sent to you at the instance of the President, who has fears in relation to the battery at Burwell's Bay, because of the liability to a land attack. Your attention is invited to that quarter. Have you any rifled guns in battery there? No time is to be lost, as the attack will probably be made this or the coming week. General Magruder has been advised of the information here communicated.

Very respectfully, your obedient servant,

S. COOPER,
Adjutant and Inspector-General.

CENTREVILLE, *December* 5, 1861.

General WHITING:

MY DEAR GENERAL: I have just heard that the road from Dumfries to Bacon Race by Greenwood Church is blocked up. I want to know precisely what roads are open and which closed. Please inform me. The enemy's movements might be such as to tempt me to go in your direction first. It is necessary to be prepared to do so at all events. That road seems to me the best for our purposes. The bridge at Bland's Ford is done. Preparations are begun for one at Davis' Ford. Should we go against your enemy it ought to be in two columns on those two routes. The infernal balloon may interfere with such success as we had with Patterson.

Yours, truly,

J. E. JOHNSTON.

RICHMOND, *December* 5, 1861.

General LORING, *Staunton, Va.:*

The exigency requires the arrival of your entire command as rapidly as possible at Winchester.

S. COOPER,
Adjutant and Inspector-General.

DUBLIN, *December* 5, 1861.

General S. COOPER, *Adjutant and Inspector General:*

I am here with part of my command, awaiting your orders. There is neither wood nor water within four miles of this point suitable for building.

Respectfully,

JOHN B. FLOYD,
Brigadier-General, Commanding.

RICHMOND, *December* 5, 1861.

Brig. Gen. JOHN B. FLOYD, *Dublin Station:*

Remove your command to any point on the railroad where you can get supplies. Your stay will be but temporary. I write by mail. Halt Donelson's command and Starke's regiment at some convenient point on the railroad for further orders.

S. COOPER,
Adjutant and Inspector-General.

RICHMOND, *December* 6, 1861.

Maj. Gen. T. J. JACKSON, *Winchester, Va.:*

SIR: I have hitherto been unable to send you any instructions relative to your command, not knowing what number of troops it would be possible to assign to your district. You will now perceive, by the inclosed copy of letter received from General Loring, that in accordance with your views, indorsed by this Department, he has commenced a movement for co-operation with you, which will place at your disposal quite an effective force for your proposed campaign, although I regret to observe that his movement cannot be made as promptly as I had hoped.

Since writing to General Loring and receiving the inclosed answer I am led, by what I deem reliable information, to conclude that a movement is contemplated by the enemy for an attack on you by a rapid concentration of Banks' division, combined with an advance of the forces at Romney, which latter are being partially re-enforced. This attack on your command is represented by our spies as part of a grand combined movement to be made on our whole army, by Banks on our left, [by ——] on our right at Evansport, and McClellan in front—the latter holding back his advance until he can hear of the success of his lieutenants on either or both wings. This may not be true, but prudence requiring that no time shall be lost, I have telegraphed General Loring to-day to move his whole force to Winchester as rapidly as possible, and if successful in joining you promptly you may be able to turn the tables handsomely on the enemy by anticipating his purpose. As soon as you are joined by General Loring's forces I shall desire a report setting forth your effective force in as much detail as possible, and shall hope thenceforward to receive the regular monthly reports required by the Army Regulations with punctuality.

It will be my pleasure at all times to use all the resources at my command in aiding your movements whenever apprised of any deficiency that our limited means may enable me to supply.

Your obedient servant,

J. P. BENJAMIN,
Secretary of War.

[Inclosure.]

HEADQUARTERS NORTHWESTERN ARMY,
Huntersville, Va., November 29, 1861.

SIR: I have the honor to acknowledge the receipt of your letter of the 24th instant, inclosing one from Major-General Jackson, when on a tour of inspection to my hospitals in rear.

The policy of marching a force from Winchester or that vicinity in the direction of Romney was the subject of conversation between General Lee and myself during the recent campaign of this army. He informed me that troops could not be had there for the purpose.

I consider a winter campaign practicable if the means of transportation sufficient to move this army can be obtained, and especially in a country where supplies are abundant, which I am informed in the communication inclosed in your letter is the case in that section of Western Virginia where it is proposed to operate. With warm clothing, good tents, and proper attention by the regimental and company officers there need be no suffering from the climate in that region.

I consider that it is proper that I should place before you the present disposition of this army, made with a view to the defense of our extended line. The passes now guarded are at Alleghany on the Staunton and at Huntersville on the Millborough turnpike, besides the approaches on the right in front of Franklin and on the left from Summersville and that section on the Lewisburg and Marling Bottom turnpike—the whole distance between one and two hundred miles. The enemy is strongly fortified on Cheat Mountain, and at Crouche's, on this turnpike, and had a short time since about 8,000 men at and near these places. To-day reliable scouts returned from the vicinity of these points, and report the enemy are moving several regiments, they (the enemy) say in the direction of Kentucky and General Floyd, but it is believed by the people their destination is Romney, in consequence of an apprehended attack from General Jackson, now at Winchester. It may be observed that a campaign from Winchester against the enemy at Romney is the subject of conversation among the people from Petersburg to this place, and yesterday I received an express from General Boggs, asking a regiment to aid him in forcing the militia of Pendleton County to turn out for that purpose. The troops here and at Alleghany have nearly completed their huts, and, as now located, it is believed could be subsisted through the winter. Owing to the difficulty of procuring means of transportation and to the present state of the roads, it will require, with every exertion, two, possibly three, weeks to remove to the rear the troops, a large sick report, and a considerable amount of munitions not needed on the campaign.

In order to conceal, as far as possible, the movements of the army, I think it best to send the troops on this line to Millborough, and thence by rail to Strasburg; those at Monterey either direct to Moorefield or to Strasburg via Staunton. The forces at Monterey will check any advance on that line, if attempted, and be in readiness to move as indicated. If the road from Strasburg is practicable, the command ordered there could act with that from Moorefield; if impracticable, with that from Winchester.

I do not think that a movement of the army could be kept fully concealed from the enemy, because the Union men have numerous relations throughout this region, and will, notwithstanding the utmost vigilance, obtain information. If the purpose of the withdrawal of this column can be disguised until that at Monterey shall have been fully prepared, the desired object may be effected by a rapid movement. I shall not, therefore, commence the march till sufficient transportation can be procured for the whole command. In the mean time (orders have been given therefor) the sick and public property not needed for the cavalry, which you suggest be left to protect the country against marauding parties, will be removed to the rear as rapidly as possible. It appears that General Jackson anticipates a sudden movement of this command. With the utmost exertion on our part it is impossible to effect it in less time than that heretofore stated. There is a large quantity of ammunition, and from two hundred and fifty to two hundred and sixty thousand pounds of subsistence stores at this depot, a reserve of ammunition at Warm Springs, and a large number of sick in hospital at the springs between this and the railroad. All of these must be transferred to Staunton, and transportation collected here, before the movement can be made.

As I consider prompt movement after starting of much importance, and as my suggestions differ somewhat from those contained in the letter of General Jackson, I deem it proper to submit these suggestions to you, and ask for them your attention and opinion before perfecting my arrangements.

If, upon consideration of affairs on this line, you should desire the proposed campaign to be prosecuted, be assured that I shall enter into it with a spirit to succeed, and will be seconded by a command as ardent in the cause as any in the country, and who will cheerfully endure all the hardships incident to a winter campaign.

With respect, I have the honor to be, your obedient servant,

W. W. LORING,
Brigadier General, Commanding.

HEADQUARTERS, *Centreville, Va., December* 6, 1861.

General S. COOPER, *Adjutant and Inspector General :*

SIR : I have just received from the Adjutant and Inspector General Special Orders, No. 252 [of 3d instant].

This order forms two brigades of Mississippi volunteers "without delay."

I would respectfully bring to the attention of the War Department the following facts, which induce me to request most urgently a suspension of the execution of this order. The carrying it into immediate effect will involve the withdrawal from the field for the space of five or six days of not less than nine effective regiments. The subtraction of so considerable a force, even for one day, at this crisis, would of itself be attended with extreme peril. Of the nine regiments of Mississippians in this army the Second and the Eleventh are in General Whiting's brigade, near Dumfries; the Thirteenth, Seventeenth, Eighteenth, and Twenty-first in General Griffith's, near Leesburg ; the Twelfth, Sixteenth, and Nineteenth near Centreville.

The forces as now arranged are perfectly familiar with their respective positions ; officers and men have become accustomed to each other, are aquainted with the nature of the ground they occupy, &c. The execution of Orders, No. 252, would work a complete revolution in the organization of the army, and necessitate a change of position of all the regiments from Leesburg to Dumfries, and from this position to Dumfries and Leesburg.

Should the enemy attack us whilst these changes of station are in process (an event by no means improbable), it would be almost impossible to avert disaster to our arms. A conviction that any sudden change of a material nature in the existing organization of this army will be of serious detriment forces me to solicit the continuance of the discretion left me in General Orders, No. 15.

The front occupied by this army extends near 50 miles, the enemy being only half that distance, and meditating (according to latest information) an immediate attack upon us at all points with immense numerical odds. I respectfully assure the Department that the mischief consequent upon the immediate enforcement of Special Orders, No. 252, cannot well be exaggerated.

As General Griffith has already a brigade of four regiments of Mississippi volunteers, I would also suggest that no injury will result from a postponement of the contemplated changes.

Most respectfully, your obedient servant,

J. E. JOHNSTON,
General.

HEADQUARTERS, *Centreville, December* 6, 1861.

Brigadier-General WHITING :

DEAR GENERAL : I am a little exercised on the subject of our communications. The blocking of the road near Greenwood Church was, I suppose, to cover your left flank. Could it be so done as to give us access to you ? Think of it, and tell us how to approach you. I don't want our communications to be interrupted either by Davis' Ford or Bland's. Should we go to you, it might be well to do so in two columns. It would be well, therefore, to observe the river as well as your strength will permit—the Occoquan, I mean.

Should you have to fall back and it is practicable, it should be towards us by Bland's or Brentsville. The batteries should not be watched when you are contending with an army coming from above; to oppose it, get all your troops together. If we beat it, we get back the guns, supposing a river party to have occupied the batteries in the mean time. The only question is, where to meet him—whether on the Occoquan or where you are. Your knowledge of localities enables you to judge better than we can do here. I suppose that if an army approaches us and another the Occoquan, lesser columns will approach by every intermediate road. It might and would be well, as far as practicable, to have a party at each crossing place to impose upon these columns and give information of them.

Yours, truly,

J. E. JOHNSTON.

CENTREVILLE, *December* 7, 1861.

General COOPER:

Cannot Brigadier-General Jackson's troops come here and General Loring re-enforce the Valley District?

J. E. JOHNSTON.

CENTREVILLE, *December* 7, 1861.

Brigadier-General WHITING:

DEAR GENERAL: I have received your note of to-day.* Your conclusion is excellent; you can do nothing better than to whip these gentlemen who are giving us such anxiety. We have heretofore been considering the matter under a single aspect—the consideration of a heavy force thrown against you; this may not be done. We must watch. You must get Hampton to look up the Telegraph road as far and as closely as possible. Should it turn out that they intend to neglect you and bring their great force to crush us, then you will have to come up to our help, and after the defeat of such an army we will go back with you and retake the batteries. We must be prepared for all contingencies. You speak of Van Dorn as if he were on your side of the Occoquan. He is not—no nearer than to have a brigade (Rodes') between us and Davis' Ford, in observation both ways. I understood that you and Hampton would observe that ford of Wolf Run.

Very truly, yours,

J. E. JOHNSTON.

P. S.—The enemy's left may follow the Telegraph road to Pohick, and then turn to Sangster's, or to Mrs. Violet's, and thence Union Mills, Wolf Run, &c. You will have to watch very closely. Do you hear anything from Maryland? Should you march up here, your men should bring nothing but their blankets (on their person), cooking implements, and ammunition. It would be well to deposit the knapsacks as safely as possible. The wagons coming up should be very light.

CAMP WIGFALL, *December* 8, 1861.

General JOHNSTON:

My DEAR GENERAL: I beg to thank you for the sword you have honored me by committing to my keeping, and I shall try to return it

---

*Not found.

untarnished. It is a beautiful one, and I trust it may do good service whilst in my hands. I have been very busy making such defenses here as I could, but my supply of tools has been so limited, that as yet only a small line of rifle-pits are completed. My main dependence here must be on rifles, for I suppose the enemy will bring such heavy guns, and so many of them, that my artillery cannot fight them very long. As there seems to be a great diversity of opinion as to the object of my being placed here and the course I should pursue, whilst there appears to be no general plan of action settled on, may I ask you to give me directions how to carry out best your wishes? My own plan was to make this place as strong as possible and to hold it as long as I can. If forced to retire, shall I fall back towards General Whiting or up in the direction of Bacon Race? I am sure that I can hold the position if attacked only in front for some hours at least, and if you want it held until re-enforcements can come up, I will do it. I have some apprehension that tugs may be able to run up close to the ferry, as there seems to be some considerable depth of water along the bay and river here. General Van Dorn, who was here to-day, thinks that the enemy should be allowed to cross the river. No line has been chosen for any of the troops to fall back on, and I think the men would fight better if they are told to keep their position. I wish you could examine this country, or that General Beauregard or General Smith could do so. We hear nothing from our scouts, except that the enemy come down almost every day to Pohick Church. Troops can be landed at Deep Hole, and there is a very large body of cleared land around that place.*

*   *   *   *   *   *   *

With my best wishes, I am, yours, very respectfully,
                                        WADE HAMPTON.

—————

                              RICHMOND, *December* 9, 1861.
General JOSEPH E. JOHNSTON,
        Commanding Department of Northern Virginia:

SIR: Your letter of 6th instant, addressed to the Adjutant-General on the subject of Order, No. 252 [of 3d instant], directing the formation of the two Mississippi brigades without delay, has been submitted to the President, who instructs me to reply that he adheres to his order, and expects you to execute it.

Fully two months have elapsed since the President's verbal expression of his desires that the will of the Congress on this subject should be obeyed. Six weeks or more have elapsed since orders were formally issued from this Department, to be executed as early as in your discretion it could be safely done, and the President now finds the Mississippi regiments scattered as far apart as it is possible to scatter them, and General Griffith sent to your extreme left, although assigned by orders to the division of General Van Dorn, which is on the right.

The President considers it necessary to re-enforce your right by adding to the strength of General Whiting's command, as already pointed out by yourself, and he therefore desires that the Thirteenth, Seventeenth, and Eighteenth Mississippi regiments be sent to General Whiting, to whose brigade they belong. You can replace the regiments thus drawn from Leesburg by any other brigade you deem proper, calling back from Leesburg the Twenty-first Mississippi, to be brigaded

———————————————————————————————————
* Some private and personal matter omitted.

with the Twelfth, Sixteenth, and Nineteenth, under command of General Griffith.

The President further desires me to inform you that he can see no reason for withdrawing from General Whiting's command any of the force now there, even after sending him the three Mississippi regiments in accordance with the foregoing instructions, inasmuch as he considers the danger of attack on your right more imminent than on your center. But on this point he does not desire to control your discretion. He confines himself to directing that his repeatedly expressed wishes and orders about the Mississippi regiments be carried into effect.

Your obedient servant,

J. P. BENJAMIN,
Secretary of War.

HEADQUARTERS VALLEY DISTRICT,
Winchester, December 9, 1861.

Hon. J. P. BENJAMIN, *Secretary of War:*

SIR: Your letter of the 6th instant has been received, and tends to confirm the apprehension that I have entertained for weeks of the Federal forces on the other side of the Potomac effecting a junction with General Kelley's troops. The forces in Romney are receiving re-enforcements. On the 5th instant Howe's battery of six pieces arrived there from Cheat Mountain, and three regiments are expected there soon from the same place. This information is from a reliable person residing in Romney. I have understood that General Loring contemplates leaving his cavalry. It appears to me very important that his force should come as a unit to this point for not only are General Kelley's forces in Hampshire County at this moment near 7,000 strong, and more expected from the West, but additional troops may at any time cross the Potomac at a lower point, and enter this district. In addition to these reasons for bringing his entire command here may be added the great importance, if successful, in recovering this district and capturing many of the enemy, and disorganizing the mass of such forces as are threatening this region of wintering on the waters of the Ohio, as expressed in my letter of the 20th ultimo. Besides the reasons given in that letter for occupying the northwestern part of Virginia this winter may now be added the inducement of organizing forces in that region this winter, in accordance with the recent ordinance of the Convention of this Commonwealth, in the event of there not being enough troops for the war.

As the Federal forces may move on this place any day, I would respectfully recommend that General Loring be directed not to postpone the marching of his troops in consequence of a desire to save a large supply of subsistence stores. The enemy may remove such stores from this district much more rapidly than General Loring can his to a place of safety. The probabilities are that his stores, after withdrawing his command, could by a quartermaster or contractor be removed before their safety would be endangered; but should the enemy advance too soon, it does appear to me that it would be economy to burn or otherwise destroy them. It does appear to me that the capture of General Kelley's army, including his munitions of war, would be of far more value to our Republic than General Loring's subsistence stores. If General Loring's entire command were here I would, with God's blessing, soon expect to see General Kelley's army, or a large portion of it, in our possession; but if General Loring is not here speedily my command may be a retreating instead of a victorious one, and the consequences of such a retreat may not have their disastrous effects limited to this district. The canal-boats have been going toward Cumberland for near a week. They have gone up empty and in large numbers. To prevent their returning to Washington with coal I attempted to turn the water around the Virginia side of Dam No. 5, but was prevented by the enemy's sharpshooters. I am still sanguine of accomplishing my purpose at another point.

The militia of the exposed counties ought to be able to protect their localities from marauding parties that might be disposed to commit depredations in the event of General Loring's cavalry being withdrawn.

Col. W. B. Taliaferro arrived yesterday with his brigade in good condition. I much need a good engineer officer.

Very respectfully, your obedient servant,
T. J. JACKSON,
Major-General, P. A. C. S., Commanding Valley District.

HEADQUARTERS NORTHWESTERN ARMY,
Staunton, Va., December 9, 1861.

General S. COOPER, *Adjutant General, &c.:*

GENERAL: I have the honor to inclose the letter of Colonel Johnson, in command on Alleghany Pass. In consequence of the insufficiency of the cavalry on both lines I think it would be best to leave a regiment of infantry, with a section of artillery, on the Staunton line, in the vicinity of Monterey. It will also be advisable to call out some of the militia on the Millborough line, to aid the cavalry to be left at Huntersville. I think that proposed will be sufficient to keep back depredating parties. Unless you think otherwise, I shall order as above stated.

With respect, I have the honor to be, your obedient servant,
W. W. LORING,
Brigadier-General, Commanding, &c.

[Inclosure.]

CAMP ON ALLEGHANY, *December 7,* 1861.

Col. C. L. STEVENSON,
Assistant Adjutant General, Army Northwest, Staunton:

SIR: If it is intended to abandon entirely this position, under the impression that the enemy have left Cheat Mountain, or that if they have not, the roads and climate, &c., will prevent their making incursions into this country, a grave mistake has been committed. The enemy are still on Cheat Mountain. Their scouts are almost daily seen. To-day my scouts chased a party of 100 from the old encampment at Greenbrier. Yesterday they were in the vicinity of Green Bank, and stole a horse or two. If this post is abandoned there will be nothing to prevent their march to Staunton, and my opinion is that they will improve the opportunity thus offered them. Moreover, if they get possession here it will be difficult to dislodge them. Our own intrenchments will afford them shelter, and additional works will make this point very strong. The cavalry to be here will be, in my opinion, of no avail against the forces of the enemy. Little reliance can be placed in the cavalry I have thus far seen. Infantry and artillery I consider essential in order to hold this position.

I have deemed it my duty to throw out these hints without making any suggestions, and without knowing upon what information in regard to the enemy the contemplated abandonment of this place is predicated. I only state what I know in regard to the immediate presence of the enemy. They have erected commodious and comfortable buildings on Cheat Mountain, as I hear from a prisoner captured a few weeks since. He furthermore states that they will annoy us all winter.

I am, sir, very respectfully, your obedient servant,

E. JOHNSON,
Colonel, Commanding Monterey Line.

PRIVATE.]   CENTREVILLE, VA., *December* 9, 1861.
General JOSEPH E. JOHNSTON:

DEAR GENERAL: To prevent spies and others from communicating to "George" our arrangements, I think it would be advisable to keep in reserve, at some safe place, our "wooden guns," to be put in position only when required. I have so instructed Longstreet for the armament of his batteries. I understand they are "preparing a case" at Richmond relative to the condition of the depot at Manassas, the bad arrangements for taking care of the sick arriving there, and of those on their way home or to other hospitals; also relative to our retreat from Fairfax Court-House, especially relative to the transportation of the sick on that occasion, and of the burning of some baggage and tents at Fairfax Station. I mention these things to you to keep you on your guard.

I hear it suggested there is in some quarter a great desire to send Bragg to command this army. So far as I am personally concerned they can do so, if they please, after our next battle, but not before. With regard to the condition of the quartermaster's department at Manassas, I think it can be remedied by sending there a competent quartermaster and putting him entirely under the control of Colonel Anderson, who should be made responsible for the proper order and system at that post.

Outside of Barbour I know of but two quartermasters who might answer for that responsible position—Bonham's and D. R. Jones' (Captains Young and Adams)—but I fear those generals would almost die before giving them up.

Yours, truly,

G. T. BEAUREGARD.

CAMP LEE, NEAR HAGUE, *December* 10, 1861.
Hon. J. P. BENJAMIN, *Secretary War:*

The extent of the obligations of the Confederate Government to Maryland is not known by me, and I feel compelled to ask for information and instruction.

Three gentlemen, with the full endorsation of the Government, captains' commissions, are here recruiting, and claiming the right to run boats to Maryland. Any man who crosses is taken in, and may go back as a hand on board the boat, and for aught I know any deserter from Sickles' brigade may come, get any desired information, and go back. A letter from your office to Colonel Arnold, of King George, I think in September, required these gentlemen to be furnished every facility to recruit, and they claim the right to send any one to Baltimore to do this. Are they under my control or not? I cannot discharge my duty as provost-marshal to the people here as my judgment directs if they have full discretion in this matter. I have permitted them to use boats, under the impression your order was imperative upon me.

A steamboat was introduced here on Saturday. Is she to pass freely? If so, I hazard little in saying that all communication with the Maryland shore will be cut off in a few days and our creeks will be blockaded by tugs.

I have forbidden the Maryland captain's boat to cross for the present because of misconduct and by request from friends in Maryland.

The desertions so far about equal the recruits.

Very respectfully, your obedient servant,

R. L. T. BEALE,
Major and Provost-Marshal.

HEADQUARTERS DISTRICT LOWER RAPPAHANNOCK,
Tappahannock, December 10, 1861.

Col. D. H. MAURY,
Assistant Adjutant General, Brooke's, Station, Va.:

COLONEL: I have the honor to state that I have, in obedience to orders from the general commanding, visited Major Beale at his post on the Potomac. After consultation we both, came to the conclusion that some strenuous and immediate measures should be taken to avoid, if possible, the contamination which might ensue. A greater portion of our loyal men, the chivalry and high-toned gentlemen of the country, have volunteered, and are far from their homes. There is a strong element among those who are left either to be non-combatants or to fall back under the old flag. I do not consider we have any time to lose. I therefore suggest that the militia of Westmoreland and Northumberland Counties be organized and relieved by other troops, they being ordered away from the dangerous ground and placed under the immediate supervision of some one able to govern them. It is impossible for me to be on both sides of the river at the same time, and I place but little confidence in the present militia ineffective system. This feeling of discontent is augmented in the Northern Neck by a report which has been circulated to the effect that the Neck is to be abandoned. These reports have come to me from various sources as having originated at the War Department and from the general commanding the district. Not having received anything to confirm or even to have suggested such a thought I have denied it, and impressed on all the persons asking for information the falsity of the rumor; for should such a step become necessary, I feel confident I should be informed of it in season to put the inhabitants, who look to me for protection, on their guard.

Your communication of the 6th instant in reference to the boats was received to-night after my return from the other side of the river. I shall forward instructions to Captain Lewis and the other officers in command in the Neck, in accordance with your orders. I inclose copy of order to Colonel [Samuel L.] Straughan on this subject.*

I cannot close this communication to the general commanding without saying that many more complaints are made by a certain class of

---

* Not found.

population than are warranted. We have to fear them most. All during a war like this must suffer, but for the good of the general service it will not do to yield to those persons who have refused to volunteer, while the proprietors of the country are actually in the field, and who plead poverty and would join the enemy should an occasion occur. It will be a mistaken leniency, and would only lead to further trouble.

I am, colonel, very respectfully, your obedient servant,

G. E. PICKETT,
Colonel P. A. C. S., Commanding.

[Indorsement.]

HEADQUARTERS AQUIA DISTRICT, *December* 13, 1861.

Respectfully referred to the Adjutant-General.

The persons referred to in the last paragraph are the poor and non-slaveholders.

TH. H. HOLMES,
Major-General, Commanding District.

DUBLIN, VA., *December* 10, 1861.

S. COOPER, *Adjutant-General:*

Donelson's brigade, 1,300 strong, moves to-day for Petersburg. Eighth and Thirteenth Tennessee, Floyd's brigade, require repose. There is no disorganization whatever. The men are in fine spirits. A paymaster should be sent up at once. They have not been paid since June 30. I estimate the amount required at 3,000 men for four months. Is this line to be re-enforced? The people are alarmed at the departure of the troops.

GEO. DEAS,
Assistant Adjutant-General.

RICHMOND, *December* 10, 1861.

Brigadier-General DONELSON, *Dublin Station, Va.:*

Proceed without delay with your brigade and Starke's regiment to Charleston, S. C., and report to General R. E. Lee.

S. COOPER,
Adjutant and Inspector General.

RICHMOND, *December* 10, 1861.

Captain J. G. PAXTON,
Quartermaster, Jackson River, Virginia:

Send the following dispatch to Colonel Davis, commanding Wise's Legion:

Proceed with your command to Lynchburg in the manner directed in instructions of the Quartermaster-General and Capt. J. G. Paxton, quartermaster at Jackson River. Further orders will be sent you at Lynchburg.

S. COOPER,
Adjutant and Inspector General.

HEADQUARTERS AQUIA DISTRICT,
December 12, 1861.

General S. COOPER,
  Adjutant and Inspector General:

GENERAL: I have from time to time received information from the lower Northern Neck that makes me apprehensive of danger in that quarter. I fear the inhibition of trade, the absence of necessaries, such as salt, coffee, &c., and the heavy stress on the women and children incident to the absence of the men on militia and volunteer duty, are beginning to tell to the prejudice of our cause among the non-slaveholders. If the enemy do not attack our batteries in a few days I think we may conclude they do not design doing so, and I respectfully submit whether it will not be better for me to withdraw a regiment from Evansport to replace Colonel Brockenbrough's very excellent regiment, which comes from that region, and send it there to substitute the militia, which should be disbanded. The regiment is in a high state of discipline, full of enthusiasm, and its presence would not fail to have a powerful moral effect on the people, and at the same time give the protection of property they are so clamorous for.

I am, general, very respectfully, your obedient servant,
TH. H. HOLMES,
Major-General, Commanding District.

HEADQUARTERS, *Centreville, December* 13, 1861.

Hon. J. P. BENJAMIN, *Secretary of War:*

SIR: I have just received your letter of the 9th instant, in which you inform me that the President "adheres to his order and expects me to execute it." You add that "six weeks or more have elapsed since orders were formally given from this Department to be executed as early as in your discretion it could be safely done, and the President now finds the Mississippi regiments scattered as far as it is possible to scatter them, and General Griffith sent to your extreme left, although assigned by orders to the division of General Van Dorn, which is on the right."

I beg leave to say in reply that there has been no time within the last six weeks when I was not ready, cheerfully and zealously, to put into operation the changes prescribed in the order referred to, had I believed "it could be safely done"; but believing an attack from the enemy imminent at any moment and at any point, and deeming any change, however judicious in itself, to be incompatible with safety, I felt confident that the exercise of the discretion vested in me would meet the entire approval of the President.

The Mississippi regiments are occupying now precisely the positions in which they were when the President last visited this army more than two months ago, except the Twenty-first, which was sent to Leesburg to make up a Mississippi brigade. This was intended as a step towards carrying out the President's plan, to be consummated whenever opportunity might permit. General Griffith was sent temporarily to the extreme left, to command that brigade until the regiments indicated could without risk be transferred to General Van Dorn's division.

I beg leave again to assure the President that in the exercise of the discretion vested in me I postponed the execution of his orders fully believing that my opinion of the danger attending their enforcement under present exigencies would meet with his concurrence and sanction.

In informing the Government that General Whiting's command needed re-enforcement, so far from intending to intimate that either the left or center could furnish the additional troops, I sought to impress upon it the fact that both are too weak.

In view of the fact that our right flank is about 25 miles from this point, the left almost as far, the enemy's center about 15 miles from it, the country full of disloyal people, our army liable to attack upon its whole front or any part of it by at least threefold numbers, I hope the President will favorably consider my appeal, earnestly and respectfully renewed, for a continuance of the discretion he has vested in me, merely as to the time of executing the orders in question.

Trusting that the President will think, as I do, that I only ask for an authority rarely withheld from a general commanding an army, I am, most respectfully, your obedient servant,

J. E. JOHNSTON,
General.

RICHMOND, *December* 13, 1861.

General S. COOPER,
    Adjutant-General C. S. Army, Richmond, Va.:

GENERAL: I have the honor to state that I have taken the liberty of leaving my command for a couple of days, in order to report to the War Department in person what I have already done by letter to Major-General Holmes, namely, the necessity of some immediate steps being taken in the District of the Lower Rappahannock in order to prevent the possibility of the disaffected element from gaining the ascendency. The landed proprietors of the Northern Neck, Essex, and Middlesex have not only most of them volunteered, but have also appropriated funds for the maintenance of the poor in those counties.

I would respectfully advise that the militia of Northumberland and Westmoreland be at once organized, sent to some other part of the Confederacy, and relieved by troops from elsewhere.

The impression is prevalent that the Northern Neck is to be abandoned. As commanding officer of that part of the country, the inhabitants look to me for protection. I do not wish to be placed in a false position. I have endeavored to quiet their apprehensions. Should the Confederacy wish to abandon the Neck, I would like to be informed at once. Two regiments could be readily and comfortably quartered there for the winter, and at the same time, by sending off this class of people, we will be actively guarding the country, and forcing into service those who have refused to volunteer, and who would undoubtedly join the enemy at the first opportunity.

Should the Rappahannock close during the winter, which is very likely to occur, then the enemy have it at their option to land from Chesapeake Bay, which will be open, and we cannot re-enforce.

It is due to the people, those who are supporting this war by direct taxation, by subscription, and in person, that their families should not be left at the mercy of these Northern marauders.

I am, general, very respectfully, your obedient servant,

GEO. E. PICKETT,
Colonel, P. A. C. S.

HEADQUARTERS FIRST CORPS, ARMY OF THE POTOMAC,
Centreville, Va., December 14, 1861.

Brig. Gen. D. H. HILL, *Commanding at Leesburg, Va.:*

GENERAL: Your letter of this date is received. The spades called for will be sent as soon as practicable.

General Johnston and myself are of the opinion that any demonstration (however strong) of the enemy against you will be made to cover an attack against the batteries blockading the Potomac, for they are more interested in relieving themselves from the blockade than in taking possession of Leesburg; and however desirable it is for us to hold the latter, we cannot send you any assistance without having to give up the plan of operations already communicated to you when you were here. You can, however, spread the rumor that we are going to send you the division of E. K. Smith, say 10,000 men, of all arms, in case of any serious demonstration against you, for which purpose you can say it has been ordered to Gum Spring. But in case you are attacked by overwhelming odds which you would not be able to prevent from crossing the Potomac, you will act as already instructed. Full discretion, however, is allowed you, as we have entire confidence in your judgment.

It is more than probable that, should the enemy intend to cross again the Potomac, he will make a strong demonstration at one point and cross at another. You will then have to determine whether to fight him along the banks of the Potomac, which is the best, if you are sufficiently strong and quick, or in rear of Goose Creek, at the points already indicated to you.

With strong hopes of your success, I remain, general, very respectfully, your obedient servant,

G. T. BEAUREGARD,
General, Commanding.

———

Report of the inspection of Floyd's brigade, near Newbern, Va.

RICHMOND, VA., *December* 14, 1861.

General S. COOPER,
Adjutant and Inspector General:

This brigade is now composed as follows:

Twenty-second, Thirty-sixth, Forty-fifth, Fiftieth, and Fifty-first Regiments Virginia Volunteers.

Twentieth Regiment Mississippi Volunteers.

Thirteenth Regiment Georgia Volunteers.

Phillips' Legion Georgia Volunteers, ten companies of infantry and four of horse.

Guy's battery of artillery, four pieces, Virginia.

Jackson's battery of artillery, four pieces, Virginia.

Adams' battery of artillery, two pieces, Virginia.

Eighth Regiment of Cavalry, Virginia.

The aggregate strength of this command present and fit for duty is about 3,500, and there are absent, sick in hospital at various places, about 1,500. Of these latter many are arriving daily, and in the course of ten days or a fortnight it may be expected that nearly a thousand will join their respective regiments. The troops have suffered a great deal of hardship and exposure during the active campaign in Western Virginia, and now feel the effects of the measles and its consequences; but they are evidently improving, and with a little rest they will soon be able to engage in any service which may be required of them. To judge of these men by what is said of them by their officers, they are certainly brave and reliable. To the eye of the critical inspector they present the appearance of raw, undisciplined levies. Their instruction in the most simple evolutions is entirely wanting. Indeed, they have had no opportunity to receive any instruction, having been constantly engaged in the most active operations since the month of August last. Yet these raw countrymen have certainly gone through a campaign which would do credit to any force however perfect in its composition, and I am told that all their hardships have been borne without a murmur.

I am not aware of what disposition it is intended to make of the command of General Floyd, but I certainly would recommend that, if it be not contemplated to remove it to any great distance, he be ordered to establish a winter camp of instruction not far from where he now is. Dublin Depot is not a good place, but the general has such a perfect acquaintance with that region of country that he could at once select a suitable place. I would recommend that the Thirteenth Georgia Regiment, Phillips' Legion, and the Twentieth Mississippi Regiment be ordered into a milder climate. The severe winters of Western Virginia will be fatal to those Southern men. The cavalry force might be reduced. It will not be necessary to keep there more than four full companies for the winter. The artillery horses are in bad order—entirely unfit for service. The horses of the transport service are in the same condition. All the horses, therefore, should be turned out to winter with responsible farmers, who can be selected by the general. In the spring, then, all these horses would be fit for service again. The wagons are in pretty good condition, but require repairs. The arms of the command are in good order, but in some of the regiments there is a mixture of rifles, flint locks, and percussion guns. This can be remedied when the time arrives for filling requisitions which have been already made. The clothing in some instances is bad, but supplies are arriving daily, both from the public stores and from private contributions. Medical supplies are deficient, and this has been the complaint throughout the campaign. The larger portion of the troops have not been paid for six months. A paymaster should be sent there at once. Many of the men have families who are really suffering for want of support. The discipline of the command seems to be good. The general impression made upon me by this inspection is, that the men having just come from a most fatiguing campaign, and having suffered considerably from camp diseases, they are just at present in a somewhat enfeebled condition, but it is evident that they will improve by repose and the improvement in their daily rations, and in a comparatively short period of time they will recover their usual healthy condition. With good instructions they could soon be made more apt in their evolutions. Without such minute instruction reliance must be placed, as heretofore, upon their steady aim and good pluck.

Respectfully submitted.

GEO. DEAS,
Assistant Inspector-General.

WAR DEPARTMENT, C. S. A.,
Richmond, December 15, 1861.

Maj. R. L. T. BEALE, *Camp Lee, near Hague:*

SIR: I am in receipt of your letter of the 10th instant. At the time the authority was given to the several Maryland captains to recruit for our service the condition of affairs on the opposite shore was very different from the present state of things, and there was a strong desire to enable our friends on the other side to cross and join us. Ample time has been given for that purpose, and you are authorized to use to the fullest extent your own discretion on the subject. Full facilities have been given, and it is no advantage to our service to continue the recruiting of Marylanders on the Lower Potomac.

The steamer was taken across to a creek within your command by my permission, given to Mr. Henry Stewart, who has been engaged in procuring some supplies for the Government; but all these permissions have been granted invariably with the understanding that they are subject to the discretion of the military commanders. Being responsible for the safety of your command and the police of that district of country, I do not desire at all to interfere with your discretion in enforcing such precautions about the crossing as may seem to you wise and prudent.

Your obedient servant,

J. P. BENJAMIN,
Secretary of War.

WAR DEPARTMENT, C. S. A.,
Richmond, December 16, 1861.

Maj. Gen. T. H. HOLMES,
Headquarters Aquia District, Fredericksburg, Va.:

SIR: I have had the honor to receive your letter of the 12th instant in regard to the condition of the Northern Neck of Virginia, in which you propose also to send a regiment to that section. This Department entirely approves of your plan, and recommends its execution as soon as, in your opinion, it can be done with safety to your command.

I am, respectfully, your obedient servant,

J. P. BENJAMIN,
Secretary of War.

P. S.—Our friends in Washington inform us that there will be a simultaneous attack at Mathias Point, Winchester, and Centreville before the end of the week.

RICHMOND, *December* 16, 1861.

General JOSEPH E. JOHNSTON,
Commanding, &c., Centreville, Va.:

GENERAL: I am directed to say, in reply to your letter of the 12th * instant, that since the date of the order you refer to (General Orders, No. 18, of November 16, 1861), the regiments named therein have been ordered by the Secretary of War to re-enforce General Jackson in the Winchester Valley.

Yours, very respectfully, &c.,

R. H. CHILTON,
Assistant Adjutant-General.

---

* Probably 13th, p. 993.

HEADQUARTERS,
Centreville, December 16, 1861.

General S. COOPER, *Adjutant and Inspector General:*

SIR: Brigadier-General Hill, commanding at Leesburg, writes that the enemy are able to sweep the ground on our side of the Potomac for 2 miles from the water with their artillery. He cannot, therefore, contest the passage of the river. With another regiment of infantry and a sufficient body of cavalry he could occupy his position, and observe the long line of the Potomac, so as to prevent surprise. He thinks it possible that a regiment of infantry might be spared from Richmond. If so, I beg that it may be sent without delay.

Colonel Jenifer, who was here to-day, thinks that his regiment, now in Western Virginia, could be very useful in Loudoun, and that the horses would gain very much by being removed to that abundant country. His minute knowledge of the country and people makes his own services there almost indispensable. I earnestly request, therefore, that his regiment may join him as soon as possible.

I need not remind the Department of the injury that would result to us from permitting the enemy to establish himself in Leesburg, nor repeat that we are too weak here to re-enforce General Hill from this body of troops. If the two brigades announced to be *en route* to it in General Orders, No. 18, may be expected soon, I shall, on their arrival, be able to strengthen Brigadier-General Hill's command sufficiently.

Most respectfully, your obedient servant,

J. E. JOHNSTON,
General.

DUMFRIES, VA., *December* 16, 1861.

R. M. SMITH, Esq.:

DEAR SIR: I was informed yesterday that our troops were destroying my houses on the river. There was a two-story, with attic, dwelling-house, with shed-rooms on the north side and a covered porch to both stories on the south side the length of the house. There were six rooms, besides two in the shed, a large, well-built kitchen, a servants' house, a meat-house, a frame office, new, and a large stable. My tenant was removed from the property two months ago. I rode down to-day, and found every plank taken from the stable, the office removed, the kitchen and servants' house all gone but the brick chimneys, the shed portion of the dwelling entirely gone, the window-sash and doors and the weather-boarding torn off and carried away, the fencing gone, and what I expected to be my future home a complete wreck. The enemy have not destroyed any man's property on the Potomac so completely as the Georgia, Texas, and Captain Frobel's company have destroyed mine. Is there no redress? Do we live under a military despotism? I found Captain Trobel at the Cockpit Point batteries, 2 miles off, erecting winter quarters out of my houses. Other portions were taken by the Eighteenth Georgia Regiment and Second Texas Regiment. My wife grieves over the vandalism, because it was her father's, and the place where she was born. We have no courts of justice, or I would prosecute the ruffians. I am between the upper and nether millstones, robbed by the Yankees in Washington and by Southern troops here. I have paid taxes on this property to the State, and the courts of the State fail to give me any protection. The country around here is treated more like an enemy's country than the homes of loyal citizens. What right has a colonel or captain, without my leave, to take my property? I would not have had it destroyed for thrice its value. I shall never be able to rebuild, and the whole place will have to be deserted.

I should not trouble you, but I must give vent to my indignation. I give up all hope of saving any of my property except the soil, and I have a wife and seven children to provide with bread.

Yours, truly,

C. W. C. DUNNINGTON.

[Indorsement.]

ENQUIRER OFFICE, *December* 19, 1861.

Hon. J. P. BENJAMIN:

The foregoing is from as true a man and as faithful to the South as breathes. He is an exile from Washington for his principles, leaving and losing thereby the most of his property. The rest is going as he states. Please protect him, and oblige his friend and yours.

Very respectfully,

R. M. SMITH.

LEESBURG, VA., *December* 16, 1861.

General G. T. BEAUREGARD:

SIR: Inclosed you will find General Stone's reply* to my letter; the real object of my correspondence being to get in the following sentence: "I will hang these villains unless forbidden by my immediate superior, General [G. W.] Smith, at Gum Spring." It is left to the consideration of the general commanding whether there ought not to be some support of this assertion.

I learn that the pickets at Dranesville fall back to Broad Run at night, and that successful foraging parties of the enemy constantly depredate around Dranesville. I have not destroyed the bridge over Broad Run, as Captain Alexander has discovered two good fords over that stream.

I returned last night from Point of Rocks. Private houses in that vicinity have been bombarded from the other side of the river; private carriages, with ladies in them, have been fired at, horses have been stolen, &c.

The remark made in my last letter was drawn out by my statement in regard to the inadequacy of our force to prevent surprise. If attacked on all sides, I thought we would lose less by a determined resistance than by a running and retreating fight. Would it not be well to let us have some guns of large caliber to cope with the enemy's heavy artillery?

With great respect,

D. H. HILL,
Brigadier-General, P. A. C. S.

HDQRS. FIRST CORPS, ARMY OF THE POTOMAC,
Centreville, December 16, 1861.

Brig. Gen. D. H. HILL,
Commanding C. S. Forces in Loudoun County, Leesburg, Va.:

GENERAL: Your letter of this morning has been received and its con-

---

* Not found.

tents communicated to the general commanding, who instructs as follows:

Let General Hill try and hang our own traitors for murder, robbery, and treason, but the Northern soldiers cannot be dealt with thus summarily. He must not make up his mind to victory or the extermination of his command, but must be reminded of the instructions already furnished him. We are too far to be able to give him assistance, after an attack is begun and too weak to send him re-enforcements whilst there is uncertainty as to the point of attack. By disposing of his heavy baggage, as already instructed, he can retreat in safety before a force too strong to be opposed successfully. I will write for an additional regiment from Richmond besides the cavalry regiment of Colonel Jenifer, but with little hope of success.

Marauders should receive no quarter; that would prevent any trouble or difficulty.

I concur fully with these views and in these instructions of General Johnston.

Very respectfully, your obedient servant,

G. T. BEAUREGARD,
General Commanding.

WAR DEPARTMENT, C. S. A.,
Richmond, December 16, 1861.

Brig. Gen. JOHN B. FLOYD, *Dublin Depot, Va.:*

SIR : It is not believed to be at all necessary that your brigade should establish itself in winter quarters while the enemy are pressing in superior force on the columns of General Lee in South Carolina and General Johnston in Kentucky. For this reason it is that the Department has ordered Anderson's [Donelson's] brigade and Starke's regiment (originally intended to re-enforce your command) to South Carolina, and has also directed that the Twentieth Mississippi, the Thirteenth Georgia, Phillips' Legion, and Waddill's battalion should be detached from your command and sent to join General Lee. Your remaining force consists of the Twenty-second, Thirty-sixth, Forty-fifth, Fiftieth, and Fifty-first Virginia, of the Eighth Virginia Cavalry, and of three batteries.

It is deemed necessary for the protection of the inhabitants of Greenbrier and Monroe Counties from the incursions of marauders, and to prevent any panic among them, that one regiment of troops accustomed to the rigors of the winter climate among the mountains should be stationed at or near Lewisburg. With this view you are requested to detach one of your regiments (selecting an officer of vigilance, activity, and discretion as commander), to be sent to Lewisburg as soon as the troops are sufficiently rested, and furnished with the necessary equipment in the way of tents, clothing, &c., there to winter for the protection of the surrounding country. You will advise the Department of the colonel you have selected and the route by which he is to be sent and the date of his departure, that the necessary supplies may be furnished in time. The remainder of your brigade, as soon as fit for active duty, will be moved, under your command, to re-enforce General A. S. Johnston at Bowling Green, Ky., and it is desired by the Department that no further delay occur in making this movement than such as may be absolutely necessary to put your troops in proper condition for movement. If your horses require a longer period than the men to be ready to move, you can leave your cavalry and artillery, with orders to follow you.

When the season approaches for the renewal of the campaign in Western Virginia it is the intention of the Department to reorganize your command for service in that region, on such a footing and with such force as will enable you to take and keep possession of the whole of Southwestern Virginia.

I am, your obedient servant,

J. P. BENJAMIN,
Secretary of War.

HEADQUARTERS ARMY OF NORTHWEST,
Staunton, Va., December 17, 1861.

Col. E. JOHNSON,
Commanding Forces on Monterey Line, Virginia:

COLONEL: General Orders, No. 17, from these headquarters,* as far as they are applicable to your command, are revoked. Instructions have been given to forward to you supplies, with those now on hand, sufficient for two months.

It is the intention to hold Alleghany Pass and the country in its vicinity, and you will please dispose of your command with a view thereto. Circumstances, however, may render it advisable to detach it for service with the forces now moving towards Winchester, and the general desires that you will keep it constantly and fully prepared for such an emergency.

*   *   *   *   *   *   *

I am, sir, respectfully, your obedient servant,

C. L. STEVENSON,
Adjutant-General.

CENTREVILLE, VA., *December* 19, 1861.

Hon. W. P. MILES:

MY DEAR SIR: As we are all greatly interested in the reorganization of the army now here, I do not hesitate to give you my views on the subject. The reorganization should be here and before the troops can get a leave of absence. Then they should be allowed a leave of absence of 30 days—one-third at a time. The bounty should be paid as they start off on leave. It would be better to reorganize the companies and regiments as they now are; that is, skeleton regiments and companies. When the companies go home I think it will be easy for them to fill up the ranks. The reorganization in companies and regiments as they now are I suppose would be best, as each company represents some particular section and each regiment some particular district.

The success of this effort will depend in a great measure, I think, upon the way in which it is started. But one of the brigades of my division belongs permanently to my command—D. R. Jones' brigade, now commanded by Colonel Jenkins. I propose to start the thing with this brigade, and think that I may be able to get nearly every man of it if it can be done as I propose, viz, make Jenkins a brigadier, and let the troops understand that it is to be his brigade, and that they are to be allowed the privileges heretofore suggested. If we are as successful with this brigade as I hope we may be, I believe that every other regiment in the army will follow handsomely. Besides being much liked by his men, Colonel Jenkins is one of the finest officers of this army. I think him as well worthy and deserving of the position of brigadier as any officer of my acquaintance.

---

*Not found.

You must not suppose that I mean to intimate that Jones is wanting in character or ability as an officer. He is a very dear friend of mine, and wanting in nothing as a gentleman or a soldier; but he has gone to Richmond to seek an exchange of brigades. This is known in his old command, and he could not now satisfy the command so completely as could Jenkins. If he is still in Richmond I would like you to consult him on this subject, and show him this letter, if you deem it at all advisable. I am satisfied that he will unite with me in my recommendation of Jenkins.

With high respect and esteem, I am, very sincerely, yours,

JAMES LONGSTREET,
Major-General, C. S. Army.

[Indorsement.]

If the plan of reorganization proposed above can be carried into effect it certainly meets with my unqualified approval, as well as the promotion of Colonel Jenkins, who has already been warmly recommended by me as a brigadier-general.

Yours, truly,

G. T. BEAUREGARD,
General, C. S. Army.

———

CAMP WIGFALL, *December* 20, 1861.

General WHITING:

MY DEAR GENERAL: I will be over to see you as soon as possible, perhaps this afternoon. Does General Johnston include Wolf Run Shoals as in my lines? This ford is too far from me to enable me to guard it with my present force, but I have always advised that artillery and infantry should be stationed there. If I am to guard this ford I would suggest that you send the battery of Captain Bachman there, and let me ask for a supporting force of infantry. The brigade which is at Davis' Ford could easily defend Wolf Run, and it would be well for a portion of that command to be on this side of the river at Davis' Ford; they can only operate by supporting the lines at Union Mills or starve down here. But the fact is, I do not think the enemy will come anywhere, and we ought to beat up his quarters.

I send you a report of our skirmish day before yesterday. It was entirely successful, as far as driving back the cavalry of the enemy was concerned, but owing to the fact of our infantry not having attained its proper position when the fight began, we failed in cutting off the detachment as I hoped to do. I should like to try these fellows again in some force, and if you will allow it, I feel sure that I can bag a large party. Yesterday they came to the church with 900 infantry, 100 cavalry, and two guns. I have arranged my ferry here so that I can carry over a large force in a few minutes, while my guns can protect the crossing. If we were to send over some infantry, a few guns, and a large force of cavalry, we could stampede the whole camp over there. My cavalry went 3 miles beyond the church and drove in some pickets. There is no chance for a fight here, so we will have to look up one.

I am yours, very respectfully and truly,

WADE HAMPTON.

HEADQUARTERS VALLEY DISTRICT,
Winchester, Va., December 21, 1861.

Major THOMAS G. RHETT,
Asst. Adjt. Gen., Hdqrs. Department of Northern Virginia:

MAJOR: Part of the Army of the Northwest has arrived here and more of it will be here early next week. I expect Brigadier-General Loring here on next Tuesday, and I would respectfully recommend that he be continued in the command of such forces as he has brought into this district, and that they be designated as the First Division of the Army of the Valley. Please let me know the decision of the commanding general as to what shall constitute General Loring's command and what shall be its designation.

Very respectfully, your obedient servant,
T. J. JACKSON,
Major-General, Commanding Valley District.

WAR DEPARTMENT, C. S. A.,
Richmond, December 23, 1861.

Brig. Gen. W. W. LORING, *Staunton:*

SIR: Your letters of the 13th instant and 17th instant* have been received, and the measures taken by you in disposing and moving your forces meet the entire approval of the Department.

You will use your own discretion as to the proper force to be left under command of Col. (now Brig. Gen.) E. Johnson, and of the length of time it will be proper to hold the pass which the enemy has made so disastrous an effort to force.

I inclose you a letter for Brigadier-General Johnson,† knowing that it cannot but be agreeable to you to be made the channel of communication of the President's approval conveyed to meritorious and gallant soldiers under your command.

I am, your obedient servant,
J. P. BENJAMIN,
Secretary of War.

RICHMOND, *December* 23, 1861.

General G. T. BEAUREGARD, *Centreville, Va.:*

I am afraid, with all my efforts, I shall not succeed in obtaining a light battery in exchange for Calhoun's battery. There are three batteries here, but neither of them complete, either in men or pieces. I am still endeavoring to complete one of them, and if I succeed will send it.

S. COOPER,
Adjutant and Inspector General.

HEADQUARTERS VALLEY DISTRICT,
Winchester, December 23, 1861.

General S. COOPER,
Adjutant and Inspector General, C. S. Army:

GENERAL: I respectfully request that such of Brig. Gen. W. W. Loring's forces as are on and near the Alleghany Mountains be ordered to

---

* Not found.   † See p. 464.

march forthwith to Moorefield, Hardy County, with a view to forming a junction with the troops now at and near this point. If it is the design of the Government to commence offensive operations against Romney soon, the troops asked for should move to my aid at once. Recent intelligence from Romney gives reason to believe that the force of the enemy in Hampshire County is about 10,000, and that re-enforcements are continuing to arrive.

I regret to say that the occupation of Hampshire by the enemy is exercising a demoralizing influence upon our people, who are gradually yielding to outward pressure and taking the oath of allegiance to the United States. There are noble spirits in and about Romney who have given up their earthly all, and are now for our cause and institutions exiles from their homes. I have endeavored to cheer them, and to deter those who remained behind from taking the oath of allegiance to the enemy by holding out to them the prospect of a speedy deliverance, but this, I fear, will prove a delusion, unless the asked-for forces or their equivalent come soon.

I fear that the forces that were recently defeated on the Alleghany will be in Romney before Colonel Johnson leaves his position.

Respectfully, your obedient servant,

T. J. JACKSON,
Major-General, P. A. C. S., Commanding.

HEADQUARTERS VALLEY DISTRICT,
Winchester, Va., December 24, 1861.

Maj. THOMAS G. RHETT,
Asst. Adjt. Gen., Hdqrs. Department of Northern Virginia:

MAJOR: I have good reason to believe that the enemy in Hampshire are nearly 10,000 strong, and that he continues to receive re-enforcements.

As yet General Loring has not arrived, and as he has not reported to me the strength of his command I am unable to give it, except by estimate based upon the number of his regiments. According to this estimate I suppose my entire volunteer command, exclusive of McDonald's cavalry, will, after General Loring's regiments, now *en route* for this place, arrive, amount to 7,500. But it must be borne in mind that the accessions from the Army of the Northwest are not well drilled, having passed the present campaign in the mountains, where the opportunities for drilling were very limited.

As I have reason to believe that the enemy has been re-enforced more rapidly than I have been, and as additional re-enforcements are expected, and they already outnumber me, I would respectfully urge upon the commanding general of the department the importance of sending me at once 5,000 good infantry and the First Virginia Cavalry, or its equivalent, and also a battery of four guns. These forces asked for can be immediately returned to their present stations after the Federal forces shall have been captured or driven out of Hampshire County. It may be thought that I am applying for too many troops; but it is a miserable policy to merely base the estimate for troops on one side for future operations upon the enemy's present strength when he is continually receiving re-enforcements.

It appears to me that General Kelley's true policy would be not to march direct from Romney upon this place, but to move first to Martinsburg, form a junction with General Banks, and then, with their united strength, move on Winchester over a road that presents no very strong defensive positions.

If this place is to be held by us, our true policy, in my opinion, is to attack the enemy in his present position before he receives additional re-enforcements, and especially never to permit a junction of their forces at or near Martinsburg.

There is reason to believe that the recent break in Dam No. 5 will destroy any vestiges of hope that might have been entertained of supplying Washington with Cumberland coal by the Chesapeake and Ohio Canal, and consequently their only prospect of procuring that coal must be the Baltimore and Ohio Railroad, and for this purpose near 25 miles of track west of Harper's Ferry must first be relaid, and this can be done under a much smaller protecting force stationed at Winchester than would be required if distributed along the railroad, and consequently I must anticipate an attempted occupation of this place by the enemy. My present force of 7,500 volunteers, 2,234 militia, and 664 (McDonald's) cavalry is insufficient for defending my position.

General Loring has arrived. He states that the Secretary of War left it optional with him whether to bring his troops from the Monterey line or not, and he has decided not to bring any more of these troops here.

I have given the subject much thought, and as the enemy appears to be continually receiving accessions, and as I may receive no more, it appears to me that my best plan is to attack him at the earliest practicable moment, and accordingly, as soon as the inspection of General Loring's forces shall be finished and the necessary munitions of war procured, I expect to march on the enemy, unless I receive orders to the contrary.

Very respectfully, your obedient servant,

T. J. JACKSON,
Major-General, Commanding Valley District.

HEADQUARTERS VALLEY DISTRICT,
Winchester, Va., December 24, 1861.

General JOSEPH E. JOHNSTON:

GENERAL: In reply to your letter of December 21 I have to state that on inquiry I learn from General Loring that there is no company of Colonel Moore's regiment in Colonel Gilham's regiment.

The regiments now here from Western Virginia are: The Twenty-third Virginia, aggregate 517; Thirty-seventh Virginia, aggregate 846; First Georgia, aggregate 918; Third Arkansas, aggregate 756.

I do not know the names and strength of the other regiments ordered here. As soon as I learn them I will report to you.

Respectfully, your obedient servant,

T. J. JACKSON,
Major-General, Commanding.

HEADQUARTERS VALLEY DISTRICT,
Winchester, Va., December 24, 1861.

Maj. THOMAS G. RHETT,
Asst. Adjt. Gen., Hdqrs. Department of Northern Virginia:

MAJOR: Brig. Gen. W. W. Loring informs me that, in his opinion, the Secretary of War designs his command to continue to be known as

the Army of the Northwest and that he should continue to be its immediate commander. This meets with my approbation, and I respectfully
request that no action be taken upon my former application for him to
command as a division such part of his forces as might be in this district.

I am, major, your obedient servant,

T. J. JACKSON,
Major-General, Commanding.

DUBLIN, *December* 24, 1861.

General S. COOPER, *Adjutant-General C. S. Army:*

The troops are going off rapidly. Neither money nor supplies have
come. Can't they be sent after us? Many of our people are without a
dollar and in great need.

JOHN B. FLOYD,
Brigadier-General, C. S. Army.

SPECIAL ORDERS, }   HEADQUARTERS AQUIA DISTRICT,
No. 203.   }   *December* 24, 1861.

I. Under instructions from the War Department, Col. John M. Brockenbrough, with the Fortieth Virginia Volunteers and Cooke's battery,
is hereby transferred from the Second Brigade, Aquia District, and will
proceed to take post at such point in the Northern Neck as will be most
convenient for its management, control, and defense.

He will assume command over all the forces in the Northern Neck
and will act in concert with Col. George E. Pickett for the defense of
the Rappahannock. He will confer with Maj. R. L. T. Beale, and afford
him every possible aid in the discharge of his duties as provost-marshal.

*   *   *   *   *   *   *

By order of Maj. Gen. T. H. Holmes:

D. H. MAURY,
Assistant Adjutant-General.

HEADQUARTERS,
Centreville, December 25, 1861.

Hon. J. P. BENJAMIN, *Secretary of War:*

SIR: I respectfully transmit herewith for your information a copy of
a letter to-day received from one of our friends in Washington, dated
23d instant, and an extract from another, also from a friend in Washington, dated 22d instant. The preceding part of the second letter is
entirely personal.

Most respectfully, your obedient servant,

J. E. JOHNSTON,
General.

[Inclosures.]

MONDAY MORNING, *December* 23, 1861.

MY DEAR COLONEL: If any confidence whatever can be placed in
anything that is said by those in high authority, an advance of the
Federal (tory) Army of the Potomac will take place between this and

the 5th of next month. Most likely it will take place this week. General Porter told a friend of mine on Saturday that an advance would in all probability be made this week. He also told him that General Burnside's fleet was all in confusion and in a general state of derangement. It is important, however, that you watch both land and water, as it is more than likely that you will be attacked both by land and water. I would advise, under all the circumstances, that you prepare for an attack this week. All of their available force on this side of the river was sent across this morning. Johnson and Etheridge, of Tennessee, are doing all they can to get Yankee thieves into Tennessee and Southwestern Virginia, to burn bridges and mills, store-houses, machine-shops, &c. A large sum of money has been set apart by the Cabinet for that special work. Watch these devils. Keep a sharp lookout for bridge-burners, &c., in every direction. Look out for an advance this week. God be with you. Colonel Thompson has been arrested; letters found on the ducker; poor fellow.

CHARLES R. CABLES.

I inclose letter just received from our friend. Address me with great care hereafter.

CHARLES R. CABLES.

I send several papers. Things are working finely in England. God is with us and no mistake.

Extract.

* * * The visit lasted some time. In the course of it I learned that an advance of McClellan's army is certainly anticipated within the next ten days, and that they wished to get rid of me on account of my daring activity. These were the words. Now, what shall I do? They may be obliged to release me here unconditionally, if at all, but it may be a long time. If I can hurt them by being kept, I will submit cheerfully, because my life belongs to our cause. Tell me what you think. I sent a letter to you by dear Canard, and you had best answer this in the same way.

HEADQUARTERS, Centreville, December 25, 1861.

General S. COOPER, *Adjutant and Inspector General:*

SIR: I respectfully transmit herewith, for the consideration of the War Department, two letters just received from Major-General Jackson.*

It is needless for me to attempt to impress upon the Administration the importance of preventing the reconstruction of the Baltimore and Ohio Railroad in Virginia, which has been increased by the breaking of Dam No. 5, above Williamsport. No one understands this subject better than the President himself.

It is of the utmost importance to us to hold the valley of the Shenandoah, but of greater consequence to hold this point. I cannot, therefore, detach 5,000 men from this army to the Valley District. We are but 15 or 18 miles from the enemy, and almost four times as far from Major-General Jackson. If it is possible to add to the forces under

---

* No inclosures found with original. Reference is probably to Jackson to Rhett, and to Johnston, December 24, pp. 1004, 1005.

Major-General Jackson, I respectfully urge that it may be done. A re-enforcement of 3,000 or 4,000 men would, if it joined to him promptly, make the force under his command strong enough to attack the enemy with confidence.

The enemy's troops beyond the Alleghany lately are supposed to be now with General Kelley. Our own, who lately confronted General Kelley's, might therefore be put under General Jackson, to oppose the same enemies on this side of the Alleghany. The operation proposed by General Jackson will require but a week or two. Troops who are merely in observation might therefore re-enforce him, and after the service he proposes return to their present stations.

If there is a probability of a junction of the troops of Kelley and Banks, General Jackson's plan of attacking the former soon is undoubt-edly most judicious. If it is possible to re-enforce him for such an object, I hope that it will be done.

Most respectfully, your obedient servant,

J. E. JOHNSTON,
General.

CENTREVILLE, *December* 26, 1861.

General D. H. HILL, *Commanding at Leesburg :*

MY DEAR FRIEND : Yours of the 23d* was received yesterday.

In regard to the affair at Dranesville, without being an important dis-aster, it was quite a serious check and rather unfortunate for us. The reports in the papers on our side are substantially correct, I believe. The Yankees, I think, must have understated their loss. We had 43 killed, 143 wounded, and 8 missing. Our troops behaved well ; retired in good order by command, and are anxious to try it again.

Your present position is one of great importance and heavy respon-sibility. I am satisfied that General Johnston and General Beauregard considered themselves and this army fortunate in having the benefit of your services on our extreme left.

In the contemplated rearrangement of brigades it is intended to give you the North Carolina regiments. In the mean time I would say, "Do the work before you"; it is difficult and important ; bide your time; all will be right.

We have rumors of an intended advance of the enemy within a few days; keep a bright eye out. I am not altogether well for a few days past, but will be better, I hope, in a day or two.

Write as often as you can. I am always delighted to hear from you. There were no letters here for you when I received your first note.

Yours, as ever,

G. W. SMITH.

WINCHESTER, VA., *December* 26, 1861.

J. P. BENJAMIN, *Secretary of War :*

DEAR SIR : I had an interview this morning with General T. J. Jack-son, and learned that most of the troops of the enemy who were at the fight on Alleghany Mountain a few days since were now at Romney, and that he was very desirous that the forces on the Alleghany, under

---

* Not found.

the command of Colonel Johnson, should be immediately sent direct to Moorefield, so as to form a junction with his troops when desired. The enemy is doing a great deal of mischief in Hampshire County, and should be driven out as soon as possible, or captured, if convenient.

Jackson mentioned that he had written a letter directed to the Adjutant-General, requesting these troops on the Alleghany to be sent to Moorefield on the 23d instant, in which his wishes are fully set out.

Having called frequently at your department on business, and observed with pleasure your promptness in attending to all calls, I, with the approbation of General Jackson, write to you to request that you will look at General Jackson's letter of the 23d, and, if advisable, adopt his recommendations. Here at Romney the enemy is concentrating all his forces from Western Virginia, leaving, as I am informed, very few troops on Cheat Mountain. Let us without delay meet them with our western forces.

I hope the deep interest I feel in this matter will be sufficient apology for my writing this letter.

With much respect, I am, yours, &c.,

T. S. HAYMOND.

RICHMOND, VA., *December* 26, 1861.

General JOHN B. FLOYD, *Dublin Station, Va.:*

Capt. R. G. Banks, quartermaster, left here yesterday with funds to pay off your command.

S. COOPER,
Adjutant and Inspector General.

ABINGDON, VA., *December* 27, 1861.

General S. COOPER, *Adjutant-General C. S. Army:*

DEAR SIR : I stopped a train to start the regiment of cavalry, which will leave the moment transportation can be gotten. I find a regiment of Virginia volunteers (the Fifty-sixth, Colonel Stuart) encamped near here, under orders, as I hear, for Pound Gap, awaiting transportation, which is slow and difficult to procure. It occurred to me that if the condition of things as represented here were known to the Department the Secretary might order this regiment probably to Bowling Green. If General Marshall is at Paintville, near Prestonburg, Ky., with his command, no force of any consequence can march upon Pound Gap without leaving General Marshall in its rear. A small force holding the gap would be amply sufficient against any band of marauders likely to advance in that direction. This regiment would be a good and efficient one, I judge, for service at Bowling Green. My command is moving well on, and with all possible speed we will be with General Johnston.

I have the honor to be, very respectfully, your obedient servant,

JOHN B. FLOYD,
Brigadier-General, C. S. Army.

[Indorsement.]

DECEMBER 30, 1861.

Respectfully submitted to Secretary of War. Colonel Deas left here this morning for Abingdon, to inspect and hasten forward this regiment

(Fifty-sixth Virginia) and that of Colonel Moore to General Marshall's command, whither they were ordered some time since.

S. COOPER,
Adjutant and Inspector General.

WAR DEPARTMENT, *December* 27, 1861.

Mr. Macfarland had the honor to call at the office of Hon. Mr. Benjamin to submit to him the inclosed letter from Mr. Price, a leading citizen of Greenbrier. From information from other sources there is no doubt the people of the country are apprehensive of another inroad, which is inevitable except it be prevented.

Mr. Macfarland will be obliged to Hon. Mr. Benjamin to be enabled to say to Mr. Price that due provision is made for the defense of the country.

[Inclosure.]

LEWISBURG, *December* 21, 1861.

WM. H. MACFARLAND, Esq.:

MY DEAR SIR: When I was in Richmond I called on the Secretary of War, and remonstrated against the withdrawal of all the troops from the Greenbrier country. The Secretary regarded the idea of an invasion by the Federal Army during the winter as absurd, upon the ground that it could not travel here on account of the badness of the roads, nor subsist if even it could reach here. He, however, said that he would "leave," "keep," or "send" here—I do not know which word he used—a sufficient mounted force to keep off raids if attempted by a force of from 20 to 100 persons. When I returned home I found the troops all leaving, and they finally all went away, not leaving a single man. You may under this state of circumstances imagine our intense concern—an army of several thousand at Gauley Bridge and 1,000 at Nicholas Court-House able and ready to approach us, without the means on our part of the slightest resistance. The Secretary had failed to "leave" or "send" a single man here, thereby making the impression upon the minds of many of our people that we were intentionally given up to the tender mercies of the enemy, but wherefore no one could tell.

On Tuesday evening last the enemy accordingly made his appearance in our county on your farm in force, varying, from information, from 150 to 300 strong. The first account we had of him was that Mr. Valk's house had been surrounded during the night and the inmates captured, not, however, including Mr. Valk or his family. He was, and I believe they were, away. Next, that they had encamped on your farm, and were still there committing depredations. A remnant of a cavalry company from Henrico, commanded by Captain Magruder, numbering about 30, which had recently passed on east, was sent for, and overtaken at or near the White Sulphur Springs. It returned here on Wednesday night, and Captain Morris' company of infantry, numbering about the same, also came back. On Thursday morning they, with such other volunteers as could be hastily collected and were willing to go, started in pursuit of the enemy. They found he had left your farm about the time the troops left Lewisburg on his way back to Nicholas. Some of the mounted men pursued him and overtook him, but for the want of an adequate force or something else he escaped them. It grieves me to think of it.

One hundred of your best sheep, your two-year-old cattle, oxen, horses, and mules, including your fine young stud-horse, were carried off. Other property, from perhaps Crallis Valk and Andrew Burns, was also taken, amounting in all to several thousand dollars' worth. Your house and furniture I understand were not injured, nor were your slaves taken away, because I understand one of them said they declined to go. Where the next raid is to be committed I cannot tell. The success of this one will inspire others.

Why is the whole of Western Virginia to be given up? Is Virginia too large in this scale of States? Is there any real desire to have Virginia dissevered and the west given over to the Federals? I am pained to think of the treatment which we have received. A small force would have prevented this humiliating result, but now the bloodhounds having fleshed their fangs it will take an army to prevent the recurrence of a like event. We must move away from our homes and give up all we possess, or be subject to the invasions and insults of these robbers.

Very truly and respectfully, yours, &c.,

SAML. PRICE.

WAR DEPARTMENT, C. S. A.,
Richmond, December 27, 1861.

General JOSEPH E. JOHNSTON,
Comdg. Department of Northern Virginia, Centreville, Va.:

SIR: I am informed by a letter from S. T. Stewart, agent Confederate States, Thoroughfare, Va., to Major Blair, Confederate States, forwarded to the Commissary General, that it is reported by J. H. Myers, agent of the commissary department for the valley, that parties near Mount Jackson and Strasburg are refusing to sell the grain, &c., necessary for the subsistence of the Government cattle and hogs purchased for the supply of the Army, except at exorbitant prices. This state of things should not be tolerated. Our Army must be fed. The supplies necessary for this purpose must be had, and those who refuse to sell them to the Government at fair and reasonable rates cannot be regarded as true friends of our cause. You are, therefore, requested to issue orders requiring the impressment of such supplies, wherever the owners refuse to dispose of them at fair market value in Confederate money. It is hoped, however, that the knowledge that such orders have been issued will prevent the necessity of executing them, otherwise the exigencies of our Army demand that they be promptly enforced.

Respectfully, your obedient servant,

J. P. BENJAMIN,
Secretary of War.

WAR DEPARTMENT, C. S. A.,
Richmond, December 27, 1861.

General JOSEPH E. JOHNSTON,
Commanding Department Northern Virginia:

SIR: The Adjutant-General has, in conformity with the request of General W. H. C. Whiting, placed his letter of the 19th instant * before the President, and I am instructed by him to make reply as follows:

The President has read with grave displeasure the very insubordinate letter of General Whiting, in which he indulges in presumptuous censure

---

* Not found.

of the orders of his commander-in-chief, and tenders unasked advice to his superiors in command. The President does not desire to force on Brigadier-General Whiting the command of the brigade which had been assigned to him and which it was supposed he would feel honored in accepting, and you are requested to issue an order relieving Brigadier-General Whiting of the command of a brigade of five Mississippi regiments as assigned to him by General Orders, Nos. 15 and 18, issued from this Department.

As there is no other brigade in the Army of the Potomac not already provided with a commander under the general orders of the Department, the services of Brigadier-General Whiting will no longer be needed for the command of troops. The President therefore further requests that Maj. W. H. C. Whiting, of the Engineer Corps of the Confederate States, be directed by your order to report for duty as engineer to Major-General Jackson, of the Valley District, where the services of this able engineer will be very useful to the Army.

In conclusion, the President requests me to say that he trusts you will hereafter decline to forward to him communications of your subordinates having so obvious a tendency to excite a mutinous and disorganizing spirit in the Army.

I am, very respectfully, your obedient servant,

J. P. BENJAMIN,
Secretary of War.

WAR DEPARTMENT, C. S. A.,
Richmond, December 27, 1861.

General JOSEPH E. JOHNSTON,
Commanding Department of Northern Virginia :

SIR : The President has received several communications from officers of regiments on your extreme right (including the Eleventh Mississippi Regiment), from which it seems that they anticipate being disturbed in their winter quarters by the effect of the General Orders, Nos. 15 and 18. The President desires me to say to you that he has not required and does not expect those troops to be disturbed in their winter quarters; he simply renews his oft-repeated request that the three regiments of Mississippians that were at Leesburg prior to General Griffith's arrival there be sent to join the two hitherto under General Whiting. These five regiments being assigned to General Van Dorn's division on the right, he knows no reason why they should not remain at the present headquarters of General Whiting's brigade, without disturbing the winter quarters of any of the regiments now under General Whiting. If the winter quarters of any of the troops are disturbed, the President must regret this unfortunate result, not of his orders, but of the unusual delay which has supervened in their execution, and which he could not have anticipated.

Your obedient servant,

J. P. BENJAMIN,
Secretary of War.

HEADQUARTERS, *Evansport, December 30,* 1861.

General S. COOPER,
Adjutant and Inspector General, Richmond, Va.:

SIR: Since the withdrawal of Colonel Fagan's First Arkansas Regiment and the Fourteenth Alabama Regiment, Colonel Judge, from my brigade, I am left here with the following troops as a repelling force near the batteries:

Twenty-second North Carolina Regiment: To-day, privates present for duty, including a company in the battery, 471.

Thirty-fifth Georgia Regiment: To-day, privates present for duty, 259.

Arkansas battalion: To-day, privates present for duty, 42.

This is the infantry force here to do the labor on the batteries and to furnish the guard at night, which should be half a regiment.

To guard the river between the Chopawamsic and Aquia Creek I have one fine regiment, the Second Tennessee (and a very weak one), the Forty-seventh Virginia, one battery of artillery, and one company of cavalry.

Two regiments, as stated, are withdrawn from my force here at hand in rear of the batteries, and I beg that other regiments be sent to me here to replace them. I ask it for this reason: The batteries as yet are entirely open in rear, except a weak picket-fence around part of No. 1 Battery, and in front, an extent of a mile between the Quantico and the Chopawamsic, there is no obstacle, natural or artificial, that can obstruct a landing except the guards. An enemy landing here or near here would rush immediately to the accomplishment of his object—the capture of the guns—and must be met instantly. Hence the force must be at hand. Landing at any other point, no such immediate object to accomplish, he would wait an attack, and it would be but the gradual meeting of opposite forces. My situation is different, requiring an immediate repelling force to act instantly.

You will further perceive that for the labor to be performed in strengthening the works by shelters and ditches, and the large guards at night required on the river front, the force is inadequate, and, considering the constant annoyance day and night from the enemy, no troops in this Confederacy are as unpleasantly situated.

Very respectfully, your obedient servant,

S. G. FRENCH,
Brigadier-General, Commanding.

P. S.—Night before last a steamer shelled the Cockpit battery; also this morning before daylight, this forenoon, and again this evening, assuming a position that the guns mounted could not reach him, and which point is to be defended by the Tredegar gun, just arrived.

[Indorsements.]

HEADQUARTERS, *Brooke's Station, December* 31, 1861.

General JOHNSTON, *Commanding Department:*

The Fourteenth Alabama Regiment, ordered to Richmond by the War Department from Evansport, belonged to General Whiting's command, and I have requested him to replace it with another. If he cannot do so conveniently, General French should recall one of the regiments under his command from the south of the Chopawamsic, one being ample for the service there. If the enemy should appear at any point below Aquia, every soldier in this vicinity would be required to prevent his landing.

Respectfully forwarded.

TH. H. HOLMES,
Major-General.

HEADQUARTERS, *Centreville, January* 2, 1862.

Respectfully forwarded. The removal of the Arkansas regiment from Evansport to replace one sent into the Northern Neck was, I understood from Major-General Holmes, made under the instructions of the War Department, and therefore beyond my control. I respectfully recommend that those regiments return to their former positions. The force near Evansport and Dumfries is now far too weak.

J. E. JOHNSTON,
General.

HEADQUARTERS, *Centreville, December* 30, 1861.

Hon. J. P. BENJAMIN, *Secretary of War:*

SIR: I respectfully ask your attention to an article in the Richmond Dispatch of this morning, by "Bohemian." [Copy following.]

The information it contains would be very valuable to the enemy, such as he would pay for liberally. I cannot suppose it innocently published. The author's name is Shepardson or Shepherdson, styled Doctor. I respectfully suggest his arrest. He is now in Richmond. I ascertained this fact by attempting yesterday to have him found, on account of a previous letter in the same paper. Could not the editor of the paper be included in the accusation?

Most respectfully, your obedient servant,

J. E. JOHNSTON,
General.

MANASSAS, *December* 27.

To-day our whole army is engaged in building log houses for winter quarters or in moving to sites already selected. Several brigades will remain where they now are, near the fortifications in Centreville, and the remainder will fall back a mile or two upon Bull Run. General Kirby Smith's brigade is at Camp Wigfall, to the right of the Orange and Alexandria road, near the run. Near by the whole of Van Dorn's division are making themselves comfortable in their little cottages, which rise rapidly day by day under diligent hands of the soldiers. A few brigades are scattered down towards the Occoquan, where wood and water is plenty, the farthest being by Davis' Ford. The artillery, with the exception of Walton's battalion, has already been located between Cub Run and Stone Bridge. The cavalry has fallen back a little and they are now building stables and houses near Centreville.

General Stuart will remain in the advance. It is probable that General Johnston will occupy the Lewis House, on the battle-field, and General Beauregard Wier's, his old headquarters. Before the 18th and 21st Longstreet's division will, if I am correctly informed, occupy the advanced position, and will remain near where it is at present.

The artillerists detailed to man the guns in the battery will also remain by the fortifications. In case of an attack by the Yankees it will take about two hours to get the main strength of the army across Bull Run. Information of an approach would be given at least two hours before an enemy could come up, and in that time we could be well prepared to resist any force that can be brought up.

That is about the situation of affairs for the winter, and it remains to be seen whether our men are to have an opportunity of a brush with the Yankees or whether they will be allowed to enjoy their new houses in quietness. When I say all are ready for an attack, I express but feebly the feeling which pervades the army.

*   *   *   *   *   *   *

BOHEMIAN.

Abstract from return of the Department of Northern Virginia, commanded by General Joseph E. Johnston, C. S. Army, for the month of December, 1861.

Commands.	Present for duty.						Effective total.	Aggregate present.	Aggregate present and absent.	Pieces of artillery.
	Infantry.		Cavalry.		Artillery.					
	Officers.	Men.	Officers.	Men.	Officers.	Men.				
Potomac District:										
First Corps............	1,123	16,554	33	584	63	1,279	*19,853	24,914	31,155	......
Second Corps.........	882	12,815	11	233	27	568	†14,543	18,301	22,132	38
Reserve Division.	416	6,428	......	....	7	170	7,163	8,278	10,139	12
Cavalry Brigade......	....	....	185	2,200	......	......	2,430	3,006	3,793	......
Artillery Corps.......	....	....	......	....	30	540	574	660	828	......
Total Potomac District........	2,421	35,795	229	3,017	127	2,557	44,563	55,165	68,047	50
Aquia District..........	400	5,418	31	400	23	439	6,597	8,244	10,050	30
Valley District	746	9,236	40	571	22	424	10,952	12,922	19,953	29
Grand total.......	3,567	50,451	300	3,988	172	3,420	62,112	76,331	98,050	109

Notes from original return :
* Effective total (2,770) near Leesburg, under Brigadier-General Hill, to be deducted.
† Effective total (7,601) near Dumfries, to be deducted.

HEADQUARTERS, *Centreville, January* 1, 1862.

Hon. J. P. BENJAMIN, *Secretary of War:*

SIR: I had the honor to receive this morning your letter of the 27th ultimo, conveying the President's orders in relation to Brigadier-General Whiting.

I beg to be allowed to intercede in this case, partly because this officer's services as brigadier-general are very important to this army, and partly because I also share the wrong. I am confident that he has in his heart neither insubordination nor disrespect. Had I returned the letter to him, pointing out the objectionable language in it, it would, I doubt not, have been promptly corrected. I regret very much that in my carelessness it was not done. No one is less disposed than I to be instrumental in putting before the President a paper offensive in its character.

Brigadier-General Whiting has a very important command—that of the troops near Evansport and on the Lower Occoquan ; is a soldier of high ability ; has studied his situation and circumstances ; his removal now might be unfortunate should the enemy attack before his successor had equally qualified himself for that command. The only officers who can be intrusted with it are in command of divisions from which they cannot be taken. I therefore beg the President to pass over this matter.

Should the President adhere to his decision, I respectfully ask that his orders may be so far modified as to place this "able engineer" on duty in this department, instead of in one of its districts. Major

Stevens has been unfit for duty for several months, and is not likely to recover soon. A skillful officer of that corps would be of great value to this army.

Most respectfully, your obedient servant,

J. E. JOHNSTON,
General.

GENERAL ORDERS, }   ADJT. AND INSP. GEN.'S OFFICE,
No. 1.   }   *Richmond, January* 1, 1862.

I. The following act of Congress, with regulations of the Secretary of War thereupon, are published for the information of the Army:

AN ACT providing for the granting of bounty and furloughs to privates and non-commissioned officers in the Provisional Army.

SECTION 1. *The Congress of the Confederate States of America do enact,* That a bounty of fifty dollars be, and the same is hereby, granted to all privates, musicians, and non-commissioned officers in the Provisional Army who shall serve continuously for three years or for the war, to be paid at the following times, to wit: To all now in the service for twelve months, to be paid at the time of volunteering or enlisting for the next two ensuing years subsequent to the expiration of their present term of service. To all now in the service for three years or for the war, to be paid at the expiration of their first year's service. To all who may hereafter volunteer or enlist for three years or for the war, to be paid at the time of entry into service.

SEC. 2. *And be it further enacted,* That furloughs, not exceeding sixty days, with transportation home and back, shall be granted to all twelve-months' men now in service who shall, prior to the expiration of their present term of service, volunteer or enlist for the next two ensuing years subsequent to the expiration of their present term of service, or for three years, or the war. Said furloughs to be issued at such times and in such numbers as the Secretary of War may deem most compatible with the public interest, the length of each furlough being regulated with reference to the distance of each volunteer from his home: *Provided,* That in lieu of a furlough the commutation value in money of the transportation hereinabove granted shall be paid to each volunteer, musician, or non-commissioned officer who may elect to receive it at such time as the furlough itself would otherwise be granted.

SEC. 3. This act shall apply to all troops who have volunteered or enlisted for a term of twelve months or more in the service of any State, who are now in the service of the said State, and who may hereafter volunteer or enlist in the service of the Confederate States under the provisions of the present act.

SEC. 4. *And be it further enacted,* That all troops revolunteering or re-enlisting shall, at the expiration of their present term of service, have the power to reorganize themselves into companies and elect their company officers; and said companies shall have the power to organize themselves into battalions or regiments and elect their field officers; and after the first election all vacancies shall be filled by promotion from the company, battalion, or regiment in which such vacancies may occur: *Provided,* That whenever a vacancy shall occur, whether by promotion or otherwise, in the lowest grade of commissioned officers of a company, said vacancy shall always be filled by election: *And provided further,* That in the case of troops which have been regularly enlisted into the service of any particular State prior to the formation of the Confederacy, and which have by such State been turned over to the Confederate Government, the officers shall not be elected, but appointed and promoted in the same manner and by the same authority as they have heretofore been appointed and promoted.

Approved December 11, 1861.

II. Captains or commanding officers of twelve-months' men will, under direction of regimental and battalion commanders, make out duplicate muster rolls of their companies, noting opposite the name of each man desiring to renew his enlistment for two years from the expiration of his present term of service the following remark, " Enlistment extended for two years; bounty due, $50," inserting the date of the remark.

As soon as the intention of each man is thus ascertained, report will be made to the commanding officer of the army in which the troops are serving. The commanding officer will thereupon cause his inspector-generals, or other officers assigned for that purpose, to verify the rolls, and muster into service for said additional term all that are fitted for service. One of the rolls thus verified, and certified by the inspecting officers, will be sent to the adjutant and inspector general. The other will be given to the company commander, from which to make out further muster rolls.

III. Whenever the number of men in a company who re-enlist shall suffice to form a new company according to the number required by law, the men thus re-enlisted shall have the right immediately to reorganize themselves into a company and elect their company officers, remaining attached to the regiment or battalion to which they belong until the expiration of the twelve months of the original enlistment.

IV. If the number of men re-enlisted in any company be insufficient to form a new company, their original organization will be preserved until within twenty days of the expiration of their term, at which date all the twelve-months' men who have re-enlisted will proceed to organize themselves afresh into new companies and elect their company officers.

V. Whenever all the companies now forming a battalion or regiment shall have reorganized themselves into new companies, they shall have the right of reorganizing themselves at once into a new battalion or regiment, as the case may be, electing their field officers, as allowed by law. But if any one company of any battalion or regiment declines to reorganize itself, the present organization will remain until within twenty days of the expiration of the present term, at which time all re-enlisted companies will proceed immediately to organize themselves into new regiments and elect their field officers, as provided by law.

VI. All re-enlisted companies which may fail within the last twenty days of their present term to reorganize themselves into regiments or battalions will be considered as independent companies re-enlisted for the war, and will be organized into battalions or regiments by the President, and their field officers appointed by him in the same manner as is provided by law for all other independent companies.

VII. The furlough allowed by law, and directed to be regulated according to the distance of each volunteer from his home, is established as follows, viz: To each volunteer there will be allowed a furlough of full thirty days at home, to which will be added by the commanding officer of the army a number of days estimated to be sufficient to allow the volunteer to travel home and back. But in no case will the furlough exceed sixty days, even for those most distant from their homes.

VIII. Commanding officers are directed to commence as soon as possible granting the furloughs allowed as above in such numbers as may be deemed compatible with the safety of their commands, giving preference, as far as practicable, to the men in the order of their re-enlistment.

IX. The bounty of $50 will be paid to each man when he receives his furlough, at which time his transportation also will be furnished.

X. Each man entitled to furlough may receive instead thereof the commutation value of his transportation in addition to the bounty of $50 provided by law.*

By order of the Secretary of War :

S. COOPER,
Adjutant and Inspector General.

---

* This order inserted here because of correspondence resulting therefrom between General Johnston and the Richmond authorities. (See Johnston to Benjamin, January 18; Benjamin to Johnston, January 25; and Johnston to Benjamin, February 1; and to Cooper, February 3; Benjamin to Johnston, February 3; and General Johnston's order of February 4, *post.*)

HEADQUARTERS VALLEY DISTRICT,
Unger's Store, Morgan County, Virginia, January 2, 1862.

General JOSEPH E. JOHNSTON,
Commanding Department of Northern Virginia:

MY DEAR GENERAL: Yours of the 31st ultimo is at hand, and tends to confirm information previously received by me that an advance was to be made on Winchester by forces from Reynolds and Banks. I am taking a position such as to prevent their junction without giving me an opportunity of striking a blow at one of them previously, should circumstances justify it.

To-morrow I hope to recover Bath, and before leaving Morgan I desire to drive the enemy out of this county and destroy the railroad bridge which has been recently constructed across the Big Cacapon. Reynolds' forces in and about Romney are estimated at about 18,000, but I think this is too large; yet I fear that it is true. At last advices General Banks' headquarters were at Fredericktown, but he has had ample time to change them since.

Very truly, your friend,

T. J. JACKSON,
[Major-General, Commanding Valley District.]

HEADQUARTERS,
Brooke's Station, January 2, 1862.

General S. COOPER, *Adjutant-General:*

GENERAL: The two regiments withdrawn from Evansport were Colonel Judge's Fourteenth Alabama and Colonel Fagan's First Arkansas, the latter some time ago, to replace Brockenbrough's, sent to the Northern Neck. The Fourteenth Alabama belonged to General Whiting's command, and I have requested him to send another to replace it. I would send one from here, but am fearful that Burnside's expedition will land below here for the purpose of marching on Fredericksburg, when the five regiments that are in this neighborhood would scarcely be able to hold him in check until re-enforcements could arrive. In the mean time I do not think the batteries are in danger, as General French has four regiments at his disposal and Whiting in easy supporting distance.

I sincerely hope you will excuse the liberty I am about to take in asking you to issue at your earliest convenience the order relative to enlistments under the new law. The troops now are in good spirits and many disposed to re-enlist, but there is a system of electioneering going on, under the belief that any man who can raise a company by re-enlistments is authorized to do so, that will result in heart-burnings and discontent. This will be avoided if the plan of furnishing each company with rolls and re-enlistments on them to be confined to the company be carried out. In this way the officers and men going on furlough will know the number of men they require to complete their reorganization, and will exert themselves to bring back from their homes the number necessary to fill the places of those who refuse to re-enlist.

I am, general, very respectfully, your obedient servant,

TH. H. HOLMES,
Major-General, Commanding District.

Memorandum for the War Department from notes received from Washington by Colonel Jordan yesterday.

(Received January 4, 1862.)

The first, dated December 28, according to which Kelley is to advance on Winchester, Stone and Banks on Leesburg, McClellan on Centreville, and Burnside's flotilla to attack the batteries. This to occur this week, and an aide-de-camp of McClellan, and Fox, of the Navy Department, the authorities.

The second, dated December 30, states that the outside pressure will force McClellan forward either this or next week; supposes he is waiting for Burnside's fleet.

The third, without date, is headed "From very high sources": "Kelley advances on Romney; Burnside's fleet against the batteries; Stone and Banks cross and advance on Leesburg. McClellan and all round Washington are to push on to Centreville. McClellan's aide-de-camp said that if the general were well enough the move would be made next week, and simultaneous ones in Kentucky and Missouri. Puts the force about Washington at from 150,000 to 300,000. Fox said Fort Pulaski would be attacked by land and water in ten days. They will make an attempt to pass the Potomac batteries in force soon."

The fourth is headed "Valuable information." The Pensacola frigate, armed with the largest Dahlgren guns, is under orders to proceed down the Potomac, with other gunboats, to force the batteries on the Virginia side. The Burnside expedition at Annapolis is also about ready, and is believed to be under orders for the Potomac, to co-operate with the expedition from Alexandria and Washington via the Potomac and Pohick Church. Reynolds has superseded Kelley at Romney. Rosecrans is in Washington. McClellan to move upon Manassas and Reynolds upon Winchester simultaneously with the attack on the batteries. This dated 28th December.

The four papers are in different handwriting. I don't know the writers.

Respectfully submitted.

J. E. JOHNSTON,
General.

[Inclosure.]

[Extract from National Intelligencer—date not known.]

General Burnside is awaiting the arrival of gunboats and transports at Annapolis. Sixteen transports, four schooners, and five floating batteries are already there. The naval rendezvous will be at Old Point Comfort, and it is said that Captain Goldsborough is assigned to the command.

Brig. Gen. J. J. Reynolds has been ordered to supersede General Kelley, and is expected to leave Indiana in a few days. The Thirteenth Indiana, Colonel Sullivan, and Fourteenth Indiana, Colonel Kimball, have gone forward to Romney from Cheat Mountain.

HEADQUARTERS FIRST CORPS, ARMY OF THE POTOMAC,
Centreville, Va., January 4, 1862.
Brig. Gen. D. H. HILL,
Commanding C. S. Forces in Loudoun County, Leesburg, Va.:

GENERAL: I send you herewith a telegram received this day from the War Department. It indicates a movement on the part of the enemy, to what point we are not yet informed, but probably to attack the batteries on the Potomac, which have so much inconvenienced him at Washington. The other movements of the enemy will probably be as supposed when you were here. If so, we still hope for a brilliant success, although so much inferior to him in numbers and equipments; but we will have to make up in rapidity of movement and concentration of forces for our inferiority in other respects.

It would be well to keep your command on the alert, and ready to move, if necessary, as already instructed. But if the works you are constructing could hold in check a large part of Banks' command until you could return to their assistance, you might leave to defend them a part of your forces and the militia of Loudoun County. The guns you called for have been asked and promised, I am informed, but I am unable to state when you will get them.

Hoping that our efforts will again meet with success, I remain, very respectfully, your obedient servant,

G. T. BEAUREGARD,
General Commanding.

[Inclosure.]

RICHMOND, *January* 3, 1862.

General JOSEPH E. JOHNSTON:

The following telegram is just received from Norfolk, Va.:

In Hampton Roads are fourteen steam gunboats; four steam ferry-boats, four guns each; three small tugs, one gun each; one large steam frigate; one large and one small sloop of war; four large barges, two with one gun each; eight large steam transports; twenty-six schooners, two brigs, and one bark. All the steamers have steam up.

S. COOPER,
Adjutant and Inspector General.

WAR DEPARTMENT, C. S. A.,
Richmond, Va., January 5, 1862.

Major-General HOLMES, *Aquia Creek, Virginia:*

SIR: The Thirty-fifth Georgia Regiment is represented to me to be in almost as bad a condition as the Alabama regiment of Colonel Judge, which I was compelled to order here in order to give them a chance of recruiting their strength, after going through the usual camp diseases.

I cannot further weaken your command, but humanity requires that I should try some way to prevent suffering and mortality among these troops just called from a southern clime and weakened by disease. Without, therefore, wishing in any way to interfere with any of the details of your command, I beg you will try, as far as you possibly can, to relieve this regiment from exposure and picket duty till the men have well recovered from the effects of the measles and other camp maladies.

Yours, respectfully,

J. P. BENJAMIN,
Secretary of War.

WAR DEPARTMENT, C. S. A.,
Richmond, Va., January 5, 1862.

General JOSEPH E. JOHNSTON, *Centreville, Va.:*

SIR: Your letters of the 30th ultimo and 1st instant have been received.

1st. The President, to whom I submitted the latter, declines making any change in his former order relative to Major Whiting.

2d. On the subject of the publication in the Richmond Dispatch of two articles signed "Bohemian," I share your indignation at such an outrageous breach of duty of both the writer and publisher. I have anxiously sought for some means of punishing the offense, but the state of the law is such as to give no remedy for this wrong through the courts of justice, and I have appealed to the Military Committee of Congress for some legislation to protect the Army and the country against the great evils resulting from such publications. Judge Harris, the chairman of the committee, has promised to report a bill for the purpose.

In this connection allow me to say that I think some of the mischief from this too-frequent offense arises from your own too lenient toleration of the presence of newspaper reporters within your lines. I will do all I can to help you, but the application of military regulations within the Army will be much more efficacious than any attempt at punishment by jury trial. I feel persuaded that this man Shepardson is a spy, and would be found guilty as such by a court-martial; and if he is caught again within your camp I trust you will bring him to prompt trial as a spy. But if I arrest him here he will at once be liberated by habeas corpus, and I will be unable to secure his proper punishment. His offense is a military one and ought to be summarily repressed by a military trial.

I beg also to call your attention to a practice that is becoming too prevalent, of sending here prisoners arrested on suspicion of being disloyal. I have no means of enforcing their confinement, and am compelled to discharge them as fast as they come, or the judges would certainly do it by habeas corpus. But military commanders have the right to arrest and keep in confinement all dangerous or suspected persons prowling about their camps. It is, I know, a little troublesome to be burdened with this class of prisoners in camp, but I see nothing else that can be done with them. They come here without definite charges against them; without any proof or witnesses, and I am utterly powerless to hold them for you. I can only, therefore, urge upon you a stricter and less lenient application of military law as the sole resource I see for repressing this growing mischief.

I am, your obedient servant,

J. P. BENJAMIN,
Secretary of War.

HEADQUARTERS FIRST CORPS, ARMY OF THE POTOMAC,
Near Centreville, January 6, 1862.

Brig. Gen. D. H. HILL, *Commanding C. S. Forces, Leesburg:*

GENERAL: Your letter of this date has been received and communicated to the general commanding, whose instructions in the premises are the following:

You are not expected to hold the works under construction, unless all three of them shall, at the time of the emergency, be so far completed as to satisfy you that they are defensible for about a week with, say, one regiment of your forces and such local volunteer troops and militia as you can muster meanwhile. There must not be an attempt to hold the works on the eve of an assault or investment before they are in a tenable condition.

An effort will be made to send an engineer to you, also a competent artillery officer.

Respectfully, your obedient servant,

THOMAS JORDAN,
Assistant Adjutant-General.

GENERAL ORDERS, }   ADJT. AND INSP. GEN.'S OFFICE,
No. 2.   }   *Richmond, January 6, 1862.*

I. The following act of Congress and regulations in reference thereto are published for the information of the Army:

AN ACT for the recruiting service of the Provisional Army of the Confederate States..

SECTION 1. *The Congress of the Confederate States do enact,* That the Secretary of War be, and he is hereby, authorized to adopt measures for recruiting and enlisting men for companies for service in the war or three years, which by the casualties of the service have been reduced by death and discharges.

SEC. 2. *And be it further enacted,* That the Secretary of War be, and he is hereby, authorized to detail the company commissioned officers for the above duty, in such numbers and at such times as in his opinion will best comport with the public service. The officers thus appointed to enlist and recruit for their respective companies.

Approved December 19, 1861.

II. Commanding officers of all war regiments, battalions, squadrons, and independent companies will detail for recruiting service, subject to approval of the commanding officer of the army with which they are serving, a subaltern and a non-commissioned officer or private from each war company below the minimum organization, with instructions to proceed to the neighborhood where his company was raised, and there enlist recruits to raise the company to the maximum organization.

III. Officers detailed for recruiting service will make requisitions on the Adjutant-General for recruiting funds, reporting the station to which they have been ordered, the company and regiment for which they have been directed to recruit, and post-town, county, and State to which letters for them should be addressed. A similar report should also be made to the Commissary and Quartermaster's Departments, in order that the required instructions may issue to the proper officers of these departments to fill the requisitions necessary for such recruiting purposes.

IV. As soon as possible after the enlistment of a recruit, he shall be inspected by a commissioned surgeon of the Confederate States, and, if unfit for service, shall be rejected. In all cases this inspection shall take place before the recruit leaves the State in which he is enlisted.

V. A commutation for rations, at the rate of twenty-five cents per ration, shall be allowed to each recruit from the date of his enlistment until he is supplied regularly with subsistence by an officer of the Commissary Department.

VI. No clothing or commutation for clothing will be allowed a recruit until after inspection. As soon as possible after inspection and muster, the recruit will be supplied with clothing or commutation therefor by the nearest quartermaster, in accordance with regulations.

VII. The time allowed for recruiting will in no case extend beyond thirty days; at the expiration whereof the recruiting party with the enlisted men will proceed to join their company.

VIII. Officers in charge of recruiting parties will keep a strict account of the disbursements made by them of moneys placed in their hands for the recruiting service, taking duplicate receipts for every item of expenditure. One set of these receipts will be retained by the officer for his security; the other set, with an account-current, will at the expiration of the recruiting term be transmitted to the Adjutant and Inspector General for final settlement at the Treasury. These vouchers and accounts-current, addressed to the Adjutant and Inspector General, will be marked on the upper right-hand corner of the envelope which covers them, "Recruiting service."*

By command of the Secretary of War:

S. COOPER,
Adjutant and Inspector General.

WAR DEPARTMENT, C. S. A.,
Richmond, Va., January 7, 1862.

General JOSEPH E. JOHNSTON, *Centreville, Va.:*

SIR: A letter from Brigadier-General French, of the 30th ultimo, with indorsements of General Holmes and yourself, has been received and submitted to the President.

The withdrawal of the Arkansas regiment was not, as you suppose, "made under the instructions of this Department" to a request of General Holmes on the subject. He was authorized, by a reply of the 16th ultimo, to move a regiment of his command to the Northern Neck "as soon as, in his opinion, it could be done with safety to his command." The reduction of the force under General French, arising from the withdrawal of this regiment (as well as of Colonel Judge's Alabama regiment, totally disabled by sickness), renders it necessary, in the opinion of the President, to strengthen that important position by a detail from your center, as there are no re-enforcements here that can be sent to Evansport. As soon as Colonel Judge's regiment is recovered from its present deplorable condition it will be returned to you, and as commander of the Department of Northern Virginia you have, of course, the power to recall from the Northern Neck the regiment sent there, if in your opinion the safety of your command requires it.

The President has ordered Brigadier-General Wayne, from Georgia, to assume command of a brigade of Georgians; and as there are only thirteen Virginia regiments in your army, already provided with three Virginia brigadiers, he does not deem it now necessary to appoint another Virginia brigadier.

The delay in organizing your army under General Orders, Nos. 15 and 18, has embarrassed me in providing the brigadier-generals appropriate to its several brigades, in accordance with the act of Congress directing that they should be assigned as far as possible according to States, and I have to request of you a statement of your present organization, indicating the separate brigade commands with the designation of the regiments comprised in each, so as to guide the Executive in selecting any additional generals that may be requisite from the States entitled to such additional nominations.

Your obedient servant,

J. P. BENJAMIN,
Secretary of War.

---

* Inserted here because of resulting correspondence between General Johnston and the Richmond authorities.

HEADQUARTERS FORTY-FIFTH VIRGINIA REGIMENT,
Camp Thorn Spring, near Dublin Depot, January 7, 1862.

Hon. J. P. BENJAMIN, *Secretary of War, C. S. A.:*

SIR: As you were advised in a dispatch from this place a few days since, I sent two scouts, with instructions to proceed to Pack's Ferry, where it was reported the enemy in some force were crossing. They have returned, and report that a few of the enemy had crossed at that point and proceeded some distance (probably 10 or 12 miles) on the road to Peterstown. They were, however, driven back by a number of the citizens of Giles and Monroe.

The information which will be communicated to your excellency through the letter which I have the honor to forward you is confirmed by reports of refugees from the county of Raleigh. The strength of the enemy at Fayetteville and Raleigh County is given by intelligent persons from that section at 3,000. The forward movement of the enemy to Raleigh Court-House in any force is very recent, and I feel confident that they have in contemplation an advance upon this road.

Deeming it proper to give you the above information, I have the honor to remain, very respectfully, your obedient servant,

WILLIAM E. PETERS,
Lieutenant-Colonel Commanding Forty-fifth Virginia Regiment.

[Inclosures.]

DUBLIN, *January 6, 1862.*

Lieutenant-Colonel PETERS:

DEAR SIR: Inclosed I send you a letter I have just received from Lieut. Col. Joseph Caldwell, of Raleigh County, giving information of the movements of the enemy.

Respectfully,

WM. H. HOWE.

MERCER COURT-HOUSE, VA., *January 3, 1862.*

Mr. WM. H. HOWE:

DEAR SIR: I am a citizen of the county of Raleigh, residing near the Court-House, and have been driven from home with a good many other citizens of the county. Having just arrived here from that county, the citizens of this village think it proper that the fact of the invasion of that county by the Federal troops should be made known, so that the citizens of the counties between that place and the railroad may adopt some policy to repel their intended raid upon the Virginia and Tennessee Railroad. Hence I am troubling you with this note, that the people may have time to organize for their own protection.

After repeated visits by the enemy in small forces, and committing depredations wherever they went by stealing property (cattle, horses, &c.) and arresting citizens pursuing their usual avocations, forcing them to take the oath or taking them to Fayetteville and holding them in confinement, on last Monday, the 30th day of December last, our village was taken possession of by at least 1,000 Federal troops, arresting the citizens that were remaining and compelling them to take the oath, or holding them prisoners. They are robbing the citizens of all their property, grain, provender, &c., leaving the families of those that have had to flee from their persecutions entirely dependent and helpless. Holding a commission as lieutenant-colonel of the militia (the colonel being a prisoner in their hands), I have issued orders to call out the militia of Raleigh County to meet to-morrow in edge of this county, but the principal portion of the county being in possession of the Federals, the number to assemble is very small, but we will assist with all our power in resisting any further advances of the enemy, hoping to have the aid of the counties interested with ourselves; and perhaps, if the facts were properly represented to our authorities, they would dispatch a regiment of volunteer forces to our assistance, for they openly avow that their destination is ultimately the railroad.

Asking pardon for troubling you (being a stranger), and hoping that you will use your influence in procuring aid, I am, very respectfully,

JOSEPH CALDWELL,
Lieutenant-Colonel of the One hundred and eighty-fourth Regiment.

| SPECIAL ORDERS, | ADJT. AND INSP. GEN.'S OFFICE, |
| No. 5. | *Richmond, January 7, 1862.* |

*　　　*　　　*　　　*　　　*　　　*　　　*

XIX. Brig. Gen. H. C. Wayne, Provisional Army, will forthwith proceed to Manassas, Va., and report for duty to General Joseph E. Johnston, commanding.

By command of the Secretary of War:

JNO. WITHERS,
Assistant Adjutant-General.

HEADQUARTERS CAVALRY BRIGADE,
Camp Qui Vive, January 9, 1862.

[General HILL:]

DEAR GENERAL: I thank you for your favor received some time since, and I assure you I am very grateful to you for the suggestions it contained.

I was desirous of sending the whole of Radford's regiment to Leesburg, but the commanding general was unwilling to spare so much cavalry. Colonel Radford, with two companies, to join the four already with you, are now *en route*, making your available cavalry amount to six companies. The picket now in sight of Dranesville is merely to notify me of any movement on Leesburg from that direction. I regret very much that you have lost the services of Colonel Jenifer, whose thorough acquaintance with the whole Potomac region must have made him invaluable as a cavalry commander.

I will require of Colonel Radford a monthly return of his regiment, and I hope you will concert with me some point of junction by pickets or patrols, so we can keep up a more rigid non-intercourse, as well as more direct communication with each other. A system of signals similar to those in use by the cavalry here is, I think, indispensable to safety from injury by friends as well as imposition by enemies. I hope to hear cheering news from Stonewall Jackson soon.

The Potomac Burnside fleet has not yet developed itself, but we are all anxiously expectant. McClellan's illness delays its operations doubtless.

Most respectfully, your obedient servant and true friend,

J. E. B. STUART,
Brigadier-General.

HEADQUARTERS,
Lewisburg, Va., January 9, 1862.

General S. COOPER, *Adjutant-General C. S. A.:*

SIR: I have the honor to report that the Twenty-second Regiment Virginia, under Lieutenant-Colonel Jackson, arrived at the White Sulphur Springs yesterday. From sickness and other causes the regiment has been reduced to about 325 effective men. Its weakness invites attack.

The country towards the Virginia and Tennessee Railroad is left entirely open. At any time the enemy's cavalry could move from Raleigh Court-House and do great damage. I would therefore urge upon the Department the necessity of sending a force to Peterstown (a strategic point), ready to move towards Union or the road leading from Raleigh Court-House to Virginia and Tennessee Railroad in case the enemy should threaten either point.

It may be some time before a sufficient force can be raised for "local defense," and as I am threatened on all sides, I respectfully call the attention of the Department to our defenseless condition and the importance of guarding not only the Virginia and Tennessee Railroad, but that of the Central Railroad and the depot of supplies at Jackson's River.

Since my return I have raised one company of cavalry, which will be organized on the 11th. I will immediately place it on duty, guarding the roads leading to this place; other companies (of infantry and one of artillery) are in process of being formed.

In case of necessity I will force out the militia; those who are not for me are against me.

Capt. R. Caskie, Wise's Legion, desires to join me with his company of cavalry. He has been operating in Mercer and Raleigh during the past summer, and he is well acquainted with the country. I hope you will gratify him, and order him to join me.

I am, sir, very respectfully, your obedient servant,

A. W. REYNOLDS,
Colonel, Commanding.

HEADQUARTERS VALLEY DISTRICT,
Morgan County, Virginia, January 10, 1862.

General JOSEPH E. JOHNSTON,
Commanding Department of Northern Virginia:

GENERAL: In accordance with instructions received from you I submit the following report respecting the location of the troops of this district. The numbers are not strictly accurate:

At Winchester, 183 infantry; at Hanging Rock, on the Northwestern turnpike, distant from Winchester 28 miles, 650 infantry and 56 cavalry; at North River Mills, on Cacapon bridge, and Frankfort turnpike, distant from Winchester 20 miles, 50 cavalry; at Martinsburg, 100 infantry and 56 cavalry; at Shepherdstown, 60 cavalry; at Duffield's Depot, on the Baltimore and Ohio Railroad, midway between Charlestown and Shepherdstown, 100 infantry and 26 cavalry; at Moorefield, distant 57 miles from Winchester and 27 from Romney, 400 infantry; at this place, on the Hampshire and Berkeley turnpike, distant 24 miles from Winchester, 8,000 infantry and 375 cavalry.

Brigadier-General Meem left here this morning for Moorefield with 545 infantry, and Brigadier-General Carson left here this morning for

Bath, a distance of 16 miles, in command of 200 infantry and 25 mounted militia. All the volunteers and regulars are stationed here.

I am, general, very respectfully, your obedient servant,

T. J. JACKSON,
Major-General, P. A. C. S., Commanding.

SPECIAL ORDERS, } HDQRS. DEP'T OF NORTHERN VIRGINIA,
No. 13. } *January* 10, 1862.

* * * * * * *

IV. In accordance with instructions from the War Department, Maj. Gen. Earl Van Dorn is relieved from duty in this department, and will report to the Secretary of War, at Richmond, Va.

V. In accordance with instructions from the War Department, Brig. Gen. Sam. Jones is relieved from duty in this department, and will report to the Secretary of War, at Richmond, Va.

By command of General Johnston:

THOS. G. RHETT,
Assistant Adjutant-General.

HEADQUARTERS FIRST CORPS, ARMY OF THE POTOMAC,
Near Centreville, January 12, 1862.

Brig. Gen. D. H. HILL, *Commanding C. S. Forces, Leesburg:*

GENERAL: Your letter of this date having been submitted to the general commanding, he approves your suggested application to the War Department for an increase of your force.

He regrets his inability to send you a suitable engineer, but has dispatched the best at his command. At least half a dozen competent engineers and as many each of topographical and ordnance officers should be with this army; but there is only one officer of engineers on duty with it.

Respectfully, your obedient servant,

THOMAS JORDAN,
Assistant Adjutant-General.

LEESBURG, VA., *January* 13, 1862.

Hon. J. P. BENJAMIN, *Secretary of War:*

SIR: With the permission of the general commanding, I address you directly upon the subject of an increase of force at this point. You are aware that our force at Centreville is scarce a third as large as it ought to be; and yet that its rout would do more to demoralize our Confederacy than the subjugation of two States. In the weak condition of that army I cannot look for aid from that quarter. Their fortifications may prevent a direct attack, and it has been a favorite scheme of the enemy to turn them by a combined movement from Point of Rocks and Edwards Ferry via Leesburg. The rashness of Colonel Baker defeated a a well-devised and well-arranged plan of general advance on the 21st October. The whole army here understand that immense masses of men had gathered then at these points to be thrown over here; the defeat and rout of the van discouraged and disheartened the main body, but the original plan has never been abandoned. In the last month the enemy has thrown up most formidable batteries to cover all the crossings.

We have constructed one most excellent fort and have two others in process of construction. These, when finished, could be held by a single regiment, and Loudoun County, the richest in the State, would be safe. If this regiment was sent from Richmond my whole available force could move to Centreville on the decisive day.

The object of my communication, then, is to ask for at least one additional regiment, for guns to be placed in the batteries and for artillerists to work them. The guns I learn can be got, and if no artillerists can be spared, I could have men trained and drilled in the re-enforcing regiment.

As " the Army of the Potomac is the rebellion," in the emphatic language of McClellan, I trust that I may be excused for troubling you on a matter materially connected with its efficiency.

With great respect,

D. H. HILL,
Brigadier-General, P. A. C. S.

[Memorandum.]

Write General Hill that one unarmed regiment can be furnished, if desired, but we have no arms.

HEADQUARTERS DEPARTMENT OF NORTHERN VIRGINIA,
Centreville, January 14, 1862.

Hon. J. P. BENJAMIN, *Secretary of War:*

SIR: I have had the honor to receive your letter of the 7th instant, and transmit herewith the statement required of the organization of the troops of the Potomac District, with partial ones of those of Aquia and the valley. These are incomplete, because the officers commanding those districts have not yet furnished the statements (similar) asked for by me some time since.

I regret to find from your last letter that the President is dissatisfied with the manner in which I have exercised the discretion with which he invested me as to the execution of Orders 15 and 18. I have assured him that there has been no time since those orders were given when i did not believe it to be utterly unsafe to attempt such reorganization, and no time when I was not, as now, anxious to carry out his wishes.

I have hitherto regarded these changes as impracticable because unsafe, and shall so regard them until the destination of the Burnside expedition is known.

Could the President see the condition of the country at this season, and that of our means of transportation, I am sure that he would regard these changes as physically impracticable now. The teams are all in constant employment, either to supply the troops with provision and fuel or themselves and the cavalry horses with food.

Since the supply in the neighborhood was exhausted the Quartermaster's Department has been unable to furnish full forage. Hay and fodder are rarely to be had, consequently our horses are in wretched condition.

I have twice asked by telegraph for an officer to take General Whiting's command, but have received no reply. No competent officer can be spared from any other part of this army.

Most respectfully, your obedient servant,

J. E. JOHNSTON,
General.

[Inclosure.]

POTOMAC DISTRICT.

General G. T. BEAUREGARD, commanding.

FIRST DIVISION.

(Late Major-General VAN DORN'S.)

Brigadier-General Bonham's brigade.

Second South Carolina Infantry.
Third South Carolina Infantry.
Seventh South Carolina Infantry.
Eighth South Carolina Infantry.
Boykin's Rangers, cavalry.
Kemper's battery (Virginia).

Brigadier-General Early's brigade.

Twentieth Georgia Infantry.
Fifth North Carolina Infantry.
Twenty-third North Carolina Infantry.
Twenty-fourth Virginia Infantry.
Jeff. Davis (Montgomery) Artillery (Alabama).

Brigadier-General Rodes' brigade.

Fifth Alabama Infantry.
Sixth Alabama Infantry.
Twelfth Alabama Infantry.

Twelfth Mississippi Infantry.
King William Artillery (Virginia).

SECOND DIVISION.

Maj. Gen. G. W. SMITH, commanding.

—— —— brigade.

Seventh Georgia Infantry.
Eighth Georgia Infantry.
Ninth Georgia Infantry.
Eleventh Georgia Infantry.
Wise Artillery (Virginia).

Brigadier-General Wilcox's brigade.

Ninth Alabama Infantry.
Tenth Alabama Infantry.
Eleventh Alabama Infantry.
Nineteenth Mississippi Infantry.
Thirty-eighth Virginia Infantry.
Thomas Artillery (Virginia).

Brigadier-General Toombs' brigade.

First Georgia (regulars) Infantry.
Second Georgia Infantry.
Fifteenth Georgia Infantry.

Seventeenth Georgia Infantry.
Blodget's battery.

THIRD DIVISION.

Major-General LONGSTREET, commanding.

Brigadier-General Ewell's brigade.

First Virginia Infantry.
Seventh Virginia Infantry.
Eleventh Virginia Infantry.
Seventeenth Virginia Infantry.
Loudoun Artillery (Virginia).

Brig. Gen. D. R. Jones' brigade.

Fourth South Carolina Infantry.
Fifth South Carolina Infantry.
Sixth South Carolina Infantry.
Ninth South Carolina Infantry.
Fauquier Artillery (Virginia).

—— —— brigade.

Eighth Virginia Infantry.
Eighteenth Virginia Infantry.
Nineteenth Virginia Infantry.

Twenty-eighth Virginia Infantry.
Latham's artillery (Virginia).

FOURTH DIVISION.

Maj. Gen. E. KIRBY SMITH, commanding.

Brigadier-General Elzey's brigade.

First Maryland Infantry.
Third Tennessee Infantry.
Thirteenth Virginia Infantry.
Sixteenth Virginia Infantry.
Baltimore Light Artillery (Maryland).

Brigadier-General Trimble's brigade.

Fifteenth Alabama Infantry.
Twenty-first Georgia Infantry.
Sixteenth Mississippi Infantry.
Twenty-first North Carolina Infantry.
Courtney's artillery (Virginia).

Brigadier-General Taylor's brigade.

Sixth Louisiana Infantry.
Seventh Louisiana Infantry.
Eighth Louisiana Infantry.

Ninth Louisiana Infantry.
First Louisiana Battalion Infantry.
Bowyer's artillery (Virginia).

FORCES NEAR DUMFRIES.

Brigadier-General WHITING, commanding.

——— ——— *brigade.*

Fourth Alabama Infantry.
Second Mississippi Infantry.
Eleventh Mississippi Infantry.
Sixth North Carolina Infantry.
First Tennessee Infantry.
Staunton Artillery (Virginia).

Brigadier-General Wigfall's brigade.

Fifth Alabama Battalion Infantry.
Eighteenth Georgia Infantry.
First Texas Infantry.
Fourth Texas Infantry.
Fifth Texas Infantry.

Colonel Hampton's brigade.

Fourteenth Georgia Infantry.
Nineteenth Georgia Infantry.
Sixteenth North Carolina Infantry.
Hampton's Legion (South Carolina).

Detachment.

Reilly's artillery (North Carolina).
Rives' battery (South Carolina).
Shannon's cavalry (South Carolina).
Thornton's cavalry (Virginia).

FORCES AT LEESBURG.

Brigadier-General HILL, commanding.

Brigadier-General Griffith's brigade.

Thirteenth Mississippi Infantry.
Seventeenth Mississippi Infantry.
Eighteenth Mississippi Infantry.
Twenty-first Mississippi Infantry.

Detachment.

Second Virginia Cavalry (four companies).
Richmond Howitzers (Virginia).

GARRISON AT MANASSAS.

Colonel ANDERSON, commanding.

Twenty-seventh Georgia Infantry.
Twenty-eighth Georgia Infantry.
Fourth North Carolina Infantry.

Forty-ninth Virginia Infantry.
Heavy Artillery Battalion.

CAVALRY BRIGADE.

Brigadier-General STUART, commanding.

First North Carolina Cavalry.
First Virginia Cavalry.
Second Virginia Cavalry.

Fourth Virginia Cavalry.
Sixth Virginia Cavalry.
Jeff. Davis Legion.*

_____

* Composed of two companies from Alabama, one from Georgia, and three from Mississippi.

RESERVE ARTILLERY.

Colonel PENDLETON, commanding.

Ashland Artillery (Virginia).
Cocke's battery (Virginia).
Coleman's battery (Virginia).
Cutts' battery (Georgia).
Dance's battery (Virginia).

Hamilton's battery (Georgia).
Holman's battery (Virginia).
Kirkpatrick's battery (Virginia).
Lane's battery (Georgia).

Major Walton's command.

Washington Light Artillery Battalion, Louisiana.

Saint Paul's Foot Rifles, Louisiana.

AQUIA DISTRICT.

Maj. Gen. T. H. HOLMES, commanding.

Brigadier-General French's brigade.

Second Arkansas Battalion Infantry.
Thirty-fifth Georgia Infantry.
Twenty-second North Carolina Infantry.
Second Tennessee Infantry.
Forty-seventh Virginia Infantry.

Braxton's artillery (Virginia).
Maryland Flying Artillery.
Caroline Light Dragoons (Virginia).
Stafford Rangers, cavalry, (Virginia).

Major-General Holmes has not given the brigade organizations of his other regiments.*

VALLEY DISTRICT.

Maj. Gen. T. J. JACKSON, commanding.

Brigadier-General Garnett's brigade.

Second Virginia Infantry.
Fourth Virginia Infantry.
Fifth Virginia Infantry.

Twenty-seventh Virginia Infantry.
Thirty-third Virginia Infantry.
McLaughlin's artillery (Virginia).

Colonel Ashby's cavalry (Virginia).

I have no report of the remaining troops of the Valley District. Have no official information, but believe there are ten regiments, under Brigadier-General Loring.

J. E. JOHNSTON.

[Addenda.]

AQUIA DISTRICT.

Maj. Gen. T. H. HOLMES, commanding.

Second brigade.

Brig. Gen. JOHN G. WALKER.

First Arkansas Regiment, batteries about Aquia and Potomac Creeks.
First Regiment North Carolina State troops, Brooke's Station.
Second Regiment North Carolina State troops, batteries about Aquia and Potomac Creeks.
Third Regiment North Carolina State troops, batteries about Aquia and Potomac Creeks.
Thirtieth Virginia Regiment, Fredericksburg.
Cooke's battery, Brooke's Station.
Walker's battery, batteries about Aquia and Potomac Creeks.

---

* See Addenda.

Not brigaded.

Fortieth Virginia Regiment, Northern Neck.
Lewis' company of cavalry, Northern Neck.
Tayloe's company of cavalry, Northern Neck.
Two companies of local volunteers, Northern Neck.
Fifty-fifth Virginia Regiment, near Tappahannock, for the defense of Fort Lowry.
Essex Cavalry, near Tappahannock, for the defense of Fort Lowry.

HEADQUARTERS,
Evansport, January 14, 1862.

General S. COOPER,
  Adjutant and Inspector General, Richmond, Va.:

GENERAL: On the morning of the 12th instant, between the hours of 4 and 5 o'clock, a vessel was discovered floating down under cover of the darkness of the night. She was then a little above the battery known as No. 1. The sentinel reported it to the corporal of the guard in the battery. He waited to see her, and then went to summon the guard for the guns always in the battery, but before they manned the guns she was so far past the battery that all the guns could not be brought to bear on her. From two guns, the new guns, and battery No. 2, a fire was opened, and it is certain she was struck several times. After she was discovered here a shot was fired from Cockpit. Had that battery seen her pass it and fired sooner, our men could have been at their guns in time; or had the corporal 'at once summoned the crews many more shots could have been fired.

The men were slow in getting to the guns until the first gun opened. As soon as fired at she put on all steam and, with the assistance of a tug, passed rapidly down. Every precaution was taken by me and by Captain Chatard, C. S. Navy.

At 9 p. m. I saw a light in an unusual place, and sent a courier down to the battery to report to Captain Peatross to observe unusual vigilance and have everything ready in case the Pensacola should attempt to run past. These instructions were given, and the men in some of the companies removed none of their clothing; these instructions were also given to the officer of the day, the officer of the guard, and the guard in the battery.

Again I directed the officer of the guard of the infantry force which guards the river at night and which acts as a supporting force against surprise to instruct the pickets, in case of anything being seen on the river, to first warn the batteries and then their main guard. This duty they performed. Between 11 and 12 o'clock at night Captain Collins and I went with our glasses and made a long and careful survey of the river up and down, but could discern nothing. But notwithstanding my taking all these precautions, the vessel was not discovered until nearly abreast of Battery No. 1. She passed Cockpit undisturbed, and I presume unobserved, and whether the darkness did completely conceal her until the moment she was reported I cannot tell. One thing is certain, the corporal should not have waited to see her before he summoned the men. I mention all this, because I am very much dissatisfied that, with the unusual precautions for the night, the men were not more prompt, and that she escaped many shots that should have been fired at her. It was the third time the men had to man the guns during the night, but that is not uncommon.

As regards the blockade of the river, not a sail has passed for weeks.

The river would be lifeless and desolate except for the eight or ten steamers always in sight above and below.

The plan of the Pensacola seems to have been, with the assistance of a tug, to float silently in the darkness by the batteries. She did not return a shot. I presume she left Alexandria and came directly down.

Very respectfully, your obedient servant,

S. G. FRENCH,
Brigadier-General, Commanding.

HEADQUARTERS VALLEY DISTRICT,
Bloomery Gap, Hampshire County, Virginia, January 14, 1862.

Hon. J. P. BENJAMIN, *Secretary of War:*

SIR: Through the blessing of God I regard this district as essentially in our possession. There is reason to believe that there are medical and other stores in Cumberland, which would, if in our possession, be of great value to our Government. If you desire them to be secured, in addition to other advantages resulting from the occupation of Cumberland and the dispersion or capture of their army near there, please send me at once 4,000 infantry and 350 cavalry. An engineer officer is much needed.

Very respectfully, your obedient servant,

T. J. JACKSON,
Major-General, P. A. C. S., Commanding.

HEADQUARTERS FIRST CORPS, ARMY OF THE POTOMAC,
Near Centreville, January 14, 1862.

Brig. Gen. D. H. HILL,
Commanding C. S. Forces, Leesburg, Va.:

GENERAL: Under the supposition that a considerable part of the Federal General Banks' forces have been diverted either to Hancock or elsewhere, and that circumstances may favor a sudden effective blow at your immediate adversary, General Stone, some clear night, when the passage of the river on the ice shall seem to you practicable and safe, I am instructed to advise you that such are the wishes of the general commanding this army corps, sanctioned by the general commanding the department.

But preliminary to so grave and important an operation I am directed to say it is essential that the utmost secrecy and circumspection should be observed in all your preparations. Several reliable and trustworthy guides must be secured, and in the mean time no means should be spared to acquire exact information of the position of General Stone's forces, his strength, and whether or not his supports have actually been diminished by diversions such as is suspected, whether towards Washington or Hancock. Nor should there be any doubt as to the soundness and strength of the ice, including its durability for the time needful for such an expedition.

In the conduct of such an expedition the general has all confidence in your discretion and military ability, but desires me to suggest that you should provide colored lights—lanterns—for signals of recognition. This can be made, you know, with flannel wrappings.

Your forces should be kept well in hand and close together; thoroughly informed, once across the river, of the aims of the expedition. Your men should be inspired with a determination to succeed and to deserve success by coolness and precaution against the casualty of mistaking and slaying friends for enemies. It may be judicious to make a slight detour to take the enemy in reverse, and your point of recrossing must be well guarded and covered by your artillery.

The ice should be littered with straw, sand, or ashes by a pioneer party. Finally, ice two inches thick will bear infantry in open order. The utmost care should be taken to prevent crowding, especially on the return.

Respectfully, your obedient servant,

THOMAS JORDAN,
Assistant Adjutant General.

HEADQUARTERS FIRST CORPS, ARMY OF THE POTOMAC,
Centreville, Va., January 16, 1862.

Brig. Gen. D. H. HILL, *Commanding at Leesburg, Va.:*

GENERAL: Your letter of the 15th instant has just been received. The movement you were ordered to make against General Stone's forces is based upon the supposition that they are not too strong in numbers and position to be attacked by you with all the probabilities of success, and that they cannot be supported in time by General Banks. Moreover, it should be on your part a surprise, and not a regular attack. We should by all means avoid undertaking any aggressive movement not likely to meet with entire success.

Very respectfully, your obedient servant,

G. T. BEAUREGARD,
General, Commanding.

HEADQUARTERS VALLEY DISTRICT,
Romney, Va., January 16, 1862.

Maj. THOMAS G. RHETT,
Assistant Adjutant-General, Hdqrs. Dept. of Northern Virginia:

MAJOR: In consequence of the weather and bad condition of the roads none of General Loring's command has yet arrived here, though last night the head of the column encamped only 8 miles distant. Garnett's brigade arrived yesterday. At last accounts the enemy were crossing the Potomac into Maryland on the railroad bridge below Cumberland. Their force in and about Cumberland is from last information about 11,000; at Hancock, 2,000; at Hagerstown, 2,000; at Fredericktown, 8,000. I have not succeeded in obtaining definite information as to the number in Williamsport.

Unless otherwise directed, I will proceed to construct winter quarters, and will station General Loring's troops and General Boggs' militia brigade in the South Branch Valley; General Garnett's brigade at Winchester; General Carson's brigade at Bath, and General Meem's brigade at Martinsburg. The cavalry will be distributed along the northern frontier at various points.

I am, major, very respectfully, your obedient servant,

T. J. JACKSON,
Major-General, P. A. C. S., Commanding.

HEADQUARTERS DEPARTMENT OF NORTHERN VIRGINIA,
Centreville, January 16, 1862.

Hon. J. P. BENJAMIN, *Secretary of War :*

SIR: I beg leave to urge the importance of filling, as soon as possible, the grades of major and brigadier general now existing in this army. The necessity of filling these offices is increasing by the absence of three brigadier-generals, two of whom are members of Congress; the other is sick.

I have twice asked, by telegraph, for an officer of ability to succeed General Whiting, but have received no reply. That command is an important one, and should be exercised by one of our best officers ; but those at my disposal who are competent to it are indispensable in their present positions.

Most respectfully, your obedient servant,

J. E. JOHNSTON,
General.

———

LEESBURG, VA., *January* 17, 1862.

General G. T. BEAUREGARD,
Commanding First Corps, Army of the Potomac :

GENERAL: A negro has been captured by our scouts, who reports that the enemy has a large force concentrated behind Harper's Ferry, and that they are talking of crossing there. I can perceive no diminution of Stone's force. He has at least 1,700 men on post every moment from Point of Rocks to Edwards Ferry, or 5,100 on sentry duty. Colonel Radford thinks this a low estimate; I have never in my life seen such a chain of sentinels. They are evidently very solicitous about the canal. Stone has not annoyed me at the fortifications since I threatened to fire at the barges if he fired any more at my forts. I forgot to mention that the captive negro says that some of the generals from Washington had been up to examine the position at Harper's Ferry.

With great respect,

D. H. HILL,
Brigadier-General.

———

HEADQUARTERS AQUIA DISTRICT,
Brooke's Station, January 17, 1862.

General JOSEPH E. JOHNSTON,
Commanding Department of Northern Virginia :

MY DEAR GENERAL : Your favor of yesterday is received, and caused me to resume my thinking-cap, which was momentarily removed when the incubus (Burnside's expedition) sailed. I do not see how I can change the position of my regiments to advantage; they are in supporting distance, and ready for action in any direction, and it glads my heart to say they are in excellent condition and spirits, except the Fourteenth Alabama, at Evansport, which has suffered greatly with measles and its concomitants. If General McClellan advances, it will certainly be irrespective of our batteries ; and if he cannot turn the position at Centreville by crossing the Occoquan he must meet that part of your command squarely, and I do not doubt you will destroy him. If, however, you wish any co-operation from my command, I can be with you at very short notice, for we can march almost at a moment's notice.

The two regiments referred to as being out of position between Evansport and Aquia are part of the Evansport command, not more than 2 or 3 miles from the batteries, and General French can move them to the batteries at his discretion.

I am, general, yours, very faithfully,

TH. H. HOLMES.

———

HEADQUARTERS VALLEY DISTRICT,
Romney, Va., January 17, 1862.
General JOSEPH E. JOHNSTON,
Commanding Department of Northern Virginia :

GENERAL : Your letter of the 16th* is at hand, and I hasten to reply that I have not enough troops for the proper defense of this district, as from the most reliable information that I have recently received the enemy's force in and about Cumberland is near 12,000—in Hancock 2,000, in Hagerstown 2,000, and in Fredericktown 8,000. Of the force in Williamsport I am not so well informed, but there is reason to believe that it is larger than in Hancock.

General Loring's command has not all arrived here from Morgan, but so soon as it does I hope to be able to leave him with his command to occupy the valley of the South Branch, while Garnett's brigade will return to Winchester and near Centreville, should you so direct; but in my opinion it should not go farther than Winchester, if the enemy are to be kept out of this district. Since leaving Winchester General Loring's command has become very much demoralized.

I have taken special pains to obtain information respecting General Banks, but I have not been informed of his having gone east. I will see what can be effected through the Catholic priests in Martinsburg.

I am establishing lines of couriers through this district. From Winchester I can send dispatches to Leesburg in three hours. I have thought that if you had a line of couriers between Leesburg and Manassas no additional one for carrying dispatches between Manassas and Winchester would be necessary; but should you desire an additional line, please indicate the route and I will have it established immediately.

I am, general, very respectfully, your obedient servant,

T. J. JACKSON,
Major-General, Commanding.

———

WAR DEPARTMENT, C. S. A.,
Richmond, Va., January 18, 1862.
General D. H. HILL, *Leesburg, Va.:*

SIR : In reply to your letter of January 13 I can only promise to send you an unarmed regiment, if you desire it; but we have no armed reenforcements or arms to spare.

Respectfully,

J. P. BENJAMIN,
Secretary of War.

———

HEADQUARTERS DEPARTMENT OF NORTHERN VIRGINIA,
Centreville, January 18, 1862.
Hon. J. P. BENJAMIN, *Secretary of War :*

SIR : A colonel of a Mississippi regiment has just informed me that you had referred him to me for information in relation to the recent act

———

* Not found.

of Congress granting bounties and furloughs to non-commissioned officers and privates of the Provisional Army. I have received no order
from the War Department directly on this subject. A copy of General
Orders, No. 1 [of 1st instant], transmitted to General Beauregard, has,
however, been laid before me.

The terms both of the law and of the order in question leave my
mind in doubt as to the time at which any person re-enlisting has the
right to expect a furlough; whether it must necessarily be granted out
of his present term of service for twelve months, or if it be competent
so to distribute the furloughs as to put off some of the men until their
new term shall have begun. As the law directs "said furloughs to be
issued at such times and in such numbers as the Secretary of War may
deem compatible with the public interests," I find myself compelled to
request further instructions on this point.

In case it be determined that these furloughs are to be granted
during the first period of a volunteer's service, I beg leave to submit for the consideration of the Department the impracticability of
granting them within the time specified in such numbers as will induce
any considerable re-enlistments among the twelve-months' regiments in
this command, for the army here is composed in large part of such
regiments, and inasmuch as the terms of service of nearly all of them
expire at no distant day, it would be necessary to grant furloughs in
very great numbers during the next few months, in order to obtain
many re-enlistments for the two years following. To grant them in
such numbers I deem incompatible with the safety of this command.

The men here now are as few as we can safely meet the enemy with;
yet there is no saying how soon he may attack us. We know that he
was not in sufficient force to meet General Jackson at Romney, and
obviously he meditates no offensive operations in that quarter. General Hill writes from Leesburg that the enemy has ceased to annoy his
working parties with his artillery, and that his pickets had reported
large quantities of baggage to be moving towards Washington. There
is a rumor that General Banks is marching to the same point, whether
true or false we do not know; but we do know that McClellan has not
put his army into winter quarters. General Jackson informs me that
a deserter, a very intelligent man, reports that the troops had been
ordered from Cincinnati to the east, supposed to Washington, all which
facts forbid any relaxation of vigilance on our part, and warn us against
any diminution of this command. If it should, on the other hand, be
decided that furloughs may be granted after as well as before the expiration of the first year's service, the principal difficulty still recurs, and
must continue to recur as long as this army shall continue of its present
size and be confronted by the forces to which we are now opposed. As
long as the existing condition of affairs continues it will be unsafe to
allow any large number of men to leave here; and without sustaining
such a loss I do not see how the object of the law can be accomplished.

In order to remove these doubts and difficulties, by which we must
otherwise be greatly embarrassed, I find myself under the necessity of
referring to you for instructions as to the government of my conduct.
The law requires me to be guided by the Secretary of War, not only as
to the "time" of granting furloughs, but also as to the number of them
to be granted.

Most respectfully, your obedient servant,

J. E. JOHNSTON,
General.

CENTREVILLE, *January* 18, 1862.

[The following] respectfully transmitted for the information of the War Department, by instructions from General Beauregard.

THOMAS JORDAN,
Assistant Adjutant-General.

DECEMBER 28, 1861.

DEAR GENERAL: I wrote you yesterday, giving you some information additional to that contained in my dispatch the day before. I omitted to say yesterday that I inclosed a dispatch from our friend Mrs. Greenhow, which I hope reached you to-day. I also inclosed one from our friend in B. To-day I have it in my power to say that Kelley is to advance on Winchester. Stone and Banks are to cross and go to Leesburg. Burnside's fleet is to engage the batteries on the Potomac, and McClellan & Co. will move on Centreville and Manassas. This move will be made next week. This information comes from one of McClellan's aides, and from Fox, of the Navy Department. As I remarked yesterday, be prepared for them on every hand and at every moment. Mason and Slidell have been given up, and the Hall clique are furious. Look out for a smash-up. I send you the papers containing Seward's letter, &c.

Now, my dear general, look out for a large army, and tell your men (God bless them!) to cut and slay until the last man is destroyed. Do not allow one to come back to tell the sad tale. No living man ever made such a desperate effort as McClellan will make. Nevertheless I believe he is a coward, and is afraid to meet you. If some excuse is not hatched up you may certainly expect an attack next week. My God! general, give them the most awful whipping that any army ever received. McClellan's army will certainly number 180,000 or 185,000 men—perhaps more. Let our next greeting be in Washington. You shall have a warm reception. I write in some haste.

From Mrs. Greenhow.

DECEMBER 26.

In a day or two 1,200 cavalry, supported by four batteries of artillery, will cross the river above to get behind Manassas and cut off railroad and other communications with our army whilst an attack is made in front. For God's sake heed this. It is positive. They are obliged to move or give up. They find me a hard bargain, and I shall be, I think, released in a few days, without condition, but to go South. A confidential member of McClellan's staff came to see me and tell me that my case should form an exception, and I only want to gain time. All my plans are nearly completed.

SPECIAL ORDERS, }   ADJT. AND INSP. GEN.'S OFFICE,
     No. 22.   }   *Richmond, January* 18, 1862.

*   *   *   *   *   *   *

XXI. Brig. Gen. H. Heth, Provisional Army, will immediately proceed to Lewisburg, Va., and assume command of all the troops in that district.

*   *   *   *   *   *   *

By command of the Secretary of War:

JNO WITHERS,
Assistant Adjutant-General.

HEADQUARTERS VALLEY DISTRICT,
                    Romney, January 20, 1862.

Hon. J. P. BENJAMIN, *Secretary of War:*

SIR: Though the enemy have retreated to the Potomac, yet they continue in possession of the frontier of this district from 7 miles below Cumberland to the Alleghany. On the 1st of this month there was not a single loyal citizen of Morgan County who in my opinion could with safety remain at home, and the same may be said respecting the most valuable portion of Hampshire County. A kind Providence has restored to us the entire county of Morgan and nearly the entire county of Hampshire, but so long as the enemy hold possession of the railroad bridge 5 miles below Cumberland and the two railroad bridges above Cumberland they can make dangerous inroads upon us.

On last Friday night I designed moving rapidly with my old brigade and one of General Loring's, for the purpose of destroying one of the railroad bridges across the North Branch of the Potomac west of Cumberland and thus cut off their supplies from the west, and consequently force them to reduce their army in front of me; but as General Loring's leading brigade, commanded by Colonel Taliaferro, was not in a condition to move, the enterprise had to be abandoned. Since leaving Winchester, on the 1st instant, the troops have suffered greatly, and General Loring has not a single brigade in a condition for active operations, though in a few days I expect they will be much improved, and will, if placed in winter quarters, be able to hold this important portion of the valley, but these quarters should be well selected and the positions strengthened, and hence the great importance of having a good engineer officer. It will not do for me to remain here much longer, lest General Banks should cross the Potomac. Consequently in a few days I expect to leave this place, taking with me Garnett's brigade. I have written to General Johnston that, unless otherwise directed, General Loring's command will go into winter quarters in the South Branch Valley, General Carson's at Bath, General Meem's at Martinsburg, and Garnett's at Winchester. The cavalry will be distributed at various points along the northern frontier. General Boggs' brigade, which principally belongs to the South Branch Valley, will be distributed over the section of country to which it belongs.

It is very desirable that the troops should go into winter quarters as soon as possible, so I trust that you will send me the best engineer officer you can, though it be for only ten days.

Very respectfully, your obedient servant,
                              T. J. JACKSON,
                    Major-General, P. A. C. S., Commanding.

HEADQUARTERS VALLEY DISTRICT,
                Romney, Va., January 21, 1862.

General JOSEPH E. JOHNSTON,
     Commanding Department of Northern Virginia:

GENERAL: Your letter of the 18th instant* has just been received, and I hasten to reply that my headquarters will continue to be in Winchester, and I am putting General Loring's three brigades into winter quarters near here. General Garnett's brigade is to be stationed at

---

* Not found.

Winchester, General Carson's at Bath, General Meem's at Martinsburg, and General Boggs' at various points in and near the South Branch Valley. Possibly I may be able to station them all in the South Branch Valley, but this must depend upon the movements of the enemy. The cavalry will be distributed along the frontier. I hope to be in Winchester this week, and will at once establish a line of couriers on any route you may indicate. The enemy are still in force on this side of the Potomac 7 miles below Cumberland and 20 miles from here.

Respectfully, your obedient servant,

T. J. JACKSON,
Major-General.

Abstract from field return, January 22, 1862, of the First Corps, Army of the Potomac, commanded by General Beauregard, near Centreville, Va.

Troops.	Present for duty.		Total present.	Aggregate present.	Total present and absent.	Aggregate present and absent.
	Officers.	Men.				
General staff	13	......	13	13	13	13
Infantry	1,120	16,570	21,321	22,645	26,948	28,674
Cavalry	38	524	672	718	912	974
Light artillery	56	1,050	1,175	1,232	1,373	1,441
Heavy artillery	13	216	259	274	277	294
Grand total	1,240	18,360	23,440	24,882	29,523	31,396

HEADQUARTERS FIRST CORPS, ARMY OF THE POTOMAC,
Centreville, Va., January 23, 1862.

Brig. Gen. D. H. HILL,
Commanding at Leesburg, Va.:

GENERAL: Your letter of yesterday * has been received. I incline to the opinion that the troops referred to by you come, not from Washington, but from Banks, at Frederick, for the purpose of repairing the damages to the railroad at and about Harper's Ferry, and then advancing on Winchester, for the purpose of cutting off General Jackson from that place, which is his true base of operations; but I hope he will yet have time to reach it before the enemy gets there. General Johnston coincides with me in these views. It would be well, however, to keep yourself and ourselves well advised of the enemy's movements in that direction. I send you herewith inclosed a telegram relative to the defeat of Crittenden's command. I hope, however, that the news is exaggerated.

Respectfully, your obedient servant,

G. T. BEAUREGARD,
General, Commanding.

ROMNEY, VA., *January 23,* 1862.

Hon. WALTER R. STAPLES:

MY DEAR SIR: I write you a few lines to enlist your influence as a public man in behalf of that portion of the Army of the Northwest now

---

* Not found.

stationed at this place. A portion of General Loring's command comprises the force here. This part of the army, during the last summer and fall, passed through a campaign in Northwestern Virginia, the character of which in point of suffering, toil, exposure, and deprivations has no parallel in this war, and scarcely can be equaled in any war. After all this hardship and exposure, and many, with much labor, had built winter huts, a call was made upon them to march some 150 miles to Winchester. This march was made about the 1st of December, in very inclement weather, but with a cheerfulness and alacrity that has seldom been witnessed under similar circumstances. After arriving at Winchester an expedition was ordered to Morgan County and to this place. This was also cheerfully undertaken by the men, as well as the officers, with the expectation on every side that after the object of the expedition was accomplished, this force, which had passed through eight months of incessant toil, would be permitted to retire to some convenient point and enjoy a short respite, preparatory to the spring campaign, rendered the more necessary by the terrible exposure since leaving Winchester, which has emaciated the force to almost a skeleton, compared to what it was on marching from that place.

Now we are ordered to remain here during the remainder of the winter. A more unfavorable spot could not be selected. We are willing to endure all that men can bear when our cause requires it; but where there is a discretion, that discretion should be exercised in favor of men who have seen such hard and continued service. This place is of no importance in a strategical point of view; the country around it has been exhausted by the enemy, and its proximity to the enemy and the Baltimore and Ohio Railroad will wear us away (already greatly reduced) by heavy picket and guard duty. Besides this, there is no suitable ground and not sufficient wood here upon and by which men can be made comfortable. We have not been in as uncomfortable a place since we entered the service.

By going to Winchester we could be much better situated and save a vast expense in the transportation of supplies; or we could go to Moorefield, in Hardy County, where there is the greatest abundance of forage, and where the Government has a large number of fat cattle. At the latter point we can effect every military object that we can effect here. We all must be impressed with the great importance of raising an army for the next summer. With the benefit of a short furlough for the men, I am satisfied that at Winchester I could have enlisted 500 of my regiment for the war. With the present prospect before them, I do not know that I could get a single man. Still, if the men could yet be placed in a position where their spirits could be revived, many of them would re-enlist for the war.

This is a public consideration that ought not to be overlooked. All of the officers of this army take the same view of the case that I have above presented, and all are endeavoring to effect the same object that I am.

I will ask you, in view of these facts, to see the Adjutant-General, the Secretary of War, and the President, if necessary, and impress these considerations upon them, and by doing so you will perform a public service as well as confer a favor upon a meritorious army.

I would say more, but deem it unnecessary. I have written to Hon. Walter Preston upon the same subject.

Yours, respectfully,

SAML. V. FULKERSON,
[*Colonel Thirty-seventh Virginia Infantry.*]

66 R R—VOL V

[Inclosure.]

HEADQUARTERS FOURTH BRIGADE NORTHWESTERN ARMY,
Camp near Romney, January 23, 1862.

MY DEAR STAPLES: Fulkerson has shown me the letter he has written you, and asks me to take it to town to mail it for him.

I take the liberty with an old friend, which I know you will pardon, to state that every word and every idea conveyed by Colonel F. in his letter to you is strictly and most unfortunately true. The best army I ever saw of its strength has been destroyed by bad marches and bad management. It is ridiculous to hold this place; it can do no good, and will subject our troops to great annoyance and exposed or picket duty, which will destroy them. Not one will re-enlist, not one of the whole army. It will be suicidal in the Government to keep this command here.

For Heaven's sake urge the withdrawal of the troops, or we will not [have] a man of this army for the spring campaign.

Very truly, your friend,

WM. B. TALIAFERRO,
Colonel, Commanding Brigade.

———

HEADQUARTERS,
Lewisburg, Va., January 23, 1862.

Hon. J. P. BENJAMIN, *Secretary of War, C. S. A.:*

SIR: Having a day or two since obtained some information of the doings and movements of the enemy in the Kanawha Valley, by means of some friends of our cause who have succeeded in getting through their lines, I hasten to submit them by the first mail for your consideration.

These men state that the enemy are actively engaged in shipping immense quantities of military stores to the Kanawha Valley; that at Point Pleasant they have three large sheds nearly 200 yards long filled; that at Charleston every store-house and deserted building has been occupied by them, besides having erected numerous sheds; that at Gauley Bridge they have also extensive sheds filled with stores, and a large number of new transportation wagons and pack mules.

These gentlemen say all along the Ohio and Kanawha Rivers the utmost activity prevails for an early and energetic campaign. I have also ascertained that the enemy have erected a new wire suspension bridge over the Gauley River, which would be completed by the 25th instant.

This information comes from men who are intelligent and known to be trustworthy, and entirely devoted to the Southern cause. From them I learn that there are between 3,000 and 4,000 of the enemy in the Kanawha Valley, besides those stationed at Sutton, Fayetteville, and Raleigh Court-House.

This activity on the part of the enemy bespeaks, in my humble opinion, an early movement.

It is a fact well worthy of being borne in mind that after a freeze in this country the roads in a very short time become smooth and transportation can be had over them very successfully. From these facts I would respectfully submit to the Department the propriety of immediately establishing depots at Jackson's River, White Sulphur Springs, and at Peterstown, or some other suitable point in that section. If it is the intention of the Government to make an early spring campaign in Western Virginia, the operations cannot be carried into effect too soon. The mild open winter is inviting, and I am fearful that unless something is not speedily done the enemy will be able to anticipate us in making the first move, which I think will be very unfortunate in a country like this.

There is another matter that I wish to bring to your consideration. It is this: That while the enemy have a regular chain of posts and scouts from the Maryland to the Kentucky line (which it is almost impossible for our friends to get through), we have but a very few troops stationed at two or three points, with little or no cavalry. By this means the enemy have a great advantage over us, as it enables them to intercept nearly all our spies and cut off all information of their doings and flood our whole Confederacy with theirs. In fact, I think that it has been through this source that they have derived the most of their information of the transactions of our Government. In my opinion the interest of the service requires that we should have a similar chain of posts and scouts to enable us to intercept all persons going out.

I am, very respectfully, your obedient servant,

A. W. REYNOLDS,
Colonel, Commanding.

RICHMOND, *January* 24, 1862.

General JOSEPH E. JOHNSTON, *Centreville:*

The President directs that you send here as promptly as possible 6,000 stands of arms out of the number reported by General Cooper as not being now in use in your army. This is very urgent.

J. P. BENJAMIN,
Secretary of War.

HEADQUARTERS VALLEY DISTRICT,
Winchester, January 24, 1862.

Hon. J. P. BENJAMIN, *Secretary of War:*

SIR: I returned to this place yesterday, still leaving the enemy in possession of our frontier from Patterson's Creek Depot westward; our operations against the Federal forces were pressed as far as in my opinion circumstances would justify.

The important valley of the South Branch of the Potomac is, with but a slight exception, in our possession, and it is very desirable that we should continue to hold it; but as the enemy are in force 7 miles below Cumberland and also are at New Creek, the former being 20 miles and the latter 18 from Romney, I am apprehensive that an attempt may be made to surprise General Loring's command at Romney; and to prevent this, I trust that you will, if practicable, send me 300 cavalry, to be stationed near Romney. An abundance of corn can be procured at 50 cents per bushel, whereas in this county it cannot be had for less than about 80 cents per bushel, and east of the Blue Ridge it is probably still dearer. I mention this comparative cost of forage for the purpose of showing how economically cavalry might be supported in Hampshire County. With a proper mounted force the enemy can, in my opinion, be deterred from advancing so near General Loring's position as to attempt a surprise.

My command is going into winter quarters as rapidly as practicable.

I have given orders for constructing a telegraphic line from Winchester to Romney, in order that I may at the earliest possible moment receive intelligence of an advance on Romney.

Respectfully, your obedient servant,

T. J. JACKSON,
Major-General, P. A. C. S.

WINCHESTER, VA., *January* 24, 1862.

General JOSEPH E. JOHNSTON,
Commanding Department of Northern Virginia:

GENERAL: I arrived here yesterday evening from Romney, where I left General Loring, with about 4,000 infantry, three companies of cavalry, and thirteen pieces of field artillery. General Garnett's brigade is *en route* for this place.

To-day I received both your letters respecting the movements of the enemy towards Harper's Ferry.* The object may be to cross at that point, but I am apprehensive that these forces are moving higher up. I fear that the enemy is determined to rebuild the railroad from Hancock westward, and I am not in a condition to prevent it, as the troops of this district will do well if they but hold their positions during the reorganization. The great desire to rebuild the railroad may be inferred not only from its importance to the grand army, but from the fact that the enemy in retreating from Romney halted on this side of the railroad bridge next below Cumberland. Notwithstanding, it gave them a bad position, and while there a loyal citizen of my acquaintance visited General Lander for the purpose of recovering property, and during their conversation General Lander said if I did any further damage to the railroad that he would burn every village in Hampshire County, and that he would burn the house of every secessionist in the county and would destroy all his property. This great desire to reconstruct the railroad shows its importance to the enemy, and I am in favor of destroying it at once, so as to put away this bone of contention. But to do this I require a regiment of cavalry for a few days. Can you not send it to me?

Respectfully, your obedient servant,

T. J. JACKSON,
Major-General.

DUBLIN, *January* 24, 1862.

General S. COOPER, *Adjutant-General:*

The enemy with a force of one regiment of infantry and some cavalry are advancing in the direction of Pack's Ferry, on New River. A regiment of infantry should be sent to Peterstown to protect the stores there. I think I can hold the enemy in check until re-enforcements arrive.

In haste, truly, yours,

W. H. JENIFER,
Colonel Eighth Virginia Cavalry.

---

* Not found.

[Indorsements.]

There is a regiment at Dublin Station. Shall it be ordered to Pack's Ferry? There are numerous stores also at Dublin. Armistead's regiment is available.

Respectfully,

R. H. CHILTON,
Assistant Adjutant-General.

RICHMOND, VA., *January 25, 1862.*

Col. WILLIAM E. PETERS, *Commanding, Dublin Station, Va.:*

Move up immediately to Pack's Ferry, with nine companies, to oppose advance of the enemy in that direction, leaving the tenth company to guard stores at Dublin. Advise Colonel Jenifer, Eighth Cavalry, of your movements.

S. COOPER.

WAR DEPARTMENT, C. S. A.,
Richmond, Va., January 25, 1862.

General JOSEPH E. JOHNSTON,
Comdg. Department of Northern Virginia, Centreville, Va.:

SIR: I am in receipt of your letter of the 18th instant. I regret that there should have been any delay in your receipt of General Orders, No. 1 [of 1st instant], relative to the bounty and re-enlistment law. In order to prevent this delay I had myself inclosed to your address a copy of the circular letter prepared for use in my correspondence, and General Cooper had mailed to your address the general order referred to, of which I now inclose another copy.

In relation to the time when the furloughs are to be granted, the VIIIth paragraph of the general order gives such instructions as were deemed prudent. I could not undertake to determine when and in what numbers the furloughs could be safely granted. I am aware that your solicitude for the safety of your command must necessarily embarrass you in giving furloughs in large numbers at present; but at the same time I beg you to observe that the eager desire for a furlough during the inclement season will form the strongest inducement for your men, and thus afford the best guarantee of your having under your orders a large force of veteran troops when active operations recommence.

It seems scarcely possible that in the present condition of the roads an attack can be make; and it is surely better to run a little risk now than to meet the certain danger of finding a large body of your men abandoning you at the expiration of their terms, now nearly about to expire. There is danger on both sides, I admit; but the hazard is the inevitable result of our comparative weakness in available resources.

I will order up a few regiments of unarmed men, who can be drilling and exercising with the arms of furloughed men, and whom you will be able to make available, to some extent, while your best troops are diminished in number. All I can say beyond what is contained in the general order is to advise, very urgently, that you go to the extreme verge of prudence in tempting your twelve-months' men by liberal furloughs, and thus secure for yourself a fine body of men for the spring operations. The rest I must leave to your own judgment. I need not add that you can much better hazard furloughs now than later, and that it is much better to lose your men for thirty or sixty days than altogether.

Your own letter presents, in a striking manner, the fact that we have but a choice of evils. I will do my best to aid you; but you can scarcely conceive the difficulties which encompass me in this task. The enormous masses of the enemy threatening us in the West; his naval expeditions hovering over the coasts of North Carolina, South Carolina, Georgia, Florida, Alabama, Mississippi, Louisiana, and Texas; his force below us on the Peninsula; the invasion of Western Virginia, all combine to assail me with hourly demands for re-enforcements, and prevents my withdrawing troops from any of the points named, and our citizens themselves, with natural weakness, refuse to volunteer for distant service while their homes are threatened.

The Department can only trust to the skill and prudence of our generals and the indomitable spirit of our people to maintain a struggle in which the disparity of numbers, already fearful, becomes still more threatening from the impossibility of adding to our stock of arms.

I am, your obedient servant,

J. P. BENJAMIN,
Secretary of War.

JANUARY 25, 1862.

Brigadier-General LORING,
Commanding Army of the Northwest:

GENERAL: The undersigned officers of your command beg leave to present their condition to your consideration as it exists at Romney.

It is unnecessary to detail to you, who participated in it all, the service performed by the Army of the Northwest during the last eight months. The unwritten (it will never be truly written) history of that remarkable campaign would show, if truly portrayed, a degree of severity, of hardship, of toil, of exposure and suffering that finds no parallel in the prosecution of the present war, if indeed it is equaled in any war. And the alacrity and good-will with which the men of your command bore all this hardship, exposure, and deprivation would have done honor to our sires in the most trying times of the Revolution.

After being worn down with unremitting toil and wasted by death and disease, the remainder were about preparing quarters to shield them from the storms of winter in a rigorous climate. Many had prepared comparatively comfortable quarters, when they were called upon to march to Winchester and join the force under General Jackson. This they did about the 1st of December, with the same alacrity which had characterized their former conduct, making a march of some 150 miles at that inclement season of the year.

After reaching Winchester, as expected, was ordered in the direction of the enemy, when all cheerfully obeyed the order, with the confident expectation that so soon as the object of the expedition was attained they would be marched to some comfortable position, where they could enjoy a short respite and recruit their wasted energies for the spring campaign.

The terrible exposure and suffering on this expedition can never be known to those who did not participate in it. When men pass night after night in the coldest period of a cold climate without tents, blankets, or even an ax to cut wood with, and without food for twenty-four hours, and with some of the men nearly two days at a time, and attended by toilsome marches, it is not to be thought strange that some regiments which left Winchester with nearly 600 men should now, short as the time has been, report less than 200 men for duty.

Instead of finding, as expected, a little repose during midwinter, we are ordered to remain at this place. Our position at and near Romney is one of the most disagreeable and unfavorable that could well be imagined. We can only get an encampment upon the worst of wet, spouty land, much of which when it rains is naught but one sheet of water and a consequent corresponding depth of mud, and this, too, without the advantage of sufficient wood, the men having to drag that indispensable article down from high up on the mountain side.

We are within a few miles of the enemy and of the Baltimore and Ohio Railroad, which imposes upon our men the continued hardship of very heavy picket duty, which will in a short time tell terribly upon their health and strength. We regard Romney as a place difficult to hold, and of no strategical importance after it is held. Besides, the country around it for some distance has already been by the enemy exhausted of its supplies. Your army could be maintained much more comfortably, and at much less expense, and with every military advantage, at almost any other place.

Another consideration we would endeavor to impress upon your mind: All must be profoundly impressed with the paramount importance of raising an army for the next summer's campaign. When we left Winchester, a very large proportion of your army, with the benefit of a short furlough, would have enlisted for the war, but now, with the present prospect before them, we doubt if one single man would re-enlist. But if they are yet removed to a position where their spirits could be revived, many, we think, will go for the war.

In view of all these considerations and many others that might be presented, we ask that you present the condition of your command to the War Department, and earnestly ask that it may be ordered to some more favorable position.

Respectfully,

WM. B. TALIAFERRO,
Colonel, Commanding Fourth Brigade Northwestern Army.
SAML. V. FULKERSON,
Colonel Thirty-seventh Virginia Volunteers.
VAN H. MANNING,
Major, Commanding Third Arkansas Volunteers.
J. W. ANDERSON,
Major, Commanding First Georgia Regiment.
A. V. SCOTT,
Captain, Commanding Twenty-third Virginia Volunteers.
JESSE S. BURKS,
Colonel, Commanding Third Brigade Northwestern Army.
D. A. LANGHORNE,
Lieutenant-Colonel, Commanding Forty-second Virginia Volunteers.
P. B. ADAMS,
Major, Forty-second Virginia Volunteers.
J. Y. JONES,
Captain, Commanding First Battalion P. A. C. S.
R. H. CUNNINGHAM, Jr.,
Captain, Commanding Twenty-first Virginia Volunteers.
JOHN A. CAMPBELL,
Colonel, Commanding Forty-eighth Virginia Volunteers.

[Indorsements.]

HEADQUARTERS ARMY OF NORTHWEST,
Romney, Va., January 26, 1862.

As this is a respectful communication, and presents for the consideration of the honorable Secretary of War the true condition of this army, and coming from so high a source, expressing the united feeling of the army, I deem it proper to respectfully forward it for his information.   I am most anxious to re-enlist this fine army, equal to any I ever saw, and am satisfied if something is not done to relieve it, it will be found impossible to induce the army to do so, but with some regard for its comfort, a large portion, if not the whole, may be prevailed upon.

At the earliest possible moment I shall write more fully.

Very respectfully, your obedient servant,
W. W. LORING,
Brigadier-General, Commanding, &c.

HEADQUARTERS VALLEY DISTRICT,
Winchester, February 4, 1862.

Respectfully forwarded, but disapproved.
T. J. JACKSON,
Major-General, Commanding.

WAR DEPARTMENT, C. S. A.,
Richmond, Va., January 26, 1862.

General JOSEPH E. JOHNSTON, *Centreville, Va.:*

SIR: Inclosed you will find an order detaching General Beauregard from the army under your command and assigning him to do duty at Columbus, Ky., which you are requested to forward him at once. Regretting that the exigencies of the public service force us to deprive you of the aid of this valuable officer, I still entertain undiminished confidence in your capacity, with the aid of the able generals who still surround you, to maintain the position which you have thus far successfully defended.

I am, your obedient servant,
J. P. BENJAMIN,
Secretary of War.

[Inclosure.]

General G. T. BEAUREGARD, *Manassas, Va.:*

SIR: Colonel Pryor has reported to the President, as the result of his interview with you, that you would cheerfully accept the command of the defenses at Columbus, Ky., and that your absence from the Army of the Potomac would not seriously impair its efficiency.   He therefore desires that you proceed at once to report to General A. S. Johnston, at Bowling Green, Ky., and thence proceed, as promptly as possible, to assume your new command at Columbus, which is threatened by a powerful force, and the successful defense of which is of vital importance.   You are authorized to take with you your present staff or such members of it as you wish to accompany you.

I am, your obedient servant,
J. P. BENJAMIN,
Secretary of War.

WAR DEPARTMENT, C. S. A.,
Richmond, Va., January 26, 1862.

General JOSEPH E. JOHNSTON, *Centreville, Va.:*

SIR: The accounts which have reached us of the condition of the army in the Valley District fill us with apprehension, especially when connected with the fact reported by you of the movement of large bodies of the enemy to Harper's Ferry. The President, therefore, requests that you will, as promptly as possible, examine for yourself into the true state of the case, take such measures as you think prudent under the circumstances, and report to the Department whether any measures are necessary on its part to restore the efficiency of that army, said to be seriously impaired.

Your obedient servant,

J. P. BENJAMIN,
Secretary of War.

WAR DEPARTMENT, C. S. A.,
Richmond, Va., January 27, 1862.

General JOSEPH E. JOHNSTON,
Comdg. Department of Northern Virginia, Centreville, Va.:

SIR: Congress has provided by law for the appointment of field officers of artillery in the Provisional Army in proportion to the number of guns in each command. You are respectfully requested to report, as early as convenient, the number of guns in each of the three armies under your command, and a list of the artillery officers in each army in the order of their merit, so as to assist the President in doing justice to your meritorious subordinates by proper promotion. It would be agreeable to us to have a like list prepared separately by the commanders of each of the three armies in relation to the officers under his command, so as to compare the estimates made of their respective merits, and thus increase the probability of doing exact justice to all.

Your obedient servant,

J. P. BENJAMIN,
Secretary of War.

HEADQUARTERS,
Centreville, January 28, 1862.

General S. COOPER, *Adjutant and Inspector General:*

SIR: I am informed that General Orders, No. 2 [of 6th instant], has been distributed to the "war regiments" of this army.

A recent order of the Secretary of War directs me to send to Richmond 6,000 of the muskets belonging to our absent sick. This deprives the different regiments of the means of arming their men who return from the hospitals, even, and of course there are no arms for recruits. I shall not, under such circumstances, permit the expense of recruiting to be incurred without additional orders.

Very respectfully, your obedient servant,

J. E. JOHNSTON,
General.

HEADQUARTERS,
Centreville, Va., January 28, 1862.

General JACKSON,
Commanding Valley District, Winchester, Va.:

GENERAL: I have to-day received your letters of 21st and 24th. I regret to be unable to re-enforce you. May not your own cavalry, Colonel Ashby's regiment, be concentrated and used for the purpose for which you apply to me for cavalry? I am an enemy to much distribution of troops. May not yours be brought together; so posted, that is to say, that you may be able to assemble them all to oppose an enemy coming from Harper's Ferry, Williamsport, or the northwest? Should the report given by General Hill prove to be correct, it would be imprudent, it seems to me, to keep your troops dispersed as they now are. Do not you think so? The enemy might not only prevent your concentrating, but interpose himself between us, which we must never permit.

Most respectfully, your obedient servant,

J. E. JOHNSTON,
General.

CENTREVILLE, *January* 29, 1862.

General S. COOPER:

What is the total number of arms of sick and absent men reported to you here?

J. E. JOHNSTON.

JANUARY 29, 1862.

General JOHNSTON:

The total number of arms of sick and absent men, according to reports handed me at Centreville, is 3,405; this is exclusive of the number of arms in depot at Manassas, which according to your indorsement on General G. W. Smith's division return is 2,430, making in all 6,830 surplus arms.

I send by mail to your address at Manassas the original reports I received at Centreville.

S. COOPER.

RICHMOND, VA., *January* 29 [?], 1862.

SECRETARY OF WAR:

It will be necessary to act promptly. Have you been notified of the return of General Jackson to Winchester and the withdrawal of the brigade with which he undertook the service from which he is reported to have retired, leaving only those who were sent to re-enforce him? Will confer with you at your pleasure.

J. D. [DAVIS.]

The petition of the officers with General Loring's indorsement is returned.*

D.

---

* Probably Taliaferro *et al.* to Loring, January 25, p. 1046.

HEADQUARTERS DEPARTMENT OF NORTHERN VIRGINIA,
Centreville, January 29, 1862.
Hon. J. P. BENJAMIN, *Secretary of War:*

SIR: I had the honor to receive by the last mail your letter of the 26th instant in relation to General Jackson's command.

Without being entirely certain that I understand the precise object of apprehension in the Valley District, I have dispatched the acting inspector general of the department to see and report without delay the condition of Major-General Jackson's troops.

Most respectfully, your obedient servant,

J. E. JOHNSTON,
General.

CENTREVILLE, *January* 29, 1862.
Hon. J. P. BENJAMIN, *Secretary of War:*

SIR: I have just had the honor to receive your letter of the 26th instant, inclosed with one to General Beauregard, assigning him to command at Columbus, Ky.

General Beauregard will be relieved from his present command to-morrow.

I regret very much that it is thought necessary to remove this distinguished officer from this district, especially at the present time, when the recent law granting bounty and furloughs, &c., is having a disorganizing effect. I fear that General Beauregard's removal from the troops he has formed may increase this effect among them.

In this connection permit me to urge the necessity of this army for the general officers I have asked for more than once.

Most respectfully, your obedient servant,

J. E. JOHNSTON,
General.

HEADQUARTERS DEPARTMENT OF NORTHERN VIRGINIA,
Centreville, January 29, 1862.
Col. S. BASSETT FRENCH,
Aide-de-Camp of Governor of Virginia:

SIR: Your letter of the 25th instant in relation to arms the property of the Commonwealth of Virginia not in the hands of the troops of the Army, and desiring me to take measures for their return to the State authorities so far as they can be found within this department of the Army of the Confederate States, has been duly received.

I am sorry that I can afford little information and less aid in relation to the important and interesting objects of your communication. The troops under my command have generally come into my department with arms in their hands. I had and have no means of ascertaining by whom the arms were furnished. I understand that Virginia does not wish to reclaim arms now in actual use. As some arms have become disposable by the death or discharges of soldiers, they have been withdrawn from my control under orders of the War Department of the Confederate States. These orders have been repeatedly issued by the Department and executed by me. Of late they have gone to the length of taking the arms of the sick. When removed from this army, the arms of course passed under the direct control of the Department of

War. To that Department I must refer you for the information which you seek of me.

There are no flint-lock muskets in the hands of my soldiers, nor have there been any since I assumed the command here. There were 500 such in the depot at Manassas when I arrived here from the valley. They were soon afterwards sent to Richmond, in accordance with the general practice in such matters above specified.

Do me the favor to express to the governor my grateful acknowledgment of his kind and patriotic message. Nothing earthly could afford me higher gratification than the fulfillment of his good wishes by this army striking a great blow for the freedom and independence of Virginia and of the South.

Most respectfully, your obedient servant,
J. E. JOHNSTON,
General.

CAVALRY CAMP,
Between Pack's Ferry and Raleigh C. H., January 29, 1862.

General S. COOPER, *Adjutant-General, Richmond, Va.:*

GENERAL: I have the honor to report that I am now between Pack's Ferry and Raleigh with my cavalry. I learn this evening that the enemy has been re-enforced at the latter place, numbering in all about 1,500 infantry, 100 cavalry, and several pieces of artillery. I do not think it is his intention to make a general advance soon, but they have been very annoying to the loyal citizens of Raleigh County, causing many to leave their homes, and arresting others and compelling them to take the oath.

The infantry regiment ordered here from Dublin five or six days ago has not yet arrived. I do not know what has detained it, unless it is the swollen condition of the streams between Peterstown and Pack's Ferry. I have ordered the commander of the regiment, when he arrives, to station two companies at Jumping Branches, which is a very important point, being 7 miles in advance of Pack's Ferry and 18 miles from Raleigh Court-House. I have also two companies of cavalry at Jumping Branches, with the advance pickets at Shady Springs, 10 miles from Raleigh Court-House. The remaining companies of the infantry regiment I have ordered to Peterstown. In placing the command at these points it makes it convenient for the advanced companies to be re-enforced, or in case it is necessary for them to fall back they can readily do so, without danger of being cut off by the enemy.

I will also report that neither the major nor surgeon of this regiment are on duty with it. The major has never yet reported.

I am, sir, very respectfully, your obedient servant,
W. H. JENIFER,
Colonel, Commanding.

UNION, *Wednesday, January* 29, 1862.

Colonel JENIFER:

DEAR SIR: It has been ascertained with certainty that 250 Yankee cavalry passed Tyree, at the foot of Big Sewell, on Monday, and that they staid at Hickman's, about 6 miles west of Meadow, on Monday night. It is reported that they were to meet 1,000 infantry at Meadow Bluff on yesterday, and that the 1,000 men were on their march by the Wilderness road from Summersville. This last-mentioned report seems to have some credit about Lewisburg. There is quite a panic at that place. They may attempt a movement by way of the Blue Sulphur and thence to the Red Sulphur, or by way of Blue Sulphur and across the Flat Top to this place. They may, and I think that most probable, stop and intrench at Meadow Bluff. I understand that the cavalry had some wagons with them; the number has not been reported.

Very respectfully, your obedient servant,

A. T. CAPERTON.

RICHMOND, VA., *January* 30, 1862.

General T. J. JACKSON, *Winchester, Va.:*

Our news indicates that a movement is being made to cut off General Loring's command. Order him back to Winchester immediately.

J. P. BENJAMIN,
Secretary of War.

GENERAL ORDERS, }   HDQRS. DEP'T OF NORTHERN VIRGINIA,
No. 17.   }   *January* 30, 1862.

In obedience to orders received from the Secretary of War, assigning him to an important position in another department, General Beauregard is relieved from the duties of his present command.

In losing the aid of this distinguished soldier the commanding general cannot withhold the expression of his sense of the eminent services by which he has achieved so much for our country, our cause, and the renown of our arms.

By command of General Johnston:

A. P. MASON,
Acting Assistant Adjutant-General.

HEADQUARTERS VALLEY DISTRICT,
Winchester, Va., January 31, 1862.

Hon. J. P. BENJAMIN, *Secretary of War:*

SIR: Your order requiring me to direct General Loring to return with his command to Winchester immediately has been received and promptly complied with.

With such interference in my command I cannot expect to be of much service in the field, and accordingly respectfully request to be ordered to report for duty to the superintendent of the Virginia Military Institute at Lexington, as has been done in the case of other professors. Should this application not be granted, I respectfully request that the President will accept my resignation from the Army.

I am, sir, very respectfully, your obedient servant,

T. J. JACKSON,
Major-General, P. A. C. S.

[Indorsement.]

HEADQUARTERS,
Centreville, February 7, 1862.

Respectfully forwarded, with great regret. I don't know how the loss of this officer can be supplied. General officers are much wanted in this department.

J. E. JOHNSTON,
General.

HEADQUARTERS,
Romney, Va., January 31, 1862.

Hon. J. P. BENJAMIN, *Secretary of War:*

SIR: I inclose the report of Colonel Barton, who acted as engineer, by order of General Jackson, in examining the defenses, &c., of Romney, and the copy of a letter inclosing it, which I sent General Jackson. I beg to call your attention to them, particularly the fact of the enemy, in force at their railroad, making it their base of operations, with Cumberland as their center, secured by Patterson's Creek Depot and the mouth of the South Branch and its bridge on the one side, and New Creek Depot and its bridge on the other, and also the large number of roads leading to our rear from various points on their railroad.

I deem it my duty to report that this command is now forced, in the depth of winter, from the requirements of our position, to a degree of service which is telling with fearful effect upon their health. In the short time since its departure from Winchester a number of our best officers and men have died, the result of exposure; and the medical men of the army tell me that the constant exposure during the recent summer in the mountains, followed by the unremitting duty in the winter, is filling the hospitals with hundreds of our sick.

It is a fine army, and should be, if possible, re-enlisted for the war. I am satisfied that unless it is given relief it will be found impossible to effect it. With some attention to their comfort most, if not all, may be induced to enter again.

It is proper for me to say that we came cheerfully to co-operate with the forces of General Jackson in the campaign, the reports of which have been sent you. All movements have some time since ceased, and General Jackson has gone to Winchester with his brigade. I now most respectfully ask, in justice to this command and myself, that it be ordered to the line to which I had the honor to be assigned. Numerous places may be selected where it can be reorganized; or, if this should not be deemed advisable, to some point where it can have the stimulant of active service.

I have the honor to be, respectfully, your obedient servant,

W. W. LORING,
Brigadier-General, Commanding.

[Inclosure No. 1.]

HEADQUARTERS ARMY OF THE NORTHWEST,
Romney, January 28, 1862.

Maj. Gen. T. J. JACKSON, *Commanding, &c.:*

GENERAL: I send a report of Colonel Barton of the means of defense and of the approaches to Romney, the position this force is ordered to hold. After a careful and thorough examination of the mountain passes, I am of the opinion that he has given a correct estimate of their strength. With the aid of the best guides of this country I have made observation of its roads, and fully concur with him in the facility with which an enemy with a large command can flank and turn our positions. He has also given a correct statement of the numerous approaches of the enemy from the railroad to our rear.

So far as our best information enables us to judge, they have at this time, near the mouth of Patterson's Creek—a railroad depot 18 miles distant—about 6,000 men; at Green Springs Depot, 19 miles, about 1,500; New Creek Depot, 18 miles, 3,000 men; Cumberland, reported to be between 2,000 and 3,000 men. Within a few hours they can concentrate their entire force at any one of these stations, or place along the line scouting and foraging parties. The total of their strength is about 12,000 men.

To oppose this army we have about 4,500 effective men and a few militia.

It will be seen that the picketing and scouting necessary to keep ourselves advised must be excessive, and when the inclement season is considered, the exposure makes the duty one of great hardship, attended with loss of life.

You are also aware that the country here and in its vicinity, occupied so long by the enemy, has been exhausted of its resources, and our supplies must be brought mostly from Winchester and Strasburg, 42 and 60 miles distant; grain from the South Branch Valley, some of it 35 miles, part of the way exposed to the enemy, necessitating large escorts.

In brief, the advantages of the enemy are in having the base of their operations at the railroad with nearly three times our force, while the position of this command is indefensible, and over 40 miles from its source of supply, with none of the roads macadamized, and which must necessarily become impassable in a short time with ordinary freight.

The recent demonstration upon the enemy in considerable numbers, having aroused their apprehension for the security of their railroad communications and its facilities, has induced them to concentrate their scattered forces from adjacent points, including Fort Pendleton.

If it is the intention to keep this command here, I am compelled to say that the force is not equal to the requirements, and I therefore respectfully but earnestly request a re-enforcement of 3,000 men to meet the immediate concentration of the enemy as well as to relieve the command of the unparalleled exposure to which they have been and are now subjected.

I am, sir, respectfully, your obedient servant,

W. W. LORING,
Brigadier-General, Commanding, &c.

[Inclosure No. 2.]

Notes on the location and approaches to Romney.

This village is situated on the Northwest turnpike, within a mile of its intersection with the South Branch of the Potomac. From its location in a valley surrounded by mountains and hills not difficult of access it is of course indefensible. The approaches are (by roads) by the Northwest turnpike east and west, the Springfield turnpike, and two roads up the South Branch to Moorefield. All of these roads connect with farm roads, which, with the nature of the surrounding country, render travel in every direction without baggage easy.

Defenses.—On the left front, a pass, through which Mill Creek runs. This is a narrow and tortuous part of the road, half a mile long, and ending at Mechanicsburg, 3½ miles from Romney. The pass is difficult to defend, the approach from the west offering no obstruction to the enemy, but affording them cover; it can also be turned on the south by a road practicable for artillery. It would be dangerous, therefore, to use artillery in or beyond this pass. The road mentioned above leads into the Moorefield grade, which passes through Romney and the pass. At Mechanicsburg, besides the Northwest turnpike, a road leads up Mill Creek, one to New Creek 18 miles, via Sheet's Mill, and another 5 miles to Fox's

Ford, of South Branch, at mouth of Hanging Rock, on Springfield grade, 4 miles. The road through this pass is at the base of a precipice on the right and on the bank of a deep stream on the left, straight 800 yards in length, and enfiladed by our guns; the mountain in our possession commands all neighboring heights. This pass can also be turned; 1st, by a ford 1 mile downstream; 2d, by another ford three-quarters of a mile farther down—these by foot troops only; 3d, by the Chain Bridge 2½ miles on Springfield grade; and 4th, by farm roads at the base of Jersey Mountain. There is also a road on the ridge of this mountain chain which falls into the Northwest turnpike 2½ miles in rear of Romney. Seven or eight roads lead from the railroad to the Winchester road in our rear. To secure our flanks and rear a large number of scouting parties and pickets are required.

For a small force this point is indefensible. For a large one (say 20,000), it could be made a strong position.

Respectfully submitted.

S. M. BARTON,
Chief Engineer.

HEADQUARTERS VALLEY DISTRICT,
February 1, 1862.
Maj. THOMAS G. RHETT,
Assistant Adjutant-General, Headquarters D. N. V.:

MAJOR: The Secretary of War stated, in the order requiring General Loring's command to fall back to this place immediately, that he had been informed that the command was in danger of being cut off. Such danger I am well satisfied does not exist, nor did it, in my opinion, exist at the time the order was given; and I therefore respectfully recommend that the order be countermanded, and that General L. be required to return with his command to the vicinity of Romney.

Respectfully, your obedient servant,

T. J. JACKSON,
Major-General, P. A. C. S., Commanding.

[Indorsement.]

HEADQUARTERS, *Centreville, February* 6, 1862.

Respectfully referred to the Secretary of War, whose orders I cannot countermand.

J. E. JOHNSTON,
General.

HEADQUARTERS DEPARTMENT OF NORTHERN VIRGINIA,
February 1, 1862.
Brig. Gen. M. L. BONHAM, *Commanding Division:*
Brig. Gen. R. S. EWELL, *Commanding Division:*

GENERAL: The general commanding directs me to say that hereafter you will command your division, reporting directly to him. All your official communications will therefore be addressed to this office.

Respectfully, your obedient servant,

A. P. MASON,
Acting Assistant Adjutant-General.

HEADQUARTERS DEPARTMENT OF NORTHERN VIRGINIA,
Centreville, February 1, 1862.

Hon. J. P. BENJAMIN, *Secretary of War:*

SIR: Your letter of the 25th ultimo, in reply to mine of the 18th, did not reach me until yesterday.

In entering upon the delicate and difficult work assigned me I shall keep in view your advice, "To go to the extreme verge of prudence in tempting the twelve-months' men by liberal furloughs to re-enlist." It is, however, indispensable to the success of the undertaking that you should remove certain difficulties which not only embarrass the execution of these particular orders, but are also causing great confusion and an approach to demoralization in this army. They result from a practice of giving orders to the army in matters of military detail which should come only from the commanding officer present. It is impossible to specify all these orders, as many of them are brought incidentally to my knowledge from the difficulties attending their execution. I allude especially to those granting leaves of absence, furloughs, discharges, and acceptances of resignations upon applications made directly to yourself, the officers concerned having had no hearing, and detailing in the same way mechanics and other soldiers to labor for contractors, ordering troops into the department without informing me of the fact, and from it without consulting me, and moving companies from point to point within it. Two of these companies were at Manassas, having been selected to man some of our heavy batteries there. They had been well instructed in that service, and of course were unpracticed as infantry. The companies that take their places will for weeks be worth less as artillery than they as infantry. If as general I cannot control such matters, our heavy guns will prove a useless expense.

The matters mentioned are purely military, and I respectfully submit should be left under the control of military officers.

I have been informed that you have already granted furloughs to four entire companies, three belonging to the same regiment, but have received but one of the orders. They are, it is said, re-enlisted as artillery. We thus lose good infantry and gain artillery having no other advantage over recruits than that of being inured to camp life. This increases the difficulty of inducing the re-enlistment of infantry as such. You will readily perceive that while you are granting furloughs on such a scale at Richmond I cannot safely grant them at all.

To execute these orders consistently and advisedly there must be a system. If the War Department continues to grant these furloughs without reference to the plans determined on here, confusion and disorganizing collisions must be the result.

I have been greatly surprised to-day to receive an order from the War Office detailing a private for a working party here. I hazard nothing in saying that in time of war a Secretary of War never before made such a detail.

In asking your attention to the mischief resulting from the orders alluded to above, be assured that I am making no point of mere official propriety. They are practical evils, which are weighing heavily upon this army. Officers laboring under the impression that I am in some way responsible for the changes which they direct complain that they are made without consulting their wishes and in opposition to their plans.

The discipline of the army cannot be maintained under such circumstances. The direct tendency of such orders is to insulate the commanding general from his troops, to diminish his moral as well as official control, and to harass him with the constant fear that his most matured plans may be marred by orders from the Government which it is impossible for him to anticipate.

I respectfully request that you will forbear to exercise your power upon these points. You intrusted to my "skill and judgment," as you kindly express it, a work full of hazards and difficulties; may I not ask that you will extend your confidence in me to those matters of minor detail which legitimately belong to my position.

I appreciate fully the demands upon your time and attention by the great pressure upon all our lines of defense which you so vividly present in your letter of the 25th ultimo. By leaving to me the exclusive control of the military arrangements appertaining to my command here you will be relieved of much that must divert your mind from that general supervision which is the part of your exalted station.

From all I can learn, the disposition to re-enlist is not very general. I will do what I can to stimulate it into activity. Care must be taken, however, not to reduce our force so much as to make its very weakness the inducement to the enemy's attack.

I have written, sir, in no spirit of captiousness, but with perfect frankness, in order to remove any causes of misunderstanding and to secure concert of action between us.

Most respectfully, your obedient servant,
J. E. JOHNSTON,
General.

HEADQUARTERS DEPARTMENT OF NORTHERN VIRGINIA,
Centreville, February 2, 1862.

General S. COOPER, *Adjutant and Inspector General:*

SIR: We are beginning to feel the want of the arms recently sent to Richmond under orders from the War Department. One regiment already has 23 men returned from hospital who are without arms. The recruiting directed in General Orders, No. 2, will give us men who cannot be armed unless a part at least of the arms referred to can be returned.

Permit me again to remind the War Department that a division and five brigades (including those of two members of Congress, Senators-elect) are without their proper generals. The great number of colonels and other field officers who are absent sick makes the want of general officers the more felt.

Several of the colonels of this army are well qualified to be brigadier-generals. Besides Cols. A. P. Hill and Forney, whom I have mentioned before, Colonels Hampton, Winder, Garland, and Mott are fully competent to command brigades.

Most respectfully, your obedient servant,
J. E. JOHNSTON,
General.

HEADQUARTERS DEPARTMENT OF NORTHERN VIRGINIA,
Centreville, February 3, 1862.

General S. COOPER, *Adjutant and Inspector General:*

SIR: The execution of War Department General Orders, No. 1, will greatly reduce the strength of the "one year" regiments of this army. They constitute about two-thirds of the whole number. I respectfully suggest that men to fill those regiments, say 20 or 30 per company, be sent to us as soon as possible.

The Secretary of War proposed to send unarmed regiments to supply the places of the men furloughed. Such regiments would be of little value for some time, but the men composing them, if distributed among our present troops and mixed with them in companies, would be valuable at once, and soon equal to the old soldiers.

Very respectfully, your obedient servant,

J. E. JOHNSTON,
General.

———

WAR DEPARTMENT, C. S. A.,
Richmond, Va., February 3, 1862.

General JOSEPH E. JOHNSTON:

SIR: * * * I have your letter about the command in the valley. I telegraphed General Jackson, at the President's instance, to order Loring's command back to Winchester at once, as we had news of a contemplated movement by McClellan to cut off Loring's command. I inclose you a memorandum received from the President for your consideration and reflection.* I fear with you (as shown by your correspondence forwarded to the Department) that General Jackson has scattered his forces quite too far apart for safety, and do not think Moorefield would be as advantageous a point for Loring as Winchester. I think the valley army ought, as far as possible, to be kept within reach of a co-operation with your left wing, which would be impossible if Loring's winter quarters were established at Moorefield. But these are mere suggestions, the decision being left to yourself.

I have heard nothing more from you on the re-enlistment question. I feel sure that you will find your true policy to be to take some risk of reducing your force now, in order to secure your trained soldiers for the rest of the war. The men in many cases really will not go home. A number of them who came here with their bounty and furloughs are going back to you at once. They came here, had a frolic with their bounty money, spent it all, and have agreed to go straight back to camp, receiving their commutation for transportation instead of furlough.

I am calling on the different States for additional troops, and will be able to re-enforce you considerably before the enemy can move through the mud.

Your obedient servant,

J. P. BENJAMIN,
Secretary of War.

———

CENTREVILLE, VA., *February* 3, 1862.

Major-General JACKSON:

MY DEAR FRIEND: I have just read, and with profound regret, your letter [of January 31] to the Secretary of War, asking to be relieved from your present command either by an order to the Virginia Military Institute or the acceptance of your resignation. Let me beg you to reconsider this matter. Under ordinary circumstances a due sense of one's own dignity, as well as care for professional character and official rights, would demand such a course as yours, but the character of this war, the great energy exhibited by the Government

———
* Not found.

of the United States, the danger in which our very existence as an independent people lies, requires sacrifices from us all who have been educated as soldiers.

I receive my information of the order of which you have such cause to complain from your letter. Is not that as great an official wrong to me as the order itself to you? Let us dispassionately reason with the Government on this subject of command, and if we fail to influence its practice, then ask to be relieved from positions the authority of which is exercised by the War Department, while the responsibilities are left to us.

I have taken the liberty to detain your letter to make this appeal to your patriotism, not merely from warm feelings of personal regard, but from the official opinion which makes me regard you as necessary to the service of the country in your present position.

Very truly, yours,

J. E. JOHNSTON.

EXECUTIVE DEPARTMENT, *February* 3, 1862.

Hon. J. P. BENJAMIN, *Secretary of War:*

SIR: From a letter received this day from Maj. Gen. T. J. Jackson, dated January 31, 1862, I make the following quotation:

I ask as a special favor that you will have me ordered back to the Institute.

In deference to his request I ask that his wish may be complied with, and the requisite order issued.

I am, truly,

JOHN LETCHER.

HEADQUARTERS DEPARTMENT OF NORTHERN VIRGINIA,
February 4, 1862.

Brig. Gen. W. H. C. WHITING,
Commanding Forces at Dumfries:

GENERAL: The general commanding directs me to say that hereafter you will report your command directly to him.

* * * * * * *

Respectfully, your obedient servant,

A. P. MASON,
Acting Assistant Adjutant-General.

GENERAL ORDERS, } HDQRS. DEP'T OF NORTHERN VIRGINIA,
No. 21.   }   *February* 4, 1862.

The commanding general calls the attention of the twelve-months' troops under his command to General Orders, No. 1 [January 1, 1862], from the War Department, on the subject of their re-enlistment under the act of Congress approved December 11, 1861.

Soldiers! your country again calls you to the defense of the noblest of human causes. To the indomitable courage already exhibited on the battle-field you have added the rarer virtues of high endurance, cheerful obedience, and self-sacrifice. Accustomed to the comforts and luxuries of home, you have met and borne the privations of camp life, the exactions of military discipline, and the rigors of a winter campaign. The rich results of your courage, patriotism, and unfaltering virtue are before you. Intrusted with the defense of this important frontier, you have driven back the immense army which the enemy had sent to invade our country and to establish his dominion over our people by the wide-spread havoc of a war inaugurated without a shadow of constitutional right and prosecuted in a spirit of ruthless vengeance. By your valor and firmness you have kept him in check until the nations of the earth have been forced to see us in our true character, not dismembered and rebellious communities, but an empire of Confederate States, with a constitution safe in the affections of the people, institutions and laws in full and unobstructed operation, a population enjoying all the comforts of life, and a citizen soldiery who laugh to scorn the threat of subjugation.

Your country now summons you to a nobler duty and a greater deed. The enemy has gathered up all his energies for a final conflict. His enormous masses threaten us in the West, his naval expeditions are assailing us upon our whole Southern coast, and upon the Potomac, within a few hours' march, he has a gigantic army, inflamed by lust and maddened by fanaticism. But the plains of Manassas are not forgotten, and he shrinks from meeting the disciplined heroes who hurled across the Potomac his grand army, routed and disgraced. He does not propose to attack this army so long as it holds its present position with undiminished numbers and unimpaired discipline; but, protected by his fortifications, he awaits the expiration of your term of service. He recollects that his own ignoble soldiery, when their term of service expired, " marched away from the scene of the conflict to the sound of the enemy's cannon," and he hopes that at that critical moment Southern men will consent to share with them this infamy.

Expecting a large portion of our army to be soon disbanded, he hopes that his immense numbers will easily overpower your gallant comrades who will be left here, and thus remove the chief obstacle to his cherished scheme of Southern subjugation. The commanding general calls upon the twelve-months' men to stand by their brave comrades who have volunteered for the war, to revolunteer at once, and thus show to the world that the patriots engaged in this struggle for independence will not swerve from the bloodiest path they may be called to tread. The enemies of your country, as well as her friends, are watching your action with deep, intense, tremulous interest. Such is your position that you can act no obscure part. Your decision, be it for honor or dishonor, will be written down in history. You cannot, will not, draw back at this solemn crisis of our struggle, when all that is heroic in the land is engaged, and all that is precious hangs trembling in the balance.

By command of General Johnston:

A. P. MASON,
Acting Assistant Adjutant-General.

GENERAL ORDERS, }   HDQRS. DEP'T OF NORTHERN VIRGINIA,
    No. 22.   }   *February 5, 1862.*

I. The division composed of the brigades of Generals Toombs and Wilcox, and that commanded by Col. G. T. Anderson, will hereafter be designated the First Division of the Army of the Potomac, under command of Maj. Gen. G. W. Smith.

II. Maj. Gen. Longstreet's division will be designated the Second, Maj. Gen. E. K. Smith's the Third, and that commanded by Brig. Gen. Early the Fourth Division of the Army of the Potomac.

By command of General Johnston:

A. P. MASON,
Acting Assistant Adjutant-General.

HEADQUARTERS DEPARTMENT OF NORTHERN VIRGINIA,
Centreville, Va., February 5, 1862.

General S. COOPER, *Adjutant and Inspector General:*

SIR: I respectfully inclose herewith a letter to the President of the Confederate States, and beg that it may be laid before him.

Most respectfully, your obedient servant,

J. E. JOHNSTON,
General.

[Inclosure.]

HEADQUARTERS DEPARTMENT OF NORTHERN VIRGINIA,
Centreville, Va., February 5, 1862.

To His Excellency the PRESIDENT:

SIR: I have just received from Major-General Jackson a copy of the letter of the Secretary of War to him, directing the evacuation of Romney and withdrawal of our troops to Winchester. On a former occasion I ventured to appeal to your excellency against such exercise of military command by the Secretary of War. Permit me now to suggest the separation of the Valley District from my command, on the ground that it is necessary for the public interest. A collision of the authority of the honorable Secretary of War with mine might occur at a critical moment. In such an event disaster would be inevitable. The responsibility of the command has been imposed upon me. Your excellency's known sense of justice will not hold me to that responsibility while the corresponding control is not in my hands. Let me assure your excellency that I am prompted in this matter by no love of privileges of position or of official rights as such, but by a firm belief that under the circumstances what I propose is necessary to the safety of our troops and cause.

Let me urge you to visit this army again as a matter of great importance. Your presence here now or soon would secure to us thousands of excellent troops, who otherwise will disperse just as the active operations of the enemy may be expected to begin and be very beneficial otherwise. The highest benefit would be your assuming the command.

Most respectfully, your obedient servant,

J. E. JOHNSTON,
General.

WINCHESTER, *February* 6, 1862.

His Excellency JOHN LETCHER, *Governor of Virginia:*

GOVERNOR: Your letter of the 4th instant was received this morning.*

If my retiring from the Army would produce that effect upon our country that you have named in your letter, I of course would not desire

---

* Not found.

to leave the service, and if, upon the receipt of this note, your opinion remains unchanged, you are authorized to withdraw my resignation, unless the Secretary of War desires that it should be accepted. My reasons for resigning were set forth in my letter of the 31st ultimo and my views remain unchanged, and if the Secretary persists in the ruinous policy complained of, I feel that no officer can serve his country better than by making his strongest possible protest against it, which, in my opinion, is done by tendering his resignation, rather than be a willful instrument in prosecuting the war upon a ruinous principle.

I am much obliged to you for requesting that I should be ordered to the Institute.

> Very truly, your friend,
>
> T. J. JACKSON.

[Indorsement.]

EXECUTIVE DEPARTMENT, *February* 10, 1862.

I have just received this letter from General Jackson, which I send for your perusal, and with the request that his resignation be sent to me. Be kind enough to return this letter.

> JOHN LETCHER.

RICHMOND, *February* 6, 1862.

General JOSEPH E. JOHNSTON:

GENERAL: I have the honor to acknowledge yours of the 3d instant, with its inclosures.

Notwithstanding the threatening position of the enemy I infer from your account of the roads and streams that his active operations must be for some time delayed, and thus I am permitted to hope that you will be able to mobilize your army by the removal of your heavy ordnance and such stores as are not required for active operations, so that whenever you are required to move it may be without public loss and without impediment to celerity. I was fully impressed with the difficulties which you presented when discussing the subject of a change of position to preserve the efficiency of your army. You will, of course, avoid all needless exposure, and when your army has been relieved of every useless incumbrance, you can have no occasion to move it whilst the roads and the weather are such as would involve serious suffering, because the same reasons must restrain the operations of the enemy. In the mean time, as I have heretofore advised you, I am making diligent effort to re-enforce your columns. It may still be that you will have the power to meet and repel the enemy, a course of action more acceptable certainly to both of us, but it is not to be disguised that your defective position and proximity to the enemy's base of operations do not permit us to be sanguine in that result.

It is therefore necessary to make all due preparations for the opposite course of events. You will be assured that in my instructions to you I did not intend to diminish the discretionary power which is essential to successful operations in the field, and that I fully rely upon your zeal and capacity to do all which is practicable. I will make inquiry, and, if it be possible to do so, will increase the amount of your railroad transportation. The letter of General Hill painfully impresses me with that which has heretofore been indicated—a want of vigilance and intelligent observation on the part of General Stuart. The officers commanding his pickets should be notified of all roads in their neighborhood, and sleepless watchfulness should be required of them. The failure to secure either of these two things renders them worse than useless to the commands which rely upon them for timely notice of the approach of an enemy.

Please keep me fully and frequently advised of your condition and give me early information if there be anything in which I can aid your operations.

Very respectfully, yours,

JEFFERSON DAVIS.

HEADQUARTERS DEPARTMENT OF NORTHERN VIRGINIA,
Centreville, Va., February 6, 1862.

Maj. Gen. T. J. JACKSON, *Commanding Valley District:*

SIR : I respectfully inclose herewith a letter containing the location and names of the proprietors of distilleries in your district. The War Department has directed the impressment of grain for military use when it cannot be purchased at fair prices. Let me suggest that whenever impressment becomes necessary the grain at the distilleries be taken first, because they generally control the grain market and less real oppression of individuals will be produced.

Most respectfully, your obedient servant,

J. E. JOHNSTON,
General.

RICHMOND, *February 7, 1862.*

General JOSEPH E. JOHNSTON *and other commanding officers, &c.:*

SIR : In view of the existing exigencies in the service it is desired to keep the armory in this city at work day and night. For this purpose the Chief of Ordnance has applied for the detail of 200 gunsmiths and machinists from the army, as the only practicable means of effecting the object in view.

By direction of the Secretary of War you are therefore requested, immediately on the receipt of this letter, to ascertain what number of such workmen, gunsmiths, and machinists may be in your command, and report their names, companies, and regiments to this office for the information of the Secretary of War.

It is desirable that this examination and report should be made without delay, and that as far as practicable those who are best qualified for the work in view should be designated.

Very respectfully, &c.,

S. COOPER,
Adjutant and Inspector General.

HEADQUARTERS DEPARTMENT OF NORTHERN VIRGINIA,
Centreville, February 7, 1862.

Hon. J. P. BENJAMIN, *Secretary of War:*

SIR : I had the honor to receive your letter of the 3d instant by the last mail. On the 2d instant I sent Lieutenant-Colonel Harrison, Virginia cavalry, with a proposition to Major-General McClellan for an exchange of prisoners of war. That officer was stopped by the enemy's pickets near Falls Church, and his dispatches carried to Brigadier-General Wadsworth, at Arlington. That officer informed Lieutenant-Colonel Harrison that they were promptly forwarded to General McClellan. He waited for the answer until yesterday, when being informed by Brigadier-General Wadsworth that he could form no opinion as to the time when it might be expected, he returned.

On receiving your letter in reply to mine in relation to re-enlistments, I directed your orders on that subject to be carried into immediate effect, furloughs to be given at the rate of 20 per cent. of the men present for duty.

The order directing recruiting for the war regiments is also in course of execution. In my opinion the position of the valley army ought, if possible, to enable it to co-operate with that of the Potomac. But it must also depend upon that of the enemy and his strength. General Jackson occupied Romney strongly because the enemy was reported to be concentrating his troops, including those supposed to be near Harper's Ferry, at New Creek. I regret very much that you did not refer this matter to me before ordering General Loring to Winchester instead of now.

I think that orders from me now, conflicting with those you have given, would have an unfortunate effect—that of making the impression that our views do not coincide, and that each of us is pursuing his own plan. This might especially be expected among General Loring's troops, if they are, as represented to me, in a state of discontent little removed from insubordination.

Troops stationed at Moorefield could not well co-operate with those in the northern part of the valley, as the President remarks.

Let me suggest that, having broken up the dispositions of the military commander, you give whatever other orders may be necessary.

Most respectfully, your obedient servant,

J. E. JOHNSTON,
General.

HEADQUARTERS DEPARTMENT OF NORTHERN VIRGINIA,
Centreville, February 7, 1862. (Received Feb. 10.)

General S. COOPER, *Adjutant and Inspector General:*

SIR: The inclosed charges against Brigadier-General Loring were received from General Jackson to-day. The official reports I have received of the condition of General Loring's command make me think the trial of this case necessary to the maintenance of discipline in the Valley District. So many officers of high rank are absent from this department, that I cannot "without manifest injury to the service" assemble an adequate court-martial.

The object of this letter is to ascertain if you can detail 4 or 5 officers, of suitable rank, for such a court.

Please return the charges.

Very respectfully, your obedient servant,

J. E. JOHNSTON,
General.

[Inclosure.]

Charges and specifications preferred by Maj. Gen. T. J. Jackson, P. A. C. S., against Brig. Gen. W. W. Loring, P. A. C. S.

CHARGE I. Neglect of duty.

Specification 1. In this, that Brig. Gen. W. W. Loring, P. A. C. S., did fail to be with his command and see that it was properly encamped and cared for on the evening of the 1st of January, 1862, near Pugh-town, Va.

Specification 2. In this, that when the command of Brig. Gen. W. W. Loring was met by a party of the enemy in the vicinity of Bath, Va., on the evening of the 3d of January, 1862, he neglected to attack and press forward with requisite promptness.

Specification 3. In this, that Brig. Gen. W. W. Loring, P. A. C. S., having the advance in moving on the enemy at Bath, Va., on the 4th January, 1862, did permit the head of his column, without sufficient cause, repeatedly to halt and lose so much time as to induce Maj. Gen. T. J. Jackson, P. A. C. S., to order forward other troops of General Loring's command for the purpose of at least securing the town of Bath before night.

Specification 4. In this, that Brig. Gen. W. W. Loring, P. A. C. S., permitted part of his command to become so demoralized as not to be in a condition for active service at Romney, Va., on the 18th of January, 1862, and thus, though the troops of other commanders were in a condition for active service, it was necessary to abandon an important expedition against the enemy in consequence of such inefficiency in Brig. Gen. W. W. Loring's command preventing his efficient co-operation.

Specification 5. In this, that Brig. Gen. W. W. Loring, P. A. C. S., did permit officers of his command, in violation of the Army Regulations, to unite in a petition against their commands being required to pass the winter in the vicinity of Romney, notwithstanding the commanding general of the Valley District had directed that Brig. Gen. W. W. Loring's command should go into winter quarters in that vicinity. All this at or near Romney, Va., on or about the 17th of January, 1862.

CHARGE II. Conduct subversive of good order and military discipline.

Specification 1. In this, that when, on the 3d of January, 1862, a staff officer delivered a message from Maj. Gen. T. J. Jackson to Brig. Gen. W. W. Loring, near Unger's Store, Va., he did state in the hearing of said staff officer, "By God, sir, this is the damnedest outrage ever perpetrated in the annals of history, keeping my men out here in the cold without food," or words to that effect.

Specification 2. In this, that Brig. Gen. W. W. Loring, P. A. C. S., did forward to the War Department, without disapproval, a petition which was united in by a number of officers of his command, notwithstanding said petition was in violation of the Army Regulations and subversive of good order and military discipline. All this at or near Romney, Va., on or about the 26th of January, 1862.*

> T. J. JACKSON,
> *Major-General, P. A. C. S.*

WAR DEPARTMENT, C. S. A.,
Richmond, Va., February 9, 1862.

General JOSEPH E. JOHNSTON, *Centreville, Va.:*

SIR: The threatening aspect of our affairs in the West has determined the President to spare no effort to check the advance of the enemy in that quarter, while the abandonment by General Jackson of the winter campaign projected by him and his retirement into winter quarters, combined with the unhappy discordance between his command

---

* See Loring to Benjamin, February 12, p. 1070.

and that of General Loring, have determined him to make such disposal of General Loring's forces as will render them more immediately effective than if retained in the Valley District. He has therefore determined to send into Tennessee the three regiments of Tennessee troops that have been longest in service, and to add to them the Georgia regiment now with General Loring, the whole to be combined, with four regiments withdrawn from General Bragg and five regiments withdrawn from General Lovell, for the defense of our line in Eastern Tennessee, left open by the defeat of General Crittenden at Somerset. The President therefore directs the following disposal of forces to be made :

1. That you send at once to Knoxville the regiments of Colonels Maney, Bate, and Vaughn, and the Georgia regiment, now with General Loring.

2. That you send to General Holmes the two remaining Tennessee regiments belonging to the brigade of General Anderson and the Arkansas regiment of Colonel Rust.

3. That you transfer to your own army (Potomac) all the remaining troops belonging to General Loring's command.

The President desires that you exercise your own discretion in sending any re-enforcements you may deem necessary to General Jackson from the Army of the Potomac; but he thinks the good of the service requires that no part of General Loring's command be left with General Jackson. You are also requested to order General Loring to report to the Adjutant-General here for orders. He is assigned to duty with General Lee, in Georgia.

You are specially requested to lose no time in sending the troops ordered to Knoxville, where we are sorely pressed, and where the danger is imminent.

I am, your obedient servant,

J. P. BENJAMIN,
Secretary of War.

HEADQUARTERS VALLEY DISTRICT,
Winchester, Va., February 9, 1862.

General JOSEPH E. JOHNSTON,
Commanding Department of Northern Virginia :

GENERAL : I return the inclosed letter, as I presume it was referred to me by mistake, Nelson County being in Eastern Virginia; but I would state in this connection that the chief commissary of the department (Major Blair) raised the price of flour in this district, and my chief quartermaster informs me that Major Barbour, of the Quartermaster's Department, has also sent an agent into this district, who has raised the price of corn from $4 to $4.50 per barrel. This increase of price is at present unnecessary and produces bad feeling on the part of those who have to take the less price. To avoid such and other bad results in future I would respectfully request that agents of the various departments of the staff, when sent into this district to make purchases, be required to report to the chief of their department in this district and to conform to his prices in making purchases. I have directed my chief quartermaster not only to impress his grain from distillers first, should impressment be necessary, but also to make purchases of them at a fair price when circumstances require it.

Respectfully, your obedient servant,

T. J. JACKSON,
Major-General, Commanding.

SPECIAL ORDERS, ⎰   ADJT. AND INSP. GEN.'S OFFICE,
    No. 33.   ⎱   *Richmond, February* 10, 1862.

*   *   *   *   *   *   *

IV. The following regiments will proceed without delay to Knoxville, Tenn., and report for duty to General A. S. Johnston, commanding Department No. 2:

Colonel Maney's First Regiment Tennessee Volunteers.
Colonel Vaughn's Third Regiment Tennessee Volunteers.
First Regiment Georgia Volunteers.

V. The following regiments will proceed at once to Fredericksburg, Va., and report for duty to Major-General Holmes, commanding Aquia District:

Seventh Regiment Tennessee Volunteers.
Fourteenth Regiment Tennessee Volunteers.
Third Regiment Arkansas Volunteers.

VI. All the remainder of the command of Brigadier-General Loring will proceed without delay to Manassas, Va., and report for duty to General Joseph E. Johnston, commanding.

*   *   *   *   *   *   *

By command of the Secretary of War.

JNO. WITHERS,
Assistant Adjutant-General.

HEADQUARTERS DEPARTMENT OF NORTHERN VIRGINIA,
Centreville, February 11, 1862.

General S. COOPER, *Adjutant and Inspector General:*

SIR: An order from the War Department removed two artillery companies which manned four of the heavy batteries at Manassas. I cannot supply their places without taking for the purpose excellent infantry, who are ignorant of artillery service.

I therefore respectfully ask that two companies may be sent to Manassas, to man the batteries in question, without delay; they might be sent without small-arms.

Let me again urge the importance of sending to this army the proper number of general officers. The great number of sick field officers makes the want of them felt the more.

Most respectfully, your obedient servant,

J. E. JOHNSTON,
General.

WINCHESTER, VA., *February* 12, 1862.

General JOSEPH E. JOHNSTON,
Commanding Department of Northern Virginia:

GENERAL: From official information the enemy have burnt several houses in Harper's Ferry near the Potomac, the Wager House being among the number.

Since the evacuation of Romney by our troops the Federal forces have returned there, and from information received this morning from Colonel Harness, the commanding officer at Moorefield, the enemy, 3,000 strong, were advancing on Moorefield.

Col. Edward H. McDonald, after General Loring left Romney, burned the South Branch Bridge, on the Northwestern turnpike.

I have authorized furloughs to be granted to re-enlisted men at the rate of one-third of the rank and file present and for duty. In Garnett's brigade the men are re-enlisting encouragingly, and yesterday it was more encouraging in the Army of the Northwest. The Twenty-third Regiment, Colonel Fulkerson's, had about 20 re-enlistments.

Respectfully, your obedient servant,

T. J. JACKSON,
Major-General.

HEADQUARTERS,
Centreville, February 12, 1862.

General HILL:

GENERAL: The Legislature of Virginia has just passed a law prescribing the mode of raising the State quota of troops for the war. It will, I suppose, supersede the Confederate law on that subject as far as Virginians are concerned. I have therefore directed here that for the present no more furloughs be given to the members of Virginia regiments until the decision of the two Governments in the case. You will oblige me by doing so in Colonel Radford's regiment.

To prevent the people living near and within the enemy's [lines] from coming within our lines, I have ordered our outposts not to permit the country people to pass. You will oblige me by giving no passes to market people or others who have not really military business here.

Very respectfully, yours, truly,

J. E. JOHNSTON.

HEADQUARTERS,
Centreville, February 12, 1862.

[General WHITING:]

MY DEAR GENERAL: I have just received your note of yesterday.[*] I think I have told you to keep down the furloughs as much below 20 per cent. as you please.

It will not do to send your arms to Richmond. You'll never see them again if you do.

As to what Burnside may or can do, it depends so much upon the preparations our Government has made, of which we know nothing, that I can't guess. Our people ought to be able to drive them away from the Roanoke if they attempt to enter it. I am glad (keep this to yourself) that B. didn't come up the Potomac.

In the event of invasion you would, of course, command the troops beyond the Occoquan. They may, therefore, now be considered as under your command, except Holmes'.

Jasper has just come in, and desires me to say that he has received a letter from your mother, which he left with his wife. All [well?]. The date January 5.

I can't comprehend how or why that expedition up the Tennessee has been permitted.

Very truly, yours,

J. E. JOHNSTON.

---

* Not found.

RICHMOND, VA., *February* 12, 1862.

Hon. J. P. BENJAMIN, *Secretary of War :*

SIR : In compliance with your request of this morning I have the honor to supply the following answer to the charges preferred against me by Maj. Gen. T. J. Jackson :*

To the 1*st specification* of 1ST CHARGE, I need only reply that on beginning the march on the 1st of January I received a note from General Jackson requesting to see me in Winchester, 4 miles in rear. Before leaving I directed my inspector-general to go forward with a field officer from each brigade and select a suitable encampment, giving him instructions as to location and comfort, and as soon as possible joined the command before its encampments were made, examined and approved the arrangements. This allegation is therefore without foundation.

2*d specification.* General Jackson and a portion of his staff were in front of the advance guard at the time and place specified, and learned before I did that the advance scouts had fallen in with the enemy's picket. The first information received by me was from an officer of his staff, directing a force to be thrown upon and over the hill on our left, to take the enemy in flank and rear. This was done in handsome style by four companies of Gilham's regiment. The evidence of the promptness of the movement is found in the fact that they killed 4—as I was informed—and took 8 prisoners of a flying picket. Simultaneously another force was thrown upon a hill on our right flank, which moved to the front in splendid style at double-quick. Night came on, and as a snow-storm was brewing, the command bivouacked on the road-side, by order of General Jackson.

3*d specification.* The halt of the head of the column mentioned in this specification was in consequence of the line of march being enfiladed by the enemy's cannon on a hill in front and flanked by a party of his infantry stationed on a wooded hill on our left. The force—militia— sent by General Jackson the evening before to attack this flank having failed to drive off the enemy, upon consultation with General Jackson I ordered a regiment to proceed at double-quick and dislodge him. This order was countermanded by General Jackson to await re-enforcements, and the delay was occasioned by him and not by me. I moved upon Bath without his orders and upon my own responsibility, notifying him of the fact.

4*th specification.* I can scarcely be held responsible for the results when I had no control over the cause. That portion of my command was rendered unfit for active service by marches of cruel severity, which prostrated it, was a fault, but can only be attributed to him who ordered it. I obeyed the instructions of my superior. While I gave every attention in my power to the march, the state of the roads and the inclemency of the weather rendered it impossible to avert the sickness and suffering of the troops. It is hardly possible that an important expedition could have been frustrated, for this inefficient part of my force, as stated, was but one-third of the whole, and only that particular force was called for.

5*th specification.* An intimate acquaintance with the Army Regulations and the customs of the service for some twenty-six years has failed to inform me of the fact that a respectful and truthful statement by commanders of the condition of their commands was other than a duty, and when it was accompanied by a request for the amelioration of their

---

*See Johnston to Cooper, February 7, p. 1065.

condition, humanity and the customs of the service require their common superior to give it his most serious consideration.

1st specification of 2D CHARGE. I have no recollection of the occurrence here stated. My staff officer, who was with me all that day, assures me that it did not take place. I do recollect perfectly that my command was kept standing in the road for several hours on the 2d, in order to allow General Jackson's old brigade to keep in advance; also owing to the mismanagement, for which none of my command was responsible, the baggage wagons, with food, tents, and bedding, did not reach camp that night, and also that the command, without any cause known to me, was kept shivering in their camp on the 3d for a long time. It is quite possible that my just indignation for this utter disregard for human suffering found expression in words. I do not recollect it.

The 2d specification has already been answered.

Should this reply be deemed not satisfactory, I respectfully request that a court-martial be ordered to ascertain the merits of the case.

Very respectfully, your obedient servant,

W. W. LORING,
Brigadier-General.

RICHMOND, VA., *February* 13, 1862.

Brig. Gen. S. R. ANDERSON, *Nashville:*

Your brigade has been ordered to Aquia Creek, except Maney's regiment, which has been ordered to East Tennessee.

J. P. BENJAMIN,
Secretary of War.

RICHMOND, VA., *February* 14, 1862.

General JOSEPH E. JOHNSTON,
Comdg. Department of Northern Virginia, Centreville, Va.:

GENERAL: I have received your letter of the 5th instant. While I admit the propriety in all cases of transmitting orders through you to those under your command, it is not surprising that the Secretary of War should, in a case requiring prompt action, have departed from this the usual method, in view of the fact that he had failed more than once in having his instructions carried out when forwarded to you in the proper manner.

You will remember that you were directed, on account of the painful reports received at the War Department in relation to the command at Romney, to repair to that place, and after the needful examination to give the orders proper in the case. You sent your adjutant [inspector] general, and I am informed that he went no farther than Winchester, to which point the commander of the expedition had withdrawn, leaving the troops for whom anxiety had been excited at Romney. Had you given your personal attention to the case, you must be'assured that the confidence reposed in you would have prevented the Secretary from taking any action before your report had been received. In the absence of such security he was further moved by what was deemed reliable information that a large force of the enemy was concentrating to capture the force at Romney, and by official report that the place had no natural strength and little strategic importance.

To insure concert of action in the defense of our Potomac frontier, it was thought best to place all the forces for this object under one command. The reasons which originally induced the adding of the Valley District to your department exist in full force at present, and I cannot therefore agree to its separation from your command.

I will visit the Army of the Potomac as soon as other engagements will permit, although I cannot realize your complimentary assurance that great good to the army will result from it, nor can I anticipate the precise time when it will be practicable to leave my duties here.

Very respectfully and truly, yours,

JEFFERSON DAVIS.

HEADQUARTERS DEPARTMENT OF NORTHERN VIRGINIA,
Centreville, February 14, 1862.

Hon. J. P. BENJAMIN, Secretary of War:

SIR: I have the honor to acknowledge your letter of the 9th instant, just received. The necessary orders have been given to Major-Generals Holmes and Jackson and E. K. Smith to send the four regiments named by you to Knoxville, Tenn., forthwith.

In a letter dated February 12, Major-General Jackson informed me that since the evacuation of Romney by your order the United States troops have returned to it, and that the officer commanding at Moorefield reported that the enemy, 3,000 strong, were approaching that place.

The reduction of our force by the operation of the furlough system makes it impracticable to re-enforce the Valley District from that of the Potomac.

Most respectfully, your obedient servant,

J. E. JOHNSTON,
General.

HEADQUARTERS DEPARTMENT OF NORTHERN VIRGINIA,
Centreville, Va., February 14, 1862.

General JACKSON:

SIR: The President, through the Secretary of War, directs that the Georgia regiment now with General Loring be sent immediately to Knoxville; that the two Tennessee regiments of General Anderson's brigade and Colonel Rust's (Arkansas) regiment be sent to report to Major-General Holmes, commanding Aquia District, and the remaining troops of General Loring's command sent to this district (of the Potomac). Please give the necessary orders for these movements, to be made in the order in which they are written above. If the regiments coming to join this army should be provided with tolerable means of transportation, they had better be sent to Manassas. Possibly some of the troops might, considering the inefficiency of the railroad, with less delay and discomfort march by the turnpike to Snicker's Gap. This will be for your decision.

Re-enlistments in the Virginia regiments must be, I think, under the recent law of the State Legislature, and no longer under the bounty and furlough law of Congress. It is so intended by the State authorities. Please, therefore, to make the necessary modifications in the mode of procedure in the Virginia regiments under your command.

Please give me any information you have of the numbers and strength of the enemy near you.

Retain any of the artillery of General Loring's command you may think necessary.

Very respectfully, your obedient servant,

J. E. JOHNSTON,
General.

P. S.—What number of troops do you think necessary in your district during the winter? How many do you suppose the enemy has upon your frontier?

HEADQUARTERS DISTRICT OF LEWISBURG,
Lewisburg, Va., February 14, 1862.

Hon. J. P. BENJAMIN, *Secretary of War:*

SIR: I beg leave to call your attention to certain statements made to me in reference to improving the navigation of the James and Jackson's Rivers from Buchanan to Covington. I am informed by reliable persons that the capacity of the Virginia Central Railroad for transportation is already greatly diminished. This diminution must increase. The James River and Kanawha Company agree, I am informed, to put these rivers in condition for navigation if they can get $15,000 advanced to them by the Government, to be deducted in tolls.

An army must be sent to this section of the country very soon. The supplies are now hauled from Jackson's River to this point. By completing bateau navigation to Covington I have 9 miles less hauling, which alone will counterbalance the loan, in addition to the great saving of expense in water over land carriage.

By this arrangement an entirely new country will be opened, from which I could draw a large amount of supplies. Grain is already scarce in this section of the country. Unless the James and Jackson's Rivers are made navigable up to Covington, in addition to the transportation of commissary supplies, ordnance, &c., over the Virginia Central Railroad, I will be compelled to transport the heavy item of forage from counties adjacent to the Virginia Central Railroad, when this forage should go to Eastern Virginia, where it is so much needed.

I write by this mail to Colonel Ellis, the president of the James River and Kanawha Company, requesting him to confer with you on the subject and make proposals for completing bateau navigation from Buchanan to Covington.

By order of General H. Heth, commanding.

I am, sir, very respectfully,

R. H. FINNEY,
Assistant Adjutant-General.

RICHMOND, *February* 15, 1862.

General JOSEPH E. JOHNSTON, *Centreville:*

Order Maj. Gen. [E.] Kirby Smith to report here immediately for assignment to other duties. I am sorry to deprive you of him, but the urgency of the service compels me. You will have additional general officers appointed for your army in a very few days. Answer.

J. P. BENJAMIN,
Secretary of War.

SPECIAL ORDERS, } HDQS. DEP'T OF NORTHERN VIRGINIA,
No. 48.   }   *February* 15, 1862.

I. Brig. Gen. R. H. Anderson, P. A. C. S., will report to Maj. Gen. J. Longstreet, commanding Second Division, for duty with a South Carolina brigade.

*   *   *   *   *   *   *

By command of General Johnston:

A. P. MASON,
Acting Assistant Adjutant-General.

HEADQUARTERS DEPARTMENT OF NORTHERN VIRGINIA,
Centreville, February 16, 1862.

His Excellency the PRESIDENT:

SIR: I have received information from a highly respectable source that Maj. Gen. G. W. Smith is to be ordered to East Tennessee. Permit me to avail myself of a privilege once given to address you directly on this subject, one, in my opinion of high importance to this army, and therefore so to the Confederacy.

This army is far weaker now than it has ever been since July 20, 1861. It has lost lately General Beauregard, Major-General Van Dorn, and five brigadier-generals. The law granting furloughs and bounty for re-enlistment has done much to disorganize it, and the furloughs given under the orders of the War Department have greatly reduced its numerical strength. More than half of it serving under the two distinguished officers first mentioned has had its efficiency impaired by their removal. More than half the remainder would be similarly affected in spirit by the loss of Maj. Gen. G. W. Smith. He is an officer of great ability, and has carefully studied our position. He is necessary here as the commander of the main body; for the necessity of defending our batteries on the Potomac, the threatening position of the troops on the opposite side of that river, and of those near Alexandria have compelled me to divide this army into two bodies. The principal one here requires such a man as Major-General Smith to direct it. It is a much larger one, and it seems to me far more important, requiring greater ability than that to be formed near Knoxville. I therefore earnestly suggest that he be permitted to remain.

We cannot retreat from this point without heavy loss. If we are beaten, this army will be broken up, and Virginia, at least, lost. General Smith's continuance here will diminish the chances against us. I cannot exercise this special command, having, besides Leesburg, a front of more than 20 miles to the right to observe. Having no competent staff, I must depend much, very much, upon the officers who command here and near the Potomac. The Secretary of War has relied upon the season to prevent action by the enemy. He controls the water, however, and can move on the Potomac as easily now as in midsummer, and a few days of cold would make the ground as firm as in that season.

The want of general officers is felt the more in this army because a very large proportion of the field officers are absent, sick.

The importance of this subject to the army is my apology for bringing it to your excellency's notice. I regard Maj. Gen. G. W. Smith as absolutely necessary to this army, and have written in the hope of convincing you of the fact.

Most respectfully, your obedient servant,

J. E. JOHNSTON,
General.

HEADQUARTERS DEPARTMENT OF NORTHERN VIRGINIA,
Centreville, February 16, 1862.

Hon. J. P. BENJAMIN, *Secretary of War:*

SIR: I have the honor to acknowledge your letter of the 11th instant, in relation to Captain Rhett, and that of Captain Dyerle to you, dated February 8, referred to me.

I think that you were mistaken in regarding General Beauregard as the commander of these troops. I have been so considered here and so styled by yourself.

More furloughs have already been granted than the condition of the army will justify. I hope, therefore, that you will not require a rule published to the army to be broken in the case of Captain Rhett's company. The army is so much weakened by loss of officers from sickness and soldiers on furlough, that I am compelled to use every man in the way in which he can serve best. It is essential that this authority should not be taken from me. Captain Dyerle's company is serving as infantry, as it engaged to do for a year. It would be useless as artillery.

The granting authority to raise artillery companies from our present force of infantry has interfered very much with the object of your order No. 1. Besides the persons having such authority, many others have been induced by their success to attempt to form such companies, and have thereby injured the reorganization of our infantry. The infantry which has been converted into artillery is excellent as such, but entirely ignorant of artillery. We therefore lose decidedly by the change.

The rules of military correspondence require that letters addressed to you by members of this army should pass through my office. Let me ask, for the sake of discipline, that you have this rule enforced. It will save much time and trouble, and create the belief in the army that I am its commander, and, moreover, will enable you to see both sides of every case (the military and personal at once).

I have just received information from General Whiting that the enemy's forces near Evansport have just been considerably increased both on land and water, and from General Jackson that from Moorefield the enemy has a graded road to Strasburg, passing a good deal to the south of Winchester.

Most respectfully, your obedient servant,

J. E. JOHNSTON,
General.

SPECIAL ORDERS, }   HDQRS. DEP'T OF NORTHERN VIRGINIA,
No. 49.   }   *February* 16, 1862.

Brig. Gen. D. R. Jones is ordered to report to Maj. Gen. G. W. Smith, commanding First Division, for duty with the brigade recently commanded by Brig. Gen. S. Jones.

By command of General Johnston:

A. P. MASON,
Acting Assistant Adjutant-General.

HEADQUARTERS VALLEY DISTRICT,
Winchester, Va., February 17, 1862.

General JOSEPH E. JOHNSTON,
Commanding Department of Northern Virginia:

GENERAL: Your letter of the 14th instant, respecting the disposition of General Loring's command, has been received.

Availing myself of your permission, I will retain Shumaker's battery; the other troops will leave for their respective destinations, via the railroad, except those directed to proceed to Manassas. They will march via Snicker's Gap.

The enemy, under General Lander, after taking possession of Bloomery Gap, on the morning of the 14th instant fell back, with the exception of some cavalry, to Paw Paw. I have reason to believe that he commands about 12,000 troops, scattered along the frontier of the district and west of Williamsport, his main force being at Paw Paw. So long as the communications by railroad with the west remain unbroken, he can supply himself from that direction. From information received he is reconstructing the railroad bridge over the Big Cacapon. From last accounts the Federal forces had left New Creek and the mouth of Patterson's Creek; their movements are towards Morgan County. Things are quiet along the frontier of Berkeley and Jefferson Counties. I have no satisfactory means of estimating the number of the enemy between Hancock and the Blue Ridge.

There should not be less than 9,000 troops under my command, for Lander may concentrate all his command at Paw Paw, seize Bloomery Pass, and by a graded road advance on this place. You know how Banks could co-operate in such a movement from Williamsport and even by Harper's Ferry.

Respectfully, your obedient servant,

T. J. JACKSON,
Major-General.

WINCHESTER, VA., *February 18, 1862.*

General JOSEPH E. JOHNSTON,
Commanding Department of Northern Virginia:

GENERAL: I have received information that there is below Washington another brigade besides Sickles', and that they are provided with pontoon trains, by which they can cross their artillery and other force in about four hours, and that they design doing so in the night at three or four different points, and that the first favorable night is the time fixed upon; that the crossing is to be followed by the occupation of Fredericksburg.

The First Tennessee leaves for Knoxville at dawn to-morrow morning; would have left this morning, but I thought it best not to move until something could be heard respecting the time when the cars could receive them, as the weather has been very bad and the troops are comfortable in their present position, and are within a day's march of Strasburg.

To-morrow at 10 a. m. the First Georgia will leave, and the regiments for General Holmes will move in time for their railroad transportation, as there is no evidence of an immediate move on this place.

I do not attach much importance to the information respecting the crossing of the Potomac below you, but I have felt it my duty to make mention of it. The information is that the crossing is to be at night.

The troops for Manassas can leave at any time via Snicker's Gap, as the boats now there will transport 250 infantry per trip; but unless I receive further instructions from you I will keep them, as you directed, until after the regiments for the Aquia District leave.

Respectfully, your obedient servant,

T. J. JACKSON,
Major-General.

SPECIAL ORDERS, }   ADJT. AND INSP. GEN.'S OFFICE,
  No. 40.   }   *Richmond, February* 18, 1862.

    *   *   *   *   *   *   *

XVIII. Brigadier-General Wise, with the Legion under his present command, exclusive of the light battery companies, will proceed with the least practicable delay to Manassas, and report to General J. E. Johnston, commanding Department of Northern Virginia.

    *   *   *   *   *   *   *

By command of the Secretary of War:

JNO. WITHERS,
Assistant Adjutant-General.

RICHMOND, VA., *February* 19, 1862.

General JOSEPH E. JOHNSTON, *Centreville, Va.:*

GENERAL: I have received your letter of the 16th instant, in reference to the reported removal of General G. W. Smith to East Tennessee.

I have not intended to withdraw General Smith from your command, and with regret have taken others.

Thanking you for the inclosures referred to in your postscript, I return them in accordance with request thereon. I am very anxious to see you. Events have cast on our arms and our hopes the gloomiest shadows, and at such a time we must show redoubled energy and resolution.

Very respectfully and truly, yours,

JEFFERSON DAVIS.

HEADQUARTERS DISTRICT OF LEWISBURG,
Lewisburg, February 20, 1862.

General S. COOPER,
    Adjutant and Inspector General, Richmond, Va.:

GENERAL: I propose to lay before the War Department all the reliable information that I have been able to gather since my arrival in this district and my views necessary for its defense.

The available force of the enemy in my front is between 4,000 and 5,000 men. At present his force is scattered, but can be concentrated at any one of the points named in from four to five days.

The headquarters of the general commanding (Cox) is at Charleston, where he has one regiment; one regiment is between that point and the mouth of the Kanawha River; one is at or near Gauley Bridge; one at Fayette Court-House; one at Raleigh Court-House; one at Summersville. Everything that I hear, and from the undoubted fact that the enemy has accumulated and is still transporting large quantities of army supplies of all descriptions, including wagons, &c., to his depot at Gauley Bridge, justifies me in concluding that he intends making an early movement in the spring; or sooner, if the roads will permit.

By examining the map, it will be seen that there are two routes leading from his depot at Gauley Bridge by which he can advance. The first (and I conceive the most important) is through Raleigh Court-House, now in his possession, to Pack's Ferry, and thence by Peterstown to Dublin Depot, on the Virginia and Tennessee Railroad, or preferably from Raleigh to Princeton, the county seat of Mercer, where the roads fork, enabling him to choose the road to Dublin via the mouth of East River and Giles Court-House, or the road leading to Wytheville. A successful advance on either of the above routes places him in command of the Virginia and Tennessee Railroad at those points. The second line will be over the James River and Kanawha turnpike, threatening Lewisburg. the White Sulphur Springs, Covington, and the Virginia Central Railroad at its present terminus—Jackson's River.

My opinion is that the enemy will make simultaneously a movement on both of the above lines. The force defending the approaches to Lewisburg can be of no assistance to that defending the roads leading to the Virginia and Tennessee Railroad, separated, as they will be, by a distance of from 60 to 80 miles, with a high range of mountains intervening. Our force in this district consists of the Eighth Virginia Cavalry (Jenifer's) and the Forty-fifth Virginia Regiment, guarding the approaches to the Virginia and Tennessee, and the Twenty-second Virginia Regiment (Patton's) at this place, numbering, all told, about 1,500 men. The enemy can, by steamboats, throw any amount of force he sees proper, or has disposable, to his depot at Gauley Bridge. To resist successfully an advance, an adequate force must be sent to protect these two lines.

Here it becomes my duty to mention a fact which only a sense of duty dictates. The people of this country show an indifference to its fate which amounts almost to apathy. A few weeks since, when Lewisburg was threatened by an advancing foe, with orders to burn, if they could not hold, the town, only two men of some 300 able to bear arms joined the regiment that advanced to defend their homes.

My plan for defending the two lines above referred to is this: As soon as I can procure the necessary tools I propose throwing up field works some 6 or 8 miles in advance of Lewisburg. I shall pursue the same policy on the approaches to the Virginia and Tennessee Railroad. I hope that this plan will give confidence to the community; it will certainly give them the opportunity of having points on which they can rally for the defense of their hearth-stones. I regret at this time, when every available regiment is required for the defense of points actually threatened, to make a call on the Department for troops. The day on which the enemy will commence a forward movement will be determined simply by the condition of the roads. I do not wish to be understood that there is an immediate necessity for additional troops in this country. The roads, which are now in very bad condition, are usually passable by the 1st of April. Anticipating by that time re-enforcements, I shall make the necessary arrangements, throwing forward supplies on the James River and Kanawha turnpike and on the approaches to the Virginia and Tennessee Railroad. I shall attempt, through the influential men of both sections, to arouse the people to a sense of their danger and the necessity of aiding in defending their homes.

Respectfully, your obedient servant,

H. HETH,
Brigadier-General, Commanding.

SPECIAL ORDERS, }   HDQRS. DEP'T OF NORTHERN VIRGINIA,
   No. 56.   }   *February* 21, 1862.

I. Maj. Gen. E. K. Smith is relieved from duty with this department, and will proceed to Richmond and report to the Secretary of War.

II. Maj. Gen. R. S. Ewell will assume command of the Third Division Army of the Potomac.

By command of General Johnston:

A. P. MASON,
Acting Assistant Adjutant-General.

HEADQUARTERS, *Manassas, February* 22, 1862.

His EXCELLENCY:

Mr. PRESIDENT: The condition of the country is even worse now than I described it to be and rain is falling fast. I fear that field artillery near the Potomac cannot be moved soon.

The enemy may not allow us much time for changes of position. He has been more active than usual lately. It is reported that a picket of 8 men was captured this morning near Fairfax Court-House. Reconnaissances on the Lower Occoquan and on the Potomac have been frequent, the latter in balloons as well as boats. Two of the three guns at Cockpit Point are bursted; one (a rifle) partially.

Let me suggest, most respectfully, that several general officers are required here. I have repeatedly reported the fact to the War Department. I beg you also to have orders expedited for the assignment of engineer officers to my command. It is of great importance that their services should commence immediately.

Most respectfully, your obedient servant,

J. E. JOHNSTON,
General.

CENTREVILLE, *February* 23, 1862.

His EXCELLENCY:

Mr. PRESIDENT: In the present condition of the country the orders you have given me cannot be executed promptly, if at all. Well-mounted officers from the neighborhood of Dumfries report that they could travel no faster than at the rate of 12 miles in 6½ hours.

I believe that the guns on the Potomac have very little effect. Vessels pass the batteries at night without much damage.

The matter which you wished to keep secret was reported at Dumfries by an officer who left Richmond on Thursday. I was informed of it in the train within 20 miles of Richmond as under discussion in the Cabinet. Major-General Jackson reported on the 20th and on the 21st that there are indications of an advance upon Winchester by the road from Bloomery Pass, north of Romney. The railroad has been repaired to Hancock, so that Lander and Williams have easy communication. Upon a similar report a week ago he was authorized to retain the Virginia regiments formerly under Brigadier-General Loring's command.

Most respectfully, your obedient servant,

J. E. JOHNSTON,
General.

[WINCHESTER VA.,] *February* 24, 1862.

General JOSEPH E. JOHNSTON:

GENERAL: First Lieutenant James K. Boswell, of the Provisional Engineers, is directed to report to me for duty. I have plenty of work for him, but if you desire additional fortifications constructed for the defense of Winchester, please state what shall be their character, and I will put him at work immediately after his arrival. The subject of fortifying is of such importance as to induce me to consult you before moving in the matter. If you think that this place will be adequately re-enforced if attacked, then it appears to me that it should be strongly fortified. I have reason to believe that the enemy design advancing on this place in large force. The Seventh and Fourteenth Tennessee Regiments left, via Snicker's Gap, for Manassas on the 22d. The remaining part of General Loring's command can move at any time, but I deem it prudent to retain them until other troops arrive, or until something further is heard from you respecting their marching. The Third Arkansas Regiment left here on the 22d for the purpose of taking the cars at 7 a. m. this morning, at Strasburg, *en route* for Fredericksburg. General Holmes requested that the Seventh and Fourteenth Tennessee Regiments should move to Manassas, where they should halt until they should receive orders to go to Evansport.

I am making arrangements to construct, if practicable, a raft bridge at Castleman's, so the troops at Leesburg and this place can co-operate with the least loss of time. If the two places were connected by telegraph several hours would be saved. From last advices 3,000 of the troops that were at Patterson's Creek had gone west, and I suppose that their destination was Kentucky. I have understood that a large force is being sent to that region from the Federal Army of the Potomac. My opinion is that Lander relies on Banks for re-enforcements since the completion of the railroad to Hancock, and that the boats of which I recently spoke to you answer the double purpose of receiving re-enforcements and also of retreating to the north side of the Potomac in case of a reverse.

From last advices there were about 600 of the enemy at New Creek and Piedmont; only guards at Cumberland, Patterson's Creek, and North Branch Railroad Bridge below Cumberland; about 400 are near the mouth of the South Branch recruiting, moving from farm to farm as they consume the forage.

Respectfully, your obedient servant,

T. J. JACKSON,
Major-General.

WAR DEPARTMENT, C. S. A.,
Richmond, Va., February 25, 1862.

To the PRESIDENT:

SIR : In response to the resolution of the House of Representatives of the 19th instant, asking that the President communicate the report of Maj. Gen. Thomas J. Jackson respecting the recent operations of the division under his command in the Valley District of Virginia; also report of Col. George Lay, inspector-general of the Department of Northern Virginia, as to the condition of the Valley District, I have the honor to report:

1st. That Major-General Jackson has made no such report to this Department as is above called for.

2d. That the report of Colonel Lay, made without actual inspection on his part of any portion of the army under General Loring's command, and composed in a great degree of *ex-parte* statements of other officers, is not of such nature as can be communicated to the House without detriment to the public service.

I am, very respectfully, your obedient servant,

J. P. BENJAMIN,
Secretary of War.

CENTREVILLE, VA., *February* 25, 1862.

General JOSEPH E. JOHNSTON:

The following dispatch just received from General Huger, at Norfolk, viz:

NORFOLK, *February* 25, 1862.

General S. COOPER:

I have just learned through a reliable person who has just arrived by flag of truce that large means of transportation have been sent from Baltimore and Hagerstown, Md., for the purpose of carrying troops to Hancock, and from thence to be thrown across the river to attack Winchester, Va., which they expect to have in a few days.

BENJ. HUGER.

You are authorized by the Department to withdraw the troops from the Valley District should you deem proper.

S. COOPER.

HEADQUARTERS,
Centreville, February 25, 1862.

His Excellency the PRESIDENT:

I respectfully inclose a copy of a report by Major-General Jackson.* Brigadier-General Whiting informs me that Brigadier-General French and Captain Chatard think it impracticable to make the desired movement by water. I submit General French's letter on the subject.† The land transportation would, it seems to me, require too much time and labor, even were the roads tolerable. They are not now practicable for our field artillery with their teams of four horses.

The army is crippled and its discipline greatly impaired by the want of general officers. The four regiments observing the fords of the Lower Occoquan are commanded by a lieutenant-colonel; and, besides, a division of five brigades is without generals; and at least half the field officers are absent—generally sick.

The accumulation of subsistence stores at Manassas is now a great evil. The Commissary-General was requested more than once to suspend those supplies. A very extensive meat-packing establishment at Thoroughfare is also a great incumbrance. The great quantities of personal property in our camps is a still greater one. Much of both kinds of property must be sacrificed in the contemplated movement.

Most respectfully, your obedient servant,

J. E. JOHNSTON,
General.

ENGINEER BUREAU,
Richmond, February 25, 1862.

General JOSEPH E. JOHNSTON,
Commanding Army of Northern Virginia:

GENERAL: I have exerted myself to supply you promptly with competent engineers, but have only partially succeeded. The greatest diffi-

---

*Probably that of February 21, of operations since November 4 in the Valley District. See p. 389.
†Not found.

culty I have not been able to overcome—that of sending you a suitable chief to direct them. After much thought I most respectfully make the following suggestion: In a matter of such importance, could not a brigadier-general be temporarily assigned to duty as your chief engineer? General Whiting, major of Engineers, C. S. A., would doubtless render great service in that capacity. Should it be too inconvenient to detail him temporarily, General R. E. Rodes is most admirably fitted for the position by talent, education, and experience. He is an engineer of great attainments, accustomed to organizing and directing engineering enterprises, and I feel perfectly certain, from personal knowledge, just such a man as you need in this crisis. He can also probably suggest to you the names of several capable engineers on other duty under your command, and thus augment the list of available officers given on the next page.

> With great respect, your obedient servant,
> A. L. RIVES,
> *Acting Chief Engineer Bureau.*

> HEADQUARTERS,
> *Centreville, February 27, 1862.*

[General W. H. C. WHITING:]

MY DEAR GENERAL: Yours of yesterday was received last [night].

Your picture is dark. I have others to look at which are so likewise; none, however, so much so as yours.

I don't know why you seem to suppose a change of intention in speaking of not putting Hood in command on the Occoquan. It seems to me during Colonel Hampton's illness that it is especially important, connected with necessary preparations. You know the matter which you came up to have explained is a measure of the Government, which I can't change, although I wish most heartily that Mc. would. If we could beat him, we might move at our leisure. In the other event all embarrassments of transportation would be removed and the way to the rear passed over expeditiously.

I am trying to get additional transportation, but the quantity must be very small. The want of an efficient staff is now more seriously felt than ever.

The time must depend upon the rate of preparation, which has, so far, been even slower than I expected. Three days absolutely lost, and enormous supplies to remove. You must prepare as well as you can. I will send you such help as I can, but hope to be able to afford little only.

In case of advance, look that we are not separated. If the enemy's army is divided, the distance between ought not to be so great as from this turnpike to the Telegraph road. The two portions would have one first object—to defeat our army. The batteries are taken thereby. Remember I have always urged the importance of your watching that they do not get between us by Wolf Run and Bacon Race. It is all-important.

In regard to the march of the Occoquan troops, if it can be expedited by taking the course you suggest, I am willing. It is a question of roads, which I cannot answer. The farther west they can strike the railroad the better.

The orders here, given by division commanders, are to put the troops in "light marching order." Suppose you give similar ones to be executed so far as your means of transportation will permit.

The troops on the Occoquan belong to your command.

The enemy is in force at Harper's Ferry, and also at Hancock and Frederick. Many wagons have been sent from Baltimore to Hagerstown. They will soon move upon Winchester, so threatening our left flank.

Tell French to make his command, so far as he can, ready to join General Holmes at a moment's notice. I write him a note to that effect. His movements must correspond in time with yours. He will receive intimation from you.

Very truly, yours,

J. E. JOHNSTON,
General.

Please inclose the accompanying note to Brigadier-General French.

Banks telegraphs new Cabinet: Benjamin, Secretary of State; Lee (R. E.), of War; General Randolph, Navy; Memminger, Treasury; H. V. Johnson, Attorney-General; Henry, Postmaster-General.

HEADQUARTERS,
Centreville, February 28, 1862.

Mr. PRESIDENT: I regret to be unable to make a favorable report of the progress of our preparations to execute your plans. The want of an efficient staff and the wretched mismanagement of the railroad are the causes and our endeavoring to save as much as possible of the great amount of public property collected here.

General Hill reported to me to-day that the enemy is in force at Harper's Ferry, having crossed the Potomac on a pontoon bridge; they occupied Charlestown yesterday; I am not informed if in force. Should they move directly upon Winchester from that point as well as from Hancock, our left would be so threatened as to compel the movement you have ordered without further delay.

General Whiting writes that it is impossible, with any means at our control, to remove the heavy guns. As I remarked to you, orally, the measure must be attended with great sacrifice of property, and perhaps much suffering.

Most respectfully, your obedient servant,

J. E. JOHNSTON,
General.

RICHMOND, VA., *February 28, 1862.*

General JOSEPH E. JOHNSTON, *Commanding Department, &c.:*

SIR: I have the honor to acknowledge yours of the 22d, 23d, and 25th, with inclosures. The last-named letter is without a signature. From these it appears that the enemy is concentrating in your front and pushing his reconnaissance closely and actively.

Your opinion that your position may be turned whenever the enemy shall choose to advance, and that he will be ready to take the field before yourself, so clearly indicate prompt effort to disencumber yourself of everything which would interfere with your rapid movement when necessary, and such thorough examination of the country in your rear as would give you exact knowledge of its roads and general topography, and enable you to select a line of greater natural advantages than that now occupied by your forces. The heavy guns at Manassas and Evansport, needed elsewhere and reported to be useless in their present position, would necessarily be abandoned in any hasty retreat. I regret that you find it impossible to move them. The subsistence stores should, when removed, be placed in position to answer your future wants; those cannot be determined until you have furnished definite information as to your plans, especially the line to which you would remove in the contingency of retiring. The Commissary-General had previously stopped further shipments to your army, and gives satisfactory reasons for the establishment of a packing establishment at Thoroughfare.

Increased effort has recently been made to raise men in this State, and it has even been promised that your force should be raised to more than 100,000 effective troops. If that were done, your present position would answer the purpose for which it seemed to me suited—a base from which to advance in co-operation with the armies of Aquia and the valley.

In the mean time, and with your present force, you cannot secure your communication from the enemy, and may at any time, when he can pass to your rear, be compelled to retreat at the sacrifice of your siege train and army stores, and without any preparation on a second line to receive your army as it retired. As heretofore stated in conversation with you, it is needful that the armies on the north, the east, and the proximate south of this capital should be so disposed as to support each other. With their present strength and position the armies under your command are entirely separated from the others.

Threatened as we are by a large force on the southeast, you must see the hazard of your position, by its liability to isolation and attack in rear, should we be beaten on the lines south and east of Richmond; and that reflection is connected with consideration of the fatal effect which the disaster contemplated would have upon the cause of the Confederacy. Two questions therefore press upon us for solution. First, how can your army best serve to prevent the advance of the enemy while the want of force compels you to stand on the defensive? Second, what dispositions can you and should you make to enable you most promptly to co-operate with other columns, in the event of disaster to their forces or to yours, and of consequent danger to the capital?

I need not urge on your consideration the value to our country of arms and munitions of war. You know the difficulty with which we have obtained our present small supply, and that to furnish heavy artillery to the advanced posts we have exhausted the supplies here, which were designed for the armament of the city defenses. Whatever can be should be done to avoid the loss of those guns. The letter of General Jackson presents the danger with which he is threatened and the force he requires to meet it. It is unnecessary for me to say that I have not the force to send, and have no other hope of his re-enforcement than by the militia of the valley. Assurances have been given to me that they were rallying to his support, but you are no doubt aware of what has been done and is doing in that regard.

Anxious as heretofore to hold and defend the valley, that object must be so pursued as to avoid the sacrifice of the army now holding it or the loss of the arms in store and in use there.

As has been my custom, I have only sought to present general purposes and views. I rely upon your special knowledge and high ability to effect whatever is practicable in this our hour of need.

Recent disasters have depressed the weak and are depriving us of the aid of the wavering; traitors show the tendencies heretofore concealed, and the selfish grow clamorous for local and personal interests. At such an hour the wisdom of the trained and the steadiness of the brave possess a double value.

The military paradox, that impossibilities must be rendered possible, had never better occasion for its application.

The engineers for whom you asked have been ordered to report to you, and further additions will be made to your list of brigadier-generals.

Let me hear from you often and fully.

Very truly and respectfully, yours,

JEFFERSON DAVIS.

CENTREVILLE, *February* 28, 1862.

General WHITING :

MY DEAR GENERAL : Yours of yesterday was received this afternoon. I inclose your statement in Major Humphrey's case; it had been mislaid.

The passage you quote from my letter of yesterday refers only to the case of our being attacked in our present position ; not to what might happen on a march. I mean by "this turnpike" that through Fairfax Court-House.

Publish nothing about the move until we are all ready. We may indeed have to start before we are ready. General Hill reports that the enemy has crossed the Potomac at Harper's Ferry on a pontoon bridge, and yesterday occupied Charlestown. His scout reported the size of the train of the latter troops seventy-two wagons. He is also occupying the Loudoun Heights. If he drives Jackson out of Winchester we shall be compelled to fall back at once. I have some apprehension that he may attempt the turning operation through Loudoun by crossing the Shenandoah and taking the road at the end of the mountain.

Your order of march is good and your arrangements judicious; only don't publish anything until it is necessary. Make no unnecessary confidences.

I propose to let G. W. [Smith] and Longstreet follow this turnpike, and the remaining troops the railroad and country road near it, using the cars to some extent for baggage wagons.

Yours, truly,

J. E. JOHNSTON,
General.

Since writing the above I have received a note from Stuart's man Burke, whom I sent up as a scout, written in Berryville yesterday. He says that the bridge at Harper's Ferry is of canal-boats; that the enemy's pickets are 3 miles out ; that a large party of their cavalry had on the 27th come within 3 miles of Charlestown, sending a party of 25 into the town, who carried off 3 prisoners.

Hurry Archie Cole. We have a few horses to distribute after his inspection.

SPECIAL ORDERS, }   HDQRS. DEP'T OF NORTHERN VIRGINIA,
No. 63.   }   *February* 28, 1862.

I. Brig. Gen. George E. Pickett, P. A. C. S., is assigned to duty with the Second Division Army of the Potomac, and will report to Maj. Gen. James Longstreet, commanding.

  *   *   *   *   *   *   *

By command of General Johnston :

A. P. MASON,

Acting Assistant Adjutant-General.

Abstract from return of the Department of Northern Virginia, General Joseph E. Johnston, C. S. Army, commanding, for the month of February, 1862.

Commands.	Present for duty.						Effective total present.	Aggregate present.	Aggregate present and absent.
	Infantry.		Cavalry.		Artillery.				
	Officers.	Men.	Officers.	Men.	Officers.	Men.			
Potomac District :									
First Division	355	6,161			9	197	6,855	7,892	10,371
Second Division	331	3,968			9	155	4,522	5,580	9,095
Third Division	304	4,321			7	128	4,918	5,597	8,838
Fourth Division	371	5,192	3	37	10	220	5,785	7,161	10,019
Dumfries	356	6,577	8	183	14	350	7,596	9,040	11,430
Manassas	100	1,758			13	206	2,067	2,404	3,208
Leesburg	122	2,279			4	85	2,460	2,912	3,600
Walton's command	7	173			17	293	482	518	617
Cavalry brigade			73	1,059			1,074	1,173	2,064
Artillery corps					35	470	508	583	820
Total Potomac District	1,946	30,429	84	1,279	118	2,104	36,267	42,860	60,062
Valley District	362	3,935	41	560	14	355	5,394	6,404	13,759
Aquia District	346	4,876	38	443	14	362	5,956	7,128	10,401
Grand total	2,654	39,240	163	2,282	146	2,821	47,617	56,392	84,222

AGGREGATE PRESENT FOR DUTY.

Infantry 41,894
Cavalry 2,445
Artillery 2,967

  Total 47,306

HEADQUARTERS,

Centreville, March 1, 1862.

Mr. PRESIDENT : I ask permission to call your attention to practices prevailing at the War Department which are disorganizing in their effects upon this army and destructive to its discipline.

Orders of the War Department are received daily granting leaves of absence and furloughs and detailing soldiers for some service away from their companies, based upon applications made directly to the honorable Secretary of War, without the knowledge of commanding officers and in violation of the Army Regulations on this subject. The object of this wholesome rule, which was to give the Government the right to be heard through its officers, is defeated, the Department acting upon mere *ex parte* statements. This is especially the case in reference to furloughs, their arrival being usually the first intimation of an application.

Of still more injury to the army, because destructive of its organization, is the practice of giving authority to officers or soldiers to raise companies in the different one-year regiments, usually, frequently at least, to be converted into artillery. In this way the reorganization of our excellent infantry is interfered with, and artillery companies organized, which will be no better than if formed of new volunteers. This is in violation, too, of the law "granting furloughs," &c., which distinctly limits the period for reorganization to the expiration of the term of the present enlistment. The terms of service of some of these regiments do not expire until July and August.

This practice is also in direct opposition to the regulations of the War Department on this subject of re-enlistments, which I am required to carry into effect. This system absolutely cultivates discontent and dissatisfaction among the men. It has been my aim, so far as practicable and the laws permitted, to preserve the present organization. The reason for this it is unnecessary to present to you, a trained soldier. But this object cannot be even approximately attained if the present practices at the War Department are continued.

The object of the Provisional Congress in authorizing persons to raise troops and giving contingent commissions was, as I understood it, to procure additional troops, new levies, and was not designed to interfere with the present organization of the army.

My object in writing to your excellency on this subject is to invoke your protection of the discipline and organization of this army. My position makes me responsible for the former, but the corresponding authority has been taken from me. Let me urge its restoration. The course of the Secretary of War has not only impaired discipline, but deprived me of the influence in the army, without which there can be little hope of success. I have respectfully remonstrated with the honorable Secretary, but without securing his notice.

Most respectfully, your obedient servant,

J. E. JOHNSTON,
General.

WINCHESTER, VA., *March* 3, 1862.

General JOSEPH E. JOHNSTON,
    Commanding Department of Virginia:

DEAR GENERAL: This morning I received your letter of the 1st instant.* I do not believe that the enemy will occupy Millwood so long as we are in possession of Winchester. Should I have to leave this place and fall back beyond the line of Strasburg and Front Royal, I will, if the condition of the roads will admit of it, follow the South Branch of the Shenandoah; if not, I will, unless otherwise directed, move along the Valley turnpike. Upon reaching New Market, which is 8 miles beyond Mount Jackson, I will have a choice of good roads, one leading to Luray, which is on the east side of the South Branch of the Shenandoah. Luray is 36 miles, I understand, from Culpeper Court-House, and the two points connected by a good road. After leaving New Market another good road can, if necessary, be followed, so as to strike the South Branch a little higher up, and passes through Madison Court-House, and so on to Gordonsville.

My position at New Market would also enable me to move on towards Staunton, if the enemy should move in that direction. My principal

---

* Not found.

depot is being established at Mount Jackson. From that point I hope to be able to move the stores in any direction required on good roads.

Shall I leave the valley and cross the Blue Ridge, if necessary for the purpose of keeping between you and the enemy? If I go up the South Branch of the Shenandoah from Front Royal, the enemy may march direct from Front Royal to Culpeper Court-House on a good road, and thus get between us, and, owing to the good condition of the road via New Market, he might get to Luray before I could, and thus cut off my escape by having possession of both ends of the road connecting Front Royal and Luray. So I am of the opinion that I had better follow the Valley turnpike towards New Market, unless you design me to cross the Blue Ridge via Front Royal, in which event please let me know at once, as my supplies should be sent on towards Luray at once from Mount Jackson, as they would be in danger of falling into the hands of the enemy, and my hospital which is being established at Woodstock should be removed.

If you will examine the roads leading from the valley across the Blue Ridge you will see the difficulty of keeping between you and the enemy and at the same time opposing his advance along the valley. For instance, if I fall back towards Front Royal or Strasburg, he might cross at Berry's Ferry; if I pass Front Royal, he may move from that point on Culpeper Court-House; if I pass New Market, he may move either to Culpeper Court-House or Gordonsville. I will keep you advised of the movements of the enemy, and be in readiness to move my command promptly in any direction that you may indicate. If the enemy take possession of Berryville, I will at once have all the boats at Castleman's Ferry destroyed.

From what I learn, the present strength of the enemy in Martinsburg is about 4,500, and a large cavalry force is said to be coming from Williamsport.

Respectfully, yours,

T. J. JACKSON.

HEADQUARTERS,
Centreville, March 3, 1862.

His Excellency JEFFERSON DAVIS:

Mr. PRESIDENT: I respectfully submit three notes from Major-General Jackson and one from Brigadier-General Hill for the information they contain of the enemy.*

Your orders for moving cannot be executed now on account of the condition of the roads and streams. The removal of public property goes on with painful slowness, because, as the officers employed in it report, sufficient number of cars and engines cannot be had. It is evident that a large quantity of it must be sacrificed or your instructions not observed. I shall adhere to them as closely as possible.

In conversation with you and before the Cabinet I did not exaggerate the difficulties of marching in this region. The suffering and sickness which would be produced can hardly be exaggerated.

Most respectfully, your obedient servant,

J. E. JOHNSTON,
General.

[Indorsement.]

Colonel Myers will read and report whether any increase can be made to the number of cars and engines.

JEFFERSON DAVIS.

---

* Inclosures not found.

SPECIAL ORDERS, }   HDQRS. DEP'T OF NORTHERN VIRGINIA,
No. 67.   }   *March* 3, 1862.

*   *   *   *   *   *   *

II. Brig. Gen. I. R. Trimble, P. A. C. S., will assume control of all
the operations now going on at Manassas, and will be furnished with
the details he may require by Major-General Ewell, Brigadier-General
Early, and Col. G. B. Anderson.

By command of General Johnston:

A. P. MASON,
Assistant Adjutant-General.

RICHMOND, VA., *March* 4, 1862.

General JOSEPH E. JOHNSTON:

DEAR SIR: Yours of the 1st instant received prompt attention, and
I am led to the conclusion that some imposition has been practiced upon
you.

The Secretary of War informs me that he has not granted leaves
of absence or furloughs to soldiers of your command for a month past,
and then only to divert the current which threatened by legislation
to destroy your army by a wholesale system of furloughs. Those which
you inform me are daily received must be spurious.

The authority to re-enlist and change from infantry to artillery, the
Secretary informs me, has been given but in four cases, three on the
recommendation of General Beauregard and specially explained to you
some time since; the remaining case was that of a company from Wheeling, which was regarded as an exceptional one. I wish therefore you
would send to the Adjutant-General the cases of recent date in which
the discipline of your troops has been interfered [with] in the two
methods stated, so that an inquiry may be made into the origin of the
papers presented.

The law in relation to re-enlistment provides for reorganization, and
was under the policy of electing the officers. The concession to army
opinions was limited to the promotion by seniority after the organization of the companies and regiments had been completed. The reorganization was not to occur before the expiration of the present term.

A subsequent law provides for filling up the twelve-months' companies
by recruits for the war, but the organization ceases with the term of the
twelve-months' men.

Be assured of my readiness to protect your proper authority, and I
do but justice to the Secretary of War in saying that he cannot desire
to interfere with the discipline and organization of your troops. He
has complained that his orders are not executed, and I regret that he
was able to present to me so many instances to justify that complaint,
which were in nowise the invasion of your prerogative as a commander
in the field.

You can command my attention at all times to any matter connected
with your duties, and I hope that full co-intelligence will secure full
satisfaction.

Very truly, yours,

JEFFERSON DAVIS.

HEADQUARTERS,
Richmond, Va., March 5, 1862.

General JOSEPH E. JOHNSTON,
Commanding, &c., Army of Northern Virginia:

GENERAL: It has been reported that some of the enemy's gunboats have reached West Point. The President is apprehensive that they may ascend the Pamunkey before the obstructions in that river are completed, and thus get possession of the grain, &c., in that valley. He thinks if you could send a good light battery, supported by infantry, to a favorable point on the Pamunkey, it would have the effect of delaying the advance of the enemy, if not of preventing him. Not knowing your position or movements, I do not know whether this is practicable. He is also anxious to receive a reply to his dispatch to you of the 1st instant. As it may not have reached you, I inclose a copy.*

I am, most respectfully, your obedient servant,
R. E. LEE,
General.

HEADQUARTERS,
Centreville, March 5, 1862.

His EXCELLENCY:

Mr. PRESIDENT: In connection with one of the subjects of my letter of the 1st instant, I respectfully submit herewith a handbill said to be circulating in our camps. Several such recruiting advertisements have been pointed out to me in newspapers. It is said that such cases are common ; that many officers profess to have letters from the honorable Secretary of War authorizing them to raise troops, endowed with special privileges, which would render them worthless as soldiers should their generals be weak enough to respect such privileges.

It is easy to perceive how ruinous to the reorganization of our excellent infantry such a system must be, and how it is calculated to produce present discontent and future mutiny.

I have just directed that a citizen should be excluded from the camps who professes to have the privilege granted by the War Department of raising troops in this army for local service in "the valley."

I beg you not to think me importunate for again addressing you on this subject. I feel simply the interest of a true citizen of the Confederacy in this army, and am conscious of no other motive.

Most respectfully, your obedient servant,
J. E. JOHNSTON,
General.

HEADQUARTERS,
Centreville, March 5, 1862.

General WHITING:

MY DEAR GENERAL: The embarrassments you mention are great. I hope that Major Barbour gave you relief which may serve until a change of situation, which will be (between us alone) in two or three days. It ought to have been four or five days ago, but the enemy being still and the country in such condition, I didn't like to sacrifice anything. If I telegraph "It is time," give your orders, and move. Hampton should

---

* Not found.

have a start of some hours. How would it do for him to start after dark, leaving pickets, and march to the road leading from Bacon Race to your camp, bivouac, and march at your hour next morning?

I will write again to-morrow.

J. E. JOHNSTON.

SPECIAL ORDERS,) HDQRS. DEP'T OF NORTHERN VIRGINIA,
No. 70.   }   *March 5, 1862.*

I. The reserve artillery corps under command of Col. W. N. Pendleton is temporarily assigned to duty with the First Division, Army of the Potomac, and will report directly to Maj. Gen. G. W. Smith, commanding division.

II. The battalion of Washington Artillery under command of Capt. B. F. Eshleman is temporarily assigned to duty with the Second Division, Army of the Potomac, and will report directly to Maj. Gen. J. Longstreet, commanding division.

By command of General Johnston:

A. P. MASON,
Assistant Adjutant-General.

HEADQUARTERS,
Centreville, March 6, 1862.

Brigadier-General HILL:

GENERAL: I have your note of yesterday. You are right to take the armed militia with you. The unarmed, however, it seems to me, would be an incumbrance. I'd leave them.

The only purpose the militia placed in the forts could serve would be to employ, or rather delay, the enemy for a few hours. Should you not have that to do, it is best to take them with you.

Unless you can burn extensively enough to harm the enemy, I should think little good would result.

I will order three days' provisions for 3,200 men to be sent to the Plains Station for you.

In crossing the railroad, destroy the bridges within reach on both sides of you. Your cavalry can do it.

Yours, truly,

J. E. JOHNSTON,
General.

HEADQUARTERS,
Centreville, March 6, 1862.

General WHITING:

MY DEAR GENERAL: I ordered forage to you, which was reported sent yesterday morning. I cannot learn from you by telegraph, as I have tried to do, if you have received it.

Cole writes that your officers are to get horses this morning. I wish that you had asked directly for what was necessary,

I have fixed upon Saturday morning for the move. Mention it to no one until necessary. To-morrow give Hampton his instructions, and confer with French, who must move about the time you do. I send a letter to him, which need not be delivered until to-morrow.

You have been more despondent lately than one gifted like you by Providence should be. You owe it to the Giver of good gifts and our cause to throw such a weight off your faculties, to leave them their full value.

Name by telegraph anything the quartermaster can send and you shall have it; it is almost too late now for anything but forage.

Hampton must move off as cunningly as possible. The river, probably, will not be fordable.

Yours, truly,

J. E. JOHNSTON.

I shall ask French to ride up to see you. Make an appointment with him by the courier who will carry this. The mode of disposing of the guns must be determined upon between you. As senior, your destination being the same, you will be commander, whenever a common one is necessary.

Report to General Holmes by letter when you start. I informed you some time since that you would join him. I send a letter to him, which need not be sent until to-morrow, or when your letters [are sent?], should it be inconvenient to send sooner.

WINCHESTER, *March* 6, 1862—6.10 a. m.

General JOSEPH E. JOHNSTON,
   Commanding Department of Northern Virginia:

GENERAL: I forward herewith a copy of a report made by Mr. Herbert Umbaugh,* who recently visited Cumberland for the purpose of procuring information respecting the enemy's movements. His information is from various sources—one from a surgeon in the United States Army through a loyal brother. It appears that Lander is still in command of his troops near Paw Paw, and that he did not go to Kentucky, as I wrote to you. The accumulation of army stores in Cumberland looks ominous. I have written to the Secretary of War favoring the raising of the force for operating against the railroad, and did not pass it through your hands, but sent Mr. U. direct with it to Richmond, as I was well satisfied that it would meet with your approval, as such a force can do more in that way towards retarding an advance and crippling the enemy than in any other way. Whilst Mr. U. is a bold man and Mr. Parsons a gentleman of character and influence, yet I do not expect so much from them as indicated, but much is to be expected.

Yesterday the enemy advanced from Martinsburg to Bunker Hill. So Leonard, the commander, has effected a junction with the Charlestown forces via the Charlestown and Smithfield road. Leonard, before leaving Martinsburg, sent his baggage in the direction of Williamsport. His column was about 2 miles long, composed of seven regiments of infantry, four companies of cavalry, and probably six pieces of artillery.

It would be dangerous for me in the present condition of the roads to attempt to move up the South Branch of the Shenandoah from Front Royal. The information that I received yesterday respecting that road makes it even worse than I had before supposed it to be.

If I move from here to Front Royal, and I should have to fall back any farther, I would join you.

---

* Not found.

Should you fail to receive a dispatch from me every day, please let me know. I received none from General Hill yesterday, and I fear that the enemy is the cause of it, as he writes to me with great regularity.

My stores and sick have been removed from here, except a few sick, who cannot be moved with safety. I am establishing a hospital of 150 beds in Woodstock. I see in the Whig of yesterday that the Washington news of the 3d states that Lander is dead and that Shields is his successor.

Respectfully, your obedient servant,

T. J. JACKSON,
Major-General.

QUARTERMASTER-GENERAL'S OFFICE,
Richmond, March 7, 1862.

To the PRESIDENT:

I have the honor to report that I have read General J. E. Johnston's letter of March 3 to you, with your indorsement, directing me to report if any increase can be made to the number of cars and engines at Manassas. All the cars belonging to the Virginia Central Railroad in running order are on the Orange road. All the engines which are acceptable, except one, are on that road; that one is kept to run the mail train between Richmond and Gordonsville. From report of conductors sent from the Central road to Manassas, I am inclined to think that there are too many trains now on that road; they are not able to pass each other on the turnouts. Some engines have been thirty-six hours making the trip from Manassas to Gordonsville. Some cars sent on Sunday night last were at Gordonsville on Thursday morning. A letter from the superintendent of the Orange road to the president of Virginia Central Railroad states that he expects to have all the stores away from Manassas this (Friday) evening.

Some pork on the Manassas road would require four or five days more for removal.

The cars and engines of the Manassas Gap road and Orange road and Virginia Central road are all, I believe, in use at Manassas. No further increase can be made.

I respectfully return General Johnston's letter, and am, your most obedient servant,

A. C. MYERS,
Quartermaster-General.

HEADQUARTERS CAMP FISHER, *March 7, 1862.*

Col. WADE HAMPTON:

MY DEAR COLONEL: I have just received notice from General Johnston, in which he tells me he has decided on Saturday morning (to-morrow) for the move. You will therefore act accordingly. For your information I send you a copy of the order I have prepared for my own brigade and which will be issued to them this evening.* In your place I would get my wagons off by all means during the night, or, what would be perhaps better, this evening, bivouacking where you are and being all ready to make your march in the morning. The movement of the wagons would not then be heard on the frozen ground, and would only be taken, if discovered, for the usual supply trains.

Let me know when your troops start from all points and keep me advised. When I am satisfied that you are well on your way, and not

* See p. 531.

till then, I will move mine. I shall endeavor to get my baggage off, of course, according to the programme which you see.

General Johnston thinks the Occoquan is not fordable. If we are not attacked, try and pass the Chopawamsic on your march. Let your pickets remain as long as they can, all day and night, if the enemy will let them. They can escape—those mounted. The infantry pickets may follow a few hours after you.

Very truly, yours,

W. H. C. WHITING,
Brigadier-General, Commanding.

HEADQUARTERS, CAMP FISHER, *March* 7, 1862.

Colonel HAMPTON:

MY DEAR COLONEL: All the baggage trains, caissons, &c., you can get off this evening, even if it is only to make a start, will be an immense gain. Pack and send off all you can to-day. We will have to bivouac for one or two days any way, and may as well begin to-night.

Send word to Lee. Your march will commence as soon after your wagons are gone as to give them a fair start. If you can get off the wagons to-night you can march early in the morning.

Yours,

W. H. C. WHITING,
Brigadier-General.

HEADQUARTERS, CAMP FISHER, *March* 7, 1862.

Col. WADE HAMPTON:

MY DEAR COLONEL: I will telegraph to Major Barbour to let you have some wagons if he can. Whether my order will get them I know not.

Your infantry pickets ought to let you get a good start, while the cavalry pickets, each one provided with a feed or two of corn, ought to remain as long as the enemy will let them and then make their escape. Your cavalry should in any event abandon the country very slowly, because it is of the utmost importance that we should have some here after we leave, to give us information of the enemy's movements. Almost all the citizens are, as you know, disaffected. Select a good officer for your picket service. When the time comes I will send you over an order I have prepared, but not yet published, for my own brigade.

As to march, starting, &c., don't you think the enemy may discover the movement of your wagons over the hills near Occoquan unless they were moved under darkness?

I shall hear from General Johnston very shortly.

Very truly, yours,

W. H. C. WHITING,
Brigadier-General.

HEADQUARTERS VALLEY DISTRICT,
Winchester, March 8, 1862.

General JOSEPH E. JOHNSTON,
Commanding Department of Northern Virginia:

GENERAL: I greatly desire to hold this place so far as may be consistent with your views and plans, and am making arrangements, by constructing works, removing forests, &c., to make a stand. Though you directed me some time since to fall back in the event of yourself or General Hill's doing so, yet as in your letter of the 5th instant you say "delay the enemy as long as you can," I have felt justified in remaining here for the present.

And now, general, that Hill has fallen back, can you not send him over here? I greatly need such an officer; one who can be sent off as occasion may offer against an exposed detachment of the enemy for the purpose of capturing it. But his command is mostly needed for holding the valley, and I believe that if you can spare Hill, and let him move here at once, you will never have any occasion to regret it. The very idea of re-enforcements coming to Winchester would, I think, be a damper to the enemy, in addition to the fine effect that would be produced on our own troops, who are already in fine spirits. But if you cannot spare Hill, can you not send me some other troops? If we cannot be successful in defeating the enemy should he advance, a kind Providence may enable us to inflict a terrible wound and effect a safe retreat in the event of having to fall back. I will keep myself on the alert with respect to the communications between us, so as to be able to join you at the earliest possible moment, if such a movement becomes necessary.

Re-enlisting and recruiting progress encouragingly.

Very truly, your friend,

T. J. JACKSON,
Major-General.

[Indorsement.]

MARCH 9, 1862.

General JOSEPH E. JOHNSTON:

GENERAL: I met the courier on the road, about a mile from Groveton, at 2.30. Opened the dispatch and read it.

Longstreet will not get beyond Broad Run to-night, and I will not get to Warrenton. I regret this the less because we will be within better supporting distance of Manassas.

Yours, truly,

G. W. SMITH.

SPECIAL ORDERS, }   ADJT. AND INSP. GEN.'S OFFICE,
    No. 54.   }   *Richmond, March 8,* 1862.

*   *   *   *   *   *   *

XIII. The following Tennessee regiments Provisional Army, viz, First, Colonel Turney; Seventh, Colonel Hatton; Fourteenth, Colonel Forbes, will constitute a brigade, under Brig. Gen. S. R. Anderson, who will proceed to Evansport and assume command of the brigade.

*   *   *   *   *   *   *

By command of the Secretary of War:

JNO. WITHERS,
Assistant Adjutant-General.

WARRENTON, *March* 9, 1862—8.30 p. m.

Brig. Gen. HILL,
    Commanding Troops on Warrenton and White Plains Road:

GENERAL: General Johnston directed me to inform you as soon as you were in close proximity to this column that you and your command were attached temporarily to the division of Major-General Longstreet, and would report accordingly. I suppose General Longstreet to be now in bivouac on the turnpike from here to Centreville, somewhere in the vicinity of Broad Run. I think it important for you to receive instructions from him to-night, as my train is beyond this place, my troops not yet up by several miles. General Longstreet's train is intended to be placed to-morrow in rear of my troops, and to avoid confusion there should be a definite understanding in advance. Our train is behaving badly; troubles and difficulties by the million; plenty of room for improvement, but no great promise of it.

Hoping to see you soon, and rejoicing that we are likely to be thrown more together in future, I remain, as of old, your friend,

G. W. SMITH.

—

MARCH 10, 1862.

General JOSEPH E. JOHNSTON, *Centreville, Va.:*

Further assurance given to me this day that you shall be promptly and adequately re-enforced, so as to enable you to maintain your position and resume first policy when the roads will permit.

JEFFERSON DAVIS.

—

WARRENTON SPRINGS, *March* 10, 1862—11 p. m.

Brig. Gen. D. H. HILL, *on road from Warrenton to Sperryville:*

MY DEAR GENERAL: Your note of 8 p. m. is received. I am fairly launched on a sea of mud. Had great difficulty to-day in crossing a weak and shaky bridge. The rear of my division crossed about 8 o'clock, and we are camped on the right bank of the North Fork of the Rappahannock. I am glad you have a turnpike. The road is said to be very bad; some good judges say it is impracticable; it may be, but we will get through safely, I hope, in good time. At any rate can't turn back now even if I wished to.

Yours, truly,

G. W. SMITH.

—

RICHMOND, *March* 11, 1862.

Maj. Gen. T. H. HOLMES, *Brooke's Station:*

GENERAL: Mr. Daniel, president of the Richmond, Fredericksburg and Potomac Railroad, has been advised by the Secretary of War to cause that part of the road between Aquia Creek and Fredericksburg to be broken up and the rails removed to some place of safety.

You are requested to give such facilities in men and means as may be in your power to accomplish this object.

Very respectfully, your obedient servant,

S. COOPER,
Adjutant and Inspector General.

—

RICHMOND, VA., *March* 11, 1862.

General T. H. HOLMES, *Fredericksburg, Va.:*

Remove all your heavy guns and munitions, preserving in front only such light rifle guns as could be readily withdrawn on approach of enemy.

J. P. BENJAMIN,
Secretary of War.

EXECUTIVE DEPARTMENT, *March* 12, 1862.

Authority is hereby given to the Confederate generals commanding within the limits of Virginia to call for such militia as are within the bounds of their commands, and muster them into service, to meet any public exigency.

JOHN LETCHER.

RICHMOND, *March* 12, 1862.

Major-General HOLMES, *Fredericksburg, Va.:*

Assign Brig. Gen. J. B. Hood to the command of the Texas Brigade (late Wigfall's).

S. COOPER,
Adjutant and Inspector General.

RICHMOND, *March* 12, 1862.

General T. H. HOLMES, *Brooke's Station:*

Send anything in the way of arms and munitions you can at once.

S. COOPER,
Adjutant and Inspector General.

SPECIAL ORDERS, }   HDQRS. DEP'T OF NORTHERN VIRGINIA,
No. 76.   }   *Culpeper Court-House, March* 12, 1862.

I. The depot quartermaster at Culpeper Court-House will take immediate steps for the removal of the ordnance, quartermaster, subsistence, and medical stores to Gordonsville, Va., and the chief quartermaster will make such arrangements with the railroad agent as will most speedily accomplish this object; the ordnance stores being moved first.

II. A sufficiency of subsistence stores for the troops will be retained at this point by the chief commissary.

III. The sick will be moved at once beyond Gordonsville, Va., under the direction of Surg. A. M. Fauntleroy, P. A. C. S.

By command of General Johnston:

A. G. MASON,
Assistant Adjutant-General.

RICHMOND, *March* 13, 1862.

General HOLMES, *Fredericksburg, Va.:*

Order General French to repair to this place for detached service.

S. COOPER,
Adjutant and Inspector General.

RAPPAHANNOCK BRIDGE, *March* 13, 1862.

General WHITING:

MY DEAR GENERAL: I have just had the pleasure to receive your note of yesterday.

Your brigade certainly marched well. I am very glad your division is concentrated; it will gain rapidly.

We were detained at Manassas until Sunday evening, late. The performance of the Winchester Railroad was pleasant to witness, compared with that of the Orange and Alexandria on this recent occasion. We destroyed nearly four days' rations for men and about as many for horses—of grain, that is to say. The depot had been filled far beyond my wishes, and some 10,000 bushels of corn were sent up just before we left.

Four brigades following the railroad crossed the river day before yesterday here; G. W.'s division on the same day by the Warrenton road. Longstreet is looking for better roads farther west, or perhaps a smaller stream. Two brigades coming by Brentsville crossed here yesterday; about the same time G. W. encamped near Culpeper Court-House. Stuart is at Warrenton, his line running down to the Brentsville road and some 10 miles in our front. A reserve depot was established at Culpeper Court-House last fall. We shall remain here to empty it, then cross the Rapidan, and communicate with you by the plank road.

D. H. Hill, with the Leesburg garrison, is with Longstreet; G. B. Anderson, with that of Manassas, is here. What is become of the Page? You should not be near Fredericksburg.

Yours, truly,

J. E. JOHNSTON.

You have read Commodore Buchanan's exploits. May it not retard enterprises of the enemy by water?

RAPPAHANNOCK BRIDGE, *March* 13, 1862.

General S. COOPER, *Adjutant and Inspector General:*

GENERAL: I have just been informed by Major-General Jackson, whose letter was written yesterday morning, that he had left Winchester and was falling back to the neighborhood of Strasburg. He expected to encamp last night near Cedar Creek.

General Jackson abandoned Winchester because threatened by greatly superior forces.

Most respectfully, your obedient servant,

J. E. JOHNSTON,
General.

RICHMOND, VA., *March* 13, 1862.

Brig. Gen. H. HETH, *Commanding, &c., Lewisburg, Va.:*

GENERAL: As far as I can ascertain from the records in the Adjutant-General's Office, the force under your command consists of the Twenty-second and Forty-fifth Virginia Regiments and the Eighth Regiment Virginia Cavalry. Please inform me of your actual force and whether you cannot increase it from the adjoining counties. Under the proclamation of the governor the present regiments must be filled up to the number designated before additional regiments can be received. I inclose authority from the governor to call out the militia in case of necessity, and you are desired to report what may be the prospect of recruiting your army in the Kanawha Valley and the counties west of the Alleghany.

I am, &c.,

R. E. LEE,
General, Commanding.

P. S.—Should the militia be called out, you will take measures not to interfere with the counties in which General H. Marshall is operating.
Official:

W. H. TAYLOR,
Assistant Adjutant-General.

GENERAL ORDERS, }   ADJT. AND INSP. GEN.'S OFFICE,
    No. 14.   }   *Richmond, March 13, 1862.*

General Robert E. Lee is assigned to duty at the seat of government; and, under the direction of the President, is charged with the conduct of military operations in the armies of the Confederacy.
By command of the Secretary of War:

S. COOPER,
Adjutant and Inspector General.

RICHMOND, VA., *March 14, 1862.*
Maj. Gen. T. H. HOLMES, *Commanding, &c., Fredericksburg, Va.:*

GENERAL: At the time the position of Fort Lowry was selected it was supposed to be the lowest point at which the river could be defended with the guns then available. I do not know what may be its present strength, or whether there may not be other points above better calculated to arrest the ascent of the Rappahannock by the enemy's boats. I request, should you not already have done so, that you will cause examinations to be made as to the best point that can be taken for this purpose. All other things being equal, the lowest point ought, in my opinion, to be preferred. But I think, in addition to the batteries that may be erected, a barrier should be placed in the bed of the river below, and close under their guns. The locality should therefore be chosen with this view. Please advise me of the condition of affairs on the river and what, in your opinion, can be done to close its navigation to the enemy.
I am, &c.,

R. E. LEE,
General, Commanding.

RICHMOND, VA., *March 14, 1862.*
Maj. Gen. T. H. HOLMES, *Commanding, &c., Fredericksburg, Va.:*

GENERAL: The retirement of your defensive line to the Rappahannock River causes me to call your attention to the propriety of securing all provisions, &c., in your front, and particularly that exposed in the Northern Neck of Virginia. I think it probable that you have already made arrangements for that purpose; but as I have experienced how difficult it is for the farmers to procure the necessary transportation to effect this object, at a time when it becomes necessary to forward their families and property to places of security, I thought it might be necessary for you to render them every facility in your power. Should it be determined to rest your right at Fort Lowry, supplies of provisions could be accumulated there for the troops in that direction, and a depot could also be formed at Fredericksburg. As to the quantity of provisions at each point you must judge; but none ought to be allowed to fall into the hards of the enemy, and to prevent which, when necessary, they must be destroyed. I presume General Johnston has informed you of his plans, and you will be able to regulate the amount of supplies by the number of troops, time, &c., he may expect to occupy that line.

I am, &c.,

R. E. LEE,
General, Commanding.

————

HEADQUARTERS AQUIA DISTRICT,
Fredericksburg, March 15, 1862.

General [LEE:]

Your letter is received. There is already in depot at Fredericksburg a large supply of commissary and quartermaster stores, and I will give direction for all that remains in the Northern Neck to be forwarded with the utmost dispatch, though I am almost certain that it will be unnecessary, as there is little doubt that the status of this part of Virginia will be fixed long before the present supply is consumed. There appears to be no doubt that Hooker's division has crossed the river at Evansport, and that a column of 5,000 or 6,000 men have reached Brentsville from the direction of Manassas. Dumfries is also occupied in force, whether from Evansport or via the Occoquan, I can't say. All of which seems to indicate a concentration by the enemy for an attack on Fredericksburg; and I am clearly of opinion that they should be met and given battle before they reach this city. I have directed Colonel Maloney to concentrate his forces for the defense of Fort Lowry, and I have also caused a battery of four guns to be placed on the Rappahannock 4 miles below here.

I am, general, very respectfully,

TH. H. HOLMES,
Major-General.

MARCH 16, 1862.

I open my letter to communicate information obtained last night. Lieutenant-Colonel Lee, who has charge of my cavalry picket of observation, reports that the enemy landed a part of their force below the Chopawamsic and marched up that creek to the point where the Telegraph road crosses it. This indicates a concentration of their forces before marching on Fredericksburg, and if they are not met before reaching here the fate of the town and depot is sealed, for they cannot be held an hour after the enemy have taken possession of the heights which command them on the opposite bank of the river.

General Johnston was yesterday at the Rappahannock Station, more than 40 miles from here. I know nothing of his plans, and have received no instructions for my guidance. I sent him an express last night with a letter from myself and one from General Whiting, urging the necessity of a concentration of our forces here to enable us to give battle before the enemy reaches here. If this town is abandoned you may expect an utter demoralization of the people, which I greatly fear will be reflected on the troops. These at present are in a high state of discipline and are most anxious to meet the enemy, but they are not veterans and cannot be relied on in a retreat. The object of the enemy is certainly an immediate advance on Richmond, and this is certainly their most direct and available route, and it will be a thousand times better for us to concentrate there at once and be prepared to meet them in a general engagement than to be separated as we are, and liable to to be beaten and demoralized in detail. The idea of deserting this noble and generous people grieves my heart beyond measure, and I am perfectly willing to sacrifice myself and every soldier that I have to protect them. Whiting and myself have together about 15,000 men, and it is for you, my dear general, who have all the lights before you, to say whether we shall fight the enemy. If so, I will make immediate preparations to meet them about the Potomac Run, some 5 miles north of here.

I send this by my aide-de-camp, Lieutenant Hinsdale, and earnestly request that you will answer it either by telegraph or through him by special train this evening.

RICHMOND, VA., *March* 15, 1862.

Brig. Gen. EDWARD JOHNSON,
  Commanding, &c., Monterey, Va.:

GENERAL : I inclose authority from the governor of Virginia to call out the militia of the counties of Highland, Pendleton, and Pocahontas, that you may be enabled to re-enforce your command when necessary.

Please send me a report of its present strength at your earliest convenience, and inform me what may be the prospect of calling to your aid volunteers from the country in which you are operating. It will depend upon your strength and that of the enemy opposed to you what plan of operations can be adopted in the ensuing campaign, and on this point I request your views and opinions, and as to the best line of defense you can take and hold so as to cover the approaches to Staunton.

  I am, &c.,

R. E. LEE,
General, Commanding.

RAPPAHANNOCK BRIDGE, *March* 15, 1862—10.40 a. m.

Brigadier-General WHITING :

MY DEAR GENERAL : I have just received the dispatches by Captain Randolph, duplicates of which were delivered yesterday by a courier, who bore a brief reply to General Holmes.

The depot at Fredericksburg, unless very small, should be broken up. A point well in rear should be chosen.

It was my intention in falling back to take a line on which the two bodies of troops could readily unite against the body of the enemy operating against either. The Government wishes us to be within reach, also, of the troops on the east and southeast of Richmond. The large force in the valley and the good roads hence to Culpeper Court-House and Gordonsville make it not impossible that McClellan, who seems not to value time especially, may repair this railroad and advance upon both routes, uniting the valley troops with his own. On every account we must be within supporting distance of each other. I can't understand why you should fight with the Rappahannock in your rear. You should, it seems to me, be on its south side. I cannot join you on the north side without crossing at Fredericksburg.

Stuart reported last night the enemy in heavy force at Cedar Run, 12 miles from here. He has made no report this morning. I am waiting for one. Should have moved to-day towards the Rapidan but for the necessity of sustaining him and avoiding the appearance to the men of falling back from the enemy.

I shall cross and be in condition to co-operate with you as soon as this railroad—worse than that at Harper's Ferry—will get off our stores.

Tell General H. not to have a depot at Fredericksburg. Depots should never be on a defensible frontier. Let him attend to that immediately.

  Yours, truly,

          J. E. JOHNSTON.

       RAPPAHANNOCK BRIDGE, *March* 15, 1862—4 p. m.

General WHITING:

MY DEAR GENERAL: The sentence of mine upon which you wrote the letter brought and delivered to me an hour ago is evidently incomplete, if you quote correctly. In sending you to Fredericksburg it seems to me that I indicated in general such principles as you advocate in your three letters which I have received here. The plan with which I left Manassas was much like that which you proposed a day or two ago. I have been delayed here by anxiety to lose or destroy no more public property and to secure in this rich neighborhood something that otherwise the enemy would get possession of. Perhaps I have been too confident of the slothful condition of our adversaries.

We may be required by the Government to place ourselves within striking distance of the armies of Yorktown and Norfolk. Jackson is compelled to abandon Winchester. He has a very large force in his front. The presence of such a force in front of our left makes it not impossible that this force may be united with the center, and advance, repairing the railroad. We ought, therefore, to be placed so as to be able to unite against the enemy's left upon the Fredericksburg route, or near this route, against his main body. "Ought not to be near Fredericksburg" should have been written "too near," merely as a matter of discipline.

Should a landing be threatened on the south shore of the Rappahannock, a line farther back would be necessary.

Stuart, 2 miles this side of Cedar Run, reports the enemy in force in his front on that stream, with skirmishers deployed on the farther bank, and looking for fords. Jackson, by last accounts, dated yesterday (a mistake probably), was at Strasburg.

I cannot see the merit of a depot of importance at Fredericksburg. I think that I have said this once, but keeping no copies of letters to my friends, I don't know. The depot ought to be emptied forthwith. Tell General Holmes so for me. I am trammeled now by having a reserve supply at Culpeper Court-House; but for it I should have been ere now much nearer to you.

  Yours, truly,

          J. E. JOHNSTON.

        RICHMOND, VA., *March* 16, 1862.

General JOSEPH E. JOHNSTON:

GENERAL: Holmes reports that Hooker's division has crossed the Potomac and occupying Dumfries, Occoquan, Evansport, and the Chopawamsic, where crossed by the Telegraph road.

A column from Manassas occupies Brentsville, he thinks.

Fredericksburg threatened; wants assistance from you before they reach Fredericksburg.

You alone can determine or direct the movements necessary.

JEFFERSON DAVIS.

RICHMOND, VA., *March* 16, 1862.

Maj. Gen. T. H. HOLMES, *Commanding, &c., Fredericksburg, Va.:*

GENERAL: I have had the honor to receive your letter of the 15th and 16th instant, by the hands of Lieutenant Hinsdale. The enemy has naturally occupied the ground from which we have withdrawn, and seems to have taken a line approaching parallelism to the position of our army. What route of approach to Richmond he will adopt does not now seem certain. His land transportation would be shortened by coming up the Rappahannock, though the route from the Potomac through Fredericksburg offers other advantages.

I do not think his advance from Dumfries, &c., can be immediate, from what I learn of the condition of the roads, but that he will advance upon our line as soon as he can, I have no doubt. To retard his movements, cut him up in detail if possible, attack him at disadvantage, and, if practicable, drive him back, will of course be your effort and study. It is not the plan of the Government to abandon any country that can be held, and it is only the necessity of the case, I presume, that has caused the withdrawal of the troops to the Rappahannock. I trust there will be no necessity of retrograding farther. The position of the main body of the Army of the Potomac seems to have been taken in reference to the reported advance of the enemy up the Shenandoah Valley. A report from General Johnston of his plans and intentions has not yet been received. His movements are doubtless regulated by those of the enemy, and he alone can say whether it is practicable to re-enforce you, to enable you to make the attack you propose or not. As advised by my dispatch of to-day, he has been informed of the contents of your letter, and as he must also have received your communication to him, he will doubtless give such directions as the case admits of.

In the uncertainty of the position of our own troops, that of the enemy, the condition of the roads, &c., the measures you propose could not safely be directed from here. A blow at the enemy at the crossing of the Chopawamsic might, it seems to me, come within the scope of your forces, provided it meets with the concurrence of General Johnston, whose directions in the matter must, of course, be had.

I very much regret to learn from your letter of the 14th that it is the opinion of yourself and officers that Fredericksburg is in itself untenable. Can it be maintained by occupying a position on the left bank of the river or in advance of the hills on that side? I request that you will cause an examination of the country to be made, should you not be sufficiently acquainted with it, both in your front and rear, with a view to take the best position the case admits of. I would also suggest that arrangements be made to break up the railroad to Aquia Creek and remove the iron as soon as in your judgment it can be done without detriment to the service. I think it certain the enemy will press his advance on Richmond in every direction.

Our troops are coming in spiritedly, and if we can gain time, I trust we shall be able to drive him back.

I am, &c.,

R. E. LEE,
General, Commanding.

RICHMOND, *March* 16, 1862.

General T. H. HOLMES, *Fredericksburg, Va.:*

GENERAL: In answer to your letter of the 14th, respecting the militia called out by the recent proclamation of the governor of Virginia, I have to state that it is the intention of the governor to use them for the purpose, either by draft or voluntary enrollment, to fill up the maximum organization of the several companies of the Virginia regiments now in service. In the mean time you can make use of such as have reported to you in such manner as your necessities may require.

The Government will proceed as rapidly as possible to arm volunteers engaged for the war, but cannot undertake to furnish arms to the militia serving as such.

Very respectfully, &c.,

S. COOPER,
Adjutant and Inspector General.

HEADQUARTERS ARMY OF THE NORTHWEST,
March 17, 1862.

S. COOPER,
Adjutant and Inspector General, Richmond, Va.:

GENERAL: I have the honor to report that from reliable sources I have information that the enemy beyond this, in the vicinity of Beverly, at Cheat Mountain, and other points, do not exceed about 3,000 in number. It is reported further that the transportation of their supplies is exceedingly difficult, by reason of the condition of the roads, and that their provisions are running short. They have recently—within the last two or three weeks—made raids into Pendleton County for the purpose of plundering.

Although they have spoken and still speak of a move in this direction, I hardly think they will attempt it for the present.

If it is in contemplation to move this command, may I request timely intimation of it?

I am, sir, very respectfully, your obedient servant,

E. JOHNSON,
Brigadier-General, Commanding.

RICHMOND, VA., *March* 17, 1862.

General T. H. HOLMES,
Commanding Aquia District, Fredericksburg, Va.:

GENERAL: Your letter of the 17th instant has been received. Should General Johnston have selected no place for the depot on your line, I would designate the junction of the Central and Richmond and Fredericksburg Railroads as a convenient position to which to send back your surplus stores. A portion of these stores by railroad could from this point, if required, be sent to General Johnston's army, for which, I understand from your letter, they were originally intended. Some shelter could doubtless be procured at the Junction and other provided. In my former letter, on the subject of drawing stores from the exposed country in your front, it was intended to draw your attention to the matter if stores were required. It was not intended for you to accumulate more than you could consume or take care of, and was based upon the supposition that you could hold the line of the Rappahannock. If that line cannot be held, it alters the case. You must therefore follow your good judgment.

Very respectfully, &c.,

R. E. LEE,
General, Commanding.

HEADQUARTERS,
Richmond, Va., March 17, 1862.

General JOSEPH E. JOHNSTON,
Commanding Army of the Potomac :

GENERAL: General Magruder has applied to be re-enforced in cavalry, and asks that the Lunenburg Cavalry from Fredericksburg be sent him, in addition to other companies which he names. Can you spare the services of this company, or is there any cavalry in your command whose services you could dispense with for this purpose? There is none unassigned with which to re-enforce him.

I am, &c.,

R. E. LEE,
General, Commanding.

RICHMOND, VA., *March* 17, 1862.

General JOSEPH E. JOHNSTON,
Commanding, &c., Culpeper Court-House, Va.:

GENERAL: I received yesterday from General Holmes a letter dated 14th instant, of which the accompanying is a copy.

I presume he has already communicated with you on the subject, but as the matter is briefly and distinctly stated, I have thought it might be convenient to you to consider it in the manner presented. In a letter of the 16th General Holmes also reports that Hooker's division had crossed the Potomac at Evansport, and that a column of 5,000 or 6,000 of the enemy had reached Brentsville from the direction of Manassas. Dumfries was occupied in force, but whether from Evansport or via Occoquan he did not know. He states that the enemy landed a part of his force below Chopawamsic, and marched up that creek to where it is crossed by the Telegraph road. He considers these movements indicate a purpose of the enemy to concentrate his force for an attack on Fredericksburg, and that unless he can be defeated before reaching it, the town could not be held an hour after the occupation of the hills on the opposite bank of the river.

From what is stated of the condition of the roads I hardly think an immediate movement against Fredericksburg can be made; nor am I aware of anything that indicates with any degree of certainty what route the enemy will adopt in his march towards Richmond.

You have doubtless considered the subject with reference to your operations, and made your arrangements as to the points to be held and defended.

I am, &c.,

R. E. LEE,
General, Commanding.

[Inclosure.]

HEADQUARTERS AQUIA DISTRICT,
Fredericksburg, March 14, 1862.

General R. E. LEE, *Commanding Army:*

GENERAL: Since the withdrawal of Generals Whiting and French from Evansport and its vicinity the enemy have crossed the river in large force, and have also advanced from the direction of Manassas as far as Brentsville. This would seem to indicate that their efforts against Richmond will be via Fredericksburg. Last night I called Generals Whiting and French and Colonels Hampton and Pettigrew in consultation. These gentlemen had served all the fall and winter between Aquia and the Occoquan, and were thus perfectly conversant with the country and everything belonging to its defense. The unanimous result of the conference was—

1st. Fredericksburg *per se* is untenable; it can only be defended by a force strong enough to attack the enemy's advance north of the Rappahannock.

2d. The present disposition of the enemy's forces would seem to indicate that his advance will be in three columns; *i. e.*, from Manassas, Evansport, and from below Potomac Creek. The two first are most serious, and if they move simultaneously absolutely necessitates the assistance of our main body to the force now about Fredericksburg; and this assistance should be given as soon as it is ascertained there is no mistake in this programme. You are aware that at Fredericksburg there is a large depot, well supplied with everything necessary for troops, which, independently of the interests of its noble, zealous, and true-hearted people, makes its preservation and defense a matter of much importance, and which can only be effected by winning a battle before the enemy arrive, the town being perfectly commanded by the heights on the opposite bank of the river.

I am, sir, very respectfully, your obedient servant,

TH. H. HOLMES,
Major-General.

INDEX.

Brigades, Divisions, Corps, and Armies are "Mentioned" under name of commanding officer; State and other organizations under their official designation.

---

*Embraces correspondence of Halleck and Scott only.

Page.

Page.

1150

*Embraces also correspondence as General-in-Chief.

Page.

McClellan, George B.—Continued.

Correspondence with

Sullivan, J. H. 587

Sumner, E. V 55, 762

Tripler, Charles S. 97, 98, 100, 101, 105, 107, 657, 664, 713

Wadsworth, J. S 57

War Department, U. S..... .... 9, 36, 42, 56, 57, 62,

342, 585–587, 598, 616, 619, 621, 727–730, 739–743, 747, 749–752, 754–758

Williams, S. 748

Williamson, R. S 625, 629

Wyman, R. H. 608

Instructions to

Banks, Nathaniel P. (*Shenandoah Valley*) 56, 59

Buell, Don Carlos. (*Kentucky and Tennessee*) 38

Burnside, A. E. (*North Carolina*) 36

Butler, Benjamin F. (*New Orleans*) 40

Halleck, H. W. (*Missouri*) 37

Sherman, T. W. (*South Atlantic Coast*) 39

Wadsworth, J. S. (*Washington and vicinity*) 57

Mentioned 5, 32, 34, 41, 46, 50,

54, 61, 63–67, 100–102, 105, 121, 153, 184, 195, 290, 334, 341–347, 428, 430,

474, 512, 514, 515, 548, 554, 560, 561, 563, 567, 574, 579, 597, 609, 613, 616,

620–622, 626, 639, 655, 685, 700, 712, 725, 730, 733, 742, 748–750, 753, 754,

757, 765, 769, 778, 790, 848, 903, 929, 953, 956, 959, 965, 978, 979, 981, 983,

990, 1007, 1019, 1025, 1028, 1035, 1037, 1038, 1059, 1064, 1065, 1082, 1101

Operations. Proposed 6, 9, 57

Reports of.

Ball's Bluff, Va. Engagement at, October 21, 1861 .... 32–35, 290

Cedar Run, Va. Reconnaissance to, March 14–16, 1862 550

Lewinsville, Va. Reconnaissance to, and action at, Sept. 11, 1861 .. 167, 168

Potomac, Army of the. Operations, July 27, 1861–March 17, 1862 5

Review of affairs, February, 1862 42–45

Statement of condition of Union Army in October, 1861 9

Suggests organization of flotilla for operations on Potomac River 36, 586

McConnell, Thomas.

Mentioned 484

Report of engagement at Dranesville, Va., December 20, 1861 .... 484, 485

McCook, Alexander McD. Mentioned 242, 412

McCook, Daniel. Mentioned 242

McCook, Robert L.

Mentioned 130, 132, 134, 143, 144, 253–255, 266, 268, 271, 272, 586, 599, 636, 657

Report of engagement Carnifix Ferry, Gauley River, W. Va., Sept. 10, 1861. 141

McCoy, Henry K. Mentioned 463

McCoy's Mill, W. Va. Report of William S. Smith of skirmish near, November 14, 1861 283

(See also *West Virginia. Operations in Kanawha region.*)

McCubbin, R. C. Mentioned 195

McDonald, Angus W., Colonel.

Correspondence with

Adjutant and Inspector General's Office, C. S. A. 926, 931

Lee, Robert E. 857

Mentioned 383, 808, 846, 851, 857, 859, 931, 942

Report of descent upon Romney, W. Va., September 23–25, 1861 ..... 200, 201

McDonald, Angus W., Lieutenant. Mentioned 201, 206, 210

Page.

Page.

---

* Potomac Home Brigade.   † Eastern Shore.

1158

INDEX.

---

*Sometimes called 9th Battery (9th N. Y. S. M.)

Page.

---

* Also called 20th N. Y. S. M.

1164 INDEX.

---

* Did not join regiment until January, 1865.   † Three-months' organization.

Page.

Pegram, William J.　Mentioned... 115
Peirpoint, Francis H.
　Correspondence with
　　Lincoln, Abraham.. 674
　　Rosecrans, W. S.. 615, 639
　　War Department, U. S 590, 691
　Mentioned 557, 674
Pendleton, A. S.　Mentioned 394
Pendleton, W. B.　Mentioned.................................. 232
Pendleton, William N.　Mentioned.................. 830, 932, 1031, 1091
Peninsular Campaign.　Preliminary operations.　Communications from
　Adjutant-General's Office, U. S. A.................................. 751
　Banks, N. P.. 750
　Dahlgren, John A... 760
　Heiss, W. H 764
　Lincoln, Abraham 58
　McClellan, George B 739–743, 748, 749, 751, 752, 754, 755, 758
　Navy Department, U. S.. 752, 753, 757
　Sumner, E. V.. 762, 763
　War Department, U. S................... 62, 739, 741, 747, 750, 752, 754, 756, 757
　Wool, John E.. 749, 753
　　　(See *Virginia. Withdrawal of Confederate forces, March 7–9, 1862.*)
Pennsylvania.　Military departments embracing 712
Pennsylvania, Department of.
　Affairs in, generally.　Communications from J. A. Dix..556, 558, 562, 565, 569, 654
　Merged into the Department of the Potomac............................ 567
Pennsylvania Troops.　Mentioned.
　Artillery—*Batteries (Independent)*: **C,*** 21; **D**, 21; **E**, 21; **F,*** 21.　*Regiments (Light)*: **1st, A**, 17, 21, 455, 473–475, 477, 480, 482, 484, 485, 487–489, 715, 719; **B**, 17, 21, 715; **C**, 20; **D**, 16, 20; **E**, 17, 20, 216, 715; **F**, 16, 20, 21, 400, 522; **G**, 17, 21, 448, 455, 715; **H**, 16.　(*Heavy*): **2d,†L, M**, 22.
　Cavalry—*Battalions:* Ringgold, 21, 379, 380, 404.　*Companies:* Reading City Guard, 17; Richards', 428, 429, 641; Washington, 220, 404.　*Regiments:* **1st**, 17, 21, 77, 81, 92, 448, 449, 455, 474, 476–481, 485, 489, 715; **2d**, 22; **3d**, 16, 19, 169, 216, 443–445, 447, 548, 715; **4th**, 15, 22; **5th**, 17, 504–510, 717; **6th**, 19; **8th**, 16, 19, 548, 549, 715; **11th**, 15, 385, 386.
　Infantry—*Regiments:‡* **1st**, 17, 21, 556, 570, 572, 715; **2d**, 17, 21, 715; **3d**, 17, 21, 715; **4th**, 17, 21, 556, 566, 572, 715; **5th**, 17, 21, 715, **6th**, 17, 21, 127, 474, 475, 478, 482, 483, 485, 489, 715; **7th, 8th**, 17, 21, 127, 715; **9 h**, 17, 21, 474, 475, 476, 478, 479, 482–485, 489, 715; **10th**, 17, 21, 92, 474, 478, 479, 483–486, 489, 715; **11th**, 17, 21, 22, 516, 715; **12th**, 17, 21, 474, 478, 483–485, 487–489, 715; **13th**, 21, 92, 228, 473, 474, 477–485, 487, 489, 715; **18th,§** 559; **23d**, 16, 20, 718; **26th**, 15, 17, 20, 22, 716; **27th**, 15, 17, 452, 716; **28th**, 16, 21, 92, 197–199, 214, 215, 239–242, 246, 472, 473, 511–517, 549, 562, 568, 574, 584, 600, 651, 719, 757; **29th**, 16, 22, 399, 400, 719, 757; **30th,‖** 16, 331, 332, 335, 337, 719; **31st**, 17, 20, 718; **32d**, 16; **33d**, 16; **35th**, 17, 92, 495, 716; **36th**, 385; **40th**, 17, 716; **45th**, 16, 385, 386; **46th**, 16, 22, 521, 522, 694, 719, 757; **47th**, 17, 717; **49th**, 17, 20, 716; **52d**, 20, 717; **53d**, 19, 720; **54th**, 22, 719; **56th**, 22; **57th**, 20; **58th**, 749; **61st**, 16, 20, 718; **62d**, 20, 84, 572, 715; **63d**, 16, 20, 518–520, 718; **69th**, 16, 19, 22, 216, 218, 714: **71st**, 16, 19, 22,

---

* Also called Hampton's and Thompson's Batteries, Maryland Artillery.
† At date mentioned were independent batteries.
‡ 1st to 13th, inclusive, designated "Reserves."
§ Militia.
‖ Designation changed to 66th Infantry, January, 1862,

---

* Originally known as 21st Pennsylvania.

† Originally known as 13th Pennsylvania.

*Includes operations in counties of Maryland bordering on; also Loudoun County, Va., Lower Shenandoah Valley, and Hampshire, Hardy, and Morgan Counties, W. Va.

1172 INDEX.

* Provisional Army.

* Region lying between the Potomac and Rappahannock Rivers.

---

* Assigned to 9th Virginia Cavalry, January 18, 1862.

† Subsequently assigned to 8th Virginia Cavalry.

*Includes operations in region between Kanawha and Upper Potomac and on line of Baltimore and Ohio Railroad west of Maryland.

*Includes operations on Greenbrier and New Rivers, also region south and west of Kanawha River.

○